America Reads Seventh Edition

Traditions in Literature

America Reads Seventh Edition

Beginnings in Literature
Alan L. Madsen
Sarah Durand Wood
Philip M. Connors

Discoveries in Literature
Edmund J. Farrell
Ruth S. Cohen
L. Jane Christensen

Explorations in Literature
Ruth S. Cohen
Nancy C. Millett
Raymond J. Rodrigues

Patterns in Literature
Edmund J. Farrell
Ouida H. Clapp
Karen J. Kuehner

Traditions in Literature
James E. Miller, Jr.
Helen McDonnell
Russell J. Hogan

The United States in Literature
The Red Badge of Courage Edition
Three Long Stories Edition
James E. Miller, Jr.
Carlota Cárdenas de Dwyer
Kerry M. Wood

England in Literature
Macbeth Edition
Hamlet Edition
Helen McDonnell
John Pfordresher
Gladys V. Veidemanis

Testbooks

Guidebooks

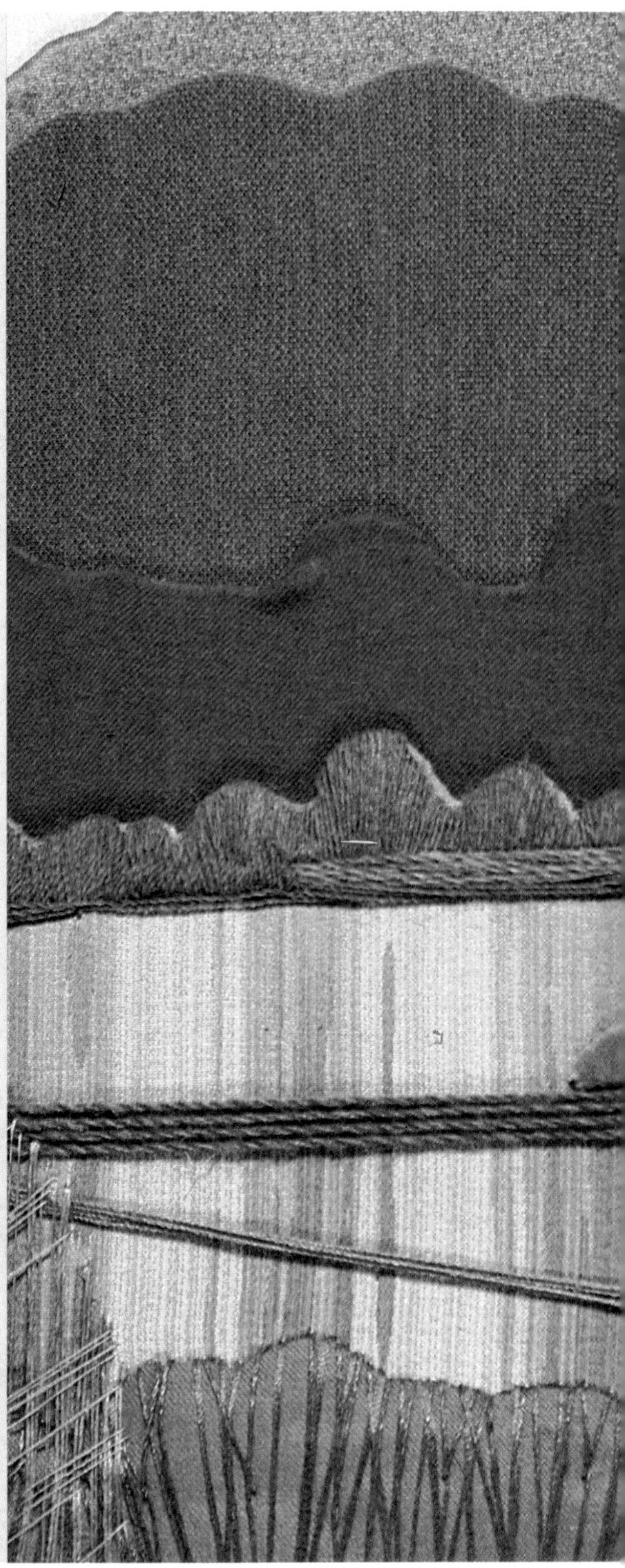

America Reads Seventh Edition

Traditions
in Literature

James E. Miller, Jr.

Helen McDonnell

Russell J. Hogan

Scott, Foresman and Company

Editorial Offices: Glenview, Illinois
Regional Offices: Palo Alto, California
Tucker, Georgia
Glenview, Illinois
Oakland, New Jersey
Dallas, Texas

James E. Miller, Jr. Professor of English and former Department Chairman, University of Chicago. Fulbright Lecturer in Naples and Rome, Italy, 1958–1959, and in Kyoto, Japan, 1968. Chairman, Commission on Literature, National Council of Teachers of English, 1967–1969. Guggenheim Fellow, 1969–1970. President, NCTE, 1970. Author of *Quests Surd and Absurd; Word, Self, and Reality; T. S. Eliot's Personal Wasteland;* and *The American Quest for a Supreme Fiction.*

Helen McDonnell English Supervisor of the Ocean Township Junior and Senior High Schools, Oakhurst, New Jersey. Formerly Chairman of the Committee on Comparative and World Literature, NCTE. Formerly member of the Commission on Literature, NCTE. Editor of *Nobel Parade* and co-author of titles in the America Reads, Fountainhead, and Gateway Series, Scott, Foresman and Company.

Russell J. Hogan Chairman of the English Department, Clayton High School, Missouri. Associate Chairman of the Committee on Comparative and World Literature of the National Council of Teachers of English. Foreign Expert, Foreign Language School, Beijing, China, 1983–1984. Contributor of an article on the poetry of François Villon to *Teachers' Guide to World Literature* (NCTE).

Cover: Panel featuring appliqué and over-embroidery. BPCC Publishing Corporation/Aldus Archive, courtesy The Embroiderers' Guild, Surrey.

ISBN: 0-673-27054-8

2345678910-RRW-93929190898887

Table of Contents

Unit 1

Experience in Fiction

Unit 2

Modern Drama

Unit 3

Poetry

*Nobel Prize winner

*Nobel Prize winner

Unit 4

Greek Drama

Unit 5

Tradition in Fiction

*Nobel Prize winner

Unit 6

Shakespearean Drama

Unit 7

Nonfiction

*Nobel Prize winner

Unit 8

The Novel

*Nobel Prize winner

Handbook of Literary Terms

Composition Guide

Unit 1
Experience in Fiction

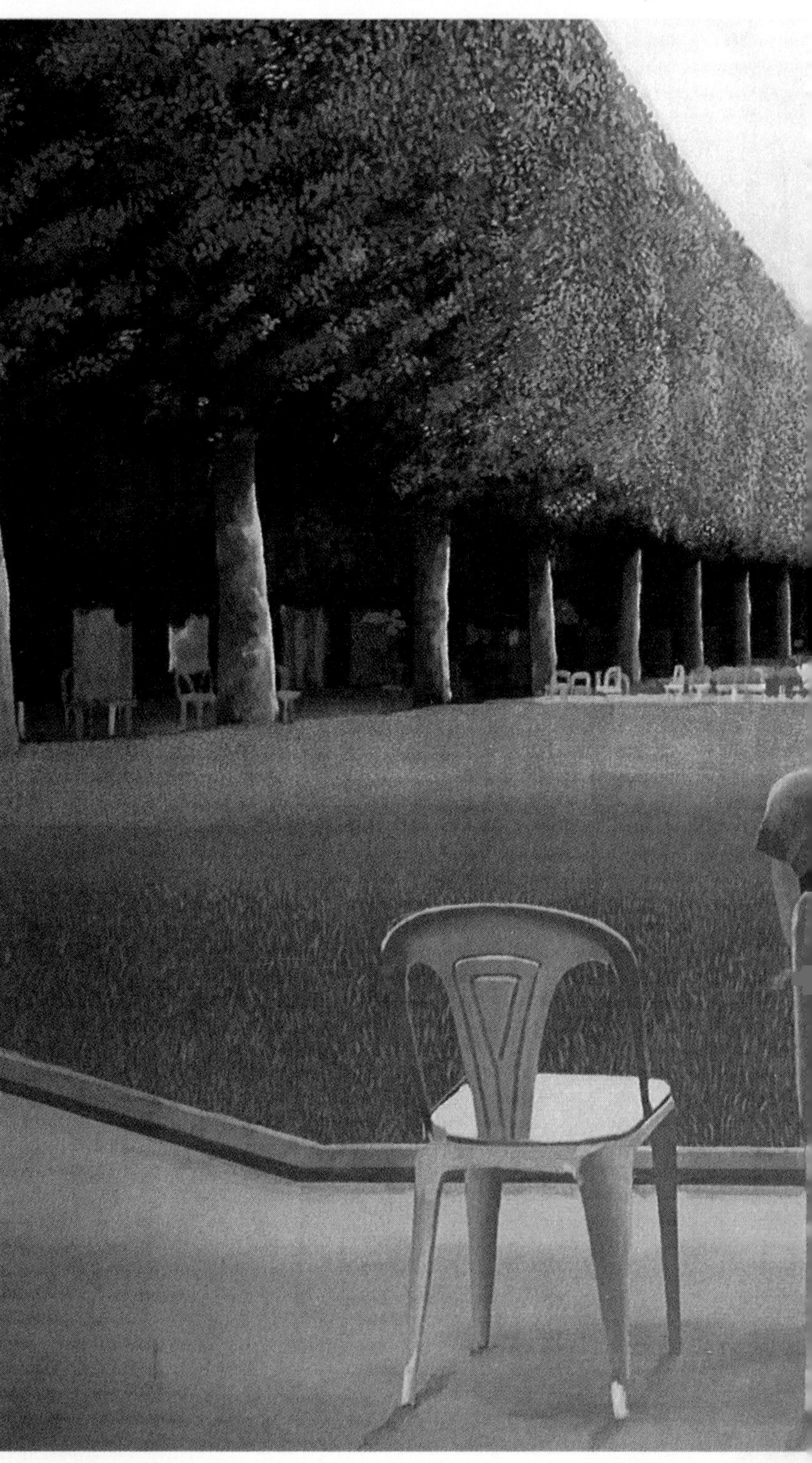

Le Parc Des Sources by David Hockney.

See **SETTING** Handbook of Literary Terms

The Boar Hunt

José Vasconcelos Mexico

The promise of adventure attracts four hunters to unexplored jungles of the Amazon. There they discover where greed and recklessness can lead.

We were four companions, and we went by the names of our respective nationalities: the Colombian, the Peruvian, the Mexican; the fourth, a native of Ecuador, was called Quito[1] for short. Unforeseen chance had joined us together a few years ago on a large sugar plantation on the Peruvian coast. We worked at different occupations during the day and met during the evening in our off time. Not being Englishmen, we did not play cards. Instead, our constant discussions led to disputes. These didn't stop us from wanting to see each other the next night, however, to continue the interrupted debates and support them with new arguments. Nor did the rough sentences of the preceding wrangles indicate a lessening of our affection, of which we assured ourselves reciprocally with the clasping of hands and a look. On Sundays we used to go on hunting parties. We roamed the fertile glens, stalking, generally with poor results, the game of the warm region around the coast, or we entertained ourselves killing birds that flew in the sunlight during the siesta hour.

We came to be tireless wanderers and excellent marksmen. Whenever we climbed a hill and gazed at the imposing range of mountains in the interior, its attractiveness stirred us and we wanted to climb it. What attracted us more was the trans-Andean region:[2] fertile plateaus extending on the other side of the range in the direction of the Atlantic toward the immense land of Brazil. It was as if primitive nature called us to her breast. The vigor of the fertile, untouched jungles promised to rejuvenate our minds, the same vigor which rejuvenates the strength and the thickness of the trees each year. At times we devised crazy plans. As with all things that are given a lot of thought, these schemes generally materialized. Ultimately nature and events are largely what our imaginations make them out to be. And so we went ahead planning and acting. At the end of the year, with arranged vacations, accumulated money, good rifles, abundant munitions, stone- and mud-proof boots, four hammocks, and a half dozen faithful Indians, our caravan descended the Andean slopes, leading to the endless green ocean.

At last we came upon a village at the edge of the Marañón River.[3] Here we changed our safari. The region we were going to penetrate had no roads. It was unexplored underbrush into which we could enter only by going down the river in a canoe. In time we came to the area where we

1. ***Ecuador*** (ek'wə dôr) . . . ***Quito*** (kē'tō). Ecuador is located in northwestern South America; Quito is its capital.
2. ***trans-Andean region,*** the area across—that is, to the east of—the Andes Mountains. The Andes run in a generally north-south direction through the length of South America.
3. ***Marañón*** (mä'rä nyôn') ***River,*** a river in Peru, flowing north and then east into the Amazon.

"The Boar Hunt" by José Vasconcelos, translated by Paul Waldorf, from *The Muse in Mexico: A Mid-Century Miscellany, Supplement to the Texas Quarterly,* Volume II, Number 1, Spring 1959, pp. 64–69. Reprinted by permission of The University of Texas Press.

José Vasconcelos (hō zā' väs kōn sā'lōs).

proposed to carry out the purpose of our journey, the hunting of wild boars.

We had been informed that boars travel in herds of several thousands, occupying a region, eating grass and staying together, exploiting the grazing areas, organized just like an army. They are very easy to kill if one attacks them when they are scattered out satisfying their appetites—an army given over to the delights of victory. When they march about hungry, on the other hand, they are usually vicious. In our search we glided down river between imposing jungles with our provisions and the company of three faithful Indian oarsmen.

One morning we stopped at some huts near the river. Thanks to the information gathered there, we decided to disembark a little farther on in order to spend the night on land and continue the hunt for the boars in the thicket the following day.

Sheltered in a backwater, we came ashore, and after a short exploration found a clearing in which to make camp. We unloaded the provisions and the rifles, tied the boat securely, then with the help of the Indians set up our camp one-half kilometer from the riverbank. In marking the path to the landing, we were careful not to lose ourselves in the thicket. The Indians withdrew toward their huts, promising to return two days later. At dawn we would set out in search of the prey.

Though night had scarcely come and the heat was great, we gathered at the fire to see each other's faces, to look instinctively for protection. We talked a little, confessed to being tired, and decided to go to bed. Each hammock had been tied by one end to a single tree, firm though not very thick in the trunk. Stretching out from this axis in different directions, the hammocks were supported by the other end on other trunks. Each of us carried his rifle, cartridges, and some provisions which couldn't remain exposed on the ground. The sight of the weapons made us consider the place where we were, surrounded by the unknown. A slight feeling of terror made us laugh, cough, and talk. But fatigue overcame us, that heavy fatigue which compels the soldier to scorn danger, to put down his rifle, and to fall asleep though the most persistent enemy pursues him. We scarcely noticed the supreme grandeur of that remote tropical night.

I don't know whether it was the light of the magnificent dawn or the strange noises which awakened me and made me sit up in my hammock and look carefully at my surroundings. I saw nothing but the awakening of that life which at night falls into the lethargy of the jungle. I called my sleeping companions and, alert and seated in our hanging beds, we dressed ourselves. We were preparing to jump to the ground when we clearly heard a somewhat distant, sudden sound of rustling branches. Since it did not continue, however, we descended confidently, washed our faces with water from our canteens, and slowly prepared and enjoyed breakfast. By about 11:00 in the morning we were armed and bold and preparing to make our way through the jungle.

But then the sound again. Its persistence and proximity in the thicket made us change our minds. An instinct made us take refuge in our hammocks. We cautiously moved our cartridges and rifles into them again, and without consulting each other we agreed on the idea of putting our provisions safely away. We passed them up into the hammocks, and we ourselves finally climbed in. Stretched out face down, comfortably suspended with rifles in hand, we did not have to wait long. Black, agile boars quickly appeared from all directions. We welcomed them with shouts of joy and well-aimed shots. Some fell immediately, giving comical snorts, but many more came out of the jungle. We shot again, spending all the cartridges in the magazine. Then we stopped to reload. Finding ourselves safe in the height of our hammocks, we continued after a pause.

We counted dozens of them. At a glance we made rapid calculations of the magnitude of the destruction, while the boars continued to come out of the jungle in uncountable numbers. Instead of going on their way or fleeing, they seemed confused. All of them emerged from the jungle where it was easy for us to shoot them. Occasionally we had to stop firing because the frequent shooting heated the barrels of our rifles. While they were cooling we were able to joke, celebrating our good fortune. The impotent anger of the boars amazed us. They raised their tusks in our direction, uselessly threatening us. We laughed at their snorts, quietly aimed at those who were near, and Bang! a dead boar. We carefully studied the angle of the shoulder blade so that the bullet would cross the heart. The slaughter lasted for hours.

At 4:00 P.M. we noticed an alarming shortage of our ammunition. We had been well supplied and had shot at will. Though the slaughter was gratifying, the boars must have numbered, as we had been informed previously, several thousands, because their hordes didn't diminish. On the contrary, they gathered directly beneath our hammocks in increasing groups. They slashed furiously at the trunk of the tree which held the four points of the hammocks. The marks of the tusks remained on the hard bark. Not without a certain fear we watched them gather compactly, tenaciously, in tight masses against the resisting trunk. We wondered what would happen to a man who fell within their reach. Our shots were now sporadic, well aimed, carefully husbanded. They did not drive away the aggressive beasts, but only redoubled their fury. One of us ironically noted that from being the attackers we had gone on the defensive. We did not laugh very long at the joke. Now we hardly shot at all. We needed to save our cartridges.

The afternoon waned and evening came upon us. After consulting each other, we decided to eat in our hammocks. We applauded ourselves for taking the food up—meat, bread, and bottles of water. Stretching ourselves on our hammocks, we passed things to each other, sharing what we needed. The boars deafened us with their angry snorts.

After eating, we began to feel calm. We lit cigars. Surely the boars would go. Their numbers were great, but they would finally leave peacefully. As we said so, however, we looked with greedy eyes at the few unused cartridges that remained. Our enemies, like enormous angry ants, stirred beneath us, encouraged by the ceasing of our fire. From time to time we carefully aimed and killed one or two of them, driving off the huge group of uselessly enraged boars at the base of the trunk which served as a prop for our hammocks.

Night enveloped us almost without our noticing the change from twilight. Anxiety also overtook us. When would the cursed boars leave? Already there were enough dead to serve as trophies to several dozen hunters. Our feat would be talked about; we had to show ourselves worthy of such fame. Since there was nothing else to do, it was necessary to sleep. Even if we had had enough bullets it would have been impossible to continue the fight in the darkness. It occurred to us to start a fire to drive the herd off with flames, but apart from the fact that we couldn't leave the place in which we were suspended, there were no dry branches in the lush forest. Finally, we slept.

We woke up a little after midnight. The darkness was profound, but the well-known noise made us aware that our enemies were still there. We imagined they must be the last ones which were leaving, however. If a good army needs several hours to break camp and march off, what can be expected of a vile army of boars but disorder and delay? The following morning we would fire upon the stragglers, but this painful thought bothered us: they were in large and apparently active numbers. What were they up to? Why didn't they leave? We thus spent long hours of worry. Dawn finally came, splendid in the sky but noisy in the jungle still enveloped inwardly in shadows. We eagerly waited for the sun to penetrate the foliage in order to survey the appearance of the field of battle of the day before.

What we finally saw made us gasp. It terrified us. The boars were painstakingly continuing the work which they had engaged in throughout the entire night. Guided by some extraordinary instinct, with their tusks they were digging out the

ground underneath the tree from which our hammocks hung; they gnawed the roots and continued to undermine them like large, industrious rats. Presently the tree was bound to fall and we with it, among the beasts. From that moment we neither thought nor talked. In desperation we used up our last shots, killing more ferocious beasts. Still, the rest renewed their activity. They seemed to be endowed with intelligence. However much we concentrated our fire against them, they did not stop their attack against the tree.

Soon our shots stopped. We emptied our pistols, and then silently listened to the tusks gnawing beneath the soft, wet, pleasant-smelling earth. From time to time the boars pressed against the tree, pushing it and making it creak, eager to smash it quickly. We looked on, hypnotized by their devilish activity. It was impossible to flee because the black monsters covered every inch in sight. It seemed to us that, by a sudden inspiration, they were preparing to take revenge on us for the ruthless nature of man, the unpunished destroyer of animals since the beginning of time. Our imagination, distorted by fear, showed us our fate as an atonement for the unpardonable crimes implicit in the struggle of biological selection. Before my eyes passed the vision of sacred India, where the believer refuses to eat meat in order to prevent the methodical killing of beasts and in order to atone for man's evil, bloody, treacherous slaughter, such as ours, for mere vicious pleasure. I felt that the multitude of boars was raising its accusing voice against me. I now understood the infamy of the hunter, but what was repentance worth if I was going to die with my companions, hopelessly devoured by that horde of brutes with demonlike eyes?

Stirred by terror and without realizing what I was doing, I hung from the upper end of my hammock, I balanced myself in the air, I swung in a long leap, I grasped a branch of a tree facing the one on which the boars were digging. From there I leaped to other branches and to others, reviving in myself habits which the species had forgotten.

The next moment a terrifying sound and unforgettable cries told me of the fall of the tree and the end of my companions. I clung to a trunk, trembling and listening to the chattering of my jaws. Later, the desire to flee gave me back my strength. Leaning out over the foliage, I looked for a path, and I saw the boars in the distance, marching in compressed ranks and holding their insolent snouts in the air. I knew that they were now withdrawing, and I got down from the tree. Horror overwhelmed me as I approached the site of our encampment, but some idea of duty made me return there. Perhaps one of my friends had managed to save himself. I approached hesitantly. Each dead boar made me tremble with fear.

But what I saw next was so frightful that I could not fix it clearly in my mind: remains of clothing—and footwear. There was no doubt; the boars had devoured them. Then I ran toward the river, following the tracks we had made two days before. I fled with great haste, limbs stiff from panic.

Running with long strides, I came upon the boat. With a great effort, I managed to row to the huts. There I went to bed with a high fever which lasted many days.

I will participate in no more hunts. I will contribute, if I have to, to the extermination of harmful beasts. But I will not kill for pleasure. I will not amuse myself with the ignoble pleasure of the hunt.

Discussion

1. (a) What first brings the four men together? **(b)** Describe their relationship with one another. **(c)** Why is it important to the meaning of the story that they all be of different nationalities?

2. (a) Where and how do the men go about setting up their camp? **(b)** Why do you think they decide to tie all four hammocks to one tree? **(c)** In what way is this decision significant to what happens later?

3. (a) List some of the descriptive details the author uses to emphasize the extent of the slaughter of the boars. **(b)** Why, in your opinion, does the author describe the slaughter so vividly?

4. (a) At what point do the men begin to change from being the attackers to being on the defensive? **(b)** At what point are they completely on the defensive?

5. By the story's end, the narrator has developed strong feelings about hunting for sport. Based on what has happened, what other strong feelings might he be experiencing?

Application

Setting

The place where this story is set is fairly specific—near the Marañón River, east of the Andes Mountains in Peru. However, what the area looks like becomes clear only gradually: details are presented throughout the story.

1. Using these details, describe the setting in your own words.

2. How important is the setting to what happens in the story—that is, would the story work as well if set elsewhere? Defend your answer.

3. What aspect of setting is never made clear? Why do you think it is not mentioned?

Vocabulary

Context, Dictionary

A. One aid in understanding a word you don't know is context—the setting in which the word appears. Read each of the following quotations from "The Boar Hunt." If there is enough information to determine the meaning of the italicized word, write what you think it means on a separate sheet of paper. If there is not enough information, write "no."

1. "The afternoon *waned* and evening came upon us."

2. "The *impotent* anger of the boars amazed us."

3. "I saw nothing but the awakening of that life which at night falls into the *lethargy* of the jungle."

4. "We shot again, spending all the cartridges in the *magazine.*"

5. "They were digging out the ground underneath the tree from which our hammocks hung; they gnawed the roots and continued to *undermine* them."

B. Check the Glossary for the meanings and pronunciations of all the italicized words; then use each in an original sentence that shows you understand its meaning.

José Vasconcelos 1882–1959

A thinker and a politician as well as an author, José Vasconcelos did much to improve the level of living in his native land of Mexico. Not long after the revolution of 1910, Vasconcelos was appointed Minister of Public Education by the new government. During this period (1920–1924) he instituted important reforms in the educational system and was responsible for the opening of many rural schools. Extending his activities to cultural matters, he commissioned the first murals for public buildings, assisted orchestras and musicians, and invited other Latin American intellectual leaders to Mexico. In 1929 he even made an unsuccessful run for the presidency.

Vasconcelos's most important literary work is undoubtedly his multi-volume autobiography, one of the best studies of culture and life in twentieth-century Mexico ever written. He also produced essays and philosophical books.

See **CHARACTERIZATION** Handbook of Literary Terms

A Visit to Grandmother

William Melvin Kelley USA

Three generations—grandmother, son, and grandson—and a long-unspoken misunderstanding that has in some way touched each one.

Chig knew something was wrong the instant his father kissed her. He had always known his father to be the warmest of men, a man so kind that when people ventured timidly into his office, it took only a few words from him to make them relax, and even laugh. Doctor Charles Dunford cared about people.

But when he had bent to kiss the old lady's black face, something new and almost ugly had come into his eyes: fear, uncertainty, sadness, and perhaps even hatred.

Ten days before in New York, Chig's father had decided suddenly he wanted to go to Nashville to attend his college class reunion, twenty years out. Both Chig's brother and sister, Peter and Connie, were packing for camp and besides were too young for such an affair. But Chig was seventeen, had nothing to do that summer, and his father asked if he would like to go along. His father had given him additional reasons: "All my running buddies got their diplomas and were snapped up by them crafty young gals, and had kids within a year—now all those kids, some of them gals, are your age."

The reunion had lasted a week. As they packed for home, his father, in a far too offhand way, had suggested they visit Chig's grandmother. "We're this close. We might as well drop in on her and my brothers."

So, instead of going north, they had gone farther south, had just entered her house. And Chig had a suspicion now that the reunion had been only an excuse to drive south, that his father had been heading to this house all the time.

His father had never talked much about his family, with the exception of his brother, GL, who seemed part con man, part practical joker, and part Don Juan; he had spoken of GL with the kind of indulgence he would have shown a cute, but ill-behaved and potentially dangerous five-year-old.

Chig's father had left home when he was fifteen. When asked why, he would answer: "I wanted to go to school. They didn't have a Negro high school at home, so I went up to Knoxville and lived with a cousin and went to school."

They had been met at the door by Aunt Rose, GL's wife, and ushered into the living room. The old lady had looked up from her seat by the window. Aunt Rose stood between the visitors.

The old lady eyed his father. "Rose, who that? Rose?" She squinted. She looked like a doll made of black straw, the wrinkles in her face running in one direction like the head of a broom. Her hair was white and coarse and grew out straight from her head. Her eyes were brown—the whites, too, seemed light brown—and were hidden behind thick glasses, which remained somehow on a tiny nose. "That Hiram?" That was another of his father's brothers. "No, it ain't

Hiram; too big for Hiram." She turned then to Chig. "Now that man, he look like Eleanor, Charles's wife, but Charles wouldn't never send my grandson to see me. I never even hear from Charles." She stopped again.

"It Charles, Mama. That who it is." Aunt Rose, between them, led them closer. "It Charles come all the way from New York to see you, and brung little Charles with him."

The old lady stared up at them. "Charles? Rose, that really Charles?" She turned away, and reached for a handkerchief in the pocket of her clean, ironed, flowered housecoat, and wiped her eyes. "God have mercy, Charles." She spread her arms up to him, and he bent down and kissed her cheek. That was when Chig saw his face, grimacing. She hugged him; Chig watched the muscles in her arms as they tightened around his father's neck. She half rose out of her chair. "How are you, son?"

Chig could not hear his father's answer.

She let him go, and fell back into her chair, grabbing the arms. Her hands were as dark as the wood, and seemed to become part of it. "Now, who that standing there? Who that man?"

"That's one of your grandsons, Mama." His father's voice cracked. "Charles Dunford, junior. You saw him once, when he was a baby, in Chicago. He's grown now."

"I can see that, boy!" She looked at Chig squarely. "Come here, son, and kiss me once." He did. "What they call you? Charles too?"

"No, ma'am, they call me Chig."

She smiled. She had all her teeth, but they were too perfect to be her own. "That's good. Can't have two boys answering to Charles in the same house. Won't nobody at all come. So you that little boy. You don't remember me, do you. I used to take you to church in Chicago, and you'd get up and hop in time to the music. You studying to be a preacher?"

"No, ma'am. I don't think so. I might be a lawyer."

"You'll be an honest one, won't you?"

"I'll try."

"Trying ain't enough! You be honest, you

hear? Promise me. You be honest like your daddy."

"All right. I promise."

"Good. Rose, where's GL at? Where's that thief? He gone again?"

"I don't know, Mama." Aunt Rose looked embarrassed. "He say he was going by his liquor store. He'll be back."

"Well, then where's Hiram? You call up those boys, and get them over here—now! You got enough to eat? Let me go see." She started to get up. Chig reached out his hand. She shook him off. "What they tell you about me, Chig? They tell you I'm all laid up? Don't believe it. They don't know nothing about old ladies. When I want help, I'll let you know. Only time I'll need help getting anywheres is when I dies and they lift me into the ground."

She was standing now, her back and shoulders straight. She came only to Chig's chest. She squinted up at him. "You eat much? Your daddy ate like two men."

"Yes, ma'am."

"That's good. That means you ain't nervous.

Your mama, she ain't nervous. I remember that. In Chicago, she'd sit down by a window all afternoon and never say nothing, just knit." She smiled. "Let me see what we got to eat."

"I'll do that, Mama." Aunt Rose spoke softly. "You haven't seen Charles in a long time. You sit and talk."

The old lady squinted at her. "You can do the cooking if you promise it ain't because you think I can't."

Aunt Rose chuckled. "I know you can do it, Mama."

"All right. I'll just sit and talk a spell." She sat again and arranged her skirt around her short legs.

Chig did most of the talking, told all about himself before she asked. His father only spoke when he was spoken to, and then only one word at a time, as if by coming back home, he had become a small boy again, sitting in the parlor while his mother spoke with her guests.

When Uncle Hiram and Mae, his wife, came, they sat down to eat. Chig did not have to ask about Uncle GL's absence; Aunt Rose volunteered an explanation: "Can't never tell where the man is at. One Thursday morning he left here and next thing we knew, he was calling from Chicago, saying he went up to see Joe Louis fight. He'll be here though; he ain't as young and footloose as he used to be." Chig's father had mentioned driving down that GL was about five years older than he was, nearly fifty.

Uncle Hiram was somewhat smaller than Chig's father; his short-cropped kinky hair was half gray, half black. One spot, just off his forehead, was totally white. Later, Chig found out it had been that way since he was twenty. Mae (Chig could not bring himself to call her Aunt) was a good deal younger than Hiram, pretty enough so that Chig would have looked at her twice on the street. She was a honey-colored woman, with long eyelashes. She was wearing a white sheath.

At dinner, Chig and his father sat on one side, opposite Uncle Hiram and Mae; his grandmother and Aunt Rose sat at the ends. The food was good; there was a lot and Chig ate a lot. All through the meal, they talked about the family as it had been thirty years before, and particularly about the young GL. Mae and Chig asked questions; the old lady answered; Aunt Rose directed the discussion, steering the old lady onto the best stories; Chig's father laughed from time to time. Uncle Hiram ate.

"Why don't you tell them about the horse, Mama?" Aunt Rose, over Chig's weak protest, was spooning mashed potatoes onto his plate. "There now, Chig."

"I'm trying to think." The old lady was holding her fork halfway to her mouth, looking at them over her glasses. "Oh, you talking about that crazy horse GL brung home that time."

"That's right, Mama." Aunt Rose nodded and slid another slice of white meat on Chig's plate.

Mae started to giggle. "Oh, I've heard this. This is funny, Chig."

The old lady put down her fork and began: Well, GL went out of the house one day with an old, no-good chair I wanted him to take over to the church for a bazaar, and he met up with this man who'd just brung in some horses from out West. Now, I reckon you can expect one swindler to be in every town, but you don't rightly think there'll be two, and heaven forbid they should ever meet—but they did, GL and his chair, this man and his horses. Well, I wished I'd-a been there; there must-a been some mighty high-powered talking going on. That man with his horses, he told GL them horses was half Arab, half Indian, and GL told that man the chair was an antique he'd stole from some rich white folks. So they swapped. Well, I was a-looking out the window and seen GL dragging this animal to the house. It looked pretty gentle and its eyes was most closed and its feet was shuffling.

"GL, where'd you get that thing?" I says.

"I swapped him for that old chair, Mama," he says. "And made myself a bargain. This is even better than Papa's horse."

Well, I'm a-looking at this horse and noticing how he be looking more and more wide-awake every minute, sort of warming up like a teakettle until, I swears to you, that horse is blowing steam out its nose.

"Come on, Mama," GL says, "come on and I'll take you for a ride." Now George, my husband, God rest his tired soul, he'd brung home this white folks' buggy which had a busted wheel and fixed it and was to take it back that day and GL says: "Come on, Mama, we'll use this fine buggy and take us a ride."

"GL," I says, "no, we ain't. Them white folks'll burn us alive if we use their buggy. You just take that horse right on back." You see, I was sure that boy'd come by that animal ungainly.

"Mama, I can't take him back," GL says.

"Why not?" I says.

"Because I don't rightly know where that man is at," GL says.

"Oh," I says. "Well, then I reckon we stuck with it." And I turned to go back into the house because it was getting late, near dinner time, and I was cooking for ten.

"Mama," GL says to my back. "Mama, ain't you coming for a ride with me?"

"Go on, boy. You ain't getting me inside kicking range of that animal." I was eying that beast and it was boiling hotter all the time. I reckon maybe that man had drugged it. "That horse is wild, GL," I says.

"No, he ain't. He ain't. That man say he is buggy and saddle broke and as sweet as the inside of an apple."

My oldest girl, Essie, had-a come out on the porch and she says: "Go on, Mama. I'll cook. You ain't been out the house in weeks."

"Sure, come on, Mama," GL says. "There ain't nothing to be fidgety about. This horse is gentle as a rose petal." And just then that animal snorts so hard it sets up a little dust storm around its feet.

"Yes, Mama," Essie says, "you can see he gentle." Well, I looked at Essie and then at that horse because I didn't think we could be looking at the same animal. I should-a figured how Essie's eyes ain't never been so good.

"Come on, Mama," GL says.

"All right," I says. So I stood on the porch and watched GL hitching that horse up to the white folks' buggy. For a while there, the animal was pretty quiet, pawing a little, but not much. And I was feeling a little better about riding with GL behind that crazy-looking horse. I could see how GL was happy I was going with him. He was scurrying around that animal buckling buckles and strapping straps, all the time smiling, and that made me feel good.

Then he was finished, and I must say, that horse looked mighty fine hitched to that buggy and I knew anybody what climbed up there would look pretty good, too. GL came around and stood at the bottom of the steps, and took off his hat and bowed and said: "Madam," and reached out his hand to me and I was feeling real elegant like a fine lady. He helped me up to the seat and then got up beside me and we moved out down our alley. And I remember how black folks came out on their porches and shook their heads, saying: "Will you *look* at Eva Dunford, the fine lady! Don't she look good sitting up there!" And I pretended not to hear and sat up straight and proud.

We rode on through the center of town, up Market Street, and all the way out where Hiram is living now, which in them days was all woods, there not being even a farm in sight, and that's when that horse must-a first realized he weren't at all broke or tame or maybe thought he was back out West again, and started to gallop.

"GL," I says, "now you ain't joking with your mama, is you? Because if you is, I'll strap you purple if I live through this."

Well, GL was pulling on the reins with all his meager strength, and yelling, "Whoa, you. Say now, whoa!" He turned to me just long enough to say, "I ain't fooling with you, Mama. Honest!"

I reckon that animal weren't too satisfied with the road, because it made a sharp right turn just then, down into a gulley and struck out across a hilly meadow. "Mama," GL yells. "Mama, do something!"

I didn't know what to do, but I figured I had to

do something so I stood up, hopped down onto the horse's back, and pulled it to a stop. Don't ask me how I did that; I reckon it was that I was a mother and my baby asked me to do something, is all.

"Well, we walked that animal all the way home; sometimes I had to club it over the nose with my fist to make it come, but we made it, GL and me. You remember how tired we was, Charles?"

"I wasn't here at the time." Chig turned to his father and found his face completely blank, without even a trace of a smile or a laugh.

"Well, of course you was, son. That happened in . . . in . . . it was a hot summer that year and—"

"I left here in June of that year. You wrote me about it."

The old lady stared past Chig at him. They all turned to him; Uncle Hiram looked up from his plate.

"Then you don't remember how we all laughed?"

"No, I don't, Mama. And I probably wouldn't have laughed. I don't think it was funny." They were staring into each other's eyes.

"Why not, Charles?"

"Because in the first place, the horse was gained by fraud. And in the second place, both of you might have been seriously injured or even killed." He broke off their stare and spoke to himself more than to any of them: "And if I'd done it, you would've beaten me good for it."

"Pardon?" The old lady had not heard him; only Chig had heard.

Chig's father sat up straight as if preparing to debate. "I said that if I had done it, if I had done just exactly what GL did, you would have beaten me good for it, Mama." He was looking at her again.

"Why you say that, son?" She was leaning toward him.

"Don't you know? Tell the truth. It can't hurt me now." His voice cracked, but only once. "If GL and I did something wrong, you'd beat me first and then be too tired to beat him. At dinner, he'd always get seconds and I wouldn't. You'd do things with him, like ride in that buggy, but if I wanted you to do something with me, you were always too busy." He paused and considered whether to say what he finally did say: "I cried when I left here. Nobody loved me, Mama. I cried all the way up to Knoxville. That was the last time I ever cried in my life."

"Oh, Charles." She started to get up, to come around the table to him.

He stopped her. "It's too late."

"But you don't understand."

"What don't I understand? I understood then; I understand now."

Tears now traveled down the lines in her face, but when she spoke, her voice was clear. "I thought you knew. I had ten children. I had to give all of them what they needed most." She nodded. "I paid more mind to GL. I had to. GL could-a ended up swinging if I hadn't. But you was smarter. You was more growed up than GL when you was five and he was ten, and I tried to show you that by letting you do what you wanted to do."

"That's not true, Mama. You know it. GL was light-skinned and had good hair and looked almost white and you loved him for that."

"Charles, no. No, son. I didn't love any one of you more than any other."

"That can't be true." His father was standing now, his fists clenched tight. "Admit it, Mama . . . please!" Chig looked at him, shocked; the man was actually crying.

"It may not-a been right what I done, but I ain't no liar." Chig knew she did not really understand what had happened, what he wanted of her. "I'm not lying to you, Charles."

Chig's father had gone pale. He spoke very softly. "You're about thirty years too late, Mama." He bolted from the table. Silverware and dishes rang and jumped. Chig heard him hurrying up to their room.

They sat in silence for a while and then heard a key in the front door. A man with a new, lacquered straw hat came in. He was wearing brown and white two-tone shoes with very pointed toes and a white summer suit. "Say now! Man! I heard my brother was in town. Where he at? Where that rascal?"

He stood in the doorway, smiling broadly, an engaging, open, friendly smile, the innocent smile of a five-year-old.

Discussion

1. Is it merely coincidental that Dr. Dunford and Chig pay a visit to Chig's grandmother? Explain.

2. (a) How does Dr. Dunford react to his mother's greeting? **(b)** Why is Chig surprised by his reaction? **(c)** What might be going on in Chig's mind as he watches his father?

3. Dr. Dunford left home when he was fifteen. In what other ways is he different from the others in his family?

4. At one point Mrs. Dunford says, "I had ten children. I had to give all of them what they needed most." **(a)** What did she feel she was giving to GL? **(b)** What did she feel she was giving to Chig's father? **(c)** How might she have been responsible for Dr. Dunford's becoming a successful physician?

5. One student has commented that this story is about a misunderstanding based on love. Do you agree? Explain.

Application

Characterization

Depending on the techniques an author uses and his or her skill at using them, sometimes the character of a figure in a story can be made clear before that character ever actually appears. GL, for example, is not introduced until the very end of "A Visit to Grandmother," but by then the reader knows him rather well.

1. What methods of characterization has the author used to accomplish this?

2. Does the information he presents about GL in the last sentence of the story change your opinion of GL? of Dr. Dunford? Explain.

3. Who would you say is the most important character in the story? Defend your answer.

Composition

Just as the account of the frantic buggy ride revealed GL's personal characteristics in the story, a particular incident can sometimes make clear the qualities of a person in real life. Reconstruct from your memory an incident that showed something significant about a person you know; if necessary, jot down the steps of the incident and why they were important. (See "Prewriting," page 655, in the Composition Guide.)

Write a three- or four-paragraph character sketch built around the incident. You may want to begin by introducing the person and perhaps giving a clue as to what the incident is going to demonstrate about him or her.

William Melvin Kelley 1937–

Although many of his stories have southern settings, William Melvin Kelley was born and raised in New York City. He was educated at Harvard University and later taught at the New School for Social Research, but most of his adult life has been involved with writing. His novels include, among others, *A Different Drummer, A Drop of Patience,* and *Dunfords Travels Everywhere;* and his short stories have appeared in numerous magazines and anthologies.

Kelley is often exasperated by reviewers who put all black writers into one category under the assumption that they speak for American blacks in general. As he has written, "I am not a sociologist or a politician or a spokesman. Such people try to give answers. A writer, I think, should ask questions. He should depict people, not symbols or ideas disguised as people."

See **PLOT** Handbook of Literary Terms

The Monkey's Paw

W. W. Jacobs Great Britain

"If I could have three wishes . . ." —the start of many a daydream. But the fulfillment of such wishes may lead to nightmarish consequences.

Without, the night was cold and wet, but in the small parlor of Lakesnam Villa the blinds were drawn and the fire burned brightly. Father and son were at chess, the former, who possessed ideas about the game involving radical changes, putting his king into such sharp and unnecessary perils that it even provoked comment from the white-haired old lady knitting placidly by the fire.

"Hark at the wind," said Mr. White, who, having seen a fatal mistake after it was too late, was amiably desirous of preventing his son from seeing it.

"I'm listening," said the latter, grimly surveying the board as he stretched out his hand. "Check."[1]

"I should hardly think that he'd come tonight," said his father, with his hand poised over the board.

"Mate," replied the son.

"That's the worst of living so far out," bawled Mr. White, with sudden and unlooked-for violence; "of all the beastly, slushy, out-of-the-way places to live in, this is the worst. Pathway's a bog, and the road's a torrent. I don't know what people are thinking about. I suppose because only two houses on the road are let, they think it doesn't matter."

"Never mind, dear," said his wife soothingly; "perhaps you'll win the next one."

Mr. White looked up sharply, just in time to intercept a knowing glance between mother and son. The words died away on his lips, and he had a guilty grin in his thin gray beard.

"There he is," said Herbert White, as the gate banged to loudly and heavy footsteps came toward the door.

The old man rose with hospitable haste, and opening the door, was heard condoling with the new arrival. The new arrival also condoled with himself, so that Mrs. White said "Tut, tut!" and coughed gently as her husband entered the room, followed by a tall burly man, beady of eye and rubicund of visage.

"Sergeant-Major Morris," he said, introducing him.

The sergeant-major shook hands, and, taking the proffered seat by the fire, watched contentedly while his host got out whiskey and tumblers and stood a small copper kettle on the fire.

At the third glass his eyes got brighter, and he began to talk, the little family circle regarding with eager interest this visitor from distant parts, as he squared his broad shoulders in the chair and spoke of strange scenes and doughty deeds, of wars and plagues and strange peoples.

---

1. ***Check,*** a call made by a chess player to warn an opponent that the opponent's king piece is in danger and must be moved. When a chess player makes the winning move that will capture the opponent's king, he or she calls "Mate."

"Twenty-one years of it," said Mr. White, nodding at his wife and son. "When he went away he was a slip of a youth in the warehouse. Now look at him."

"He don't look to have taken much harm," said Mrs. White politely.

"I'd like to go to India myself," said the old man, "just to look round a bit, you know."

"Better where you are," said the sergeant-major, shaking his head. He put down the empty glass and, sighing softly, shook it again.

"I should like to see those old temples and

fakirs and jugglers,'' said the old man. ''What was that you started telling me the other day about a monkey's paw or something, Morris?''

''Nothing,'' said the soldier hastily. ''Leastways, nothing worth hearing.''

''Monkey's paw?'' said Mrs. White curiously.

''Well, it's just a bit of what you might call magic, perhaps,'' said the sergeant-major offhandedly.

His three listeners leaned forward eagerly. The visitor absent-mindedly put his empty glass to his lips and then set it down again. His host filled it for him.

''To look at,'' said the sergeant-major, fumbling in his pocket, ''it's just an ordinary little paw, dried to a mummy.''

He took something out of his pocket and proffered it. Mrs. White drew back with a grimace, but her son, taking it, examined it curiously.

''And what is there special about it?'' inquired Mr. White, as he took it from his son and, having examined it, placed it upon the table.

''It had a spell put on it by an old fakir,'' said the sergeant-major, ''a very holy man. He wanted to show that fate ruled people's lives, and that those who interfered with it did so to their sorrow. He put a spell on it so that three separate men could each have three wishes from it.''

His manner was so impressive that his hearers were conscious that their light laughter jarred somewhat.

''Well, why don't you have three, sir?'' said Herbert White cleverly.

The soldier regarded him in the way that middle age is wont to regard presumptuous youth. ''I have,'' he said quietly, and his blotchy face whitened.

''And did you really have the three wishes granted?'' asked Mrs. White.

''I did,'' said the sergeant-major, and his glass tapped against his strong teeth.

''And has anybody else wished?'' inquired the old lady.

''The first man had his three wishes, yes,'' was the reply. ''I don't know what the first two were, but the third was for death. That's how I got the paw.''

His tones were so grave that a hush fell upon the group.

''If you've had your three wishes, it's no good to you now, then, Morris,'' said the old man at last. ''What do you keep it for?''

The soldier shook his head. ''Fancy, I suppose,'' he said slowly. ''I did have some idea of selling it, but I don't think I will. It has caused enough mischief already. Besides, people won't buy. They think it's a fairy tale, some of them, and those who do think anything of it want to try it first and pay me afterward.''

''If you could have another three wishes,'' said the old man, eying him keenly, ''would you have them?''

''I don't know,'' said the other. ''I don't know.''

He took the paw, and dangling it between his front finger and thumb, suddenly threw it upon the fire. White, with a slight cry, stooped down and snatched it off.

''Better let it burn,'' said the soldier solemnly.

''If you don't want it, Morris,'' said the old man, ''give it to me.''

''I won't,'' said his friend doggedly. ''I threw it on the fire. If you keep it, don't blame me for what happens. Pitch it on the fire again, like a sensible man.''

The other shook his head and examined his new possession closely. ''How do you do it?'' he inquired.

''Hold it up in your right hand and wish aloud,'' said the sergeant-major, ''but I warn you of the consequences.''

''Sounds like the *Arabian Nights,*''[2] said Mrs. White, as she rose and began to set the supper. ''Don't you think you might wish for four pairs of hands for me?''

Her husband drew the talisman from his pocket and then all three burst into laughter as

---

2. *the Arabian Nights,* a collection of old tales from Arabia, Persia, and India, dating from the tenth century.

the sergeant-major, with a look of alarm on his face, caught him by the arm.

"If you must wish," he said gruffly, "wish for something sensible."

Mr. White dropped it back into his pocket, and placing chairs, motioned his friend to the table. In the business of supper the talisman was partly forgotten, and afterward the three sat listening in an enthralled fashion to a second installment of the soldier's adventures in India.

"If the tale about the monkey's paw is not more truthful than those he has been telling us," said Herbert, as the door closed behind their guest, just in time for him to catch the last train, "we shan't make much out of it."

"Did you give him anything for it, Father?" inquired Mrs. White, regarding her husband closely.

"A trifle," said he, coloring slightly. "He didn't want it, but I made him take it. And he pressed me again to throw it away."

"Likely," said Herbert, with pretended horror. "Why, we're going to be rich, and famous, and happy. Wish to be an emperor, Father, to begin with; then you can't be henpecked."

He darted round the table, pursued by the maligned Mrs. White armed with an antimacassar.[3]

Mr. White took the paw from his pocket and eyed it dubiously. "I don't know what to wish for, and that's a fact," he said slowly. "It seems to me I've got all I want."

"If you only cleared the house,[4] you'd be quite happy, wouldn't you?" said Herbert, with his hand on his shoulder. "Well, wish for two hundred pounds,[5] then; that'll just do it."

His father, smiling shamefacedly at his own credulity, held up the talisman, as his son, with a solemn face somewhat marred by a wink at his mother, sat down at the piano and struck a few impressive chords.

"I wish for two hundred pounds," said the old man distinctly.

A fine crash from the piano greeted the words, interrupted by a shuddering cry from the old man. His wife and son ran toward him.

"It moved," he cried, with a glance of disgust at the object as it lay on the floor. "As I wished, it twisted in my hands like a snake."

"Well, I don't see the money," said his son, as he picked it up and placed it on the table, "and I bet I never shall."

"It must have been your fancy, Father," said his wife, regarding him anxiously.

He shook his head. "Never mind, though; there's no harm done, but it gave me a shock all the same."

They sat down by the fire again while the two men finished their pipes. Outside, the wind was higher than ever, and the old man started nervously at the sound of a door banging upstairs. A silence unusual and depressing settled upon all three, which lasted until the old couple rose to retire for the night.

"I expect you'll find the cash tied up in a big bag in the middle of your bed," said Herbert, as he bade them good night, "and something horrible squatting up on top of the wardrobe watching you as you pocket your ill-gotten gains."

In the brightness of the wintry sun next morning as it streamed over the breakfast table, Herbert laughed at his fears. There was an air of prosaic wholesomeness about the room which it had lacked on the previous night, and the dirty, shriveled little paw was pitched on the sideboard with a carelessness which betokened no great belief in its virtues.

"I suppose all old soldiers are the same," said Mrs. White. "The idea of our listening to such nonsense! How could wishes be granted in these days? And if they could, how could two hundred pounds hurt you, Father?"

"Might drop on his head from the sky," said the frivolous Herbert.

"Morris said the things happened so natur-

---

3. ***antimacassar*** (an′ti mə kas′ər), small covering to protect the back or arms of a chair or sofa from soiling.

4. ***cleared the house,*** paid the money that was still owing on the purchase of a house.

5. ***two hundred pounds.*** At the time of the story, this amount in English money was worth about one thousand American dollars.

ally," said his father, "that you might if you wished attribute it to coincidence."

"Well, don't break into the money before I come back," said Herbert, as he rose from the table. "I'm afraid it'll turn you into a mean, avaricious man, and we shall have to disown you."

His mother laughed, and following him to the door, watched him down the road, and returning to the breakfast table, was very happy at the expense of her husband's credulity. All of which did not prevent her from scurrying to the door at the postman's knock, nor prevent her from referring somewhat shortly to retired sergeant-majors of bibulous habits when she found that the post brought a tailor's bill.

"Herbert will have some more of his funny remarks, I expect, when he comes home," she said as they sat at dinner.

"I dare say," said Mr. White, pouring himself out some beer; "but for all that, the thing moved in my hand; that I'll swear to."

"You thought it did," said the old lady soothingly.

"I say it did," replied the other. "There was no thought about it; I had just—What's the matter?"

His wife made no reply. She was watching the mysterious movements of a man outside, who, peering in an undecided fashion at the house, appeared to be trying to make up his mind to enter. In mental connection with the two hundred pounds, she noticed that the stranger was well dressed and wore a silk hat of glossy newness. Three times he paused at the gate and then walked on again. The fourth time he stood with his hand upon it, and then with sudden resolution flung it open and walked up the path. Mrs. White at the same moment placed her hands behind her and hurriedly unfastening the strings of her apron, put that useful article of apparel beneath the cushion of her chair.

She brought the stranger, who seemed ill at ease, into the room. He gazed furtively at Mrs. White, and listened in a preoccupied fashion as the old lady apologized for the appearance of the room, and her husband's coat, a garment which he usually reserved for the garden. She then waited as patiently as her sex would permit for him to broach his business, but he was at first strangely silent.

"I—was asked to call," he said at last, and stooped and picked a piece of cotton from his trousers. "I come from Maw and Meggins."

The old lady started. "Is anything the matter?" she asked breathlessly. "Has anything happened to Herbert? What is it? What is it?"

Her husband interposed. "There, there, Mother," he said hastily. "Sit down, and don't jump to conclusions. You've not brought bad news, I'm sure, sir," and he eyed the other wistfully.

"I'm sorry—" began the visitor.

"Is he hurt?" demanded the mother.

The visitor bowed in assent. "Badly hurt," he said quietly, "but he is not in any pain."

"Oh, thank God!" said the old woman, clasping her hands. "Thank God for that! Thank—"

She broke off suddenly as the sinister meaning of the assurance dawned upon her and she saw the awful confirmation of her fears in the other's averted face. She caught her breath, and turning to her slower-witted husband, laid her trembling old hand upon his. There was a long silence.

"He was caught in the machinery," said the visitor at length, in a low voice.

"Caught in the machinery," repeated Mr. White, in a dazed fashion, "yes."

He sat staring blankly out of the window, and taking his wife's hand between his own, pressed it as he had been wont to do in their old courting days nearly forty years before.

"He was the only one left to us," he said, turning gently to the visitor. "It is hard."

The other coughed, and rising, walked slowly to the window. "The firm wished me to convey their sincere sympathy with you in your great loss," he said, without looking round. "I beg that you will understand I am only their servant and merely obeying orders."

There was no reply; the old woman's face was white, her eyes staring, and her breath inaudible; on the husband's face was a look such as his friend the sergeant might have carried into his first action.

"I was to say that Maw and Meggins disclaim all responsibility," continued the other. "They admit no liability at all, but in consideration of your son's services they wish to present you with a certain sum as compensation."

Mr. White dropped his wife's hand, and rising to his feet, gazed with a look of horror at his visitor. His dry lips shaped the words, "How much?"

"Two hundred pounds," was the answer.

Unconscious of his wife's shriek, the old man smiled faintly, put out his hands like a sightless man, and dropped, a senseless heap, to the floor.

In the huge new cemetery, some two miles distant, the old people buried their dead, and came back to a house steeped in shadow and silence. It was all over so quickly that at first they could hardly realize it and remained in a state of expectation as though of something else to happen—something else which was to lighten this load, too heavy for old hearts to bear. But the days passed, and expectation gave place to resignation—the hopeless resignation of the old, sometimes miscalled apathy. Sometimes they hardly exchanged a word, for now they had nothing to talk about, and their days were long to weariness.

It was about a week after that that the old man, waking suddenly in the night, stretched out his hand and found himself alone. The room was in darkness, and the sound of subdued weeping came from the window. He raised himself in bed and listened.

"Come back," he said tenderly. "You will be cold."

"It is colder for my son," said the old woman and wept afresh.

The sound of her sobs died away on his ears. The bed was warm, and his eyes heavy with sleep. He dozed fitfully, and then slept until a sudden wild cry from his wife awoke him with a start.

"The monkey's paw!" she cried wildly. "The monkey's paw!"

He started up in alarm. "Where? Where is it? What's the matter?"

She came stumbling across the room toward him. "I want it," she said quietly. "You've not destroyed it?"

"It's in the parlor, on the bracket," he replied, marveling. "Why?"

She cried and laughed together, and bending over, kissed his cheek.

"I only just thought of it," she said hysterically. "Why didn't I think of it before? Why didn't you think of it?"

"Think of what?" he questioned.

"The other two wishes," she replied rapidly. "We've only had one."

"Was not that enough?" he demanded fiercely.

"No," she cried triumphantly; "we'll have one more. Go down and get it quickly, and wish our boy alive again."

The man sat up in bed and flung the bedclothes from his quaking limbs. "You are mad!" he cried, aghast.

"Get it," she panted; "get it quickly, and wish—Oh, my boy, my boy!"

Her husband struck a match and lit the candle. "Get back to bed," he said unsteadily. "You don't know what you are saying."

"We had the first wish granted," said the old woman feverishly; "why not the second?"

"A coincidence," stammered the old man.

"Go and get it and wish," cried the old woman, and dragged him toward the door.

He went down in the darkness, and felt his way to the parlor, and then to the mantelpiece. The talisman was in its place, and a horrible fear that the unspoken wish might bring his mutilated son before him ere he could escape from the room seized upon him, and he caught his breath as he found that he had lost the direction of the door. His brow cold with sweat, he felt his way round the table, and groped along the wall until he found himself in the small passage with the unwholesome thing in his hand.

Even his wife's face seemed changed as he entered the room. It was white and expectant, and to his fears seemed to have an unnatural look upon it. He was afraid of her.

"Wish!" she cried, in a strong voice.

"It is foolish and wicked," he faltered.

"Wish!" repeated his wife.

He raised his hand. "I wish my son alive again."

The talisman fell to the floor, and he regarded it shudderingly. Then he sank trembling into a chair as the old woman, with burning eyes, walked to the window and raised the blind.

He sat until he was chilled with the cold, glancing occasionally at the figure of the old woman peering through the window. The candle end, which had burned below the rim of the china candlestick, was throwing pulsating shadows on the ceiling and walls, until, with a flicker larger than the rest, it expired. The old man, with an unspeakable sense of relief at the failure of the talisman, crept back to his bed, and a minute or two afterward the old woman came silently and apathetically beside him.

Neither spoke, but both lay silently listening to the ticking of the clock. A stair creaked, and a squeaky mouse scurried noisily through the wall. The darkness was oppressive, and after lying for some time screwing up his courage, the husband took the box of matches and striking one went downstairs for a candle.

At the foot of the stairs the match went out, and he paused to strike another, and at the same moment a knock, so quiet and stealthy as to be scarcely audible, sounded on the front door.

The matches fell from his hand. He stood motionless, his breath suspended until the knock was repeated. Then he turned and fled swiftly back to his room and closed the door behind him. A third knock sounded through the house.

"*What's that?*" cried the old woman, starting up.

"A rat," said the old man, in shaking tones—"a rat. It passed me on the stairs."

His wife sat up in bed listening. A loud knock resounded through the house.

"It's Herbert!" she screamed. "It's Herbert!"

She ran to the door, but her husband was before her, and catching her by the arm, held her tightly.

"What are you going to do?" he whispered hoarsely.

"It's my boy; it's Herbert!" she cried, struggling mechanically. "I forgot it was two miles away. What are you holding me for? Let go. I must open the door."

"For heaven's sake don't let it in," cried the old man, trembling.

"You're afraid of your own son," she cried, struggling. "Let me go. I'm coming, Herbert; I'm coming."

There was another knock, and another. The old woman with a sudden wrench broke free and ran from the room. Her husband followed to the landing, and called after her appealingly as she hurried downstairs. He heard the chain rattle back and the bottom bolt drawn slowly and stiffly from the socket. Then the old woman's voice, strained and panting.

"The bolt," she cried loudly. "Come down. I can't reach it."

But her husband was on his hands and knees groping wildly on the floor in search of the paw. If he could only find it before the thing outside got in. A perfect fusillade of knocks reverberated through the house, and he heard the scraping of a chair as his wife put it down in the passage against the door. He heard the creaking of the bolt as it came slowly back, and at the same moment he found the monkey's paw and frantically breathed his third and last wish.

The knocking ceased suddenly, although the echoes of it were still in the house. He heard the chair drawn back and the door opened. A cold wind rushed up the staircase, and a long loud wail of disappointment and misery from his wife gave him courage to run down to her side, and then to the gate beyond. The street lamp flickering opposite shone on a quiet and deserted road.

Discussion

1. Contrast the scene outside the Whites' home with the scene in the living room as the Whites await Sergeant-Major Morris's arrival. What does the author intend your attitude toward the White family to be?

2. (a) In what ways does Morris indicate his fear of the monkey's paw? **(b)** Do the Whites share his fear? Why do you think they feel as they do? **(c)** What is significant about Herbert's comment after his father wishes for two hundred pounds?

3. (a) What do Mr. and Mrs. White assume the knocking at their door to be? **(b)** If, as Morris told Mr. White, the monkey's paw fulfills wishes "so naturally that you might . . . attribute [them] to coincidence," could the Whites' assumption about the knocking be right? If not, then how would *you* account for the knocking?

4. What is Mr. White's third wish? Why do you think he makes it?

5. Before he made his first wish, Mr. White said, "I don't know what to wish for, and that's a fact. It seems to me I've got all I want." Comment on this statement in the light of what happens later.

Application
Plot

You have learned that in most short stories the plot is advanced through some conflict. What you may not have realized, however, is that often a story will have two or even three conflicts, and that sometimes one can be the cause of another.

1. At what point does the conflict between Mr. White and the paw actually begin? Explain.

2. When Mr. White begins to deal with the monkey's paw, what internal conflict is initiated in his mind?

3. What is the climax of the story?

Vocabulary
Etymology

At the end of most dictionary entries is the word's etymology—an explanation of its origin and history. Etymologies generally give the language and the original word or words in that language that the entry word is derived from, as well as the meaning of the original word. If an original word or a meaning is not given, you may assume that that element is the same as in English.

Check the Glossary for the etymologies of the following words. For each, list the language the word is derived from and the meaning of the original word.

1. bog; **2.** rubicund; **3.** wont; **4.** fakir; **5.** fusillade.

W. W. Jacobs 1863–1943

Jacobs was born in Wapping, near Tower Bridge, in the ship-docking section of London. There his father was employed as a wharf manager, and there Jacobs gathered the raw material for many of his later stories. Educated privately, Jacobs became a clerk in the Civil Service in 1883, and during the next sixteen years served in a department of the General Post Office. In 1896 his first book, *Many Cargoes,* was published, followed by one-act plays, novels, and short stories. When Jacobs was certain he could support himself by his writing, he left the Civil Service.

The influence of Jacobs's early life around the London docks is reflected in many of his book titles, such as *Light Freights, The Lady of the Barge* (in which "The Monkey's Paw" appeared), and *Deep Waters,* and in the plots of a number of his short stories.

In addition to stories about seamen, Jacobs wrote macabre tales and stories dealing with country village life. Elements of the last two appear in "The Monkey's Paw."

The Parachutist

D'Arcy Niland Australia

"The kitten knew that it had no place here in the heart of space, and its terrified instincts told it that its only contact with solidity and safety was the thing that held it."

The hurricane came down from Capricorn,[1] and for two days and a night it rained.

In the darkness of the second night, softening away to dawn, there was silence. There was only the gurgle and drip of the wet world, and the creatures that lived on the earth began to appear, freed from the tyranny of the elements.

The hawk, ruffled in misery, brooding in ferocity, came forth in hunger and hate. It struck off into the abyss of space, scouring the earth for some booty of the storm—the sheep lying like a heap of wet kapok in the sodden paddocks, the bullock like a dark bladder carried down on the swollen stream and washing against a tree on the river flats, the rabbit, driven from its flooded warren and squeezed dead against a log.

With practiced eye it scrutinized the floating islands of rubble and the wracks of twigs lying askew on the banks for sign of lizard or snake, dead or alive. But there was nothing. Once, in the time before, there had been a rooster, draggled, forlorn, derelict, riding a raft of flotsam: too weak to fight and too sick to care about dying or the way it died.

The hawk rested on a crag of the gorge and conned the terrain with a fierce and frowning eye. The lice worried its body with the sting of nettles. Savagely it plucked with its beak under the fold of its wings, first on one side, then on the other. It rasped its bill on the jagged stone, and dropped over the lip. It climbed in a gliding circle, widening its field of vision.

The earth was yellow and green. On the flats were chains of lagoons as if the sky had broken and fallen in sheets of blue glass. The sun was hot and the air heavy and humid.

Swinging south, the hawk dropped over a vast graveyard of dead timber. The hurricane had ravaged the gaunt trees, splitting them, felling them, tearing off their naked arms and strewing the ground with pieces, like a battlefield of bones, gray with exposure and decay.

A rabbit sprang twenty yards like a bobbing wheel, and the sight drew the hawk like a plummet, but the rabbit vanished in a hollow log, and stayed there, and there was no other life.

Desperate, weak, the hawk alighted on a bleak limb and glared in hate. The sun was a fire on its famished body. Logs smoked with steam and the brightness of water on the earth reflected like mirrors. The telescopic eye inched over the ground—crawled infallibly over the ground, and stopped. And then suddenly the hawk swooped to the ground and tore at the body of a dead field mouse—its belly bloated and a thin vapor drifting from the gray, plastered pelt.

The hawk did not sup as it supped on the hot running blood of the rabbit in the trap—squealing in eyeless terror; it did not feast in stealthy leisure as it did on the sheep paralyzed in the drought, tearing out bit by bit its steaming entrails. Voraciously it ripped at the mouse, swallowing fast and finishing the meal in a few seconds.

---

1. ***Capricorn,*** that is, the Tropic of Capricorn, an imaginary circle around the earth south of the equator, representing the point farthest south at which the sun shines directly overhead. The hurricane came "down" from there because this story is set in the Southern Hemisphere.

D'Arcy Niland (där'sē nī'lənd).

But the food was only a tantalization, serving to make the hawk's appetite more fierce, more lusty. It flew into a tree, rapaciously scanning the countryside. It swerved into space and climbed higher and higher in a vigilant circle, searching the vast expanse below, even to its uttermost limits.

Hard to the west something moved on the earth, a speck: and the hawk watched it: and the speck came up to a walnut, and up to a plum, and up to a ball striped with white and gray.

The hawk did not strike at once. Obedient to instinct, it continued to circle, peering down at the farmhouse and the outbuildings, suspicious; seeing the draught horses in the yard and the fowls in the hen coop, the pigs in the sty, and the windmill twirling, and watching for human life in their precincts.

Away from them all, a hundred yards or more, down on the margin of the fallowed field, the kitten played, leaping and running and tumbling, pawing at a feather and rolling on its back biting at the feather between its forepaws.

Frenzied with hunger, yet ever cautious, the hawk came down in a spiral, set itself, and swooped. The kitten propped and froze with its head cocked on one side, unaware of danger but startled by this new and untried sport. It was no more than if a piece of paper had blown past it in a giant brustle of sound. But in the next moment the hawk fastened its talons in the fur and the fat belly of the kitten, and the kitten spat and twisted, struggling against the power that was lifting it.

Its great wings beating, paddling with the rhythm of oars, the hawk went up a slope of space with its cargo, and the kitten, airborne for the first time in its life, the earth running under it in a blur, wailed in shrill terror. It squirmed frantically as the world fell away in the distance, but the hawk's talons were like the grabs of an iceman.

The air poured like water into the kitten's eyes and broke against its triangular face, streaming back against its rippling furry sides. It howled in infinite fear, and gave a sudden desperate twist, so that the hawk was jolted in its course and dropped to another level, a few feet below the first.

Riding higher and higher on the wind, the hawk went west by the dam like a button of silver far below. The kitten cried now with a new note. Its stomach was wambling. The air gushing into its mouth and nostrils set up a humming in its ears and an aching dizziness in its head. As the hawk turned on its soundless orbit, the sun blazed like flame in the kitten's eyes, leaving its sight to emerge from a blinding grayness.

The kitten knew that it had no place here in the heart of space, and its terrified instincts told it that its only contact with solidity and safety was the thing that held it.

Then the hawk was ready to drop its prey. It was well practiced. Down had gone the rabbit, a whistle in space, to crash in a quiver of death on the ruthless earth. And the hawk had followed to its gluttonous repast.

Now there at two thousand feet the bird hovered. The kitten was alarmingly aware of the change, blinking at the pulsations of beaten air as the wings flapped, hearing only that sound. Unexpectedly, it stopped, and the wings were still—outstretched, but rigid, tilting slightly with the poised body, only the fanned tail lifting and lowering with the flow of the currents.

The kitten felt the talons relax slightly, and that was its warning. The talons opened, but in the first flashing shock of the movement the kitten completed its twist and slashed at the hawk's legs and buried its claws in the flesh like fishhooks. In the next fraction of a second the kitten had consolidated its position, securing its hold, jabbing in every claw except those on one foot which thrust out in space, pushing against insupportable air. And then the claws on this foot were dug in the breast of the hawk.

With a cry of pain and alarm the bird swooped crazily, losing a hundred feet like a dropping stone. And then it righted itself, flying in a drunken sway that diminished as it circled.

Blood from its breast beaded and trickled down the paw of the kitten and spilled into one eye. The kitten blinked, but the blood came and congealed, warm and sticky. The kitten could not turn its head. It was frightened to risk a change of position. The blood slowly built over its eye a blinding pellicle.[2]

The hawk felt a spasm of weakness, and out of it came an accentuation of its hunger and a lust to kill at all costs the victim it had claimed and carried to this place of execution. Lent an excess of power by its ferocity, it started to climb again, desperately trying to dislodge the kitten. But the weight was too much and it could not ascend. A great tiredness came in its dragging body, an ache all along the frames of its wings. The kitten clung tenaciously, staring down at the winding earth and mewling in terror.

For ten minutes the hawk gyrated on a level, defeated and bewildered. All it wanted to do now was to get rid of the burden fastened to its legs and body. It craved respite, a spell on the tallest trees, but it only flew high over these trees, knowing it was unable to perch. Its beak gaped under the harsh ruptures of its breath. It descended three hundred feet. The kitten, with the wisdom of instinct, never altered its position, but rode down like some fantastic parachutist.

In one mighty burst the hawk with striking beak and a terrible flapping of its wings tried finally to cast off its passenger—and nearly suc-

---

2. *pellicle* (pel′ə kəl), a very thin skin; membrane.

ceeded. The kitten miauled[3] in a frenzy of fear at the violence of the sound and the agitation. Its back legs dangled in space, treading air, and like that it went around on the curves of the flight for two minutes. Then it secured a foothold again, even firmer than the first.

In a hysterical rage, the hawk tried once more to lift itself, and almost instantly began to sweep down in great, slow, gliding eddies that became narrower and narrower.

The kitten was the pilot now and the hawk no longer the assassin of the void, the lord of the sky, and the master of the wind. The ache coiled and throbbed in its breast. It fought against the erratic disposition of its wings and the terror of its waning strength. Its heart bursting with the strain, its eyes dilated wild and yellow, it came down until the earth skimmed under it; and the kitten cried at the silver glare of the roofs not far off, and the expanding earth, and the brush of the grass.

The hawk lobbed and flung over, and the kitten rolled with it. And the hawk lay spraddled in exhaustion, its eyes fiercely, cravenly aware of the danger of its forced and alien position.

The kitten staggered giddily, unhurt, toward the silver roofs, wailing loudly as if in answer to the voice of a child.

---

3. ***miauled,*** meowed.

Discussion

1. (a) Describe the land the hawk flies over as it searches for prey. **(b)** What is the reason for the bird's great hunger?

2. (a) How does the hawk plan to kill the kitten? **(b)** What makes the kitten aware of the hawk's intentions?

3. In this story, the hawk is in conflict with something else besides the kitten. **(a)** Identify this source of conflict. **(b)** Explain how the setting has contributed to it.

4. In your opinion, is the climax when the kitten learns how to hold on, or when the hawk finally returns to earth? Give reasons for your answer.

5. One reader has commented that the title adds much to the story. Do you agree or disagree? Why?

D'Arcy Niland 1920–1967

A native of Australia, D'Arcy Niland produced an amazing number of short stories—over five hundred of them. Before becoming a full-time writer, Niland worked as a magazine editor and as a journalist; in addition to short stories, he also wrote novels and television scripts. His first novel, *The Shiralee* (1955), was translated into twelve languages and then made into a successful motion picture. He and his wife, Ruth Park, who is also an author, collaborated on an autobiographical work, *The Drums Go Bang* (1956), and Niland himself wrote several other novels. A short story like "The Parachutist" shows his universality: except for a few terms native to Australia, the story could have taken place almost anywhere else in the world. Niland died suddenly of a heart attack in 1967.

Comment: The Plot-Centered, Suspenseful Story

A most popular form of short story among all readers is the plot-centered, suspenseful account that quickly establishes a conflict, carries the reader along breathlessly, and ends with a sudden, sometimes totally unexpected climax. In dramatic form these are the stories that made the television presentations of Alfred Hitchcock and, to a lesser extent, films like *Raiders of the Lost Ark* famous.

Though they may deal with death or violence, these stories generally leave no sympathetic feelings in the reader. This is because the author carefully underplays characterization and concentrates instead either exclusively on plot, or on setting as well insofar as it helps heighten the mood of the plot. Of the stories you have read, two—"The Boar Hunt" and "The Monkey's Paw"—definitely fit into the plot-centered, suspense-filled category; a third, "The Parachutist," though ultimately a survival-of-the-fittest animal tale, contains elements of it as well.

The first thing stories like these have in common is their abbreviated length: it is impossible to maintain edge-of-the-chair suspense for any extended length of time. Necessary setting and background are quickly painted in and the conflict is established as soon as possible. The author's next step is to arouse suspense and keep the reader hanging on every word, then speedily bring the story to its climax and tie up any loose ends.

Analyze the three selections mentioned earlier to see how well they fit into this category, or subgenre, of short story. How long does it take to establish the main conflict in each? Do any give a hint of the ending before or while the conflict is presented? What sort of background and setting does each use, and how important are these elements in the development of plot? Which has the most unexpected ending? Which, if any, leave you wanting to know more about what happens later to the characters?

The American short-story writer Edgar Allan Poe once said that every word in a story had to contribute to a single effect—in other words, no character, description, or episode should be there without reason. This rule of thumb applies particularly to suspense stories, where in many ways the plot *is* the effect.

The Piano

Aníbal Monteiro Machado Brazil

When the owner looked at his piano, he saw a piece of family history. Others saw a piece of junk.

Rosália!'' shouted João de Oliveira[1] to his wife, who was upstairs, ''I told the guy to get out. What a nerve! He laughed at it. He said it wasn't worth even five hundred cruzeiros.''[2]

''It's an old trick,'' she replied. ''He wants to get it for nothing and then sell it to somebody else. That's how these fellows get rich.''

But Rosália and Sara looked somewhat alarmed as they came downstairs. The family approached the old piano respectfully, as if to console it after the insult.

''We'll get a good price for it, you'll see,'' asserted Oliveira, gazing at the piano with a mixture of affection and apprehension. ''They don't make them like this anymore.''

''Put an ad in the paper,'' said Rosália, ''and they'll come flocking. The house will be like *this* with people.'' She joined the tips of the fingers of her right hand in customary token of an immense crowd. ''It's a pity to have to give it up.''

''Ah, it's a love of a piano!'' said João. ''Just looking at it you think you hear music.'' He caressed its oaken case.

''Well, come on, João. Let's put the ad in.''

It had to be sold so that the little parlor could be made into a bedroom for Sara and her intended, a lieutenant in the artillery. Besides, the price would pay for her trousseau.

Three mornings later, the piano was adorned with flowers for the sacrifice, and the house was ready to receive prospective buyers.

The first to arrive were a lady and her daughter. The girl opened the piano and played a few chords.

''It's no good at all, Mama.''

The lady stood up, looked at it, and noticed that the ivory was missing from some of the keys. She took her daughter by the hand and walked out, muttering as she went: ''Think of coming all this distance to look at a piece of junk.''

The Oliveira family had no time to feel resentment, for three new candidates appeared, all at the same time: an elderly lady who smelled like a rich widow, a young girl wearing glasses and carrying a music portfolio, and a redheaded man in a worn, wrinkled suit.

''I was here ahead of you,'' said the young girl to the old lady. ''It doesn't really matter. I only came because my mother wanted me to. There must be plenty of others for sale. But I'd just like to say that I was ringing the doorbell while you were still getting off the bus. We came in together but I got here first.''

This rivalry for priority pleased the Oliveiras. They thought it wise, however, to break up the argument, so they smiled at everyone and offered them all coffee. The young girl went over to the piano, while the redheaded man stood at a distance and evaluated it with a cool eye. At this moment a lady entered holding a schoolgirl by the hand. They sat down distrustfully.

Suddenly the young girl began to play, and the whole room hung on the notes that she extracted from the keyboard. Off-pitch, metallic, horrible notes. The Oliveiras anxiously studied the faces of their visitors. The redheaded man remained utterly impassive. The others glanced at one another as if seeking a common understanding. The newly arrived lady made a wry face. The per-

1. ***Rosália*** (rō sä′lyä) . . . ***João de Oliveira*** (zhwoun dā ō le vā′rə).
2. ***five hundred cruzeiros*** (crü zer′ōs), at the time of the story, an amount about equivalent to thirty American dollars.

Aníbal Monteiro Machado (ä nē′bäl mōn tā′rō mä shä′dō).

fumed old lady seemed more tolerant and looked indulgently at the old piano case.

It was a jury trial and the piano was the accused. The young girl continued to play, as if she were wringing a confession from it. The timbre suggested that of a decrepit, cracked-voiced soprano with stomach trouble. Some of the notes did not play at all. Doli joined in with her barking, a well-considered verdict. A smile passed around the room. No one was laughing, however. The girl seemed to be playing now out of pure malice, hammering at the dead keys and emphasizing the cacophony. It was a dreadful situation.

"There's something you ought to know about this piano," explained João de Oliveira. "It's very sensitive to the weather. It changes a great deal with variations in temperature."

The young girl stopped abruptly. She rose, put on some lipstick, and picked up her music portfolio.

"I don't know how you had the nerve to advertise this horror," she said, speaking to João but looking disdainfully at Rosália as if she had been the horror.

And she left.

João said nothing for a moment. After all, the insult had been directed at the old piano, not at him. Nevertheless, he felt constrained to declare that it was a genuine antique.

"They don't make them like this anymore," he said emphatically. "They just don't make them."

There was a long silence. The status of the piano had reached its nadir. Finally the red-headed man spoke: "What are you asking for it?"

In view of what had happened, João de Oliveira lowered substantially the price he had had in mind.

"Five contos,"[3] he said timidly.

He looked at everyone to see the effect. There was a silent response. Oliveira felt cold. Was the price monstrously high? Only the old lady showed any delicacy at all: she said she would think it over. But, through her veil of mercy, João perceived her decision.

As they all were leaving, a man about to enter stepped out of their way.

"Did you come about the piano?" asked one of them. "Well, you'll . . ."

But Oliveira interrupted.

"Come in," he said cheerfully. "It's right here. Lots of people have been looking at it."

The man was middle-aged, with a shock of grayish hair. He lifted the lid of the piano and examined the instrument at length. "Probably a music teacher," thought João.

The man did not ask the price. "Thank you," he said and left.

The house was empty again. Sara returned to her room. Rosália and João looked at each other in disappointment.

"Nobody understands its value," commented João sadly. "If I can't get a decent price for it, I'd rather not sell it at all."

"But how about Sara's trousseau?" said Rosália.

"I'll borrow the money."

"You'd never be able to pay it back out of your salary."

"We'll postpone the marriage."

"They love each other, João. They'll want to get married no matter what, trousseau or no trousseau."

At this moment, Sara could be heard shouting from her room that she could not possibly get married without two new slips and so forth.

"The thing is," Rosália went on, "this house is about the size of a matchbox. Where can we put the newlyweds? We'll have to give up the piano to make room for them. Nobody nowadays has enough room."

Sara's voice was heard again: "No, don't sell the piano. It's so pretty. . . ."

"It's also so silent," interrupted her mother. "You never play it anymore. All you ever play is the Victrola."[4]

She went to her daughter's room to speak further with her. Strange that Sara should talk like

---

3. ***Five contos,*** approximately three hundred dollars.
4. ***Victrola,*** trademark for an early kind of phonograph.

that. Rosália put the dilemma flatly: "A husband or a piano. Choose."

"Oh, a husband!" replied Sara with conviction. "Of course."

She hugged her pillow.

"So . . . ?"

"You're always against it, Rosália," shouted João de Oliveira.

"Against what?"

"Our piano."

"Oh, João, how can you say such a thing!"

The next day, as soon as he got back from work, João de Oliveira asked about the piano.

"Did any people answer the ad, Rosália?"

Yes, there had been several telephone calls for information about the piano, and an old man had come and looked at it. Also, the redheaded man had come again.

"Did any of them say anything about buying it?" asked João.

"No. But the two men who came to the house looked at it a long time."

"They did? Did they look at it with interest? With admiration?"

"It's hard to say."

"Yes, they admired it," said Sara. "Especially the old man. He almost ate it with his eyes."

João de Oliveira was touched. It was no longer a matter of price. He just wanted his piano to be treated with consideration and respect, that's all. Maybe it wasn't worth a lot of money, but it certainly deserved some courteous attention. He was sorry he hadn't been there, but what his daughter told him of the old man's respectful attitude consoled him for the contumely of the day before. That man must understand the soul of antique furniture.

"Did he leave his address, Sara? No? Oh, well . . . he'll probably be back."

He rose from his chair and walked around the old instrument. He smiled at it lovingly.

"My piano," he said softly. He ran his hand over the varnished wood as if he were caressing an animal.

No candidate the next day. Only a voice with a foreign accent asking if it was new. Rosália replied that it wasn't but that they had taken such good care of it that it almost looked like new.

"Tomorrow is Saturday," thought Oliveira. "There's bound to be a lot of people."

There were two, a man and a little girl, and they came in a limousine. The man looked at the modest house of the Oliveira family and considered it useless to go in. Nevertheless, he went to the door and asked the make and age of the piano.

"Thank you. There's no need for me to see it," he replied to João's insistence that he look at it. "I thought it would be a fairly new piano. Good luck. . . ."

And he went away.

João was grief stricken. Ever since he had inherited the piano he had prized it dearly. He had never thought he would have to part with it. Worst of all, no one appreciated it; no one understood its value.

No one, except possibly the fellow who came the next Wednesday. He praised the piano in the most enthusiastic terms, said it was marvelous, and refused to buy. He said that if he paid so low a price for it he would feel he was stealing it, and that João and Rosália were virtually committing a crime in letting this precious thing get out of their hands. Oliveira did not exactly understand.

"Does he mean what he says?" he asked Rosália.

"I think he's just trying to be funny," she replied.

"I don't know. Maybe not."

Rosália was the first to lose hope. Her main concern now, when her husband came home from work, was to alleviate his suffering.

"How many today?"

"Nobody. Two telephone calls. They didn't give their names but they said they'd probably come and look at it."

Her voice was calm, soothing.

"How about the redheaded fellow?"

"I'm sure he'll be back."

For several days no one came or telephoned. João de Oliveira's feelings may be compared to those of a man who sees his friend miss a train: he is sad for his friend's sake and he is happy because he will continue for a time to have the pleasure of his company. João sat down near the piano and enjoyed these last moments with it. He admired its dignity. He confided his thoughts to it. Three generations had played it. How many people it had induced to dream or to dance! All this had passed away, but the piano remained. It was the only piece of furniture that bespoke the presence of his forebears. It was sort of eternal. It and the old oratory upstairs.

"Sara, come and play that little piece by Chopin.[5] See if you remember it."

"I couldn't, Papa. The piano sounds terrible."

"Don't say that," Rosália whispered. "Can't you see how your father feels?"

Whenever Sara's eyes lit on the piano, they transformed it into a nuptial bed.

For days and days no prospective buyer appeared. Nothing but an occasional telephone call from the redheaded man, as if he had been a doctor verifying the progress of a terminal case. The advertisement was withdrawn.

"Well, João, what are we going to do about it?"

"What are we going to do about what, Rosália?"

"The piano!"

"I'm not going to sell it," João shouted. "These leeches don't care about the piano; they just want a bargain. I'd rather give it away to someone who'll take good care of it, who knows what it represents."

He was walking back and forth agitatedly. Suddenly the expression of his face changed.

"Listen, Rosália. Let's phone our relatives in Tijuca."[6]

Rosália understood his purpose and was pleased.

"Hello! Is Messias there? He went out? Oh, is this Cousin Miquita?[7] Look . . . I want to give you our piano as a present. . . . Yes, as a present. . . . No, it's not a joke. . . . Really. . . . Right. . . . Exactly. . . . So it won't go out of the family. . . . Fine. Have it picked up here sometime soon. . . . You're welcome. I'm glad to do it. . . ."

After he had hung up he turned to his wife.

"You know what? She didn't believe me at first. She thought it was All Fools' Day."

Rosália was delighted. João walked over to the old piano as if to confer with it about what he had just done.

"My conscience is clear," he thought. "You will not be rejected. You will stay in the family, with people of the same blood. My children's children will know and respect you; you will play for them. I'm sure you understand and won't be angry with us."

"When will they come for it?" interrupted Rosália, eager to get the room ready for the bridal couple.

The next day Messias telephoned his relatives in Ipanema.[8] Did they really mean to give him a piano? It was too much. He was grateful but they really shouldn't. When his wife told him, he could hardly believe it.

"No, it's true, Messias. You know, our house is about as big as a nutshell. We can't keep the piano here, and João doesn't want it to fall into the hands of strangers. If you people have it, it's almost the same as if it were still with us. Are you going to send for it soon?"

Several days went by. No moving van came. Mr. and Mrs. Oliveira thought the silence of their relatives in Tijuca extremely odd.

"Something's wrong. Telephone them, Rosália."

Cousin Miquita answered. She was embarrassed. The moving men asked a fortune for the job.

"I guess it's the gasoline shortage. . . . Wait a few more days. Messias will arrange something. We're delighted about getting the piano. We think of nothing else, Rosália."

---

5. ***Chopin*** (shō′pan), Frédéric François (fräN swä′) Chopin, 1810–1849, Polish composer and pianist.
6. ***Tijuca*** (tē zhü′kä), a hill suburb of Rio de Janeiro, about eight miles southwest of the city center.
7. ***Messias*** (mes ē′äs) . . . ***Miquita*** (mē kē′tä).
8. ***Ipanema*** (ē pä nē′mä), a seafront district of Rio de Janeiro; the area where the Oliveiras live.

This last sentence struck a false note, thought Rosália. After a week, João de Oliveira telephoned again.

"Do you want it or don't you, Messias?"

"João, you can't imagine how terrible we feel about this," came the stammered reply. "You give us a fine present and we can't accept it. They're asking an arm and a leg to move it here. And, anyway, we really have no room for it. We haven't even got enough room for the stuff we have now. We should have thought of this before. Miquita feels awful about it."

"In short, you don't want the piano."

"We want it. . . . But we don't . . . we can't . . ."

João de Oliveira hung up. He was beginning to understand.

"You see, Rosália. We can't even give the piano away. We can't even give it away."

"What can you do, João! Everything ends up with nobody wanting it."

After a few minutes of silent despondence, they were aroused by Sara, who interspersed her sobs with words of bitter desperation. Her mother comforted her.

"Don't worry, child. It'll be all right. We'll sell it for whatever we can get."

"I want it out right away, Mama. In a few days I'm to be married and my room isn't even ready yet. None of our things are in here. Only that terrible piano ruining my life, that piano that nobody wants."

"Speak softly, dear. Your father can hear you."

"I want him to hear me," she cried, with another sob. She wiped her eyes.

João de Oliveira slept little that night. He was meditating about life. His thoughts were confused and generally melancholy. They induced in him a fierce rage against both life and the piano. He left the house early and went to a nearby bar, where he talked with several men.

"What is my husband doing in a place like that?" Rosália asked herself. João was never a drinker.

Oliveira came back accompanied by a shabbily dressed black and two husky Portuguese in work clothes. He showed them the piano. They hefted it and said they doubted if they could handle it, just the three of them.

Rosália and Sara looked on in amazement.

"Have you found a buyer?" asked Rosália.

"No, wife. Nobody will buy this piano."

"You're giving it away?"

"No, wife. Nobody wants it even for free."

"Then what are you doing, João? What in the world are you doing?"

João's eyes watered but his face hardened.

"I'm going to throw it into the ocean."

"Oh, no, Papa!" exclaimed Sara. "That's crazy!"

The Oliveiras could not see the ocean from their windows, but they could smell it and hear it, for they were only three blocks from the avenue that ran along the beach.

The men were waiting, talking among themselves.

"What a courageous thing to do, João!" said his wife. "But shouldn't we talk it over first? Is there no other way out? People will think it funny, throwing a piano into the water."

"What else can we do, Rosália? Lots of ships go to the bottom of the ocean. Some of them have pianos on board."

This irrefutable logic silenced his wife. João seemed to take heart.

"Okay, you fellows," he cried. "Up with it! Let's go!"

One of the Portuguese came forward and said humbly, on behalf of his colleagues and himself, that they couldn't do it. They hoped he would excuse them, but it would hurt their conscience to throw something like that in the sea. It almost seemed like a crime.

"Boss, why don't you put an ad in the paper? The piano is in such good condition."

"Yes, I know," replied Oliveira ironically. "You may go."

The men left. For a moment the shabbily dressed one entertained the idea that he might take the piano for himself. He stared at it. He was fascinated by the idea of owning something, and a fine, luxurious thing at that. It was a dream that could become an immediate reality. But where would he take it? He had no house.

Rosália rested her head on her husband's shoulder and fought back the tears.

"Ah, João, what a decision you have made!"

"But if nobody wants it, and if it can't stay here . . ."

"I know, João. But I can't help feeling sad. It's always been with us. Doesn't it seem cruel, after all these years, to throw it in the ocean? Look at it, standing there, knowing nothing about what's going to happen to it. It's been there almost twenty years, in that corner, never doing any harm. . . ."

"We must try to avoid sentimentality, Rosália."

She looked at him with admiration.

"All right, João. Do what you must."

Groups of young boys, ragged but happy, start out from the huts at Pinto and Latolandia[9] where they live, and stroll through the wealthy neighborhoods. One can always find them begging nickels for ice cream, gazing in rapture at the posters outside the movie houses, or rolling on the sand in Leblon.[10]

That morning a southwester was whipping the Atlantic into a fury. The piano, needless to say, remained as tranquil as ever. And imposing in the severity of its lines.

Preparations for the departure were underway. João de Oliveira asked his wife and daughter to remove the parts that might possibly be useful. Accordingly, the bronze candlesticks were taken off, then the pedals and metal ornaments, and finally the oak top.

"Ugh!" exclaimed Sara. "It looks so different."

Without mentioning it to his family, João de Oliveira had recruited a bunch of the young boys. They were waiting impatiently outside the door. Oliveira now told them to come in, the strongest ones first.

It was twenty after four in the afternoon when the funeral cortege started out. A small crowd on the sidewalk made way for it. The piano moved slowly and irregularly. Some people came up to observe it more closely. Rosália and her daughter contemplated it sadly from the porch, their arms around each other's shoulders. They could not bring themselves to accompany it. The cook was wiping her eyes on her apron.

"Which way?" asked the boys when the procession reached the corner. They were all trying to hold the piano at the same time, with the result that it almost fell.

"Which way?" they repeated.

"To the sea!" cried João de Oliveira. And with the grand gesture of a naval commander he pointed toward the Atlantic.

"To the sea! To the sea!" echoed the boys in chorus.

They began to understand that the piano was going to be destroyed, and this knowledge excited them. They laughed and talked animatedly among themselves. The hubbub inspired the little dog Doli to leap in the air and bark furiously.

The balconies of the houses were crowded, chiefly with young girls.

"Mother of heaven!" they exclaimed. "What is it?" And, incredulously, "A piano!"

"It came from ninety-nine," cried an urchin, running from house to house to inform the families.

"Why, that's where Sara lives!"

"It's João de Oliveira's house."

An acquaintance ran out to learn the facts from Oliveira himself.

"What's wrong, João?"

"Nothing's wrong. I know what I'm doing. Just everybody keep out of the way."

"But why don't you sell it?"

"I'll sell it, all right. I'll sell it to the Atlantic Ocean. See it there? The ocean . . ."

With the air of a somewhat flustered executioner, he resumed his command.

"More to the left, fellows. . . . Careful, don't

9. ***Pinto and Latolandia,*** poor districts of Rio de Janeiro.
10. ***Leblon,*** a seafront district just west of Ipanema.

John Slobodnik

let it drop. . . . Just the big boys now, everybody else let go.''

From time to time one of the boys would put his arm inside the piano and run his hand along the strings. The sound was a sort of death rattle.

A lady on a balcony shouted at João, ''Would you sell it?''

''No, madam, it's not for sale. I'll give it away. You want it?''

The lady reddened, felt offended, and went into her house. João made his offer more general.

''Anyone around here want a piano?''

At number forty-three a family of Polish refugees accepted. They were astounded, but they accepted.

''Then it's yours,'' shouted João de Oliveira.

The Polish family came down and stood around the piano.

''We'll take it, all right. . . . But . . . our house is very small. Give us a couple of days to get ready for it.''

''Now or never!'' replied Oliveira. ''Here it is, right outside your house. You don't want it? Okay, fellows, let's go.''

The piano moved closer and closer to the sea. It swayed like a dead cockroach carried by ants.

João de Oliveira distinguished only a few of the exclamations coming from the doors, windows, and balconies of the houses.

''This is the craziest thing I ever heard of,'' someone shouted from a balcony.

''Crazy?'' replied João de Oliveira, looking up at the speaker. ''Okay, then you take it. Take it. . . .''

Farther on, the scene was repeated. Everyone thought it was a crazy thing to do and everyone wanted the piano; but as soon as the owner offered immediate possession, there was just embarrassed silence. After all, who is prepared to receive a piano at a moment's notice?

João de Oliveira proceeded resolutely, accompanied by a buzz of comments and lamentations. He decided to make no more replies.

A group of motorcycle policemen stopped the procession and surrounded the old piano. João de Oliveira gave a detailed explanation. They asked to see his documents. He went back to the house and got them. He thought the requirement natural enough, for the nation was at war. But he resented having had to give an explanation, for he was acting pursuant to a personal decision for which he was accountable to no one outside the family. He certainly had a right to throw away his own property. This thought reawakened his affection for the instrument. Placing his hand on the piano as if on the forehead of a deceased friend, he felt deeply moved and began to discourse on its life.

''It's an antique, one of the oldest pianos in Brazil.''

It had belonged to his grandparents, who had been in the service of the Empire.[11]

''It was a fine piano, you may believe me. Famous musicians played on it. They say that Chopin preferred it over all others. But what does this matter? No one appreciates it anymore. Times have changed. . . . Sara, my daughter, is getting married. She'll live with us. The house is small. What can I do? No one wants it. This is the only way out.''

And he nodded toward the sea.

The boys were growing impatient with the interruptions. They were eager to see the piano sink beneath the waves. Almost as impatient as these improvised movers were the people who had joined the procession, including delivery men, messenger boys, a few women, and a great many children.

The police examined the interior of the piano but found nothing suspicious. They returned Oliveira's papers and suggested that he hurry so that traffic would not be impeded.

A photographer asked some of the people to form a group and snapped their picture. João de Oliveira was on the left side in a pose expressing sadness. Then he became annoyed with all these interruptions that prolonged the agony of his piano.

Night fell rapidly. A policeman observed that

---

11. ***the Empire,*** Brazil was ruled by emperors from 1821 to 1889.

after six o'clock they would not be permitted to go on. They would have to wait till the next day.

The boys dispersed. They were to be paid later, at Oliveira's house. People were amazed that evening at the number of young boys strolling around with small, ivory-plated pieces of wood in their hands.

The piano remained there on the street where they had left it, keeled over against the curb. A ridiculous position. Young men and women on their evening promenade soon surrounded it and made comments.

When he got home, João de Oliveira found some of Sara's girlfriends there, eagerly questioning her about the piano.

It was still dark when João and his wife awoke to the loud sound of rain. Wind, rain, and the roar of the surf. They lit the light and looked at each other.

"I was thinking about the piano, Rosália."

"So was I, João. Poor thing! Out in the rain there . . . and it's so cold!"

"The water must be getting into the works and ruining everything . . . the felt, the strings. It's terrible, isn't it, Rosália?"

"We did an ungrateful thing, João."

"I don't even like to think about it, Rosália."

João de Oliveira looked out the window. Flashes of lightning illuminated the trees, revealing branches swaying wildly in the wind. João went back to bed and slept fitfully. He awoke again and told his wife that he had been listening to the piano.

"I heard everything that was ever played on it. Many different hands. My grandmother's hands, my mother's, yours, my aunt's, Sara's. More than twenty hands, more than a hundred white fingers were pressing the keys. I never heard such pretty music. It was sublime, Rosália. The dead hands sometimes played better than the live ones. Lots of young girls from earlier generations were standing around the piano, listening. Couples who later got married were sitting nearby, holding hands. I don't know why, but after a while they all looked at me—with contempt. Suddenly the hands left the piano, but it kept on playing. The Funeral March. Then the piano shut by itself. . . . There was a torrent of water. The piano let itself get swept along . . . toward the ocean. I shouted to it but it wouldn't listen to me. It seemed to be offended, Rosália, and it just kept on going. . . . I stood there in the street, all alone. I began to cry. . . ."

João de Oliveira was breathing hard. The mysterious concert had left him in a state of emotion. He felt remorseful.

The rain stopped. As soon as it was light, João went out to round up the boys. All he wanted now was to get the thing over with as quickly as possible.

The wind was still strong, and the ocean growled as if it were digesting the storm of the night before. The boys came, but in smaller numbers than before. Several grown men were among them. João de Oliveira, in a hoarse voice, assumed command again.

On the beach the piano moved more slowly. Finally the long tongues of the waves began to lick it.

Some families stood on the sidewalk, watching the spectacle. Oliveira's crew carried and pushed the piano far enough for the surf to take charge and drag it out to sea. Two enormous waves broke over it without effect. The third made it tremble. The fourth carried it away forever.

João de Oliveira stood there, knee-deep in water, with his mouth open. The sea seemed enormously silent. No one could tell that he was crying, for the tears on his cheeks were indistinguishable from the drops of spray.

Far off, he saw Sara with her head resting on the lieutenant's shoulder. Doli was with her, her snout expressing inquiry and incipient dismay; she had always slept next to the piano. João was glad that Rosália had not come.

Many people appeared later on the beach, asking one another what had happened. It seemed at first that an entire Polish family had drowned. Subsequently, it was learned that only one person had drowned. Some said it was a child. Others insisted that it was a lady who had had an unhappy love affair. Only later was it generally known that the person who had drowned was a piano.

People posted themselves at their windows to watch João de Oliveira come back from the beach.

"That's the man!" someone announced.

Oliveira walked slowly, staring at the ground. Everyone felt respect for him.

"It's gone, Rosália," he said as he entered the house. "It has passed the point of no return."

"Before we talk about it, João, go change your clothes."

"Our piano will never come back, Rosália."

"Of course it won't come back. That's why you threw it in the sea."

"Who knows," said Sara. "Maybe it'll be washed up on a beach somewhere."

"Let's not think about it anymore. It's over. It's finished. Sara, it's time you did your room."

There was a pause, after which João resumed his lamentation.

"I saw the waves swallow it."

"Enough, my husband. Enough!"

"It came back to the surface twice."

"It's all over! Let's not think about it anymore."

"I didn't mention it to anybody so they wouldn't think I went crazy . . . though they're beginning to think I'm crazy anyway. . . . The fact is, I'm probably the most rational man in the whole neighborhood. . . . But a little while ago I clearly heard the piano play the Funeral March."

"That was in your dream last night," Rosália reminded him.

"No, it was there by the sea, in broad daylight. Didn't you hear it, Sara? Right afterward, it was covered all with foam, and the music stopped."

He nodded his head, expressing hopelessness before the inevitable. He was talking as if to himself.

"It must be far away by now. Under the water, moving along past strange sights. The wrecks of ships. Submarines. Fishes. Until yesterday it had never left this room. . . . Years from now it will be washed up on some island in an ocean on the other side of the world. And when Sara, Rosália, and I are dead, it will still remember the music it made in this house."

He left the room. Sara, alone, looked at the place where the piano had been. She felt a little guilty.

Her thoughts were interrupted by a knock at the door. A fellow came in with an official notice. Some unidentified person had told the police that a secret radio was hidden in the piano and that her father had wanted to get rid of it. He was to appear at the district police station and answer questions. Well, it was the sort of thing you had to expect in wartime. Nothing anyone could do about it.

Oliveira spent the rest of the day at the police station. He came home late.

"What a life, Rosália!" he said as he fell dejected into the armchair. "What a life! We can't even throw away things that belong to us."

João felt oppressed, stifled. He meditated awhile and then spoke again.

"Have you ever noticed, Rosália, how people hate to get rid of old things? How they cling to them?"

"Not only old things," replied Rosália. "Old ideas too."

Doli was sniffing the area where the piano had been. She wailed a little and fell asleep.

The doorbell rang. A man entered and drew some papers from a briefcase. He said he came from the Port Captain's office.

"Are you João de Oliveira?"

"Yes, I am João de Oliveira."

"What did you cast in the sea this morning?"

Oliveira was stupefied.

"Out here we're not in that port, my dear sir. It's ocean."

"Are you going to give me a vocabulary lesson, Mr. Oliveira?"

The man repeated his previous question and explained that regulations now forbade the placing of objects in or on the sea without a license.

"Have you a license?"

Oliveira humbly asked whether what he had done was in any way offensive or bad.

"That's not the question. Don't you know that we're at war? That our coasts must be protected? That the Nazis are always watching for an opportunity?"

"But it was just a piano, sir."

"It's still a violation. Anyway, was it really a piano? Are you absolutely sure?"

"I think I am," João blurted, looking at his daughter and his wife. "Wasn't it a piano, Rosália? Wasn't it, Sara?"

"Where's your head, João?" exclaimed Rosália. "You know it was a piano."

Her husband's doubt surprised everyone. He seemed to be musing.

"I thought a person could throw anything in the ocean that he wanted to."

"No, indeed! That's all we need. . . ."

João arose. He looked delirious.

"Suppose I want to throw myself in the sea. Can I?"

"It all depends," replied the man from the Port Captain's office.

"Depends on whom? On me and nobody else! I'm a free man. My life belongs to me."

"Much less than you think," said the man.

Sara broke into the smile with which she always greeted the lieutenant, who had just come in. She ran to kiss him.

"See our room, darling. It looks good now, doesn't it?"

"Yes, real good. Where are you going to put the new one?"

"The new one?"

"Yes. Aren't you going to get another?"

Sara and her mother exchanged glances of amazement.

"I'm crazy for a piano," said Sara's fiancé. "You have no idea how it relaxes me. All day long I have to hear guns shooting. A little soft music in the evening . . ."

Sara had a fit of coughing. João de Oliveira went out the door. He felt suffocated; he needed to breathe.

Who else would come out of the night and make new demands of him? How could he have known that a piano hidden from the world, living in quiet anonymity, was really an object of public concern? Why hadn't he just left it where it was?

It was miles away now, traveling. . . . Far away, riding the southern seas. . . . And free. More so than he or Sara or Rosália. It was he, João de Oliveira, who now felt abandoned. For himself and for his family. It wasn't their piano anymore. It was a creature loose in the world. Full of life and pride, moving boldly through the seven seas. Sounding forth. Embraced by all the waters of the world. Free to go where it wished, to do what it wished.

Beneath the trees in front of the house, the young boys were waiting for their second day's pay. They had worked hard. It was so dark that he could scarcely distinguish their shaved heads. In the midst of them he saw a vaguely familiar form. The person opened the garden gate and asked permission to enter.

With some difficulty João recognized the red-headed man, but he was wholly unprepared for what the man was about to say:

"I've come back about the piano. I think I can make you a reasonable offer."

Discussion

1. (a) For what two reasons does the piano have to be sold? **(b)** Compare João's feeling about the instrument with those of the people who come to examine it.

2. In many places in the story, the piano is described as though it were a living creature. Find at least five examples of this technique, and explain what you think the author was trying to accomplish by using it.

3. By the end of the story, the piano has become almost superhuman, making the tale a combination of humor, fantasy, and bittersweet sadness. Which feeling, in your opinion, is uppermost? Explain your answer.

4. None of the following people or situations is all that important in itself, but they all add color to the plot. Explain in what way each makes the basic story more interesting: **(a)** the redheaded man; **(b)** the reactions of the relatives in Tijuca; **(c)** the street urchins who move the piano; **(d)** the involvement of the police and of the Port Captain's employee.

5. Is João a realistic character? Is Rosália? Sara? Why do you feel as you do?

Composition

As the saying goes, "Beauty is in the eye of the beholder"—an object one person cherishes may have no value to another. Choose a treasured item now in your possession that probably holds no meaning for anyone else, such as a worn piece of clothing, a good-luck charm, an old letter. Think about what it looks like and why it is important to you.

Write a two- or three-paragraph composition about the object, first describing it in some detail, then telling the reasons or the circumstances that have made you treasure it. Or follow the same procedure with an object that used to be important to you: describe it, explain why it once mattered, and tell why you no longer care about it.

Aníbal Monteiro Machado 1895–1964

A Brazilian from the area around the city of Belo Horizonte, Machado was originally trained as a lawyer. However, he only practiced law for a short time, finding the profession not well suited to his temperament. He later held positions as a teacher and a public official, both in his native area and in Rio de Janeiro.

Through most of his life Machado was also a writer, primarily of short stories. He developed a reputation first through pieces he submitted to magazines, later through collections he published of his work. Early on he became associated with the Latin American literary movement known as Modernism, which attempted to throw off the influence of European literature and forge its own way. "The Piano" illustrates an area of interest of the particular Modernist group Machado was associated with: the episodic and social side of urban life.

See **POINT OF VIEW** Handbook of Literary Terms

Forgiveness in Families

Alice Munro Canada

Mother had a way of viewing my brother's faults as virtues. I, however, found his list of shortcomings too long.

I've often thought, suppose I had to go to a psychiatrist, and he would want to know about my family background, naturally, so I would have to start telling him about my brother, and he wouldn't even wait till I was finished, would he, the psychiatrist, he'd commit me.

I said that to Mother; she laughed. "You're hard on that boy, Val."

"Boy," I said. *"Man."*

She laughed, she admitted it. "But remember," she said, "the Lord loves a lunatic."

"How do you know," I said, "seeing you're an atheist?"

Some things he couldn't help. Being born, for instance. He was born the week I started school, and how's that for timing? I was scared, it wasn't like now when the kids have been going to playschool and kindergarten for years. I was going to school for the first time and all the other kids had their mothers with them and where was mine? In the hospital having a baby. The embarrassment to me. There was a lot of shame about those things then. . . .

I will skip over what he did between getting born and throwing up at my wedding except to say that he had asthma and got to stay home from school weeks on end, listening to soap operas. Sometimes there was a truce between us, and I would get him to tell me what happened every day on "Big Sister" and "Road of Life" and the one with Gee-Gee and Papa David. He was very good at remembering all the characters and getting all the complications straight, I'll say that, and he did read a lot in *Gateways to Bookland,* that lovely set Mother bought for us and that he later sneaked out of the house and sold, for ten dollars, to a secondhand-book dealer. Mother said he could have been brilliant at school if he wanted to be. That's a deep one, your brother, she used to say, he's got some surprises in store for us. She was right, he had.

He started staying home permanently in Grade Ten after a little problem of being caught in a cheating ring that was getting math tests from some teacher's desk. One of the janitors was letting him back in the classroom after school because he said he was working on a special project. So he was, in his own way. Mother said he did it to make himself popular, because he had asthma and couldn't take part in sports.

Now. Jobs. The question comes up, what is such a person as my brother— and I ought to give him a name at least, his name is Cam, for Cameron, Mother thought that would be a suitable name for a university president or honest tycoon (which was the sort of thing she planned for him to be)—what is he going to do, how is he going to make a living? Until recently the country did not pay you to sit on your uppers and announce that you had adopted a creative lifestyle. He got a job first as a movie usher. Mother got it for him, she knew the manager, it was the old International Theater over on Blake Street. He had to quit, though, because he got this darkness phobia. All the people sitting in the dark he said gave him a crawly feeling, very peculiar. It only interfered with him working as an usher, it didn't interfere with him going to the movies on his own. He got very fond of movies. In fact, he spent whole days sitting in movie houses, sitting through every show twice, then going to another theater and sitting through what was there. He had to do something with his time, because Mother and all of us believed he was working then in the office of the Greyhound Bus Depot. He went off to work at the right time every morning and came home at the right time every night, and he told all about the cranky old man in charge of the office and the woman with curvature of the spine who had been there since 1919 and how mad she got at the young girls chewing gum, oh, a lively story, it would have worked up to something as good as the soap operas if Mother hadn't phoned up to complain about the way they were withholding his paycheck—due to a technical error in the spelling of his name, he said—and found out he'd quit in the middle of his second day.

Well. Sitting in movies was better than sitting in beer parlors, Mother said. At least he wasn't on the street getting in with criminal gangs. She asked him what his favorite movie was and he said *Seven Brides for Seven Brothers*. See, she said, he is interested in an outdoor life,[1] he is not suited to office work. So she sent him to work for some cousins of hers who have a farm in the Fraser Valley. I should explain that my father, Cam's and mine, was dead by this time, he died away back when Cam was having asthma and listening to soap operas. It didn't make much difference, his dying, because he worked as a conductor on the P.G.E. when it started at Squamish, and he lived part of the time in Lillooet.[2] Nothing changed. Mother went on working at Eaton's as she always had, going across on the ferry and then on the bus; I got supper, she came trudging up the hill in the winter dark.

Cam took off from the farm, he complained that the cousins were religious and always after his soul. Mother could see his problem, she had after all brought him up to be a freethinker. He hitchhiked east. From time to time a letter came. A request for funds. He had been offered a job in northern Quebec if he could get the money together to get up there. Mother sent it. He sent word the job had folded, but he didn't send back the money. He and two friends were going to start a turkey farm. They sent us plans, estimates. They were supposed to be working on contract for the Purina Company, nothing could go wrong. The turkeys were drowned in a flood, after Mother had sent him money and we had too against our better judgment. Everywhere that boy hits turns into a disaster area, Mother said. If you read it in a book you wouldn't believe it, she said. It's so terrible it's funny.

She knew. I used to go over to see her on Wednesday afternoon—her day off—pushing the stroller with Karen in it, and later Tommy in it and Karen walking beside, up Lonsdale and down King's Road, and what would we always end up talking about? That boy and I, we are getting a divorce, she said. I am definitely going to write him off. What good will he ever be until he stops relying on me, she asked. I kept my mouth shut, more or less. She knew my opinion. But she ended up every time saying, "He was a nice fellow to have around the house, though. Good company. That boy could always make me laugh."

Or, "He had a lot to contend with, his asthma and no dad. He never did intentionally hurt a soul."

"One good thing he did," she said, "you could really call it a good turn. That girl."

Referring to the girl who came and told us she had been engaged to him, in Hamilton, Ontario, until he told her he could never get married because he had just found out there was hereditary fatal kidney disease in his family. He wrote her a letter. And she came looking for him to tell

---

1. ***Seven Brides . . . outdoor life.*** The movie, a 1954 musical, celebrated outdoor life in that it was set in the Oregon backwoods.
2. ***P.G.E. . . . Lillooet*** (lil′ü ət). The P.G.E. is the Pacific Grand Eastern Railway Company; Squamish and Lillooet are towns in the Canadian province of British Columbia.

him it didn't matter. Not at all a bad-looking girl. She worked for the Bell Telephone. Mother said it was a lie told out of kindness, to spare her feelings when he didn't want to marry her. I said it was a kindness, anyway, because she would have been supporting him for the rest of his life.

Though it might have eased things up a bit on the rest of us.

But that was then and now is now and as we all know times have changed. Cam is finding it easier. He lives at home, off and on, has for a year and a half. His hair is thin in front, not surprising in a man thirty-four years of age, but shoulder-length behind, straggly, graying. He wears a sort of rough brown robe that looks as if it might be made out of a sack (is that what sackcloth is supposed to be, I said to my husband Haro, I wouldn't mind supplying the ashes),[3] and hanging down on his chest he has all sorts of chains, medallions, crosses, elk's teeth, or whatnot. Rope sandals on his feet. Some friend of his makes them. He collects welfare. Nobody asks him to work. Who could be so crude? If he has to write down his occupation he writes priest.

It's true. There is a whole school of them, calling themselves priests, and they have a house over in Kitsilano,[4] Cam stays there too sometimes. They're in competition with the Hare Krishna bunch,[5] only these ones don't chant, they just walk around smiling. He has developed this voice I can't stand, a very thin, sweet voice, all on one level. It makes me want to stand in front of him and say, "There's an earthquake in Chile, two hundred thousand people just died, they've burned up another village in Vietnam, famine as usual in India." Just to see if he'd keep saying, "Ve-ery ni-ice, ve-ery ni-ice," that sweet way. He won't eat meat, of course, he eats whole-grain cereals and leafy vegetables. He came into the kitchen where I was slicing beets—beets being forbidden, a root vegetable—and, "I hope you understand that you're committing murder," he said.

"No," I said, "but I'll give you sixty seconds to get out of here or I may be."

So as I say he's home part of the time now and he was there on the Monday night when Mother got sick. She was vomiting. A couple of days before this he had started her on a vegetarian diet—she was always promising him she'd try it—and he told her she was vomiting up all the old poisons stored up in her body from eating meat and sugar and so on. He said it was a good sign, and when she had it all vomited out she'd feel better. She kept vomiting, and she didn't feel better, but he had to go out. Monday nights is when they have the weekly meeting at the priests' house, where they chant and burn incense or celebrate the black mass, for all I know. He stayed out most of the night, and when he got home he found Mother unconscious on the bathroom floor. He got on the phone and phoned *me*.

"I think you better come over here and see if you can help Mom, Val."

"What's the matter with her?"

"She's not feeling very well."

"What's the matter with her? Put her on the phone."

"I can't."

"Why can't you?"

I swear he tittered. "Well, I'm afraid she's passed out."

I called the ambulance and sent them for her, that was how she got to the hospital, five o'clock in the morning. I called her family doctor, he got over there, and he got Dr. Ellis Bell, one of the best-known heart men in the city, because that was what they had decided it was, her heart. I got dressed and woke Haro and told him and then I drove myself over to the Lions Gate Hospital. They wouldn't let me in till ten o'clock. They had her in Intensive Care. I sat outside Intensive Care in their slick little awful waiting room. They had red slippery chairs, cheap covering, and a stand full of pebbles with green plastic leaves growing up. I sat there hour after hour and read *The Reader's Digest*. The jokes. Thinking this is how it is,

---

3. ***sackcloth . . . ashes.*** Wearing sackcloth and ashes (that is, putting ashes on one's head) is a sign of mourning or penitence.
4. ***Kitsilano*** (kit'si lä'nō).
5. ***Hare Krishna*** (hä'rə krish'nä) ***bunch.*** Hare Krishna is the popular name of a religious sect founded in India in 1954 that has attracted young members worldwide.

this is it, really, she's dying. Now, this moment, behind those doors, dying. Nothing stops or holds off for it the way you somehow and against all your sense believe it will. I thought about Mother's life, the part of it I knew. Going to work every day, first on the ferry, then on the bus. Shopping at the old Red-and-White, then at the new Safeway—new, fifteen years old! Going down to the Library one night a week, taking me with her, and we would come home on the bus with our load of books and a bag of grapes we bought at the Chinese place, for a treat. Wednesday afternoons too when my kids were small and I went over there to drink coffee. And I thought, all these things don't seem that much like life, when you're doing them, they're just what you do, how you fill up your days, and you think all the time something is going to crack open, and you'll find yourself, *then* you'll find yourself, in life. It's not even that you particularly want this to happen, this cracking open, you're comfortable enough the way things are, but you do expect it. Then you're dying, Mother is dying, and it's just the same plastic chairs and plastic plants and ordinary day outside with people getting groceries and what you've had is all there is, and going to the Library, just a thing like that, coming back up the hill on the bus with books and a bag of grapes seems now worth wanting, oh doesn't it, you'd break your heart wanting back there.

When they let me in to see her she was bluish-gray in the face and her eyes were not all-the-way closed, but they had rolled up, the slit that was open showed the whites. She always looked terrible with her teeth out, anyway, wouldn't let us see her. Cam teased her vanity. They were out now. So all the time, I thought, all the time even when she was young it was in her that she was going to look like this.

They didn't hold out hope. Haro came and took a look at her and put his arm around my shoulders and said, "Val, you'll have to be prepared." He meant well but I couldn't talk to him. It wasn't his mother and he couldn't remember anything. That wasn't his fault but I didn't want to talk to him, I didn't want to listen to him telling me I better be prepared. We went and ate something in the hospital cafeteria.

"You better phone Cam," Haro said.

"Why?"

"He'll want to know."

"Why do you think he'll want to know? He left her alone last night and he didn't know enough to get an ambulance when he came in and found her this morning."

"Just the same. He has a right. Maybe you ought to tell him to get over here."

"He is probably busy this moment preparing to give her a hippie funeral."

But Haro persuaded me as he always can and I went and phoned. No answer. I felt better because I had phoned, and justified in what I had said because of Cam not being in. I went back and waited, by myself.

About seven o'clock that night Cam turned up. He was not alone. He had brought along a tribe of co-priests, I suppose they were, from that house. They all wore the same kind of outfit he did, the brown sacking nightgown and the chains and crosses and holy hardware, they all had long hair, they were all a good many years younger than Cam, except for one old man, really old, with a curly gray beard and bare feet—in March, bare feet—and no teeth. I swear this old man didn't have a clue what was going on. I think they picked him up down by the Salvation Army and put that outfit on him because they needed an old man for a kind of mascot, or extra holiness, or something.

Cam said, "This is my sister Valerie. This is Brother Michael. This is Brother John, this is Brother Louis." Etc., etc.

"They haven't said anything to give me hope, Cam. She is dying."

"We hope not," said Cam with his secret smile. "We spent the day working for her."

"Do you mean praying?" I said.

"Work is a better word to describe it than praying, if you don't understand what it is."

Well of course, I never understand.

"Real praying is work, believe me," says

Cam and they all smile at me, his way. They can't keep still, like children who have to go to the bathroom they're weaving and jiggling and doing little steps.

"Now where's her room?" says Cam in a practical tone of voice.

I thought of Mother dying and through that slit between her lids—who knows, maybe she can see from time to time—seeing this crowd of dervishes celebrating around her bed. Mother who lost her religion when she was thirteen and went to the Unitarian Church and quit when they had the split about crossing God out of the hymns, Mother having to spend her last conscious minutes wondering what had happened, if she was transported back in history to where loonies cavorted around in their crazy ceremonies, trying to sort her last reasonable thoughts out in the middle of their business.

Thank God the nurse said no. The intern was brought and he said no. Cam didn't insist, he smiled and nodded at them as if they were granting permission and then he brought the troupe back into the waiting room and there, right before my eyes, they started. They put the old man in the center, sitting down with his head bowed and his eyes shut—they had to tap him and remind him how to do that—and they squatted in a rough sort of circle round him, facing in and out, in and out, alternately. Then, eyes closed, they started swaying back and forth moaning some words very softly, only not the same words, it sounded as if each one of them had got different words, and not in English of course but Swahili or Sanskrit[6] or something. It got louder, gradually it got louder, a pounding singsong, and as it did they rose to their feet, all except the old man who stayed where he was and looked as if he might have gone to sleep, sitting, and they began a shuffling kind of dance where they stood, clapping, not very well in time. They did this for a long while, and the noise they were making, though it was not terribly loud, attracted the nurses from their station and nurses' aides and orderlies and a few people like me who were waiting, and nobody seemed to know what to do, because it was so unbelievable, so crazy in that ordinary little waiting room. Everybody just stared as if they were asleep and dreaming and expecting to wake up. Then a nurse came out of Intensive Care and said, "We can't have this disturbance. What do you think you're doing here?"

She took hold of one of the young ones and shook him by the shoulder, else she couldn't have got anybody to stop and pay attention.

"We're working to help a woman who's very sick," he told her.

"I don't know what you call working, but you're not helping anybody. Now I'm asking you to clear out of here. Excuse me. I'm not asking. I'm telling."

"You're very mistaken if you think the tones of our voices are hurting or disturbing any sick person. This whole ceremony is pitched at a level which will reach and comfort the unconscious mind and draw the demonic influences out of the body. It's a ceremony that goes back five thousand years."

"Good lord," said the nurse, looking stupefied as well she might. "Who are these people?"

I had to go and enlighten her, telling her that it was my brother and what you might call his friends, and I was not in on their ceremony. I asked about Mother, was there any change.

"No change," she said. "What do we have to do to get them out of here?"

"Turn the hose on them," one of the orderlies said, and all this time, the dance, or ceremony, never stopped, and the one who had stopped and done the explaining went back to dancing too, and I said to the nurse, "I'll phone in to see how she is, I'm going home for a little while." I walked out of the hospital and found to my surprise that it was dark. The whole day in there, dark to dark. In the parking lot I started to cry. Cam has turned this into a circus for his own benefit, I said to myself, and said it out loud when I got home.

Haro made me a drink.

"It'll probably get into the papers," I said. "Cam's chance for fame."

Haro phoned the hospital to see if there was any news and they said there wasn't. "Did they have—was there any difficulty with some young people in the waiting room this evening? Did they leave quietly?" Haro is ten years older than I am, a cautious man, too patient with everybody. I used to think he was sometimes giving Cam money I didn't know about.

"They left quietly," he said. "Don't worry about the papers. Get some sleep."

I didn't mean to but I fell asleep on the couch, after the long day. I woke up with the phone ringing and day lightening the room. I stumbled into the kitchen dragging the blanket Haro had put over me and saw by the clock on the wall it was a quarter to six. She's gone, I thought.

It was her own doctor.

He said he had encouraging news. He said she was much better this morning.

I dragged over a chair and collapsed in it, both arms and my head too down on the kitchen counter. I came back on the phone to hear him saying she was still in a critical phase and the next

6. ***Swahili*** (swä hē'lē) . . . ***Sanskrit*** (san'skrit). Swahili is spoken in much of eastern Africa; Sanskrit, the ancient sacred and literary language of India, is now extinct.

forty-eight hours would tell the story, but without raising my hopes too high he wanted me to know she was responding to treatment. He said that this was especially surprising in view of the fact that she had been late getting to hospital and the things they did to her at first did not seem to have much effect, though of course the fact that she survived the first few hours at all was a good sign. Nobody had made much of this good sign to me yesterday, I thought.

I sat there for an hour at least after I had hung up the phone. I made a cup of instant coffee and my hands were shaking so I could hardly get the water into the cup, then couldn't get the cup to my mouth. I let it go cold. Haro came out in his pajamas at last. He gave me one look and said, "Easy, Val. Has she gone?"

"She's some better. She's responding to treatment."

"The look of you I thought the other."

"I'm so amazed."

"I wouldn't've given five cents for her chances yesterday noon."

"I know. I can't believe it."

"It's the tension," Haro said. "I know. You build yourself up ready for something bad to happen and then when it doesn't, it's a queer feeling, you can't feel good right away, it's almost like a disappointment."

Disappointment. That was the word that stayed with me. I was so glad, really, grateful, but underneath I was thinking, so Cam didn't kill her after all, with his carelessness and craziness and going out and neglecting her he didn't kill her, and I was, yes, I was, sorry in some part of me to find out that was true. And I knew Haro knew this but wouldn't speak of it to me, ever. That was the real shock to me, why I kept shaking. Not whether Mother lived or died. It was what was so plain about myself.

Mother got well, she pulled through beautifully. After she rallied she never sank back. She was in the hospital three weeks and then she came home, and rested another three weeks, and after that went back to work, cutting down a bit and working ten to four instead of full days, what they call the housewives' shift. She told everybody about Cam and his friends coming to the hospital. She began to say things like, "Well, that boy of mine may not be much of a success at anything else but you have to admit he has a knack of saving lives." Or, "Maybe Cam should go into the miracle business, he certainly pulled it off with me." By this time Cam was saying, he is saying now, that he's not sure about that religion, he's getting tired of the other priests and all that not eating meat or root vegetables. It's a stage, he says now, he's glad he went through it, self-discovery. One day I went over there and found he was trying on an old suit and tie. He says he might take advantage of some of the adult education courses, he is thinking of becoming an accountant.

I was thinking myself about changing into a different sort of person from the one I am. I do think about that. I read a book called *The Art of Loving*.[7] A lot of things seemed clear while I was reading it but afterwards I went back to being more or less the same. What has Cam ever done that actually hurt me, anyway, as Haro once said. And how am I better than he is after the way I felt the night Mother lived instead of died? I made a promise to myself I would try. I went over there one day taking them a bakery cake—which Cam eats now as happily as anybody else—and I heard their voices out in the yard—now it's summer, they love to sit in the sun—Mother saying to some visitor, "Oh yes I was, I was all set to take off into the wild blue yonder, and Cam here, this *idiot*, came and danced outside my door with a bunch of his hippie friends—"

"My lord, woman," roared Cam, but you could tell he didn't care now, "members of an ancient holy discipline."

I had a strange feeling, like I was walking on coals and trying a spell so I wouldn't get burned.

Forgiveness in families is a mystery to me, how it comes or how it lasts.

---

7. ***The Art of Loving,*** a philosophical work arguing that love is a feeling of universal brotherhood as much as anything else, by psychoanalyst Erich Fromm.

Discussion

1. (a) How does Val feel about Cam as the story opens? **(b)** List some of the things Cam has done that make Val feel as she does.

2. Describe the religious group Cam gets involved with. Does it surprise you that most of the members are much younger than Cam? Why or why not?

3. (a) What are Val's thoughts as she waits outside her mother's hospital room? **(b)** Do you think her frame of mind at this point is what causes her negative reaction to Cam and his friends' "ceremony"? Explain. **(c)** How did *you* react to the ceremony?

4. (a) Why might Val have been disappointed in some part of her to find out that Cam hadn't really killed their mother after all? **(b)** Later, what does she think of herself for feeling this sense of disappointment?

5. What does Val mean by the last line of the story?

Application

Point of View

Authors generally use minor characters as first-person narrators when they want someone in the story to stand slightly apart from the action and comment on it. However, when authors decide to have a major character tell the story, they often choose their most important major character. Since the story is mostly about this character, it is helpful to know directly what he or she is thinking, feeling, and so on.

1. Why do you think the author made Val, rather than Cam, the narrator? Isn't the story more about him than about her? Explain.

2. How would you expect Cam to describe himself if he were telling the story? How might he characterize his sister?

3. What advantage, if any, do you think the author has gained by having Val as narrator?

Vocabulary

Dictionary

Using the Glossary, determine if the following statements about the italicized words are true or false. On separate paper write "T" or "F" after the number of each statement. Be sure you can spell each italicized word.

1. *Tycoon* comes from Chinese words meaning "great lord."

2. A synonym for *stupefy* is "astound."

3. A *freethinker* is a person who solves problems for others without charging for his or her services.

4. A *dervish* would be unlikely to *cavort.*

5. The words *phobia* and *atheist* come originally from Greek.

Alice Munro 1931–

Recognized for her refreshing portrayals of the Canadian small-town experience, Alice Munro was born and educated in Ontario. While working in the Vancouver [British Columbia] Public Library in the early 1950s, she began to have some of her short stories published by various small magazines. Her first collection, *Dance of the Happy Shades* (1968), received the Governor General's Award for Literature. Her keen eye for detail and the murkier depths of the human personality is evidenced in many of her works, including the novel *Lives of Girls and Women* (1971), the story collections *Something I've Been Meaning to Tell You* (1974) and *Beggar Maid* (1982), and the short stories that frequently appear in such prominent magazines as *The New Yorker* and *The Atlantic.* She still resides in Ontario.

Lamb to the Slaughter

Roald Dahl Great Britain

"It's the old story. Get the weapon, and you've got the man."

The room was warm and clean, the curtains drawn, the two table lamps alight—hers and the one by the empty chair opposite. On the sideboard behind her, two tall glasses, soda water, whiskey. Fresh ice cubes in the Thermos bucket.

Mary Maloney was waiting for her husband to come home from work.

Now and again she would glance up at the clock, but without anxiety, merely to please herself with the thought that each minute gone by made it nearer the time when he would come. There was a slow smiling air about her, and about everything she did. The drop of the head as she bent over her sewing was curiously tranquil. Her skin—for this was her sixth month with child—had acquired a wonderful translucent quality, the mouth was soft, and the eyes, with their new placid look, seemed larger, darker than before.

When the clock said ten minutes to five, she began to listen, and a few moments later, punctually as always, she heard the tires on the gravel outside, and the car door slamming, the footsteps passing the window, the key turning in the lock. She laid aside her sewing, stood up, and went forward to kiss him as he came in.

"Hullo, darling," she said.

"Hullo," he answered.

She took his coat and hung it in the closet. Then she walked over and made the drinks, a strongish one for him, a weak one for herself; and soon she was back again in her chair with the sewing, and he in the other, opposite, holding the tall glass with both his hands, rocking it so the ice cubes tinkled against the side.

For her, this was always a blissful time of day. She knew he didn't want to speak much until the first drink was finished, and she, on her side, was content to sit quietly, enjoying his company after the long hours alone in the house. She loved to luxuriate in the presence of this man, and to feel—almost as a sunbather feels the sun—that warm male glow that came out of him to her when they were alone together. She loved him for the way he sat loosely in a chair, for the way he came in a door, or moved slowly across the room with long strides. She loved the intent, far look in his eyes when they rested on her, the funny shape of the mouth, and especially the way he remained silent about his tiredness, sitting still with himself until the whiskey had taken some of it away.

"Tired, darling?"

"Yes," he said. "I'm tired." And as he spoke, he did an unusual thing. He lifted his glass and drained it in one swallow although there was still half of it, at least half of it left. She wasn't really watching him, but she knew what he had done because she heard the ice cubes falling back against the bottom of the empty glass when he lowered his arm. He paused a moment, leaning forward in the chair, then he got up and went slowly over to fetch himself another.

"I'll get it!" she cried, jumping up.

"Sit down," he said.

When he came back, she noticed that the new drink was dark amber with the quantity of whiskey in it.

"Darling, shall I get your slippers?"

"No."

She watched him as he began to sip the dark yellow drink, and she could see little oily swirls in the liquid because it was so strong.

"I think it's a shame," she said, "that when a policeman gets to be as senior as you, they keep him walking about on his feet all day long."

He didn't answer, so she bent her head again and went on with her sewing; but each time he lifted the drink to his lips, she heard the ice cubes clinking against the side of the glass.

"Darling," she said. "Would you like me to get you some cheese? I haven't made any supper because it's Thursday."

"No," he said.

"If you're too tired to eat out," she went on, "it's still not too late. There's plenty of meat and stuff in the freezer, and you can have it right here and not even move out of the chair."

Her eyes waited on him for an answer, a smile, a little nod, but he made no sign.

"Anyway," she went on, "I'll get you some cheese and crackers first."

"I don't want it," he said.

She moved uneasily in her chair, the large eyes still watching his face. "But you *must* have supper. I can easily do it here. I'd like to do it. We can have lamb chops. Or pork. Anything you want. Everything's in the freezer."

"Forget it," he said.

"But darling, you *must* eat! I'll fix it anyway, and then you can have it or not, as you like."

She stood up and placed her sewing on the table by the lamp.

"Sit down," he said. "Just for a minute, sit down."

It wasn't till then that she began to get frightened.

"Go on," he said. "Sit down."

She lowered herself back slowly into the chair, watching him all the time with those large, bewildered eyes. He had finished the second drink and was staring down into the glass, frowning.

"Listen," he said. "I've got something to tell you."

"What is it, darling? What's the matter?"

He had now become absolutely motionless, and he kept his head down so that the light from the lamp beside him fell across the upper part of his face, leaving the chin and mouth in shadow. She noticed there was a little muscle moving near the corner of his left eye.

"This is going to be a bit of a shock to you, I'm afraid," he said. "But I've thought about it a good deal and I've decided the only thing to do is tell you right away. I hope you won't blame me too much."

And he told her. It didn't take long, four or five minutes at most, and she sat very still through it all, watching him with a kind of dazed horror as he went further and further away from her with each word.

"So there it is," he added. "And I know it's kind of a bad time to be telling you, but there simply wasn't any other way. Of course I'll give you money and see you're looked after. But there needn't really be any fuss. I hope not anyway. It wouldn't be very good for my job."

Her first instinct was not to believe any of it, to reject it all. It occurred to her that perhaps he hadn't even spoken, that she herself had imagined the whole thing. Maybe, if she went about her business and acted as though she hadn't been listening, then later, when she sort of woke up again, she might find none of it had ever happened.

"I'll get the supper," she managed to whisper, and this time he didn't stop her.

When she walked across the room she couldn't feel her feet touching the floor. She couldn't feel anything at all—except a slight nausea and a desire to vomit. Everything was automatic now—down the steps to the cellar, the light switch, the deep freeze, the hand inside the cabinet taking hold of the first object it met. She lifted it out, and looked at it. It was wrapped in paper, so she took off the paper and looked at it again.

A leg of lamb.

All right then, they would have lamb for supper. She carried it upstairs, holding the thin bone-end of it with both her hands, and as she went through the living room, she saw him standing over by the window with his back to her, and she stopped.

"For heaven's sake," he said, hearing her, but not turning round. "Don't make supper for me. I'm going out."

At that point, Mary Maloney simply walked up behind him and without any pause she swung the big frozen leg of lamb high in the air and brought it down as hard as she could on the back of his head.

She might just as well have hit him with a steel club.

She stepped back a pace, waiting, and the funny thing was that he remained standing there for at least four or five seconds, gently swaying. Then he crashed to the carpet.

The violence of the crash, the noise, the small table overturning, helped bring her out of the shock. She came out slowly, feeling cold and surprised, and she stood for a while blinking at the body, still holding the ridiculous piece of meat tight with both hands.

All right, she told herself. So I've killed him.

It was extraordinary, now, how clear her mind became all of a sudden. She began thinking very fast. As the wife of a detective, she knew quite well what the penalty would be. That was fine. It made no difference to her. In fact, it would be a relief. On the other hand, what about the child? What were the laws about murderers with unborn children? Did they kill them both—mother and child? Or did they wait until the tenth month? What did they do?

Mary Maloney didn't know. And she certainly wasn't prepared to take a chance.

She carried the meat into the kitchen, placed it in a pan, turned the oven on high, and shoved it inside. Then she washed her hands and ran upstairs to the bedroom. She sat down before the mirror, tidied her hair, touched up her lips and face. She tried a smile. It came out rather peculiar. She tried again.

"Hullo, Sam," she said brightly, aloud.

The voice sounded peculiar too.

"I want some potatoes please, Sam. Yes, and I think a can of peas."

That was better. Both the smile and the voice were coming out better now. She rehearsed it several times more. Then she ran downstairs, took her coat, went out the back door, down the garden, into the street.

It wasn't six o'clock yet and the lights were still on in the grocery shop.

"Hullo, Sam," she said brightly, smiling at the man behind the counter.

"Why, good evening, Mrs. Maloney. How're *you?*"

"I want some potatoes please, Sam. Yes, and I think a can of peas."

The man turned and reached up behind him on the shelf for the peas.

"Patrick's decided he's tired and doesn't want to eat out tonight," she told him. "We usually go out Thursdays, you know, and now he's caught me without any vegetables in the house."

"Then how about meat, Mrs. Maloney?"

"No, I've got meat, thanks. I got a nice leg of lamb from the freezer."

"Oh."

"I don't much like cooking it frozen, Sam, but I'm taking a chance on it this time. You think it'll be all right?"

"Personally," the grocer said, "I don't believe it makes any difference. You want these Idaho potatoes?"

"Oh, yes, that'll be fine. Two of those."

"Anything else?" The grocer cocked his head on one side, looking at her pleasantly. "How about afterwards? What you going to give him for afterwards?"

"Well—what would you suggest, Sam?"

The man glanced around his shop. "How about a nice big slice of cheesecake? I know he likes that."

"Perfect," she said. "He loves it."

And when it was all wrapped and she had paid, she put on her brightest smile and said, "Thank you, Sam. Goodnight."

"Goodnight, Mrs. Maloney. And thank *you.*"

And now, she told herself as she hurried back, all she was doing now, she was returning home to her husband and he was waiting for his supper; and she must cook it good, and make it as tasty as possible because the poor man was tired, and if, when she entered the house, she happened to find anything unusual, or tragic, or terrible, then naturally it would be a shock and she'd become frantic with grief and horror. Mind you, she wasn't *expecting* to find anything. She was just going home with the vegetables. Mrs. Patrick Maloney going with the vegetables on Thursday evening to cook supper for her husband.

That's the way, she told herself. Do everything right and natural. Keep things absolutely natural and there'll be no need for any acting at all.

Therefore, when she entered the kitchen by the back door, she was humming a little tune to herself and smiling.

"Patrick!" she called. "How are you, darling?"

She put the parcel down on the table and went through into the living room; and when she saw him lying there on the floor with his legs doubled up and one arm twisted back underneath his body, it really was rather a shock. All the old love and longing for him welled up inside her, and she ran over to him, knelt down beside him, and began to cry her heart out. It was easy. No acting was necessary.

A few minutes later she got up and went to the phone. She knew the number of the police station, and when the man at the other end answered, she cried to him, "Quick! Come quick! Patrick's dead!"

"Who's speaking?"

"Mrs. Maloney. Mrs. Patrick Maloney."

"You mean Patrick Maloney's dead?"

"I think so," she sobbed. "He's lying on the floor and I think he's dead."

"Be right over," the man said.

The car came very quickly, and when she opened the front door, two policemen walked in. She knew them both—she knew nearly all the men at that precinct—and she fell right into Jack Noonan's arms, weeping hysterically. He put her gently into a chair, then went over to join the other one, who was called O'Malley, kneeling by the body.

"Is he dead?" she cried.

"I'm afraid he is. What happened?"

Briefly, she told her story about going out to the grocer and coming back to find him on the floor. While she was talking, crying and talking, Noonan discovered a small patch of congealed blood on the dead man's head. He showed it to O'Malley, who got up at once and hurried to the phone.

Soon, other men began to come into the house. First a doctor, then two detectives, one of whom she knew by name. Later, a police photographer arrived and took pictures, and a man who knew about fingerprints. There was a great deal of whispering and muttering beside the corpse, and the detectives kept asking her a lot of questions. But they always treated her kindly. She told her story again, this time right from the beginning, when Patrick had come in, and she was sewing, and he was tired, so tired he hadn't wanted to go out for supper. She told how she'd put the meat in the oven—"it's there now, cooking"—and how she'd slipped out to the grocer for vegetables, and come back to find him lying on the floor.

"Which grocer?" one of the detectives asked.

She told him, and he turned and whispered something to the other detective, who immediately went outside into the street.

In fifteen minutes he was back with a page of notes, and there was more whispering, and through her sobbing she heard a few of the whispered phrases—". . . acted quite normal . . . very cheerful . . . wanted to give him a good supper . . . peas . . . cheesecake . . . impossible that she . . ."

After a while, the photographer and the doctor departed and two other men came in and took the corpse away on a stretcher. Then the fingerprint man went away. The two detectives re-

mained, and so did the two policemen. They were exceptionally nice to her, and Jack Noonan asked if she wouldn't rather go somewhere else, to her sister's house perhaps, or to his own wife, who would take care of her and put her up for the night.

No, she said. She didn't feel she could move even a yard at the moment. Would they mind awfully if she stayed just where she was until she felt better. She didn't feel too good at the moment, she really didn't.

Then hadn't she better lie down on the bed? Jack Noonan asked.

No, she said. She'd like to stay right where she was, in this chair. A little later perhaps, when she felt better, she would move.

So they left her there while they went about their business, searching the house. Occasionally one of the detectives asked her another question. Sometimes Jack Noonan spoke to her gently as he passed by. Her husband, he told her, had been killed by a blow on the back of the head administered with a heavy blunt instrument, almost certainly a large piece of metal. They were looking for the weapon. The murderer may have taken it with him, but on the other hand he may've thrown it away or hidden it somewhere on the premises.

"It's the old story," he said. "Get the weapon, and you've got the man."

Later, one of the detectives came up and sat beside her. Did she know, he asked, of anything in the house that could've been used as the weapon? Would she mind having a look around to see if anything was missing—a very big spanner,[1] for example, or a heavy metal vase.

They didn't have any heavy metal vases, she said.

---

1. ***spanner,*** wrench. [*British*]

"Or a big spanner?"

She didn't think they had a big spanner. But there might be some things like that in the garage.

The search went on. She knew that there were other policemen in the garden all around the house. She could hear their footsteps on the gravel outside, and sometimes she saw the flash of a torch through a chink in the curtains. It began to get late, nearly nine she noticed by the clock on the mantel. The four men searching the rooms seemed to be growing weary, a trifle exasperated.

"Jack," she said, the next time Sergeant Noonan went by. "Would you mind giving me a drink?"

"Sure I'll give you a drink. You mean this whiskey?"

"Yes, please. But just a small one. It might make me feel better."

He handed her the glass.

"Why don't you have one yourself," she said. "You must be awfully tired. Please do. You've been very good to me."

"Well," he answered. "It's not strictly allowed, but I might take just a drop to keep me going."

One by one the others came in and were persuaded to take a little nip of whiskey. They stood around rather awkwardly with the drinks in their hands, uncomfortable in her presence, trying to say consoling things to her. Sergeant Noonan wandered into the kitchen, came out quickly and said, "Look, Mrs. Maloney. You know that oven of yours is still on, and the meat still inside."

"Oh, *dear* me!" she cried. "So it is!"

"I better turn it off for you, hadn't I?"

"Will you do that, Jack. Thank you so much."

When the sergeant returned the second time, she looked at him with her large, dark, tearful eyes. "Jack Noonan," she said.

"Yes?"

"Would you do me a small favor—you and these others?"

"We can try, Mrs. Maloney."

"Well," she said. "Here you all are, and good friends of dear Patrick's too, and helping to catch the man who killed him. You must be terrible hungry by now because it's long past your suppertime, and I know Patrick would never forgive me, God bless his soul, if I allowed you to remain in his house without offering you decent hospitality. Why don't you eat up that lamb that's in the oven. It'll be cooked just right by now."

"Wouldn't dream of it," Sergeant Noonan said.

"Please," she begged. "Please eat it. Personally I couldn't touch a thing, certainly not what's been in the house when he was here. But it's all right for you. It'd be a favor to me if you'd eat it up. Then you can go on with your work again afterwards."

There was a good deal of hesitating among the four policemen, but they were clearly hungry, and in the end they were persuaded to go into the kitchen and help themselves. The woman stayed where she was, listening to them through the open door, and she could hear them speaking among themselves, their voices thick and sloppy because their mouths were full of meat.

"Have some more, Charlie?"

"No. Better not finish it."

"She *wants* us to finish it. She said so. Be doing her a favor."

"Okay then. Give me some more."

"That's a big club the guy must've used to hit poor Patrick," one of them was saying. "The doc says his skull was smashed all to pieces just like from a sledgehammer."

"That's why it ought to be easy to find."

"Exactly what I say."

"Whoever done it, they're not going to be carrying a thing like that around with them longer than they need."

One of them belched.

"Personally, I think it's right here on the premises."

"Probably right under our very noses. What you think, Jack?"

And in the other room Mary Maloney began to giggle.

Discussion

1. (a) What preparations has Mary Maloney made for her husband's return from work? **(b)** What indications are there that she loves him very much? **(c)** Explain her various reactions after he tells her his news.

2. (a) Do you find Mary's calmness and care in working out her alibi after the crime believable? Why or why not? **(b)** How do the police check her alibi? What is the result?

3. This story is told by a limited omniscient narrator who knows the thoughts of only one character—Mary. **(a)** What significant information might have been made clear if Patrick's thoughts were also presented? **(b)** Why do you think the author chose not to have this information communicated?

4. Does the proverbial meaning of "lamb to the slaughter"—an innocent victim sacrificed for some purpose—apply to this story? Does the literal meaning (exactly what the words say)? Explain.

5. The last sentence of the story seems to be out of place—or is it? What do you think the author intends to show about Mary?

Roald Dahl 1916–

Born in Llandaff, South Wales, Roald Dahl spent his early career, from 1932 to 1939, with an oil company in East Africa. After Hitler invaded Poland in 1939, Dahl joined the Royal Air Force of Britain and served for six years.

The short-story collections *Over to You* (1946) and *Someone Like You* (1953), plus regular appearances in *The New Yorker,* acquainted American readers with Dahl's growing talents. *Kiss, Kiss* (1960), another story anthology, added to his reputation. Dahl has also produced a number of children's books and written or collaborated on several screenplays, including the original story for the film *Willie Wonka and the Chocolate Factory.*

Of Dahl's adult stories, the most successful contain a mixture of the humorous and the bizarre, as does "Lamb to the Slaughter." He has twice received the Edgar Allan Poe Award ("Edgar") of Mystery Writers of America.

See **INFERENCE** Handbook of Literary Terms

The Other Wife

Colette France

"Why didn't you ever tell me that she had blue eyes too?"

"For two? This way, *monsieur* and *madame,* there's still a table by the bay window, if *madame* and *monsieur* would like to enjoy the view."

Alice followed the *maître d'hôtel.*[1]

"Oh yes, come on, Marc, we'll feel we're having lunch on a boat at sea. . . ."

Her husband restrained her, passing his arm through hers.

"We'll be more comfortable there."

"There? In the middle of all those people? I'd much prefer . . . "

"Please, Alice."

He tightened his grip in so emphatic a way that she turned round.

"What's the matter with you?"

He said "shh" very quietly, looking at her intently, and drew her towards the table in the middle.

"What is it, Marc?"

"I'll tell you, darling. Let me order lunch. Would you like shrimps? Or eggs in aspic?"

"Whatever *you* like, as you know."

They smiled at each other, wasting the precious moments of an overworked, perspiring maître d'hôtel who stood near to them, suffering from a kind of St. Vitus' dance.[2]

"Shrimps," ordered Marc. "And then eggs and bacon. And cold chicken with cos lettuce salad. Cream cheese? *Spécialité de la maison?*[3] We'll settle for the *spécialité.* Two very strong coffees. Please give lunch to my chauffeur; we'll be leaving again at two o'clock. Cider? I don't trust it. . . . Dry champagne."

He sighed as though he had been moving a wardrobe, gazed at the pale noonday sea, the nearly white sky, then at his wife, finding her pretty in her little Mercury-type hat[4] with its long hanging veil.

"You're looking well, darling. And all this sea-blue color gives you green eyes, just imagine! And you put on weight when you travel. . . . It's nice, up to a point, but only up to a point!"

Her rounded bosom swelled proudly as she leaned over the table.

"Why did you stop me taking that place by the bay window?"

It did not occur to Marc Séguy[5] to tell a lie.

"Because you'd have sat next to someone I know."

"And whom I don't know?"

"My ex-wife."

She could not find a word to say and opened her blue eyes wider.

"What of it, darling? It'll happen again. It's not important."

Alice found her tongue again and asked the inevitable questions in their logical sequence.

"Did she see you? Did she know that you'd seen her? Point her out to me."

---

1. ***maître d'hôtel*** (mā'trə dō tel'), headwaiter. [*French*]
2. ***St. Vitus'*** (sānt vī'təs) ***dance,*** a nervous disease characterized by involuntary twitching of the muscles.
3. ***Spécialité de la maison*** (spā syal ē tā' də la mā zon'), specialty of the house. [*French*]
4. ***Mercury-type hat,*** the god Mercury is characteristically pictured wearing a rounded hat with small wings.
5. ***Séguy*** (sā gē').

"Don't turn round at once, I beg you; she must be looking at us. A lady with dark hair, without a hat; she must be staying at this hotel. . . . On her own, behind those children in red. . . ."

"Yes, I see."

Sheltered behind broad-brimmed seaside hats, Alice was able to look at the woman who fifteen months earlier had still been her husband's wife. "Incompatibility," Marc told her. "Oh, it was total incompatibility! We divorced like well-brought-up people, almost like friends, quietly and quickly. And I began to love you, and you were able to be happy with me. How lucky we are that in our happiness there haven't been any guilty parties or victims!"

The woman in white, with her smooth, lustrous hair over which the seaside light played in blue patches, was smoking a cigarette, her eyes half closed. Alice turned back to her husband, took some shrimps and butter, and ate composedly.

"Why didn't you ever tell me," she said after a moment's silence, "that she had blue eyes too?"

"But I'd never thought about it!"

He kissed the hand that she stretched out to the bread basket and she blushed with pleasure. Dark-skinned and plump, she might have seemed slightly earthy, but the changing blue of her eyes, and her wavy golden hair, disguised her as a fragile and soulful blond. She showed overwhelming gratitude to her husband. She was immodest without knowing it and her entire person revealed overconspicuous signs of extreme happiness.

They ate and drank with good appetite and each thought that the other had forgotten the woman in white. However, Alice sometimes laughed too loudly and Marc was careful of his posture, putting his shoulders back and holding his head up. They waited some time for coffee, in silence. An incandescent stream, a narrow reflection of the high and invisible sun, moved slowly over the sea and shone with unbearable brilliance.

"She's still there, you know," Alice whispered suddenly.

"Does she embarrass you? Would you like to have coffee somewhere else?"

"Not at all! It's she who ought to be embarrassed! And she doesn't look as though she's having a madly gay time, if you could see her. . . ."

"It's not necessary. I know that look of hers."

"Oh, was she like that?"

He breathed smoke through his nostrils and wrinkled his brows.

"Was she like that? No. To be frank, she wasn't happy with me."

"Well, my goodness!"

"You're delightfully generous, darling, madly

generous. . . . You're an angel, you're . . . You love me. . . . I'm so proud, when I see that look in your eyes . . . yes, the look you have now. . . . She . . . No doubt I didn't succeed in making her happy. That's all there is to it, I didn't succeed."

"She's hard to please!"

Alice fanned herself irritably, and cast brief glances at the woman in white, her head leaning against the back of the cane chair, her eyes closed with an expression of satisfied lassitude.

Marc shrugged his shoulders modestly.

"That's it," he admitted. "What can one do? We have to be sorry for people who are never happy. As for us, we're so happy. . . . Aren't we, darling?"

She didn't reply. She was looking with furtive attention at her husband's face, with its good color and regular shape, at his thick hair, with its occasional thread of white silk, at his small, well-cared-for hands. She felt dubious for the first time, and asked herself: "What more did she want, then?"

And until they left, while Marc was paying the bill, asking about the chauffeur and the route, she continued to watch, with envious curiosity, the lady in white, that discontented, hard-to-please, superior woman. . . .

Discussion

1. (a) Compare the appearance of Alice with that of Marc's first wife. **(b)** Why might Marc have married Alice, who seems so different?

2. (a) How is Marc made to seem older and somehow superior to Alice? **(b)** How does Alice feel about the difference between them?

3. (a) Whose idea was the breakup between Marc and his first wife? **(b)** Does Marc seem to have any feelings about this one way or the other? Explain.

4. What is achieved by having the first wife say nothing and merely be part of the environment?

5. To which of the two wives do you think the title of the story applies? Explain your answer.

Application

Inference

In order to infer the point of a brief story like this one, in which the only thing going on is interaction between characters, it may be necessary to put yourself in the place of those characters.

1. What things about Marc's first wife might secretly impress Alice?

2. What sorts of criticisms of Marc is the first wife likely to have had?

3. How might the things she has learned about the other two characters have made Alice feel "dubious for the first time"?

Colette 1873–1954

Thoroughly French in every respect, Colette (full name: Sidonie Gabrielle Claudine Colette) was born in the Burgundy region and died in Paris. She enjoyed a happy and creative childhood in her small village, growing extremely close to her mother. Memories of her childhood and her mother are preserved in the book *My Mother's House* (1923).

Married to a man considerably older than herself, Colette collaborated with him on the *Claudine* series of novels. Later she established herself independently as a major novelist with the publication of such works as *Cheri* (1920) and *Gigi* (1944). Concentrating on characterization rather than plot, Colette often places her protagonist in a crisis situation, delicately showing the changes in mood and the emotional subtleties as the character confronts the situation and reacts to it. This is what happens in "The Other Wife," when Alice first views her predecessor in Marc's affections.

See **FORESHADOWING** Handbook of Literary Terms

Life Is Sweet at Kumansenu[1]

Abioseh Nicol Sierra Leone

Bola could not overcome vague suspicions about her son's secret visit. Perhaps it was because mystery had marked his life from the beginning.

The sea and the wet sand to one side of it; green tropical forest on the other; above it the slow tumbling clouds. The clean round blinding disc of sun and the blue sky covered and surrounded the small African village, Kameni.[2]

A few square mud houses with roofs like helmets, here thatched and there covered with corrugated zinc where the prosperity of cocoa and trading had touched the head of the family.

The widow Bola stirred her palm-oil stew and thought of nothing in particular. She chewed a kola nut[3] rhythmically with her strong toothless jaws and soon unconsciously she was chewing in rhythm with the skipping of Asi, her granddaughter. She looked idly at Asi as the seven-year-old brought the twisted palm-leaf rope smartly over her head and jumped over it, counting in English each time the rope struck the ground and churned up a little red dust. Bola herself did not understand English well, but she could count easily up to twenty in English for market purposes. Asi shouted six and then said nine, ten. Bola called out that after six came seven. And I should know, she sighed. Although now she was old, there was a time when she bore children regularly every two years. Six times she had borne a boy child and six times they had died. Some had swollen up and with weak plaintive cries had faded away. Others had shuddered in sudden convulsions, with burning skins, and had rolled up their eyes and died. They had all died. Or rather he had died, Bola thought, because she knew it was one child all the time whose spirit had crept up restlessly into her womb to be born and to mock her.[4] The sixth time Musa, the village magician whom time had transformed into a respectable Muslim, had advised her and her husband to break the bones of the quiet little corpse and mangle it so that it couldn't come back to torment them alive again. But she held on to the child, and refused to let them handle it. Secretly she had marked it with a sharp pointed stick at the left buttock before it was wrapped in a mat and they had taken it away. When, the seventh time she had borne a son, and the purification ceremonies had taken place, she had turned it slyly to see whether the mark was there. It was. She showed it to the old woman who was the midwife and asked her what that was, and she had forced herself to believe the other who said it was an accidental scratch made whilst the child was being

1. ***Kumansenu*** (kü män sā′nü).
2. ***Kameni*** (kä mā′nē).
3. ***kola nut,*** the bitter seed of an African evergreen tree, used in making medicines and soft drinks.
4. ***one child . . . to mock her,*** a reference to a West African belief in a spirit-child who does not live to maturity but returns in a series of rebirths.

Abioseh Nicol (ä′bē ōs′ə nik ol′).

scrubbed. But this child had stayed. Meji,[5] he had been called. And he was now thirty years of age and a second-class clerk in government offices in a town ninety miles away. Asi, his daughter, had been left with her to do the things an old woman wanted a small child for, to run and take messages to the neighbors, to fetch a cup of water from the earthenware pot in the kitchen, to sleep with her and be fondled.

She threw the washed and squeezed cassava[6] leaves into the red boiling stew, putting in a finger's pinch of salt, and then went indoors, carefully stepping over the threshold to look for the dried red pepper. She found it, and then dropped it, leaning against the wall with a little cry. He turned round from the window and looked at her with a twisted half smile of love and sadness. In his short-sleeved, open-necked white shirt and gray gabardine trousers, a gold wristwatch and brown suede shoes, he looked like the pictures in African magazines of a handsome clerk who would get to the top because he ate the correct food, or regularly took the correct laxative, which was being advertised. His skin was grayish brown and he had a large handkerchief tied round his neck.

"Meji, God be praised," Bola cried. "You gave me quite a turn. My heart is weak and I can no longer take surprises. When did you come? How did you come? By lorry,[7] by fishing boat? And how did you come into the house? The front door was locked. There are so many thieves nowadays. I'm so glad to see you, so glad," she mumbled and wept, leaning against his breast.

Meji's voice was hoarse, and he said: "I am glad to see you too, Mother," beating her back affectionately.

Asi ran in and cried, "Papa, Papa," and was rewarded with a lift and a hug.

"Never mind how I came, Mother," Meji said, laughing. "I'm here, and that's all that matters."

"We must make a feast, we must have a big feast. I must tell the neighbors at once. Asi, run this very minute to Mr. Addai,[8] the catechist, and tell him your papa is home. Then to Mami Gbera to ask her for extra provisions, and to Pa Babole[9] for drummers and musicians . . ."

"Stop," said Meji raising his hand. "This is all quite unnecessary. I don't want to see *anyone*, no one at all; I wish to rest quietly and completely. No one is to know I'm here."

Bola looked very crestfallen. She was proud of Meji, and wanted to show him off. The village would never forgive her for concealing such an important visitor. Meji must have sensed this because he held her shoulder comfortingly and said: "They will know soon enough. Let us enjoy each other, all three of us, this time. Life is too short."

Bola turned to Asi, picked up the packet of pepper, and told her to go and drop a little into the boiling pot outside, taking care not to go too near the fire or play with it. After the child had gone, Bola said to her son, "Are you in trouble? Is it the police?"

He shook his head. "No," he said, "it's just that I like returning to you. There will always be this bond of love and affection between us, and I don't wish to share it. It is our private affair and that is why I've left my daughter with you," he ended up irrelevantly; "girls somehow seem to stay with relations longer."

"And don't I know it," said Bola. "But you look pale," she continued, "and you keep scraping your throat. Are you ill?" She laid her hand on his brow. "And you're cold, too."

"It's the cold wet wind," he said, a little harshly. "I'll go and rest now if you can open and dust my room for me. I'm feeling very tired. Very tired indeed. I've traveled very far today and it has not been an easy journey."

"Of course, my son, of course," Bola replied, bustling away hurriedly but happily.

Meji slept all afternoon till evening, and his mother brought his food to his room, later took the empty basins away. Then he slept again till morning.

---

5. ***Meji*** (mā'jē).
6. ***cassava*** (kä sä'vä), a tropical plant with starchy roots.
7. ***lorry,*** truck. *[British]*
8. ***Addai*** (ä dī').
9. ***Mami Gbera*** (mä'mē gə be'rä) . . . ***Pa Babole*** (pä bä bō'lē).

The next day, Saturday, was a busy one, and after further promising Meji that she would tell no one he was about, Bola went off to market. Meji took Asi for a long walk through a deserted path and up into the hills. She was delighted. They climbed high until they could see the village below in front of them, and the sea in the distance, and the boats with their wide white sails. Soon the sun had passed its zenith and was halfway towards the west. Asi had eaten all the food, the dried fish and the flat tapioca pancakes and the oranges. Her father said he wasn't hungry, and this had made the day perfect for Asi, who had chattered, eaten, and then played with her father's fountain pen and other things from his pocket. They soon left for home because he had promised they would be back before dark; he had carried her down some steep boulders and she had held on to his shoulders because he had said his neck hurt so and she must not touch it. She had said: "Papa, I can see behind you and you haven't got a shadow. Why?"

He had then turned her round to face the sun. Since she was getting drowsy, she had started asking questions, and her father had joked with her and humored her. "Papa, why has your watch stopped at twelve o'clock?" "Because the world ends at noon." Asi had chuckled at that. "Papa, why do you wear a scarf always round your neck?" "Because my head would fall off if I didn't." She had laughed out loud at that. But soon she had fallen asleep as he bore her homewards.

Just before nightfall, with his mother dressed

in her best, they had all three, at her urgent request, gone to his father's grave, taking a secret route and avoiding the main village. It was a small cemetery, not more than twenty years or so old, started when the Rural Health Department had insisted that no more burials take place in the backyards of households. Bola took a bottle of wine and a glass and four split halves of kola, each a half sphere, two red and two white. They reached the graveside and she poured some wine into the glass. Then she spoke to the dead man softly and caressingly. She had brought his son to see him, she said. This son whom God had given success, to the confusion and discomfiture of their enemies. Here he was, a man with a pensionable clerk's job and not a farmer, fisherman, or a mechanic. All the years of their married life people had said she was a witch because her children had died young. But this boy of theirs had shown that she was a good woman. Let her husband answer her now, to show that he was listening. She threw the four kola nuts up into the air and they fell on the grave. Three fell with the flat face upwards and one with its flat face downwards. She picked them up again and conversed with him once more and threw the kola nuts up again. But still there was an odd one or sometimes two.

They did not fall with all four faces up, or with all four faces down, to show that he was listening and was pleased. She spoke endearingly, she cajoled, she spoke sternly. But all to no avail. Then she asked Meji to perform. He crouched by the graveside and whispered. Then he threw the kola nuts and they rolled a little, Bola following them eagerly with her sharp old eyes. They all ended up face downwards. Meji emptied the glass of wine on the grave and then said that he felt nearer his father at that moment than he had ever done before in his life.

It was sundown, and they all three went back silently home in the short twilight. That night, going outside the house near her son's room window, she found, to her sick disappointment, that he had been throwing away all the cooked food out there. She did not mention this when she went to say goodnight, but she did sniff and say that there was a smell of decay in the room. Meji said he thought there was a dead rat up in the rafters, and he would clear it away after she had gone to bed.

That night it rained heavily, and sheet lightning turned the darkness into brief silver daylight for one or two seconds at a time. Then the darkness again and the rain. Bola woke soon after midnight and thought she could hear knocking. She went to Meji's room to ask him to open the door, but he wasn't there. She thought he might have gone out for a while and been locked out by mistake. She opened the door quickly, holding an oil lamp upwards. He stood on the veranda, curiously unwet, and refused to come in.

"I have to go away," he said hoarsely, coughing.

"Do come in," she said.

"No," he said, "I have to go, but I wanted to thank you for giving me a chance."

"What nonsense is this?" she said. "Come in out of the rain."

"I did not think I should leave without thanking you."

The rain fell hard, the door creaked, and the wind whistled.

"Life is sweet, Mother dear, good-by, and thank you."

He turned round and started running.

There was a sudden diffuse flash of lightning and she saw that the yard was empty. She went back heavily, and fell into a restless sleep. Before she slept she said to herself that she must see Mr. Addai next morning, Sunday, or, better still, Monday, and tell him about this in case Meji was in trouble. She hoped Meji would not be annoyed. He was such a good son.

But it was Mr. Addai who came instead, on Sunday afternoon, quiet and grave, and saw Bola sitting on an old stool in the veranda, dressing Asi's hair in tight thin plaits.

Mr. Addai sat down and, looking away, he said: "The Lord giveth and the Lord taketh away." And soon half the village were sitting round the veranda and in the yard.

"But I tell you, he was here on Friday and left Sunday morning," Bola said. "He couldn't have died on Friday."

Bola had just recovered from a fainting fit after being told of her son's death in town. His wife, Asi's mother, had come with the news, bringing some of his property. She said Meji had died instantly at noon on Friday and had been buried on Saturday at sundown. They would have brought him to Kameni for the burial. He had always wished that. But they could not do so in time as bodies did not last much after a day.

"He was here, he was here," Bola said, rubbing her forehead and weeping.

Asi sat by quietly. Mr. Addai said comfortingly, "Hush, hush, he couldn't have been, because no one in the village saw him."

"He said we were to tell no one," Bola said.

The crowd smiled above Bola's head, and shook their heads. "Poor woman," someone said, "she is beside herself with grief."

"He died on Friday," Mrs. Meji repeated, crying. "He was in the office and he pulled up the window to look out and call the messenger. Then the sash broke. The window fell, broke his neck, and the sharp edge almost cut his head off; they say he died at once."

"My papa had a scarf around his neck," Asi shouted suddenly.

"Hush," said the crowd.

Mrs. Meji dipped her hand into her bosom and produced a small gold locket and put it round Asi's neck, to quieten her. "Your papa had this made last week for your Christmas present. You may as well have it now."

Asi played with it and pulled it this way and that.

"Be careful, child," Mr. Addai said, "it was your father's last gift."

"I was trying to remember how he showed me yesterday to open it," Asi said.

"You have never seen it before," Mrs. Meji said, sharply, trembling with fear mingled with anger.

She took the locket and tried to open it.

"Let me have it," said the village goldsmith, and he tried whispering magic words of incantation. Then he said, defeated, "It must be poor-quality gold; it has rusted. I need tools to open it."

"I remember now," Asi said in the flat complacent voice of childhood.

The crowd gathered round quietly and the setting sun glinted on the soft red African gold of the dangling trinket. The goldsmith handed the locket over to Asi and asked in a loud whisper: "How did he open it?"

"Like so," Asi said and pressed a secret catch. It flew open and she spelled out gravely the word inside: "ASI."

The silence continued.

"His neck, poor boy," Bola said a little wildly, "that is why he could not eat the lovely meals I cooked for him."

Mr. Addai announced a service of intercession after vespers that evening. The crowd began to leave quietly.

Musa, the magician, was one of the last to leave. He was now very old and bent. In times of grave calamity, it was known that even Mr. Addai did not raise objection to Musa being consulted.

He bent over further and whispered in Bola's ear: "You should have had his bones broken and mangled thirty-one years ago when he went for the sixth time and then he would not have come back to mock you all these years by pretending to be alive. I told you so. But you women are naughty and stubborn."

Bola stood up, her black face held high, her eyes terrible with maternal rage and pride.

"I am glad I did not," she said, "and that is why he came back specially to thank me before he went for good."

She clutched Asi to her. "I am glad I gave him the opportunity to come back, for life is sweet. I do not expect you to understand why I did so. After all, you are only a man."

Discussion

1. (a) What ritual did Musa advise Bola to perform after her first six sons had died in infancy? **(b)** Why did Musa make this recommendation? Why do you think Bola refused to follow it? **(c)** Did she ever again see the mark she had placed on the body of the sixth dead child? Explain.

2. (a) How is the sadness of Bola's sons' deaths healed by the birth and growth of Meji? **(b)** How is Meji's visit a particular sign of his gratitude for his mother's care?

3. What is the significance of Meji's walk with his daughter and his visit to his father's grave?

4. (a) How has Meji made it difficult for the villagers to believe he has actually visited? **(b)** What finally convinces them that he has been there?

5. Meji and Bola each use the phrase "Life is sweet"—Meji when he says good-by to his mother, and Bola at the end of the story. Explain the special meanings of the phrase for each of them.

Application

Foreshadowing

You have seen that in a carefully constructed story every statement and episode is there for a reason. This is particularly true in a story that contains foreshadowing, a device that often is not noticed by the reader until he or she thinks about the story afterwards.

1. How do Bola's recollections of her earlier children set the stage for a supernatural element in the story?

2. Reread the various things Meji does and says during his visit. Point out at least five examples that give a clue to what has actually happened to him.

Composition

Any story that contains elements of fantasy—that is, unreal or otherworldly characters or occurrences—often raises a question in the reader's mind: can a story that features the unbelievable be capable of conveying a believable message? Review "Life Is Sweet at Kumansenu" to determine what the author's basic message is; then decide whether you think his use of the supernatural adds to or detracts from it, and why.

Write a two- or three-paragraph composition identifying the message and discussing specific reasons why the supernatural helps or hurts in conveying it.

Abioseh Nicol 1924–

Abioseh Nicol (real name: Davidson Sylvester Hector Willoughby Nicol) has had a varied career as administrator, teacher, and doctor as well as writer. As a child he was educated in both his native Sierra Leone and in Nigeria; he later received a medical degree from Cambridge University, England. He has worked as a physician in both England and Africa and as a school administrator in Sierra Leone; he has also held various posts in the United Nations.

Although he had published many articles on medical subjects, education, and politics, it was largely through the efforts of the late American writer Langston Hughes that his creative writing began to appear in print. Nicol has written poetry as well as short stories; his story collections include *The Truly Married Woman and Other Stories,* and *Two African Tales.* Many of his stories involve a mixture of the old and new in Africa—tribal life is shown side by side with the more European style of living in the cities.

Comment: The Oldest Ghost Story?

Stories in which the dead walk the earth in some form may be as old as the human race itself. Certainly the ancient Egyptians and Greeks believed that spirits could return to the world of the living. The tale that follows was included in a letter from the Roman writer Pliny (plin′ē) the Younger, A.D. 62?–A.D.113, and may be one of the earliest written-down ghost stories. Even this translation of it is old, having been done by the Englishman John Henley in 1724:

"There was a house at Athens large and capacious, but forsaken and of a very ill name. In the depth of night, a noise was heard in it, and if you listened closer the rattling of chains, first at a distance, then very near you. Presently appeared a spectre in the shape of an old man, worn out with age, meagre, and dejected, with a long beard and bristled hair; he wore fetters on his legs and chains on his hands, and shook them. On this, the inhabitants of the house passed several uneasy and melancholy nights; want of sleep brought a distemper upon them, and this, redoubling their terror, was followed by death. For in the day time, though the phantasm was absent, the memory of the appearance was still before their eyes, and their past fear produced a longer.

"Upon that, the house was quitted, and left entire to the phantasm. Yet an advertisement was put upon it, for the selling or letting it, if any stranger was inclined to the bargain.

"Athenodorus (a thē′nō dôr′əs) the philosopher came to Athens, he read the inscription; hearing the price and suspecting the lowness of the terms, he enquires, and is informed of every circumstance, and yet takes it, indeed the more readily upon that account.

"About evening he orders a bed in the fore-part of the house, calls for his writing-tables, his pencil, and a light. He dismisses all his family to the inner part of it, then he applies himself closely to writing, that his mind should not be vacant and form to itself imaginary fears and appearances. At first a profound silence reigned throughout the house as at other times; then the shaking of irons and the clink of chains began. He did not raise his eyes or lay down his pencil, but confirmed his resolution and was content only to listen.

"Then the noise increased and approached nearer, and sometimes was heard as at the entrance of the door, and sometimes within it. He looks back, sees it, and owns the shape as it was described to him. It stood still and beckoned with the finger as if it called him. He made a sign with his hand that it should stay a little and again set himself to his writing. The spectre renewed the noise of his chains and rattled them about the ears of the philosopher. He looked back, it beckoned again as before. So, without more delay, he takes up the light and follows it. It stalked along with a slow pace, as if it were over laden with the chains, turned into a court belonging to the house, and vanished.

"When he was left alone Athenodorus laid some weeds and leaves, which he pulled off for the purpose, for a mark upon the place. The next day he went to the magistrates and advised them to give an order for digging up the spot. Several bones were found in it, bound up and entangled with chains which the body, putrefied by the length of time and lying in the ground, had left behind it, bare: for the flesh had been eaten off by the irons.

"They were gathered up and buried publicly, and the house afterwards was free from the apparition, after this last duty was paid to it by a solemn interment."

Pliny, *Epistles,* Book VII, number xxvi. Translated by John Henley, 1724.

See **THEME** Handbook of Literary Terms

Through the Tunnel

Doris Lessing

Rhodesia (Zimbabwe)

"He looked down into the blue well of water. He knew he must find his way through that cave, or hole, or tunnel, and out the other side."

Going to the shore on the first morning of the vacation, the young English boy stopped at a turning of the path and looked down at a wild and rocky bay, and then over to the crowded beach he knew so well from other years. His mother walked on in front of him, carrying a bright striped bag in one hand. Her other arm, swinging loose, was very white in the sun. The boy watched that white, naked arm, and turned his eyes, which had a frown behind them, toward the bay and back again to his mother. When she felt he was not with her, she swung around. "Oh, there you are, Jerry!" she said. She looked impatient, then smiled. "Why, darling, would you rather not come with me? Would you rather—" She frowned, conscientiously worrying over what amusements he might secretly be longing for, which she had been too busy or too careless to imagine. He was very familiar with that anxious, apologetic smile. Contrition sent him running after her. And yet, as he ran, he looked back over his shoulder at the wild bay; and all morning, as he played on the safe beach, he was thinking of it.

Next morning, when it was time for the routine of swimming and sunbathing, his mother said, "Are you tired of the usual beach, Jerry? Would you like to go somewhere else?"

"Oh, no!" he said quickly, smiling at her out of that unfailing impulse of contrition—a sort of chivalry. Yet, walking down the path with her, he blurted out, "I'd like to go and have a look at those rocks down there."

She gave the idea her attention. It was a wild-looking place, and there was no one there; but she said, "Of course, Jerry. When you've had enough, come to the big beach. Or just go straight back to the villa, if you like." She walked away, that bare arm, now slightly reddened from yesterday's sun, swinging. And he almost ran after her again, feeling it unbearable that she could go by herself, but he did not.

She was thinking. Of course he's old enough to be safe without me. Have I been keeping him too close? He mustn't feel he ought to be with me. I must be careful.

He was an only child, eleven years old. She was a widow. She was determined to be neither possessive nor lacking in devotion. She went worrying off to her beach.

As for Jerry, once he saw that his mother had gained her beach, he began the steep descent to the bay. From where he was, high up among red-brown rocks, it was a scoop of moving bluish green fringed with white. As he went lower, he saw that it spread among small promontories and inlets of rough, sharp rock, and the crisping, lapping surface showed stains of purple and darker

---

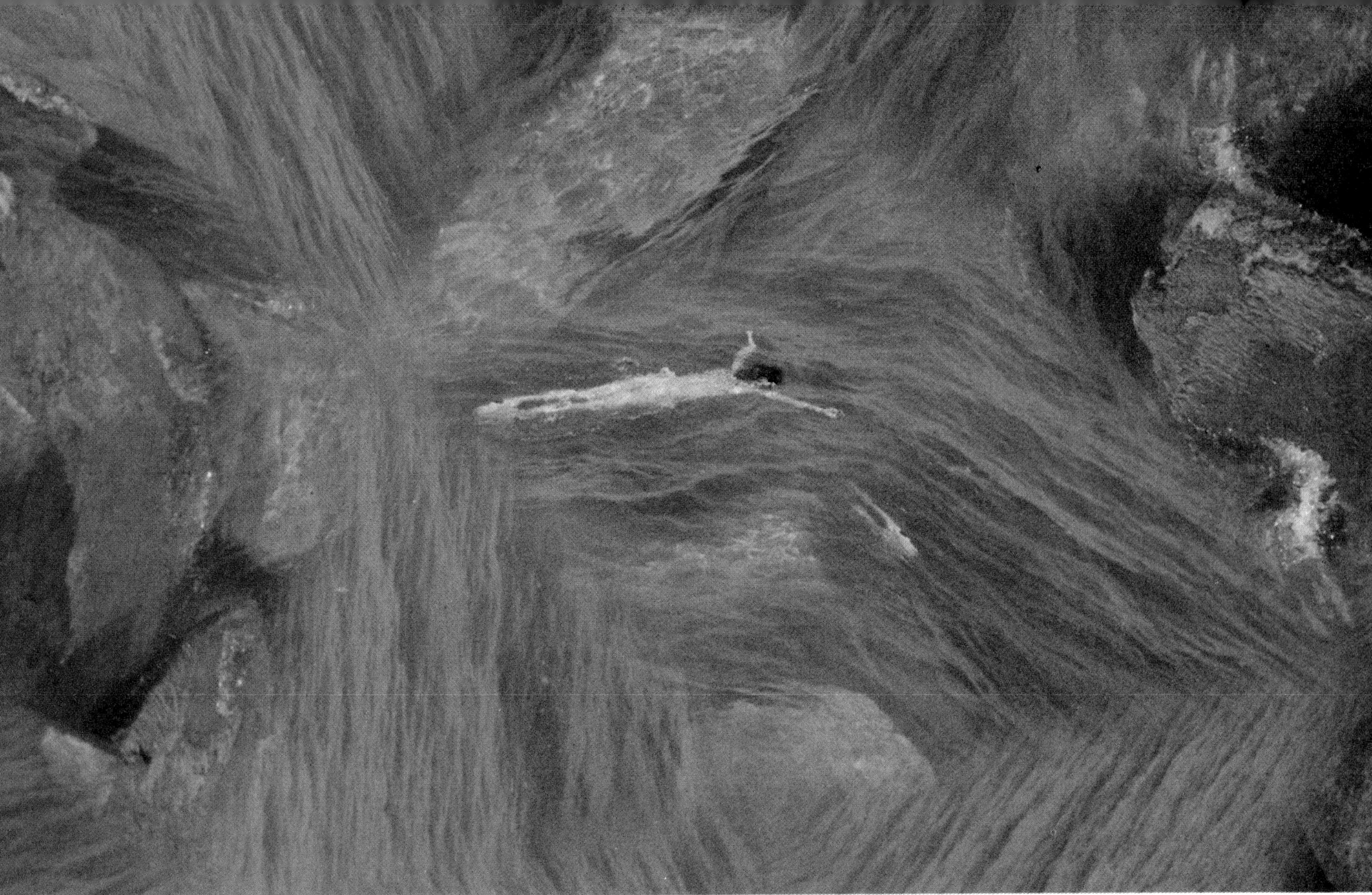

blue. Finally, as he ran sliding and scraping down the last few yards, he saw an edge of white surf and the shallow, luminous movement of water over white sand, and, beyond that, a solid, heavy blue.

He ran straight into the water and began swimming. He was a good swimmer. He went out fast over the gleaming sand, over a middle region where rocks lay like discolored monsters under the surface, and then he was in the real sea—a warm sea where irregular cold currents from the deep water shocked his limbs.

When he was so far out that he could look back not only on the little bay but past the promontory that was between it and the big beach, he floated on the buoyant surface and looked for his mother. There she was, a speck of yellow under an umbrella that looked like a slice of orange peel. He swam back to shore, relieved at being sure she was there, but all at once very lonely.

On the edge of a small cape that marked the side of the bay away from the promontory was a loose scatter of rocks. Above them, some boys were stripping off their clothes. They came running, naked, down to the rocks. The English boy swam toward them, but kept his distance at a stone's throw. They were of that coast; all of them were burned smooth dark brown and speaking a language he did not understand. To be with them, of them, was a craving that filled his whole body. He swam a little closer; they turned and watched him with narrowed, alert dark eyes. Then one smiled and waved. It was enough. In a minute, he had swum in and was on the rocks beside them, smiling with a desperate, nervous supplication. They shouted cheerful greetings at him; and then, as he preserved his nervous, uncomprehending smile, they understood that he was a foreigner strayed from his own beach, and they proceeded to forget him. But he was happy. He was with them.

They began diving again and again from a high point into a well of blue sea between rough, pointed rocks. After they had dived and come up, they swam around, hauled themselves up, and waited their turn to dive again. They were big boys—men, to Jerry. He dived, and they watched him; and when he swam around to take his place, they made way for him. He felt he was accepted and he dived again, carefully, proud of himself.

Soon the biggest of the boys poised himself, shot down into the water, and did not come up. The others stood about, watching. Jerry, after waiting for the sleek brown head to appear, let out a yell of warning; they looked at him idly and turned their eyes back toward the water. After a long time, the boy came up on the other side of a big dark rock, letting the air out of his lungs in a sputtering gasp and a shout of triumph. Immediately the rest of them dived in. One moment, the morning seemed full of chattering boys; the next, the air and the surface of the water were empty. But through the heavy blue, dark shapes could be seen moving and groping.

Jerry dived, shot past the school of underwater swimmers, saw a black wall of rock looming at him, touched it, and bobbed up at once to the surface, where the wall was a low barrier he could see across. There was no one visible; under him, in the water, the dim shapes of the swimmers had disappeared. Then one, and then another of the boys came up on the far side of the barrier of rock, and he understood that they had swum through some gap or hole in it. He plunged down again. He could see nothing through the stinging salt water but the blank rock. When he came up the boys were all on the diving rock, preparing to attempt the feat again. And now, in a panic of failure, he yelled up, in English, "Look at me! Look!" and he began splashing and kicking in the water like a foolish dog.

They looked down gravely, frowning. He knew the frown. At moments of failure, when he clowned to claim his mother's attention, it was with just this grave, embarrassed inspection that she rewarded him. Through his hot shame, feeling the pleading grin on his face like a scar that he could never remove, he looked up at the group of big brown boys on the rock and shouted, "*Bonjour! Merci! Au revoir! Monsieur, monsieur!*"[1] while he hooked his fingers round his ears and waggled them.

Water surged into his mouth; he choked, sank, came up. The rock, lately weighted with boys, seemed to rear up out of the water as their weight was removed. They were flying down past him, now, into the water; the air was full of falling bodies. Then the rock was empty in the hot sunlight. He counted one, two, three. . . .

At fifty, he was terrified. They must all be drowning beneath him, in the watery caves of the rock! At a hundred, he stared around him at the empty hillside, wondering if he should yell for help. He counted faster, faster, to hurry them up, to bring them to the surface quickly, to drown them quickly—anything rather than the terror of counting on and on into the blue emptiness of the morning. And then, at a hundred and sixty, the water beyond the rock was full of boys blowing like brown whales. They swam back to the shore without a look at him.

He climbed back to the diving rock and sat down, feeling the hot roughness of it under his thighs. The boys were gathering up their bits of clothing and running off along the shore to another promontory. They were leaving to get away from him. He cried openly, fists in his eyes. There was no one to see him, and he cried himself out.

It seemed to him that a long time had passed, and he swam out to where he could see his mother. Yes, she was still there, a yellow spot under an orange umbrella. He swam back to the big rock, climbed up, and dived into the blue pool among the fanged and angry boulders. Down he went, until he touched the wall of rock again. But the salt was so painful in his eyes that he could not see.

He came to the surface, swam to shore, and went back to the villa to wait for his mother. Soon she walked slowly up the path, swinging her striped bag, the flushed, naked arm dangling be-

1. ***"Bonjour!*** (bôn zhür′) ***Merci!*** (mer sē′) ***Au revoir!*** (ō rə vwär′) ***Monsieur . . . "*** (mə syėr′), French terms meaning "good morning," "thank you," "good-by," and "mister" or "sir."

side her. "I want some swimming goggles," he panted, defiant and beseeching.

She gave him a patient inquisitive look as she said casually, "Well, of course, darling."

But now, now, now! He must have them this minute, and no other time. He nagged and pestered until she went with him to a shop. As soon as she had bought the goggles, he grabbed them from her hand as if she were going to claim them for herself, and was off, running down the steep path to the bay.

Jerry swam out to the big barrier rock, adjusted the goggles, and dived. The impact of the water broke the rubber-enclosed vacuum, and the goggles came loose. He understood that he must swim down to the base of the rock from the surface of the water. He fixed the goggles tight and firm, filled his lungs, and floated, face down, on the water. Now, he could see. It was as if he had eyes of a different kind—fish eyes that showed everything clear and delicate and wavering in the bright water.

Under him, six or seven feet down, was a floor of perfectly clean, shining white sand, rippled firm and hard by the tides. Two grayish shapes steered there, like long, rounded pieces of wood or slate. They were fish. He saw them nose toward each other, poise motionless, make a dart forward, swerve off, and come around again. It was like a water dance. A few inches above them the water sparkled as if sequins were dropping through it. Fish again—myriads of minute fish, the length of his fingernail, were drifting through the water, and in a moment he could feel the innumerable tiny touches of them against his limbs. It was like swimming in flaked silver. The great rock the big boys had swum through rose sheer out of the white sand—black, tufted lightly with greenish weed. He could see no gap in it. He swam down to its base.

Again and again he rose, took a big chestful of air, and went down. Again and again he groped over the surface of the rock, feeling it, almost hugging it in the desperate need to find the entrance. And then, once, while he was clinging to the black wall, his knees came up and he shot his feet out forward and they met no obstacle. He had found the hole.

He gained the surface, clambered about the stones that littered the barrier rock until he found a big one, and, with this in his arms, let himself down over the side of the rock. He dropped, with the weight, straight to the sandy floor. Clinging tight to the anchor of stone, he lay on his side and looked in under the dark shelf at the place where his feet had gone. He could see the hole. It was an irregular, dark gap; but he could not see deep into it. He let go of his anchor, clung with his hands to the edges of the hole, and tried to push himself in.

He got his head in, found his shoulders jammed, moved them in sidewise, and was inside as far as his waist. He could see nothing ahead. Something soft and clammy touched his mouth; he saw a dark frond moving against the grayish rock, and panic filled him. He thought of octopuses, of clinging weed. He pushed himself out backward and caught a glimpse, as he retreated, of a harmless tentacle of seaweed drifting in the mouth of the tunnel. But it was enough. He reached the sunlight, swam to shore, and lay on the diving rock. He looked down into the blue well of water. He knew he must find his way through that cave, or hole, or tunnel, and out the other side.

First, he thought, he must learn to control his breathing. He let himself down into the water with another big stone in his arms, so that he could lie effortlessly on the bottom of the sea. He counted. One, two, three. He counted steadily. He could hear the movement of blood in his chest. Fifty-one, fifty-two . . . His chest was hurting. He let go of the rock and went up into the air. He saw that the sun was low. He rushed to the villa and found his mother at her supper. She said only "Did you enjoy yourself?" and he said "Yes."

All night the boy dreamed of the water-filled cave in the rock, and as soon as breakfast was over he went to the bay.

That night, his nose bled badly. For hours he had been underwater, learning to hold his breath, and now he felt weak and dizzy. His mother said, "I shouldn't overdo things, darling, if I were you."

That day and the next, Jerry exercised his lungs as if everything, the whole of his life, all that he would become, depended upon it. Again his nose bled at night, and his mother insisted on his coming with her the next day. It was a torment to him to waste a day of his careful self-training, but he stayed with her on that other beach, which now seemed a place for small children, a place where his mother might lie safe in the sun. It was not his beach.

He did not ask for permission, on the following day, to go to his beach. He went, before his mother could consider the complicated rights and wrongs of the matter. A day's rest, he discovered, had improved his count by ten. The big boys had made the passage while he counted a hundred and sixty. He had been counting fast, in his fright. Probably now, if he tried, he could get through that long tunnel, but he was not going to try yet. A curious, most unchildlike persistence, a controlled impatience, made him wait. In the meantime, he lay underwater on the white sand, littered now by stones he had brought down from the upper air, and studied the entrance to the tunnel. He knew every jut and corner of it, as far as it was possible to see. It was as if he already felt its sharpness about his shoulders.

He sat by the clock in the villa, when his mother was not near, and checked his time. He was incredulous and then proud to find he could hold his breath without strain for two minutes. The words "two minutes," authorized by the clock, brought close the adventure that was so necessary to him.

In another four days, his mother said casually one morning, they must go home. On the day before they left, he would do it. He would do it if it killed him, he said defiantly to himself. But two days before they were to leave—a day of triumph when he increased his count by fifteen—his nose bled so badly that he turned dizzy and had to lie limply over the big rock like a bit of seaweed, watching the thick red blood flow on the rock and trickle slowly down to the sea. He was frightened. Supposing he turned dizzy in the tunnel? Supposing he died there, trapped? Supposing—his head went around, in the hot sun, and he almost gave up. He thought he would return to the house and lie down, and next summer, perhaps, when he had another year's growth in him—*then* he would go through the hole.

But even after he had made the decision, or thought he had, he found himself sitting up on the rock and looking down into the water; and he knew that now, this moment, when his nose had only just stopped bleeding, when his head was still sore and throbbing—this was the moment when he would try. If he did not do it now, he never would. He was trembling with fear that he would not go; and he was trembling with horror at that long, long tunnel under the rock, under the sea. Even in the open sunlight, the barrier rock seemed very wide and very heavy; tons of rock pressed down on where he would go. If he died there, he would lie until one day—perhaps not before next year—those big boys would swim into it and find it blocked.

He put on his goggles, fitted them tight, tested the vacuum. His hands were shaking. Then he chose the biggest stone he could carry and slipped over the edge of the rock until half of him was in the cool, enclosing water and half in the hot sun. He looked up once at the empty sky, filled his lungs once, twice, and then sank fast to the bottom with the stone. He let it go and began to count. He took the edges of the hole in his hands and drew himself into it, wriggling his shoulders in sidewise as he remembered he must, kicking himself along with his feet.

Soon he was clear inside. He was in a small rock-bound hole filled with yellowish-gray water. The water was pushing him up against the roof. The roof was sharp and pained his back. He pulled himself along with his hands—fast, fast—and used his legs as levers. His head knocked against something; a sharp pain dizzied him. Fifty, fifty-one, fifty-two . . . He was without light, and the water seemed to press upon him with the weight of rock. Seventy-one, seventy-two . . . There was no strain on his lungs. He felt like an inflated balloon, his lungs were so light and easy, but his head was pulsing.

He was being continually pressed against the sharp roof, which felt slimy as well as sharp. Again he thought of octopuses, and wondered if the tunnel might be filled with weed that could tangle him. He gave himself a panicky, convulsive kick forward, ducked his head, and swam. His feet and hands moved freely, as if in open water. The hole must have widened out. He thought he must be swimming fast, and he was frightened of banging his head if the tunnel narrowed.

A hundred, a hundred and one . . . The water paled. Victory filled him. His lungs were beginning to hurt. A few more strokes and he would be out. He was counting wildly; he said a hundred and fifteen, and then, a long time later, a hundred and fifteen again. The water was a clear jewel-green all around him. Then he saw, above his head, a crack running up through the rock. Sunlight was falling through it, showing the clean, dark rock of the tunnel, a single mussel shell, and darkness ahead.

He was at the end of what he could do. He looked up at the crack as if it were filled with air and not water, as if he could put his mouth to it to draw in air. A hundred and fifteen, he heard himself say inside his head—but he had said that long ago. He must go on into the blackness ahead, or he would drown. His head was swelling, his lungs cracking. A hundred and fifteen, a hundred and fifteen pounded through his head, and he feebly clutched at rocks in the dark, pulling himself forward, leaving the brief space of sunlit water behind. He felt he was dying. He was no longer quite conscious. He struggled on in the darkness between lapses into unconsciousness. An immense, swelling pain filled his head, and then the darkness cracked with an explosion of green light. His hands, groping forward, met nothing; and his feet, kicking back, propelled him out into the open sea.

He drifted to the surface, his face turned up to the air. He was gasping like a fish. He felt he would sink now and drown; he could not swim the few feet back to the rock. Then he was clutching it and pulling himself up onto it. He lay face down, gasping. He could see nothing but a red-veined, clotted dark. His eyes must have burst, he thought; they were full of blood. He tore off his goggles and a gout of blood went into the sea. His nose was bleeding, and the blood had filled the goggles.

He scooped up handfuls of water from the cool, salty sea, to splash on his face, and did not know whether it was blood or salt water he tasted. After a time, his heart quieted, his eyes cleared, and he sat up. He could see the local boys diving and playing half a mile away. He did not want them. He wanted nothing but to get back home and lie down.

In a short while, Jerry swam to shore and climbed slowly up the path to the villa. He flung himself on his bed and slept, waking at the sound of feet on the path outside. His mother was coming back. He rushed to the bathroom, thinking she must not see his face with bloodstains, or tearstains, on it. He came out of the bathroom and met her as she walked into the villa, smiling, her eyes lighting up.

"Have a nice morning?" she asked, laying her hand on his warm brown shoulder a moment.

"Oh, yes, thank you," he said.

"You look a bit pale." And then, sharp and anxious, "How did you bang your head?"

"Oh, just banged it," he told her.

She looked at him closely. He was strained; his eyes were glazed looking. She was worried. And then she said to herself, Oh, don't fuss! Nothing can happen. He can swim like a fish.

They sat down to lunch together.

"Mummy," he said, "I can stay underwater for two minutes—three minutes, at least." It came bursting out of him.

"Can you, darling?" she said. "Well, I shouldn't overdo it. I don't think you ought to swim anymore today."

She was ready for a battle of wills, but he gave in at once. It was no longer of the least importance to go to the bay.

Discussion

1. (a) Describe the relationship between Jerry and his mother as the story opens. **(b)** To what extent do you think the relationship is a consequence of Jerry's being fatherless?

2. (a) Explain how the attitude of the older boys toward Jerry changes during the time he is with them. **(b)** What is Jerry's reaction to the surprising feat the boys are able to perform? **(c)** Why do you suppose he reacts as he does?

3. (a) Describe the preparations Jerry makes to conquer the underwater tunnel. **(b)** What health risks do these preparations involve? **(c)** What is significant about his choosing to make the swim at a point when he really doubts he can do it?

4. Describe Jerry's internal and external conflicts while swimming through the tunnel. Which, in your opinion, have more effect on him, and why?

5. After the swim, Jerry sees the older boys and thinks that he "did not want them," that he "wanted nothing but to get back home and lie down." How is this a change in his attitude?

Application

Theme

Though it would be harder if the plot were more complicated or the characters more numerous, determining the theme of this story might still give you pause. One approach might be to think through the events of the plot and then decide what overall effect they've had on the characters, particularly the main character. Another is to keep in mind all the things that theme is *not.*

Choose the best theme statement from the following, and explain what is wrong with the others.

1. To be treated as an adult, act like one!

2. An eleven-year-old boy puts himself through strict training to swim successfully through a long underwater tunnel.

3. The successful accomplishment of a difficult task through one's own will and effort can be an important step in growing up.

Vocabulary

Roots, Context

Certain Latin and Greek words, or parts of them, form the roots of dozens of English words. An example is the Latin verb *lucere,* "to shine," and its related noun *lumen,* "light."

The italicized words in the following sentences are derived from one or the other of these roots. Using context clues as well, write the meaning of each.

1. A spotlight under the water made the whole pool *luminous.*

2. How can you expect two candles to *illuminate* a big room like this?

3. *Luminaries* from sports and the theater made the banquet the place to be that night.

4. Since no one could understand the poem, I offered to *elucidate* it.

5. As he got over his morning grogginess, his remarks became more *lucid.*

Doris Lessing 1919–

The daughter of an army captain, Lessing was actually born in Iran; soon afterwards, however, her family moved to Southern Rhodesia (now Zimbabwe). At age thirty she left Rhodesia for England, but Africa remained a dominant influence on her writing.

Her first novel, *The Grass Is Singing* (1950), was highly acclaimed. In 1952 she began a series of novels called *Children of Violence* dealing with the problems of blacks and whites in rapidly changing African society. When she revisited Rhodesia she was so angered by the inequalities there that she incorporated her experiences in a book, *Going Home* (1957).

African Stories (1964), a collection, contains some of her best portrayals of the problems of southern Africa. But her most famous work is probably her novel *The Golden Notebook* (1962).

The Story of the Widow's Son

Mary Lavin Ireland

Which is more painful: the death of love or the death of a loved one?

This is the story of a widow's son, but it is a story that has two endings.

There was once a widow, living in a small neglected village at the foot of a steep hill. She had only one son, but he was the meaning of her life. She lived for his sake. She wore herself out working for him. Every day she made a hundred sacrifices in order to keep him at a good school in the town, four miles away, because there was a better teacher there than the village dullard that had taught herself.

She made great plans for Packy, but she did not tell him about her plans. Instead she threatened him, day and night, that if he didn't turn out well, she would put him to work on the roads, or in the quarry under the hill.

But as the years went by, everyone in the village, and even Packy himself, could tell by the way she watched him out of sight in the morning, and watched to see him come into sight in the evening, that he was the beat of her heart, and that her gruff words were only a cover for her pride and her joy in him.

It was for Packy's sake that she walked for hours along the road, letting her cow graze the long acre of the wayside grass, in order to spare the few poor blades that pushed up through the stones in her own field. It was for his sake she walked back and forth to the town to sell a few cabbages as soon as ever they were fit. It was for his sake that she got up in the cold dawning hours to gather mushrooms that would take the place of foods that had to be bought with money. She bent her back daily to make every penny she could, and as often happens, she made more by industry, out of her few bald acres, than many of the farmers around her made out of their great bearded meadows. Out of the money she made by selling eggs alone, she paid for Packy's clothes and for the greater number of his books.

When Packy was fourteen, he was in the last class in the school, and the master had great hopes of his winning a scholarship to a big college in the city. He was getting to be a tall lad, and his features were beginning to take a strong cast. His character was strengthening too, under his mother's sharp tongue. The people of the village were beginning to give him the same respect they gave to the sons of the farmers who came from their fine colleges in the summer, with blue suits and bright ties. And whenever they spoke to the widow they praised him up to the skies.

One day in June, when the air was so heavy the scent that rose up from the grass was imprisoned under the low clouds and hung in the air, the widow was waiting at the gate for Packy. There had been no rain for some days and the hens and chickens were pecking irritably at the dry ground and wandering up and down the road in bewilderment.

A neighbor passed.

"Waiting for Packy?" said the neighbor, pleasantly, and he stood for a minute to take off his hat and wipe the sweat of the day from his face. He was an old man.

"It's a hot day!" he said. "It will be a hard push for Packy on that battered old bike of his. I wouldn't like to have to face into four miles on a day like this!"

"Packy would travel three times that distance if there was a book at the other end of the road!"

"The Story of the Widow's Son" by Mary Lavin from *Irish Harvest*. Reprinted by permission of the author.

said the widow, with the pride of those who cannot read more than a line or two without wearying.

The minutes went by slowly. The widow kept looking up at the sun.

"I suppose the heat is better than the rain!" she said, at last.

"The heat can do a lot of harm too, though," said the neighbor, absent-mindedly, as he pulled a long blade of grass from between the stones of the wall and began to chew the end of it. "You could get sunstroke on a day like this!" He looked up at the sun. "The sun is a terror," he said. "It could cause you to drop down dead like a stone!"

The widow strained out further over the gate. She looked up the hill in the direction of the town.

"He will have a good cool breeze on his face coming down the hill, at any rate," she said.

The man looked up the hill. "That's true. On the hottest day of the year you would get a cool breeze coming down that hill on a bicycle. You would feel the air streaming past your cheeks like silk. And in the winter it's like two knives flashing to either side of you, and peeling off your skin like you'd peel the bark off a sally-rod."[1] He chewed the grass meditatively. "That must be one of the steepest hills in Ireland," he said. "That hill is a hill worthy of the name of a hill." He took the grass out of his mouth. "It's my belief," he said, earnestly looking at the widow—"it's my belief that that hill is to be found marked with a name in the Ordnance Survey map!"[2]

"If that's the case," said the widow, "Packy will be able to tell you all about it. When it isn't a book he has in his hand it's a map."

"Is that so?" said the man. "That's interesting. A map is a great thing. A map is not an ordinary thing. It isn't everyone can make out a map."

The widow wasn't listening.

"I think I see Packy!" she said, and she opened the wooden gate and stepped out into the roadway.

At the top of the hill there was a glitter of spokes as a bicycle came into sight. Then there was a flash of blue jersey as Packy came flying downward, gripping the handlebars of the bike, with his bright hair blown back from his forehead. The hill was so steep, and he came down so fast, that it seemed to the man and woman at the bottom of the hill that he was not moving at all, but that it was the bright trees and bushes, the bright ditches and wayside grasses that were streaming away to either side of him.

The hens and chickens clucked and squawked and ran along the road looking for a safe place in the ditches. They ran to either side with feminine fuss and chatter. Packy waved to his mother. He came nearer and nearer. They could see the freckles on his face.

"Shoo!" cried Packy at the squawking hens that had not yet left the roadway. They ran with their long necks straining forward.

"Shoo!" said Packy's mother, lifting her apron and flapping it in the air to frighten them out of his way.

It was only afterwards, when the harm was done, that the widow began to think that it might, perhaps, have been the flapping of her own apron that frightened the old clucking hen and sent her flying out over the garden wall into the middle of the road.

The old hen appeared suddenly on top of the grassy ditch and looked with a distraught eye at the hens and chickens as they ran to right and left. Her own feathers began to stand out from her. She craned her neck forward and gave a distracted squawk, and fluttered down into the middle of the hot dusty road.

Packy jammed on the brakes. The widow screamed. There was a flurry of white feathers and a spurt of blood. The bicycle swerved and fell. Packy was thrown over the handlebars.

It was such a simple accident that, although the widow screamed, and although the old man looked around to see if there was help near, nei-

---

1. ***sally-rod,*** a willow twig.
2. ***Ordnance Survey map,*** a very complete and detailed map of a limited area, prepared by the British Royal Engineers. (Britain at one time controlled Ireland.)

ther of them thought that Packy was very badly hurt, but when they ran over and lifted his head, and saw that he could not speak, they wiped the blood from his face and looked around, desperately, to measure the distance they would have to carry him.

It was only a few yards to the door of the cottage, but Packy was dead before they got him across the threshold.

"He's only in a weakness!" screamed the widow, and she urged the crowd that had gathered outside the door to do something for him. "Get a doctor!" she cried, pushing a young laborer towards the door. "Hurry! Hurry! The doctor will bring him around."

But the neighbors that kept coming in the door, quickly, from all sides, were crossing themselves, one after another, and falling on their knees, as soon as they laid eyes on the boy, stretched out flat on the bed, with the dust and dirt and the sweat marks of life on his dead face.

When at last the widow was convinced that her son was dead, the other women had to hold her down. She waved her arms and cried out aloud, and wrestled to get free. She wanted to wring the neck of every hen in the yard.

"I'll kill every one of them. What good are they to me, now? All the hens in the world aren't worth one drop of human blood. That old clucking hen wasn't worth more than six shillings,[3] at the very most. What is six shillings? Is it worth poor Packy's life?"

But after a time she stopped raving, and looked from one face to another.

"Why didn't he ride over the old hen?" she asked. "Why did he try to save an old hen that wasn't worth more than six shillings? Didn't he know he was worth more to his mother than an old hen that would be going into the pot one of these days? Why did he do it? Why did he put on the brakes going down one of the worst hills in the country? Why? Why?"

The neighbors patted her arm.

"There now!" they said. "There now!" and that was all they could think of saying, and they said it over and over again. "There now! There now!"

And years afterwards, whenever the widow spoke of her son Packy to the neighbors who dropped in to keep her company for an hour or two, she always had the same question to ask, the same tireless question.

"Why did he put the price of an old clucking hen above the price of his own life?"

And the people always gave the same answer.

"There now!" they said, "there now!" And they sat as silently as the widow herself, looking into the fire.

But surely some of those neighbors must have been stirred to wonder what would have happened had Packy not yielded to his impulse of fear, and had, instead, ridden boldly over the old clucking hen? And surely some of them must have stared into the flames and pictured the scene of the accident again, altering a detail here and there as they did so, and giving the story a different end. For these people knew the widow, and they knew Packy, and when you know people well it is as easy to guess what they would say and do in certain circumstances as it is to remember what they actually did say and do in other circumstances. In fact it is sometimes easier to invent than to remember accurately, and were this not so two great branches of creative art would wither in an hour: the art of the storyteller and the art of the gossip. So, perhaps, if I try to tell you what I myself think might have happened had Packy killed that cackling old hen, you will not accuse me of abusing my privileges as a writer. After all, what I am about to tell you is no more of a fiction than what I have already told, and I lean no heavier now upon your credulity than, with your full consent, I did in the first instance.

And moreover, in many respects the new story is the same as the old.

It begins in the same way too. There is the widow grazing her cow by the wayside, and walking the long roads to the town, weighted down with sacks of cabbages that will pay for Packy's schooling. There she is, fussing over Packy in the mornings in case he would be late for school. There she is in the evening watching the battered clock on the dresser for the hour when he will appear on the top of the hill at his return. And there too, on a hot day in June, is the old laboring man coming up the road, and pausing to talk to her, as she stood at the door. There he is dragging a blade of grass from between the stones of the wall, and putting it between his teeth to chew, before he opens his mouth.

And when he opens his mouth at last it is to utter the same remark.

"Waiting for Packy?" said the old man, and then he took off his hat and wiped the sweat from his forehead. It will be remembered that he was an old man. "It's a hot day," he said.

---

3. ***twelve shillings.*** At the time of this story, this amount was worth about $1.20.

"It's very hot," said the widow, looking anxiously up the hill. "It's a hot day to push a bicycle four miles along a bad road with the dust rising to choke you, and sun striking spikes off the handlebars!"

"The heat is better than the rain, all the same," said the old man.

"I suppose it is," said the widow. "All the same, there were days when Packy came home with the rain dried into his clothes so bad they stood up stiff like boards when he took them off. They stood up stiff like boards against the wall, for all the world as if he was still standing in them!"

"Is that so?" said the old man. "You may be sure he got a good petting on those days. There is no son like a widow's son. A ewe lamb!"

"Is it Packy?" said the widow, in disgust. "Packy never got a day's petting since the day he was born. I made up my mind from the first that I'd never make a soft one out of him."

The widow looked up the hill again, and set herself to raking the gravel outside the gate as if she were in the road for no other purpose. Then she gave another look up the hill.

"Here he is now!" she said, and she rose such a cloud of dust with the rake that they could hardly see the glitter of the bicycle spokes, and the flash of blue jersey as Packy came down the hill at a breakneck speed.

Nearer and nearer he came, faster and faster, waving his hand to the widow, shouting at the hens to leave the way!

The hens ran for the ditches, stretching their necks in gawky terror. And then, as the last hen squawked into the ditch, the way was clear for a moment before the whirling silver spokes.

Then, unexpectedly, up from nowhere it seemed, came an old clucking hen and, clucking despairingly, it stood for a moment on the top of the wall and then rose into the air with the clumsy flight of a ground fowl.

Packy stopped whistling. The widow screamed. Packy yelled and the widow flapped her apron. Then Packy swerved the bicycle, and a cloud of dust rose from the braked wheel.

For a minute it could not be seen what exactly had happened, but Packy put his foot down and dragged it along the ground in the dust till he brought the bicycle to a sharp stop. He threw the bicycle down with a clatter on the hard road and ran back. The widow could not bear to look. She threw her apron over her head.

"He's killed the clucking hen!" she said. "He's killed her! He's killed her!" and then she let the apron fall back into place, and began to run up the hill herself. The old man spat out the blade of grass that he had been chewing and ran after the woman.

"Did you kill it?" screamed the widow, and as she got near enough to see the blood and feathers she raised her arm over her head, and her fist was clenched till the knuckles shone white. Packy cowered down over the carcass of the fowl and hunched up his shoulders as if to shield himself from a blow. His legs were spattered with blood, and the brown and white feathers of the dead hen were stuck to his hands, and stuck to his clothes, and they were strewn all over the road. Some of the short white inner feathers were still swirling with the dust in the air.

"I couldn't help it, Mother. I couldn't help it. I didn't see her till it was too late!"

The widow caught up the hen and examined it all over, holding it by the bone of the breast, and letting the long neck dangle. Then, catching it by the leg, she raised it suddenly above her head, and brought down the bleeding body on the boy's back, in blow after blow, spattering the blood all over his face and his hands, over his clothes and over the white dust of the road around him.

"How dare you lie to me!" she screamed, gaspingly, between the blows. "You saw the hen. I know you saw it. You stopped whistling! You called out! We were watching you. We saw." She turned upon the old man. "Isn't that right?" she demanded. "He saw the hen, didn't he? He saw it?"

"It looked that way," said the old man, uncertainly, his eye on the dangling fowl in the widow's hand.

"There you are!" said the widow. She threw

the hen down on the road. "You saw the hen in front of you on the road, as plain as you see it now," she accused, "but you wouldn't stop to save it because you were in too big a hurry home to fill your belly! Isn't that so?"

"No, Mother. No! I saw her all right but it was too late to do anything."

"He admits now that he saw it," said the widow, turning and nodding triumphantly at the onlookers who had gathered at the sound of the shouting.

"I never denied seeing it!" said the boy, appealing to the onlookers as to his judges.

"He doesn't deny it!" screamed the widow. "He stands there as brazen as you like, and admits for all the world to hear that he saw the hen as plain as the nose on his face, and he rode over it without a thought!"

"But what else could I do?" said the boy, throwing out his hand; appealing to the crowd now, and now appealing to the widow. "If I'd put on the brakes going down the hill at such a speed I would have been put over the handlebars!"

"And what harm would that have done you?" screamed the widow. "I often saw you taking a toss when you were wrestling with Jimmy Mack and I heard no complaints afterwards, although your elbows and knees would be running blood, and your face scraped like a gridiron!" She turned to the crowd. "That's as true as God. I often saw him come in with his nose spouting blood like a pump, and one eye closed as tight as the eye of a corpse. My hand was often stiff for a week from sopping out wet cloths to put poultices on him and try to bring his face back to rights again." She swung back to Packy again. "You're not afraid of a fall when you go climbing trees, are you? You're not afraid to go up on the roof after a cat, are you? Oh, there's more in this than you want me to know. I can see that. You killed that hen on purpose—that's what I believe! You're tired of going to school. You want to get out of going away to college. That's it! You think if you kill the few poor hens we have there will be no money in the box when the time comes to pay for books and classes. That's it!" Packy began to redden.

"It's late in the day for me to be thinking of things like that," he said. "It's long ago I should have started those tricks if that was the way I felt. But it's not true. I want to go to college. The reason I was coming down the hill so fast was to tell you that I got the scholarship. The teacher told me as I was leaving the schoolhouse. That's why I was pedaling so hard. That's why I was whistling. That's why I was waving my hand. Didn't you see me waving my hand from once I came in sight at the top of the hill?"

The widow's hands fell to her sides. The wind of words died down within her and left her flat and limp. She didn't know what to say. She could feel the neighbors staring at her. She wished that they were gone away about their business. She wanted to throw out her arms to the boy, to drag him against her heart and hug him like a small child. But she thought of how the crowd would look at each other and nod and snigger. A ewe lamb! She didn't want to satisfy them. If she gave in to her feelings now they would know how much she had been counting on his getting the scholarship. She wouldn't please them! She wouldn't satisfy them!

She looked at Packy, and when she saw him standing there before her, spattered with the furious feathers and crude blood of the dead hen, she felt a fierce disappointment for the boy's own disappointment, and a fierce resentment against him for killing the hen on this day of all days, and spoiling the great news of his success.

Her mind was in confusion. She started at the blood on his face, and all at once it seemed as if the blood was a bad omen of the future that was for him. Disappointment, fear, resentment, and above all defiance raised themselves within her like screeching animals. She looked from Packy to the onlookers.

"Scholarship! Scholarship!" she sneered, putting as much derision as she could into her voice and expression.

"I suppose you think you are a great fellow now? I suppose you think you are independent now? I suppose you think you can go off with yourself now, and look down on your poor slave of a mother who scraped and sweated for you with her cabbages and her hens? I suppose you think to yourself that it doesn't matter now whether the hens are alive or dead? Is that the way? Well, let me tell you this! You're not as independent as you think. The scholarship may pay for your books and your teacher's fees but who will pay for your clothes? Ah-ha, you forgot that, didn't you?" She put her hands on her hips. Packy hung his head. He no longer appealed to the gawking neighbors. They might have been able to save him from blows but he knew enough about life to know that no one could save him from shame.

The widow's heart burned at sight of his shamed face, as her heart burned with grief, but her temper too burned fiercer and fiercer, and she came to a point at which nothing could quell the blaze till it had burned itself out. "Who'll buy your suits?" she yelled. "Who'll buy your boots?" She paused to think of more humiliating accusations. "Who'll buy your breeches?" She paused again and her teeth bit against each other. What would wound deepest? What shame could she drag upon him? "Who'll buy your nightshirts or will you sleep in your skin?"

The neighbors laughed at that, and the tension was broken. The widow herself laughed. She held her sides and laughed, and as she laughed everything seemed to take on a newer and simpler significance. Things were not as bad as they seemed a moment before. She wanted Packy to laugh too. She looked at him. But as she looked at Packy her heart turned cold with a strange new fear.

"Get into the house!" she said, giving him a push ahead of her. She wanted him safe under her own roof. She wanted to get him away from the gaping neighbors. She hated them, man, woman, and child. She felt that if they had not been there things would have been different. And she wanted to get away from the sight of the blood on the road. She wanted to mash a few potatoes and make a bit of potato cake for Packy. That would comfort him. He loved that.

Packy hardly touched the food. And even after he had washed and scrubbed himself there were stains of blood turning up in the most unexpected places: behind his ears, under his fingernails, inside the cuff of his sleeve.

"Put on your good clothes," said the widow, making a great effort to be gentle, but her manners had become as twisted and as hard as the branches of the trees across the road from her, and even the kindly offers she made sounded harsh. The boy sat on the chair in a slumped position that kept her nerves on edge, and set up a further conflict of irritation and love in her heart. She hated to see him slumping there in the chair, not asking to go outside the door, but still she was uneasy whenever he as much as looked in the direction of the door. She felt safe while he was under the roof; inside the lintel; under her eyes.

Next day she went in to wake him for school, but his room was empty; his bed had not been slept in, and when she ran out into the yard and called him everywhere there was no answer. She ran up and down. She called at the houses of the neighbors but he was not in any house. And she thought she could hear sniggering behind her in each house that she left, as she ran to another one. He wasn't in the village. He wasn't in the town. The master of the school said that she should let the police have a description of him. He said he never met a boy as sensitive as Packy. A boy like that took strange notions into his head from time to time.

The police did their best but there was no news of Packy that night. A few days later there was a letter saying that he was well. He asked his mother to notify the master that he would not be coming back, so that some other boy could claim the scholarship. He said that he would send the price of the hen as soon as he made some money.

Another letter in a few weeks said that he had got a job on a trawler, and that he would not be able to write very often but that he would put aside some of his pay every week and send it to his mother whenever he got into port. He said that he wanted to pay her back for all she had done for him. He gave no address. He kept his promise about the money but he never gave any address when he wrote.

. . . And so the people may have let their thoughts run on, as they sat by the fire with the widow, many a night, listening to her complaining voice saying the same thing over and over. "Why did he put the price of an old hen above the price of his own life?" And it is possible that their version of the story has a certain element of truth about it too. Perhaps all our actions have this double quality about them; this possibility of alternative, and that it is only by careful watching and absolute sincerity that we follow the path that is destined for us, and, no matter how tragic that may be, it is better than the tragedy we bring upon ourselves.

Discussion

1. The setting for the accident is the same in each version of the story. Describe this setting, explaining in what way it is a cause of what happens.

2. **(a)** In the first version, another cause of the tragedy is the widow's flapping her apron at the chickens. Explain. **(b)** How is the widow even more responsible for the tragedy in the second version?

3. **(a)** Through what means does the author show Packy's character in the first version? in the second version? **(b)** In which version do you learn more about him? Explain. **(c)** Would you say the widow has done a good job in molding his character? Why or why not?

4. According to the author, the neighbors know the widow and Packy well, and it is they who picture the accident again, altering details and giving the story a different ending. **(a)** What does this say about the widow's character? **(b)** Are there any hints in the first version of these aspects of her character? Explain.

5. At the end of the story, regarding the need to follow the path that is destined for us, the author says, "No matter how tragic that may be, it is better than the tragedy we bring upon ourselves." **(a)** How do the two endings illustrate this theme? **(b)** Which ending do you think is more tragic for the widow? Why?

Composition

One point made by the two endings to this story is that people tend to look for new possibilities in past, unchangeable events. Imagine that someone objects to the second ending on the basis that it does not really support this point. Reread the second version, noting ways the author shows that it does offer "new possibilities."

In a short composition argue in favor of the use of the second ending, citing evidence that shows how the author uses it to accomplish her purpose.

Mary Lavin 1912–

Although she was born in Walpole, Massachusetts, Mary Lavin must be counted as an Irish author, for she was born of Irish parents and as a child moved to Ireland, where she has since lived.

At first she looked forward to a career in literary research—she received her master's degree from the National University of Ireland for a thesis on Jane Austen—but the publication of one of her short stories changed the direction of her work to the writing of fiction. The detour has resulted in works in which she combines the gifts of a born storyteller with a penetrating insight into the human heart. They include *Tales from Bective Bridge* (1942), *A Memory and Other Stories* (1972), and her critically acclaimed novels *The House in Clewe Street* (1945) and *Mary O'Grady* (1950).

Unit 1 Review: Experience in Fiction

Content Review

1. In both "Lamb to the Slaughter" and "The Piano," a nonliving object is used as an important part of the plot and as the basis for an unusual or unexpected ending. Identify this object in each story; then explain how it is involved in the plot and what happens to it at the end.

2. Both "The Boar Hunt" and "The Parachutist" deal with survival in the world of nature. Compare and contrast the two in regard to the main conflict each contains and the way it is resolved. Which story do you find more believable? Why?

3. In both "A Visit to Grandmother" and "Forgiveness in Families," a major character is a brother who is a source of family disagreement. Identify the two characters; then compare their status in their respective families. Consider such things as the mothers' feelings for their sons, and the reactions of the others in the family toward these brothers.

4. "The Story of the Widow's Son" and "Through the Tunnel" both deal with the attitudes of widows toward their sons. Compare and contrast these attitudes. Which woman behaved more unselfishly toward her son? Explain.

5. Sometimes a short story requires us to make inferences as to what a character has learned about life in general or about another character in the story. Discuss what Alice and Val have realized, or at least partly realized, at the end of "The Other Wife" and "Forgiveness in Families." Explain why you think these new insights will be helpful or harmful to the characters in the future.

6. Both "The Monkey's Paw" and "Life Is Sweet at Kumansenu" contain elements of the supernatural that require what is sometimes called a "willing suspension of disbelief"—that is, although logically we know better, while we are reading the story we are willing to accept the author's use of the supernatural. Identify how the foreshadowing in each story prepares you for the supernatural element and how each author uses it to make a point or convey a lesson.

Concept Review: Interpretation of New Material

Read the short story that follows. Then use the questions that come after it to review your understanding of the concepts and literary terms presented in this unit.

Shaving • *Leslie Norris* Great Britain

Earlier, when Barry had left the house to go to the game, an overnight frost had still been thick on the roads, but the brisk April sun had soon dispersed it, and now he could feel the spring warmth on his back through the thick tweed of his coat. His left arm was beginning to stiffen up where he'd jarred it in a tackle, but it was nothing serious. He flexed his shoulders against the tightness of his jacket and was surprised again by the unexpected weight of his muscles, the thickening strength of his body. A few years back, he thought, he had been a small, unimportant boy, one of a swarming gang laughing and jostling to school, hardly aware that he possessed an

---

identity. But time had transformed him. He walked solidly now, and often alone. He was tall, strongly made, his hands and feet were adult and heavy, the rooms in which all his life he'd moved had grown too small for him. Sometimes a devouring restlessness drove him from the house to walk long distances in the dark. He hardly understood how it had happened. Amused and quiet, he walked the High Street among the morning shoppers.

He saw Jackie Bevan across the road and remembered how, when they were both six years old, Jackie had swallowed a pin. The flustered teachers had clucked about Jackie as he stood there, bawling, cheeks awash with tears, his nose wet. But now Jackie was tall and suave, his thick, pale hair sleekly tailored, his gray suit enviable. He was talking to a girl as golden as a daffodil.

"Hey, hey!" called Jackie. "How's the athlete, how's Barry boy?"

He waved a graceful hand at Barry.

"Come and talk to Sue," he said.

Barry shifted his bag to his left hand and walked over, forming in his mind the answers he'd make to Jackie's questions.

"Did we win?" Jackie asked. "Was the old Barry Stanford magic in glittering evidence yet once more this morning? Were the invaders sent hunched and silent back to their hovels in the hills? What was the score? Give us an epic account, Barry, without modesty or delay. This is Sue, by the way."

"I've seen you about," the girl said.

"You could hardly miss him," said Jackie. "Four men, roped together, spent a week climbing him—they thought he was Everest. He ought to carry a warning beacon, he's a danger to aircraft."

"Silly," said the girl, smiling at Jackie. "He's not much taller than you are."

She had a nice voice too.

"We won," Barry said. "Seventeen points to three, and it was a good game. The ground was hard, though."

He could think of nothing else to say.

"Let's all go for a frivolous cup of coffee," Jackie said. "Let's celebrate your safe return from the rough fields of victory. We could pour libations all over the floor for you."

"I don't think so," Barry said. "Thanks. I'll go straight home."

"Okay," said Jackie, rocking on his heels so that the sun could shine on his smile. "How's your father?"

"No better," Barry said. "He's not going to get better."

"Yes, well," said Jackie, serious and uncomfortable, "tell him my mother and father ask about him."

"I will," Barry promised. "He'll be pleased."

Barry dropped the bag in the front hall and moved into the room which had been the dining room until his father's illness. His father lay in the white bed, his long body gaunt, his still head scarcely denting the pillow. He seemed asleep, thin blue lids covering his eyes, but when Barry turned away he spoke.

"Hullo, son," he said. "Did you win?"

His voice was a dry, light rustling, hardly louder than the breath which carried it. Its sound moved Barry to a compassion that almost unmanned him, but he stepped close to the bed and looked down at the dying man.

"Yes," he said. "We won fairly easily. It was a good game."

His father lay with his eyes closed, inert, his breath irregular and shallow.

"Did you score?" he asked.

"Twice," Barry said. "I had a try in each half."

He thought of the easy certainty with which he'd caught the ball before his second try; casually, almost arrogantly he had taken it on the tips of his fingers, on his full burst for the line, breaking the full-back's tackle. Nobody could have stopped him. But watching his father's weakness he felt humble and ashamed, as if the morning game, its urgency and effort, was not worth talking about. His father's face, fine-skinned and pallid, carried a dark stubble of beard, almost a week's growth, and his obstinate, strong hair stuck out over his brow.

"Good," said his father, after a long pause. "I'm glad it was a good game."

Barry's mother bustled about the kitchen, a tempest of orderly energy.

"Your father's not well," she said. "He's down today, feels depressed. He's a particular man, your father. He feels dirty with all that beard on him."

She slammed shut the stove door.

"Mr. Cleaver was supposed to come up and shave him," she said, "and that was three days ago. Little things have always worried your father, every detail must be perfect for him."

Barry filled a glass with milk from the refrigerator. He was very thirsty.

"I'll shave him," he said.

His mother stopped, her head on one side.

"Do you think you can?" she asked. "He'd like it if you can."

"I can do it," Barry said.

He washed his hands as carefully as a surgeon. His father's razor was in a blue leather case, hinged at the broad edge and with one hinge broken. Barry unfastened the clasp and took out the razor. It had not been properly cleaned after its last use and lather had stiffened into hard yellow rectangles between the teeth of the guard. There were water-shaped rust stains, brown as chocolate, on the surface of the blade. Barry removed it, throwing it in the wastebin. He washed the razor until it glistened, and dried it on a soft towel, polishing the thin handle, rubbing its metal head to a glittering shine. He took a new blade from its waxed envelope, the paper clinging to the thin metal. The blade was smooth and flexible to the touch, the little angles of its cutting clearly defined. Barry slotted it into the grip of the razor, making it snug and tight in the head.

The shaving soap, hard, white, richly aromatic, was kept in a wooden bowl. Its scent was immediately evocative and Barry could almost see his father in the days of his health, standing before his mirror, thick white lather on his face and neck. As a little boy Barry had loved the generous perfume of the soap, had waited for his father to lift the razor to his face, for one careful stroke to take away the white suds in a clean revelation of the skin. Then his father would renew the lather with a few sweeps of his brush, one with an ivory handle and the bristles worn, which he still used.

His father's shaving mug was a thick cup, plain and serviceable. A gold line ran outside the rim of the cup, another inside, just below the lip. Its handle was large and sturdy, and the face of the mug carried a portrait of the young Queen Elizabeth II, circled by a wreath of leaves, oak perhaps, or laurel. A lion and unicorn balanced precariously on a scroll above her crowned head, and the Union Jack, the Royal Standard, and other flags were furled each side of the portrait. And beneath it all, in small black letters, ran the legend: "Coronation June 2nd 1953." The cup was much older than Barry. A pattern of faint translucent cracks, fine as a web, had worked itself haphazardly, invisibly almost, through the white glaze. Inside, on the bottom, a few dark bristles were lying, loose and dry. Barry shook them out, then held the cup in his hand, feeling its solidness. Then he washed it ferociously, until it was clinically clean.

Methodically he set everything on a tray, razor, soap, brush, towels. Testing the hot water with a finger, he filled the mug and put that, too, on the tray. His care was absorbed, ritualistic. Satisfied that his preparations were complete, he went downstairs, carrying the tray with one hand.

His father was waiting for him. Barry set the tray on a bedside table and bent over his father, sliding an arm under the man's thin shoulders, lifting him without effort so that he sat against the high pillows.

"You're strong. . . ." his father said. He was as breathless as if he'd been running.

"So are you," said Barry.

"I was," his father said. "I used to be strong once."

He sat exhausted against the pillows.

"We'll wait a bit," Barry said.

"You could have used your electric razor," his father said. "I expected that."

"You wouldn't like it," Barry said. "You'll get a closer shave this way."

He placed the large towel about his father's shoulders.

"Now," he said, smiling down.

The water was hot in the thick cup. Barry wet the brush and worked up the lather. Gently he built up a covering of soft foam on the man's chin, on his cheeks and his stark cheekbones.

"You're using a lot of soap," his father said.

"Not too much," Barry said. "You've got a lot of beard."

His father lay there quietly, his wasted arms at his sides.

"It's comforting," he said. "You'd be surprised how comforting it is."

Barry took up the razor, weighing it in his hand, rehearsing the angle at which he'd use it. He felt confident.

"If you have prayers to say, . . ." he said.

"I've said a lot of prayers," his father answered.

Barry leaned over and placed the razor delicately against his father's face, setting the head accurately on the clean line near the ear where the long hair ended. He held the razor in the tips of his fingers and drew the blade sweetly through the lather. The new edge moved light as a touch over the hardness of the upper jaw and down to the angle of the chin, sliding away the bristles so easily that Barry could not feel their release. He sighed as he shook the razor in the hot water, washing away the soap.

"How's it going?" his father asked.

"No problem," Barry said. "You needn't worry."

It was as if he had never known what his father really looked like. He was discovering under his hands the clear bones of the face and head; they became sharp and recognizable under his fingers. When he moved his father's face a gentle inch to one side, he touched with his fingers the frail temples, the blue veins of his father's life. With infinite and meticulous care he took away the hair from his father's face.

"Now for your neck," he said. "We might as well do the job properly."

"You've got good hands," his father said. "You can trust those hands, they won't let you down."

Barry cradled his father's head in the crook of his left arm, so that the man could tilt back his head, exposing the throat. He brushed fresh lather under the chin and into the hollows alongside the stretched tendons. His father's throat was fleshless and vulnerable, his head was a hard weight on the boy's arm. Barry was filled with unreasoning protective love. He lifted the razor and began to shave.

"You don't have to worry," he said. "Not at all. Not about anything."

He held his father in the bend of his strong arm and they looked at each other. Their heads were very close.

"How old are you?" his father said.

"Seventeen," Barry said. "Near enough seventeen."

"You're young," his father said, "to have this happen."

"Not too young," Barry said. "I'm bigger than most men."

"I think you are," his father said.

He leaned his head tiredly against the boy's shoulder. He was without strength, his face was cold and smooth. He had let go all his authority, handed it over. He lay back on his pillow, knowing his weakness and his mortality, and looked at his son with wonder, with a curious humble pride.

"I won't worry then," he said. "About anything."

"There's no need," Barry said. "Why should you worry?"

He wiped his father's face clean of all soap with a damp towel. The smell of illness was everywhere, overpowering even the perfumed lather. Barry settled his father down and took away the shaving tools, putting them by with the same ceremonial precision with which he'd prepared them: the cleaned and glittering razor in its broken case; the soap, its bowl wiped and dried, on the shelf between the brush and the coronation mug; all free of taint. He washed his hands and scrubbed his nails. His hands were firm and broad, pink after their scrubbing. The fingers were short and strong, the little fingers slightly crooked, and soft dark hair grew on the backs of his hands and his fingers just above the knuckles. Not long ago they had been small bare hands, not very long ago.

Barry opened wide the bathroom window. Already, although it was not yet two o'clock, the sun was retreating and people were moving briskly, wrapped in their heavy coats against the cold that was to come. But now the window was full in the beam of the dying sunlight, and Barry stood there, illuminated in its golden warmth for a whole minute, knowing it would soon be gone.

1. The setting for this story is **(a)** the U.S. in early spring; **(b)** England in early spring; **(c)** England in early fall; **(d)** Australia in early fall.

2. The story is told from the point of view of **(a)** Barry; **(b)** his mother; **(c)** his father; **(d)** Jackie.

3. As the story opens, Barry is coming home from **(a)** school; **(b)** the hospital; **(c)** a part-time job; **(d)** a sports event.

4. Which of the following best describes Barry's physical appearance? **(a)** short and muscular; **(b)** thin and wiry; **(c)** tall and strong; **(d)** average height and overweight.

5. Why is Jackie "uncomfortable" when Barry answers his question about Barry's father's health?

6. Is shaving his father a task that is usually Barry's? Explain.

7. Barry probably makes such elaborate preparations for the shaving because **(a)** he loves his father and knows he is a particular person; **(b)** he wants to show up Mr. Cleaver; **(c)** he is dreading the job and wants to put it off; **(d)** his mother has told him to be very careful.

8. What does Barry mean when he says to his father, "If you have prayers to say, . . ."?

9. What is the most important message communicated between Barry and his father during the shaving ritual? **(a)** that Barry will shave his father carefully; **(b)** that Barry has become a good athlete; **(c)** that his father is afraid to die; **(d)** that his father shouldn't worry about the family or the future.

10. Name two things Barry has to feel good about at the end of the day.

Composition Review

From the assignments that follow choose one to write about.

1. Suppose you have been asked to choose three stories from this unit to make up a "mini-unit" for other students to use. Go through the unit and select the three stories that you think would most interest your audience, jotting down reasons for your choices.

Write a brief description of the unit for your students. Begin by introducing the three stories; then deal with each in more detail. Remember that your goal is to interest students in reading the unit.

2. Choose what you feel is either the most believable or most unbelievable character in the unit. Review that character's actions and how they help make him or her a likely or unlikely figure.

Write a short essay discussing the character and explaining why you find him or her believable or unbelievable. If you are writing about the most unbelievable character, explain also whether the lack of believability interferes with or increases your enjoyment of the story.

3. Imagine that you are one of the characters listed below. Decide what your thoughts would be at some key point in the story and what sort of language you would use to express them.

Write a first-person account of your thoughts, trying to sound as much like the character as possible.

—the grandmother in "A Visit to Grandmother"
—the husband in "Lamb to the Slaughter"
—the mother in "Forgiveness in Families"
—the son in "The Story of the Widow's Son"
—the son in "Shaving"

4. Select a story from the unit that gives a clear picture of what life in the place it is set is like. Review the story, noting details that make life in the country particularly interesting and/or different from life in the United States.

Write an essay explaining in detail what insights you have gained into life in that area of the world.

Unit 2
Modern Drama

See **PROTAGONIST/ANTAGONIST** Handbook of Literary Terms

Twelve Angry Men

Reginald Rose USA

DESCRIPTIONS OF JURORS

FOREMAN. *A small, petty man who is impressed with the authority he has and handles himself quite formally. Not overly bright, but dogged.*

JUROR NUMBER TWO. *A meek, hesitant man who finds it difficult to maintain any opinions of his own. Easily swayed and usually adopts the opinion of the last person to whom he has spoken.*

JUROR NUMBER THREE. *A very strong, very forceful, extremely opinionated man within whom can be detected a streak of sadism. A humorless man who is intolerant of opinions other than his own and accustomed to forcing his wishes and views upon others.*

JUROR NUMBER FOUR. *Seems to be a man of wealth and position. A practiced speaker who presents himself well at all times. Seems to feel a little bit above the rest of the jurors. His only concern is with the facts in this case, and he is appalled at the behavior of the others.*

JUROR NUMBER FIVE. *A naïve, very frightened young man who takes his obligations in this case very seriously, but who finds it difficult to speak up when his elders have the floor.*

JUROR NUMBER SIX. *An honest but dull-witted man who comes upon his decisions slowly and carefully. A man who finds it difficult to create positive opinions, but who must listen to and digest and accept those opinions offered by others which appeal to him most.*

JUROR NUMBER SEVEN. *A loud, flashy, glad-handed salesman type who has more important things to do than to sit on a jury. He is quick to show temper, quick to form opinions on things about which he knows nothing. Is a bully and, of course, a coward.*

JUROR NUMBER EIGHT. *A quiet, thoughtful, gentle man. A man who sees all sides of every question and constantly seeks the truth. A man of strength tempered with compassion. Above all, a man who wants justice to be done and will fight to see that it is.*

JUROR NUMBER NINE. *A mild, gentle old man, long since defeated by life and now merely waiting to die. A man who recognizes himself for what he is and mourns the days when it would have been possible to be courageous without shielding himself behind his many years.*

JUROR NUMBER TEN. *An angry, bitter man. A man who antagonizes almost at sight. A bigot who places no values on any human life save his own. A man who has been nowhere and is going nowhere and knows it deep within him.*

JUROR NUMBER ELEVEN. *A refugee from Europe who had come to this country in 1941. A man who speaks with an accent and who is ashamed, humble, almost subservient to the people around him, but who will honestly seek justice because he has suffered through so much injustice.*

JUROR NUMBER TWELVE. *A slick, bright advertising man who thinks of human beings in terms of percentages, graphs, and polls and has no real understanding of people. A superficial snob, but trying to be a good fellow.*

Act One

Fade in[1] on a jury box. Twelve men are seated in it, listening intently to the voice of the JUDGE *as he charges them.[2] We do not see the* JUDGE. *He speaks in slow, measured tones and his voice is grave. The camera drifts over the faces of the* JURYMEN *as the* JUDGE *speaks and we see that most of their heads are turned to camera's left.* SEVEN *looks down at his hands.* THREE *looks off in another direction, the direction in which the defendant would be sitting.* TEN *keeps moving his head back and forth nervously. The* JUDGE *drones on.*

JUDGE. Murder in the first degree—premeditated homicide—is the most serious charge tried in our criminal courts. You've heard a long and complex case, gentlemen, and it is now your duty to sit down to try and separate the facts from the fancy. One man is dead. The life of another is at stake. If there is a reasonable doubt in your minds as to the guilt of the accused . . . then you must declare him not guilty. If, however, there is no reasonable doubt, then he must be found guilty. Whichever way you decide, the verdict must be unanimous. I urge you to deliberate honestly and thoughtfully. You are faced with a grave responsibility. Thank you, gentlemen.

(There is a long pause.)

CLERK *(droning).* The jury will retire.

(And now, slowly, almost hesitantly, the members of the jury begin to rise. Awkwardly, they file out of the jury box and off camera to the left. Camera holds on jury box, then fades out.

Fade in on a large, bare, unpleasant-looking room. This is the jury room in the county criminal court of a large Eastern city. It is about 4:00 P.M. *The room is furnished with a long conference table and a dozen chairs. The walls are bare, drab, and badly in need of a fresh coat of paint. Along one wall is a row of windows which look out on the skyline of the city's financial district. High on another wall is an electric clock. A washroom opens off the jury room. In one corner of the room is a water fountain. On the table are pads, pencils, ashtrays. One of the windows is open. Papers blow across the table and onto the floor as the door opens. Lettered on the outside of the door are the words "Jury Room." A uniformed* GUARD *holds the door open. Slowly, almost self-consciously, the twelve* JURORS *file in. The* GUARD *counts them as they enter the door, his lips moving, but no sound coming forth. Four or five of the* JURORS *light cigarettes as they enter the room.* FIVE *lights his pipe, which he smokes constantly throughout the play.* TWO *and* TWELVE *go to the water fountain.* NINE *goes into the washroom, the door of which is lettered "Men." Several of the* JURORS *take seats at the table. Others stand awkwardly around the room. Several look out the windows. These are men who are ill at ease, who do not really know each other to talk to, and who wish they were anywhere but here.* SEVEN, *standing at window, takes out a pack of gum, takes a piece, and offers it around. There are no takers. He mops his brow.)*

SEVEN *(to* SIX*).* Y'know something? It's hot. *(*SIX *nods.)* You'd think they'd at least air-condition the place. I almost dropped dead in court.

*(*SEVEN *opens the window a bit wider. The* GUARD *looks them over and checks his count. Then, satisfied, he makes ready to leave.)*

GUARD. Okay, gentlemen. Everybody's here. If there's anything you want, I'm right outside. Just knock.

(He exits, closing the door. Silently they all look at the door. We hear the lock clicking.)

FIVE. I never knew they locked the door.

TEN *(blowing nose).* Sure, they lock the door. What did you think?

FIVE. I don't know. It just never occurred to me.

(Some of the JURORS *are taking off their jack-*

---

1. ***Fade in,*** term used in television to indicate that the picture or scene is slowly brought into focus. When the camera "fades out," the picture disappears.
2. ***he charges them,*** he tells them what their duties are as jurors.

ets. Others are sitting down at the table. They still are reluctant to talk to each other. FOREMAN *is at head of table, tearing slips of paper for ballots. Now we get a close shot of* EIGHT. *He looks out the window. We hear* THREE *talking to* TWO.*)*

THREE. Six days. They should have finished it in two. Talk, talk, talk. Did you ever hear so much talk about nothing?

TWO *(nervously laughing).* Well . . . I guess . . . they're entitled.

THREE. Everybody gets a fair trial. *(He shakes his head.)* That's the system. Well, I suppose you can't say anything against it.

*(*TWO *looks at him nervously, nods, and goes over to water cooler. Cut*[3] *to shot of* EIGHT *staring out window. Cut to table.* SEVEN *stands at the table, putting out a cigarette.)*

SEVEN *(to* TEN*).* How did you like that business about the knife? Did you ever hear a phonier story?

TEN *(wisely).* Well, look, you've gotta expect that. You know what you're dealing with.

SEVEN. Yeah, I suppose. What's the matter, you got a cold?

TEN *(blowing).* A lulu. These hot-weather colds can kill you.

*(*SEVEN *nods sympathetically.)*

FOREMAN *(briskly).* All right, gentlemen. Let's take seats.

SEVEN. Right. This better be fast. I've got tickets to *The Seven Year Itch*[4] tonight. I must be the only guy in the whole world who hasn't seen it yet. *(He laughs and sits down.)* Okay, your honor, start the show.

(They all begin to sit down. The FOREMAN *is seated at the head of the table.* EIGHT *continues to look out the window.)*

FOREMAN *(to* EIGHT*).* How about sitting down? *(*EIGHT *doesn't hear him.)* The gentleman at the window.

*(*EIGHT *turns, startled.)*

FOREMAN. How about sitting down?

EIGHT. Oh, I'm sorry. *(He heads for a seat.)*

TEN *(to* SIX*).* It's tough to figure, isn't it? A kid kills his father. Bing! Just like that. Well, it's the element. They let the kids run wild. Maybe it serves 'em right.

FOREMAN. Is everybody here?

TWELVE. The old man's inside.

(The FOREMAN *turns to the washroom just as the door opens.* NINE *comes out, embarrassed.)*

FOREMAN. We'd like to get started.

NINE. Forgive me, gentlemen. I didn't mean to keep you waiting.

FOREMAN. It's all right. Find a seat.

*(*NINE *heads for a seat and sits down. They look at the* FOREMAN *expectantly.)*

FOREMAN. All right. Now, you gentlemen can handle this any way you want to. I mean, I'm not going to make any rules. If we want to discuss it first and then vote, that's one way. Or we can vote right now to see how we stand.

SEVEN. Let's vote now. Who knows, maybe we can all go home.

TEN. Yeah. Let's see who's where.

THREE. Right. Let's vote now.

FOREMAN. Anybody doesn't want to vote? *(He looks around the table. There is no answer.)* Okay, all those voting guilty raise your hands. *(Seven or eight hands go up immediately. Several others go up more slowly. Everyone looks around the table. There are two hands not raised,* NINE*'s and* EIGHT*'s.* NINE*'s hand goes up slowly now as the* FOREMAN *counts.)*

FOREMAN. . . . Nine . . . ten . . . eleven . . . That's eleven for guilty. Okay. Not guilty? *(*EIGHT*'s hand is raised.)* One. Right. Okay. Eleven to one, guilty. Now we know where we are.

THREE. Somebody's in left field. *(To* EIGHT*)* You think he's not guilty?

EIGHT *(quietly).* I don't know.

THREE. I never saw a guiltier man in my life. You sat right in court and heard the same thing I did. The man's a dangerous killer. You could see it.

---

3. ***Cut,*** indicates an immediate switch from one camera to another to show what is happening on another part of the television stage.
4. ***The Seven Year Itch,*** a comedy that opened on Broadway in 1952.

EIGHT. He's nineteen years old.

THREE. That's old enough. He knifed his own father. Four inches into the chest. An innocent little nineteen-year-old kid. They proved it a dozen different ways. Do you want me to list them?

EIGHT. No.

TEN *(to* EIGHT*)*. Well, do you believe his story?

EIGHT. I don't know whether I believe it or not. Maybe I don't.

SEVEN. So what'd you vote not guilty for?

EIGHT. There were eleven votes for guilty. It's not so easy for me to raise my hand and send a boy off to die without talking about it first.

SEVEN. Who says it's easy for me?

EIGHT. No one.

SEVEN. What, just because I voted fast? I think the guy's guilty. You couldn't change my mind if you talked for a hundred years.

EIGHT. I don't want to change your mind. I just want to talk for a while. Look, this boy's been kicked around all his life. You know, living in a slum, his mother dead since he was nine. That's not a very good head start. He's a tough, angry kid. You know why slum kids get that way? Because we knock 'em on the head once a day, every day. I think maybe we owe him a few words. That's all.

(He looks around the table. Some of them look back coldly. Some cannot look at him. Only NINE *nods slowly.* TWELVE *doodles steadily.* FOUR *begins to comb his hair.)*

TEN. I don't mind telling you this, mister. We don't owe him a thing. He got a fair trial, didn't he? You know what that trial cost? He's lucky he got it. Look, we're all grownups here. You're not going to tell us that we're supposed to believe him, knowing what he is. I've lived among 'em all my life. You can't believe a word they say. You know that.

NINE *(to* TEN *very slowly)*. I don't know that. What a terrible thing for a man to believe! Since when is dishonesty a group characteristic? You have no monopoly on the truth—

THREE *(interrupting)*. All right. It's not Sunday. We don't need a sermon.

NINE. What this man says is very dangerous—

*(*EIGHT *puts his hand on* NINE*'s arm and stops him. Somehow his touch and his gentle expression calm the old man. He draws a deep breath and relaxes.)*

FOUR. I don't see any need for arguing like this. I think we ought to be able to behave like gentlemen.

SEVEN. Right!

FOUR. If we're going to discuss this case, let's discuss the facts.

FOREMAN. I think that's a good point. We have a job to do. Let's do it.

ELEVEN *(with accent)*. If you gentlemen don't mind, I'm going to close the window. *(He gets up and does so.) (Apologetically)* It was blowing on my neck. *(*TEN *blows his nose fiercely.)*

TWELVE. I may have an idea here. I'm just thinking out loud now, but it seems to me that it's up to us to convince this gentleman—*(Indicating* EIGHT*)*—that we're right and he's wrong. Maybe if we each took a minute or two, you know, if we sort of try it on for size—

FOREMAN. That sounds fair enough. Supposing we go once around the table.

SEVEN. Okay, let's start it off.

FOREMAN. Right. *(To* TWO*)* I guess you're first.

TWO *(timidly)*. Oh. Well . . . *(Long pause)* I just think he's guilty. I thought it was obvious. I mean nobody proved otherwise.

EIGHT *(quietly)*. Nobody has to prove otherwise. The burden of proof is on the prosecution. The defendant doesn't have to open his mouth. That's in the Constitution. The Fifth Amendment.[5] You've heard of it.

TWO *(flustered)*. Well, sure, I've heard of it. I know what it is. I . . . what I meant . . . well, anyway, I think he was guilty.

THREE. Okay, let's get to the facts. Number one, let's take the old man who lived on the second floor right underneath the room where the murder took place. At ten minutes after twelve on

---

5. ***The Fifth Amendment,*** the amendment that guarantees that a person on trial for a criminal offense cannot be forced to testify against himself or herself.

the night of the killing he heard loud noises in the upstairs apartment. He said it sounded like a fight. Then he heard the kid say to his father, "I'm gonna kill you." A second later he heard a body falling, and he ran to the door of his apartment, looked out, and saw the kid running down the stairs and out of the house. Then he called the police. They found the father with a knife in his chest.

FOREMAN. And the coroner fixed the time of death at around midnight.

THREE. Right. Now what else do you want?

FOUR. The boy's entire story is flimsy. He claimed he was at the movies. That's a little ridiculous, isn't it? He couldn't even remember what pictures he saw.

THREE. That's right. Did you hear that? *(To* FOUR*)* You're absolutely right.

TEN. Look, what about the woman across the street? If her testimony don't prove it, then nothing does.

TWELVE. That's right. She saw the killing, didn't she?

FOREMAN. Let's go in order.

TEN *(loud)*. Just a minute. Here's a woman who's lying in bed and can't sleep. It's hot, you know. *(He gets up and begins to walk around, blowing his nose and talking.)* Anyway, she looks out the window, and right across the street she sees the kid stick the knife into his father. She's known the kid all his life. His window is right opposite hers, across the el tracks, and she swore she saw him do it.

EIGHT. Through the windows of a passing elevated train.

TEN. Okay. And they proved in court that you can look through the windows of a passing el train at night and see what's happening on the other side. They proved it.

EIGHT. I'd like to ask you something. How come you believed her? She's one of "them," too, isn't she?

*(*TEN *walks over to* EIGHT.*)*

TEN. You're a pretty smart fellow, aren't you?

FOREMAN *(rising)*. Now take it easy.

*(*THREE *gets up and goes to* TEN.*)*

THREE. Come on. Sit down. *(He leads* TEN *back to his seat.)* What're you letting him get you all upset for? Relax.

*(*TEN *and* THREE *sit down.)*

FOREMAN. Let's calm down now. *(To* FIVE*)* It's your turn.

FIVE. I'll pass it.

FOREMAN. That's your privilege. *(To* SIX*)* How about you?

SIX *(slowly)*. I don't know. I started to be convinced, you know, with the testimony from those people across the hall. Didn't they say something about an argument between the father and the boy around seven o'clock that night? I mean, I can be wrong.

ELEVEN. I think it was eight o'clock. Not seven.

EIGHT. That's right. Eight o'clock. They heard the father hit the boy twice and then saw the boy walk angrily out of the house. What does that prove?

SIX. Well, it doesn't exactly prove anything. It's just part of the picture. I didn't say it proved anything.

FOREMAN. Anything else?

SIX. No.

*(*SIX *goes to the water fountain.)*

FOREMAN *(to* SEVEN*)*. All right. How about you?

SEVEN. I don't know, most of it's been said already. We can talk all day about this thing, but I think we're wasting our time. Look at the kid's record. At fifteen he was in reform school. He stole a car. He's been arrested for mugging. He was picked up for knife-fighting. I think they said he stabbed somebody in the arm. This is a very fine boy.

EIGHT. Ever since he was five years old his father beat him up regularly. He used his fists.

SEVEN. So would I! A kid like that.

THREE. You're right. It's the kids. The way they are—you know? They don't listen. *(Bitter)* I've got a kid. When he was eight years old he ran away from a fight. I saw him. I was so ashamed, I told him right out, "I'm gonna make a man out of you or I'm gonna bust you

up into little pieces trying." When he was fifteen he hit me in the face. He's big, you know. I haven't seen him in three years. Rotten kid! You work your heart out. . . . *(Pause)* All right. Let's get on with it. *(Looks away embarrassed)*

FOUR. We're missing the point here. This boy—let's say he's a product of a filthy neighborhood and a broken home. We can't help that. We're not here to go into reasons why slums are breeding grounds for criminals. They are. I know it. So do you. The children who come out of slum backgrounds are potential menaces to society.

TEN. You said it there. I don't want any part of them, believe me.

(There is a dead silence for a moment, and then FIVE *speaks haltingly.)*

FIVE. I've lived in a slum all my life—

TEN. Oh, now wait a second!

FIVE. I used to play in a backyard that was filled with garbage. Maybe it still smells on me.

FOREMAN. Now let's be reasonable. There's nothing personal—*(*FIVE *stands up.)*

FIVE. There is something personal!

(Then he catches himself and, seeing everyone looking at him, sits down, fists clenched.)

THREE *(persuasively)*. Come on, now. He didn't

mean you, feller. Let's not be so sensitive. . . .

(There is a long pause.)

ELEVEN. I can understand this sensitivity.

FOREMAN. Now let's stop the bickering. We're wasting time. *(To* EIGHT*)* It's your turn.

EIGHT. All right. I had a peculiar feeling about this trial. Somehow I felt that the defense counsel never really conducted a thorough cross-examination. I mean, he was appointed by the court to defend the boy. He hardly seemed interested. Too many questions were left unasked.

THREE *(annoyed).* What about the ones that were asked? For instance, let's talk about that cute little switch-knife.[6] You know, the one that fine upright kid admitted buying.

EIGHT. All right. Let's talk about it. Let's get it in here and look at it. I'd like to see it again, Mr. Foreman.

(The FOREMAN *looks at him questioningly and then gets up and goes to the door. During the following dialogue the* FOREMAN *knocks, the* GUARD *comes in, the* FOREMAN *whispers to him, the* GUARD *nods and leaves, locking the door.)*

THREE. We all know what it looks like. I don't see why we have to look at it again. *(To* FOUR*)* What do you think?

FOUR. The gentleman has a right to see exhibits in evidence.

THREE *(shrugging).* Okay with me.

FOUR *(to* EIGHT*).* This knife is a pretty strong piece of evidence, don't you agree?

EIGHT. I do.

FOUR. The boy admits going out of his house at eight o'clock after being slapped by his father.

EIGHT. Or punched.

FOUR. Or punched. He went to a neighborhood store and bought a switch-knife. The storekeeper was arrested the following day when he admitted selling it to the boy. It's a very unusual knife. The storekeeper identified it and said it was the only one of its kind he had in stock. Why did the boy get it? *(Sarcastically)* As a present for a friend of his, he says. Am I right so far?

EIGHT. Right.

THREE. You bet he's right. *(To all)* Now listen to this man. He knows what he's talking about.

FOUR. Next, the boy claims that on the way home the knife must have fallen through a hole in his coat pocket, that he never saw it again. Now there's a story, gentlemen. You know what actually happened. The boy took the knife home and a few hours later stabbed his father with it and even remembered to wipe off the fingerprints.

(The door opens and the GUARD *walks in with an oddly designed knife with a tag on it.* FOUR *gets up and takes it from him. The* GUARD *exits.)*

FOUR. Everyone connected with the case identified this knife. Now are you trying to tell me that someone picked it up off the street and went up to the boy's house and stabbed his father with it just to be amusing?

EIGHT. No, I'm saying that it's possible that the boy lost the knife and that someone else stabbed his father with a similar knife. It's possible.

*(*FOUR *flips open the knife and jams it into the table.)*

FOUR. Take a look at that knife. It's a very strange knife. I've never seen one like it before in my life. Neither had the storekeeper who sold it to him.

*(*EIGHT *reaches casually into his pocket and withdraws an object. No one notices this. He stands up quietly.)*

FOUR. Aren't you trying to make us accept a pretty incredible coincidence?

EIGHT. I'm not trying to make anyone accept it. I'm just saying it's possible.

THREE *(shouting).* And I'm saying it's not possible.

*(*EIGHT *swiftly flicks open the blade of a switch-knife and jams it into the table next to the first one. They are exactly alike. There are several*

6. ***switch-knife,*** switchblade knife.

gasps and everyone stares at the knife. There is a long silence.)

THREE *(slowly, amazed)*. What are you trying to do?

TEN *(loud)*. Yeah, what is this? Who do you think you are?

FIVE. Look at it! It's the same knife!

FOREMAN. Quiet! Let's be quiet.

(They quiet down.)

FOUR. Where did you get it?

EIGHT. I got it last night in a little junk shop around the corner from the boy's house. It cost two dollars.

THREE. Now listen to me! You pulled a real smart trick here, but you proved absolutely zero. Maybe there are ten knives like that, so what?

EIGHT. Maybe there are.

THREE. The boy lied and you know it.

EIGHT. He may have lied. *(To* TEN*)* Do you think he lied?

TEN *(violently)*. Now that's a stupid question. Sure he lied!

EIGHT *(to* FOUR*)*. Do you?

FOUR. You don't have to ask me that. You know my answer. He lied.

EIGHT *(to* FIVE*)*. Do you think he lied?

*(*FIVE *can't answer immediately. He looks around nervously.)*

FIVE. I . . . I don't know.

SEVEN. Now wait a second. What are you, the guy's lawyer? Listen, there are still eleven of us who think he's guilty. You're alone. What do you think you're gonna accomplish? If you want to be stubborn and hang this jury,[7] he'll be tried again and found guilty, sure as he's born.

EIGHT. You're probably right.

SEVEN. So what are you gonna do about it? We can be here all night.

NINE. It's only one night. A man may die.

*(*SEVEN *glares at* NINE *for a long while, but has no answer.* EIGHT *looks closely at* NINE *and we can begin to sense a rapport between them. There is a long silence. Then suddenly everyone begins to talk at once.)*

THREE. Well, whose fault is that?

SIX. Do you think maybe if we went over it again? What I mean is—

TEN. Did anyone force him to kill his father? *(To* THREE*)* How do you like him? Like someone forced him!

ELEVEN. Perhaps this is not the point.

FIVE. No one forced anyone. But listen—

TWELVE. Look, gentlemen, we can spitball all night here.

TWO. Well, I was going to say—

SEVEN. Just a minute. Some of us've got better things to do than sit around a jury room.

FOUR. I can't understand a word in here. Why do we all have to talk at once?

FOREMAN. He's right. I think we ought to get on with it.

*(*EIGHT *has been listening to this exchange closely.)*

THREE *(to* EIGHT*)*. Well, what do you say? You're the one holding up the show.

EIGHT *(standing)*. I've got a proposition to make.

(We catch a close shot of FIVE *looking steadily at him as he talks.* FIVE, *seemingly puzzled, listens closely.)*

EIGHT. I want to call for a vote. I want you eleven men to vote by secret ballot. I'll abstain. If there are still eleven votes for guilty, I won't stand alone. We'll take in a guilty verdict right now.

SEVEN. Okay. Let's do it.

FOREMAN. That sounds fair. Is everyone agreed?

(They all nod their heads. EIGHT *walks over to the window, looks out for a moment, and then faces them.)*

FOREMAN. Pass these along.

(The FOREMAN *passes ballot slips to all of them, and now* EIGHT *watches them tensely as they begin to write.)*

(Fade out)

---

7. ***hang this jury,*** keep this jury from reaching a verdict. A jury that fails to reach a verdict is called a "hung" jury.

Discussion

1. (a) Who is the defendant in this case and what is his crime? **(b)** What specific instructions does the judge give the jurors before they go into the jury room?

2. (a) How might the jury room, the time, and the weather affect the jurors? **(b)** Which juror is particularly anxious to make a quick decision? Why?

3. (a) What is the result of the first vote? **(b)** Which juror seems least confident of his vote? **(c)** What reasons does Juror Eight give for *his* vote? **(d)** How do the others react to Eight's statements?

4. (a) In discussing the facts of the case, what testimony from witnesses is mentioned by Three? by Ten? by Six? **(b)** Do the comments about the defendant made by Seven, Three, and Four have any bearing on the case? Explain. **(c)** How does Five react to these comments?

5. (a) What was the defendant's testimony about the switch-knife? **(b)** Why is the knife considered an important piece of evidence?

6. (a) How does the knife figure in the climax of Act One? **(b)** Why might some of the jurors begin to have doubts after this point? **(c)** How do you think Four, Three, Five, and Nine will vote on the second ballot? Give reasons for your answer.

Vocabulary

Dictionary

If you were a juror deciding the guilt or innocence of the accused, you would need to understand the meanings of many words as used in a court of law—and understand them with absolute precision. Use the Glossary to write answers to the following questions.

1. What is the difference between *homicide* and *premeditated homicide?*

2. A defendant must be found innocent if a "reasonable doubt" of his or her guilt exists in the minds of the jurors. What is significant about the meaning of *reasonable* in this phrase?

3. *Evidence, testimony,* and *proof* have fairly similar meanings in a trial setting. Use the synonym study following *testimony* in the Glossary to explain the difference between the words.

Composition

A familiar form of external conflict is the kind that pits one person against a group, as Juror Eight is pitted against his fellow jurors in Act One. Think about the problems of the individual vs. the group as demonstrated either in the play thus far or in a real-life situation you have seen or experienced. Consider these questions: Why is it easier to join the group than to stand alone? Do personal feelings sometimes overshadow the real issues? What might an individual do to get the opposition at least to consider his or her side of the conflict?

Write a three- or four-paragraph essay, first describing the specifics of the individual-vs.-group conflict you've thought about, then presenting your views on at least one of the questions mentioned above. (See "Defending Your Position," page 663, in the Composition Guide.)

Act Two

Fade in on same scene, no time lapse. EIGHT *stands tensely watching as the* JURORS *write on their ballots. He stays perfectly still as one by one they fold the ballots and pass them along to the* FOREMAN. *The* FOREMAN *takes them, riffles through the folded ballots, counts eleven, and now begins to open them. He reads each one out loud and lays it aside. They watch him quietly, and all we hear is his voice and the sound of* TWO *sucking on a cough drop.*

FOREMAN. Guilty. Guilty. Guilty. Guilty. Guilty. Guilty. Guilty. Guilty. Guilty. *(He pauses at the tenth ballot and then reads it.)* Not Guilty. (THREE *slams down hard on the table. The* FOREMAN *opens the last ballot.)* Guilty.

TEN *(angry).* How do you like that!

SEVEN. Who was it? I think we have a right to know.

ELEVEN. Excuse me. This was a secret ballot. We agreed on this point, no? If the gentleman wants it to remain secret—

THREE *(standing up angrily).* What do you mean? There are no secrets in here! I know who it was. *(He turns to* FIVE.*)* What's the matter with you? You come in here and you vote guilty and then this slick preacher starts to tear your heart out with stories about a poor little kid who just couldn't help becoming a murderer. So you change your vote. If that isn't the most sickening—

(FIVE *stares at* THREE, *frightened at this outburst.)*

FOREMAN. Now hold it.

THREE. Hold it? We're trying to put a guilty man into the chair where he belongs—and all of a sudden we're paying attention to fairy tales.

FIVE. Now just a minute—

ELEVEN. Please. I would like to say something here. I have always thought that a man was entitled to have unpopular opinions in this country. This is the reason I came here. I wanted to have the right to disagree. In my own country, I am ashamed to say—

TEN. What do we have to listen to now—the whole history of your country?

SEVEN. Yeah, let's stick to the subject. *(To* FIVE*)* I want to ask you what made you change your vote.

(There is a long pause as SEVEN *and* FIVE *eye each other angrily.)*

NINE *(quietly).* There's nothing for him to tell you. He didn't change his vote. I did. *(There is a pause.)* Maybe you'd like to know why.

THREE. No, we wouldn't like to know why.

FOREMAN. The man wants to talk.

NINE. Thank you. *(Pointing at* EIGHT*)* This gentleman chose to stand alone against us. That's his right. It takes a great deal of courage to stand alone even if you believe in something very strongly. He left the verdict up to us. He gambled for support and I gave it to him. I want to hear more. The vote is ten to two.

TEN. That's fine. If the speech is over, let's go on.

(FOREMAN *gets up, goes to door, knocks, hands* GUARD *the tagged switch-knife and sits down again.)*

THREE *(to* FIVE*).* Look, buddy, I was a little excited. Well, you know how it is. I . . . I didn't mean to get nasty. Nothing personal. (FIVE *looks at him.)*

SEVEN *(to* EIGHT*).* Look, supposing you answer me this. If the kid didn't kill him, who did?

EIGHT. As far as I know, we're supposed to decide whether or not the boy on trial is guilty. We're not concerned with anyone else's motives here.

NINE. Guilty beyond a reasonable doubt. This is an important thing to remember.

THREE *(to* TEN*).* Everyone's a lawyer. *(To* NINE*)* Supposing you explain what your reasonable doubts are.

NINE. This is not easy. So far, it's only a feeling I have. A feeling. Perhaps you don't understand.

TEN. A feeling! What are we gonna do, spend the night talking about your feelings? What about the facts?

THREE. You said a mouthful. *(To* NINE*)* Look, the

old man heard the kid yell, "I'm gonna kill you." A second later he heard the father's body falling, and he saw the boy running out of the house fifteen seconds after that.

TWELVE. That's right. And let's not forget the woman across the street. She looked into the open window and saw the boy stab his father. She saw it. Now if that's not enough for you . . .

EIGHT. It's not enough for me.

SEVEN. How do you like him? It's like talking into a dead phone.

FOUR. The woman saw the killing through the windows of a moving elevated train. The train had five cars, and she saw it through the windows of the last two. She remembers the most insignificant details.

(Cut to close shot of TWELVE, *who doodles a picture of an el train on a scrap of paper.)*

THREE. Well, what have you got to say about that?

EIGHT. I don't know. It doesn't sound right to me.

THREE. Well, supposing you think about it. *(To* TWELVE*)* Lend me your pencil.

*(*TWELVE *gives it to him. He draws a tick-tack-toe square on the same sheet of paper on which* TWELVE *has drawn the train. He fills in an X, hands the pencil to* TWELVE.*)*

THREE. Your turn. We might as well pass the time.

*(*TWELVE *takes the pencil.* EIGHT *stands up and snatches the paper away.* THREE *leaps up.)*

THREE. Wait a minute!

EIGHT *(hard)*. This isn't a game.

THREE *(angry)*. Who do you think you are?

SEVEN *(rising)*. All right, let's take it easy.

THREE. I've got a good mind to walk around this table and belt him one!

FOREMAN. Now, please. I don't want any fights in here.

THREE. Did ya see him? The nerve! The absolute nerve!

TEN. All right. Forget it. It don't mean anything.

SIX. How about sitting down.

THREE. This isn't a game. Who does he think he is?

(He lets them sit him down. EIGHT *remains standing, holding the scrap of paper. He looks at it closely now and seems to be suddenly interested in it. Then he throws it back toward* THREE. *It lands in center of table.* THREE *is angered again at this, but* FOUR *puts his hand on his arm.* EIGHT *speaks now and his voice is more intense.)*

EIGHT *(to* FOUR*)*. Take a look at that sketch. How long does it take an elevated train going at top speed to pass a given point?

FOUR. What has that got to do with anything?

EIGHT. How long? Guess.

FOUR. I wouldn't have the slightest idea.

EIGHT *(to* FIVE*)*. What do you think?

FIVE. About ten or twelve seconds, maybe.

EIGHT. I'd say that was a fair guess. Anyone else?

ELEVEN. I would think about ten seconds, perhaps.

TWO. About ten seconds.

FOUR. All right. Say ten seconds. What are you getting at?

EIGHT. This. An el train passes a given point in ten seconds. That given point is the window of the room in which the killing took place. You can almost reach out of the window of that room and touch the el. Right? *(Several of them nod.)* All right. Now let me ask you this. Did anyone here ever live right next to the el tracks? I have. When your window is open and the train goes by, the noise is almost unbearable. You can't hear yourself think.

TEN. Okay. You can't hear yourself think. Will you get to the point?

EIGHT. The old man heard the boy say, "I'm going to kill you," and one second later he heard a body fall. One second. That's the testimony, right?

TWO. Right.

EIGHT. The woman across the street looked through the windows of the last two cars of the el and saw the body fall. Right? The *last two* cars.

TEN. What are you giving us here?

EIGHT. An el takes ten seconds to pass a given point or two seconds per car. That el had been going by the old man's window for at least six seconds, and maybe more, before the body fell, according to the woman. The old man would have had to hear the boy say, "I'm going to kill you," while the front of the el was roaring past his nose. It's not possible that he could have heard it.

THREE. What d'ya mean! Sure he could have heard it.

EIGHT. Could he?

THREE. He said the boy yelled it out. That's enough for me.

NINE. I don't think he could have heard it.

TWO. Maybe he didn't hear it. I mean with the el noise—

THREE. What are you people talking about? Are you calling the old man a liar?

FIVE. Well, it stands to reason.

THREE. You're crazy. Why would he lie? What's he got to gain?

NINE. Attention, maybe.

THREE. You keep coming up with these bright sayings. Why don't you send one in to a newspaper? They pay two dollars.

(EIGHT *looks hard at* THREE *and then turns to* NINE.)

EIGHT *(softly)*. Why might the old man have lied? You have a right to be heard.

NINE. It's just that I looked at him for a very long time. The seam of his jacket was split under the arm. Did you notice that? He was a very old man with a torn jacket, and he carried two canes. I think I know him better than anyone here. This is a quiet, frightened, insignificant man who has been nothing all his life, who has never had recognition—his name in the newspapers. Nobody knows him after seventy-five years. That's a very sad thing. A man like this needs to be recognized. To be questioned, and listened to, and quoted just once. This is very important.

TWELVE. And you're trying to tell us he lied about a thing like this just so that he could be important?

NINE. No, he wouldn't really lie. But perhaps he'd make himself believe that he heard those words and recognized the boy's face.

THREE *(loud)*. Well, that's the most fantastic story I've ever heard. How can you make up a thing like that? What do you know about it?

NINE *(low)*. I speak from experience. *(There is a long pause. Then the* FOREMAN *clears his throat.)*

FOREMAN *(to* EIGHT*)*. All right. Is there anything else?

*(*EIGHT *is looking at* NINE. TWO *offers the* FOREMAN *a box of cough drops. The* FOREMAN *pushes it away.)*

TWO *(hesitantly)*. Anybody . . . want a cough . . . drop?

FOREMAN *(sharply)*. Come on. Let's get on with it.

EIGHT. I'll take one. *(*TWO *almost gratefully slides him one along the table.)* Thanks. *(*TWO *nods and* EIGHT *puts the cough drop into his mouth.)*

EIGHT. Now. There's something else I'd like to point out here. I think we proved that the old man couldn't have heard the boy say, "I'm going to kill you," but supposing he really did hear it? This phrase: how many times has each of you used it? Probably hundreds. "If you do that once more, Junior, I'm going to murder you." "Come on, Rocky, kill him!" We say it every day. This doesn't mean that we're going to kill someone.

THREE. Wait a minute. The phrase was "I'm going to kill you," and the kid screamed it out at the top of his lungs. Don't try and tell me he didn't mean it. Anybody says a thing like that the way he said it—they mean it.

TEN. And how they mean it!

EIGHT. Well, let me ask you this. Do you really think the boy would shout out a thing like that so the whole neighborhood would hear it? I don't think so. He's much too bright for that.

TEN *(exploding)*. Bright! He's a common, ignorant slob. He don't even speak good English!

ELEVEN *(slowly)*. He *doesn't* even speak good English.

*(*TEN *stares angrily at* ELEVEN, *and there is silence for a moment. Then* FIVE *looks around the table nervously.)*

FIVE. I'd like to change my vote to not guilty.

*(*THREE *gets up and walks to the window, furious, but trying to control himself.)*

FOREMAN. Are you sure?

FIVE. Yes. I'm sure.

FOREMAN. The vote is nine to three in favor of guilty.

SEVEN. Well, if that isn't the end. *(To* FIVE*)* What are you basing it on? Stories this guy—*(Indicating* EIGHT*)*—made up! He oughta write for *Amazing Detective Monthly*. He'd make a fortune. Listen, the kid had a lawyer, didn't he? Why didn't his lawyer bring up all these points?

FIVE. Lawyers can't think of everything.

SEVEN. Oh, brother! *(To* EIGHT*)* You sit in here and pull stories out of thin air. Now we're supposed to believe that the old man didn't get up out of bed, run to the door, and see the kid beat it downstairs fifteen seconds after the killing. He's only saying he did to be important.

FIVE. Did the old man say he ran to the door?

SEVEN. Ran. Walked. What's the difference? He got there.

FIVE. I don't remember what he said. But I don't see how he could run.

FOUR. He said he went from his bedroom to the front door. That's enough, isn't it?

EIGHT. Where was his bedroom again?

TEN. Down the hall somewhere. I thought you remembered everything. Don't you remember that?

EIGHT. No. Mr. Foreman, I'd like to take a look at the diagram of the apartment.

SEVEN. Why don't we have them run the trial over just so you can get everything straight?

EIGHT. Mr. Foreman—

FOREMAN *(rising)*. I heard you.

(The FOREMAN *gets up, goes to door during following dialogue. He knocks on door,* GUARD *opens it, he whispers to* GUARD, GUARD *nods and closes door.)*

THREE *(to* EIGHT*)*. All right. What's this for? How come you're the only one in the room who wants to see exhibits all the time?

FIVE. I want to see this one, too.

THREE. And I want to stop wasting time.

FOUR. If we're going to start wading through all that nonsense about where the body was found . . .

EIGHT. We're not. We're going to find out how a man who's had two strokes in the past three years, and who walks with a pair of canes, could get to his front door in fifteen seconds.

THREE. He said twenty seconds.

TWO. He said fifteen.

THREE. How does he know how long fifteen seconds is? You can't judge that kind of a thing.

NINE. He said fifteen. He was positive about it.

THREE *(angry)*. He's an old man. You saw him. Half the time he was confused. How could he be positive about . . . anything?

*(*THREE *looks around sheepishly, unable to cover up his blunder. The door opens and the* GUARD *walks in, carrying a large pen-and-ink diagram of the apartment. It is a railroad flat.*[1] *A bedroom faces the el tracks. Behind it is a series of rooms off a long hall. In the front bedroom is a diagram of the spot where the body was found. At the back of the apartment we see the entrance into the apartment hall from the building hall. We see a flight of stairs in the building hall. The diagram is clearly labeled and included in the information on it are the dimensions of the various rooms. The* GUARD *gives the diagram to the* FOREMAN.*)*

GUARD. This what you wanted?

FOREMAN. That's right. Thank you.

(The GUARD *nods and exits.* EIGHT *goes to* FOREMAN *and reaches for it.)*

EIGHT. May I?

(The FOREMAN *nods.* EIGHT *takes the diagram and sets it up on a chair so that all can see it.* EIGHT *looks it over. Several of the* JURORS *get up to see it better.* THREE, TEN, *and* SEVEN, *however, barely bother to look at it.)*

SEVEN *(to* TEN*)*. Do me a favor. Wake me up when this is over.

EIGHT *(ignoring him)*. All right. This is the apartment in which the killing took place. The old man's apartment is directly beneath it and exactly the same. *(Pointing)* Here are the el tracks. The bedroom. Another bedroom. Living room. Bathroom. Kitchen. And this is the hall. Here's the front door to the apartment. And here are the steps. *(Pointing to front bedroom and then front door)* Now the old man was in bed in this room. He says he got up, went out into the hall, down the hall to the front door, opened it, and looked out just in time to see the boy racing down the stairs. Am I right?

THREE. That's the story.

EIGHT. Fifteen seconds after he heard the body fall.

ELEVEN. Correct.

EIGHT. His bed was at the window. It's—*(Looking closer)*—twelve feet from his bed to the bedroom door. The length of the hall is forty-three feet, six inches. He had to get up out of bed, get his canes, walk twelve feet, open the bedroom door, walk forty-three feet, and open the front door—all in fifteen seconds. Do you think this possible?

TEN. You know it's possible.

ELEVEN. He can only walk very slowly. They had to help him into the witness chair.

THREE. You make it sound like a long walk. It's not.

*(*EIGHT *gets up, goes to the end of the room, and takes two chairs. He puts them together to indicate a bed.)*

---

1. ***railroad flat,*** long, narrow apartment with rooms joined in a line.

NINE. For an old man who uses canes, it's a long walk.

THREE *(to* EIGHT*).* What are you doing?

EIGHT. I want to try this thing. Let's see how long it took him. I'm going to pace off twelve feet—the length of the bedroom. *(He begins to do so.)*

THREE. You're crazy. You can't re-create a thing like that.

ELEVEN. Perhaps if we could see it . . . this is an important point.

THREE *(mad).* It's a ridiculous waste of time.

SIX. Let him do it.

EIGHT. Hand me a chair. *(Someone pushes a chair to him.)* All right. This is the bedroom door. Now how far would you say it is from here to the door of this room?

SIX. I'd say it was twenty feet.

TWO. Just about.

EIGHT. Twenty feet is close enough. All right, from here to the door and back is about forty feet. It's shorter than the length of the hall, wouldn't you say that?

NINE. A few feet, maybe.

TEN. Look, this is absolutely insane. What makes you think you can—

EIGHT. Do you mind if I try it? According to you, it'll only take fifteen seconds. We can spare that. *(He walks over to the two chairs now and lies down on them.)* Who's got a watch with a second hand?

TWO. I have.

EIGHT. When you want me to start, stamp your foot. That'll be the body falling. Time me from there. *(He lies down on the chairs.)* Let's say he keeps his canes right at his bedside. Right?

TWO. Right!

EIGHT. Okay. I'm ready.

(They all watch carefully. TWO *stares at his watch, waiting for the second hand to reach sixty. Then, as it does, he stamps his foot loudly.* EIGHT *begins to get up. Slowly he swings his legs over the edges of the chairs, reaches for imaginary canes, and struggles to his feet.* TWO *stares at the watch.* EIGHT *walks as a crippled old man would walk, toward the chair which is serving as the bedroom door. He gets to it and pretends to open it.)*

TEN *(shouting).* Speed it up. He walked twice as fast as that.

*(*EIGHT, *not having stopped for this outburst, begins to walk the simulated forty-foot hallway.)*

ELEVEN. This is, I think, even more quickly than the old man walked in the courtroom.

EIGHT. If you think I should go faster, I will.

(He speeds up his pace slightly. He reaches the door and turns now, heading back, hobbling as an old man would hobble, bent over his imaginary canes. They watch him tensely. He hobbles back to the chair, which also serves as the front door. He stops there and pretends to unlock the door. Then he pretends to push it open.)

EIGHT *(loud).* Stop.

TWO. Right.

EIGHT. What's the time?

TWO. Fifteen . . . twenty . . . thirty . . . thirty-one seconds exactly.

ELEVEN. Thirty-one seconds.

(Some of the JURORS *adlib*[2] *their surprise to each other.)*

EIGHT. It's my guess that the old man was trying to get to the door, heard someone racing down the stairs, and assumed that it was the boy.

SIX. I think that's possible.

THREE *(infuriated).* Assumed? Now, listen to me, you people. I've seen all kinds of dishonesty in my day . . . but this little display takes the cake. *(To* FOUR*)* Tell him, will you?

*(*FOUR *sits silently.* THREE *looks at him and then he strides over to* EIGHT.*)*

THREE. You come in here with your heart bleeding all over the floor about slum kids and injustice and you make up these wild stories, and you've got some soft-hearted old ladies listening to you. Well I'm not. I'm getting real sick of it. *(To all)* What's the matter with you people? This kid is guilty! He's got to burn! We're

2. ***adlib,*** make up words that are not in the script.

letting him slip through our fingers here.

EIGHT *(calmly).* Our fingers. Are you his executioner?

THREE *(raging).* I'm one of 'em.

EIGHT. Perhaps you'd like to pull the switch.

THREE *(shouting).* For this kid? You bet I'd like to pull the switch!

EIGHT. I'm sorry for you.

THREE *(shouting).* Don't start with me.

EIGHT. What it must feel like to want to pull the switch!

THREE. Shut up!

EIGHT. You're a sadist.

THREE *(louder).* Shut up!

EIGHT *(strong).* You want to see this boy die because you personally want it—not because of the facts.

THREE *(shouting).* Shut up!

(He lunges at EIGHT, *but is caught by two of the* JURORS *and held. He struggles as* EIGHT *watches calmly.)*

THREE *(screaming).* Let me go! I'll kill him. I'll kill him!

EIGHT *(softly).* You don't really mean you'll kill me, do you?

*(*THREE *stops struggling now and stares at* EIGHT. *All the* JURORS *watch in silence as we fade out.)*

Discussion

1. (a) Which juror begins the discussion of who changed his ballot on the second vote? **(b)** Which juror immediately jumps into the conversation in an angry manner? **(c)** Why do Five, Eleven, and Nine take offense at this juror's anger?

2. (a) What evidence does Eight offer first to discount the old man's testimony? **(b)** What is the connection between the el-train's noise and the old man's testimony?

3. Reread the comments Nine makes about the old man. Are these comments based on fact or do they reflect Nine's personal feelings? Explain.

4. (a) What is the significance of Ten's comment that the defendant "don't even speak good English"? **(b)** How does this comment affect Eleven? Five? **(c)** Is the comment consistent with Ten's previous behavior? Explain.

5. How does Eight interpret the result of his timed experiment?

6. (a) By the end of Act Two, Three has contradicted some of his earlier views. In what ways? **(b)** How do you think each juror would vote at the end of this act?

Application

Protagonist/Antagonist

In a longer work like *Twelve Angry Men,* it may take some time to get a clear idea of just who is at odds with whom. For instance, it was fairly obvious even in Act One that Juror Eight is the protagonist, but at that point you may have felt that all the other jurors were antagonists. Now, however, having read further, you have probably begun to reassess this opinion.

1. Which juror has emerged as the main antagonist by the end of Act Two?

2. Contrast the attitudes of this juror with those of Juror Eight.

Comment: The Story Behind the Play

Reginald Rose says the following about his thoughts and motivations as he set about writing *Twelve Angry Men:*

Twelve Angry Men is the only play I've written which has any relation at all to actual personal experience. A month or so before I began the play I sat on the jury of a manslaughter case in New York's General Sessions Court. This was my first experience on a jury, and it left quite an impression on me. The receipt of my jury notice activated many grumblings and mutterings, most of which began with lines like "Eight million people in New York and they have to call me!" All the prospective jurors I met in the waiting room the first day I appeared had the same grim, horribly persecuted attitude. But, strangely, the moment I walked into the courtroom to be empaneled and found myself facing a strange man whose fate was suddenly more or less in my hands, my entire attitude changed. I was hugely impressed with the almost frightening stillness of the courtroom, the impassive, masklike face of the judge, the brisk, purposeful scurrying of the various officials in the room, and the absolute finality of the decision I and my fellow jurors would have to make at the end of the trial. I doubt whether I have ever been so impressed in my life with a role I had to play, and I suddenly became so earnest that, in thinking about it later, I probably was unbearable to the eleven other jurors.

It occurred to me during the trial that no one anywhere ever knows what goes on inside a jury room but the jurors, and I thought then that a play taking place entirely within a jury room might be an exciting and possibly moving experience for an audience.

Actually, the outline of *Twelve Angry Men,* which I began shortly after the trial ended, took longer to write than the script itself. The movements in the play were so intricate that I wanted to have them down on paper to the last detail before I began the construction of the dialogue. I worked on the idea and outline for a week and was stunned by the time I was finished to discover that the outline was twenty-seven typewritten pages long. The average outline is perhaps five pages long, and many are as short as one or two pages. This detailed setting down of the moves of the play paid off, however. The script was written in five days and could have been done in four had I not written it approximately fifteen pages too long.

In writing *Twelve Angry Men* I attempted to blend four elements which I had seen at work in the jury room during my jury service. These elements are: (a) the evidence as remembered and interpreted by each individual juror (the disparities here were incredible); (b) the relationship of juror to juror in the life-and-death situation; (c) the emotional pattern of each individual juror; and (d) physical problems such as the weather, the time, the uncomfortable room, etc. All of these elements are of vital importance in any jury room, and all of them presented excellent dramatic possibilities.

Act Three

Fade in on same scene. No time lapse. THREE *glares angrily at* EIGHT. *He is still held by two* JURORS. *After a long pause, he shakes himself loose and turns away. He walks to the windows. The other* JURORS *stand around the room now, shocked by this display of anger. There is silence. Then the door opens and the* GUARD *enters. He looks around the room.*

GUARD. Is there anything wrong, gentlemen? I heard some noise.

FOREMAN. No. There's nothing wrong. *(He points to the large diagram of the apartment.)* You can take that back. We're finished with it.

(The GUARD *nods and takes the diagram. He looks curiously at some of the* JURORS *and exits. The* JURORS *still are silent. Some of them slowly begin to sit down.* THREE *still stands at the window. He turns around now. The* JURORS *look at him.)*

THREE *(loud).* Well, what are you looking at?

(They turn away. He goes back to his seat now. Silently the rest of the JURORS *take their seats.* TWELVE *begins to doodle.* TEN *blows his nose, but no one speaks. Then, finally—)*

FOUR. I don't see why we have to behave like children here.

ELEVEN. Nor do I. We have a responsibility. This is a remarkable thing about democracy. That we are . . . what is the word? . . . Ah, notified! That we are notified by mail to come down to this place and decide on the guilt or innocence of a man we have not known before. We have nothing to gain or lose by our verdict. This is one of the reasons why we are strong. We should not make it a personal thing.

(There is a long, awkward pause.)

TWELVE. Well—we're still nowhere. Who's got an idea?

SIX. I think maybe we should try another vote. Mr. Foreman?

FOREMAN. It's all right with me. Anybody doesn't want to vote? *(He looks around the table.)*

SEVEN. All right, let's do it.

THREE. I want an open ballot. Let's call out our votes. I want to know who stands where.

FOREMAN. That sounds fair. Anyone object? *(No one does.)* All right. I'll call off your jury numbers.

(He takes a pencil and paper and makes marks now in one of two columns after each vote.)

FOREMAN. I vote guilty. Number Two?

TWO. Not guilty.

FOREMAN. Number Three?

THREE. Guilty.

FOREMAN. Number Four?

FOUR. Guilty.

FOREMAN. Number Five?

FIVE. Not guilty.

FOREMAN. Number Six?

SIX. Not guilty.

FOREMAN. Number Seven?

SEVEN. Guilty.

FOREMAN. Number Eight?

EIGHT. Not guilty.

FOREMAN. Number Nine?

NINE. Not guilty.

FOREMAN. Number Ten?

TEN. Guilty.

FOREMAN. Number Eleven?

ELEVEN. Not guilty.

FOREMAN. Number Twelve?

TWELVE. Guilty.

FOUR. Six to six.

TEN *(mad).* I'll tell you something. The crime is being committed right in this room.

FOREMAN. The vote is six to six.

THREE. I'm ready to walk into court right now and declare a hung jury. There's no point in this going on anymore.

SEVEN. I go for that, too. Let's take it in to the judge and let the kid take his chances with twelve other guys.

FIVE *(to* SEVEN*).* You mean you still don't think there's room for reasonable doubt?

SEVEN. No, I don't.

ELEVEN. I beg your pardon. Maybe you don't understand the term "reasonable doubt."

SEVEN *(angry).* What do you mean I don't understand it? Who do you think you are to talk to me like that? *(To all)* How do you like this guy? He comes over here running for his life, and before he can even take a big breath he's telling us how to run the show. The arrogance of him!

FIVE *(to* SEVEN*)*. Wait a second. Nobody around here's asking where you came from.

SEVEN. I was born right here.

FIVE. Or where your father came from. . . . *(He looks at* SEVEN, *who doesn't answer but looks away.)* Maybe it wouldn't hurt us to take a few tips from people who come running here! Maybe they learned something we don't know. We're not so perfect!

ELEVEN. Please—I am used to this. It's all right. Thank you.

FIVE. It's not all right!

SEVEN. Okay, okay, I apologize. Is that what you want?

FIVE. That's what I want.

FOREMAN. All right. Let's stop the arguing. Who's got something constructive to say?

TWO *(hesitantly)*. Well, something's been bothering me a little . . . this whole business about the stab wound and how it was made, the downward angle of it, you know?

THREE. Don't tell me we're gonna start that. They went over it and over it in court.

TWO. I know they did—but I don't go along with it. The boy is five feet eight inches tall. His father was six two. That's a difference of six inches. It's a very awkward thing to stab *down* into the chest of someone who's half a foot taller than you are.

*(*THREE *jumps up, holding the knife.)*

THREE. Look, you're not going to be satisfied till you see it again. I'm going to give you a demonstration. Somebody get up.

(He looks around the table. EIGHT *stands up and walks toward him.* THREE *closes the knife and puts it in his pocket. They stand face to face and look at each other for a moment.)*

THREE. Okay. *(To* TWO*)* Now watch this. I don't want to have to do it again. *(He crouches down now until he is quite a bit shorter than* EIGHT.*)* Is that six inches?

TWELVE. That's more than six inches.

THREE. Okay, let it be more.

(He reaches into his pocket and takes out the knife. He flicks it open, changes its position in his hand, and holds the knife aloft, ready to stab. He and EIGHT *look steadily into each other's eyes. Then he stabs downward, hard.)*

TWO *(shouting)*. Look out!

(He stops short just as the blade reaches EIGHT*'s chest.* THREE *laughs.)*

SIX. That's not funny.

FIVE. What's the matter with you?

THREE. Now just calm down. Nobody's hurt, are they?

EIGHT *(low)*. No. Nobody's hurt.

THREE. All right. There's your angle. Take a look at it. Down and in. That's how I'd stab a taller man in the chest, and that's how it was done. Take a look at it and tell me I'm wrong.

*(*TWO *doesn't answer.* THREE *looks at him for a moment, then jams the knife into the table, and sits down. They all look at the knife.)*

SIX. Down and in. I guess there's no argument.

*(*EIGHT *picks the knife out of the table and closes it. He flicks it open and, changing its position in his hand, stabs downward with it.)*

EIGHT *(to* SIX*)*. Did you ever stab a man?

SIX. Of course not.

EIGHT *(to* THREE*)*. Did you?

THREE. All right, let's not be silly.

EIGHT. Did you?

THREE *(loud)*. No, I didn't!

EIGHT. Where do you get all your information about how it's done?

THREE. What do you mean? It's just common sense.

EIGHT. Have you ever seen a man stabbed?

THREE *(pauses and looks around the room nervously)*. No.

EIGHT. All right. I want to ask you something. The boy was an experienced knife fighter. He was even sent to reform school for knifing someone, isn't that so?

TWELVE. That's right.

EIGHT. Look at this. *(*EIGHT *closes the knife, flicks it open, and changes the position of the*

knife so that he can stab overhanded.) Doesn't it seem like an awkward way to handle a knife?

THREE. What are you asking me for?

(EIGHT closes the blade and flicks it open, holds it ready to slash underhanded.)

FIVE. Wait a minute! What's the matter with me? Give me that. *(He reaches out for the knife.)*

EIGHT. Have you ever seen a knife fight?

FIVE. Yes, I have.

EIGHT. In the movies?

FIVE. In my backyard. On my stoop. In the vacant lot across the street. Too many of them. Switch-knives came with the neighborhood where I lived. Funny I didn't think of it before. I guess you try to forget those things. *(Flicking the knife open)* Anyone who's ever used a switch-knife would never have stabbed downward. You don't handle a switch-knife that way. You use it underhanded.

EIGHT. Then he couldn't have made the kind of wound which killed his father.

FIVE. No. He couldn't have. Not if he'd ever had any experience with switch-knives.

THREE. I don't believe it.

TEN. Neither do I. You're giving us a lot of mumbo jumbo.

EIGHT *(to* TWELVE*)*. What do you think?

TWELVE *(hesitantly)*. Well . . . I don't know.

EIGHT *(to* SEVEN*)*. What about you?

SEVEN. Listen, I'll tell you something. I'm a little sick of this whole thing already. We're getting nowhere fast. Let's break it up and go home. I'm changing my vote to not guilty.

THREE. You're what?

SEVEN. You heard me. I've had enough.

THREE. What do you mean, you've had enough? That's no answer.

ELEVEN *(angry)*. I think perhaps you're right. This is not an answer. *(To* SEVEN*)* What kind of a man are you? You have sat here and voted guilty with everyone else because there are some theater tickets burning a hole in your pocket. Now you have changed your vote for the same reason. I do not think you have the right to play like this with a man's life. This is an ugly and terrible thing to do.

SEVEN. Now wait a minute . . . you can't talk like that to me.

ELEVEN *(strong)*. I can talk like that to you! If you want to vote not guilty, then do it because you are convinced the man is not guilty. If you believe he is guilty, then vote that way. Or don't you have the . . . the . . . guts—the guts to do what you think is right?

SEVEN. Now listen . . .

ELEVEN. Is it guilty or not guilty?

SEVEN *(hesitantly)*. I told you. Not . . . guilty.

ELEVEN *(hard)*. Why?

SEVEN. I don't have to—

ELEVEN. You have to! Say it! Why?

(They stare at each other for a long while.)

SEVEN *(low)*. I . . . don't think . . . he's guilty.

EIGHT *(fast)*. I want another vote.

FOREMAN. Okay, there's another vote called for. I guess the quickest way is a show of hands. Anybody object? *(No one does.)* All right. All those voting not guilty, raise your hands.

*(*TWO, FIVE, SIX, SEVEN, EIGHT, NINE, *and* ELEVEN *raise their hands immediately. Then, slowly,* TWELVE *raises his hand. The* FOREMAN *looks around the table carefully and then he too raises his hand. He looks around the table, counting silently.)*

FOREMAN. Nine. *(The hands go down.)* All those voting guilty.

*(*THREE, FOUR, *and* TEN *raise their hands.)*

FOREMAN. Three. *(They lower their hands.)* The vote is nine to three in favor of acquittal.

TEN. I don't understand you people. How can you believe this kid is innocent? Look, you know how those people lie. I don't have to tell you. They don't know what the truth is. And lemme tell you, they—*(*FIVE *gets up from table, turns his back to it, and goes to window.)*—don't need any real big reason to kill someone either. You know, they get drunk, and *bang,* someone's lying in the gutter. Nobody's blaming them. That's how they are. You know what I mean? Violent! *(*NINE *gets up and does the same. He is followed by* ELEVEN.*)*

TEN. Human life don't mean as much to them as it does to us. Hey, where are you going? Look, these people are drinking and fighting all the time, and if somebody gets killed, so somebody gets killed. They don't care. Oh, sure, there are some good things about them, too. Look, I'm the first to say that. *(*EIGHT *gets up, and then* TWO *and* SIX *follow him to the window.)*

TEN. I've known a few who were pretty decent, but that's the exception. Most of them, it's like they have no feelings. They can do anything. What's going on here?

(The FOREMAN *gets up and goes to the window, followed by* SEVEN *and* TWELVE.*)*

TEN. I'm speaking my piece, and you—Listen to me! They're no good. There's not a one of 'em who's any good. We better watch out. Take it from me. This kid on trial . . .

*(*THREE *sits at table toying with the knife and* FOUR *gets up and starts for the window. All have their backs to* TEN.*)*

TEN. Well, don't you know about them? Listen to me! What are you doing? I'm trying to tell you something. . . .

*(*FOUR *stands over him as he trails off. There is a dead silence. Then* FOUR *speaks softly.)*

FOUR. I've had enough. If you open your mouth again, I'm going to split your skull.

*(*FOUR *stands there and looks at him. No one moves or speaks.* TEN *looks at him, then looks down at the table.)*

TEN *(softly)*. I'm only trying to tell you. . . .

(There is a long pause as FOUR *stares down at* TEN.*)*

FOUR *(to all)*. All right. Sit down, everybody.

(They all move back to their seats. When they are all seated, FOUR *then sits down.)*

FOUR *(quietly).* I still believe the boy is guilty of murder. I'll tell you why. To me, the most damning evidence was given by the woman across the street who claimed she actually saw the murder committed.

THREE. That's right. As far as I'm concerned, that's the most important testimony.

EIGHT. All right. Let's go over her testimony. What exactly did she say?

FOUR. I believe I can recount it accurately. She said that she went to bed at about eleven o'clock that night. Her bed was next to the open window, and she could look out of the window while lying down and see directly into the window across the street. She tossed and turned for over an hour, unable to fall asleep. Finally she turned toward the window at about twelve-ten and, as she looked out, she saw the boy stab his father. As far as I can see, this is unshakable testimony.

THREE. That's what I mean. That's the whole case.

*(*FOUR *takes off his eyeglasses and begins to polish them, as they all sit silently watching him.)*

FOUR *(to the* JURY*).* Frankly, I don't see how you can vote for acquittal. *(To* TWELVE*)* What do you think about it?

TWELVE. Well . . . maybe . . . there's so much evidence to sift.

THREE. What do you mean, maybe? He's absolutely right. You can throw out all the other evidence.

FOUR. That was my feeling.

*(*TWO*, polishing his glasses, squints at clock, can't see it.* SIX *watches him closely.)*

TWO. What time is it?

ELEVEN. Ten minutes of six.

TWO. It's late. You don't suppose they'd let us go home and finish it in the morning. I've got a kid with mumps.

FIVE. Not a chance.

SIX *(to* TWO*).* Pardon me. Can't you see the clock without your glasses?

TWO. Not clearly. Why?

SIX. Oh, I don't know. Look, this may be a dumb thought, but what do you do when you wake up at night and want to know what time it is?

TWO. What do you mean? I put on my glasses and look at the clock.

SIX. You don't wear them to bed.

TWO. Of course not. No one wears eyeglasses to bed.

TWELVE. What's all this for?

SIX. Well, I was thinking. You know the woman who testified that she saw the killing wears glasses.

THREE. So does my grandmother. So what?

EIGHT. Your grandmother isn't a murder witness.

SIX. Look, stop me if I'm wrong. This woman wouldn't wear her eyeglasses to bed, would she?

FOREMAN. Wait a minute! Did she wear glasses at all? I don't remember.

ELEVEN *(excited).* Of course she did. The woman wore bifocals. I remember this very clearly. They looked quite strong.

NINE. That's right. Bifocals. She never took them off.

FOUR. She did wear glasses. Funny. I never thought of it.

EIGHT. Listen, she wasn't wearing them in bed. That's for sure. She testified that in the midst of her tossing and turning she rolled over and looked casually out the window. The murder was taking place as she looked out, and the lights went out a split second later. She couldn't have had time to put on her glasses. Now maybe she honestly thought she saw the boy kill his father. I say that she saw only a blur.

THREE. How do you know what she saw? Maybe she's farsighted. *(He looks around. No one answers.)*

THREE *(loud).* How does he know all these things?

(There is silence.)

EIGHT. Does anyone think there still is not a reasonable doubt?

(He looks around the room, then squarely at TEN. TEN *looks down and shakes his head no.)*

THREE *(loud).* I think he's guilty.

EIGHT *(calmly).* Does anyone else?

FOUR *(quietly).* No. I'm convinced.

EIGHT *(to* THREE*).* You're alone.

THREE. I don't care whether I'm alone or not! I have a right.

EIGHT. You have a right.

(There is a pause. They all look at THREE.*)*

THREE. Well, I told you I think the kid's guilty. What else do you want?

EIGHT. Your arguments. *(They all look at* THREE.*)*

THREE. I gave you my arguments.

EIGHT. We're not convinced. We're waiting to hear them again. We have time.

*(*THREE *runs to* FOUR *and grabs his arm.)*

THREE *(pleading).* Listen. What's the matter with you? You're the guy. You made all the arguments. You can't turn now. A guilty man's gonna be walking the streets. A murderer. He's got to die! Stay with me.

FOUR. I'm sorry. There's a reasonable doubt in my mind.

EIGHT. We're waiting.

*(*THREE *turns violently on him.)*

THREE *(shouting).* Well, you're not going to intimidate me! *(They all look at* THREE.*)* I'm entitled to my opinion! *(No one answers him.)* It's gonna be a hung jury! That's it!

EIGHT. There's nothing we can do about that, except hope that some night, maybe in a few months, you'll get some sleep.

FIVE. You're all alone.

NINE. It takes a great deal of courage to stand alone.

*(*THREE *looks around at all of them for a long time. They sit silently, waiting for him to speak, and all of them despise him for his stubbornness. Then, suddenly, his face contorts as if he is about to cry, and he slams his fist down on the table.)*

THREE *(thundering).* All right!

*(*THREE *turns his back on them. There is silence for a moment and then the* FOREMAN *goes to the door and knocks on it. It opens. The* GUARD *looks in and sees them all standing. The* GUARD *holds the door for them as they begin slowly to file out.* EIGHT *waits at the door as the others file past him. Finally he and* THREE *are the only ones left.* THREE *turns around and sees that they are alone. Slowly he moves toward the door. Then he stops at the table. He pulls the switch-knife out of the table and walks over to* EIGHT *with it. He holds it in the approved knife-fighter fashion and looks long and hard at* EIGHT, *pointing the knife at his belly.* EIGHT *stares back. Then* THREE *turns the knife around.* EIGHT *takes it by the handle.* THREE *exits.* EIGHT *closes the knife, puts it away, and, taking a last look around the room, exits, closing the door. The camera moves in close on the littered table in the empty room, and we clearly see a slip of crumpled paper on which are scribbled the words "Not guilty.")*

(Fade out)

Discussion

1. At the beginning of Act Three, the jurors vote for the third time. **(a)** What is the result of the third vote? **(b)** Which jurors have changed their votes?

2. Five provides information that discounts an important piece of testimony. **(a)** What information does Five provide? **(b)** Is he qualified to speak as an expert? Why or why not? **(c)** Is Five's ability to provide this information too coincidental to be believable? Explain.

3. (a) In what way is Seven's willingness to change his vote consistent with his earlier behavior? **(b)** Why does Eleven question Seven so closely?

4. (a) How do the other jurors react to Ten's statements about "those people"? **(b)** Does the fact that they all seem to have the same opinion surprise you? Why or why not?

5. (a) What is the result of the fourth vote? **(b)** Why does Four feel that he still cannot vote for acquittal? **(c)** What significant observation does Six make at this point?

6. (a) At the end of the play, has the jury proven the defendant not guilty? Explain. **(b)** Do you think Three was pressured into agreeing with the majority? Why or why not?

Vocabulary

Pronunciation

A. Write the letter of the correct pronunciation for each of the following words. Then use each word in a sentence that shows you understand its meaning.

1. sadism: **(a)** si dish′ən **(b)** sā′diz′əm

2. bigot: **(a)** big′ət **(b)** bi get′

3. appall: **(a)** ə pôl′ **(b)** ə pēl′

4. prosecution: **(a)** pėr′sə kyü′shən **(b)** pros′ə-kyü′shən

5. rapport: **(a)** ra pôr′ **(b)** ri pôrt′

B. Copy the following words; then divide them into syllables and put the stress marks after each accented syllable. Finally, use each word in a meaningful sentence.

1. simulate; **2.** unanimous; **3.** superficial; **4.** subservient; **5.** insignificant

Reginald Rose 1920–

A native New Yorker, Rose was a publicity writer and advertising copywriter during the early 1950s. He sold his first television script, which he had written in his spare time, in 1951. He wrote *Twelve Angry Men* in 1954 for television; later he wrote the script for the motion-picture version and then another script for the stage version. Among his numerous awards are three Emmys, one for *Twelve Angry Men* and two for the television series *The Defenders,* another work that dealt with the American legal system. Now living in England, Rose has written feature films as well as television plays.

The Romancers

Edmond Rostand France

CHARACTERS

SYLVETTE
PERCINET (per sē nā′)
STRAFOREL (strȧ fô rel′)
BERGAMIN (ber gä maN′), *Percinet's father*
PASQUINOT (pȧ skē nō′), *Sylvette's father*
A WALL, *silent figurant*
SWORDSMEN, MUSICIANS, MOORS, TORCHBEARERS

The action can take place anywhere, as long as the costumes are attractive.

The stage is cut in half by an old moss-grown wall completely covered with lush vines, creepers, and flowers. At the right, a corner of the BERGAMIN *park, at the left a corner of the* PASQUINOT *park. A bench is placed on each side of the wall. As the curtain goes up,* PERCINET *is sitting atop the wall. He has a book in his lap and is reading to* SYLVETTE, *who listens attentively. She is standing on the bench on the other side and leaning against the wall.*

SYLVETTE. Oh! *Monsieur* Percinet, how beautiful!

PERCINET. Yes, isn't it? Listen to Romeo's reply.

(He reads.)
It was the lark, the herald of the morn;
No nightingale. Look, love, what envious streaks
Do lace the severing clouds in yonder East.
Night's candles are burnt out, and jocund day
Stands tiptoe on the misty mountaintops.[1]

SYLVETTE *(suddenly straining her ear).* Hush!

PERCINET *(listening for a moment, then).* There's no one coming, *Mademoiselle.* You mustn't take fright like the sparrow that flutters from a branch at the slightest sound. . . . Listen to the Immortal Lovers speak:

JULIET.
Yond light is not daylight; I know it, I;
It is some meteor that the sun exhales,
To be to thee this night a torchbearer
And light thee on thy way to Mantua.
Therefore stay yet; thou need'st not to be gone.
ROMEO.
Let me be ta'en, let me be put to death;
I am content, so thou wilt have it so. . . .
Come, death, and welcome!

---

1. ***It was the lark . . . misty mountaintops,*** lines from Act Three, Scene 5 of William Shakespeare's tragic play *Romeo and Juliet.* The title characters, members of two feuding families in Verona, Italy, die for their love.

Edmond Rostand (ed môN rôs täN′).

SYLVETTE. Oh no! I don't want him to talk about that! If he does, I'll start crying. . . .

PERCINET. All right, then let's stop there: we'll close our book until tomorrow, and for your sake we'll let gentle Romeo live on. *(He shuts the book and looks around.)* What a wonderful spot. I think it's the perfect place to indulge in the beautiful verses of the Great Bard.[2]

SYLVETTE. Yes, those lines are so beautiful, and the divine murmur of the leaves and the boughs is really a fine accompaniment, and the setting of this green shade is just right. Yes, indeed, *Monsieur* Percinet, those verses *are* lovely. But what makes their beauty even more poignant is the way you recite them in your melodious voice.

PERCINET. You terrible flatterer, you!

SYLVETTE *(sighing)*. Ah! The poor lovers! How cruel their destiny, how wretched the world was to them! *(With a sigh)* Ah! . . .

PERCINET. What are you thinking about?

SYLVETTE *(sharply)*. Nothing!

PERCINET. But all at once, something made you turn crimson.

SYLVETTE *(sharply)*. Nothing!

PERCINET. You little liar. . . . Your eyes are too transparent! I can see what you're thinking about! *(Lowering his voice)* Our parents!

SYLVETTE. Perhaps . . .

PERCINET. Your father and mine, and the hatred that divides them!

SYLVETTE. Well, yes, that's what distresses me and often makes me weep in secret. Last month, when I came home from the convent

2. ***the Great Bard,*** Shakespeare. *Bard* here means "poet."

my father showed me your father's park and said, "My dear child, there you see the lair of my old mortal enemy Bergamin. Keep away from that wretch and that son of his; and I'll disown you unless you promise me to regard those people as your everlasting enemies, for since time immemorial their family has execrated ours." I gave him my word. . . . And you see, *Monsieur,* how I keep it.

PERCINET. And didn't I also promise my father to hate you forever, Sylvette?—And I love you!

SYLVETTE. Oh, goodness me!

PERCINET. And I love you, my darling.

SYLVETTE. How sinful.

PERCINET. Very sinful . . . but who can blame us? The more you're kept from loving someone, the more you *want* to love. Sylvette, kiss me!

SYLVETTE. Never! *(She jumps off the bench and moves away from the wall.)*

PERCINET. But you *do* love me!

SYLVETTE. What did he say?

PERCINET. My darling, I said something that your heart is still struggling against, but it would be foolish to deny it any longer. I said . . . the very same thing you said. Yes, you, Sylvette, when you compared us to the Lovers of Verona.

SYLVETTE. I never compared—

PERCINET. You did so! You likened my father and yours to those of Romeo and Juliet, my darling! That's why *we* are Romeo and Juliet, and that's why we're so madly in love! And despite all their intense hatred, I'll defy both Pasquinot-Capulet and Bergamin-Montague![3]

SYLVETTE *(drawing a bit closer to the wall).* So then we're in love? But *Monsieur* Percinet, how did it happen so quickly?

PERCINET. Love comes when it has to, and no one can say how or why. I would often see you passing by my window. . . .

SYLVETTE. And I saw you passing, too. . . .

PERCINET. And our eyes conversed in code.

SYLVETTE. One day, I was here, gathering nuts near the wall, and by chance . . .

PERCINET. I happened to be reading Shakespeare; and see how all things conspired to unite two hearts. . . .

SYLVETTE. Whoosh! The wind blew my ribbon over to you!

PERCINET. I climbed up on the bench to retrieve it. . . .

SYLVETTE *(climbing).* I climbed up on the bench. . . .

PERCINET. And ever since then, my darling, I've been waiting for you every day, and every day my heart beats faster when—oh, blessed signal—your gentle fledgling laughter rises from behind the wall, and it doesn't stop until your head emerges from the trembling tangle of vines and ivy.

SYLVETTE. Since we're in love, we ought to be engaged.

PERCINET. I was just thinking the very same thing.

SYLVETTE *(solemnly).* I, the last of the Pasquinots, do pledge myself to you, the last of the Bergamins.

PERCINET. What noble folly!

SYLVETTE. They'll speak of us in future ages!

PERCINET. Oh! Tenderhearted children of two callous fathers!

SYLVETTE. But, darling, who knows? Perhaps the time's at hand when Heaven will use us to wipe out their hatred.

PERCINET. I don't think so.

SYLVETTE. Well, I have faith. I can foresee five or six highly possible solutions.

PERCINET. Really? Tell me.

SYLVETTE. Just suppose—I've read of similar things in lots of old romances—just suppose the Reigning Prince were to ride by one day. . . . I would hurry over to him, throw myself at his feet, tell him about our love and the old feud dividing our fathers. . . . After all, a king married Don Rodrigo and Ximene[4]—The Prince will summon our fathers and reconcile them.

---

3. ***Pasquinot-Capulet and Bergamin-Montague.*** The family names of Sylvette and Percinet are paired respectively with the family names of Juliet and Romeo.

4. ***Don Rodrigo and Ximene*** (ksē mān′), characters in Pierre Corneille's play *The Cid* (1636). Their dutifulness to their fathers presents an obstacle to their love; however, they overcome it.

PERCINET. And he'll give me your hand!

SYLVETTE. Or else it will happen the same way as in *The Donkey's Skin*.[5] You'll be at the point of death, a stupid doctor will despair of your life. . . .

PERCINET. My father, panic-stricken, will ask me, "What do you want?"

SYLVETTE. You'll say, "I want Sylvette!"

PERCINET. And his stubborn pride will be forced to yield!

SYLVETTE. Or else, here's another possibility: an old duke, seeing my portrait, falls in love with me, sends a magnificent equerry to me in his name, and offers to make me a duchess. . . .

PERCINET. And you answer "No!"

SYLVETTE. This infuriates him. One lovely evening, as I wander, lost in dreams, down a dark garden path, strange men seize me! . . . I scream! . . .

PERCINET. And I'm at your side immediately. Trusting in my sword, I fight like a lion, slice up—

SYLVETTE. Three or four men. My father runs up, flings his arms about you. You tell him your name. His heart softens. He gives me to my rescuer. And your father is so proud of your valor that he consents!

PERCINET. And we live happily ever after!

SYLVETTE. And none of this seems the least bit unlikely.

PERCINET *(hearing a noise)*. Someone's coming!

SYLVETTE *(losing her head)*. Kiss me good-by!

PERCINET *(kisses her)*. And tonight, when the bell rings for Mass, will you be here? Tell me.

SYLVETTE. No.

PERCINET. Yes.

SYLVETTE *(vanishing behind the wall)*. Your father!

*(*PERCINET *leaps down from the wall.* SYLVETTE, *having stepped down, can't be seen by* BERGAMIN.*)*

BERGAMIN. Ah! So I've caught you daydreaming again, all alone in this corner of the park?

PERCINET. Father, I love . . . this part of the park! I love sitting on this bench, sheltered by the overhanging vines on the wall! . . . Isn't the vine graceful? Look at those arabesque festoons.[6] It's so good to breathe pure air in this spot.

BERGAMIN. In front of that wall?

PERCINET. I love this wall.

BERGAMIN. I don't see anything lovable about it.

SYLVETTE *(aside)*. How can he?

PERCINET. Why, it's a wonderful old wall. Look at its grassy top; look at the scarlet creeper, and the green ivy, and the long flossy clusters of the mauve wisteria, and the honeysuckle and the woodbine over there. This ancient, crumbling wall is studded with tiny flowers and filled with cracks that hang strange red hair into the sunshine. And the moss is so thick and rich that like a velvet backdrop it turns the humble bench into a royal throne!

BERGAMIN. Now, now, you young pup, do you really expect me to believe that you come here just to feast your eyes on the wall?

PERCINET. To feast my eyes on the eyes of the wall! . . . *(Facing the wall)* Such lovely eyes, fresh azure smiles, gentle blue crannies, deep flowers, limpid eyes, to feast my eyes upon. And if ever any tears dim your hue, I'll kiss them away at once.

BERGAMIN. But the wall hasn't got any eyes.

PERCINET. It's got these morning glories. *(And quickly breaking one off, he gracefully presents it to* BERGAMIN.*)*

SYLVETTE. Oh, he's so clever!

BERGAMIN. What a dunce! But I know why you're all wrought up. *(*PERCINET *and* SYLVETTE *start.)* You come here to read on the sly! *(He takes the book jutting out of* PERCINET*'s pocket and glances at the title.)* Plays! *(He opens it and, horrified, drops it.)* In verse! Verse. That's why your brain's in a whirl. No wonder you roam about dreaming, avoiding other people. No wonder you carry on about wisteria; no

5. ***The Donkey's Skin,*** a French fairy tale in which the heroine hides her beauty in the skin of a donkey.

6. ***arabesque*** (ar′ə besk′) ***festoons,*** a reference to the vine. It is an elaborate design of leaves and flowers (arabesque) hung in curves (festoons).

wonder you see blue eyes in the wall! Walls don't need to be attractive; they have to be sturdy! I'm going to have all that green junk removed; it may be concealing some open gaps. And for better protection against that insolent neighbor, I'm going to remortar the whole surface and build a fine white wall. Very white, very smooth, and very clean. And there'll be no wisteria. I'll cut notches into the plaster on top for broken bottle ends, a sharp and jagged battalion of them in serried ranks.

PERCINET. Have pity, Father!

BERGAMIN. Never! I hereby issue a decree: up and down and all along the top.

SYLVETTE *and* **PERCINET** *(aghast).* Ohh!

BERGAMIN *(sitting down on the bench).* Now then, it's time you and I had a chat! *(He gets up again and, as if suspecting something, steps back from the wall.)* Hmmm! . . . Walls may not have eyes, but they do have ears! *(He is about to mount the bench.* PERCINET *is terror stricken.* SYLVETTE, *hearing the noise, crouches against the wall. However,* BERGAMIN, *grimacing because of some chronic pain, changes his mind and motions to his son to climb up instead and have a look.)* Just see if anyone's eavesdropping. . . .

*(*PERCINET *hops lithely onto the bench and leans over the wall.* SYLVETTE *stands up and he murmurs to her.)*

PERCINET. Till tonight!

SYLVETTE *(letting him kiss her hand, whispers back).* I'll come before the hour strikes.

PERCINET *(whispering).* I'll be here.

SYLVETTE *(whispering).* I love you.

BERGAMIN *(to* PERCINET*).* Well?

PERCINET *(jumping back down, says aloud).* Well, nobody there!

BERGAMIN *(feeling reassured, sits down again).* Fine, then let's have our little talk. . . . Percinet, I want you to get married.

SYLVETTE. Ohh!

BERGAMIN. What was that?

PERCINET. Nothing.

BERGAMIN. I heard a feeble cry.

PERCINET *(looking up).* Some fledgling must have hurt itself—*(*SYLVETTE *sighs.)*—in the branches.

BERGAMIN. At any rate, my boy, after careful consideration, I've settled on a wife for you.

*(*PERCINET *walks upstage, whistling.)*

BERGAMIN *(after choking for an instant, follows him).* I'm a stubborn man, sir, and I'll force you to—

*(*PERCINET *returns, whistling.)*

BERGAMIN. Will you stop that whistling, you magpie! . . . The woman I've chosen is still young and she's very rich—a gem of a girl.

PERCINET. Who cares about your gem!

BERGAMIN. Just you wait! I'll show you, you scamp. . . .

PERCINET *(pushing back his father's raised cane).* Spring has filled the bushes with the fluttering of wings, Father, and near the forest brooks tiny birds swoop down as loving couples. . . .

BERGAMIN. You're indecent!

PERCINET. All creatures are blithely welcoming April. The butterflies—

BERGAMIN. You rascal!

PERCINET. —are flocking through the countryside to marry all the flowers that they love! . . . Love—

BERGAMIN. You villain!

PERCINET. —is making all hearts blossom. . . . And you expect me to marry for money!

BERGAMIN. Of course, you little cur!

PERCINET *(in a vibrant voice).* Well, then, no, Father, no! I swear—by this wall—I hope it can hear me—that my marriage will be more romantic than the wildest romance in any of the old romances. *(He dashes away.)*

BERGAMIN *(running after him).* Oh, when I catch him!

(Exeunt.)

SYLVETTE *(alone).* Honestly, now I understand why Daddy hates that nasty old—

PASQUINOT *(entering left).* Well, what are you doing here, young lady?

SYLVETTE. Nothing. Just strolling about.

PASQUINOT. Here! All by yourself? Why, you silly thing! . . . Aren't you afraid?

SYLVETTE. I'm not the nervous kind.

PASQUINOT. All by yourself near that wall! . . . Didn't I order you never to go near it? You foolhardy child, just take a good look at that park: it's the lair of my old mortal enemy—

SYLVETTE. I know, Father.

PASQUINOT. And yet you deliberately expose yourself to insults, or even . . . ? There's no telling what those people are capable of! If that wretched neighbor of mine or his son knew that my daughter comes all alone to this arbor to daydream—Oh! It makes me shiver just to think of it. Why, I'll cover that wall with armor, I'll bard it, I'll caparison it.[7] I'll put a row of spikes on top to impale any invader, to disembowel anyone trying to climb over it, to slash anyone who even comes near it!

SYLVETTE. He'll never do it; it would cost too much. Daddy's a bit stingy.

PASQUINOT. Get back in the house—and quickly!

(She exits; he stares after her angrily.)

BERGAMIN *(in the wings).* Take this letter to *Monsieur* Straforel immediately.

PASQUINOT *(dashes over to the wall and climbs up).* Bergamin!

BERGAMIN *(following suit).* Pasquinot!

(They embrace.)

PASQUINOT. How *are* you?

BERGAMIN. Not bad.

PASQUINOT. How's your gout?

BERGAMIN. Better. And how's your head cold?

PASQUINOT. The thing won't go away.

BERGAMIN. Well, the marriage is settled!

PASQUINOT. What?

BERGAMIN. I was hidden in the foliage and I heard everything. They're madly in love.

PASQUINOT. Wonderful!

BERGAMIN. Now, we've got to bring matters to a head! *(Rubbing his hands)* Ha! Ha! Both of us widowers, and fathers to boot. My son had a slightly overromantic mother who named him Percinet.

PASQUINOT. Yes, it does sound grotesque.

BERGAMIN. And your daughter Sylvette is a daydreaming little maid from school, with an ethereal soul. What was our sole aim?

PASQUINOT. To tear down the wall.

BERGAMIN. To live together—

PASQUINOT. And merge our two estates into one.

BERGAMIN. A scheme of old friends—

PASQUINOT. And landowners.

BERGAMIN. How could we do it?

PASQUINOT. If our children married each other.

BERGAMIN. Exactly! But could we have succeeded if they had so much as suspected our wishes and our agreement? A prearranged marriage is not very enticing for two young poetic canaries. Which is why, taking advantage of their living far away, we hushed up our matrimonial plans. But then, his boarding school and her convent came to an end this year. I thought that if we prevented them from meeting they'd be sure to seek one another out and fall in love surreptitiously and sinfully. And so I concocted this marvelous hatred! . . . Remember, you were worried that such an extraordinary plan might not succeed? Well, now all we have to do is give our consent.

PASQUINOT. Fine! But how? How can we be foxy to say "Yes" without arousing their suspicions? After all, I called you a wretch, an idiot—

BERGAMIN. An idiot? "Wretch" would have been enough. Don't say any more than you have to.

PASQUINOT. Yes, but what pretext can we use? . . .

BERGAMIN. Listen! Your daughter herself gave me the idea. As she spoke, my plan for a final stratagem took shape. They're meeting here tonight. Percinet is coming first. The moment Sylvette appears, men in black will burst out of hiding and seize her. She'll scream, and my young hero will leap upon the kidnappers and attack them with his sword. They'll pretend to flee, you turn up suddenly, so do I, your daughter and her honor will be safe and sound, you're overjoyed, you shed a few tears and

---

7. ***bard it . . . caparison it,*** drape it with leather armor and other ornamental trappings, as one would cover a horse.

bless the rescuing hero, I relent: tableau and curtain!

PASQUINOT. Why, that's brilliant! . . . That's absolutely brilliant. . . .

BERGAMIN *(modestly).* Well, yes . . . if I do say so myself. Hush! Look who's coming! It's Straforel, the famous bravo. I just dropped him a line about my project. He's the one who's going to stage our kidnapping.

(STRAFOREL, gorgeously bedizened as a bravo, appears upstage and moves forward majestically.)

BERGAMIN *(descending from the wall and bowing).* Ahem! First of all, may I introduce my friend Pasquinot. . . .

STRAFOREL *(bowing). Monsieur* . . .

(Upon straightening up, he is astonished not to see PASQUINOT.)

BERGAMIN *(pointing to* PASQUINOT *astride the wall).* There he is, on the wall.

STRAFOREL *(aside).* An amazing exercise for a man of his years!

BERGAMIN. What do you think of my plan, Straforel?

STRAFOREL. There'll be no problems.

BERGAMIN. Good; you know how to grasp things quickly and act swiftly—

STRAFOREL. And hold my tongue.

BERGAMIN. A make-believe abduction and a sham swordfight, have you got that?

STRAFOREL. It's all clear.

BERGAMIN. Use skillful swordsmen who won't wound my little boy. I love him. He's my only child.

STRAFOREL. I'll attend to the operation personally.

BERGAMIN. Excellent. In that case, I needn't worry. . . .

PASQUINOT *(in a low voice to* BERGAMIN*).* Listen, ask him how much it's going to cost us.

BERGAMIN. How much do you charge for an abduction, *Monsieur* Straforel?

STRAFOREL. It all depends on what's involved, *Monsieur.* And the prices vary accordingly. But I gather that you don't care about the expense. So if I were you, *Monsieur,* I'd take a—first-class abduction!

BERGAMIN. Oh! You've got more than one class?

STRAFOREL. Why of course, *Monsieur!* We offer an abduction with two men in black; a commonplace abduction by carriage—it's one of our least popular items. A midnight abduction. A daytime abduction. A pomp-and-circumstance abduction, by royal coach, with powdered and bewigged lackeys—there's an extra charge for the wigs—and with mutes, Moors, sbirri, brigands, musketeers[8]—all included in the price! Then we offer an abduction by post chaise, two horses, or three, four, five—as many as you like. A discreet abduction in a berlin coach—it's a bit somber. Then a humorous abduction, in a sack. A romantic abduction by boat—except we'd need a lake! A Venetian abduction by gondola—but we'd have to have a canal! An abduction by the dark of the moon—moonlight is so much in demand nowadays that the cost is slightly higher! A sinister abduction with flashes of lightning, stamping of feet, screams and shouts, dueling, clash of swords, wide-brimmed hats, and gray cloaks. A brutal abduction. A polite abduction. A torchlight abduction—it's very lovely! A so-called classical abduction in masks. A gallant abduction, to a musical accompaniment. An abduction by sedan chair,[9] the gayest, the most modern, *Monsieur,* and by far the most distinguished!

BERGAMIN *(scratching his head, to* PASQUINOT*).* Well, what do you think?

PASQUINOT. Uh . . . I don't know, what do you think?

BERGAMIN. I think we've got to overwhelm their imagination! Money can be no object! . . . We need a bit of everything! . . . Let's have—

STRAFOREL. Everything! Why not?

---

8. ***mutes, Moors, sbirri*** (sbē'rē), ***brigands, musketeers,*** all mentioned here as attendants and helpers. Moors are Moslems from northwestern Africa; sbirri are police officers from Italy; brigands are highway robbers.

9. ***sedan chair,*** a covered chair for one person, carried on poles by two bearers.

BERGAMIN. Give us something memorable for our young romancers. A sedan chair, cloaks, torches, music, masks!

STRAFOREL *(jotting down notes in a memo book).* To combine these diverse elements, we'll have a first-class abduction—with all the trimmings.

BERGAMIN. Wonderful!

STRAFOREL. I'll be back soon. *(Pointing to* PASQUINOT*)* But he'll have to leave the gate to his park ajar. . . .

BERGAMIN. He will, don't worry.

STRAFOREL *(bowing).* Gentlemen, I wish you the very best! *(Before exiting)* A first-class abduction with all the paraphernalia. *(Exit.)*

PASQUINOT. Off he goes, a gentleman and a scholar, with his high-and-mighty manner . . . and he didn't even set the price.

BERGAMIN. Never mind, the whole thing's settled! We're going to knock down the wall and have only one home.

PASQUINOT. And during the winter, only one rent to pay in town.

BERGAMIN. We'll do entrancing things in the park!

PASQUINOT. We'll trim the yew trees!

BERGAMIN. We'll gravel the paths.

PASQUINOT. In the middle of each flower bed, we'll intertwine our monograms in floral calligraphy!

BERGAMIN. And since this greenery is a bit too severe—

PASQUINOT. We'll brighten it up with decorations!

BERGAMIN. We'll have fish in a brand-new pond!

PASQUINOT. We'll have a fountain with a stone egg dancing on the peak of the spray! We'll have a mass of rock! What do you think of that!

BERGAMIN. All our wishes are coming true.

PASQUINOT. We'll grow old together.

BERGAMIN. And your daughter's provided for.

PASQUINOT. And so is your son.

BERGAMIN. Ah, good old Pasquinot!

PASQUINOT. Ah, good old Bergamin!

*(*SYLVETTE *and* PERCINET *suddenly enter on their respective sides.)*

SYLVETTE *(seeing her father holding* BERGAMIN*).* Oh!

BERGAMIN *(to* PASQUINOT, *upon noticing* SYLVETTE*).* Your daughter.

PERCINET *(seeing his father holding* PASQUINOT*).* Oh!

PASQUINOT *(to* BERGAMIN, *upon noticing* PERCINET*).* Your son!

BERGAMIN *(sotto voce*[10] *to* PASQUINOT*).* Let's fight. *(They turn their hug into a scuffle.)* You blackguard!

PASQUINOT. You wretch!

SYLVETTE *(pulling at her father's coattails).* Daddy! . . .

PERCINET *(pulling at his father's coattails).* Dad! . . .

BERGAMIN. Leave us alone, you little brats.

PASQUINOT. He started it; he insulted me!

BERGAMIN. He hit me!

PASQUINOT. Coward!

SYLVETTE. Daddy!

BERGAMIN. Swindler!

PERCINET. Dad!!

PASQUINOT. Robber!

SYLVETTE. Daddy!!

(The children manage to separate them.)

PERCINET *(dragging his father off).* Let's go home; it's getting late.

BERGAMIN *(trying to come back).* I'm in a towering rage!

*(*PERCINET *takes him away.)*

PASQUINOT *(likewise with* SYLVETTE*).* I'm boiling!

SYLVETTE. It's getting cool out. Think of your rheumatism!

(All exeunt.)

(Twilight is beginning to set in. The stage is empty for a moment. Then STRAFOREL *and his* SWORDSMEN, MUSICIANS, *et al., enter the park.)*

STRAFOREL. There's already one star out in the clear sky; the day is dying. . . . *(He places his men in their positions.)* You stay there. . . . And you, here. . . . And you, over there.

---

10. ***sotto voce*** (sot'ō vō'chē), in a low tone.

Evening Mass will be starting any moment. She'll appear as soon as the bell rings, and then I'll whistle. . . . *(He looks at the moon.)* The moon? . . . Wonderful! We won't omit a single effect tonight! *(Looking at the extravagant cloaks of his bravos)* The cloaks are excellent! . . . Let them ride up a bit more on the rapiers: bear down on the hilts. *(A sedan chair is brought in.)* Put the chair over here, in the shade. *(Staring at the chairmen)* Ah! The Moors! Not bad at all! *(Speaking into the wings)* Don't forget to bring out the torches when I signal. *(The back of the stage is tinged with the dim pink reflections of the torches from behind the trees. The* MUSICIANS *enter.)* The musicians? There, against a background of rosy light. *(He positions them upstage.)* Grace, tenderness! Vary your poses! Will the mandolinist please stand up, and the violinist sit down! Just as in Watteau's *Rustic Concert!*[11] *(In a severe tone, to a bravo)* Masked man, number one: stop slouching! Is that what you call bearing?—Fine.—Instruments, *con sordini!*[12] Please tune up. . . . Very good! Sol, mi, sol. *(He puts on his mask.)*

PERCINET *(enters slowly. As he declaims the following lines, the night grows darker and the stars emerge).* My father's calmed down. . . . I've managed to come here. . . . The twilight is settling. . . . The air is redolent with the heady fragrance of the elder trees. . . . The gray shadows are making the flowers close.

STRAFOREL *(sotto voce to the violins).* Music! *(The* MUSICIANS *play softly until the end of the act.)*

PERCINET. I'm trembling like a reed. What's wrong with me? . . . She'll be here soon!

STRAFOREL *(to the* MUSICIANS*). Amoroso!*[13] . . .

PERCINET. This is my first evening rendezvous. . . . Oh! I feel faint! . . . The breeze is rustling like a silken gown. . . . I can't see the flowers anymore . . . there are tears in my eyes. . . . I can't see the flowers . . . but I can smell their fragrance! Oh! That tall tree with a star on top! . . . But who's playing here? The night has come—

Now old desire doth in his deathbed lie,
And young affection gapes to be his heir;
That fair for which love groaned for and would die,
With tender Juliet matched, is now not fair.
Now Romeo is beloved and loves again,
Alike bewitched by the charm of looks;
But to his foe supposed he must complain,
And she steal love's sweet bait from fearful hooks.
Being held a foe, he may not have access
To breathe such vows as lovers use to swear,
And she as much in love, her means much less
To meet her new belovèd anywhere;
But passion lends them power, time means, to meet,
Temp'ring extremities with extreme sweet.

(A bell peals in the distance.)

SYLVETTE *(appearing at the sound of the bell).* The bell! He must be waiting. *(A whistle.* STRAFOREL *looms up before her; the torches appear.)* Oh! *(The bravos seize her and thrust her into the sedan chair.)* Help!

PERCINET. Good lord!

SYLVETTE. Percinet, I'm being abducted!

PERCINET. I'm coming. *(He leaps over the wall, draws his sword, and fences with a few of the bravos.)* Take that . . . and that . . . and that.

STRAFOREL *(to the* MUSICIANS*).* Tremolo![14] *(The violins surge up in a dramatic tremolo. The bravos dash off.* STRAFOREL*, in a theatrical voice)* Zounds! That lad's a devil! *(Duel between* STRAFOREL *and* PERCINET. STRAFOREL *clutches his chest.)* That blow . . . is mortal. *(He falls.)*

PERCINET *(running over to* SYLVETTE*).* Sylvette! *(Tableau. She is in the sedan chair, he is kneeling beside her.)*

SYLVETTE. My hero!

PASQUINOT *(appearing).* Bergamin's son a hero? Your rescuer? . . . Let me shake his hand.

---

11. ***Watteau's Rustic Concert,*** a painting by French artist Jean Antoine Watteau, 1684–1721.
12. ***con sordini*** (kon sôr dē'nē), (in music) used to indicate a softening or muffling of sound. [*Italian*]
13. ***Amoroso*** (ä mə rō'so), loving, fond; (in music) perform lyrically and romantically. [*Italian*]
14. ***Tremolo*** (trem'ə lō), a rapid repetition of musical notes, causing a trembling or vibrating effect.

SYLVETTE *and* **PERCINET.** Oh joy!

*(***BERGAMIN** *enters on his side, followed by torch-bearing servants.)*

PASQUINOT *(to* **BERGAMIN**, *who appears on top of the wall).* Bergamin, your son is a hero! . . . Let's put an end to our feud and make our children happy!

BERGAMIN *(solemnly).* My hatred is allayed.

PERCINET. Sylvette, we must be dreaming. Sylvette, speak low, or else the sound of our voices will awaken us! . . .

BERGAMIN. Hatred always ends in a wedding. Peace is upon us. *(Pointing to the wall)* Down with the Pyrenees![15]

PERCINET. Who would have dreamed that my father could change?

SYLVETTE *(naïvely).* Didn't I tell you it would all work out in the end?

(As the lovers go upstage with **PASQUINOT**, **STRAFOREL** *rises and hands* **BERGAMIN** *a slip of paper.)*

BERGAMIN *(in a low voice).* What? What's this piece of paper with your signature on it?

STRAFOREL *(bowing). Monsieur,* this is my bill. *(He drops back to the ground.)*

---

15. ***Pyrenees*** (pir′ə nēz′), the wall is compared to the Pyrenees, a mountain range between France and Spain.

Discussion

1. Early in the play, Percinet tells Sylvette his heart beats faster when "your gentle fledgling laughter rises from behind the wall, and it doesn't stop until your head emerges from the trembling tangle of vines and ivy." Sylvette says later, commenting on their quarreling fathers, "Perhaps the time's at hand when Heaven will use us to wipe out their hatred." **(a)** How is their style of speaking similar to the speeches they have just enjoyed from *Romeo and Juliet?* **(b)** What does their style of speaking reveal about their relationship?

2. As Sylvette and Percinet ponder their situation, Sylvette can see "five or six highly possible solutions." **(a)** Describe the three solutions she actually proposes. **(b)** Do they seem realistic? Why or why not? **(c)** In what way is her final solution different from the others?

3. **(a)** Who sees the wall as more of a barrier to the progress of the love relationship—Sylvette and Percinet themselves, or their fathers? Explain. **(b)** Which father does more to move the plot along? Give examples.

4. **(a)** Which of the abductions that Straforel proposes contain elements that he may not be able to furnish? **(b)** What elements do he and the fathers decide to include in Sylvette's abduction? **(c)** How do they expect this abduction to "overwhelm" the lovers' imaginations?

5. **(a)** Identify the climax of the play. **(b)** What effect is achieved by closing the play with Straforel giving Bergamin the bill?

6. Is Straforel best described as an idealistic romantic, a practical realist, or a combination of the two? Defend your answer.

Vocabulary
Combined Skills

Check the meaning of each numbered word below in the Glossary. Then from the lists that follow, choose first a synonym (word that means the same) and then an antonym (word that means the opposite) for each italicized word. Write each set of three words. You will not use all the words.

1. insolent; **2.** poignant; **3.** diverse; **4.** lithe; **5.** redolent

varied	supple	courteous
fragrant	odorless	unfelt
intense	rude	stiff
jealous	similar	attractive

Edmond Rostand 1868–1918

When Edmond Rostand began writing for the theater in the 1890s, most dramatists were producing somber works about the realities and difficulties of modern life. Rostand's romantic liveliness and vague optimism offered a refreshing alternative.

Born in Marseilles, France, Rostand studied to be a lawyer, but abandoned that career in 1890 when he published a small volume of poems. In that same year he wrote *The Romancers,* which was immediately successful. Later he tried to add more acts to the play, but the expanded form never achieved popularity. It was the original version that was the inspiration for *The Fantastiks,* a comedy that set records as one of New York's longest-running plays.

Rostand's best-known work is probably *Cyrano de Bergerac* (sir′ə no′ də bėr′zhə rak′), a comedy set in the seventeenth century about a young man with an enormous nose. Though Rostand wrote poetry and other plays, he never equaled the success of *Cyrano* and *The Romancers.*

Comment: The Romantic Comedy

A romantic comedy may be defined as a play that features love as the central motivating force and that ends happily once the lovers have overcome all the obstacles to their love. Such a play is *The Romancers.*

Shakespeare's *Romeo and Juliet,* had it ended happily, would have been a romantic comedy; however, the deaths of Romeo and Juliet make it a tragedy. Clearly *The Romancers* has been patterned after Shakespeare's play, but the plot is reversed. Instead of the families of the lovers scheming to keep the two apart, they scheme to bring them together by pretending to want to keep them apart. And the lovers finally "live happily ever after"—as they must in romantic comedy.

But *The Romancers* must be considered a romantic comedy with a difference. The flowery language and ridiculous plot complications, compared as they are with more serious works involving lovers like *Romeo and Juliet* and *The Cid,* make clear that the writer not only knows the romantic comedy form; he is also poking gentle fun at it. Early in the play, a trite abduction plot is described by Sylvette; then it is painstakingly enacted with showy display. As a result, the action of the play seems to mock the conventional action of the traditional romantic comedy. And we end by laughing as much at a play that seems to make fun of itself—or of its genre—as at the comic characters and events.

See **FLASHBACK** Handbook of Literary Terms

Our Town

Thornton Wilder USA

CHARACTERS *(in the order of their appearance)*

STAGE MANAGER
DR. GIBBS
JOE CROWELL
HOWIE NEWSOME
MRS. GIBBS
MRS. WEBB
GEORGE GIBBS
REBECCA GIBBS
WALLY WEBB
EMILY WEBB
PROFESSOR WILLARD
MR. WEBB
WOMAN IN THE BALCONY
MAN IN THE AUDITORIUM
LADY IN THE BOX
SIMON STIMSON
MRS. SOAMES
CONSTABLE WARREN
SI CROWELL
THREE BASEBALL PLAYERS
SAM CRAIG
JOE STODDARD

The entire play takes place in Grover's Corners, New Hampshire.

Act One

No curtain.

No scenery.

The audience, arriving, sees an empty stage in half-light.

Presently the STAGE MANAGER, *hat on and pipe in mouth, enters and begins placing a table and three chairs downstage left, and a table and three chairs downstage right. He also places a low bench at the corner of what will be the Webb house, left.*

"Left" and "right" are from the point of view of the actor facing the audience. "Up" is toward the back wall.

As the house lights go down he has finished setting the stage and leaning against the right proscenium pillar watches the late arrivals in the audience.

When the auditorium is in complete darkness he speaks:

STAGE MANAGER. This play is called *Our Town*. It was written by Thornton Wilder; produced and directed by A. . . . (or: produced by A. . . .; directed by B. . . .). In it you will see Miss C. . . .; Miss D. . . .; Miss E. . . .; and Mr. F. . . .; Mr. G. . . .; Mr. H. . . .; and many others. The name of the town is Grover's Corners, New Hampshire—just across the Massachusetts line: latitude 42 degrees 40 minutes; longitude 70 degrees 37 minutes. The First Act shows a day in our town. The day is May 7, 1901. The time is just before dawn. *(A rooster crows.)* The sky is beginning to show some streaks of light over in the East there, behind our mount'in. The morning star always gets wonderful bright the minute before it has to go—doesn't it? *(He stares at it for a moment, then goes upstage.)*

Well, I'd better show you how our town lies. Up here—*(That is: parallel with the back wall)* is Main Street. Way back there is the railway station; tracks go that way. Polish Town's across the tracks, and some Canuck[1] families. *(Toward the left)* Over there is the Congregational Church; across the street's the Presbyterian. Methodist and Unitarian are over there. Baptist is down in the holla' by the river. Catholic Church is over beyond the tracks. Here's the Town Hall and Post Office combined; jail's in the basement. Bryan[2] once made a speech from these very steps here. Along here's a row of stores. Hitching posts and horse blocks in front of them. First automobile's going to come along in about five years—belonged to Banker Cartwright, our richest citizen . . . lives in the big white house up on the hill. Here's the grocery store and here's Mr. Morgan's drugstore. Most everybody in town manages to look into those two stores once a day. Public School's over yonder. High School's still farther over. Quarter of nine mornings, noontimes, and three o'clock afternoons, the hull town can hear the yelling and screaming from those schoolyards. *(He approaches the table and chairs downstage right.)* This is our doctor's house—Doc Gibbs's. This is the back door. *(Two arched trellises, covered with vines and flowers, are pushed out, one by each proscenium pillar.)* There's some scenery for those who think they have to have scenery. This is Mrs. Gibbs's garden. Corn . . . peas . . . beans . . . hollyhocks . . . heliotrope . . . and a lot of burdock. *(Crosses the stage)* In those days our newspaper come out twice a week—the Grover's Corners *Sentinel*—and this is Editor Webb's house. And this is Mrs. Webb's garden. Just like Mrs. Gibbs's, only it's got a lot of sunflowers, too. *(He looks upward, center stage.)* Right here . . .'s a big butternut tree. *(He returns to his place by the right proscenium pillar and looks at the audience for a minute.)*

Nice town, y'know what I mean? Nobody very remarkable ever come out of it, s'far as we know. The earliest tombstones in the cemetery up there on the mountain say 1670–1680—they're Grovers and Cartwrights and

---

1. ***Canuck*** (kə nuk′), Canadian. [*Slang*]
2. ***Bryan,*** William Jennings Bryan, 1860–1925, American political leader and orator.

Gibbses and Herseys—same names as are around here now. Well, as I said: it's about dawn. The only lights on in town are in a cottage over by the tracks where a Polish mother's just had twins. And in the Joe Crowell house, where Joe Junior's getting up so as to deliver the paper. And in the depot, where Shorty Hawkins is gettin' ready to flag the 5:45 for Boston. *(A train whistle is heard. The* STAGE MANAGER *takes out his watch and nods.)* Naturally, out in the country—all around—there've been lights on for some time, what with milkin's and so on. But town people sleep late.

So—another day's begun. There's Doc Gibbs comin' down Main Street now, comin' back from that baby case. And here's his wife comin' downstairs to get breakfast.

(MRS. GIBBS, *a plump, pleasant woman in the middle thirties, comes "downstairs" right. She pulls up an imaginary window shade in her kitchen and starts to make a fire in her stove.)*

Doc Gibbs died in 1930. The new hospital's named after him. Mrs. Gibbs died first—long time ago, in fact. She went out to visit her daughter, Rebecca, who married an insurance man in Canton, Ohio, and died there—pneumonia—but her body was brought back here. She's up in the cemetery there now—in with a whole mess of Gibbses and Herseys—she was Julia Hersey 'fore she married Doc Gibbs in the Congregational Church over there. In our town we like to know the facts about everybody. There's Mrs. Webb, coming downstairs to get her breakfast, too.—That's Doc Gibbs. Got that call at half-past one this morning. And there comes Joe Crowell, Jr., delivering Mr. Webb's *Sentinel.*

(DR. GIBBS *has been coming along Main Street from the left. At the point where he would turn to approach his house, he stops, sets down his—imaginary—black bag, takes off his hat, and rubs his face with fatigue, using an enormous handkerchief.*

MRS. WEBB, *a thin, serious, crisp woman, has entered her kitchen, left, tying on an apron. She goes through the motions of putting wood into a stove, lighting it, and preparing breakfast.*

Suddenly, JOE CROWELL, JR., *eleven, starts down Main Street from the right, hurling imaginary newspapers into doorways.)*

JOE CROWELL, JR. Morning, Doc Gibbs.

DR. GIBBS. Morning, Joe.

JOE CROWELL, JR. Somebody been sick, Doc?

DR. GIBBS. No. Just some twins born over in Polish Town.

JOE CROWELL, JR. Do you want your paper now?

DR. GIBBS. Yes, I'll take it.—Anything serious goin' on in the world since Wednesday?

JOE CROWELL, JR. Yessir. My schoolteacher, Miss Foster,'s getting married to a fella over in Concord.

DR. GIBBS. I declare.—How do you boys feel about that?

JOE CROWELL, JR. Well, of course, it's none of my business—but I think if a person starts out to be a teacher, she ought to stay one.

DR. GIBBS. How's your knee, Joe?

JOE CROWELL, JR. Fine, Doc, I never think about it at all. Only like you said, it always tells me when it's going to rain.

DR. GIBBS. What's it telling you today? Goin' to rain?

JOE CROWELL, JR. No, sir.

DR. GIBBS. Sure?

JOE CROWELL, JR. Yessir.

DR. GIBBS. Knee ever make a mistake?

JOE CROWELL, JR. No, sir. *(*JOE *goes off.* DR. GIBBS *stands reading his paper.)*

STAGE MANAGER. Want to tell you something about that boy Joe Crowell there. Joe was awful bright—graduated from high school here, head of his class. So he got a scholarship to Massachusetts Tech. Graduated head of his class there, too. It was all wrote up in the Boston paper at the time. Goin' to be a great engineer, Joe was. But the war broke out and he died in France.—All that education for nothing.

HOWIE NEWSOME *(off left).* Giddap, Bessie! What's the matter with you today?

STAGE MANAGER. Here comes Howie Newsome, deliverin' the milk.

*(*HOWIE NEWSOME, *about thirty, in overalls, comes along Main Street from the left, walking beside an invisible horse and wagon and carrying an imaginary rack with milk bottles. The sound of clinking milk bottles is heard. He leaves some bottles at* MRS. WEBB*'s trellis, then, crossing the stage to* MRS. GIBBS*'s, he stops center to talk to* DR. GIBBS.*)*

HOWIE NEWSOME. Morning, Doc.

DR. GIBBS. Morning, Howie.

HOWIE NEWSOME. Somebody sick?

DR. GIBBS. Pair of twins over to Mrs. Goruslawski's.

HOWIE NEWSOME. Twins, eh? This town's gettin' bigger every year.

DR. GIBBS. Goin' to rain, Howie?

HOWIE NEWSOME. No, no. Fine day—that'll burn through. Come on, Bessie.

DR. GIBBS. Hello, Bessie. *(He strokes the horse, which has remained up center.)* How old is she, Howie?

HOWIE NEWSOME. Going on seventeen. Bessie's all mixed up about the route ever since the Lockharts stopped takin' their quart of milk every day. She wants to leave 'em a quart just the same—keeps scolding me the hull trip. *(He reaches* MRS. GIBBS*'s back door. She is waiting for him.)*

MRS. GIBBS. Good morning, Howie.

HOWIE NEWSOME. Morning, Mrs. Gibbs. Doc's just comin' down the street.

MRS. GIBBS. Is he? Seems like you're late today.

HOWIE NEWSOME. Yes. Somep'n went wrong with the separator. Don't know what 'twas. *(He passes* DR. GIBBS *up center.)* Doc!

DR. GIBBS. Howie!

MRS. GIBBS *(calling upstairs).* Children! Children! Time to get up.

HOWIE NEWSOME. Come on, Bessie! *(He goes off right.)*

MRS. GIBBS. George! Rebecca!

*(*DR. GIBBS *arrives at his back door and passes through the trellis into his house.)*

MRS. GIBBS. Everything all right, Frank?

DR. GIBBS. Yes. I declare—easy as kittens.

MRS. GIBBS. Bacon'll be ready in a minute. Set down and drink your coffee. You can catch a couple hours' sleep this morning, can't you?

DR. GIBBS. Hm! . . . Mrs. Wentworth's coming at eleven. Guess I know what it's about, too. Her stummick ain't what it ought to be.

MRS. GIBBS. All told, you won't get more'n three hours' sleep. Frank Gibbs, I don't know what's goin' to become of you. I do wish I could get you to go away someplace and take a rest. I think it would do you good.

MRS. WEBB. Emileeee! Time to get up! Wally! Seven o'clock!

MRS. GIBBS. I declare, you got to speak to George. Seems like something's come over him lately. He's no help to me at all. I can't even get him to cut me some wood.

DR. GIBBS *(washing and drying his hands at the sink.* MRS. GIBBS *is busy at the stove).* Is he sassy to you?

MRS. GIBBS. No. He just whines! All he thinks about is that baseball—George! Rebecca! You'll be late for school.

DR. GIBBS. M-m-m . . .

MRS. GIBBS. George!

DR. GIBBS. George, look sharp!

GEORGE'S VOICE. Yes, Pa!

DR. GIBBS *(as he goes off the stage).* Don't you hear your mother calling you? I guess I'll go upstairs and get forty winks.

MRS. WEBB. Walleee! Emileee! You'll be late for school! Walleee! You wash yourself good or I'll come up and do it myself.

REBECCA GIBBS'S VOICE. Ma! What dress shall I wear?

MRS. GIBBS. Don't make a noise. Your father's been out all night and needs his sleep. I washed and ironed the blue gingham for you special.

REBECCA. Ma, I hate that dress.

MRS. GIBBS. Oh, hush-up-with-you.

REBECCA. Every day I go to school dressed like a sick turkey.

MRS. GIBBS. Now, Rebecca, you always look *very* nice.

REBECCA. Mama, George's throwing soap at me.

MRS. GIBBS. I'll come and slap the both of you—that's what I'll do.

(A factory whistle sounds. The CHILDREN *dash in and take their places at the tables. Right,* GEORGE, *about sixteen, and* REBECCA, *eleven. Left,* EMILY *and* WALLY, *same ages. They carry strapped schoolbooks.)*

STAGE MANAGER. We've got a factory in our town too—hear it? Makes blankets. Cartwrights own it and it brung 'em a fortune.

MRS. WEBB. Children! Now I won't have it. Breakfast is just as good as any other meal and I won't have you gobbling like wolves. It'll stunt your growth—that's a fact. Put away your book, Wally.

WALLY. Aw, Ma! By ten o'clock I got to know all about Canada.

MRS. WEBB. You know the rule's well as I do—no books at table. As for me, I'd rather have my children healthy than bright.

EMILY. I'm both, Mama: you know I am. I'm the brightest girl in school for my age. I have a wonderful memory.

MRS. WEBB. Eat your breakfast.

WALLY. I'm bright, too, when I'm looking at my stamp collection.

MRS. GIBBS. I'll speak to your father about it when he's rested. Seems to me twenty-five cents a week's enough for a boy your age. I declare I don't know how you spend it all.

GEORGE. Aw, Ma—I gotta lotta things to buy.

MRS. GIBBS. Strawberry phosphates—that's what you spend it on.

GEORGE. I don't see how Rebecca comes to have so much money. She has more'n a dollar.

REBECCA *(spoon in mouth, dreamily).* I've been saving it up gradual.

MRS. GIBBS. Well, dear, I think it's a good thing to spend some every now and then.

REBECCA. Mama, do you know what I love most in the world—do you?—Money.

MRS. GIBBS. Eat your breakfast.

THE CHILDREN. Mama, there's first bell.—I gotta hurry.—I don't want any more.—I gotta hurry.

(The CHILDREN *rise, seize their books, and dash out through the trellises. They meet, down center, and chattering, walk to Main Street, then turn left. The* STAGE MANAGER *goes off, unobtrusively, right.)*

MRS. WEBB. Walk fast, but you don't have to run. Wally, pull up your pants at the knee. Stand up straight, Emily.

MRS. GIBBS. Tell Miss Foster I send her my best congratulations—can you remember that?

REBECCA. Yes, Ma.

MRS. GIBBS. You look real nice, Rebecca. Pick up your feet.

ALL. Good-by.

*(*MRS. GIBBS *fills her apron with food for the chickens and comes down to the footlights.)*

MRS. GIBBS. Here, chick, chick, chick. No, go away, you. Go away. Here, chick, chick, chick. What's the matter with *you?* Fight, fight, fight—that's all you do. Hm . . . *you* don't belong to me. Where'd you come from? *(She shakes her apron.)* Oh, don't be so scared. Nobody's going to hurt you. *(*MRS. WEBB *is sitting on the bench by her trellis, stringing beans.)* Good morning, Myrtle. How's your cold?

MRS. WEBB. Well, I still get that tickling feeling in my throat. I told Charles I didn't know as I'd go to choir practice tonight. Wouldn't be any use.

MRS. GIBBS. Have you tried singing over your voice?

MRS. WEBB. Yes, but somehow I can't do that and stay on the key. While I'm resting myself I thought I'd string some of these beans.

MRS. GIBBS *(rolling up her sleeves as she crosses the stage for a chat).* Let me help you. Beans have been good this year.

MRS. WEBB. I've decided to put up forty quarts if it kills me. The children say they hate 'em, but I notice they're able to get 'em down all winter. *(Pause. Brief sound of chickens cackling)*

MRS. GIBBS. Now, Myrtle. I've got to tell you something, because if I don't tell somebody I'll burst.

MRS. WEBB. Why, Julia Gibbs!

MRS. GIBBS. Here, give me some more of those

beans. Myrtle, did one of those secondhand-furniture men from Boston come to see you last Friday?

MRS. WEBB. No-o.

MRS. GIBBS. Well, he called on me. First I thought he was a patient wantin' to see Dr. Gibbs. 'N he wormed his way into my parlor, and, Myrtle Webb, he offered me three hundred and fifty dollars for Grandmother Wentworth's highboy, as I'm sitting here!

MRS. WEBB. Why, Julia Gibbs!

MRS. GIBBS. He did! That old thing! Why, it was so big I didn't know where to put it and I almost give it to Cousin Hester Wilcox.

MRS. WEBB. Well, you're going to take it, aren't you?

MRS. GIBBS. I don't know.

MRS. WEBB. You don't know—three hundred and fifty dollars! What's come over you?

MRS. GIBBS. Well, if I could get the Doctor to take the money and go away someplace on a real trip, I'd sell it like that.—Y'know, Myrtle, it's been the dream of my life to see Paris, France.—Oh, I don't know. It sounds crazy, I suppose, but for years I've been promising myself that if we ever had the chance—

MRS. WEBB. How does the Doctor feel about it?

MRS. GIBBS. Well, I did beat about the bush a little and said that if I got a legacy—that's the way I put it—I'd make him take me somewhere.

MRS. WEBB. M-m-m . . . What did he say?

MRS. GIBBS. You know how he is. I haven't heard a serious word out of him since I've known him. No, he said, it might make him discontented with Grover's Corners to go traipsin' about Europe; better let well enough alone, he says. Every two years he makes a trip to the battlefields of the Civil War and that's enough treat for anybody, he says.

MRS. WEBB. Well, Mr. Webb just *admires* the way Dr. Gibbs knows everything about the Civil War. Mr. Webb's a good mind to give up Napoleon and move over to the Civil War, only Dr. Gibbs being one of the greatest experts in the country just makes him despair.

MRS. GIBBS. It's a fact! Dr. Gibbs is never so happy as when he's at Antietam or Gettysburg. The times I've walked over those hills, Myrtle, stopping at every bush and pacing it all out, like we were going to buy it.

MRS. WEBB. Well, if that secondhand man's really serious about buyin' it, Julia, you sell it. And then you'll get to see Paris, all right. Just keep droppin' hints from time to time—that's how I got to see the Atlantic Ocean, y'know.

MRS. GIBBS. Oh, I'm sorry I mentioned it. Only it seems to me that once in your life before you die you ought to see a country where they don't talk in English and don't even want to.

(The STAGE MANAGER *enters briskly from the right. He tips his hat to the ladies, who nod their heads.)*

STAGE MANAGER. Thank you, ladies. Thank you very much. *(*MRS. GIBBS *and* MRS. WEBB *gather up their things, return into their homes, and disappear.)* Now we're going to skip a few hours. But first we want a little more information about the town, kind of a scientific account, you might say. So I've asked Professor Willard of our State University to sketch in a few details of our past history here. Is Professor Willard here? *(*PROFESSOR WILLARD, *a rural savant, pince-nez on a wide satin ribbon, enters from the right with some notes in his hand.)* May I introduce Professor Willard of our State University. A few brief notes, thank you, Professor—unfortunately our time is limited.

PROFESSOR WILLARD. Grover's Corners . . . let me see. . . . Grover's Corners lies on the old Pleistocene granite of the Appalachian range. I may say it's some of the oldest land in the world. We're very proud of that. A shelf of Devonian basalt crosses it with vestiges of Mesozoic[3] shale, and some sandstone outcroppings; but that's all more recent: two hundred, three hundred million years old. Some highly

---

3. ***Pleistocene*** (plī'stə sēn') . . . ***Devonian*** (də vō'nē ən) . . . ***Mesozoic*** (mes'ə zō'ik), geological time periods, all predating the emergence of civilized human beings, when granite, basalt, and shale, respectively, were formed.

interesting fossils have been found . . . I may say: unique fossils . . . two miles out of town, in Silas Peckham's cow pasture. They can be seen at the museum in our University at any time—that is, at any reasonable time. Shall I read some of Professor Gruber's notes on the meteorological situation—mean precipitation, et cetera?

STAGE MANAGER. Afraid we won't have time for that, Professor. We might have a few words on the history of man here.

PROFESSOR WILLARD. Yes . . . anthropological data: Early Amerindian stock. Cotahatchee[4] tribes . . . no evidence before the tenth century of this era . . . hm . . . now entirely disappeared . . . possible traces in three families. Migration toward the end of the seventeenth century of English brachiocephalic blue-eyed stock . . . for the most part. Since then some Slav and Mediterranean—

STAGE MANAGER. And the population, Professor Willard?

PROFESSOR WILLARD. Within the town limits: 2,640.

STAGE MANAGER. Just a moment, Professor. *(He whispers into the* PROFESSOR'*s ear.)*

PROFESSOR WILLARD. Oh, yes, indeed?—The population, *at the moment,* is 2,642. The Postal District brings in 507 more, making a total of 3,149.—Mortality and birth rates: constant.—By MacPherson's gauge: 6.032.

STAGE MANAGER. Thank you very much, Professor. We're all very much obliged to you, I'm sure.

PROFESSOR WILLARD. Not at all, sir; not at all.

STAGE MANAGER. This way, Professor, and thank you again. *(Exit* PROFESSOR WILLARD.*)* Now the political and social report: Editor Webb.—Oh, Mr. Webb?

*(*MRS. WEBB *appears at her back door.)*

MRS. WEBB. He'll be here in a minute. . . . He just cut his hand while he was eatin' an apple.

STAGE MANAGER. Thank you, Mrs. Webb.

MRS. WEBB. Charles! Everybody's waitin'. *(Exit* MRS. WEBB.*)*

STAGE MANAGER. Mr. Webb is Publisher and Editor of the Grover's Corners *Sentinel.* That's our local paper, y'know.

*(*MR. WEBB *enters from his house, pulling on his coat. His finger is bound in a handkerchief.)*

MR. WEBB. Well . . . I don't have to tell you that we're run here by a Board of Selectmen.—All males vote at the age of twenty-one. Women vote indirect. We're lower middle class: sprinkling of professional men . . . ten percent illiterate laborers. Politically, we're eighty-six percent Republicans; six percent Democrats; four percent Socialists; rest, indifferent. Religiously, we're eighty-five percent Protestants; twelve percent Catholics; rest, indifferent.

STAGE MANAGER. Have you any comments, Mr. Webb?

MR. WEBB. Very ordinary town, if you ask me. Little better behaved than most. Probably a lot duller. But our young people here seem to like it well enough. Ninety percent of 'em graduating from high school settle down right here to live—even when they've been away to college.

STAGE MANAGER. Now, is there anyone in the audience who would like to ask Editor Webb anything about the town?

WOMAN IN THE BALCONY. Is there much drinking in Grover's Corners?

MR. WEBB. Well, ma'am, I wouldn't know what you'd call *much.* Satiddy nights the farmhands meet down in Ellery Greenough's[5] stable and holler some. We've got one or two town drunks, but they're always having remorses every time an evangelist comes to town. No, ma'am, I'd say likker ain't a regular thing in the home here, except in the medicine chest. Right good for snake bite, y'know—always was.

BELLIGERENT MAN AT BACK OF AUDITORIUM. Is there no one in town aware of—

STAGE MANAGER. Come forward, will you, where we can all hear you.—What were you saying?

---

4. ***Amerindian*** (am'ə rin'dē ən) . . . ***Cotahatchee*** (kō'ta ha'chē). Amerindian here refers to American Indians.
5. ***Greenough's*** (grē'nōz).

BELLIGERENT MAN. Is there no one in town aware of social injustice and industrial inequality?

MR. WEBB. Oh, yes, everybody is—somethin' terrible. Seems like they spend most of their time talking about who's rich and who's poor.

BELLIGERENT MAN. Then why don't they do something about it? *(He withdraws without waiting for an answer.)*

MR. WEBB. Well, I dunno. . . . I guess we're all hunting like everybody else for a way the diligent and sensible can rise to the top and the lazy and quarrelsome can sink to the bottom. But it ain't easy to find. Meanwhile, we do all we can to help those that can't help themselves and those that can we leave alone.—Are there any other questions?

LADY IN A BOX. Oh, Mr. Webb? Mr. Webb, is there any culture or love of beauty in Grover's Corners?

MR. WEBB. Well, ma'am, there ain't much—not in the sense you mean. Come to think of it, there's some girls that play the piano at High School Commencement; but they ain't happy about it. No, ma'am, there isn't much culture; but maybe this is the place to tell you that we've got a lot of pleasures of a kind here: we like the sun comin' up over the mountain in the morning, and we all notice a good deal about the birds. We pay a lot of attention to them. And we watch the change of the seasons; yes, everybody knows about them. But those other things—you're right, ma'am—there ain't much.—*Robinson Crusoe* and the Bible; and Handel's "Largo," we all know that; and Whistler's "Mother"[6]—those are just about as far as we go.

LADY IN A BOX. So I thought. Thank you, Mr. Webb.

STAGE MANAGER. Thank you, Mr. Webb. (MR. WEBB *retires.)* Now, we'll go back to the town. It's early afternoon. All 2,642 have had their dinners and all the dishes have been washed. (MR. WEBB, *having removed his coat, returns and starts pushing a lawn mower to and fro beside his house.)* There's an early-afternoon calm in our town: a buzzin' and a hummin' from the school buildings; only a few buggies on Main Street—the horses dozing at the hitching posts; you all remember what it's like. Doc Gibbs is in his office, tapping people and making them say "ah." Mr. Webb's cuttin' his lawn over there; one man in ten thinks it's a privilege to push his own lawn mower. No, sir. It's later than I thought. There are the children coming home from school already.

(Shrill girls' voices are heard, off left. EMILY *comes along Main Street, carrying some books. There are some signs that she is imagining herself to be a lady of startling elegance.)*

EMILY. I *can't,* Lois. I've got to go home and help my mother. I *promised.*

MR. WEBB. Emily, walk simply. Who do you think you are today?

EMILY. Papa, you're terrible. One minute you tell me to stand up straight and the next minute you call me names. I just don't listen to you. *(She gives him an abrupt kiss.)*

MR. WEBB. Golly, I never got a kiss from such a great lady before. *(He goes out of sight.* EMILY *leans over and picks some flowers by the gate of her house.)*

(GEORGE GIBBS *comes careening down Main Street. He is throwing a ball up to dizzying heights, and waiting to catch it again. This sometimes requires his taking six steps backward. He bumps into an* OLD LADY *invisible to us.)*

GEORGE. Excuse me, Mrs. Forrest.

STAGE MANAGER *(as* MRS. FORREST*).* Go out and play in the fields, young man. You got no business playing baseball on Main Street.

GEORGE. Awfully sorry, Mrs. Forrest.—Hello, Emily.

EMILY. H'lo.

GEORGE. You made a fine speech in class.

---

6. ***Robinson Crusoe . . . Whistler's "Mother,"*** familiar works of art. *Robinson Crusoe* is an English novel by Daniel Defoe about a man surviving on a desert island. Handel's "Largo" is a slow, stately composition by English composer George Handel that is often played on solemn occasions like weddings (see Act Three). Whistler's "Mother" is the common name for a painting by American artist James Abbot McNeill Whistler that is actually entitled *Arrangement in Gray and Black: Portrait of the Artist's Mother.*

EMILY. Well . . . I was really ready to make a speech about the Monroe Doctrine, but at the last minute Miss Corcoran made me talk about the Louisiana Purchase instead. I worked an awful long time on both of them.

GEORGE. Gee, it's funny, Emily. From my window up there I can just see your head nights when you're doing your homework over in your room.

EMILY. Why, can you?

GEORGE. You certainly do stick to it, Emily. I don't see how you can sit still that long. I guess you like school.

EMILY. Well, I always feel it's something you have to go through.

GEORGE. Yeah.

EMILY. I don't mind it really. It passes the time.

GEORGE. Yeah.—Emily, what do you think? We might work out a kinda telegraph from your window to mine; and once in a while you could give me a kinda hint or two about one of those algebra problems. I don't mean the answers, Emily, of course not . . . just some little hint. . . .

EMILY. Oh, I think *hints* are allowed.—So—ah—if you get stuck, George, you whistle to me; and I'll give you some hints.

GEORGE. Emily, you're just naturally bright, I guess.

EMILY. I figure that it's just the way a person's born.

GEORGE. Yeah. But, you see, I want to be a farmer, and my Uncle Luke says whenever I'm ready I can come over and work on his farm and if I'm any good I can just gradually have it.

EMILY. You mean the house and everything?

(Enter MRS. WEBB *with a large bowl and sits on the bench by her trellis.)*

GEORGE. Yeah. Well, thanks . . . I better be getting out to the baseball field. Thanks for the talk, Emily.—Good afternoon, Mrs. Webb.

MRS. WEBB. Good afternoon, George.

GEORGE. So long, Emily.

EMILY. So long, George.

MRS. WEBB. Emily, come and help me string these beans for the winter. George Gibbs let himself have a real conversation, didn't he? Why, he's growing up. How old would George be?

EMILY. I don't know.

MRS. WEBB. Let's see. He must be almost sixteen.

EMILY. Mama, I made a speech in class today and I was very good.

MRS. WEBB. You must recite it to your father at supper. What was it about?

EMILY. The Louisiana Purchase. It was like silk off a spool. I'm going to make speeches all my life.—Mama, are these big enough?

MRS. WEBB. Try and get them a little bigger if you can.

EMILY. Mama, will you answer me a question, serious?

MRS. WEBB. Seriously, dear—not serious.

EMILY. Seriously—will you?

MRS. WEBB. Of course, I will.

EMILY. Mama, am I good-looking?

MRS. WEBB. Yes, of course you are. All my children have got good features; I'd be ashamed if they hadn't.

EMILY. Oh, Mama, that's not what I mean. What I mean is: am I *pretty?*

MRS. WEBB. I've already told you, yes. Now that's enough of that. You have a nice young pretty face. I never heard of such foolishness.

EMILY. Oh, Mama, you never tell us the truth about anything.

MRS. WEBB. I *am* telling you the truth.

EMILY. Mama, were *you* pretty?

MRS. WEBB. Yes, I was, if I do say it. I was the prettiest girl in town next to Mamie Cartwright.

EMILY. But, Mama, you've got to say *some*thing about me. Am I pretty enough . . . to get anybody . . . to get people interested in me?

MRS. WEBB. Emily, you make me tired. Now stop it. You're pretty enough for all normal purposes.—Come along now and bring that bowl with you.

EMILY. Oh, Mama, you're no help at all.

STAGE MANAGER. Thank you. Thank you! That'll

do. We'll have to interrupt again here. Thank you, Mrs. Webb; thank you, Emily. *(*MRS. WEBB *and* EMILY *withdraw.)* There are some more things we want to explore about this town. *(He comes to the center of the stage. During the following speech the lights gradually dim to darkness, leaving only a spot on him.)* I think this is a good time to tell you that the Cartwright interests have just begun building a new bank in Grover's Corners—had to go to Vermont for the marble, sorry to say. And they've asked a friend of mine what they should put in the cornerstone for people to dig up . . . a thousand years from now. . . . Of course, they've put in a copy of the *New York Times* and a copy of Mr. Webb's *Sentinel*. . . . We're kind of interested in this because some scientific fellas have found a way of painting all that reading matter with a glue—a silicate glue—that'll make it keep a thousand—two thousand years. We're putting in a Bible . . . and the Constitution of the United States—and a copy of William Shakespeare's plays. What do you say, folks? What do you think? Y'know—Babylon once had two million people in it, and all we know about 'em is the names of the kings and some copies of wheat contracts . . . and contracts for the sale of slaves. Yet every night all those families sat down to supper, and the father came home from his work, and the smoke went up the chimney—same as here. And even in Greece and Rome, all we know about the *real* life of the people is what we can piece together out of the joking poems and the comedies they wrote for the theater back then. So I'm going to have a copy of this play put in the cornerstone and the people a thousand years from now'll know a few simple facts about us—more than the Treaty of Versailles and the Lindbergh flight.[7] See what I mean? So—people a thousand years from now—this is the way we were in the provinces north of New York at the beginning of the twentieth century.—This is the way we were: in our growing up and in our marrying and in our living and in our dying. *(A choir partially concealed in the orchestra pit has begun singing "Blessed Be the Tie That Binds."* SIMON STIMSON *stands directing them. Two ladders have been pushed onto the stage; they serve as indication of the second story in the* GIBBS *and* WEBB *houses.* GEORGE *and* EMILY *mount them, and apply themselves to their schoolwork.* DR. GIBBS *has entered and is seated in his kitchen reading.)* Well!—good deal of time's gone by. It's evening. You can hear choir practice going on in the Congregational Church. The children are at home doing their schoolwork. The day's running down like a tired clock.

SIMON STIMSON. Now look here, everybody. Music come into the world to give pleasure.—Softer! Softer! Get it out of your heads that music's only good when it's loud. You leave loudness to the Methodists. You couldn't beat 'em, even if you wanted to. Now again. Tenors!

GEORGE. Hssst! Emily!

EMILY. Hello.

GEORGE. Hello.

EMILY. I can't work at all. The moonlight's so *terrible*.

GEORGE. Emily, did you get the third problem?

EMILY. Which?

GEORGE. The *third?*

EMILY. Why, yes, George—that's the easiest of them all.

GEORGE. I don't see it. Emily, can you give me a hint?

EMILY. I'll tell you one thing: the answer's in yards.

GEORGE. ! ! ! In yards? How do you mean?

EMILY. In *square* yards.

GEORGE. Oh . . . in square yards.

EMILY. Yes, George, don't you see?

GEORGE. Yeah.

EMILY. In square yards of *wallpaper*.

GEORGE. Wallpaper—oh, I see. Thanks a lot, Emily.

---

7. *Treaty of Versailles* (ver sī′) . . . ***Lindbergh flight.*** The Treaty of Versailles (1919) ended World War I; the (Charles) Lindbergh flight (1927) was the first solo flight across the Atlantic.

EMILY. You're welcome. My, isn't the moonlight *terrible?* And choir practice going on.—I think if you hold your breath you can hear the train all the way to Contoocook. Hear it?

GEORGE. M-m-m—What do you know!

EMILY. Well, I guess I better go back and try to work.

GEORGE. Good night, Emily. And thanks.

EMILY. Good night, George.

SIMON STIMSON. Before I forget it: how many of you will be able to come in Tuesday afternoon and sing at Fred Hersey's wedding?—show your hands. That'll be fine; that'll be right nice. We'll do the same music we did for Jane Trowbridge's last month.—Now we'll do: "Art Thou Weary; Art Thou Languid?" It's a question, ladies and gentlemen, make it talk. Ready.

DR. GIBBS. Oh, George, can you come down a minute?

GEORGE. Yes, Pa. *(He descends the ladder.)*

DR. GIBBS. Make yourself comfortable, George; I'll only keep you a minute. George, how old are you?

GEORGE. I? I'm sixteen, almost seventeen.

DR. GIBBS. What do you want to do after school's over?

GEORGE. Why, you know, Pa. I want to be a farmer on Uncle Luke's farm.

DR. GIBBS. You'll be willing, will you, to get up early and milk and feed the stock . . . and you'll be able to hoe and hay all day?

GEORGE. Sure, I will. What are you . . . what do you mean, Pa?

DR. GIBBS. Well, George, while I was in my office today I heard a funny sound . . . and what do you think it was? It was your mother chopping wood. There you see your mother—getting up early; cooking meals all day long; washing and ironing—and still she has to go out in the backyard and chop wood. I suppose she just got tired of asking you. She just gave up and decided it was easier to do it herself. And you eat her meals, and put on the clothes she keeps nice for you, and you run off and play baseball—like she's some hired girl we keep around the house but that we don't like very much. Well, I knew all I had to do was call your attention to it. Here's a handkerchief, son. George, I've decided to raise your spending money twenty-five cents a week. Not, of course, for chopping wood for your mother, because that's a present you give her, but because you're getting older—and I imagine there are lots of things you must find to do with it.

GEORGE. Thanks, Pa.

DR. GIBBS. Let's see—tomorrow's your payday. You can count on it.—Hmm. Probably Rebecca'll feel she ought to have some more, too. Wonder what could have happened to your mother. Choir practice never was as late as this before.

GEORGE. It's only half-past eight, Pa.

DR. GIBBS. I don't know why she's in that old choir. She hasn't any more voice than an old crow. . . . Traipsin' around the streets at this hour of the night. . . . Just about time you retired, don't you think?

GEORGE. Yes, Pa. *(GEORGE mounts to his place on the ladder.)*

(Laughter and good nights can be heard on stage left and presently MRS. GIBBS, MRS. SOAMES, and MRS. WEBB come down Main Street. When they arrive at the corner of the stage they stop.)

MRS. SOAMES. Good night, Martha. Good night, Mr. Foster.

MRS. WEBB. I'll tell Mr. Webb; I *know* he'll want to put it in the paper.

MRS. GIBBS. My, it's late!

MRS. SOAMES. Good night, Irma.

MRS. GIBBS. Real nice choir practice, wa'n't it? Myrtle Webb! Look at that moon, will you! Tsk-tsk-tsk. Potato weather, for sure. *(They are silent a moment, gazing up at the moon.)*

MRS. SOAMES. Naturally I didn't want to say a word about it in front of those others, but now we're alone—really, it's the worst scandal that ever was in this town!

MRS. GIBBS. What?

MRS. SOAMES. Simon Stimson!

MRS. GIBBS. Now, Louella!

MRS. SOAMES. But, Julia! To have the organist of a church *drink* and *drunk* year after year. You know he was drunk tonight.

MRS. GIBBS. Now, Louella! We all know about Mr. Stimson, and we all know about the troubles he's been through, and Dr. Ferguson knows too, and if Dr. Ferguson keeps him on there in his job the only thing the rest of us can do is just not to notice it.

MRS. SOAMES. *Not to notice it!* But it's getting worse.

MRS. WEBB. No, it isn't, Louella. It's getting better. I've been in that choir twice as long as you have. It doesn't happen anywhere near so often. . . . My, I hate to go to bed on a night like this.—I better hurry. Those children'll be sitting up till all hours. Good night, Louella. *(They all exchange good nights. She hurries downstage, enters her house, and disappears.)*

MRS. GIBBS. Can you get home safe, Louella?

MRS. SOAMES. It's as bright as day. I can see Mr. Soames scowling at the window now. You'd think we'd been to a dance the way the menfolk carry on.

(More good nights. MRS. GIBBS arrives at her home and passes through the trellis into the kitchen.)

MRS. GIBBS. Well, we had a real good time.

DR. GIBBS. You're late enough.

MRS. GIBBS. Why, Frank, it ain't any later 'n usual.

DR. GIBBS. And you stopping at the corner to gossip with a lot of hens.

MRS. GIBBS. Now, Frank, don't be grouchy. Come out and smell the heliotrope in the moonlight. *(They stroll out arm in arm along the footlights.)* Isn't that wonderful? What did you do all the time I was away?

DR. GIBBS. Oh, I read—as usual. What were the girls gossiping about tonight?

MRS. GIBBS. Well, believe me, Frank—there is something to gossip about.

DR. GIBBS. Hmm! Simon Stimson far gone, was he?

MRS. GIBBS. Worst I've ever seen him. How'll that end, Frank? Dr. Ferguson can't forgive him forever.

DR. GIBBS. I guess I know more about Simon Stimson's affairs than anybody in this town. Some people ain't made for small-town life. I don't know how that'll end; but there's nothing we can do but just leave it alone. Come, get in.

MRS. GIBBS. No, not yet. . . . Frank, I'm worried about you.

DR. GIBBS. What are you worried about?

MRS. GIBBS. I think it's my duty to make plans for you to get a real rest and change. And if I get that legacy, well, I'm going to insist on it.

DR. GIBBS. Now, Julia, there's no sense in going over that again.

MRS. GIBBS. Frank, you're just *unreasonable!*

DR. GIBBS *(starting into the house).* Come on, Julia, it's getting late. First thing you know you'll catch cold. I gave George a piece of my mind tonight. I reckon you'll have your wood chopped for a while anyway. No, no, start getting upstairs.

MRS. GIBBS. Oh, dear. There's always so many things to pick up, seems like. You know, Frank, Mrs. Fairchild always locks her front door every night. All those people up that part of town do.

DR. GIBBS *(blowing out the lamp).* They're all getting citified, that's the trouble with them. They haven't got nothing fit to burgle and everybody knows it. *(They disappear.)*

*(*REBECCA *climbs up the ladder beside* GEORGE.*)*

GEORGE. Get out, Rebecca. There's only room for one at this window. You're always spoiling everything.

REBECCA. Well, let me look just a minute.

GEORGE. Use your own window.

REBECCA. I did, but there's no moon there. . . . George, do you know what I think, do you? I think maybe the moon's getting nearer and nearer and there'll be a big 'splosion.

GEORGE. Rebecca, you don't know anything. If the moon were getting nearer, the guys that sit up all night with telescopes would see it first and they'd tell about it, and it'd be in all the newspapers.

REBECCA. George, is the moon shining on South America, Canada, and half the whole world?

GEORGE. Well—prob'ly is.

(The STAGE MANAGER *strolls on. Pause. The sound of crickets is heard.)*

STAGE MANAGER. Nine thirty. Most of the lights are out. No, there's Constable Warren trying a few doors on Main Street. And here comes Editor Webb, after putting his newspaper to bed.

*(*MR. WARREN, *an elderly policeman, comes along Main Street from the right,* MR. WEBB *from the left.)*

MR. WEBB. Good evening, Bill.

CONSTABLE WARREN. Evenin', Mr. Webb.

MR. WEBB. Quite a moon!

CONSTABLE WARREN. Yepp.

MR. WEBB. All quiet tonight?

CONSTABLE WARREN. Simon Stimson is rollin' around a little. Just saw his wife movin' out to hunt for him so I looked the other way—there he is now.

*(*SIMON STIMSON *comes down Main Street from the left, only a trace of unsteadiness in his walk.)*

MR. WEBB. Good evening, Simon. . . . Town seems to have settled down for the night pretty well. . . . *(*SIMON STIMSON *comes up to him and pauses a moment and stares at him, swaying slightly.)* Good evening. . . . Yes, most of the town's settled down for the night, Simon. . . . I guess we better do the same. Can I walk along a ways with you? *(*SIMON STIMSON *continues on his way without a word and disappears at the right.)* Good night.

CONSTABLE WARREN. I don't know how that's goin' to end, Mr. Webb.

MR. WEBB. Well, he's seen a peck of trouble, one thing after another. . . . Oh, Bill . . . if you see my boy smoking cigarettes, just give him a word, will you? He thinks a lot of you, Bill.

CONSTABLE WARREN. I don't think he smokes no cigarettes, Mr. Webb. Leastways, not more'n two or three a year.

MR. WEBB. Hm . . . I hope not.—Well, good night, Bill.

CONSTABLE WARREN. Good night, Mr. Webb. *(Exit.)*

MR. WEBB. Who's that up there? Is that you, Myrtle?

EMILY. No, it's me, Papa.

MR. WEBB. Why aren't you in bed?

EMILY. I don't know. I just can't sleep yet, Papa. The moonlight's so *won*-derful. And the smell of Mrs. Gibbs's heliotrope. Can you smell it?

MR. WEBB. Hm . . . Yes. Haven't any troubles on your mind, have you, Emily?

EMILY. *Troubles,* Papa? *No.*

MR. WEBB. Well, enjoy yourself, but don't let your mother catch you. Good night, Emily.

EMILY. Good night, Papa.

*(*MR. WEBB *crosses into the house, whistling "Blessed Be the Tie That Binds," and disappears.)*

REBECCA. I never told you about that letter Jane Crofut got from her minister when she was sick. He wrote Jane a letter and on the envelope the address was like this: It said: Jane Crofut; The Crofut Farm; Grover's Corners; Sutton County; New Hampshire; United States of America.

GEORGE. What's funny about that?

REBECCA. But listen, it's not finished: the United States of America; Continent of North America; Western Hemisphere; the Earth; the Solar System; the Universe; the Mind of God—that's what it said on the envelope.

GEORGE. What do you know!

REBECCA. And the postman brought it just the same.

GEORGE. What do you know!

STAGE MANAGER. That's the end of the First Act, friends. You can go and smoke now, those that smoke.

Discussion

1. The Stage Manager in *Our Town* has a leading part, but he does not play a major character in the plot. Citing examples from the play, describe his various functions as **(a)** a source of information about the town and its people; **(b)** a mover or manipulator of the action; **(c)** a player of minor parts.

2. Rather early in the first act it becomes clear that the playwright wishes to focus on the Gibbs and Webb households. **(a)** Point out the differences between the two families, particularly their professions and family members. **(b)** Discuss the similarities between the families. **(c)** Give possible reasons for the playwright's intermingling the family scenes, shifting focus from one side of the stage to another as the families engage in similar activities.

3. By the end of Act One Emily Webb and George Gibbs are established as major characters. Find evidence in the following scenes that their relationship will be of concern throughout the play: **(a)** the scene in which George suggests they "work out a kinda telegraph" to communicate between their windows; **(b)** the scene in which Emily helps George with an arithmetic problem.

4. (a) In the scene where the town is discussed, what kind of information does Professor Willard present? **(b)** What is its relevance to the play? **(c)** What do Mr. Webb's replies to the questions of the "audience" tell about the town? **(d)** How do the replies compare to your image of Grover's Corners?

5. At one point the Stage Manager tells what items are to be placed in the new bank's cornerstone, to be opened in a thousand years. **(a)** What are the items? **(b)** What would they reveal to the future about the town and the country? **(c)** Why does the Stage Manager include a copy of *Our Town?*

6. Describe the following minor characters and

the function of each in Act One: **(a)** Joe Crowell, Jr.; **(b)** Howie Newsome; **(c)** Simon Stimson; **(d)** Mrs. Soames.

7. At the end of the act Rebecca Gibbs tells George about the peculiar address the minister used in his letter to Jane Crofut. **(a)** What is George's reaction to his sister's story? **(b)** How does the story suggest that the play is about more than just Grover's Corners?

Composition

Assume that people in your community are suggesting items to go in the cornerstone of a new public building. Choose three items you think would convey to future generations what everyday life in your area is like.

Write a three- or four-paragraph composition describing the items, explaining why you included them, and predicting what conclusions someone in the future might draw from each.

Act Two

The tables and chairs of the two kitchens are still on the stage.

The ladders and the small bench have been withdrawn. The STAGE MANAGER *has been at his accustomed place watching the audience return to its seats.*

STAGE MANAGER. Three years have gone by. Yes, the sun's come up over a thousand times. Summers and winters have cracked the mountains a little bit more and the rains have brought down some of the dirt. Some babies that weren't even born before have begun talking regular sentences already; and a number of people who thought they were right young and spry have noticed that they can't bound up a flight of stairs like they used to, without their heart fluttering a little. All that can happen in a thousand days. Nature's been pushing and contriving in other ways, too: a number of young people fell in love and got married. Yes, the mountain got bit away a few fractions of an inch; millions of gallons of water went by the mill; and here and there a new home was set up under a roof. Almost everybody in the world gets married—you know what I mean? In our town there aren't hardly any exceptions. Most everybody in the world climbs into their graves married.

The First Act was called the Daily Life. This act is called Love and Marriage. There's another act coming after this: I reckon you can guess what that's about.

So: It's three years later. It's 1904. It's July 7th, just after High School Commencement. That's the time most of our young people jump up and get married. Soon as they've passed their last examinations in solid geometry and Cicero's Orations,[1] looks like they suddenly feel themselves fit to be married. It's early morning. Only this time it's been raining. It's been pouring and thundering. Mrs. Gibbs's garden, and Mrs. Webb's here: drenched. All those bean poles and pea vines: drenched. All yesterday over there on Main Street, the rain looked like curtains being blown along. Hm . . . it may begin again any minute. There! You can hear the 5:45 for Boston.

(MRS. GIBBS *and* MRS. WEBB *enter their kitchens and start the day as in the First Act.)*

And there's Mrs. Gibbs and Mrs. Webb come down to make breakfast, just as though it were an ordinary day. I don't have to point out to the women in my audience that those ladies they see before them, both of those ladies cooked three meals a day—one of 'em for

1. ***Cicero's Orations,*** speeches of ancient Roman orator Marcus Tullius Cicero that students translate from Latin to English.

twenty years, the other for forty—and no summer vacation. They brought up two children apiece, washed, cleaned the house—and *never a nervous breakdown.*

It's like what one of those Middle West poets said: You've got to love life to have life, and you've got to have life to love life. . . . It's what they call a vicious circle.

HOWIE NEWSOME *(offstage left).* Giddap, Bessie!

STAGE MANAGER. Here comes Howie Newsome delivering the milk. And there's Si Crowell delivering the papers like his brother before him.

*(*SI CROWELL *has entered hurling imaginary newspapers into doorways;* HOWIE NEWSOME *has come along Main Street with Bessie.)*

SI CROWELL. Morning, Howie.

HOWIE NEWSOME. Morning, Si.—Anything in the papers I ought to know?

SI CROWELL. Nothing much, except we're losing about the best baseball pitcher Grover's Corners ever had—George Gibbs.

HOWIE NEWSOME. Reckon he is.

SI CROWELL. He could hit and run bases, too.

HOWIE NEWSOME. Yep. Mighty fine ballplayer.—Whoa! Bessie! I guess I can stop and talk if I've a mind to!

SI CROWELL. I don't see how he could give up a thing like that just to get married. Would you, Howie?

HOWIE NEWSOME. Can't tell, Si. Never had no talent that way. *(*CONSTABLE WARREN *enters. They exchange good mornings.)* You're up early, Bill.

CONSTABLE WARREN. Seein' if there's anything I can do to prevent a flood. River's been risin' all night.

HOWIE NEWSOME. Si Crowell's all worked up here about George Gibbs's retiring from baseball.

CONSTABLE WARREN. Yes, sir; that's the way it goes. Back in '84 we had a player, Si—even George Gibbs couldn't touch him. Name of Hank Todd. Went down to Maine and become a parson. Wonderful ballplayer.—Howie, how does the weather look to you?

HOWIE NEWSOME. Oh, 'tain't bad. Think maybe it'll clear up for good. *(*CONSTABLE WARREN *and* SI CROWELL *continue on their way.* HOWIE NEWSOME *brings the milk first to* MRS. GIBBS*'s house. She meets him by the trellis.)*

MRS. GIBBS. Good morning, Howie. Do you think it's going to rain?

HOWIE NEWSOME. Morning, Mrs. Gibbs. It rained so heavy, I think maybe it'll clear up.

MRS. GIBBS. Certainly hope it will.

HOWIE NEWSOME. How much did you want today?

MRS. GIBBS. I'm going to have a houseful of relations, Howie. Looks to me like I'll need three-a-milk and two-a-cream.

HOWIE NEWSOME. My wife says to tell you we both hope they'll be very happy, Mrs. Gibbs. Know they *will.*

MRS. GIBBS. Thanks a lot, Howie. Tell your wife I hope she gits there to the wedding.

HOWIE NEWSOME. Yes, she'll be there; she'll be there if she kin. *(*HOWIE NEWSOME *crosses to* MRS. WEBB*'s house.)* Morning, Mrs. Webb.

MRS. WEBB. Oh, good morning, Mr. Newsome. I told you four quarts of milk, but I hope you can spare me another.

HOWIE NEWSOME. Yes'm . . . and the two of cream.

MRS. WEBB. Will it start raining again, Mr. Newsome?

HOWIE NEWSOME. Well. Just sayin' to Mrs. Gibbs as how it may lighten up. Mrs. Newsome told me to tell you as how we hope they'll both be very happy, Mrs. Webb. Know they *will.*

MRS. WEBB. Thank you, and thank Mrs. Newsome and we're counting on seeing you at the wedding.

HOWIE NEWSOME. Yes, Mrs. Webb. We hope to git there. Couldn't miss that. Come on, Bessie. *(Exit* HOWIE NEWSOME.*)*

*(*DR. GIBBS *descends in shirtsleeves, and sits down at his breakfast table.)*

DR. GIBBS. Well, Ma, the day has come. You're losin' one of your chicks.

MRS. GIBBS. Frank Gibbs, don't you say another word. I feel like crying every minute. Sit down and drink your coffee.

DR. GIBBS. The groom's up shaving himself—only there ain't an awful lot to shave. Whistling and singing, like he's glad to leave us.—Every now and then he says "I do" to the mirror, but it don't sound convincing to me.

MRS. GIBBS. I declare, Frank, I don't know how he'll get along. I've arranged his clothes and seen to it he's put warm things on—Frank! they're too *young*. Emily won't think of such things. He'll catch his death of cold within a week.

DR. GIBBS. I was remembering my wedding morning, Julia.

MRS. GIBBS. Now don't start that, Frank Gibbs.

DR. GIBBS. I was the scaredest young fella in the State of New Hampshire. I thought I'd make a mistake for sure. And when I saw you comin' down that aisle I thought you were the prettiest girl I'd ever seen, but the only trouble was that I'd never seen you before. There I was in the Congregational Church marryin' a total stranger.

MRS. GIBBS. And how do you think I felt!—Frank, weddings are perfectly awful things. Farces—that's what they are! *(She puts a plate before him.)* Here, I've made something for you.

DR. GIBBS. Why, Julia Hersey—French toast!

MRS. GIBBS. 'Tain't hard to make and I had to do *some*thing. *(Pause.* DR. GIBBS *pours on the syrup.)*

DR. GIBBS. How'd you sleep last night, Julia?

MRS. GIBBS. Well, I heard a lot of the hours struck off.

DR. GIBBS. Ye-e-s! I get a shock every time I think of George setting out to be a family man—that great gangling thing!—I tell you, Julia, there's nothing so terrifying in the world as a *son*. The relation of father and son is the darndest, awkwardest—

MRS. GIBBS. Well, mother and daughter's no picnic, let me tell you.

DR. GIBBS. They'll have a lot of troubles, I suppose, but that's none of our business. Everybody has a right to their own troubles.

MRS. GIBBS *(at the table, drinking her coffee, meditatively)*. Yes . . . people are meant to go through life two by two. 'Tain't natural to be lonesome. *(Pause.* DR. GIBBS *starts laughing.)*

DR. GIBBS. Julia, do you know one of the things I was scared of when I married you?

MRS. GIBBS. Oh, go along with you!

DR. GIBBS. I was afraid we wouldn't have material for conversation more'n'd last us a few weeks. *(Both laugh.)* I was afraid we'd run out and eat our meals in silence, that's a fact.—Well, you and I been conversing for twenty years now without any noticeable barren spells.

MRS. GIBBS. Well—good weather, bad weather—'tain't very choice, but I always find something to say. *(She goes to the foot of the stairs.)* Did you hear Rebecca stirring around upstairs?

DR. GIBBS. No. Only day of the year Rebecca hasn't been managing everybody's business up there. She's hiding in her room.—I got the impression she's crying.

MRS. GIBBS. Lord's sakes!—This has got to stop.—Rebecca! Rebecca! Come and get your breakfast.

*(*GEORGE *comes rattling down the stairs, very brisk.)*

GEORGE. Good morning, everybody. Only five more hours to live. *(Makes the gesture of cutting his throat, and a loud "k-k-k," and starts through the trellis)*

MRS. GIBBS. George Gibbs, where are you going?

GEORGE. Just stepping across the grass to see my girl.

MRS. GIBBS. Now, George! You put on your overshoes. It's raining torrents. You don't go out of this house without you're prepared for it.

GEORGE. Aw, Ma. It's just a *step!*

MRS. GIBBS. George! You'll catch your death of cold and cough all through the service.

DR. GIBBS. George, do as your mother tells you! *(*DR. GIBBS *goes upstairs.)*

*(*GEORGE *returns reluctantly to the kitchen and pantomimes putting on overshoes.)*

MRS. GIBBS. From tomorrow on you can kill yourself in all weathers, but while you're in my house you'll live wisely, thank you.—Maybe

Mrs. Webb isn't used to callers at seven in the morning.—Here, take a cup of coffee first.

GEORGE. Be back in a minute. *(He crosses the stage, leaping over the puddles.)* Good morning, Mother Webb.

MRS. WEBB. Goodness! You frightened me!—Now, George, you can come in a minute out of the wet, but you know I can't ask you in.

GEORGE. Why not—?

MRS. WEBB. George, you know's well as I do: the groom can't see his bride on his wedding day, not until he sees her in church.

GEORGE. Aw!—that's just a superstition.—Good morning, Mr. Webb.

(Enter MR. WEBB.*)*

MR. WEBB. Good morning, George.

GEORGE. Mr. Webb, you don't believe in that superstition, do you?

MR. WEBB. There's a lot of common sense in some superstitions, George. *(He sits at the table, facing right.)*

MRS. WEBB. Millions have folla'd it, George, and you don't want to be the first to fly in the face of custom.

GEORGE. How is Emily?

MRS. WEBB. She hasn't waked up yet. I haven't heard a sound out of her.

GEORGE. Emily's *asleep!!!*

MRS. WEBB. No wonder! We were up 'til all hours, sewing and packing. Now I'll tell you what I'll do; you set down here a minute with Mr. Webb and drink this cup of coffee; and I'll go upstairs and see she doesn't come down and surprise you. There's some bacon, too; but don't be long about it. *(Exit* MRS. WEBB.*)*

(Embarrassed silence. MR. WEBB *dunks doughnuts in his coffee. More silence)*

MR. WEBB *(suddenly and loudly).* Well, George, how are you?

GEORGE *(startled, choking over his coffee).* Oh, fine, I'm fine. *(Pause)* Mr. Webb, what sense could there be in a superstition like that?

MR. WEBB. Well, you see—on her wedding morning a girl's head's apt to be full of . . . clothes and one thing and another. Don't you think that's probably it?

GEORGE. Ye-e-s. I never thought of that.

MR. WEBB. A girl's apt to be a mite nervous on her wedding day. *(Pause)*

GEORGE. I wish a fellow could get married without all that marching up and down.

MR. WEBB. Every man that's ever lived has felt that way about it, George; but it hasn't been any use. It's the womenfolk who've built up weddings, my boy. For a while now the women have it all their own. A man looks pretty small at a wedding, George. All those good women standing shoulder to shoulder making sure that the knot's tied in a mighty public way.

GEORGE. But . . . you *believe* in it, don't you, Mr. Webb?

MR. WEBB *(with alacrity).* Oh, yes; *oh, yes.* Don't you misunderstand me, my boy. Marriage is a wonderful thing—wonderful thing. And don't you forget that, George.

GEORGE. No, sir.—Mr. Webb, how old were you when you got married?

MR. WEBB. Well, you see: I'd been to college and I'd taken a little time to get settled. But Mrs. Webb—she wasn't much older than what Emily is. Oh, age hasn't much to do with it, George—not compared with . . . uh . . . other things.

GEORGE. What were you going to say, Mr. Webb?

MR. WEBB. Oh, I don't know.—Was I going to say something? *(Pause)* George, I was thinking the other night of some advice my father gave me when I got married. Charles, he said, Charles, start out early showing who's boss, he said. Best thing to do is to give an order, even if it don't make sense; just so she'll learn to obey. And he said: if anything about your wife irritates you—her conversation, or anything—just get up and leave the house. That'll make it clear to her, he said. And, oh, yes! he said never, *never* let your wife know how much money you have, never.

GEORGE. Well, Mr. Webb . . . I don't think I could . . .

MR. WEBB. So I took the opposite of my father's advice and I've been happy ever since. And let

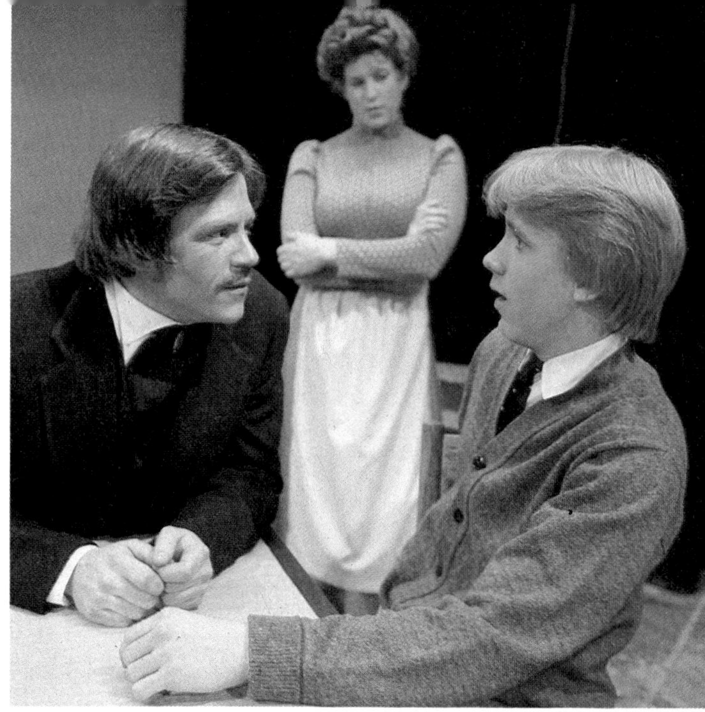

that be a lesson to you, George, never to ask advice on personal matters.—George, are you going to raise chickens on your farm?

GEORGE. What?

MR. WEBB. Are you going to raise chickens on your farm?

GEORGE. Uncle Luke's never been much interested, but I thought—

MR. WEBB. A book came into my office the other day, George, on the Philo System of raising chickens. I want you to read it. I'm thinking of beginning in a small way in the backyard, and I'm going to put an incubator in the cellar— *(Enter* MRS. WEBB.*)*

MRS. WEBB. Charles, are you talking about that old incubator again? I thought you two'd be talking about things worthwhile.

MR. WEBB *(bitingly).* Well, Myrtle, if you want to give the boy some good advice, I'll go upstairs and leave you alone with him.

MRS. WEBB *(pulling* GEORGE *up).* George, Emily's got to come downstairs and eat her breakfast. She sends you her love but she doesn't want to lay eyes on you. Good-by.

GEORGE. Good-by.

*(*GEORGE *crosses the stage to his own home, bewildered and crestfallen. He slowly dodges a puddle and disappears into his house.)*

MR. WEBB. Myrtle, I guess you don't know about that older superstition.

MRS. WEBB. What do you mean, Charles?

MR. WEBB. Since the cavemen: no bridegroom should see his father-in-law on the day of the wedding, or near it. Now remember that.

(Both leave the stage.)

STAGE MANAGER. Thank you very much, Mr. and Mrs. Webb.—Now I have to interrupt again here. You see, we want to know how all this began—this wedding, this plan to spend a lifetime together. I'm awfully interested in how big things like that begin. You know how it is: you're twenty-one or twenty-two and you make some decisions; then whisssh! you're seventy: you've been a lawyer for fifty years, and that white-haired lady at your side has eaten over fifty thousand meals with you. How do such things begin? George and Emily are going to show you now the conversation they had when they first knew that . . . that . . . as the saying goes . . . they were meant for one another. But before they do it I want you to try and remember what it was like to have been very young. And particularly the days when you were first in love; when you were like a person sleepwalking, and you didn't quite see the street you were in, and didn't quite hear everything that was said to you. You're just a little bit crazy. Will you remember that, please? Now they'll be coming out of high school at three o'clock. George has just been elected President of the Junior Class, and as it's June, that means he'll be President of the Senior Class all next year. And Emily's just been elected Secretary and Treasurer. I don't have to tell you how important that is. *(He places a board across the backs of two chairs, which he takes from those at the* GIBBS *family's table. He brings two high stools from the wings and places them behind the board. Persons sitting on the stools will be facing the audience. This is the counter of* MR. MORGAN*'s drugstore. The sounds of young people's voices are heard off left.)* Yepp—there they are coming down Main Street now.

*(*EMILY, *carrying an armful of—imaginary—schoolbooks, comes along Main Street from the left.)*

EMILY. I can't, Louise. I've got to go home. Good-by. Oh, Ernestine! Ernestine! Can you come over tonight and do Latin? Isn't that Cicero the worst thing—! Tell your mother you *have* to. G'by. G'by, Helen. G'by, Fred.

*(*GEORGE, *also carrying books, catches up with her.)*

GEORGE. Can I carry your books home for you, Emily?

EMILY *(coolly).* Why . . . uh . . . Thank you. It isn't far. *(She gives them to him.)*

GEORGE. Excuse me a minute, Emily.—Say, Bob, if I'm a little late, start practice anyway. And give Herb some long high ones.

EMILY. Good-by, Lizzy.

GEORGE. Good-by, Lizzy.—I'm awfully glad you were elected, too, Emily.

EMILY. Thank you.

(They have been standing on Main Street, almost against the back wall. They take the first steps toward the audience when GEORGE *stops and says:)*

GEORGE. Emily, why are you mad at me?

EMILY. I'm not mad at you.

GEORGE. You've been treating me so funny lately.

EMILY. Well, since you ask me, I might as well say it right out, George—*(She catches sight of a teacher passing.)* Good-by, Miss Corcoran.

GEORGE. Good-by, Miss Corcoran.—Wha—what is it?

EMILY *(not scoldingly; finding it difficult to say).* I don't like the whole change that's come over you in the last year. I'm sorry if that hurts your feelings, but I've got to—tell the truth and shame the devil.

GEORGE. A *change?*—Wha—what do you mean?

EMILY. Well, up to a year ago I used to like you a lot. And I used to watch you as you did everything . . . because we'd been friends so long . . . and then you began spending all your time at *baseball* . . . and you never stopped to speak to anybody anymore. Not even to your own family you didn't . . . and, George, it's a fact, you've got awful conceited and stuck-up, and all the girls say so. They may not say so to your face, but that's what they say about you behind your back, and it hurts me to hear them say it, but I've got to agree with them a little. I'm sorry if it hurts your feelings . . . but I can't be sorry I said it.

GEORGE. I . . . I'm glad you said it, Emily. I never thought that such a thing was happening to me. I guess it's hard for a fella not to have faults creep into his character.

(They take a step or two in silence, then stand still in misery.)

EMILY. I always expect a man to be perfect and I think he should be.

GEORGE. Oh . . . I don't think it's possible to be perfect, Emily.

EMILY. Well, my *father* is, and as far as I can see *your* father is. There's no reason on earth why you shouldn't be, too.

GEORGE. Well, I feel it's the other way round. That men aren't naturally good; but girls are.

EMILY. Well, you might as well know right now that I'm not perfect. It's not as easy for a girl to be perfect as a man, because we girls are more—more—nervous.—Now I'm sorry I said all that about you. I don't know what made me say it.

GEORGE. Emily—

EMILY. Now I can see it's not the truth at all. And I suddenly feel that it isn't important, anyway.

GEORGE. Emily . . . would you like an ice-cream soda, or something, before you go home?

EMILY. Well, thank you. . . . I would.

(They advance toward the audience and make an abrupt right turn, opening the door of MORGAN'*s drugstore. Under strong emotion,* EMILY *keeps her face down.* GEORGE *speaks to some passers-by.)*

GEORGE. Hello, Stew—how are you?—Good afternoon, Mrs. Slocum.

(The STAGE MANAGER, *wearing spectacles and assuming the role of* MR. MORGAN, *enters*

abruptly from the right and stands between the audience and the counter of his soda fountain.)

STAGE MANAGER. Hello, George. Hello, Emily.—What'll you have?—Why, Emily Webb—what you been crying about?

GEORGE *(he gropes for an explanation).* She . . . she just got an awful scare, Mr. Morgan. She almost got run over by that hardware-store wagon. Everybody says that Tom Huckins drives like a crazy man.

STAGE MANAGER *(drawing a drink of water).* Well, now! You take a drink of water, Emily. You look all shook up. I tell you, you've got to look both ways before you cross Main Street these days. Gets worse every year.—What'll you have?

EMILY. I'll have a strawberry phosphate, thank you, Mr. Morgan.

GEORGE. No, no, Emily. Have an ice-cream soda with me. Two strawberry ice-cream sodas, Mr. Morgan.

STAGE MANAGER *(working the faucets).* Two strawberry ice-cream sodas, yes sir. Yes, sir. There are a hundred and twenty-five horses in Grover's Corners this minute I'm talking to you. State Inspector was in here yesterday. And now they're bringing in these automobiles, the best thing to do is to just stay home. Why, I can remember when a dog could go to sleep all day in the middle of Main Street and nothing come along to disturb him. *(He sets the imaginary glasses before them.)* There they are. Enjoy 'em. *(He sees a customer, right.)* Yes, Mrs. Ellis. What can I do for you? *(He goes out right.)*

EMILY. They're so expensive.

GEORGE. No, no—don't you think of that. We're celebrating our election. And then do you know what else I'm celebrating?

EMILY. N-no.

GEORGE. I'm celebrating because I've got a friend who tells me all the things that ought to be told me.

EMILY. George, *please* don't think of that. I don't know why I said it. It's not true. You're—

GEORGE. No, Emily, you stick to it. I'm glad you spoke to me like you did. But you'll *see:* I'm going to change so quick—you bet I'm going to change. And, Emily, I want to ask you a favor.

EMILY. What?

GEORGE. Emily, if I go away to State Agriculture College next year, will you write me a letter once in a while?

EMILY. I certainly will. I certainly will, George. . . . *(Pause. They start sipping the sodas through the straws.)* It certainly seems like being away three years you'd get out of touch with things. Maybe letters from Grover's Corners wouldn't be so interesting after a while. Grover's Corners isn't a very important place when you think of all—New Hampshire; but I think it's a very nice town.

GEORGE. The day wouldn't come when I wouldn't want to know everything that's happening here. I know *that's* true, Emily.

EMILY. Well, I'll try to make my letters interesting. *(Pause)*

GEORGE. Y'know, Emily, whenever I meet a farmer I ask him if he thinks it's important to go to Agriculture School to be a good farmer.

EMILY. Why, George—

GEORGE. Yeah, and some of them say that it's even a waste of time. You can get all those things, anyway, out of the pamphlets the government sends out. And Uncle Luke's getting old—he's about ready for me to start in taking over his farm tomorrow, if I could.

EMILY. My!

GEORGE. And, like you say, being gone all that time . . . in other places and meeting other people . . . Gosh, if anything like that can happen I don't want to go away. I guess new people aren't any better than old ones. I'll bet they almost never are. Emily . . . I feel that you're as good a friend as I've got. I don't need to go and meet the people in other towns.

EMILY. But, George, maybe it's very important for you to go and learn all that about—cattle judging and soils and those things. . . . Of course, I don't know.

GEORGE *(after a pause, very seriously).* Emily, I'm going to make up my mind right now. I won't go. I'll tell Pa about it tonight.

EMILY. Why, George, I don't see why you have to decide right now. It's a whole year away.

GEORGE. Emily, I'm glad you spoke to me about that . . . that fault in my character. What you said was right; but there was *one* thing wrong in it, and that was when you said that for a year I wasn't noticing people, and . . . you, for instance. Why, you say you were watching me when I did everything. . . . I was doing the same about you all the time. Why, sure—I always thought about you as one of the chief people I thought about. I always made sure where you were sitting on the bleachers, and who you were with, and for three days now I've been trying to walk home with you; but something's always got in the way. Yesterday I was standing over against the wall waiting for you, and you walked home with *Miss Corcoran.*

EMILY. George! . . . Life's awful funny! How could I have known that? Why, I thought—

GEORGE. Listen, Emily, I'm going to tell you why I'm not going to Agriculture School. I think that once you've found a person that you're very fond of . . . I mean a person who's fond of you, too, and likes you enough to be interested in your character . . . Well, I think that's just as important as college is, and even more so. That's what I think.

EMILY. I think it's awfully important, too.

GEORGE. Emily.

EMILY. Y-yes, George.

GEORGE. Emily, if I *do* improve and make a big change . . . would you be . . . I mean: *could* you be . . .

EMILY. I . . . I am now; I always have been.

GEORGE *(pause).* So I guess this is an important talk we've been having.

EMILY. Yes . . . yes.

GEORGE *(takes a deep breath and straightens his back).* Wait just a minute and I'll walk you home. *(With mounting alarm he digs into his pockets for the money. The* STAGE MANAGER *enters, right.* GEORGE, *deeply embarrassed, but direct, says to him)* Mr. Morgan, I'll have to go home and get the money to pay you for this. It'll only take a minute.

STAGE MANAGER *(pretending to be affronted).* What's that? George Gibbs, do you mean to tell me—!

GEORGE. Yes, but I had reasons, Mr. Morgan.—Look, here's my gold watch to keep until I come back with the money.

STAGE MANAGER. That's all right. Keep your watch. I'll trust you.

GEORGE. I'll be back in five minutes.

STAGE MANAGER. I'll trust you ten years, George—not a day over.—Got all over your shock, Emily?

EMILY. Yes, thank you, Mr. Morgan. It was nothing.

GEORGE *(taking up the books from the counter).* I'm ready.

(They walk in grave silence across the stage and pass through the trellis at the WEBBS' *back door and disappear. The* STAGE MANAGER *watches them go out, then turns to the audience, removing his spectacles.)*

STAGE MANAGER. Well—*(He claps his hands as a signal.)* Now we're ready to get on with the wedding. *(He stands waiting while the set is prepared for the next scene.* STAGEHANDS *remove the chairs, tables, and trellises from the* GIBBS *and* WEBB *houses. They arrange the pews for the church in the center of the stage. The congregation will sit facing the back wall. The aisle of the church starts at the center of the back wall and comes toward the audience. A small platform is placed against the back wall on which the* STAGE MANAGER *will stand later, playing the minister. The image of a stained-glass window is cast from a lantern slide upon the back wall. When all is ready the* STAGE MANAGER *strolls to the center of the stage, down front, and musingly, addresses the audience.)* There are a lot of things to be said about a wedding; there are a lot of thoughts that go on during a wedding. We can't get them all into one wedding, naturally, and especially not into a wedding at Grover's Corners, where they're awfully plain and short. In this wedding I play the minister. That gives me the right to say a few more things about it. For a while now, the play gets pretty serious. Y'see, some churches say that marriage is a sacrament. I don't quite know what that means, but I can guess. Like Mrs. Gibbs said a few minutes ago: People were made to live two-by-two. This is a good wedding, but people are so put together that even at a good wedding there's a lot of confusion way down deep in people's minds and we thought that that ought to be in our play, too.

The real hero of this scene isn't on the stage at all, and you know who that is. It's like what one of those European fellas said: every child born into the world is nature's attempt to make a perfect human being. Well, we've seen nature pushing and contriving for some time now. We all know that nature's interested in quantity; but I think she's interested in quality, too—that's why I'm in the ministry. And don't forget all the other witnesses at this wedding—the ancestors. Millions of them. Most of them set out to live two-by-two, also. Millions of them.

Well, that's all my sermon. 'Twan't very long, anyway.

(The organ starts playing Handel's "Largo." The congregation streams into the church and sits in silence. Church bells are heard. MRS. GIBBS *sits in the front row, the first seat on the aisle, the right section; next to her are* REBECCA *and* DR. GIBBS. *Across the aisle* MRS. WEBB, WALLY, *and* MR. WEBB. *A small choir takes its place, facing the audience under the stained-glass window.* MRS. WEBB, *on the way to her place, turns back and speaks to the audience.)*

MRS. WEBB. I don't know why on earth I should be crying. I suppose there's nothing to cry about. It came over me at breakfast this morning; there was Emily eating her breakfast as she's done for seventeen years and now she's going off to eat it in someone else's house. I suppose that's it. And Emily! She suddenly said: I can't eat another mouthful, and she put her head down on the table and *she* cried. *(She starts toward her seat in the church, but turns back and adds)* Oh, I've got to say it: you know, there's something downright cruel about sending our girls out into marriage this way. I hope some of her girlfriends have told her a thing or two. It's cruel, I know, but I couldn't bring myself to say anything. I went into it blind as a bat myself. *(In half-amused exasperation)* The whole world's wrong, that's what's the matter. There they come. *(She hurries to her place in the pew.)*

*(*GEORGE *starts to come down the right aisle of the theater, through the audience. Suddenly* THREE MEMBERS *of his baseball team appear by the right proscenium pillar and start whistling and catcalling to him. They are dressed for the ball field.)*

THE BASEBALL PLAYERS. Eh, George, George! Hsst—yaow! Look at him, fellas—he looks scared to death. Yaow! George, don't look so innocent, you old geezer. We know what you're thinking. Don't disgrace the team, big boy. Whoo-oo-oo.

STAGE MANAGER. All right! All right! That'll do. That's enough of that. *(Smiling, he pushes them off the stage. They lean back to shout a few more catcalls.)* There used to be an awful lot to that kind of thing at weddings in the old days—Rome, and later. We're more civilized now—so they say.

(The choir starts singing "Love Divine, All Love Excelling—" GEORGE *has reached the stage. He stares at the congregation a moment, then takes a few steps of withdrawal, toward the right proscenium pillar. His mother, from the front row, seems to have felt his confusion. She leaves her seat and comes down the aisle quickly to him.)*

MRS. GIBBS. George! George! What's the matter?

GEORGE. Ma, I don't want to grow old. Why's everybody pushing me so?

MRS. GIBBS. Why, George . . . you wanted it.

GEORGE. No, Ma, listen to me—

MRS. GIBBS. No, no, George—you're a man now.

GEORGE. Listen, Ma—for the last time I ask you . . . All I want to do is to be a fella—

MRS. GIBBS. George! If anyone should hear you! Now stop. Why, I'm ashamed of you!

GEORGE *(he comes to himself and looks over the scene)*. What? Where's Emily?

MRS. GIBBS *(relieved)*. George! You gave me such a turn.

GEORGE. Cheer up, Ma. I'm getting married.

MRS. GIBBS. Let me catch my breath a minute.

GEORGE *(comforting her)*. Now, Ma, you save Thursday nights. Emily and I are coming over to dinner every Thursday night . . . you'll see. Ma, what are you crying for? Come on; we've got to get ready for this.

*(*MRS. GIBBS, *mastering her emotion, fixes his tie and whispers to him. In the meantime,* EMILY, *in white and wearing her wedding veil, has come through the audience and mounted onto the stage. She too draws back, frightened, when she sees the congregation in the church. The choir begins: "Blessed Be the Tie That Binds.")*

EMILY. I never felt so alone in my whole life. And George over there, looking so . . . ! I *hate* him. I wish I were dead. Papa! Papa!

MR. WEBB *(leaves his seat in the pews and comes toward her anxiously)*. Emily! Emily! Now don't get upset. . . .

EMILY. But, Papa—I don't want to get married. . . .

MR. WEBB. Sh—sh—Emily. Everything's all right.

EMILY. Why can't I stay for a while just as I am? Let's go away—

MR. WEBB. No, no, Emily. Now stop and think a minute.

EMILY. Don't you remember that you used to say—all the time you used to say—all the time: that I was *your* girl! There must be lots of places we can go to. I'll work for you. I could keep house.

MR. WEBB. Sh . . . You mustn't think of such things. You're just nervous, Emily. *(He turns and calls:)* George! George! Will you come here a minute? *(He leads her toward* GEORGE.*)* Why, you're marrying the best young fellow in the world. George is a fine fellow.

EMILY. But Papa—

*(*MRS. GIBBS *returns unobtrusively to her seat.* MR. WEBB *has one arm around his daughter. He places his hand on* GEORGE*'s shoulder.)*

MR. WEBB. I'm giving away my daughter, George. Do you think you can take care of her?

GEORGE. Mr. Webb, I want to . . . I want to try. Emily, I'm going to do my best. I love you, Emily. I need you.

EMILY. Well, if you love me, help me. All I want is someone to love me.

GEORGE. I will, Emily. Emily, I'll try.

EMILY. And I mean for*ever*. Do you hear? Forever and ever.

(They fall into each other's arms. The "March" from Lohengrin is heard. The STAGE MANAGER, *as* CLERGYMAN, *stands on the box, up center.)*

MR. WEBB. Come, they're waiting for us. Now you know it'll be all right. Come, quick.

*(*GEORGE *slips away and takes his place beside the* STAGE MANAGER-CLERGYMAN. EMILY *proceeds up the aisle on her father's arm.)*

STAGE MANAGER. Do you, George, take this woman, Emily, to be your wedded wife, to have . . .

*(*MRS. SOAMES *has been sitting in the last row of the congregation. She now turns to her neighbors and speaks in a shrill voice. Her chatter drowns out the rest of the* CLERGYMAN*'s words.)*

MRS. SOAMES. Perfectly lovely wedding! Loveliest wedding I ever saw. Oh, I do love a good wedding, don't you? Doesn't she make a lovely bride?

GEORGE. I do.

STAGE MANAGER. Do you, Emily, take this man, George, to be your wedded husband—

(Again his further words are covered by those of MRS. SOAMES.*)*

MRS. SOAMES. Don't know *when* I've seen such a lovely wedding. But I always cry. Don't know why it is, but I always cry. I just like to see young people happy, don't you? Oh, I think it's lovely.

(The ring. The kiss. The stage is suddenly arrested into silent tableau. The STAGE MANAGER, *his eyes on the distance, as though to himself:)*

STAGE MANAGER. I've married over two hundred couples in my day. Do I believe in it? I don't know. M. . . . marries N. . . . millions of them. The cottage, the go-cart, the Sunday-afternoon drives in the Ford, the first rheumatism, the grandchildren, the second rheumatism, the deathbed, the reading of the will— *(He now looks at the audience for the first time, with a warm smile that removes any sense of cynicism from the next line.)* Once in a thousand times it's interesting.

—Well, let's have Mendelssohn's "Wedding March"!

(The organ picks up the "March." The BRIDE *and* GROOM *come down the aisle, radiant, but trying to be very dignified.)*

MRS. SOAMES. Aren't they a lovely couple? Oh, I've never been to such a nice wedding. I'm sure they'll be happy. I always say: *happiness*, that's the great thing! The important thing is to be happy.

(The BRIDE *and* GROOM *reach the steps leading into the audience. A bright light is thrown upon them. They descend into the auditorium and run up the aisle joyously.)*

STAGE MANAGER. That's all the Second Act, folks. Ten minutes' intermission.

Discussion

1. In his opening speech the Stage Manager states that Act One is called "Daily Life" and Act Two "Love and Marriage." Then he says, "There's another act coming after this: I reckon you can guess what that's about." **(a)** How and why are these titles appropriate? **(b)** What do you think Act Three will be about? Why?

2. (a) Compare and contrast the brief, early appearances of the paperboy and milkman with their similar roles in Act One. **(b)** What is achieved by having them in both acts?

3. Describe the nature of the advice that Mr. Webb gives to George, his future son-in-law, on the morning of the wedding.

4. (a) In the scene showing how their love began, what does Emily's frank criticism of George reveal about each of them? **(b)** Why does George decide soon after that he does not want to go to college? **(c)** Do you think he makes the right decision? Explain.

5. Just before the wedding neither Emily nor George seems to want to go through with it. **(a)** Why are they suddenly reluctant? **(b)** How do they overcome these feelings?

6. (a) Do Mrs. Soames's chatter and comments during the wedding strike you as unusual? Explain. **(b)** What effect, if any, do they have on the solemnity of the occasion?

7. Near the end of the act the Stage Manager makes a few final remarks, using the word "millions" to number the weddings that have preceded George and Emily's. **(a)** Which of his lines implies that life is cyclical, with events occurring again and again with little variation? **(b)** Does he seem to expect anything different for George and Emily? Give reasons for your answer.

Application

Flashback

As the Handbook article demonstrates, flashbacks are common in novels and short stories, where the story is told rather than acted out. They do not occur very often in stage plays, however, where it is more difficult to show movement backward in time.

1. Why does the flashback not seem unexpected or out of place in this play?

2. Could the information in the flashback have been communicated as effectively if it had just been explained by one of the characters? Why or why not?

Act Three

During the intermission the audience has seen the STAGEHANDS *arranging the stage. On the right-hand side, a little right of the center, ten or twelve ordinary chairs have been placed in three openly spaced rows facing the audience.*

These are graves in the cemetery.

Toward the end of the intermission the ACTORS *enter and take their places. The front row contains: toward the center of the stage, an empty chair; then* MRS. GIBBS*;* SIMON STIMSON.

The second row contains, among others, MRS. SOAMES. *The third row has* WALLY WEBB.

The dead do not turn their heads or their eyes to right or left, but they sit in a quiet without stiffness. When they speak their tone is matter-of-fact, without sentimentality and, above all, without lugubriousness.

The STAGE MANAGER *takes his accustomed place and waits for the house lights to go down.*

STAGE MANAGER. This time nine years have gone by, friends—summer, 1913. Gradual changes in Grover's Corners. Horses are getting rarer. Farmers coming into town in Fords. Everybody locks their house doors now at night. Ain't been any burglars in town yet, but everybody's heard about 'em. You'd be surprised, though—on the whole, things don't change much around here.

This is certainly an important part of Grover's Corners. It's on a hilltop—a windy hilltop—lots of sky, lots of clouds—often lots of sun and moon and stars. You come up here on a fine afternoon and you can see range on range of hills—awful blue they are—up there by Lake Sunapee and Lake Winnipesaukee . . . and way up, if you've got a glass, you can see the White Mountains and Mt. Washington—where North Conway and Conway is. And, of course, our favorite mountain, Mt. Monadnock,[1]'s right here—and all these towns that lie around it: Jaffrey, 'n East Jaffrey, 'n Peterborough, 'n Dublin; and *(Then pointing down in the audience)* there, quite a ways down, is Grover's Corners. Yes, beautiful spot up here. Mountain laurel and li-lacks. I often wonder why people like to be buried in Woodlawn and Brooklyn when they might pass the same time up here in New Hampshire. Over there—*(Pointing to stage left)* are the old stones—1670, 1680. Strong-minded people that come a long way to be independent. Summer people walk around there laughing at the funny words on the tombstones . . . it don't do any harm. And genealogists come up from Boston—get paid by city people for looking up their ancestors. They want to make sure they're Daughters of the American Revolution and of the *Mayflower*. . . . Well, I guess that don't do any harm, either. Wherever you come near the human race, there's layers and layers of nonsense. . . .

Over there are some Civil War veterans. Iron flags on their graves . . . New Hampshire boys . . . had a notion that the Union ought to be kept together, though they'd never seen more than fifty miles of it themselves. All they knew was the name, friends—the United States of America. The United States of America. And they went and died about it.

This here is the new part of the cemetery. Here's your friend Mrs. Gibbs. 'N let me see—here's Mr. Stimson, organist at the Congregational Church. And Mrs. Soames who enjoyed the wedding so—you remember? Oh, and a lot of others. And Editor Webb's boy, Wallace, whose appendix burst while he was on a Boy Scout trip to Crawford Notch. Yes, an awful lot of sorrow has sort of quieted down up here. People just wild with grief have brought their relatives up to this hill. We all know how it is . . . and then time . . . and sunny days . . . and rainy days . . . 'n snow . . . We're all glad they're in a beautiful place and we're coming up here ourselves when our fit's over.

Now there are some things we all know, but we don't take'm out and look at'm very often.

---

1. ***Monadnock*** (mə näd'nok).

We all know that *something* is eternal. And it ain't houses and it ain't names, and it ain't earth, and it ain't even the stars . . . everybody knows in their bones that *something* is eternal, and that something has to do with human beings. All the greatest people ever lived have been telling us that for five thousand years and yet you'd be surprised how people are always losing hold of it. There's something way down deep that's eternal about every human being. *(Pause)*

You know as well as I do that the dead don't stay interested in us living people for very long. Gradually, gradually, they lose hold of the earth . . . and the ambitions they had . . . and the pleasures they had . . . and the things they suffered . . . and the people they loved. They get weaned away from earth—that's the way I put it—weaned away. And they stay here while the earth part of 'em burns away, burns out; and all that time they slowly get indifferent to what's goin' on in Grover's Corners. They're waitin' for something that they feel is comin'. Something important, and great. Aren't they waitin' for the eternal part in them to come out clear? Some of the things they're going to say maybe'll hurt your feelings—but that's the way it is: mother 'n daughter . . . husband 'n wife . . . enemy 'n enemy . . . money 'n miser . . . all those terribly important things kind of grow pale around here. And what's left when memory's gone, and your identity, Mrs. Smith? *(He looks at the audience a minute, then turns to the stage.)* Well! There are some *living* people. There's Joe Stoddard, our undertaker, supervising a new-made grave. And here comes a Grover's Corners boy, that left town to go out West.

*(*JOE STODDARD *has hovered about in the background.* SAM CRAIG *enters left, wiping his forehead from the exertion. He carries an umbrella and strolls front.)*

SAM CRAIG. Good afternoon, Joe Stoddard.

JOE STODDARD. Good afternoon, good afternoon. Let me see now: do I know you?

SAM CRAIG. I'm Sam Craig.

JOE STODDARD. Gracious sakes' alive! Of all people! I should'a knowed you'd be back for the funeral. You've been away a long time, Sam.

SAM CRAIG. Yes, I've been away over twelve years. I'm in business out in Buffalo now, Joe. But I was in the East when I got news of my cousin's death, so I thought I'd combine things a little and come and see the old home. You look well.

JOE STODDARD. Yes, yes, can't complain. Very sad, our journey today, Samuel.

SAM CRAIG. Yes.

JOE STODDARD. Yes, yes. I always say I hate to supervise when a young person is taken. They'll be here in a few minutes now. I had to come here early today—my son's supervisin' at the home.

SAM CRAIG *(reading stones)*. Old Farmer McCarty, I used to do chores for him—after school. He had the lumbago.

JOE STODDARD. Yes, we brought Farmer McCarty here a number of years ago now.

SAM CRAIG *(staring at* MRS. GIBBS*'s knees)*. Why, this is my Aunt Julia. . . . I'd forgotten that she'd . . . of course, of course.

JOE STODDARD. Yes, Doc Gibbs lost his wife two-three years ago . . . about this time. And today's another pretty bad blow for him, too.

MRS. GIBBS *(to* SIMON STIMSON, *in an even voice)*. That's my sister Carey's boy, Sam . . . Sam Craig.

SIMON STIMSON. I'm always uncomfortable when *they're* around.

MRS. GIBBS. Simon.

SAM CRAIG. Do they choose their own verses much, Joe?

JOE STODDARD. No . . . not usual. Mostly the bereaved pick a verse.

SAM CRAIG. Doesn't sound like Aunt Julia. There aren't many of those Hersey sisters left now. Let me see: where are . . . I wanted to look at my father's and mother's . . .

JOE STODDARD. Over there with the Craigs . . . Avenue F.

SAM CRAIG *(reading* SIMON STIMSON*'s epitaph)*.

He was organist at church, wasn't he?—Hm, drank a lot, we used to say.

JOE STODDARD. Nobody was supposed to know about it. He'd seen a peck of trouble. *(Behind his hand)* Took his own life, y'know?

SAM CRAIG. Oh, did he?

JOE STODDARD. Hung himself in the attic. They tried to hush it up, but of course it got around. He chose his own epy-taph. You can see it there. It ain't a verse exactly.

SAM CRAIG. Why, it's just some notes of music—what is it?

JOE STODDARD. Oh, I wouldn't know. It was wrote up in the Boston papers at the time.

SAM CRAIG. Joe, what did she die of?

JOE STODDARD. Who?

SAM CRAIG. My cousin.

JOE STODDARD. Oh, didn't you know? Had some trouble bringing a baby into the world. 'Twas her second, though. There's a little boy 'bout four years old.

SAM CRAIG *(opening his umbrella).* The grave's going to be over there?

JOE STODDARD. Yes, there ain't much more room over here among the Gibbses, so they're opening a whole new Gibbs section over by Avenue B. You'll excuse me now. I see they're comin'.

(From left to center, at the back of the stage, comes a procession. FOUR MEN *carry a casket, invisible to us. All the rest are under umbrellas. One can vaguely see:* DR. GIBBS, GEORGE, *the* WEBBS, *etc. They gather about a grave in the back center of the stage, a little to the left of center.)*

MRS. SOAMES. Who is it, Julia?

MRS. GIBBS *(without raising her eyes).* My daughter-in-law, Emily Webb.

MRS. SOAMES *(a little surprised, but no emotion).* Well, I declare! The road up here must have been awful muddy. What did she die of, Julia?

MRS. GIBBS. In childbirth.

MRS. SOAMES. Childbirth. *(Almost with a laugh)* I'd forgotten all about that. My, wasn't life awful—*(With a sigh)* and wonderful.

SIMON STIMSON *(with a sideways glance).* Wonderful, was it?

MRS. GIBBS. Simon! Now, remember!

MRS. SOAMES. I remember Emily's wedding. Wasn't it a lovely wedding! And I remember her reading the class poem at Graduation Exercises. Emily was one of the brightest girls ever graduated from High School. I've heard Principal Wilkins say so time after time. I called on them at their new farm, just before I died. Perfectly beautiful farm.

A WOMAN FROM AMONG THE DEAD. It's on the same road we lived on.

A MAN AMONG THE DEAD. Yepp, right smart farm.

(They subside. The group by the grave starts singing "Blessed Be the Tie That Binds.")

A WOMAN AMONG THE DEAD. I always liked that hymn. I was hopin' they'd sing a hymn.

(Pause. Suddenly EMILY *appears from among the umbrellas. She is wearing a white dress. Her hair is down her back and tied by a white ribbon like a little girl. She comes slowly, gazing wonderingly at the dead, a little dazed. She stops halfway and smiles faintly. After looking at the mourners for a moment, she walks slowly to the vacant chair beside* MRS. GIBBS *and sits down.)*

EMILY *(to them all, quietly, smiling).* Hello.

MRS. SOAMES. Hello, Emily.

A MAN AMONG THE DEAD. Hello, M's Gibbs.

EMILY *(warmly).* Hello, Mother Gibbs.

MRS. GIBBS. Emily.

EMILY. Hello. *(With surprise)* It's raining. *(Her eyes drift back to the funeral company.)*

MRS. GIBBS. Yes . . . They'll be gone soon, dear. Just rest yourself.

EMILY. It seems thousands and thousands of years since I . . . Papa remembered that that was my favorite hymn. Oh, I wish I'd been here a long time. I don't like being new here.—How do you do, Mr. Stimson?

SIMON STIMSON. How do you do, Emily.

(EMILY continues to look about her with a wondering smile; as though to shut out from her mind the thought of the funeral company she starts speaking to MRS. GIBBS with a touch of nervousness.)

EMILY. Mother Gibbs, George and I have made that farm into just the best place you ever saw. We thought of you all the time. We wanted to show you the new barn and a great long cement drinking fountain for the stock. We bought that out of the money you left us.

MRS. GIBBS. I did?

EMILY. Don't you remember, Mother Gibbs—the legacy you left us? Why, it was over three hundred and fifty dollars.

MRS. GIBBS. Yes, yes, Emily.

EMILY. Well, there's a patent device on the drinking fountain so that it never overflows, Mother Gibbs, and it never sinks below a certain mark they have there. It's fine. *(Her voice trails off and her eyes return to the funeral group.)* It won't be the same to George without me, but it's a lovely farm. *(Suddenly she looks directly at MRS. GIBBS.)* Live people don't understand, do they?

MRS. GIBBS. No, dear—not very much.

EMILY. They're sort of shut up in little boxes, aren't they? I feel as though I knew them last a thousand years ago. . . . My boy is spending the day at Mrs. Carter's. *(She sees MR. CARTER among the dead.)* Oh, Mr. Carter, my little boy is spending the day at your house.

MR. CARTER. Is he?

EMILY. Yes, he loves it there—Mother Gibbs, we have a Ford, too. Never gives any trouble. I don't drive, though. Mother Gibbs, when does this feeling go away?—Of being . . . one of *them?* How long does it . . . ?

MRS. GIBBS. Sh! dear. Just wait and be patient.

EMILY *(with a sigh)*. I know.—Look, they're finished. They're going.

MRS. GIBBS. Sh—

(The umbrellas leave the stage. DR. GIBBS has come over to his wife's grave and stands before it a moment. EMILY looks up at his face. MRS. GIBBS does not raise her eyes.)

EMILY. Look! Father Gibbs is bringing some of my flowers to you. He looks just like George, doesn't he? Oh, Mother Gibbs, I never realized before how troubled and how . . . how in the dark live persons are. Look at him. I loved him so. From morning till night, that's all they are—troubled. *(DR. GIBBS goes off.)*

THE DEAD. Little cooler than it was.—Yes, that rain's cooled it off a little. Those northeast winds always do the same thing, don't they? If it isn't a rain, it's a three-day blow.

(A patient calm falls on the stage. The STAGE MANAGER appears at his proscenium pillar, smoking. EMILY sits up abruptly with an idea.)

EMILY. But, Mother Gibbs, one can go back; one can go back there again . . . into living. I feel it. I know it. Why just then for a moment I was thinking about . . . about the farm . . . and for a minute I *was* there, and my baby was on my lap as plain as day.

MRS. GIBBS. Yes, of course you can.

EMILY. I can go back there and live all those days over again . . . why not?

MRS. GIBBS. All I can say is, Emily, don't.

EMILY *(she appeals urgently to the STAGE MANAGER)*. But it's true, isn't it? I can go and live . . . back there . . . again.

STAGE MANAGER. Yes, some have tried—but they soon come back here.

MRS. GIBBS. Don't do it, Emily.

MRS. SOAMES. Emily, don't. It's not what you think it'd be.

EMILY. But I won't live over a sad day. I'll choose a happy one—I'll choose the day I first knew I loved George. Why should that be painful?

(They are silent. Her question turns to the STAGE MANAGER.*)*

STAGE MANAGER. You not only live it; but you watch yourself living it.

EMILY. Yes?

STAGE MANAGER. And as you watch it, you see the thing that they—down there—never know. You see the future. You know what's going to happen afterwards.

EMILY. But is that—painful? Why?

MRS. GIBBS. That's not the only reason why you shouldn't do it, Emily. When you've been here longer you'll see that our life here is to forget all that, and think only of what's ahead, and be ready for what's ahead. When you've been here longer you'll understand.

EMILY *(softly)*. But, Mother Gibbs, how can I *ever* forget that life? It's all I know. It's all I had.

MRS. SOAMES. Oh, Emily. It isn't wise. Really, it isn't.

EMILY. But it's a thing I must know for myself. I'll choose a happy day, anyway.

MRS. GIBBS. *No!*—At least, choose an unimportant day. Choose the least important day in your life. It will be important enough.

EMILY *(to herself)*. Then it can't be since I was married; or since the baby was born. *(To the* STAGE MANAGER, *eagerly)* I can choose a birthday at least, can't I?— I choose my twelfth birthday.

STAGE MANAGER. All right. February 11th, 1899. A Tuesday.—Do you want any special time of day?

EMILY. Oh, I want the whole day.

STAGE MANAGER. We'll begin at dawn. You remember it had been snowing for several days; but it had stopped the night before, and they had begun clearing the roads. The sun's coming up.

EMILY *(with a cry; rising)*. There's Main Street . . . why, that's Mr. Morgan's drugstore before he changed it! . . . And there's the livery stable. *(The stage at no time in this act has been very dark; but now the left half of the stage gradually becomes very bright—the brightness of a crisp winter morning.* EMILY *walks toward Main Street.)*

STAGE MANAGER. Yes, it's 1899. This is fourteen years ago.

EMILY. Oh, that's the town I knew as a little girl. And, *look,* there's the old white fence that used to be around our house. Oh, I'd forgotten that! Oh, I love it so! Are they inside?

STAGE MANAGER. Yes, your mother'll be coming downstairs in a minute to make breakfast.

EMILY *(softly)*. Will she?

STAGE MANAGER. And you remember: your father had been away for several days; he came back on the early-morning train.

EMILY. No . . . ?

STAGE MANAGER. He'd been back to his college to make a speech—in western New York, at Clinton.

EMILY. Look! There's Howie Newsome. There's our policeman. But he's *dead;* he *died.*

(The voices of HOWIE NEWSOME, CONSTABLE WARREN, *and* JOE CROWELL, JR., *are heard at the left of the stage.* EMILY *listens in delight.)*

HOWIE NEWSOME. Whoa, Bessie!—Bessie! 'Morning, Bill.

CONSTABLE WARREN. Morning, Howie.

HOWIE NEWSOME. You're up early.

CONSTABLE WARREN. Been rescuin' a party; darn near froze to death, down by Polish Town thar. Got drunk and lay out in the snowdrifts. Thought he was in bed when I shook'm.

EMILY. Why, there's Joe Crowell. . . .

JOE CROWELL. Good morning, Mr. Warren. 'Morning, Howie.

*(*MRS. WEBB *has appeared in her kitchen, but* EMILY *does not see her until she calls.)*

MRS. WEBB. Chil-*dren!* Wally! Emily! . . . Time to get up.

EMILY. Mama, I'm here! Oh! how young Mama looks! I didn't know Mama was ever that young.

MRS. WEBB. You can come and dress by the kitchen fire, if you like; but hurry. *(*HOWIE NEWSOME *has entered along Main Street and brings the milk to* MRS. WEBB*'s door.)* Good morning, Mr. Newsome. Whhhh—it's cold.

HOWIE NEWSOME. Ten below by my barn, Mrs. Webb.

MRS. WEBB. Think of it! Keep yourself wrapped up. *(She takes her bottles in, shuddering.)*

EMILY *(with an effort).* Mama, I can't find my blue hair ribbon anywhere.

MRS. WEBB. Just open your eyes, dear, that's all. I laid it out for you special—on the dresser, there. If it were a snake it would bite you.

EMILY. Yes, yes . . .

(She puts her hand on her heart. MR. WEBB *comes along Main Street, where he meets* CONSTABLE WARREN. *Their movements and voices are increasingly lively in the sharp air.)*

MR. WEBB. Good morning, Bill.

CONSTABLE WARREN. Good morning, Mr. Webb. You're up early.

MR. WEBB. Yes, just been back to my old college in New York State. Been any trouble here?

CONSTABLE WARREN. Well, I was called up this mornin' to rescue a Polish fella—darn near froze to death he was.

MR. WEBB. We must get it in the paper.

CONSTABLE WARREN. 'Twan't much.

EMILY *(whispers).* Papa.

*(*MR. WEBB *shakes the snow off his feet and enters his house.* CONSTABLE WARREN *goes off, right.)*

MR. WEBB. Good morning, Mother.

MRS. WEBB. How did it go, Charles?

MR. WEBB. Oh, fine, I guess. I told'm a few things.—Everything all right here?

MRS. WEBB. Yes—can't think of anything that's happened, special. Been right cold. Howie Newsome says it's ten below over to his barn.

MR. WEBB. Yes, well, it's colder than that at Hamilton College. Students' ears are falling off. It ain't Christian.—Paper have any mistakes in it?

MRS. WEBB. None that I noticed. Coffee's ready when you want it. *(He starts upstairs.)* Charles! Don't forget; it's Emily's birthday. Did you remember to get her something?

MR. WEBB *(patting his pocket).* Yes, I've got something here. *(Calling up the stairs)* Where's my girl? Where's my birthday girl? *(He goes off left.)*

MRS. WEBB. Don't interrupt her now, Charles. You can see her at breakfast. She's slow enough as it is. Hurry up, children! It's seven o'clock. Now, I don't want to call you again.

EMILY *(softly, more in wonder than in grief).* I can't bear it. They're so young and beautiful. Why did they ever have to get old? Mama, I'm here. I'm grown up. I love you all, everything.—I can't look at everything hard enough. *(She looks questioningly at the* STAGE MANAGER, *saying or suggesting: "Can I go in?" He nods briefly. She crosses to the inner door to the kitchen, left of her mother, and as though entering the room, says, suggesting the voice of a girl of twelve)* Good morning, Mama.

MRS. WEBB *(crossing to embrace and kiss her; in her characteristic matter-of-fact manner).* Well, now, dear, a very happy birthday to my girl and many happy returns. There are some surprises waiting for you on the kitchen table.

EMILY. Oh, Mama, you *shouldn't* have. *(She throws an anguished glance at the* STAGE MANAGER.*)* I can't—I can't.

MRS. WEBB *(facing the audience, over her stove).* But birthday or no birthday, I want you to eat your breakfast good and slow. I want you to grow up and be a good strong girl. That in the blue paper is from your Aunt Carrie; and I reckon you can guess who brought the postcard album. I found it on the doorstep when I brought in the milk—George Gibbs . . . must have come over in the cold pretty early . . . right nice of him.

EMILY *(to herself).* Oh, George! I'd forgotten that. . . .

MRS. WEBB. Chew that bacon good and slow. It'll help keep you warm on a cold day.

EMILY *(with mounting urgency).* Oh, Mama, just look at me one minute as though you really saw me. Mama, fourteen years have gone by. I'm dead. You're a grandmother, Mama. I married George Gibbs, Mama. Wally's dead, too. Mama, his appendix burst on a camping trip to

North Conway. We felt just terrible about it—don't you remember? But, just for a moment now we're all together. Mama, just for a moment we're happy. *Let's look at one another.*

MRS. WEBB. That in the yellow paper is something I found in the attic among your grandmother's things. You're old enough to wear it now, and I thought you'd like it.

EMILY. And this is from you. Why, Mama, it's just lovely and it's just what I wanted. It's beautiful!

(She flings her arms around her mother's neck. Her mother goes on with her cooking, but is pleased.)

MRS. WEBB. Well, I hoped you'd like it. Hunted all over. Your Aunt Norah couldn't find one in Concord, so I had to send all the way to Boston. *(Laughing)* Wally has something for you, too. He made it at manual-training class and he's very proud of it. Be sure you make a big fuss about it.—Your father has a surprise for you, too; don't know what it is myself. Sh—here he comes.

MR. WEBB *(offstage).* Where's my girl? Where's my birthday girl?

EMILY *(in a loud voice to the* STAGE MANAGER*).* I can't. I can't go on. It goes so fast. We don't have time to look at one another. *(She breaks down sobbing. The lights dim on the left half of the stage.* MRS. WEBB *disappears.)* I didn't realize. So all that was going on and we never noticed. Take me back—up the hill—to my grave. But first: Wait! One more look. Good-by. Good-by, world. Good-by, Grover's Corners . . . Mama and Papa. Good-by to clocks ticking . . . and Mama's sunflowers. And food and coffee. And new-ironed dresses and hot baths . . . and sleeping and waking up. Oh, earth, you're too wonderful for anybody to realize you. *(She looks toward the* STAGE MANAGER *and asks abruptly, through her tears)* Do any human beings ever realize life while they live it?—every, every minute?

STAGE MANAGER. No. *(Pause)* The saints and poets, maybe—they do some.

EMILY. I'm ready to go back.

(She returns to her chair beside MRS. GIBBS. *Pause)*

MRS. GIBBS. Were you happy?

EMILY. No . . . I should have listened to you. That's all human beings are! Just blind people.

MRS. GIBBS. Look, it's clearing up. The stars are coming out.

EMILY. Oh, Mr. Stimson, I should have listened to them.

SIMON STIMSON *(with mounting violence; bitingly).* Yes, now you know. Now you know! That's what it was to be alive. To move about in a cloud of ignorance; to go up and down trampling on the feelings of those . . . of those about you. To spend and waste time as though you had a million years. To be always at the mercy of one self-centered passion, or another. Now you know—that's the happy existence you wanted to go back to. Ignorance and blindness.

MRS. GIBBS *(spiritedly).* Simon Stimson, that ain't the whole truth and you know it. Emily, look at that star. I forget its name.

A MAN AMONG THE DEAD. My boy Joel was a sailor—knew 'em all. He'd set on the porch evenings and tell 'em all by name. Yes, sir, wonderful!

ANOTHER MAN AMONG THE DEAD. A star's mighty good company.

A WOMAN AMONG THE DEAD. Yes. Yes, 'tis.

SIMON STIMSON. Here's one of *them* coming.

THE DEAD. That's funny. 'Tain't no time for one of them to be here.—Goodness sakes.

EMILY. Mother Gibbs, it's George.

MRS. GIBBS. Sh, dear. Just rest yourself.

EMILY. It's George.

*(*GEORGE *enters from the left, and slowly comes toward them.)*

A MAN FROM AMONG THE DEAD. And my boy, Joel, who knew the stars—he used to say it took millions of years for that speck o' light to git to the earth. Don't seem like a body could believe it, but that's what he used to say—millions of years.

*(*GEORGE *sinks to his knees, then falls full length at* EMILY*'s feet.)*

A WOMAN AMONG THE DEAD. Goodness! That ain't no way to behave!

MRS. SOAMES. He ought to be home.

EMILY. Mother Gibbs?

MRS. GIBBS. Yes, Emily?

EMILY. They don't understand, do they?

MRS. GIBBS. No, dear. They don't understand. *(The* STAGE MANAGER *appears at the right, one hand on a dark curtain which he slowly draws across the scene. In the distance a clock is heard striking the hour very faintly.)*

STAGE MANAGER. Most everybody's asleep in Grover's Corners. There are a few lights on: Shorty Hawkins, down at the depot, has just watched the Albany train go by. And at the livery stable somebody's setting up late and talking.—Yes, it's clearing up. There are the stars—doing their old, old crisscross journeys in the sky. Scholars haven't settled the matter yet, but they seem to think there are no living beings up there. Just chalk . . . or fire. Only this one is straining away, straining away all the time to make something of itself. The strain's so bad that every sixteen hours everybody lies down and gets a rest. *(He winds his watch.)* Hm. . . . Eleven o'clock in Grover's Corners.—You get a good rest, too. Good night.

THE END

Discussion

1. In his introductory remarks the Stage Manager describes how the living, after a first wild grief, tend gradually to forget the dead. Then he describes how one might imagine the dead being gradually "weaned away from earth." Explain the parallels the Stage Manager draws between the response of the dead to the living and that of the living to the dead.

2. The first living characters appearing in Act Three are new—Sam Craig and Joe Stoddard. **(a)** What bits of information do you learn from their conversation? **(b)** Which information advances the dramatic action of the play?

3. One hymn, "Blessed Be the Tie That Binds," is heard over and over again in the play. **(a)** What are the scenes in which it is heard? **(b)** What is the effect of the repetition of the hymn in these scenes?

4. When the dead Emily appears in the cemetery, she says, "Live people don't understand, do they?" and she adds, "They're sort of shut up in little boxes." What does she mean?

5. Against the advice of her mother-in-law Emily decides to relive one day of her past life. **(a)** Why does she choose her twelfth birthday? **(b)** How is George involved in her return? **(c)** Is this scene a flashback? Why or why not?

6. On her day of return Emily exclaims to her mother, "Oh, Mama, just look at me one minute as though you really saw me. Mama, fourteen years have gone by. I'm dead. You're a grandmother, Mama. I married George Gibbs, Mama. Wally's dead, too." **(a)** What is Mrs. Webb's reaction to this speech? **(b)** In what way is the speech the turning point of Emily's day of return?

7. When Emily returns to the dead, Simon Stimson blurts out, "Now you know—that's the happy existence you wanted to go back to. Ignorance and blindness." Mrs. Gibbs chimes in, "Simon Stimson, that ain't the whole truth and you know it." **(a)** Who is right? Explain. **(b)** Did the appearance of George, falling at Emily's feet at the close of the play, affect your answer? If so, how?

8. Thornton Wilder has said that his play is not a "picture of life in a New Hampshire village" nor an explanation of the "conditions of life after death," but rather an "attempt to find a value above all price for the smallest events in our daily life." Review the entire action of the play. Does Wilder's statement conform to your sense of the play and its overall effect? Discuss.

Vocabulary

Combined Skills

tableau	exertion
epitaph	torrent
traipse	bereave
diligent	cynicism

Check your Glossary for the meanings of the words listed above; then use the words to complete the following sentences. In each case, however, the form of the word must be changed by the addition (or subtraction) of a prefix, suffix, or plural, or by a change of tense. Do not use the words as they appear above without altering their form to fit the meaning of the sentences. You will not use all the words.

1. Everyone ______ the utmost effort at the last drive, but the fund is still too low.

2. Although they worked ______, they were unable to finish the dissection before the end of class.

3. Her hobby is searching out unusual ______ in old burial grounds.

4. While ______ around in southwestern Colorado, we discovered many unusual and fascinating rock formations.

5. People usually experience a period of ______ following the death of a loved one.

Composition

Think about what the Stage Manager might say in an epilogue or afterword to this play—about George, his son, and his farm, for example; or about Grover's Corners or any of the other characters. Think also about the language the Stage Manager would use in communicating his message.

Now write a two- or three-paragraph epilogue for the Stage Manager to speak.

Thornton Wilder 1897–1975

The works of Thornton Wilder presented universally recognized insights in ways that were unconventional and innovative. He was not a follower of fashions in literature, but an originator.

Born in Madison, Wisconsin, Wilder attended schools in China, the U.S. (where he took degrees at Yale and Princeton), and in Rome. Beginning his writing career as a novelist, he published his first book, *The Cabala,* in 1926, stirring scarcely a ripple. However, his next book, *The Bridge of San Luis Rey,* a story weaving the complex relationships of a group of people who die in a bridge collapse, brought him worldwide attention and a Pulitzer Prize in 1927.

Our Town established Wilder as an important playwright. When it was first tried out in Boston in 1938, its reception was so cool that the run was shortened and the play moved to New York. There it received rave reviews, winning the Pulitzer Prize in drama for the year. The play, with its unusual use of time and lack of scenery, departed from traditional forms and introduced new methods of presentation for modern theater.

In 1942, Wilder won his third Pulitzer Prize for his play *Skin of Our Teeth.* His following success, *The Matchmaker* (1954), a reworking of a Broadway flop of 1938 (*The Merchant of Yonkers*), is remembered primarily as the basis for the highly popular musical comedy *Hello, Dolly!*

In his later years Wilder turned from drama back to the novel. His books, like the Pulitzer Prize-winning *The Eighth Day* (1967), attracted both critical readers and popular audiences. At the end of his career he could look back with the satisfaction of a writer who was a remarkably independent—and totally committed—artist in words.

Unit 2 Review: Modern Drama

Content Review

1. As dramatists set their major conflicts in motion, they provide whatever background information their audiences need to understand characters and actions. Such explanatory information is called the *exposition* of the play, and it generally occurs fairly early in the action. **(a)** In *Twelve Angry Men,* what information about the trial does Rose provide after the jurors vote for the first time? **(b)** In *The Romancers,* what information is provided in the first episode in which Bergamin and Pasquinot find themselves alone together? **(c)** Who provides most of the background for the action in *Our Town?* Where does this information occur in the play?

2. When first performed in 1938, *Our Town* struck theatergoers as revolutionary in conception and design. Instead of occurring on a realistic set, the actions flowed between scenes on a bare stage on which the curtain never closed, and the audience used its imagination to fill in whatever was missing in the setting. Explain what props are used to suggest places and events in each of the following scenes: **(a)** the scene at the windows in Act One, in which George and Emily discuss their homework; **(b)** the drugstore scene in Act Two, with Emily and George discovering their love for each other; **(c)** the burial scene in Act Three, with Emily moving from the world of the living to the world of the dead. What might have been the author's purpose in not re-creating scenes in a realistic fashion?

3. Explain why you agree or disagree with each of the following statements about *The Romancers.* **(a)** The fluffy characterizations and flamboyant decorations of the play do not disguise its heavy, realistic subject. **(b)** The wall serves more as a backdrop for unity than a means of separation in the play. **(c)** From beginning to end, the play is nothing more than Rostand's updated version of Shakespeare's *Romeo and Juliet.*

4. *Twelve Angry Men* is written in the form of a television script. **(a)** How are its stage directions different from those of a play designed for presentation on a stage? Give examples. **(b)** Do the various time requirements of television—length of the total program, breaks required for commercials, and so on—seem to have any effect on the development of the action? Explain.

5. Different time periods and personalities aside, the Stage Manager in *Our Town,* Juror Eight in *Twelve Angry Men,* and Bergamin in *The Romancers* perform a similar function. Compare these characters.

6. Playwrights often use suspense to sustain interest in their dramas. Examine the suspense in *Twelve Angry Men, The Romancers,* and *Our Town.* What is it audiences want to know as each play moves from episode to episode?

Concept Review: Interpretation of New Material

Read the introduction and scene from the play. Then use the questions following it to review your understanding of the concepts and terms presented in this unit.

from A Doll's House • *Henrik Ibsen* Norway

A Doll's House takes place in a town in Norway in the nineteenth century. Nora and Torvald Helmer have been married several years, but Torvald, a newly appointed bank manager, has always treated Nora like a child, a doll-wife. Some years back, when Torvald was desperately ill and told by his doctor to go abroad, Nora had secretly borrowed money for him by forging her ill father's name to a document. She worked and saved to pay this money back, but had not been able to do so completely. The man who had lent Nora the money, finding himself about to be fired by Torvald Helmer from his job at the bank, threatens to expose Nora's forgery and ruin both her and her husband. When Torvald reads the letter from the lender about his wife's forgery and imagines himself ruined, he accuses Nora of having betrayed her family and her religion, of being a criminal and a liar and unfit to bring up their children. Shocked by these accusations, Nora sees for the first time the shallowness of Torvald's love. Although his attitude changes when he receives another letter from the lender promising not to expose the forgery, it is too late. Torvald has shown himself to Nora as hypocritical and self-centered, concerned more for his own fate than for hers. It is a wiser, sadder, and rapidly maturing Nora who, in the following scene, insists that she and her husband have a serious talk.

NORA *(looking at her watch).* It is not so very late. Sit down here, Torvald. You and I have much to say to one another. *(She sits down at one side of the table.)*

HELMER. Nora—what is this?—this cold, set face?

NORA. Sit down. It will take some time; I have a lot to talk over with you.

HELMER *(sits down at the opposite side of the table).* You alarm me, Nora!—and I don't understand you.

NORA. No, that is just it. You don't understand me, and I have never understood you either—before tonight. No, you mustn't interrupt me. You must simply listen to what I say. Torvald, this is a settling of accounts.

HELMER. What do you mean by that?

NORA *(after a short silence).* Isn't there one thing that strikes you as strange in our sitting here like this?

HELMER. What is that?

NORA. We have been married now eight years. Does it not occur to you that this is the first time we two, you and I, husband and wife, have had a serious conversation?

HELMER. What do you mean by serious?

NORA. In all these eight years—longer than that—from the very beginning of our acquaintance, we have never exchanged a word on any serious subject.

HELMER. Was it likely that I would be continually and forever telling you about worries that you could not help me to bear?

NORA. I am not speaking about business matters. I say that we have never sat down in earnest together to try and get at the bottom of anything.

HELMER. But, dearest Nora, would it have been any good to you?

NORA. That is just it; you have never understood me. I have been greatly wronged, Torvald—first by Papa and then by you.

HELMER. What! By us two—by us two, who have loved you better than anyone else in the world?

NORA *(shaking her head).* You have never loved me. You have only thought it pleasant to be in love with me.

HELMER. Nora, what do I hear you saying?

NORA. It is perfectly true, Torvald. When I was at home with Papa, he told me his opinion about everything, and so I had the same opinions; and if I differed from him I concealed the fact, because he would not have liked it. He called me his doll-child, and he played with me just as I used to play with my dolls. And when I came to live with you—

HELMER. What sort of an expression is that to use about our marriage?

NORA *(undisturbed).* I mean that I was simply transferred from Papa's hands into yours. You arranged everything according to your own taste, and so I got the same tastes as you—or else I pretended to, I am really not quite sure which—I think sometimes the one and sometimes the other. When I look back on it, it seems to me as if I had been living here like a poor woman—just from hand to mouth. I have existed merely to perform tricks for you, Torvald. But you would have it so. You and Papa have committed a great sin against me. It is your fault that I have made nothing of my life.

HELMER. How unreasonable and how ungrateful you are, Nora! Have you not been happy here?

NORA. No, I have never been happy. I thought I was, but it has never really been so.

From *A Doll's House* by Henrik Ibsen, translated by R. Farquharson Sharp, Everyman's Library series. Reprinted by permission of J. M. Dent & Sons Ltd.

HELMER. Not—not happy!

NORA. No, only merry. And you have always been so kind to me. But our home has been nothing but a playroom. I have been your doll-wife, just as at home I was Papa's doll-child; and here the children have been my dolls. I thought it great fun when you played with me, just as they thought it great fun when I played with them. That is what our marriage has been, Torvald.

HELMER. There is some truth in what you say—exaggerated and strained as your view of it is. But for the future it shall be different. Playtime shall be over, and lesson-time shall begin.

NORA. Whose lessons? Mine, or the children's?

HELMER. Both yours and the children's, my darling Nora.

NORA. Alas, Torvald, you are not the man to educate me into being a proper wife for you.

HELMER. And you can say that!

NORA. And I—how am I fitted to bring up the children?

HELMER. Nora!

NORA. Didn't you say so yourself a little while ago—that you dare not trust me to bring them up?

HELMER. In a moment of anger! Why do you pay any heed to that?

NORA. Indeed, you were perfectly right. I am not fit for the task. There is another task I must undertake first. I must try and educate myself—you are not the man to help me in that. I must do that for myself. And that is why I am going to leave you now.

HELMER *(springing up).* What do you say?

NORA. I must stand quite alone, if I am to understand myself and everything about me. It is for that reason that I cannot remain with you any longer.

HELMER. Nora! Nora!

NORA. I am going away from here now, at once. I am sure my friend Christine will take me in for the night—

HELMER. You are out of your mind! I won't allow it! I forbid you!

NORA. It is no use forbidding me anything any longer. I will take with me what belongs to myself. I will take nothing from you, either now or later.

HELMER. What sort of madness is this!

NORA. Tomorrow I shall go home—I mean, to my old home. It will be easiest for me to find something to do there.

HELMER. You blind, foolish woman!

NORA. I must try and get some sense, Torvald.

HELMER. To desert your home, your husband, and your children! And you don't consider what people will say!

NORA. I cannot consider that at all. I only know that it is necessary for me.

HELMER. It's shocking. This is how you would neglect your most sacred duties.

NORA. What do you consider my most sacred duties?

HELMER. Do I need to tell you that? Are they not your duties to your husband and your children?

NORA. I have other duties just as sacred.

HELMER. That you have not. What duties could those be?

NORA. Duties to myself.

HELMER. Before all else, you are a wife and a mother.

NORA. I don't believe that any longer. I believe that before all else I am a reasonable human being, just as you are—or, at all events, that I must try and become one. I know quite well, Torvald, that most people would think you right, and that views of that kind are to be found in books; but I can no longer content myself with what most people say, or with what is found in books. I must think over things for myself and get to understand them.

HELMER. Can you not understand your place in your own home? Let me try and awaken your conscience. I suppose you have some moral sense? Or—answer me—am I to think you have none?

NORA. I assure you, Torvald, that is not an easy question to answer. I really don't know. The thing perplexes me altogether. I only know that you and I look at it in quite a different light. I am learning, too, that the law is quite another thing from what I supposed; but I find it impossible to convince myself that the law is right. According to it a woman has no right to spare her old dying father, or to save her husband's life. I can't believe that.

HELMER. You talk like a child. You don't understand the conditions of the world in which you live.

NORA. No, I don't. But now I am going to try. I am going to see if I can make out who is right, the world or I.

1. In the three or four speeches opening this scene, which of the following appears to characterize Nora's feelings? **(a)** gaiety and merriment; **(b)** uncertainty and hesitation; **(c)** certainty and firmness of purpose; **(d)** fear and confusion.

2. In these same speeches, which of the following seems best to characterize Torvald's state? **(a)** puzzlement and alarm; **(b)** amused interest; **(c)** sympathetic understanding; **(d)** seething rage.

3. How long have Nora and Torvald been married?

4. When Nora states that she and Torvald have never had a "serious conversation," Torvald believes she is referring to **(a)** politics; **(b)** religion; **(c)** their marriage and life together; **(d)** his business affairs.

5. Who else besides Torvald does Nora blame for the state her mind is in?

6. Nora tells Torvald she must leave him because **(a)** she no longer loves him; **(b)** what she has to do, she must do by herself; **(c)** he won't share his business interests with her; **(d)** he doesn't love her anymore.

7. Where does Nora expect to live if she leaves Torvald?

8. Torvald's first reaction to Nora's announcement that she is leaving is to **(a)** declare his love; **(b)** declare that he won't allow her to leave; **(c)** appeal to her sense of honor; **(d)** apologize for his behavior.

9. Torvald reminds Nora of her "sacred duties," which according to him are to **(a)** her husband and children; **(b)** God; **(c)** herself; **(d)** the community.

10. At the end of the scene, Torvald clearly has not undergone any change because he still believes that Nora **(a)** loves him; **(b)** behaves like a child; **(c)** would be bored by his business affairs; **(d)** does not love the children.

Composition Review

From the assignments that follow choose one to write about.

1. *Our Town* and *The Romancers* portray two different worlds. The world of *Our Town* is that of the small town, offering a simple life and simple pleasures. *The Romancers* portrays a world of more sophistication and gaiety, not only in the basic action but particularly in the long speech by Straforel listing his various kinds of mock-abductions. Which of these two worlds would you prefer to inhabit? Think of specific details of what living in that world would be like.

Write an essay setting forth your preferences and describing the life you would imagine you might live in such a world.

2. Emily of *Our Town* is enabled to relive one day in her life on earth. If the same privilege were granted to you, what day would you choose? Recollect the day in your mind and decide on specific reasons you would want to relive it.

Write a letter to a friend explaining the choice of that particular day.

3. The jury system has sometimes been assailed as a burdensome system that does not always result in justice being done. Some critics have argued that the number of jurors should be fewer (perhaps six), that individuals should be required to have a certain level of education to qualify as jurors, or that all cases should be decided by judges alone. What is your view on these questions? You may form your opinions based on *Twelve Angry Men* as well as on anything else you know about the jury system.

In a short essay argue your opinion on one or more of the questions. Use examples to back up the points you make.

4. Nora of *A Doll's House,* Sylvette of *The Romancers,* and Emily of *Our Town* display such qualities as determination, imagination, and perceptiveness. Which of these characters is most admirable? If necessary, review the play the character appears in for evidence to support your view.

Write an essay identifying the character and discussing reasons for your admiration.

Unit 3
Poetry

The Four Seasons (1974) mosaic of stone + glass fragments
Jewish emigré Marc Chagall (1887–
This was his 'gift' to Chicago

Story Poems

Poems do many things—describe, portray, celebrate, question. They even tell stories. Poems can, with a few lines or many, convey the magic of "Once upon a time . . ."

See **NARRATIVE POETRY** Handbook of Literary Terms

My Father & The Figtree

Naomi Shihab USA

For other fruits my father was indifferent.
He'd point at the cherry trees and say,
"See those? I wish they were figs."
In the evenings he sat by my bed
weaving folktales like vivid little scarves.
They always involved a figtree.
Even when it didn't fit, he'd stick it in.
Once Joha was walking down the road & he saw a figtree.
Or, he tied his camel to a figtree & went to sleep.
Or, later when they caught & arrested him,
his pockets were full of figs.

At age six I ate a dried fig & shrugged.
"That's not what I'm talking about!" he said,
"I'm talking about a fig straight from the earth,
gift of Allah![1]—on a branch so heavy it touches the ground."
"I'm talking about picking the largest fattest sweetest fig
in the world & putting it in my mouth."
(Here he'd stop and close his eyes.)

---

1. ***Allah*** (al′ə), the Moslem name for God.

"My Father & The Figtree" by Naomi Shihab Nye published in *A Geography of Poets* edited by Edward Field (Bantam Books, 1978) and *Different Ways to Pray* by Naomi Shihab Nye (Breitenbush Books, 1980). Reprinted by permission of the author.

Naomi Shihab (shē′hab).

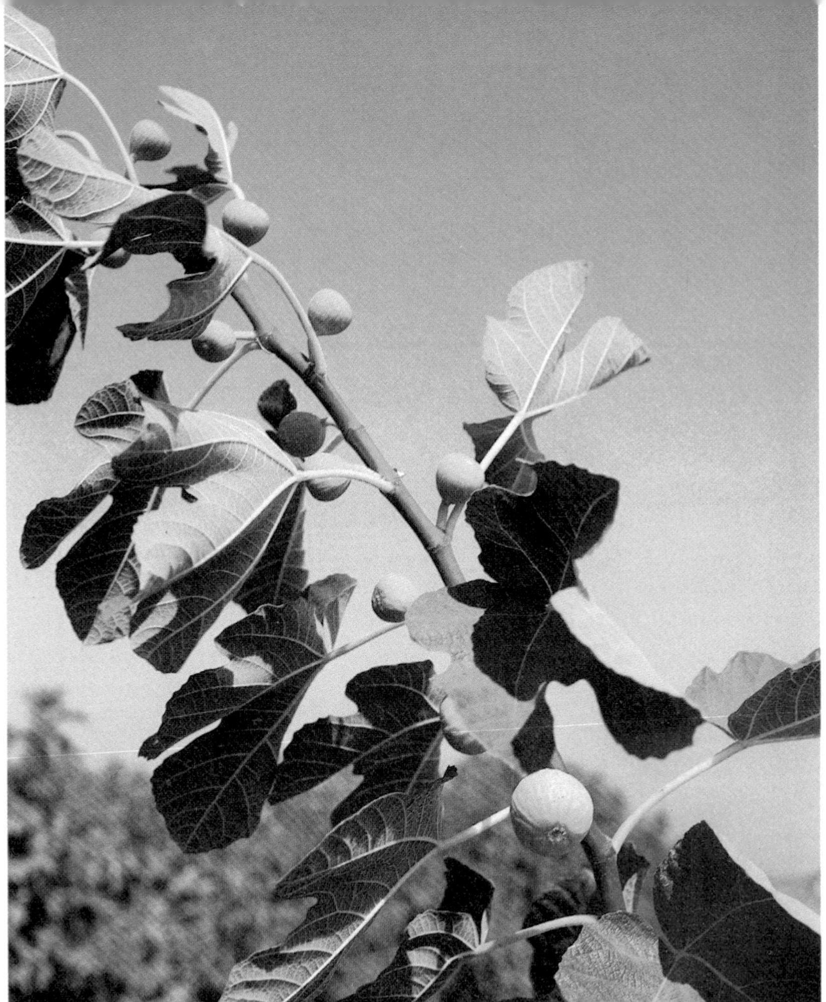

Years passed, we lived in many houses, none had figtrees.
We had lima beans, zucchini, parsley, beets.
Plant one! my mother said, but my father never did.
He tended garden halfheartedly, forgot to water,
let the okra get too big.
"What a dreamer he is. Look how many things he starts
and doesn't finish."

The last time he moved, I got a phonecall.
My father, in Arabic, chanting a song I'd never heard.
"What's that?" I said.
"Wait till you see."

He took me out back to the new yard.
There, in the middle of Dallas, Texas,
a tree with the largest, fattest, sweetest figs in the world.
"It's a figtree song!" he said,
plucking his fruits like ripe tokens,
emblems, assurance
of a world that was always his own.

See **RHYTHM** Handbook of Literary Terms

The Stone

Wilfrid Wilson Gibson Great Britain

"And will you cut a stone for him,
To set above his head?
And will you cut a stone for him—
A stone for him?" she said.

Three days before, a splintered rock
Had struck her lover dead—
Had struck him in the quarry dead,
Where, careless of the warning call,
He loitered, while the shot was fired—
A lively stripling, brave and tall,
And sure of all his heart desired . . .
A flash, a shock,
A rumbling fall . .
And, broken 'neath the broken rock,
A lifeless heap, with face of clay,
And still as any stone he lay,
With eyes that saw the end of all.

I went to break the news to her:
And I could hear my own heart beat
With dread of what my lips might say;
But some poor fool had sped before;
And, flinging wide her father's door,
Had blurted out the news to her,
Had struck her lover dead for her,
Had struck the girl's heart dead in her,
Had struck life, lifeless, at a word,
And dropped it at her feet:
Then hurried on his witless way,
Scarce knowing she had heard.
And when I came, she stood alone—
A woman, turned to stone:
And, though no word at all she said,
I knew that all was known.
Because her heart was dead,
She did not sigh nor moan.
His mother wept:
She could not weep.
Her lover slept:
She could not sleep.
Three days, three nights,
She did not stir:
Three days, three nights,
Were one to her,
Who never closed her eyes
From sunset to sunrise,
From dawn to evenfall—
Her tearless, staring eyes,
That, seeing naught, saw all.

The fourth night when I came from work,
I found her at my door.
"And will you cut a stone for him?"
She said: and spoke no more:
But followed me, as I went in,
And sank upon a chair;
And fixed her grey eyes on my face,
With still, unseeing stare.
And, as she waited patiently,
I could not bear to feel
Those still, grey eyes that followed me,
Those eyes that plucked the heart from me,
Those eyes that sucked the breath from me
And curdled the warm blood in me,
Those eyes that cut me to the bone,
And pierced my marrow like cold steel.

And so I rose, and sought a stone;
And cut it, smooth and square:
And, as I worked, she sat and watched,
Beside me, in her chair.
Night after night, by candlelight,
I cut her lover's name:
Night after night, so still and white,
And like a ghost she came;
And sat beside me, in her chair,
And watched with eyes aflame.
She eyed each stroke,
And hardly stirred:
She never spoke
A single word:
And not a sound or murmur broke
The quiet, save the mallet-stroke.

With still eyes ever on my hands,
With eyes that seemed to burn my hands,
My wincing, overwearied hands,
She watched, with bloodless lips apart,
And silent, indrawn breath:
And every stroke my chisel cut,
Death cut still deeper in her heart:
The two of us were chiselling,
Together, I and death.

And when at length the job was done,
And I had laid the mallet by,
As if, at last, her peace were won,
She breathed his name; and, with a sigh,
Passed slowly through the open door;
And never crossed my threshold more.

Next night I labored late, alone,
To cut her name upon the stone.

Phoebus and Boreas[1]

La Fontaine France translated by Marianne Moore

The sun and the north wind observed a traveler
Who was cloaked with particular care
Because fall had returned; for when autumn has come,
What we wear must be warm or we dare not leave home.
Both rain and rainbow as the sun shines fitfully,
Warn one to dress warily
In these months when we don't know for what to prepare,
An uncertain time in the Roman calendar.
Though our traveler was fortified for a gale,
With interlined cloak which the rain could not penetrate,
The wind said, "This man thinks himself impregnable
And his cloak is well sewn, but my force can prevail
As he'll find in the blast I create,
No button has held. Indeed before I am through,
I may waft the whole mantle away.
The battle could afford us amusement, I'd say.
Do you fancy a contest?" The sun said, "I do.
Mere words are unprofitable,
Let us see which can first unfasten the mantle
Protecting the pedestrian.
Begin: I shall hide; you uncloak him if you can."
Then our blower swelled, swallowed what wind he could,
To form a balloon, and with the wager to win,
Made demoniacal din.
Puffed, snorted, and sighed till the blast that he brewed
Left ships without a sail and homes without a roof
Because a mantle proved stormproof.
It was a triumph for the man to have withstood
The onslaught of wind that had rushed in,
As he somehow stood firm. The wind roared his chagrin—
A defeated boaster since his gusts had been borne.
Controlling clasp and skirt required dexterity,

---

1. ***Phoebus*** (fē'bəs), ***Boreas*** (bôr'ē əs), in Greek myths, the sun and the north wind, respectively.

La Fontaine (lȧ fôɴ ten').

But the wind found nothing torn
And must stop punctually.
The cloud had made it cool
Till the sun's genial influence caused the traveler to give way,
And perspiring because wearing wool,
He cast off a wrap too warm for the day
Though the sun had not yet shone with maximum force.

Clemency may be our best resource.

See **RHYME** Handbook of Literary Terms

A *Poison Tree*

William Blake Great Britain

I was angry with my friend:
I told my wrath, my wrath did end.
I was angry with my foe:
I told it not, my wrath did grow.

And I water'd it in fears,
Night & morning with my tears;
And I sunnèd it with smiles,
And with soft deceitful wiles.

And it grew both day and night,
Till it bore an apple bright.
And my foe beheld it shine,
And he knew that it was mine,

And into my garden stole,
When the night had veil'd the pole;[1]
In the morning glad I see
My foe outstretch'd beneath the tree.

---

1. ***night had veil'd the pole,*** night had covered one half of the earth, including the North Pole.

William Blake, "A Poison Tree," from *Songs of Experience,* 1794.

The Man Who Spilled Light

David Wagoner USA

The man who spilled light wasn't to blame for it.
He was in a hurry to bring it home to the city
Where, everyone said, there was too much darkness:
"Look at those shadows," they said. "They're dangerous.
Who's there? What's that?" and crouching, "Who are *you?*"
So he went and scraped up all the light he could find.

But it was too much to handle and started spilling:
Flakes and star marks, shafts of it splitting
To ring light and light gone slack or jagged,
Clouds folded inside out, whole pools
And hummocks and domes of light,
Egg light, light tied in knots or peeled in swatches,
Daylight as jumbled as jackstraws falling.

Then everything seemed perfectly obvious
Wherever they looked. There was nothing they couldn't see.
The corners and alleys all looked empty,
And no one could think of anything terrible
Except behind their backs, so they all lined up
With their backs to walls and felt perfectly fine.
And the man who'd spilled it felt fine for a while,
But then he noticed people squinting.

They should have been looking at everything, and everything
Should have been perfectly clear, and everyone
Should have seemed perfectly brilliant, there was so much
Dazzle: people were dazzled, they were dazzling,
But they were squinting, trying to make darkness
All over again in the cracks between their eyelids.
So he swept up all the broken light
For pity's sake and put it back where it came from.

Discussion

My Father & The Figtree

1. What part of the world is the speaker's father from? How do you know?

2. What are some ways the father demonstrates his yearning for figs and figtrees?

3. (a) When the father finally gets his figtree, what do you think it reminds him of? **(b)** How do his actions show that the tree is a dream fulfilled?

The Stone

1. (a) Who is the speaker in this poem? **(b)** Does he seem to have any special feeling for the woman? Discuss.

2. (a) What is suggested by the last three lines? **(b)** Do you think the rest of the poem prepares you for this? Explain.

3. What are some of the various things to which the title of the poem might refer?

Phoebus and Boreas

1. Both Phoebus and Boreas are characterized in the poem by their speeches and actions. Describe their personalities.

2. (a) What is the object of the contest that the two are involved in? **(b)** Who wins? Explain.

3. The story in this poem is really a fable—a tale involving animals or things as characters and told to convey a lesson or moral. **(a)** Which line states the moral of this poem? **(b)** How does the moral relate to the action of the story?

A Poison Tree

1. What does the first stanza suggest about the nature of unexpressed anger?

2. (a) What is the "it" referred to in the second and third stanzas? **(b)** How does this "it" tie in with the title of the poem? **(c)** What is the connection between the apple and the speaker's foe?

The Man Who Spilled Light

1. (a) Why was the man carrying light in the first place? **(b)** How did it look when it spilled?

2. (a) After the man spilled light, people "lined up with their backs to walls." Explain. **(b)** Then they began squinting. Why?

3. What might the story in this poem mean if the light stood for truth?

Application 

Narrative Poetry

As you have seen, story or narrative poems can be of various types. Discuss the following.

1. In your opinion, which poem in this section sounds most like a narrative should? Explain. Which other poems tell complete stories?

2. Narratives can also express emotions. What emotion is expressed in "My Father & The Figtree"? in "The Stone"?

3. What specifics might you use to flesh out the story in "A Poison Tree"? in "The Man Who Spilled Light"?

Rhythm, Rhyme

Rhythm and rhyme are two of the most common devices in poetry, but there are many variations in how they are used. For instance, though all poems have rhythm, that rhythm may or may not be the kind that falls into a regular metrical pattern. Similarly, rhyme may occur in a regular, easy-to-identify rhyme scheme or a more subtle one—or it may not be present in a poem at all.

1. Identify the meter in "The Stone" and "A Poison Tree." In which poem does the number of feet per line vary more? Give examples.

2. What is the rhyme scheme of stanzas 1 and 2 of "A Poison Tree"? of stanza 2 of "The Stone"?

3. Do "Phoebus and Boreas" and "My Father & The Figtree" contain recognizable metrical patterns? Does either use rhyme? Explain.

Vocabulary

Context

The numbered sentences in the paragraph below contain italicized words that don't make sense in context. Check the Glossary for the meanings of the words; then write the word that best fits the context of each sentence.

1. An air of excited anticipation seemed to *wrath* over the spectators. **2.** The opposing players had lost bitterly to our hockey team in last season's championship game, but we felt prepared to deal with their *naught.* **3.** Our star goalie, whose ability to catch flying pucks is amazing, was said to have more *chagrin* than theirs. **4.** He blocked countless shots throughout the game, but his valiant efforts were all for *waft.* **5.** Much to the *dexterity* of the home crowd, the opposing left wing slapshot the winning goal past him.

Naomi Shihab 1952–

Naomi Shihab was born in St. Louis and now lives in San Antonio. She participates there in the "poets-in-the-schools" program. She has published several books of poetry, including *Eye-to-Eye* (1978), *Different Ways to Pray* (1980), and *Hugging the Jukebox* (1982).

Wilfrid Wilson Gibson 1878–1962

Gibson was a prolific poet who began as a romantic verse-writer and turned, in midstream, to become a poet of the people. His origins, Hexham, in the north of England, gave him the background to write about nature and country people; yet he first wrote about knights and historical characters. In 1910, his book *Daily Bread* turned to everyday life, and thereafter he concerned himself with that subject.

William Blake 1757–1827

Blake's only formal education was in art. He studied in London, his birthplace, and at fourteen was apprenticed as an engraver. At this time he also began writing verse. He is best known for his poetry collections *Songs of Innocence* (1789) and *Songs of Experience* (1794), which he also illustrated with watercolor-painted engravings. Virtually unknown in his lifetime, Blake was recognized as an artistic and poetic genius only in the twentieth century.

La Fontaine 1621–1695

La Fontaine grew up in the French countryside but spent most of his adult life in Paris. A learned man, he did translations as well as wrote poetry and fiction. But his fame rests on his *Fables,* tales adapted not only from the Greek stories of Aesop but also from later collections done in other cultures. Volumes of his fables appeared in 1668, 1678, and 1694.

David Wagoner 1926–

Wagoner was born in Ohio and went to school at Pennsylvania State University and Indiana University. He has been characterized as a nature poet since many of his poems are given natural settings; his characters also display a strong sense of self-reliance. He has published several volumes of poems, including *A Place to Stand* (1958), *Staying Alive* (1966), and *In Broken Country* (1979). He teaches at the University of Washington in Seattle.

Portraits

Poems often depict characters—characters who make us angry, make us think, make us wonder, make us laugh, or maybe even make us cry. . . .

See **LYRIC** Handbook of Literary Terms

Who Is Silvia?

William Shakespeare Great Britain

Who is Silvia? what is she,
  That all our swains commend her?
Holy, fair, and wise is she;
  The heaven such grace did lend her,
That she might admired be.

Is she kind as she is fair?
  For beauty lives with kindness:
Love doth to her eyes repair
  To help him of his blindness;
And being help'd, inhabits there.

Then to Silvia let us sing
  That Silvia is excelling;
She excels each mortal thing
  Upon the dull earth dwelling.
To her let us garlands bring.

See **FIGURATIVE LANGUAGE** Handbook of Literary Terms

Those Winter Sundays

Robert Hayden USA

Sundays too my father got up early
and put his clothes on in the blueblack cold,
then with cracked hands that ached
from labor in the weekday weather made
banked fires blaze. No one ever thanked him.

I'd wake and hear the cold splintering, breaking.
When the rooms were warm, he'd call,
and slowly I would rise and dress,
fearing the chronic angers of that house,

Speaking indifferently to him,
who had driven out the cold
and polished my good shoes as well.
What did I know, what did I know
of love's austere and lonely offices?

William Shakespeare, "Who Is Silvia?" from Act Four, Scene 2 of *Two Gentlemen of Verona*.

To Julia de Burgos

Julia de Burgos Puerto Rico

The word is out that I am your enemy
that in my poetry I am giving you away.

They lie, Julia de Burgos. They lie, Julia de Burgos.
That voice that rises in my poems is not yours: it is my voice;
you are the covering and I the essence;
and between us lies the deepest chasm.

You are the frigid doll of social falsehood,
and I, the virile sparkle of human truth.

You are honey of courtly hypocrisy, not I;
I bare my heart in all my poems.

You are selfish, like your world, not I;
I gamble everything to be what I am.

You are but the grave lady, ladylike;
not I; I am life, and strength, and I am woman.

You belong to your husband, your master, not I;
I belong to no one or to everyone, because to all, to all
I give myself in pure feelings and in my thoughts.

Your curl your hair, and paint your face, not I;
I am curled by the wind, painted by the sun.

You are lady of the house, resigned and meek,
tied to the prejudices of men, not I;
smelling the horizons of the justice of God.
I am Rocinante,[1] running headlong.

---

1. ***Rocinante*** (rô THē nän′te), the broken-down but spirited horse of Don Quixote (don ki hō′tē) in the classic Spanish novel of the same name.

"To Julia de Burgos" by Julia de Burgos, translated by Maria Arrillaga, 1971. Reprinted by permission of Maria Consuelo Saez Burgos.

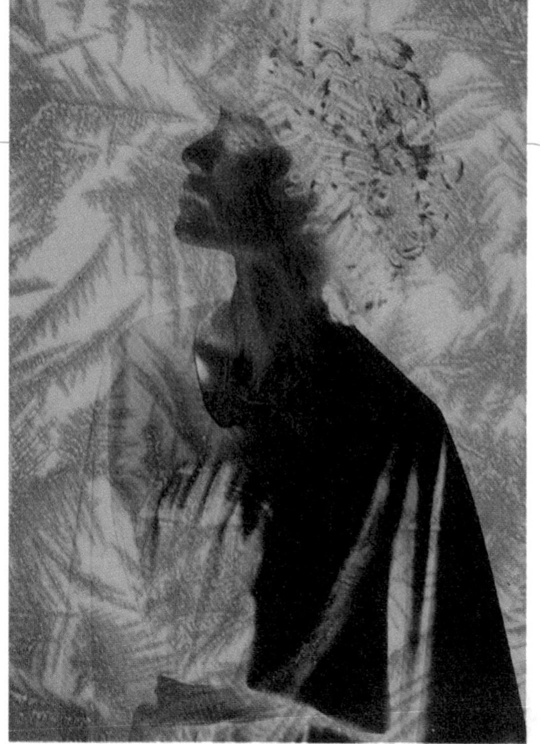

Comment: The Speaker and the Poet

Poems often portray someone speaking in the first person—"I"—and readers often wonder whether the "I" is really the poet speaking. The answer is complicated, as is evident in "To Julia de Burgos."

A close reading of this poem reveals that Julia de Burgos is thinking of herself as double. The speaker in the poem, the "I," is separated from the living Julia de Burgos by the "deepest chasm." The latter is possessed by the social world, her husband, and the demands of everyday life; the former belongs to "no one or to everyone," and is free to deal in truth and bare her heart. Thus the poem demonstrates a truth about all poetry—that the speaker in the poem, even when mentioned by name as the same person as the writer, is different from the living author in many subtle ways. No absolute identification can necessarily be made between the two.

In many poems, of course, there is little reason to confuse the speaker and the writer. A work like Wilfrid Wilson Gibson's "The Stone," for example, has a speaker—the stonecutter—who has clearly been created by the writer for a dramatic role in the poem. But in poems like Naomi Shihab's "My Father & The Figtree," the author may seem to be speaking in her own voice. Yet even if she is doing so, she is presenting only one aspect of herself—her role in relation to her father—and is no doubt shaping and thus in some sense inventing that aspect of herself.

When going through collections of poems by the same poet, as you yourself will do later in this unit, a reader can often detect a "voice" that runs through many poems, giving them the poet's personal stamp. There may be, for example, characteristic patterns of speech, thought, and style that help the reader identify the writer even when no by-line is provided. But it is still best not to assume that the "I" in any poem is the same "I" speaking in the writer's other poems or that this "I" can be matched with facts in the author's biography. The American poet Emily Dickinson once said in a letter to a critic, "When I state myself, as the representative of the verse, it does not mean me, but a supposed person."

We may assume that all poets would caution readers in similar ways: the "I" in the poem is a "supposed person." It is, of course, all right to refer to this "I," when it seems to be the author's voice, by the author's name—as long as it is understood that it encompasses only the author's identity as portrayed in this poem. To avoid confusion, it may be better to identify "I" simply as "the speaker."

See **HYPERBOLE** Handbook of Literary Terms

For Anne Gregory

William Butler Yeats Ireland

"Never shall a young man,
Thrown into despair
By those great honey-coloured
Ramparts at your ear,
Love you for yourself alone
And not your yellow hair."

"But I can get a hair-dye
And set such colour there,
Brown, or black, or carrot,
That young men in despair
May love me for myself alone
And not my yellow hair."

"I heard an old religious man
But yesternight declare
That he had found a text to prove
That only God, my dear,
Could love you for yourself alone
And not your yellow hair."

Going Blind

Rainer Maria Rilke Germany

She sat quite like the others there at tea.
It seemed to me at first she grasped her cup
a little differently from the rest.
Once she gave a smile. It almost hurt.

And when people finally stood up and spoke
and slowly and as chance brought it about
moved through many rooms (they talked and
laughed),
I saw her. She was moving after the others,

withheld, as one who in a moment
will have to sing and before many people;
upon her bright eyes, that rejoiced,
was light from outside as upon a pool.

She followed slowly, taking a long time,
as though something had not yet been
surmounted;
and yet as though, after a crossing over,
she would no longer walk, but fly.

William Butler Yeats (yāts).

Rainer Maria Rilke (rī′nər mä rē′ä ril′kə).

Yevgeny Yevtushenko (yef gyā′nē yef′tü shen′kō).

See **ASSONANCE** Handbook of Literary Terms

Schoolmaster

Yevgeny Yevtushenko USSR

The window gives onto the white trees.
The master looks out of it at the trees,
for a long time, he looks for a long time
out through the window at the trees,
breaking his chalk slowly in one hand.
And it's only the rules of long division.
And he's forgotten the rules of long division.
Imagine not remembering long division!
A mistake on the blackboard, a mistake.
We watch him with a different attention
needing no one to hint to us about it,
there's more than difference in this attention.
The schoolmaster's wife has gone away,
we do not know where she has gone to,
we do not know why she has gone,
what we know is his wife has gone away.

His clothes are neither new nor in the fashion;
wearing the suit which he always wears
and which is neither new nor in the fashion
the master goes downstairs to the cloakroom.
He fumbles in his pocket for a ticket.
"What's the matter? Where is that ticket?
Perhaps I never picked up my ticket.
Where is the thing?" Rubbing his forehead.
"Oh, here it is. I'm getting old.
Don't argue auntie dear, I'm getting old.
You can't do much about getting old."
We hear the door below creaking behind him.

The window gives onto the white trees.
The trees there are high and wonderful,
but they are not why we are looking out.
We look in silence at the schoolmaster.
He has a bent back and clumsy walk,
he moves without defenses, clumsily,
worn out I ought to have said, clumsily.
Snow falling on him softly through silence
turns him to white under the white trees.
He whitens into white like the trees.
A little longer will make him so white
we shall not see him in the whitened trees.

The Crazy Woman

Gwendolyn Brooks USA

I shall not sing a May song.
A May song should be gay.
I'll wait until November
And sing a song of gray.

I'll wait until November.
That is the time for me.
I'll go out in the frosty dark
And sing most terribly.

And all the little people
Will stare at me and say,
"That is the Crazy Woman
Who would not sing in May."

Wood sculpture by Chris Carsten (1863–1956).

Almost an Epigram

Salvatore Quasimodo Italy

The contortionist in the bar, a gypsy
and a melancholy fellow, got up abruptly
from a corner and put on a rapid
scene. He threw off his coat and in his coarse
red sweater, bent over backwards
and like a dog he seized a dirty handkerchief
between his teeth. The shirtless bridge
performed the act twice over, then bowed
with his plastic plate. With his
ferret's eyes, he wished good luck
in the lottery, and disappeared.
Atomic civilization at its apex.

Salvatore Quasimodo (säl vä tô′rā kwä zē′mō dō).

Discussion

Who Is Silvia?

1. Line 3 suggests different kinds of beauty Silvia possesses. If "fair" means she is beautiful physically, what sorts of beauty do "holy" and "wise" attribute to her?

2. (a) If, as the saying goes, "Love is blind," why does Love "repair," or go, to Silvia? **(b)** What does this say about the quality of Silvia's love?

Those Winter Sundays

1. (a) What does the word "too" in line 1 tell you? **(b)** Why do you think "no one ever thanked him"?

2. (a) What do phrases like "fearing the chronic angers" and "speaking indifferently to him" tell about the speaker's attitude toward his father? **(b)** How do the last two lines suggest his attitude has changed?

3. This poem is a portrait of the speaker's father, but it tells something about the son as well. What impression do you get of each character?

To Julia de Burgos

1. Two Julia de Burgoses appear in the poem, one speaking and one being addressed. Which is which? Discuss.

2. The speaker says to the living Julia, "You are the covering and I the essence." Explain how this generalization relates to the rest of the poem and its meaning.

3. The speaker seems angry with the living Julia. Is her attitude fair? Why or why not?

For Anne Gregory

1. This poem is a dialogue. Who seems to be speaking in stanza 1? in stanza 2?

2. Look up *ramparts* in the Glossary. In what way might the speaker's hair look like "honey-coloured ramparts"?

3. (a) What opinion is presented in stanza 1? **(b)** What added twist is given to that opinion in stanza 3?

Going Blind

1. (a) What movements does the woman make that suggest to the speaker that she might be losing her sight? **(b)** Do you think these movements are noticed by the others she is with? Discuss.

2. In what way are lines 11–12 an apt description of how the eyes of a blind person might appear?

3. What seems to be the woman's attitude toward her approaching blindness? Give examples to support your answer.

Schoolmaster

1. (a) Who is speaking in this poem? **(b)** In your opinion, what perspectives do we get from this speaker that we might not get from one closer in age to the schoolmaster?

2. Find examples showing each of the following characteristics of the schoolmaster: **(a)** absent-minded; **(b)** out-of-date; **(c)** aging.

3. (a) What feelings does the speaker seem to have about the schoolmaster? **(b)** What feelings do *you* have for him? Discuss.

The Crazy Woman

1. Why does the speaker decide to sing not a May song but a song of November?

2. Does this decision necessarily mean she is crazy? Why or why not?

Almost an Epigram

1. Describe the contortionist and his act.

2. (a) What is an "apex"? **(b)** Is line 12 simply a comment on the contortionist's act? Discuss.

3. Check the meaning of *epigram* in the Glossary; then explain the title.

Application

Lyric

Because it is actually a song from a play, "Who Is Silvia?" expresses not so much the poet's direct feelings as those of the character in the play who sings or speaks the lines.

1. What emotion is that character expressing?

2. Which other poems in this section would you classify as lyrics? Discuss.

Figurative Language

It is fairly easy to spot figurative language that makes or suggests a clear comparison between two unlike things. Less obvious, however, are figurative expressions containing only a noun and a modifier, in which unlike qualities are subtly combined.

1. How can "cold" be "blueblack," as described in line 2 of "Those Winter Sundays"? Does the time of day mentioned help you understand the comparison? Discuss.

2. What subtle comparison is suggested by the figurative description of cold in line 6 of the same poem?

3. In line 7 of "Almost an Epigram," who or what is the "shirtless bridge"? Explain the comparison suggested by the words.

Hyperbole

Hyperbole, a specific type of figurative language, is particularly effective when it changes the reader's overall reaction to a piece of writing. Identify the hyperbole in "For Anne Gregory," and explain how it affects the general feeling the poem communicates.

Assonance

The style used in "Schoolmaster" involves repetition of certain words and phrases. In the last few lines this repetitive quality is expanded to include assonance as well.

1. What vowel sound is dominant in lines 36–39?

2. Do you think the repetition of this sound adds to the effectiveness of what is being described? If so, in what way?

William Shakespeare 1564–1616

(See biography on page 455.)

Robert Hayden 1913–1980

Born and raised in the Detroit area, Hayden later taught at both the University of Michigan and Fisk University in Nashville. He received little early recognition for his poetry, but beginning in the 1960s he won several awards, including a National Book Award in 1971 for his collection *Words in the Mourning Time.* Though Hayden's writing frequently reflects his black heritage, it often extends far beyond it, revealing his love and compassion for all humanity.

Julia de Burgos 1914–1953

The oldest of thirteen children, Julia de Burgos was born in Carolina, Puerto Rico, and educated at the University of Puerto Rico. She published her first book in 1938, taught briefly at the University of Havana, and in 1940 came to the United States, where she suffered from bouts of illness and poverty. She died there, virtually unknown as a poet. Since her death, her poetic force has been recognized, and her *Collected Works* appeared in 1961.

William Butler Yeats 1865–1939

Yeats was born of Anglo-Irish parents in Dublin, and at an early age began to write poetry. Moving frequently between London and Dublin in the 1890s, he published a number of volumes during that time, including many poems influenced by his study of Irish folklore. He helped found the famous Abbey Theatre in Dublin in 1904 and for a time concentrated on writing plays, but turned again to poetry as he grew older, writing much about the frustrations of aging. In 1923, when at the height of his poetic powers, he was awarded the Nobel Prize for Literature.

Rainer Maria Rilke 1875–1926

One of the greatest German poets, Rilke was born in Prague (now in Czechoslovakia) of German parents. Dedicating himself to poetry at an early age, he was able to travel widely and learn from other writers: the Russian novelist Tolstoy, for example, imparted to him the concept of "spiritual openness." Rilke's poems are filled with mystical insights and sometimes display intricate symbolism. Among his best-known works are *Sonnets to Orpheus* (1923) and *Duino Elegies* (1923).

Yevgeny Yevtushenko 1933–

Yevtushenko's poetry is distinctive in the ease with which it moves from the personal realm to the public. Sometimes called a "middle-brow" writer because of his mass appeal, his poetry readings have drawn huge crowds both in Russia and the West. He was born in remote Zima, a place that has figured prominently in his poetry. His first book of poems, *Prospects of the Future,* was published in 1952. Soviet authorities have criticized him for his candor about Russian life, but his popularity has only increased.

Gwendolyn Brooks 1917–

Although she was born in Topeka, Kansas, Brooks grew up in Chicago and identifies closely with the city in her poetry. She published her first book of poems, *A Street in Bronzeville,* and in 1950 won a Pulitzer Prize for *Annie Allen.* In 1968, she was named Poet Laureate of Illinois. Her poetry is vivid in both diction and image, often evoking a slum apartment or street scene in a few short lines. A collection of her work appeared in 1971, entitled *The World of Gwendolyn Brooks.*

Salvatore Quasimodo 1901–1968

Quasimodo was born in Sicily and trained as an engineer, but gave up engineering for his real love—literature. His first book of poems, *Waters and Lands,* appeared in 1930, and many volumes followed, including *The Incomparable Earth* (1958). His early poetry is often difficult, but the brutalities of World War II brought a deeper human concern into his writing. In 1959, Quasimodo was awarded the Nobel Prize for Literature.

All Creatures

Some poems turn to the animal world and find there perplexing mysteries—and even wit and wisdom—in all creatures, great and small. . . .

The Zoo

Stevie Smith Great Britain

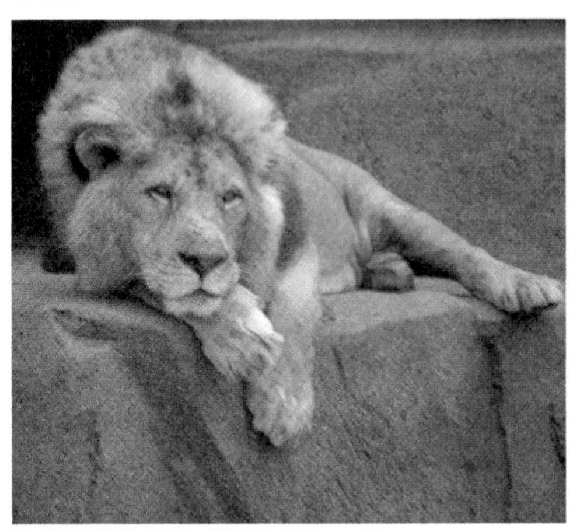

The lion sits within his cage,
Weeping tears of ruby rage,
He licks his snout, the tears fall down
And water dusty London town.

He does not like you, little boy,
It's no use making up to him,
He does not like you any more
Than he likes Nurse, or Baby Jim.

Nor would you do if you were he,
And he were you, for dont you see
God gave him lovely teeth and claws
So that he might eat little boys.

So that he might
In anger slay
The little lambs
That skip and play
Pounce down upon their placid dams[1]
And make dams flesh to pad his hams.

So that he might
Appal the night
With crunching bones
And awful groans
Of antelope and buffalo,
And the unwary hunter whose "Hallo"
Tells us his life is over here below.
There's none to help him, fear inspired,
Who shouts because his gun misfired.

All this the lion sees, and pants
Because he knows the hot sun slants
Between the rancid jungle-grass,
Which never more shall part to let him pass
Down to the jungle drinking-hole,
Whither the zebra comes with her sleek foal.

The sun is hot by day and has his swink,[2]
And sops up sleepy lions' and tigers' stink,
But not this lion's stink, poor carnivore,
He's on the shady shelf for ever more.

His claws are blunt, his teeth fall out,
No victim's flesh consoles his snout,
And that is why his eyes are red
Considering his talents are misusèd.

---

1. ***dams,*** the female parents of the sheep.
2. ***swink,*** an archaic term for labor or toil. [*British*]

See **FREE VERSE** Handbook of Literary Terms

Porcupine Fish

Raquel Chalfi Israel

Apparently a fish like you and me.
But there is something nail-like about him.

Slowly he glides,
examining himself in that great mirror called water
and asking why,
why these nails planted in his flesh,
why this need for endless wariness
that sharpens him, keeps him from being one
with the blue enfolding softness.

And then
the waters breathe,
something moves,
something alien perhaps,
certainly malign.
His spines bristle.
He turns into something else—
a swollen ball,
a small mountain of fear—
all roar, if one could hear.
His mouth—small, tight, rectangular—
distorts into a smile.
And his eyes, tiny pools in a suddenly vast forehead,
whirl violent images in his brain.

This time, however,
it was nothing really.

And he subsides
into the rigid destiny
of his nail-like self.

See **ALLITERATION** Handbook of Literary Terms

A *Parrot*

May Sarton USA

My parrot is emerald green,
His tail feathers, marine.
He bears an orange half-moon
Over his ivory beak.
He must be believed to be seen,
This bird from a Rousseau[1] wood.
When the urge is on him to speak,
He becomes too true to be good.

He uses his beak like a hook
To lift himself up with or break
Open a sunflower seed,
And his eye, in a bold white ring,
Has a lapidary look.
What a most astonishing bird,
Whose voice when he chooses to sing
Must be believed to be heard.

That stuttered staccato scream
Must be believed not to seem
The shriek of a witch in the room.
But he murmurs some muffled words
(Like someone who talks through a dream)
When he sits in the window and sees
The to-and-fro wings of wild birds
In the leafless improbable trees.

1. ***Rousseau*** (rü sō′), French primitive painter Henri Rousseau, 1844–1910, who painted jungle scenes in vivid colors.

See **ONOMATOPOEIA** Handbook of Literary Terms

Cheers

Eve Merriam USA

The frogs and the serpents each had a football team,
and I heard their cheer leaders in my dream:

"Bilgewater, bilgewater," called the frog,
"Bilgewater, bilgewater,
Sis, boom, bog!
Roll 'em off the log,
Slog 'em in the sog,
Swamp 'em, swamp 'em
Muck mire quash!"

"Sisyphus, Sisyphus,"[1] hissed the snake,
"Sibilant, syllabub,
Syllable-loo-ba-lay.
Scylla and Charybdis,[2]
Sumac, asphodel,
How do you spell Success?
With an S-S-S!"

1. ***Sisyphus*** (sis′ə fəs), a king in Greek myth.
2. ***Scylla*** (sil′ə), ***Charybdis*** (kə rib′dis), a dangerous rock on and whirlpool near the tip of Italy, respectively.

The Naming of Cats

T. S. Eliot Great Britain

The Naming of Cats is a difficult matter,
  It isn't just one of your holiday games;
You may think at first I'm as mad as a hatter
When I tell you, a cat must have THREE DIFFERENT NAMES.
First of all, there's the name that the family use daily,
  Such as Peter, Augustus, Alonzo or James,
Such as Victor or Jonathan, George or Bill Bailey—
  All of them sensible everyday names.
There are fancier names if you think they sound sweeter,
  Some for the gentlemen, some for the dames:
Such as Plato, Admetus, Electra, Demeter[1]—
  But all of them sensible everyday names.
But I tell you, a cat needs a name that's particular,
  A name that's peculiar, and more dignified,
Else how can he keep up his tail perpendicular,
  Or spread out his whiskers, or cherish his pride?
Of names of this kind, I can give you a quorum,
  Such as Munkustrap, Quaxo, or Coricopat,
Such as Bombalurina, or else Jellylorum[2]—
  Names that never belong to more than one cat.
But above and beyond there's still one name left over,
  And that is the name that you never will guess;
The name that no human research can discover—
  But THE CAT HIMSELF KNOWS, and will never confess.
When you notice a cat in profound meditation,
  The reason, I tell you, is always the same:
His mind is engaged in a rapt contemplation
  Of the thought, of the thought, of the thought of his name:
    His ineffable effable
    Effanineffable[3]
Deep and inscrutable singular Name.

---

1. ***Plato . . . Demeter,*** names from Greek history or mythology.
2. ***Munkustrap . . . Jellylorum,*** names made up by the poet.
3. ***effanineffable,*** a made-up word combining *effable* and *ineffable.*

Discussion

The Zoo

1. The speaker is explaining the facts of animal life to a little boy. What do you suppose the boy has been doing before the poem begins?

2. What does the speaker say that might frighten the little boy?

3. What is the lion's present condition? Is he really a threat? Explain.

Porcupine Fish

1. (a) How does the point of view in this poem change after the first two lines? **(b)** What might have been the poet's purpose in making this change?

2. (a) What makes the fish frightened? **(b)** Does this fear surprise you, considering that the fish is, in fact, armed? Discuss.

3. In the final stanza, does "rigid destiny" refer only to the makeup of the fish's body, or to its total existence as well? Explain.

A Parrot

1. The first few lines in each stanza focus on a different aspect of the parrot. What does each group of lines emphasize?

2. The last line of stanza 1 appears to reverse a usual saying: "too good to be true." **(a)** Does the reversal make sense? Explain. **(b)** Find other similar reversals in the poem and discuss whether they have any particular meaning.

3. In stanza 3, what is the parrot likely to be thinking or murmuring about as it looks out the window?

4. (a) Which two stanzas use a similar rhyme scheme? **(b)** What is that rhyme scheme?

Cheers

1. In general, how do the sounds in stanzas 2 and 3 differ from each other?

2. What do you think the author's intent was in writing this poem?

The Naming of Cats

1. What is the nature of the first two names the speaker says a cat needs?

2. (a) What purpose does the third name serve? **(b)** Does the description of how cats react to this name correspond with what you know about cats' habits? Discuss.

3. What, in your opinion, is added to this poem by the use of rhyme?

Application

Free Verse

Using free verse allows a poet to vary line length to create certain effects.

1. Explain how the lines in stanza 3 of "Porcupine Fish" are set up to develop suspense.

2. What other free-verse poems have you read in this unit? Choose one, and explain why you think its free-verse form is preferable to a more rigid structure.

Alliteration, Onomatopoeia

Though onomatopoeia is generally more closely related to the meaning of a piece of writing than alliteration is, both are devices used to make sound more interesting.

1. Find three examples of alliteration in "A Parrot." Select one that you think has an effect on the meaning, and explain what that effect is.

2. The second stanza of "Cheers" contains both alliteration and onomatopoeia. Explain how one device reinforces the other.

Vocabulary

Etymology

Some words came into English through several different languages, others through several forms in one language. In an etymology the symbol [<], meaning "derived from," is placed before each source of the word. The most recent source is listed first and the earliest source last.

Check the Glossary for the etymologies of the italicized words that follow to determine if the statements in which they appear are true or false. On your paper write "T" after the number of each true statement and correct each false one.

1. *Quorum* comes from an Italian word.

2. The original source for *lapidary* is "stone."

3. *Foal* is derived from an Old English word.

4. In its original language *staccato* means "detached."

5. The original source of *inscrutable* is Late Latin.

Stevie Smith 1902–1971

Her real name was Florence Margaret Smith, but she adopted her nickname "Stevie" for her poetry. Born in Yorkshire, England, she began working at a publishing house soon after high school and lived all her life with an aunt. Her first book of poems, *A Good Time Was Had by All,* appeared in 1937, and others followed, including what is probably her best known, *Not Waving But Drowning,* in 1957. Hers is a warm and witty, sometimes sharp and incisive, poetic voice.

Raquel Chalfi 1923–

Raquel Chalfi currently teaches at the University of Tel Aviv, Israel. Her academic field is film and television, and she has written film documentaries and plays. "Porcupine Fish" was taken from her book *Submarine and Other Poems.*

May Sarton 1912–

Sarton was born in Belgium but came to the United States with her father, who was appointed to teach history of science at Harvard. The author of over thirty volumes of fiction, autobiography, and poetry, her books of poems include *Encounter in April* (1937) and *Cloud, Stone, Sun, Vine* (1961). Her poems tend to portray private moments, but they can also comment on public events. Many, like "A Parrot," derive from meticulous, penetrating observation.

Eve Merriam 1916–

Merriam has written advertising copy, radio scripts, newspaper and magazine columns, and she has lectured to various audiences. But she is probably best known for her poetry. Among her recent books is *Growing Up Female in America.*

A devoted outdoorswoman, she keeps fit through walking, biking, and skating.

T. S. Eliot 1888–1965

Eliot was born in St. Louis, but went to England when World War I broke out and lived there for the rest of his life, becoming a British citizen in 1927. He had begun to write poetry while a student at Harvard, including the famous "The Love Song of J. Alfred Prufrock." His great poem *The Waste Land,* expressing the acute modern feeling of futility, appeared in 1922. Though Eliot's poetry was generally serious, there were always comic or absurd elements in it. In 1939 he published an entire volume of light verse about cats, which was the basis of the Broadway musical *Cats* and from which "The Naming of Cats" is taken. In 1948 he received the Nobel Prize for Literature.

Landscapes

Sometimes a poet finds a landscape that inspires a poem. The landscape can be any scene in any place—in the mountains, the city, the farmlands, even the back lot of a hospital. . . .

Improved Farm Land

Carl Sandburg USA

Tall timber stood here once, here on a corn belt farm along the Monon.[1]
Here the roots of a half mile of trees dug their runners deep
in the loam for a grip and a hold against wind storms.
Then the axmen came and the chips flew to the zing of steel and handle—
the lank railsplitters cut the big ones first, the beeches and
the oaks, then the brush.
Dynamite, wagons and horses took the stumps—the plows sunk their teeth in—
now it is first class corn land—improved property—and the hogs
grunt over the fodder crops.
It would come hard now for this half mile of improved farm land along
the Monon corn belt, on a piece of Grand Prairie, to remember
once it had a great singing family of trees.

1. ***Monon,*** the Monon Railroad runs in a generally north-south direction through western Indiana.

See **IMAGERY** Handbook of Literary Terms

Drought

Oumar Ba Senegal

The frail scorched grasses are stripped now
Of their green hues and compared to the
Hot sun. The evil dryness poisons the heart
Of the unconquerable branching rivers and
The harsh shriveling winds burrow under ground,
Muddied with filth—the forest next,
Now birds give up their songs, and the dug-out
Canoes are lodged in the banks of sand.
Now the somber salvation from dryness,
A time of gaiety, celebration, but
Stripped of its leaves and useful shrubs,
Nature, after the moist sorrow of the
Fatal loss, weeps like a mother
Bereft of her children, the adornments.
Parched with thirst, the whole tribe of birds,
Song ravaged by unending drought,
Strength pillaged by pain—the tumult dies
Now the somber salvation from dryness,
The natural fatality of existence.

Alpine Afternoon

Giosuè Carducci

Italy

In the great circle of the Alps, over granite
Bleak and drab, over glaciers brightly glowing,
Rules serene, intense and infinite
In its immense silence the noon of day.

Pines and firs, not a gust of wind blowing,
Stand erect in the penetrating sunlight;
One hears the lyre-like prattle only, ever so slight,
Of water that among stones thinly made its way.

See **SIMILE** Handbook of Literary Terms

Sunset

Mbuyiseni Oswald Mtshali

South Africa

The sun spun like
a tossed coin.
It whirled on the azure sky,
it clattered into the horizon,
it clicked in the slot,
and neon-lights popped
and blinked "Time expired,"
as on a parking meter.

Giosuè Carducci (jyō sü ā′ kär dü′chē).

Afterglow

Jorge Luis Borges

Argentina

Sunset is always disturbing
whether theatrical or muted,
but still more disturbing
is that last desperate glow
that turns the plain to rust
when on the horizon nothing is left
of the pomp and clamor of the setting sun.
How hard holding on to that light, so tautly drawn and different,
that hallucination which the human fear of the dark
imposes on space
and which ceases at once
the moment we realize its falsity,
the way a dream is broken
the moment the sleeper knows he is dreaming.

Jorge Luis Borges (hôr'hā lü ēs' bôr'hes).

Comment: The Art of Translation 1

There are some who believe poetry cannot be successfully translated. The American poet Robert Frost, for instance, once said that poetry was what got *lost* in translation.

It is true that certain elements of poetry may cause problems for a less-than-skillful translator. A good many poems, as you have seen, contain figurative language; to translate it literally would in many cases render the translated poem ridiculous. Beyond this, however, there is the question of what even literally used words mean. People who share a language as a mother tongue in a particular period of history share more than simple definitions of words. They also share feelings that words arouse because of the aura of emotion that builds up around them. This aura of emotion is likely to fade away in translation—unless it can be captured in new ways by the imaginative translator.

A literal translation, then, may give us what the poet really said, but not necessarily what he or she really meant. And, in fact, the literal translation is the one most likely to lose the poetic quality as well—the rhythm, the harmony of sounds, the imagery.

Thus, an imaginative translator of poetry is in effect a poet. (Think of the poetic devices used in some of the translated works you have read so far.) Such a translator can re-create the poem in the new language so that it approximates (*not* duplicates) the effect of the poem in its original words. This process may leave the literal translation far behind—in order to reproduce something in the nature of, but not exactly like, the original in sound and sense.

The following are two English translations of the opening lines of "Mi Prima Agueda" ("My Cousin Agueda") by Mexican poet Ramón López Velarde, one by Willis Knapp Jones, the other by Cheli Duran. Each is in some parts literal, in others beyond-the-literal; one adds rhyme not in the original. By comparing the versions, you can see how differently two translators interpret the same poetic lines.

My Cousin Agueda

My godmother often invited my cousin Agueda
To come and spend the day.
My cousin used to arrive
Appearing in a mixed-up way,
Suggesting starch and fearful
Mourning of a funereal day.

Agueda would appear rustling
With starch, and with her eyes green,

And her rosy cheeks
Protecting me against the mourning
That I'd seen.

I was a kid
And knew nothing at all,
And Agueda, who was moving
Tamely and persistently in the hall,
With her rustling brought excitement
About which I knew nothing at all.

(I even think she is responsible
For my mad habit of talking to myself.)

My Cousin Agatha

to Jesús Villalpando

My godmother used to ask my cousin Agatha
to spend the day with us,
and my cousin used to arrive
wrapped in a contradictory magic
of starch and odious ritual
mourning.

Agatha entered, rustling
starch, and her green eyes
and warm red cheeks
protected me from the dreadful
black. . .
I was only a child
who knew the O by its roundness,
and Agatha, who knitted
mildly, persistently, in the echoing corridor,
sent little unknown shivers
up my spine.

(I think I owe her, too, my crazy
but heroic habit of talking alone.)

See **METAPHOR** Handbook of Literary Terms

Water Picture

May Swenson USA

In the pond in the park
all things are doubled:
Long buildings hang and
wriggle gently. Chimneys
are bent legs bouncing
on clouds below. A flag
wags like a fishhook
down there in the sky.

The arched stone bridge
is an eye, with underlid
in the water. In its lens
dip crinkled heads with hats
that don't fall off. Dogs go by,
barking on their backs.
A baby, taken to feed the
ducks, dangles upside-down,
a pink balloon for a buoy.

Treetops deploy a haze of
cherry bloom for roots,
where birds coast belly-up
in the glass bowl of a hill;
from its bottom a bunch
of peanut-munching children
is suspended by their
sneakers, waveringly.

A swan, with twin necks
forming the figure three,
steers between two dimpled
towers doubled. Fondly
hissing, she kisses herself,
and all the scene is troubled:
water-windows splinter,
tree-limbs tangle, the bridge
folds like a fan.

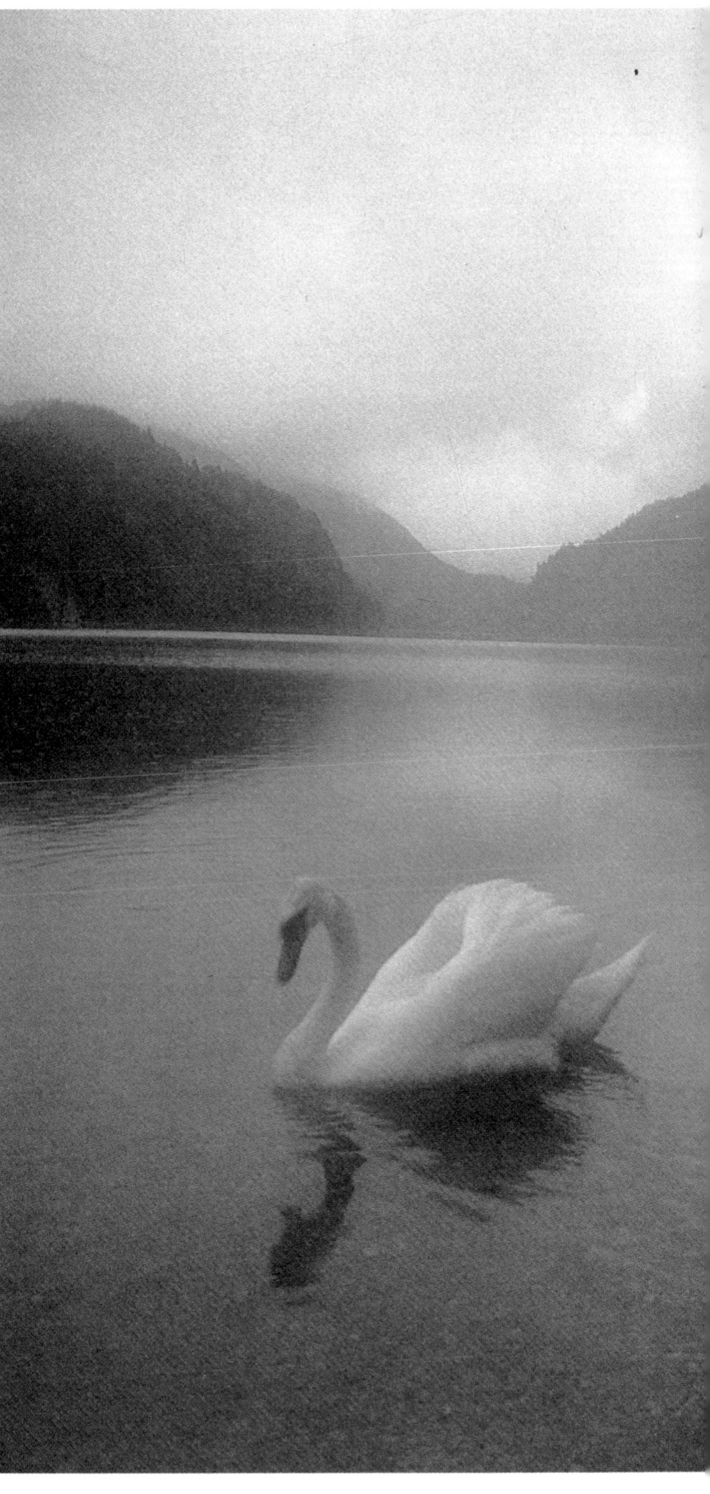

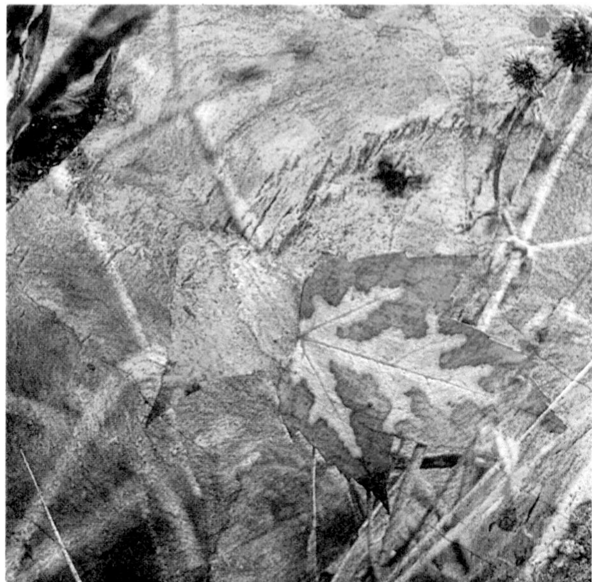

See **PERSONIFICATION** Handbook of Literary Terms

Wind

Suyama Hisayo Japan

Tree leaves—where are they going, scuffling
Along the endless road,
Dragging their dry crackling steps
Driven onwards by the gales of wind?

Despite the breath of spring
The chill sound strikes at
The secret heart of earth, that is breaking, but
Obstinately refuses to give a sign of life.

In swirling wind, black raindrops vainly
Catch at the old throat with dry coughings
Till trembling water-splashes weep in darkness.

Driven by the gale, they keep shuffling
Feeble feet along the earth in the drenched dark,
Keep playing their eerie tune in
Endless whirlpools of vexed anxiety.

Suyama Hisayo (sü yä′mä hē sä′yō).

Between Walls

William Carlos Williams USA

the back wings
of the

hospital where
nothing

will grow lie
cinders

in which shine
the broken

pieces of a green
bottle

Discussion

Improved Farm Land

1. In general, how would you characterize the actions of the axmen; the dynamite, wagons, and horses; and the plows?

2. The speaker imagines what this landscape was like before it became a farm. Why does he entitle the poem "Improved Farm Land" instead of "Great Singing Family of Trees"?

Drought

1. How does the sequence of descriptions in the first eight lines present a widening pattern of devastation?

2. **(a)** What would be the "salvation from dryness" mentioned in line 9? **(b)** How do lines 10–14 show in what way the salvation is "somber" in this case?

3. In the last five lines the birds' song is referred to as "tumult." What "somber salvation from dryness" do lines 18–19 suggest that the birds receive?

Alpine Afternoon

1. Describe in your own words the scene presented in the poem.

2. Choose one word to summarize the overall feeling you think the scene conveys.

Sunset

1. Do you think by describing the sunset as he does that the poet has made it a less mysterious occurrence? Why or why not?

2. What might the "neon-lights" be?

Afterglow

1. The afterglow of the sunset is described as "tautly drawn and different" from the "pomp and clamor" of the sunset. Explain.

2. This poem is not only a description of a scene; it is also a view of human fears. **(a)** Why is the sunset "always disturbing"? **(b)** In what way does its afterglow become a "hallucination"?

Water Picture

1. At what point did you realize what the poem is about? Did the illustration help? Discuss.

2. **(a)** List at least two unusual pictures the mirror effect causes. **(b)** What makes the mirror effect disappear?

Wind

1. **(a)** What two seasons figure in this poem? **(b)** Is the passage from one to the next easy or difficult? Explain.

2. Name two effects the wind has on the scene.

Between Walls

1. "Between Walls" may be considered "minimalist poetry"—poetry made out of a minimal number of words and images. Out of twenty-four words (counting the title), the poet has not only created a picture, but also suggested a larger one. **(a)** Describe the actual picture in the poem. **(b)** Describe the larger picture the poem suggests.

2. Write the poem in a continuous line. What, in your opinion, is lost by dropping the line divisions and stanzas?

Application

Imagery

If the imagery in a poem is strong enough, a thoughtful reader can often go beyond it to imagine details that are not specifically described.

1. What sense or senses are appealed to in the first eight lines of "Drought"? in the two stanzas of "Alpine Afternoon"?

2. Let the imagery in each set of lines suggest at least one detail appealing to a different sense that you think the poet could have included.

Simile, Metaphor, Personification

As with imagery, figures of speech like these three involve vivid ways of seeing or perceiving things. But what makes figurative language in general distinctive from imagery is that it describes things in such a way that they appear different from what they literally are.

1. Identify the two similes in "Sunset" and discuss their effect.

2. Stanza 1 of "Water Picture" contains both a simile and a metaphor. Name them, and find one other example of each figure in the poem.

3. Identify one human quality the leaves, earth, and rain are said to have in "Wind."

Composition

Choose a landscape (or cityscape or seascape) familiar to you, and go there and see it as if for the first time. As you look at it, jot down any images or figures of speech that you think will make the place sound unique or special.

Use your jottings to create a short descriptive essay or poem that will evoke a picture of the scene for your reader. (See "Writing a Description," page 658, in the Composition Guide.)

Carl Sandburg 1878–1967

Born of Swedish immigrants in Galesburg, Illinois, Sandburg left school at thirteen for a series of jobs out West, then returned to attend Lombard College. He worked as a newspaperman in Chicago and there began to publish his poems in *Poetry* magazine, receiving wide attention. His many books include *Chicago Poems* (1916), *Slabs of the Sunburnt West* (1922), and *The American Songbag* (1927). He often gave public poetry readings, accompanying himself on guitar.

Oumar Ba

Oumar Ba is a woman poet living in Senegal, a country of West Africa where droughts have been common and devastating. "Drought" was published in the *Penguin Book of Women Poets,* a collection of poetry by women from all over the world.

Giosuè Carducci 1835–1907

Italian scholar and poet, Carducci became professor of Italian literature at Bologna University in 1860, and a senator in Parliament in 1890. He devoted as much time to political activities as to poetry, working for a free and united Italy. But poetry was his first love and he wrote many volumes, treating themes of self and country in a style fusing romantic and classical elements. He won the Nobel Prize for Literature in 1906.

Mbuyiseni Oswald Mtshali 1940–

Mtshali was born in South Africa and lives in Johannesburg, where he has been under house arrest. His work has been collected and published under the title *Sounds of a Cowhide Drum.*

Jorge Luis Borges 1899–

Borges is perhaps the best known of the contemporary South American writers. He was born in Buenos Aires into a well-educated family and learned English as a youth; he received his college education in Switzerland. His first book of poetry, *Fervor de Buenos Aires,* was published in 1923; it was followed by several others, and by many collections of uniquely conceived short stories and parables, often set in a fantasy world of his own creation. After gradually losing his sight over a period of years, Borges is now totally blind.

May Swenson 1919–

A noted modern American poet, Swenson was born in Logan, Utah, and took a degree from the University of Utah. Her first book of poems was *Another Animal: Poems* (1954); in this and in subsequent collections, such as *Half Sun Half Sleep* (1967) and *More Poems to Solve* (1971), she shows a tendency to play with language, combining words in original and unusual ways. She has received many distinguished awards, including a Guggenheim Fellowship and membership in the National Institute of Arts and Letters.

Suyama Hisayo 1882– ?

Suyama Hisayo became a poet late in life, joining a local *haiku* society in the Hiroshima area after World War II. Her first volume of poems, *Tomorrow!,* was published in 1966 (when she was in her middle seventies), followed by *Acorn* in 1967.

William Carlos Williams 1883–1963

Williams advised the poet to write on "things with which he is familiar, simple things—at the same time to detach them from ordinary experience to the imagination." He also adopted as a kind of poetic credo, "no idea but in things." Williams spent his life as a doctor in Rutherford, New Jersey, writing his poetry in his free moments. In addition to producing several volumes of short poems, he spent many of his later years writing his long masterpiece, *Paterson.*

Moods and Emotions

Most poetry grows out of emotion. A poem can explode out of anger, dance out of joy or love, shoot straight to a target in a mood of frustration, sag in anguish, or soar in eloquence. . . .

See **MOOD** Handbook of Literary Terms

Gift

Czeslaw Milosz Poland

A day so happy.
Fog lifted early, I worked in the garden.
Hummingbirds were stopping over honeysuckle flowers.
There was no thing on earth I wanted to possess.
I knew no one worth my envying him.
Whatever evil I had suffered, I forgot.
To think that once I was the same man did not embarrass me.
In my body I felt no pain.
When straightening up, I saw the blue sea and sails.

Sorrow

Chu Shu Chen China

The white moon gleams through scudding
Clouds in the cold sky of the Ninth
Month. The white frost weighs down the
Leaves and the branches bend low
Over the freezing water.
All alone I sit by my
Window. The crushing burden
Of the passing days never
Grows lighter for an instant.
I write poems, change and correct them,
And finally throw them away.
Gold chrysanthemums wither
Along the balcony. Hard
Cries of migrating storks fall
Heavily from the icy sky.
All alone by my window
Hidden in my empty room,
All alone, I burn incense,
And dream in the smoke, all alone.

Hope

Lisel Mueller USA

It hovers in dark corners
before the lights are turned on,
it shakes sleep from its eyes
and drops from mushroom gills,
it explodes in the starry heads
of dandelions turned sages,
it sticks to the wings of green angels
that sail from the tops of maples.

It sprouts in each occluded eye
of the many-eyed potato,
it lives in each earthworm segment,
surviving cruelty,
it is the motion that runs
from the eyes to the tail of a dog,
it is the mouth that inflates the lungs
of the child that has just been born.

It is the singular gift
we cannot destroy in ourselves,
the argument that refutes death,
the genius that invents the future,
all we know of God.

It is the serum which makes us swear
not to betray one another;
it is in this poem, trying to speak.

Czeslaw Milosz (ches′wäf mē′wôsh).

Sky Diving

Nikki Giovanni   USA

I hang on the edge
of this universe
singing off-key
talking too loud
embracing myself
to cushion the fall

I shall tumble
into deep space
never in this form
or with this feeling
to return to earth

It is not tragic

I will spiral
through that Black hole
losing skin   limbs
internal organs
searing
my naked soul

Landing
in the next galaxy
with only my essence
embracing myself
as

I dream of you

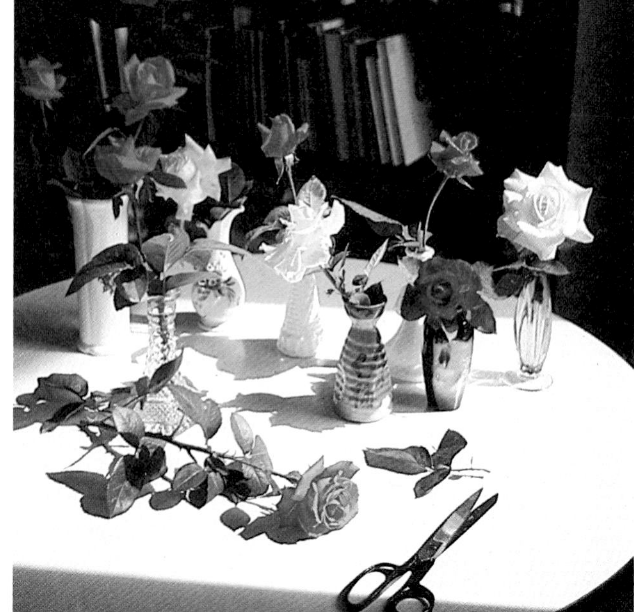

See **TONE** Handbook of Literary Terms

One Perfect Rose

Dorothy Parker   USA

A single flow'r he sent me, since we met.
All tenderly his messenger he chose;
Deep-hearted, pure, with scented dew still wet—
One perfect rose.

I knew the language of the floweret;
"My fragile leaves," it said, "his heart enclose."
Love long has taken for his amulet
One perfect rose.

Why is it no one ever sent me yet
One perfect limousine, do you suppose?
Ah no, it's always just my luck to get
One perfect rose.

The Street

Octavio Paz Mexico

The street is very long and filled with silence.
I walk in shadow and I trip and fall,
And then get up and walk with unseeing feet
Over the silent stones and the dry leaves,
And someone close behind, tramples them, too.
If I slow down and stop, he also stops.
If I run, so does he. I look. No one!
The whole street seems so dark, with no way out,
And though I turn and turn, I can't escape.
I always find myself on the same street
Where no one waits for me and none pursues.
Where I pursue, a man who trips and falls
Gets up and seeing me, keeps saying: "No one!"

Comment: On "The Street"

"The Street" may most easily be read as a dream, with the speaker encountering the kind of unreal world we all encounter in our dreams—especially those that frighten us. The place is without geographical location—simply a street, long and without sound of any kind. There seem to be no buildings or houses along the street—at least the speaker does not refer to them. And there seems to be little or no light, the darkness thus deepening the mystery and increasing the fear. The speaker trips and falls, gets up and goes on, and then hears someone behind him trampling the same "stones and . . . dry leaves" he has passed over. If the speaker runs, so does the pursuer; if he stops, so does the pursuer. The speaker looks—and sees no one. The street turns into a kind of labyrinth or maze, with many turns but no way out. And, perplexingly, the speaker always finds himself on the same street, with no one waiting for him, and no one pursuing. At the end of the poem the earlier incident involving pursued and pursuer is repeated, but this time, the speaker becomes the pursuer, a change not unusual in dreams. He is running after a man who trips and falls; who, on getting up and looking back, says "No one!"

As with all dreams, the content of this dream-poem stands for something, and we may guess at what. The speaker is really both the pursued and the pursuer. The maze of streets, without escape, represents an unbearable situation, mental entanglement, or emotional strain from which the speaker can find no exit. In first being pursued by himself, and then later becoming the pursuer pursuing himself, the speaker appears to be divided or torn within. He is uncertain of his identity, his direction, his purpose. In this state of uncertainty, the speaker may be seen to stand for modern humanity, filled with fear and anxiety as to the nature of the self and the meaning of life.

The Traveller's Curse After Misdirection

Robert Graves Great Britain

May they stumble, stage by stage
On an endless pilgrimage,
Dawn and dusk, mile after mile,
At each and every step, a stile;
At each and every step withal
May they catch their feet and fall;
At each and every fall they take
May a bone within them break;
And may the bone that breaks within
Not be, for variation's sake,
Now rib, now thigh, now arm, now shin,
But always, without fail THE NECK.

Discussion

Gift

1. **(a)** What ideas or attitudes does the speaker mention that might have kept him from being happy in the past? **(b)** What about this particular day makes him happy?

2. Would you agree that happiness can be the absence of negative things as well as the presence of positive things? Discuss.

Sorrow

1. It is difficult to read these lines without feeling their coldness. What in the poem evokes this feeling?

2. **(a)** What evidence is there that the speaker feels sorrowful? **(b)** What might be the cause of her sorrow?

Hope

1. What is the "It" mentioned in line 1?

2. **(a)** Find two examples in stanzas 1 and 2 that show the influence "it" has on the existence of living things. **(b)** Identify one use of personification in the stanzas.

3. (a) In stanzas 3 and 4, what does the speaker say "it" gives to human beings? **(b)** What does the last line of the poem mean?

Sky Diving

1. (a) What is causing the emotion expressed in this poem? **(b)** What effect does the author create by not revealing this cause until the final line?

2. (a) Explain the connection between the title and the descriptions used throughout. **(b)** What effect does the speaker expect the "Black hole" to have?

3. In what way is the entire poem an example of hyperbole?

One Perfect Rose

1. What is the "messenger" in stanza 1?

2. Does the speaker accept the idea that a rose generally stands for love? Discuss.

The Street

1. What situations or events in this poem resemble those you have encountered in a dream?

2. How is the poem relevant to the fears and concerns of people in today's world?

The Traveller's Curse After Misdirection

1. (a) Who are the "they" being cursed by the traveller? **(b)** In what way is the curse suitable as revenge?

2. Notice that the words "step," "fall," "bone," and "break" are repeated. **(a)** How does the curse change with each repetition of one of these words? **(b)** How does the use of end rhyme add to the overall effect?

Application

Mood

Particularly in poetry, where ideas are usually presented in brief, compressed form, setting can play a large part in establishing a mood. It may be, in fact, that certain settings represent or help create certain moods in people's minds.

1. Do you think the author of "Gift" would have used the same details of setting if he intended to convey a mood of sorrow or anger?

2. How does the setting in "Sorrow" contribute to the poem's mood? Discuss.

Tone

Though not every part of a piece of writing has a clearly recognizable tone, when an author does use a specific tone it can change the mood of the selection as well.

1. Where and how does the author adopt a clear tone in "One Perfect Rose"? What is the tone?

2. How does the use of this tone affect the mood of the poem?

3. Is the writer's tone in "The Traveller's Curse After Misdirection" simply one of anger? Do you think the tone helps create a mood? Discuss.

Vocabulary

Combined Skills

Use the Glossary to answer the following questions. Be sure you know the meaning and pronunciation of each word.

1. From what language is *refute* derived?

2. Where is the accent in *amulet?*

3. Does the vowel sound of the last syllable of *pilgrimage* sound like the *a* in *hat* or the *i* in *hit?*

4. Is *scud* derived from Danish or Old English?

5. Is the accent in *occlude* on the first or second syllable?

Czeslaw Milosz 1911–

Born in Lithuania, Milosz became one of the leaders of the new poetry movement in Poland during the 1930s, and then fought in the Resistance against the Nazis in World War II. After serving in the diplomatic service for Poland during the post-war years, he came to the United States to teach at the University of California, Berkeley. He continued to write throughout his various careers. One critic has described Milosz's poetry as offering a "sober version of stoicism which does not ignore reality, however absurd and horrendous." He was awarded the Nobel Prize for Literature in 1980.

Chu Shu Chen

Almost nothing is known about the writer called "the Poetess Chu Shu Chen." It is, however, fairly certain that she lived some time during the Sung dynasty, 960–1280, a period noted for its achievements in literature and the arts.

Lisel Mueller 1924–

Born in Hamburg, Germany, Mueller fled from the country with her family in 1939 and settled in Indiana. After graduating from college, she married and raised a family. Writing poetry came to her much later and grew to be a major interest. Her book, *The Private Life,* won the Lamont Poetry Prize in 1976.

Nikki Giovanni 1943–

Nikki Giovanni graduated from Fisk University in 1967 and immediately began her poetic career with the publication of *Black Feeling, Black Talk* in 1968. She early won a Ford Foundation grant, which enabled her to devote time to writing. She has published a great many books, including *The Women and the Men* (1975) and *Those Who Ride the Night Winds* (1983). She made a record in 1971 *(Truth Is on Its Way)* reading her poems to gospel music.

Dorothy Parker 1893–1967

Parker delighted the reading public with her witty, often cynical verse for many years. Early in her career as a critic in New York she became friendly with humorist Robert Benchley and playwright Robert Sherwood, and together they formed the nucleus of a witty and influential group of writers and critics known as the Algonquin Round Table. The titles of some of Parker's books of poetry suggest the wry humor that she favored: *Enough Rope* (1926), *Death and Taxes* (1931), and *Collected Poems: Not So Deep as a Well* (1936). She also wrote short stories.

Octavio Paz 1914–

One of the Latin American poets best known outside that region, Paz was a precocious youth who published his first volume of poems before he was twenty. He served in a number of diplomatic posts for Mexico, and while in Europe was influenced by the surrealists, writers who used dream-imagery techniques. (See also the Comment on page 230.) One of his best-known collections is *La estación violenta* (1958), which contains his ambitious poem "The Sun Stone," based on the engraved stone calendar of the Aztec Indians.

Robert Graves 1895–

Poet, novelist, and scholar, Graves fought in World War I at a young age and began to publish poetry at the same time. Reported dead in battle, he read his own obituary in the London *Times.* After the war he taught for a time in Egypt, but then decided to devote himself entirely to writing. He has published several historical novels, such as *I, Claudius* (1934), and many volumes of poems characterized by wit, melancholy, and robust bravado alternating with lyric tenderness.

Choices

Poems, like life, sometimes seem full of choices—which road to take, which line to stand in, which friend to share with . . . which life to lead. . . .

Ordinance on Lining Up

Naomi Lazard USA

A line will form to the right
and one to the left. You must join
one of them. After careful consideration
choose the line you are most attracted to;
stand at the end of it.
Both lines are serpentine. However,
if you look closely
you will see subtle differences.
The one to the right moves more quickly,
the left line at a more leisurely pace
which may prove beneficial
to certain dispositions.
Try to see where the lines go;
this is your option.
Everything possible is being done
to protect your privileges.
A factor to keep in mind:
in joining the line to the right
you will end life as a beggar.
If you decide on the line to the left
everything you believe will become nonsense.
You will be spending
a great deal of time on whichever one
you choose. Choose wisely.
No changing from one line to the other
once you have joined.
Common sense
will tell you that you will become
an indispensable link
in the line of your choice.
Good luck to you.

The Enemy

Alice Walker USA

in gray, scarred Leningrad[1]
a tiny fist unsnapped to show
crumpled heads
of pink and yellow flowers
snatched hurriedly on the go
in the cold spring shower—

consent or not
countries choose
cold or hot
win or lose
to speak of wars
yellow and red
but there is much
let it be said
for children.

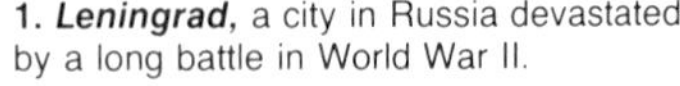

1. ***Leningrad,*** a city in Russia devastated by a long battle in World War II.

Don't Ask Me What to Wear

Sappho Greece

Don't ask me what to wear

I have no embroidered
headband from Sardis[1] to
give you, Cleis,[2] such as
I wore
        and my mother
always said that in her
day a purple ribbon
looped in the hair was thought
to be high style indeed

but we were dark:
                a girl
whose hair is yellower than
torchlight should wear no
headdress but fresh flowers

1. ***Sardis,*** capital of Lydia, the chief kingdom in Asia Minor.
2. ***Cleis*** (klē'is), Sappho's daughter.

Yoke and Star

José Martí Cuba

When I was born, my mother said to me:
"My son, Homagno, Flower of my breast,
Reflected sum of me and of the world,
Fish that to bird and horse and man has turned,
See these two signs of life I offer you
With hope and sorrow. Look and make your choice.
This is a yoke. He who accepts it lives.
By it the ox is tamed, and since he gives
Full service to his master, in warm straw
He sleeps and eats good and abundant oats.
But this, O Mystery sprung from my womb
As peaks from lofty mountain range take shape,
This thing that gleams and slays, this is a star!
All sinners flee from one who bears its mark,
And from its spreading light; and so in life,
As though the one who wears it were a beast
Burdened with crimes, he will be shunned by all.
The man who imitates the care-free ox
Becomes himself a dumb, submissive brute
And has to start again the eternal climb.
But he who, confident, shall choose a star
To be his symbol, grows.
When for Mankind
The living person freely pours his cup;
When for the bloody human festival
The good man sacrificed his beating heart
Quickly and gravely; when to wandering winds
Of North and South, he gave his sacred words;
The Star, a mantle now, envelops him
And the clear air is bright, as in festive days,
And the living man, who did not fear to live,
Knows he is not alone in dark and death."

"Give me the yoke, O Mother, so that I
Can stamp it under foot, then let the Star
That lights and kills glow brightly on my brow!"

José Martí (hō zā′ mär tē′).

See **PARADOX** Handbook of Literary Terms

The Soul of Goodness in Things Evil

Rumi Persia

Fools take false coins because they are like the true.
If in the world no genuine minted coin
Were current, how would forgers pass the false?
Falsehood were nothing unless truth were there,
To make it specious. 'Tis the love of right
Lures men to wrong. Let poison but be mixed
With sugar, they will cram it into their mouths.
Oh, cry not that all creeds are vain! Some scent
Of truth they have, else they would not beguile.
Say not, "How utterly fantastical!"
No fancy in the world is all untrue.
Amidst the crowd of dervishes hides one,
One true fakir. Search well and thou wilt find!

A Round Shape Water Takes Inside the Gourd

Nguyen Trai Vietnam

A round shape water takes inside the gourd.
For good or ill, all fit some frame or mold.
Live near the rich—you'll munch on crackly rice.
Fall in with thieves—you'll rue it and eat stick.
Befriend a fool—you'll join the pack of fools.
Meet clever men—you'll learn some clever tricks.
Mix with low folk—you'll stoop to their low plane.
Get black near ink, get red near cinnabar.

Nguyen Trai (nə win′ trī).

Harlem

Langston Hughes USA

What happens to a dream deferred?

Does it dry up
like a raisin in the sun?
Or fester like a sore—
And then run?
Does it stink like rotten meat?
Or crust and sugar over—
like a syrupy sweet?

Maybe it just sags
like a heavy load.

Or does it explode?

Discussion

Ordinance on Lining Up

1. An ordinance is a rule or law issued by an authority. What in the poem itself reveals that it is an ordinance?

2. The poem offers you a choice of joining one of two lines. **(a)** Which line would you choose? **(b)** What are the differences between the two lines?

3. Can the choices between the lines be related to choices faced in life in some way? Discuss.

The Enemy

1. What choice does this poem focus on?

2. What contrast is set up by mentioning children at the beginning and then again at the end of the poem?

Don't Ask Me What to Wear

1. What do you imagine has preceded this statement from the mother to the daughter?

2. The mother implies in line 1 that she won't advise her daughter on what to wear. **(a)** Does she advise her? Discuss. **(b)** Do the mother's comments sound like those of a modern-day mother? Why or why not?

Yoke and Star

1. **(a)** What, literally, are the two choices the mother offers the son? **(b)** What sort of life does each possible choice stand for?

2. Why is it that selecting one of the choices will cause a person to be "shunned by all"?

3. Is the choice presented in the poem relevant to any countries of the twentieth century? Discuss.

The Soul of Goodness in Things Evil

1. The basic argument in this poem is that nothing can exist without its opposite and that thus, in a sense, everything contains the seeds of its opposite. Explain how the examples of the coin and of truth and falsehood are used to support this argument.

2. **(a)** Of the various religious "creeds" that exist, the author says, "No fancy in the world is all untrue." Explain. **(b)** In what way do "dervishes" and "fakir" stand for these creeds?

A Round Shape Water Takes Inside the Gourd

1. **(a)** What is the meaning of line 1? **(b)** How does it relate to the rest of the poem?

2. **(a)** Do you think the message of the poem is true? Discuss. **(b)** If it is true, what choice does it seem to leave people with?

Harlem

1. Check the meaning of *deferred* in the Glossary; then explain the kind of dream the speaker is talking about in line 1.

2. In what sense does the last line of the poem offer a choice?

3. What is the author's tone throughout the poem?

Application

Paradox

A piece of writing dealing with philosophical ideas or beliefs, as does "The Soul of Goodness in Things Evil," is a likely place to find paradoxical statements. Explain why " 'Tis the love of right lures men to wrong" is a paradox; then use your understanding of the poem's general message to explain what the line means.

Naomi Lazard 1936–

Born in Philadelphia, Lazard attended the City College of New York, where she took an M.A. in 1964. Prior to the 1967 publication of her first collection, *Cry of the Peacocks,* Lazard's poems had appeared in many magazines. Her works include *Ordinances* (1977) and *The Moonlit Upper Deckerina* (1977). In 1978, she was elected president of the Poetry Society of America.

Alice Walker 1944–

Walker was born in Eatonton, Georgia, and attended Sarah Lawrence College, graduating in 1966. By the age of twenty-nine she had written five books. Also a novelist and teacher, Walker has taught creative writing and black literature at several colleges nationwide. Her volumes of poetry include *Once* (1968) and *Revolutionary Petunias and Other Poems* (1973), which was nominated for the National Book Award. In 1983, she won an American Book Award for her widely acclaimed novel *The Color Purple.*

Sappho 610 B.C.—? B.C.

Although stories about Sappho have been passed on through the ages, little is known for certain about her life. Her poems are said to have filled nine books, but only fragments have survived; these indicate that her family was aristocratic. Her poems are noted tor their simplicity and perfection of form. The ancients ranked Sappho with such honored writers as Homer, and called her the "Tenth Muse." Even today she is probably the most famous Greek woman poet.

José Martí 1853–1895

Martí was born and educated in Cuba at a time when it was ruled by Spain. In 1868, at the age of sixteen, he was arrested in an uprising and sentenced to six years of hard labor. This experience inspired him to become not only a Cuban patriot but a writer. As a kind of wandering exile, Martí lived in many countries and produced articles about their political situations. His poetry expresses an interest in the common man and was innovative in both technique and subject. He published many collections of poems.

Rumi 1207–1273

Jala-uddin, called "Rumi" because he came from a Roman-controlled area, founded the religious group called Maulana. The little-understood Maulana, commonly called whirling dervishes, attempt to gain Oneness with God through a dance that starts slowly and becomes a whirling frenzy. Rumi's most famous work is the beautifully poetic *Mathnawi,* one of Persia's great mystical works.

Nguyen Trai 1380–1442

Nguyen Trai was born in the capital of Vietnam, present-day Hanoi, and in 1400 won a doctoral degree. Caught up in the wars between Vietnam and China, Trai was imprisoned for a time, but escaped to fight with fellow Vietnamese for national independence. When the Chinese were driven out, he wrote the poem for the victory celebration. He is looked upon by the Vietnamese as an important figure in their history and literature.

Langston Hughes 1902–1967

Although Hughes is best known as a poet, his novels, short stories, plays, and translations, as well as his poems, have given voice to the concerns of minorities. Born in Joplin, Missouri, Hughes became known to the literary world during the 1920s. Works such as *The Weary Blues* (1926), *The Dream Keeper* (1932), and *The Panther and the Lash* (1967) reflected the changing role of blacks in American society. Toward the end of his career, he devoted his energies to helping young writers.

Edgar Lee Masters USA

Poetry can bring to life the many and varied people of a small town, even if it means calling them forth from their graves, as in Edgar Lee Masters's *Spoon River Anthology*. . . .

Comment: On *Spoon River Anthology*

The characters speaking in the following poems—Mrs. Kessler, Hortense Robbins, Samuel Gardner, Dow Kritt, Cooney Potter, and Walter Simmons—are all dead and speaking from beyond the grave. It is as though the tombstones above their graves speak. They are all buried in the same graveyard of a little community in rural Illinois called Spoon River (not a real town, but one incorporating features of two small towns Masters had known as a youth). They lived their lives in Spoon River in the late 1800s and early 1900s.

These characters are but six examples from a total of 244 portrayed in Edgar Lee Masters's book of poems *Spoon River Anthology,* published in 1915. Taken together, the poems gave readers candid glimpses into the life of a small town at the turn of the century. There was enough variety in the characters, diversity in their occupations and interests, and range in their social status to give the impression of an entire community—a universal portrait of Small Town, USA. In reading *Spoon River Anthology,* readers recognized themselves and their own villages.

The inhabitants of the Spoon River graveyard speak the truth, confessing their own sins or weaknesses. For example, Walter Simmons reveals that his problem was that he "didn't have the brains" to do what others expected of him, while Cooney Potter states that the real cause of his death was bolting down his food as he drove himself with his ambitions. These and similar revelations created a sensation when *Spoon River Anthology* was published, because many of the portraits were based on real people who had been involved in one scandal or another.

Though there are portraits of happy, fulfilled people in *Spoon River Anthology,* there are probably more that convey sadness and melancholy—for wasted or twisted lives, for unfulfilled dreams, or for dreams turned bitter even when fulfilled. And yet the overall effect of the collection is not morbid. The reader feels sad at misfortunes and happy or amused with successes, but tends to forget after a while that all these people are supposed to be dead. The poems become, in essence, fascinating character sketches of the various individuals in a town.

Mrs. Kessler

Mr. Kessler, you know, was in the army,
And he drew six dollars a month as a pension,
And stood on the corner talking politics,
Or sat at home reading Grant's Memoirs;[1]
And I supported the family by washing,
Learning the secrets of all the people
From their curtains, counterpanes, shirts and skirts.
For things that are new grow old at length,
They're replaced with better or none at all:
People are prospering or falling back.
And rents and patches widen with time;
No thread or needle can pace decay,
And there are stains that baffle soap,
And there are colors that run in spite of you,
Blamed though you are for spoiling a dress.
Handkerchiefs, napery, have their secrets—
The laundress, Life, knows all about it.
And I, who went to all the funerals
Held in Spoon River, swear I never
Saw a dead face without thinking it looked
Like something washed and ironed.

---

1. ***Grant's Memoirs,*** the book of memories and recollections written by Ulysses S. Grant, U.S. President from 1869 to 1877.

Hortense Robbins

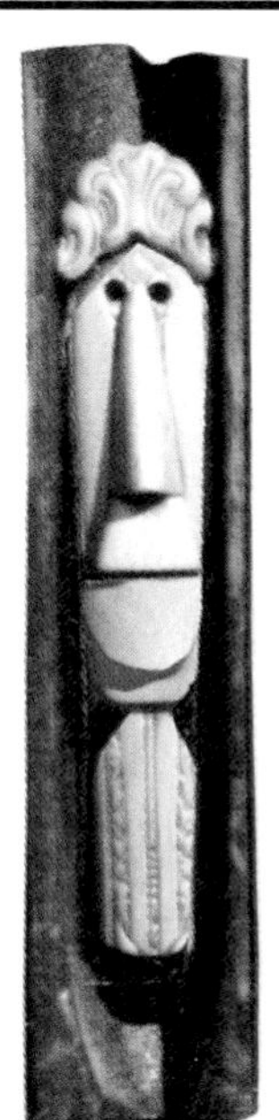

My name used to be in the papers daily
As having dined somewhere,
Or traveled somewhere,
Or rented a house in Paris,
Where I entertained the nobility.
I was forever eating or traveling,
Or taking the cure at Baden-Baden.[1]
Now I am here to do honor
To Spoon River, here beside the family whence I sprang.
No one cares now where I dined,
Or lived, or whom I entertained,
Or how often I took the cure at Baden-Baden!

---

1. ***Baden-Baden*** (bäd'n-bäd'n), a famous health resort with curative waters in southwestern Germany.

Samuel Gardner

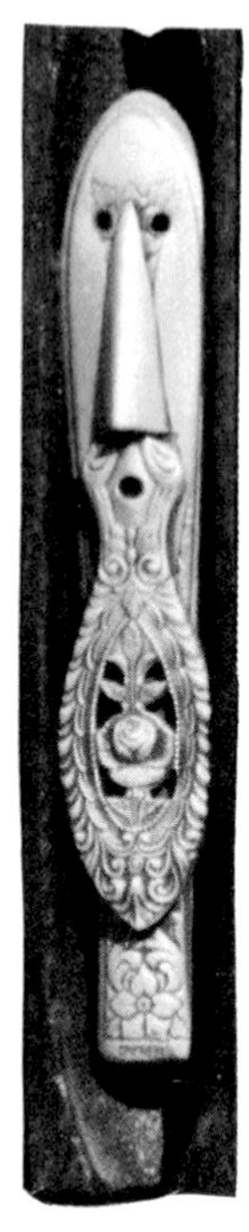

I who kept the greenhouse,
Lover of trees and flowers,
Oft in life saw this umbrageous elm,
Measuring its generous branches with my eye,
And listened to its rejoicing leaves
Lovingly patting each other
With sweet æolian whispers.
And well they might:
For the roots had grown so wide and deep
That the soil of the hill could not withhold
Aught of its virtue, enriched by rain,
And warmed by the sun;
But yielded it all to the thrifty roots,
Through which it was drawn and whirled to the trunk,
And thence to the branches, and into the leaves,
Wherefrom the breeze took life and sang.
Now I, an under-tenant of the earth, can see
That the branches of a tree
Spread no wider than its roots.
And how shall the soul of a man
Be larger than the life he has lived?

Dow Kritt

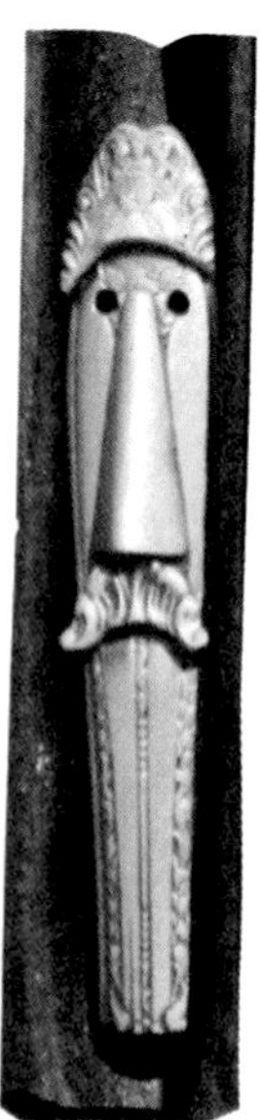

Samuel is forever talking of his elm—
But I did not need to die to learn about roots:
I, who dug all the ditches about Spoon River.
Look at my elm!
Sprung from as good a seed as his,
Sown at the same time,
It is dying at the top:
Not from lack of life, nor fungus,
Nor destroying insect, as the sexton thinks.
Look, Samuel, where the roots have struck rock,
And can no further spread.
And all the while the top of the tree
Is tiring itself out, and dying,
Trying to grow.

Cooney Potter

I inherited forty acres from my Father
And, by working my wife, my two sons and two daughters
From dawn to dusk, I acquired
A thousand acres. But not content,
Wishing to own two thousand acres,
I bustled through the years with axe and plow,
Toiling, denying myself, my wife, my sons, my daughters.
Squire Higbee wrongs me to say
That I died from smoking Red Eagle cigars.
Eating hot pie and gulping coffee
During the scorching hours of harvest time
Brought me here ere I had reached my sixtieth year.

Walter Simmons

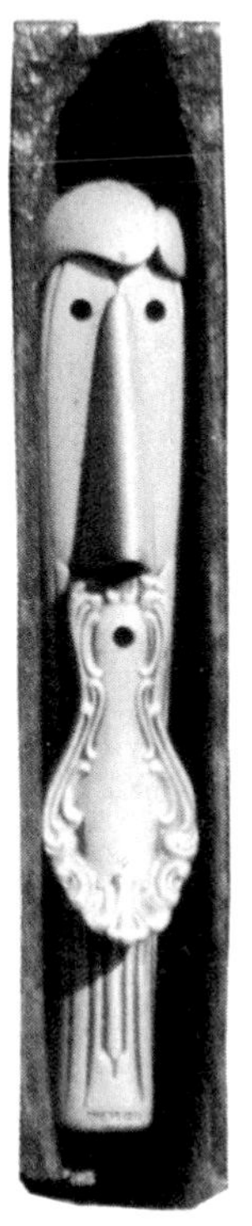

My parents thought that I would be
As great as Edison or greater:
For as a boy I made balloons
And wondrous kites and toys with clocks
And little engines with tracks to run on
And telephones of cans and thread.
I played the cornet and painted pictures,
Modeled in clay and took the part
Of the villain in the "Octoroon."[1]
But then at twenty-one I married
And had to live, and so, to live
I learned the trade of making watches
And kept the jewelry store on the square,
Thinking, thinking, thinking, thinking,—
Not of business, but of the engine
I studied the calculus to build.
And all Spoon River watched and waited
To see it work, but it never worked.
And a few kind souls believed my genius
Was somehow hampered by the store.
It wasn't true. The truth was this:
I didn't have the brains.

---

1. ***the "Octoroon,"*** popular play about slavery written by Dion Boucicault (bü′sē kôlt′), first produced in 1859.

Discussion

Mrs. Kessler, Hortense Robbins

1. Describe and contrast the main interests in life of Mrs. Kessler and Hortense Robbins.

2. How do the two women differ in attitude as they recall their lives and their fates?

Samuel Gardner, Dow Kritt

1. (a) What occupation did each of these men have in life? **(b)** How did their occupations acquaint them with certain parts of trees?

2. (a) How do the elms that the two men are buried under differ? **(b)** Would you say that their personalities, as revealed in the poems, fit their respective trees? Why or why not?

3. What do the last four lines of Samuel Gardner's poem mean?

Cooney Potter

1. Does Cooney Potter sound happy about the sort of life he has led? Discuss.

2. (a) What really caused his death? **(b)** Does this sound like the kind of death you would expect for a man who lived as he did? Why or why not?

Walter Simmons

1. Why did Walter's parents and others believe that as a boy he had great promise of major achievement?

2. Later, after he became a jeweler on the town square, "all Spoon River watched and waited." Why?

3. How are the townspeople ("a few kind souls") deceived?

Composition

The lives of Mrs. Kessler and Hortense Robbins were obviously quite different; how might they have viewed each other when their paths did cross? Imagine you are Mrs. Kessler and have just picked up some laundry from Hortense Robbins, who has recently returned from a trip. Consider what your conversation with Robbins must have been like, the kind of clothing she has given you to launder, and what you might deduce about her life from the garments.

As Mrs. Kessler, write a three- or four-paragraph account of what you think of Robbins and the life she leads, including some of the points mentioned above. When you finish, evaluate your composition. (See "Revising," page 656, in the Composition Guide.)

Edgar Lee Masters 1868–1950

Edgar Lee Masters became famous overnight with the publication of *Spoon River Anthology* in 1915. By that time he was in his forties and had written many books of poems and essays, but was virtually unknown as an author. He had also been a lawyer. Admitted to the Illinois bar in 1891, he practiced law in Chicago for almost thirty years.

But in 1920, famous as the author of *Spoon River Anthology,* he gave up his law practice and devoted himself to writing. During his career he published over fifty volumes, including another collection on Spoon River—*The New Spoon River* (1924). But he never again was able to capture the public imagination as he had in *Spoon River Anthology.* When he wrote his autobiography in 1936, he entitled it *Across Spoon River.*

Spoon River Anthology has been translated into many languages, including Arabic, Korean, and Chinese. And it has strong affinities with Thornton Wilder's *Our Town,* set in New England, and with many other works that deal with small-town life.

A. E. Housman Great Britain

A. E. Housman presents a gallery of portraits that seem to speak with one melancholy voice. . . .

Far in a Western Brookland

Far in a western brookland
  That bred me long ago
The poplars stand and tremble
  By pools I used to know.

There, in the windless night-time,
  The wanderer, marvelling why,
Halts on the bridge to hearken
  How soft the poplars sigh.

He hears: no more remembered
  In fields where I was known,
Here I lie down in London
  And turn to rest alone.

There, by the starlit fences,
  The wanderer halts and hears
My soul that lingers sighing
  About the glimmering weirs.

Oh, When I Was in Love with You

Oh, when I was in love with you,
  Then I was clean and brave,
And miles around the wonder grew
  How well did I behave.

And now the fancy passes by,
  And nothing will remain,
And miles around they'll say that I
  Am quite myself again.

See **INVERSION** Handbook of Literary Terms

White in the Moon the Long Road Lies

White in the moon the long road lies,
  The moon stands blank above;
White in the moon the long road lies
  That leads me from my love.

Still hangs the hedge without a gust,
  Still, still the shadows stay:
My feet upon the moonlit dust
  Pursue the ceaseless way.

The world is round, so travellers tell,
  And straight though reach the track,
Trudge on, trudge on, 'twill all be well,
  The way will guide one back.

But ere the circle homeward hies
  Far, far must it remove:
White in the moon the long road lies
  That leads me from my love.

When First My Way to Fair I Took

When first my way to fair I took
  Few pence in purse had I,
And long I used to stand and look
  At things I could not buy.

Now times are altered: if I care
  To buy a thing, I can;
The pence are here and here's the fair,
  But where's the lost young man?

—To think that two and two are four
  And neither five nor three
The heart of man has long been sore
  And long 'tis like to be.

An Epitaph

Stay, if you list, O passer by the way;
Yet night approaches: better not to stay.
  I never sigh, nor flush, nor knit the brow,
  Nor grieve to think how ill God made me, now.
Here, with one balm for many fevers found,
Whole of an ancient evil, I sleep sound.

Discussion

Far in a Western Brookland

1. The speaker is longingly remembering the place where he grew up. Where is he now, and what details does he recall?

2. The speaker imagines a wanderer going through his homeland. **(a)** Why does the wanderer pause? **(b)** What do you think he actually hears in the last stanza?

3. Analyze the meter of stanzas 1 and 2.

Oh, When I Was in Love with You

1. The two stanzas show different states of feeling in the speaker. **(a)** What has happened to bring about the state in stanza 2? **(b)** How has the speaker changed as well?

2. What is the tone of this poem?

White in the Moon the Long Road Lies

1. Why might the speaker be going on the road leading him from his love?

2. **(a)** What do "travellers tell" the speaker about the road? **(b)** Is it likely that their prediction will come true? Explain.

When First My Way to Fair I Took

1. **(a)** What has the speaker gained since he first went to fair? **(b)** What has he lost?

2. Discuss the meaning of the last stanza.

An Epitaph

1. What kind of man do you think would have such an epitaph as this?

2. What is the "ancient evil" from which the speaker of the epitaph has apparently found "balm"?

Application

Inversion

Besides emphasizing certain words, inversion can also be effective, if not used excessively, in regularizing the meter of a line of poetry.

1. What words does the inversion "White in the moon the long road lies" emphasize? Without the inversion, how would the line fit the poem?

2. Reword lines 1 and 2 of "When First My Way to Fair I Took" to eliminate the inversion.

A. E. Housman 1859–1936

A. E. Housman is widely recognized as a poet who wrote a small number of deeply moving poems about certain melancholy themes—unfulfilled love, dashed hopes, thwarted ambitions, death at a young age before a life is lived, the longing for a land of no return. His poems often bring a lump to the throat, but they are not sentimental. Their very brevity and brilliantly turned phrases guard against gush.

Housman was born in the British county of Worcestershire (wůs′tər shər)—not in Shropshire, the locale made famous by his poems. He had two ambitions, to become a poet and a classical scholar, and was successful in both. He taught at University College, London, and later at Cambridge University, dedicating most of his scholarly life to editing the poetry of Latin writer Manilius.

In 1896 his poetic career was launched with publication of *A Shropshire Lad,* which was very popular and made him famous. He published more poems later in life, including a volume in 1922, but his total poetic output was just over one hundred works, most of them written in the early 1890s. All had been written in the conviction that poetry should be "more physical than intellectual" and should "entangle the reader in a net of thoughtless delight."

Emily Dickinson USA

Emily Dickinson's poetic voice is unmistakable, whether expressing a sudden joy or a deep hurt, or marveling at the mystery of a well. . . .

Dear March, Come In!

Dear March, come in!
How glad I am!
I looked for you before.
Put down your hat—
You must have walked—
How out of breath you are!
Dear March, how are you?
And the rest?
Did you leave Nature well?
Oh, March, come right upstairs with me,
I have so much to tell!

I got your letter, and the bird's;
The maples never knew
That you were coming,—I declare,
How red their faces grew!
But, March, forgive me—
And all those hills
You left for me to hue;
There was no purple suitable,
You took it all with you.

Who knocks? That April!
Lock the door!
I will not be pursued!
He stayed away a year, to call
When I am occupied.
But trifles look so trivial
As soon as you have come,
That blame is just as dear as praise
And praise as mere as blame.

See **CONSONANCE** Handbook of Literary Terms

Hope Is the Thing with Feathers

Hope is the thing with feathers
That perches in the soul,
And sings the tune without the words
And never stops at all,

And sweetest in the gale is heard;
And sore must be the storm
That could abash the little bird
That kept so many warm.

I've heard it in the chillest land,
And on the strangest sea;
Yet, never, in extremity,
It asked a crumb of me.

The Grass So Little Has to Do

The grass so little has to do,—
A sphere of simple green,
With only butterflies to brood,
And bees to entertain,

And stir all day to pretty tunes
The breezes fetch along,
And hold the sunshine in its lap
And bow to everything;

And thread the dews all night, like pearls,
And make itself so fine,—
A duchess were too common
For such a noticing.

And even when it dies, to pass
In odors so divine,
As lowly spices gone to sleep,
Or amulets of pine.

And then to dwell in sovereign barns,
And dream the days away,—
The grass so little has to do,
I wish I were the hay!

What Mystery Pervades a Well!

What mystery pervades a well!
The water lives so far,
Like neighbor from another world
Residing in a jar.

The grass does not appear afraid;
I often wonder he
Can stand so close and look so bold
At what is dread to me.

Related somehow they may be,—
The sedge stands next the sea,
Where he is floorless, yet of fear
No evidence gives he.

But nature is a stranger yet;
The ones that cite her most
Have never passed her haunted house,
Nor simplified her ghost.

To pity those that know her not
Is helped by the regret
That those who know her, know her less
The nearer her they get.

Comment: On "What Mystery Pervades a Well!"

Imagine a well common in the nineteenth century, usually in the backyard of a farmhouse, with a bucket suspended over it for pulling up water from the cool depths below. The surface of the water gleams, reflecting what little light finds its way so far down.

Such a well must be what Emily Dickinson is thinking of. The water "lives so far" down that it is as mysterious as a foreigner living in similar remoteness in a huge jar. The grass, which grows boldly close to the edge of the well, is not afraid of this distant water that inspires "dread" in the poet.

In stanza 3, Dickinson speculates that the bold grass may be related in some mysterious way to the well. In a similar way, sedge (grassy plants growing in marshy places) springs up next to the sea, in places where it is watery ("floorless"), yet shows no fear of the ocean.

In stanza 4, Dickinson drops reference to the well and, moving from the particular to the general, speaks of "nature" (thus the well as standing for nature). Nature remains a stranger, with all the mystery of a stranger; yet, ironically, those who speak of her most have never experienced her mystery directly ("Have never passed her haunted house") nor analyzed the essence of that mystery ("simplified her ghost").

Stanza 5 leaves us with a paradox. Since we feel "pity" for those who do not know nature at all (like those who "cite her most" in stanza 4), we might expect the opposite of pity, perhaps pleasure, for those who do know her. But no—for them we feel "regret" (close to pity!) because those who do know nature "know her less the nearer her they get." In other words, they have a knowledge that is even more baffling—because of nature's mysteries—than the total ignorance of those who "know her not" at all.

A Thought Went Up My Mind To-day

A thought went up my mind to-day
That I have had before,
But did not finish,—some way back,
I could not fix the year,

Nor where it went, nor why it came
The second time to me,
Nor definitely what it was,
Have I the art to say.

But somewhere in my soul, I know
I've met the thing before;
It just reminded me—'twas all—
And came my way no more.

Discussion

Dear March, Come In!

1. (a) How does the speaker treat March? Explain. **(b)** What figure of speech is used in this treatment?

2. In line 12, what might the "letter" from March and from the bird be?

3. (a) How is April treated in lines 21–25? **(b)** Why do you think April's arrival will wipe out distinctions between praise and blame as described in lines 26–30?

Hope Is the Thing with Feathers

1. Explain the central metaphor around which this poem is built.

2. Does the poet feel hope can be easily lost? Do you agree with her? Discuss.

The Grass So Little Has to Do

1. What is the speaker's attitude toward the grass throughout the poem?

2. Speculate on the meanings of the following phrases: **(a)** line 3: "only butterflies to brood"; **(b)** line 16: "amulets of pine"; **(c)** line 17: "dwell in sovereign barns."

What Mystery Pervades a Well!

1. When the poet speaks of the "mystery" of a well, does she think of it as a puzzle to be solved or as something for the reader simply to meditate on? Discuss.

2. Does the poet's tone come clearly through this poem? If so, what is it?

A Thought Went Up My Mind To-day

1. How long ago was it that the speaker had the thought before?

2. How would meaning be changed if "soul" in line 9 were changed to "mind"?

3. Is the experience described in the poem unique or common? Discuss.

Application

Consonance

There are many examples of half rhyme involving consonance in Dickinson's poetry, but in some cases the lines started out as perfect rhymes. The change is because the pronunciations of some words have altered slightly in the last hundred years.

Find three examples of half rhyme involving consonance in the poems in this section.

Emily Dickinson 1830–1886

Although Emily Dickinson constantly wrote poems—over 1,750 total—she published only seven of them in her lifetime. Rarely has a poet of such genius remained so nearly unknown among his or her contemporaries. Her complete poetic works did not appear in print until 1955, over seventy years after her death; they show her poetry to be much ahead of its time in both form and substance.

Dickinson grew up in Amherst, Massachusetts, the daughter of a well-known lawyer. For college education she had one year at Mount Holyoke Female Seminary. To all outward appearance, little of interest happened to her. She lived at the family home in Amherst, traveled very little, and never married. In the latter part of her life she tended to dress in white. And she was so acutely sensitive that she would often talk with visitors from behind a door. But obviously much happened in her inner life, the source of her poetry. Through her imagination she lived through the full range of emotional and spiritual experiences recorded in her poems. She found more in her private garden to inspire her wonder and passion than many people find wandering all over the world.

Robert Frost USA

Robert Frost's keen Yankee wisdom comes through all his poems, whether wondering about the road not taken or confessing terror in the self's desert places. . . .

The Road Not Taken

Two roads diverged in a yellow wood,
And sorry I could not travel both
And be one traveler, long I stood
And looked down one as far as I could
To where it bent in the undergrowth;

Then took the other, as just as fair,
And having perhaps the better claim,
Because it was grassy and wanted wear;
Though as for that, the passing there
Had worn them really about the same,

And both that morning equally lay
In leaves no step had trodden black.
Oh! I kept the first for another day!
Yet knowing how way leads on to way,
I doubted if I should ever come back.

I shall be telling this with a sigh
Somewhere ages and ages hence:
Two roads diverged in a wood, and I—
I took the one less traveled by,
And that has made all the difference.

The Exposed Nest

You were forever finding some new play.
So when I saw you down on hands and knees
In the meadow, busy with the new-cut hay,
Trying, I thought, to set it up on end,
I went to show you how to make it stay,
If that was your idea, against the breeze,
And, if you asked me, even help pretend
To make it root again and grow afresh.
But 'twas no make-believe with you today,
Nor was the grass itself your real concern,
Though I found your hand full of wilted fern,
Steel-bright June-grass, and blackening heads of clover.
'Twas a nest full of young birds on the ground
The cutter-bar had just gone champing over
(Miraculously without tasting flesh)
And left defenseless to the heat and light.
You wanted to restore them to their right
Of something interposed between their sight
And too much world at once—could means be found.
The way the nest-full every time we stirred
Stood up to us as to a mother-bird
Whose coming home has been too long deferred,
Made me ask would the mother-bird return
And care for them in such a change of scene
And might our meddling make her more afraid.
That was a thing we could not wait to learn.
We saw the risk we took in doing good,
But dared not spare to do the best we could
Though harm should come of it; so built the screen
You had begun, and gave them back their shade.
All this to prove we cared. Why is there then
No more to tell? We turned to other things.
I haven't any memory—have you?—
Of ever coming to the place again
To see if the birds lived the first night through,
And so at last to learn to use their wings.

Neither Out Far Nor In Deep

The people along the sand
All turn and look one way.
They turn their back on the land.
They look at the sea all day.

As long as it takes to pass
A ship keeps raising its hull;
The wetter ground like glass
Reflects a standing gull.

The land may vary more;
But wherever the truth may be—
The water comes ashore,
And the people look at the sea.

They cannot look out far.
They cannot look in deep.
But when was that ever a bar
To any watch they keep?

Desert Places

Snow falling and night falling fast, oh, fast
In a field I looked into going past,
And the ground almost covered smooth in snow,
But a few weeds and stubble showing last.

The woods around it have it—it is theirs.
All animals are smothered in their lairs.
I am too absent-spirited to count;
The loneliness includes me unawares.

And lonely as it is that loneliness
Will be more lonely ere it will be less—
A blanker whiteness of benighted snow
With no expression, nothing to express.

They cannot scare me with their empty spaces
Between stars—on stars where no human race is.
I have it in me so much nearer home
To scare myself with my own desert places.

The Secret Sits

We dance round in a ring and suppose,
But the Secret sits in the middle and knows.

Discussion

The Road Not Taken

1. **(a)** How does the speaker decide which of the two roads to take? **(b)** What do the two roads seem to stand for in his mind?

2. Explain lines 13–15.

The Exposed Nest

1. **(a)** What does the speaker at first believe his friend is busy with? **(b)** What is the friend trying to do instead?

2. **(a)** How do the birds react to the movements of the humans around them? **(b)** Explain how line 27 relates to the action in the latter part of the poem.

3. Why do you think the story is left unconcluded, with the birds' fate uncertain?

Neither Out Far Nor In Deep

1. Which offers more variety for the observer, the sea or the land? Does this make a difference to people? Discuss.

2. Explain the meaning of the title as it relates to stanzas 3 and 4.

Desert Places

1. In stanza 2, what is the speaker referring to when he says, "The loneliness includes me unawares"?

2. What does the speaker foresee in stanza 3, particularly in the last line?

3. **(a)** What are the "desert places" referred to in the last line of the poem? **(b)** How are these related to the mood developed earlier?

The Secret Sits

1. What does the description in line 1 remind you of?

2. How might the poem be a description of life? Discuss.

Composition

"The Exposed Nest" is typical of much of Frost's poetry in that it reads as easily as prose, yet is composed in precise poetic form. Review the poem to get a feel for its subject matter, language, rhyme, meter, and theme.

Write a several-paragraph essay discussing and analyzing these five elements of the poem. Conclude with a paragraph explaining why you did or did not like the poem.

Robert Frost 1874–1963

Although we seem to hear a shrewd Yankee or New England voice in Frost's poetry, he was actually born in San Francisco. However, he moved to Massachusetts at the age of eleven, and his poems tend to be set in New England, especially on the farm or in the rural areas.

Frost married at twenty, studied at Harvard for two years, and then supported himself at a number of odd jobs before settling down on a New Hampshire farm. After eleven years of farming and writing poetry, Frost had little success to show: his farm was a failure and only the local newspaper would accept his poems for publication. In a discouraged mood he moved to England and offered his collected work to a publisher. The book came out as *A Boy's Will* in 1913 and was immediately recognized for its fresh, original poetry. Frost followed this with *North of Boston* (1914).

Now famous, Frost returned home in 1915. He was to become one of the most popular poets in America. In 1924 he won the first of several Pulitzer Prizes for his poetry. In 1961 he was invited to read a poem at the inauguration ceremonies of President John F. Kennedy.

Federico García Lorca Spain

García Lorca's poems inhabit a strange world uniquely his, a world in which clocks fly apart and collide with stars, and guitars lament as waters weep. . . .

Half Moon

The moon goes over the water.
How tranquil the sky is!
She goes scything slowly
the old shimmer from the river;
meanwhile a young frog
takes her for a little mirror.

The Moon Rising

When the moon rises,
the bells hang silent,
and impenetrable footpaths
appear.

When the moon rises,
the sea covers the land,
and the heart feels
like an island in infinity.

Nobody eats oranges
under the full moon.
One must eat fruit
that is green and cold.

When the moon rises,
moon of a hundred equal faces,
the silver coinage
sobs in the pocket.

Comment: Surrealistic Imagery

García Lorca's poetry, as you have seen, contains startling and unexpected images, and many critics see a direct connection between these and the paintings of Salvador Dali, a famous Spanish artist with whom Lorca was friendly. Dali was a surrealist, a painter who believed that art should try to show what takes place in the subconscious mind. His paintings represent the startling juxtapositions found in dreams—a gigantic ear standing upright in a desert, an oversized watch melting on a rocky plain. After reading Lorca's poetry, the influence of surrealism on it seems unmistakable.

In "Half Moon," for instance, the moon is presented as a scythe—not cutting grass as scythes usually do, but moving over the "shimmer from the river." In "The Moon Rising," the startling imagery involves not only sight, but sound and touch as well, ending with "silver coinage" sobbing "in the pocket," apparently in ecstatic appreciation of the rising of the moon.

The remaining García Lorca poems that you will read contain similar imagery. In "Pause of the Clock," we find a "white silence"—a color given to a sound (or its absence)—and stars colliding with the black numerals of a clock, a surrealistic picture highly suggestive of dreams. Even the fairly conventional "Song" concludes with an image of the wind with its "gray arm" around a girl's waist.

In "The Guitar," the "lament" of the instrument evokes a succession of surrealistic images. The "glasses of the dawn are broken" by the lament (dawn's light streaking the sky, suggesting cracked glasses, perhaps). The "sands of the warm South" seek "white camellias." The "first bird" is "dead upon the branch." And the heart is "pierced through with five swords." In calling forth these images the lament of the guitar apparently reaches into the same unconscious that is the source of dreams.

Such strange and exotic combinations of images tend to make us uneasy, even uncomfortable. They jar us out of our easy ways of thinking. Perhaps they even startle us into a new awareness of things and their possible relationships, into new ways of seeing the reality around us.

Pause of the Clock

I sat down
in a space of time.
It was a backwater
of silence,
a white silence,
a formidable ring
wherein the stars
collided with the twelve floating
black numerals.

Song

The girl of beautiful face
goes gathering olives.
The wind, that suitor of towers,
grasps her round the waist.
Four riders have passed
on Andalusian ponies,[1]
with suits of azure and green,
and long dark cloaks.
"Come to Córdoba, lass."
The girl pays no heed.
Three young bullfighters have passed,
their waists are slender,
their suits orange-colored,
their swords of antique silver.
"Come to Seville, lass."
The girl pays no heed.
When the evening became
purple, with diffused light,
a youth passed by bringing
roses and myrtles of the moon.
"Come to Granada, lass."
But the girl pays no heed.
The girl of beautiful face
still goes on gathering olives,
with the gray arm of the wind
encircling her waist.

1. ***Andalusian ponies,*** ponies from Andalusia (än′dä lü′ᴛʜē ä), the region in southern Spain where all the cities mentioned later in the poem—Córdoba (kôr′ᴛʜō vä), Seville, and Granada—are located.

The Guitar

The lament
of the guitar begins.
The glasses of the dawn
are broken.
The lament
of the guitar begins.
It is useless
to hush it.
It is impossible
to hush it.
Monotonously weeping
as the water weeps,
as the wind weeps
over the snowfall.
It is impossible
to hush it.
Weeping for things
far away.
Sands of the warm South
seeking white camellias.
It weeps, like an arrow without a target,
evening without morning,
and the first bird dead
upon the branch.
Oh guitar!
Heart pierced through
with five swords.

Discussion

Half Moon

1. Describe in your own words the picture created in this poem.

2. Do you think the frog is actually using the moon's reflection for a mirror? If not, what might have been the poet's reason for including this image?

The Moon Rising

1. Each stanza of the poem indicates what happens "when the moon rises." How would you describe, in general, the effect of the rising moon?

2. Why do you think the speaker holds the opinion he does in stanza 3?

Pause of the Clock

1. Why is the phrase "a space of time" a paradox? Discuss.

2. What possibly has happened to the speaker, causing him to sit in a "backwater" of "white silence"?

3. How do space and time come together in the last four lines of the poem?

Song

1. What story is narrated in this poem? Does it seem realistic? Why or why not?

2. Why do you think the girl stays at her work? Discuss.

3. In what way is the wind a "suitor of towers"?

The Guitar

1. How would you describe the mood created by the lament of the guitar?

2. (a) Discuss the effect of the closing image in the poem. **(b)** Choose one other unusual image and explain the picture or idea it brings to your mind.

Federico García Lorca 1899–1936

When the Spanish Civil War broke out in 1936, Federico García Lorca, the leading young poet of Spain, fled from the capital city of Madrid to the place where he grew up, the city of Granada in Andalusia. There he was arrested and executed without trial by Fascist supporters of General Francisco Franco. He was no doubt judged guilty because of his sympathy for the poor and his support of the common people. His death was a loss to world literature.

García Lorca was, at his death, a widely read and popular poet in Spain. By the time he was twenty he had published his first book—*Landscape Impressions,* a work in prose. His first volume of poems appeared in 1921, followed by *Canciones (Songs)* in 1927. But the work that brought him international fame was *Gypsy Ballads* (1928), eighteen poems that combined the folk ballads so popular in his native Andalusia with the startling imagery he had developed in his association with surrealism. (See the Comment on page 230.)

García Lorca continued to write poetry; a trip to the United States resulted in *Poet in New York,* a collection not published until 1940. But his interest turned more and more toward drama: he founded a group of wandering players who brought classical theater to the working people, and he wrote several plays of his own. Among the most popular are *The Blood Wedding* and *The House of Bernarda Alba,* both frequently produced in the United States. These plays blend humor and melancholy in actions that are starkly tragic.

Unit 3 Review: *Poetry*

Content Review

1. Some poems in the "Story Poems" section present a fairly traditional narrative with regular plot and character development, while others have a less well-developed story or a story that stands for something else. Group the poems according to these two types and explain what elements in each poem led you to place it in the group you did.

2. Poets use several techniques to reveal the characters they are portraying: the character's own speech; his or her actions or thoughts; a description of the character; the speaker's attitude toward the character; other characters' attitudes toward the character. Select three poems from the "Portraits" section and explain the way or ways the main character in each is developed.

3. Describe the attitude of the speaker in each poem in the "All Creatures" section toward the animal or animals in the poem.

4. Choose one poem from the "Landscapes" section and one from "Moods and Emotions" that you feel do a particularly good job of making you see or feel their subjects clearly. Explain why you think each poem is especially effective, quoting lines to support your opinion.

5. Compare and contrast the kinds of choices presented in "Ordinance on Lining Up" and "Yoke and Star." With what set of choices would you prefer to be confronted? Give reasons for your answer.

6. Both Edgar Lee Masters and A. E. Housman have been described as generally creating sad and melancholy characters in their poems. Compare and contrast the overall impressions created by the speakers in the Masters poems with those of the speakers in the Housman poems.

7. Analyze the following pairs of poems in terms of their overall message, the mood they create, and/or the techniques they use to create that mood: **(a)** Emily Dickinson's "The Grass So Little Has to Do" and Oumar Ba's "Drought"; **(b)** Dickinson's "Hope Is the Thing with Feathers" and Lisel Mueller's "Hope"; **(c)** Robert Frost's "Desert Places" and Octavio Paz's "The Street"; **(d)** García Lorca's "The Guitar" and Chu Shu Shen's "Sorrow."

Concept Review: Interpretation of New Material

Read the poem that follows. Then use the questions that come after it to review your understanding of the concepts and literary terms presented in this unit.

The Rabbit • *Edna St. Vincent Millay* USA

Hearing the hawk squeal in the high sky
I and the rabbit trembled.
Only the dark small rabbits newly kittled in their neatly dissembled
Hollowed nest in the thicket thatched with straw
Did not respect his cry.
At least, not that I saw.

Continued

But I have said to the rabbit with rage and a hundred times, "Hop!
Streak it for the bushes! Why do you sit so still?
You are bigger than a house, I tell you, you are bigger than a hill, you are a beacon for air-planes!
O indiscreet!
And the hawk and all my friends are out to kill!
Get under cover!" But the rabbit never stirred; she never will.

And I shall see again and again the large eye blaze
With death, and gently glaze;
The leap into the air I shall see again and again, and the kicking feet;
And the sudden quiet everlasting, and the blade of grass green in the strange mouth of the interrupted grazer.

1. Is this poem a lyric or a narrative? Give a reason for your answer.

2. On hearing the hawk squeal in the sky, who is afraid? **(a)** only the speaker; **(b)** all the rabbits; **(c)** the speaker and one rabbit; **(d)** all the animals in the thicket.

3. When the speaker refers to respecting the hawk's cry in line 5, she means **(a)** appreciating the harmony of the cry; **(b)** knowing that the cry might signal attack and death; **(c)** understanding what the hawk is trying to say; **(d)** liking the hawk as a fellow creature.

4. The incident described **(a)** has never happened before; **(b)** has happened once before; **(c)** happens once a year; **(d)** has happened many times before.

5. The speaker believes that rabbits **(a)** attract hawks by their noise; **(b)** should guard their young more carefully; **(c)** tend to be invisible to hawks; **(d)** are more than big enough to attract hawks' attention.

6. What is the speaker's tone in stanza 2?

7. Find one example of hyperbole in stanza 2.

8. What was the rabbit doing when it was killed?

9. In this poem the speaker is most concerned about **(a)** people dying; **(b)** nature versus people; **(c)** the extinction of hawks; **(d)** rabbits that do not hide from those who prey on them.

10. Which of the following best describes the metrical pattern of stanzas 2 and 3? **(a)** no rhythm but regular rhyme; **(b)** no rhythm and irregular rhyme; **(c)** regular rhythm and regular rhyme; **(d)** irregular rhythm and irregular rhyme.

Composition Review

Choose one of the following assignments.

1. Review the "All Creatures" section of this unit and decide what other creature you would have included in it. Make a list of the various features and characteristics of the creature you've chosen.

Write a two- or three-paragraph essay explaining why your creature should be honored by a poem in "All Creatures." Be sure to emphasize those aspects of the creature that you find particularly impressive.

2. If you could choose one of the poets in the "Portraits" section to write a poem about you or someone you know, which poet would you select? Make your decision based on how that poet portrayed the character in the poem you read—word choice, descriptions used, ideas expressed.

Write a three- or four-paragraph essay explaining your choice of poet, using examples from the poem you read to back up your opinion.

3. Suppose all the poems in the "Choices" section were submitted to a poetry contest for which you are the judge. Review the poems, analyzing them for such things as originality of thought, effective use of language, and appropriate imagery.

In a three-paragraph composition explain your reasons for awarding first and second prizes.

4. You have read a number of the poems of Masters, Housman, Dickinson, Frost, and García Lorca. Select the poet from this group that most appealed to you; reread all of his or her poems and the biographical note, attempting to get a feel for this poet's "voice."

Write a letter to a friend recommending the poet and trying to persuade him or her to read the poet's works. Set forth your reasons for liking the poet, including such things as technique, subject matter, and voice, and quoting favorite lines to make your points.

Unit 4

Greek Drama

Medea

Background

Origins

Classical Greek drama, the form from which modern drama as we know it developed, had its origins in the early religious rituals of ancient Greece. By the fifth century B.C. these rituals had evolved into dramatic presentations and were a central feature of the annual festival held in Athens to honor Dionysus (dī'ə nī'səs), the god of wine and fertility. The dramas were presented in three-day contests that attracted the finest playwrights in Greece. Competing for prizes with other dramatists, each presented four plays: three tragedies and one *satyr* (sā'tər) play, a short, comic version of a Greek myth. A prestigious ivy wreath was awarded to the playwright deemed best by a citizen panel of five judges. The contests produced some of the world's greatest dramatists, most notedly Aeschylus (es'kə ləs), Sophocles (sof'ə klēz'), and Euripides (yů rip'ə dēz'), and Greek tragedy flowered as a dramatic form.

The Greek Theater

The enormous open-air amphitheater of Athens, built into the slope of a hillside, held thousands of people. A playgoer in Athens saw a statue of Dionysus sitting on a special altar waiting to "witness" the dramatic contests. Because of the religious and civic nature of the festival of Dionysus, everyone was invited and encouraged to attend. On the days of performance, businesses and law courts were closed. The admission charge was refunded for those who could not afford it, and others were compensated for wages lost.

In the approximately fifty-five rows of seats were most of the citizens of Athens: a number of school-age boys, most of the voting population, some of the better-educated slaves, and even women (usually barred from most public events). The spectators looked down from their seats in the natural, horseshoe-shaped amphitheater to the *orchestra,* the circular area where the chorus, an important part of any Greek drama, would perform. (See the illustration of the theater at Epidaurus, a typical example of an ancient Greek theater.) Behind the orchestra was a raised platform that functioned as the stage, and a building called a *skene* (skē'nē), used for costume changes and storing scenery. It was in front of this small structure that the scenes in many Greek tragedies took place, as they did in *Medea.* In fact, in *Medea,* the skene served as Medea's house.

The Actors

Playwrights often directed and acted in their own plays, which they wrote in poetry and presented with music and dance. Because the outdoor theater was so vast, they and the other actors, who were all men, had to make themselves appear larger than life to communicate mood and feeling to the distant spectators. One way they did this was by wearing masks; these were made of linen, cork, or wood, and some had a different expression on each side. The use of masks permitted actors to portray several different roles (including female characters), even though there were never more than three masked characters on stage at once. To balance the visual effect of the large masks, actors also wore thick-soled boots and great robes with huge sleeves.

Although the amphitheater had excellent acoustics, the actors were carefully trained in formal speaking, for they had to be heard by an immense and sometimes noisy audience. To help project the actors' voices, the mouths of their masks were funnel-shaped and thus were able to serve as small megaphones.

Primitive Ancestor of Greek Drama

The Dionysian festivals had not always revolved around dramatic contests. At first, in fact, the dramatic presentations at the festivals were simply choral songs to honor the god and were performed by a fifty-member chorus. The choral songs evolved into the dramatic form Euripides and the other playwrights knew with the help of an actor-producer named Thespis. About 534 B.C. Thespis separated himself from the chorus, in effect creating a character. This separation of chorus and character made dialogue possible between them. Thus Greek drama was born.

Tragedy

The tragedies were based on the numerous stories and characters of Greek mythology that the Greek audiences knew well. However, the religious nature of the Dionysian festival required the tragedies to be morally instructive as well as entertaining. They were not just solemn stories of unhappy persons; rather, they were complex studies of the nature of human beings in conflict with themselves, with society, and with the gods.

Tragedies often depicted high-born persons whose display of *hubris* (hyü′bris)—insolent pride or arrogance—offended the gods and led to disastrous consequences. *Medea* is such a play.

What the Audience Knew

Spectators at the Greek plays tended to know the background and the action of the play inasmuch as the plots were taken from well-known legends and myths. They knew, for example, that Medea had committed violent deeds in the service of Jason, the famous hero and leader of the adventurers known as the Argonauts. These deeds made it necessary for Medea to leave her homeland and flee with Jason to Corinth, where they lived for several years. As the play opens, Jason has abandoned Medea to marry King Creon's daughter. Medea is outraged and seeks revenge. The spectators already know what will happen—and what horrible deeds will follow—but they are interested in how the playwright will dramatize the familiar events.

See **ALLUSION** Handbook of Literary Terms

Medea

Euripides Greece

translated by Robinson Jeffers

CHARACTERS

THE NURSE	CREON (krē'on)
THE TUTOR	JASON
THE CHORUS	AEGEUS (ē'jē əs)
FIRST WOMAN OF CORINTH	THE TWO SONS OF JASON AND MEDEA
SECOND WOMAN OF CORINTH	JASON'S SLAVE
THIRD WOMAN OF CORINTH	ATTENDANTS TO MEDEA
MEDEA (mi dē'ə)	SOLDIERS

The entire action of the play occurs before MEDEA'*s house in Corinth.*

Act One

The NURSE *comes from the doorsteps toward the front of the stage.*

THE NURSE. I wish the long ship *Argo* had never passed that
perilous channel between the Symplegades,
I wish the pines that made her mast and her oars still waved in
the wind on Mount Pelion, and the gray fishhawk
Still nested in them, the great adventurers had never voyaged
Into the Asian sunrise to the shores of morning for the Golden
Fleece.
For then my mistress Medea
Would never have seen Jason nor loved and saved him, nor cut
herself off from home to come with him

Into this country of the smiling chattering Greeks and the roofs of Corinth:[1] over which I see evil
Hang like a cloud. For she is not meek but fierce, and the daughter of a king.
Yet at first all went well.
The folk of Corinth were kind to her, they were proud of her beauty, and Jason loved her. Happy is the house
Where the man and the woman love and are faithful.
Now all is changed; all is black hatred. For Jason
Has turned from her; he calls the old bond a barbarian mating, not a Greek marriage; he has cast her off
And wedded the yellow-haired child of Creon, the ruler here. He wants worldly advantage, fine friends,
And a high place in Corinth. For these he is willing to cast Medea like a harlot, and betray the children
That she has borne him. He is not wise, I think.
But Medea
Lies in the house, broken with pain and rage; she will neither eat nor drink, except her own tears;
She turns her face toward the earth, remembering her father's house and her native land, which she abandoned
For the love of this man: who now despises her.
And if I try to speak comfort to her she only stares at me, great eyes like stones. She is like a stone on the shore
Or a wave of the sea, and I think she hates
Even her children. She is learning what it is to be a foreigner, cast out, alone, and despised.
She will never learn to be humble; she will never learn to drink insult
Like harmless water. O I'm in terror of her: whether she'll thread a knife through her own heart,
Or whether she'll hunt the bridegroom and his new bride, or what more dreadful evil stalks in the forest
Of her dark mind. I know that Jason would have been wiser to tempt a lioness, or naked-handed
Steal the whelps of a tiger.
(She sees MEDEA'*s* SONS *coming with their* TUTOR.*)*
Here come the happy children. Little they know
Of their mother's grief.

THE TUTOR *(entering with the two little* BOYS*).* Old servant of my lady, why do you stand out here, keeping watch in solitude
With those grim eyes? Is it some trouble of your own that you are lamenting? I should think Medea
Would need your care.

1. ***I wish . . . the roofs of Corinth.*** Jason met Medea while seeking the legendary Golden Fleece, a closely guarded treasure of Medea's father, King Aeëtes (ē ē′tēz) of Colchis (kol′kis). While journeying east to Colchis and the "shores of morning" on his ship the *Argo,* Jason and his companions faced many dangers, among them the Clashing Rocks, or Symplegades (sim pleg′ə dēz′), which roll continuously against one another and threaten to crush whatever comes between them. When "the great adventurers" finally arrived at Colchis, a barbarian country on the Black Sea, Aeëtes set Jason an impossible series of tasks as the price of winning the Golden Fleece. The goddesses Hera and Aphrodite sent down Cupid to inflame Medea with love for Jason; as a result, Medea used magic to help Jason win the Fleece and then fled with him, ending up eventually in the Greek city of Corinth.

THE NURSE. It is all one to Medea, whether I am there or here. Yes, it is mine.
My trouble. My lady's grief is my grief. And it has hurt me
So that I had to come out and speak it to the earth and sky.

THE TUTOR. Is she still in that deep despair?

THE NURSE. You are lucky,
Old watchdog of Jason's boys. I envy you,
You do not see her. This evil is not declining, it is just at dawn. I dread the lion-eyed
Glare of its noon.

THE TUTOR. Is she so wrought? Yet neither you nor Medea
Knows the latest and worst.

THE NURSE. What? What?

THE TUTOR. I shouldn't have spoken.
No, it is nothing.

THE NURSE. Tell me the truth, old man. You and I are two slaves, we can trust each other.
We can keep secrets.

THE TUTOR. I heard them saying—when we walked beside the holy fountain Peirene,[2]
Where the old men sit in the sun on the stone benches—they were saying that Creon, the lord of this land,
Intends to drive out Medea and the children with her, these innocent boys, out of this house
And out of Corinth, and they must wander through the wild world
Homeless and helpless.

THE NURSE. I don't believe it. Ah, no! Jason may hate the mother, but he would hardly
Let his sons be cast out.

THE TUTOR. Well . . . he has made a new alliance. He is not a friend of this house.

THE NURSE. If this were true!—Listen: I hear her voice. Take the children away, keep them away from her.
Take them to the other door. Quickly.

(They go out, toward a rear door of the house. The NURSE *looks after them, wringing her hands.)*

MEDEA *(within the house. She is Asiatic and laments loudly).*[3] Death. Death is my wish. For myself, my enemies, my children. Destruction.
That's the word. Grind, crush, burn. Destruction. Ai . . . Ai . . .

THE NURSE *(wringing her hands).* This is my terror:
To hear her always harking back to the children, like a fierce hound at fault. O unhappy one,
They're not to blame.

2. ***Peirene*** (pi ren′).

3. ***She is Asiatic and laments loudly.*** The Greeks prided themselves on their rational, civilized behavior, which generally included avoiding excessive shows of emotion.

MEDEA *(within).* If any god hears me: let me die. Ah, rotten, rotten, rotten: death is the only
Water to wash this dirt.
(CHORUS is coming in, but the NURSE does not yet notice them. She is intent on MEDEA's cries and her own thoughts.)
THE NURSE. Oh, it's a bad thing
To be born of high race, and brought up willful and powerful in a great house, unruled
And ruling many: for then if misfortune comes it is unendurable; it drives you mad. I say that poor people
Are happier: the little commoners and humble people, the poor in spirit: they can lie low
Under the wind and live: while the tall oaks and cloud-raking mountain pines go mad in the storm,
Writhe, groan, and crash. This is the wild and terrible justice of God: it brings on great persons
The great disasters.
(She becomes aware of the WOMEN OF THE CHORUS who have come in, and is startled from her reverie.)
What do you want?
FIRST WOMAN. I hear her crying again: it is dreadful.
SECOND WOMAN. Her lamentation.
She is beautiful and deep in grief: we couldn't help coming.
THIRD WOMAN. We are friends of this house and its trouble hurts us.
THE NURSE. You are right, friends; it is not a home. It is broken.
A house of grief and of weeping.
MEDEA *(within).* Hear me, God, let me die.
What I need: all dead, all dead, all dead,
Under the great cold stones. For a year and a thousand years and another thousand: cold as the stones, cold,
But noble again, proud, straight, and silent, crimson-cloaked
In the blood of our wounds.
FIRST WOMAN. O shining sky, divine earth,
Harken not to the song that this woman sings.
It is not her mind's music; her mind is not here.
She does not know what she prays for.
Pain and wrath are the singers.
SECOND WOMAN. Unhappy one,
Never pray for death, never pray for death,
He is here all too soon.
He strikes from the clear sky like a hawk,
He hides behind green leaves, or he waits
Around the corner of the wall.
O never pray for death, never pray for death—

Because that prayer will be answered.

MEDEA *(the rise and fall of her voice indicate that she is prowling back and forth beyond the doorway, like a caged animal).* I know poisons. I know the bright teeth of steel. I know fire. But I will not be mocked by my enemies,
And I will not endure pity. Pity and contempt are sister and brother, twin-born. I will not die tamely.
I will not allow blubber-eyed pity, nor contempt either, to snivel over the stones of my tomb.
I am not a Greek woman.

THIRD WOMAN. No, a barbarian woman from savage Colchis, at the bitter end
Of the Black Sea. Does she boast of that?

SECOND WOMAN. She doesn't know what she is saying.

MEDEA *(in the house).* Poisons. Death-magic. The sharp sword. The hemp rope. Death-magic. Death . . .

SECOND WOMAN. I hate Jason, who made this sorrow.

FIRST WOMAN *(to the* NURSE*).* Old and honored servant of a great house, do you think it is wise
To leave your lady alone in there, except perhaps a few slaves, building that terrible acropolis
Of deadly thoughts? We Greeks believe that solitude is very dangerous, great passions grow into monsters
In the dark of the mind; but if you share them with loving friends they remain human, they can be endured.
I think you ought to persuade Medea to come from the dark dwelling and speak with us, before her heart breaks,
Or she does harm to herself. She has lived among us, we've learned to love her, we'd gladly tell her so.
It might comfort her spirit.

THE NURSE. Do you think so? She wouldn't listen. —Oh, oh, she is coming!
Speak carefully to her; make your words a soft music.

*(*MEDEA *comes through the doorway, propping herself against one of the pillars, and stands staring.)*

THE NURSE. Oh, my dear, my poor child. *(She hurries toward* MEDEA.*)*

SECOND WOMAN *(whispering).* They say she is dangerous. Look at her eyes.

FIRST WOMAN. She is a witch, but not evil. She can make old men young again: she did it for Jason's father.[4]

THIRD WOMAN. All the people of her country are witches. They know about drugs and magic. They are savages, but they have a wild wisdom.

4. She is a witch . . . Jason's father. Medea was, in fact, a sorceress or witch, and had once prepared, at Jason's request, a special potion that made his father forty years younger.

SECOND WOMAN. Poor soul, it hasn't helped this one much.

MEDEA *(she does not see the gaping and whispering* WOMEN*).* I will look at the light of the sun, this last time. I wish from that blue sky the white wolf of lightning
Would leap, and burst my skull and my brain, and like a burning babe cling to these breasts. . . .
(She checks and looks fiercely at the WOMEN *below.)*
Someone is here?
(Her hostile eyes range back and forth; she sees the WOMEN *clearly now, and assumes full self-control. Her voice is cautious and insincere.)* I did not know I had visitors. . . . Women of Corinth,
If anything has been spoken too loudly here, consider
That I believed I was alone; and I have some provocation. You've come—let me suppose
With love and sympathy—to peer at my sorrow. I understand well enough
That nothing is ever private in a Greek city; whoever withholds anything
Is thought sullen or proud . . .
(With irony) undemocratic
I think you call it. This is not always just, but we know that justice, at least on earth,
Is a name, not a fact; and as for me, I wish to avoid any appearance
Of being . . . proud. Of what? Of affliction? I will show you my naked heart. You know that my lord Jason
Has left me and made a second marriage, with the bright-haired child
Of wealth and power. I too was a child of power, but not in this country; and I spent my power
For love of Jason. I poured it out before him like water; I made him drink it like wine. I gave him
Success and fame; I saved him his precious life, not once, many times. You may have heard what I did for him:
I betrayed my father for him, I killed my brother to save him; I made my own land to hate me forever;
And I fled west with Jason in the Greek ship, under the thunder of the sail, weeping and laughing,
That huge journey through the Black Sea and the Bosporus, where the rocks clang together, through the Sea of Marmora,
And through the Hellespont, watched by the spearmen of wealthy Troy, and home to Greek water:[5] his home, my exile,
My endless exile. And here I have loved him and borne him sons; and this . . . man . . .
Has left me and taken Creon's daughter, to enjoy her fortune, and put aside her soft yellow hair

5. ***I betrayed my father . . . to Greek water.*** Medea not only gave Jason magical charms and potions to help him accomplish the near-impossible tasks Aeëtes had demanded he perform in return for the Golden Fleece; she also took her younger brother along on the *Argo*'s flight from Colchis and had him killed as a way of delaying Aeëtes' pursuit of her and Jason. The journey to Greece took Jason and Medea southwest through the Black Sea and the Sea of Marmora to the Aegean Sea; the Bosporus (bos′pər əs) and the Hellespont (hel′i spont) are straits connecting Marmora with the Black Sea and the Aegean, respectively. The "wealthy" city of Troy, later destroyed in the Trojan War, was near the banks of the Hellespont (now called the Dardanelles).

And kiss her young mouth.

*(*MEDEA *stands rigid, struggling for self-control.)*

FIRST WOMAN. She is terrible. Stone with stone eyes.

SECOND WOMAN. Look: the foam-flake on her lip, that flickers with her breathing.

THIRD WOMAN. She is pitiable: she is under great injuries.

MEDEA *(low-voiced).* I do not know what other women . . . I do not know how much a Greek woman

Will endure. The people of my race are somewhat rash and intemperate. As for me, I want simply to die.

But Jason is not to smile at his bride over my grave, nor that great man Creon

Hang wreaths and make a feast day in Corinth. Or let the wreaths be bright blinding fire, and the songs a high wailing,

And the wine, blood.

FIRST WOMAN. Daughter of sorrow, beware.

It is dangerous to dream of wine; it is worse

To speak of wailing or blood:

For the images that the mind makes

Find a way out, they work into life.

MEDEA. Let them work into life!

FIRST WOMAN. There are evils that cannot be cured by evil.

Patience remains, and the gods watch all.

MEDEA *(dully, without hope).* Let them watch my enemies go down in blood.

SECOND WOMAN. Medea, beware!

Some great person is coming.—It is Creon himself!

THIRD WOMAN. Creon is coming.

THE NURSE. He is dark with anger. O my lady . . . my child . . . bend in this wind,

And not be broken!

*(*CREON *comes in, with* MEN *attending him. The* WOMEN OF THE CHORUS *move to one side. He speaks to* MEDEA, *with an angry gesture toward* CHORUS.*)*

CREON. You have admirers, I see. Abate your pride: these people will not be with you where you are going.

(A pause. MEDEA *does not answer.* CREON *brings his wrath under control.)*

Medea, woman of the stone forehead and hate-filled eyes: I have made my decision. I have decided

That you must leave this land at once and go into banishment, you with your children. I intend to remove

A root of disturbance out of the soil of Corinth. I am here to see to it. I will not return home

Until it is done.

MEDEA. You mean . . . banishment?

CREON. Exile: banishment:
go where you may, Medea, but here
You abide no more.
MEDEA. . . . I with my children?
CREON. I will not take them
away from you.
MEDEA. Because we have suffered evil
We are to suffer more evil. Death was my wish.
CREON. Ha? Words.
You'll not be hindered: you can have death
While there are ropes to hang by or waves to drown in. Only
make haste
And leave this land.
MEDEA. The children, my lord . . .
(Her lips move angrily, but the voice is not heard.)
CREON. What are you
muttering?
MEDEA. Nothing . . . I am praying to my gods for wisdom.
And you for mercy. My sons are still very young, tender and
helpless. You know, my lord,
What exile means—to wander with fear and famine for guide and
driver, through all the wild winter storms
And the rage of the sun; and beg a bread crust and be derided;
pelted with stones in the villages,

Held a little lower than the scavenger dogs, kicked, scorned, and slaved—the children, my lord,
Are Jason's children. Your chosen friend, I believe, and now
Even closer bound. And as for me, your servant, O master of Corinth, what have I done? Why
Must I be cast?

CREON. I will tell you frankly: because you nourish rancorous ill will toward persons
Whom I intend to protect: I send you out before you've time to do harm here. And you are notorious
For occult knowledge: sorcery, poisons, magic. Men say you can even sing down the moon from heaven,
And make the holy stars to falter and run backward, against the purpose
And current of nature. Ha? As to that I know not: I know you are dangerous. You threaten my daughter: you have to go.

MEDEA. But I wish her well, my lord! I wish her all happiness. I hope that Jason may be as kind to her
As . . . to me.

CREON *(fiercely)*. That is your wish?

MEDEA. I misspoke. I thought of . . . old days. . . .

(She seems to weep.)

CREON. I acknowledge, Medea,
That you have some cause for grief. I all the more must guard against your dark wisdom and bitter heart.

MEDEA. You misjudge me cruelly. It is true that I have some knowledge of drugs and medicines: I can sometimes cure sickness:
Is that a crime? These dark rumors, my lord,
Are only the noise of popular gratitude. You must have observed it often: if any person
Knows a little more than the common man, the people suspect him. If he brings a new talent,
How promptly the hateful whispers begin. But you are not a common man, lord of Corinth, you
Will not fear knowledge.

CREON. No. Nor change my decision. I am here to see you leave this house and the city:
And not much time. Move quickly, gather your things and go. I pity you, Medea,
But you must go.

MEDEA. You pity me? You . . . pity me?

(She comes close to him, wild with rage.)

I will endure a dog's pity or a wart-grown toad's. May God who hears me . . . We shall see in the end

Who's to be pitied.

CREON *(shocked, recovering his dignity).* This is good. This is what I desire. Unmask the livid face of your hatred
And I see whom I deal with. Serpent and wolf: a wolf from Asia: I'd rather have you rage now
Than do harm later. Now, Medea: out of here.
Before my men drive you out.

MEDEA *(controls her fury, then speaks).* You see a woman driven half mad with sorrow, laboring to save
Her little children. No wolf, my lord. And though I was born in far-off Asia: call that misfortune,
Not vice. The races of Asia are human too,
As the bright Greeks are. And our hearts are as brittle: if you hurt us we cry. And we have children and love them,
As Greeks do. You have a daughter, sir—

CREON. Yes, and I'll keep her safe of your female hatred: therefore I send you
Out of this land.

MEDEA. It is not true, I am not jealous. I never hated her.
Jealous for the sake of Jason? I am far past wanting Jason, my lord. You took him and gave him to her,
And I will say you did well, perhaps wisely. Your daughter is loved by all: she is beautiful: if I were near her
I should soon love her.

CREON. You can speak sweetly enough, you can make honey in your mouth like a brown bee
When it serves your turn.

MEDEA. Not honey: the truth.

CREON. Trust you or not, you are going out of this country, Medea.
What I decide is fixed; it is like the firm rocks of Acrocorinth,[6] which neither earthquake can move
Nor a flood of tears melt. Make ready quickly: I have a guest in my house. I should return to him.

THE NURSE *(comes beside* MEDEA *and speaks to her).* What guest? O my lady, ask him
Who is the guest? If powerful and friendly
He might be a refuge to us in bitter exile. . . .

MEDEA *(pays no attention to her. Kneels to* CREON*).* I know that your will is granite. But even on the harsh face of a granite mountain some flowers of mercy
May grow in season. Have mercy on my little sons, Creon,
Though there is none for me.

(She reaches to embrace his knees. He steps backward from her.)

CREON. How long, woman? This is decided; done; finished.

6. ***Acrocorinth*** (from the Greek *akros*, meaning "top" or "peak," + *Corinth*), a high rock on which was built a citadel and a temple of Aphrodite.

MEDEA *(rising from her knees, turns half away from him)*. I am not a beggar.
I will not trouble you. I shall not live long.
(She turns to him again.)
Sire: grant me a few hours yet, one day to prepare in, one little day
Before I go out of Corinth forever.
CREON. What? No! I told you. The day is today, Medea, this day.
And the hour is now.
MEDEA. There are no flowers on this mountain: not one violet, not one anemone.
Your face, my lord, is like flint. If I could find the right words, if some god would lend me a touch of eloquence,
I'd show you my heart. I'd lift it out of my breast and turn it over in my hands; you'd see how pure it is
Of any harm or malice toward you or your household.
(She holds out her hands to him.) Look at it: not a speck: look, my lord. They call mercy
The jewel of kings. I am praying
To you as to one of the gods: destroy us not utterly. To go out with no refuge, nothing prepared,
Is plain death: I would rather kill myself quickly and here. If I had time but to ask the slaves
And strolling beggars where to go, how to live: and I must gather some means: one or two jewels
And small gold things I have, to trade them for bread and goat's milk. Wretched, wretched, wretched I am,
I and my boys.
(She kneels again.)
I beseech you, Creon,
By the soft yellow hair and cool smooth forehead and the white knees
Of that young girl who is now Jason's bride: lend me this inch of time: one day—half a day,
For this one is now half gone—and I will go my sad course and vanish in the morning quietly as dew
That drops on the stones at dawn and is dry at sunrise. You will never again be troubled by any word
Or act of mine. And this I pray you for your dear child's sake. O Creon, what is half a day
In all the rich years of Corinth?
CREON. I will think of it. I am no tyrant.
I have been merciful to my own hurt, many times. Even to myself I seem to be foolish
If I grant you this thing. . . . No, Medea,

I will not grant it.
(She has been kneeling with bowed head. Silently she raises her imploring face toward him.)
Well . . . We shall watch you: as a hawk does a viper. What harm could she do
In the tail of one day? A ruler ought to be ruthless, but I am not. I am a fool
In my own eyes, whatever the world may think. I can be gruff with warriors; a woman weeping
Floods me off course.—Take it, then. Make your preparations.
But if tomorrow's sun shines on you here—Medea, you die. . . . Enough words. Thank me not. I want my hands
Washed of this business.
(He departs quickly, followed by his MEN. MEDEA *rises from her knees.)*
MEDEA. I will thank you.
And the whole world will hear of it.
FIRST WOMAN. I have seen this man's arrogance, I watched and heard him.
I am of Corinth, and I say that Corinth
Is not well ruled.
SECOND WOMAN. The city where even a woman, even a foreigner,
Suffers unjustly the rods of power
Is not well ruled.
FIRST WOMAN. Unhappy Medea, what haven, what sanctuary, where will you wander?
Which of the gods, Medea,
Drives you through waves of woe, the mooring broken, the hawsers and the anchor-head,
Hopeless from harbor?
MEDEA. . . . This man . . . this barking dog . . . this gulled fool . . . gods of my father's country,
You saw me low on my knees before the great dog of Corinth; humble, holding my heart in my hands
For a dog to bite—break this dog's teeth!
Women: it is a bitter thing to be a woman.
A woman is weak for warfare, she must use cunning. Men boast their battles: I tell you this, and we know it:
It is easier to stand in battle three times, in the front line, in the stabbing fury, than to bear one child.
And a woman, they say, can do no good but in childbirth. It may be so. She can do evil, she can do evil.
I wept before that tall dog, I wept my tears before him, I degraded my knees to him, I gulled and flattered him:
O triple fool, he has given me all that I needed: a little time, a

space of time. Death is dearer to me
Than what I am now; and if today by sunset the world has not turned, and turned sharp too—let your dog Creon
Send two or three slaves to kill me and a cord to strangle me: I will stretch out
My throat to it. But I have a bitter hope, women. I begin to see light
Through the dark wood, between the monstrous trunks of the trees, at the end of the tangled forest an eyehole,
A pinpoint of light: I shall not die perhaps
As a pigeon dies. Nor like an innocent lamb, that feels a hand on its head and looks up from the knife
To the man's face and dies. No, like some yellow-eyed beast that has killed its hunters let me lie down
On the hounds' bodies and the broken spears.—Then how to strike them? What means to use? There are so many
Doors through which painful death may glide in and catch . . . which one, which one?

(She stands meditating. The NURSE *comes from behind her and speaks to the* FIRST WOMAN OF THE CHORUS.*)*

THE NURSE. Tell me: do you know what guest
Is in Creon's house?

FIRST WOMAN. What?—Oh. An Athenian ship came from the north last night: it is Aegeus,[7]
The lord of Athens.

THE NURSE. Aegeus! My lady knows him: I believe he will help us. Some god has brought him here,
Some savior god.

FIRST WOMAN. He is leaving, I think, today.

THE NURSE *(hobbling back toward* MEDEA*).* My lady! Lord Aegeus
Is here in Corinth, Creon's guest. Aegeus of Athens.

*(*MEDEA *looks at her silently, without attention.)*

If you will see him and speak him fairly,
We have a refuge.

MEDEA. I have things in my hand to do. Be quiet.

THE NURSE. Oh, listen to me!
You are driven out of Corinth; you must find shelter. Aegeus of Athens is here.

*(*MEDEA *turns from her and moves to reenter the house. The* NURSE *catches at her clothing, servile but eager, slave and mother at the same time.)*

MEDEA *(angrily turning on her).* What's that to me?

THE NURSE. I lifted you in my arms when you were . . . this long.

7. ***Aegeus,*** a legendary Athenian king and the father of Theseus.

I gave you milk from these breasts, that are now dead leaves.
I saw the little beautiful body straighten and grow tall: Oh . . . child . . . almost my child . . . how can I
Not try to save you? Life is better than death—

MEDEA. Not now.

THE NURSE. Time's running out!

MEDEA. I have time. Oh, I have time.
It would be good to sit here a thousand years and think of nothing
But the deaths of three persons.

THE NURSE. Ai! There's no hope then.
Ai, child, if you could do this red thing you dream of, all Corinth
Would pour against you.

MEDEA. After my enemies are punished and I have heard the last broken moan—Corinth?
What's that? I'll sleep well. I am alone against all, and so weary
That it is pitiful.

(The NURSE *stands wringing her hands.* MEDEA *goes slowly up to the door of the house. Some of the* CORINTHIAN WOMEN *are watching her; others gaze into the distance.)*

FIRST WOMAN. Look: who is coming? I see the sunlight glitter on lanceheads.

SECOND WOMAN. Oh, it is Jason!

THIRD WOMAN. Jason! Medea's worst enemy, who should have been
Her dearest protector.

*(*MEDEA *leans wearily against one of the pillars of the doorway, her back to the stage, unconscious of what they are saying.* JASON *enters in haste, followed by armed attendants, and speaks angrily.)*

JASON. What business have you here, you women
Clustered like buzzing bees at the hive-door?
Where is Medea?

(They do not answer for a moment, but look involuntarily toward MEDEA, *and* JASON *sees her. She jerks and stiffens at the sound of his voice, but does not turn.)*

FIRST WOMAN *(pointing)*. There: mourning for what you have done.

JASON. Ha? What she has done.
Not I. Not by my will she and my sons are exiled.

*(*MEDEA *slowly turns and faces him, her head high, rigid with inner violence.)*

MEDEA. Is there another dog here?

JASON. So, Medea,
You have once more affronted and insulted the head of Corinth. This is not the first time
I've seen what a fool anger is. You might have lived here happily,

secure and honored—I hoped you would—
By being just a little decently respectful toward those in power.
Instead, you had to go mad with anger
And talk yourself into exile. To me it matters little what you say
about me, but rulers are sensitive.
Time and again I've smoothed down Creon's indignation, then
you like a madwoman, like a possessed imbecile,
Wag your head and let the words flow again; you never cease
From speaking evil against him and his family. So now—you've
got it. Call yourself lucky, Medea,
Not to get worse than exile. In spite of all this, I have your
interest at heart and am here to help you.
Exile's a bitter business; I want to make some provision for you.
I wish you no harm,
Although you hate me.
(He waits for her to speak, but she is silent. He continues:)
And in particular the children; my sons;
our sons. You might have been decent enough
To have thought of our sons.
MEDEA *(slowly).* Did you consider them
When you betrayed this house?
JASON. Certainly I considered them.
It was my hope that they would grow up here,
And I, having married power, could protect and favor them. And
if perhaps, after many years, I become
Dynast of Corinth—for that is Creon's desire, to make me his
heir—our sons
Would have been a king's sons. . . . I hope to help them,
wherever they go: but now of course must look forward
To younger children.
MEDEA *(trembling).* Ah . . . it's enough. Something might happen.
It is . . . likely that . . . something might happen
To the bride and the marriage.
JASON. I'll guard against it. But evidently
Creon is right to be rid of you.
MEDEA. Have you finished now? I thought I would let you speak
on and spread out your shamelessness
Before these women: the way a Tyrian trader unrolls his rare
fabrics:[8] "Do you like it, ladies?" It is the
Dog's daughter's husband. It is a brave person: it has finally got
up its courage—with a guard of spears—
To come and look me in the face.
O Jason: how have you pulled
me down
To this hell of vile thoughts? I did not used to talk like a common
woman. I loved you once:

8. ***the way a Tyrian*** (tir'ē ən) ***trader unrolls his rare fabrics,*** the people of Tyre (tīr) in Phoenicia were the greatest merchants of the ancient world.

And I am ashamed of it: but there are some things
That ought to be remembered by you and me. That blue day when we drove through the Hellespont
Into Greek sea,[9] and the great-shouldered heroes were singing at the oars, and those birds flying
Through the blown foam: that day was too fine I suppose
For Creon's daughter's man to remember—but you might remember
Whether I cheated my father for you and tamed the fire-breathing
Brazen-hoofed bulls; and whether I saved your life in the field of the teeth; and you might remember
Whether I poisoned the great serpent and got you the Golden Fleece; and fled with you, and killed my brother
When he pursued us, making myself abominable
In my own home; and then in yours I got your enemy Pelias hacked to death
By his own daughters' hands[10]—whatever these fine Corinthian friends of yours
May say against my rapid and tricky wisdom: you it has served,
You it has served well: here are five times, if I counted right—and all's not counted—
That your adventure would have been dusty death
If I'd not saved you—but now you think that your adventures are over; you are safe and high placed in Corinth,
And will need me no more.
It is a bit of a dog, isn't it, women? It is well qualified
To sleep with the dog's daughter. But for me, Jason, me driven by the hairy snouts from the quadruped marriage-bed,
What refuge does your prudent kindness advise? Shall I fly home to Colchis—
To put my neck in the coil of a knotted rope, for the crimes
I served you with? Or shall I go and kneel to the daughters of Pelias? They would indeed be happy
To lay their hands on my head: holding the very knives and the cleavers
That carved their sire. The world is a little closed to me, ah?
By the things I have done for you.

(Meanwhile the NURSE *has come forward on the stage, and stands this side of* CHORUS, *listening, wringing her hands. Now she speaks.)*

THE NURSE. I'll go to the palace
And seek for Aegeus. There is no other hope.

(She hurries out in that direction.)

JASON *(slowly).* I see, Medea,
You have been a very careful merchant of benefits. You forget

9. ***That blue day . . . into Greek sea,*** the day Medea and Jason, fleeing the wrath of her father and homeland, went to Greece.

10. ***Whether I cheated . . . his own daughters' hands.*** Medea recalls the magic she worked to help Jason win and keep the Golden Fleece. The tasks Aeëtes had given Jason were to yoke two bronze-footed, fire-breathing bulls and then to use them to sow dragons' teeth into the ground, from which would spring a crop of armed men. Medea provided him with an ointment to protect him and a charm to help him subdue the bulls; she also showed him a trick to confuse the armed men and keep them from attacking him. The "great serpent"—that is, the dragon that guarded the Golden Fleece—Medea put to sleep with a magic potion. Having thus secured the Fleece, Jason returned with it to Iolcos (ī ōl′kəs), his home city, and gave it to his Uncle Pelias (pē′lē əs), who had usurped the throne of the city from Jason's father. When Pelias still refused to return the throne to Jason, Medea avenged the wrong by persuading Pelias's daughters that they could rejuvenate their father if they dismembered his body while he slept. They did as Medea told them, but Medea let him die. Then she and Jason fled to Corinth.

none, you keep a strict reckoning. But—
Some little things that I on my side have done for you
Ought to be in the books too: as, for example, that I carried you
Out of the dirt and superstition of Asiatic Colchis into the rational
Sunlight of Greece, and the marble music of the Greek temples: is that no benefit? And I have brought you
To meet the first minds of our time, and to speak as an equal with the great heroes and the rulers of cities:
Is that no benefit? And now—this grievous thing that you hate me for:
That I have married Creon's young daughter, little Creüsa:[11] do you think I did it like a boy or a woman,
Out of blind passion? I did it to achieve power here; and I'd have used that power to protect
You and our sons, but your jealous madness has muddled everything. And finally:
As to those acts of service you so loudly boast—whom do I thank for them? I thank divine Venus,[12] the goddess
Who makes girls fall in love. You did them because you had to do them; Venus compelled you; I
Enjoyed her favor. A man dares things, you know, he makes his adventure
In the cold eye of death; and if the gods care for him
They appoint an instrument to save him; if not, he dies. You were that instrument.

MEDEA. Here it is: the lowest,
The obscene dregs; the slime and the loathing; the muddy bottom of a mouthed cup: when a scoundrel begins
To invoke the gods. You had better go, Jason. Vulgarity
Is a contagious disease; and in a moment what could I do but spit at you like a peasant, or curse you
Like a drunken slave? You had better take yourself back to . . .
"Little Creüsa."

JASON. I came to help you and save you if possible.

MEDEA. Your help
Is not wanted. Go. Go.

JASON. If I could see my boys . . .

MEDEA. Go quickly.

JASON. Yours the regret then. *(Exit.)*

(Watching him go, MEDEA *strokes her wrist and hand to the tips of the spread fingers, as if she were scraping off slime.)*

MEDEA. This is it. I did not surely know it: loathing is all. This flesh
He has touched and fouled. These hands that wrought for him, these knees

11. ***Creüsa*** (krē ü'sə).

12. ***Venus,*** Roman name of the goddess of love Aphrodite.

That ran his errands. This body that took his . . . what they call love, and made children of it. If I could peel off
The flesh, the children, the memory . . .
(Again she scarifies one hand with the other. She looks at her hand.)
Poor misused hand: poor defiled arm: your bones
Are not unshapely. If I could tear off the flesh and be bones, naked bones;
Salt-scoured bones on the shore
At home in Colchis . . .
(She stands staring, thinking of home perhaps.)
FIRST CORINTHIAN WOMAN. God keep me from fire and the hunger of the sword,
Save me from the hateful sea and the jagged lightning,
And the violence of love.
SECOND WOMAN. A little love is a joy in the house,
A little fire is a jewel against frost and darkness.
FIRST WOMAN. A great love is a fire
That burns the beams of the roof.
The doorposts are flaming and the house falls.
A great love is a lion in the cattle-pen,
The herd goes mad, the heifers run bawling,
And the claws are in their flanks.
Too much love is an armed robber in the treasury;
He has killed the guards and he walks in blood.

SECOND WOMAN. And now I see the black end,
The end of great love, and God save me from it:
The unburied horror, the unbridled hatred,
The vultures tearing a corpse:
God keep me clean of those evil beaks.
THIRD WOMAN. What is she doing, that woman,
Staring like stone, staring?
Oh, she has moved now.
MEDEA. Annihilation. The word is pure music: annihilation. To annihilate the past—
Is not possible: but its fruit in the present . . .
Can be nipped off. Am I to look in my sons' eyes
And see Jason's forever? How could I endure the endless defilement, those lives
That mix Jason and me? Better to be clean
Bones on the shore. Bones have no eyes at all; how could they weep? White bones
On the Black Sea shore . . .
Oh, but that's far. Not yet. Corinth must howl first.
(She stands meditating.)
FIRST WOMAN. The holy fountains flow up from the earth,
The smoke of sacrifice flows up from the earth,
The eagle and the wild swan fly up from the earth,
Righteousness also
Has flown up from the earth to the feet of God.
It is not here, but up there; peace and pity are departed;
Hatred is here; hatred is heavy, it clings to the earth.
Love blows away, hatred remains.
SECOND WOMAN. Women hate war, but men will wage it again.
Women may hate their husbands, and sons their fathers,
But women will never hate their own children.
FIRST WOMAN. But as for me, I will do good to my husband,
I will love my sons and daughters, and adore the gods.
MEDEA. If I should go into the house with a sharp knife
To the man and his bride . . .
Or if I could fire the room they sleep in, and hear them
Wake in the white of the fire, and cry to each other, and howl like dogs,
And howl and die . . .
But I might fail; I might be cut down first;
The knife might turn in my hand, or the fire not burn, and my enemies could laugh at me.
No: I have subtler means, and more deadly cruel; I have my dark art
That fools call witchcraft. Not for nothing I have worshipped the

wild gray goddess that walks in the dark, the wise one,
The terrible one, the sweet huntress, flower of night, Hecate,[13]
In my house at my hearth.

THE NURSE *(has entered, and hurries toward* MEDEA*).* My lady: he was leaving Creon's door: he is coming.

*(*MEDEA *pays no attention; the* NURSE *kneels, catches her hand.)*

Aegeus is coming!
The power of Athens.

MEDEA. I will not see him. Go back and tell him so.

(The NURSE *retreats behind* CHORUS. MEDEA *prays:)*

Ancient goddess to whom I and my people
Make the sacrifice of black lambs and black female hounds,
Holy one, haunter of crossroads, queen of night, Hecate,
Help me now: to remember in my mind the use of the venomous fire, the magic song,
And the sharp gems.

(She sits on the steps in deep thought.)

*(*AEGEUS *comes in, with* ATTENDANTS. *His servants are not armed; they have a look of travel and the sea.)*

FIRST CORINTHIAN WOMAN. He is here, Medea.
Athens is here.

*(*MEDEA *pays no attention.)*

AEGEUS *(comes near to her).* Medea, rejoice! There is no fairer greeting from friend to friend.

(She ignores him. He speaks more loudly.)

Hail and rejoice, Medea!

(She lifts her head and stares at him.)

MEDEA. "Rejoice?" It may be so. It may be I shall . . . rejoice
Before the sun sets.

AEGEUS. Medea! What has happened to you?

MEDEA. Nothing.

AEGEUS. Your eyes are cavernous!
And your mouth twitches.

MEDEA. Nothing: I am quite well: fools trouble me.—Where are you traveling from,
Aegeus?

AEGEUS. From Delphi, where I went to consult
The ancient oracle of Apollo.[14]

MEDEA *(abstractedly).* Oh . . . Delphi . . . Did you get a good answer?

AEGEUS. An obscure one.
Some god or other has made me unable to beget a child: that is my trouble: but the oracle
Never gives plain responses. I tell you these things because you are skilled in mysteries, and you might help me

13. ***Hecate*** (hek′ə tē), the goddess of the underworld; associated with magic and witchcraft.

14. ***Delphi*** (del′fī) . . . ***oracle of Apollo.*** Delphi is a city in Greece where a temple of Apollo, the god of truth, was located. An oracle is a place where prophecies, believed to be the words of a god, were spoken by priests or priestesses; Delphi was one of the most famous and trustworthy oracles.

To the god's meaning.
MEDEA *(wearily).* You want a child! What did Apollo
Say to you?
AEGEUS. That I must not unloose the hanging foot of the wineskin until I return
To the hearth of my fathers.
MEDEA *(without interest).* The hanging foot of the wineskin. You have never had a child?
AEGEUS. No.
And it is bitterness.
MEDEA. But when misfortune comes it is bitter to have children, and watch their starlike
Faces grow dim to endure it.
AEGEUS. When death comes, Medea,
It is, for a childless man, utter despair, darkness, extinction. One's children
Are the life after death.
MEDEA *(excited).* Do you feel it so? Do you feel it so?
Then—if you had a dog-eyed enemy and needed absolute vengeance—you'd kill
The man's children first. Unchild him, ha?
And then unlife him.
AEGEUS. I do not care to think of such horrors.
I have no complete enemy.
(He stares, and slightly recoils from her.)
What is it? What is the matter, Medea? You are trembling; wild fever
Flames in your eyes.
MEDEA. I am well enough. . . . Fools trouble me, and dogs; but not that—Oh . . .
(She collapses on the steps and weeps.)
AEGEUS. What has happened to you?
THE NURSE *(crouches by her, trying to comfort her).* My dear . . . my love . . .
MEDEA *(pushes her gently aside, looks up at* AEGEUS*).* I would not hurt my children. Their father hurts them.
AEGEUS. What do you mean, Medea? Jason? What has Jason done?
MEDEA. He has betrayed and denied
Both me and them.
AEGEUS. Jason has done that? Why? Why?
MEDEA. He has cast me off and married Creon's young daughter.
And Creon, this very day, is driving us
Into black exile.
AEGEUS. Jason consents to that?

MEDEA. He is glad of it.

AEGEUS. Why—it's atrocious, it's past belief.

THE NURSE *(says in* MEDEA*'s ear).* Ask him for refuge! Ask him to receive you in Athens!

MEDEA *(stands up, straight and rigid).* Do you think such men ought to be punished, Aegeus?

AEGEUS. You mean you are driven out into exile?

MEDEA. Into homeless exile.

AEGEUS. Why that?

MEDEA. Because our presence here is embarrassing
To the young bride—Do you not think such men ought to be punished, Aegeus?

AEGEUS. I think it is villainous.
They told me nothing of this.

MEDEA. Do you not think such men ought to be punished, Aegeus?

AEGEUS. It's bad.
Where will you go?

MEDEA *(solemnly).* If there is any rightness on earth or in heaven, they will be punished.

AEGEUS. Where
Will you go to, Medea?

MEDEA. What? To death, of course.

THE NURSE. Oh . . . She is all bewildered, sir,
In the deep storm and ocean of grief, or she would ask of you
Refuge in Athens.

MEDEA *(in bitter mockery, seeing* AEGEUS *hesitate).* Ah? So I should. That startled the man.—Aegeus:
Will you shelter me in Athens?

AEGEUS. Why . . . yes. Yes . . . I will not take you from Corinth, it would not be right.
I want no trouble with Creon; I am his guest here. If you by your own means come to Athens
I will take care of you.

MEDEA. I could repay you for it. I know the remedies that would make a dry stick
Flame into flower and fruit.

AEGEUS *(eagerly).* You'd cure my sterility?

MEDEA. I could do so.

AEGEUS. You are famous for profound knowledge
Of drugs and charms.
(Eagerly) You'll come to Athens?

MEDEA. If I choose. If the

gods decide it so. But, Aegeus,
Would you protect me if I came? I have certain enemies. If
powerful enemies came, baying for my blood,
Would you protect me?

AEGEUS. Why . . . yes. What enemies? . . . Yes.
Athens protects.

MEDEA. I should need peace and a free mind
While I prepared the medicines to make you well.

AEGEUS. You'll have
them, you'll have them, Medea. You've seen the huge stones
In the old sacred war-belt of Athens.[15] Come the four ends of the
world, they will not break in: you're safe there:
I am your pledge.

MEDEA. Will you swear it, Aegeus?

AEGEUS. Ah? Why? I
promised.

MEDEA. I trust you: the oath is formal: your cure
Depends on it. You swear by the fruitful earth and high shining
heaven that you will protect me in Athens
Against all men. Swear it.

AEGEUS. I swear by the fruitful earth and high
shining heaven to protect you in Athens
Against all men.

MEDEA. And if you should break this oath?

AEGEUS. I will not
break it.

MEDEA. If you should break it, the earth
Will give you no bread but death, and the sky no light
But darkness.

AEGEUS *(visibly perturbed).* I will not break it.

MEDEA. You must repeat the
words, Aegeus.

AEGEUS. If I break it, the earth
Will give me no bread but death, and the sky no light
But darkness.

MEDEA. You have sworn: the gods have heard you.

AEGEUS *(uneasily).* When
will you come to Athens?

MEDEA. To . . . Athens? Oh,
To Athens. Why—if I come, if I live—it will be soon. The yoke's
On the necks of the horses.—I have some things to do
That men will talk of afterwards with hushed voices: while I and
my children
Safe in Athens laugh. Is that it? Farewell, Aegeus.
(She turns abruptly from him; goes slowly, deep in thought, into the house.)

15. ***the huge stones . . . of Athens,*** the stones in an ancient wall around the city, used for protection.

AEGEUS *(staring after her).* May the gods
comfort you, Medea.—To you also farewell,
Ladies of Corinth.
FIRST WOMAN. Fair be the gale behind you, sir, and the way
ahead.
(She turns to her companions.)
What is she plotting in her deep mind?
She is juggling with death and life, as a juggler
With a black ball and a white ball.
SECOND WOMAN. No: she is like some distracted city
Sharpening its weapons. Embassies visit her;
The heads of state come to her door;
She receives them darkly.
THE NURSE. I beseech you, women,
Not to speak words against my lady whom I love. You know
what wicked injustice she has to suffer.
(She prays.)
O God, protector of exiles, lord of the holy sky, lead us
To the high rock that Athena loves, and the olive
Garland of Athens.[16]
FIRST WOMAN. Athens is beautiful
As a lamp on a rock.
The temples are marble-shafted; light shines and lingers there,
Honey-color among the carved stones
And silver-color on the leaves of the olives.
The maidens are crowned with violets; Athens and Corinth
Are the two crowns of time.
SECOND WOMAN. Mycenae for spears and armor; Sparta
For the stern men and the tall blonde women; and Thebes I
remember,
Old Thebes and the seven gates in the gray walls—
But rather I praise Athena, the ivory, the golden,
The gray-eyed virgin, her city.
And also I praise Corinth of the beautiful fountains,[17]
On the fair plain between the two gulfs.
FIRST WOMAN. God-favored cities of the Greek world.
Fortunate those that dwell in them, happy that behold them.
SECOND WOMAN. How can one wish to die? How can that woman
Be drowned in sorrow and bewildered with hatred?
(She does not see MEDEA, *who comes from the door and stands between the pillars.)*
For only to be alive and to see the light
Is beautiful. Only to see the light;
To see a blade of young grass,
Or the gray face of a stone.
FIRST WOMAN *(pointing toward* MEDEA*).* Hush.

16. *the high rock . . . of Athens.* The "high rock" is the Acropolis of Athens, the fortified high part of the city on which was built a temple to the goddess Athena, protectress of cities and of Athens in particular. It was for Athens that Athena created the olive tree, thereafter considered sacred by its citizens.

17. *Mycenae . . . the beautiful fountains.* The various cities of Greece are invoked and characterized: Mycenae (mī sē′nē), known for its weapons; Sparta, for its warriors; Thebes, for its gates; Athens, for its patroness Athena, the "gray-eyed virgin"; and Corinth, for its fountains.

MEDEA *(proudly and falsely).* As you say. What a marvelous privilege it is
Merely to be alive. And how foolish it would be
To spend the one day of life that remains to me—at least in Corinth—this tag end of one day
On tears and hatred! Rather I should rejoice, and sing, and give gifts; and as to my enemies—
I will be reconciled with them.

FIRST WOMAN *(amazed).* Reconciled with them!

MEDEA. As you say. Reconciled. Why should they hate me?
Surely I can appease those people.
They say that gold will buy anything, even friendship, even love: at least in Greece,
Among you civilized people, you reasonable and civilized Hellenes.[18] In fact,
We've seen it happen. They bought Jason; Jason's love. Well . . .
I shall buy theirs.
I still have two or three of the treasures that I brought from home, things of pure precious gold, which a god
Gave to the kings my ancestors.
(The light darkens, a cloud passing over the sun.)
Is it late? It seems to me
That the light darkens.
(To the NURSE*)* Is it evening?

THE NURSE *(trembling).* No . . . No . . . A cloud.

MEDEA. I hope for thunder: let the sky rage: my gifts
Will shine the brighter.—Listen, old woman: I want you
To go to Jason and tell him . . . tell him . . . tell him that I am sick of hating and weary of evil!
I wish for peace.
I wish to send precious gifts to that pale girl with the yellow hair
Whom he has married: tell him to come and take them—and to kiss his boys
Before we go into exile. Tell him to come speedily. Now run, run, find him.

THE NURSE. Oh, I'll go. I'll run.
(Tremulously, to CHORUS*)*
Let me pass, please.
*(*MEDEA *stands looking after her. The* NURSE *turns back at the limit of the scene, and says, wringing her hands:)*
But I am terrified. I do not know. . . . I am terrified. Pray to the gods, women, to keep
Evil birds from our hearts!
(She hurries away. MEDEA *goes into the house.)*

18. ***Hellenes*** (hel′ēnz), Greeks.

Discussion

Act One

1. In her opening speech, Medea's nurse sets forth the essential background for the play. **(a)** What has happened that the audience must know immediately? **(b)** How does the nurse describe Medea's reaction to Jason's abandonment? **(c)** What does she say about Medea's temperament? **(d)** Which of her statements might foreshadow coming events?

2. What important news does the tutor share with the nurse concerning the two sons of Medea and Jason?

3. (a) What basic feeling toward Medea's situation do the chorus of Corinthian women express as they listen to her talking offstage? **(b)** Do the Corinthian women have the same expectation about Medea's future actions as her nurse does? Explain. **(c)** According to the Corinthian women and Medea, what are the differences between the people of Greece and the people of Colchis?

4. (a) When Creon goes to Medea to present his demand, why does he particularly fear Medea? **(b)** When Creon tells Medea he pities her, what does her reaction reveal to him? **(c)** Why does he finally allow Medea to remain in Corinth until the next morning? **(d)** Based on what Creon knows about Medea, do you think he acts reasonably in submitting to her plea? Why or why not?

5. Medea is brought to her knees during her confrontation with Creon. **(a)** What is her attitude immediately following his departure? **(b)** What does this reveal about her character?

6. (a) According to Jason, why is Medea the object of Creon's disfavor? **(b)** Do Medea and Jason share the same view of their past relationship? Explain. **(c)** When Jason offers Medea some provision for her and her children, is she justified in refusing him? Discuss.

7. (a) In his discussion with Medea, which of Aegeus's complaints about his childlessness particularly stirs Medea's interest? Why? **(b)** How does Medea convince Aegeus to shelter her in Athens? **(c)** What might be Medea's reasons for making Aegeus swear he will shelter her? **(d)** Why is Aegeus so insistent that Medea must escape from Corinth by her own means?

Vocabulary

Combined Skills

A. Use your Glossary to find the meanings and pronunciations of the following words. Then use five of them to complete the statements about the characters in Act One.

occult	dynast	snivel
writhe	reconcile	rash
reverie	sanctuary	prudent

1. The other characters regard Medea's nature as ________.

2. Jason's desire is to eventually become ________ of Corinth.

3. The nurse urges Medea to ask Aegeus for ________.

4. Aegeus has respect for Medea's ________ knowledge.

5. Medea unexpectedly decides to ________ with Jason.

B. Form a derivative with each root word below by combining it with the correct suffix. If necessary, use your Glossary for reference: the spelling of some roots may change. Then use each derivative in a sentence of your own to show you understand its meaning.

arrogant	-ous
provoke	-ence
peril	-ion
afflict	-ance
eloquent	-ation

Comment: The Greek Chorus

As you have learned, Greek drama evolved from the ritualistic performances of a chorus at the Dionysian festivals. After the actor Thespis stepped out of the chorus and began a dialogue with it, other characters soon followed suit, and the chorus's role gradually diminished in size (from fifty members to fifteen) and importance. Playwrights kept the chorus as a significant element in their dramas, but its functions were necessarily more limited.

Robinson Jeffers, who translated this version of *Medea,* has also retained the chorus, but has modified its nature slightly. Instead of having it speak in unison, he has assigned speeches to individual members. Nevertheless, the chorus still plays a prominent part and fills the traditional functions of a chorus in Greek tragedy.

Many of these functions were merely technical. For instance, the chorus often announced the entrances and exits of characters or foreshadowed events in the action. It also recounted or interpreted past events for the purpose of clarifying the plot. These functions aided the movement of the story.

The chorus also had several well-defined dramatic functions. One was to sing and dance during the interludes between dialogues. Another, more significant function was to create or add to the emotional atmosphere of a play. One of the main ways it did this was to take on the important role of "ideal spectator." In this role, the chorus embodied the moral ideals of society and often admonished the characters against breaking these moral laws. In Act One, you saw how the chorus, in the roles of the Corinthian women, carried out this function by commenting on Medea's situation and behavior. As you read Act Two, observe how the chorus responds to Medea's further actions.

Act Two

MEDEA *is sitting on one of the upper doorsteps. A cloak of woven gold lies across her knee and down the stone steps. Beside her are two open cases of dark leather. From one she takes a coronet of golden vine leaves, looks at it, and replaces it.*

Two SERVING-WOMEN *stand in the doorway behind her. The* NURSE *stands below her, to one side of the steps. On the other side, at some distance, the* CORINTHIAN WOMEN *are huddled, like sheep in a storm.*

The scene is darker than it was, and the gold cloth shines.

MEDEA. These are the gifts I am sending to the young bride: this golden wreath
And this woven-gold veil. They are not without value; there is nothing like them in the whole world, or at least
The Western world; the god of the sun[1] gave them to my father's father, and I have kept them
In the deep chest for some high occasion: which has now come.
I have great joy in giving these jewels to Creon's daughter, for the glory of life consists in being generous
To one's friends, and . . . merciless to one's enemies. . . . You know what a friend she has been to me. All Corinth knows.
The slaves talk of it. The old stones in the walls
Have watched and laughed.

*(*MEDEA *looks at the gold cloth, and strokes it cautiously with her hand. It seems to scorch her fingers.* CHORUS *has come nearer to look; now starts backward.)*

MEDEA. See, it is almost alive. Gold is a living thing: such pure gold.
But when her body has warmed it, how it will shine!

(To the NURSE*)*

Why doesn't he come? What keeps him?

THE NURSE *(evidently terrified).* Oh, my lady: presently.
I have but now returned from him. He was beyond the gate, watching the races—where a monstrous thing
Had happened: a young mare broke from the chariot
And tore with her teeth a stallion.

*(*MEDEA *stands up, shakes out the golden cloak, which again smolders. She folds it cautiously, lays it in the leather case. The light has darkened again; she looks anxiously at the clouded sun.)*

MEDEA. He takes his time, ah? It is intolerable
To sit and wait.

(To the SERVING-WOMEN*)*

1. ***god of the sun,*** Helios (hē′lē os), an ancestor of Medea.

Take these into the house. Keep them at hand
For when I call.
(They take them in. MEDEA *moves restlessly, under extreme nervous tension. Speaks to the* NURSE*)*
You say that a mare attacked a stallion?
THE NURSE. She tore
him cruelly.
I saw him being led away: a black racer: his blood ran down
From the throat to the fetlocks.
MEDEA. You're sure he's coming? You're
sure?
THE NURSE. He said he would.
MEDEA. Let him make haste then!
SECOND CORINTHIAN WOMAN. Frightening irrational things
Have happened lately; the face of nature is flawed with omens.
FIRST WOMAN. Yesterday evening a slave
Came up to the harbor-gate, carrying a basket
Of new-caught fish: one of the fish took fire
And burned in the wet basket with a high flame: the thing was
witnessed
By many persons.
THIRD WOMAN. And a black leopard was seen
Gliding through the marketplace. . . .
MEDEA *(abruptly, approaching the* WOMEN*)*. You haven't told me
yet: do you not think that Creon's daughter
Will be glad of those gifts?
FIRST WOMAN. O Medea, too much wealth
Is sometimes dreadful.
MEDEA. She'll be glad, however. She'll take them
and put them on, she'll wear them, she'll strut in them,
She'll peacock in them.—I see him coming now.—The whole
palace will admire her.—Stand away from me, women,
While I make my sick peace.
(She goes across the scene to meet JASON, *but more and more slowly, and stops. Her attitude indicates her aversion.)*
JASON *(entering)*. Well, I have come. I tell you plainly,
Not for your sake: the children's. Your woman says that you
have your wits again, and are willing
To look beyond your own woes.
*(*MEDEA *is silent.* JASON *observes her and says:)*
It appears doubtful.
—Where are the boys? I have made inquiry: I can find fosterage
for them
In Epidaurus;[2] or any other of several cities
That are Creon's friends. I'll visit them from time to time, and
watch

2. *fosterage . . . Epidaurus,* that is, a foster home or place of refuge in Epidaurus (ep′i dôr′əs), a city to the southeast of Corinth and southwest of Athens.

That they're well kept.
MEDEA *(with suppressed violence).* You mean . . . take them from me!
Be careful, Jason, I am not patient yet.
(More quietly) I am the one who labored in pain to bear them, I cannot
Smile while I lose them. But I am learning; I am learning.—No, Jason: I will not give up my little ones
To the cold care of strangers. It would be better for them to be drowned in the sea than to live with those
Who do not love them, hard faces, harsh hands. It will be far better for them to share
My wandering ocean of beggary and bleak exile: they'll still be loved;
And when the sky rages I'll hold them warm
Against my heart. I love them, Jason. Only if you would keep them and care for them here in Corinth,
I might consent.
JASON. Gladly—but they are exiled.
MEDEA. —In your own house.
JASON. Gladly I'd do it—but you understand
They are exiled, as you are.
MEDEA. Innocent; for my rebellion. That's black.
(She reaches her hands toward him.)
Forgive me, Jason,
As I do you. We have had too much wrath, and our acts
Are closing on us. On me I mean. Retribution is from the gods, and it breaks our hearts: but you
Feel no guilt, you fear nothing, nothing can touch you. It is wonderful to stand serene above fate
While earthlings wince. If it lasts. It does not always last.—Do you love them, Jason?
JASON. Ha? Certainly. The children? Certainly!
I am their father.
MEDEA. Oh, but that's not enough. If I am to give them up to you—be patient with me,
I must question you first. And very deeply; to the quick. If anything happened to them,
Would you be grieved?
JASON. Nothing will happen to them, Medea, if in my care. Rest your mind on it.
MEDEA. You must pardon me: it is not possible to be certain of that. If they were . . . killed and their blood

Ran on the floor of the house or down the deep earth—
Would you be grieved?
JASON. You have a sick mind. What a weak thing
a woman is, always dreaming of evil.
MEDEA. Answer me!
JASON. Yes, after I'd cut their killer into red
collops[3]—I'd be grieved.
MEDEA. That is true: vengeance
Makes grief bearable. And knowing that . . . Creon's daughter,
your wife . . . no doubt will breed
Many other boys. But, if something should happen to . . . Creon's
daughter . . .
JASON. Enough, Medea. Too much.
Be silent!
MEDEA. I am to conclude that you love . . . Creon's daughter . . .
More than your sons. They'll have to take the sad journey with
me.
(To the NURSE*)*
Tell the boys to come out
And bid their father farewell.
(The NURSE *goes into the house.)*
JASON. I could take them from you
By force, Medea.
MEDEA *(violently).* Try it, you!
(Controlling herself) No, Creon decided otherwise: he
said they will share my exile.—Come, Jason,
Let's be friends at last! I know you love them. If they could stay
here in Corinth I'd be content.
JASON. I asked it,
And he refused it.
MEDEA. You asked him to take
My children from me!
(The CHILDREN *come out with their* TUTOR, *followed by the* NURSE.*)*
I am quite patient now; I have learned.—
Come, boys: come,
Speak to your father.
(They shrink back.)
No, no, we're friends again. We're not angry
anymore.
*(*JASON *has gone eagerly to meet them on the steps. He drops to one knee to be more nearly level with them, but they are shy and reluctant.)*
JASON. Big boys. Tall fellows, ha?
You've grown up since I saw you.
MEDEA. Smile for him, children.
Give him your hands.

3. ***collops,*** small pieces, as of meat.

(She turns, and stands rigidly turned away, her face sharp with pain.)

THE NURSE *(to* JASON*).* I think he's afraid of your helmet, sir.

JASON *(to the* YOUNGER BOY*).* What?
What? You'll learn, my man,
Not to fear helmets. The enemy will run from yours
When you grow up to size.
(To the ELDER BOY*)* And you, Captain,
How would you like a horn-tipped bow to hunt rabbits with?
Wolves, I mean.

(He plays with the CHILDREN*. They are less shy of him now.)*

FIRST CORINTHIAN WOMAN *(coming close to* MEDEA*).* Don't give them to him,
Medea. If you do, it will ache forever.

SECOND WOMAN. You have refuge: take them there.
Athens is beautiful. . . .

MEDEA *(fiercely).* Be silent!
Look at him: he loves them—ah? Therefore his dear children
Are not going to that city but a darker city, where no games are played, no music is heard. Do you think
I am a cow lowing after the calf? Or a bitch with pups, licking
The hand that struck her? Watch and see. Watch this man, women: he is going to weep. I think
He is going to weep blood, and quite soon, and much more
Than I have wept. Watch and keep silence.
(She goes toward the group on the steps.) Jason,
Are the boys dear to you? I think I am satisfied that you love them. . . .
(She weeps, covering her face.)
Oh, Oh, Oh . . .

*(*JASON *stands up and turns to her, one of the* BOYS *clinging to each of his hands. He has made friends with them.)*

JASON. These two young heroes . . . God's hand, Medea, what is it?
What is the matter?

MEDEA *(makes with both hands a gesture of pushing down something, and flings her head back proudly).* Nothing. It is hard to let them go.
Are they very sweet to you? You love them dearly?—This I have thought of:
You shall take them to . . . Creon's daughter, your wife . . . and make them kneel to her, and ask her
To ask her father to let them stay here in Corinth. He'll grant it, he is growing old, he denies her nothing.
Even that hard king loves his only child.

What she asks is done. You will go with the boys, Jason, and
speak for them—they are not skillful yet
In supplication—and I'll send gifts. I'll put gifts in their hands.
People say that gifts
Will persuade even the gods.—Is it well thought of?
Will she listen to us?
JASON. Why, if I ask it! She'd hardly refuse me
anything. And I believe that you're right,
She can rule Creon.
MEDEA *(to the* NURSE*)*. Bring me those gold things.
(To the CHILDREN*)* Dear ones,
brave little falcons . . . little pawns of my agony . . .
Go ask that proud breastless girl of her bitter charity
Whether she will let you nest here until your wings fledge, while
far your mother
Flies the dark storm. . . .
(She weeps again.)
JASON. I'm sorry for you. Parting is hard.
MEDEA. I can
bear it.
And worse too.
(The NURSE *and a* SERVING-WOMAN *bring the gifts.)*
Oh, here: here are the things: take them, darlings,
Into your little hands.
(Giving them to the CHILDREN*)*
Hold carefully by the cases: don't touch the
gold,
Or it might . . . tarnish.
JASON. Why! These are king's treasures. You
shouldn't, Medea: it's too much. Creon's house
Has gold enough of its own.
MEDEA. Oh—if she'll wear them. What should
I want
With woven golden vanities? Black is my wear. The woman ought
to be very happy
With such jewels—and such a husband—ah? Her sun is rising,
mine going down—I hope
To a red sunset.—The little gold wreath is pretty, isn't it?
JASON *(doubtfully)*. It looks
like fire. . . .
MEDEA. Vine leaves: the flashing
Arrow-sharp leaves. They have weight, though.
(She takes the cases from the CHILDREN*, gives them to the* NURSE
and the TUTOR.*)* Gold is too heavy
a burden for little hands. Carry them, you,
Until you come to the palace.—Farewell, sweet boys: brave little

trudging pilgrims from the black wave
To the white desert: take the stuff in; be sure you lay it in her own hands.
Come back and tell me what happens.
(She turns abruptly away from them.) Tell me what happens.
(The CHILDREN *go out reluctantly,* JASON *holding their hands. The* NURSE *and the* TUTOR *have gone ahead.* MEDEA *hides her face, weeping; then lifts her head proudly, and walks toward* CHORUS.*)*
Rejoice, women. The gifts are given; the bait is laid.
The gods roll their great eyes over Creon's house and quietly smile: for no rat nor cony
Would creep into the open undisguised traps
That take the proud race of man. They snap at a shiny bait; they'll believe anything. I too
Have been fooled in my time: now I shall triumph. That robe of bright-flowing gold, that bride-veil, that fish-net
To catch a young slender salmon—not mute, she'll sing: her delicate body writhes in the meshes,
The golden wreath binds her bright head with light: she'll dance, she'll sing loudly:
Would I were there to hear it, that proud one howling.—Look, the sun's out again, the clouds are gone,
All's gay and clear. I wish the deep earth would open and swallow us—
Before I do what comes next.
I wish all life would perish, and the holy gods in high heaven die, before my little ones
Come home to my hands.

FIRST CORINTHIAN WOMAN. It would be better for you, Medea, if the earth
Opened her jaws and took you down into darkness.
But one thing you will not do, for you cannot,
You will not hurt your own children, though wrath like plague-boils
Aches, your mind in a fire-haze
Bites the purple apples of pain. No blood-lapping
Beast of the field, she-bear nor lioness,
Nor the lean wolf-bitch,
Hurts her own tender whelps; nor the yellow-eyed,
Scythe-beaked, and storm-shouldered
Eagle that tears the lambs has ever made prey
Of the fruit of her own tree—

MEDEA. How could that girl's death slake me?

THIRD WOMAN *(coming forward from the others).* I am sick with terror.

I'll run to the palace, I'll warn them.
MEDEA. Will you?—Go. Go, if you will.
God and my vengeful goddess[4] are doing these things: you cannot prevent them, but you could easily fall
In the same fire.
THIRD WOMAN *(retreating).* I am afraid to go.
MEDEA. You are wise. Anyone
Running between me and my justice will reap
What no man wants.
FIRST WOMAN. Not justice: vengeance.
You have suffered evil; you wish to inflict evil.
MEDEA. I do according to nature what I have to do.
FIRST WOMAN. I have heard evil
Answering evil as thunder answers the lightning,
A great waste voice in the hollow sky,
And all that they say is death. I have heard vengeance
Like an echo under a hill answering vengeance,
Great hollow voices: all that they say is death.
SECOND WOMAN. The sword speaks
And the spear answers: the city is desolate.
The nations remember old wrongs and destroy each other,
And no man binds up their wounds.
FIRST WOMAN. But justice
Builds a firm house.
MEDEA. The doors of her house are vengeance.
SECOND WOMAN. I dreamed that someone
Gave good for evil, and the world was amazed.
MEDEA. Only a coward or a madman gives good for evil.—Did you hear a thin music
Like a girl screaming? Or did I perhaps imagine it? Hark, it is music.
THIRD WOMAN. Let me go, Medea!
I'll be mute, I'll speak to no one. I cannot bear—
Let me go to my house!
MEDEA. You will stay here,
And watch the end.
(The WOMEN *are beginning to mill like scared cattle, huddled and circular.)*
You will be quiet, you women. You came to see
How the barbarian woman endures betrayal: watch and you'll know.
SECOND WOMAN. My heart is a shaken cup

4. ***my vengeful goddess,*** Hecate. Medea was a priestess of Hecate.

Of terror: the thin black wine
Spills over all my flesh down to my feet.
FIRST WOMAN. She fled from her father's house in a storm of blood,
In a blood-storm she flew up from Thessaly,[5]
Now here and dark over Corinth she widens
Wings to ride up the twisted whirlwind
And talons to hold with—
Let me flee this dark place and the pillared doorway.
SECOND WOMAN. I hear the man-wolf on the snow hill
Howl to the soaring moon—
THIRD WOMAN. The demon comes in through the locked door
And strangles the child—
SECOND WOMAN. Blood is the seed of blood, hundredfold the harvest;
The gleaners that follow it, their feet are crimson—
FIRST WOMAN. I see the whirlwind hanging from the black sky
Like a twisted rope,
Like an erect serpent, its tail tears the earth,
It is braided of dust and lightning,
Who will fly in it? Let me hide myself
From these night-shoring pillars and the dark door.
MEDEA. Have patience, women. Be quiet.
I am quite sure something has happened; presently someone
Will bring us news.
THIRD WOMAN. Look! The children are coming.
SECOND WOMAN. They have bright things in their hands: their faces are clear and joyous: was all that fear
A dream, a dream?
(The TUTOR *enters with the* CHILDREN. *The* ELDER CHILD *carries a decorated bow and arrows; the* YOUNGER CHILD *has a doll, a brightly painted wooden warrior.* MEDEA, *gazing at the* CHILDREN, *retreats slowly backward from them.)*
THE TUTOR. Rejoice, Medea, I bring good news. The princess graciously
Received your presents and smiled: it is peace between you. She has welcomed the little boys, they are safe from exile.
They'll be kept here. Their father is joyful.
MEDEA *(coldly, her hands clenched in the effort of self-control).* Yes?
THE TUTOR. All Creon's house is well pleased. When we first went in
The serving-women came and fondled the children; it was rumored through all the household that you and Jason
Were at peace again: like word of a victory

5. ***In a blood-storm . . . Thessaly.*** Iolcos, home of Jason's Uncle Pelias, whom Medea caused his own daughters to kill, was in the eastern district of Greece known as Thessaly.

Running through a wide city, when people gather in the streets to be glad together: and we brought the boys
Into the hall; we put those costly gifts in their hands; then Jason
Led them before the princess. At first she looked angrily at them and turned away, but Jason said,
"Don't be angry at your friends. You ought to love
Those whom I love. Look what they've brought you, dear," and she looked and saw
In the dark boxes the brilliant gold: she smiled then,
And marveled at it. Afterward she caressed the children; she even said that this little one's
Hair was like fine-spun gold. Then Jason gave them these toys and we came away.

MEDEA. Yes.—If this
Were all. If this were all, old man—
I'd have your bony loins beaten to a blood-froth
For the good news you bring.

THE TUTOR. My lady—!

MEDEA. There's more, however.
It will soon come.

(She moves restlessly in the direction they have come from; stands gazing; returns toward the doorsteps. The CHILDREN *shyly approach her and show their toys. She, with violent self-constraint, looks at them; but folds her hands in her cloak, not to touch them.)*

THE ELDER CHILD *(drawing the little bow).* Look, Mother.

MEDEA *(suddenly weeping).* Take them away from me!
I cannot bear. I cannot bear.

(She sits on the steps, and draws the cloak over her face.)

THE TUTOR. Children, come quickly.

(He shepherds them up the steps and disappears in the house; but they turn back and stand in the doorway.)

FIRST WOMAN. If there is any mercy or forbearance in heaven
Let it reach down and touch that dark mind
To save it from what it dreams—

(A young SLAVE *dashes in, panting and distraught.*[6] *He has run from* CREON'*s house.)*

THE SLAVE. Where is Medea?

SECOND WOMAN. What has happened? What horror drives you?
Are spears hunting behind you?

THE SLAVE *(he sees* MEDEA, *still sitting on the steps, her face and head hidden).* Flee for your life, Medea! I am Jason's man, but you were good to me
While I was here in the house. Can you hear me? Escape, Medea!

6. ***slave . . . panting and distraught.*** The slave, and later the nurse, will provide the details of the horrifying events at Creon's house. Violence was usually not shown directly on the Greek stage.

MEDEA *(slowly, drawing the cloak slowly from her head, and still sitting).* I hear you. Draw breath; say quietly
What you have seen. It must have been something notable, the way your eyes
Bulge in the whites.
THE SLAVE. If you have horses, Medea, drive! Or a boat on the shore,
Sail!
MEDEA. But first you must tell me about that beautiful girl who was lately married: your great man's daughter:
Are they all quite well?
THE SLAVE. My ears ring with the crying, my eyes are scalded. She put on the gold garments—
Did you do it, Medea?
MEDEA. I did it. Speak quietly.
THE SLAVE. You are avenged.
You are horribly avenged. It is too much.
The gods will hate you.
MEDEA *(avid, but still sitting).* That is my care. Did anyone die with her?
THE SLAVE. Creon!
MEDEA *(solemnly, standing up).* Where is pride now?
Tell me all that you saw. Speak slowly.
THE SLAVE. He tried to save her—he died! Corinth is masterless.
All's in amazed confusion, and some are looting, but they'll avenge him—
(He hears someone coming behind him.)
I'm going on!
Someone is going to die.
(He runs to the far side of the scene, and exits while MEDEA *speaks. Meanwhile the light has been changing, and soon the sun will set.)*
MEDEA. Here comes a more stable witness.
(The NURSE *enters.)*
Old friend:
Catch your breath; take your time. I want the whole tale, every gesture and cry. I have labored for this.
THE NURSE. Death is turned loose! I've hobbled and run, and fallen—
MEDEA. Please, Nurse: I am very happy: go slowly.
Tell me these things in order from the beginning.
As when you used to dress me, when I was little, in my father's house: you used to say
"One thing at a time; one thing and then the next."

(The light has changed to a flare of sunset.)

THE NURSE. My eyes are blistered,
My throat's like a dry straw. . . . There was a long mirror on the wall, and when her eyes saw it—
After the children had gone with Jason—she put her hands in the cases and took those gold things—and I
Watched, for I feared something might happen to her, but I never thought

So horribly—she placed on her little head the bright golden wreath, she gathered the flowing gold robe
Around her white shoulders,
And slender flanks,
And gazed at the golden girl in the metal mirror, going back and forth
On tiptoe almost; and swung her leg from the hip, to see the flexible gold
Molding the thigh. But suddenly horror began. I . . . Oh, Oh . . .
MEDEA. You are not suffering.
You saw it, you did not feel it. Speak plainly.
THE NURSE. Her face went white;
She staggered a few steps, bending over, and fell
Into the great throne-chair; then a serving-woman
Began to call for water thinking she had fainted, but saw the foam
Start on her lips, and the eyes rolling, and screamed instead. Then some of them
Ran after Jason, others ran to fetch Creon: and that doomed girl
Frightfully crying started up from the chair; she ran, she was like a torch, and the gold crown
Like a comet streamed fire; she tore at it but it clung to her head; the golden cloak
Was white-hot, flaying the flesh from the living bones; blood mixed with fire ran down, she fell, she burned
On the floor, writhing. Then Creon came and flung himself on her, hoping to choke
That rage of flame, but it ran through him, his own agony
Made him forget his daughter's. The fire stuck to the flesh, it glued him to her; he tried to stand up,
He tore her body and his own. The burned flesh broke
In lumps from the bones.
(She covers her eyes with her hands.)
I have finished. They lie there.
Eyeless, disfaced, untouchable; middens[7] of smoking flesh laced with molten gold. . . .
(Nearly a scream) No! I have finished.
I have no more.
MEDEA. I want all.
Had they died when you came away?
THE NURSE. I am not able . . . have mercy. . . . No, the harsh tides of breath
Still whistled in the black mouths. No one could touch them.
Jason stood in their smoke, and his hands tore
His unhelmeted hair.

7. ***middens,*** pieces of garbage or refuse.

MEDEA. You have told good news well: I'll reward you.
As for those people, they will soon die. Their woes are over too soon. Mine are not.
Jason's are not.
(She turns abruptly from her, toward the CHILDREN *who have been standing by the doorway, fascinated, not comprehending but watching.)*
My little falcons! Listen to me: laugh and be glad: we nave accomplished it.
Our enemies were great and powerful, they were full of cold pride, they ruled all this country—they are down in the ashes,
Crying like dogs, cowering in the ashes, in their own ashes. They went down with the sun, and the sun will rise
And not see them again. He will think, "Perhaps they are sleeping, they feasted late.
At noon they will walk in the garden." Oh, no, oh, no!
They will not walk in the garden. No one has ever injured me but suffered more
Than I had suffered.
(She turns from the CHILDREN.*)*
Therefore this final sacrifice I intended glares in my eyes
Like a lion on a ridge.
(Turning back to the CHILDREN*)*
We still hate, you know: a person nearer than these, more vile, more contemptible,
Whom I . . . I cannot. If he were my own hands I would cut him off, or my eyes, I would gouge him out—
But not you: that was madness.
(She turns from them.) So Jason will be able to say, "I have lost much,
But not all: I have children: my sons are well." That too is unbearable.
(She stands staring, agonized, one hand picking at the other.)
I want him crushed, boneless, crawling. . . .
I have no choice.
(Resolutely, to CHORUS*)*
You there! You thought me soft and submissive like a common woman—who takes a blow
And cries a little, and she wipes her face
And runs about the housework, loving her master? I am not such a woman.
FIRST WOMAN. Awake, Medea!
Awake from the evil dream. Catch up your children and flee.

Farther than Athens, farther than Thrace[8] or Spain, flee to the world's end.
Fire and death have done your bidding.
Are you not fed full with evil?
Is it not enough?

MEDEA. No. Loathing is endless.
Hate is a bottomless cup. I will pour and pour.
(She turns fiercely to the CHILDREN.*)* Children—
(Suddenly melting) O my little ones!
What was I dreaming?—My babes, my own!
(She kneels to them, taking their hands.) Never, never, never, never
Shall my own babes be hurt. Not if every war-hound and spear-slave in headless Corinth
Were on the track.
(Still kneeling, to CHORUS*)*
Look, their sweet lips are trembling: look, women, the little mouths: I frightened them
With those wild words: they stood and faced me, they never flinched.
Look at their proud young eyes! My eaglets, my golden ones!
(She kisses them, then holds them off and gazes at them.) O sweet small faces . . . like the pale wild roses
That bloom where the cliff breaks toward the brilliant sea: the delicate form and color, the dear, dear fragrance
Of your sweet breath . . .
(She continues gazing at them; her face changes.)

THE NURSE. My lady, make haste, haste!
Take them and flee. Flee away from here! Someone will come soon.
*(*MEDEA *still gazes at the* CHILDREN. *The* NURSE *clutches her shoulder.)*
Oh—listen to me.
Spears will come, death will come. All Corinth is in confusion and headless anarchy, unkinged and amazed
Around that horror you made: therefore they linger: yet in a moment
Its avengers come!
*(*MEDEA *looks up from staring at the* CHILDREN. *Her face has changed; the love has gone out of it. She speaks in a colorless tired voice.)*

MEDEA. I have a sword in the house.
I can defend you.
(She stands up stiffly and takes the CHILDREN *by their shoulders;*

8. ***Thrace,*** once a country to the northeast of Greece; now part of Greece, Bulgaria, and Turkey.

holds the ELDER BOY *in front of her, toward* CHORUS*; speaks with cold intensity.)*

Would you say that this child
Has Jason's eyes?

(The WOMEN *are silent, in terror gazing at her.)*

. . . They are his cubs. They have his blood.
As long as they live I shall be mixed with him.

(She looks down at the CHILDREN, *speaks tenderly but hopelessly.)*

Children:
It is evening. See, evening has come. Come, little ones,
Into the house. Evening brings all things home. It brings the bird to the bough and the lamb to the fold—
And the child to the mother. We must not think too much: people go mad
If they think too much.

(She has pushed the CHILDREN *gently into the house. In the doorway, behind them, she flings up her hands as if to tear her hair out by the roots; then quietly goes in. The great door closes; the iron noise of the bolt is driven home.)*

THE NURSE. No! No!

(She rushes toward the door, but sinks down on the steps, helpless, her hand reaching up and beating feebly against the foot of the door.) No . . .

FIRST WOMAN. What has happened?

SECOND WOMAN. That crown of horrors . . .

(They speak like somnambulists, and stand frozen. There is a moment of silence.)

CHILD'S VOICE *(in the house, shrill, broken off).* Mother! Ai—!

(The WOMEN *press toward the door, crying more or less simultaneously.)*

THE WOMEN. Medea, no!
Prevent her! Save them!
Open the door—

(They listen for an answer.)

ELDER CHILD'S VOICE. You've hurt him! The blood. The blood. Oh, Mother!

THIRD WOMAN *(below the steps, farthest from the door).* A god is here, Medea, he calls to you, he forbids you—

(The NURSE *has risen, and beats feebly on the door, stooping and bent over.* FIRST WOMAN *stands beside her very erect, with her back against the door, covering her ears with her hands. They are silent.)*

ELDER CHILD'S VOICE *(clear, but as if hypnotized).* She is hunting me. . . .
She is hunting me. . . . She is hunting. . . . Aah!

(Lamentation—keening[9]—is heard in the house. It rises and falls, and continues to the end, but often nearly inaudible. It is now twilight.)

THE NURSE *(limps down the steps and says).* There is no hope in heaven or earth. It is done.
It was destined when she was born, now it is done.
(Wailing) Oh, Oh, Oh.

THIRD WOMAN *(with terror, looking into the shadows).* Who is coming?
Someone is running at us!

FIRST WOMAN *(quietly).* The accursed man.
Jason.

SECOND WOMAN. He has a sword!

FIRST WOMAN. I am more afraid of the clinging contagion of his misfortunes.
A man the gods are destroying.

JASON *(enters rapidly, disheveled and shaking, a drawn sword in his hand).* Where is that murderess? Here in the house?
Or has she fled? She'll have to hide in the heavy metal darkness and caves of the earth—and there
I'll crawl and find her.
(No answer. The WOMEN *draw away from him as he moves toward the door. He stops and turns on them, drawing his left hand across his face, as if his eyes were bewildered.)*
Are you struck dumb? Are you shielding her?
Where is Medea?

FIRST WOMAN. You caused these things. She was faithful to you and you broke faith.
Horror is here.

JASON. Uncaused. There was no reason. . . . Tell me at least
Whether she took my boys with her? Creon's people would kill them for what she has done: I'd rather save them
Than punish her. Help me in this.

THE NURSE *(wailing).* Oh, Oh, Oh . . .

JASON *(looking sharply at the* NURSE*).* So she has killed herself.
Good. She never lacked courage. . . . I'll take my sons away to the far end of the earth, and never
Speak of these things again.

THE NURSE *(wailing).* Oh, Oh, Oh . . .
(Lamentation from the house answers.)

JASON *(with a queer slyness, for he is trying to cheat himself out*

9. ***keening,*** loud, sorrowful wailing for the dead.

of believing what he dreads. He glances at the door, furtively, over his shoulder). Is she lying in there?
Honorable at least in her death. I might have known it.
(They remain silent.) Well, answer!

FIRST WOMAN *(pointing toward* CREON*'s house).* Death is there; death is here.
But you are both blind and deaf: how can I tell you?

JASON *(is silent, then says slowly).* But . . . the . . . children are well?

FIRST WOMAN. I do not know
Whether Medea lives or is dead.

JASON *(stares at her; turns suddenly to the door and hammers on it with his sword-hilt).* Open! Open! Open!
(He flings down the sword and sets his shoulder against the door; pushes in vain; returns halfway down the steps, and says pitiably) Women, I am alone. Help me.
Help me to break the bolt.

SECOND WOMAN. Our shoulders?

JASON. Go and find help. . . .
(The door opens behind him. It is now fairly dark; the interior of the house is lighted. Two SERVING-WOMEN *come from behind the door-jambs, and place two flickering lamps just outside the door, at the bases of the pillars, and withdraw themselves. They move symmetrically, like mirror-images of each other, one right-handed, one left-handed.* CHORUS *draws back in fear;* JASON *stands on the steps, bewildered.* MEDEA *comes into the doorway; her hand and clothing are bloodmarked.)*

MEDEA. What feeble night-bird overcome by misfortunes beats at my door? Can this be that great adventurer,
The famous lord of the seas and delight of women, the heir of rich Corinth—this crying drunkard
On the dark doorstep? Yet you've not had enough. You have come to drink the last bitter drops.
I'll pour them for you.

JASON. What's that stain on your hand?

MEDEA. The wine I was pouring for you spilled on my hand.
Dear were the little grapes that were crushed to make it; dear were the vineyards.

JASON. I came to kill you, Medea,
Like a caught beast, like a crawling viper. Give me my sons, that I may save them from Creon's men,
I'll go quietly away.

MEDEA. Hush, they are sleeping. Perhaps I will let
you look at them: you cannot have them.
But the hour is late, you ought to go home to that high-born
bride; the night has fallen, surely she longs for you.
Surely her flesh is not crusted black, nor her mouth a horror.
(JASON kneels on the steps, painfully groping for his sword.)
She
is very young,
But surely she will be fruitful.—Your sword you want?
There it is. Not that step, the next lower. No, the next higher.
JASON *(finds it and stands erect)*. I'll kill you first and then find
my sons.
MEDEA. You must be careful, Jason. Do you see the two
fire-snakes
That guard this door?
(Indicating the two lamps)
Here and here: one on each side: two
serpents. Their throats are swollen with poison,
Their eyes are burning coals, and their tongues are fire. They are
coiled ready to strike: if you come near them,
They'll make you what Creon is. But stand there very quietly, I'll
let you
Look at your sons.
(She speaks to someone in the house, behind the left door-jamb.)
Bring them across the doorway that he may
see them.
(She stands back, and two SERVING-WOMEN pass within the doorway from left to right, bearing the slain CHILDREN on a litter between them. It stands a moment in the gape of the door, and passes.)
JASON *(dropping the sword, flinging his hands to his temples)*. I
knew it already.
I knew it before I saw it. No wild beast could have done it.
MEDEA. I have
done it: because I loathed you more
Than I loved them. Mine is the triumph.
JASON. Your triumph. No
iron-fleshed demon of those whom your father worships
In that blood-crusted temple—did you feel nothing, no pity; are
you pure evil? I should have killed you
The day I saw you.
MEDEA. I tore my own heart and laughed: I was
tearing yours.
JASON Will you laugh while I strangle you?
MEDEA. I would still laugh.—Beware my door-holders, Jason!
these eager serpents.—I'd still be joyful

To know that every bone of your life is broken; you are left hopeless, friendless, mateless, childless,
Avoided by gods and men, unclean with awful excess of grief—childless—

JASON *(exhausted).* It is no matter now
Who lives, or who dies.

MEDEA. Go down to your ship *Argo* and weep beside it, that rotting hulk on the harbor-beach
Drawn dry astrand, never to be launched again—even the weeds and barnacles on the warped keel
Are dead and stink—that's your last companion—
And only hope: for sometime one of the rotting timbers
Will fall on your head and kill you[10]—meanwhile sit there and mourn, remembering the infinite evil, and the good
That has turned evil.

JASON. Exult in evil, gloat your fill, have your glory.

MEDEA. My heart's blood bought it.

JASON. Enjoy it then.
Only give me my boys: the little pitiful violated bodies: that I may bury them
In some kind place.

MEDEA. To you? You would betray even the little bodies: coin them for silver,
Sell them for power. No.

JASON *(kneeling).* Let me touch their dear flesh, let me touch their hair!

MEDEA. No. They are mine.
They are going with me: the chariot is in the gate. You had love and betrayed it; now of all men
You are utterly the most miserable. As I of women. But I, a woman, a foreigner, alone
Against you and the might of Corinth—have met you throat for throat, evil for evil. Now I go forth
Under the cold eyes of the weakness-despising stars:—not me they scorn.

(She goes out of sight behind the right door-jamb, following the dead CHILDREN. JASON *stumbles up the steps to follow her, and falls between the two flickering lamps. The door remains open, the light in the house is partially extinguished. A music of mixed triumph and lamentation is heard to pass from the house, and diminish into the distance beyond it.)*

10. ***one of the rotting timbers . . . kill you,*** a prophecy about Jason's death that later came true.

Discussion

Act Two

1. As Medea sits waiting for Jason at the opening of the act, the chorus describes omens that have been appearing in Corinth. **(a)** What are the omens? **(b)** Do they appear to suggest specific events of the play? Discuss.

2. When Jason enters, Medea tells him she forgives him and then questions him closely on his feelings for his sons. If they were killed, she asks, would he be grieved? **(a)** What is Jason's reaction to Medea's question? **(b)** What do you think is Medea's purpose in questioning Jason in this way? **(c)** Does Medea ever actually intend to leave their sons with him? Explain.

3. How does Euripides introduce suspense in the scene in which Medea sends the children off to the royal palace with their father?

4. When the tutor reports the success of the children at the palace, Medea replies: "If this were all, old man—I'd have your bony loins beaten to a blood-froth for the good news you bring." Why does she respond in this way?

5. **(a)** Who is the first to bring Medea the news she wishes to hear? **(b)** How does she respond to the warnings this messenger gives her? **(c)** When her old nurse returns, what do Medea's responses to the detailed account she hears reveal about her character?

6. After hearing the consequences of her plot, Medea turns to her children and briefly appears to have lost her resolve to harm them. Then suddenly she changes her mind. What causes her to change from a loving mother back into an avenging wife?

7. As Medea departs, leaving Jason "the most miserable" of men, she says: "Now I go forth under the cold eyes of the weakness-despising stars:—not me they scorn." Explain how this final remark fits Medea's character.

Application

Allusion

The allusions you encounter in literature textbooks should generally cause you no problems, for most of them are explained in footnotes or sidenotes. Nevertheless, there are times when it is interesting to speculate on what an author's purpose in using certain allusions might be.

1. Review the sidenotes involving allusions that accompany this play. What, in general, is the subject they most often deal with?

2. Why do you think this subject is alluded to as often as it is?

Composition

The women of Corinth accuse Medea of wanting "not justice: vengeance." As a native of neither Corinth nor Colchis, you may have your own view about her motives. Be sure you understand the distinction between the two feelings; then review Medea's actions and focus on any statements she makes about what she does. Also consider the offenses she thinks Jason has committed and notice how others react to them. Then decide whether you agree with the Corinthian women's opinion.

Write a three- or four-paragraph essay stating and defending your opinion, citing specific lines or incidents from the play as evidence. (See "Evaluating Your Evidence," page 662, in the Composition Guide.)

Euripides 480? B.C.–406? B.C.

The main image of Euripides to come down from classic times is that of a recluse who lived in a cave by the sea, where he wrote plays revealing the violent emotions of the human heart. Thus, he appears as strangely unsociable, as someone who has peered too long into the darkness of the soul and knows too much of the treachery of human behavior.

Euripides was born on the Greek island of Salamis into a middle-class landholding family. A distinguished member of Athenian society, he lived at a time when Greece was at the height of its political power and creativity in the arts and philosophy. He was a friend of the great philosopher Socrates, who reportedly was an enthusiastic admirer of his works.

Not only was Euripides a successful and productive playwright, he was also an accomplished athlete. Because his parents had received a prophecy that he would win crowns of victory, he was given gymnastic training, and did indeed achieve several athletic victories. As a young man, Euripides served in the army and held a priesthood position in the rites of the Delphian Apollo.

As an adult, Euripides avoided society and political life. He lived with his wife on an estate on Salamis, where he wrote a number of his many plays. Although he produced between eighty and ninety works, only nineteen have survived in relatively complete form.

About 408 B.C., Euripides was accused of being a traitor because he opposed the war party and questioned traditional religious beliefs. He went into voluntary exile, dying shortly after at the age of seventy-four.

Euripides, along with Aeschylus and Sophocles, is known as one of the great triad of Greek tragic writers. All contributed to the development of the tragic form, elevating it to a status that has endured 2,500 years. Of the three, Euripides was the least respectful of the Olympian gods, the most insistent in his social criticism, and the most modern in his appeal. In his long active career, he was awarded the prize for the best drama in the Dionysian competition only four times; however, he subsequently was to become the most popular tragic poet of Greece, whose plays were the most frequently revived, translated, and adapted.

Robinson Jeffers 1887–1962

The translator of *Medea,* Robinson Jeffers was a modern American poet whose poems often strike the reader as tragic and bitter, focusing—like the plays of Euripides—on the darker side of human behavior. Among his well-known poems are "Shine, Perishing Republic" (1925), *Tamar* (1924), *Roan Stallion* (1925), and his Pulitzer-Prize-winning collection *Hungerfield and Other Poems* (1954).

Born in Pittsburgh, Jeffers pursued an interest in classical language and literature, graduating from Occidental College in Los Angeles in 1905. He settled in Carmel, California, a starkly beautiful and isolated coastal region, where he found dramatic inspiration and produced most of his work.

Jeffers has written about his translation of *Medea:* "The endeavor was to present Euripides' tragedy in a form and in poetry that might be interesting to an intelligent but not learned contemporary audience. There is much in any Greek play that would seem dull or absurd to anyone but a classical scholar; I tried to omit all this and to emphasize the essential values of the play."

Jeffers translated *Medea* for the accomplished actress Judith Anderson, who appeared in the play's triumphant initial run in 1947. In a successful revival of the play in the early 1980s, Zoe Caldwell assumed the title role, supported by Judith Anderson as Medea's nurse. The illustrations in this unit are from that production.

Unit 4 Review: Greek Drama

Content Review

1. Briefly identify each of the following:

Creon	Dionysus	Colchis
Thespis	Hecate	Delphi
Golden Fleece	*Argo*	Athena

2. Though *Medea* portrays the conflict between a husband and wife in a specific situation, the play at times suggests a more basic conflict between men and women generally. **(a)** Review Medea's long speech after Creon leaves in Act One and explain how her views about the condition of women relate to her own behavior in the play. **(b)** Review Jason's long speech to Medea just before his exit in Act One. In what ways do his assumptions about the nature of women differ from Medea's?

3. Review the article about the chorus; then cite three passages in *Medea* that represent three different functions of the chorus.

4. Medea is a good example of a character who is "larger than life." Her gigantic emotions and extravagant deeds seem to come from a superhuman force within her. How would you characterize this force? Cite lines and incidents from the play to support your view.

5. In *Medea,* as in many of Euripides' plays, the intervention of the gods in the affairs of mortals is acknowledged, but there is also recognition of the fact that humans can exercise freedom of choice. For example, in Act One, Medea criticizes Jason for invoking the gods to rationalize how she (and later Creüsa) came to love him; yet in Act Two, she explains her own actions to the chorus by saying, "I do according to nature what I have to do." **(a)** Are statements like this one indications that Medea's actions are inevitable and beyond her control, or are they merely excuses? **(b)** Would the play be as effective if the element of human choice were not included? Discuss.

6. In Act One of *Medea,* the sun stands for the light of reason: Jason speaks of the "rational sunlight of Greece." Find another reference to sunlight that is connected to one of Medea's deeds, and explain why it does or doesn't fit in with Jason's view of the sun.

Concept Review: Interpretation of New Material

Read the introduction and scene from the play. Then use the questions that come after it to review your understanding of the concepts presented in this unit.

from Alcestis • *Euripides* Greece

This excerpt, from the earliest play of Euripides in existence, presents the predicament of Admetus (ad me′təs), king of the region called Thessaly, who has been told by the gods that he must die. However, the god Apollo has arranged that if Admetus finds a suitable substitute, his life will be spared. Among his friends, courtiers, and family he finds only his wife Alcestis (al ses′təs) willing to take his place. She gives some of her reasons for doing so as she lies dying.

ALCESTIS. Somebody has me, somebody takes me away, do you see,
don't you see, to the courts
of dead men. He frowns from under dark
brows. He has wings. It is Death.

Let me go, what are you doing, let go.
Such is the road
most wretched I have to walk.
ADMETUS. Sorrow for all who love you, most of all for me
and for the children. All of us share in this grief.
ALCESTIS. Let me go now, let me down,
flat. I have no strength to stand.
Death is close to me.
The darkness creeps over my eyes. O children,
my children, you have no mother now,
not any longer. Daylight is yours,
my children. Look on it and be happy.
ADMETUS. Ah, a bitter word for me to hear,
heavier than any death of my own.
Before the gods, do not be so harsh
as to leave me, leave your children forlorn.
No, up, and fight it.
There would be nothing left of me if you died.
All rests in you, our life, our not
having life. Your love is our worship.
ALCESTIS. Admetus, you can see how it is with me. Therefore,
I wish to have some words with you before I die.
I put you first, and at the price of my own life
made certain you would live and see the daylight. So
I die, who did not have to die, because of you.
I could have taken any man in Thessaly
I wished and lived in queenly state here in this house.
But since I did not wish to live bereft of you
and with our children fatherless, I did not spare
my youth, although I had so much to live for. Yet
your father, and the mother who bore you, gave you up,
though they had reached an age when it was good to die
and good to save their son and end it honorably.
You were their only one, and they had no more hope
of having other children if you died. That way
I would be living and you would live the rest of our time,
and you would not be alone and mourning for your wife
and tending motherless children. No, but it must be
that some god has so wrought that things shall be this way.
So be it. But swear now to do, in recompense,
what I shall ask you—not enough, oh, never enough,
since nothing is enough to make up for a life,

---

but fair, and you yourself will say so, since you love
these children as much as I do; or at least you should.
Keep them as masters in my house, and do not marry
again and give our children to a stepmother
who will not be so kind as I, who will be jealous
and raise her hand to your children and mine. Oh no,
do not do that, do not. That is my charge to you.
For the new-come stepmother hates the children born
to a first wife, no viper could be deadlier.
The little boy has his father for a tower of strength.
(He can talk with him and be spoken to in turn.)
But you, my darling, what will your girlhood be like,
how will your father's new wife like you? She must not
make shameful stories up about you, and contrive
to spoil your chance of marriage in the blush of youth,
because your mother will not be there to help you
when you are married, not be there to give you strength
when your babies are born, when only a mother's help will do.
For I must die. It will not be tomorrow, not
the next day, or this month, the horrible thing will come,
but now, at once, I shall be counted among the dead.
Good-by, be happy, both of you. And you, my husband,
can boast the bride you took made you the bravest wife,
and you, children, can say, too, that your mother was brave.

CHORUS. Fear nothing; for I dare to speak for him. He will
do all you ask. If he does not, the fault is his.

ADMETUS. It shall be so, it shall be, do not fear, since you
were mine in life, you still shall be my bride in death
and you alone, no other girl in Thessaly
shall ever be called wife of Admetus in your place.
There is none such, none so marked out in pride of birth
nor beauty's brilliance, nor in anything else. I have
these children, they are enough; I only pray the gods
grant me the bliss to keep them as we could not keep you.
I shall go into mourning for you, not for just
a year, but all my life while it still lasts, my dear,
and hate the woman who gave me birth always, detest
my father. These were called my own people. They were not.
You gave what was your own and dear to buy my life
and saved me. Am I not to lead a mourning life
when I have lost a wife like you? I shall make an end
of revelry and entertainment in my house,
the flowers and the music that were found here once.

1. From her opening lines, do you think Alcestis finds the presence of death comforting? Explain.

2. List two reasons Alcestis gives for dying in Admetus's place.

3. In return for her sacrifice, Alcestis requests that Admetus **(a)** give thanks to the gods; **(b)** build a great monument in her memory; **(c)** not remarry; **(d)** put aside memories of their life together.

4. Alcestis fears that her little girl would not **(a)** wish to marry because of her parents' ordeal; **(b)** get over the grief of her mother's death; **(c)** remember what Alcestis was like; **(d)** be treated kindly by a stepmother.

5. Alcestis wishes to be remembered as **(a)** generous; **(b)** proud; **(c)** brave; **(d)** beautiful.

6. The chorus speaks only once in this passage. Does it approve or disapprove of the requests Alcestis makes?

7. Reread lines 16–21. Is Admetus satisfied that his wife is his substitute? Explain.

8. In response to his wife's last requests, Admetus tells her **(a)** it would displease the gods to follow them; **(b)** his family would pressure him to ignore them; **(c)** he will follow them; **(d)** in order to follow them, he must leave Thessaly.

9. The first four lines contain a figure of speech. Identify it.

10. The focus of this passage from *Alcestis* is on the **(a)** love between husband and wife; **(b)** unpredictable nature of death; **(c)** inability of mortals to escape the influence of the gods; **(d)** tragic consequences of hubris.

Composition Review

From the following assignments choose one to write about.

1. Assume that you are Aegeus. Now that the story of Medea's crime is out, you feel it necessary to explain your decision to shelter her in your kingdom. Think through the reasons you had for helping her—your friendship, her plight, the favor she promised you—and decide on the proper tone a monarch's statement should take.

Write a two-paragraph press release admitting your decision and then providing a justification for it.

2. The classical Greek theater required a play to have one plot occurring on one day in one place. In analyzing *Medea* in terms of this requirement, consider the following questions: How are the actions that take place before the play opens incorporated into the play? How does the plot effectively use the rule that the play take place in one day?

Now write a three- or four-paragraph essay discussing how well *Medea* adheres to the one-plot, one-day, one-place requirement. (You may want to deal with each aspect of the requirement separately.) Use examples to support what you say.

3. On the surface, Medea and Alcestis appear totally unlike; upon closer examination, however, they may be seen to have a few similarities. Review the selections to obtain information about the following: their status in the societies in which they live; their views on a woman's role in marriage; how each regards her husband; their attitudes toward their children; any other areas in which they might be compared.

Write a two- or three-paragraph essay comparing and contrasting the two characters.

Unit 5
Tradition in Fiction

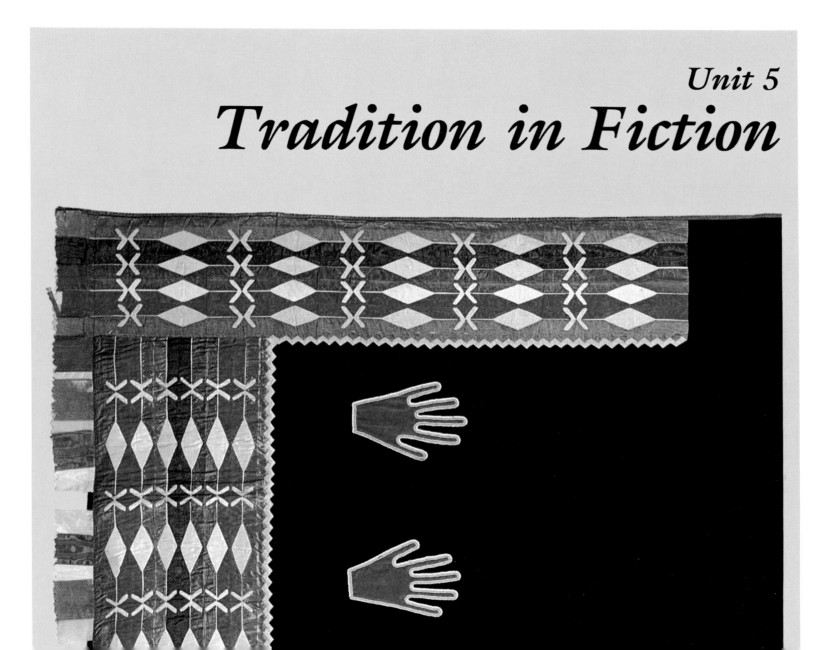

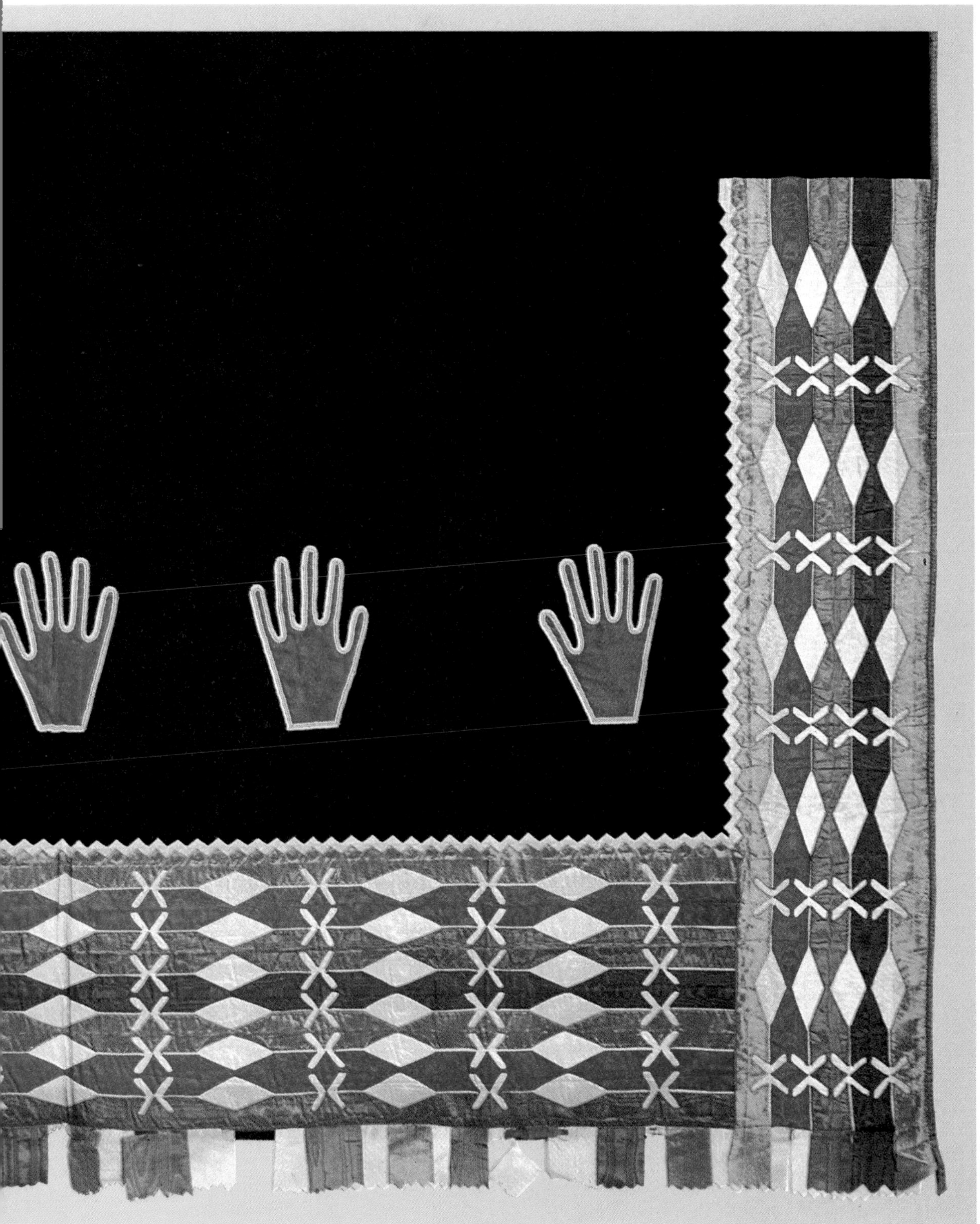

See **IRONY** Handbook of Literary Terms

The Necklace

Guy de Maupassant France

It was dazzlingly beautiful—and more costly than anyone could have imagined.

She was one of those pretty, charming young ladies, born, as if through an error of destiny, into a family of clerks. She had no dowry, no hopes, no means of becoming known, appreciated, loved, and married by a man either rich or distinguished; and she allowed herself to marry a petty clerk in the office of the Board of Education.

She was simple, not being able to adorn herself, but she was unhappy, as one out of her class; for women belong to no caste, no race; their grace, their beauty, and their charm serving them in the place of birth and family. Their inborn finesse, their instinctive elegance, their suppleness of wit are their only aristocracy, making some daughters of the people the equal of great ladies.

She suffered incessantly, feeling herself born for all delicacies and luxuries. She suffered from the poverty of her apartment, the shabby walls, the worn chairs, and the faded stuffs. All these things, which another woman of her station would not have noticed, tortured and angered her. The sight of the little Breton,[1] who made this humble home, awoke in her sad regrets and desperate dreams. She thought of quiet antechambers with their Oriental hangings lighted by high bronze torches, and of the two great footmen in short trousers who sleep in the large armchairs, made sleepy by the heavy air from the heating apparatus. She thought of large drawing rooms hung in old silks, of graceful pieces of furniture carrying bric-a-brac of inestimable value, and of the little perfumed coquettish apartments made for five o'clock chats with most intimate friends, men known and sought after, whose attention all women envied and desired.

When she seated herself for dinner before the round table, where the tablecloth had been used three days, opposite her husband who uncovered the tureen with a delighted air, saying: "Oh! the good potpie! I know nothing better than that," she would think of the elegant dinners, of the shining silver, of the tapestries peopling the walls with ancient personages and rare birds in the midst of fairy forests; she thought of the exquisite food served on marvelous dishes, of the whispered gallantries, listened to with the smile of the Sphinx while eating the rose-colored flesh of the trout or a chicken's wing.

She had neither frocks nor jewels, nothing. And she loved only those things. She felt that she was made for them. She had such a desire to please, to be sought after, to be clever and courted.

She had a rich friend, a schoolmate at the convent, whom she did not like to visit; she suffered so much when she returned. And she wept for whole days from chagrin, from regret, from despair and disappointment.

---

1. ***Breton*** (bret′n), a native of Brittany, a coastal region in western France.

Guy de Maupassant (gē də mō pá säɴ′).

One evening her husband returned, elated, bearing in his hand a large envelope.

"Here," he said, "here is something for you."

She quickly tore open the wrapper and drew out a printed card on which were inscribed these words:

The Minister of Public Instruction and Madame George Ramponneau ask the honor of M. and Mme. Loisel's[2] *company Monday evening, January 18, at the Minister's residence.*

Instead of being delighted, as her husband had hoped, she threw the invitation spitefully upon the table, murmuring:

"What do you suppose I want with that?"

"But, my dearie, I thought it would make you happy. You never go out, and this is an occasion, and a fine one! I had a great deal of trouble to get it. Everybody wishes one, and it is very select; not many are given to employees. You will see the whole official world there."

She looked at him with an irritated eye and declared impatiently:

"What do you suppose I have to wear to such a thing as that?"

He had not thought of that; he stammered:

"Why, the dress you wear when we go to the theater. It seems very pretty to me."

He was silent, stupefied, in dismay, at the sight of his wife weeping. Two great tears fell slowly from the corners of her eyes toward the corners of her mouth; he stammered:

"What is the matter? What is the matter?"

By a violent effort she had controlled her vexation and responded in a calm voice, wiping her moist cheeks:

"Nothing. Only I have no dress and consequently I cannot go to this affair. Give your card to some colleague whose wife is better fitted out than I."

He was grieved but answered:

"Let us see, Matilda. How much would a suitable costume cost, something that would serve for other occasions, something very simple?"

She reflected for some seconds, making estimates and thinking of a sum that she could ask for without bringing with it an immediate refusal and a frightened exclamation from the economical clerk.

Finally she said in a hesitating voice:

"I cannot tell exactly, but it seems to me that four hundred francs[3] ought to cover it."

He turned a little pale, for he had saved just this sum to buy a gun that he might be able to join some hunting parties the next summer, on the plains at Nanterre,[4] with some friends who went to shoot larks up there on Sunday. Nevertheless, he answered:

"Very well. I will give you four hundred francs. But try to have a pretty dress."

The day of the ball approached, and *Mme.* Loisel seemed sad, disturbed, anxious. Nevertheless, her dress was nearly ready. Her husband said to her one evening:

"What is the matter with you? You have acted strangely for two or three days."

And she responded: "I am vexed not to have a jewel, not one stone, nothing to adorn myself with. I shall have such a poverty-laden look. I would prefer not to go to this party."

He replied: "You can wear some natural flowers. At this season they look very chic. For ten francs you can have two or three magnificent roses."

She was not convinced. "No," she replied, "there is nothing more humiliating than to have a shabby air in the midst of rich women."

Then her husband cried out: "How stupid we are! Go and find your friend *Madame* Forestier[5] and ask her to lend you her jewels. You are well enough acquainted with her to do this."

She uttered a cry of joy. "It is true!" she said. "I had not thought of that."

The next day she took herself to her friend's

---

2. ***Ramponneau*** (râm pə nō′) . . . ***M. and Mme. Loisel's*** (lwä zelz′). *M.* and *Mme.* are the abbreviations for *Monsieur* and *Madame*, respectively.

3. ***four hundred francs,*** about $240 in United States currency at the time of the story. The franc itself was worth about sixty cents.

4. ***Nanterre*** (nän ter′).

5. ***Forestier*** (fôr es tyā′).

house and related her story of distress. *Mme.* Forestier went to her closet with the glass doors, took out a large jewel case, brought it, opened it, and said: "Choose, my dear."

She saw at first some bracelets, then a collar of pearls, then a Venetian cross of gold and jewels and of admirable workmanship. She tried the jewels before the glass, hesitated, but could neither decide to take them nor leave them. Then she asked:

"Have you nothing more?"

"Why, yes. Look for yourself. I do not know what will please you."

Suddenly she discovered in a black satin box a superb necklace of diamonds, and her heart beat fast with an immoderate desire. Her hands trembled as she took them up. She placed them about her throat, against her dress, and remained in ecstasy before them. Then she asked in a hesitating voice full of anxiety:

"Could you lend me this? Only this?"

"Why, yes, certainly."

She fell upon the neck of her friend, embraced her with passion, then went away with her treasure.

The day of the ball arrived. *Mme.* Loisel was a great success. She was the prettiest of all, elegant, gracious, smiling, and full of joy. All the men noticed her, asked her name, and wanted to be presented. All the members of the Cabinet wished to waltz with her. The Minister of Education paid her some attention.

She danced with enthusiasm, with passion, intoxicated with pleasure, thinking of nothing, in the triumph of her beauty, in the glory of her success, in a kind of cloud of happiness that came of all this homage and all this admiration, of all these awakened desires and this victory so complete and sweet to the heart of woman.

She went home toward four o'clock in the morning. Her husband had been half asleep in one of the little salons since midnight with three other gentlemen whose wives were enjoying themselves very much.

He threw around her shoulders the wraps they had carried for the coming home, modest garments of everyday wear, whose poverty clashed with the elegance of the ball costume. She felt this and wished to hurry away in order not to be noticed by the other women who were wrapping themselves in rich furs.

Loisel detained her. "Wait," said he. "You will catch cold out there. I am going to call a cab."

But she would not listen and descended the steps rapidly. When they were in the street they found no carriage, and they began to seek for one, hailing the coachmen whom they saw at a distance.

They walked along toward the Seine,[6] hopeless and shivering. Finally they found on the dock one of those old nocturnal coupés that one sees in Paris after nightfall, as if they were ashamed of their misery by day.

It took them as far as their door in Martyr Street, and they went wearily up to their apartment. It was all over for her. And on his part he remembered that he would have to be at the office by ten o'clock.

She removed the wraps from her shoulders before the glass for a final view of herself in her glory. Suddenly she uttered a cry. Her necklace was not around her neck.

Her husband, already half undressed, asked: "What is the matter?"

She turned toward him excitedly:

"I have—I have—I no longer have *Madame* Forestier's necklace."

He arose in dismay: "What! How is that? It is not possible."

And they looked in the folds of the dress, in the folds of the mantle, in the pockets, everywhere. They could not find it.

He asked: "You are sure you still had it when we left the house?"

"Yes, I felt it in the vestibule as we came out."

"But if you had lost it in the street we should have heard it fall. It must be in the cab."

6. ***Seine*** (sān), river that flows through the center of Paris.

"Yes. It is probable. Did you take the number?"

"No. And you, did you notice what it was?"

"No."

They looked at each other, utterly cast down. Finally Loisel dressed himself again.

"I am going," said he, "over the track where we went on foot, to see if I can find it."

And he went. She remained in her evening gown, not having the force to go to bed, stretched upon a chair, without ambition or thoughts.

Toward seven o'clock her husband returned. He had found nothing.

He went to the police and to the cab offices and put an advertisement in the newspapers, offering a reward; he did everything that afforded them a suspicion of hope.

She waited all day in a state of bewilderment before this frightful disaster. Loisel returned at evening, with his face harrowed and pale, and had discovered nothing.

"It will be necessary," said he, "to write to your friend that you have broken the clasp of the necklace and that you will have it repaired. That will give us time to turn around."

She wrote as he dictated.

At the end of a week they had lost all hope. And Loisel, older by five years, declared:

"We must take measures to replace this jewel."

The next day they took the box which had enclosed it to the jeweler whose name was on the inside. He consulted his books.

"It is not I, *Madame*," said he, "who sold this necklace; I only furnished the casket."

Then they went from jeweler to jeweler, seeking a necklace like the other one, consulting their memories, and ill, both of them, with chagrin and anxiety.

In a shop of the Palais-Royal[7] they found a chaplet of diamonds which seemed to them exactly like the one they had lost. It was valued at forty thousand francs. They could get it for thirty-six thousand.

They begged the jeweler not to sell it for three days. And they made an arrangement by which they might return it for thirty-four thousand francs if they found the other one before the end of February.

Loisel possessed eighteen thousand francs which his father had left him. He borrowed the rest.

He borrowed it, asking for a thousand francs of one, five hundred of another, five louis[8] of this one, and three louis of that one. He gave notes, made ruinous promises, took money of usurers and the whole race of lenders. He compromised his whole existence, in fact, risked his signature without even knowing whether he could make it good or not, and, harrassed by anxiety for the future, by the black misery which surrounded him, and by the prospect of all physical privations and moral torture, he went to get the new necklace, depositing on the merchant's counter thirty-six thousand francs.

When *Mme*. Loisel took back the jewels to *Mme*. Forestier the latter said to her in a frigid tone:

"You should have returned them to me sooner, for I might have needed them."

She did open the jewel box as her friend feared she would. If she should perceive the substitution what would she think? What should she say? Would she take her for a robber?

Mme. Loisel now knew the horrible life of necessity. She did her part, however, completely, heroically. It was necessary to pay this frightful debt. She would pay it. They sent away the maid; they changed their lodgings; they rented some rooms under a mansard roof.

She learned the heavy cares of a household, the odious work of a kitchen. She washed the dishes, using her rosy nails upon the greasy pots and the bottoms of the stew pans. She washed the soiled linen, the chemises and dishcloths, which she hung on the line to dry; she took down the refuse to the street each morning and brought up

---

7. ***Palais-Royal*** (pȧ lä' rwä yal'), a Parisian shopping district.
8. ***louis*** (lü'ē), a French gold coin equal in value to twenty francs. At the time of the story, five louis were worth about sixty dollars.

the water, stopping at each landing to breathe. And, clothed like a woman of the people, she went to the grocer's, the butcher's, and the fruiterer's with her basket on her arm, shopping, haggling to the last sou[9] her miserable money.

Every month it was necessary to renew some notes, thus obtaining time, and to pay others.

The husband worked evenings, putting the books of some merchants in order, and nights he often did copying at five sous a page.

And this life lasted for ten years.

At the end of ten years they had restored all, all, with interest of the usurer, and accumulated interest, besides.

Mme. Loisel seemed old now. She had become a strong, hard woman, the crude woman of the poor household. Her hair badly dressed, her skirts awry, her hands red, she spoke in a loud tone and washed the floors in large pails of water. But sometimes, when her husband was at the office, she would seat herself before the window and think of that evening party of former times, of that ball where she was so beautiful and so flattered.

How would it have been if she had not lost that necklace? Who knows? Who knows? How singular is life and how full of changes! How small a thing will ruin or save one!

One Sunday, as she was taking a walk in the Champs Élysées[10] to rid herself of the cares of the week, she suddenly perceived a woman walking with a child. It was *Mme*. Forestier, still young, still pretty, still attractive. *Mme*. Loisel was affected. Should she speak to her? Yes, certainly. And now that she had paid, she would tell her all. Why not?

She approached her. "Good morning, Jeanne."

Her friend did not recognize her and was astonished to be so familiarly addressed by this common personage. She stammered:

"But, *Madame*—I do not know—You must be mistaken."

"No, I am Matilda Loisel."

Her friend uttered a cry of astonishment: "Oh! My poor Matilda! How you have changed."

"Yes, I have had some hard days since I saw you, and some miserable ones—and all because of you."

"Because of me? How is that?"

"You recall the diamond necklace that you loaned me to wear to the Minister's ball?"

"Yes, very well."

"Well, I lost it."

"How is that, since you returned it to me?"

"I returned another to you exactly like it. And it has taken us ten years to pay for it. You can understand that it was not easy for us who have nothing. But it is finished, and I am decently content."

Mme. Forestier stopped short. She said:

"You say that you bought a diamond necklace to replace mine?"

"Yes. You did not perceive it then? They were just alike."

And she smiled with a proud and simple joy. *Mme*. Forestier was touched and took both her hands as she replied:

"Oh, my poor Matilda! Mine were false. They were not worth over five hundred francs!"

---

9. *sou* (sü), a former French coin that was worth one-twentieth of a franc, or about a penny.
10. *Champs Élysées* (shäɴ zā lē zā'), a famous avenue in Paris.

Discussion

1. (a) What is Matilda Loisel's family background? **(b)** Describe her feelings about her situation in life as the story opens.

2. (a) What two "problems" make Matilda unwilling to go to the party? **(b)** How is each taken care of? **(c)** Contrast the characters of Matilda and her husband as shown through their dealings with these problems.

3. (a) How does Matilda happen to lose the necklace? **(b)** How does her husband help to delay *Mme*. Forestier's discovery of the loss?

4. When using a surprise ending, an author must provide clues anticipating it or risk being accused of falsely manipulating his or her material. **(a)** What clues give a hint to the surprise ending of this story? **(b)** How does the point of view the author uses help to keep the secret?

5. In your opinion, are the things that happen to Matilda the result of fate or coincidence, or are they caused by her own character? Give reasons for your answer.

6. Is the ending of the story happy or unhappy? Discuss.

Application

Irony

The ending of this story, as with many surprise endings, turns on irony of situation: after working all those years to replace the necklace, Matilda finds out it was worthless. But there are many small ironies throughout the story that make this ending even more poignant. Discuss the irony in each of the following.

1. Matilda's friend *Mme.* Forestier, whom she admires for her wealth, lends her a paste necklace.

2. Matilda is ecstatic at the party because it is her first glimpse of a lifestyle she earnestly desires for herself.

3. Matilda tells the story of replacing the lost necklace with dignity and pride.

Vocabulary

Context

Using context clues, determine the meaning of the italicized word in each sentence that follows. Then write the letter of the definition that best fits the sentence.

1. There is rarely a moment of silence in that house; everyone in the family seems to talk *incessantly.* **(a)** calmly; **(b)** continually; **(c)** argumentatively; **(d)** persuasively.

2. There is practically no sign of raccoons in our neighborhood during the day; however, their *nocturnal* activities—which often awaken us—never let us forget their presence. **(a)** unnoticeable; **(b)** mid-morning; **(c)** remarkably quiet; **(d)** nighttime.

3. Because he had always been able to pay someone to do it for him, having to shovel the snow himself seemed particularly *odious* now. **(a)** hateful; **(b)** easy; **(c)** entertaining; **(d)** fair.

4. The *harrowed* look on her face suggested that the incident had bothered her more than she had admitted. **(a)** delighted; **(b)** distressed; **(c)** confused; **(d)** confident.

5. By polishing his boots regularly, he had preserved the *suppleness* of the leather even after years of wear. **(a)** ability to bend easily; **(b)** ability to keep out cold; **(c)** color; **(d)** up-to-date style.

Guy de Maupassant 1850–1893

Called one of the most productive writers of all time, de Maupassant is best known as a master of short fiction. He is credited with the invention of the "whiplash ending," one that is both surprising and cruel, which he cunningly employs in "The Necklace."

Born in Normandy, France, de Maupassant was raised by a cultivated mother who knew the novelist Gustave Flaubert (flō ber′). At seventeen, the young man began what was to be a ten-year apprenticeship with the noted author, learning the craft of writing. He developed his skills so precisely that his first published story, "Ball of Wax" (1880), immediately established his reputation as an accomplished artist.

Just as Flaubert's instruction influenced him, de Maupassant's hundreds of short stories became examples of the form to readers worldwide. Often portraying the conflicts of average people, they are characterized by the author's detached tone, irony, and pessimism.

The Interlopers

Saki Great Britain

"Each had a rifle in his hand; each had hate in his heart and murder uppermost in his mind."

In a forest of mixed growth somewhere on the eastern spurs of the Carpathians,[1] a man stood one winter night watching and listening, as though he waited for some beast of the woods to come within the range of his vision, and later, of his rifle. But the game for whose presence he kept so keen an outlook was none that figured in the sportsman's calendar as lawful and proper for the chase; Ulrich von Gradwitz[2] patrolled the dark forest in quest of a human enemy.

The forest lands of Gradwitz were of wide extent and well stocked with game; the narrow strip of precipitous woodland that lay on its outskirts was not remarkable for the game it harbored or the shooting it afforded, but it was the most jealously guarded of all its owner's territorial possessions. A famous lawsuit, in the days of his grandfather, had wrested it from the illegal possession of a neighboring family of petty landowners; the dispossessed party had never acquiesced in the judgment of the courts, and a long series of poaching affrays and similar scandals had embittered the relationships between the families for three generations. The neighbors' feud had grown into a personal one since Ulrich had come to be head of his family; if there was a man in the world whom he detested and wished ill to, it was Georg Znaeym,[3] the inheritor of the quarrel and the tireless game snatcher and raider of the disputed border forest.

The feud might, perhaps, have died down or been compromised if the personal ill will of the two men had not stood in the way: as boys they had thirsted for one another's blood; as men each prayed that misfortune might fall on the other; and this wind-scourged winter night Ulrich had banded together his foresters to watch the dark forest, not in quest of four-footed quarry, but to keep a lookout for the prowling thieves whom he suspected of being afoot from across the land boundary. The roebuck, which usually kept in the sheltered hollows during a storm-wind, were running like driven things tonight; and there was movement and unrest among the creatures that were wont to sleep through the dark hours. Assuredly there was a disturbing element in the forest, and Ulrich could guess the quarter from whence it came.

He strayed away by himself from the watchers whom he had placed in ambush on the crest of the hill, and wandered far down the steep slopes amid the wild tangle of undergrowth, peering through the tree trunks and listening through the whistling and skirling of the wind and the restless beating of the branches for sight or sound of the

---

1. ***Carpathians*** (kär pā'thē ənz), mountain chain extending from northern Rumania to Czechoslovakia.
2. ***Ulrich von Gradwitz*** (ül'rik fən gräd'vits).
3. ***Georg Znaeym*** (gā'ôrg znä'im).

marauders. If only on this wild night, in this dark, lone spot, he might come across Georg Znaeym, man to man, with none to witness—that was the wish that was uppermost in his thoughts. And as he stepped round the trunk of a huge beech, he came face to face with the man he sought.

The two enemies stood glaring at one another for a long, silent moment. Each had a rifle in his hand; each had hate in his heart and murder uppermost in his mind. The chance had come to give full play to the passions of a lifetime. But a man who has been brought up under the code of a restraining civilization cannot easily nerve himself to shoot down his neighbor in cold blood and without a word spoken, except for an offense against his hearth and honor. And before the moment of hesitation had given way to action, a deed of nature's own violence overwhelmed them both. A fierce shriek of the storm had been answered by a splitting crash over their heads; and ere they could leap aside, a mass of falling beech tree had thundered down on them. Ulrich von Gradwitz found himself stretched on the ground, one arm numb beneath him and the other held almost as helpless in a tight tangle of forked branches, while both legs were pinned beneath the fallen mass. His heavy shooting boots had saved his feet from being crushed to pieces; but if his fractures were not so serious as they might have been, at least it was evident that he could not move from his present position till someone came to release him. The descending twigs had slashed the skin of his face, and he had to wink away some drops of blood from his eyelashes before he could take in a general view of the disaster. At his side, so near that under ordinary circumstances he could almost have touched him, lay Georg Znaeym, alive and struggling, but obviously as helplessly pinioned down as himself. All round them lay a thick-strewn wreckage of splintered branches and broken twigs.

Relief at being alive and exasperation at his captive plight brought a strange medley of pious thank offerings and sharp curses to Ulrich's lips. Georg, who was nearly blinded with the blood which trickled across his eyes, stopped his struggling for a moment to listen and then gave a short, snarling laugh.

"So you're not killed, as you ought to be; but you're caught, anyway," he cried; "caught fast. Ho, what a jest, Ulrich von Gradwitz snared in his stolen forest. There's real justice for you!"

And he laughed again, mockingly and savagely.

"I'm caught in my own forest land," retorted Ulrich. "When my men come to release us, you will wish, perhaps, that you were in a better plight than caught poaching on a neighbor's land. Shame on you!"

Georg was silent for a moment; then he answered quietly:

"Are you sure that your men will find much to release? I have men, too, in the forest tonight, close behind me; and *they* will be here first and do the releasing. When they drag me out from under these branches, it won't need much clumsiness on their part to roll this mass of trunk right over on the top of you. Your men will find you dead under a fallen tree. For form's sake I shall send my condolences to your family."

"It is a useful hint," said Ulrich fiercely. "My men had orders to follow in ten minutes' time, seven of which must have gone by already; and when they get me out—I will remember the hint. Only as you will have met your death poaching on my lands, I don't think I can decently send any message of condolence to your family."

"Good," snarled Georg, "good. We'll fight this quarrel out to the death—you and I and our foresters, with no cursed interlopers to come between us. Death to you, Ulrich von Gradwitz!"

"The same to you, Georg Znaeym, forest thief, game snatcher!"

Both men spoke with the bitterness of possible defeat before them, for each knew that it might be long before his men would seek him out or find him; it was a bare matter of chance which party would arrive first on the scene.

Both had now given up the useless struggle to free themselves from the mass of wood that held them down; Ulrich limited his endeavors to an effort to bring his one partially free arm near enough to his outer coat pocket to draw out his wine flask. Even when he had accomplished that operation, it was long before he could manage the unscrewing of the stopper or get any of the liquid down his throat. But what a Heaven-sent draft it seemed! It was an open winter, and little snow had fallen as yet, hence the captives suffered less from the cold than might have been the case at that season of the year; nevertheless, the wine was warming and reviving to the wounded man, and he looked across with something like a throb of pity to where his enemy lay, barely keeping the groans of pain and weariness from crossing his lips.

"Could you reach this flask if I threw it over to you?" asked Ulrich suddenly. "There is good wine in it, and one may as well be as comfortable as one can. Let us drink, even if tonight one of us dies."

"No. I can scarcely see anything, there is so much blood caked round my eyes," said Georg; "and in any case I don't drink wine with an enemy."

Ulrich was silent for a few minutes and lay listening to the weary screeching of the wind. An idea was slowly forming and growing in his brain, an idea that gained strength every time that he looked across at the man who was fighting so grimly against pain and exhaustion. In the pain and languor that Ulrich himself was feeling, the old fierce hatred seemed to be dying down.

"Neighbor," he said presently, "do as you please if your men come first. It was a fair compact. But as for me, I've changed my mind. If my men are the first to come, you shall be the first to be helped, as though you were my guest. We have quarreled like devils all our lives over this stupid strip of forest where the trees can't even stand upright in a breath of wind. Lying here tonight, thinking, I've come to think that we've been rather fools; there are better things in life than getting the better of a boundary dispute. Neighbor, if you will help me to bury the old quarrel I—I will ask you to be my friend."

Georg Znaeym was silent for so long that Ulrich thought, perhaps, he had fainted with the pain of his injuries. Then he spoke slowly and in jerks:

"How the whole region would stare and gabble if we rode into the market square together. No one living can remember seeing a Znaeym and a Von Gradwitz talking to one another in friendship. And what peace there would be among the forester folk if we ended our feud tonight. And if we choose to make peace among our people, there is none other to interfere, no interlopers from outside. . . . You would come and keep the Sylvester night[4] beneath my roof, and I would come and feast on some high day at your castle. . . . I would never fire a shot on your land, save when you invited me as a guest; and you should come and shoot with me down in the marshes where the wild fowl are. In all the countryside there are none that could hinder if we willed to make peace. I never thought to have wanted to do other than hate you all my life; but I think I have changed my mind about things, too, this last half-hour. And you offered me your wine flask. . . . Ulrich von Gradwitz, I will be your friend."

For a space both men were silent, turning over in their minds the wonderful changes that this dramatic reconciliation would bring about. In the cold, gloomy forest, with the wind tearing in fitful gusts through the naked branches and whistling around the tree trunks, they lay and waited for the help that would now bring release and succor to both parties. And each prayed a private prayer that his men might be the first to arrive, so that he might be the first to show honorable attention to the enemy that had become a friend.

Presently, as the wind dropped for a moment, Ulrich broke silence.

"Let's shout for help," he said; "in this lull our voices may carry a little way."

"They won't carry far through the trees and undergrowth," said Georg; "but we can try. Together, then."

The two raised their voices in a prolonged hunting call.

---

4. ***Sylvester night,*** New Year's Eve. Festivities honor St. Sylvester.

"Together again," said Ulrich a few minutes later, after listening in vain for an answering halloo.

"I heard something that time, I think," said Ulrich.

"I heard nothing but the pestilential wind," said Georg hoarsely.

There was silence again for some minutes, and then Georg gave a joyful cry.

"I can see figures coming through the wood. They are following in the way I came down the hillside."

Both men raised their voices in as loud a shout as they could muster.

"They hear us! They've stopped. Now they see us. They're running down the hill toward us," cried Ulrich.

"How many of them are there?" asked Georg.

"I can't see distinctly," said Ulrich; "nine or ten."

"Then they are yours," said Georg; "I had only seven out with me."

"They are making all the speed they can, brave lads," said Ulrich gladly.

"Are they your men?" asked Georg. "Are they your men?" he repeated impatiently as Ulrich did not answer.

"No," said Ulrich with a laugh, the idiotic chattering laugh of a man unstrung with hideous fear.

"Who are they?" asked Georg quickly, straining his eyes to see what the other would gladly not have seen.

"Wolves!"

Discussion

1. (a) What was the original cause of the feud between Ulrich's and Georg's families? **(b)** What seemed to assure that the feud would continue?

2. (a) Describe the setting of the story. **(b)** Does the setting help to establish the mood? **(c)** What is Ulrich doing outdoors in such a situation?

3. (a) What two things keep Georg and Ulrich from killing each other when they meet? **(b)** How and why does Ulrich change his feelings about his old enemy? **(c)** Does his change of heart seem believable? Discuss.

4. (a) What is ironic about the end of the story? **(b)** Find wording early in the story that foreshadows this ending. **(c)** How are Georg's two uses of the word *interlopers* also ironic in view of what happens?

5. Identify three different conflicts in the story. Which ultimately proves to be the most important? Explain.

Saki 1870–1916

British writer H. H. Munro adopted the pen name "Saki" while writing political sketches for the *Westminster Gazette.* However, the name became widely known in connection with his short stories. *Reginald* (1904), *The Chronicles of Clovis* (1911), and *Beasts and Super Beasts* (1914), all successful collections, displayed Munro's satirical humor as well as his fascination with the unusual.

Munro was born in Akyab (now Sittwe), Burma, where his father was a colonel in the Bengal Staff Corps. He was sent home to England to the care of relatives at the age of two, following the death of his mother. In 1893 he returned to Burma, but poor health led him back to England and a career as both a journalist and short-story writer. He also produced his only novel, *The Unbearable Bassington* (1912).

He joined the army as a private at the beginning of World War I and went to France in 1915. Within a year he was killed in battle.

The Man from Kabul[1]

Rabindranath Tagore India

A friendship becomes a faded memory; however, the bond of affection somehow endures.

My five-year-old daughter, Mini, cannot live without chattering. I really believe that in all her life she has not wasted a minute in silence. Her mother is often vexed at this, and would like to stop her prattle, but I would not. For Mini to be quiet is unnatural, and I cannot bear it long. And so my own talk with her is always lively.

One morning, for instance, when I was in the midst of the seventeenth chapter of my new novel, my little Mini stole into the room, and putting her hand into mine, said, "Father! Ramdayal,[2] the doorkeeper, calls a crow a crew! He doesn't know anything, does he?"

Before I could explain to her the difference between one language and another in this world, she had embarked on the full tide of another subject. "What do you think, Father? Bhola says there is an elephant in the clouds, blowing water out of his trunk, and that is why it rains!"

And then, darting off anew, while I sat still, trying to think of some reply to this: "Father, what relation is Mother to you?"

With a grave face I contrived to say, "Go and play with Bhola, Mini! I am busy!"

The window of my room overlooks the road. The child had seated herself at my feet near my table, and was playing softly, drumming on her knees. I was hard at work on my seventeenth chapter, in which Pratap Singh, the hero, has just caught Kanchanlata,[3] the heroine, in his arms, and is about to escape with her by the third-story window of the castle, when suddenly Mini left her play and ran to the window, crying, "A Kabuliwallah! A Kabuliwallah!"[4] And indeed, in the street below, there was a man from Kabul, walking slowly along. He wore the loose, soiled clothing of his people, and a tall turban; he carried a bag on his back and boxes of grapes in his hands.

I cannot tell what my daughter's feelings were when she saw this man, but she began to call him loudly. "Ah!" thought I. "He will come in, and my seventeenth chapter will never be finished!" At that very moment the Kabuliwallah turned and looked up at the child. When she saw this, she was overcome by terror, and running to her mother's protection, disappeared. She had a blind belief that inside the bag which the big man carried there were perhaps two or three other children like herself. The peddler meanwhile entered my doorway and greeted me with a smile.

So precarious was the position of my hero and my heroine that my first impulse was to stop and buy something, since Mini had called the man to the house. I made some small purchases, and we began to talk about Abdur Rahman, the Russians, the English, and the Frontier Policy.[5]

As he was about to leave, he asked, "And where is the little girl, sir?"

And then, thinking that Mini must get rid of her false fear, I had her brought out.

---

1. ***Kabul*** (kä'bül), capital of Afghanistan, a country bordering on Pakistan to the northwest of India.
2. ***Ramdayal*** (räm'dä yäl).
3. ***Pratap Singh*** (prə täp' sin'hə) . . . ***Kanchanlata*** (kun'chən lä'tə).
4. ***Kabuliwallah*** (kä'bül ē wä'lə).
5. ***Abdur Rahman*** (əb dür' ra män') . . . ***Frontier Policy,*** a political figure and issues of the time. Abdur Rahman became ruler of Afghanistan in 1880, a period when England and Russia were rivals for its control. Afghanistan's attempts to avoid the influence of the two powers, and England's foreign-policy aim to expand into Kabul, resulted in a war between England and Afghanistan.

Rabindranath Tagore (rä bēn'drā nät' tə gôr').

She stood by my chair and looked at the Kabuliwallah and his bag. He offered her nuts and raisins, but she would not be tempted, and only clung the closer to me, with all her doubts increased.

This was their first meeting.

A few mornings later, however, as I was leaving the house, I was startled to find Mini seated on a bench near the door, laughing and talking, with the great Kabuliwallah at her feet. In all her life, it appeared, my small daughter had never found so patient a listener, save her father. And already the corner of her little sari was stuffed with almonds and raisins, the gift of her visitor. "Why did you give her those?" I said, and taking out an eight-anna piece,[6] I handed it to him. The man accepted the money without demur and put it into his pocket.

Alas, on my return, an hour later, I found the unfortunate coin had made twice its own worth of trouble! For the Kabuliwallah had given it to Mini; and her mother, catching sight of the bright round object, had pounced on the child with: "Where did you get that eight-anna piece?"

"The Kabuliwallah gave it to me," said Mini cheerfully.

"The Kabuliwallah gave it to you!" cried her mother, greatly shocked. "Oh, Mini! How could you take it from him?"

I entered at that moment, and saving her from impending disaster, proceeded to make my own inquiries.

It was not the first or the second time, I found, that the two had met. The Kabuliwallah had overcome the child's first terror by a judicious bribe of nuts and almonds, and the two were now great friends.

They had many quaint jokes, which amused them greatly. Mini would seat herself before him, look down on his gigantic frame in all her tiny dignity, and with her face rippling with laughter, would begin: "O Kabuliwallah! Kabuliwallah! What have you got in your bag?"

And he would reply, in the nasal accents of the mountaineer, "An elephant!" Not much cause for merriment, perhaps; but how they both enjoyed the fun! And for me, this child's talk with a grown-up man had always in it something strangely fascinating.

Then the Kabuliwallah, not to be behindhand, would take his turn: "Well, little one, and when are you going to your father-in-law's house?"

Now, nearly every small Bengali maiden had heard long ago about her father-in-law's house; but we were a little newfangled,[7] and had kept these things from our child, so that Mini at this question must have been a trifle bewildered. But she would not show it, and with ready tact replied, "Are *you* going there?"

Amongst men of the Kabuliwallah's class, however, it is well-known that the words "father-in-law's house" have a double meaning. It is a euphemism for jail, the place where we are well cared for, at no expense to ourselves. In this sense would the sturdy peddler take my daughter's question. "Oh," he would say, shaking his fist at an invisible policeman, "I will thrash my father-in-law!" Hearing this, and picturing the poor discomfited relative, Mini would go off into peals of laughter in which her formidable friend would join.

These were autumn mornings, the very time of year when kings of old went forth to conquest; and I, without stirring from my little corner in Calcutta,[8] would let my mind wander over the whole world. At the very name of another country, my heart would go out to it, and at the sight of a foreigner in the streets, I would fall to weaving a network of dreams—the mountains, the glens, and the forests of his distant land, with his cottage in their midst, and the free and independent life, or faraway wilds. Perhaps scenes of travel are conjured up before me and pass and

---

6. ***eight-anna piece.*** An anna was a coin once used in India and Pakistan that at the time of the story was worth approximately one penny. An eight-anna piece was worth eight cents.

7. ***Bengali maiden . . . newfangled.*** A Bengali was a native of Bengal, a former province of India; traditionally, the joining of an Indian woman to her husband's family through marriage meant that she was no longer considered part of her own family. This view was less rigidly held, however, as Indian society became influenced by "newfangled" Western culture.

8. ***Calcutta.*** The story takes place in this seaport city in eastern India that at that time was the country's capital.

repass in my imagination all the more vividly because I lead an existence so like a vegetable that a call to travel would fall upon me like a thunderbolt. In the presence of this Kabuliwallah, I was immediately transported to the foot of arid mountain peaks, with narrow little defiles twisting in and out amongst their towering heights. I could see the string of camels bearing the merchandise, and the company of turbaned merchants, some carrying their queer old firearms, and some their spears, journeying downward toward the plains. I could see— But at some such point, Mini's mother would intervene, and implore me to "Beware of that man."

Mini's mother is unfortunately very timid. Whenever she hears a noise in the street, or sees people coming toward the house, she always jumps to the conclusion that they are either thieves, or drunkards, or snakes, or tigers, or malaria, or cockroaches, or caterpillars. Even after all these years of experience, she is not able to overcome her terror. So she was full of doubts about the Kabuliwallah, and used to beg me to keep a watchful eye on him.

If I tried to laugh her fear gently away, she would turn around seriously, and ask me solemn questions:

Were children never kidnapped?

Was it not true that there was slavery in Kabul?

Was it so very absurd that this big man should be able to carry off a tiny child?

I urged that though not impossible, it was very improbable. But this was not enough, and her dread persisted. But as it was a very vague dread, it did not seem right to forbid the man the house, and the intimacy went on unchecked.

Once a year, in the middle of January, Rahman the Kabuliwallah used to return to his own country, and as the time approached, he would be very busy, going from house to house collecting his debts. This year, however, he could always find time to come and see Mini. It might have seemed to a stranger that there was some conspiracy between the two, for when he could not come in the morning, he would appear in the evening.

Even to me it was a little startling, now and then, suddenly to surprise this tall, loose-garmented man, laden with his bags, in the corner of a dark room; but when Mini ran in, smiling, with her "O Kabuliwallah! Kabuliwallah!" and the two friends, so far apart in age, subsided into their old laughter and their old jokes, I felt reassured.

One morning, a few days before he had made up his mind to go, I was correcting proof sheets in my study. The weather was chilly. Through the window the rays of the sun touched my feet, and the slight warmth was very welcome. It was nearly eight o'clock, and early pedestrians were returning home with their heads covered. Suddenly I heard an uproar in the street, and looking out, saw Rahman being led away bound between two policemen, and behind them a crowd of inquisitive boys. There were bloodstains on his clothes, and one of the policemen carried a knife. I hurried out, and stopping them, inquired what it all meant. Partly from one, partly from another, I gathered that a certain neighbor had owed the peddler something for a Rampuri shawl,[9] but had denied buying it, and that in the course of the quarrel, Rahman had struck him. Now, in his excitement, the prisoner began calling his enemy all sorts of names, when suddenly in a veranda of my house appeared my little Mini, with her usual exclamation: "O Kabuliwallah! Kabuliwallah!" Rahman's face lighted up as he turned to her. He had no bag under his arm today, so that she could not talk about the elephant with him. She therefore at once proceeded to the next question: "Are you going to your father-in-law's house?" Rahman laughed and said, "That is just where I am going, little one!" Then, seeing that the reply did not amuse the child, he held up his fettered hands. "Ah!" he said, "I would have thrashed that old father-in-law, but my hands are bound!"

On a charge of murderous assault, Rahman was sentenced to several years' imprisonment.

Time passed, and he was forgotten. Our accustomed work in the accustomed place went on, and the thought of the once-free mountaineer spending his years in prison seldom or never occurred to us. Even my lighthearted Mini, I am ashamed to say, forgot her old friend. New companions filled her life. As she grew older, she spent more of her time with girls. So much, indeed, did she spend with them that she came no more, as she used to do, to her father's room, so that I rarely had any opportunity of speaking to her.

Years had passed away. It was once more autumn, and we had made arrangements for our Mini's marriage. It was to take place during the Puja holidays.[10] The light of our home would depart to her husband's house, and leave her father's in shadow.

The morning was bright. After the rains, it seemed as though the air had been washed clean and the rays of the sun looked like pure gold. So bright were they that they made even the sordid brick walls of our Calcutta lanes radiant. Since

---

9. ***Rampuri shawl,*** an item from Rampur, an Indian town.
10. ***Puja holidays,*** a religious festival observed by Hindus.

early dawn the wedding pipes had been sounding, and at each burst of sound my own heart throbbed. The wail of the tune, "Bhairavi," seemed to intensify the pain I felt at the approaching separation.[11] My Mini was to be married that night.

From early morning, noise and bustle had pervaded the house. In the courtyard there was the canopy to be slung on its bamboo poles; there were chandeliers with their tinkling sound to be hung in each room and veranda. There was endless hurry and excitement. I was sitting in my study, looking through the accounts, when someone entered, saluting respectfully, and stood before me. It was Rahman the Kabuliwallah. At first I did not recognize him. He carried no bag, his long hair was cut short, and his old vigor seemed to have gone. But he smiled, and I knew him again.

"When did you come, Rahman?" I asked him.

"Last evening," he said, "I was released from jail."

The words struck harshly upon my ears. I had never before talked with one who had wounded his fellow man, and my heart shrank within itself when I realized this; for I felt that the day would have been better omened had he not appeared.

"There are ceremonies going on," I said, "and I am busy. Perhaps you could come another day?"

He immediately turned to go; but as he reached the door, he hesitated, and said, "May I not see the little one, sir, for a moment?" It was his belief that Mini was still the same. He had pictured her running to him as she used to do, calling, "O Kabuliwallah! Kabuliwallah!" He had imagined, too, that they would laugh and talk together, just as of old. Indeed, in memory of former days, he had brought, carefully wrapped up in a paper, a few almonds and raisins and grapes, obtained somehow or other from a countryman; for what little money he had, had gone.

I repeated, "There is a ceremony in the house, and you will not be able to see anyone today."

The man's face fell. He looked wistfully at me for a moment, then said, "Good morning," and went out.

I felt a little sorry, and would have called him back, but I found he was returning of his own accord. He came close up to me and held out his offerings with the words: "I have brought these few things, sir, for the little one. Will you give them to her?"

I took them, and was going to pay him, but he caught my hand and said, "You are very kind, sir! Keep me in your memory. Do not offer me money! You have a little girl; I, too, have one like her in my own home. I think of her, and bring this fruit to your child—not to make a profit for myself."

Saying this, he put his hand inside his big loose robe and brought out a small and dirty piece of paper. Unfolding it with great care, he smoothed it out with both hands on my table. It bore the impression of a little hand. Not a photograph. Not a drawing. Merely the impression of an ink-smeared hand laid flat on the paper. This touch of the hand of his own little daughter he had carried always next to his heart, as he had come year after year to Calcutta to sell his wares in the streets.

Tears came to my eyes. I forgot that he was a poor Kabuli fruit-seller, while I was— But no, what was I more than he? He also was a father.

That impression of the hand of his little Parvati in her distant mountain home reminded me of my own little Mini.

I sent for Mini immediately from the inner apartment. Many difficulties were raised, but I swept them aside. Clad in the red silk of her wedding day, with the sandal paste on her forehead, and adorned as a young bride, Mini came and stood modestly before me.

The Kabuliwallah seemed amazed at the apparition. He could not revive their old friendship. At last he smiled and said, "Little one, are you going to your father-in-law's house?"

---

11. ***"Bhairavi"*** (bī rä'vē) . . . ***approaching separation.*** The tune appropriately underscores Mini's departure; its title is the name of an Indian goddess believed to assist souls in departing to heaven.

But Mini now understood the meaning of the word "father-in-law," and she could not answer him as of old. She blushed at the question and stood before him with her bridelike face bowed down.

I remembered the day when the Kabuliwallah and my Mini had first met, and I felt sad. When she had gone, Rahman sighed deeply and sat down on the floor. The idea had suddenly come to him that his daughter, too, must have grown up while he had been away so long, and that he would have to make friends anew with her, also. Assuredly he would not find her as she was when he left her. And besides, what might not have happened to her in these eight years?

The marriage pipes sounded, and the mild autumn sunlight streamed around us. But Rahman sat in the little Calcutta lane and saw before him the barren mountains of Afghanistan.

I took out a currency note, gave it to him, and said, "Go back to your daughter, Rahman, in your own country, and may the happiness of your meeting bring good fortune to my child!"

Having made this present, I had to curtail some of the festivities. I could not have the electric lights I had intended, nor the military band, and the ladies of the house were despondent about it. But to me the wedding feast was all the brighter for the thought that in a distant land a long-lost father had met again his only child.

Discussion

1. (a) What characteristics of Mini can be seen in the opening paragraphs of the story? **(b)** Why do you think the Kabuliwallah seems drawn to her? **(c)** Contrast her mother's and father's attitudes about her chattering.

2. (a) Explain the double meaning of "going to your father-in-law's house." **(b)** Why does Mini not understand that the Kabuliwallah says it to tease her? **(c)** In what ways does the phrase foreshadow the action of the story?

3. (a) How does the Kabulliwallah get himself into trouble? **(b)** Do his actions fit in with what you know about him thus far? Discuss.

4. When the Kabuliwallah returns from prison, he presents himself to Mini's father. **(a)** Why does the father change his mind about letting the Kabuliwallah see Mini? **(b)** Contrast the Kabuliwallah's expectations about Mini with what he actually finds. **(c)** Does Mini's reaction surprise you? Why or why not?

5. In what ways is this story about lost love?

Rabindranath Tagore 1861–1941

Tagore was the eldest of seven sons of an extremely wealthy family of Calcutta, India (his surname was actually a title of nobility). Educated by tutors and private schools, he showed early promise as a poet. In 1890 he was put in charge of the family's rural estates, where he came to know the sufferings of the poor. The experience prompted Tagore to work for social reform in his homeland.

Already acclaimed in India for his poems, he attracted a following in England by publishing translations of his works. In 1913 Tagore became the first non-Westerner to win the Nobel Prize for Literature. In an action characteristic of his devotion to India's improvement, he donated the prize money to a school he had founded there.

Among Tagore's best-known works are a novel, *The Home and the World* (1916), and the short-story collections *The Hungry Stones* (1916) and *The Supreme Right* (1919). Much of his writing contains elements of humor, satire, and mysticism.

See **SYMBOL** Handbook of Literary Terms

The Sentimentality of William Tavener

Willa Cather USA

"The strategic contest had gone on so long that it had almost crowded out the memory of a closer relationship."

It takes a strong woman to make any sort of success of living in the West, and Hester undoubtedly was that. When people spoke of William Tavener as the most prosperous farmer in McPherson County, they usually added that his wife was a "good manager." She was an executive woman, quick of tongue and something of an imperatrix.[1] The only reason her husband did not consult her about his business was that she did not wait to be consulted.

It would have been quite impossible for one man, within the limited sphere of human action, to follow all Hester's advice, but in the end William usually acted upon some of her suggestions. When she incessantly denounced the "shiftlessness" of letting a new threshing machine stand unprotected in the open, he eventually built a shed for it. When she sniffed contemptuously at his notion of fencing a hog corral with sod walls, he made a spiritless beginning on the structure—merely to "show his temper," as she put it—but in the end he went off quietly to town and bought enough barbed wire to complete the fence. When the first heavy rains came on, and the pigs rooted down the sod wall and made little paths all over it to facilitate their ascent, he heard his wife relate with relish the story of the little pig that built a mud house, to the minister at the dinner table, and William's gravity never relaxed for an instant. Silence, indeed, was William's refuge and his strength.

William set his boys a wholesome example to respect their mother. People who knew him very well suspected that he even admired her. He was a hard man towards his neighbors, and even towards his sons: grasping, determined, and ambitious.

There was an occasional blue day about the house when William went over the store bills, but he never objected to items relating to his wife's gowns or bonnets. So it came about that many of the foolish, unnecessary little things that Hester bought for her boys she had charged to her personal account.

One spring night Hester sat in a rocking chair by the sitting-room window, darning socks. She rocked violently and sent her long needle vigorously back and forth over her gourd,[2] and it took only a very casual glance to see that she was wrought up over something. William sat on the other side of the table reading his farm paper. If he had noticed his wife's agitation, his calm, clean-shaven face betrayed no sign of concern. He must have noticed the sarcastic turn of her remarks at the supper table, and he must have noticed the moody silence of the older boys as they ate. When supper was but half over little Billy, the youngest, had suddenly pushed back

---

1. ***imperatrix*** (im′pə rā′trix), an empress or woman who rules.
2. ***sent her long needle . . . gourd.*** Because a small gourd easily conforms to the inside of small articles of clothing, it is a handy tool for darning.

his plate and slipped away from the table, manfully trying to swallow a sob. But William Tavener never heeded ominous forecasts in the domestic horizon, and he never looked for a storm until it broke.

After supper the boys had gone to the pond under the willows in the big cattle corral to get rid of the dust of plowing. Hester could hear an occasional splash and a laugh ringing clear through the stillness of the night as she sat by the open window. She sat silent for almost an hour reviewing in her mind many plans of attack. But she was too vigorous a woman to be much of a strategist, and she usually came to her point with directness. At last she cut her thread and suddenly put her darning down, saying emphatically:

"William, I don't think it would hurt you to let the boys go to that circus in town tomorrow."

William continued to read his farm paper, but it was not Hester's custom to wait for an answer. She usually divined his arguments and assailed them one by one before he uttered them.

"You've been short of hands all summer, and you've worked the boys hard, and a man ought use his own flesh and blood as well as he does his hired hands. We're plenty able to afford it, and it's little enough our boys ever spend. I don't see how you can expect 'em to be steady and hard workin', unless you encourage 'em a little. I never could see much harm in circuses, and our boys have never been to one. Oh, I know Jim Howley's boys get drunk an' carry on when they go, but our boys ain't that sort, an' you know it, William. The animals are real instructive, an' our boys don't get to see much out here on the prairie. It was different where we were raised, but the boys have got no advantages here, an' if you don't take care, they'll grow up to be greenhorns."

Hester paused a moment, and William folded up his paper, but vouchsafed no remark. His sisters in Virginia had often said that only a quiet man like William could ever have lived with Hester Perkins. Secretly, William was rather proud of his wife's "gift of speech," and of the fact that she could talk in prayer meeting as fluently as a man. He confined his own efforts in that line to a brief prayer at Covenant meetings.

Hester shook out another sock and went on.

"Nobody was ever hurt by goin' to a circus. Why, law me! I remember I went to one myself once, when I was little. I had most forgot about it. It was over at Pewtown, an' I remember how I had set my heart on going. I don't think I'd ever forgiven my father if he hadn't taken me, though that red-clay road was in a frightful way after the rain. I mind they had an elephant and six poll parrots, an' a Rocky Mountain lion, an' a cage of monkeys, an' two camels. My! but they were a sight to me then!"

Hester dropped the black sock and shook her head and smiled at the recollection. She was not expecting anything from William yet, and she was fairly startled when he said gravely, in much the same tone in which he announced the hymns in prayer meeting:

"No, there was only one camel. The other was a dromedary."

She peered around the lamp and looked at him keenly.

"Why, William, how come you to know?"

William folded his paper and answered with some hesitation, "I was there, too."

Hester's interest flashed up. "Well, I never, William! To think of my finding it out after all these years! Why, you couldn't have been much bigger'n our Billy then. It seems queer I never saw you when you was little, to remember about you. But then you Back Creek folks never have anything to do with us Gap people. But how come you to go? Your father was stricter with you than you are with your boys."

"I reckon I shouldn't 'a gone," he said slowly, "but boys will do foolish things. I had done a good deal of fox hunting the winter before, and Father let me keep the bounty money. I hired Tom Smith's Tap to weed the corn for me, an' I slipped off unbeknownst to Father an' went to the show."

Hester spoke up warmly: "Nonsense, William! It didn't do you no harm, I guess. You was always worked hard enough. It must have been a

big sight for a little fellow. That clown must have just tickled you to death."

William crossed his knees and leaned back in his chair.

"I reckon I could tell all that fool's jokes now. Sometimes I can't help thinkin' about 'em in meetin' when the sermon's long. I mind I had on a pair of new boots that hurt me like the mischief, but I forgot all about 'em when that fellow rode the donkey. I recall I had to take them boots off as soon as I got out of sight o' town, and walked home in the mud barefoot."

"O poor little fellow!" Hester ejaculated, drawing her chair nearer and leaning her elbows on the table. "What cruel shoes they did use to make for children. I remember I went up to Back Creek to see the circus wagons go by. They came down from Romney, you know. The circus men stopped at the creek to water the animals, an' the elephant got stubborn an' broke a big limb off the yellow willow tree that grew there by the toll-house porch,[3] an' the Scribners were 'fraid as death he'd pull the house down. But this much I saw him do; he waded in the creek an' filled his trunk with water and squirted it in at the window and nearly ruined Ellen Scribner's pink lawn dress that she had just ironed an' laid out on the bed ready to wear to the circus."

"I reckon that must have been a trial to Ellen," chuckled William, "for she was mighty prim in them days."

Hester drew her chair still nearer William's. Since the children had begun growing up, her conversation with her husband had been almost wholly confined to questions of economy and expense. Their relationship had become purely a business one, like that between landlord and ten-

3. ***toll-house porch.*** It was once customary for tollgate operators to live in houses situated near the gate.

ant. In her desire to indulge her boys she had unconsciously assumed a defensive and almost hostile attitude towards her husband. No debtor ever haggled with his usurer more doggedly than did Hester with her husband in behalf of her sons. The strategic contest had gone on so long that it had almost crowded out the memory of a closer relationship. This exchange of confidences tonight, when common recollections took them unawares and opened their hearts, had all the miracle of romance. They talked on and on; of old neighbors, of old familiar faces in the valley where they had grown up, of long-forgotten incidents of their youth—weddings, picnics, sleighing parties, and baptizings. For years they had talked of nothing else but butter and eggs and the prices of things, and now they had as much to say to each other as people who meet after a long separation.

When the clock struck ten, William rose and went over to his walnut secretary and unlocked it. From his red leather wallet he took out a ten-dollar bill and laid it on the table beside Hester.

"Tell the boys not to stay late, an' not to drive the horses hard," he said quietly, and went off to bed.

Hester blew out the lamp and sat still in the dark a long time. She left the bill lying on the table where William had placed it. She had a painful sense of having missed something, or lost something; she felt that somehow the years had cheated her.

The little locust trees that grew by the fence were white with blossoms. Their heavy odor floated in to her on the night wind and recalled a night long ago, when the first whippoorwill of the spring was heard, and the rough, buxom girls of Hawkins Gap had held her laughing and struggling under the locust trees, and searched in her bosom for a lock of her sweetheart's hair, which is supposed to be on every girl's breast when the first whippoorwill sings. Two of those same girls had been her bridesmaids. Hester had been a very happy bride. She rose and went softly into the room where William lay. He was sleeping heavily, but occasionally moved his hand before his face to ward off the flies. Hester went into the parlor and took the piece of mosquito net from the basket of wax apples and pears that her sister had made before she died. One of the boys had brought it all the way from Virginia, packed in a tin pail, since Hester would not risk shipping so precious an ornament by freight. She went back to the bedroom and spread the net over William's head. Then she sat down by the bed and listened to his deep, regular breathing until she heard the boys returning. She went out to meet them and warn them not to waken their father.

"I'll be up early to get your breakfast, boys. Your father says you can go to the show." As she handed the money to the eldest, she felt a sudden throb of allegiance to her husband and said sharply, "And you be careful of that, an' don't waste it. Your father works hard for his money."

The boys looked at each other in astonishment and felt that they had lost a powerful ally.

Discussion

1. (a) In what ways does Hester display the qualities of an imperatrix? **(b)** Is her husband's personality, by contrast, soft and easygoing? Explain. **(c)** What evidence is there early in the story of the soft side of both characters' nature?

2. (a) Before Hester brings up the subject of the circus, what signs indicate that she is upset about something? **(b)** Do you think she actually has reason to think William won't agree with her plan, or is it just her nature to react strongly? Discuss.

3. What kind of argument might Hester be anticipating from William for each of her following comments? **(a)** "a man ought use his own flesh and blood as well as he does his hired hands"; **(b)** "it's little enough our boys ever spend"; **(c)** "how [can you] expect 'em to be steady and hard workin', unless you encourage 'em a little."

4. (a) When and how does William show his "sentimentality"? **(b)** When and how does Hester show hers? **(c)** What will be the immediate and long-range effects on their sons?

5. In describing William and Hester's new relationship, the author refers to the "miracle of romance." Is the word *miracle* appropriate or not? Explain.

Application

Symbol

Though some literary symbols are complicated and make the reader look beyond the immediate context of a selection for their meaning, others seem to grow naturally out of the context and thus are not difficult to notice and understand.

1. As Hester and William reminisce, what does the circus come to stand for in their minds?

2. Do you think the circus will symbolize anything more when they remember the conversation of this night four or five years later? Discuss.

3. What is symbolic about Hester's removing the netting from the wax fruit and putting it over William's head?

Composition

Details of the setting presented in the story, as well as comments made in their discussion, give a fairly clear idea of the lifestyle of William and Hester. From these details, decide in what ways their lives were similar to or different from those of people living in rural areas today.

Write a three- or four-paragraph composition comparing and contrasting rural life then and now. (See "Making Comparisons and Contrasts," page 657, in the Composition Guide.)

Willa Cather 1873–1947

Cather's cherished memories of the prairie frontier determined her literary direction. In her first writings she had attempted to follow the sophisticated trends that were popular with Eastern writers, but finally found her best material at home, out of her own youthful experiences and observations.

Born in Gore, Virginia, Cather moved with her family to a ranch in Red Cloud, Nebraska, in 1883. She grew up there among immigrant farmers from Scandinavia and Bohemia. In a style that was noted for its accuracy and simplicity, she portrayed their struggle to adapt to the frontier in her first story collection, *The Troll Garden* (1905), and in her novels *O Pioneers!* (1913) and *My Antonia* (1918). The optimism behind these works began fading during World War I, when Cather started having doubts about the future of the human race. Her Pulitzer Prize-winning novel, *One of Ours* (1922), reflected this disillusionment. However, she recaptured the spirit of the pioneer in *Death Comes for the Archbishop* (1927), a historical novel regarded as an American masterpiece.

The Rocking-Horse Winner

D. H. Lawrence Great Britain

To meet the ceaseless demands of a troubled household, Paul turned in desperation to his wooden rocking horse.

There was a woman who was beautiful, who started with all the advantages, yet she had no luck. She married for love, and the love turned to dust. She had bonny children, yet she felt they had been thrust upon her, and she could not love them. They looked at her coldly, as if they were finding fault with her. And hurriedly she felt she must cover up some fault in herself. Yet what it was that she must cover up she never knew. Nevertheless, when her children were present, she always felt the center of her heart go hard. This troubled her, and in her manner she was all the more gentle and anxious for her children, as if she loved them very much. Only she herself knew that at the center of her heart was a hard little place that could not feel love, no, not for anybody. Everybody else said of her: "She is such a good mother. She adores her children." Only she herself, and her children themselves, knew it was not so. They read it in each other's eyes.

There was a boy and two little girls. They lived in a pleasant house, with a garden, and they had discreet servants, and felt themselves superior to anyone in the neighborhood.

Although they lived in style, they felt always an anxiety in the house. There was never enough money. The mother had a small income, and the father had a small income, but not nearly enough for the social position which they had to keep up. The father went into town to some office. But though he had good prospects, these prospects never materialized. There was always the grinding sense of the shortage of money, though the style was always kept up.

At last the mother said: "I will see if *I* can't make something." But she did not know where to begin. She racked her brains and tried this thing and the other, but could not find anything successful. The failure made deep lines come into her face. Her children were growing up, they would have to go to school. There must be more money, there must be more money. The father, who was always very handsome and expensive in his tastes, seemed as if he never *would* be able to do anything worth doing. And the mother, who had a great belief in herself, did not succeed any better, and her tastes were just as expensive.

And so the house came to be haunted by the unspoken phrase: There *must* be more money! There *must* be more money! The children could hear it all the time, though nobody said it aloud. They heard it at Christmas, when the expensive and splendid toys filled the nursery. Behind the shining modern rocking horse, behind the smart doll's house, a voice would start whispering: "There *must* be more money! There *must* be more money!" And the children would stop playing, to listen for a moment. They would look into each other's eyes, to see if they had all heard. And each one saw in the eyes of the other two that they, too, had heard. "There *must* be more money! There *must* be more money!"

It came whispering from the springs of the still-swaying rocking horse, and even the horse, bending his wooden, champing head, heard it. The big doll, sitting so pink and smirking in her new pram, could hear it quite plainly, and seemed to be smirking all the more self-consciously because of it. The foolish puppy, too, that took the place of the teddy bear, he was looking so extraordinarily foolish for no other reason but that he heard the secret whisper all over the house: "There *must* be more money!"

Yet nobody ever said it aloud. The whisper was everywhere, and therefore no one spoke it. Just as no one ever says: "We are breathing!" in spite of the fact that breath is coming and going all the time.

"Mother," said the boy Paul one day, "why don't we keep a car of our own? Why do we always use Uncle's, or else a taxi?"

"Because we're the poor members of the family," said the mother.

"But why *are* we, Mother?"

"Well—I suppose," she said slowly and bitterly, "it's because your father has no luck."

The boy was silent for some time.

"Is luck money, Mother?" he asked, rather timidly.

"No, Paul. Not quite. It's what causes you to have money."

"Oh!" said Paul vaguely. "I thought when Uncle Oscar said *filthy lucker,* it meant money."

"*Filthy lucre* does mean money," said the mother. "But it's lucre, not luck."

"Oh!" said the boy. "Then what is luck, Mother?"

"It's what causes you to have money. If you're lucky you have money. That's why it's better to be born lucky than rich. If you're rich, you may lose your money. But if you're lucky, you will always get more money."

"Oh! Will you? And is Father not lucky?"

"Very unlucky, I should say," she said bitterly.

The boy watched her with unsure eyes.

"Why?" he asked.

"I don't know. Nobody ever knows why one person is lucky and another unlucky."

"Don't they? Nobody at all? Does nobody know?"

"Perhaps God. But He never tells."

"He ought to, then. And aren't you lucky either, Mother?"

"I can't be, if I married an unlucky husband."

"But by yourself, aren't you?"

"I used to think I was, before I married. Now I think I am very unlucky indeed."

"Why?"

"Well—never mind! Perhaps I'm not really," she said.

The child looked at her, to see if she meant it. But he saw, by the lines of her mouth, that she was only trying to hide something from him.

"Well, anyhow," he said stoutly, "I'm a lucky person."

"Why?" said his mother, with a sudden laugh.

He stared at her. He didn't even know why he had said it. "God told me," he asserted, brazening it out.

"I hope He did, dear!" she said, again with a laugh, but rather bitter.

"He did, Mother!"

"Excellent!" said the mother, using one of her husband's exclamations.

The boy saw she did not believe him; or, rather, that she paid no attention to his assertion. This angered him somewhat, and made him want to compel her attention.

He went off by himself, vaguely, in a childish way, seeking for the clue to "luck." Absorbed, taking no heed of other people, he went about with a sort of stealth, seeking inwardly for luck. He wanted luck, he wanted it, he wanted it. When the two girls were playing dolls in the nursery, he would sit on his big rocking horse, charging madly into space, with a frenzy that made the little girls peer at him uneasily. Wildly the horse careered, the waving dark hair of the boy tossed, his eyes had a strange glare in them. The little girls dared not speak to him.

When he had ridden to the end of his mad little journey, he climbed down and stood in front of his rocking horse, staring fixedly into its lowered face. Its red mouth was slightly open, its big eye was wide and glassy bright.

"Now!" he would silently command the snorting steed. "Now, take me to where there is luck! Now take me."

And he would slash the horse on the neck with the little whip he had asked Uncle Oscar for. He *knew* the horse could take him to where there was luck, if only he forced it. So he would mount again, and start on his furious ride, hoping at last to get there. He knew he could get there.

"You'll break your horse, Paul!" said the nurse.

"He's always riding like that! I wish he'd leave off!" said his elder sister Joan.

But he only glared down on them in silence. Nurse gave him up. She could make nothing of him. Anyhow he was growing beyond her.

One day his mother and his Uncle Oscar came in when he was on one of his furious rides. He did not speak to them.

"Hallo, you young jockey! Riding a winner?" said his uncle.

"Aren't you growing too big for a rocking horse? You're not a very little boy any longer, you know," said his mother.

But Paul only gave a blue glare from his big, rather close-set eyes. He would speak to nobody when he was in full tilt. His mother watched him with an anxious expression on her face.

At last he suddenly stopped forcing his horse into the mechanical gallop, and slid down. "Well, I got there!" he announced fiercely, his blue eyes still flaring, and his sturdy long legs straddling apart.

"Where did you get to?" asked his mother.

"Where I wanted to go," he flared back at her.

"That's right, son!" said Uncle Oscar. "Don't you stop till you get there. What's the horse's name?"

"He doesn't have a name," said the boy.

"Gets on without all right?" asked the uncle.

"Well, he has different names. He was called Sansovino last week."

"Sansovino, eh? Won the Ascot.[1] How did you know his name?"

"He always talks about horse races with Bassett," said Joan.

The uncle was delighted to find that his small nephew was posted with all the racing news. Bassett, the young gardener, who had been wounded in the left foot in the war and had got his present job through Oscar Cresswell, whose batman[2] he had been, was a perfect blade of the "turf." He lived in the racing events, and the small boy lived with him.

Oscar Cresswell got it all from Bassett.

"Master Paul comes and asks me, so I can't do more than tell him, sir," said Bassett, his face terribly serious, as if he were speaking of religious matters.

"And does he ever put anything on a horse he fancies?"

"Well—I don't want to give him away—he's a young sport, a fine sport, sir. Would you mind asking him himself? He sort of takes a pleasure in it, and perhaps he'd feel I was giving him away, sir, if you don't mind."

Bassett was serious as a church.

The uncle went back to his nephew, and took him off for a ride in the car.

"Say, Paul, old man, do you ever put anything on a horse?" the uncle asked.

The boy watched the handsome man closely.

"Why, do you think I oughtn't to?" he parried.

"Not a bit of it! I thought perhaps you might give me a tip for the Lincoln."

The car sped on into the country, going down to Uncle Oscar's place in Hampshire.

"Honor bright?" said the nephew.

"Honor bright, son!" said the uncle.

"Well, then. Daffodil."

"Daffodil! I doubt it, sonny. What about Mirza?"

"I only know the winner," said the boy. "That's Daffodil."

"Daffodil, eh?"

There was a pause. Daffodil was an obscure horse comparatively.

"Uncle!"

"Yes, son?"

"You won't let it go any further, will you? I promised Bassett."

"Bassett be . . . , old man! What's he got to do with it?"

"We're partners. We've been partners from the first. Uncle, he lent me my first five shillings,[3] which I lost. I promised him, honor bright, it was only between me and him; only you gave me that ten-shilling note I started winning with, so I thought you were lucky. You won't let it go any further, will you?"

The boy gazed at his uncle from those big, hot, blue eyes, set rather close together. The uncle stirred and laughed uneasily.

"Right you are, son! I'll keep your tip private. Daffodil, eh! How much are you putting on him?"

"All except twenty pounds,"[4] said the boy. "I keep that in reserve."

The uncle thought it a good joke.

"You keep twenty pounds in reserve, do you, you young romancer? What are you betting, then?"

"I'm betting three hundred," said the boy gravely. "But it's between you and me, Uncle Oscar! Honor bright?"

The uncle burst into a roar of laughter.

"It's between you and me all right, you young Nat Gould,"[5] he said, laughing. "But where's your three hundred?"

"Bassett keeps it for me. We're partners."

"You are, are you! And what is Bassett putting on Daffodil?"

---

1. ***Ascot,*** a horse race. Other races mentioned are Lincoln (the shortened name for Lincolnshire), Leger, Grand National, and Derby (där′bē).
2. ***batman.*** Bassett had been Cresswell's servant while the latter served in the army.
3. ***five shillings.*** At the time of this story, this amount in English money was worth about $1.25.
4. ***twenty pounds.*** The English pound was worth nearly five dollars in United States currency; thus, twenty pounds was worth almost one hundred dollars.
5. ***Nat Gould,*** journalist, author, and highly respected racing authority.

"He won't go quite as high as I do, I expect. Perhaps he'll go a hundred and fifty."

"What, pennies?" laughed the uncle.

"Pounds," said the child, with a surprised look at his uncle. "Bassett keeps a bigger reserve than I do."

Between wonder and amusement Uncle Oscar was silent. He pursued the matter no further, but he determined to take his nephew with him to the Lincoln races.

"Now son," he said, "I'm putting twenty on Mirza, and I'll put five for you on any horse you fancy. What's your pick?"

"Daffodil, Uncle."

"No, not the fiver on Daffodil!"

"I should if it was my own fiver," said the child.

"Good! Good! Right you are! A fiver for me and a fiver for you on Daffodil."

The child had never been to a race meeting before, and his eyes were blue fire. He pursed his mouth tight, and watched. A Frenchman just in front had put his money on Lancelot. Wild with excitement, he flayed his arms up and down, yelling *"Lancelot! Lancelot!"* in his French accent.

Daffodil came in first, Lancelot second, Mirza third. The child, flushed and with eyes blazing, was curiously serene. His uncle brought him four five-pound notes, four to one.

"What am I to do with these?" he cried, waving them before the boy's eyes.

"I suppose we'll talk to Bassett," said the boy. "I expect I have fifteen hundred now; and twenty in reserve; and this twenty."

His uncle studied him for some moments.

"Look here, son!" he said. "You're not serious about Bassett and that fifteen hundred, are you?"

"Yes, I am. But it's between you and me, Uncle. Honor bright!"

"Honor bright all right, son! But I must talk to Bassett."

"If you'd like to be a partner, Uncle, with Bassett and me, we could all be partners. Only, you'd have to promise, honor bright, Uncle, not to let it go beyond us three. Bassett and I are lucky, and you must be lucky, because it was your ten shillings I started winning with. . . ."

Uncle Oscar took both Bassett and Paul into Richmond Park[6] for an afternoon, and there they talked.

"It's like this, you see, sir," Bassett said. "Master Paul would get me talking about racing events, spinning yarns, you know, sir. And he was always keen on knowing if I'd made or if I'd lost. It's about a year since, now, that I put five shillings on Blush of Dawn for him—and we lost. Then the luck turned, with that ten shillings he had from you, that we put on Singhalese. And since that time it's been pretty steady, all things considering. What do you say, Master Paul?"

"We're all right when we're sure," said Paul. "It's when we're not quite sure that we go down."

"Oh, but we're careful then," said Bassett.

"But when you are *sure?"* smiled Uncle Oscar.

"It's Master Paul, sir," said Bassett, in a secret, religious voice. "It's as if he had it from heaven. Like Daffodil, now, for the Lincoln. That was as sure as eggs."

"Did you put anything on Daffodil?" asked Oscar Cresswell.

"Yes, sir. I made my bit."

"And my nephew?"

Bassett was obstinately silent, looking at Paul.

"I made twelve hundred, didn't I, Bassett? I told Uncle I was putting three hundred on Daffodil."

"That's right," said Bassett, nodding.

"But where's the money?" asked the uncle.

"I keep it safe locked up, sir. Master Paul he can have it any minute he likes to ask for it."

"What, fifteen hundred pounds?"

"And twenty! And *forty,* that is, with the twenty he made on the course."

"It's amazing!" said the uncle.

"If Master Paul offers you to be partners, sir,

---

6. ***Richmond Park,*** a deer park just outside of London.

I would if I were you; if you'll excuse me," said Bassett.

Oscar Cresswell thought about it.

"I'll see the money," he said.

They drove home again, and sure enough, Bassett came round to the garden house with fifteen hundred pounds in notes. The twenty pounds reserve was left with Joe Glee, in the Turf Commission deposit.[7]

"You see, it's all right, Uncle, when I'm *sure!* Then we go strong, for all we're worth. Don't we, Bassett?"

"We do that, Master Paul."

"And when are you sure?" said the uncle, laughing.

"Oh, well, sometimes I'm *absolutely* sure, like about Daffodil," said the boy; "and sometimes I have an idea; and sometimes I haven't even an idea, have I, Bassett? Then we're careful, because we mostly go down."

"You do, do you! And when you're sure, like about Daffodil, what makes you sure, sonny?"

"Oh, well, I don't know," said the boy uneasily. "I'm sure, you know, Uncle; that's all."

"It's as if he had it from heaven, sir," Bassett reiterated.

"I should say so!" said the uncle.

But he became a partner. And when the Leger was coming on, Paul was "sure" about Lively Spark, which was a quite inconsiderable horse. The boy insisted on putting a thousand on the horse, Bassett went for five hundred, and Oscar Cresswell two hundred. Lively Spark came in first, and the betting had been ten to one against him. Paul had made ten thousand.

"You see," he said, "I was absolutely sure of him."

Even Oscar Cresswell had cleared two thousand.

"Look here, son," he said, "this sort of thing makes me nervous."

---

7. ***Turf Commission deposit,*** a type of bank in which English bettors deposit betting funds.

"It needn't, Uncle! Perhaps I shan't be sure again for a long time."

"But what are you going to do with your money?" asked the uncle.

"Of course," said the boy, "I started it for Mother. She said she had no luck, because Father is unlucky, so I thought if *I* was lucky, it might stop whispering."

"What might stop whispering?"

"Our house. I *hate* our house for whispering."

"What does it whisper?"

"Why—why"—the boy fidgeted—"why, I don't know. But it's always short of money, you know, Uncle."

"I know it, son, I know it."

"You know people send Mother writs,[8] don't you, Uncle?"

"I'm afraid I do," said the uncle.

"And then the house whispers, like people laughing at you behind your back. It's awful, that is! I thought if I was lucky . . ."

"You might stop it," added the uncle.

The boy watched him with big blue eyes that had an uncanny cold fire in them, and he said never a word.

"Well, then!" said the uncle. "What are we doing?"

"I shouldn't like Mother to know I was lucky," said the boy.

"Why not, son?"

"She'd stop me."

"I don't think she would."

"Oh!"—and the boy writhed in an odd way—"I *don't* want her to know, Uncle."

"All right, son! We'll manage it without her knowing."

They managed it very easily. Paul, at the other's suggestion, handed over five thousand pounds to his uncle, who deposited it with the family lawyer, who was then to inform Paul's mother that a relative had put five thousand pounds into his hands, which sum was to be paid out a thousand pounds at a time, on the mother's birthday, for the next five years.

"So she'll have a birthday present of a thousand pounds for five successive years," said Uncle Oscar. "I hope it won't make it all the harder for her later."

Paul's mother had her birthday in November. The house had been "whispering" worse than ever lately, and, even in spite of his luck, Paul could not bear up against it. He was very anxious to see the effect of the birthday letter, telling his mother about the thousand pounds.

When there were no visitors, Paul now took his meals with his parents, as he was beyond the nursery control. His mother went into town nearly every day. She had discovered that she had an odd knack of sketching furs and dress materials, so she worked secretly in the studio of a friend who was the chief "artist" for the leading drapers.[9] She drew the figures of ladies in furs and ladies in silk and sequins for the newspaper advertisements. This young woman artist earned several thousand pounds a year, but Paul's mother only made several hundred, and she was again dissatisfied. She so wanted to be first in something, and she did not succeed, even in making sketches for drapery advertisements.

She was down to breakfast on the morning of her birthday. Paul watched her face as she read her letters. He knew the lawyer's letter. As his mother read it, her face hardened and became more expressionless. Then a cold, determined look came on her mouth. She hid the letter under the pile of others, and said not a word about it.

"Didn't you have anything nice in the post for your birthday, Mother?" said Paul.

"Quite moderately nice," she said, her voice cold and absent.

She went away to town without saying more.

But in the afternoon Uncle Oscar appeared. He said Paul's mother had had a long interview with her lawyer, asking if the whole five thousand could not be advanced at once, as she was in debt.

---

8. ***writs,*** legal documents. Here the term is used to mean that legal action is about to be taken to collect unpaid bills.
9. ***drapers,*** a dealer in cloth or dry goods. [*British*]

"What do you think, Uncle?" said the boy.

"I leave it to you, son."

"Oh, let her have it, then! We can get some more with the other," said the boy.

"A bird in the hand is worth two in the bush, laddie!" said Uncle Oscar.

"But I'm sure to *know* for the Grand National; or the Lincolnshire; or else the Derby. I'm sure to know for *one* of them," said Paul.

So Uncle Oscar signed the agreement, and Paul's mother touched the whole five thousand. Then something very curious happened. The voices in the house suddenly went mad, like a chorus of frogs on a spring evening. There were certain new furnishings, and Paul had a tutor. He was *really* going to Eton, his father's school, in the following autumn. There were flowers in the winter, and a blossoming of the luxury Paul's mother had been used to. And yet the voices in the house, behind the sprays of mimosa and almond blossom, and from under the piles of iridescent cushions, simply trilled and screamed in a sort of ecstasy. "There *must* be more money! Oh-h-h; there *must* be more money! Oh, now, now-w! Now-w-w—there *must* be more money!—more than ever! More than ever!"

It frightened Paul terribly. He studied away at his Latin and Greek with his tutors. But his intense hours were spent with Bassett. The Grand National had gone by: he had not "known," and had lost a hundred pounds. Summer was at hand. He was in agony for the Lincoln. But even for the Lincoln he didn't "know," and he lost fifty pounds. He became wild-eyed and strange, as if something were going to explode in him.

"Let it alone, son! Don't you bother about it!" urged Uncle Oscar. But it was as if the boy couldn't really hear what his uncle was saying.

"I've got to know for the Derby! I've got to know for the Derby!" the child reiterated, his big blue eyes blazing with a sort of madness.

His mother noticed how overwrought he was.

"You'd better go to the seaside. Wouldn't you like to go now to the seaside, instead of waiting? I think you'd better," she said, looking down at him anxiously, her heart curiously heavy because of him.

But the child lifted his uncanny blue eyes.

"I couldn't possibly go before the Derby, Mother!" he said. "I couldn't possibly!"

"Why not?" she said, her voice becoming heavy when she was opposed. "Why not? You can still go from the seaside to see the Derby with your Uncle Oscar, if that's what you wish. No need for you to wait here. Besides, I think you care too much about these races. It's a bad sign. My family has been a gambling family, and you won't know till you grow up how much damage it has done. But it has done damage. I shall have to send Bassett away, and ask Uncle Oscar not to talk racing to you, unless you promise to be reasonable about it; go away to the seaside and forget it. You're all nerves!"

"I'll do what you like, Mother, so long as you don't send me away till after the Derby," the boy said.

"Send you away from where? Just from this house?"

"Yes," he said, gazing at her.

"Why, you curious child, what makes you care about this house so much, suddenly? I never knew you loved it."

He gazed at her without speaking. He had a secret within a secret, something he had not divulged, even to Bassett or to his Uncle Oscar.

But his mother, after standing undecided and a little bit sullen for some moments, said:

"Very well, then! Don't go to the seaside till after the Derby, if you don't wish it. But promise me you won't let your nerves go to pieces. Promise you won't think so much about horse racing and *events* as you call them!"

"Oh, no," said the boy casually. "I won't think much about them, Mother. You needn't worry. I wouldn't worry, Mother, if I were you."

"If you were me and I were you," said his mother, "I wonder what we *should* do!"

"But you know you needn't worry, Mother, don't you?" the boy repeated.

"I should be awfully glad to know it," she said wearily.

"Oh, well, you *can,* you know. I mean, you *ought* to know you needn't worry," he insisted.

"Ought I? Then I'll see about it," she said.

Paul's secret of secrets was his wooden horse, that which had no name. Since he was emancipated from a nurse and a nursery-governess, he had had his rocking horse removed to his own bedroom at the top of the house.

"Surely, you're too big for a rocking horse!" his mother had remonstrated.

"Well, you see, Mother, till I can have a *real* horse, I like to have *some* sort of animal about," had been his quaint answer.

"Do you feel he keeps you company?" she laughed.

"Oh, yes! He's very good, he always keeps me company, when I'm there," said Paul.

So the horse, rather shabby, stood in an arrested prance in the boy's bedroom.

The Derby was drawing near, and the boy grew more and more tense. He hardly heard what was spoken to him, he was very frail, and his eyes were really uncanny. His mother had sudden strange seizures of uneasiness about him. Sometimes, for half an hour, she would feel a sudden anxiety about him that was almost anguish. She wanted to rush to him at once, and know he was safe.

Two nights before the Derby, she was at a big party in town, when one of her rushes of anxiety about her boy, her first-born, gripped her heart till she could hardly speak. She fought with the feeling, might and main, for she believed in common sense. But it was too strong. She had to leave the dance and go upstairs to telephone to the country. The children's nursery-governess was terribly surprised and startled at being rung up in the night.

"Are the children all right, Miss Wilmot?"

"Oh, yes, they are quite all right."

"Master Paul? Is he all right?"

"He went to bed as right as a trivet. Shall I run up and look at him?"

"No," said Paul's mother reluctantly. "No! Don't trouble. It's all right. Don't sit up. We shall be home fairly soon." She did not want her son's privacy intruded upon.

"Very good," said the governess.

It was about one o'clock when Paul's mother and father drove up to their house. All was still. Paul's mother went to her room and slipped off her white fur cloak. She had told her maid not to wait up for her. She heard her husband downstairs, mixing a whiskey-and-soda.

And then, because of the strange anxiety at her heart, she stole upstairs to her son's room. Noiselessly she went along the upper corridor. Was there a faint noise? What was it?

She stood, with arrested muscles, outside his door, listening. There was a strange, heavy, and yet not loud noise. Her heart stood still. It was a soundless noise, yet rushing and powerful. Something huge, in violent, hushed motion. What was it? What in God's name was it? She ought to know. She felt that she knew the noise. She knew what it was.

Yet she could not place it. She couldn't say what it was. And on and on it went, like a madness.

Softly, frozen with anxiety and fear, she turned the door handle.

The room was dark. Yet in the space near the window, she heard and saw something plunging to and fro. She gazed in fear and amazement.

Then suddenly she switched on the light, and saw her son, in his green pajamas, madly surging on the rocking horse. The blaze of light suddenly lit him up, as he urged the wooden horse, and lit her up, as she stood, blonde, in her dress of pale green and crystal, in the doorway.

"Paul!" she cried. "Whatever are you doing?"

"It's Malabar!" he screamed, in a powerful, strange voice. "It's Malabar!"

His eyes blazed at her for one strange and senseless second, as he ceased urging his wooden horse. Then he fell with a crash to the ground, and she, all her tormented motherhood flooding upon her, rushed to gather him up.

But he was unconscious, and unconscious he

remained, with some brain fever. He talked and tossed, and his mother sat stonily by his side.

"Malabar! It's Malabar! Bassett, Bassett, I *know!* It's Malabar!"

So the child cried, trying to get up and urge the rocking horse that gave him his inspiration.

"What does he mean by Malabar?" asked the heart-frozen mother.

"I don't know," said the father stonily.

"What does he mean by Malabar?" she asked her brother Oscar.

"It's one of the horses running for the Derby," was the answer.

And, in spite of himself, Oscar Cresswell spoke to Bassett, and himself put a thousand on Malabar: at fourteen to one.

The third day of the illness was critical: they were waiting for a change. The boy, with his rather long, curly hair, was tossing ceaselessly on the pillow. He neither slept nor regained consciousness, and his eyes were like blue stones. His mother sat, feeling her heart had gone, turned actually into a stone.

In the evening, Oscar Cresswell did not come, but Bassett sent a message, saying could he come up for one moment, just one moment? Paul's mother was very angry at the intrusion, but on second thought she agreed. The boy was the same. Perhaps Bassett might bring him to consciousness.

The gardener, a shortish fellow with a little brown mustache, and sharp little brown eyes, tiptoed into the room, touched his imaginary cap to Paul's mother, and stole to the bedside, staring with glittering, smallish eyes, at the tossing, dying child.

"Master Paul!" he whispered. "Master Paul! Malabar came in first all right, a clean win. I did as you told me. You've made over seventy thousand pounds, you have; you've got over eighty thousand. Malabar came in all right, Master Paul."

"Malabar! Malabar! Did I say Malabar, Mother? Did I say Malabar? Do you think I'm lucky, Mother? I knew Malabar, didn't I? Over eighty thousand pounds! I call that lucky, don't you, Mother? Over eighty thousand pounds! I knew, didn't I know I knew? Malabar came in all right. If I ride my horse till I'm sure, then I tell you, Bassett, you can go as high as you like. Did you go for all you were worth, Bassett?"

"I went a thousand on it, Master Paul."

"I never told you, Mother, that if I can ride my horse, and *get* there, then I'm absolutely sure—oh, absolutely! Mother, did I ever tell you? I *am* lucky!"

"No, you never did," said the mother.

But the boy died in the night.

And even as he lay dead, his mother heard her brother's voice saying to her: "My God, Hester, you're eighty-odd thousand to the good, and a poor devil of a son to the bad. But, poor devil, poor devil, he's best gone out of a life where he rides his rocking horse to find a winner."

Discussion

1. (a) How is the mother characterized in the opening lines of this story? **(b)** Why do you think the lack of money in the household particularly troubles her? **(c)** Though seemingly a minor character, what important role does the father play in the plot?

2. (a) What is the connection between the whispering Paul hears and his determination to have luck? **(b)** How does he go about getting luck?

3. (a) What does the lawyer's letter inform Paul's mother of? **(b)** Why does her face grow hard and determined as she reads it? **(c)** Why do you think the whispering grows even louder after this? What effect does it have on Paul?

4. Shortly before Paul dies, his mother hears

him on his rocking horse. What similarities exist between the effect of the noise made by the rocking horse on her and the effect of the house's whispering on Paul?

5. Reread the passages dealing with Paul's eyes, paying special attention to the adjectives used to describe them. How do the feelings reflected in his eyes show the changes he undergoes?

6. **(a)** Explain what the whispering and the rocking horse symbolize. **(b)** Does the fact that both these elements involve fantasy strengthen or weaken the story? Discuss.

7. Defend or criticize this statement: "Money is the root of all evil" is an adequate statement of the theme of "The Rocking-Horse Winner."

Vocabulary

Context, Dictionary

Look up the words listed below in the Glossary. When you have determined their meanings, rewrite each sentence to include the appropriate word in the place of the italicized word or phrase. Be sure you can spell and pronounce each word. You will not use all the words.

parry	overwrought
discreet	remonstrate
reiterate	uncanny

1. Because completing the project on time was really everyone's responsibility, I resented having to *repeat again and again* my requests for help.

2. She is a sensible person, and we can depend upon her to be *cautious* in this rather delicate matter of the company's merger.

3. The celebrity managed to *turn aside* the interviewer's prying questions without appearing cross.

4. Chloe maintains that there is nothing *supernatural* in her ability to sense when the telephone is about to ring.

5. Uncle Ralph used to try to *reason* with his disobedient children, but Aunt Kate's method was to send them to their rooms to think over their offenses privately.

D(avid) H(erbert) Lawrence 1885–1930

The son of a coal miner, Lawrence was born in the small provincial town of Eastwood, England, where he endured a miserable childhood. His strong-willed mother urged him to become a teacher, a profession he took up at the age of twenty and followed for a number of years. During this period he also wrote and, with the publication of his first work and the death of his mother, left teaching to write full time. In nearly twenty years of writing, he produced over forty volumes of fiction, poetry, drama, literary criticism, and travel description. His novels and short stories came to be regarded as early examples of modern psychological fiction.

Long threatened by tuberculosis, Lawrence traveled widely in search of healthful environments. He and his wife resided briefly in many European locations and at a retreat in Taos, New Mexico, that became famous for his presence. Lawrence was only forty-four when he died of the disease.

The Needle

Isaac Bashevis Singer

Poland/USA

Some might take extreme measures in choosing the right mate, but according to the teller of this tale, "Everything depends on luck."

My good people, nowadays all marriages are arranged by Mr. Love. Young folks fall in love and begin to date. They go out together until they start to quarrel and hate each other. In my time we relied on father and mother and the matchmaker. I myself did not see my Todie until the wedding ceremony, when he lifted the veil from my face. There he stood with his red beard and disheveled sidelocks. It was after Pentecost,[1] but he wore a fur coat as if it were winter. That I didn't faint dead away was a miracle from heaven. I had fasted through the long summer day. Still, I wish my best friends no worse life than I had with my husband, he should intercede for me in the next world. Perhaps I shouldn't say this, but I can't wait until our souls are together again.

"Yes, love-shmuv. What does a young boy or girl know about what is good for them? Mothers used to know the signs. In Krasnostaw[2] there lived a woman called Reitze Leah,[3] and when she was looking for brides for her sons she made sure to drop in on her prospective in-laws early in the morning. If she found that the bed linens were dirty and the girl in question came to the door with uncombed hair, wearing a sloppy dressing gown, that was it. Before long everybody in the neighboring villages was on to her, and when she was seen in the marketplace early in the morning, all the young girls made sure their doors were bolted. She had six able sons. None of the matches she made for them was any good, but that is another story. A girl may be clean and neat before the wedding, but afterwards she becomes a slattern. Everything depends on luck.

"But let me tell you a story. In Hrubyeshow there lived a rich man, Reb Lemel Wagmeister.[4] In those days we didn't use surnames, but Reb

1. ***sidelocks . . . Pentecost.*** Sidelocks are worn by Jewish male Hasidim (has′i dim), members of a religious movement founded in the 1700s in Poland; Pentecost is a religious festival observed during the spring.
2. ***Krasnostaw*** (krus′nü stäf), a village in Poland. Other places mentioned are Hrubyeshow (hrü byesh′üf), Zamosc (zä′mosh), Lublin (lü′blēn), and Warsaw, all cities in Poland; and Vienna, the capital of Austria.
3. ***Reitze Leah*** (rī′tzə lā′ə).
4. ***Reb Lemel Wagmeister*** (reb′ lā′məl väg′mī′stər). *Reb* is a title of respect meaning "rabbi" or "mister."

Isaac Bashevis Singer (bə shev′is).

Lemel was so rich that he was always called Wagmeister. His wife's name was Esther Rosa, and she came from the other side of the Vistula.[5] I see her with my own eyes: a beautiful woman, with a big-city air. She always wore a black-lace mantilla over her wig. Her face was as white and smooth as a girl's. Her eyes were dark. She spoke Russian, Polish, German, and maybe even French. She played the piano. Even when the streets were muddy, she wore high-heeled patent-leather shoes. One autumn I saw her hopping from stone to stone like a bird, lifting her skirt with both hands, a real lady. They had an only son, Ben Zion. He was as like his mother as two drops of water. We were distant relatives, not on her side but on her husband's. Ben Zion—Benze, he was called—had every virtue: he was handsome, clever, learned. He studied the Torah[6] with the rabbi in the daytime and in the evening a teacher of secular subjects took over. Benze had black hair and a fair complexion, like his mother. When he took a walk in the summertime wearing his elegant gaberdine with a fashionable slit in the back, and his smart kid boots, all the girls mooned over him through the windows. Although it is the custom to give dowries only to daughters, Benze's father set aside for his son a sum of ten thousand rubles.[7] What difference did it make to him? Benze was his only heir. They tried to match him with the richest girls in the province, but Esther Rosa was very choosy. She had nothing to do, what with three maids, a manservant, and a coachman in addition. So she spent her time looking for brides for Benze. She had already inspected the best-looking girls in half of Poland, but not one had she found without some defect. One wasn't beautiful enough; another, not sufficiently clever. But what she was looking for most was nobility of character. 'Because,' she said, 'if a woman is coarse, it is the husband who suffers. I don't want any woman to vent her spleen on my Benze.' I was already married at the time. I married when I was fifteen. Esther Rosa had no real friend in Hrubyeshow and I became a frequent visitor to her house. She taught me how to knit and embroider and do needlepoint. She had golden hands. When the fancy took her, she could make herself a dress or even a cape. She once made me a dress, just for the fun of it. She had a good head for business as well. Her husband hardly took a step without consulting her. Whenever she told him to buy or sell a property, Reb Lemel Wagmeister immediately sent for Lippe the agent and said: 'My wife wants to buy or sell such-and-such.' She never made a mistake.

"Well, Benze was already nineteen, and not even engaged. In those days nineteen was considered an old bachelor. Reb Lemel Wagmeister complained that the boy was being disgraced by his mother's choosiness. Benze developed pimples on his forehead.

"One day I came to see Esther Rosa to borrow a ball of yarn. And she said to me: 'Zeldele,[8] would you like to ride to Zamosc with me?'

" 'What will I do in Zamosc?' I asked.

" 'What difference does it make?' she replied. 'You'll be my guest.'

"Esther Rosa had her own carriage, but this time she went along with someone else who was going to Zamosc. I guessed that the journey had something to do with looking over a bride, but Esther Rosa's nature was such that one didn't ask questions. If she were willing to talk, well and good. If not, you just waited. To make it short, I went to tell my mother about the trip. No need to ask my husband. He sat in the study house all day long. When he came home in the evening, my mother served him his supper. In those days a young Talmud scholar[9] barely knew he had a wife. I don't believe that he would have recognized me if he met me on the street. I packed a dress and a pair of bloomers—I beg your par-

---

5. ***Vistula*** (vis′chə lə), the longest river in Poland.
6. ***Benze*** (ben′tsə) ***. . . studied the Torah.*** The young man was studying the first five books of the Old Testament.
7. ***ten thousand rubles.*** At the time of the story, this amount in Russian money was worth about five thousand dollars in United States currency.
8. ***Zeldele*** (zel′də lə).
9. ***Talmud scholar.*** It was once customary for all young Jewish men to study the Talmud, a collection of sixty-three volumes containing Jewish civil and church law in the form of interpretation and expansion of Old Testament teachings.

don—and I was ready for the trip. We were traveling in a nobleman's carriage and he did the driving himself. Two horses like lions. The road was dry and smooth as a table. When we arrived in Zamosc, he let us off not at the marketplace but on a side street where the Gentiles live. Esther Rosa thanked him and he tipped his hat and waved his whip at us good-naturedly. It all looked arranged.

"As a rule, when Esther Rosa traveled anyplace she dressed as elegantly as a countess. This time she wore a simple cotton dress, and a kerchief over her wig. It was summer and the days were long. We walked to the marketplace and she inquired for Berish Lubliner's dry-goods store. A large store was pointed out to us. Nowadays in a dry-goods store you can only buy yard goods, but in those days they sold everything: thread, wool for knitting, and odds and ends. What didn't they sell? It was a store as big as a forest, filled with merchandise to the ceiling. At a high desk-stand a man sat writing in a ledger, as they do in the big cities. I don't know what he was, the cashier or a bookkeeper. Behind a counter stood a girl with black eyes that burned like fire. We happened to be the only customers in the store, and we approached her. 'What can I do for you?' she asked. 'You seem to be strangers.'

" 'Yes, we are strangers,' said Esther Rosa.

" 'What would you like to see?' the girl asked.

" 'A needle,' said Esther Rosa.

"The moment she heard the word 'needle,' the girl's face changed. Her eyes became angry. 'Two women for one needle,' she said.

"Merchants believe that a needle is unlucky. Nobody ever dared to buy a needle at the beginning of the week, because they knew it meant the whole week would be unlucky. Even in the middle of the week the storekeepers did not like to sell needles. One usually bought a spool of thread, some buttons, and the needle was thrown in without even being mentioned. A needle costs only half a groshen and it was a nuisance to make such small change.

" 'Yes,' said Esther Rosa. 'All I need is a needle.'

"The girl frowned but took out a box of needles. Esther Rosa searched through the box and said: 'Perhaps you have some other needles?'

" 'What's wrong with these?' the girl asked impatiently.

" 'Their eyes are too small,' Esther Rosa said. 'It will be difficult to thread them.'

" 'These are all I have,' the girl said angrily. 'If you can't see well, why don't you buy yourself a pair of eyeglasses.'

"Esther Rosa insisted. 'Are you sure you have no others? I must have a needle with a larger eye.'

"The girl reluctantly pulled out another box and slammed it down on the counter. Esther Rosa examined several needles and said: 'These too have small eyes.'

"The girl snatched away the box and screamed: 'Why don't you go to Lublin and order yourself a special needle with a big eye.'

"The man at the stand began to laugh. 'Perhaps you need a sackcloth needle,' he suggested. 'Some nerve,' the girl chimed in, 'to bother people over a half-groshen sale.'

"Esther Rosa replied: 'I have no use for sackcloth or for girls who are as coarse as sackcloth.' Then she turned to me and said: 'Come, Zeldele, they are not our kind.'

"The girl turned red in the face and said loudly, 'What yokels! Good riddance!'

"We went out. The whole business had left a bad taste in my mouth. A woman passed by and Esther Rosa asked her the way to Reb Zelig Izbitzer's dry-goods store. 'Right across the street,' she said, pointing. We crossed the marketplace and entered a store that was only a third of the size of the first one. Here too there was a young saleswoman. This one wasn't dark; she had red hair. She was not ugly but she had freckles. Her eyes were as green as gooseberries. Esther Rosa asked if she sold needles. And the girl replied, 'Why not? We sell everything.'

" 'I'm looking for a needle with a large eye, because I have trouble threading needles,' Esther Rosa said.

" 'I'll show you every size we have and you

can pick the one that suits you best,' the girl replied.

"I had already guessed what was going on and my heart began to beat like a thief's. The girl brought out about ten boxes of needles. 'Why should you stand?' she said. 'Here is a stool. Please be seated.' She also brought a stool for me. It was perfectly clear to me that Esther Rosa was going to test her too.

" 'Why are the needles all mixed together?' Esther Rosa complained. 'Each size should be in a different box.'

" 'When they come from the factory, they are all sorted out,' the girl said apologetically. 'But they get mixed up.' I saw Esther Rosa was doing her best to make the girl lose her temper. 'I don't see too well,' Esther Rosa said. 'It's dark here.'

" 'Just one moment and I'll move the stools to the door. There is more light there,' the girl replied.

" 'Does it pay you to make all this effort just to sell a half-penny needle?' Esther Rosa asked. And the girl answered: 'First of all, a needle costs only a quarter of a penny, and then as the Talmud says, the same law applies to a penny as it does to a hundred guilders.[10] Besides, today you buy a needle and tomorrow you may be buying satins for a trousseau.'

" 'Is that so? Then how come the store is empty?' Esther Rosa wanted to know. 'Across the street, Berish Lubliner's store is so full of customers you can't find room for a pin between them. I bought my materials there but I decided to come here for the needle.'

"The girl became serious. I was afraid that Esther Rosa had overdone it. Even an angel can lose patience. But the girl said, 'Everything according to God's will.' Esther Rosa made a move to carry her stool to the door, but the girl stopped her. 'Please don't trouble yourself. I'll do it.' Esther Rosa interrupted. 'Just a moment. I want to tell you something.'

" 'What do you want to tell me?' the girl said, setting down the stool.

" 'My daughter, *Mazel Tov!*'[11] Esther Rosa called out.

"The girl turned as white as chalk. 'I don't understand,' she said.

" 'You will be my daughter-in-law,' Esther Rosa announced. 'I am the wife of Reb Lemel Wagmeister of Hrubyeshow. I have come here to look for a bride for my son. Not to buy a needle. Reb Berish's daughter is like a straw mat and you are like silk. You will be my Benze's wife, God willing.'

"That the girl didn't faint dead away was a miracle from heaven. Everybody in Zamosc had heard of Reb Lemel Wagmeister. Zamosc is not Lublin. Customers came in and saw what was happening. Esther Rosa took a string of amber beads out of her basket. 'Here is your engagement gift. Bend your head.' The girl lowered her head submissively and Esther Rosa placed the beads around her neck. Her father and mother came running into the store. There was kissing, embracing, crying. Someone immediately rushed to tell the story to Reb Berish's daughter. When she heard what had happened, she burst into tears. Her name was Itte.[12] She had a large dowry and was known as a shrewd saleswoman. Zelig Izbitzer barely made a living.

"My good people, it was a match. Esther Rosa wore the pants in the family. Whatever she said went. And as I said, in those days young people were never asked. An engagement party was held and the wedding soon after. Zelig Izbitzer could not afford a big wedding. He barely could give his daughter a dowry, for he also had two other daughters and two sons who were studying in the yeshiva.[13] But, as you know, Reb Lemel Wagmeister had little need for her dowry. I went to the engagement party and I danced at the wedding. Esther Rosa dressed the girl like a princess. She became really beautiful. When good luck shines, it shows on the face. Whoever did not see that couple standing under the wedding canopy and later dancing the virtue dance

---

10. ***a hundred guilders,*** about twenty dollars.
11. ***Mazel Tov*** (ma'zəl tôv), congratulations. [*Hebrew*]
12. ***Itte*** (ē'tə).
13. ***yeshiva*** (yə shē'və), a Jewish school for higher studies, often a rabbinical seminary.

will never know what it means to have joy in children. Afterwards they lived like doves. Exactly to the year, she bore a son.

"From the day Itte discovered that Esther Rosa had come to test her, she began to ail. She spoke about the visit constantly. She stopped attending customers. Day and night she cried. The matchmakers showered her with offers, but first she wouldn't have anyone else and second what had happened had given her a bad name. You know how people exaggerate. All kinds of lies were invented about her. She had insulted Esther Rosa in the worst way, had spat in her face, had even beaten her up. Itte's father was stuffed with money and in a small town everybody is envious of his neighbor's crust of bread. Now his enemies had their revenge. Itte had been the real merchant and without her the store went to pieces. After a while she married a man from Lublin. He wasn't even a bachelor. He was divorced. He came to Zamosc and took over his father-in-law's store. But he was as much a businessman as I am a musician.

"That is how things are. If luck is with you, it serves you well. And when it stops serving you, everything goes topsy-turvy. Itte's mother became so upset she developed gallstones, or maybe it was jaundice. Her face became as yellow as saffron. Itte no longer entered the store. She became a stay-at-home. It was hoped that when she became pregnant and had a child, she would forget. But twice she miscarried. She became half crazy, went on cursing Frieda Gittel—that is what Benze's wife was called—and insisted that the other had connived against her. Who knows what goes on in a madwoman's head? Itte also foretold that Frieda Gittel would die and that she, Itte, would take her place. When Itte became pregnant for the third time, her father took her to a miracle-worker. I've forgotten to mention that by this time her mother was already dead. The miracle-worker gave her potions and talismans, but she miscarried again. She began to run to doctors and to imagine all kinds of illnesses.

"Now listen to this. One evening Itte was sitting in her room sewing. She had finished her length of thread and wanted to rethread her needle. While getting the spool she placed the needle between her lips. Suddenly she felt a stab in her throat and the needle vanished. She searched all over for it, but—what is the saying—'Who can find a needle in a haystack?' My dear people, Itte began to imagine that she had swallowed the needle. She felt a pricking in her stomach, in her breast, her legs. There is a saying 'A needle wanders.' She visited the leech,[14] but what does a leech know? She went to doctors in Lublin and even in Warsaw. One doctor said one thing; another, something different. They poked her stomach but could find no needle. God preserve us. Itte lay in bed and screamed that the needle was pricking her. The town was in a turmoil. Some said that she had swallowed the needle on purpose to commit suicide. Others, that it was a punishment from God. But why should she have been punished? She had already suffered enough for her rudeness. Finally she went to Vienna to a great doctor. And he found the way out. He put her to sleep and made a cut in her belly. When she woke up he showed her the needle that he was supposed to have removed from her insides. I wasn't there. Perhaps he really found a needle, but that's not what people said. When she returned from Vienna, she was her former self again. The store had gone to ruin. Her father was already in the other world. Itte, however, opened a new store. In the new store she succeeded again, but she never had any children.

"I've forgotten to mention that after what happened between Esther Rosa and the two girls, the salesgirls of Zamosc became the souls of politeness, not only to strangers, but even to their own townspeople. For how could one know whether a customer had come to buy or to test? The book peddler did a fine trade in books on etiquette, and when a woman came to buy a ball of yarn, she was offered a chair.

"I can't tell you what happened later, because I moved away from Zamosc. In the big cities one

14. ***the leech,*** one who applies leeches—bloodsucking worms—to draw blood from wounds.

forgets about everything, even about God. Reb Lemel Wagmeister and Esther Rosa have long since passed away. I haven't heard from Benze or his wife for a long time. Yes, a needle. Because of a rooster and a chicken a whole town was destroyed in the Holy Land,[15] and because of a needle a match was spoiled. The truth is that everything is fated from heaven. You can love someone until you burst, but if it's not destined, it will come to naught. A boy and a girl can be keeping company for seven years, and a stranger comes along and breaks everything up. I could tell you a story of a boy who married his girl's best friend out of spite, and she, to spite him, kept to her bed for twenty years. Tell it? It's too late. If I were to tell you all the stories I know, we'd be sitting here for seven days and seven nights."

15. ***Because . . . Holy Land.*** It was an ancient Jewish custom to carry a chicken and rooster before the bride and groom in a wedding procession to symbolize a fruitful union. According to the Talmud, when a contingent of Roman soldiers once happened upon such a scene in a town near Jerusalem, a skirmish took place that was reported to Roman authorities as a rebellion. As a result, Roman forces destroyed the town.

Discussion

1. **(a)** What major complaint does Zeldele, the narrator of the story, make about marriages nowadays as compared with the old days? **(b)** Does her story about Reitze Leah support her point? Discuss. **(c)** What evidence is there that her own marriage was a success?

2. **(a)** What makes Zeldele think Esther Rosa's trip to Zamosc has a hidden purpose? **(b)** What qualities in a young woman is Esther Rosa's test designed to bring out? **(c)** Does the test work? Explain.

3. **(a)** In what ways is Itte's life unhappy after she fails the test? **(b)** What particular problem does she have with a needle? **(c)** How is the problem resolved?

4. Zeldele's style in narrating this story is so distinctive that the effect is more like listening to her talk than reading her words. Find at least two examples of each of the following characteristics of informal speech: **(a)** remarks addressed directly to the audience; **(b)** rhetorical questions (questions asked only for effect, not for information); **(c)** brief statements or anecdotes that interrrupt the basic story line; **(d)** exaggerations.

5. According to Zeldele, what is the ultimate cause of human destiny? Do you agree with her? Discuss.

6. What might the needle symbolize to each of the following characters? **(a)** Esther Rosa; **(b)** Itte; **(c)** Frieda Gittel.

Isaac Bashevis Singer 1904–

Singer's writings are rooted in his Polish-Jewish background. Born in Radzymin (räd zi′mēn), Poland, he came from a family of rabbis and received an intensely religious education; however, he came to share his older brother's strong interest in nonreligious writings. Following his brother to Warsaw in the 1920s, Singer became an editor and short-story contributor to a literary magazine. In 1935 he settled in the United States, producing fiction in Yiddish for a newspaper. He gained a wider audience and much critical praise when these works were translated into English. In 1978 his tales won him the Nobel Prize.

An old-fashioned storyteller in a modern age, Singer is best known for his short stories. A few of his collections are *Gimpel the Fool* (1957), *The Spinoza of Market Street* (1961), *A Crown of Feathers* (1973), and *Old Love* (1979). A book for young people, *A Day of Pleasure: Stories of a Boy Growing Up in Warsaw* (1969), is a reflection of his own youth that won the 1970 National Book Award.

See **ANALOGY** Handbook of Literary Terms

The Rat Trap

Selma Lagerlöf Sweden

The peddler's outlook on life had been shaped by his experiences. Then there came a chance to take on the experiences of someone else.

Once upon a time there was a man who went around selling small rat traps of wire. He made them himself at odd moments, from material he got by begging in the stores or at the big farms. But even so, the business was not especially profitable, so he had to resort to both begging and petty thievery to keep body and soul together. Even so, his clothes were in rags, his cheeks were sunken, and hunger gleamed in his eyes.

No one can imagine how sad and monotonous life can appear to such a vagabond, who plods along the road, left to his own meditations. But one day this man had fallen into a line of thought which really seemed to him entertaining. He had naturally been thinking of his rat traps when suddenly he was struck by the idea that the whole world about him—the whole world with its lands and seas, its cities and villages—was nothing but a big rat trap. It had never existed for any other purpose than to set baits for people. It offered riches and joys, shelter and food, heat and clothing, exactly as the rat trap offered cheese and pork, and as soon as anyone let himself be tempted to touch the bait, it closed in on him, and then everything came to an end.

The world had, of course, never been very kind to him, so it gave him unwonted joy to think ill of it in this way. It became a cherished pastime of his, during many dreary ploddings, to think of people he knew who had let themselves be caught in the dangerous snare, and of others who were still circling around the bait.

One dark evening as he was trudging along the road he caught sight of a little gray cottage by the roadside, and he knocked on the door to ask shelter for the night. Nor was he refused. Instead of the sour faces which ordinarily met him, the owner, who was an old man without wife or child, was happy to get someone to talk to in his loneliness. Immediately he put the porridge pot on the fire and gave him supper; then he carved off such a big slice from his tobacco roll that it was enough for both the stranger's pipe and his own. Finally he got out an old pack of cards and played *mjölis*[1] with his guest until bedtime.

The old man was just as generous with his confidences as with his porridge and tobacco. The guest was informed at once that in his days of prosperity his host had been a crofter at the Ramsjö Ironworks[2] and had worked on the land. Now that he was no longer able to do day labor, it was his cow which supported him. Yes, that bossy was extraordinary. She could give milk for the creamery every day, and last month he had received all of thirty kronor[3] in payment.

---

1. ***mjölis*** (myu'lis), a Swedish card game.
2. ***crofter at the Ramsjö*** (räm'shu) ***Ironworks.*** A crofter is a person who cultivates a very small farm (croft), usually as a tenant of someone else—in this case, of the Ramsjö Ironworks.
3. ***thirty kronor.*** A krona is a silver and copper coin that is the Swedish monetary unit; thirty kronor at the time amounted to six dollars in United States currency.

Selma Lagerlöf (lä'gər ləv).

The stranger must have seemed incredulous, for the old man got up and went to the window, took down a leather pouch which hung on a nail in the very window frame, and picked out three wrinkled ten-kronor bills. These he held up before the eyes of his guest, nodding knowingly, and then stuffed them back into the pouch.

The next day both men got up in good season. The crofter was in a hurry to milk his cow, and the other man probably thought he should not stay in bed when the head of the house had gotten up. They left the cottage at the same time. The crofter locked the door and put the key in his pocket. The man with the rat traps said good-by and thank you, and thereupon each went his own way.

But half an hour later the rat-trap peddler stood again before the door. He did not try to get in, however. He only went up to the window, smashed a pane, stuck in his hand, and got hold of the pouch with the thirty kronor. He took the money and thrust it into his own pocket. Then he hung the leather pouch very carefully back in its place and went away.

As he walked along with the money in his pocket he felt quite pleased with his smartness. He realized, of course, that at first he dared not continue on the public highway, but must turn off the road, into the woods. During the first few hours this caused him no difficulty. Later in the day it became worse, for it was a big and confusing forest which he had gotten into. He tried, to be sure, to walk in a definite direction, but the paths twisted back and forth so strangely! He walked and walked, without coming to the end of the wood, and finally he realized that he had only been walking around in the same part of the forest. All at once he recalled his thoughts about the world and the rat trap. Now his own turn had come. He had let himself be fooled by a bait and had been caught. The whole forest, with its trunks and branches, its thickets and fallen logs, closed in upon him like an impenetrable prison from which he could never escape.

It was late in December. Darkness was already descending over the forest. This increased the danger, and increased also his gloom and despair. Finally he saw no way out, and he sank down on the ground, tired to death, thinking that his last moment had come. But just as he laid his head on the ground, he heard a sound—a hard, regular thumping. There was no doubt as to what that was. He raised himself. "Those are the hammer strokes from an iron mill," he thought. "There must be people nearby." He summoned all his strength, got up, and staggered in the direction of the sound.

The Ramsjö Ironworks, which are now closed down, was, not so long ago, a large plant, with smelter, rolling mill, and forge. In the summertime long lines of heavily loaded barges and scows slid down the canal, which led to a large inland lake, and in the wintertime the roads near the mill were black from all the coal dust which sifted down from the big charcoal crates.

During one of the long dark evenings just before Christmas, the master smith and his helper sat in the dark forge near the furnace waiting for the pig iron, which had been put in the fire, to be ready to put on the anvil. Every now and then one of them got up to stir the glowing mass with a long iron bar, returning in a few moments, dripping with perspiration, though, as was the custom, he wore nothing but a long shirt and a pair of wooden shoes.

All the time there were many sounds to be heard in the forge. The big bellows groaned and the burning coal cracked. The fire boy shoveled charcoal into the maw of the furnace with a great deal of clatter. Outside roared the waterfall, and a sharp north wind whipped the rain against the brick-tiled roof.

It was probably on account of all this noise that the blacksmith did not notice that a man had opened the gate and entered the forge, until he stood close up to the furnace.

Surely it was nothing unusual for poor vagabonds without any better shelter for the night to be attracted to the forge by the glow of light which escaped through the sooty panes, and to come in to warm themselves in front of the fire. The blacksmiths glanced only casually and indifferently at the intruder. He looked the way people of his type usually did, with a long beard, dirty, ragged, and with a bunch of rat traps dangling on his chest.

He asked permission to stay, and the master blacksmith nodded a haughty consent without honoring him with a single word.

The tramp did not say anything, either. He had not come there to talk but only to warm himself and sleep.

In those days the Ramsjö iron mill was owned by a very prominent ironmaster, whose greatest ambition was to ship out good iron to the market. He watched both night and day to see that the work was done as well as possible, and at this very moment he came into the forge on one of his nightly rounds of inspection.

Naturally the first thing he saw was the tall ragamuffin who had eased his way so close to the furnace that steam rose from his wet rags. The ironmaster did not follow the example of the blacksmiths, who had hardly deigned to look at the stranger. He walked close up to him, looked him over very carefully, then tore off his slouch hat to get a better view of his face.

"But of course it is you, Nils Olof!" he said. "How do you look!"

The man with the rat traps had never before seen the ironmaster of Ramsjö and did not even know what his name was. But it occurred to him that if the fine gentleman thought he was an old acquaintance, he might perhaps throw him a couple of kronor. Therefore he did not want to undeceive him all at once.

"Yes, God knows things have gone downhill with me," he said.

"You should not have resigned from the regiment," said the ironmaster. "That was the mistake. If only I had still been in the service at the time, it never would have happened. Well, now of course you will come home with me."

To go along up to the manor house and be received by the owner like an old regimental comrade—that, however, did not please the tramp.

"No, I couldn't think of it!" he said, looking quite alarmed.

He thought of the thirty kronor. To go up to the manor house would be like throwing himself voluntarily into the lions' den. He only wanted a chance to sleep here in the forge and then sneak away as inconspicuously as possible.

The ironmaster assumed that he felt embarrassed because of his miserable clothing.

"Please don't think that I have such a fine home that you cannot show yourself there," he said. "Elizabeth is dead, as you may already have heard. My boys are abroad, and there is no one at home except my oldest daughter and myself. We were just saying that it was too bad we didn't have any company for Christmas. Now come along with me and help us make the Christmas food disappear a little faster."

But the stranger said no, and no, and again no, and the ironmaster saw that he must give in.

"It looks as though Captain von Ståhle prefers to stay with you tonight, Stjernström,"[4] he said to the master blacksmith, and turned on his heel.

But he laughed to himself as he went away, and the blacksmith, who knew him, understood very well that he had not said his last word.

It was not more than half an hour before they heard the sound of carriage wheels outside the forge, and a new guest came in, but this time it was not the ironmaster. He had sent his daughter, apparently hoping that she would have better powers of persuasion than he himself.

She entered, followed by a valet, carrying on his arm a big fur coat. She was not at all pretty, but seemed modest and quite shy. In the forge everything was just as it had been earlier in the evening. The master blacksmith and his apprentice still sat on their bench, and iron and charcoal still glowed in the furnace. The stranger had

---

4. ***von Ståhle*** (fôn stō'lə) . . . ***Stjernström*** (styern'strum).

stretched himself out on the floor and lay with a piece of pig iron under his head and his hat pulled down over his eyes. As soon as the young girl caught sight of him she went up and lifted his hat. The man was evidently used to sleeping with one eye open. He jumped up abruptly and seemed to be quite frightened.

"My name is Edla Willmansson," said the young girl. "My father came home and said that you wanted to sleep here in the forge tonight, and then I asked permission to come and bring you home to us. I am so sorry, Captain, that you are having such a hard time."

She looked at him compassionately, with her heavy eyes, and then she noticed that the man was afraid. "Either he has stolen something or else he has escaped from jail," she thought, and added quickly, "You may be sure, Captain, that you will be allowed to leave us just as freely as you came. Only please stay with us over Christmas Eve."

She said this in such a friendly manner that the rat-trap peddler must have felt confidence in her.

"It would never have occurred to me that you would bother with me yourself, miss," he said. "I will come at once."

He accepted the fur coat, which the valet handed him with a deep bow, threw it over his rags, and followed the young lady out to the carriage, without granting the astonished blacksmiths so much as a glance.

But while he was riding up to the manor house he had evil forebodings.

"Why the devil did I take that fellow's money?" he thought. "Now I am sitting in the trap and will never get out of it."

The next day was Christmas Eve, and when the ironmaster came into the dining room for breakfast he probably thought with satisfaction of his old regimental comrade whom he had run across so unexpectedly.

"First of all we must see to it that he gets a little flesh on his bones," he said to his daughter, who was busy at the table. "And then we must see that he gets something else to do than to run around the country selling rat traps."

"It is queer that things have gone downhill with him as badly as that," said the daughter. "Last night I did not think there was anything about him to show that he had once been an educated man."

"You must have patience, my little girl," said the father. "As soon as he gets clean and dressed up, you will see something different. Last night he was naturally embarrassed. The tramp manners will fall away from him with the tramp clothes."

Just as he said this the door opened and the stranger entered. Yes, now he was truly clean and well dressed. The valet had bathed him, cut his hair, and shaved him. Moreover, he was dressed in a good-looking suit of clothes which belonged to the ironmaster. He wore a white shirt and a starched collar and whole shoes.

But although his guest was now so well-groomed, the ironmaster did not seem pleased. He looked at him with puckered brow, and it was easy enough to understand that when he had seen the strange fellow in the uncertain reflection from the furnace he might have made a mistake, but that now, when he stood there in broad daylight, it was impossible to mistake him for an old acquaintance.

"What does this mean?" he thundered.

The stranger made no attempt to dissimulate. He saw at once that all the splendor had come to an end.

"It is not my fault, sir," he said. "I never pretended to be anything but a poor trader, and I pleaded and begged to be allowed to stay in the forge. But no harm has been done. At worst I can put on my rags again and go away."

"Well," said the ironmaster, hesitating a little, "it was not quite honest, either. You must admit that, and I should not be surprised if the sheriff would like to have something to say in the matter."

The tramp took a step forward and struck the table with his fist.

"Now I am going to tell you, Mr. Ironmaster, how things are," he said. "This whole world is nothing but a big rat trap. All the good things that are offered you are nothing but cheese rinds and bits of pork, set out to drag a poor fellow into trouble. And if the sheriff comes now and locks me up for this, then you, Mr. Ironmaster, must remember that a day may come when you yourself may want to get a big piece of pork, and then you will get caught in the trap."

The ironmaster began to laugh.

"That was not so badly said, my good fellow. Perhaps we should let the sheriff alone on Christmas Eve. But now get out of here as fast as you can."

But just as the man was opening the door, the daughter said, "I think he ought to stay with us today. I don't want him to go." And with that she went and closed the door.

"What in the world are you doing?" said the father.

The daughter stood there quite embarrassed and hardly knew what to answer. That morning she had felt so happy when she thought how homelike and Christmassy she was going to make things for the poor hungry wretch. She could not get away from the idea all at once, and that was why she had interceded for the vagabond.

"I am thinking of this stranger here," said the young girl. "He walks and walks the whole year long, and there is probably not a single place in the whole country where he is welcome and can feel at home. Wherever he turns he is chased away. Always he is afraid of being arrested and cross-examined. I should like to have him enjoy a day of peace with us here—just one in the whole year."

The ironmaster mumbled something in his beard. He could not bring himself to oppose her.

"It was all a mistake, of course," she continued. "But anyway I don't think we ought to chase away a human being whom we have asked to come here, and to whom we have promised Christmas cheer."

"You do preach worse than a parson," said the ironmaster. "I only hope you won't have to regret this."

The young girl took the stranger by the hand and led him up to the table.

"Now sit down and eat," she said, for she could see that her father had given in.

The man with the rat traps said not a word; he only sat down and helped himself to the food. Time after time he looked at the young girl who had interceded for him. Why had she done it? What could the crazy idea be?

After that, Christmas Eve at Ramsjö passed just as it always had. The stranger did not cause any trouble because he did nothing but sleep. The whole forenoon he lay on the sofa in one of the guest rooms and slept at one stretch. At noon they woke him up so that he could have his share of the good Christmas fare, but after that he slept again. It seemed as though for many years he had not been able to sleep as quietly and safely as here at Ramsjö.

In the evening, when the Christmas tree was lighted, they woke him up again, and he stood for a while in the drawing room, blinking as though the candlelight hurt him, but after that he disappeared again. Two hours later he was aroused once more. He then had to go down into the dining room and eat the Christmas fish[5] and porridge.

As soon as they got up from the table he went around to each one present and said thank you and good night, but when he came to the young girl she gave him to understand that it was her father's intention that the suit which he wore was to be a Christmas present—he did not have to return it; and if he wanted to spend next Christmas Eve in a place where he could rest in peace, and be sure that no evil would befall him, he would be welcomed back again.

The man with the rat traps did not answer anything to this. He only stared at the young girl in boundless amazement.

The next morning the ironmaster and his daughter got up in good season to go to the early Christmas service. Their guest was still asleep, and they did not disturb him.

When, at about ten o'clock, they drove back from church, the young girl sat and hung her head even more dejectedly than usual. At church she had learned that one of the old crofters of the ironworks had been robbed by a man who went around selling rat traps.

"Yes, that was a fine fellow you let into the house," said her father. "I only wonder how many silver spoons are left in the cupboard by this time."

The wagon had hardly stopped at the front steps when the ironmaster asked the valet whether the stranger was still there. He added that he had heard at church that the man was a thief. The valet answered that the fellow had gone and that he had not taken anything with him at all. On the contrary, he had left behind a little package which Miss Willmansson was to be kind enough to accept as a Christmas present.

The young girl opened the package, which was so badly done up that the contents came into view at once. She gave a little cry of joy. She found a small rat trap, and in it lay three wrinkled ten-kronor notes. But that was not all. In the rat trap lay also a letter written in large, jagged characters:

Honored and noble Miss:

Since you have been so nice to me all day long, as if I was a captain, I want to be nice to you, in return, as if I was a real captain: for I do not want you to be embarrassed at this Christmas season by a thief; but you can give back the money to the old man on the roadside, who has the money pouch hanging on the window frame as a bait for poor wanderers.

The rat trap is a Christmas present from a rat who would have been caught in this world's rat trap if he had not been raised to captain, because in that way he got power to clear himself.

Written with friendship and high regard,

Captain von Ståhle.

5. ***Christmas fish,*** probably lutefisk (lüd′ə fisk), which is served in Sweden traditionally on the eve of Christmas.

Discussion

1. (a) As the story opens, what reasons does the tramp have for feeling so pessimistic about the world? **(b)** Do you get the impression that he desires material possessions? Explain.

2. (a) What motivates the old crofter to receive the tramp into his cottage? **(b)** Is the crofter in any way to blame for the theft of his money? Discuss.

3. (a) How does the tramp happen to end up at the Ramsjö Ironworks? **(b)** Explain the circumstances through which he goes to the ironmaster's house. **(c)** What do these circumstances show about the character of the ironmaster? of his daughter?

4. (a) When the ironmaster reassures his daughter that "the tramp manners will fall away from him with the tramp clothes," what assumption about clothes is he making? **(b)** Do you think he is justified in getting angry when he realizes the tramp is not who he thought he was? Discuss. **(c)** Why is the tramp allowed to stay with the family anyway?

5. (a) In his letter, what does the tramp reveal has given him the strength to return the money and "to clear himself"? **(b)** Do you think he intends to assume the identity of Captain von Ståhle from this time on? Why or why not?

Application

Analogy

When an author introduces an analogy as early in a story as the rat-trap analogy is introduced in this one, the reader can fairly assume that the analogy will be important throughout the story.

1. Complete the analogy: Rat trap is to rat as ______ is to ______.

2. (a) What "bait" awaits the tramp at the crofter's? at the ironmaster's? **(b)** Does each bait get the tramp into trouble? Explain.

3. In what way has the tramp escaped the rat trap by the end of the story?

Vocabulary

Roots, Affixes

Some Latin roots are used widely in English words because they combine easily with so many prefixes. An example is *ced* (sometimes spelled *cede* or *ceed*), which comes from the Latin word *cedere,* "to go."

Using the prefixes listed below, form words with *ced* that fit the context of each of the following sentences. Check a dictionary to make sure you have spelled each word correctly. You will not use all the prefixes.

re-: "back; again"
inter-: "together; between"
ex-: "out; from"
pre-: "before in place, time, order, or rank"
ac- (ad-): "to; toward"
pro-: "forward, forth; out; in favor of"

1. Since neither management nor labor can settle the bitter strike, an outside party should ______.

2. As we watched the tide ______, we were able to see more and more shoreline.

3. If you are certain that your plan can't work, don't ______ with it.

4. Because it is her brother's birthday, she intends to ______ to all his wishes.

5. The total cost of the junior prom may ______ the amount presently in the class treasury.

Selma Lagerlöf 1858–1940

Lagerlöf's sympathetic interpretation of Swedish folklore won her an international audience. It also won her the 1909 Nobel Prize for Literature, making her the first woman to be so honored.

Born on the family estate in the province of Värmland, Lagerlöf grew up fascinated with the old legends of the area. She began publishing her writings during her years as a country schoolteacher, never dreaming of fame. Yet in 1891 the publication of *The Story of Gösta Berling,* her first novel, made her the most well-known Scandinavian storyteller since Hans Christian Andersen. Its success allowed Lagerlöf to devote all her time to writing. Her works from this productive period include *Jerusalem* (1901–1902), an epic novel of men who travel to the Holy Land, and *The Wonderful World of Nils* (1906–1907), a two-volume young people's classic. Many of her writings, which contain themes of reconciliation and goodness triumphing over the forces of low-mindedness and cruelty, have been adapted for the stage and screen.

Comment: An Artist Shares His Family Life

The inviting scene on page 339, which gives one the impression of having just walked into a story, is the work of noted Swedish artist Carl Larsson, 1853–1919. Though the painting is, in fact, a depiction of a celebration in Larsson's own living room, it perfectly captures the spirit of warmth and sharing that is such an important element in "The Rat Trap."

Larsson's dreary early life in Stockholm led him to turn to drawing as an escape. By the 1880s the diversion had become a successful career; he was one of his country's leading book illustrators and mural painters. In 1889 his wife's family gave them a rundown little house in the village of Sundborn. Now in a position to provide his seven children with the cheerful atmosphere he had not known, Larsson set out to rebuild their new residence. The result—a whimsical showplace with portraits painted on doors, unusual passages, and wood-carved dragons on the rooftops—was a structure so original in design that it remains one of Europe's most famous handcrafted homes.

The dwelling was not only a work of architectural art; it was the backdrop for many of Larsson's best-loved paintings. Acting on his wife's suggestion during one rainy and confining summer, he turned to his cozy surroundings for his subjects. From then on he devoted himself to creating delicately detailed watercolors of his family. Such images as his wife sewing, his children playing dress-up, and his dog sleeping were collected and published in *A Home* in 1899 and have been in publication ever since.

Larsson was a contemporary of Selma Lagerlöf, and each contributed greatly to Swedish cultural history. His warm depictions of home and her richly romantic tales celebrating Swedish life are regarded as national treasures.

The Jay

Kawabata Yasunari Japan

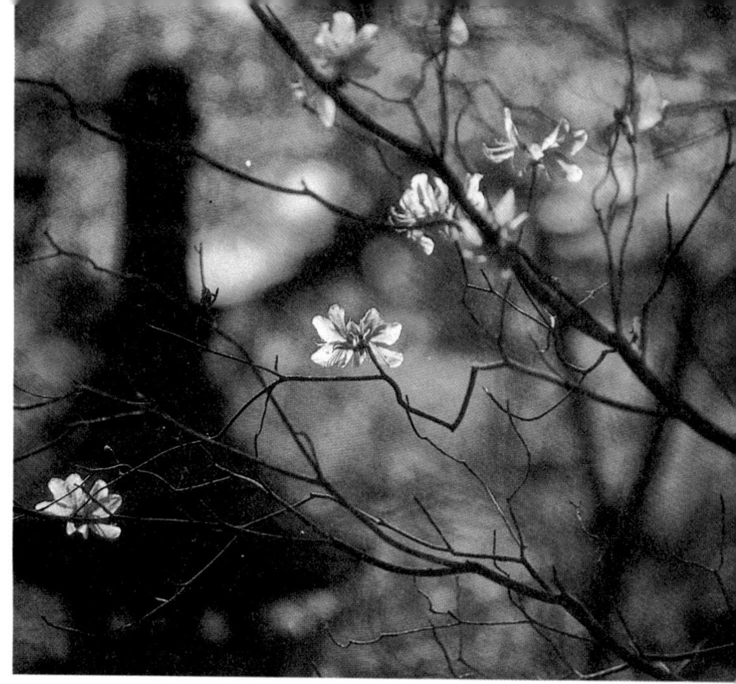

"Because of what her father had been through she had been frightened of marriage, but now that it was coming it did not seem so frightening after all."

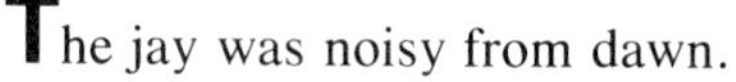

The jay was noisy from dawn.

It seemed to have flown from a lower branch of the pine tree as Yoshiko[1] was opening the shutters and then come back again. They could hear its wings from the breakfast table.

"What a racket," said her brother, starting to get up.

"Leave it alone," said her grandmother. "I think the little one must have fallen from the nest yesterday. I could still hear the mother last night after dark. I suppose she couldn't find it. And isn't that nice, here she is back again this morning."

"Are you sure?" asked Yoshiko.

Save for a liver attack some ten years before, her grandmother had never been ill, but she had suffered from cataracts ever since she was very young. Now she could barely see, and with the left eye only. She had to be handed her food. She could grope her way around the house, but she never went out alone into the garden.

She would sometimes stand or sit at the glass door and gaze at her fingers, spread out in the sunlight. Her whole life seemed to be concentrated in the gaze.

Yoshiko would be afraid of her. She would want to call from behind, and then she would slip away.

Yoshiko was filled with admiration that her blind grandmother could talk about the jay as if she had seen it.

When she went out to do the breakfast dishes, the jay was calling from the roof next door.

There were a chestnut and several persimmons in the backyard. She could see against them that a gentle rain was falling, so gentle that she could not make it out except against the dark background.

The jay flew to the chestnut, skimmed the ground, and flew back again, calling out all the while.

Would the nestling still be near, that the mother was so reluctant to leave?

Yoshiko went to her room. She must be ready by noon.

Her mother and father would be bringing her fiancé's mother.

As she sat down before the mirror she glanced at the white dots on her fingernails. They were

1. ***Yoshiko*** (yōsh'kō).

"The Jay" by Kawabata Yasunari, translated by Edward Seidensticker from *Contemporary Japanese Literature*, edited by Howard Hibbet (Alfred A. Knopf, 1977). Reprinted by permission of Edward Seidensticker.

Kawabata Yasunari (kä wä bä'tä yä sü nä'rē).

said to be a sign that someone would come with gifts, but she had read in a newspaper that they really showed a deficiency in vitamin C or something of the sort. She was pleased with her face when she had finished making herself up. She thought her eyebrows and lips rather charming. She liked the set of her kimono.

She had thought she would wait for her mother to help her, and then she was glad that she had dressed by herself.

Her father and mother, actually her stepmother, did not live with them.

Her father had divorced her mother when Yoshiko was four and her brother two. It was said that her mother had been gaudy and extravagant, but Yoshiko suspected that there had been deeper causes.

Her father had said nothing when her brother had found a picture of their mother and shown it to him. He had frowned and torn the picture to pieces.

When Yoshiko was thirteen her new mother came into the house. Later Yoshiko was to think it rather remarkable of her father to have waited almost ten years. Her new mother was a kind woman and they lived a quiet, happy life.

When her brother entered high school and went to live in a dormitory, it was plain to all of them that his attitude toward his stepmother was changing.

"I've seen Mother," he said to Yoshiko. "She is married and living in Azabu.[2] She is very beautiful. She was glad to see me."

Yoshiko was too startled to answer. She was sure that she had turned white, and she was trembling.

Her stepmother came in from the next room. "It's all right. There's nothing wrong at all with his seeing his own mother. It's only natural. I knew it would happen. It doesn't bother me at all."

Her stepmother seemed drained of strength, and so tiny that Yoshiko felt somehow protective.

Her brother got up and went out. Yoshiko wanted to slap him.

"You are not to say anything, Yoshiko," said her stepmother softly. "It would only make things worse."

Yoshiko was in tears.

Her father brought her brother home from the dormitory. She thought that would be the end of the matter; and then her father and stepmother moved away.

She was frightened. She felt that she had had the full force of—a man's anger, perhaps, or vengefulness? She wondered if she and her brother had something of the same thing in them. She had felt certain, as he had left the room, that her brother had inherited that terrible masculine something.

Yet she felt too that she knew her father's loneliness those ten years he had waited to take a new wife.

She was startled when her father came with talk of a prospective bridegroom.

"You have had a hard time of it, Yoshiko, and I am sorry. I have told his mother that I want you to have the girlhood you never had."

There were tears in Yoshiko's eyes.

With Yoshiko married, there would be no one to take care of her grandmother and brother, and so it was decided that they would live with her father and stepmother. The decision was what touched Yoshiko most. Because of what her father had been through she had been frightened of marriage, but now that it was coming it did not seem so frightening after all.

She went to her grandmother when she had finished dressing.

"Can you see the red,[3] Grandmother?"

"I can see that there is something red." She pulled Yoshiko to her and looked intently at her kimono and obi.[4] "I have forgotten what you look like, Yoshiko. How nice if I could see you again."

Embarrassed, Yoshiko put her hand to her grandmother's head.

---

2. ***Azabu*** (ə zä'bü).
3. ***the red.*** Red is a traditional part of the Japanese bridal costume.
4. ***obi*** (ō'bē), a long, broad sash worn by Japanese around the waist of a kimono.

She went out into the garden. She wanted to run and meet her father and stepmother. She opened a hand, but the rain was scarcely enough to wet it. Lifting her skirts she looked through the shrubs and bamboo, and found the nestling jay in the grass under the *hagi*.[5]

She stole up to it. Head pulled in, it was a tight little ball. It seemed without strength and she had no trouble taking it. She looked around but could not find the mother.

She ran to the house.

"I've found it, Grandmother. It seems very weak."

"Really? You must give it water."

Her grandmother was very calm.

She brought a cup of water and put its beak in, and it drank most prettily, swelling its small throat.

"Kikikikiki." It quickly revived.

Hearing, the mother jay called from a power line.

"Kikiki." The nestling struggled in Yoshiko's hand.

"How very nice," said her grandmother. "You must give it back."

Yoshiko went into the garden. The mother jay left the power line and sat watching Yoshiko from the cherry tree.

Raising her hand to show the nestling, Yoshiko put it on the ground.

She watched from inside the glass door. The nestling called forlornly up. The mother came nearer and then was at the lower branches of the pine tree just above. The nestling flapped its wings as if it were about to take flight, and fell forward, calling out to its mother.

Very cautious, the mother still did not alight.

Then, in a swoop, it was beside the nestling, whose joy was boundless. The head shook, the outstretched wings were trembling, it was like a spoiled child. The mother seemed to be feeding it.

Yoshiko wished that her father and stepmother would hurry. She wanted them to see.

---

5. ***hagi*** (hä'gē), a bush clover that grows in Japan.

Discussion

1. (a) What is the reason for the jay's noisiness as the story opens? **(b)** Contrast Yoshiko's, her brother's, and her grandmother's response to the disturbance. **(c)** Does the brother's reaction fit in with what you learn about him later? Discuss.

2. Explain the reason for the conflict between Yoshiko's brother and father.

3. (a) How would you characterize Yoshiko's stepmother? **(b)** What makes the father move away with her? **(c)** How does Yoshiko react to the move?

4. (a) Do you agree that Yoshiko has "never had" a normal girlhood? Why or why not? **(b)** How does her father propose to remedy this? **(c)** What is to happen to the brother and grandmother?

5. At the end of the story the mother jay and the nestling are reunited. **(a)** Do you see an analogy between this and what is happening in Yoshiko's own family? Explain. **(b)** In what ways is the analogy not perfect?

Kawabata Yasunari 1899–1972

The air of melancholy present in "The Jay" is characteristic of much of the author's work and probably originates from his lonely life. Kawabata (by the way, the usual order of Japanese names is the surname *before* the first one) was born in Osaka and orphaned not long after. A grandfather assumed the role of parent but died before Kawabata reached fifteen. In 1924 he received a degree in

Japanese literature from Tokyo Imperial University. He soon landed a writing position with a new literary magazine, which became a showcase for his works. His very brief but intriguing short stories—called "palm-of-the-hand stories"—and his autobiographical tale, *The Izu Dancer* (1926), placed Kawabata at the forefront of a new literary movement and launched his long career.

Kawabata's writing style conveys a keenness of perception and delicate sensitivity. He won the Nobel Prize for Literature in 1968 for, as the citation reads, "his narrative mastery, which with great sensibility expresses the essence of the Japanese mind."

Comment: Alternatives to the Plot-Oriented Story

Many readers demand from a short story an exciting plot with a definite ending and are confused and disappointed when this expectation is not met. Before assuming that stories with little surface action have nothing to say, however, serious readers ought at least to be aware of what writers of such stories are trying to do and what historical influences are working on them.

In most nineteenth-century stories, such as "The Necklace," the greatest emphasis was on plot—on action. The average writer saw progress and development throughout society and generally expected that same sort of progress and development in the affairs of individuals. The belief was widespread not only that people could improve themselves and their lot in life, but that outward behavior made clear a person's inner character. Thus action in these early stories was not so much an end in itself; it was intended to be an illustration of what characters believed and felt and how they were growing and changing.

At some point in the early twentieth century—certainly by the end of World War I—this confidence in the efforts of single individuals began to diminish. The war had affected the lives of millions, who seemed at the mercy of events beyond their control. The development of industry had indeed changed the world, but in the process had made people feel like cogs in machines, doubting their own abilities and worth. People could no longer assume that the external world held all the answers and, prompted as well by the research of psychoanalysts like Sigmund Freud (froid), began to look into their own minds for solutions.

As outlooks on life changed, so did the general focus of short stories. Writers were still engaged in a search for truth, but this search led them increasingly to a study of the inner workings of human nature. And just as, for example, people in the real world sometimes find that small, seemingly insignificant events have considerable impact on them, writers became more inclined to focus their stories on such events. While this sort of focus often precluded a great deal of action or plot development, it just as often led to a greater understanding of character. "The Jay," which you have just read, is an example of this kind of story.

Talented contemporary writers did not, of course, confine themselves entirely to stories that provided psychological views of characters. "Action Will Be Taken," the next story you will read, reacts to a work- and machine-oriented society by making fun of it; and "Tuesday Siesta," which comes a bit later, puts as much emphasis on setting and mood as on character. Nevertheless, you will find in general that the remaining stories in the unit are short on action and long on feeling, reaction, and insight. In reading them, you will get a good overview of the concerns—and skills—of some of today's best writers.

See **SATIRE** Handbook of Literary Terms

Action Will Be Taken

Heinrich Böll Germany

Is action the same thing as productivity? It all depends. . . .

Probably one of the strangest interludes in my life was the time I spent as an employee in Alfred Wunsiedel's[1] factory. By nature I am inclined more to pensiveness and inactivity than to work, but now and again prolonged financial difficulties compel me—for pensiveness is no more profitable than inactivity—to take on a so-called job. Finding myself once again at a low ebb of this kind, I put myself in the hands of the employment

1. ***Wunsiedel's*** (vün′zē′dlz).

Heinrich Böll (hīn′rik bœl).

office and was sent with seven other fellow-sufferers to Wunsiedel's factory, where we were to undergo an aptitude test.

The exterior of the factory was enough to arouse my suspicions: the factory was built entirely of glass brick, and my aversion to well-lit buildings and well-lit rooms is as strong as my aversion to work. I became even more suspicious when we were immediately served breakfast in the well-lit, cheerful coffee shop: pretty waitresses brought us eggs, coffee, and toast; orange juice was served in tastefully designed jugs; goldfish pressed their bored faces against the sides of pale-green aquariums. The waitresses were so cheerful that they appeared to be bursting with good cheer. Only a strong effort of will—so it seemed to me—restrained them from singing away all day long. They were as crammed with unsung songs as chickens with unlaid eggs.

Right away I realized something that my fellow-sufferers evidently failed to realize: that this breakfast was already part of the test; so I chewed away reverently, with the full appreciation of a person who knows he is supplying his body with valuable elements. I did something which normally no power on earth can make me do: I drank orange juice on an empty stomach, left the coffee and egg untouched, as well as most of the toast, got up, and paced up and down the coffee shop, pregnant with action.

As a result I was the first to be ushered into the room where the questionnaires were spread out on attractive tables. The walls were done in a shade of green that would have summoned the word "delightful" to the lips of interior-decoration enthusiasts. The room appeared to be empty, and yet I was so sure of being observed that I behaved as someone pregnant with action behaves when he believes himself unobserved: I ripped my pen impatiently from my pocket, unscrewed the top, sat down at the nearest table and pulled the questionnaire toward me, the way irritable customers snatch at the bill in a restaurant.

Question No. 1: Do you consider it right for a human being to possess only two arms, two legs, eyes, and ears?

Here for the first time I reaped the harvest of my pensive nature and wrote without hesitation: "Even four arms, legs, and ears would not be adequate for my driving energy. Human beings are very poorly equipped."

Question No. 2: How many telephones can you handle at one time?

Here again the answer was as easy as simple arithmetic: "When there are only seven telephones," I wrote, "I get impatient; there have to be nine before I feel I am working to capacity."

Question No. 3: How do you spend your free time?

My answer: "I no longer acknowledge the term free time—on my fifteenth birthday I eliminated it from my vocabulary, for in the beginning was the act."

I got the job. Even with nine telephones I really didn't feel I was working to capacity. I shouted into the mouthpieces: "Take immediate action!" or: "Do something!—We must have some action—Action will be taken—Action has been taken—Action should be taken." But as a rule—for I felt this was in keeping with the tone of the place—I used the imperative.

Of considerable interest were the noon-hour breaks, when we consumed nutritious foods in an atmosphere of silent good cheer. Wunsiedel's factory was swarming with people who were obsessed with telling you the story of their lives, as indeed vigorous personalities are fond of doing. The story of their lives is more important to them than their lives; you have only to press a button, and immediately it is covered with spewed-out exploits.

Wunsiedel had a right-hand man called Broschek,[2] who had in turn made a name for himself by supporting seven children and a paralyzed wife by working night shifts in his student days, and successfully carrying on four business agencies, besides which he had passed two examinations with honors in two years. When asked by

---

2. ***Broschek*** (brō'shek).

reporters: "When do you sleep, Mr. Broschek?" he had replied: "It's a crime to sleep!"

Wunsiedel's secretary had supported a paralyzed husband and four children by knitting, at the same time graduating in psychology and German history as well as breeding shepherd dogs, and she had become famous as a night-club singer where she was known as *Vamp Number Seven.*

Wunsiedel himself was one of those people who every morning, as they open their eyes, make up their minds to act. "I must act," they think as they briskly tie their bathrobe belts around them. "I must act," they think as they shave, triumphantly watching their beard hairs being washed away with the lather: these hirsute vestiges are the first daily sacrifices to their driving energy. Action has been taken. Bread gets eaten, eggs are decapitated.

With Wunsiedel, the most trivial activity looked like action: the way he put on his hat, the way—quivering with energy—he buttoned up his overcoat, the kiss he gave his wife, everything was action.

When he arrived at his office he greeted his secretary with a cry of "Let's have some action!" And in ringing tones she would call back: "Action will be taken!" Wunsiedel then went from department to department, calling out his cheerful: "Let's have some action!" Everyone would answer: "Action will be taken!" And I would call back to him too, with a radiant smile, when he looked into my office: "Action will be taken!"

Within a week I had increased the number of telephones on my desk to eleven, within two weeks to thirteen, and every morning on the streetcar I enjoyed thinking up new imperatives, or chasing the words *take action* through various tenses and modulations: for two whole days I kept saying the same sentence over and over again because I thought it sounded so marvelous: "Action ought to have been taken"; for another two days it was: "Such action ought not to have been taken."

So I was really beginning to feel I was working to capacity when there actually was some action. One Tuesday morning—I had hardly settled down at my desk—Wunsiedel rushed into my office crying his "Let's have some action!" But an inexplicable something in his face made me hesitate to reply, in a cheerful gay voice as the rules dictated: "Action will be taken!" I must have paused too long, for Wunsiedel, who seldom raised his voice, shouted at me: "Answer! Answer, you know the rules!" And I answered, under my breath, reluctantly, like a child who is forced to say: I am a naughty child. It was only by a great effort that I managed to bring out the sentence: "Action will be taken," and hardly had I uttered it when there really was some action: Wunsiedel dropped to the floor. As he fell he rolled over onto his side and lay right across the open doorway. I knew at once, and I confirmed it when I went slowly around my desk and approached the body on the floor: he was dead.

Shaking my head I stepped over Wunsiedel, walked slowly along the corridor to Broschek's office, and entered without knocking. Broschek was sitting at his desk, a telephone receiver in each hand; between his teeth a ballpoint pen with which he was making notes on a writing pad, while with his bare feet he was operating a knitting machine under the desk. In this way he helps to clothe his family. "We've had some action," I said in a low voice.

Broschek spat out the ballpoint pen, put down the two receivers, reluctantly detached his toes from the knitting machine.

"What action?" he asked.

"Wunsiedel is dead," I said.

"No," said Broschek.

"Yes," I said, "come and have a look!"

"No," said Broschek, "that's impossible," but he put on his slippers and followed me along the corridor.

"No," he said, when we stood beside Wunsiedel's corpse, "no, no!" I did not contradict him. I carefully turned Wunsiedel over onto his back, closed his eyes, and looked at him pensively.

I felt something like tenderness for him, and

realized for the first time that I had never hated him. On his face was that expression which one sees on children who obstinately refuse to give up their faith in Santa Claus, even though the arguments of their playmates sound so convincing.

"No," said Broschek, "no."

"We must take action," I said quietly to Broschek.

"Yes," said Broschek, "we must take action."

Action was taken: Wunsiedel was buried, and I was delegated to carry a wreath of artificial roses behind his coffin, for I am equipped with not only a penchant for pensiveness and inactivity but also a face and figure that go extremely well with dark suits. Apparently as I walked along behind Wunsiedel's coffin carrying the wreath of artificial roses I looked superb. I received an offer from a fashionable firm of funeral directors to join their staff as a professional mourner. "You are a born mourner," said the manager, "your outfit would be provided by the firm. Your face—simply superb!"

I handed in my notice to Broschek, explaining that I had never really felt I was working to capacity there; that, in spite of the thirteen telephones, some of my talents were going to waste. As soon as my first professional appearance as a mourner was over I knew: This is where I belong, this is what I am cut out for.

Pensively I stand behind the coffin in the funeral chapel, holding a simple bouquet, while the organ plays Handel's *Largo*,[3] a piece that does not receive nearly the respect it deserves. The cemetery café is my regular haunt; there I spend the intervals between my professional engagements, although sometimes I walk behind coffins which I have not been engaged to follow, I pay for flowers out of my own pocket and join the welfare worker who walks behind the coffin of some homeless person. From time to time I also visit Wunsiedel's grave, for after all I owe it to him that I discovered my true vocation, a vocation in which pensiveness is essential and inactivity my duty.

It was not till much later that I realized I had never bothered to find out what was being produced in Wunsiedel's factory. I expect it was soap.

---

3. ***Handel's Largo,*** a musical composition by English composer George Handel that is often played on solemn occasions.

Discussion

1. (a) What two qualities does the narrator claim are part of his nature? **(b)** Is there a difference between them? Discuss. **(c)** What forces him to seek employment?

2. (a) What details about the factory suggest that effort has been made to make working there pleasant? **(b)** How does the narrator show his enthusiasm for the "breakfast test"? the written test? **(c)** What do you think the questions on the written test are trying to determine?

3. (a) Describe the industriousness of Broschek and of Wunsiedel's secretary. **(b)** What seems to be the main activity the narrator engages in? **(c)** What is the only really significant action that occurs in the story?

4. (a) What qualities does the narrator say make him just right to act as a professional mourner? **(b)** What is absurd about these qualifications? **(c)** Why does the narrator enjoy his new job more than his former one?

5. The narrator thinks Wunsiedel's factory made soap. Perhaps the author uses soap as a symbol for modern civilized industry, suggesting that it is useful, clean, necessary, universal, and so forth. What other products might work well as symbols of industry? Give reasons for your choices.

Application

Satire

In order to successfully satirize something so broad and general as modern industry, a writer needs first to satirize various distinct aspects of it. Thus, he or she may use irony to present one aspect, exaggeration to describe another, and in this way work to create an overall satiric effect.

Explain the satire in each of the following, and decide what satiric device(s) has been used to communicate it.

1. the narrator's interest in variations of "Action will be taken"

2. Wunsiedel's early-morning activities

3. the industriousness of Broschek and of Wunsiedel's secretary

4. the factory's modern, cheery cafeteria

Composition

Select an event or occurrence familiar to you and your classmates that you think could be satirized in an amusing rather than cruel way. (Possibilities include such things as an annual class outing, the superior attitude of a certain group of students, the hype that precedes a big sports event like the World Series or the Super Bowl.) Then think of details related to the event that should be included and decide how you can satirize them most effectively—through exaggeration, humor, or whatever.

Write a three- or four-paragraph composition satirizing the event. You may either make your subject clear right away or build up to it throughout the composition. (See "Developing Your Style," page 660, in the Composition Guide.)

Heinrich Böll 1917–1985

Böll spent most of his life in his native city of Cologne, Germany, where he witnessed the shattering effects of two world wars. In 1939 he was drafted into the infantry, fighting but wanting Germany to lose in World War II. At its end he returned to Cologne to attend the university there and to begin his writing career.

Through his writings, Böll did much to revive interest in German literature, which prior to the war had been reduced to a tool of the Nazi regime. Such works as *The Train Was on Time* (1949) and *Traveller, If You Come to the Spa* (1950) described soldiers' wartime experiences. He later shifted his focus to satiric portraits—of which "Action Will Be Taken" is an example—of the generations of Germans who have survived World War II.

Böll's contribution to the rebirth of German literature won him the Nobel Prize in 1972. An active defender of freedom of literature, he donated part of the prize money to aid writers imprisoned for their political beliefs. He died near Bonn at the age of 67.

See **STEREOTYPE** Handbook of Literary Terms

Enemies

Nadine Gordimer South Africa

What are the most effective ways of escaping an enemy? Clara Hansen thought she knew them all.

When Mrs. Clara Hansen travels, she keeps herself to herself. This is usually easy, for she has money, has been a baroness and a beauty, and has survived dramatic suffering. The crushing presence of these states in her face and bearing is nearly always enough to stop the loose mouths of people who find themselves in her company. It is only the very stupid, the senile, or the self-obsessed who blunder up to assail that face, withdrawn as a castle, across the common ground of a public dining room.

Last month, when Mrs. Hansen left Cape Town for Johannesburg[1] by train, an old lady occupying the adjoining compartment tried to make of her apologies, as she pressed past in the corridor loaded with string bags and paper parcels, an excuse to open one of those pointless conversations between strangers which arise in the nervous moments of departure. Mrs. Hansen was giving last calm instructions to Alfred, her Malay[2] chauffeur and manservant, whom she was leaving behind, and she did not look up. Alfred had stowed her old calf cases from Europe firmly and within reach in her compartment, which, of course, influence with the reservation office had ensured she would have to herself all the way. He had watched her put away in a special pocket in her handbag her train ticket, a ticket for her deluxe bed, a book of tickets for her meals. He had made sure that she had her two yellow sleeping pills and the red pills for that feeling of pressure in her head, lying in cotton wool in her silver pillbox. He himself had seen that her two pairs of spectacles, one for distance, one for reading, were in her overnight bag, and had noted that her lorgnette hung below the diamond bow on the bosom of her dress. He had taken down the folding table from its niche above the washbasin in the compartment, and placed on it the three magazines she had sent him to buy at the bookstall, along with the paper from Switzerland that, this week, had been kept aside, unread, for the journey.

For a full fifteen minutes before the train left, he and his employer were free to ignore the to-and-fro of voices and luggage, the heat and confusion. Mrs. Hansen murmured down to him; Alfred, chauffeur's cap in hand, dusty sunlight the color of beer dimming the oil shine of his black hair, looked up from the platform and made low assent. It was hardly speech; now and then it sank away altogether into the minds of each, but the sounds of the station did not well up in its place. Alfred dangled the key of the car on his little finger. The old face beneath the toque noted it, and the lips, the infinitely weary corners of the eyes drooped in the indication of a smile. Would he really put the car away into the garage for six weeks after he'd seen that it was oiled and greased?

Unmindful of the finger, his face empty of the

1. ***left Cape Town for Johannesburg*** (jō han′is bėrg′). Cape Town, sometimes referred to as "the Cape," and Johannesburg are cities in South Africa, about eight hundred miles apart.
2. ***Malay,*** person from—or whose ancestors were from—Malaysia, a country in Southeast Asia.

satisfaction of a month's wages in advance in his pocket, two friends waiting to be picked up in a house in the Malay quarter of the town, he said, "I must make a note that I mustn't send Madam's letters on after the twenty-sixth."

"No. Not later than the twenty-sixth."

Did she know? With that face that looked as if it knew everything, could she know, too, about the two friends in the house in the Malay quarter?

She said—and neither of them listened—"In case of need, you've always got Mr. Van Dam." Van Dam was her lawyer. This remark, like a stone thrown idly into a pool to pass the time, had fallen time and again between them into the widening hiatus of parting. They had never questioned or troubled to define its meaning. In ten years, what need had there ever been that Alfred couldn't deal with himself, from a burst pipe in the flat to a jammed fastener on Mrs. Hansen's dress?

Alfred backed away from the ice-cream carton a vendor thrust under his nose; the last untidy lump of canvas luggage belonging to the woman next door thumped down like a dusty animal at Mrs. Hansen's side; the final bell rang.

As the train ground past out of the station, Alfred stood quite still with his cap between his hands, watching Mrs. Hansen. He always stood like that when he saw her off. And she remained at the window, as usual, smiling slightly, inclining her head slightly, as if in dismissal. Neither waved. Neither moved until the other was borne out of sight.

When the station was gone and Mrs. Hansen turned slowly to enter her compartment to the quickening rhythm of the train, she met the gasping face of the old woman next door. Fat overflowed not only from her jowl to her neck, but from her ankles to her shoes. She looked like a pudding that had risen too high and run down the sides of the dish. She was sprinkling cologne onto a handkerchief and hitting with it at her face as if she were trying to kill something. "Rush like that, it's no good for you," she said. "Something went wrong with my son-in-law's car, and what a job to get a taxi! *They* don't care—get you here today or tomorrow. I thought I'd never get up those steps."

Mrs. Hansen looked at her. "When one is no longer young, one must always give oneself exactly twice as much time as one needs. I have learned that. I beg your pardon." And she passed before the woman into her compartment.

The woman stopped her in the doorway. "I wonder if they're serving tea yet? Shall we go along to the dining car?"

"I always have my tea brought to me in my compartment," said Mrs. Hansen, in the low, dead voice that had been considered a pity in her day but that now made young people who could have been her grandchildren ask if she had been an actress. And she slid the door shut.

Alone, she stood a moment in the secretive privacy, where everything swayed and veered in obedience to the gait of the train. She began to look anxiously over the stacked luggage, her lips moving, but she had grown too set to adjust her balance from moment to moment, and suddenly she found herself sitting down. The train had dumped her out of the way. Good thing, too, she thought, chastising herself impatiently—counting the luggage, fussing, when in ten years Alfred's never forgotten anything. Old fool, she told herself, old fool. Her aging self often seemed to her an enemy of her real self, the self that had never changed. The enemy was a stupid one, fortunately; she merely had to keep an eye on it in order to keep it outwitted. Other selves that had arisen in her life had been much worse; how terrible had been the struggle with some of *them!*

She sat down with her back to the engine, beside the window, and put on her reading glasses and took up the newspaper from Switzerland. But for some minutes she did not read. She heard again inside herself the words *alone, alone,* just the way she had heard them fifty-nine years ago when she was twelve years old and crossing France by herself for the first time. As she had sat there, bolt upright in the corner of a carriage, her green velvet fur-trimmed cloak around her, her hamper beside her, and the locket with the picture of her grandfather hidden in her hand, she had felt a swelling terror of exhilaration, the dark, drowning swirl of cutting loose, had tasted the strength to be brewed out of self-pity and the calm to be lashed together out of panic that belonged to other times and other journeys approaching her from the distance of her future. *Alone, alone.* This that her real self had known years before it happened to her—before she had lived the journey that took her from a lover, or those others that took her from the alienated faces of madness and death—that same self remembered years after those journeys had dropped behind into the past. Now she was alone, lonely, lone—whatever you liked to call it—all the time. There is nothing of the drama of an occasion about it, for me, she reminded herself dryly. Still, there was no denying it, *alone* was not the same as *lonely;* even the Old Fool could not blur the distinction of that. The blue silk coat quivered where Alfred had hung it, the bundle of magazines edged along the table, and somewhere above her head a loose strap tapped. She felt again aloneness as the carapace that did not shut her off but shielded her strong sense of survival—against it, and all else.

She opened the paper from Switzerland, and, with her left foot (the heat had made it a little swollen) up on the seat opposite, she began to read. She felt lulled and comfortable and was not even irritated by the thuds and dragging noises coming from the partition behind her head; it was clear that that was the woman next door—*she* must be fussing with her luggage. Presently a steward brought a tea tray, which Alfred had ordered before the train left. Mrs. Hansen drew in her mouth with pleasure at the taste of the strong tea, as connoisseurs do when they drink old brandy, and read the afternoon away.

She took her dinner in the dining car because she had established in a long experience that it was not a meal that could be expected to travel train corridors and remain hot, and also because there was something shabby, something *petit bourgeois,*[3] about taking meals in the stuffy cubicle in which you were also to sleep. She tidied her hair around the sides of her toque—it was a beautiful hat, one of four, always the same shape, that she had made for herself every second year in Vienna—took off her rings and washed her hands, and powdered her nose, pulling a critical, amused face at herself in the compact mirror. Then she put on her silk coat, picked up her handbag, and went with upright dignity, despite the twitchings and lurchings of the train, along the corridors to the dining car. She seated herself at an empty table for two beside a window, and, of course, although it was early and there were many other seats vacant, the old woman from the compartment next door, entering five minutes later, came straight over and sat down opposite her.

Now it was impossible not to speak to the woman, and Mrs. Hansen listened to her with the distant patience of an adult giving half an ear to a child, and answered her when necessary, with a dry simplicity calculated to be far above her head. Of course, Old Fool was tempted to unbend, to lapse into the small boastings and rivalries usual between two old ladies. But Mrs. Hansen would not allow it and certainly not with this woman—this acquaintance thrust upon her in a train. It was bad enough that, only the week before, Old Fool had led her into one of these pathetic pieces of senile nonsense, cleverly disguised—Old Fool could be wily enough—but, just the same, unmistakably the kind of thing that people found boring. It was about her teeth. At seventy-one they were still her own, which was a self-evident miracle. Yet she had allowed herself, at a dinner party given by some young friends who were obviously impressed by her, to tell a funny story (not quite true, either) about how, when she was a weekend guest in a house with an oversolicitous hostess, the jovial host had hoaxed his wife by impressing upon her the importance of providing a suitable receptacle for their guest's teeth when she took them out overnight. There was a glass beside the jug of water

3. ***petit bourgeois*** (pet'ē bu̇r zhwä'), the lower middle class.

on the bedside table; the hostess appeared, embarrassedly, with another. "But, my dear, what is the other glass for?" The denouement, laughter, etc. Disgusting. Good teeth as well as bad aches and pains must be kept to oneself; when one is young, one takes the first for granted, and does not know the existence of the others.

So it was that when the menu was held before the two women Mrs. Hansen ignored the consternation into which it seemed to plunge her companion, forestalled the temptation to enter, by contributing her doctor's views, into age's passionate preoccupation with diet, and ordered fish.

"D'you think the fish'll be all right? I always wonder, on a train, you know. . . ." said the woman from the next compartment.

Mrs. Hansen merely confirmed her order to the waiter by lowering her eyes and settling her chin slightly. The woman decided to begin at the beginning, with soup. "Can't go far wrong with soup, can you?"

"Don't wait, please," said Mrs. Hansen when the soup came.

The soup was watery, the woman said. Mrs. Hansen smiled her tragic smile, indulgently. The woman decided that she'd keep Mrs. Hansen company, and risk the fish, too. The fish lay beneath a pasty blanket of white sauce, and while Mrs. Hansen calmly pushed aside the sauce and ate, the woman said, "There's nothing like the good, clean food cooked in your own kitchen."

Mrs. Hansen put a forkful of fish to her mouth and, when she had finished it, spoke at last. "I'm afraid it's many years since I had my own kitchen for more than a month or two a year."

"Well, of course, if you go about a lot, you get used to strange food, I suppose. I find I can't eat half the stuff they put in front of you in hotels. Last time I was away, there were some days I didn't know what to have at all for lunch. I was in one of the best hotels in Durban and all there was was this endless curry—curry this, curry that—and a lot of dried-up cold meats."

Mrs. Hansen shrugged. "I always find enough for my needs. It does not matter much."

"What can you do? I suppose this sauce is the wrong thing for me, but you've got to take what you get when you're traveling," said the woman. She broke off a piece of bread and passed it swiftly around her plate to scoop up what was left of the sauce. "Starchy," she added.

Mrs. Hansen ordered a cutlet, and, after a solemn study of the menu, the other woman asked for the item listed immediately below the fish—oxtail stew. While they were waiting she ate bread and butter and, shifting her mouthful comfortably from one side of her mouth to the other, accomplished a shift of her attention, too, as if her jaw and her brain had some simple mechanical connection. "You're not from here, I suppose?" she asked, looking at Mrs. Hansen with the appraisal reserved for foreigners and the license granted by the tacit acceptance of old age on both sides.

"I have lived in the Cape, on and off, for some years," said Mrs. Hansen. "My second husband was Danish, but settled here."

"I could have married again. I'm not boasting, I mean, but I did have the chance, if I'd've wanted to," said the woman. "Somehow, I couldn't face it, after losing my first—fifty-two, that's all, and you'd have taken a lease on his life. Ah, those doctors. No wonder I feel I can't trust them a minute."

Mrs. Hansen parted the jaws of her large, elegant black bag to take out a handkerchief; the stack of letters that she always had with her—new ones arriving to take the place of old with every airmail—lay exposed. Thin letters, fat letters, big envelopes, small ones; the torn edges of foreign stamps, the large, sloping, and small, crabbed hands of foreigners writing foreign tongues. The other woman looked down upon them like a tourist, curious, impersonally insolent, envious. "Of course, if I'd been the sort to run about a lot, I suppose it might have been different. I might have met someone really *congenial.* But there's my daughters. A mother's responsibility is never over—that's what I say. When they're little, it's little troubles. When they're grown up, it's big ones. They're all nicely married, thank God, but you know, it's always something—one of them sick, or one of the grandchildren, bless them. . . . I don't suppose you've got any children. Not even from your first, I mean?"

"No," said Mrs. Hansen. "No." And the lie, as always, came to her as a triumph against that arrogant boy (Old Fool persisted in thinking of him as a gentle-browed youth bent over a dachshund puppy, though he was a man of forty-five by now) whom truly she had made, as she had warned she would, no son of hers. When the lie was said it had the effect of leaving her breathless, as if she had just crowned a steep rise. Firmly and calmly, she leaned forward and poured herself a glass of water, as one who has deserved it.

"My, it does look fatty," the other woman was saying over the oxtail, which had just been placed before her. "My doctor'd have a fit if he knew I was eating this." But eat it she did, and cutlet and roast turkey to follow. Mrs. Hansen never knew whether or not her companion rounded off the meal with rhubarb pie (the woman had remarked, as she saw it carried past, that it looked soggy), because she herself had gone straight from cutlet to coffee, and, her meal finished, excused herself before the other was through the turkey course. Back in her compartment, she took off her toque at last and tied a gray chiffon scarf around her head. Then she waited for the man to come and convert her seat into the deluxe bed Alfred had paid for in advance.

It seemed to Mrs. Hansen that she did not sleep very well during the early part of the night, though she did not quite know what it was that made her restless. She was awakened, time and again, apparently by some noise that had ceased by the time she was conscious enough to identify it. The third or fourth time this happened, she woke to silence and a sense of absolute cessation, as if the world had stopped turning. But it was only the train that had stopped. Mrs. Hansen lay and listened. They must be at some deserted siding in the small hours; there were no lights shining in through the shuttered window, no footsteps, no talk. The voice of a cricket, like a fingernail screeching over glass, sounded, providing, beyond the old woman's closed eyes, beyond the dark compartment and the shutters, a landscape of grass, dark, and telephone poles.

Suddenly the train gave a terrific reverberating jerk, as if it had been given a violent push. All was still again. And in the stillness, Mrs. Hansen became aware of groans coming from the other side of the partition against which she lay. The groans came, bumbling and nasal, through the wood and leather; they sounded like a dog with its head buried in a cushion, worrying at the feathers. Mrs. Hansen breathed out once, hard, in annoyance, and turned over; the greedy old pig, now she was suffering agonies of indigestion from that oxtail, of course. The groans continued at intervals. Once there was a muffled tinkling sound, as if a spoon had been dropped. Mrs. Hansen lay tense with irritation, waiting for the train to move on and drown the woman's noise. At last, with a shake that quickly settled into a fast clip, they were off again, lickety-lack, lickety-lack, past (Mrs. Hansen could imagine) the endless telephone poles, the dark grass, the black-coated cricket. Under the dialogue of the train, she was an unwilling eavesdropper to the vulgar intimacies next door; then either the groans stopped or she fell asleep in spite of them, for she heard nothing till the steward woke her with the arrival of early-morning coffee.

Mrs. Hansen sponged herself, dressed, and had a quiet breakfast, undisturbed by anyone, in the dining car. The man sitting opposite her did not even ask her so much as to pass the salt. She was back in her compartment, reading, when the ticket examiner came in to take her ticket away (they would be in Johannesburg soon), and of course, she knew just where to lay her hand on it, in her bag. He leaned against the doorway while she got it out. "Hear what happened?" he said.

"What happened?" she said uncertainly, screwing up her face because he spoke indistinctly, like most young South Africans.

"Next door," he said. "The lady next door, elderly lady. She died last night."

"She died? That woman died?" She stood up and questioned him closely, as if he were irresponsible.

"Yes," he said, checking the ticket on his list. "The bed boy found her this morning, dead in her bed. She never answered when the steward came round with coffee, you see."

"My God," said Mrs. Hansen. "My God. So she died, eh?"

"Yes, lady." He held out his hand for her ticket; he had the tale to tell all up and down the train.

With a gesture of futility, she gave it to him.

After he had gone, she sank down on the seat, beside the window, and watched the veld go by, the grasses streaming past in the sun like the long black tails of the widow birds blowing where they swung upon the fences. She had finished her paper and magazines. There was no sound but the sound of the hurrying train.

When they reached Johannesburg she had all her luggage trimly closed and ready for the porter from the hotel at which she was going to stay. She left the station with him within five minutes of the train's arrival, and was gone before the doctor, officials, and, she supposed, newspaper reporters came to see the woman taken away from the compartment next door. What could I have said to them? she thought, pleased with her sensible escape. Could I tell them she died of greed? Better not to be mixed up in it.

And then she thought of something. Newspaper reporters. No doubt there would be a piece in the Cape papers tomorrow. ELDERLY WOMAN FOUND DEAD IN CAPE–JOHANNESBURG TRAIN.

As soon as she had signed the register at the hotel she asked for a telegram form. She paused a moment, leaning on the marble-topped reception desk, looking out over the heads of the clerks. Her eyes, which were still handsome, crinkled at the corners; her nostrils lifted; her mouth, which was still so shapely because of her teeth, turned its sad corners lower in her reluctant, calculating smile. She printed Alfred's name and the address of the flat in Cape Town, and then wrote quickly, in the fine hand she had mastered more than sixty years ago: "It was not me. Clara Hansen."

Discussion

1. **(a)** Where does Clara Hansen's journey begin and end? **(b)** What details in the opening paragraphs help establish her social background?

2. During the fifteen minutes before the train leaves, Mrs. Hansen and her chauffeur Alfred engage in small talk. **(a)** What is each of them thinking about? **(b)** What can you infer about their relationship from their thoughts?

3. **(a)** What simile does the author use to describe the old woman in the next compartment? **(b)** How does Mrs. Hansen get rid of her the first time? the second time?

4. Mrs. Hansen sometimes thinks of her "Old Fool" self as opposed to her "real" self. **(a)** Under what circumstances did her real self learn to find strength and pleasure in being alone? **(b)** Would the Old Fool self be likely to feel lonely? Explain. **(c)** What other sorts of things does the Old Fool self like to do?

5. **(a)** Describe the meal shared by Mrs. Hansen and the old woman. **(b)** Do the woman's comments about non-home-cooked food fit her actions? Explain. **(c)** Why does Mrs. Hansen lie about her son?

6. **(a)** What is Mrs. Hansen's reaction to the woman's overnight distress? **(b)** What do her actions after she learns of the woman's death reveal about her character? **(c)** Do her earlier thoughts and actions prepare you for this? Discuss.

7. Does the author intend you to pity Mrs. Hansen, to censure her, or both? Justify your answer.

Application

Stereotype

By definition a stereotyped character is one-dimensional and therefore unlikely to arouse much interest or sympathy. In this story, however, the author lulls the reader into regarding the woman in the next compartment as a stereotype, then dramatically forces a reconsideration of that view.

1. Discuss which of the following characteristics of the old woman are stereotypical. **(a)** carrying "string bags and paper parcels"; **(b)** overeating; **(c)** discussing her doctor's views on diet and health; **(d)** worrying about her children and grandchildren; **(e)** talking to strangers.

2. When and how does the woman become a three-dimensional character?

Nadine Gordimer 1923–

Believing that the purpose of a writer is to "make sense of life," Nadine Gordimer has used her writings to explore the complexity of human relationships. In her numerous novels and short stories, she has described many sides of contemporary life—the private, the social, and the political—and has provided insights rather than judgments.

Gordimer's birthplace is a small town near Johannesburg, South Africa. Reading, her favorite youthful activity, increased her awareness of the world and led her to become a writer. Her principal works are the short-story collections *The Soft Voice of the Serpent* (1952) and *Livingstone's Companions* (1971), and the novel *A Guest of Honor* (1970). Her fiction reflects themes of exile and aloneness, and frequently presents characters who are strangers in their own land.

Because Gordimer's writings usually touch upon her country's troubling racial and social problems, they are not allowed to be published there; however, they have earned her wide recognition elsewhere. She has lectured abroad and in recent years been involved in adapting her stories for film.

Tuesday Siesta

Gabriel García Márquez Colombia

"Two big rusty keys hung on the inside of the door; the girl imagined . . . that they were Saint Peter's keys."

The train emerged from the quivering tunnel of sandy rocks, began to cross the symmetrical, interminable banana plantations, and the air became humid and they couldn't feel the sea breeze anymore. A stifling blast of smoke came in the car window. On the narrow road parallel to the railway there were oxcarts loaded with green bunches of bananas. Beyond the road, in uncultivated spaces set at odd intervals there were offices with electric fans, red-brick buildings, and residences with chairs and little white tables on the terraces among dusty palm trees and rosebushes. It was eleven in the morning, and the heat had not yet begun.

"You'd better close the window," the woman said. "Your hair will get full of soot."

The girl tried to, but the shade wouldn't move because of the rust.

They were the only passengers in the lone third-class car. Since the smoke of the locomotive kept coming through the window, the girl left her seat and put down the only things they had with them: a plastic sack with some things to eat and a bouquet of flowers wrapped in newspaper. She sat on the opposite seat, away from the window, facing her mother. They were both in severe and poor mourning clothes.

The girl was twelve years old, and it was the first time she'd ever been on a train. The woman seemed too old to be her mother, because of the blue veins on her eyelids and her small, soft, and shapeless body, in a dress cut like a cassock. She was riding with her spinal column braced firmly against the back of the seat, and held a peeling patent-leather handbag in her lap with both hands. She bore the conscientious serenity of someone accustomed to poverty.

By twelve the heat had begun. The train stopped for ten minutes to take on water at a station where there was no town. Outside, in the mysterious silence of the plantations, the shadows seemed clean. But the still air inside the car smelled like untanned leather. The train did not pick up speed. It stopped at two identical towns with wooden houses painted bright colors. The woman's head nodded and she sank into sleep. The girl took off her shoes. Then she went to the washroom to put the bouquet of flowers in some water.

Gabriel García Márquez (gä bryel′ gär sē′ä mär′kās).

When she came back to her seat, her mother was waiting to eat. She gave her a piece of cheese, half a cornmeal pancake, and a cookie, and took an equal portion out of the plastic sack for herself. While they ate, the train crossed an iron bridge very slowly and passed a town just like the ones before, except that in this one there was a crowd in the plaza. A band was playing a lively tune under the oppressive sun. At the other side of town the plantations ended in a plain which was cracked from the drought.

The woman stopped eating.

"Put on your shoes," she said.

The girl looked outside. She saw nothing but the deserted plain, where the train began to pick up speed again, but she put the last piece of cookie into the sack and quickly put on her shoes. The woman gave her a comb.

"Comb your hair," she said.

The train whistle began to blow while the girl was combing her hair. The woman dried the sweat from her neck and wiped the oil from her face with her fingers. When the girl stopped combing, the train was passing the outlying houses of a town larger but sadder than the earlier ones.

"If you feel like doing anything, do it now," said the woman. "Later, don't take a drink anywhere even if you're dying of thirst. Above all, no crying."

The girl nodded her head. A dry, burning wind came in the window, together with the locomotive's whistle and the clatter of the old cars. The woman folded the plastic bag with the rest of the food and put it in the handbag. For a moment a complete picture of the town, on that bright August Tuesday, shone in the window. The girl wrapped the flowers in the soaking-wet newspapers, moved a little farther away from the window, and stared at her mother. She received a pleasant expression in return. The train began to whistle and slowed down. A moment later it stopped.

There was no one at the station. On the other side of the street, on the sidewalk shaded by the almond trees, only the pool hall was open. The town was floating in the heat. The woman and the girl got off the train and crossed the abandoned station—the tiles split apart by the grass growing up between—and over to the shady side of the street.

It was almost two. At that hour, weighted down by drowsiness, the town was taking a siesta. The stores, the town offices, the public school were closed at eleven, and didn't reopen until a little before four, when the train went back. Only the hotel across from the station, with its bar and pool hall, and the telegraph office at one side of the plaza stayed open. The houses, most of them built on the banana company's model, had their doors locked from inside and their blinds drawn. In some of them it was so hot that the residents ate lunch in the patio. Others leaned a chair against the wall, in the shade of the almond trees, and took their siesta right out in the street.

Keeping to the protective shade of the almond trees, the woman and the girl entered the town without disturbing the siesta. They went directly to the parish house. The woman scratched the metal grating on the door with her fingernail, waiting a moment, and scratched again. An electric fan was humming inside. They did not hear the steps. They hardly heard the slight creaking of a door, and immediately a cautious voice, right next to the metal grating: "Who is it?" The woman tried to see through the grating.

"I need the priest," she said.

"He's sleeping now."

"It's an emergency," the woman insisted.

Her voice showed a calm determination.

The door was opened a little way, noiselessly, and a plump, older woman appeared, with very pale skin and hair the color of iron. Her eyes seemed too small behind her thick eyeglasses.

"Come in," she said, and opened the door all the way.

They entered a room permeated with an old smell of flowers. The woman of the house led them to a wooden bench and signaled them to sit down. The girl did so, but her mother remained standing, absent-mindedly, with both hands clutching the handbag. No noise could be heard above the electric fan.

The woman of the house reappeared at the door at the far end of the room. "He says you should come back after three," she said in a very low voice. "He just lay down five minutes ago."

"The train leaves at three-thirty," said the woman.

It was a brief and self-assured reply, but her voice remained pleasant, full of undertones. The woman of the house smiled for the first time.

"All right," she said.

When the far door closed again, the woman sat down next to her daughter. The narrow waiting room was poor, neat, and clean. On the other side of the wooden railing which divided the room, there was a worktable, a plain one with an oilcloth cover, and on top of the table a primitive typewriter next to a vase of flowers. The parish records were beyond. You could see that it was an office kept in order by a spinster.

The far door opened and this time the priest appeared, cleaning his glasses with a handkerchief. Only when he put them on was it evident that he was the brother of the woman who had opened the door.

"How can I help you?" he asked.

"The keys to the cemetery," said the woman.

The girl was seated with the flowers in her lap and her feet crossed under the bench. The priest looked at her, then looked at the woman, and then through the wire mesh of the window at the bright, cloudless sky.

"In this heat," he said. "You could have waited until the sun went down."

The woman moved her head silently. The priest crossed to the other side of the railing, took out of the cabinet a notebook covered in oilcloth, a wooden penholder, and an inkwell, and sat down at the table. There was more than enough hair on his hands to account for what was missing on his head.

"Which grave are you going to visit?" he asked.

"Carlos Centeno's," said the woman.

"Who?"

"Carlos Centeno," the woman repeated.

The priest still did not understand.

"He's the thief who was killed here last week," said the woman in the same tone of voice. "I am his mother."

The priest scrutinized her. She stared at him with quiet self-control, and the Father blushed. He lowered his head and began to write. As he filled the page, he asked the woman to identify herself, and she replied unhesitatingly, with precise details, as if she were reading them. The Father began to sweat. The girl unhooked the buckle of her left shoe, slipped her heel out of it, and rested it on the bench rail. She did the same with the right one.

It had all started the Monday of the previous week, at three in the morning, a few blocks from there. Rebecca, a lonely widow who lived in a house full of odds and ends, heard above the sound of the drizzling rain someone trying to force the front door from outside. She got up, rummaged around in her closet for an ancient revolver that no one had fired since the days of Colonel Aureliano Buendía,[1] and went into the living room without turning on the lights. Orienting herself not so much by the noise at the lock as by a terror developed in her by twenty-eight years of loneliness, she fixed in her imagination not only the spot where the door was but also the exact height of the lock. She clutched the weapon with both hands, closed her eyes, and squeezed the trigger. It was the first time in her life that she had fired a gun. Immediately after the explosion, she could hear nothing except the murmur of the drizzle on the galvanized roof. Then she heard a little metallic bump on the cement porch, and a very low voice, pleasant but terribly exhausted: "Ah, Mother." The man they found dead in front of the house in the morning, his nose blown to bits, wore a flannel shirt with colored stripes, everyday pants with a rope for a belt, and was barefoot. No one in town knew him.

"So his name was Carlos Centeno," murmured the Father when he finished writing.

---

1. ***Aureliano Buendía*** (ou'rā lyä'nō bwān dē'ä).

"Centeno Ayala,"[2] said the woman. "He was my only boy."

The priest went back to the cabinet. Two big rusty keys hung on the inside of the door; the girl imagined, as her mother had when she was a girl and as the priest himself must have imagined at some time, that they were Saint Peter's keys. He took them down, put them on the open notebook on the railing, and pointed with his forefinger to a place on the page he had just written, looking at the woman.

"Sign here."

The woman scribbled her name, holding the handbag under her arm. The girl picked up the flowers, came to the railing shuffling her feet, and watched her mother attentively.

The priest sighed.

"Didn't you ever try to get him on the right track?"

The woman answered when she finished signing.

"He was a very good man."

The priest looked first at the woman and then at the girl, and realized with a kind of pious amazement that they were not about to cry. The woman continued in the same tone:

"I told him never to steal anything that anyone needed to eat, and he minded me. On the other hand, before, when he used to box, he used to spend three days in bed, exhausted from being punched."

"All his teeth had to be pulled out," interrupted the girl.

"That's right," the woman agreed. "Every mouthful I ate those days tasted of the beatings my son got on Saturday nights."

"God's will is inscrutable," said the Father.

But he said it without much conviction, partly because experience had made him a little skeptical and partly because of the heat. He suggested that they cover their heads to guard against sunstroke. Yawning, and now almost completely asleep, he gave them instructions about how to find Carlos Centeno's grave. When they came back, they didn't have to knock. They should put the key under the door; and in the same place, if they could, they should put an offering for the Church. The woman listened to his directions with great attention, but thanked him without smiling.

The Father had noticed that there was someone looking inside, his nose pressed against the metal grating, even before he opened the door to the street. Outside was a group of children. When the door was opened wide, the children scattered. Ordinarily, at that hour there was no one in the street. Now there were not only children. There were groups of people under the almond trees. The Father scanned the street swimming in the heat and then he understood. Softly, he closed the door again.

"Wait a moment," he said without looking at the woman.

His sister appeared at the far door with a black jacket over her nightshirt and her hair down over her shoulders. She looked silently at the Father.

"What was it?" he asked.

"The people have noticed," murmured his sister.

"You'd better go out by the door to the patio," said the Father.

"It's the same there," said his sister. "Everybody is at the windows."

The woman seemed not to have understood until then. She tried to look into the street through the metal grating. Then she took the bouquet of flowers from the girl and began to move toward the door. The girl followed her.

"Wait until the sun goes down," said the Father.

"You'll melt," said his sister, motionless at the back of the room. "Wait and I'll lend you a parasol."

"Thank you," replied the woman. "We're all right this way."

She took the girl by the hand and went into the street.

---

2. ***Centeno Ayala*** (ä yä'lä). In Spanish-speaking countries a person's first name and surname are customarily followed by his or her mother's maiden name. Thus, the young man's full name was Carlos Centeno Ayala.

Discussion

1. (a) What details presented during the train ride help you to visualize a rural, twentieth-century, South American setting? **(b)** What details convey the poverty of the mother and daughter?

2. The description of the mother "riding with her spinal column braced firmly against the back of the seat" suggests certain things about her character. Explain what qualities you infer she possesses, and discuss how she shows these qualities in the following: **(a)** her warning to her daughter as they get off the train; **(b)** her statements when the priest's sister opens the door; **(c)** her reaction to the priest's tale about her son's death; **(d)** her actions at the end of the story.

3. (a) What opinion does the priest seem to have of the dead son? **(b)** What details does the mother mention to back up *her* opinion of him? **(c)** Might both characters' opinions be right? Discuss.

4. (a) What do you think causes the townspeople to gather in the street? Justify your answer. **(b)** Do you think the woman anticipated that something like this might happen? Why or why not? **(c)** How does the priest show consideration for the woman at this point?

5. Mood is a very important element in this story. Explain how the writer creates it by **(a)** the various details of setting that he presents; **(b)** keeping the purpose of the mother's journey secret until fairly late in the story.

Composition

The use of imagery contributes to the mood of a written work by helping the reader to experience what he or she is reading. Review the selection for any words or phrases that appeal to the senses. Consider that the writer may have wanted to evoke various sensations or one in particular. Recall your reactions as you read the story. Do you think you "felt" anything that helped you to identify with what the characters were feeling? Does the imagery communicate a pleasant or unpleasant atmosphere?

In a brief essay analyze the author's use of imagery and its effectiveness.

Gabriel García Márquez 1928–

The sweltering setting of "Tuesday Siesta" may be based on the small Caribbean town of Aracataca (är ä kä tä'kä), Colombia, the birthplace of the author. To mold his fictional view of Latin American life and conflicts, García Márquez has drawn material from actual locations and history. In doing so, he has advanced—and revived interest in—his continent's literary tradition. In 1982 he was awarded the Nobel Prize for Literature.

A writer since childhood, García Márquez began his career as a reporter for a newspaper. Encouraged by his well-received short stories, which appeared in the paper's literary section, he published his first novel, *Leaf Storm,* in 1955. His major work is *One Hundred Years of Solitude* (1967), regarded on one level as a family saga and on another as the history of Latin America. His writings often feature a blend of reality and fantasy.

My Old Home

Lu Xun China

A final journey home brings forth past acquaintances—and new realizations.

Braving the bitter cold, I traveled more than seven hundred miles back to the old home I had left over twenty years before.

It was late winter. As we drew near my former home the day became overcast and a cold wind blew into the cabin of our boat, while all one could see through the chinks in our bamboo awning were a few desolate villages, void of any sign of life, scattered far and near under the somber yellow sky. I could not help feeling depressed.

Ah! Surely this was not the old home I had remembered for the past twenty years?

The old home I remembered was not in the least like this. My old home was much better. But if you asked me to recall its peculiar charm or describe its beauties, I had no clear impression, no words to describe it. And now it seemed this was all there was to it. Then I rationalized the matter to myself, saying: Home was always like this, and although it has not improved, still it is not so depressing as I imagine; it is only my mood that has changed, because I am coming back to the country this time with no illusions.

This time I had come with the sole object of saying good-by. The old house our clan had lived in for so many years had already been sold to another family and was to change hands before the end of the year. I had to hurry there before New Year's Day to say good-by forever to the familiar old house, and to move my family to another place where I was working, far from my old home town.

At dawn on the second day I reached the gateway of my home. Broken stems of withered grass on the roof, trembling in the wind, made very clear the reason why this old house could not avoid changing hands. Several branches of our clan had probably already moved away, so it was unusually quiet. By the time I reached the house my mother was already at the door to welcome me, and my eight-year-old nephew, Hung-erh,[1] rushed out after her.

Though Mother was delighted, she was also trying to hide a certain feeling of sadness. She told me to sit down and rest and have some tea, letting the removal wait for the time being. Hung-erh, who had never seen me before, stood watching me at a distance.

But finally we had to talk about the removal. I said that rooms had already been rented elsewhere, and I had bought a little furniture; in addition, it would be necessary to sell all the furniture in the house in order to buy more things. Mother agreed, saying that the luggage was nearly all packed, and about half the furniture that could not easily be moved had already been sold. Only it was difficult to get people to pay up.

"You must rest for a day or two and call on our relatives, and then we can go," said Mother.

"Yes."

"Then there is Jun-tu. Each time he comes here he always asks after you, and wants very much to see you again. I told him the probable date of your return home, and he may be coming any time."

---

1. ***Hung-erh*** (hůng′är′).

From *Selected Stories of Lu Xun,* translated by Yang Hsien-yi and Gladys Yang, published by Oriole Editions. Reprinted by permission of The Moretus Press, Inc. Slightly adapted.

Lu Xun (lü′ shʏn′).

At this point a strange picture suddenly flashed into my mind: a golden moon suspended in a deep blue sky and beneath it the seashore, planted as far as the eye could see with jade-green watermelons, while in their midst a boy of eleven or twelve, wearing a silver necklet and grasping a steel pitchfork in his hand, was thrusting with all his might at a *cha* which dodged the blow and escaped between his legs.

This boy was Jun-tu. When I first met him he was just over ten—that was thirty years ago, and at that time my father was still alive and the family well off, so I was really a spoiled child. That year it was our family's turn to take charge of a big ancestral sacrifice, which came round only once in thirty years, and hence was an important one. In the first month the ancestral images were presented and offerings made, and since the sacrificial vessels were very fine and there was such a crowd of worshippers, it was necessary to guard against theft. Our family had only one part-time laborer. (In our district we divide laborers into three classes: those who work all the year for one family are called full-timers; those who are hired by the day are called dailies; and those who farm their own land and only work for one family at New Year, during festivals, or when rents are being collected are called part-timers.) And since there was so much to be done, he told my father that he would send for his son Jun-tu to look after the sacrificial vessels.

When my father gave his consent I was overjoyed, because I had long since heard of Jun-tu and knew that he was about my own age, born in the intercalary month,[2] and when his horoscope

2. ***intercalary month.*** The Chinese lunar calendar has 360 days to a year, and each month has 29 or 30 days, never 31. So every few years a thirteenth or intercalary month is added to the calendar.

was told it was found that of the five elements that of earth was lacking,[3] so his father called him Jun-tu (Intercalary Earth). He could set traps and catch small birds.

I looked forward every day to New Year, for New Year would bring Jun-tu. At last, when the end of the year came, one day Mother told me that Jun-tu had come, and I flew to see him. He was standing in the kitchen. He had a round, crimson face and wore a small felt cap on his head and a gleaming silver necklet around his neck, showing that his father doted on him and, fearing he might die, had made a pledge with the gods and buddhas, using the necklet as a talisman. He was very shy, and I was the only person he was not afraid of. When there was no one else there, he would talk with me, so in a few hours we were fast friends.

I don't know what we talked of then, but I remember that Jun-tu was in high spirits, saying that since he had come to town he had seen many new things.

The next day I wanted him to catch birds.

"Can't be done," he said. "It's only possible after a heavy snowfall. On our sands, after it snows, I sweep clear a patch of ground, prop up a big threshing basket with a short stick, and scatter husks of grain beneath. When the birds come there to eat, I tug a string tied to the stick, and the birds are caught in the basket. There are all kinds: wild pheasants, woodcocks, wood pigeons, 'blue-backs'. . . ."

Accordingly I looked forward very eagerly to snow.

"Just now it is too cold," said Jun-tu another time, "but you must come to our place in summer. In the daytime we'll go to the seashore to look for shells. There are green ones and red ones, besides 'scare-devil' shells and 'buddha's hands.' In the evening when Dad and I go to see to the watermelons, you shall come too."

"Is it to look out for thieves?"

"No. If passers-by are thirsty and pick a watermelon, folk down our way don't consider it as stealing. What we have to look out for are badgers, hedgehogs, and *cha*. When under the moonlight you hear the crunching sound made by the *cha* when it bites the melons, then you take your pitchfork and creep steathily over. . . ."

I had no idea then what this thing called *cha* was—and I am not much clearer now for that matter—but somehow I felt it was something like a small dog, and very fierce.

"Don't they bite people?"

"You have a pitchfork. You go across, and when you see it you strike. It's a very cunning creature and will rush towards you and get away between your legs. Its fur is as slippery as oil. . . ."

I had never known that all these strange things existed: at the seashore there were shells all colors of the rainbow; watermelons were exposed to such danger, yet all I had known of them before was that they were sold in the greengrocer's.

"On our shore, when the tide comes in, there are lots of jumping fish, each with two legs like a frog. . . ."

Jun-tu's mind was a treasure house of such strange lore, all of it outside the ken of my former friends. They were ignorant of all these things and, while Jun-tu lived by the sea, they like me could see only the four corners of the sky above the high courtyard wall.

Unfortunately, a month after New Year Jun-tu had to go home. I burst into tears and he took refuge in the kitchen, crying and refusing to come out, until finally his father carried him off. Later he sent me by his father a packet of shells and a few very beautiful feathers, and I sent him presents once or twice, but we never saw each other again.

Now that my mother mentioned him, this childhood memory sprang into life like a flash of lightning, and I seemed to see my beautiful old home. So I answered:

"Fine! And he—how is he?"

"He? . . . He's not at all well off either," said Mother. And then, looking out of the door:

---

3. ***of the five elements . . . lacking.*** Earth, fire, wood, metal, and water were regarded by the ancient Chinese as the five basic elements.

"Here come those people again. They say they want to buy our furniture; but actually they just want to see what they can pick up. I must go and watch them."

Mother stood up and went out. The voices of several women could be heard outside. I called Hung-erh to me and started talking to him, asking him whether he could write, and whether he would be glad to leave.

"Shall we be going by train?"

"Yes, we shall go by train."

"And boat?"

"We shall take a boat first."

"Oh! Like this! With such a long mustache!" A strange shrill voice suddenly rang out.

I looked up with a start, and saw a woman of about fifty with prominent cheekbones and thin lips. With her hands on her hips, not wearing a skirt but with her trousered legs apart, she stood in front of me just like the compass in a box of geometrical instruments.

I was flabbergasted.

"Don't you know me? Why, I have held you in my arms!"

I felt even more flabbergasted. Fortunately my mother came in just then and said:

"He has been away so long, you must excuse him for forgetting. You should remember," she said to me, "this is Mrs. Yang from across the road. . . . She has a beancurd shop."

Then, to be sure, I remembered. When I was a child there was a Mrs. Yang who used to sit nearly all day long in the beancurd shop across the road, and everybody used to call her Beancurd Beauty. She used to powder herself, and her cheekbones were not so prominent then nor her lips so thin; moreover she remained seated all the time, so that I had never noticed this resemblance to a compass. In those days people said that, thanks to her, that beancurd shop did very good business. But, probably on account of my age, she had made no impression on me, so that later I forgot her entirely. However, the Compass was extremely indignant and looked at me most contemptuously, just as one might look at a Frenchman who had never heard of Napoleon or an American who had never heard of Washington, and smiling sarcastically she said:

"You had forgotten? Naturally I am beneath your notice. . . ."

"Certainly not . . . I . . ." I answered nervously, getting to my feet.

"Then you listen to me, Master Xun. You have grown rich, and they are too heavy to move, so you can't possibly want these old pieces of furniture anymore. You had better let me take them away. Poor people like us can do with them."

"I haven't grown rich. I must sell these in order to buy . . ."

"Oh, come now, you have been made the intendant of a circuit,[4] how can you still say you're not rich? Whenever you go out it is in a big sedan chair with eight bearers. Do you still say you're not rich? Hah! You can't hide anything from me."

Knowing there was nothing I could say, I remained silent.

"Come now, really, the more money people have the more miserly they get, and the more miserly they are the more money they get. . . ." remarked the Compass, turning indignantly away and walking slowly off, casually picking up a pair of Mother's gloves and stuffing them into her pocket as she went out.

After this a number of relatives in the neighborhood came to call. In the intervals between entertaining them I did some packing, and so three or four days passed.

One very cold afternoon, I sat drinking tea after lunch when I was aware of someone coming in, and turned my head to see who it was. At the first glance I gave an involuntary start, hastily stood up, and went over to welcome him.

The newcomer was Jun-tu. But although I knew at a glance that this was Jun-tu, it was not the Jun-tu I remembered. He had grown to twice his former size. His round face, once crimson, had become sallow and acquired deep lines and

---

4. ***intendant of a circuit,*** an administrator of a judicial district.

wrinkles; his eyes too had become like his father's, the rims swollen and red, a feature common to most peasants who work by the sea and are exposed all day to the wind from the ocean. He wore a shabby felt cap and just one very thin padded jacket, with the result that he was shivering from head to foot. He carried a paper package and a long pipe, nor was his hand the plump red hand I remembered, but coarse and clumsy and chapped, like the bark of a pine tree.

Delighted as I was, I did not know how to express myself, and could only say:

"Oh! Jun-tu—so it's you? . . ."

After this there were so many things I wanted to talk about, they should have poured out like a string of beads: woodcocks, jumping fish, shells, *cha*. . . . But I was tongue-tied, unable to put all I was thinking into words.

He stood there, mixed joy and sadness showing on his face. His lips moved, but not a sound did he utter. Finally, assuming a respectful attitude, he said clearly:

"Master! . . ."

I felt a shiver run through me; for I knew then what a lamentably thick wall had grown up between us. Yet I could not say anything.

He turned his head to call:

"Shui-sheng,[5] bow to the master." Then he pulled forward a boy who had been hiding behind his back, and this was just the Jun-tu of twenty years before, only a little paler and thinner, and he had no silver necklet.

"This is my fifth," he said. "He's not used to company, so he's shy and awkward."

Mother came downstairs with Hung-erh, probably after hearing our voices.

"I got your letter some time ago, Madam," said Jun-tu. "I was really so pleased to know the master was coming back. . . ."

"Now, why are you so polite? Weren't you playmates together in the past?" said Mother gaily. "You had better still call him Brother Xun as before."

"Oh, you are really too . . . What bad manners that would be. I was a child then and didn't understand." As he was speaking Jun-tu motioned Shui-sheng to come and bow, but the child was shy, and stood stock-still behind his father.

"So he is Shui-sheng? Your fifth?" asked Mother. "We are all strangers; you can't blame him for feeling shy. Hung-erh had better take him out to play."

When Hung-erh heard this he went over to Shui-sheng, and Shui-sheng went out with him, entirely at his ease. Mother asked Jun-tu to sit down, and after a little hesitation he did so; then leaning his long pipe against the table he handed over the paper package, saying:

"In winter there is nothing worth bringing; but these few beans we dried ourselves, if you will excuse the liberty, sir."

When I asked him how things were with him, he just shook his head.

"In a very bad way. Even my sixth can do a little work, but still we haven't enough to eat . . . and then there is no security . . . all sorts of people want money, there is no fixed rule . . . and the harvests are bad. You grow things, and when you take them to sell you always have to pay several taxes and lose money, while if you don't try to sell, the things may go bad. . . ."

He kept shaking his head; yet, although his face was lined with wrinkles, not one of them moved, just as if he were a stone statue. No doubt he felt intensely bitter, but could not express himself. After a pause he took up his pipe and began to smoke in silence.

From her chat with him, Mother learned that he was busy at home and had to go back the next day; and since he had had no lunch, she told him to go to the kitchen and fry some rice for himself.

After he had gone out, Mother and I both shook our heads over his hard life: many children, famines, taxes, soldiers, bandits, officials, and landed gentry, all had squeezed him as dry as a mummy. Mother said that we should offer him all the things we were not going to take away, letting him choose for himself.

---

5. ***Shui-sheng*** (shwā'shung').

That afternoon he picked out a number of things: two long tables, four chairs, an incense burner and candlesticks, and one balance. He also asked for all the ashes from the stove (in our part we cook over straw, and the ashes can be used to fertilize sandy soil), saying that when we left he would come to take them away by boat.

That night we talked again, but not of anything serious; and the next morning he went away with Shui-sheng.

After another nine days it was time for us to leave. Jun-tu came in the morning. Shui-sheng did not come with him—he had just brought a little girl of five to watch the boat. We were very busy all day, and had no time to talk. We also had quite a number of visitors, some to see us off, some to fetch things, and some to do both. It was nearly evening when we left by boat, and by that time everything in the house, however old or shabby, large or small, fine or coarse, had been cleared away.

As we set off, in the dusk, the green mountains on either side of the river became deep blue, receding toward the stern of the boat.

Hung-erh and I, leaning against the cabin window, were looking out together at the indistinct scene outside, when suddenly he asked:

"Uncle, when shall we go back?"

"Go back? Do you mean that before you've left you want to go back?"

"Well, Shui-sheng has invited me to his home. . . ." He opened wide his black eyes in anxious thought.

Mother and I both felt rather sad, and so Jun-tu's name came up again. Mother said that ever since our family started packing up, Mrs. Yang from the beancurd shop had come over every day, and the day before in the ash heap she had unearthed a dozen bowls and plates, which after some discussion she insisted must have been buried there by Jun-tu, so that when he came to remove the ashes he could take them home at the same time. After making this discovery Mrs. Yang was very pleased with herself, and flew off taking the dog-teaser with her. (The dog-teaser is used by poultry keepers in our parts. It is a wooden cage inside which food is put, so that hens can stretch their necks in to eat but dogs can only look on furiously.) And it was a marvel, considering the size of her feet, how fast she could run.

I was leaving the old house farther and farther behind, while the hills and rivers of my old home were also receding gradually ever farther in the distance. But I felt no regret. I only felt that all around me was an invisible high wall, cutting me off from my fellows, and this depressed me thoroughly. The vision of that small hero with the silver necklet among the watermelons had formerly been as clear as day, but now it suddenly blurred, adding to my depression.

Mother and Hung-erh fell asleep.

I lay down, listening to the water rippling beneath the boat, and knew that I was going my way. I thought: although there is such a barrier between Jun-tu and myself, the children still have much in common, for wasn't Hung-erh thinking of Shui-sheng just now? I hope they will not be like us, that they will not allow a barrier to grow up between them. But again I would not like them, because they want to be akin, all to have a treadmill existence like mine, nor to suffer like Jun-tu until they become stupefied, nor yet, like others, to devote all their energies to dissipation. They should have a new life, a life we have never experienced.

The access of hope made me suddenly afraid. When Jun-tu asked for the incense burner and candlesticks I had laughed up my sleeve at him, to think that he still worshipped idols and could not put them out of his mind. Yet what I now called hope was no more than an idol I had created myself. The only difference was that what he desired was close at hand, while what I desired was less easily realized.

As I dozed, a stretch of jade-green seashore spread itself before my eyes, and above a round golden moon hung in a deep blue sky. I thought: hope cannot be said to exist, nor can it be said not to exist. It is just like roads across the earth. For actually the earth had no roads to begin with, but when many men pass one way, a road is made.

Discussion

1. (a) Why does the narrator return to his old home? **(b)** Why is he not happy when he sees it? **(c)** How does he rationalize his feelings?

2. (a) Why was the narrator looking forward to seeing Jun-tu again? **(b)** What words begin and end the flashback that deals with him? **(c)** What opinions do you form of the narrator and Jun-tu as they are presented in the flashback?

3. (a) To what does the narrator compare Mrs. Yang when he meets her again? **(b)** What does she probably look like?

4. (a) What differences seem to exist between the narrator now and when he first left home? **(b)** How does Mrs. Yang react to the differences? **(c)** How does Jun-tu react? **(d)** Which character's reaction bothers the narrator more? Explain.

5. (a) How do Hung-erh's and Shui-sheng's lives parallel those of their elders? **(b)** What point does the author make in creating these parallels? **(c)** In what ways does the narrator hope the boys' lives will be better than his and Jun-tu's?

6. Is the ending of this story optimistic or pessimistic? Give reasons for your answer.

Vocabulary

Etymology

void	flabbergast
talisman	vessel
illusion	ken

Refer to the Glossary for the etymologies of the words listed above. Then write the number of each of the following statements and the word from the list that it best fits. You will not use all the words.

1. Has an origin that can be traced back to a Latin root and prefix.

2. Has an uncertain origin.

3. Comes from a Greek word with a similar spelling.

4. Comes from an Old English word.

5. Has an Old French origin for which no word is given.

Lu Xun 1881–1936

The writings of Lu Xun realistically portrayed Chinese rural life, customs, and beliefs, and dealt with the problems of poverty, ignorance, superstition, and injustice. Often called the greatest writer of modern China, he aimed his works at social reform.

He was born Chou Shu-jen in the province of Chekiang (che'kyang'), where he experienced both wealth and poverty. His family survived great financial loss through the efforts of his mother, whose family name, Lu, he later adopted as a pen name.

Lu Xun was educated in the traditional Chinese way, but exposure to Western literature and science impressed him with the need for China to modernize. In his novels, short stories (upon which his fame was built), essays, and critical writings, he met his own challenge to Chinese writers to "take off their masks, look life honestly, penetratingly, and boldly in the face, and write of flesh and blood."

Unit 5 Review: *Tradition in Fiction*

Content Review

1. In both "The Sentimentality of William Tavener" and "The Needle" a mother is looking after her offspring's best interest. Identify the mothers and compare and contrast their backgrounds; then explain what each considers her offspring's "best interest" to be and how she goes about getting it.

2. The narrators in both "The Man from Kabul" and "My Old Home" meet again with friends they have not seen in years. Tell in each case who the friend was and under what circumstances the narrator had last seen him. Next, explain the realization each narrator took from the meeting.

3. To what extent are the main characters in "The Necklace," "The Interlopers," and "The Rat Trap" to blame for the predicaments they find themselves in? To what extent are their problems caused by fate or coincidence? Explain the role character vs. fate plays in each story. In which do you think fate is strongest? Why?

4. Contrast the train rides of Mrs. Hansen in "Enemies" and the mother in "Tuesday Siesta" in terms of their destinations, the purposes of their journeys, their relative comfort, and so on. Do you think each woman will remember her train ride equally vividly? Why or why not?

5. Growing up was not a happy experience for either Paul in "The Rocking-Horse Winner" or Yoshiko in "The Jay." Locate a symbol in each story that the character would say stands for him or her; then explain how that symbol is related to the story's happy or sad ending.

6. Read these statements about the stories in the unit that are listed below. Explain which story fits best with each statement, and why. You will not use all the stories. **(a)** A statement made in jest to a child foreshadows the future for both the child and the speaker; **(b)** The setting plays a large part in creating the oppressive mood; **(c)** The ending is a good example of irony of situation; **(d)** The satire in this story is amusing rather than cruel; **(e)** "The kindness and good example of a stranger can change a person's negative outlook on life" is the theme.

The Necklace	The Rat Trap
The Needle	The Man from Kabul
Tuesday Siesta	Action Will Be Taken

Concept Review: Interpretation of New Material

Read the short story that follows. Then use the questions that come after it to review your understanding of the concepts and literary terms presented in this unit.

The Death of the Dauphin[1] • *Alphonse Daudet* France

The little Dauphin is ill; the little Dauphin is dying. In all the churches of the kingdom the Holy Sacrament remains exposed night and day, and great tapers burn, for the recovery of the royal child. The streets of the old capital are sad and silent, the bells ring no more, the carriages slacken their pace. In the neighborhood of the palace the curious townspeople gaze through the railings upon the beadles with gilded paunches, who converse in the courts and put on important airs.

---

1. ***Dauphin*** (dô′fən), the oldest son of the king of France, used as a title from 1349 to 1830.

"The Death of the Dauphin" by Alphonse Daudet from *Treasury of World Literature,* edited by Dagobert D. Runes. Reprinted by permission of Philosophical Library, Publishers.

Alphonse Daudet (dō dā′).

All the castle is in a flutter. Chamberlains and major-domos run up and down the marble stairways. The galleries are full of pages and of courtiers in silken apparel, who hurry from one group to another, begging in low tones for news. Upon the wide perrons the maids of honor, in tears, exchange low courtesies and wipe their eyes with daintily embroidered handkerchiefs.

A large assemblage of robed physicians has gathered in the Orangery.[2] They can be seen through the panes waving their long black sleeves and inclining their periwigs with professional gestures. The governor and the equerry of the little Dauphin walk up and down before the door awaiting the decision of the Faculty. Scullions pass by without saluting them. The equerry swears like a pagan; the governor quotes verses from Horace.[3]

And meanwhile, over there, in the direction of the stables, is heard a long and plaintive neighing; it is the little Dauphin's sorrel, forgotten by the hostlers, and calling sadly before his empty manger.

And the King? Where is his highness the King? The King has locked himself up in a room at the other end of the castle. Majesties do not like to be seen weeping. For the Queen it is different. Sitting by the bedside of the little Dauphin, she bows her fair face, bathed in tears, and sobs very loudly before everybody, like a mere draper's wife.

On the bed embroidered with lace the little Dauphin, whiter than the pillows on which he is extended, lies with closed eyes. They think that he is asleep; but no, the little Dauphin is not asleep. He turns towards his mother, and seeing her tears, he asks:

"*Madame la Reine,*[4] why do you weep? Do you really believe that I am going to die?"

The Queen tries to answer. Sobs prevent her from speaking.

"Do not weep, *Madame la Reine.* You forget that I am the Dauphin, and that Dauphins cannot die thus."

The Queen sobs more violently, and the little Dauphin begins to feel frightened.

"Holloa!" says he, "I do not want Death to come and take me away, and I know how to prevent him from coming here. Order up on the spot forty of the strongest lansquenets[5] to keep guard around our bed! Have a hundred big cannons watch day and night, with lighted fuses, under our windows! And woe to Death if he dares to come near us!"

In order to humor the royal child, the Queen makes a sign. On the spot the great cannons are heard rolling in the courts, and forty tall lansquenets, with halberds in their fists, draw up around the room. They are all veterans, with grizzly mustaches. The little Dauphin claps his hands on seeing them. He recognizes one, and calls,

"Lorrain! Lorrain!"

The veteran makes a step towards the bed.

"I love you well, my old Lorrain. Let me see your big sword. If Death wants to fetch me, you will kill him, won't you?"

Lorrain answers:

"Yes, *Monseigneur.*"[6]

And two great tears roll down his tanned cheeks.

At that moment the chaplain approaches the little Dauphin and, pointing to the crucifix, talks to him in low tones. The little Dauphin listens with astonished air; then, suddenly interrupting him,

"I understand well what you are saying, *Monsieur l'Abbé;*[7] but still, couldn't my little friend Beppo die in my place, if I gave him plenty of money?"

The chaplain continues to talk to him in low tones, and the little Dauphin looks more and more astonished.

When the chaplain has finished, the little Dauphin resumes, with a heavy sigh:

"What you have said is all very sad, *Monsieur l'Abbé*; but one thing consoles me, and that is that up there, in the Paradise of the stars, I shall still be the Dauphin. I know that the good God is my cousin, and cannot fail to treat me according to my rank."

Then he adds, turning towards his mother:

"Bring me my fairest clothes, my doublet of white

---

2. ***Orangery*** (ôr′inj rē), an elaborately styled greenhouse built to house the delicate greenery of a palatial estate.
3. ***Horace,*** Roman poet and satirist, 65 B.C.–8 B.C.
4. ***Madame la Reine*** (lä ren′), Madam Queen. [*French*]
5. ***lansquenets*** (län skə nā′), German mercenary soldiers in service to another country, such as France.
6. ***Monseigneur*** (môɴ se nyær′), title of honor given to princes, bishops, and other persons of importance. [*French*]
7. ***Monsieur l'Abbé*** (lȧ bā′), title of respect given to a priest. [*French*].

ermine, and my pumps of velvet! I wish to look brave to the angels, and to enter Paradise in the dress of a Dauphin."

A third time the chaplain bends over the little Dauphin, and talks to him in low tones. In the midst of his discourse the royal child interrupts him angrily.

"Why, then," he cries, "to be Dauphin is nothing at all!"

And refusing to listen to anything more, the little Dauphin turns towards the wall and weeps bitterly.

---

1. Identify one clue in the first paragraph that the story is set in the past.

2. Which word best describes the mood of the workers in the palace? **(a)** prayerful; **(b)** plotting; **(c)** frantic; **(d)** resigned.

3. The Dauphin's horse **(a)** will be put to sleep after its master dies; **(b)** is brought outside the Dauphin's window; **(c)** threw the Dauphin and seriously injured him; **(d)** is ignored in all the activity.

4. What is similar about the reactions of the King and Queen? **(a)** Both weep; **(b)** Both pray in the chapel; **(c)** Both sit at the Dauphin's bedside; **(d)** Both wish to supervise the funeral arrangements.

5. What is the first reason the Dauphin gives for believing that he will not die?

6. Why does the Dauphin ask for forty lansquenets and a hundred cannon? **(a)** to show he is Dauphin; **(b)** to frighten the physicians into curing him; **(c)** to impress his friend Beppo; **(d)** to frighten Death away.

7. Which lansquenet does he speak to specifically?

8. Why doesn't the author tell you exactly what the chaplain says to the Dauphin? **(a)** He feels the chaplain's comments are meant for the Dauphin's ears only; **(b)** The reader can infer what the chaplain says from the Dauphin's responses; **(c)** The author doesn't want to give the ending away; **(d)** The author doesn't want to make the chaplain too important a character.

9. What thought consoles the Dauphin when he is convinced he is dying? **(a)** that everyone has to die sometime; **(b)** that he will be with God; **(c)** that he will be able to wear his best clothes; **(d)** that he will keep his rank in heaven.

10. What irony of life does the Dauphin finally come to realize?

Composition Review

Choose one of the following assignments.

1. Neither "The Interlopers" nor "Tuesday Siesta" has an absolutely clear ending: we think we know what happened to the characters, but we're not positive. Choose one of the stories and decide what you would say if you could add three more paragraphs to the end of it. Make sure your ending fits the context.

Write the three paragraphs, making them sound as much like the author's style as possible.

2. Both "Action Will Be Taken" and "The Rat Trap" involve factories, but those factories are presented quite differently. Review the stories, noting differences between the factories and determining reasons for the differences, such as the time, the location, or the purpose of the story.

Write a three- or four-paragraph composition contrasting the two factories and explaining why you think they are so different.

3. Can a very short story be as effective as a longer one? Think about what the authors of "The Rocking-Horse Winner" (the longest story in the unit) and "The Death of the Dauphin" (the shortest) were trying to accomplish and how well each met his goals. Then decide which story you think is more successful.

Write a three-paragraph composition beginning "A very short [long] story can be just as effective as a very long [short] one." Back up that statement with specifics from the story you've chosen.

Unit 6

Shakespearean Drama

Julius Caesar

Background

Date and Source

Julius Caesar is a play of political intrigue, assassination, and revenge set against the backdrop of the Roman Empire. It features not one but two possible heroes out of its four major characters and ultimately depicts the downfall of both of them. It makes clear the temptations and effects of power even on those who desire it least.

Written by William Shakespeare in 1599, *Julius Caesar* was among the first plays to be presented at the new Globe Theater, the home of Shakespeare's acting company since earlier that year. The play is generally regarded to have been written just after *Henry IV,* a history play, and just before *As You Like It,* a comedy. It was the first tragedy Shakespeare wrote after *Romeo and Juliet* (1597); his next tragedy, *Hamlet,* did not appear until 1603.

Shakespeare drew on Plutarch's *Lives of the Noble Greeks and Romans,* translated from Latin by Sir Thomas North, for most of the material in the play. "The Life of Caesar" gave him much of the basic plot; "The Life of Brutus" provided characterization, especially of Brutus and Cassius; and "The Life of Mark Antony" gave him background on Antony (as well as the idea for another tragedy, *Antony and Cleopatra,* 1606).

Major Characters

Julius Caesar 100 B.C.–44 B.C.

A great conqueror, soldier, and politician, Caesar was popular because he gained territory for Rome and because he frequently sent money back to the city to be used for public works or to help the common people. Because of his conquests he was ultimately given the honor of ruling Rome for as long as he lived, but he was still not satisfied; many suspected that he wanted to set up a monarchy so that power would pass to his heirs as well. Caesar was married to Calpurnia, but thus far she had borne him no children.

Marcus Brutus 85 B.C.–42 B.C.

A descendant of Lucius Junius Brutus, who had driven out the Tarquin kings and made Rome a republic, Brutus was a quiet, idealistic man who enjoyed reading and study. At one time he had supported Pompey, one of Caesar's chief rivals for power, and fought with him against Caesar. After Pompey's defeat Caesar pardoned Brutus and the two resumed an interrupted friendship. Though Brutus liked Caesar, he feared that Caesar's ambition endangered the future of the republic. Brutus was married to Portia, whose father had killed himself rather than submit to Caesar's rule.

Caius Cassius ? B.C.–42 B.C.

Cassius, who had married Brutus' sister Tertia and thus was Brutus' brother-in-law, was a thin, quick-tempered, practical man with a personal grudge against Caesar. With Brutus, he had supported Pompey in his war against Caesar. After Brutus was pardoned, Caesar, at his request, also pardoned Cassius.

Mark Antony 83 B.C.–30 B.C.

A young man notorious for his wild living, Antony had fought under Caesar and supported his ambitious schemes. A holder of various public offices, including that of tribune, Antony understood the commoners and their general instability, and knew just how to speak to them to control their actions.

The Globe Theater

The theater in which *Julius Caesar* was introduced was located across the Thames (temz) River from

London, in an area called the Bankside. A detailed model of the Globe, constructed by Dr. J. C. Adams of Hofstra University and located at the Folger Shakespeare Library in Washington, D.C., provides much useful information about the place where many of Shakespeare's plays were first staged.

The Globe Theater was octagonal in shape, three stories high, and constructed of oak timbers and white plaster walls. Rising above the thatched roof were three attached "huts" and a tower from which a flag flew on days when a play was to be presented. Playgoers could see this flag from London and would hurry to be ferried across the river for the 2:00 P.M. performance. (Without electricity, of course, no plays could be presented at night.)

Within the theater were three galleries, or seating areas for spectators, each projecting slightly beyond the one beneath it. The galleries and the area behind the stage were roofed, as was the stage itself, but the rest of the interior was open to the elements. This unprotected area, necessary to allow light and air into the crowded theater, was where the groundlings—apprentices and others who could afford only a penny to see the play—stood.

At one end of this unroofed area, or yard, was the performing area. This consisted of a *platform stage* (1) that projected well out into the audience area. Two ornate pillars, one at either end of the front of the stage, supported a *canopy* (2), on which rested the *huts* (3) and the playhouse *turret* (4). On the under part of the canopy, which was painted blue, were pictures of the sun, the moon, and the signs of the zodiac: this area was referred to as the *Heavens.*

Under the platform stage, and sometimes used for acting, was an area where stage props were stored known as *Hell* (5). In the center of the platform stage was a large *trap door* (6) that provided access from this lower area. The trap door was not visible to the audience until it was opened from below.

Behind the platform stage, and serving as a background, was a three-storied structure called the *tiring house.* On its first level it contained a curtained *inner stage* (7), sometimes called the *study,* which was flanked at right and left by *doors* (8). The second level held the *balcony stage* (9) and, behind it, a second curtained area known as the *chamber.* The balcony stage projected slightly over the platform and was flanked by *bay-window stages* (10). The curtained *music gallery* (11), on the third level, could also function as a stage.

The platform-level inner stage and the balcony-level chamber were almost identical. When the front curtains of either stage were drawn apart, the inner area suggested the interior of a room. The side walls were made of tapestry hangings that could be changed between scenes, and each rear wall had a door and a window with similar tapestry hangings in between. The doors were connected by a stairway allowing access from one level to the next, but both they and the windows could be completely covered with tapestries if the scene required it. By using appropriate wall coverings throughout, the inner stage could represent a variety of enclosed scenes.

Nearly all parts of the performing area were used in a production of *Julius Caesar.* Most outdoor scenes took place on the platform and most indoor ones on the inner stage or balcony stage, but there are also scenes where the platform and inner stage were used simultaneously, and even one using the trap door. To help you visualize the action, notes at the beginning of each scene tell the main parts of the performing area on which it was acted.

As the Play Opens

For many years Caesar had been struggling with Pompey, once his ally, for control of Rome and its territories. Eventually warfare broke out between them, and in 48 B.C. Caesar, a superb military man, defeated Pompey at the Battle of Pharsalus (fär sā′ləs). Fleeing to Egypt for safety, Pompey was murdered there by a servant of the ruler, but the war was taken up by his two sons. They, however, were also defeated by Caesar—in 45 B.C. at the Battle of Munda in Spain—and one was killed.

Returning to Rome, Caesar was first named dictator and then dictator for life. Many Romans, including Brutus' brother-in-law Cassius, became suspicious of Caesar's growing power and feared that he meant to put an end to their republic, which had been in existence since the last of the Tarquin kings was overthrown in 509 B.C. Still other Romans were angry that Caesar wished to celebrate a public triumph over Pompey's sons, who were not foreigners but Romans like themselves.

The action begins on February 15, 44 B.C., the feast of the Lupercalia (lü′pər kā′lē ə) and the day that Caesar has selected to celebrate his triumph.

See **BLANK VERSE** Handbook of Literary Terms

Julius Caesar

William Shakespeare Great Britain

CHARACTERS

JULIUS CAESAR

OCTAVIUS CAESAR, MARK ANTONY, M. AEMILIUS LEPIDUS — *triumvirs° after the death of Julius Caesar*

CICERO, PUBLIUS, POPILIUS LENA — *senators*

MARCUS BRUTUS, CASSIUS, CASCA, TREBONIUS, CAIUS LIGARIUS, DECIUS BRUTUS, METELLUS CIMBER, CINNA — *conspirators against Julius Caesar*

FLAVIUS *and* MARULLUS, *tribunes°*

ARTEMIDORUS OF CINDOS, *a teacher of rhetoric*

SOOTHSAYER

CINNA, *a poet*

Another POET

LUCILIUS, TITINIUS, MESSALA, YOUNG CATO, VOLUMNIUS, FLAVIUS — *officers under Brutus and Cassius*

VARRO, CLITUS, CLAUDIUS, DARDANIUS — *soldiers in Brutus' army*

STRATO, LUCIUS — *servants and slaves to Brutus*

PINDARUS, *servant and slave to Cassius*

CALPURNIA, *wife to Caesar*

PORTIA, *wife to Brutus*

SENATORS, CITIZENS, GUARDS, ATTENDANTS, *etc.*

triumvirs (trī um′vərz), joint rulers.

tribunes, elected officials who serve as spokesmen for the commoners and protect them from the government if necessary.

Slightly abridged.

Act One

Scene 1: Rome. A street. (Played on the Platform.)
It is February fifteenth, the festival of Lupercalia. The COMMONERS *are in a holiday mood, eager to celebrate* CAESAR*'s victory over* POMPEY*'s sons.*

A crowd of excited COMMONERS, *dressed in holiday garments, rush onto the platform at left door. All talk at once and look expectantly toward the right, the direction from which* CAESAR*'s procession will appear. Offstage shouts and cheers, indications that* CAESAR *draws closer, send the* COMMONERS *scurrying for vantage points.*

Meanwhile, the tribunes FLAVIUS *and* MARULLUS *have entered at inner-stage curtains. As they stride briskly forward, it is apparent that they disapprove of the general holiday mood.* FLAVIUS *addresses the* COMMONERS *angrily.*

FLAVIUS. Hence! Home, you idle creatures, get you home!
Is this a holiday? What, know you not,
Being mechanical,° you ought not walk
Upon a laboring day without the sign
Of your profession?° *(Singling one out)* Speak, what trade art thou?[1]

CARPENTER. Why, sir, a carpenter.

MARULLUS. Where is thy leather apron and thy rule?
What dost thou with thy best apparel on?
(To another) You, sir, what trade are you?

COBBLER. Truly, sir, in respect of a fine workman, I am but, as you would say, a cobbler.°

MARULLUS *(impatiently).* But what trade art thou? Answer me directly.

COBBLER. A trade, sir, that I hope I may use with a safe conscience, which is indeed, sir, a mender of bad soles.[2]

(The COMMONERS *laugh at the pun.)*

FLAVIUS. What trade, thou knave? Thou naughty knave, what trade?

COBBLER. Nay, I beseech you, sir, be not out with me.° Yet if you be out, sir, I can mend you.

FLAVIUS. What mean'st thou by that? Mend me, thou saucy fellow?

COBBLER. Why, sir, cobble you.

FLAVIUS *(scowling).* Thou art a cobbler, art thou?

COBBLER. Truly, sir, all that I live by is with the awl. I meddle with no trademan's matters, nor women's matters; but withal° I am indeed, sir, a surgeon to old shoes. When they are in great danger, I recover them. As proper men as ever trod upon neat's leather° have gone upon my handiwork.

mechanical, workingmen.

you ought not . . . profession, a reference to a law of Shakespeare's own time requiring workers to wear their laboring clothes and carry the tools of their profession.

1. How are the opening lines of the play effective in getting audience attention?

cobbler. In Shakespeare's time this word meant a clumsy workman and did not refer only to a mender of soles. That explains Marullus' next question.

2. Shakespeare usually has characters from upper social levels, like Marullus and Flavius, speak in blank verse; the commoners speak prose. What other indication is there that Marullus and Flavius outrank the commoners?

be not . . . me, a pun. *To be out* means "out of temper" and also "having worn-out soles."

withal, yet. This is also a pun on "with awl" (a shoemaker's tool).

as ever . . . leather, as ever wore shoes.

FLAVIUS. But wherefore art not in thy shop today?
Why dost thou lead these men about the streets?
COBBLER *(grinning)*. Truly, sir, to wear out their shoes, to get myself into more work. But indeed, sir, we make holiday to see Caesar and to rejoice in his triumph.
(The mob shouts its agreement.)
MARULLUS *(addressing the mob)*. Wherefore rejoice? What
conquest brings he home?
What tributaries° follow him to Rome,
To grace in captive bonds his chariot-wheels?
(The shouting of the mob grows louder.)
You blocks, you stones, you worse than senseless things!
O you hard hearts, you cruel men of Rome,
Knew you not Pompey?° Many a time and oft
Have you climbed up to walls and battlements,
To towers and windows, yea, to chimney-tops,°
Your infants in your arms, and there have sat
The livelong day, with patient expectation,
To see great Pompey pass the streets of Rome.
And when you saw his chariot but appear,
Have you not made an universal shout,
That Tiber° trembled underneath her banks
To hear the replication° of your sounds
Made in her concave shores?
And do you now put on your best attire?
And do you now cull out a holiday?
And do you now strew flowers in his way
That comes in triumph over Pompey's blood?°
(The mob, subdued by MARULLUS' *words, is silent now.)*
Be gone!
Run to your houses, fall upon your knees,
Pray to the gods to intermit° the plague
That needs must light on this ingratitude.[3]
FLAVIUS. Go, go, good countrymen, and, for this fault,
Assemble all the poor men of your sort;
Draw them to Tiber banks, and weep your tears
Into the channel, till the lowest stream
Do kiss the most exalted shores of all.°
(The COMMONERS, *singly or in pairs, file off the platform at left.)*
(To MARULLUS*)* See whether their basest metal be not moved.
They vanish tongue-tied in their guiltiness.
(There is a loud flourish of trumpets offstage.)
Go you down that way towards the Capitol;
This way will I. Disrobe the images°
If you do find them decked with ceremonies.
MARULLUS *(cautiously)*. May we do so?

tributaries, captives who must pay tribute to Rome for their freedom.

Knew . . . Pompey? Not long before, the fickle mob had been cheering this enemy of Caesar.

chimney-tops. Ancient Rome did not have chimney-tops, but Shakespeare's England did. An error such as this, deliberate or otherwise, is called an anachronism (ə nak′rə niz′əm). The play contains a number of others; look for them as you read.

Tiber (tī′bər), a river flowing through Rome.

replication, echo.

Pompey's blood, Pompey's sons.

intermit, withhold.

3. Why does Marullus want the commoners to stop their celebrating?

weep your tears . . . of all, weep enough tears to bring the lowest waterline up to the highest.

Disrobe the images, take down the decorations that have been placed on Caesar's statues.

You know it is the feast of Lupercal.°
FLAVIUS. It is no matter. Let no images
Be hung with Caesar's trophies. I'll about,
And drive away the vulgar° from the streets.
So do you too, where you perceive them thick.
These growing feathers° plucked from Caesar's wing
Will make him fly an ordinary pitch,
Who else would soar above the view of men
And keep us all in servile fearfulness.[4]
(The TRIBUNES *exit, going in different directions.)*

the feast of Lupercal, celebrated in honor of Lupercus, god of fertility. The young priest-celebrants ran a specified course, striking people who stood in their way with goatskin thongs. Women desiring children purposely sought to be struck as a cure for barrenness.

the vulgar, the commoners.

These growing feathers, Caesar's new followers. Falconers sometimes clip their birds' wings to keep them from flying too great a height, or pitch. So Caesar, without the help of the commoners, would be checked in his ambition to rise.

4. What conflict has already been set up in this first scene?

Scene 2: Rome. A public place. (Played on the Platform.)
Groups of COMMONERS *run onto the platform, looking offstage at* CAESAR'*s approaching procession.* SOLDIERS *march on at right door and force people back so the procession can pass. There is a loud flourish of trumpets; and* CAESAR *appears at right, accompanied by* ANTONY, CALPURNIA, PORTIA, DECIUS, CICERO, BRUTUS, CASSIUS, *and* CASCA. *More* COMMONERS *follow, among them a* SOOTHSAYER. *Last come* FLAVIUS *and* MARULLUS, *watching but saying nothing. Amid cheers,* CAESAR *leads the procession well onto the platform, then stops. All bow, rendering* CAESAR *homage.*

CAESAR. Calpurnia!
CASCA. Peace, ho! Caesar speaks.
CAESAR. Calpurnia!
CALPURNIA *(stepping forward).* Here, my lord.
CAESAR. Stand you directly in Antonius' way,
When he doth run his course.° Antonius!
*(*ANTONY *hurries forward and stands before* CAESAR.*)*
ANTONY. Caesar, my lord?
CAESAR. Forget not, in your speed, Antonius,
To touch Calpurnia; for our elders say,
The barren, touchèd in this holy chase,
Shake off their sterile curse.
ANTONY. I shall remember.
When Caesar says, "Do this," it is performed. *(He steps back.)*
CAESAR. Set on, and leave no ceremony out.[5]
(The trumpets flourish; the procession starts forward.)
SOOTHSAYER *(in awesome tones).* Caesar!
CAESAR *(stopping).* Ha?° Who calls?
(The crowd murmurs, wondering who thus has accosted CAESAR.*)*
CASCA. Bid every noise be still. Peace yet again!
CAESAR. Who is it in the press that calls on me?
I hear a tongue, shriller than all the music,
Cry "Caesar!" Speak. Caesar is turned to hear.[6]
SOOTHSAYER *(ominously).* Beware the ides of March.°

When he doth run his course. Antony, as one of the priests of Lupercus, is one of the young nobles making the run through the streets.

5. *Lines 6–10.* Why does Caesar want Antony to touch Calpurnia? How will those Romans who think Caesar wants to be king react to his words to Antony?

Ha? an expression of surprise rather than laughter.

6. This is the first hint of Caesar's deafness, something not mentioned in Shakespeare's source, Plutarch. Why might Shakespeare have included it as part of his characterization of Caesar?

the ides (īdz) ***of March,*** March 15.

CAESAR *(looking to right and left).* What man is that?
BRUTUS. A soothsayer bids you beware the ides of March.
CAESAR. Set him before me; let me see his face.
CASSIUS *(stepping forward).* Fellow, come from the throng. Look upon Caesar.

(SOLDIERS drag the SOOTHSAYER before CAESAR.)

CAESAR. What sayest thou to me now? Speak once again.
SOOTHSAYER. Beware the ides of March.

(For a moment CAESAR, looking disturbed, stares at the SOOTHSAYER; then he turns to ANTONY, who begins to laugh. When others join in, CAESAR with a gesture dismisses the SOOTHSAYER.)

CAESAR. He is a dreamer. Let us leave him. Pass.[7]

(The trumpets flourish; the procession and the crowd go out at left, BRUTUS and CASSIUS remaining behind. BRUTUS stands at one side, lost in thought. CASSIUS approaches him.)

CASSIUS. Will you go see the order of the course?
BRUTUS. Not I.
CASSIUS. I pray you, do.
BRUTUS. I am not gamesome. I do lack some part
Of that quick spirit° that is in Antony.
Let me not hinder, Cassius, your desires;
I'll leave you.

7. How does Caesar respond to the Soothsayer's warning? Do you think the presence of the crowd influenced his response? Explain.

quick spirit, lively disposition.

CASSIUS. Brutus, I do observe you now of late.
I have not from your eyes that gentleness
And show of love as I was wont to have.°
You bear too stubborn and too strange a hand
Over your friend that loves you.

BRUTUS. Cassius,
Be not deceived. If I have veiled my look,
I turn the trouble of my countenance
Merely upon myself.° Vexed I am
Of late with passions of some difference,
Conceptions only proper to myself,
Which give some soil, perhaps, to my behaviors.
But let not therefore my good friends be grieved—
Among which number, Cassius, be you one—
Nor construe any further my neglect,
Than that poor Brutus, with himself at war,
Forgets the shows of love to other men.[8]

CASSIUS. Then, Brutus, I have much mistook your passion,
By means whereof this breast of mine hath buried
Thoughts of great value, worthy cogitations.°
Tell me, good Brutus, can you see your face?

BRUTUS. No, Cassius, for the eye sees not itself
But by reflection, by some other things.

(He moves toward front platform; CASSIUS *follows.)*

CASSIUS. 'Tis just.
And it is very much lamented, Brutus,
That you have no such mirrors as will turn
Your hidden worthiness into your eye,
That you might see your shadow. I have heard
Where many of the best respect in Rome,
Except immortal Caesar, speaking of Brutus
And groaning underneath this age's yoke,
Have wished that noble Brutus had his eyes.

BRUTUS *(facing* CASSIUS*).* Into what dangers would you lead me, Cassius,
That you would have me seek into myself
For that which is not in me?

CASSIUS. Therefore, good Brutus, be prepared to hear;
And since you know you cannot see yourself
So well as by reflection, I, your glass,
Will modestly discover to yourself
That of yourself which you yet know not of.
And be not jealous on me, gentle Brutus.
Were I a common laughter,° or did use
To stale with ordinary oaths my love
To every new protester; if you know

as I was wont to have, that I customarily had.

I turn . . . upon myself. Brutus is troubled by his own thoughts, not by anything Cassius has done to him.

8. *Lines 32–47.* Cassius complains of Brutus' unusual behavior. How does he describe it? What is Brutus' response?

Then . . . worthy cogitations. Here Cassius hints at the thoughts (cogitations) locked in his own breast and begins sounding out Brutus to see whether he has the same thoughts and will join with the conspirators.

a common laughter, a buffoon laughed at or scorned by everyone.

That I do fawn on men and hug them hard
And after scandal them, or if you know
That I profess myself in banqueting
To all the rout,° then hold me dangerous.

the rout, the rabble; worthless people.

(There is a flourish of trumpets offstage, then loud cheers.
BRUTUS *and* CASSIUS *look up.)*

BRUTUS. What means this shouting? I do fear the people
Choose Caesar for their king.
CASSIUS. Ay, do you fear it?
Then must I think you would not have it so.[9]

9. Upon what statement of Brutus' does Cassius pounce? What does this reveal about Cassius' feelings toward Caesar?

BRUTUS. I would not, Cassius, yet I love him well.
But wherefore do you hold me here so long?
What is it that you would impart to me?
If it be aught toward the general good,
Set honor in one eye and death in the other,
And I will look on both indifferently;°
For let the gods so speed me as I love
The name of honor more than I fear death.

If it be . . . indifferently. If what Cassius has in mind is for the public welfare and is honorable, Brutus will do it even if it means death.

CASSIUS. I know that virtue to be in you, Brutus,
As well as I do know your outward favor.
Well, honor is the subject of my story.
I cannot tell what you and other men
Think of this life; but, for my single self,
I had as lief not be as live to be
In awe of such a thing as I myself.
I was born free as Caesar; so were you.
We both have fed as well, and we can both
Endure the winter's cold as well as he.
For once, upon a raw and gusty day,
The troubled Tiber chafing with her shores,
Caesar said to me, "Darest thou, Cassius, now
Leap in with me into this angry flood,
And swim to yonder point?" Upon the word,
Accoutered° as I was, I plungèd in
And bade him follow; so indeed he did.

Accoutered (ə kü'tərd) ***as I was.*** Cassius was fully dressed.

The torrent roared, and we did buffet it,
With lusty sinews throwing it aside
And stemming it with hearts of controversy;
But ere we could arrive the point proposed,
Caesar cried, "Help me, Cassius, or I sink!"
Ay, as Aeneas, our great ancestor,
Did from the flames of Troy upon his shoulder
The old Anchises bear,° so from the waves of Tiber
Did I the tired Caesar. *(Angrily)* And this man
Is now become a god, and Cassius is
A wretched creature and must bend his body

as Aeneas (i nē'əs) ***. . . Anchises*** (an kī'sēz) ***bear.*** Aeneas, carrying his aged father Anchises and leading his little son, escaped from burning Troy and wandered for years. Finally he reached the banks of the Tiber, where his descendants founded Rome.

If Caesar carelessly but nod on him. *(He pauses.)*
He had a fever when he was in Spain,
And when the fit was on him, I did mark
How he did shake. 'Tis true, this god did shake.
His coward lips did from their color fly,°
And that same eye whose bend doth awe the world
Did lose his° luster. I did hear him groan.
Ay, and that tongue of his that bade the Romans
Mark him and write his speeches in their books,
"Alas," it cried, "Give me some drink, Titinius,"
As a sick girl. Ye gods, it doth amaze me
A man of such a feeble temper° should
So get the start of the majestic world
And bear the palm° alone.[10]
(Loud shouts and the flourish of trumpets heard offstage)
BRUTUS *(crossing to right pillar).* Another general shout?
I do believe that these applauses are
For some new honors that are heaped on Caesar.
CASSIUS *(following).* Why, man, he doth bestride the narrow world
Like a Colossus,° and we petty men
Walk under his huge legs and peep about
To find ourselves dishonorable graves.
Men at some time are masters of their fates.
The fault, dear Brutus, is not in our stars,
But in ourselves, that we are underlings.[11]
Brutus and Caesar. What should be in that "Caesar"?
Why should that name be sounded more than yours?
Write them together, yours is as fair a name;
Sound them, it doth become the mouth as well;
Weigh them, it is as heavy; conjure with 'em,
"Brutus" will start a spirit° as soon as "Caesar."
Now, in the names of all the gods at once,
Upon what meat doth this our Caesar feed
That he is grown so great? Age, thou art shamed!
Rome, thou hast lost the breed of noble bloods!
When went there by an age, since the great flood,
But it was famed with more than with one man?
When could they say, till now, that talked of Rome,
That her wide walks encompassed but one man?
Now is it Rome indeed and room enough,
When there is in it but one only man.
O, you and I have heard our fathers say
There was a Brutus once that would have brooked
The eternal devil to keep his state in Rome
As easily as a king.[12]
(Loud shouts and the flourish of trumpets offstage)

His coward lips . . . fly. His lips became white.

his, *its* in modern usage.

A man . . . feeble temper. The Romans worshipped physical strength, and here Cassius paints Caesar as a physical weakling.

the palm, symbol of victory.

10. *Lines 100–131.* What physical weaknesses does Cassius say Caesar has? How suitable are these to a great public hero and conqueror?

Like a Colossus (kə los′əs). The Colossus was a huge statue of Apollo at Rhodes. According to legend, it was so enormous that it bestrode the entrance to the harbor, and ships passed between its legs.

11. *Lines 140–141.* These lines are often quoted. Explain in your own words what they mean.

start a spirit, call forth a ghost from the spirit world.

12. *Lines 159–161.* Cassius suggests that Brutus' ancestor Lucius Junius Brutus, the founder of the republic, would have allowed the devil to set up his throne in Rome as easily as he would have allowed a king to. Why might Cassius be reminding his friend of this earlier Brutus?

BRUTUS. That you do love me, I am nothing jealous.
What you would work me to, I have some aim.
How I have thought of this, and of these times,
I shall recount hereafter. For this present,
I would not, so with love I might entreat you,
Be any further moved. What you have said
I will consider; what you have to say
I will with patience hear, and find a time
Both meet to hear and answer such high things.
Till then, my noble friend, chew upon this:
Brutus had rather be a villager
Than to repute himself a son of Rome
Under these hard conditions as this time
Is like to lay upon us.

CASSIUS. I am glad that my weak words
Have struck but thus much show of fire from Brutus.

(The sounds of approaching people are heard from offstage.)

BRUTUS. The games are done and Caesar is returning.

CASSIUS. As they pass by, pluck Casca by the sleeve,
And he will, after his sour fashion, tell you
What hath proceeded worthy note today.

(CAESAR and his followers reenter at left and start across the platform, ANTONY on CAESAR's left, CASCA following at rear.)

BRUTUS. I will do so. But, look you, Cassius,
The angry spot doth glow on Caesar's brow,
And all the rest look like a chidden train.°
Calpurnia's cheek is pale, and Cicero
Looks with such ferret and such fiery eyes°
As we have seen him in the Capitol,
Being crossed in conference by some senators.[13]

CASSIUS. Casca will tell us what the matter is.

(CAESAR stops before he reaches center platform and looks speculatively at CASSIUS.)

CAESAR. Antonius!

ANTONY. Caesar?

CAESAR. Let me have men about me that are fat,
Sleek-headed men, and such as sleep o' nights.
Yond Cassius has a lean and hungry look.
He thinks too much. Such men are dangerous.[14]

ANTONY. Fear him not, Caesar; he's not dangerous.
He is a noble Roman, and well given.

CAESAR. Would he were fatter! But I fear him not.
Yet if my name were liable to fear,
I do not know the man I should avoid
So soon as that spare Cassius. He reads much,
He is a great observer, and he looks

like a chidden train, like a group of people who were harshly scolded.

such ferret . . . eyes, red and angry-looking eyes, like a weasel's.

13. By their appearance, Caesar and his followers have undergone a radical change of mood. How do they now feel?

14. What reason does Caesar give for calling Cassius dangerous? Do you agree with Caesar's opinion? Why might Cassius be so opposed to Caesar?

Quite through the deeds of men. He loves no plays,
As thou dost, Antony; he hears no music.
Seldom he smiles, and smiles in such a sort
As if he mocked himself and scorned his spirit
That could be moved to smile at anything.
Such men as he be never at heart's ease
Whiles they behold a greater than themselves,
And therefore are they very dangerous.
I rather tell thee what is to be feared
Than what I fear; for always I am Caesar.[15]
Come on my right hand, for this ear is deaf,
And tell me truly what thou think'st of him.

*(*ANTONY *steps to* CAESAR*'s right. The trumpets sound and the procession, with* CASCA *still at rear, moves slowly out at right. When* CASCA *reaches center platform he is detained by* BRUTUS *and* CASSIUS.*)*

CASCA. You pulled me by the cloak. Would you speak with me?

BRUTUS. Ay, Casca. Tell us what hath chanced today,
That Caesar looks so sad.

CASCA. Why, you were with him, were you not?

BRUTUS. I should not then ask Casca what had chanced.

CASCA. Why, there was a crown offered him, and being offered him, he put it by with the back of his hand, thus; and then the people fell a-shouting.[16]

BRUTUS. What was the second noise for?

CASCA. Why, for that too.

CASSIUS. They shouted thrice. What was the last cry for?

CASCA. Why, for that too.

BRUTUS *(incredulously).* Was the crown offered him thrice?

CASCA. Ay, marry,° was't, and he put it by thrice, every time gentler than other, and at every putting-by mine honest neighbors shouted.

CASSIUS. Who offered him the crown?

CASCA. Why, Antony.

BRUTUS. Tell us the manner of it, gentle Casca.

CASCA. I can as well be hanged as tell the manner of it. It was mere foolery; I did not mark it. I saw Mark Antony offer him a crown—yet 'twas not a crown neither, 'twas one of these coronets—and, as I told you, he put it by once; but, for all that, to my thinking, he would fain have had it. Then he offered it to him again; then he put it by again; but, to my thinking, he was very loath to lay his fingers off it. And then he offered it the third time. He put it the third time by, and still as he refused it, the rabblement hooted and clapped their chapped hands, and threw up their sweaty nightcaps,° and uttered such a deal of stinking breath because Caesar refused the crown that it

15. *Lines 211–212.* What insight into Caesar's character do these lines give? Note the two lines that follow; how do they contradict Caesar's opinion of himself?

16. Note that Casca speaks here in prose, not blank verse. How might what Cassius says in lines 179–181 about Casca's manner of speaking account for this?

marry, a mild oath.

nightcaps, an anachronism.

had almost choked Caesar, for he swounded and fell down at it. And for mine own part I durst not laugh, for fear of opening my lips and receiving the bad air.[17]

CASSIUS. But, soft, I pray you. What, did Caesar swoon?

CASCA. He fell down in the market-place, and foamed at mouth, and was speechless.

BRUTUS. 'Tis very like. He hath the falling sickness.

CASSIUS. No, Caesar hath it not, but you and I,
And honest Casca, we have the falling sickness.

CASCA. I know not what you mean by that, but I am sure Caesar fell down. If the tag-rag people did not clap him and hiss him, according as he pleased and displeased them, as they use to do the players in the theater, I am no true man.

BRUTUS. What said he when he came unto himself?

CASCA. Marry, before he fell down, when he perceived the common herd was glad he refused the crown, he plucked me ope his doublet° and offered them his throat to cut. An° I had been a man of any occupation, if I would not have taken him at a word, I would I might go to hell among the rogues. And so he fell. When he came to himself again, he said, If he had done or said anything amiss, he desired their worships to think it was his infirmity. Three or four wenches, where I stood, cried, "Alas, good soul!" and forgave him with all their hearts. But there's no heed to be taken of them. If Caesar had stabbed their mothers, they would have done no less.

BRUTUS. And after that, he came thus sad away?

CASCA. Ay.

CASSIUS. Did Cicero say anything?

CASCA. Ay, he spoke Greek.

CASSIUS. To what effect?

CASCA. Nay, an I tell you that, I'll ne'er look you i' th' face again. But those that understood him smiled at one another and shook their heads; but, for mine own part, it was Greek to me.° I could tell you more news too. Marullus and Flavius, for pulling scarfs off Caesar's images, are put to silence.° Fare you well. There was more foolery yet, if I could remember it.

CASSIUS. Will you sup with me tonight, Casca?

CASCA. No, I am promised forth.

CASSIUS. Will you dine with me tomorrow?

CASCA. Ay, if I be alive, and your mind hold, and your dinner worth the eating.

CASSIUS. Good. I will expect you.

CASCA. Do so. Farewell, both. *(He exits at inner-stage curtains.)*

BRUTUS. What a blunt fellow is this grown to be!
He was quick mettle° when he went to school.

CASSIUS. So is he now in execution

17. Based on Casca's description, how do you think the commoners felt about Caesar being given a crown?

doublet, a man's close-fitting jacket. Doublets were not worn until about the 1400s; hence, another anachronism.

An, if

it was Greek to me, a saying popular even today when a person is unable to understand something—and Shakespeare never does tell what Cicero said.

put to silence, deprived of their rank as tribunes, which permitted them to speak for the people.

quick mettle, easily stirred to action.

Of any bold or noble enterprise,
However he puts on this tardy form.
This rudeness is a sauce to his good wit,
Which gives men stomach to digest his words
With better appetite.

BRUTUS. And so it is. For this time I will leave you.
Tomorrow, if you please to speak with me,
I will come home to you; or, if you will,
Come home to me, and I will wait for you.

CASSIUS. I will do so. Till then, think of the world.
(BRUTUS exits at left.)
Well, Brutus, thou art noble. Yet I see
Thy honorable metal may be wrought
From that it is disposed.° Therefore it is meet°
That noble minds keep ever with their likes;
For who so firm that cannot be seduced?
Caesar doth bear me hard,° but he loves Brutus.
If I were Brutus now and he were Cassius,
He should not humor me.° I will this night,
In several hands,° in at his windows, throw,
As if they came from several citizens,
Writings, all tending to the great opinion
That Rome holds of his name, wherein obscurely
Caesar's ambition shall be glancèd at.°
And after this let Caesar seat him sure,
For we will shake him, or worse days endure.[18]
(He exits at inner-stage curtains.)

Scene 3: Rome. A street. (Played on the Platform.)
It is the night before the ides of March. A month has gone by since CASSIUS first spoke to BRUTUS about CAESAR. Unperturbed by this wild night, CICERO enters at left. There is lightning and thunder as CASCA, his sword drawn, enters at right.

CICERO *(calmly).* Good even,° Casca. Brought you Caesar home?
Why are you breathless? And why stare you so?

CASCA. Are not you moved, when all the sway of earth
Shakes like a thing unfirm? O Cicero,
I have seen tempests when the scolding winds
Have rived the knotty oaks, and I have seen
The ambitious ocean swell and rage and foam
To be exalted with the threatening clouds;
But never till tonight, never till now,
Did I go through a tempest dropping fire.
(More thunder, then a scream. CASCA darts to left pillar.)
Either there is a civil strife in heaven,

Thy honorable . . . disposed, your spirit can be turned from its natural inclination.

meet, fitting; appropriate.

Caesar . . . hard, Caesar hates me.

humor me, win me over to his opinions.

In several hands, in different handwritings.

glancèd at, hinted at.

18. *Lines 301–315.* This is the play's first soliloquy (sə lil′ə kwē)—a speech in which a character expresses honestly to the audience his or her inmost thoughts. Explain in your own words what Cassius is saying.

even, evening.

Or else the world, too saucy with the gods,
Incenses them to send destruction.
CICERO *(drawing closer).* Why, saw you anything more wonderful?
CASCA. A common slave—you know him well by sight—
Held up his left hand, which did flame and burn
Like twenty torches joined, and yet his hand,
Not sensible of fire,° remained unscorched.
Besides—I had not since put up my sword—
Against° the Capitol I met a lion,
Who glazed° upon me, and went surly by
Without annoying me. And there were drawn
Upon a heap a hundred ghastly women,
Transformèd with their fear, who swore they saw
Men, all in fire, walk up and down the streets.
And yesterday the bird of night did sit
Even at noon-day upon the market-place,
Hooting and shrieking.[19] When these prodigies
Do so conjointly meet, let not men say
"These are their reasons, they are natural,"
For I believe they are portentous things
Unto the climate that they point upon.°
CICERO. Indeed, it is a strange-disposèd time.
But men may construe things after their fashion,
Clean from the purpose of the things themselves.°
Comes Caesar to the Capitol tomorrow?
CASCA. He doth; for he did bid Antonius
Send word to you he would be there tomorrow.
CICERO. Good night then, Casca. This disturbèd sky
Is not to walk in.
CASCA. Farewell, Cicero.
(CICERO *exits at right. There is another flash of lightning and*

Not sensible of fire, not feeling the fire.

Against, opposite; nearby.

glazed, peered; stared.

19. What unusual sights has Casca seen?

When these prodigies . . . upon. Though some may try to explain these marvels (prodigies) as natural, Casca regards them as omens foretelling disaster for Rome.

But men . . . themselves. Cicero thinks men who are inclined that way will often read undue significance into happenings such as these.

CASCA *retreats to rear platform, where he takes shelter under the projecting balcony.* CASSIUS *enters at left.)*

CASSIUS. Who's there?
CASCA. A Roman.
CASSIUS. Casca, by your voice.

(He joins CASCA *under the balcony.)*

CASCA. Your ear is good. Cassius, what night° is this!

what night, what a night.

CASSIUS. A very pleasing night to honest men.
CASCA. Who ever knew the heavens menace so?
CASSIUS. Those that have known the earth so full of faults.
For my part, I have walked about the streets,
Submitting me unto the perilous night,
And, thus unbracèd,° Casca, as you see,
Have bared my bosom to the thunder-stone;
And when the cross blue lightning seemed to open
The breast of heaven, I did present myself
Even in the aim and very flash of it.

thus unbracèd. Cassius opens his garment at the neck, exposing his chest to the thunderbolts.

CASCA. But wherefore did you so much tempt the heavens?
It is the part of men to fear and tremble,
When the most mighty gods by tokens send
Such dreadful heralds to astonish us.
CASSIUS. You are dull, Casca, and those sparks of life
That should be in a Roman you do want,
Or else you use not. You look pale, and gaze,
And put on fear, and cast yourself in wonder,
To see the strange impatience of the heavens.
But if you would consider the true cause
Why all these fires, why all these gliding ghosts,
Why birds and beasts from quality and kind,
Why old men, fools, and children calculate,°
Why all these things change from their ordinance,°
Their natures, and preformed faculties,
To monstrous quality—why, you shall find
That heaven hath infused them with these spirits
To make them instruments of fear and warning
Unto some monstrous state.
Now could I, Casca, name to thee a man
Most like this dreadful night,
That thunders, lightens, opens graves, and roars
As doth the lion in the Capitol—
A man no mightier than thyself or me
In personal action, yet prodigious grown
And fearful, as these strange eruptions are.[20]

calculate, prophesy.

ordinance, accustomed ways.

20. How do you know whom Cassius is referring to?

CASCA. 'Tis Caesar that you mean, is it not, Cassius?
CASSIUS. Let it be who it is. For Romans now
Have thews and limbs like to their ancestors;

But, woe the while, our fathers' minds are dead,
And we are governed with our mothers' spirits.
Our yoke and sufferance show us womanish.

CASCA. Indeed, they say the senators tomorrow
Mean to establish Caesar as a king,
And he shall wear his crown by sea and land,
In every place, save here in Italy.

CASSIUS. I know where I will wear this dagger then;
Cassius from bondage will deliver Cassius.
Therein, ye gods, you make the weak most strong;
Therein, ye gods, you tyrants do defeat.
Nor stony tower, nor walls of beaten brass,
Nor airless dungeon, nor strong links of iron,
Can be retentive to the strength of spirit;
But life, being weary of these worldly bars,
Never lacks power to dismiss itself.
If I know this, know all the world besides,
That part of tyranny that I do bear
I can shake off at pleasure.[21]

21. What does Cassius say he will do if Caesar becomes king?

(The thunder rumbles; the two men gradually move forward.)

CASCA. So can I.
So every bondman in his own hand bears
The power to cancel his captivity.

CASSIUS. And why should Caesar be a tyrant then?
Poor man, I know he would not be a wolf,
But that he sees the Romans are but sheep;
He were no lion, were not Romans hinds.°
Those that with haste will make a mighty fire
Begin it with weak straws. What trash is Rome,
What rubbish and what offal, when it serves
For the base matter to illuminate
So vile a thing as Caesar! But, O grief,
Where hast thou led me? I perhaps speak this
Before a willing bondman; then I know
My answer must be made. But I am armed,
And dangers are to me indifferent.

He were . . . hinds. Caesar's ambition would not be so great had he less chance of attaining it. The Romans are so weak that they made Caesar appear lionlike by contrast.

CASCA. You speak to Casca, and to such a man
That is no fleering° tell-tale. *(Offering his hand)* Hold, my hand.
Be factious for redress of all these griefs,°
And I will set this foot of mine as far
As who goes farthest.[22]

fleering, deceitful.

Be factious . . . griefs, be ready to join Casca to right the grievances Romans have suffered at Caesar's hands.

22. How does Casca react to Cassius' dangerous words about Caesar?

CASSIUS. There's a bargain made.
Now know you, Casca, I have moved already
Some certain of the noblest-minded Romans
To undergo with me an enterprise
Of honorable-dangerous consequence;

And I do know, by this, they stay for me
In Pompey's porch.° For now, this fearful night,
There is no stir or walking in the streets,
And the complexion of the element
In favor's° like the work we have in hand,
Most bloody, fiery, and most terrible.

(Hurrying footsteps are heard offstage at right.)

CASCA. Stand close awhile, for here comes one in haste.

CASSIUS. 'Tis Cinna; I do know him by his gait.
He is a friend.

(CINNA enters in haste.)

Cinna, where haste you so?

CINNA. To find out you. *(Moving forward)* Who's that? Metellus Cimber?

CASSIUS. No, it is Casca; one incorporate
To our attempts.° Am I not stayed for, Cinna?

CINNA. I am glad on't. What a fearful night is this!
There's two or three of us have seen strange sights.

CASSIUS. Am I not stayed for? Tell me.

CINNA. Yes, you are. O Cassius, if you could
But win the noble Brutus to our party—

CASSIUS. Be you content. Good Cinna, take this paper,
And look you lay it in the praetor's chair,°
Where Brutus may but find it. And throw this
In at his window. Set this up with wax
Upon old Brutus'° statue.[23] All this done,
Repair to Pompey's porch, where you shall find us.
Is Decius Brutus and Trebonius there?

CINNA *(stopping)*. All but Metellus Cimber; and he's gone
To seek you at your house. Well, I will hie,
And so bestow these papers as you bade me.

CASSIUS. That done, repair to Pompey's theater.

(CINNA runs off at right as CASSIUS turns to CASCA.)

Come, Casca, you and I will yet ere day
See Brutus at his house. Three parts of him
Is ours already, and the man entire
Upon the next encounter yields him ours.°

CASCA. O, he sits high in all the people's hearts;
And that which would appear offense in us,
His countenance, like richest alchemy,
Will change to virtue and to worthiness.[24]

CASSIUS. Him and his worth, and our great need of him,
You have right well conceited.° Let us go,
For it is after midnight, and ere day
We will awake him and be sure of him.

(He and CASCA exit at right.)

stay . . . porch, wait for me on the porch of Pompey's theater.

the element . . . favor's, the sky is in appearance.

one incorporate . . . attempts, one who knows our plans and is in sympathy with them.

in the praetor's chair. Brutus at this time was a praetor (prē′tər), a Roman judge or magistrate.

old Brutus', Lucius Junius Brutus'.

23. What are these papers that Cassius wants positioned for Brutus to find?

Three parts . . . ours. Brutus is almost persuaded to join the conspirators; when they next meet with him, they will undoubtedly win him over completely.

24. Why are the conspirators so eager to have Brutus join them?

conceited, estimated.

Discussion

Scene 1

1. Shakespeare portrays the commoners as being easily swayed by emotion or by smooth talkers. **(a)** What feelings do they express for Caesar as the scene opens? **(b)** What does Marullus' long speech force them to recall?

2. What two contrasting opinions of Caesar do you get from this scene?

Scene 2

1. Characterize Caesar as he appears in the opening lines of the scene.

2. In the lengthy discussion between Brutus and Cassius, how does Cassius manage to make the following points: **(a)** that Rome is suffering under the tyranny of Caesar, who is no better a man than he or Brutus; **(b)** that not to oppose Caesar is to be disloyal to Rome; **(c)** that Brutus is an honorable man whose country needs him.

3. How might Casca's description of the encounter between Caesar and Antony add to the "fear" Brutus earlier said he had?

4. **(a)** How does this scene clarify the main conflict of the play? **(b)** On which side do you think Brutus will decide to be?

Scene 3

1. **(a)** Contrast Cassius' and Casca's reactions to the strange events occurring that night. **(b)** In what way do the two men agree about what is about to happen?

2. In what way does the conspiracy become more solidified in this scene?

Application

Blank Verse

Though writers of lengthy works in blank verse will sometimes insert short lines for dramatic effect, there are other ways to make blank verse more flexible.

1. A grave accent (`) can be used to add an extra syllable to a line. In "Indeed, it is a strange-disposèd time," *disposèd* is pronounced in three syllables, thus giving the line the correct meter. Find another line using a grave accent in Act One and read it aloud.

2. Blank-verse lines are less choppy if they flow into each other with no punctuation at the end of them to make the reader pause. Act One, Scene 2, lines 135–138 is a good example of a sentence that runs four lines without an end-stop. Locate these lines and read them aloud; then find another similar example in Act One.

Vocabulary

Context

Read the listed words within their context in the play. After determining their meanings, rewrite the sentences following the list to include the appropriate words. You will not use all the words.

servile (Scene 1, line 75)
countenance (Scene 2, line 38)
repute (Scene 2, line 173)
loath (Scene 2, line 240)
portentous (Scene 3, line 31)
prodigious (Scene 3, line 77)

1. Trying to set a new record, the student swallowed an amazing number of goldfish.

2. We were all extremely reluctant to ford the river, but there was no other way across.

3. Michael and Tony the police consider to be the leaders of the gang.

4. He interpreted the three hawks circling over the campfire as indicating evil to come.

5. She refuses to put herself in such a slavelike position.

Act Two

Scene 1: Rome. Brutus' orchard.° (Played on the Platform, Inner Stage, and Bay-Window Stage.)

orchard, garden.

It is a few hours later. The scene opens as the curtains of the inner stage are drawn apart to reveal BRUTUS *in a secluded corner of his garden. He is seated, deep in thought, on a small bench which is flanked by a pair of trees.* BRUTUS *has spent a wakeful night, and now begins to walk restlessly back and forth. Suddenly he strides forward, onto the platform, and calls to his* SERVING BOY, *who is asleep just inside the upper-right window.*

BRUTUS *(at the window).* What, Lucius, ho!
(To himself) I cannot, by the progress of the stars,
Give guess how near to day. *(Calling)* Lucius, I say!
I would it were my fault to sleep so soundly.
When, Lucius, when? Awake, I say! What, Lucius!

*(*LUCIUS *appears at the window, opens the casement, and leans out.)*

LUCIUS *(sleepily).* Called you, my lord?

BRUTUS. Get me a taper in my study, Lucius.
When it is lighted, come and call me here.

LUCIUS. I will, my lord.

(As LUCIUS *withdraws,* BRUTUS *resumes his restless pacing. He is alone with his thoughts, which he now speaks.)*

BRUTUS. It must be by his° death. And, for my part,
I know no personal cause to spurn at him,
But for the general.° He would be crowned.
How that might change his nature, there's the question.
It is the bright day that brings forth the adder,
And that craves wary walking. Crown him that,
And then I grant we put a sting in him
That at his will he may do danger with.
The abuse of greatness is when it disjoins
Remorse° from power. And, to speak truth of Caesar,
I have not known when his affections swayed
More than his reason. But 'tis a common proof
That lowliness is young ambition's ladder,
Whereto the climber-upward turns his face;
But when he once attains the upmost round,
He then unto the ladder turns his back,
Looks in the clouds, scorning the base degrees
By which he did ascend. So Caesar may.
Then, lest he may, prevent.° And, since the quarrel
Will bear no color for the thing he is,
Fashion it thus: that what he is, augmented,

his, Caesar's.

I know no personal . . . general. Though Brutus has no personal reason for striking at Caesar, he nevertheless feels he should do so for the public (general) good.

Remorse, pity.

prevent, he must be prevented.

Would run to these and these extremities.
And therefore think him as a serpent's egg
Which, hatched, would, as his kind, grow mischievous,
And kill him in the shell.[25]

25. *Lines 10–34.* What reasons does Brutus consider for assassinating Caesar? [Note that this is the first of four, fairly short, related soliloquies; to keep his audience's—including the groundlings'—attention, Shakespeare usually avoided very long speeches.]

*(*LUCIUS*, yawning, enters the platform at right door. He carries a letter—a small scroll.)*

LUCIUS. The taper burneth in your closet,° sir.
Searching the window for a flint, I found
This paper, thus sealed up, and I am sure
It did not lie there when I went to bed.

closet, study; room.

(He gives BRUTUS *the letter.)*

BRUTUS. Get you to bed again. It is not day.
*(*LUCIUS *starts to leave.)*
Is not tomorrow, boy, the ides of March?
LUCIUS. I know not, sir.
BRUTUS. Look in the calendar, and bring me word.
LUCIUS. I will, sir. *(He exits at right.)*
BRUTUS. The exhalations whizzing in the air°
Give so much light that I may read by them.

The exhalations . . . air, the falling stars.

(He opens the letter and reads.)
"Brutus, thou sleepest; awake, and see thyself!
Shall Rome, etc. Speak, strike, redress!
Brutus, thou sleepest; awake!"
Such instigations have been often dropped
Where I have took them up.
"Shall Rome, etc." Thus must I piece it out:
Shall Rome stand under one man's awe? What, Rome?
My ancestors did from the streets of Rome
The Tarquin° drive, when he was called a king.
"Speak, strike, redress!" Am I entreated
To speak and strike? *(He raises a clenched fist.)* O Rome, I make thee promise,
If the redress will follow, thou receivest
Thy full petition at the hand of Brutus![26]

The Tarquin, Tarquinius Superbus, the last Roman king.

26. How does Brutus react to Cassius' carefully placed letter?

*(*LUCIUS *reenters.)*
LUCIUS. Sir, March is wasted fifteen days.
(There is a knock at left.)
BRUTUS. 'Tis good. Go to the gate; somebody knocks.
*(*LUCIUS *hurries to open the door at left.)*
Since Cassius first did whet me against Caesar,
I have not slept.
Between the acting of a dreadful thing
And the first motion, all the interim is
Like a phantasma, or a hideous dream.
The Genius and the mortal instruments°
Are then in council; and the state of man,

The Genius . . . instruments, the soul and the body.

Like to a little kingdom, suffers then
The nature of an insurrection.[27]

27. *Lines 61–69.* What do these lines show about Brutus' conscience? What figure of speech is used in lines 67–69? Explain its meaning.

LUCIUS *(rejoining* BRUTUS*).* Sir, 'tis your brother° Cassius at the door,
Who doth desire to see you.

brother, that is, brother-in-law. Cassius was married to Brutus' sister.

BRUTUS. Is he alone?
LUCIUS. No, sir, there are moe° with him.

moe, more.

BRUTUS. Do you know them?
LUCIUS. No, sir; their hats are plucked about their ears,
And half their faces buried in their cloaks,°
That by no means I may discover them
By any mark of favor.°

hats . . . cloaks. Both are anachronisms.

any mark of favor, any features by which they can be recognized.

BRUTUS. Let 'em enter.
*(*LUCIUS *hurries to open the door at left.)*
They are the faction. O conspiracy,
Sham'st thou to show thy dangerous brow by night,
When evils are most free? O, then by day
Where wilt thou find a cavern dark enough
To mask thy monstrous visage?[28] Seek none, conspiracy!
Hide it in smiles and affability;
For if thou path, thy native semblance on,
Not Erebus itself were dim enough
To hide thee from prevention.°

28. What do these lines reveal of Brutus' feelings about the conspiracy?

For if thou . . . prevention. If the conspirators walk about (path) wearing their natural appearance (not assuming false smiles and affability), not even Erebus (er'ə bəs) would be dark (dim) enough to keep them from detection. Erebus, according to Greek and Roman mythology, was a dark, gloomy place through which the dead passed en route to Hades.

*(*LUCIUS *ushers in the* CONSPIRATORS—CASSIUS, CASCA, DECIUS, CINNA, METELLUS CIMBER, LIGARIUS, *and* TREBONIUS. *While the* CONSPIRATORS *are approaching* BRUTUS, LUCIUS *exits at right.)*

CASSIUS *(stepping forward).* I think we are too bold upon your rest.
Good morrow, Brutus. Do we trouble you?
BRUTUS. I have been up this hour, awake all night.
Know I these men that come along with you?
CASSIUS. Yes, every man of them, and no man here
But honors you; and every one doth wish
You had but that opinion of yourself
Which every noble Roman bears of you.
This is Trebonius.
BRUTUS *(extending his hand).* He is welcome hither.
CASSIUS. This, Decius Brutus.
BRUTUS. He is welcome too.
CASSIUS. This, Casca; this, Cinna; and this, Metellus Cimber.
BRUTUS. They are all welcome.[29]
What watchful cares do interpose themselves
Betwixt your eyes and night?

29. Does Brutus' courteous behavior toward the conspirators agree with what he said in lines 81–85? Explain.

CASSIUS. Shall I entreat a word?
*(*BRUTUS *and* CASSIUS *step back to speak privately. The other* CONSPIRATORS *talk idly.)*
DECIUS. Here lies the east. Doth not the day break here?

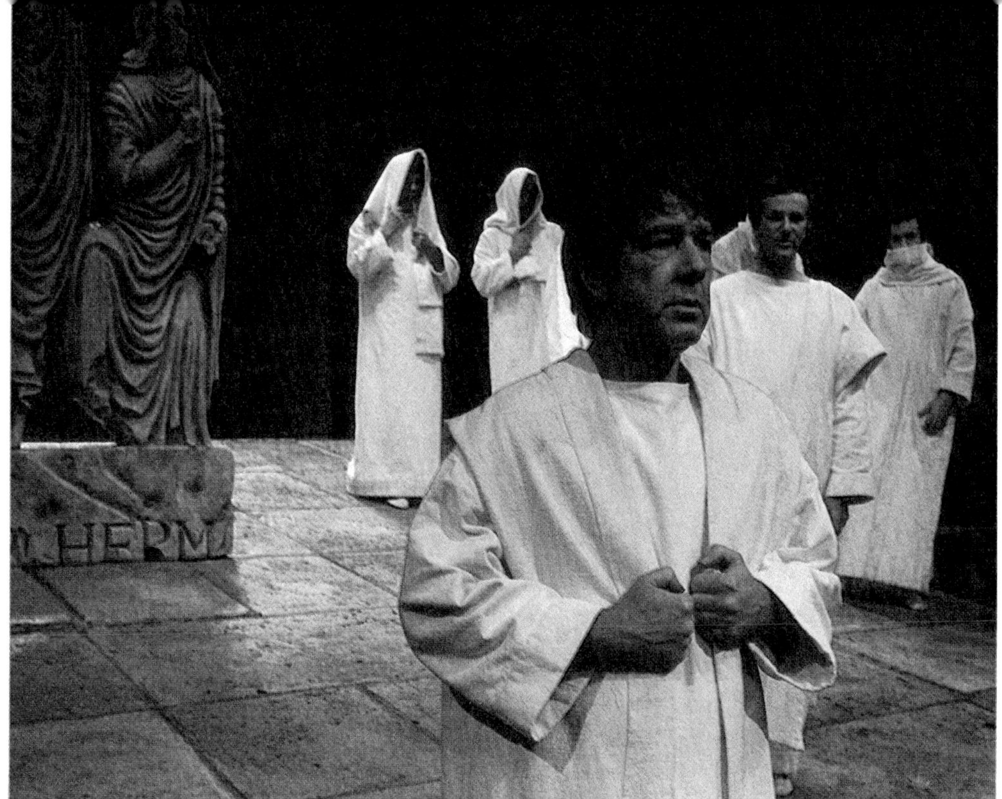

CASCA. No.
CINNA. O, pardon, sir, it doth; and yon gray lines
That fret the clouds are messengers of day.
CASCA. You shall confess that you are both deceived.
Here, as I point my sword, the sun arises,
Which is a great way growing on° the south,
Weighing the youthful season of the year.
Some two months hence, up higher toward the north
He first presents his fire; and the high east
Stands, as the Capitol, directly here.
*(*BRUTUS *and* CASSIUS *rejoin the group.)*
BRUTUS. Give me your hands all over, one by one.
CASSIUS. And let us swear our resolution.
BRUTUS. No, not an oath. If not the face of men,
The sufferance of our souls, the time's abuse—
If these be motives weak, break off betimes,
And every man hence to his idle bed;
So let high-sighted tyranny range on,
Till each man drop by lottery.° But if these,
As I am sure they do, bear fire enough
To kindle cowards and to steel with valor
The melting spirits of women, then, countrymen,
What need we any spur but our own cause
To prick us to redress? What other bond
Than secret Romans, that have spoke the word,
And will not palter?° And what other oath

growing on, toward.

If not the face . . . by lottery. If the wrongs the conspirators see about them are not sufficient to bind them to firm purpose, then let each man go his own way, become a weakling, and die when it suits a tyrant's whims.

palter, talk insincerely.

Than honesty to honesty engaged
That this shall be, or we will fall for it?
Swear priests and cowards, and men cautelous,°
Old feeble carrions, and such suffering souls
That welcome wrongs; unto bad causes swear
Such creatures as men doubt; but do not stain
The even virtue of our enterprise,
Nor the insuppressive mettle of our spirits,
To think that or our cause or° our performance
Did need an oath.[30] . . .

CASSIUS. But what of Cicero? Shall we sound him?
I think he will stand very strong with us.

CASCA. Let us not leave him out.

CINNA. No, by no means.

METELLUS. O, let us have him, for his silver hairs
Will purchase us a good opinion
And buy men's voices to commend our deeds.
It shall be said his judgment ruled our hands;
Our youths and wildness shall no whit appear,
But all be buried in his gravity.

BRUTUS. O, name him not. Let us not break with him;°
For he will never follow anything
That other men begin.[31]

CASSIUS. Then leave him out.

CASCA. Indeed he is not fit.

DECIUS. Shall no man else be touched but only Caesar?

CASSIUS. Decius, well urged. I think it is not meet
Mark Antony, so well beloved of Caesar,
Should outlive Caesar. We shall find of him
A shrewd contriver; and you know, his means,
If he improve° them, may well stretch so far
As to annoy° us all. Which to prevent,
Let Antony and Caesar fall together.

BRUTUS. Our course will seem too bloody, Caius Cassius,
To cut the head off and then hack the limbs,
Like wrath in death and envy afterwards;
For Antony is but a limb of Caesar.[32]
Let's be sacrificers, but not butchers, Caius.
We all stand up against the spirit of Caesar,
And in the spirit of men there is no blood.
O, that we then could come by Caesar's spirit,
And not dismember Caesar! But, alas,
Caesar must bleed for it. And, gentle friends,
Let's kill him boldly, but not wrathfully;
Let's carve him as a dish fit for the gods,
Not hew him as a carcass fit for hounds.

cautelous, deceitful.

or . . . or, either . . . or.

30. What are Brutus' reasons for not wanting the conspirators to swear loyalty oaths? How practical is his viewpoint?

break with him, break the news of the conspiracy to him.

31. *Lines 137–148.* Note the practical reasons the conspirators mention for having Cicero, a well-known statesman, join them; and how Brutus, always an idealist, goes against their advice. From now on Cassius will let Brutus assume the leadership of the conspiracy and go along with his wishes, and Brutus will continue to make errors in judgment such as this. What reason does Brutus give for his decision?

improve, exploit; make good use of.

annoy, harm.

32. Subsequent events will prove that this is Brutus' second error in judgment. What are his reasons for not wanting to kill Antony?

And let our hearts, as subtle masters do,
Stir up their servants° to an act of rage,
And after seem to chide them. This shall make
Our purpose necessary, and not envious;
Which so appearing to the common eyes,
We shall be called purgers, not murderers.[33]
And for Mark Antony, think not of him;
For he can do no more than Caesar's arm
When Caesar's head is off.

CASSIUS *(still unconvinced).* Yet I fear him,
For in the ingrafted love he bears to Caesar—

BRUTUS. Alas, good Cassius, do not think of him.
If he love Caesar, all that he can do
Is to himself—take thought and die for Caesar.
And that were much he should, for he is given
To sports, to wildness, and much company.

TREBONIUS. There is no fear in him.° Let him not die,
For he will live, and laugh at this hereafter.

(A clock offstage begins to strike.)

BRUTUS. Peace! Count the clock.°

CASSIUS. The clock hath stricken three.

TREBONIUS. 'Tis time to part.

CASSIUS. But it is doubtful yet
Whether Caesar will come forth today, or no;
For he is superstitious grown of late,
Quite from the main opinion he held once
Of fantasy, of dreams, and ceremonies.
It may be these apparent prodigies,
The unaccustomed terror of this night,
And the persuasion of his augurers°
May hold him from the Capitol today.[34]

DECIUS. Never fear that. If he be so resolved,
I can o'ersway him; for he loves to hear
That unicorns may be betrayed with trees,
And bears with glasses, elephants with holes,
Lions with toils,° and men with flatterers;
But when I tell him he hates flatterers,
He says he does, being then most flattered.
Let me work;
For I can give his humor the true bent,
And I will bring him to the Capitol.

CASSIUS. Nay, we will all of us be there to fetch him.

BRUTUS. By the eighth hour. Is that the uttermost?

CINNA. Be that the uttermost, and fail not then.

METELLUS. Caius Ligarius doth bear Caesar hard,
Who rated° him for speaking well of Pompey.

their servants, our hands.

33. Do you think the commoners will understand the distinction Brutus is making? Discuss.

There is no fear in him, there is no reason to fear Antony.

Count the clock, one of the most famous anachronisms in the play. Yet Shakespeare had to have some way of conveying to his audience what time it was.

augurers (ô'gər ərz), priests who predicted the future by reading signs. Also called *augurs.*

34. What reasons does Cassius give for the possibility of Caesar's not going to the Capitol?

That unicorns . . . toils, methods thought effective for capturing animals. The mythological unicorn was incited to charge; the hunter stepped behind a nearby tree, and the unicorn, unable to stop, drove his horn into the trunk. A bear could supposedly be distracted by putting a mirror in its paws; fascinated by its reflection, it was easy prey for a hunter. Elephants were captured in pits, and lions were sometimes rendered helpless by nets (toils).

rated, berated; angrily rebuked.

I wonder none of you have thought of him.
BRUTUS. Now, good Metellus, go along by him.
He loves me well, and I have given him reasons;
Send him but hither, and I'll fashion him.
CASSIUS. The morning comes upon's. We'll leave you, Brutus.
And, friends, disperse yourselves; but all remember
What you have said, and show yourselves true Romans.
BRUTUS. Good gentlemen, look fresh and merrily;
Let not our looks put on° our purposes,
But bear it as our Roman actors do,
With untired spirits and formal constancy.
And so good morrow to you every one.
(The CONSPIRATORS *exit at left. For a moment* BRUTUS *stands lost in thought; then he crosses to window at upper right and calls.)*
Boy! Lucius! Fast asleep? It is no matter.
Enjoy the honey-heavy dew of slumber.
Thou hast no figures nor no fantasies
Which busy care draws in the brains of men;
Therefore thou sleepest so sound.
*(*PORTIA, *wearing a night robe, enters at right. Her face is pale and worried as she follows* BRUTUS *to the inner stage.)*
PORTIA. Brutus, my lord!
BRUTUS. Portia, what mean you? Wherefore rise you now?
It is not for your health thus to commit
Your weak condition to the raw cold morning.
PORTIA. Nor for yours neither. You've ungently, Brutus,
Stole from my bed. And yesternight, at supper,
You suddenly arose, and walked about,
Musing and sighing, with your arms across,
And when I asked you what the matter was,
You stared upon me with ungentle looks.
I urged you further; then you scratched your head,
And too impatiently stamped with your foot.
Yet I insisted, yet you answered not,
But, with an angry wafture of your hand,
Gave sign for me to leave you.[35] So I did,
Fearing to strengthen that impatience
Which seemed too much enkindled, and withal°
Hoping it was but an effect of humor,°
Which sometime hath his hour with every man.
It will not let you eat, nor talk, nor sleep,
And could it work so much upon your shape
As it hath much prevailed on your condition,
I should not know you, Brutus. *(Pleadingly)* Dear my lord,
Make me acquainted with your cause of grief.
BRUTUS. I am not well in health, and that is all.

put on, betray.

35. What does Portia's thumbnail description of Brutus indicate about his state of mind?

withal, in addition to this.

an effect of humor, a whim.

PORTIA. Brutus is wise, and, were he not in health,
He would embrace the means to come by it.
BRUTUS. Why, so I do. *(He seats himself wearily on the nearby bench.)* Good Portia, go to bed.
PORTIA *(drawing closer).* Is Brutus sick? And is it physical
To walk unbracèd and suck up the humors
Of the dank morning? What, is Brutus sick,
And will he steal out of his wholesome bed
To dare the vile contagion of the night,
And tempt the rheumy and unpurgèd air°
To add unto his sickness? No, my Brutus,
You have some sick offense within your mind,
Which by the right and virtue of my place
I ought to know of. And, upon my knees *(Kneeling)*
I charm you, by my once-commended beauty,
By all your vows of love, and that great vow
Which did incorporate and make us one,
That you unfold to me, your self, your half,
Why you are heavy, and what men tonight
Have had resort to you; for here have been
Some six or seven, who did hide their faces
Even from darkness.
BRUTUS. Kneel not, gentle Portia. *(He raises her.)*
PORTIA. I should not need, if you were gentle Brutus.
Within the bond of marriage, tell me, Brutus,

the rheumy (rü′mē) ***. . . air,*** air that causes colds because it has not yet been purified (purged) by the sun.

Is it excepted I should know no secrets
That appertain to you?° Am I yourself
But, as it were, in sort or limitation,
To keep with you at meals, comfort your bed,
And talk to you sometimes? Dwell I but in the suburbs
Of your good pleasure?

Is it excepted . . . you? Portia is asking if an exception was made in the marriage vows so that she would have no legal right to inquire into Brutus' affairs.

BRUTUS. You are my true and honorable wife,
As dear to me as are the ruddy drops
That visit my sad heart.
PORTIA. If this were true, then should I know this secret.
I grant I am a woman, but withal
A woman that Lord Brutus took to wife.
I grant I am a woman, but withal
A woman well-reputed, Cato's daughter.
Think you I am no stronger than my sex,
Being so fathered° and so husbanded?
Tell me your counsels, I will not disclose 'em.
I have made strong proof of my constancy,
Giving myself a voluntary wound
Here, in the thigh. Can I bear that with patiènce,
And not my husband's secrets? . . .

Being so fathered. Portia's father, Cato, had killed himself rather than submit to Caesar's tyranny. He was Brutus' uncle as well as his father-in-law.

BRUTUS *(to the heavens).* O ye gods,
Render me worthy of this noble wife! *(There is a knock at left.)*
Hark, hark! One knocks. Portia, go in awhile,
And by and by thy bosom shall partake
The secrets of my heart.
All my engagements I will construe° to thee,
All the charactery° of my sad brows.
Leave me with haste.
*(*PORTIA *hastens to right door and exits.)*
Lucius, who's that knocks?

construe, explain.

charactery, lines of worry.

*(*LUCIUS *goes to open door at left and admits* CAIUS LIGARIUS, *who is wearing a kerchief.)*
LUCIUS. Here is a sick man that would speak with you.
BRUTUS. Caius Ligarius, that Metellus spake of.
Boy, stand aside. *(*LUCIUS *exits.)* Caius Ligarius, how?°
LIGARIUS. Vouchsafe good morrow from a feeble tongue.
BRUTUS. O, what a time have you chose out, brave Caius,
To wear a kerchief! Would you were not sick![36]

how? how are you?

36. Caius Ligarius' illness is taken directly from Shakespeare's source, Plutarch. What dramatic effect might Shakespeare have been trying to achieve by including it? Note that wearing a kerchief to combat a cold is another anachronism.

LIGARIUS. I am not sick, if Brutus have in hand
Any exploit worthy the name of honor.
BRUTUS. Such an exploit have I in hand, Ligarius,
Had you a healthful ear to hear of it.
LIGARIUS. By all the gods that Romans bow before,
I here discard my sickness! Soul of Rome! *(He removes kerchief.)*
Brave son, derived from honorable loins!

Thou, like an exorcist, hast conjured up
My mortified spirit.° Now bid me run,
And I will strive with things impossible,
Yea, get the better of them. What's to do?

BRUTUS. A piece of work that will make sick men whole.

LIGARIUS. But are not some whole that we must make sick?

BRUTUS. That must we also. What it is, my Caius,
I shall unfold to thee as we are going
To whom it must be done.

LIGARIUS. Set on your foot,
And with a heart new-fired I follow you,
To do I know not what; but it sufficeth
That Brutus leads me on. *(A clap of thunder sounds.)*

BRUTUS. Follow me, then. *(They exit.)*

conjured . . . spirit, brought to life my deadened spirit.

Scene 2: Rome. Caesar's house. (Played in the Balcony-Stage Chamber.)

It is early morning on the ides of March. Several hours have elapsed since the CONSPIRATORS *met in* BRUTUS' *garden. The curtains of the balcony stage (above) are drawn open just as* CAESAR *enters at right. Speaking to himself, he crosses to the left, where his street robe is draped across a high-backed chair.*

CAESAR. Nor heaven nor earth have been at peace tonight.
Thrice hath Calpurnia in her sleep cried out,
"Help, ho, they murder Caesar!" Who's within? *(He claps.)*

(A SERVANT *enters at left.)*

SERVANT. My lord?

CAESAR. Go bid the priests do present sacrifice
And bring me their opinions of success.°

SERVANT. I will, my lord.

(He exits at the door in the rear wall of the balcony stage as CALPURNIA, *who is clad in her night robe, enters at right.)*

CALPURNIA. What mean you, Caesar? Think you to walk forth?
You shall not stir out of your house today.

CAESAR. Caesar shall forth. The things that threatened me
Ne'er looked but on my back. When they shall see
The face of Caesar, they are vanishèd.[37]

CALPURNIA. Caesar, I never stood on ceremonies,°
Yet now they fright me. There is one within,°
Besides the things that we have heard and seen,
Recounts most horrid sights seen by the watch.
A lioness hath whelpèd in the streets,
And graves have yawned and yielded up their dead;
Fierce fiery warriors fight upon the clouds,
In ranks and squadrons and right form of war,

Go bid the priests . . . success. Caesar wishes to consult the augurers.

37. How do these lines show Caesar's egotism?

never stood on ceremonies, never believed greatly in signs and portents.

one within, a servant.

Which drizzled blood upon the Capitol;
The noise of battle hurtled in the air,
Horses did neigh, and dying men did groan,
And ghosts did shriek and squeal about the streets.
O Caesar, these things are beyond all use,°
And I do fear them.

CAESAR. What can be avoided
Whose end is purposed by the mighty gods?°
Yet Caesar shall go forth; for these predictions
Are to the world in general as to Caesar.

CALPURNIA. When beggars die, there are no comets seen;
The heavens themselves blaze forth the death of princes.[38]

CAESAR. Cowards die many times before their deaths;
The valiant never taste of death but once.[39]
Of all the wonders that I yet have heard,
It seems to me most strange that men should fear,
Seeing that death, a necessary end,
Will come when it will come.

(The SERVANT *reenters.)*

What say the augurers?

SERVANT. They would not have you to stir forth today.
Plucking the entrails of an offering forth,
They could not find a heart within the beast.°

CAESAR. The gods do this in shame of cowardice.
Caesar should be a beast without a heart,
If he should stay at home today for fear.
No, Caesar shall not. Danger knows full well
That Caesar is more dangerous than he.
We° are two lions littered in one day,
And I the elder and more terrible;
And Caesar shall go forth.

CALPURNIA *(going to him).* Alas, my lord,
Your wisdom is consumed in confidence.
Do not go forth today! Call it my fear
That keeps you in the house, and not your own.
We'll send Mark Antony to the Senate-house,
And he shall say you are not well today.
Let me, upon my knee, prevail in this. *(She kneels.)*

CAESAR *(raising her).* Mark Antony shall say I am not well,
And for thy humor I will stay at home.

*(*DECIUS *enters at rear door.)*

Here's Decius Brutus. He shall tell them so.

DECIUS *(bowing).* Caesar, all hail! Good morrow, worthy Caesar.
I come to fetch you to the Senate-house.

CAESAR. And you are come in very happy time
To bear my greeting to the senators

beyond all use, not customary; supernatural.

What can be . . . gods? Note Caesar's belief in fatalism, the idea that fate controls everything that happens.

38. What does Calpurnia mean by this statement?

39. These are often-quoted lines. Explain their meaning.

Plucking . . . the beast. The arrangement of the inner parts (entrails) of an animal was considered significant in foretelling the future.

We, Caesar and danger.

And tell them that I will not come today.
Cannot, is false, and that I dare not, falser;
I will not come today. Tell them so, Decius.
CALPURNIA. Say he is sick.
CAESAR *(loudly).* Shall Caesar send a lie?
Have I in conquest stretched mine arm so far,
To be afeard to tell graybeards the truth?
Decius, go tell them Caesar will not come.
DECIUS. Most mighty Caesar, let me know some cause,
Lest I be laughed at when I tell them so.
CAESAR. The cause is in my will. I will not come;
That is enough to satisfy the Senate.
But for your private satisfaction,
Because I love you, I will let you know.
Calpurnia here, my wife, stays me at home.
She dreamt tonight she saw my statuë,°
Which, like a fountain with an hundred spouts,
Did run pure blood; and many lusty Romans
Came smiling, and did bathe their hands in it.°
And these does she apply for warnings and portents
And evils imminent, and on her knee
Hath begged that I will stay at home today.

statuë (stach′ü ə), pronounced in three syllables for the sake of the meter.

She dreamt . . . hands in it. These lines foreshadow future events. Keep them in mind as you read further.

DECIUS. This dream is all amiss interpreted;
It was a vision fair and fortunate.
Your statue spouting blood in many pipes,
In which so many smiling Romans bathed,
Signifies that from you great Rome shall suck
Reviving blood, and that great men shall press
For tinctures, stains, relics, and cognizance.
This by Calpurnia's dream is signified.
CAESAR. And this way have you well expounded it.
DECIUS. I have, when you have heard what I can say;
And know it now. The Senate have concluded
To give this day a crown to mighty Caesar.
If you shall send them word you will not come,
Their minds may change. Besides, it were a mock
Apt to be rendered,° for some one to say,
"Break up the Senate till another time
When Caesar's wife shall meet with better dreams."
If Caesar hide himself, shall they not whisper
"Lo, Caesar is afraid"?[40]
Pardon me, Caesar, for my dear dear love
To your proceeding bids me tell you this;
And reason to my love is liable.
CAESAR. How foolish do your fears seem now, Calpurnia!
I am ashamèd I did yield to them.

it were a mock . . . rendered, people would likely sneer at Caesar's excuse.

40. Decius said in the previous scene (lines 198–207) that he knew how to handle Caesar. How does he interpret Calpurnia's dream? What other incentives does he give Caesar to go to the Capitol?

Give me my robe, for I will go.
(While DECIUS *is assisting* CAESAR *with his robe,* PUBLIUS, BRUTUS, LIGARIUS, METELLUS, CASCA, TREBONIUS, *and* CINNA *enter at rear door. Each man, in turn, bows to* CAESAR.*)*
And look where Publius is come to fetch me.
PUBLIUS. Good morrow, Caesar.
CAESAR *(in a dignified manner).* Welcome, Publius.
What, Brutus, are you stirred so early too?
Good morrow, Casca. Caius Ligarius,
Caesar was ne'er so much your enemy
As that same ague° which hath made you lean.
What is 't o'clock?
BRUTUS. Caesar, 'tis strucken eight.
CAESAR. I thank you for your pains and courtesy.
*(*ANTONY *enters at rear door.)*
See, Antony, that revels long o' nights,
Is notwithstanding up. Good morrow, Antony.
ANTONY *(bowing).* So to most noble Caesar.
CAESAR. Bid them prepare within.°
I am to blame to be thus waited for.
Now, Cinna. Now, Metellus. What, Trebonius!
I have an hour's talk in store for you;
Remember that you call on me today.
Be near me, that I may remember you.
TREBONIUS. Caesar, I will. *(Aside)* And so near will I be
That your best friends shall wish I had been further.
CAESAR. Good friends, go in, and taste some wine with me,
And we, like friends, will straightway go together.
BRUTUS *(aside).* That every like is not the same, O Caesar,
The heart of Brutus earns to think upon!°
*(*CAESAR, *followed by the others, exits at rear door.* CALPURNIA *waits a moment, then exits as balcony-stage curtains are closed.)*

ague (ā'gyü), fever.

prepare within, set out refreshments in another room.

That every . . . think upon. Brutus' heart grieves that everyone who appears to be a friend is not a friend.

Scene 3: Rome. A street near the Capitol. (Played on the Platform.)
ARTEMIDORUS, *a teacher of rhetoric, enters at left. In his hands he carries a paper which he intends to present to* CAESAR. *Moving slowly across the platform, he reads to himself in a low tone.*

ARTEMIDORUS. "Caesar, beware of Brutus; take heed of Cassius; come not near Casca; have an eye to Cinna; trust not Trebonius; mark well Metellus Cimber; Decius Brutus loves thee not; thou hast wronged Caius Ligarius. There is but one mind in all these men, and it is bent against Caesar. If thou beest not immortal, look about you. Security gives way to conspiracy.° The mighty gods defend thee! Thy lover,° ARTEMIDORUS."[41]
Here will I stand till Caesar pass along,

Security . . . conspiracy, overconfidence eases the way for conspirators.

lover, Shakespeare often used this word to mean "friend."

41. How much does Artemidorus know about the conspiracy?

And as a suitor will I give him this.
My heart laments that virtue cannot live
Out of the teeth of emulation.
If thou read this, O Caesar, thou mayest live;
If not, the Fates with traitors do contrive. *(He exits at right.)*

Scene 4: Rome. Another part of the same street, before the house of Brutus. (Played on the Platform.)
It is now nearly nine o'clock on the morning of the ides of March. Though BRUTUS *left for the Capitol only a short time ago,* PORTIA*'s anxiety has become almost unbearable. She enters the platform at inner-stage curtains, followed by* LUCIUS.

PORTIA. I prithee, boy, run to the Senate-house.
(LUCIUS *starts to speak, but* PORTIA *continues.)*
Stay not to answer me, but get thee gone.
Why dost thou stay?
LUCIUS *(in bewilderment).* To know my errand, madam.
PORTIA. I would have had thee there and here again
Ere I can tell thee what thou shouldst do there.—
(Aside) O constancy,° be strong upon my side,
Set a huge mountain 'tween my heart and tongue!
I have a man's mind, but a woman's might.
How hard it is for women to keep counsel!°—
Art thou here yet?
LUCIUS. Madam, what should I do?
Run to the Capitol, and nothing else?
And so return to you, and nothing else?
PORTIA. Yes, bring me word, boy, if thy lord look well,
For he went sickly forth; and take good note
What Caesar doth, what suitors press to him.
Hark, boy, what noise is that?
LUCIUS. I hear none, madam.
PORTIA. Prithee, listen well.
I heard a bustling rumor, like a fray,°
And the wind brings it from the Capitol.[42]
LUCIUS. Sooth,° madam, I hear nothing.
(The SOOTHSAYER *enters at left.)*
PORTIA *(eagerly).* Come hither, fellow; which way hast thou been?
SOOTHSAYER. At mine own house, good lady.
PORTIA. What is 't o'clock?
SOOTHSAYER. About the ninth hour, lady.
PORTIA. Is Caesar yet gone to the Capitol?
SOOTHSAYER. Madam, not yet. I go to take my stand,
To see him pass on to the Capitol.
PORTIA. Thou hast some suit to Caesar, hast thou not?

constancy, self-control.

to keep counsel, to keep a secret.

like a fray, like fighting.

42. *Lines 1–19.* What is Portia's state of mind? What might account for it?

Sooth, in truth.

SOOTHSAYER. That I have, lady, if it will please Caesar
To be so good to Caesar as to hear me:
I shall beseech him to befriend himself.
PORTIA. Why, know'st thou any harm's intended towards him?[43]
SOOTHSAYER. None that I know will be, much that I fear may
chance.
Good morrow to you. Here the street is narrow.
The throng that follows Caesar at the heels,
Of senators, of praetors, common suitors,
Will crowd a feeble man almost to death.
I'll get me to a place more void,° and there
Speak to great Caesar as he comes along. *(He exits at right.)*
PORTIA. I must go in. Ay me, how weak a thing
The heart of woman is! O Brutus,
The heavens speed thee in thine enterprise![44]
(Aside) Sure, the boy heard me.
(Speaking breathlessly to LUCIUS*)*—Brutus hath a suit
That Caesar will not grant.—O, I grow faint.—
Run, Lucius, and commend me to my lord;
Say I am merry. Come to me again,
And bring me word what he doth say to thee.
*(*LUCIUS *runs off at right;* PORTIA *exits at inner-stage curtains.)*

43. Why might Portia ask the Soothsayer this question?

more void, more empty; less crowded.

44. This line seems to prove that Brutus has told Portia of his plans. Why is she immediately afraid that Lucius has heard her? How does the rest of the speech show her agitation?

Discussion

Scene 1

1. Review Brutus' four short soliloquies at the beginning of the scene. **(a)** Why do you think he decides to join the conspirators? **(b)** Is he totally happy with his decision? Discuss.

2. After assuming the leadership of the conspiracy, Brutus makes two mistakes. **(a)** What are they? **(b)** Which seems more dangerous? Why?

3. Portia is concerned about Brutus' welfare and makes a request of him. **(a)** What is her request? **(b)** What does Brutus ultimately promise her? **(c)** What opinion do you form of their relationship from this discussion?

4. Who else joins the conspiracy in this scene? Explain the circumstances.

Scene 2

1. (a) Compare Calpurnia's request of Caesar with Portia's request of Brutus in the previous scene. **(b)** How do the men's responses differ?

2. (a) Why is Decius the first of the conspirators to arrive at Caesar's house? **(b)** How does he show his understanding of Caesar's personality during their conversation? **(c)** Why does he finally get his way?

3. In what way is this scene significant in furthering the action of the play?

Scenes 3 and 4

1. (a) How does Artemidorus' letter differ from the warnings in earlier scenes? **(b)** Who else expresses an intention to warn Caesar? **(c)** Why do you think Shakespeare placed these warning episodes where he did?

2. (a) Why can you conclude that Portia has learned Brutus' secret? **(b)** Do you think she approves of the plot? Discuss.

Composition

Act One of a Shakespearean tragedy generally introduces the main characters and establishes the conflict; in Act Two one or more of these characters makes a no-turning-back decision. Choose either act to analyze; then review it with this stated function in mind.

Write a five- or six-paragraph composition explaining what the act you've chosen should accomplish and using examples to show how well Shakespeare has fulfilled that goal.

Comment: Putting the Plays on Stage

To fully understand and appreciate any of Shakespeare's plays, it is important to be familiar with as many aspects of the theater of his day as possible. You have already seen how the stage of a playhouse like the Globe was designed to accommodate a variety of settings and actions; you should also know something about by whom and under what general circumstances plays were actually presented.

Under Queen Elizabeth I the acting profession in England was just beginning to become respectable. Since laws still existed for the imprisonment of "rogues, vagabonds, and strolling players," acting companies were taken under the protection of the country's great lords, who issued warrants permitting them to travel throughout England. Shakespeare's own acting company was first known as the Lord Chamberlain's Men ("Men" because all women's roles were played by young male apprentices). Then, when James I became king in 1603, the company was taken under his royal protection and became the King's Men.

The acting companies of the day were more similar to business partnerships than to today's acting groups. Major actors owned shares in their companies and often belonged to them for life; most of the members of Shakespeare's company, for instance, were already with the group when he joined it and stayed on after he retired. Such an arrangement gave Shakespeare the advantage of being able to write parts for specific actors, tailoring roles to their particular strengths and weaknesses. Thus the role of Brutus was probably designed for Richard Burbage, the "star" of the company; to John Heminges, who usually portrayed older men, most likely went the part of Julius Caesar; thin and sallow Richard Cowley may have played Cassius, he of the "lean and hungry look." Shakespeare himself generally played minor roles in his plays; in *Julius Caesar* he probably took the part of Cinna the poet, who appears in Act Three.

Another difference between acting groups then and now is the number of plays they performed in. Whereas currently the general practice is for one play to be presented daily until the end of its run, in Shakespeare's time acting companies performed in repertory—that is, a different play was produced each day. Records from the period indicate that an acting company might present eleven different plays on eleven consecutive days, a feat that does not seem too remarkable until you realize that the same actors were probably in all the performances.

Interestingly, modern groups devoted to staging Shakespeare's plays follow many of the practices of that earlier period. Contemporary Shakespearean playhouses, for example, are nearly always modeled on the Globe. In Shakespearean acting companies it is not uncommon for an actor to stay with the group for several years. And the plays are usually presented in repertory, though five or six plays per season tends to be the limit. These practices are followed not simply to slavishly imitate Shakespeare's era, but because they have been judged effective in their own right.

Act Three

Scene 1: Rome. Before the Capitol. (Played on the Platform and Inner Stage.)

*Today—the ides of March—*CAESAR *is to meet with the* SENATORS. ARTEMIDORUS *and the* SOOTHSAYER *enter at left among a crowd of well-wishers. The crowd bursts into cheers as* CAESAR *enters at right, followed by* ANTONY, POPILIUS, PUBLIUS, *and the* CONSPIRATORS. CAESAR *approaches the* SOOTHSAYER, *and speaks defiantly.*

CAESAR. The ides of March are come.
SOOTHSAYER. Ay, Caesar, but not gone.[45]

45. What might Shakespeare's purpose be in opening the scene with this exchange between Caesar and the Soothsayer?

(CAESAR, *waving the* SOOTHSAYER *aside, is approached by* ARTEMIDORUS, *who presents his paper.)*
ARTEMIDORUS. Hail, Caesar! Read this schedule.°

schedule, document.

(DECIUS, *waving another paper, pushes* ARTEMIDORUS *aside.)*
DECIUS. Trebonius doth desire you to o'er-read,
At your best leisure, this his humble suit.
ARTEMIDORUS. O Caesar, read mine first, for mine's a suit
That touches Caesar nearer. Read it, great Caesar.
CAESAR. What touches us ourself shall be last served.
ARTEMIDORUS. Delay not, Caesar. *(He thrusts his paper in* CAESAR'*s face.)* Read it instantly.[46]

46. What is the content of the paper Artemidorus wants Caesar to read?

CAESAR. What, is the fellow mad?
(PUBLIUS *and* CASSIUS *force* ARTEMIDORUS *aside.)*
PUBLIUS. Sirrah, give place.
CASSIUS. What, urge you your petitions in the street?
Come to the Capitol.[47]

47. Why do you think both Cassius and, in lines 4–5, Decius try to interrupt Artemidorus?

(CASSIUS *points toward inner stage, where curtains are slowly being drawn apart to reveal the interior of the Senate-house. Some* SENATORS *are already seated on the stage; a statue of* POMPEY *stands forward at left.* CAESAR *moves onto inner stage, followed by* ANTONY, PUBLIUS, METELLUS, TREBONIUS, *and* CAIUS LIGARIUS.*)*
POPILIUS *(passing* CASSIUS*).* I wish your enterprise today may thrive.
CASSIUS *(innocently).* What enterprise, Popilius?[48]
POPILIUS. Fare you well.

48. Cassius answers the senator Popilius "innocently." How would an actor playing Cassius show that Popilius' words have meaning for him?

(He joins CAESAR.*)*
BRUTUS *(fearfully).* What said Popilius Lena?
CASSIUS. He wished today our enterprise might thrive.
I fear our purpose is discovered.[49]

49. By this point, how many people besides the conspirators know or suspect something is about to happen to Caesar? Name them, and explain (if possible) where they got their information.

BRUTUS. Look, how he makes to Caesar.° Mark him.

makes to Caesar, presses toward Caesar.

CASSIUS. Casca, be sudden, for we fear prevention.
Brutus, what shall be done? If this be known,
Cassius or Caesar never shall turn back,
For I will slay myself.
BRUTUS *(with relief).* Cassius, be constant.

Popilius Lena speaks not of our purposes;
For, look, he smiles, and Caesar doth not change.
(ANTONY and TREBONIUS leave the inner stage and move off the platform at right.)
CASSIUS. Trebonius knows his time; for, look you, Brutus,
He draws Mark Antony out of the way.[50]
DECIUS. Where is Metellus Cimber? Let him go
And presently prefer his suit° to Caesar.
BRUTUS. He is addressed.° Press near and second him.
CINNA. Casca, you are the first that rears your hand.
(BRUTUS, CASSIUS, CASCA, DECIUS, and CINNA cross to the inner stage, where CAESAR is calling the group to order.)
CAESAR. Are we all ready? What is now amiss
That Caesar and his Senate must redress?
METELLUS. Most high, most mighty, and most puissant Caesar,
Metellus Cimber throws before thy seat
An humble heart—*(He falls on his knees.)*
CAESAR. I must prevent thee, Cimber.
These couchings° and these lowly courtesies
Might fire the blood of ordinary men,
And turn preordinance and first decree
Into the law of children.° Be not fond°
To think that Caesar bears such rebel blood
That will be thawed from the true quality
With that which melteth fools—I mean, sweet words,
Low-crooked curtsies, and base spaniel fawning.
Thy brother° by decree is banishèd.
If thou dost bend and pray and fawn for him,
I spurn thee like a cur out of my way.
(He pushes METELLUS aside.)
Know, Caesar doth not wrong, nor without cause
Will he be satisfied.
METELLUS. Is there no voice more worthy than my own,
To sound more sweetly in great Caesar's ear
For the repealing of my banished brother?
BRUTUS *(kneeling)*. I kiss thy hand, but not in flattery, Caesar,
Desiring thee that Publius Cimber may
Have an immediate freedom of repeal.
CAESAR *(in surprise)*. What, Brutus!
CASSIUS *(kneeling also)*. Pardon, Caesar! Caesar, pardon!
As low as to thy foot doth Cassius fall,
To beg enfranchisement for Publius Cimber.°
(One by one, the other CONSPIRATORS kneel.)
CAESAR. I could be well moved, if I were as you.
If I could pray to move, prayers would move me:
But I am constant as the northern star,

50. Why does Trebonius draw Antony aside?

presently . . . his suit, immediately present his petition.

addressed, ready.

couchings, kneelings.

And turn . . . children, and turn established laws and procedures into the whims of children.

fond, here meaning "foolish enough."

Thy brother. Publius Cimber, who had incurred Caesar's wrath.

To beg enfranchisement (en fran′chīz-mənt) ***. . . Cimber,*** to ask that Publius Cimber be allowed to return to Rome and be given again his full rights as a citizen.

Of whose true-fixed and resting quality
There is no fellow in the firmament.
The skies are painted with unnumbered sparks,
They are all fire and every one doth shine,
But there's but one in all doth hold his place.
So in the world: 'tis furnished well with men,
And men are flesh and blood, and apprehensive;°
Yet in the number I do know but one
That unassailable holds on his rank,
Unshaked of motion. And that I am he,
Let me a little show it, even in this—
That I was constant Cimber should be banished,
And constant do remain to keep him so.

CINNA. O Caesar—

CAESAR. Hence! Wilt thou lift up Olympus?[51]

DECIUS. Great Caesar—

CAESAR. Doth not Brutus bootless° kneel?

CASCA *(leaping up).* Speak, hands, for me! *(He stabs* CAESAR.*)*

(The other CONSPIRATORS, *daggers in hand, spring to their feet. They surge forward, and all but* BRUTUS *stab* CAESAR. CAESAR, *crying out, tries to ward off the blows until he sees* BRUTUS' *uplifted dagger, then covers his face with his cloak and submits.)*

CAESAR. *Et tu, Brutè!*° Then fall, Caesar!

*(*CAESAR *staggers forward and dies at the foot of* POMPEY'*s statue.)*[52]

CINNA *(shouting).* Liberty! Freedom! Tyranny is dead!
Run hence, proclaim, cry it about the streets.

CASSIUS. Some to the common pulpits,° and cry out
"Liberty, freedom, and enfranchisement."

(The CONSPIRATORS *move onto the platform, where the people stand as if stunned by the sudden attack on* CAESAR. *Then the crowd, including* ARTEMIDORUS *and the* SOOTHSAYER, *begin to flee in panic.)*

BRUTUS *(calling out).* People and senators, be not affrighted.
Fly not; stand still. Ambition's debt is paid.

CASCA. Go to the pulpit, Brutus.

DECIUS. And Cassius too.

BRUTUS. Where's Publius?°

CINNA. Here, quite confounded with this mutiny.

METELLUS. Stand fast together, lest some friend of Caesar's
Should chance—

BRUTUS. Talk not of standing. *(Extending his hand)* Publius, good cheer.
There is no harm intended to your person,
Nor to no Roman else. So tell them, Publius.

CASSIUS. And leave us, Publius, lest that the people,

apprehensive, aware of what is going on.

51. Olympus was a high mountain in Greece considered the home of the gods. How does this allusion, as well as the content of his speeches in lines 35–48 and 58–73, show Caesar's egotism? Why might Shakespeare have placed these speeches right before the murder?

bootless, in vain.

Et tu, Brutè (brü′tā), "And you, Brutus!" [*Latin*] The betrayal completely overwhelms Caesar.

52. What is ironic about where Caesar dies?

common pulpits, elevated areas where public debates were held.

Publius, an elderly senator who is stunned by what has just occurred.

Rushing on us, should do your age some mischief.
BRUTUS. Do so, and let no man abide this deed°
But we the doers.
*(*PUBLIUS, *accompanied by* POPILIUS, *moves off at left just as* TREBONIUS *reenters at right.)*
CASSIUS. Where is Antony?
TREBONIUS. Fled to his house amazed.
Men, wives, and children stare, cry out, and run
As it were doomsday.
BRUTUS *(resignedly).* Fates,° we will know your pleasures.
That we shall die, we know; 'tis but the time,
And drawing days out, that men stand upon.°
CASSIUS. Why, he that cuts off twenty years of life
Cuts off so many years of fearing death.
BRUTUS. Grant that, and then is death a benefit.
So are we Caesar's friends, that have abridged
His time of fearing death. Stoop, Romans, stoop,
And let us bathe our hands in Caesar's blood
Up to the elbows, and besmear our swords.
Then walk we forth, even to the market-place,
And, waving our red weapons o'er our heads,
Let's all cry, "Peace, freedom, and liberty!"
CASSIUS. Stoop, then, and wash. *(The* CONSPIRATORS *kneel and begin to dip their hands and weapons in* CAESAR*'s blood.)*[53]
How many ages hence
Shall this our lofty scene be acted over
In states unborn and accents yet unknown![54]
BRUTUS. How many times shall Caesar bleed in sport,
That now on Pompey's basis° lies along
No worthier than the dust!
CASSIUS. So oft as that shall be,
So often shall the knot of us be called
The men that gave their country liberty.
(They rise.)
DECIUS. What, shall we forth?
CASSIUS. Aye, every man away;
Brutus shall lead; and we will grace his heels
With the most boldest and best hearts of Rome.
(A SERVANT *of* ANTONY *enters at right.)*
BRUTUS. Soft! Who comes here? A friend of Antony's?
SERVANT *(kneeling).* Thus, Brutus, did my master bid me kneel.
Thus did Mark Antony bid me fall down;
And, being prostrate, thus he bade me say:
Brutus is noble, wise, valiant, and honest;
Caesar was mighty, bold, royal, and loving.
Say I love Brutus, and I honor him;

abide this deed, answer for this deed.

Fates, the three goddesses who were thought to control human destinies.

stand upon, are concerned with.

53. How do you think the commoners will react to this display?

54. How accurate is Cassius' prophecy? What is ironic about it and the two short speeches following it?

on Pompey's basis, at the foot of Pompey's statue.

Say I feared Caesar, honored him, and loved him.
If Brutus will vouchsafe that Antony
May safely come to him, and be resolved°
How Caesar hath deserved to lie in death,
Mark Antony shall not love Caesar dead
So well as Brutus living, but will follow
The fortunes and affairs of noble Brutus
Through the hazards of this untrod state°
With all true faith. So says my master Antony.

BRUTUS. Thy master is a wise and valiant Roman;
I never thought him worse.
Tell him, so please him come unto this place,
He shall be satisfied and, by my honor,
Depart untouched.°

SERVANT. I'll fetch him presently. *(SERVANT exits.)*

BRUTUS. I know that we shall have him well to friend.

CASSIUS. I wish we may. But yet have I a mind
That fears him much; and my misgiving still
Falls shrewdly to the purpose.

(ANTONY, reentering at right, strides toward CAESAR's body.)

BRUTUS. But here comes Antony.—Welcome, Mark Antony.

ANTONY *(ignoring BRUTUS)*. O mighty Caesar! Dost thou lie so low?
Are all thy conquests, glories, triumphs, spoils,
Shrunk to this little measure? Fare thee well.—
(To the CONSPIRATORS) I know not, gentlemen, what you intend,
Who else must be let blood, who else is rank;°
If I myself, there is no hour so fit
As Caesar's death hour, nor no instrument
Of half that worth as those your swords, made rich
With the most noble blood of all this world.
I do beseech ye, if you bear me hard,
Now, whilst your purpled hands do reek and smoke,
Fulfill your pleasure. Live a thousand years,
I shall not find myself so apt° to die;
No place will please me so, no mean° of death,
As here by Caesar, and by you cut off,
The choice and master spirits of this age.

BRUTUS *(disturbed)*. O Antony, beg not your death of us.
Though now we must appear bloody and cruel,
As, by our hands and this our present act
You see we do, yet see you but our hands
And this the bleeding business they have done.
Our hearts you see not. They are pitiful;
And pity to the general wrong of Rome—
As fire drives out fire, so pity pity°—
Hath done this deed on Caesar. For your part,

be resolved, have it explained to him.

untrod state, new and unfamiliar state of affairs.

Thy master . . . untouched. In tragedies of Shakespeare's day the fortunes of the hero reach their height, and then occurs a scene, called the dramatic reverse, where they begin to fall. Critics who see Brutus as the hero of the play (see Comment on page 430 for a fuller discussion of this) often claim that the dramatic reverse occurs when Brutus agrees to see Antony and explain Caesar's assassination to him. Note, by contrast, Cassius' "misgiving" in lines 145–147.

Who else must . . . rank, who else must be destroyed.

apt, ready.

mean, method.

so pity pity, so pity for the wrongs Rome has endured from Caesar overshadows pity for his death.

To you our swords have leaden points, Mark Antony.
Our arms in strength of malice, and our hearts
Of brothers' temper, do receive you in
With all kind love, good thoughts, and reverence.

CASSIUS. Your voice shall be as strong as any man's
In the disposing of new dignities.[55]

BRUTUS. Only be patient till we have appeased
The multitude, beside themselves with fear,
And then we will deliver you the cause
Why I, that did love Caesar when I struck him,
Have thus proceeded.

ANTONY *(extending his hand).* I doubt not of your wisdom.
Let each man render me his bloody hand.
First, Marcus Brutus, will I shake with you;
Next, Caius Cassius, do I take your hand;
Now, Decius Brutus, yours; now yours, Metellus;
Yours, Cinna; and, my valiant Casca, yours;
Though last, not least in love, yours, good Trebonius.
Gentlemen all—alas, what shall I say?
My credit now stands on such slippery ground
That one of two bad ways you must conceit° me,
Either a coward or a flatterer.
(Addressing CAESAR*'s body)* That I did love thee, Caesar, O,
'tis true!°
If then thy spirit look upon us now,
Shall it not grieve thee dearer than thy death
To see thy Antony making his peace,
Shaking the bloody fingers of thy foes—
Most noble!—in the presence of thy corse?°
Had I as many eyes as thou hast wounds,
Weeping as fast as they stream forth thy blood,
It would become me better than to close
In terms of friendship with thine enemies.
Pardon me, Julius! Here wast thou bayed, brave hart,°
Here didst thou fall, and here thy hunters stand,
Signed in thy spoil, and crimsoned in thy lethe.°
O world, thou wast the forest to this hart,
And this, indeed, O world, the heart of thee!
How like a deer, strucken by many princes,
Dost thou here lie!

CASSIUS *(sharply).* Mark Antony—

ANTONY. Pardon me, Caius Cassius.
The enemies of Caesar shall say this;
Then, in a friend, it is cold modesty.

CASSIUS. I blame you not for praising Caesar so,
But what compact mean you to have with us?

55. In offering Antony a say in handing out new government positions (dignities), Cassius is offering him power. What has Brutus offered him? Contrast the two men's approaches.

conceit, consider.

That I did love . . . true. In this speech, as in his preceding one, Antony cleverly alternates between placating the conspirators and revealing his true feelings about Caesar's death.

corse, corpse.

hart, Antony here puns on *hart* ("stag") and *heart.*

lethe (lē′thē), death.

Will you be pricked in number of our friends,°
Or shall we on, and not depend on you?
ANTONY. Therefore I took your hands, but was indeed
Swayed from the point, by looking down on Caesar.
Friends am I with you all and love you all,
Upon this hope, that you shall give me reasons
Why and wherein Caesar was dangerous.
BRUTUS. Or else were this a savage spectacle.
Our reasons are so full of good regard°
That were you, Antony, the son of Caesar,
You should be satisfied.
ANTONY. That's all I seek,
And am moreover suitor that I may
Produce his body to the market-place,
And in the pulpit, as becomes a friend,
Speak in the order° of his funeral.
BRUTUS. You shall, Mark Antony.
CASSIUS *(very much disturbed).* Brutus, a word with you.
(Taking BRUTUS *aside)* You know not what you do. Do not consent
That Antony speak in his funeral.
Know you how much the people may be moved
By that which he will utter?
BRUTUS. By your pardon;
I will myself into the pulpit first,
And show the reason of our Caesar's death.
What Antony shall speak, I will protest°
He speaks by leave and by permission,
And that we are contented Caesar shall
Have all true rites and lawful ceremonies.
It shall advantage more than do us wrong.
CASSIUS *(dubiously).* I know not what may fall; I like it not.[56]
*(*BRUTUS *and* CASSIUS *rejoin* ANTONY *and the others.)*
BRUTUS. Mark Antony, here, take you Caesar's body.
You shall not in your funeral speech blame us,
But speak all good you can devise of Caesar,
And say you do 't by our permission.°
Else shall you not have any hand at all
About his funeral. And you shall speak
In the same pulpit whereto I am going,
After my speech is ended.
ANTONY. Be it so.
I do desire no more.
BRUTUS. Prepare the body then, and follow us.
(The CONSPIRATORS *follow* BRUTUS *out at right.* ANTONY *gazes at* CAESAR, *then slowly covers the body with the dead man's cloak.)*

pricked . . . friends, numbered among our friends.

good regard, merit.

order, ceremony.

protest, announce.

56. *Lines 227–244.* Here Brutus makes another mistake. What is it? What is Cassius' reaction?

You shall not . . . permission. Keep these lines in mind to see whether Antony obeys them when speaking to the commoners.

ANTONY. Oh, pardon me, thou bleeding piece of earth,
That I am meek and gentle with these butchers!
Thou are the ruins of the noblest man
That ever livèd in the tide of times.
Woe to the hand that shed this costly blood!
Over thy wounds now do I prophesy—
Which, like dumb mouths, do ope their ruby lips
To beg the voice and utterance of my tongue—
A curse shall light upon the limbs of men;
Domestic fury and fierce civil strife
Shall cumber all the parts of Italy;
Blood and destruction shall be so in use
And dreadful objects° so familiar
That mothers shall but smile when they behold
Their infants quartered° with the hands of war,
All pity choked with custom of fell deeds;
And Caesar's spirit, ranging for revenge,
With Ate° by his side come hot from hell,
Shall in these confines with a monarch's voice
Cry "Havoc"° and let slip the dogs of war,°
That this foul deed shall smell above the earth
With carrion men, groaning for burial.
(A SERVANT *enters at left.)*
You serve Octavius Caesar, do you not?
SERVANT. I do, Mark Antony.
ANTONY. Caesar did write for him to come to Rome.
SERVANT. He did receive his letters, and is coming,
And bid me say to you by word of mouth—*(He sees the body.)*
O Caesar!
ANTONY. Thy heart is big. Get thee apart and weep.
Passion, I see, is catching, for mine eyes,
Seeing those beads of sorrow stand in thine,
Began to water. Is thy master coming?
SERVANT. He lies tonight within seven leagues of Rome.°
ANTONY. Post back with speed, and tell him what hath chanced.
Here is a mourning Rome, a dangerous Rome,
No Rome of safety for Octavius yet;
Hie hence, and tell him so. *(The* SERVANT *starts to leave.)* Yet, stay awhile.
Thou shalt not back till I have borne this corse
Into the market-place. There shall I try,
In my oration, how the people take
The cruel issue of these bloody men,
According to the which thou shalt discourse
To young Octavius of the state of things.
Lend me your hand.

objects, sights.

quartered, torn to pieces.

Ate (ā'tē), Greek goddess of vengeance.

"Havoc," a command, which could be given only by a king, which meant "Kill all! Take no prisoners."

let slip the dogs of war, let loose fire, sword, and famine.

He lies . . . Rome. With the news that Caesar's grandnephew Octavius is within seven leagues (twenty-one miles) of Rome, Antony's side is strengthened, for Caesar had recently made Octavius his adopted son and heir. He would thus attract Caesar's supporters.

*(*ANTONY *and the* SERVANT *pick up* CAESAR*'s body and proceed to carry it off at right door. At the same time the curtains of the inner stage are drawn closed.)*

Scene 2: Rome. The Forum. (Played on the Platform and Balcony Stage.)

BRUTUS *and* CASSIUS, *with groups of indignant* CITIZENS *at their heels, enter at left. The* CITIZENS *are clamoring for an explanation of* CAESAR*'s assassination. It is apparent from their threatening gestures and shouts that the people will become violent unless* BRUTUS *speaks to them. He does so from the balcony, which represents a raised pulpit in this scene.*

CITIZENS *(angrily).* We will be satisfied! Let us be satisfied!°

We . . . satisfied. Note how throughout this scene the commoners are easily swayed to support either side.

BRUTUS. Then follow me, and give me audience, friends.
Cassius, go you into the other street,
And part the numbers.°
(Loudly) Those that will hear me speak, let 'em stay here;
Those that will follow Cassius, go with him;
And public reasons shall be rendered
Of Caesar's death.

part the numbers, divide the crowd.

*(*BRUTUS *exits at inner-stage curtains to ascend the pulpit.)*

FIRST CITIZEN. I will hear Brutus speak.

SECOND CITIZEN. I will hear Cassius; and compare their reasons,
When severally° we hear them rendered.

severally, separately.

*(*CASSIUS *moves off at right, accompanied by various* CITIZENS *who clamor loudly.* BRUTUS *appears above at the balcony railing.)*

THIRD CITIZEN. The noble Brutus is ascended. Silence!

BRUTUS *(speaking earnestly).* Be patient till the last. *(Pause)*
Romans, countrymen, and lovers!

(There are shouts from the mob.)

Hear me for my cause,[57] and be silent, that you may hear. Believe me for mine honor, and have respect to mine honor, that you may believe. Censure me in your wisdom, and awake your senses, that you may the better judge. If there be any in this assembly, any dear friend of Caesar's, to him I say, that Brutus' love to Caesar was no less than his. If then that friend demand why Brutus rose against Caesar, this is my answer: Not that I loved Caesar less, but that I loved Rome more. Had you rather Caesar were living and die all slaves, than that Caesar were dead, to live all free men? As Caesar loved me, I weep for him; as he was fortunate, I rejoice at it; as he was valiant, I honor him; but, as he was ambitious, I slew him. There is tears for his love; joy for his fortune; honor for his valor; and death for his ambition. Who is here so base that would be a bondman? If any, speak, for him have I offended.

57. Note that Brutus' speech is in prose—brief, unadorned, and to the point. Throughout, he gives logical reasons for the assassination, appealing to his audience's minds rather than their emotions. What does he mean by "Not that I loved Caesar less, but that I loved Rome more" (line 21)?

Who is here so rude that would not be a Roman? If any, speak, for him have I offended. Who is here so vile that will not love his country? If any, speak, for him have I offended. I pause for a reply.

ALL *(shouting)*. None, Brutus, none.

BRUTUS. Then none have I offended. I have done no more to Caesar than you shall do to Brutus. The question of his death is enrolled° in the Capitol; his glory not extenuated,° wherein he was worthy, nor his offenses enforced, for which he suffered death.

(ANTONY enters at left. Behind him come ATTENDANTS carrying CAESAR's bier.)

Here comes his body, mourned by Mark Antony, who, though he had no hand in his death, shall receive the benefit of his dying, a place in the commonwealth, as which of you shall not? With this I depart, that, as I slew my best lover for the good of Rome, I have the same dagger for myself, when it shall please my country to need my death.

ALL *(shouting)*. Live, Brutus, live, live!

(BRUTUS exits at balcony curtains to descend from the pulpit.)

FIRST CITIZEN. Bring him with triumph home unto his house.

SECOND CITIZEN. Give him a statue with his ancestors.

THIRD CITIZEN. Let him be Caesar.[58]

FOURTH CITIZEN. Caesar's better parts
Shall be crowned in Brutus.

FIRST CITIZEN. We'll bring him to his house with shouts and clamors.

(The mob greets BRUTUS with cheers as he reenters the platform at inner-stage curtains.)

BRUTUS. My countrymen—

(The crowd cheers wildly.)

SECOND CITIZEN *(shouting)*. Peace, silence! Brutus speaks.

FIRST CITIZEN. Peace, ho!

BRUTUS. Good countrymen, let me depart alone,
And, for my sake, stay here with Antony.
Do grace to Caesar's corpse, and grace his speech
Tending to Caesar's glories, which Mark Antony,
By our permission, is allowed to make.
I do entreat you, not a man depart,
Save I alone, till Antony have spoke. *(He exits alone at right.)*

FIRST CITIZEN. Stay, ho, and let us hear Mark Antony.

THIRD CITIZEN. Let him go up into the public chair.
We'll hear him. Noble Antony, go up.

(There are murmurs from the mob.)

ANTONY. For Brutus' sake, I am beholding to you.

(ANTONY exits at inner-stage curtains to ascend the pulpit. His ATTENDANTS place CAESAR's body well forward on platform.)

The question . . . is enrolled, the reason for Caesar's death is recorded.

his glory not extenuated (ek sten′yü āt-əd), his fame has not been detracted from because of the manner of his dying.

58. What does this line tell about how well the commoners have understood Brutus' speech?

FOURTH CITIZEN. What does he say of Brutus?
THIRD CITIZEN. He says, for Brutus' sake
He finds himself beholding to us all.
FOURTH CITIZEN. 'Twere best he speak no harm of Brutus here.
FIRST CITIZEN. This Caesar was a tyrant.
THIRD CITIZEN. Nay, that's certain.
We are blest that Rome is rid of him.
(ANTONY appears above at the balcony railing.)
SECOND CITIZEN. Peace! Let us hear what Antony can say.
ANTONY. You gentle Romans—
(The crowd is not yet quiet.)
CITIZENS. Peace, ho! Let us hear him.
ANTONY. Friends, Romans, countrymen, lend me your ears.
I come to bury Caesar, not to praise him.
The evil that men do lives after them;
The good is oft interrèd with their bones.
So let it be with Caesar. The noble Brutus
Hath told you Caesar was ambitious.
If it were so, it was a grievous fault,
And grievously hath Caesar answered it.
Here, under leave of Brutus and the rest—
(The mob murmurs angrily.)
For Brutus is an honorable man;°
So are they all, all honorable men—
Come I to speak in Caesar's funeral.
He was my friend, faithful and just to me;
But Brutus says he was ambitious,
And Brutus is an honorable man.
He° hath brought many captives home to Rome,
Whose ransoms did the general coffers fill.°
Did this in Caesar seem ambitious?
When that the poor have cried, Caesar hath wept;
Ambition should be made of sterner stuff.
Yet Brutus said he was ambitious,
And Brutus is an honorable man.°
You all did see that on the Lupercal
I thrice presented him a kingly crown,
Which he did thrice refuse. Was this ambition?°
Yet Brutus says he was ambitious,
And, sure, he is an honorable man.
I speak not to disprove what Brutus spoke,
But here I am to speak what I do know.
You all did love him once, not without cause.
What cause withholds you then, to mourn for him?
O judgment! Thou art fled to brutish beasts,
And men have lost their reason. *(He pauses.)* Bear with me;

Brutus is an honorable man. The crowd's anger at words against Brutus makes Antony quick to express his admiration for the man—and for the other conspirators.

He, Caesar.

the general coffers fill, Caesar hadn't kept the ransom money for himself.

Brutus is an honorable man. Note the tinge of irony beginning to creep in.

on the Lupercal . . . ambition. Compare this explanation of Caesar's reaction with Casca's view of it in Act One, Scene 2 (lines 235–245).

My heart is in the coffin there with Caesar,
And I must pause till it come back to me. *(He weeps openly.)*[59]

FIRST CITIZEN *(soberly).* Methinks there is much reason in his sayings.

SECOND CITIZEN. If thou consider rightly of the matter,
Caesar has had great wrong.

THIRD CITIZEN. Has he, masters?
I fear there will a worse come in his place.

FOURTH CITIZEN. Marked ye his words? He would not take the crown;
Therefore 'tis certain he was not ambitious.

FIRST CITIZEN. If it be found so, some will dear abide° it.

SECOND CITIZEN. Poor soul! His eyes are red as fire with weeping.

THIRD CITIZEN. There's not a nobler man in Rome than Antony.

FOURTH CITIZEN *(pointing).* Now mark him, he begins again to speak.

ANTONY. But yesterday the word of Caesar might
Have stood against the world. Now lies he there,
And none so poor to do him reverence.°
O masters! If I were disposed to stir
Your hearts and minds to mutiny and rage,
I should do Brutus wrong, and Cassius wrong,
Who, you all know, are honorable men.[60]

(There is derisive laughter from the mob.)

I will not do them wrong; I rather choose
To wrong the dead, to wrong myself and you,
Than I will wrong such honorable men. *(He pulls a scroll from his garment.)*
But here's a parchment with the seal of Caesar;
I found it in his closet,° 'tis his will.
Let but the commons hear this testament—
Which, pardon me, I do not mean to read—
And they would go and kiss dead Caesar's wounds
And dip their napkins° in his sacred blood,
Yea, beg a hair of him for memory,
And, dying, mention it within their wills,
Bequeathing it as a rich legacy
Unto their issue.

FOURTH CITIZEN. We'll hear the will! Read it, Mark Antony.

ALL *(shouting).* The will, the will! We will hear Caesar's will.

ANTONY. Have patience, gentle friends, I must not read it.
It is not meet you know how Caesar loved you.[61]

(He puts the will away.)

You are not wood, you are not stones, but men;
And, being men, hearing the will of Caesar,
It will inflame you, it will make you mad.

59. Here Antony is overcome with grief and finds himself unable to go on. Do you think he realizes the effectiveness of this pause? Are his tears genuine?

abide, pay for.

And none . . . reverence, the dead Caesar is now poorer (lower in estate) than the poorest Roman.

60. By this point, what tone of voice is Antony using when he repeats this phrase?

closet, study; private chamber.

napkins, handkerchiefs.

61. What might be behind Antony's refusing to read the will?

(There are cries of "No! No!")

'Tis good you know not that you are his heirs,
For, if you should, O, what would come of it!

FOURTH CITIZEN. Read the will! We'll hear it, Antony.
(There are cries of "Yes! Yes!")
You shall read us the will, Caesar's will.

ANTONY. Will you be patient? Will you stay awhile?
I have o'ershot myself° to tell you of it.
I fear I wrong the honorable men
Whose daggers have stabbed Caesar; I do fear it.
(There are angry shouts from the mob.)

FOURTH CITIZEN. They were traitors. *(Sarcastically)* Honorable men!

ALL *(clamoring)*. The will! The testament!

SECOND CITIZEN. They were villains, murderers. The will! Read
the will!
(There are cries of "Read! Read!")

ANTONY. You will compel me then to read the will?
Then make a ring about the corpse of Caesar,
And let me show you him that made the will.
Shall I descend? And will you give me leave?

SEVERAL CITIZENS. Come down.

SECOND CITIZEN. Descend.

THIRD CITIZEN. You shall have leave.
(ANTONY exits at balcony curtains in order to descend from the pulpit; the crowd circles CAESAR's body.)

FOURTH CITIZEN. A ring; stand round.

FIRST CITIZEN. Stand from the hearse,° stand from the body.

I have . . . myself. Antony has said more than he intended, or pretends so.

hearse, bier.

(The crowd moves back when ANTONY *reenters the platform.)*

SECOND CITIZEN. Room for Antony, most noble Antony.

ANTONY. Nay, press not so upon me. Stand far off.

SEVERAL CITIZENS. Stand back! Room! Bear back!

ANTONY. If you have tears, prepare to shed them now.
You all do know this mantle. *(Pointing to* CAESAR'*s cloak)* I remember
The first time ever Caesar put it on;
'Twas on a summer's evening, in his tent,
That day he overcame the Nervii.°
Look, in this place ran Cassius' dagger through.
See what a rent the envious Casca made.
Through this the well-beloved Brutus stabbed,[62]
And, as he plucked his cursèd steel away,
Mark how the blood of Caesar followed it;
As rushing out of doors, to be resolved
If Brutus so unkindly knocked or no;
For Brutus, as you know, was Caesar's angel.
Judge, O you gods, how dearly Caesar loved him!
This was the most unkindest cut of all;
For when the noble Caesar saw him stab,
Ingratitude, more strong than traitors' arms,
Quite vanquished him. Then burst his mighty heart,
And, in his mantle muffling up his face,
E'en at the base of Pompey's statuë,
Which all the while ran blood, great Caesar fell.
O, what a fall was there, my countrymen!
Then I, and you, and all of us fell down,
Whilst bloody treason flourished over us.
O, now you weep, and I perceive you feel
The dint° of pity. These are gracious drops.
Kind souls, what weep you when you but behold
Our Caesar's vesture wounded?° *(He flings* CAESAR'*s cloak aside.)* Look you here,
Here is himself, marred, as you see, with traitors.[63]

(The CITIZENS *cry out in horror.)*

FIRST CITIZEN. O piteous spectacle!

SECOND CITIZEN. O noble Caesar!

THIRD CITIZEN. O woeful day!

FOURTH CITIZEN. O traitors, villains!

FIRST CITIZEN. O most bloody sight!

SECOND CITIZEN. We will be revenged.

ALL *(shouting)*. Revenge! About! Seek! Burn! Fire! Kill! Slay!
Let not a traitor live! *(They start to leave.)*

ANTONY *(commandingly)*. Stay, countrymen.

FIRST CITIZEN. Peace there! Hear the noble Antony.

Nervii (nėr′vē ī), a warlike tribe against whom Caesar led the decisive charge.

62. There is no way Antony could have known which conspirator was responsible for which wound. What is his purpose in identifying the cuts in Caesar's cloak with individual conspirators?

dint, effect.

Caesar's vesture wounded, the cuts in Caesar's clothing.

63. What effect is Antony trying to achieve by showing the body? How have his previous words led up to it?

SECOND CITIZEN. We'll hear him, we'll follow him, we'll die with him!

(The mob returns to ANTONY.*)*

ANTONY. Good friends, sweet friends, let me not stir you up
To such a sudden flood of mutiny.
They that have done this deed are honorable.
What private griefs° they have, alas, I know not,
That made them do it. They are wise and honorable,
And will no doubt with reasons answer you.
I come not, friends, to steal away your hearts.
I am no orator, as Brutus is,
But, as you know me all, a plain, blunt man,
That love my friend; and that they know full well
That gave me public leave to speak of him.
For I have neither wit, nor words, nor worth,
Action, nor utterance, nor the power of speech
To stir men's blood. I only speak right on.[64]
I tell you that which you yourselves do know,
Show you sweet Caesar's wounds, poor poor dumb mouths,
And bid them speak for me. But were I Brutus,
And Brutus Antony, there were an Antony
Would ruffle up your spirits, and put a tongue
In every wound of Caesar that should move
The stones of Rome to rise and mutiny.

(The mob are now nearly uncontrollable and shout wildly.)

ALL. We'll mutiny!

FIRST CITIZEN. We'll burn the house of Brutus.

THIRD CITIZEN. Away, then! Come, seek the conspirators.

(Again the mob starts to leave.)

ANTONY. Yet hear me, countrymen. Yet hear me speak.

ALL *(turning).* Peace, ho! Hear Antony. Most noble Antony!

ANTONY. Why, friends, you go to do you know not what.
Wherein hath Caesar thus deserved your loves?
Alas, you know not! I must tell you, then,
You have forgot the will I told you of.

(He takes the will from his garment.)

ALL *(returning to him).* Most true. The will! Let's stay and hear the will.

ANTONY *(showing it).* Here is the will, and under Caesar's seal.

(He breaks the seal, unrolls the scroll, and reads.)

To every Roman citizen he gives,
To every several° man, seventy-five drachmas.°

(The mob murmurs its approval.)

SECOND CITIZEN. Most noble Caesar! We'll revenge his death.

THIRD CITIZEN. O royal Caesar!

ANTONY. Hear me with patience.

private griefs, personal reasons.

64. *Lines 213–220.* Is what Antony says in these lines true?

several, individual.

seventy-five drachmas (drak′məz). Authorities disagree in estimating this amount; the figures vary from $10 to $100. Regardless, the purchasing power of any money was far greater then than it is now.

ALL. Peace, ho!
ANTONY. Moreover, he hath left you all his walks,
His private arbors and new-planted orchards,
On this side Tiber; he hath left them you,
And to your heirs forever—common pleasures,
To walk abroad and recreate yourselves.
Here was a Caesar! When comes such another?
FIRST CITIZEN. Never, never! Come, away, away!
We'll burn his body in the holy place,
And with the brands fire the traitors' houses.
Take up the body.
(A group of CITIZENS *take up* CAESAR'*s bier.)*
SECOND CITIZEN. Go fetch fire!
THIRD CITIZEN. Pluck down benches!
FOURTH CITIZEN. Pluck down forms,° windows, anything!

forms, public benches.

(The CITIZENS, *bearing* CAESAR'*s body aloft, exit at right door.)*
ANTONY. Now let it work. Mischief, thou art afoot,
Take thou what course thou wilt!
(A SERVANT *of* OCTAVIUS CAESAR *enters at left.)*
How now, fellow?
SERVANT. Sir, Octavius is already come to Rome.
ANTONY. Where is he?
SERVANT. He and Lepidus are at Caesar's house.
ANTONY. And thither will I straight to visit him.
He comes upon a wish. Fortune is merry,
And in this mood will give us anything.
SERVANT. I heard him say, Brutus and Cassius
Are rid° like madmen through the gates of Rome.

Are rid, have ridden. Brutus and Cassius are fleeing from the wrath of the mob.

ANTONY. Belike they had some notice of the people,
How I had moved them. Bring me to Octavius.
*(*ANTONY *leads his* ATTENDANTS *and the* SERVANT *out at left door.)*

Scene 3: Rome. A street near the Forum. (Played on the Platform.)
CINNA *the poet enters through right door.* CITIZENS *follow, gesturing and looking at him suspiciously.*

CINNA *(thoughtfully).* I dreamt tonight° that I did feast with Caesar,

tonight, last night.

And things unluckily charge my fantasy.
I have no will to wander forth of doors,
Yet something leads me forth.
FIRST CITIZEN *(to* CINNA*).* What is your name?
SECOND CITIZEN. Whither are you going?
THIRD CITIZEN. Where do you dwell?
FOURTH CITIZEN. Are you a married man or a bachelor?
SECOND CITIZEN. Answer every man directly.
FIRST CITIZEN. Ay, and briefly.

FOURTH CITIZEN. Ay, and wisely.

THIRD CITIZEN. Ay, and truly, you were best.

(The CITIZENS *surround* CINNA *threateningly.)*

CINNA *(surprised).* What is my name? Whither am I going? Where do I dwell? Am I a married man or a bachelor? Then, to answer every man directly and briefly, wisely and truly: wisely I say, I am a bachelor.

SECOND CITIZEN. That's as much as to say, they are fools that marry. You'll bear me a bang for that, I fear. Proceed directly.

CINNA. Directly, I am going to Caesar's funeral.

FIRST CITIZEN. As a friend or an enemy?

CINNA. As a friend.

SECOND CITIZEN. That matter is answered directly.

FOURTH CITIZEN. For your dwelling—briefly.

CINNA. Briefly, I dwell by the Capitol.

THIRD CITIZEN. Your name, sir, truly.

CINNA. Truly, my name is Cinna.

*(*CITIZENS *start back in anger, then take hold of* CINNA*'s arms and begin shaking him.)*

FIRST CITIZEN. Tear him to pieces! He's a conspirator!

CINNA *(desperately).* I am Cinna the poet, I am Cinna the poet!

FOURTH CITIZEN. Tear him for his bad verses, tear him for his bad verses!

CINNA *(pleadingly).* I am not Cinna the conspirator.

FOURTH CITIZEN. It is no matter, his name's Cinna. Pluck but his name out of his heart, and turn him going.

THIRD CITIZEN. Tear him, tear him! Come, brands, ho! Firebrands! To Brutus', to Cassius'; burn all! Some to Decius' house, and some to Casca's; some to Ligarius'. Away, go![65]

*(*CITIZENS *exit to the left, dragging off the struggling* CINNA.*)*

65. What does this scene show about the nature of the commoners?

Discussion

Scene 1

1. How would you describe the mood of the conspirators before Caesar begins the Senate proceedings? Use specifics to support your answer.

2. (a) Describe the events leading up to Caesar's assassination. **(b)** Would you say that Shakespeare's overall portrayal of Caesar, including his death, is favorable or unfavorable? Discuss.

3. (a) How do Antony's speeches to the conspirators show they should hesitate to trust him? **(b)** How does Brutus think he can overcome the danger of Antony's speaking to the people? **(c)** When and how does Antony reveal his true motives? What are they?

Scenes 2 and 3

1. (a) Summarize in your own words the reasons Brutus gives the crowd for the assassination of Caesar. **(b)** How do the people react to what Brutus says?

2. If Antony is to change the people's feelings, he must choose his words carefully. Give examples from his speech that appeal to each of the following feelings of the crowd: **(a)** their emotions about ambition and honor; **(b)** their greed; **(c)** their compassion; **(d)** their capacity for hatred and revenge.

3. How does Scene 3 offer evidence of the success of Antony's speech?

Vocabulary

Etymology

A. Check the Glossary for the etymology of each listed word. Then for each numbered statement that follows the list, write the word that the statement best describes. You will not use all the words.

parchment	sirrah
inter	discourse
prostrate	bequeath

1. This word is derived from a Latin word meaning "a running about."

2. This word, now archaic, probably originated as a compound.

3. This word comes originally from a place name.

4. This word is derived from Latin words meaning "in earth."

5. This word comes from two Old English words.

B. Now use each listed word in an original sentence that shows you understand its meaning.

Comment: *Julius Caesar* and the Tragic Hero

According to Aristotle's *Poetics,* an influential work on the nature of poetry and tragedy, a tragic hero is a man of high rank or station in life who possesses a tragic flaw that leads to his downfall. Though we have no hard evidence that Shakespeare ever read Aristotle, we do know that his tragic heroes tend to fit snugly into this definition.

A major problem arises, however, in dealing with *Julius Caesar:* who is the tragic hero, Caesar or Brutus? Since both characters can be seen to have tragic flaws—Caesar his arrogant ambition and Brutus his idealistic, impractical nature—each man has supporters who can advance convincing arguments in favor of their candidate.

Proponents of Caesar argue that since the play is named for him, he therefore must be its hero. They refute the argument that a character killed in Act Three cannot be a tragic hero by pointing out that Caesar's ghost or spirit pervades Acts Four and Five. Both Brutus and Cassius invoke his name at their hour of greatest travail, making clear that even though he is dead, his influence is still strong.

Those who maintain that Brutus is the tragic hero point out that audience interest centers on his inner conflict as Cassius seeks to draw him into the conspiracy; that it is to him that Caesar speaks his final dying words; that his subsequent actions remain the almost constant focus of audience attention; and that it is his corpse over which the final eulogy is said—an honor traditionally reserved for the tragic hero. To these arguments may be added another: Shakespeare uses the soliloquy to help his audience understand the mental state of his major characters, and in *Julius Caesar* Brutus has several soliloquies while Caesar has none at all. This is a clear indication that Shakespeare at least wished to focus the attention and sympathy of his audience on Brutus.

By the time you finish the play, you should have your own definite ideas as to whom Shakespeare intended to be his tragic hero, Caesar or Brutus.

Act Four

Scene 1: A house in Rome. (Played in the Balcony-Stage Chamber.) *For many months after* CAESAR*'s death in March, 44* B.C.*, chaos has reigned in Rome. The leading* CONSPIRATORS *have fled east to Greece and Asia Minor.* MARK ANTONY *has attempted to make himself virtual dictator of Rome, but has been opposed by young* OCTAVIUS CAESAR, *grandnephew and political heir of* JULIUS CAESAR*; and a devastating civil war has broken out. In October, 43* B.C., ANTONY *and* OCTAVIUS *agree to combine forces, and invite* M. AEMILIUS LEPIDUS, *one of* JULIUS CAESAR*'s former lieutenants, to join them. Together they will control Rome—and rule the world.*

The scene begins as the curtains of the balcony stage are drawn apart to reveal ANTONY, OCTAVIUS, *and* LEPIDUS *seated around a table. They are scrutinizing a wax tablet which lists the names of those Romans who might oppose them. The three men are making plans to crush all opposition to their scheme.*

ANTONY. These many, then, shall die. Their names are pricked.°
OCTAVIUS. Your brother too must die. Consent you, Lepidus?
LEPIDUS. I do consent—
OCTAVIUS. Prick him down, Antony.
LEPIDUS. Upon condition Publius shall not live,
Who is your sister's son, Mark Antony.
ANTONY *(picking up the stylus).*° He shall not live. Look, with a spot I damn him.°
But, Lepidus, go you to Caesar's house.
Fetch the will hither, and we shall determine
How to cut off some charge in legacies.°
LEPIDUS. What, shall I find you here?
OCTAVIUS. Or here, or at the Capitol.
*(*LEPIDUS *leaves at the door in the rear wall of the balcony stage.)*
ANTONY. This is a slight unmeritable man,
Meet to be sent on errands. Is it fit,
The threefold world divided, he should stand
One of the three to share it?[66]
OCTAVIUS. So you thought him,
And took his voice who should be pricked to die
In our black sentence and proscription.
ANTONY. Octavius, I have seen more days than you;
And though we lay these honors on this man,
To ease ourselves of divers° sland'rous loads,
He shall but bear them as the ass bears gold,
To groan and sweat under the business,
Either led or driven, as we point the way;

These many . . . pricked, the names of many men on the list are marked for death.

stylus (stī′ləs), a pointed instrument for writing on wax.

with a spot I damn him, my mark condemns him to death.

we shall determine . . . legacies. Antony wishes to find a way to reduce the amount Caesar has bequeathed each Roman.

66. By this point in the scene, Antony has been involved in three questionable activities. What are they? What, if anything, in earlier acts has foreshadowed this behavior?

divers, various.

And having brought our treasure where we will,
Then take we down his load, and turn him off,
Like to the empty ass, to shake his ears
And graze in commons.°

commons, public pastures.

OCTAVIUS. You may do your will;
But he's a tried and valiant soldier.

ANTONY. So is my horse, Octavius, and for that
I do appoint him store of provender.°
It is a creature that I teach to fight,
To wind, to stop, to run directly on,
His corporal motion governed by my spirit.
And, in some taste, is Lepidus but so.
He must be taught, and trained, and bid go forth—
A barren-spirited fellow, one that feeds
On objects, arts, and imitations,
Which, out of use and staled by other men,
Begin his fashion. Do not talk of him
But as a property.[67] And now, Octavius,
Listen great things. Brutus and Cassius
Are levying powers. We must straight make head.°
Therefore let our alliance be combined,
Our best friends made, our means stretched;
And let us presently go sit in council
How covert matters may be best disclosed,
And open perils surest answered.°

appoint . . . provender, provide him with food.

67. What do you expect will ultimately happen to Lepidus?

Brutus and Cassius . . . head. Brutus and Cassius were in Greece and Asia Minor, gathering forces; so must Antony and his associates.

How covert . . . answered, how hidden (covert) dangers may be discovered, and dangers already known be met.

OCTAVIUS. Let us do so, for we are at the stake,
And bayed about with many enemies;
And some that smile have in their hearts, I fear,
Millions of mischiefs.

(As ANTONY *and* OCTAVIUS *exit, the curtains of the balcony stage are drawn closed.)*

Scene 2: Brutus' camp at Sardis, a city in Asia Minor. In front of Brutus' tent. (Played on the Platform and the Inner Stage.)

Several months have passed since ANTONY *and* OCTAVIUS *made their plans. Far from Rome,* BRUTUS *awaits the arrival of* CASSIUS, *whose actions have so troubled* BRUTUS *that he has asked him here for a conference.*

The scene begins as LUCIUS *enters the platform at inner-stage curtains. He then draws the curtains aside, revealing the interior of* BRUTUS' *tent. The interior is sparsely furnished with a table, some low stools, and a few cushions.*

While LUCIUS *busies himself within the tent,* BRUTUS *and a group of his* SOLDIERS *enter the platform at left door.* LUCILIUS *and* TITINIUS, *friends of* BRUTUS, *enter the platform at right. They*

have just returned from CASSIUS' *camp and are accompanied by his servant* PINDARUS.

BRUTUS *(raising his arm in salute).* Stand, ho!°
LUCILIUS. Give the word, ho!° And stand.
BRUTUS. What now, Lucilius. Is Cassius near?
LUCILIUS. He is at hand, and Pindarus is come
To do you salutation° from his master.
BRUTUS. He greets me well. Your master, Pindarus,
In his own change, or by ill officers,°
Hath given me some worthy cause to wish
Things done, undone; but if he be at hand,
I shall be satisfied.°
PINDARUS. I do not doubt
But that my noble master will appear
Such as he is, full of regard and honor.
BRUTUS. He is not doubted. *(Motioning* LUCILIUS *aside)* A word, Lucilius,
How he received you; let me be resolved.°
LUCILIUS. With courtesy and with respect enough,
But not with such familiar instances,°
Nor with such free and friendly conference,
As he hath used of old.

Stand, ho! Halt!

Give the word, ho! Tell the soldiers to halt.

To do you salutation, to bring you greeting.

In his own . . . officers, by his own change of heart or by bad advice from troublemakers.

be satisfied, find out.

A word . . . resolved. Not content with Pindarus' assurance of Cassius' loyalty, Brutus wishes further report from Lucilius, his own man.

familiar instances, signs of friendship.

BRUTUS. Thou hast described
A hot friend cooling.[68] Ever note, Lucilius,
When love begins to sicken and decay,
It useth an enforcèd ceremony.°
There are no tricks in plain and simple faith,
But hollow men, like horses hot at hand,
Make gallant show and promise of their mettle;
But when they should endure the bloody spur,
They fall their crests, and, like deceitful jades,
Sink in the trial. Comes his army on?

LUCILIUS. They mean this night in Sardis to be quartered.
The greater part, the horse in general,°
Are come with Cassius.

(Martial music is heard offstage, followed by a SENTRY*'s ringing challenge and the murmured answer.)*

BRUTUS. Hark, he is arrived.

*(*CASSIUS*, with a group of his* SOLDIERS*, enters at right.)*

CASSIUS *(saluting).* Stand, ho!

BRUTUS *(returning the salute).* Stand, ho! Speak the word along.

FIRST SOLDIER. Stand!

SECOND SOLDIER. Stand!

THIRD SOLDIER. Stand!

CASSIUS. Most noble brother, you have done me wrong.

BRUTUS. Judge me, you gods! Wrong I mine enemies?
And, if not so, how should I wrong a brother?

CASSIUS. Brutus, this sober form of yours hides wrongs;
And when you do them—

BRUTUS *(interrupting).* Cassius, be content;
Speak your griefs softly. I do know you well.
Before the eyes of both our armies here,
Which should perceive nothing but love from us,
Let us not wrangle. Bid them move away.
Then in my tent, Cassius, enlarge your griefs,
And I will give you audience.

CASSIUS *(to his servant).* Pindarus,
Bid our commanders lead their charges off
A little from this ground.

*(*PINDARUS*, followed by* CASSIUS' SOLDIERS*, departs at right.)*

BRUTUS. Lucilius, do you the like, and let no man
Come to our tent till we have done our conference.
Let Lucius and Titinius guard our door.[69]

*(*BRUTUS *watches as his* SOLDIERS *follow* LUCILIUS *off at left. Then he and* CASSIUS *move to the inner stage.)*

68. What has happened to the relationship between Brutus and Cassius?

enforcèd ceremony, forced politeness.

the horse in general, the regular cavalry.

69. Why does Brutus take Cassius into his tent and have the door guarded? How is this scene similar to what occurred between Antony and Octavius in the preceding scene?

Scene 3: Sardis. Within Brutus' tent. (Played in the Inner Stage and on the Platform.)

Only a few seconds have elapsed since the preceding scene. LUCIUS *and* TITINIUS *guard the entrance to* BRUTUS' *tent.* BRUTUS *and* CASSIUS *stand facing each other on the inner stage.* CASSIUS *is very angry.*

CASSIUS. That you have wronged me doth appear in this:
You have condemned and noted° Lucius Pella
For taking bribes here of the Sardians,°
Wherein my letters, praying on his side,
Because I knew the man, were slighted off.
BRUTUS. You wronged yourself to write in such a case.
CASSIUS. In such a time as this it is not meet
That every nice offense should bear his comment.°
BRUTUS. Let me tell you, Cassius, you yourself
Are much condemned to have an itching palm,°
To sell and mart° your offices for gold
To undeservers.[70]
CASSIUS *(hotly).* I an itching palm?
You know that you are Brutus that speaks this,
Or, by the gods, this speech were else your last!
BRUTUS. The name of Cassius honors this corruption,
And chastisement doth therefore hide his head.°
CASSIUS. Chastisement!
BRUTUS. Remember March, the ides of March remember.
Did not great Julius bleed for justice' sake?
What villain touched his body that did stab
And not for justice? What, shall one of us,
That struck the foremost man of all this world
But for supporting robbers,° shall we now
Contaminate our fingers with base bribes,
And sell the mighty space of our large honors
For so much trash as may be graspèd thus?
I had rather be a dog, and bay the moon,
Than such a Roman.
CASSIUS. Brutus, bait not me!
I'll not endure it. You forget yourself
To hedge me in.° I am a soldier, I,
Older in practice, abler than yourself
To make conditions.°
BRUTUS. Go to! You are not, Cassius.[71]
CASSIUS. I am.
BRUTUS *(firmly).* I say you are not.
CASSIUS. Urge me no more, I shall forget myself.
Have mind upon your health. Tempt me no further.

noted, disgraced.

For taking . . . Sardians (sär′dē ənz). Brutus had, on the Sardians' complaints, publicly accused Lucius Pella of embezzling public money and, finding him guilty, had condemned him. Cassius, by contrast, had pardoned two of his friends similarly accused.

That every . . . comment, that every minor offense should be criticized.

to have an itching palm, to be greedy for money.

mart, market.

70. Of what is Brutus accusing Cassius?

The name of Cassius . . . head. If anyone but Cassius had been guilty of these deeds, he would have received severe punishment.

That struck . . . robbers, who killed Caesar for protecting dishonest public figures.

hedge me in, interfere with me.

To make conditions, to plan the campaign and tend to its details.

71. Note that here and in the next few lines Brutus and Cassius resort to childish argument and name-calling. How should the actors playing their parts deliver the lines?

BRUTUS *(unconcernedly).* Away, slight man!
CASSIUS *(in amazement).* Is't possible?
BRUTUS. Hear me, for I will speak.
Must I give way and room to your rash choler?°
Shall I be frighted when a madman stares?
CASSIUS. O ye gods, ye gods! Must I endure all this?
BRUTUS. All this! Ay, more. Fret till your proud heart break.
Go show your slaves how choleric you are,
And make your bondmen tremble. Must I budge?
Must I observe you? Must I stand and crouch
Under your testy humor? By the gods,
You shall digest the venom of your spleen
Though it do split you; for, from this day forth,
I'll use you for my mirth, yea, for my laughter,
When you are waspish.[72]
CASSIUS *(in disbelief).* Is it come to this?
BRUTUS. You say you are a better soldier.
Let it appear so; make your vaunting true,
And it shall please me well. For mine own part,
I shall be glad to learn of noble men.
CASSIUS *(pleading).* You wrong me every way! You wrong me, Brutus.
I said, an elder soldier, not a better.
Did I say "better"?
BRUTUS *(indifferently).* If you did, I care not.
CASSIUS. When Caesar lived, he durst not thus have moved me.
BRUTUS. Peace, peace! You durst not so have tempted him.
CASSIUS. I durst not!
BRUTUS. No.
CASSIUS. What, durst not tempt him?
BRUTUS. For your life you durst not.
CASSIUS *(hand on dagger).* Do not presume too much upon my love.
I may do that I shall be sorry for.
BRUTUS. You have done that you should be sorry for.
There is no terror, Cassius, in your threats,
For I am armed so strong in honesty
That they pass by me as the idle wind,
Which I respect not. I did send to you
For certain sums of gold—which you denied me—
For I can raise no money by vile means.
By heaven, I had rather coin my heart
And drop my blood for drachmas than to wring
From the hard hands of peasants their vile trash
By any indirection.° I did send
To you for gold to pay my legions,

rash choler (kol'ər), violent temper.

72. *Lines 42–50.* Of what is Brutus accusing Cassius? Is it only Cassius who is displaying the qualities mentioned in the lines? Discuss.

indirection, devious or hidden means.

Which you denied me. Was that done like Cassius?
Should I have answered Caius Cassius so?
When Marcus Brutus grows so covetous
To lock such rascal counters° from his friends,
Be ready, gods, with all your thunderbolts;
Dash him to pieces![73]
CASSIUS. I denied you not.
BRUTUS. You did.
CASSIUS. I did not; he was but a fool that brought
My answer back. Brutus hath rived° my heart.
A friend should bear his friend's infirmities,
But Brutus makes mine greater than they are.
BRUTUS. I do not, till you practice them on me.
CASSIUS. You love me not.
BRUTUS *(coldly).* I do not like your faults.
CASSIUS. A friendly eye could never see such faults.
BRUTUS. A flatterer's would not, though they do appear
As huge as high Olympus.
CASSIUS *(tragically).* Come, Antony, and young Octavius, come,
Revenge yourselves alone on Cassius,
For Cassius is aweary of the world;
Hated by one he loves, braved by his brother,
Checked like a bondman, all his faults observed,
Set in a notebook, learned, and conned by rote,°
To cast into my teeth. Oh, I could weep
My spirit from mine eyes! *(He unsheathes his dagger.)* There is my dagger,
And here my naked breast; within, a heart
Dearer than Pluto's mine,° richer than gold.
If that thou be'st a Roman, take it forth.
I, that denied thee gold, will give my heart.
Strike, as thou didst at Caesar; for I know,
When thou didst hate him worst, thou lovedst him better
Than ever thou lovedst Cassius.[74]
BRUTUS *(his good humor returning).* Sheathe your dagger.
Be angry when you will, it shall have scope;
Do what you will, dishonor shall be humor.°
O Cassius, you are yokèd with a lamb
That carries anger as the flint bears fire,
Who, much enforcèd, shows a hasty spark,
And straight is cold again.
CASSIUS *(misunderstanding).* Hath Cassius lived
To be but mirth and laughter to his Brutus,
When grief and blood ill-tempered vexeth him?
BRUTUS. When I spoke that, I was ill-tempered too.
CASSIUS. Do you confess so much? Give me your hand.

rascal counters, worthless coins.

73. *Lines 65–82.* Brutus here displays another side of his character. Of what does he boast? Why does he need Cassius' aid? Where do you suppose Cassius might get the gold?

rived, broken.

conned by rote, memorized until letter-perfect.

Pluto's mine. Pluto, the god of the underworld, is here confused with Plutus, the Greek god of riches.

74. *Lines 93–107.* Cassius here gives up the argument. What does he ask Brutus to do, and why?

dishonor shall be humor, when you dishonor me by insults, I shall consider it merely your whim.

BRUTUS. And my heart too.
CASSIUS *(with emotion).* O Brutus!
BRUTUS. What's the matter?
CASSIUS. Have not you love enough to bear with me,
When that rash humor which my mother gave me
Makes me forgetful?
BRUTUS. Yes, Cassius; and, from henceforth,
When you are over-earnest with your Brutus,
He'll think your mother chides, and leave you so.

(POET enters through front of inner stage, followed by LUCIUS, TITINIUS, and LUCILIUS.)

POET *(pleadingly).* Let me go in to see the generals.°
There is some grudge between 'em, 'tis not meet
They be alone.
LUCILIUS *(firmly).* You shall not come to them.
POET. Nothing but death shall stay me.
CASSIUS. How now? What's the matter?
POET *(chidingly).* For shame, you generals! What do you mean?
Love and be friends, as two such men should be;
For I have seen more years, I'm sure, than ye.
CASSIUS *(amused).* Ha, ha, how vilely doth this cynic rhyme!
BRUTUS *(impatiently).* Get you hence, sirrah. Saucy fellow, hence!
CASSIUS. Bear with him, Brutus. 'Tis his fashion.
BRUTUS. I'll know his humor, when he knows his time.
What should the wars do with these jigging fools?
Companion, hence! *(He turns away.)*
CASSIUS. Away, away, be gone!

(POET exits hastily through front of inner stage.)

BRUTUS. Lucilius and Titinius, bid the commanders
Prepare to lodge their companies tonight.
CASSIUS. And come yourselves, and bring Messala with you
Immediately to us.

(LUCILIUS and TITINIUS exit at left.)

BRUTUS. Lucius, a bowl of wine!

(LUCIUS crosses to the table, where he lights a taper and pours a bowl of wine for BRUTUS.)

CASSIUS *(wryly).* I did not think you could have been so angry.
BRUTUS. O Cassius, I am sick of many griefs.
CASSIUS. Of your philosophy you make no use,°
If you give place to accidental evils.
BRUTUS. No man bears sorrow better. Portia is dead.
CASSIUS. Ha! Portia?
BRUTUS. She is dead.
CASSIUS. How 'scaped I killing when I crossed you so?
O insupportable and touching loss!
Upon what sickness?

Let me . . . generals. Some readers claim there is no reason for this episode, which ends on line 137, being in the play. However, Shakespeare may have included it as a comic interlude between the tension caused by Brutus and Cassius' argument and the emotion brought forth by the news that Brutus will reveal shortly after the poet leaves.

Of your philosophy . . . use. Brutus was a Stoic (stō'ik). Believers in this philosophy thought that people should rise above emotional upsets and be unmoved by any of life's happenings.

BRUTUS. Impatient of my absence,
And grief that young Octavius with Mark Antony
Have made themselves so strong—for with her death
That tidings came—with this she fell distract,
And, her attendants absent, swallowed fire.°

swallowed fire. Portia reportedly snatched some burning charcoal from a fire and, holding it in her closed mouth, stifled herself and thus died.

CASSIUS. And died so?
BRUTUS *(nodding).* Even so.
CASSIUS. O ye immortal gods!
BRUTUS. Speak no more of her.[75] Give me a bowl of wine.
In this I bury all unkindness, Cassius. *(He drinks.)*

75. Is Brutus as unfeeling as these words suggest? Explain.

CASSIUS. My heart is thirsty for that noble pledge.
Fill, Lucius, till the wine o'erswell the cup;
I cannot drink too much of Brutus' love.
*(*LUCIUS *pours a bowl of wine for* CASSIUS. *As he does so,* BRUTUS *greets* TITINIUS, *who has reentered the platform at left.* TITINIUS *is accompanied by* MESSALA, *a friend of* BRUTUS.*)*
BRUTUS. Come in, Titinius! Welcome, good Messala.
Now sit we close about this taper here,
And call in question our necessities.° *(They all sit at the table.)*

call in question our necessities, discuss our problems.

CASSIUS *(aside).* Portia, art thou gone?
BRUTUS *(aside, to* CASSIUS*).* No more, I pray you.
(To MESSALA*)* Messala, I have here receivèd letters,
That young Octavius and Mark Antony
Come down upon us with a mighty power,
Bending their expedition toward Philippi.° *(He unrolls a scroll.)*

Philippi (fə lip'ī).

MESSALA. Myself have letters of the selfsame tenor.°

of the selfsame tenor, bearing the same tidings.

BRUTUS. With what addition?
MESSALA. That by proscription and bills of outlawry°
Octavius, Antony, and Lepidus
Have put to death an hundred senators.

bills of outlawry, public notices declaring certain persons no longer protected by Roman law. As enemies of the state they may be killed.

BRUTUS. Therein our letters do not well agree;
Mine speak of seventy senators that died
By their proscriptions, Cicero being one.
CASSIUS *(in disbelief).* Cicero one![76]

76. Why might Cassius be surprised at Cicero's death?

MESSALA. Cicero is dead,
And by that order of proscription.
Had you your letters from your wife, my lord?
BRUTUS *(flatly).* No, Messala.
MESSALA. Nor nothing in your letters writ of her?
BRUTUS. Nothing, Messala.
MESSALA. That, methinks, is strange.
BRUTUS. Why ask you? Hear you aught of her in yours?
MESSALA. No, my lord.
BRUTUS *(showing interest).* Now, as you are a Roman, tell me true.
MESSALA. Then like a Roman bear the truth I tell:

For certain she is dead, and by strange manner.[77]
BRUTUS *(stoically).* Why, farewell, Portia. We must die, Messala.
With meditating that she must die once,
I have the patience to endure it now.
MESSALA. Even so great men great losses should endure.
CASSIUS *(emotionally).* I have as much of this in art as you,
But yet my nature could not bear it so.
BRUTUS. Well, to our work alive. What do you think
Of marching to Philippi presently?°
CASSIUS. I do not think it good.
BRUTUS. Your reason?
CASSIUS. This it is:
'Tis better that the enemy seek us.
So shall he waste his means, weary his soldiers,
Doing himself offense; whilst we, lying still,
Are full of rest, defense, and nimbleness.
BRUTUS. Good reasons must of force give place to better.
The people 'twixt Philippi and this ground
Do stand but in a forced affection,
For they have grudged us contribution.
The enemy, marching along by them,
By them shall make a fuller number up,
Come on refreshed, new-added, and encouraged;
From which advantage shall we cut him off
If at Philippi we do face him there,
These people at our back.
CASSIUS *(pleading).* Hear me, good brother.
BRUTUS. Under your pardon. You must note beside
That we have tried the utmost of our friends,
Our legions are brimfull, our cause is ripe.
The enemy increaseth every day;
We, at the height, are ready to decline.
There is a tide in the affairs of men,
Which, taken at the flood, leads on to fortune;
Omitted, all the voyage of their life
Is bound in shallows and in miseries.
On such a full sea are we now afloat,
And we must take the current when it serves,
Or lose our ventures.
CASSIUS *(resignedly).* Then, with your will, go on.[78]
We'll along ourselves, and meet them at Philippi.
BRUTUS. The deep of night is crept upon our talk,
And nature must obey necessity,
Which we will niggard° with a little rest.
There is no more to say?
CASSIUS. No more. Good night.

77. Some scholars think this retelling of the news of Portia's death was the episode Shakespeare actually wanted to use in the play, but that he forgot to take out the earlier episode dealing with it. Others argue that the earlier episode provides a perfect reason for Brutus' uncharacteristic emotional tirade and that he shows his stoicism as he listens to Messala bring up the subject again. Do you think Shakespeare intended to keep one or both episodes?

presently, immediately.

78. *Lines 195–223.* Here again Brutus makes an error in judgment, but Cassius lets him have his way. Why does Brutus think they should go to Philippi? Why does Cassius disagree?

we will niggard, we will satisfy somewhat.

Early tomorrow will we rise, and hence.
BRUTUS *(standing)*. Lucius! My gown. *(To the three others)*
Farewell, good Messala.
Good night, Titinius. Noble, noble Cassius,
Good night, and good repose.
CASSIUS. O my dear brother!
This was an ill beginning of the night.
Never come such division 'tween our souls!
Let it not, Brutus.
BRUTUS. Everything is well.
CASSIUS. Good night, my lord.
BRUTUS. Good night, good brother.
TITINIUS *and* **MESSALA.** Good night, Lord Brutus.
BRUTUS. Farewell,
everyone.
*(*CASSIUS, TITINIUS, *and* MESSALA *move from the inner stage to the platform and exit at right.* LUCIUS *unfolds his master's night robe.)*
Give me the gown. Where is thy instrument?°
LUCIUS. Here in the tent.
BRUTUS. What, thou speak'st drowsily?
Poor knave,° I blame thee not; thou art o'erwatched.°
Call Claudius and some other of my men;
I'll have them sleep on cushions in my tent.
LUCIUS *(moving onto platform)*. Varro and Claudius!
*(*VARRO *and* CLAUDIUS, *entering at left, cross to inner stage.)*
VARRO. Calls my lord?
BRUTUS. I pray you, sirs, lie in my tent and sleep.
It may be I shall raise you by and by
On business to my brother Cassius.
VARRO. So please you, we will stand and watch your pleasure.
BRUTUS. I will not have it so. Lie down, good sirs.
It may be I shall otherwise bethink me.
*(*VARRO *and* CLAUDIUS *lie down.)*
Look, Lucius, here's the book I sought for so;
I put it in the pocket of my gown.
LUCIUS. I was sure your lordship did not give it me.
BRUTUS. Bear with me, good boy, I am much forgetful.
Canst thou hold up thy heavy eyes awhile,
And touch thy instrument a strain or two?
LUCIUS. Ay, my lord, an't° please you.
BRUTUS. It does, my boy.
I trouble thee too much, but thou art willing.
LUCIUS. It is my duty, sir.
BRUTUS. I should not urge thy duty past thy might;
I know young bloods look for a time of rest. *(He seats himself.)*

thy instrument, thy lute.

knave, lad.

thou art o'erwatched. Lucius has been up too long and is exhausted.

an't, if it.

LUCIUS. I have slept, my lord, already.

BRUTUS. It was well done; and thou shalt sleep again;
I will not hold thee long. If I do live,
I will be good to thee.

(LUCIUS sits on some cushions near the table and plays and sings, gradually falling asleep.)

BRUTUS. This is a sleepy tune. O murderous slumber,
Layest thou thy leaden mace° upon my boy,
That plays thee music? Gentle knave, good night;
I will not do thee so much wrong to wake thee.
If thou dost nod, thou break'st thy instrument;
I'll take it from thee. And, good boy, good night.

(He removes LUCIUS' instrument.)

Let me see, let me see; is not the leaf turned down°
Where I left reading? Here it is, I think. *(He begins to read.)*

(The GHOST OF CAESAR slowly ascends through the trap door in the floor of the inner stage.)[79]

How ill this taper burns! Ha! Who comes here?
I think it is the weakness of mine eyes
That shapes this monstrous apparition.
It comes upon me. Art thou any thing?
Art thou some god, some angel, or some devil,
That mak'st my blood cold and my hair to stare?
Speak to me what thou art.

GHOST *(in sepulchral tones)*. Thy evil spirit, Brutus.

BRUTUS. Why com'st thou?

GHOST. To tell thee thou shalt see me at Philippi.

BRUTUS. Well; then I shall see thee again?

GHOST. Ay, at Philippi.

BRUTUS. Why, I will see thee at Philippi, then.

(The GHOST descends.)

Now I have taken heart thou vanishest.
Ill spirit, I would hold more talk with thee.
Boy, Lucius! Varro! Claudius! Sirs, awake!
Claudius!

LUCIUS *(still half-asleep)*. The strings, my lord, are false.

BRUTUS. He thinks he still is at his instrument.
Lucius, awake!

LUCIUS. My lord?

BRUTUS. Didst thou dream, Lucius, that thou so criedst out?

LUCIUS. My lord, I do not know that I did cry.

BRUTUS. Yes, that thou didst. Didst thou see anything?

LUCIUS. Nothing, my lord.

BRUTUS. Sleep again, Lucius. Sirrah Claudius!
(To VARRO) Fellow thou, awake!

thy leaden mace. Morpheus (môr′fē əs), the Greek god of dreams, carried a leaden club with which he cast the spell of slumber.

the leaf turned down, an anachronism. Roman books were in the form of scrolls; there were no pages to turn down.

79. In Shakespeare's source, Plutarch, what appeared to Brutus was a ghost calling itself Brutus' "evil genius." How has Shakespeare heightened the dramatic effect by changing this to the ghost of Caesar?

VARRO. My lord?
CLAUDIUS. My lord?
BRUTUS. Why did you so cry out, sirs, in your sleep?
VARRO *and* CLAUDIUS. Did we, my lord?
BRUTUS. Ay. Saw you anything?[80]
VARRO. No, my lord, I saw nothing.
CLAUDIUS. Nor I, my lord.
BRUTUS. Go and commend me to my brother Cassius.
Bid him set on his powers betimes before,°
And we will follow.
VARRO *and* CLAUDIUS. It shall be done, my lord.
(VARRO and CLAUDIUS move from the inner stage to the platform and exit at right. BRUTUS and LUCIUS remain on the inner stage as the curtains are drawn closed.)

80. Why might Brutus have awakened these others to ask if they had seen anything?

set on . . . before, start his forces moving ahead.

Discussion

Scene 1

1. (a) What is the reason for the disagreement between Antony and Octavius? **(b)** What points does Antony make in winning the argument? **(c)** Does Antony's general ruthlessness surprise you? Why or why not?

2. What significant decision do the two men make at the end of the scene?

Scenes 2 and 3

1. Review the episode where Cassius first arrives outside Brutus' tent. Is the conduct of each man consistent with what you have learned of his personality up to this point? Discuss.

2. (a) What less-than-praiseworthy qualities of Brutus are revealed during his argument with Cassius? **(b)** What does he finally say is the reason for his ill temper? **(c)** Does this reason affect your overall feelings about him? Why or why not?

3. (a) What plan of action do Brutus and Cassius decide on after their quarrel? **(b)** Considering their opposing opinions of this plan, do you think they have made the right decision? Discuss.

4. Things seem to be looking up for Brutus after his meeting with Cassius. How does what happens then change all this?

Vocabulary

Affixes, Inflected Forms

The Latin prefix *en-* means "to cause to be," as in *enfeeble,* or "to put on or in," as in *enthrone.* Form new words using *en-* and the words listed here. Then choose the correct new words to complete the sentences that follow, changing tenses or forms as necessary. You will not use all the words.

circle rich
large shrine
live venom
noble

1. The student council's treasury was greatly ______ from the profits of the car wash.

2. This photograph is so good that we want to have it ______ to hang on the wall.

3. The swimming pool at the club is completely ______ with flowers and shrubs.

4. The local headhunters used to ______ their darts with the juice of a native plant.

5. Roberto's presence always ______ a party.

Act Five

Scene 1: The Plains of Philippi. (Played on the Platform.)
The combined armies of BRUTUS *and* CASSIUS *are about to engage the combined forces of* ANTONY *and* OCTAVIUS. *Offstage can be heard occasional battle sounds. There is a brief silence; then* OCTAVIUS *enters at right, followed by* ANTONY *and a few* OFFICERS.

OCTAVIUS. Now, Antony, our hopes are answered.
You said the enemy would not come down,
But keep the hills and upper regions.
It proves not so. Their battles° are at hand;
They mean to warn° us at Philippi here,
Answering before we do demand of them.
ANTONY. Tut, I am in their bosoms,° and I know
Wherefore they do it. They could be content
To visit other places,° and come down
With fearful bravery, thinking by this face
To fasten in our thoughts that they have courage;
But 'tis not so.
(A MESSENGER *enters from left.)*
MESSENGER. Prepare you, generals.
The enemy comes on in gallant show;
Their bloody sign° of battle is hung out,
And something to be done immediately.
ANTONY. Octavius, lead your battle softly on
Upon the left hand of the even field.
OCTAVIUS. Upon the right hand I; keep thou the left.
ANTONY *(angrily)*. Why do you cross me in this exigent?
OCTAVIUS *(stubbornly)*. I do not cross you; but I will do so.[81]
(Drum beat. BRUTUS, CASSIUS, LUCILIUS, TITINIUS, MESSALA, *and certain troops enter at left. The two armies stand facing.)*
BRUTUS *(to* CASSIUS*)*. They stand, and would have parley.
CASSIUS *(to* TITINIUS*)*. Stand fast, Titinius. We must out and talk.
*(*BRUTUS *and* CASSIUS *move toward* ANTONY *and* OCTAVIUS.*)*
OCTAVIUS *(nervously)*. Mark Antony, shall we give sign of battle?
ANTONY. No, Caesar, we will answer on their charge.°
Make forth.° The generals would have some words.
(He goes to BRUTUS *and* CASSIUS.*)*
OCTAVIUS *(to his men)*. Stir not until the signal. *(He joins* ANTONY.*)*
BRUTUS. Words before blows. Is it so, countrymen?
OCTAVIUS *(jeeringly)*. Not that we love words better, as you do.
BRUTUS. Good words are better than bad strokes, Octavius.
ANTONY. In your bad strokes, Brutus, you give good words.
Witness the hole you made in Caesar's heart,
Crying "Long live! Hail, Caesar!"

battles, armies.

warn, challenge.

bosoms, secret councils.

They could . . . places, they would prefer to be elsewhere.

bloody sign, red flag.

81. Has the relationship between Antony and Octavius changed much since they last appeared? Discuss.

answer . . . charge, fight when they attack us.

Make forth, step out ahead of the troops.

CASSIUS. Antony,
The posture of your blows are yet unknown;
But for your words, they rob the Hybla bees,°
And leave them honeyless.

ANTONY. Not stingless too?

BRUTUS. O, yes, and soundless too.
For you have stolen their buzzing, Antony,
And very wisely threat before you sting.

ANTONY *(furious)*. Villains! You did not so, when your vile daggers
Hacked one another in the sides of Caesar.
You showed your teeth like apes, and fawned like hounds,
And bowed like bondmen, kissing Caesar's feet,
Whilst damnèd Casca, like a cur, behind
Struck Caesar on the neck. O you flatterers!

CASSIUS *(to* BRUTUS, *angrily)*. Flatterers? Now, Brutus, thank yourself!
This tongue had not offended so today
If Cassius might have ruled.[82]

OCTAVIUS. Come, come, the cause. If arguing make us sweat,
The proof of it will turn to redder drops.
Look, *(He draws.)*
I draw a sword against conspirators.
When think you that the sword goes up again?
Never, till Caesar's three and thirty wounds
Be well avenged, or till another Caesar
Have added slaughter to the sword of traitors.

BRUTUS. Caesar, thou canst not die by traitors' hands,
Unless thou bring'st them with thee.

OCTAVIUS *(smugly)*. So I hope.
I was not born to die on Brutus' sword.

BRUTUS *(angrily)*. O, if thou wert the noblest of thy strain,°
Young man, thou couldst not die more honorable.

CASSIUS *(jeeringly)*. A peevish schoolboy, worthless of such honor,
Joined with a masker and a reveler!

ANTONY. Old Cassius still.

OCTAVIUS. Come, Antony, away!
Defiance, traitors, hurl we in your teeth.
If you dare fight today, come to the field;
If not, when you have stomachs.

*(*ANTONY, OCTAVIUS, *and the armies turn and leave at right.)*

CASSIUS. Why, now, blow wind, swell billow, and swim bark!
The storm is up, and all is on the hazard.

BRUTUS. Ho, Lucilius! Hark, a word with you.

LUCILIUS *(comes up to* BRUTUS*)*. My lord?

(They converse apart.)

CASSIUS. Messala!

Hybla (hī'blə) ***bees,*** bees from Hybla, an area in ancient Sicily famous for its honey.

82. What is Cassius referring to?

strain, lineage.

MESSALA *(comes up to* CASSIUS*)*. What says my general?

CASSIUS. Messala,
This is my birthday; as this very day
Was Cassius born. Give me thy hand, Messala.
Be thou my witness that against my will,
As Pompey was, am I compelled to set
Upon one battle all our liberties.
You know that I held Epicurus° strong
And his opinion. Now I change my mind,
And partly credit things that do presage.
Coming from Sardis, on our former ensign°
Two mighty eagles fell, and there they perched,
Gorging and feeding from our soldiers' hands,
Who to Philippi here consorted us.
This morning are they fled away and gone,
And in their steads do ravens, crows, and kites
Fly o'er our heads, and downward look on us,
As we were sickly prey. Their shadows seem
A canopy most fatal, under which
Our army lies, ready to give up the ghost.[83]

MESSALA. Believe not so.

CASSIUS. I but believe it partly,
For I am fresh of spirit, and resolved
To meet all perils very constantly.

BRUTUS *(ending the conversation)*. Even so, Lucilius.

CASSIUS. Now, most noble Brutus,
The gods today stand friendly, that we may,
Lovers in peace, lead on our days to age!°
But since the affairs of men rest still incertain,
Let's reason with the worst that may befall.
If we do lose this battle, then is this
The very last time we shall speak together.
What are you then determinèd to do?

BRUTUS. Even by the rule of that philosophy
By which I did blame Cato for the death
Which he did give himself°—I know not how,
But I do find it cowardly and vile,
For fear of what might fall, so to prevent
The time of life°—arming myself with patience
To stay the providence of some high powers
That govern us below.°

CASSIUS *(unbelievingly)*. Then, if we lose this battle,
You are contented to be led in triumph
Through the streets of Rome?

BRUTUS. No, Cassius, no; think not, thou noble Roman,

Epicurus (ep′ə kyür′əs), Greek philosopher who did not believe in omens or superstitions.

former ensign, foremost or forwardmost standard bearer.

83. What reasons does Cassius give for being pessimistic about the outcome of the battle?

Now . . . days to age, Cassius hopes that the gods will be on their side so that the two men will end their days as friends in peaceful times.

Even by . . . give himself. Stoicism, the philosophy Brutus followed, did not favor suicide; thus Brutus blamed his father-in-law Cato for killing himself.

prevent the time of life, cut short one's own life by suicide.

To stay . . . below, to await (stay) a normal death to be sent when the gods so decree.

That ever Brutus will go bound to Rome;
He bears too great a mind. But this same day
Must end that work the ides of March begun;
And whether we shall meet again I know not.
Therefore, our everlasting farewell take.
Forever, and forever, farewell, Cassius!
If we do meet again, why, we shall smile;
If not, why then this parting was well made.

CASSIUS. Forever, and forever, farewell, Brutus!
If we do meet again, we'll smile indeed;
If not, 'tis true this parting was well made.

BRUTUS. Why, then, lead on. O, that a man might know
The end of this day's business ere it come!
But it sufficeth that the day will end,
And then the end is known. Come, ho! Away![84]

(BRUTUS and CASSIUS move off at right.)

84. *Lines 92–125.* These lines show that Brutus and Cassius have gotten over their earlier quarrel. Why might they now be so friendly? What do the lines reveal about their characters in the face of danger?

Scene 2: The field of battle. (Played on the Platform.)

The battle is well under way. BRUTUS and his followers form the left flank of the combined army and face the forces of OCTAVIUS; CASSIUS and his men form the right flank and are opposed to ANTONY. BRUTUS, with MESSALA following, enters at left. He has prepared various dispatches which he must send to CASSIUS.

BRUTUS. Ride, ride, Messala, ride, and give these bills
Unto the legions on the other side.
(Loud alarums are heard offstage.)
Let them set on at once; for I perceive
But cold demeanor in Octavius' wing,
And sudden push gives them the overthrow.
Ride, ride, Messala. Let them all come down.[85]

(BRUTUS and MESSALA exit, going in different directions.)

85. Brutus sees signs of faltering (cold demeanor) in Octavius' men and thinks one strong attack will overcome them. What is in the message he sends to Cassius?

Scene 3: A hill in another part of the battlefield. (Played on the Platform and the Balcony.)

It is now late afternoon. Several SOLDIERS, weary from the fighting, enter at right and group themselves near the left pillar. As offstage alarums sound, CASSIUS and TITINIUS enter at right. CASSIUS, carrying a broken standard, speaks angrily.

CASSIUS *(pointing to right).* Oh, look, Titinius, look, the villains fly!
Myself have to mine own turned enemy;°
This ensign here of mine was turning back;
I slew the coward, and did take it° from him.

TITINIUS. O Cassius, Brutus gave the word too early,
Who, having some advantage on Octavius,

Myself . . . enemy. Cassius has had to turn on some of his own men who were deserting. Even an ensign was in headlong flight.

it, the ensign's standard.

Took it too eagerly. His soldiers fell to spoil,°
Whilst we by Antony are all enclosed.[86]

fell to spoil, began plundering Octavius' camp.

86. How is it Brutus' fault that Cassius' men have been encircled (enclosed) by Antony's forces?

*(*CASSIUS *tosses the broken standard to the* SOLDIERS. *As they move off at left,* PINDARUS, CASSIUS' *servant, runs on at right.)*

PINDARUS. Fly further off, my lord, fly further off!
Mark Antony is in your tents, my lord.
Fly, therefore, noble Cassius, fly far off.

CASSIUS. This hill is far enough. Look, look, Titinius!
Are those my tents where I perceive the fire?

TITINIUS. They are, my lord.

CASSIUS. Titinius, if thou lovest me,
Mount thou my horse, and hide thy spurs in him,
Till he have brought thee up to yonder troops
And here again, that I may rest assured
Whether yond troops are friend or enemy.°

TITINIUS. I will be here again, even with a thought.°

that I may . . . enemy. Cassius wonders if the horsemen he sees approaching are from his army or are Antony's men.

even . . . thought, quick as a thought.

(He exits at right.)

CASSIUS *(pointing to balcony).* Go, Pindarus, get higher on that hill.
My sight was ever thick. Regard Titinius,
And tell me what thou not'st about the field.

*(*PINDARUS *exits at inner-stage curtains to ascend the hill.)*

This day I breathèd first. Time is come round,
And where I did begin, there shall I end.°
My life is run his compass. Sirrah, what news?

This day . . . end, I shall die on the same day I was born.

PINDARUS *(appearing above).* O my lord!

CASSIUS. What news?

PINDARUS. Titinius is enclosèd round about
With horsemen, that make to him on the spur;
Yet he spurs on. Now they are almost on him.
Now, Titinius! Now some light.° Oh, he
Lights too. He's ta'en.

light, dismount.

(There are shouts offstage.)

And, hark! They shout for joy.

CASSIUS. Come down, behold no more.
Oh, coward that I am, to live so long,
To see my best friend ta'en before my face![87]

87. What does Cassius think has happened to his friend Titinius?

*(*PINDARUS *exits at balcony curtains in order to descend from the hill. In a moment he rejoins* CASSIUS.)

Come hither, sirrah.
In Parthia° did I take thee prisoner;
And then I swore thee, saving of thy life,
That whatsoever I did bid thee do,
Thou shouldst attempt it. Come now, keep thine oath.
Now be a freeman, and with this good sword,
That ran through Caesar's bowels, search this bosom.°
Stand not to answer. Here, take thou the hilts;

Parthia (pär′thē ə), an ancient country in Asia.

Now be . . . bosom, Cassius will give Pindarus his freedom if Pindarus will kill Cassius.

And, when my face is covered, as 'tis now,
Guide thou the sword.
*(*PINDARUS *obeys and stabs* CASSIUS.*)*
Caesar, thou art revenged.
Even with the sword that killèd thee. *(*CASSIUS *dies.)*[88]

88. What is ironic about Cassius' manner of death?

PINDARUS. So, I am free; yet would not so have been,
Durst I have done my will. O Cassius!
Far from this country Pindarus shall run,
Where never Roman shall take note of him.
*(*PINDARUS, *leaving* CASSIUS' *sword behind, hastens to left door and exits. Then* TITINIUS, *with* MESSALA, *reenters at right. On his head* TITINIUS *wears a garland signifying victory.)*
MESSALA. It is but change,° Titinius; for Octavius
Is overthrown by noble Brutus' power,
As Cassius' legions are by Antony.

but change, a fair exchange.

TITINIUS. These tidings will well comfort Cassius.
MESSALA. Where did you leave him?
TITINIUS. All disconsolate,
With Pindarus his bondman, on this hill.
MESSALA. Is not that he that lies upon the ground?
TITINIUS *(running forward).* He lies not like the living. O my heart!
MESSALA. Is not that he?
TITINIUS *(sadly).* No, this was he, Messala,
But Cassius is no more. O setting sun,
As in thy red rays thou dost sink tonight,
So in his red blood Cassius' day is set!
The sun of Rome is set. Our day is gone;
Clouds, dews, and dangers come; our deeds are done!
Mistrust of my success hath done this deed.
MESSALA. Mistrust of good success hath done this deed.
O hateful error, melancholy's child,
Why dost thou show to the apt thoughts of men
The things that are not?° O error, soon conceived,
Thou never com'st unto a happy birth,
But kill'st the mother that engendered thee!

Why dost thou . . . not? Why do men so readily accept things as true when they are really not?

TITINIUS *(calling).* What, Pindarus? Where art thou, Pindarus?
MESSALA. Seek him, Titinius, whilst I go to meet
The noble Brutus, thrusting this report
Into his ears. I may say "thrusting" it;
For piercing steel and darts envenomèd
Shall be as welcome to the ears of Brutus
As tidings of this sight.
TITINIUS. Hie, you, Messala,
And I will seek for Pindarus the while.
(As MESSALA *exits at left,* TITINIUS *kneels beside* CASSIUS.*)*
Why didst thou send me forth, brave Cassius?

Did I not meet thy friends?° And did not they
Put on my brows this wreath of victory,
And bid me give it thee? Didst thou not hear their shouts?
Alas, thou hast misconstrued everything![89]
But, hold thee, take this garland on thy brow.

(He places the wreath on CASSIUS' *head.)*

Thy Brutus bid me give it thee, and I
Will do his bidding. *(He rises.)* Brutus, come apace,
And see how I regarded Caius Cassius. *(He takes* CASSIUS' *sword.)*
By your leave, gods!—This is a Roman's part.°
Come, Cassius' sword, and find Titinius' heart. *(Kills himself.)*

(Alarums offstage. MESSALA *reenters at left with* BRUTUS, YOUNG CATO, STRATO, VOLUMNIUS, LUCILIUS, *and several* SOLDIERS.*)*

BRUTUS. Where, where, Messala, doth his body lie?

MESSALA. Lo, yonder, and Titinius mourning it.

BRUTUS. Titinius' face is upward.

CATO *(going to* TITINIUS*).* He is slain.

BRUTUS. O Julius Caesar, thou art mighty yet!
Thy spirit walks abroad, and turns our swords
In our own proper entrails.[90]

(There are low alarums offstage.)

CATO. Brave Titinius!
Look whether he have not crowned dead Cassius!

BRUTUS. Are yet two Romans living such as these?
The last of all the Romans, fare thee well!
It is impossible that ever Rome
Should breed thy fellow. Friends, I owe moe tears
To this dead man than you shall see me pay.
I shall find time, Cassius, I shall find time.

(He motions to the SOLDIERS, *who pick up the bodies of* CASSIUS *and* TITINIUS.*)*

Come, therefore, and to Thasos° send his body.
His funerals shall not be in our camp,
Lest it discomfort us. Lucilius, come,
And come, young Cato, let us to the field.
We shall try fortune in a second fight. *(All exit at left.)*

Scene 4: Another part of the battlefield. (Played on the Platform.) *Alarum.* BRUTUS, *exhausted, runs on from right, sword in hand, followed by* MESSALA, YOUNG CATO, LUCILIUS, *and* FLAVIUS.

BRUTUS *(encouragingly).* Yet, countrymen, O, yet hold up your heads! *(He,* MESSALA, *and* FLAVIUS *run off left.)*

CATO. Who will go with me?
I will proclaim my name about the field:
I am the son of Marcus Cato, ho!

thy friends, that is, Brutus' man Messala and his army.

89. What really happened to Titinius?

This is a Roman's part. The Romans prided themselves on being freemen, and traditionally preferred death at their own hands to acknowledging another man their master.

90. What does Brutus mean in these lines?

Thasos (thā'sôs), an island in the Aegean Sea.

A foe to tyrants, and my country's friend.
I am the son of Marcus Cato, ho!

(ANTONY'S SOLDIERS run on from right, fight with LUCILIUS and YOUNG CATO.)

LUCILIUS *(hitting his chest).* And I am Brutus, Marcus Brutus I!
Brutus, my country's friend! Know me for Brutus!

(YOUNG CATO is slain by ANTONY'S SOLDIERS.)

O young and noble Cato, art thou down?
Why, now thou diest as bravely as Titinius,
And mayst be honored, being Cato's son. *(He stands mourning.)*

FIRST SOLDIER. Yield, or thou diest.

LUCILIUS. Only I yield to die.°

(Handing over his sword)

There is so much that thou wilt kill me straight;
Kill Brutus, and be honor'd in his death.[91]

FIRST SOLDIER. We must not. A noble prisoner!

SECOND SOLDIER. Room, ho! Tell Antony, Brutus is ta'en.

(ANTONY enters from left.)

FIRST SOLDIER. I'll tell the news. Here comes the general.
Brutus is ta'en, Brutus is ta'en, my lord.

ANTONY. Where is he?

LUCILIUS *(pleased with his ruse).* Safe, Antony; Brutus is safe enough.
I dare assure thee that no enemy
Shall ever take alive the noble Brutus.
The gods defend him from so great a shame!
When you do find him, or alive or dead,
He will be found like Brutus, like himself.

ANTONY. This is not Brutus, friend, but, I assure you,
A prize no less in worth. Keep this man safe;
Give him all kindness. I had rather have
Such men my friends than enemies. Go on,
And see whe'er Brutus be alive or dead;
And bring us word unto Octavius' tent
How every thing is chanced.

(SOLDIERS lead LUCILIUS through inner-stage curtains; ANTONY exits right.)

Scene 5: Another part of the battlefield. (Played on the Platform.)
As the scene begins, a large rock is raised through the trap door in the center of the platform. Then VOLUMNIUS, carrying a lighted torch, enters at left. He is followed by BRUTUS, CLITUS, DARDANIUS, and STRATO. All are overcome with fatigue and a sense of defeat.

BRUTUS. Come, poor remains of friends, rest on this rock.

CLITUS. Statilius showed the torchlight, but, my lord,

Only I . . . die, I yield only to die immediately.

91. Why might Lucilius be claiming to be Brutus?

He came not back. He is or ta'en or slain.°
BRUTUS. Sit thee down, Clitus. Slaying is the word.
It is a deed in fashion. Hark thee, Clitus. *(Whispers to* CLITUS*)*
CLITUS. What, I, my lord? No, not for all the world.
BRUTUS. Peace then. No words.
CLITUS *(with fervor).* I'll rather kill myself.
BRUTUS. Hark thee, Dardanius. *(Again he whispers his request.)*
DARDANIUS *(aghast).* Shall I do such a deed?
*(*BRUTUS *walks away from the men.)*
CLITUS. O Dardanius!
DARDANIUS. O Clitus!
CLITUS. What ill request did Brutus make to thee?
DARDANIUS. To kill him, Clitus. Look, he meditates.
CLITUS. Now is that noble vessel full of grief,
That it runs over even at his eyes.
BRUTUS. Come hither, good Volumnius; list a word.
VOLUMNIUS *(bowing).* What says my lord?
BRUTUS. Why this, Volumnius:
The ghost of Caesar hath appeared to me
Two several times by night; at Sardis once,
And, this last night, here in Philippi fields.
I know my hour is come.[92]
VOLUMNIUS. Not so, my lord.
BRUTUS. Nay, I am sure it is, Volumnius.
Thou seest the world, Volumnius, how it goes;
Our enemies have beat us to the pit.°
(Low alarums signal the approach of ANTONY *and* OCTAVIUS.*)*

Statilius (stə til'ē əs) ***. . . slain.*** Statilius had volunteered to slip through the enemy's lines and observe their camp; later, if all was well with him, he would signal with a torch. He did signal, but never returned. It was thought he was killed shortly after he flashed the signal.

92. What new information does Brutus reveal? Why might Shakespeare have chosen to reveal it in this way?

Our enemies . . . pit, an allusion to the method of forming a large circle around a wild animal and beating on drums to drive it into a pit, where it can be captured.

It is more worthy to leap in ourselves,
Than tarry till they push us. Good Volumnius,
Thou know'st that we two went to school together.
Even for that our love of old, I prithee,°
Hold thou my sword-hilts, whilst I run on it.[93]

VOLUMNIUS. That's not an office for a friend, my lord.

(More alarums are sounded, this time louder.)

CLITUS. Fly, fly, my lord! There is no tarrying here.

BRUTUS *(going to each in turn).* Farewell to you; and you; and
you, Volumnius.
Strato, thou hast been all this while asleep;
Farewell to thee too, Strato. Countrymen,
My heart doth joy that yet in all my life
I found no man but he was true to me.
I shall have glory by this losing day
More than Octavius and Mark Antony
By this vile conquest shall attain unto.
So fare you well at once; for Brutus' tongue
Hath almost ended his life's history.
Night hangs upon mine eyes; my bones would rest.
That hath but labored to attain this hour.

(The alarum grows urgent, accompanied by cries of "Fly, fly!")

CLITUS. Fly, my lord, fly!

BRUTUS. Hence! I will follow.

(CLITUS, DARDANIUS, and VOLUMNIUS hurry off at right. STRATO, awake now, starts to follow them.)

I prithee, Strato, stay thou by thy lord.
Thou art a fellow of a good respect;
Thy life hath had some smatch° of honor in it.
Hold then my sword, and turn away thy face,
While I do run upon it. Wilt thou, Strato?

STRATO. Give me your hand first. Fare you well, my lord.

BRUTUS. Farewell, good Strato.

(STRATO takes the sword and holds it with the blade exposed. As STRATO averts his face, BRUTUS runs upon the naked blade.)

Caesar, now be still.
I killed not thee with half so good a will. *(BRUTUS dies.)*[94]

(Offstage trumpets sound retreat as two SOLDIERS with torches enter at left. They light the way for ANTONY and OCTAVIUS. More SOLDIERS follow, among them MESSALA and LUCILIUS, now prisoners. All see STRATO standing over the dead BRUTUS.)

OCTAVIUS. What man is that?

MESSALA. My master's man. Strato, where is thy master?

STRATO. Free from the bondage you are in, Messala.
The conquerors can but make a fire of him,°
For Brutus only overcame himself,

prithee, pray thee.

93. What is Brutus asking of Volumnius? How does this apparently differ from what he asked Clitus and Dardanius? Why might he have changed his mind? What is Volumnius' response?

smatch, taste; touch.

94. In what respect do Brutus' last words resemble those of Cassius?

The conquerors . . . him, a reference to the Roman custom of burning the dead.

And no man else hath honor by his death.°
LUCILIUS. So Brutus should be found. I thank thee, Brutus,
That thou has proved Lucilius' saying true.°
OCTAVIUS. All that served Brutus, I will entertain them.°
Fellow, wilt thou bestow thy time with me?
STRATO. Ay, if Messala will prefer° me to you.
OCTAVIUS. Do so, good Messala.
MESSALA. How died my master, Strato?
STRATO. I held the sword, and he did run on it.
MESSALA. Octavius, then take him to follow thee,
That did the latest service to my master.
ANTONY *(looking at the body).* This was the noblest Roman of
them all.
All the conspirators save only he
Did that they did in envy of great Caesar;
He, only in a general honest thought
And common good to all, made one of them.°
His life was gentle, and the elements°
So mixed in him that Nature might stand up
And say to all the world, "This was a man!"[95]
(ANTONY removes his cloak and covers BRUTUS with it. He then signals to the SOLDIERS, who lift BRUTUS' body onto their shields.)
OCTAVIUS. According to his virtue let us use him,
With all respect and rites of burial.
Within my tent his bones tonight shall lie,
Most like a soldier, ordered honorably.
So call the field to rest; and let's away,
To part the glories° of this happy day.
(All exit at right to the solemn accompaniment of offstage drums beating a death march.)

no man . . . death, no one can claim the honor of defeating him in combat.

Lucilius' . . . true. Lucilius had said that Brutus' enemies would never take him alive.

I will . . . them, I will take all of Brutus' servants and make them my own.

prefer, recommend.

made one of them, joined them.

elements, the four basic elements—earth, air, fire, and water. According to Antony, they were mixed in Brutus in ideal proportions.

95. Do you agree with Antony's assessment of Brutus? Discuss.

part the glories, divide the honors.

Discussion

Scenes 1 and 2

1. (a) Contrast Antony and Octavius' relationship in Scene 1 with that of Brutus and Cassius. **(b)** What might account for the difference in how the pairs are getting along?

2. Brutus explains his feelings about suicide to Cassius, but then seems to contradict himself a few lines later. **(a)** With what words does he describe the act of taking one's own life? **(b)** What does he then say to suggest that he has not entirely ruled out this option?

3. (a) What plan of attack does Brutus want to put into action in Scene 2? **(b)** What might have been Shakespeare's purpose in including this very short scene?

Scene 3

1. (a) What is Cassius' mood as the scene opens? **(b)** What reasons does he have for feeling as he does?

2. What does Pindarus see that causes him to misinterpret what has happened to Titinius?

3. **(a)** How are Cassius' decision to die and the manner of his death in keeping with his character? **(b)** What effect does his death have on Titinius? on Brutus?

Scenes 4 and 5

1. What qualities do the followers of Brutus show in Scene 4? in their refusal to kill Brutus in Scene 5?

2. Bidding his friends farewell, Brutus says he has found "no man but he was true to me." **(a)** Who did take unfair advantage of Brutus' trust? Under what circumstances? **(b)** What does the remark show about Brutus' character?

3. **(a)** How sincere do you think Antony is in making his remarks over Brutus' body? **(b)** What role do you expect he and Octavius will play in Rome's future?

Composition

Choose one of the following to write about.

1. After reaching their highest point in Act Three, the fortunes of the protagonist of a Shakespearean tragedy go steadily downhill through Act Five, where the character finally dies. Review Acts Three to Five to see how this pattern is followed in *Julius Caesar.*

Write a four- or five-paragraph composition describing the decline in the fortunes of Brutus. Include his own mistakes as well as things done to him by others.

2. Some critics claim that it was really Julius Caesar (or his spirit) that defeated Brutus and Cassius at Philippi. Do you agree with this view? Go through Act Five and pertinent parts of Act Four for evidence to help you first form and then support your opinion.

Write a three- or four-paragraph essay in which you present your view and the reasons you have for holding it. (See "Defending Your Position," page 663, in the Composition Guide.)

William Shakespeare 1564–1616

The first reference to William Shakespeare is a baptismal record for April 26, 1564, at Holy Trinity Church in Stratford-on-Avon. Since at the time it was customary for infants to be baptized when three days old, it is generally assumed that Shakespeare was born on April 23. His father was John Shakespeare, a glovemaker and farm-product dealer who during William's boyhood was elected to various offices, becoming in time high bailiff or mayor. Once William could read and write English, a requirement then for going to school, he undoubtedly was enrolled in Stratford's excellent grammar school, taught by an Oxford University graduate. There he learned Latin and a little Greek.

In 1577 John Shakespeare suffered financial reverses, and it is assumed that William dropped out of school. He is next heard of in 1582, when he married Anne Hathaway from the neighboring hamlet of Shottery. Their first child was born in 1583, followed two years later by twins.

Records are scarce on Shakespeare until 1592, but by then he was in London, where there was a performance of *Harry the Sixth* (apparently Shakespeare's *Henry VI, Part I*) on March 3. Later that year he is mentioned as a playwright in a pamphlet by Robert Greene. From at least 1592 to 1610 Shakespeare lived primarily in London, writing two or more plays a year for his acting company. By 1597 he was wealthy enough to buy New Place, one of the largest houses in Stratford, which he made his principal residence in 1610, traveling to London only when necessary.

When Shakespeare died on April 23, 1616, he left the world thirty-seven plays, a number of long poems, and a collection of sonnets. Recognizing the importance of his plays, his fellow actors John Heminges and Henry Condell arranged to have them collected and published in 1623 in a large volume known today as the First Folio.

Unit 6 Review: *Shakespearean Drama*

Content Review

1. Characterize the four main figures in *Julius Caesar,* including for each at least three details Shakespeare uses to make the character seem realistic. Do you think each of the characters deserves his final fate? Explain.

2. Contrast the characters of Portia and Calpurnia. Which seems to have a more satisfactory relationship with her husband? Give examples to support your answer.

3. Most critics agree that the commoners play a very important role in the play. Analyze each scene in which they or their reactions are featured (One, 1; One, 2; Three, 2; Three, 3) and explain how each of these portrayals of them advances or complicates the plot.

4. All of the conspirators except Cassius and Brutus disappear from the play after Act Three. What might have been Shakespeare's purpose in doing this?

5. In addition to a tragic hero and a major conflict, many Shakespearean tragedies also feature the following elements. Give one example of each in *Julius Caesar,* and explain its effect on the plot: **(a)** desire for revenge; **(b)** use of humor to relieve a somber mood; **(c)** supernatural occurrence; **(d)** chance happening that causes a tragic catastrophe.

6. Shakespeare is sometimes thought to have played the parts of Cinna the poet and of the unnamed poet in Act Four. Review the dialogue in each case; then explain how Shakespeare's presence would have added humor to the scene.

Concept Review: Interpretation of New Material

Read the introduction and scene from the play. Then use the questions following it to review your understanding of the terms and concepts dealt with in the unit.

from Henry IV, Part II • *William Shakespeare* Great Britain

Henry IV is a history play dealing with the reign of the English king of the same name. Since Henry obtained the throne in a rebellion rather than by being born to it, his fellow nobles have constantly questioned his authority; and the apparent indifference of his son and heir Prince Harry to the affairs of state makes Henry despair that the country will ever be ruled in an orderly manner.

Just before the scene presented here, the prince, sitting alone at his seriously ill father's bedside, thinks the king has died. Deeply grieved, he takes up the crown pledging to defend the honor which has descended to him, and leaves the room. When the king awakes, he misses his son and angrily asks for him. The prince reenters the room.

PRINCE. I never thought to hear you speak again.
KING HENRY. Thy wish was father, Harry, to that thought:
I stay too long by thee,° I weary thee.
Dost thou so hunger for my empty chair
That thou wilt needs invest thee with mine honors

by thee, in your opinion.

Before thy hour be ripe? O foolish youth!
Thou seek'st the greatness that will overwhelm thee.
Stay but a little; for my cloud of dignity
Is held from falling with so weak a wind
That it will quickly drop: my day is dim.
Thou hast stol'n that which after some few hours
Were thine without offense; and at my death
Thou hast sealed up° my expectation:
Thy life did manifest thou lovedst me not,
And thou wilt have me die assured of it.
Thou hidest a thousand daggers in thy thoughts,
Which thou hast whetted on thy stony heart,
To stab at half an hour of my life.
What! canst thou not forbear me half an hour?
Then get thee gone and dig my grave thyself,
And bid the merry bells ring to thine ear
That thou art crowned, not that I am dead. . . .
Pluck down my officers, break my decrees;
For now a time is come to mock at form:°
Harry the Fifth is crowned! up, vanity!
Down, royal state! all you sage counsellors, hence!
And to the English court assemble now,
From every region, apes of idleness! . . .
For the fifth Harry from curbed license° plucks
The muzzle of restraint, and the wild dog
Shall flesh° his tooth in every innocent.
O my poor kingdom! sick with civil blows!°. . .
O, thou wilt be a wilderness again,
Peopled with wolves, thy old inhabitants!

PRINCE. O, pardon me, my liege! but for my tears,
The moist impediments unto my speech,
I had forestalled this dear° and deep rebuke
Ere you with grief had spoke and I had heard
The course of it so far. There is your crown;
And He that wears the crown immortally
Long guard it yours! If I affect° it more
Than as your honor and as your renown,
Let me no more from this obedience° rise. . . .
God witness with me, when I here came in,
And found no course of breath within your majesty,
How cold it struck my heart! If I do feign,
O, let me in my present wildness die
And never live to show the incredulous world
The noble change that I have purposèd!
Coming to look on you, thinking you dead,
And dead almost, my liege, to think you were,

sealed up, finally confirmed.

form, order.

curbed license, restrained vice.

flesh, imbed in flesh; bite.

civil blows, civil wars.

dear, earnest.

affect, desire.

obedience, act of obedience, i.e., kneeling.

I spake unto this crown as having sense,
And thus upbraided it: "The care on thee depending
Hath fed upon the body of my father;
Therefore, thou best of gold art worst of gold:
Other, less fine in carat,° is more precious,
Preserving life in medicine potable:°
But thou most fine, most honored, most renowned,
Hast eat thy bearer up." Thus, my most royal liege,
Accusing it, I put it on my head,
To try with it, as with an enemy
That had before my face murdered my father,
The quarrel of a true inheritor.
But if it did infect my blood with joy,
Or swell my thoughts to any strain of pride; . . .
Let God for ever keep it from my head,
And make me as the poorest vassal° is
That doth with awe and terror kneel to it!

KING HENRY. O my son,
God put it in thy mind to take it hence,
That thou mightst win the more thy father's love,
Pleading so wisely in excuse of it!
Come hither, Harry: sit thou by my bed;
And hear, I think, the very latest° counsel
That ever I shall breathe. God knows, my son,
By what by-paths and indirect crooked ways
I met° this crown; and I myself know well
How troublesome it sat upon my head:
To thee it shall descend with better quiet,
Better opinion, better confirmation;
For all the soil of the achievement° goes
With me into the earth. It seemed in me
But as an honor snatched with boisterous hand,
And I had many living to upbraid
My gain of it by their assistances;
Which daily grew to quarrel and to bloodshed,
Wounding supposed° peace: all these bold fears
Thou seest with peril I have answered; . . .
Yet, though thou standest more sure than I could do,
Thou art not firm enough, since griefs are green;°
And all my friends, which thou must make thy friends,
Have but their stings and teeth newly ta'en out;
By whose fell working° I was first advanced,
And by whose power I well might lodge a fear
To be again displaced: which to avoid,
I cut them off; and had a purpose now,
To lead out many to the Holy Land,

carat, a measure of the purity of gold.

medicine potable, refers to *aurum potabile,* a liquid medicine containing gold, thought suitable for curing illness by primitive physicians.

vassal, slave.

latest, last.

met, gained.

soil . . . achievement, the shame of the winning.

supposed, imaginary.

griefs are green, griefs are fresh.

fell working, fierce labors.

Lest rest and lying still might make them look
Too near unto my state.° Therefore, my Harry,
Be it thy course to busy giddy minds
With foreign quarrels; that action, hence borne out,
May waste the memory of the former days.
More would I, but my lungs are wasted so
That strength of speech is utterly denied me.
How I came by the crown, O God forgive;
And grant it may with thee in true peace live!

PRINCE. My gracious liege,
You won it, wore it, kept it, gave it me;
Then plain and right must my possession be:
Which I with more than with a common pain
'Gainst all the world will rightfully maintain.

look . . . state, examine my claims to the throne too closely.

---

1. When Harry enters, the king accuses him of **(a)** wishing him dead; **(b)** plotting his death; **(c)** indifference to his death; **(d)** false grief over his death.

2. What does the king mean by "the greatness that will overwhelm" Harry?

3. Lines 16–18 contain an example of **(a)** allusion; **(b)** analogy; **(c)** extended metaphor; **(d)** irony.

4. In lines 23–26 the king predicts for Harry a reign that is **(a)** prosperous; **(b)** war-filled; **(c)** confused and lawless; **(d)** uneventful.

5. Describe in your own words the sort of people the king fears will fill the court (lines 26–28).

6. Explain the allusion used in lines 39–41.

7. The prince says the crown "hast eat . . . up" the king. In this context the crown is a symbol of **(a)** corruption; **(b)** the demands of kingship; **(c)** Harry's indifference; **(d)** Harry's desire for power.

8. The king thinks this quarrel has **(a)** severed them forever; **(b)** strained his wits; **(c)** brought them closer together; **(d)** wasted too much time.

9. The king's final hope is that the crown will **(a)** always stay in his family; **(b)** make his son a better person; **(c)** provide his son a peaceful reign; **(d)** remain near his bed until he dies.

10. A line that is *not* perfect blank verse is line **(a)** 6; **(b)** 54; **(c)** 75; **(d)** 97.

Composition Review

Choose one of the following assignments.

1. Caesar is often said to have a private character that makes him behave naturally and a public character concerned only with projecting an image of greatness. Review the play to find examples of both these aspects of the man.

Write an essay in which you contrast Caesar's private and public characters.

2. There are those who say Cassius is a better person than his role as conspirator suggests; there are also those who call Brutus a stuffed shirt and a windbag. Choose either view; then decide whether you agree with it by analyzing what you have seen of the character in the play.

Write an essay giving specific reasons why you accept or reject the view you've chosen.

3. According to Sir J.E.E. Dalberg, "Power tends to corrupt and absolute power corrupts absolutely." Apply this quote to both plays in the unit, considering **(a)** how power affects the major characters in *Julius Caesar,* and **(b)** the moves Henry IV found necessary to keep the throne.

Write an essay showing how Dalberg's view seems to be one Shakespeare could accept.

Unit 7
Nonfiction

See CONNOTATION/DENOTATION Handbook of Literary Terms

The Secret Room

Corrie ten Boom the Netherlands

(with John and Elizabeth Sherrill)

Corrie ten Boom's predicament called for desperate but careful steps: more and more Jews were turning to her to escape the Nazis, whose eyes and ears were everywhere.

When Nazi armies invaded Corrie ten Boom's homeland in 1940, she and her fellow citizens observed many dreadful changes. Living in the Holland province city of Haarlem (här′ləm) with her sister, Betsie, and elderly father, she tried to maintain the appearance of an ordinary life, working as a watchmaker at the Beje (bāy′yāy), their combined home and shop. But as the following excerpt makes clear, there was also an unseen side to her life.

Other family members introduced in Corrie's story are Peter, her nephew; Willem (vil′əm), her minister brother (who ran a home for the aged at Hilversum that he used as an escape route for fleeing Jews); Tine and Kik, Willem's wife and son; and Nollie, Peter's mother and another sister of Corrie's.

It was Sunday, May 10, 1942, exactly two years after the fall of Holland. The sunny spring skies, the flowers in the lamppost boxes, did not at all reflect the city's mood. German soldiers wandered aimlessly through the streets, some looking as if they had not yet recovered from a hard Saturday night.

Each month the occupation seemed to grow harsher, restrictions more numerous. The latest heartache for Dutchmen was an edict making it a crime to sing the "Wilhelmus,"[1] our national anthem.

Father, Betsie, and I were on our way to the Dutch Reformed church in Velsen,[2] a small town not far from Haarlem, where Peter had won the post of organist in competition against forty older and more experienced musicians. The organ at Velsen was one of the finest in the country; though the train seemed slower each time, we went frequently.

Peter was already playing, invisible in the tall organ loft, when we squeezed into the crowded pew. That was one thing the occupation had done for Holland: churches were packed.

After hymns and prayers came the sermon, a good one today, I thought. The closing prayers were said. And then, electrically, the whole church sat at attention. Without preamble, every stop pulled out to full volume, Peter was playing the "Wilhelmus"!

Father, at eighty-two, was the first one on his feet. Now everyone was standing. From somewhere in back of us a voice sang out the words.

1. ***"Wilhelmus"*** (vil′helm əs).
2. ***Velsen*** (vel′zən). Other Netherlands locations mentioned in the selection are Rotterdam, Amsterdam, Utrecht (yü′trekt), and Aerdenhout (er′dən hout′).

Another joined in, and another. Then we were all singing together, the full voice of Holland singing her forbidden anthem. We sang at the top of our lungs, sang our oneness, our hope, our love for Queen and country. On this anniversary of defeat it seemed almost for a moment that we were victors.

Afterward we waited for Peter at the small side door of the church. It was a long time before he was free to come away with us, so many people wanted to embrace him, to shake his hand and thump his back. Clearly he was enormously pleased with himself.

But now that the moment had passed I was, as usual, angry with him. The Gestapo[3] was certain to hear about it, perhaps already had: their eyes and ears were everywhere. For what had Peter risked so much? Not for people's lives but for a gesture. For a moment's meaningless defiance.

At Bos en Hoven Straat,[4] however, Peter was a hero as one by one his family made us describe again what had happened. The only members of the household who felt as I did were the two Jewish women staying at Nollie's. One of these was an elderly Austrian lady whom Willem had sent into hiding here.

The other woman was a young, blonde, blue-eyed Dutch Jew with flawless false identity papers supplied by the Dutch national underground itself. The papers were so good and Annaliese looked so unlike the Nazi stereotype of a Jew that she went freely in and out of the house, shopping and helping out at the school, giving herself out to be a friend of the family whose husband had died in the bombing of Rotterdam.

I spent an anxious afternoon, tensing at the sound of every motor, for only the police, Germans, and NSBers[5] had automobiles nowadays. But the time came to go home to the Beje and still nothing had happened.

3. ***Gestapo*** (gə stä′pō), an official group of secret police created during the Nazi regime, known for its brutality.
4. ***Straat*** (strät), street. [*Dutch*]
5. ***NSBers.*** The letters stand for the Dutch name of the National Socialist Movement. The members of this Dutch political party collaborated with the Nazis.

I worried two more days, then decided either Peter had not been reported or that the Gestapo had more important things to occupy them. It was Wednesday morning just as Father and I were unlocking our workbenches that Peter's little sister Cocky burst into the shop.

"Opa! Tante Corrie![6] They came for Peter! They took him away!"

"Who? Where?"

But she didn't know and it was three days before the family learned that he had been taken to the federal prison in Amsterdam.

It was 7:55 in the evening, just a few minutes before the new curfew hour of 8:00. Peter had been in prison for two weeks. Father and Betsie and I were seated around the dining-room table, Father replacing watches in their pockets and Betsie doing needlework, our big, black, slightly Persian cat curled contentedly in her lap. A knock on the alley door made me glance in the window mirror. There in the bright spring twilight stood a woman. She carried a small suitcase and—odd for the time of year—wore a fur coat, gloves, and a heavy veil.

I ran down and opened the door. "Can I come in?" she asked. Her voice was high-pitched in fear.

"Of course." I stepped back. The woman looked over her shoulder before moving into the little hallway.

"My name is Kleermaker. I'm a Jew."

"How do you do?" I reached out to take her bag, but she held on to it. "Won't you come upstairs?"

Father and Betsie stood up as we entered the dining room. "Mrs. Kleermaker, my father and my sister."

"I was about to make some tea!" cried Betsie. "You're just in time to join us!"

Father drew out a chair from the table and Mrs. Kleermaker sat down, still gripping the suitcase. The "tea" consisted of old leaves which had been crushed and reused so often they did little more than color the water. But Mrs. Kleermaker accepted it gratefully, plunging into the story of how her husband had been arrested some months before, her son gone into hiding. Yesterday the S.D.—the political police who worked under the Gestapo—had ordered her to close the family clothing store. She was afraid now to go back to the apartment above it. She had heard that we had befriended a man on this street. . . .

"In this household," Father said, "God's people are always welcome."

"We have four empty beds upstairs," said Betsie. "Your problem will be choosing which one to sleep in!"

Just two nights later the same scene was repeated. The time was again just before 8:00 on another bright May evening. Again there was a furtive knock at the side door. This time an elderly couple was standing outside.

"Come in!"

It was the same story: the same tight-clutched possessions, the same fearful glance and tentative tread. The story of neighbors arrested, the fear that tomorrow their turn would come.

That night after prayer time the six of us faced our dilemma. "This location is too dangerous," I told our three guests. "We're half a block from the main police headquarters. And yet I don't know where else to suggest."

Clearly it was time to visit Willem again. So the next day I repeated the difficult trip to Hilversum. "Willem," I said, "we have three Jews staying right at the Beje. Can you get places for them in the country?"

Willem pressed his fingers to his eyes and I noticed suddenly how much white was in his beard. "It's getting harder," he said. "Harder every month. They're feeling the food shortage now even on the farms. I still have addresses, yes, a few. But they won't take anyone without a ration card."

"Without a ration card! But Jews aren't issued ration cards!"

"I know." Willem turned to stare out the window. For the first time I wondered how he and

---

6. ***Opa*** (ō′pä), ***Tante*** (tän′tə) ***Corrie.*** Grandfather, Auntie Corrie.

Tine were feeding the elderly men and women in their care.

"I know," he repeated. "And ration cards can't be counterfeited. They're changed too often and they're too easy to spot. Identity cards are different. I know several printers who do them. Of course you need a photographer."

A photographer? Printers? What was Willem talking about? "Willem, if people need ration cards and there aren't any counterfeit ones, what do they do?"

Willem turned slowly from the window. He seemed to have forgotten me and my particular problem. "Ration cards?" He gestured vaguely. "You steal them."

I stared at this Dutch Reformed clergyman. "Then, Willem, could you steal . . . I mean . . . could you get three stolen cards?"

"No, Corrie! I'm watched! Don't you understand that? Every move I make is watched!"

He put an arm around my shoulder and went on more kindly. "Even if I can continue working for a while, it will be far better for you to develop your own sources. The less connection with me—the less connection with anyone else—the better."

Joggling home on the crowded train, I turned Willem's words over and over in my mind. "Your own sources." That sounded so—so professional. How was I going to find a source of stolen ration cards? Who in the world did I know? . . .

And at that moment a name appeared in my mind.

Fred Koornstra.

Fred was the man who used to read the electric meter at the Beje. The Koornstras had a retarded daughter, now a grown woman, who attended the "church" I had been conducting for the feeble-minded for some twenty years. And now Fred had a new job working for the Food Office. Wasn't it in the department where ration books were issued?

That evening after supper I bumped over the brick streets to the Koornstra house. The tires on my faithful old bicycle had finally given out and I joined the hundreds clattering about town on metal wheel rims. Each bump reminded me jarringly of my fifty years.

Fred, a bald man with a military bearing, came to the door and stared at me blankly when I said I wanted to talk to him about the Sunday service. He invited me in, closed the door, and said, "Now Corrie, what is it you really came to see me about?"

("Lord," I prayed silently, "if it is not safe to confide in Fred, stop this conversation now before it is too late.") "I must first tell you that we've had some unexpected company at the Beje. First it was a single woman, then a couple, when I got back this afternoon, another couple." I paused for just an instant. "They are Jews."

Fred's expression did not change.

"We can provide safe places for these people but they must provide something too. Ration cards."

Fred's eyes smiled. "So. Now I know why you came here."

"Fred, is there any way you can give out extra cards? More than you report?"

"None at all, Corrie. Those cards have to be accounted for a dozen ways. They're checked and double-checked."

The hope that had begun to mount in me tumbled. But Fred was frowning.

"Unless—" he began.

"Unless?"

"Unless there should be a holdup. The Food Office in Utrecht was robbed last month—but the men were caught."

He was silent a while. "If it happened at noon," he said slowly, "when just the record clerk and I are there . . . and if they found us tied and gagged . . ." He snapped his fingers. "And I know just the man who might do it! Do you remember the—"

"Don't!" I said, remembering Willem's warning. "Don't tell me who. And don't tell me how. Just get the cards if you possibly can."

Fred stared at me a moment. "How many do you need?"

I opened my mouth to say, "Five." But the

number that unexpectedly and astonishingly came out instead was, "One hundred."

When Fred opened the door to me just a week later, I gasped at the sight of him. Both eyes were a greenish purple, his lower lip cut and swollen.

"My friend took very naturally to the part," was all he would say.

But he had the cards. On the table in a brown manila envelope were one hundred passports to safety. Fred had already torn the "continuing coupon" from each one. This final coupon was presented at the Food Office the last day of each month in exchange for the next month's card. With these coupons Fred could "legally" continue to issue us one hundred cards.

We agreed that it would be risky for me to keep coming to his house each month. What if he were to come to the Beje instead, dressed in his old meterman uniform?

The meter in the Beje was in the back hall at the foot of the stairs. When I got home that afternoon I pried up the tread of the bottom step, as Peter had done higher to hide a radio, and found a hollow space inside. Peter would be proud of me, I thought as I worked—and was flooded by a wave of lonesomeness for that brave and cocksure boy. The hinge was hidden deep in the wood, the ancient riser undisturbed. I was ridiculously pleased with it.

We had our first test of the system on July 1. Fred was to come in through the shop as he always had, carrying the cards beneath his shirt. He would come at 5:30, when Betsie would have the back hall free of callers. To my horror at 5:25 the shop door opened and in stepped a policeman.

He was a tall man with close-cropped orange-red hair whom I knew by name—Rolf van Vliet—but little else. Rolf had brought in a watch that needed cleaning, and he seemed in a mood to talk. My throat had gone dry, but Father chatted cheerfully as he took off the back of Rolf's watch and examined it. What were we going to do? There was no way to warn Fred Koornstra. Promptly at 5:30 the door of the shop opened and in he walked, dressed in his blue workclothes. It seemed to me that his chest was too thick by a foot at least.

With magnificent aplomb Fred nodded to Father, the policeman, and me. "Good evening." Courteous but a little bored.

He strode through the door at the rear of the shop and shut it behind him. My ears strained to hear him lift the secret lid. There! Surely Rolf must have heard it too.

The door behind us opened again. So great was Fred's control that he had not ducked out the alleyway exit, but came strolling back through the shop.

"Good evening," he said again.

"Evening."

He reached the street door and was gone. We had got away with it this time, but somehow, some way, we were going to have to work out a warning system.

For meanwhile, in the weeks since Mrs. Kleermaker's unexpected visit, a great deal had happened at the Beje. Supplied with ration cards, Mrs. Kleermaker and the elderly couple and the next arrivals and the next had found homes in safer locations. But still the hunted people kept coming, and the needs were often more complicated than ration cards and addresses. If a Jewish woman became pregnant, where could she go to have her baby? If a Jew in hiding died, how could he be buried?

"Develop your own sources," Willem had said. And from the moment Fred Koornstra's name had popped into my mind, an uncanny realization had been growing in me. We were friends with half of Haarlem! We knew nurses in the maternity hospital. We knew clerks in the Records Office. We knew someone in every business and service in the city.

We didn't know, of course, the political views of all these people. But—and here I felt a strange leaping of my heart—God did! I knew I was not clever or subtle or sophisticated; if the Beje was becoming a meeting place for need and supply, it was through some strategy far higher than mine.

A few nights after Fred's first "meterman"

visit the alley bell rang long after curfew. I sped downstairs, expecting another sad and stammering refugee. Betsie and I had already made up beds for four new overnight guests that evening: a Jewish woman and her three small children.

But to my surprise, close against the wall of the dark alley, stood Kik. "Get your bicycle," he ordered with his usual young abruptness. "And put on a sweater. I have some people I want you to meet."

"Now? After curfew?" But I knew it was useless to ask questions. Kik's bicycle was tireless too, the wheel rims swathed in cloth. He wrapped mine also to keep down the clatter, and soon we were pedaling through the blacked-out streets of Haarlem at a speed that would have scared me even in daylight.

"Put a hand on my shoulder," Kik whispered. "I know the way."

We crossed dark side streets, crested bridges, wheeled round invisible corners. At last we crossed a broad canal and I knew we had reached the fashionable suburb of Aerdenhout.

We turned into a driveway beneath shadowy trees. To my astonishment Kik picked up my bicycle and carried both his and mine up the front steps. A serving girl with starched white apron and ruffled cap opened the door. The entrance hall was jammed with bicycles.

Then I saw him. One eye smiling at me, the other at the door, his vast stomach hastening ahead of him. Pickwick![7]

He led Kik and me into the drawing room where, sipping coffee and chatting in small groups, was the most distinguished-looking group of men and women I had ever seen. But all my attention, that first moment, was on the inexpressibly fragrant aroma in that room. Surely, was it possible, they were drinking real coffee?

Pickwick drew me a cup from the silver urn on the sideboard. It was coffee. After two years, rich, black, pungent Dutch coffee. He poured himself a cup too, dropping in his usual five lumps of sugar as though rationing had never been invented. Another starched and ruffled maid was passing a tray heaped high with cakes.

Gobbling and gulping I trailed about the room after Pickwick, shaking the hands of the people he singled out. They were strange introductions for no names were mentioned, only, occasionally, an address, and "Ask for Mrs. Smit." When I had met my fourth Smit, Kik explained with a grin, "It's the only last name in the underground."

So this was really and truly the underground! But—where were these people from? I had never laid eyes on any of them. A second later I realized with a shiver down my spine that I was meeting the national group.

Their chief work, I gleaned from bits of conversation, was liaison with England and the Free Dutch forces fighting elsewhere on the continent. They also maintained the underground route through which downed Allied plane crews reached the North Sea coast.

But they were instantly sympathetic with my efforts to help Haarlem's Jews. I blushed to my hair roots to hear Pickwick describe me as "the head of an operation here in this city." A hollow space under the stairs and some haphazard friendships were not an operation. The others here were obviously competent, disciplined, and professional.

But they greeted me with grave courtesy, murmuring what they had to offer as we shook hands. False identity papers. The use of a car with official government plates. Signature forgery.

In a far corner of the room Pickwick introduced me to a frail-appearing little man with a wispy goatee. "Our host informs me," the little man began formally, "that your headquarters building lacks a secret room. This is a danger for all, those you are helping as well as yourselves and those who work with you. With your permission I will pay you a visit in the coming week. . . ."

Years later I learned that he was one of the most famous architects in Europe. I knew him only as Mr. Smit.

---

7. *Pickwick.* The author recognizes one of her wealthy Dutch customers who looks like Pickwick, the Dickens character.

Just before Kik and I started our dash back to the Beje, Pickwick slipped an arm through mine. "My dear, I have good news. I understand that Peter is about to be released." . . .

So he was, three days later, thinner, paler, and not a whit daunted by his two months in a concrete cell. Nollie, Tine, and Betsie used up a month's sugar ration baking cakes for his welcome-home party.

And one morning soon afterward the first customer in the shop was a small thin-bearded man named Smit. Father took his jeweler's glass from his eye. If there was one thing he loved better than making a new acquaintance, it was discovering a link with an old one.

"Smit," he said eagerly. "I know several Smits in Amsterdam. Are you by any chance related to the family who—"

"Father," I interrupted, "this is the man I told you about. He's come to, ah, inspect the house."

"A building inspector? Then you must be the Smit with offices in the Grote Hout Straat. I wonder that I haven't—"

"Father!" I pleaded, "he's not a building inspector, and his name is not Smit."

"Not Smit?"

Together Mr. Smit and I attempted to explain, but Father simply could not understand a person's being called by a name not his own. As I led Mr. Smit into the back hall we heard him musing to himself, "I once knew a Smit on Koning Straat. . . ."

Mr. Smit examined and approved the hiding place for ration cards beneath the bottom step. He also pronounced acceptable the warning system we had worked out. This was a triangle-shaped wooden sign advertising "Alpina Watches" which I had placed in the dining-room window. As long as the sign was in place, it was safe to enter.

But when I showed him a cubbyhole behind the corner cupboard in the dining room, he shook his head. Some ancient redesigning of the house had left a crawl space in that corner and we'd been secreting jewelry, silver coins, and other valuables there since the start of the occupation. Not only the rabbi had brought us his library but other Jewish families had brought their treasures to the Beje for safekeeping. The space was large enough that we had believed a person could crawl in there if necessary, but Mr. Smit dismissed it without a second glance.

"First place they'd look. Don't bother to change it though. It's only silver. We're interested in saving people, not things."

He started up the narrow corkscrew stairs, and as he mounted so did his spirits. He paused in delight at the odd-placed landings, pounded on the crooked walls, and laughed aloud as the floor levels of the two old houses continued out of phase.

"What an impossibility!" he said in an awe-struck voice. "What an improbable, unbelievable, unpredictable impossibility! Miss ten Boom, if all houses were constructed like this one, you would see before you a less worried man."

At last, at the very top of the stairs, he entered my room and gave a little cry of delight. "This is it!" he exclaimed.

"You want your hiding place as high as possible," he went on eagerly. "Gives you the best chance to reach it while the search is on below." He leaned out the window, craning his thin neck, the little faun's beard pointing this way and that.

"But . . . this is my bedroom. . . ."

Mr. Smit paid no attention. He was already measuring. He moved the heavy, wobbly old wardrobe away from the wall with surprising ease and pulled my bed into the center of the room. "This is where the false wall will go!" Excitedly he drew out a pencil and drew a line along the floor thirty inches from the back wall. He stood up and gazed at it moodily.

"That's as big as I dare," he said. "It will take a cot mattress, though. Oh, yes. Easily!"

I tried again to protest, but Mr. Smit had forgotten I existed. Over the next few days he and his workmen were in and out of our house constantly. They never knocked. At each visit each man carried in something. Tools in a folded news-

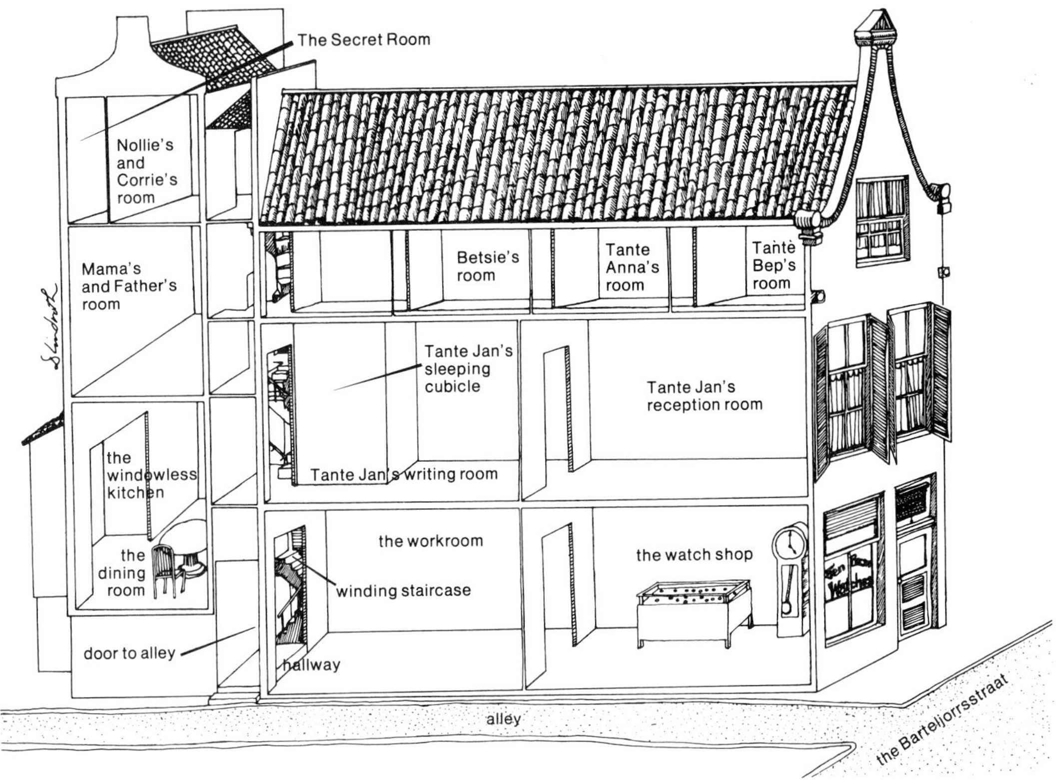

paper. A few bricks in a briefcase. "Wood!" he exclaimed when I ventured to wonder if a wooden wall would not be easier to build. "Wood sounds hollow. Hear it in a minute. No, no. Brick's the only thing for false walls."

After the wall was up, the plasterer came, then the carpenter, finally the painter. Six days after he had begun, Mr. Smit called Father, Betsie, and me to see.

We stood in the doorway and gaped. The smell of fresh paint was everywhere. But surely nothing in this room was newly painted! All four walls had that streaked and grimy look that old rooms got in coal-burning Haarlem. The ancient molding ran unbroken around the ceiling, chipped and peeling here and there, obviously undisturbed for a hundred and fifty years. Old water stains streaked the back wall, a wall that even I, who had lived half a century in this room, could scarcely believe was not the original, but set back a precious two-and-a-half feet from the true wall of the building.

Built-in bookshelves ran along this false wall, old, sagging shelves whose blistered wood bore the same water stains as the wall behind them. Down in the far lefthand corner, beneath the bottom shelf, a sliding panel, two feet high and two wide, opened into the secret room.

Mr. Smit stooped and silently pulled this panel up. On hands and knees Betsie and I crawled into the narrow room behind it. Once inside we could stand up, sit, or even stretch out one at a time on the single mattress. A concealed vent, cunningly let into the real wall, allowed air to enter from outside.

"Keep a water jug there," said Mr. Smit, crawling in behind us. "Change the water once a week. Hardtack and vitamins keep indefinitely. Anytime there is anyone in the house whose presence is unofficial, all possessions except the clothes actually on his back must be stored in here."

Dropping to our knees again, we crawled single file out into my bedroom. "Move back into this room," he told me. "Everything exactly as before."

With his fist he struck the wall above the bookshelves.

"The Gestapo could search for a year," he said. "They'll never find this one."

Discussion

1. **(a)** Why did Peter's playing of the "Wilhelmus" arouse such intense feelings in the audience? **(b)** Why did the Germans treat his act so harshly? **(c)** How does this episode set the mood for what follows?

2. Willem suggested that Corrie steal ration cards, develop her own sources for that purpose, and have as few connections as possible with anyone. **(a)** What is ironic about his first suggestion? **(b)** How did Corrie's ongoing volunteer work provide her with a contact? **(c)** How did Fred Koornstra's method of covering up the fake robbery of the Food Office illustrate the wisdom of Willem's advice?

3. The author indirectly describes the dangers of the underground work she was doing. **(a)** What were some of these? **(b)** Explain her reactions and those of the national underground leaders when she finally meets them.

4. **(a)** Describe the hiding place. **(b)** Which details of its construction most surprised Corrie? **(c)** Why was the architect Smit so sure the Gestapo would never discover it?

5. What does each quote reveal about the following characters? **(a)** Mr. ten Boom, in saying to the Jewish refugee, "In this household, God's people are always welcome." **(b)** Betsie, in saying to the refugee, "We have four empty beds upstairs. Your problem will be choosing which one to sleep in!" **(c)** Corrie, in thinking of Peter's action in the church, "For what had Peter risked so much? Not for people's lives but for a gesture. For a moment's meaningless defiance."

Application

Connotation/Denotation

In this account the author was set on a specific course of action once she grasped the significance of a simple phrase. Phrases as well as single words can take on connotations. This is particularly true in a society where speech is not free and statements often must suggest more than they actually say.

1. How does Corrie originally react to being told that she should "develop her own sources"?

2. What does the phrase eventually connote to her in terms of her involvement with the underground?

Composition

Obviously, the risks Corrie and her associates took to help others showed courage. However, her narrative implies that other qualities such as cool-headedness, cooperation, and ingenuity were just as important in the defense against the Nazis. Review the selection for evidence of these.

Write a two- or three-paragraph composition describing how some of the characters displayed these traits. You might also argue for or against their necessity in situations that are not dangerous.

Corrie ten Boom 1892–1983

Corrie ten Boom was fifty-two years old when the Nazis, suspecting the family of hiding Jews, arrested them. Imprisoned, her father was the first to die; then Betsie, who along with Corrie had endured unspeakable torments in the concentration camp at Ravensbruck.

As the result of a clerical error, ten Boom was released close to the end of World War II instead of being sent to the gas chambers. She returned to her home, regained health, and went on to establish a home for other victims of Nazi purges. Providing care not only for the tormented but also for some who had been their tormentors, ten Boom even set up a rehabilitation camp for Germans in a former concentration camp. Details of her remarkable experiences are recorded in *The Hiding Place,* the source for this selection.

I Escape from the Boers **Winston Churchill** Great Britain

Fleeing across the vast South African territory, young Churchill finds that his own basic qualities and the stars overhead are all he can rely on.

The year was 1899. A longstanding land- and political-rights dispute flared into war between British immigrants in South Africa, who had been pouring in since the early 1800s, and the Boers (bôrz), the descendants of Dutch farmers who had settled in South Africa in the mid-1600s. Battle lines of the Boer War were drawn quickly: Great Britain backed the cause of its former subjects by sending troops to British-controlled Cape Colony; the South African Republic, based in the Transvaal (trans väl′) province, was joined by the neighboring Orange Free State in protecting its borders from the British.

Twenty-five-year-old Winston Churchill, known only as the son of an English lord, set out eagerly for South Africa as a soldier and war correspondent for the Morning Post. *This dual role enabled him to participate in and report on the action. Within a month after Churchill's arrival, he took part in the daring rescue of an armored train that had been ambushed by the Boers. Although he aided in the escape of several wounded soldiers, he was captured by the enemy and taken to a prison camp in Pretoria, their capital city. The following is Churchill's descriptive account of his escape from the prison, a feat that catapulted him into public life.*

The State Model Schools[1] stood in the midst of a quadrangle, and were surrounded on two sides by an iron grille and on two by a corrugated-iron fence about ten feet high. These boundaries offered little obstacle to anyone who possessed the activity of youth, but the fact that they were guarded on the inside by sentries, fifty yards apart, armed with rifle and revolver, made them a well-nigh insuperable barrier. No walls are so hard to pierce as living walls.

After anxious reflection and continual watching, it was discovered by several of the prisoners that when the sentries along the eastern side walked about on their beats they were at certain moments unable to see the top of a few yards of the wall near a small circular lavatory office. The electric lights in the middle of the quadrangle brilliantly lighted the whole place, but the eastern wall was in shadow. The first thing was therefore to pass the two sentries near the office. It was necessary to hit off the exact moment when both their backs should be turned together. After the wall was scaled we should be in the garden of the villa next door. There the plan came to an end. Everything after this was vague and uncertain. How to get out of the garden, how to pass unnoticed through the streets, how to evade the patrols that surrounded the town, and above all how to cover the two hundred and eighty miles to the Portuguese frontier,[2] were questions which would arise at a later stage.

Together with two British officers I made an abortive attempt, not pushed with any decision, on December 11. There was no difficulty in getting into the circular office. But to climb out of it

1. ***State Model Schools,*** Churchill's place of confinement.
2. ***Portuguese frontier,*** the border of Portuguese East Africa (now Mozambique), northeast of South Africa and a place of safety.

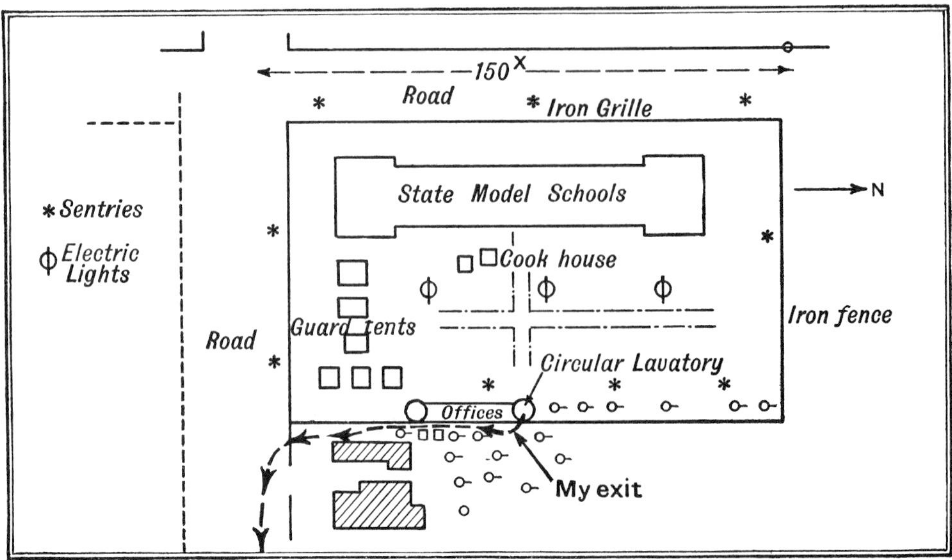

over the wall was a hazard of the sharpest character. Anyone doing so must at the moment he was on the top of the wall be plainly visible to the sentries fifteen yards away, if they were in the right place and happened to look! Whether the sentries would challenge or fire depended entirely upon their individual dispositions, and no one could tell what they would do. Nevertheless I was determined that nothing should stop my taking the plunge the next day. As the twelfth wore away my fears crystallized more and more into desperation. In the evening, after my two friends had made an attempt but had not found the moment propitious, I strolled across the quadrangle and secreted myself in the circular office. Through an aperture in the metal casing of which it was built I watched the sentries. For some time they remained stolid and obstructive. Then all of a sudden one turned and walked up to his comrade, and they began to talk. Their backs were turned.

Now or never! I stood on a ledge, seized the top of the wall with my hands, and drew myself up. Twice I let myself down again in sickly hesitation, and then with a third resolve scrambled up and over. My waistcoat got entangled with the ornamental metalwork on the top. I had to pause for an appreciable moment to extricate myself. In this posture I had one parting glimpse of the sentries still talking with their backs turned fifteen yards away. One of them was lighting his cigarette, and I remember the glow on the inside of his hands as a distinct impression which my mind recorded. Then I lowered myself lightly down into the adjoining garden and crouched among the shrubs. I was free! The first step had been taken, and it was irrevocable. It now remained to await the arrival of my comrades. The bushes in the garden gave a good deal of cover, and in the moonlight their shadows fell dark on the ground. I lay there for an hour in great impatience and anxiety. People were continually moving about in the garden, and once a man came and apparently looked straight at me only a few yards away. Where were the others? Why did they not make the attempt?

Suddenly I heard a voice from within the quadrangle say, quite loud, "All up." I crawled back to the wall. Two British officers were walking up and down inside, laughing and talking all manner of nonsense—amid which I caught my name. I risked a cough. One of the officers immediately began to chatter alone. The other said, slowly and clearly, "They cannot get out. The sentry suspects. It's all up. Can you get back again?" But now all my fears fell from me at once. I said to the officers, "I shall go on alone."

Now I was in the right mood for these undertakings—failure being almost certain, no odds against success affected me. The gate which led into the road was only a few yards from another sentry. I said to myself, "*Toujours de l'audace,*"[3] put my hat on my head, strode into the middle of the garden, walked past the windows of the house without any attempt at concealment, and so went through the gate and turned to the left. I passed the sentry at less than five yards. Most of them knew me by sight. Whether he looked at me or not I do not know, for I never turned my head. I restrained with the utmost difficulty an impulse to run. But after walking a hundred yards and hearing no challenge, I knew that the second obstacle had been surmounted. I was at large in Pretoria.

I walked on leisurely through the night, humming a tune and choosing the middle of the road. The streets were full of burghers,[4] but they paid no attention to me. Gradually I reached the suburbs, and on a little bridge I sat down to reflect and consider. I was in the heart of the enemy's country. I knew no one to whom I could apply for succor. Nearly three hundred miles stretched between me and Delagoa Bay.[5] My escape must be known at dawn. Pursuit would be immediate. Yet all exits were barred. The town was picketed, the country was patrolled, the trains were searched, the line was guarded. I wore a civilian brown flannel suit. I had seventy-five pounds[6] in my pocket and four slabs of chocolate, but the compass and the map which might have guided me, the meat lozenges which should have sustained me, were in my friends' pockets in the State Model Schools. Worst of all, I could not speak a word of Dutch or Kaffir,[7] and how was I to get food or direction?

But when hope had departed, fear had gone as well. I formed a plan. I would find the Delagoa Bay Railway. Without map or compass, I must follow that in spite of the pickets. I looked at the stars. Orion shone brightly. Scarcely a year before he had guided me when lost in the desert to the banks of the Nile. He had given me water. Now he should lead to freedom. I could not endure the want of either.

After walking south for half a mile I struck the railroad. Was it the line to Delagoa Bay or the Pietersburg[8] branch? If it were the former, it should run east. But, so far as I could see, this line ran northwards. Still, it might be only winding its way out among the hills. I resolved to follow it. The night was delicious. A cool breeze fanned my face, and a wild feeling of exhilaration took hold of me. At any rate, I was free, if only for an hour. That was something. The fascination of the adventure grew. Unless the stars in their courses fought for me, I could not escape. Where, then, was the need of caution? I marched briskly along the line. Here and there the lights of a picket fire gleamed. Every bridge had its watchers. But I passed them all, making very short detours at the dangerous places, and really taking scarcely any precautions. Perhaps that was the reason I succeeded.

As I walked I extended my plan. I could not march three hundred miles to the frontier. I would board a train in motion and hide under the seats, on the roof, on the couplings—anywhere. What train should I take? The first, of course. After walking for two hours I perceived the signal lights of a station. I left the line, and circling round it, hid in the ditch by the track about two hundred yards beyond the platform. I argued that the train would stop at the station and that it would not have got up too much speed by the time it reached me. An hour passed. I began to grow impatient. Suddenly I heard the whistle and the approaching rattle. Then the great yellow headlights of the engine flashed into view. The train waited five minutes at the station, and started again with much noise and steaming. I crouched by the track. I rehearsed the act in my mind. I must wait until the engine had passed, otherwise I should be seen. Then I must make a dash for the carriages.

---

3. ***"Toujours de l'audace"*** (tü zhur′ də lō dȧs′), boldness always pays. [*French*]
4. ***burghers*** (bėr′gərz), Dutch settlers in South Africa and their descendants.
5. ***Delagoa Bay,*** bay just inside the Portuguese East Africa border.
6. ***seventy-five pounds.*** At that time, this amount in English money was worth about three hundred dollars.
7. ***Kaffir*** (kaf′ər), the language of the Kaffirs, a Bantu native group in South Africa.
8. ***Pietersburg*** (pē′tərz bėrg′), a South African city about two hundred miles north of Pretoria.

The train started slowly, but gathered speed sooner than I had expected. The flaring lights drew swiftly near. The rattle became a roar. The dark mass hung for a second above me. Then I hurled myself on the trucks, clutched at something, missed, clutched again, missed again, grasped some sort of handhold, was swung off my feet—my toes bumping on the line, and with a struggle seated myself on the couplings of the fifth truck from the front of the train. It was a goods train, and the trucks were full of sacks, soft sacks covered with coal dust. They were in fact bags filled with empty coal bags going back to their colliery.[9] I crawled on top and burrowed in among them. In five minutes I was completely buried. The sacks were warm and comfortable. Perhaps the engine driver had seen me rush up to the train and would give the alarm at the next station; on the other hand, perhaps not. Where was the train going to? Where would it be unloaded? Would it be searched? Was it on the Delagoa Bay line? What should I do in the morning? Ah, never mind that. Sufficient for the night was the luck thereof. Fresh plans for fresh contingencies. I resolved to sleep, nor can I imagine a more pleasing lullaby than the clatter of the train that carries an escaping prisoner at twenty miles an hour away from the enemy's capital.

How long I slept I do not know, but I woke up suddenly with all feelings of exhilaration gone, and only the consciousness of oppressive difficulties heavy on me. I must leave the train before daybreak, so that I could drink at a pool and find some hiding place while it was still dark. I would not run the risk of being unloaded with the coal bags. Another night I would board another train. I crawled from my cozy hiding place among the sacks and sat again on the couplings. The train was running at a fair speed, but I felt it was time to leave it. I took hold of the iron handle at the back of the truck, pulled strongly with my left hand, and sprang. My feet struck the ground in two gigantic strides, and the next instant I was sprawling in the ditch, considerably shaken but unhurt. The train, my faithful ally of the night, hurried on its journey.

It was still dark. I was in the middle of a wide valley, surrounded by low hills, and carpeted with high grass drenched in dew. I searched for water in the nearest gully, and soon found a clear pool. I was very thirsty, but long after I had quenched my thirst I continued to drink, that I might have sufficient for the whole day.

Presently the dawn began to break, and the sky to the east grew yellow and red, slashed across with heavy black clouds. I saw with relief that the railway ran steadily towards the sunrise. I had taken the right line, after all.

Having drunk my fill, I set out for the hills, among which I hoped to find some hiding place, and as it became broad daylight I entered a small grove of trees which grew on the side of a deep ravine. Here I resolved to wait till dusk. I had one consolation: no one in the world knew where I was—I did not know myself. It was now four o'clock. Fourteen hours lay between me and the night. My impatience to proceed while I was still strong doubled their length. At first it was terribly cold, but by degrees the sun gained power, and by ten o'clock the heat was oppressive. My sole companion was a gigantic vulture, who manifested an extravagant interest in my condition, and made hideous and ominous gurglings from time to time. From my lofty position I commanded a view of the whole valley. A little tin-roofed town lay three miles to the westward. Scattered farmsteads, each with a clump of trees, relieved the monotony of the undulating ground. At the foot of a hill stood a Kaffir kraal,[10] and the figures of its inhabitants dotted the patches of cultivation or surrounded the droves of goats and cows which fed on the pasture. . . . During the day I ate one slab of chocolate, which, with the heat, produced a violent thirst. The pool was hardly half a mile away, but I dared not leave the shelter of the little wood, for I could see the figures of white men riding or walking occasionally across the valley, and once a Boer came and fired two shots at birds close to

---

9. *colliery* (kol′yər ē), a coal-mining complex.
10. *kraal* (kräl), an enclosed village of South African natives.

my hiding place. But no one discovered me.

The elation and the excitement of the previous night had burned away, and a chilling reaction followed. I was very hungry, for I had had no dinner before starting, and chocolate, though it sustains, does not satisfy. I had scarcely slept, but yet my heart beat so fiercely and I was so nervous and perplexed about the future that I could not rest. I thought of all the chances that lay against me; I dreaded and detested more than words can express the prospect of being caught and dragged back to Pretoria. I realized with awful force that no exercise of my own feeble wit and strength could save me from my enemies, and I prayed long and earnestly for help and guidance. My prayer, as it seems to me, was swiftly and wonderfully answered.

During the day I had watched the railway with attention. I saw two or three trains pass along it each way. I argued that the same number would pass at night. I resolved to board one of these. I thought I could improve on my procedure of the previous evening. I had observed how slowly the trains, particularly long goods-trains, climbed some of the steep gradients. Sometimes they were hardly going at a foot's pace. It would probably be easy to choose a point where the line was not only on an upgrade but also on a curve. Thus I could board some truck on the convex side of the train when both the engine and the guard's van were bent away, and when consequently neither the engine driver nor the guard would see me. This plan seemed to me in every respect sound. I saw myself leaving the train again before dawn, having been carried forward another sixty or seventy miles during the night. That would be scarcely one hundred and fifty miles from the frontier. And why should not the process be repeated? Where was the flaw? I could not see it. With three long bounds on three successive nights I could be in Portuguese territory. Meanwhile I still had two or three slabs of chocolate and a pocketful of crumbled biscuit—enough, that is to say, to keep body and soul together at a pinch without running the awful risk of recapture entailed by accosting a single human being. In this mood I watched with increasing impatience the arrival of darkness.

The long day reached its close at last. The western clouds flushed into fire; the shadows of the hills stretched out across the valley; a ponderous Boer wagon with its long team crawled slowly along the track towards the township; the Kaffirs collected their herds and drew them round their kraal; the daylight died, and soon it was quite dark. Then, and not until then, I set forth. I hurried to the railway line, scrambling along through the boulders and high grass and pausing on my way to drink at a stream of sweet cold water. I made my way to the place where I had seen the trains crawling so slowly up the slope, and soon found a point where the curve of the track fulfilled all the conditions of my plan. Here, behind a little bush, I sat down and waited hopefully. An hour passed; two hours passed; three hours—and yet no train. Six hours had now elapsed since the last, whose time I had carefully noted, had gone by. Surely one was due.

Another hour slipped away. Still no train! My plan began to crumble and my hopes to ooze out of me. After all, was it not quite possible that no trains ran on this part of the line during the dark hours? This was in fact the case, and I might well have continued to wait in vain till daylight. However, between twelve and one in the morning, I lost patience and started along the track, resolved to cover at any rate ten or fifteen miles of my journey. I did not make much progress. Every bridge was guarded by armed men; every few miles were huts. At intervals there were stations with tin-roofed villages clustering around them. All the veldt was bathed in the bright rays of the full moon, and to avoid these dangerous places I had to make wide circuits and even to creep along the ground. Leaving the railroad I fell into bogs and swamps, brushed through high grass dripping with dew, and waded across the streams over which the bridges carried the railway. I was soon drenched to the waist. I had been able to take very little exercise during my month's imprisonment, and I was quickly tired with walking and with want of food and sleep. Presently I approached a station. It was a mere platform in the veldt, with two or three buildings and huts around it. But laid up on the sidings, obviously for the night, were three long goods-trains. Evidently the flow of traffic over the railway was uneven. These three trains, motionless in the moonlight, confirmed my fears that traffic was not maintained by night on this part of the line. Where, then, was my plan which in the afternoon had looked so fine and sure?

It now occurred to me that I might board one of these stationary trains immediately, and hiding amid its freight be carried forward during the next day—and night too if all were well. On the other hand, where were they going to? Where would they stop? Where would they be unloaded? Once I entered a wagon my lot would be cast. It was necessary at all costs before taking such a step to find out where these trains were going. To do this I must penetrate the station, examine the labels on the trucks or on the merchandise, and see if I could extract any certain guidance from them. I crept up to the platform and got between two of the long trains on the siding. I was proceeding to examine the markings on the trucks when loud voices rapidly approaching on the outside of the trains filled me with fear. Several Kaffirs were laughing and shouting in their unmodulated tones, and I heard, as I thought, a European voice arguing or ordering. At any rate, it was enough for me. I retreated between the two trains to the extreme end of the siding, and slipped stealthily but rapidly into the grass of the illimitable plain.

There was nothing for it but to plod on—but in an increasingly purposeless and hopeless manner. I felt very miserable when I looked around and saw here and there the lights of houses and thought of the warmth and comfort within them, but knew that they meant only danger to me. Far off on the moonlit horizon there presently began to shine the row of six or eight big lights which marked either Witbank or Middleburg station. Out in the darkness to my left gleamed two or three fires. I was sure they were not the lights of houses, but how far off they were or what they were I could not be certain. The idea formed in my mind that they were the fires of a Kaffir kraal. Then I began to think that the best use I could make of my remaining strength would be to go to these Kaffirs. I had heard that they hated the Boers and were friendly to the British. At any rate, they would probably not arrest me. They might give me food and a dry corner to sleep in. Although I could not speak a word of their language, yet I thought perhaps they might understand the value of a British bank note. They might even be induced to help me. A guide, a pony—but, above all, rest, warmth, and food—such were the promptings which dominated my mind. So I set out towards the fires.

I must have walked a mile or so in this resolve before a realization of its weakness and imprudence took possession of me. Then I turned back again to the railway line and retraced my steps perhaps half the distance. Then I stopped and sat down, completely baffled, destitute of any idea what to do or where to turn. Suddenly without the slightest reason all my doubts disappeared. It was certainly by no process of logic that they were dispelled. I just felt quite clear that I would go to the Kaffir kraal.

I walked on rapidly towards the fires, which I had in the first instance thought were not more than a couple of miles from the railway line. I soon found they were much farther away than that. After about an hour or an hour and a half they still seemed almost as far off as ever. But I persevered, and presently between two and three o'clock in the morning I perceived that they were not the fires of a Kaffir kraal. The angular outline of buildings began to draw out against them, and soon I saw that I was approaching a group of houses around the mouth of a coal mine. The wheel which worked the winding gear was plainly visible, and I could see that the fires which had led me so far were from the furnaces of the engines. Hard by, surrounded by one or two slighter structures, stood a small but substantial stone house two stories high.

I halted in the wilderness to survey this scene and to resolve my action. It was still possible to turn back. But in that direction I saw nothing but the prospect of further futile wanderings terminated by hunger, fever, discovery, or surrender. On the other hand, here in front was a chance. I had heard it said before I escaped that in the mining district of Witbank and Middleburg there were a certain number of English residents who had been suffered to remain in the country in order to keep the mines working. Had I been led to one of these? What did this house which frowned dark and inscrutable upon me contain? A Briton or a Boer; a friend or a foe?

The odds were heavy against me, and it was with faltering and reluctant steps that I walked out of the shimmering gloom of the veldt into the light of the furnace fires, advanced towards the silent house, and struck with my fist upon the door.

There was a pause. Then I knocked again. And almost immediately a light sprang up above and an upper window opened.

"*Wer ist da?*"[11] cried a man's voice.

I felt the shock of disappointment and consternation to my fingers.

"I want help; I have had an accident," I replied.

Some muttering followed. Then I heard steps descending the stairs, the bolt of the door was drawn, the lock was turned. It was opened abruptly, and in the darkness of the passage a tall man hastily attired, with a pale face and dark mustache, stood before me.

"What do you want?" he said, this time in English.

I had now to think of something to say. I wanted above all to get into parley with this man, to get matters in such a state that instead of raising an alarm and summoning others he would discuss things quietly.

"I am a burgher," I began. "I have had an accident. I was going to join my commando at Komati Poort.[12] I have fallen off the train. We were skylarking. I have been unconscious for hours. I think I have dislocated my shoulder."

It is astonishing how one thinks of these things. This story leaped out as if I had learned it by heart. Yet I had not the slightest idea what I was going to say or what the next sentence would be.

The stranger regarded me intently, and after some hesitation said at length, "Well, come in." He retreated a little into the darkness of the passage, threw open a door on one side of it, and pointed with his left hand into a dark room. I walked past him and entered, wondering if it was to be my prison. He followed, struck a light, lit a lamp, and set it on the table at the far side of which I stood. I was in a small room, evidently a dining room and office in one. I noticed, besides the large table, a roll desk, two or three chairs, and one of those machines for making sodawater. On his end of the table my host had laid a revolver, which he had hitherto presumably been holding in his right hand.

"I think I'd like to know a little more about this railway accident of yours," he said, after a considerable pause.

"I think," I replied, "I had better tell you the truth."

"I think you had," he said, slowly.

So I took the plunge and threw all I had upon the board.

"I am Winston Churchill, War Correspondent of the *Morning Post*. I escaped last night from Pretoria. I am making my way to the frontier." (Making my way!) "I have plenty of money. Will you help me?"

There was another long pause. My companion rose from the table slowly and locked the door. After this act, which struck me as unpromising, and was certainly ambiguous, he advanced upon me and suddenly held out his hand.

"Thank God you have come here! It is the only house for twenty miles where you would not have been handed over. But we are all British here, and we will see you through."

It is easier to recall across the gulf of years the spasm of relief which swept over me than it is to describe it. A moment before I had thought my-

---

11. *"Wer ist da?"* "Who is there?"; a phrase in Afrikaans (af′rə-käns′), the language related to Dutch and spoken by the Boers.
12. *Komati Poort* (kō mä′tē pôrt′), a South African city on the border of Portuguese East Africa.

self trapped; and now friends, food, resources, aid were all at my disposal. I felt like a drowning man pulled out of the water and informed he has won the Derby!

My host now introduced himself as Mr. John Howard, manager of the Transvaal Collieries. He had become a naturalized burgher of the Transvaal some years before the war. But out of consideration for his British race and some inducements which he had offered to the local Field Cornet, he had not been called up to fight against the British. Instead he had been allowed to remain with one or two others on the mine, keeping it pumped out and in good order until coal cutting could be resumed. He had with him at the mine-head, besides his secretary, who was British, an engineman from Lancashire and two Scottish miners. All these four were British subjects and had been allowed to remain only upon giving their parole to observe strict neutrality. He himself as burgher of the Transvaal Republic would be guilty of treason in harboring me, and liable to be shot if caught at the time or found out later on.

"Never mind," he said, "we will fix it up somehow." And added, "The Field Cornet was round here this afternoon asking about you. They have got the hue and cry out all along the line and all over the district."

I said that I did not wish to compromise him. Let him give me food, a pistol, a guide, and if possible a pony, and I would make my own way to the sea, marching by night across country far away from the railway line or any habitation.

He would not hear of it. He would fix up something. But he enjoined the utmost caution. Spies were everywhere. He had two Dutch servant-maids actually sleeping in the house. There were many Kaffirs employed about the mine premises and on the pumping machinery of the mine. Surveying these dangers he became very thoughtful.

Then: "But you are famishing."

I did not contradict him. In a moment he had bustled off into the kitchen. He returned after an interval with the best part of a cold leg of mutton and various other delectable commodities, and, leaving me to do full justice to these, quitted the room and let himself out of the house by a back door.

Nearly an hour passed before Mr. Howard returned. In this period my physical well-being had been brought into harmony with the improvement in my prospects. I felt confident of success and equal to anything.

"It's all right," said Mr. Howard. "I have seen the men, and they are all for it. We must put you down the pit tonight, and there you will have to stay till we can see how to get you out of the country. One difficulty," he said, "will be the *skoff* (food). The Dutch girl sees every mouthful I eat. The cook will want to know what has happened to her leg of mutton. I shall have to think it all out during the night. You must get down the pit at once. We'll make you comfortable enough."

Accordingly, just as the dawn was breaking, I followed my host across a little yard into the enclosure in which stood the winding-wheel of the mine. Here a stout man, introduced as Mr. Dewsnap, of Oldham, locked my hand in a grip of crushing vigor.

A door was opened and I entered the cage. Down we shot into the bowels of the earth. At the bottom of the mine were the two Scottish miners with lanterns and a big bundle which afterwards proved to be a mattress and blankets. We walked for some time through the pitchy labyrinth, with frequent turns, twists, and alterations of level, and finally stopped in a sort of chamber where the air was cool and fresh. Here my guide set down his bundle, and Mr. Howard handed me a couple of candles, a bottle of whiskey, and a box of cigars.

"There's no difficulty about these," he said. "I keep them under lock and key. Now we must plan how to feed you tomorrow."

"Don't you move from here, whatever happens," was the parting injunction. "There will be Kaffirs about the mine after daylight, but we shall be on the lookout that none of them wanders this way. None of them has seen anything so far."

My four friends trooped off with their lanterns, and I was left alone. Viewed from the velvety darkness of the pit, life seemed bathed in rosy light. After the perplexity and even despair through which I had passed I counted upon freedom as certain. Speeded by intense fatigue, I soon slept the sleep of the weary—but of the triumphant.

I do not know how many hours I slept, but the following afternoon must have been far advanced when I found myself thoroughly awake. I put out my hand for the candle, but could feel it nowhere. I did not know what pitfalls these mining galleries might contain, so I thought it better to lie quiet on my mattress and await developments. Several hours passed before the faint gleam of a lantern showed that someone was coming. It proved to be Mr. Howard himself, armed with a chicken and other good things. He also brought several books. He asked me why I had not lighted my candle. I said I couldn't find it.

"Didn't you put it under the mattress?" he asked.

"No."

"Then the rats must have got it."

He told me there were swarms of rats in the mine, that some years ago he had introduced a particular kind of white rat, which was an excellent scavenger, and that these had multiplied and thriven exceedingly. He told me he had been to the house of an English doctor twenty miles away to get the chicken. He was worried at the attitude of the two Dutch servants, who were very inquisitive about the depredations upon the leg of mutton for which I had been responsible. If he could not get another chicken cooked for the next day, he would have to take double helpings on his own plate and slip the surplus into a parcel for me while the servant was out of the room. He said that inquiries were being made for me all over the district by the Boers, and that the Pretoria Government was making a tremendous fuss about my escape. The fact that there were a number of English remaining in the Middleburg mining region indicated it as a likely place for me to have

turned to, and all persons of English origin were more or less suspect.

I again expressed my willingness to go on alone with a Kaffir guide and a pony, but this he utterly refused to entertain. It would take a lot of planning, he said, to get me out of the country, and I might have to stay in the mine for quite a long time.

"Here," he said, "you are absolutely safe. Mac" (by which he meant one of the Scottish miners) "knows all the disused workings and places that no one else would dream of. There is one place here where the water actually touches the roof for a foot or two. If they searched the mine, Mac would dive under that with you into the workings cut off beyond the water. No one would ever think of looking there."

He stayed with me while I dined, and then departed, leaving me, among other things, half-a-dozen candles which, duly warned, I tucked under my pillow and mattress.

I slept again for a long time, and woke suddenly with a feeling of movement about me. Something seemed to be pulling at my pillow. I put out my hand quickly. There was a perfect scurry. The rats were at the candles. I rescued the candles in time, and lighted one. Luckily for me, I have no horror of rats as such, and being reassured by their evident timidity, I was not particularly uneasy. All the same, the three days I passed in the mine were not among the most pleasant which my memory reillumines. The patter of little feet and a perceptible sense of stir and scurry were continuous. Once I was waked up from a doze by one actually galloping across me. On the candle being lighted these beings became invisible.

The next day—if you can call it day—arrived in due course. This was December 14, and the third day since I had escaped from the State Model Schools. It was relieved by a visit from the two Scottish miners, with whom I had a long confabulation. I then learned, to my surprise, that the mine was only about two hundred feet deep.

On the fifteenth Mr. Howard announced that the hue and cry seemed to be dying away. No trace of the fugitive had been discovered throughout the mining district. The talk among the Boer officials was now that I must be hiding at the house of some British sympathizer in Pretoria. They did not believe that it was possible I could have got out of the town. In these circumstances he thought that I might come up and have a walk on the veldt that night, and that if all was quiet the next morning I might shift my quarters to the back room of the office. On the one hand he seemed reassured, and on the other increasingly excited by the adventure. Accordingly, I had a fine stroll in the glorious fresh air and moonlight, and thereafter, anticipating slightly our program, I took up my quarters behind packing cases in the inner room of the office. Here I remained for three more days, walking each night on the endless plain with Mr. Howard or his assistant.

On the sixteenth, the fifth day of escape, Mr. Howard informed me he had made a plan to get me out of the country. The mine was connected with the railway by a branch line. In the neighborhood of the mine there lived a Dutchman, Burgener by name, who was sending a consignment of wool to Delagoa Bay on the nineteenth. This gentleman was well disposed to the British. He had been approached by Mr. Howard, had been made a party to our secret, and was willing to assist. Mr. Burgener's wool was packed in great bales and would fill two or three large trucks. These trucks were to be loaded at the mine's siding. The bales could be so packed as to leave a small place in the center of the truck in which I could be concealed. A tarpaulin would be fastened over each truck after it had been loaded, and it was very unlikely indeed that, if the fastenings were found intact, it would be removed at the frontier. Did I agree to take this chance?

I was more worried about this than almost anything that had happened to me so far in my adventure. When by extraordinary chance one has gained some great advantage or prize and actually had it in one's possession and been enjoying it for several days, the idea of losing it becomes almost insupportable. I had really come to count upon freedom as a certainty, and the idea of having to put myself in a position in which I should be perfectly helpless, without a move of any kind, absolutely at the caprice of a searching party at the frontier, was profoundly harassing. Rather than face this ordeal I would much have preferred to start off on the veldt with a pony and a guide, and far from the haunts of man to make my way march by march beyond the wide territories of the Boer Republic. However, in the end I accepted the proposal of my generous rescuer, and arrangements were made accordingly.

I should have been still more anxious if I could have read some of the telegrams which were reaching English newspapers. For instance:

Pretoria, December 13.—Though Mr. Churchill's escape was cleverly executed there is little chance of his being able to cross the border.

Pretoria, December 14.—It is reported that Mr.

Winston Churchill has been captured at the border railway station of Komati Poort.

Lourenço Marques,[13] December 16.—It is reported that Mr. Churchill has been captured at Waterval Boven.

London, December 16.—With reference to the escape from Pretoria of Mr. Winston Churchill, fears are expressed that he may be captured again before long and if so may probably be shot;

or if I had read the description of myself and the reward for my recapture which were now widely distributed or posted along the railway line. I am glad I knew nothing of all this.

The afternoon of the eighteenth dragged slowly away. To be a fugitive, to be a hunted man, to be "wanted," is a mental experience by itself. The risks of the battlefield, the hazards of the bullet or the shell are one thing. Having the police after you is another. The need for concealment and deception breeds an actual sense of guilt very undermining to morale. Feeling that at any moment the officers of the law may present themselves or any stranger may ask the questions, "Who are you?" "Where do you come from?" "Where are you going?"—to which questions no satisfactory answer could be given—gnawed the structure of self-confidence. I dreaded in every fiber the ordeal which awaited me at Komati Poort and which I must impotently and passively endure if I was to make good my escape from the enemy.

In this mood I was startled by the sound of rifle shots close at hand, one after another at irregular intervals. A sinister explanation flashed through my mind. The Boers had come! Howard and his handful of Englishmen were in open rebellion in the heart of the enemy's country! I had been strictly enjoined upon no account to leave my hiding place behind the packing cases in any circumstances whatever, and I accordingly remained there in great anxiety. Presently it became clear that the worst had not happened. The sounds of voices and presently of laughter came from the office. Evidently a conversation amicable, sociable in its character was in progress. At last the voices died away, and then after an interval my door was opened and Mr. Howard's pale, somber face appeared, suffused by a broad grin. He relocked the door behind him and walked delicately towards me, evidently in high glee.

"The Field Cornet has been here," he said. "No, he was not looking for you. He says they caught you at Waterval Boven yesterday. But I didn't want him messing about, so I challenged him to a rifle match at bottles. He won two pounds off me and has gone away delighted.

"It is all fixed up for tonight," he added.

"What do I do?" I asked.

"Nothing. You simply follow me when I come for you."

At two o'clock on the morning of the nineteenth I awaited, fully dressed, the signal. The door opened. My host appeared. He beckoned. Not a word was spoken on either side. He led the way through the front office to the siding where three large bogie trucks[14] stood. Three figures, evidently Dewsnap and the miners, were strolling about in different directions in the moonlight. A gang of Kaffirs were busy lifting an enormous bale into the rearmost truck. Howard strolled along to the first truck and walked across the line past the end of it. As he did so he pointed with his left hand. I nipped on to the buffers and saw before me a hole between the wool bales and the end of the truck, just wide enough to squeeze into. From this there led a narrow tunnel formed of wool bales into the center of the truck. Here was a space wide enough to lie in, high enough to sit up in. In this I took up my abode.

Three or four hours later, when gleams of daylight had reached me through the interstices of my shelter and through chinks in the boards of the floorings of the truck, the noise of an approaching engine was heard. Then came the bumping and banging of coupling up. And again,

---

13. ***Lourenço Marques*** (lô ren′sō mär′kes), a city near the head of Delagoa Bay.

14. ***bogie trucks,*** low, strong, four-wheeled trucks or carts. [*British*]

after a further pause, we started rumbling off on our journey into the unknown.

I now took stock of my new abode and of the resources in munitions and supplies with which it was furnished. First there was a revolver. This was a moral support, though it was not easy to see in what way it could helpfully be applied to any problem I was likely to have to solve. Secondly, there were two roast chickens, some slices of meat, a loaf of bread, a melon, and three bottles of cold tea. The journey to the sea was not expected to take more than sixteen hours, but no one could tell what delay might occur to ordinary commercial traffic in time of war.

There was plenty of light now in the recess in which I was confined. There were many crevices in the boards composing the sides and floor of the truck, and through these the light found its way between the wool bales. Working along the tunnel to the end of the truck, I found a chink which must have been nearly an eighth of an inch in width, and through which it was possible to gain a partial view of the outer world. To check the progress of the journey I had learned by heart beforehand the names of all the stations on the route. I can remember many of them today: Witbank, Middleburg, Bergendal, Belfast, Dalmanutha, Machadodorp, Waterval Boven, Waterval Onder, Elands, Nooidgedacht,[15] and so on to Komati Poort. We had by now reached the first of these. At this point the branch line from the mine joined the railway. Here, after two or three hours' delay and shunting, we were evidently coupled up to a regular train, and soon started off at a superior and very satisfactory pace.

All day long we traveled eastward through the Transvaal, and when darkness fell we were laid up for the night at a station which, according to my reckoning, was Waterval Boven. We had accomplished nearly half of our journey. But how long should we wait on this siding? It might be for days; it would certainly be until the next morning. During all the dragging hours of the day I had lain on the floor of the truck occupying my mind as best I could, painting bright pictures of the pleasures of freedom, of the excitement of rejoining the army, of the triumph of a successful escape—but haunted also perpetually by anxieties about the search at the frontier, an ordeal inevitable and constantly approaching. Now another apprehension laid hold upon me. I wanted to go to sleep. Indeed, I did not think I could possibly keep awake. But if I slept I might snore! And if I snored while the train was at rest in the silent siding, I might be heard. And if I were heard! I decided in principle that it was only prudent to abstain from sleep, and shortly afterwards fell into a blissful slumber from which I was awakened the next morning by the banging and jerking of the train as the engine was again coupled to it.

All this day, we rattled through the enemy's country, and late in the afternoon we reached the dreaded Komati Poort. Peeping through my chink, I could see this was a considerable place, with numerous tracks of rails and several trains standing on them. Numbers of people were moving about. There were many voices and much shouting and whistling. After a preliminary inspection of the scene I retreated, as the train pulled up, into the very center of my fastness, and covering myself up with a piece of sacking lay flat on the floor of the truck and awaited developments with a beating heart.

Three or four hours passed, and I did not know whether we had been searched or not. Several times people had passed up and down the train talking in Dutch. But the tarpaulins had not been removed, and no special examination seemed to have been made of the truck. Meanwhile darkness had come on, and I had to resign myself to an indefinite continuance of my uncertainties. It was tantalizing to be held so long in jeopardy after all these hundreds of miles had been accomplished, and I was now within a few hundred yards of the frontier. Again I wondered about the dangers of snoring. But in the end I slept without mishap.

We were still stationary when I awoke. Per-

---

15. ***Machadodorp*** (mä'chä do'dôrp) . . . ***Nooidgedacht*** (nü'it kü-däkt').

haps they were searching the train so thoroughly that there was consequently a great delay! Alternatively, perhaps we were forgotten on the siding and would be left there for days or weeks. I was greatly tempted to peer out, but I resisted. At last, at eleven o'clock, we were coupled up, and almost immediately started. If I had been right in thinking that the station in which we had passed the night was Komati Poort, I was already in Portuguese territory. But perhaps I had made a mistake. Perhaps I had miscounted. Perhaps there was still another station before the frontier. Perhaps the search still impended. But all these doubts were dispelled when the train arrived at the next station. I peered through my chink and saw the uniform caps of the Portuguese officials on the platform and the name Resana Garcia[16] painted on a board. I restrained all expression of my joy until we moved on again. Then, as we rumbled and banged along, I pushed my head out of the tarpaulin and sang and shouted and crowed at the top of my voice. Indeed, I was so carried away by thankfulness and delight that I fired my revolver two or three times in the air as a *feu de joie*.[17] None of these follies led to any evil results.

It was late in the afternoon when we reached Lourenço Marques. My train ran into a goods yard, and a crowd of Kaffirs advanced to unload it. I thought the moment had now come for me to quit my hiding place, in which I had passed nearly three anxious and uncomfortable days. I had already thrown out every vestige of food and had removed all traces of my occupation. I now slipped out at the end of the truck between the couplings, and mingling unnoticed with the Kaffirs and loafers in the yard—which my slovenly and unkempt appearance well fitted me to do—I strolled my way towards the gates and found myself in the streets of Lourenço Marques.

Burgener was waiting outside the gates. We exchanged glances. He turned and walked off into the town, and I followed twenty yards behind. We walked through several streets and turned a number of corners. Presently he stopped and stood for a moment gazing up at the roof of the opposite house. I looked in the same direction, and there—blessed vision!—I saw floating the gay colors of the Union Jack. It was the British Consulate.

The secretary of the British Consul evidently did not expect my arrival.

"Be off," he said. "The Consul cannot see you today. Come to his office at nine tomorrow, if you want anything."

At this I became so angry, and repeated so loudly that I insisted on seeing the Consul personally at once, that that gentleman himself looked out of the window and finally came down to the door and asked me my name. From that moment every resource of hospitality and welcome was at my disposal. A hot bath, clean clothing, an excellent dinner, means of telegraphing—all I could want.

I devoured the file of newspapers which was placed before me. Great battles had taken place since I had climbed the wall of the States Model Schools, and casualties on a scale unknown to England since the Crimean War. All this made me eager to rejoin the army, and the Consul himself was no less anxious to get me out of Lourenço Marques, which was full of Boers and Boer sympathizers. Happily the weekly steamer was leaving for Durban[18] that very evening; in fact, it might almost be said it ran in connection with my train. On this steamer I decided to embark.

The news of my arrival had spread like wildfire through the town, and while we were at dinner the Consul was at first disturbed to see a group of strange figures in the garden. These, however, turned out to be Englishmen, fully armed, who had hurried up to the Consulate determined to resist any attempt at my recapture. Under the escort of these patriotic gentlemen I marched safely through the streets to the quay, and at about ten o'clock was on salt water in the steamship *Induna*.

I reached Durban to find myself a popular

---

16. ***Resana Garcia,*** a border town within Portuguese East Africa.
17. ***feu de joie*** (fœ də zhwä'), a rapid-fire rifle salute on an occasion of rejoicing. [*French*]
18. ***Durban,*** an east-coast South African city founded by the British.

hero. I was received as if I had won a great victory. The harbor was decorated with flags. Bands and crowds thronged the quays. The Admiral, the General, the Mayor pressed on board to grasp my hand. I was nearly torn to pieces by enthusiastic kindness. Whirled along on the shoulders of the crowd, I was carried to the steps of the town hall, where nothing would content them but a speech, which after a becoming reluctance I was induced to deliver. Sheaves of telegrams from all parts of the world poured in upon me, and I started that night for the army in a blaze of triumph.

Discussion

1. Early in his account Churchill states, "No walls are so hard to pierce as living walls." **(a)** How does this figurative expression relate to his situation at the opening of the selection? **(b)** Describe his escape from the State Model Schools.

2. Churchill's spirits were high at the outset of his escape. What were his feelings at the point he decided to go toward the fires of the Kaffir kraal?

3. **(a)** What part did luck play in Churchill's stumbling upon the home of John Howard? **(b)** Describe the risks Howard took for Churchill.

4. In the course of escaping, how did Churchill cope with the following conditions? **(a)** the long hours in hiding; **(b)** the lack of water; **(c)** the lack of a map or compass; **(d)** the rats in the coal mine.

5. **(a)** What do the series of telegrams included in the account reveal about the danger Churchill faced? **(b)** Why do you think that some of the facts were inaccurate?

6. Churchill was not totally comfortable with the escape method provided by the British sympathizer. Point out aspects of it that were at odds with his take-charge nature.

Composition

In giving his own account of a long-recorded event, Churchill probably had to consider how to most accurately portray himself. He knew that he could handle his subject in a completely factual and unemotional manner or personalize it by including some of his feelings. Review his chronicle to judge the following: his reliance on facts, his reference to any outside sources of information, and his tone. Then decide whether it is a fair account or one that unnecessarily overplays or underplays his role.

Write a short composition discussing the tone of the selection.

Winston Churchill 1874–1965

A member of one of England's most distinguished families, Churchill showed no intellectual promise as a youth. To compensate for this, his father, Lord Randolph, sent him to Sandhurst, the British military school. His studies improved there and he received his commission in the army in 1895. Finding himself with much free time, he read the works of the great philosophers, historians, and essayists, thus contributing to his own education.

Churchill became both a maker and recorder of history. The effect of his sensational part in the Boer War was twofold: it boosted his country's morale in a conflict that didn't end until 1902, and it helped to start his illustrious career as a statesman, orator, and historian.

A member of Parliament at various times, Churchill filled his time away from the political arena with writing novels, accounts of his wartime experiences, and a biography of his father. In the bleakest days of World War II, he became England's Prime Minister. His stubborn courage and stirring speeches helped to restore British faith and pride. *The Second World War* (1948–1954), his six-volume history, is regarded as his greatest literary achievement. In 1953 he was awarded the Nobel Prize for Literature.

The Backpacker

Patrick F. McManus USA

Weighing the merits of the old and new schools of backpacking can lead to heavy consequences.

Strange, the things that suddenly become fashionable. Take backpacking for instance.

I know people who five years ago had never climbed anything higher than a tall barstool. Now you can scarcely name a mountain within three hundred miles they haven't hoofed up in their Swiss-made waffle-stompers.

They used to complain about the price of sirloin steak. Now they complain about the price of beef jerky (which is about three times that of Maine lobster in Idaho).

Their backpacking is a refined sport, noted for lightness. The gear consists of such things as silk packs, magnesium frames, dainty camp stoves. Their sleeping bags are filled with the down of unborn goose, their tents made of waterproof smoke. They carry two little packets from which they can spread out a nine-course meal. One packet contains the food and the other a freeze-dried French chef.

Well, it wasn't like that back in the old days, before backpacking became fashionable. These latecomers don't know what real backpacking was like.

The rule of thumb for the old backpacking was that the weight of your pack should equal the weight of yourself and the kitchen range combined. Just a casual glance at a full pack sitting on the floor could give you a double hernia and fuse four vertebrae. After carrying the pack all day, you had to remember to tie one leg to a tree before you dropped it. Otherwise, you would float off into space. The pack eliminated the need for any special kind of ground-gripping shoes, because your feet would sink a foot and a half into hard-packed earth, two inches into solid rock. Some of the new breed of backpackers occasionally wonder what caused a swath of fallen trees on the side of a mountain. That is where one of the old backpackers slipped off a trail with a full pack.

My packboard alone met the minimum weight requirement. It was a canvas and plywood model, surplus from the Second World War. These packboards apparently were designed with the idea that a number of them could be hooked together to make an emergency bridge for Sherman tanks. The first time you picked one up you thought maybe someone had forgotten to remove his tank.

My sleeping bag looked like a rolled-up mattress salvaged from a fire in a skid-row hotel. Its filling was sawdust, horsehair, and No. 6 bird shot. Some of today's backpackers tell me their sleeping bags are so light they scarcely know they're there. The only time I scarcely knew my sleeping bag was there was when I was in it at 2 A.M. on a cold night. It was freckled from one end to the other with spark holes, a result of my efforts to stay close enough to the fire to keep warm. The only time I was halfway comfortable was when it was ablaze. It was the only sleeping bag I ever heard of which you could climb into in the evening with scarcely a mark on you and wake up in the morning bruised from head to toe.

That was because two or three times a night my companions would take it upon themselves to jump up and stomp out my sleeping-bag fires—in their haste neglecting to first evacuate the occupant. Since I was the camp cook, I never knew whether they were attempting to save me from immolation or getting in a few last licks for what they thought might be terminal indigestion.

Our provisions were not distinguished by variety. Dehydrated foods were considered effeminate. A man could ruin his reputation for life by getting caught on a pack trip with a dried apple. If you wanted apples, brother, you carried them with the water still in them. No one could afford such delicacies as commercial beef jerky. What you carried was a huge slab of bacon. It was so big that if the butcher had left on the legs, it could have walked behind you on a leash.

A typical meal consisted of fried bacon, potatoes and onions fried in bacon grease, a pan of beans heated in bacon grease, bacon-grease gravy, some bread fried in bacon grease, and cowboy coffee (made by boiling an old cowboy in bacon grease). After meals, indigestion went through our camp like a sow grizzly with a toothache. During the night coyotes sat in nervous silence on surrounding hills and listened to the mournful wailing from our camp.

There were a few bad things, too, about backpacking in the old style, but I loved all of it. I probably would never have thought of quitting if it hadn't been for all those geophysical changes that took place in the Western Hemisphere a few years ago.

The first thing I noticed was a distinct hardening of the earth. This occurred wherever I happened to spread out my sleeping bag, so I knew that the condition was widespread. (Interestingly enough, my children, lacking their father's scientific training, were unable to detect the phenomenon.)

A short while later it became apparent to me that the nights in the mountains had become much colder than any I could remember in the past. The chill would sink its fangs into my bones in the pre-dawn hours and hang on like a terrier until the sun was high. I thought possibly that the drop in temperature was heralding a new ice age.

Well, I could put up with the hard and the cold but then the air started getting thinner. The only way you could get sufficient oxygen to lug a pack the size of an adolescent pachyderm was by gasping and wheezing. (Some of my wheezes were sufficient to strip small pine trees bare of their needles.) My trail speed became so slow it posed a dangerous threat to my person. If we were in fact at the onset of a new ice age, there was a good chance I might be overtaken and crushed by a glacier.

The final straw was the discovery that a trail I had traveled easily and often in my youth had undergone a remarkable transformation. In the intervening years since I had last hiked it, the darn thing had nearly doubled in length. I must admit that I was puzzled, since I didn't know that trails could stretch or grow. The fact that it now took me twice as long to hike it, however, simply did not allow for any other explanation. I asked a couple of older friends about it, and they said that they had seen the same thing happen. They said probably the earth shifted on its axis every once in a while and caused trails to stretch. I suggested that maybe that was also the cause for the ground getting harder, the nights colder, and the air thinner. They said that sounded like a plausible theory to them. (My wife had another theory, but it was so wild and farfetched that I won't embarrass her by mentioning it here.)

Anyway, one day last fall while I was sitting at home fretting about the environment, a couple of friends telephoned and invited me along on a pack trip they were taking into the Cascades.[1] Both of them are of the new school of backpacking, and I thought I owed it to them to go along. They could profit considerably by watching an old trail hand in action.

When I saw the packs R.B. and Charley showed up with I almost had to laugh. Neither pack was large enough to carry much more than a

1. ***Cascades,*** mountain range in northwest United States.

cheese sandwich. I carried more bicarbonate of soda than they had food. I didn't know what they planned to sleep in, but it certainly couldn't be in those tidy little tote bags they had perched on top of their packs. Anyway, I didn't say anything. I just smiled and got out my winch and they each got a pry pole and before you knew it we had my pack out of the car and on my shoulders. As we headed up the trail I knew it was going to be a rough trip. Already a few flakes of snow had fallen on my eyeballs.

The environment on that trip was even harsher than I had remembered. The trails were steeper, the air thinner, the ground harder, the nights colder. Even my trail speed was slower. Several porcupines shot past me like I was standing still.

R.B. and Charley showed obvious signs of relief when I made it into camp that first night.

"You probably thought I wouldn't make it with all the food," I chided them.

"No," R.B. said. "It was just that for a moment there we didn't recognize you. We thought we were being attacked by a giant snail."

I explained to them that we old-time backpackers made a practice of traveling the last mile or so on our hands and knees in order to give our feet a rest.

It was disgusting to see them sitting there so relaxed and cheerful after a hard day's hike. They didn't seem to have any notion at all what backpacking was about. I could hardly stand it when they whipped out a little stove and boiled up some dried chunks of leather and sponge for supper. It probably would have hurt their feelings if I had got out the slab of bacon, so I didn't mention it. I just smiled and ate their food—four helpings in fact, just to make my act convincing. I never told them, but the Roast Baron of Beef was not quite rare enough for my taste and they had forgotten the cream sauce for the asparagus tips. And I have certainly tasted better Baked Alaska[2] in my day, too.

Well, they can have their fashionable new-

---

2. ***Baked Alaska,*** ice cream covered with meringue and baked.

school backpacking if they want it. I'm sticking with the old way. Oh, I'm making a few concessions to a harsher environment, but that's all. When I got back from that trip, I did order a new pack frame. It was designed by nine aeronautical engineers, three metallurgists, and a witch doctor, and weighs slightly less than the down of a small thistle. My new sleeping bag weighs nine ounces, including the thermostatic controls. If I want to sleep in, my new cook kit gets up and puts on the coffee. Then I bought a few boxes of that dried leather and sponge. But that's all. I'm certainly not going to be swept along on the tides of fashion.

Discussion

1. Discuss the narrator's tone as he begins to describe the latest trend of backpacking, its followers, and the new equipment created for it.

2. According to the narrator, the new backpackers "don't know what real backpacking was like." **(a)** Contrast the features of the newer style with those of the older style he prefers. **(b)** Which style is described more satirically?

3. **(a)** How had certain so-called "geophysical changes" affected the narrator's backpacking experience? **(b)** Point out a more credible factor and identify who mentioned it. **(c)** Does the narrator accept this different view? Explain.

4. **(a)** On a backpacking trip with friends, how does the narrator show his resistance to change? **(b)** Do you think he changes anyway? Give reasons for your answer.

Patrick F. McManus 1933–

A love of the outdoors and of outrageous humor is conveyed in the sketches of Patrick McManus. His boyhood memories of camping, hunting, and fishing, combined with his insights into human nature, have earned him popularity as an American humorist.

The Sandpoint, Idaho, native now lives in Spokane, Washington, and works as both an English professor and an associate editor of *Field & Stream.* His hilarious descriptions of open-air activities have appeared there as well as in *Sports Illustrated* and *Reader's Digest.*

The Summit

Maurice Herzog France

"That brown rock, the highest of them all, that ridge of ice—were these the goals of a lifetime? Or were they, rather, the limits of man's pride?"

When Maurice Herzog (her′tsōk) and Louis "Biscante" Lachenal (läsh näl′) stood atop Annapurna on June 3, 1950, they were the first mountaineers to conquer so high a summit. Annapurna is one of fourteen peaks over 8,000 meters (26,000 feet) in the Himalaya Mountains. Often called "the roof of the world," the Himalayas stretch for sixteen hundred miles along the northern border of India, their major peaks being in Nepal.

The French Himalayan Expedition, led by Herzog, arrived in Nepal in April, 1950. Since the summer monsoon was predicted for early June, they had only two months to accomplish their task. By mid-May, they had located Annapurna and had decided that the most practical route to the summit lay along its northwest flank. Racing against time, the mountaineers began their laborious assault. They worked in two-man teams to establish a series of five camps between the mountain base and the summit. The highest of these camps, Camp V, was set up by Herzog and Lachenal, who spent the night of June 2 there. Their tent was perched on a dangerously steep slope of Annapurna at 24,600 feet. The wind threatened to blow them off the mountain and heavy snows nearly crushed them where they lay.

As this account begins, Herzog and Lachenal have just achieved the goal of the Expedition: reaching the summit. Soon afterwards they must face a new challenge: coming down.

We were on top of Annapurna! Eight thousand seventy-five meters, 26,493 feet.

Our hearts overflowed with an unspeakable happiness.

"If only the others could know . . ."

If only everyone could know!

The summit was a corniced crest of ice, and the precipices on the far side which plunged vertically down beneath us were terrifying, unfathomable. There could be few other mountains in the world like this. Clouds floated halfway down, concealing the gentle, fertile valley of Pokhara, 23,000 feet below. Above us there was nothing!

Our mission was accomplished. But at the same time we had accomplished something infinitely greater. How wonderful life would now become! What an inconceivable experience it is to attain one's ideal and, at the very same moment, to fulfill oneself. I was stirred to the depths of my being. Never had I felt happiness like this—so intense and yet so pure. That brown rock, the highest of them all, that ridge of ice—were these the goals of a lifetime? Or were they, rather, the limits of man's pride?

"Well, what about going down?"

Lachenal shook me. What were his own feelings? Did he simply think he had finished another climb, as in the Alps? Did he think one could just go down again like that, with nothing more to it?

"One minute. I must take some photographs."

"Hurry up!"

I fumbled feverishly in my sack, pulled out the camera, took out the little French flag which was right on the bottom, and the pennants. Useless gestures, no doubt, but something more than symbols—eloquent tokens of affection and good

---

will. I tied the strips of material—stained by sweat and by the food in the sacks—to the shaft of my ice ax, the only flagstaff at hand. Then I focused my camera on Lachenal.

"Now, will you take me?"

"Hand it over—hurry up!" said Lachenal.

He took several pictures and then handed me back the camera. I loaded a color film and we repeated the process to be certain of bringing back records to be cherished in the future.

"Are you mad?" asked Lachenal. "We haven't a minute to lose: we must go down at once."

And in fact a glance round showed me that the weather was no longer gloriously fine as it had been in the morning. Lachenal was becoming impatient.

"We must go down!"

He was right. His was the reaction of the mountaineer who knows his own domain. But I just could not accustom myself to the idea that we had won our victory. It seemed inconceivable that we should have trodden those summit snows.

It was impossible to build a cairn; there were no stones; everything was frozen. Lachenal stamped his feet; he felt them freezing. I felt mine freezing too, but paid little attention. The highest mountain to be climbed by man lay under our feet!

My joy was touched with humility. It was not just one party that had climbed Annapurna today, but a whole expedition. I thought of all the others in the camps perched on the slopes at our feet, and I knew it was because of their efforts and their sacrifices that we had succeeded.

"Come on, straight down," called Lachenal.

He had already done up his sack and started going down. I did up my sack, put on my gloves and my glasses, seized my ice ax; one look around and I, too, hurried down the slope. Before disappearing into the couloir[1] I gave one last look at the summit which would henceforth be all our joy and all our consolation.

Lachenal was already far below; he had reached the foot of the couloir. I hurried down in his tracks. I went as fast as I could, but it was dangerous going. At every step one had to take care that the snow did not break away beneath one's weight. Lachenal, going faster than I thought he was capable of, was now on the long traverse. It was my turn to cross the area of mixed rock and snow. At last I reached the foot of the rock band. I had hurried and I was out of breath. I undid my sack. What had I been going to do? I couldn't say.

"My gloves!"

Before I had time to bend over, I saw them slide and roll. They went farther and farther, straight down the slope. I remained where I was, quite stunned. I watched them rolling down slowly, with no appearance of stopping. The movement of those gloves was engraved in my sight as something irredeemable, against which I was powerless. The consequences might be most serious. What was I to do?

"Quickly, down to Camp V."

Our associates Rébuffat and Terray should be there.[2] My concern dissolved like magic. I now had a fixed objective again: to reach the camp. Never for a minute did it occur to me to use as gloves the socks which I always carry in reserve for just such a mishap as this.

On I went, trying to catch up with Lachenal. It had been two o'clock when we reached the summit; we had started out at six in the morning, but I had to admit I had lost all sense of time. I felt as if I were running, whereas in actual fact I was walking normally, perhaps rather slowly, and I had to keep stopping to get my breath. The sky was now covered with clouds; everything had become gray and dirty-looking. An icy wind sprang up, boding no good. We must push on! But where was Lachenal? I spotted him a couple of hundred yards away, looking as if he was never going to stop. And I had thought he was in indifferent form!

The clouds grew thicker and came right down

---

1. ***couloir*** (kül wär′), a gorge on a mountainside.
2. ***Rébuffat*** (rā bʏ fä′) ***and Terray*** (tə rā′) ***should be there.*** Gaston Rébuffat and Lionel Terray were scheduled to advance from Camp IV to Camp V the same day.

over us; the wind blew stronger, but I did not suffer from the cold. Perhaps the descent had restored my circulation. Should I be able to find the tents in the mist?

Lachenal disappeared from time to time, and then the mist was so thick that I lost sight of him altogether. I kept going at the same speed, as fast as my breathing would allow.

The slope was now steeper; a few patches of bare ice followed the smooth stretches of snow. A good sign—I was nearing the camp. How difficult to find one's way in thick mist! I kept the course which I had set by the steepest angle of the slope. The ground was broken; with my crampons[3] I went straight down walls of bare ice. There were some patches ahead—a few more steps. It was the camp all right, but there were *two tents!*

So Rébuffat and Terray had come up. What a mercy! I should be able to tell them that we had been successful, that we were returning from the top. How thrilled they would be!

I got there, dropping down from above. The platform had been extended, and the two tents were facing each other. I tripped over one of the guy ropes of the first tent; there was movement inside, they had heard me. Rébuffat and Terray put their heads out.

"We've made it. We're back from Annapurna!"

Rébuffat and Terray received the news with great excitement.

"But what about Biscante?" asked Terray anxiously.

"He won't be long. He was just in front of me! What a day—started out at six this morning—didn't stop . . . got up at last."

Words failed me. I had so much to say. The sight of familiar faces dispelled the strange feeling that I had experienced since morning, and I became, once more, just a mountaineer.

Terray, who was speechless with delight, wrung my hands. Then the smile vanished from his face: "Maurice—your hands!" There was an uneasy silence. I had forgotten that I had lost my gloves; my fingers were violet and white and hard as wood. The other two stared at them in dismay—they realized the full seriousness of the injury. But, still blissfully floating on a sea of joy remote from reality, I leaned over toward Terray and said confidentially, "You're in such splendid form, and you've done so marvelously, it's absolutely tragic you didn't come up there with us!"

"What I did was for the Expedition, my dear Maurice, and anyway you've got up, and that's a victory for the whole lot of us."

I nearly burst with happiness. How could I tell him all that his answer meant to me? The rapture I had felt on the summit, which might have seemed a purely personal, egotistical emotion, had been transformed by his words into a complete and perfect joy with no shadow upon it. His answer proved that this was a victory for us all, a victory for mankind itself.

"Hi! Help! Help!"

"Biscante!" exclaimed the others.

Still half-intoxicated and remote from reality, I had heard nothing. Terray felt a chill at his heart. Putting his head out, and seeing Lachenal clinging to the slope a hundred yards lower down, he dressed in frantic haste.

Out he went. But the slope was bare now; Lachenal had disappeared. Terray was horribly frightened, and he could only utter unintelligible cries. It was a ghastly moment for him. A violent wind sent the mist tearing by. Under the stress of emotion Terray had not realized how it falsified distances.

"Biscante! Biscante!"

He had spotted him, through a rift in the mist, lying on the slope much lower down than he had thought. Terray set his teeth and glissaded down like a madman[4] and with a jump turn he stopped beside Lachenal, who was suffering from concussion after his tremendous fall. In a state of collapse, with no ice ax, balaclava,[5] or gloves, and only one crampon, he gazed vacantly around him.

---

3. ***crampons,*** spiked, iron plates that mountaineers fasten to their boots to prevent slipping.
4. ***Terray . . . like a madman.*** Terray made a sliding descent of the snow slope while in a standing position.
5. ***balaclava*** (bä'lə klä'və), a knitted cap that covers the head, neck, and shoulders.

"My feet are frostbitten. Take me down . . . take me down, so that Oudot[6] can see to me."

"It can't be done," said Terray sorrowfully. "Can't you see we're in the middle of a storm? . . . It'll be dark soon."

But Lachenal was obsessed by the fear of amputation. With a gesture of despair he tore the ax out of Terray's hands and tried to force his way down, but soon saw the futility of his action and resolved to climb up to the camp. While Terray cut steps without stopping, Lachenal, ravaged and exhausted as he was, dragged himself along on all fours.

Meanwhile I had gone into Rébuffat's tent. He was appalled at the sight of my hands and, as rather incoherently I told him what we had done, he took a piece of rope and began flicking my fingers. Then he took off my boots with great difficulty, for my feet were swollen, and beat my feet and rubbed me. We soon heard Terray giving Lachenal the same treatment in the other tent.

For our comrades it was a tragic moment: Annapurna was conquered, and the first eight-thousander had been climbed. Every one of us had been ready to sacrifice everything for this. Yet, as they looked at our feet and hands, what can Terray and Rébuffat have felt?

Outside the storm howled and the snow was still falling. The mist grew thick and darkness came, and we had to cling to the poles to prevent the tents being carried away by the wind. The only two air mattresses were given to Lachenal and myself while Terray and Rébuffat both sat on ropes, rucksacks, and provisions to keep themselves off the snow. They rubbed, slapped, and beat us with a rope. Sometimes the blows fell on living flesh, and howls arose from both tents. Rébuffat persevered; it was essential to continue, painful as it was. Gradually life returned to my feet as well as to my hands, and circulation started again. Lachenal, too, found that feeling was returning.

Lying half-unconscious, I was scarcely aware of the passage of time. There were moments when I was able to see our situation in its true dramatic light, but the rest of the time I was plunged in an inexplicable stupor with no thought for the consequences of our victory.

As the night wore on the snow lay heavier on the tent, and I had the frightful feeling of being slowly and silently asphyxiated. I tried, with all the strength of which I was capable, to push off with both forearms the mass that was crushing me. These fearful exertions left me gasping for breath and I fell back into the same exhausted state.

"Rébuffat! Gaston! Gaston!"

I recognized Terray's voice.

"Time to be off!"

I heard the sounds without grasping their meaning. Was it light already?

Outside the storm redoubled in violence. The tent shook and the fabric flapped alarmingly. It had usually been fine in the mornings: did this mean the monsoon was upon us? We knew it was not far off—could this be its first onslaught?

"Gaston! Are you ready?" Terray called again.

"One minute," answered Rébuffat. He did not have an easy job: he had to put my boots on and do everything to get me ready. I let myself be handled like a baby. In the other tent Terray finished dressing Lachenal, whose feet were still swollen and would not fit into his boots. So Terray gave him his own, which were bigger. To get Lachenal's onto his own feet he had to make slits in them. As a precaution he put a sleeping bag and some food into his sack and shouted to us to do the same. Were his words lost in the storm? Or were we too intent on leaving this hellish place to listen to his instructions?

Lachenal and Terray were already outside.

"We're going down!" they shouted.

Then Rébuffat tied me on the rope and we went out. There were only two ice axes for the four of us, so Rébuffat and Terray took them as a matter of course. For a moment as we left the two tents of Camp V, I felt childishly ashamed at leaving all this good equipment behind.

Already the first rope seemed a long way down below us. We were blinded by the squalls

---

6. ***Oudot*** (u dō'), Jacques Oudot, the Expedition's doctor.

of snow and we could not hear each other a yard away.

Ahead of us the other two were losing no time. Lachenal went first and, safeguarded by Terray, he forced the pace in his anxiety to get down. There were no tracks to show us the way, but it was engraved on all our minds—straight down the slope for four hundred yards, then traverse to the left for one hundred fifty to two hundred yards to get to Camp IV. The snow was thinning and the wind less violent. Was it going to clear? We hardly dared to hope so. A wall of seracs[7] brought us up short.

"It's to the left," I said. "I remember perfectly."

Somebody else thought it was to the right. We started going down again. The wind had dropped completely, but the snow fell in big flakes. The mist was thick, and, not to lose each other, we walked in line: I was third and I could barely see Lachenal, who was first. It was impossible to recognize any of the pitches. We were all experienced enough mountaineers to know that even on familiar ground it is easy to make mistakes in such weather. Distances are deceptive; one cannot tell whether one is going up or down. We kept colliding with hummocks which we had taken for hollows. The mist, the falling snowflakes, the carpet of snow, all merged into the same whitish tone and confused our vision. The towering outlines of the seracs took on fantastic shapes and seemed to move slowly around us.

Our situation was not desperate; we were certainly not lost. We would have to go lower down; the traverse must begin further on—I remembered the serac which served as a milestone. The snow stuck to our *cagoules,*[8] and turned us into white phantoms noiselessly flitting against a background equally white.

Were we too high or too low? No one could tell. Perhaps we had better try slanting over to the left! The snow was in a dangerous condition, but we did not seem to realize it. We were forced to admit that we were not on the right route, so we retraced our steps and climbed up above the serac which overhung us. No doubt, we decided, we should be on the right level now. With Rébuffat leading, we went back over the way which had cost us such an effort. I followed him jerkily, saying nothing, and determined to go on to the end. If Rébuffat had fallen I could never have held him.

We went doggedly on from one serac to another. Each time we thought we had recognized the right route, and each time there was a

---

7. ***seracs*** (sə raks′), ice pinnacles among the crevices of a glacier.
8. ***cagoules*** (kä gülz′), hoods. [*French*]

fresh disappointment. If only the mist would lift, if only the snow would stop for a second! On the slope it seemed to be growing deeper every minute. Only Terray and Rébuffat were capable of breaking the trail, and they relieved each other at regular intervals without a word and without a second's hesitation.

We were well and truly lost.

The weather did not seem likely to improve. A minute ago we had still had ideas about which way to go—now we had none. This way or that.

Perhaps if we called, someone would hear us? Lachenal gave the signal, but snow absorbs sound and his shout seemed to carry only a few yards. All four of us called out together: "One . . . two . . . three . . . *Help!*"

We got the impression that our united shout carried a long way, so we began again: "One . . . two . . . three . . . *Help!*" Not a sound in reply!

Now and again Terray took off his boots and rubbed his feet; the sight of our frostbitten limbs had made him aware of the danger, and he had the strength of mind to do something about it. Like Lachenal, he was haunted by the idea of amputation. For me, it was too late: my feet and hands, already affected from yesterday, were beginning to freeze up again.

We had eaten nothing since the day before, and we had been on the go the whole time, but men's resources of energy in face of death are inexhaustible. When the end seems imminent, there still remain reserves, though it needs tremendous will power to call them up.

Time passed, but we had no idea how long. Night was approaching, and we were terrified, though none of us made any complaint. Rébuffat and I found a way that we thought we remembered, but were brought to a halt by the extreme steepness of the slope—the mist turned it into a vertical wall. We were to find next day that at that moment we had been only thirty yards from the camp, and that the wall was the very one that sheltered the tent which would have been our salvation.

"We must find a crevasse."[9]

"We can't stay here all night!"

"A hole—it's the only thing."

"We'll all die in it."

Night had suddenly fallen, and it was essential to come to a decision without wasting another minute; if we remained on the slope, we should be dead before morning.

With his ax Terray began to dig a hole. Lachenal went over a snow-filled crevasse a few yards further on, then suddenly let out a yell and disappeared before our eyes. We stood helpless: should we, or rather would Terray and Rébuffat, have enough strength for all the maneuvers with the rope that would be needed to get him out? The crevasse was completely blocked up save for the one little hole which Lachenal had fallen through.

"Lachenal!" called Terray.

A voice, muffled by many thicknesses of ice and snow, came up to us. It was impossible to make out what it was saying.

"Lachenal!"

Terray jerked the rope violently; this time we could hear.

"I'm here!"

"Anything broken?"

"No! It'll do for the night! Come along."

This shelter was heaven sent. None of us would have had the strength to dig a hole big enough to protect the lot of us from the wind. Without hesitation Terray let himself drop into the crevasse, and a loud "Come on!" told us he had arrived safely. In my turn I let myself go; it was a regular toboggan slide. I shot down a sort of twisting tunnel, very steep, and about thirty feet long. I came out at great speed into the opening beyond and was literally hurled to the bottom of the crevasse. We let Rébuffat know he could come by giving a tug on the rope.

The intense cold of this minute grotto shriveled us up, the enclosing walls of ice were damp and the floor a carpet of fresh snow; by huddling together there was just room for the four of us. Icicles hung from the ceiling, and we broke some of them off to make more head room and kept

9. ***crevasse*** (krə vas'), deep crack or crevice in the ice of a glacier.

little bits to suck—it was a long time since we had anything to drink.

That was our shelter for the night. At least we should be protected from the wind, and the temperature would remain fairly even, though the damp was extremely unpleasant. We settled ourselves in the dark as best we could. As always in a bivouac[10] we took off our boots; without this precaution the constriction would cause immediate frostbite. Terray unrolled the sleeping bag which he had had the foresight to bring, and settled himself in relative comfort. We put on everything warm that we had, and to avoid contact with the snow I sat on the movie camera. We huddled close up to each other in our search for a hypothetical position in which the warmth of our bodies could be combined without loss, but we couldn't keep still for a second.

We did not open our mouths—signs were less of an effort than words. Every man withdrew into himself and took refuge in his own inner world. Terray massaged Lachenal's feet; Rébuffat felt his feet freezing, too, but he had sufficient strength to rub them himself. I remained motionless, unseeing. My feet and hands went on freezing, but what could be done? I attempted to forget suffering by withdrawing into myself; trying to forget the passing of time, trying not to feel the devouring and numbing cold which insidiously gained upon us.

Terray shared his sleeping bag with Lachenal, putting his feet and hands inside the precious eiderdown. At the same time he went on rubbing.

Anyhow the frostbite won't spread further, he was thinking.

None of us could make any movement without upsetting the others, and the positions we had taken up with such care were continually being altered so that we had to start all over again. This kept us busy. Rébuffat persevered with his rubbing and complained of his feet; like Terray he was thinking: We mustn't look beyond tomorrow—afterward we'll see. But he was not blind to the fact that "afterward" was one big question mark.

Terray generously tried to give me part of his sleeping bag. He had understood the seriousness of my condition, and knew why it was that I said nothing and remained quite passive; he realized that I had abandoned all hope for myself. He massaged me for nearly two hours; his feet, too, might have frozen, but he didn't appear to give the matter a thought. I found new courage simply in contemplating his unselfishness; he was doing so much to help me that it would have been ungrateful of me not to go on struggling to live. Though my heart was like a lump of ice itself, I was astonished to feel no pain. Everything material about me seemed to have dropped away. I seemed to be quite clear in my thoughts and yet I floated in a kind of peaceful happiness. There was still a breath of life in me, but it dwindled steadily as the hours went by. Terray's massage no longer had any effect upon me. All was over, I thought. Wasn't this cavern the most beautiful grave I could hope for? Death caused me no grief, no regret—I smiled at the thought.

After hours of torpor a voice mumbled "Daylight!"

This made some impression on the others. I only felt surprised—I had not thought that daylight would penetrate so far down.

"Too early to start," said Rébuffat.

A ghastly light spread through our grotto and we could just vaguely make out the shapes of each other's heads. A queer noise from a long way off came down to us—a sort of prolonged hiss. The noise increased. Suddenly I was buried, blinded, smothered beneath an avalanche of new snow. The icy snow spread over the cavern, finding its way through every gap in our clothing. I ducked my head between my knees and covered myself with both arms. The snow flowed on and on. There was a terrible silence. We were not completely buried, but there was snow everywhere. We got up, taking care not to bang our heads against the ceiling of ice, and tried to shake ourselves. We were all in our stockinged feet in the snow. The first thing to do was to find our boots.

Rébuffat and Terray began to search and real-

---

10. ***bivouac*** (biv'wak), an outdoor camp without tents.

ized at once that they were blind.[11] Yesterday they had taken off their glasses to lead us down and now they were paying for it. Lachenal was the first to lay hands upon a pair of boots. He tried to put them on, but they were Rébuffat's. Rébuffat attempted to climb up the chute down which we had come yesterday, and which the avalanche had followed in its turn.

"Hi, Gaston! What's the weather like?" called up Terray.

"Can't see a thing. It's blowing hard."

We were still groping for our things. Terray found his boots and put them on awkwardly, unable to see what he was doing. Lachenal helped him, but he was all on edge and fearfully impatient, in striking contrast to my immobility. Terray then went up the icy channel, puffing and blowing, and at last reached the outer world. He was met by terrible gusts of wind that cut right through him and lashed his face.

Bad weather, he said to himself; this time it's the end. We're lost . . . we'll never come through.

Lachenal decided to go out without his boots. He called frantically, hauled himself up on the rope, trying to get a hold or to wiggle his way up, digging his toes into the snow walls. Terray from outside pulled as hard as he could. I watched him go; he gathered speed and disappeared.

When he emerged from the opening he saw the sky was clear and blue, and he began to run like a madman, shrieking, "It's fine, it's fine!"

I set to work again to search the cave. The boots *had* to be found, or Lachenal and I were done for. On all fours, with nothing on my hands or feet I raked the snow, stirring it around this way and that, hoping every second to come upon something hard. I was no longer capable of thinking—I reacted like an animal fighting for its life.

I found one boot! The other was tied to it—a pair! Having ransacked the whole cave, I at last found the other pair. But in spite of all my efforts I could not find the movie camera, and gave up in despair. There was no question of putting my boots on—my hands were like lumps of wood and I could hold nothing in my fingers; my feet were very swollen—I should never be able to get boots on them. I twisted the rope around the boots as well as I could and called up the chute:

"Lionel. . . . Boots!"

There was no answer, but he must have heard, for with a jerk the precious boots shot up. Soon after the rope came down again. My turn. I wound the rope around me. I could not pull it tight so I made a whole series of little knots. Their combined strength, I hoped, would be enough to hold me. I had no strength to shout again. I gave a great tug on the rope, and Terray understood.

At the first step I had to kick a notch in the hard snow for my toes. Further on I expected to be able to get up more easily by wedging myself across the tunnel. I wriggled up a few yards like this and then I tried to dig my hands and my feet into the wall. My hands were stiff and hard right up to the wrists and my feet had no feeling up to the ankles; the joints were inflexible, and this hampered me greatly.

Somehow or other I succeeded in working my way up, while Terray pulled so hard he nearly choked me. I began to see more distinctly and so knew I must be nearing the opening. Often I fell back, but I clung on and wedged myself in again as best I could. My heart was bursting and I was forced to rest. A fresh wave of energy enabled me to crawl to the top. I pulled myself out by clutching Terray's legs; he was just about all in and I was in the last stages of exhaustion. Terray was close to me and I whispered:

"Lionel . . . I'm dying!"

He supported me and helped me away from the crevasse. Lachenal and Rébuffat were sitting in the snow a few yards away. The instant Lionel let go of me I sank down and dragged myself along on all fours.

The weather was perfect. Quantities of snow had fallen the day before and the mountains were resplendent. Never had I seen them look so beautiful—our last day would be magnificent.

Rébuffat and Terray were completely blind;

---

11. ***Rébuffat and Terray . . . blind.*** They were experiencing snow blindness, a temporary condition caused by the reflection of sunlight on snow or ice.

as he came along with me Terray knocked into things and I had to direct him. Rébuffat too could not move a step without guidance. It was terrifying to be blind when there was danger all around. Lachenal's frozen feet affected his nervous system. His behavior was disquieting—he was possessed by the most fantastic ideas:

"I tell you we must go down . . . down there. . . ."

"You've nothing on your feet!"

"Don't worry about that."

"You're off your head. The way's not there . . . it's to the left!"

He was already standing up; he wanted to go straight down to the bottom of the glacier. Terray held him back, made him sit down, and though he couldn't see, helped Lachenal put his boots on.

Behind them I was living in my own private dream. I knew the end was near, but it was the end that all mountaineers wish for—an end in keeping with their ruling passion. I was consciously grateful to the mountains for being so beautiful for me that day, and as awed by their silence as if I had been in church. I was in no pain, and had no worry. My utter calmness was alarming. Terray came staggering toward me, and I told him: "It's all over for me. Go on . . . you have a chance . . . you must take it . . . over to the left . . . that's the way."

I felt better after telling him that. But Terray would have none of it: "We'll help you. If we get away, so will you."

At this moment Lachenal shouted: "Help! Help!"

Obviously he didn't know what he was doing. . . . Or did he? He was the only one of the four of us who could see Camp II down below. Perhaps his calls would be heard.

I joined in with the others: "One . . . two . . . three . . . *Help!* One . . . two . . . three . . . *Help!*" We tried to shout together, but without much success; our voices could not have carried more than ten feet. The noise I made was more of a whisper than a shout. Terray insisted that I should put my boots on, but my hands were dead. Neither Rébuffat nor Terray, who were unable to see, could help much, so I said to Lachenal: "Come and help me to put my boots on."

"Don't be silly, we must go down!"

And off he went once again in the wrong direction, straight down.

Terray resolutely got out his knife, and with fumbling hands slit the uppers of my boots back and front. Split in two like this I could get them on, but it was not easy and I had to make several attempts. Soon I lost heart—what was the use of it all anyway since I was going to stay where I was? But Terray pulled violently and finally he succeeded. He laced up my now-gigantic boots, missing half the hooks. I was ready now. But how was I going to walk with my stiff joints?

"To the left, Lionel!"

"You're crazy, Maurice," said Lachenal, "it's to the right, straight down."

Terray did not know what to think of these conflicting views. He had not given up like me; he was going to fight, but what, at the moment, could he do? The three of them discussed which way to go.

I remained sitting in the snow. Gradually my mind lost grip—why should I struggle? I would just let myself drift. I saw pictures of shady slopes, peaceful paths, there was a scent of resin. It was pleasant—I was going to die in my own mountains. My body had no feeling—everything was frozen.

"Aah . . . aah!"

Was it a groan or a call? I gathered my strength for one cry: "They're coming!" The others heard me and shouted for joy. What a miraculous apparition! "Schatz[12] . . . it's Schatz!"

Barely two hundred yards away Marcel Schatz, waist-deep in snow, was coming slowly toward us like a boat on the surface of the slope. I found this vision of a strong and invincible deliverer inexpressibly moving. I expected everything of him. The shock was violent, and quite shattered

---

12. *Schatz* (shätz), Marcel Schatz, who had moved from Camp III to Camp IV the day before. On the third of June he unexpectedly decided to make a track between Camp IV and Camp V to guide Herzog and Lachenal on their descent. Thus he happened to be on the right spot at the right moment to rescue the lost party.

me. Death clutched at me, and I gave myself up.

When I came to again the wish to live returned and I experienced a violent revulsion of feeling. All was not lost! As Schatz came nearer my eyes never left him for a second—twenty yards—ten yards—he came straight toward me. Why? Without a word he leaned over me, held me close, hugged me, and his warm breath revived me.

I could not make the slightest movement—I was like marble. My heart was overwhelmed by such tremendous feelings and yet my eyes remained dry.

"It is wonderful—what you have done!"

Discussion

1. **(a)** Contrast Herzog's and Lachenal's feelings as they stand on the summit. **(b)** Why is Herzog so happy about Terray's later comment that the conquest of the mountain was "a victory for the whole lot of us"?

2. **(a)** Describe Herzog and Lachenal's descent to Camp V. **(b)** Why do you think Herzog did not react sensibly to the loss of his gloves? **(c)** How do his friends at the camp try to help him?

3. Describe the condition and concerns of the following as they spend the night in the crevasse: **(a)** Herzog; **(b)** Lachenal; **(c)** Terray; **(d)** Rébuffat.

4. In aiding their teammates, Terray and Rébuffat unintentionally create an additional hardship for the four the next morning. Explain.

5. **(a)** Who is the first to discover the approach of Schatz? **(b)** Given this person's physical and mental state, why is his noticing Schatz ironic?

6. **(a)** Explain some of the dangers mountaineers face in high-altitude climbing. **(b)** Give at least three examples of how cooperation helped the men of this expedition deal with their dangers.

7. **(a)** Would you agree or disagree that Herzog regards the conquest of Annapurna as an act of heroism? **(b)** Which climber do you think comes the closest to displaying heroic qualities? Explain.

Vocabulary

Context, Dictionary

Look up the words in the next column in the Glossary. Choose the correct word to complete each sentence. You will not use all the words, but be sure you can pronounce and spell them all.

domain	resplendent	hypothetical
insidious	unintelligible	persevere

1. Within the ______ of criminal investigation, Manuela Ortiz is the best.

2. Manuela's success demonstrates that one must ______ to reach a difficult goal.

3. She has the imagination to construct endless ______ situations to explain a criminal's motives or actions.

4. She can also understand clues that seem ______ to others.

5. In one rare interview, Manuela stated, "I understand completely the ______ workings of the criminal mind, and I have no patience with misdirected intelligence."

Maurice Herzog 1919–

Born in Lyons, France, Herzog spent his boyhood on the dizzy heights of the Alps. His skill in rock, ice, and snow climbing earned him the leadership of the French Himalayan Expedition when he was thirty-one. An engineer by profession, Herzog also holds a law degree and a degree in business administration. He commanded mountain troops during World War II.

Herzog began writing *Annapurna,* the book from which this selection is taken, in 1951, while recovering from the severe injuries he incurred on the descent from the summit. The book had to be dictated, for Annapurna had cost Herzog his fingers and toes.

PEOPLE

The Letter "A"

Christy Brown   Ireland

A simple, impulsive act lifts a barrier that separated Christy Brown from his family and the world.

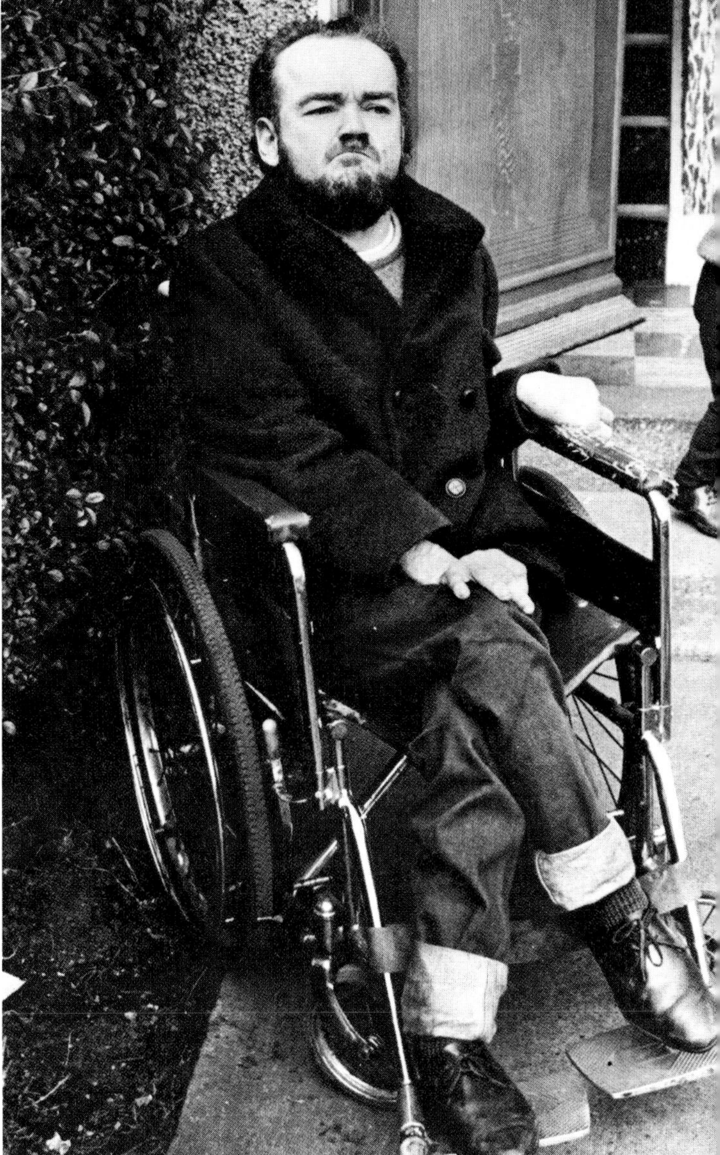

I was born in the Rotunda Hospital,[1] on June 5th, 1932. There were nine children before me and twelve after me, so I myself belong to the middle group. Out of this total of twenty-two, seventeen lived, but four died in infancy, leaving thirteen still to hold the family fort.

Mine was a difficult birth, I am told. Both mother and son almost died. A whole army of relations queued up outside the hospital until the small hours of the morning, waiting for news and praying furiously that it would be good.

After my birth Mother was sent to recuperate for some weeks and I was kept in the hospital while she was away. I remained there for some time, without name, for I wasn't baptized until my mother was well enough to bring me to church.

It was Mother who first saw that there was something wrong with me. I was about four months old at the time. She noticed that my head had a habit of falling backward whenever she tried to feed me. She attempted to correct this by placing her hand on the back of my neck to keep it steady. But when she took it away, back it would drop again. That was the first warning sign. Then she became aware of other defects as I got older. She saw that my hands were clenched nearly all of the time and were inclined to twine behind my back; my mouth couldn't grasp the teat of the bottle because even at that early age my jaws would either lock together tightly, so that it was impossible for her to open them, or they would suddenly become limp and fall loose, dragging my whole mouth to one side. At six months I could not sit up without having a mountain of pillows around me. At twelve months it was the same.

Very worried by this, Mother told my father her fears, and they decided to seek medical advice without any further delay. I was a little over a year old when they began to take me to

---

1. ***Rotunda Hospital,*** a hospital in Dublin, Ireland.

hospitals and clinics, convinced that there was something definitely wrong with me, something which they could not understand or name, but which was very real and disturbing.

Almost every doctor who saw and examined me labeled me a very interesting but also a hopeless case. Many told Mother very gently that I was mentally defective and would remain so. That was a hard blow to a young mother who had already reared five healthy children. The doctors were so very sure of themselves that Mother's faith in me seemed almost an impertinence. They assured her that nothing could be done for me.

She refused to accept this truth, the inevitable truth—as it then seemed—that I was beyond cure, beyond saving, even beyond hope. She could not and would not believe that I was an imbecile, as the doctors told her. She had nothing in the world to go by, not a scrap of evidence to support her conviction that, though my body was crippled, my mind was not. In spite of all the doctors and specialists told her, she would not agree. I don't believe she knew why—she just knew, without feeling the smallest shade of doubt.

Finding that the doctors could not help in any way beyond telling her not to place her trust in me, or, in other words, to forget I was a human creature, rather to regard me as just something to be fed and washed and then put away again, Mother decided there and then to take matters into her own hands. I was *her* child, and therefore part of the family. No matter how dull and incapable I might grow up to be, she was determined to treat me on the same plane as the others, and not as the "queer one" in the back room who was never spoken of when there were visitors present.

That was a momentous decision as far as my future life was concerned. It meant that I would always have my mother on my side to help me fight all the battles that were to come, and to inspire me with new strength when I was almost beaten. But it wasn't easy for her because now the relatives and friends had decided otherwise. They contended that I should be taken kindly, sympathetically, but not seriously. That would be a mistake. "For your own sake," they told her, "don't look to this boy as you would to the others; it would only break your heart in the end." Luckily for me, Mother and Father held out against the lot of them. But Mother wasn't content just to say that I was not an idiot: she set out to prove it, not because of any rigid sense of duty, but out of love. That is why she was so successful.

At this time she had the five other children to look after besides the "difficult one," though as yet it was not by any means a full house. They were my brothers, Jim, Tony, and Paddy, and my two sisters, Lily and Mona, all of them very young, just a year or so between each of them, so that they were almost exactly like steps of stairs.

Four years rolled by and I was now five, and still as helpless as a newly born baby. While my father was out at bricklaying, earning our bread and butter for us, Mother was slowly, patiently pulling down the wall, brick by brick, that seemed to thrust itself between me and the other children, slowly, patiently penetrating beyond the thick curtain that hung over my mind, separating it from theirs. It was hard, heartbreaking work, for often all she got from me in return was a vague smile and perhaps a faint gurgle. I could not speak or even mumble, nor could I sit up without support on my own, let alone take steps. But I wasn't inert or motionless. I seemed, indeed, to be convulsed with movement, wild, stiff, snakelike movement that never left me, except in sleep. My fingers twisted and twitched continually, my arms twined backwards and would often shoot out suddenly this way and that, and my head lolled and sagged sideways. I was a queer, crooked little fellow.

Mother tells me how one day she had been sitting with me for hours in an upstairs room, showing me pictures out of a great big storybook that I had got from Santa Claus last Christmas and telling me the names of the different animals and flowers that were in them, trying without success to get me to repeat them. This had gone on for hours while she talked and laughed with me. Then at the end of it she leaned over me and said gently into my ear:

"Did you like it, Chris? Did you like the bears and the monkeys and all the lovely flowers? Nod your head for yes, like a good boy."

But I could make no sign that I had understood her. Her face was bent over mine hopefully. Suddenly, involuntarily, my queer hand reached up and grasped one of the dark curls that fell in a thick cluster about her neck. Gently she loosened the clenched fingers, though some dark strands were still clutched between them.

Then she turned away from my curious stare and left the room, crying. The door closed behind her. It all seemed hopeless. It looked as though there was some justification for my relatives' contention that I was an idiot and beyond help.

They now spoke of an institution.

"Never!" said my mother almost fiercely, when this was suggested to her. "I know my boy is not an idiot; it is his body that is shattered, not his mind. I'm sure of that."

Sure? Yet inwardly, she prayed God would give her some proof of her faith. She knew it was one thing to believe but quite another thing to prove.

I was now five, and still I showed no real sign of intelligence. I showed no apparent interest in things except with my toes—more especially those of my left foot. Although my natural habits were clean, I could not aid myself, but in this respect my father took care of me. I used to lie on my back all the time in the kitchen or, on bright warm days, out in the garden, a little bundle of crooked muscles and twisted nerves, surrounded by a family that loved me and hoped for me and that made me part of their own warmth and humanity. I was lonely, imprisoned in a world of my own, unable to communicate with others, cut off, separated from them as though a glass wall stood between my existence and theirs, thrusting me beyond the sphere of their lives and activities. I longed to run about and play with the rest, but I was unable to break loose from my bondage.

Then, suddenly, it happened! in a moment everything was changed, my future life molded into a definite shape, my mother's faith in me rewarded, and her secret fear changed into open triumph.

It happened so quickly, so simply after all the years of waiting and uncertainty, that I can see and feel the whole scene as if it had happened last week. It was the afternoon of a cold, gray December day. The streets outside glistened with snow, the white sparkling flakes stuck and melted on the windowpanes and hung on the boughs of the trees like molten silver. The wind howled dismally, whipping up little whirling columns of snow that rose and fell at every fresh gust. And over all, the dull, murky sky stretched like a dark canopy, a vast infinity of grayness.

Inside, all the family were gathered round the big kitchen fire that lit up the little room with a warm glow and made giant shadows dance on the walls and ceiling.

In a corner Mona and Paddy were sitting, huddled together, a few torn school primers before them. They were writing down little sums onto an old chipped slate, using a bright piece of yellow chalk. I was close to them, propped up by a few pillows against the wall, watching.

It was the chalk that attracted me so much. It was a long, slender stick of vivid yellow. I had never seen anything like it before, and it showed up so well against the black surface of the slate that I was fascinated by it as much as if it had been a stick of gold.

Suddenly, I wanted desperately to do what my sister was doing. Then—without thinking or knowing exactly what I was doing, I reached out and took the stick of chalk out of my sister's hand—with my left foot.

I do not know why I used my left foot to do this. It is a puzzle to many people as well as to myself, for, although I had displayed a curious interest in my toes at an early age, I had never attempted before this to use either of my feet in any way. They could have been as useless to me as were my hands. That day, however, my left foot, apparently by its own volition, reached out and very impolitely took the chalk out of my sister's hand.

I held it tightly between my toes, and, acting on an impulse, made a wild sort of scribble with it on the slate. Next moment I stopped, a bit dazed, surprised, looking down at the stick of yellow chalk stuck between my toes, not knowing what to do with it next, hardly knowing how it got there. Then I looked up and became aware that everyone had stopped talking and was staring at me silently. Nobody stirred. Mona, her black curls framing her chubby little face, stared at me with great big eyes and open mouth. Across the open hearth, his face lit by flames, sat my father, leaning forward, hands outspread on his knees, his shoulders tense. I felt the sweat break out on my forehead.

My mother came in from the pantry with a steaming pot in her hand. She stopped midway between the table and the fire, feeling the tension flowing through the room. She followed their stare and saw me in the corner. Her eyes looked from my face down to my foot, with the chalk gripped between my toes. She put down the pot.

Then she crossed over to me and knelt down beside me, as she had done so many times before.

"I'll show you what to do with it, Chris," she said, very slowly and in a queer, choked way, her face flushed as if with some inner excitement.

Taking another piece of chalk from Mona, she hesitated, then very deliberately drew, on the floor in front of me, *the single letter "A."*

"Copy that," she said, looking steadily at me. "Copy it, Christy."

I couldn't.

I looked about me, looked around at the faces that were turned towards me, tense, excited faces that were at that moment frozen, immobile, eager, waiting for a miracle in their midst.

The stillness was profound. The room was full of flame and shadow that danced before my eyes and lulled my taut nerves into a sort of waking sleep. I could hear the sound of the water tap dripping in the pantry, the loud ticking of the clock on the mantel shelf, and the soft hiss and crackle of the logs on the open hearth.

I tried again. I put out my foot and made a wild jerking stab with the chalk which produced a very crooked line and nothing more. Mother held the slate steady for me.

"Try again, Chris," she whispered in my ear. "Again."

I did. I stiffened my body and put my left foot out again, for the third time. I drew one side of the letter. I drew half the other side. Then the stick of chalk broke and I was left with a stump. I wanted to fling it away and give up. Then I felt my mother's hand on my shoulder. I tried once more. Out went my foot. I shook, I sweated and strained every muscle. My hands were so tightly clenched that my fingernails bit into the flesh. I set my teeth so hard that I nearly pierced my lower lip. Everything in the room swam till the faces around me were mere patches of white. But—I drew it—*the letter "A."* There it was on the floor before me. Shaky, with awkward, wobbly sides and a very uneven center line. But it *was* the letter "A." I looked up. I saw my mother's face for a moment, tears on her cheeks. Then my father stooped and hoisted me onto his shoulder.

I had done it! It had started—the thing that was to give my mind its chance of expressing itself. True, I couldn't speak with my lips. But now I would speak through something more lasting than spoken words—written words.

That one letter, scrawled on the floor with a broken bit of yellow chalk gripped between my toes, was my road to a new world, my key to mental freedom. It was to provide a source of relaxation to the tense, taut thing that was I, which panted for expression behind a twisted mouth.

Discussion

1. **(a)** What were the first signs of Christy Brown's physical condition? **(b)** What did the doctors advise? **(c)** How did his mother respond?

2. Did Brown's position as "the difficult one" set him totally apart from the other children? Discuss.

3. **(a)** At what point in his account does Brown stop relying on his mother's memory and start relying on his own? **(b)** Do you think the first part of his story would have been more or less convincing if he had based it on his own memory? Explain.

4. **(a)** Describe Brown's first indication to the world that he is not an imbecile and his parents' reactions to it. **(b)** How responsible was his mother for this moment of triumph? Discuss.

5. Brown implies that his breakthrough had a different meaning for him than for his family. Describe both.

Vocabulary

Combined Skills

For the italicized words in the next column choose first the synonym and then the antonym from the list that comes after them. Write each group of three words on your paper. Use the Glossary for reference. Be sure you can spell each italicized word.

1. *inert*
2. *recuperate*
3. *momentous*
4. *impertinence*
5. *murky*
6. *molten*
7. *taut*
8. *clench*

still	dark	politeness	trivial
sicken	melted	active	release
solid	sassiness	slack	recover
tight	clear	close (tightly)	important

Christy Brown 1932–1981

Christy Brown, as he wrote in "The Letter 'A,' " was born in Dublin, Ireland, the tenth child of the twenty-two his mother would bear. Soon after his birth he was discovered to have cerebral palsy. But the steadfast faith of his mother encouraged him to struggle with his condition and to overcome it.

With the help of physical therapy, he enabled himself to write and type with his feet. Through this difficult method he wrote his autobiography, *My Left Foot* (1954). Then, in 1970, he finished a novel, *Down All the Days,* which brought him world fame. He became a serious student of human nature. "I've had no choice but to be an observer," he said, "always on the outside looking in."

See **STYLE** Handbook of Literary Terms

Five Letters

USA

Dolley Madison 1768–1849

This letter describes two tense days in the life of the First Lady during the War of 1812. In the summer of 1814, while President Madison was with his troops, she was forced to flee the then-called President's House to escape a British invasion of Washington. Along with the valuables mentioned in her letter, she took the original copy of the Declaration of Independence, which might have been destroyed in the fire set by the enemy.

Tuesday, August 23rd, 1814

My dear Sister:

My husband left me yesterday to join General Winder. . . . I have since received two dispatches from him . . . he desires that I should be ready at a moment's warning to enter my carriage and leave the city . . . I am accordingly ready; I have pressed as many Cabinet Papers into trunks as will fill one carriage; our private property must be sacrificed, as it is impossible to procure wagons for its transportation. I am determined not to go myself until I see Mr. Madison safe. . . .

My friends and acquaintances are all gone—even Colonel C, with his hundred men, who was stationed as a guard. . . . French John,[1] *with his usual activity and resolution, offers to spike the cannon at the gates, and to lay a train of powder which would blow up the British should they enter the house . . .*

Wednesday, 3 o'clock . . . We have had a battle near Bladensburg[2] *and I am still here, within sound of the cannon! Mr. Madison comes not; may God protect him! Two messengers, covered with dust, bid me fly; but I wait for him. . . . At this late hour a wagon has been procured; I have had it filled with the plate and most valuable portable articles belonging to the house. . . .*

---

1. ***French John,*** John Sioussat (syü sä'), a loyal servant.
2. ***Bladensburg,*** a town in Maryland.

From *Our First Ladies*, 5th edition, by Jane and Burt McConnell. Thomas Y. Crowell Company, 1969.

Our kind friend, Mr. Carroll, has come to hasten my departure, and is in a very bad humor with me because I insist on waiting until the large picture of General Washington[3] *is secured, and it requires to be unscrewed from the wall. This process was found to be too tedious for these perilous moments. I have [therefore] ordered the frame to be broken, and the canvas taken out; it is done—and the precious portrait placed in the hands of two gentlemen from New York for safe keeping.*

And now, dear sister, I must leave this house. . . . When I shall see or write you, or where I shall be tomorrow, I cannot tell.

---

3. ***picture of General Washington,*** the famous Gilbert Stuart portrait that is now displayed in the White House.

James Thurber 1894–1961

In this letter, one of America's greatest humorists turns down a speaking invitation at a women's college. You may know Thurber from his short story "The Secret Life of Walter Mitty" or some of the drawings of shaggy dogs for which he was noted before blindness ended that phase of his career.

West Cornwall,
Connecticut
July 8, 1949

Miss Ada Laura Fonda Snell
Mount Holyoke College
South Hadley, Massachusetts

Dear Miss Snell:

. . . Fifteen years ago and more, I sometimes talked briefly to English classes at Ohio State, on which frightening occasions my nervousness made the class nervous, setting up a nervous cycle. We were both glad when it was over. Since 1940, when I lost the ability to read and to get around by myself, I have had to abandon what one friend called my public apparitions. . . .

I was pleased and honored, so was Helen, to receive your invitation, and I am distressed that I have to decline, since I love Mount Holyoke. The idea of

---

addressing the flower of American womanhood would terrify me even if I could see. I am like the tough American soldier, loose in no-man's-land during the First War, who had invaded a dozen enemy trenches with a lone companion, capturing a hundred Germans, and who suddenly came upon a dark, mysterious, and deep hole in the ground. He peered into it cautiously. "You goin' down there, Mac?" asked his friend. Mac looked at the hole again. "I wouldn't go down there," he said, "if they was Fig Newtons down there."

Your name is like a waving flag and should never be furled in abbreviation. Helen joins me in thanking you for your invitation, and we send you our joint regrets. I hope that I will have the pleasure someday of meeting you.

Cordially yours,
James Thurber

Bartolomeo Vanzetti 1888–1927

Writing this letter on the eve of his execution, Italian immigrant Vanzetti directed his statements to the young son of his co-defendant, protesting his own innocence and that of the boy's father, Nicola Sacco. Considered radicals at an anti-radical time, the two were convicted of robbing and murdering two shoe-factory employees in the Boston area in 1920. Their trial and deaths led to international debate over their guilt or innocence, a question that to this date has not been settled.

August 21, 1927

My dear Dante:

I still hope, and we will fight until the last moment, to revindicate our right to live and to be free, but all the forces of the State and of the money and reaction are deadly against us because we are libertarians or anarchists.

I write little of this because you are now and yet too young to understand these things and other things of which I would like to reason with you.

But, if you do well, you will grow and understand

your father's and my case and your father's and my principles, for which we will soon be put to death.

I tell you now that all that I know of your father, he is not a criminal, but one of the bravest men I ever knew. Some day you will understand what I am about to tell you. That your father has sacrificed everything dear and sacred to the human heart and soul for his fate in liberty and justice for all. That day you will be proud of your father, and if you come brave enough, you will take his place in the struggle between tyranny and liberty and you will vindicate his (our) names and our blood.

If we have to die now, you shall know, when you will be able to understand this tragedy in its fullest, how good and brave your father has been with you, your father and I, during these eight years of struggle, sorrow, passion, anguish and agony. . . .

I would like you to remember me as a comrade and friend to your father, your mother and Ines, Susie and you, and I assure you that neither have I been a criminal, that I have committed no robbery and no murder, but only fought modestly to abolish crimes from among mankind and for the liberty of all.

Remember Dante, each one who will say otherwise of your father and I, is a liar, insulting innocent dead men who have been brave in their life. Remember and know also, Dante, that if your father and I would have been cowards and hypocrites and renegades of our faith, we would not have been put to death. They would not even have convicted a leprous dog; not even executed a deadly poisoned scorpion on such evidence as that they framed against us. They would have given a new trial to a matricide and habitual felon on the evidence we presented for a new trial.

Remember, Dante, remember always these things; we are not criminals; they convicted us on a frame-up; they denied us a new trial; and if we will be executed after seven years, four months and seventeen days of unspeakable tortures and wrong, it is for what I have already told you; because we were for the poor and against the exploitation and oppression of the man by the man.

The documents of our case, which you and other ones will collect and preserve, will prove to you that your father, your mother, Ines, my family, and I have been sacrificed by and to a State Reason of the American Plutocratic reaction.

The day will come when you will understand the atrocious cause of the above written words, in all its fullness. Then you will honor us.

Now Dante, be brave and good always. I embrace you. . . .

Bartolomeo

Anne Morrow Lindbergh 1906–

In 1929 the bride of world-famous aviator Charles Lindbergh wrote this letter to her mother during a stopover on her flying honeymoon.

Hotel Chase, Saint Louis, June 28th

Mother darling--

I tried to write you from Indianapolis, but it has been very hurried. We haven't slept twice at one place, flying every day so far. But we are staying here today and tomorrow because something in the plane is being looked over. . . .

Yesterday was the most thrilling day. Flying from Indianapolis, about sunset we started to climb. There was a rainbow behind us, a glorious bow that was much bigger and brighter than those on the ground. We saw more than a half circle. It was so real and yet so vanishing--about to vanish--that it reminded me of the visions one reads about. Do you remember the poor monk who had a vision of an angel and then heard the monastery doorbell ring and was torn between his duty and the vision, finally went to the door, and came back to find it still there? It was so beautiful with great piled-up golden clouds behind, and I thought of your saying to me in Mexico that first morning, "Anne, you'll have the sky--the sky!" It was glorious of you.

Then we went up, up above the clouds, at dusk, fifteen thousand feet. At about eight thousand, looking down, there was a blue mist over the flat land so that a new horizon was made. It looked as though we were on a sea and the land, patchworked below the mist, looked sunk in many depths of blue water. Then up further through mist, it was very cold and suddenly out on a plateau of blue-gray clouds, as far as one could see, and the sky bright blue above us. It is an indescribable feeling--those cold blue motionless stretches of cotton wool. Like ice in their motionless stillness, but soft and piled up like feathers. I think it is more like a mammoth bed of gray feathers than anything else. Then we dove down out of this bright cold blue into sudden warmth and <u>dark</u>. The earth was dark and lights of towns peppered the ground. We came into Saint Louis at night but you could still see those two great rivers[1] and where they joined, broad, peaceful, and gleaming between the dark shores. It was thrilling.

---

1. ***two great rivers,*** the Missouri and the Mississippi.

Harry S. Truman 1884–1972

President Truman wrote faithfully to his wife from Berlin, even though he was heavily involved in the Potsdam Conference, a meeting of world leaders following Germany's defeat in World War II.

Berlin
July 20, 1945

Dear Bess:

It was an experience to talk to you from my desk here in Berlin night before last. It sure made me homesick. . . .[1] You never saw as completely ruined a city. But they did it. I am most comfortably fixed and the palace where we meet is one of two intact palaces left standing. . . .

We had a tough meeting yesterday. I reared up on my hind legs and told 'em where to get off and they got off. I have to make it perfectly plain to them at least once a day that so far as this President is concerned Santa Claus is dead and that my first interest is U.S.A., then I want the . . . War won[2] and I want 'em both[3] in it. Then I want peace--world peace and will do what can be done by us to get it. But certainly am not going to set up another [illegible] here in Europe, pay reparations, feed the world, and get nothing for it but a nose thumbing. They are beginning to awake to the fact that I mean business.

It was my turn to feed 'em at a formal dinner last night. Had Churchill on my right, Stalin[4] on my left. We toasted the British King, the Soviet President, the U.S. President, the two honor guests, the foreign ministers, one at a time, etc. etc. ad lib. Stalin felt so friendly that he toasted the pianist when he played a Tskowsky (you spell it) piece[5] especially for him. The old man loves music. He told me he'd import the greatest Russian pianist for me tomorrow. Our boy was good. His name is List and he played Chopin, Von Weber, Schubert, and all of them.

The ambassadors and Jim Byrnes said the party was a success. Anyway they left in a happy frame of mind. I gave each of them a fine clock, specially made for them, and a set of that good, navy luggage. Well I'm hoping to get done in a week. I'm sick of the whole business--but we'll bring home the bacon.

Kiss Margie, lots and lots of love,
Harry

---

1. ***homesick. . . .*** The series of periods indicates an editorial deletion.
2. ***I want the . . . War won,*** another editorial deletion. The reference is to the yet-unsettled war with Japan.
3. ***'em both,*** England and Russia.
4. ***Stalin,*** Joseph Stalin, 1879–1953, dictator of the Soviet Union from 1929 to 1953.
5. ***a Tskowsky . . . piece,*** a misspelled reference to Russian composer Peter Ilich Tchaikovsky, 1840–1893.

Discussion

1. Madison makes no mention of her own patriotism and bravery, but they are nonetheless conveyed in her letter. Give examples.

2. (a) What reasons does Thurber give for declining the speaking invitation? **(b)** How does he manage to make his refusal gracious?

3. In writing to young Dante Sacco, what major point was Vanzetti trying to make?

4. Lindbergh refers to a story about a monk who sees a vision to draw an analogy to something she experienced. Describe what she experienced and the effect created by the comparison.

5. (a) Which comments in Truman's letter show him as a loving husband and father? **(b)** Which show him as a down-to-earth observer of a formal event?

Application

Style

You need not be an experienced writer to produce letters that are insightful as well as informative. Though the style of a letter arises naturally from an individual's unique thoughts and feelings, it can be shaped by the circumstances in which it is created.

1. James Thurber presented his reason for not visiting Mt. Holyoke in a charming fashion, but what underlying reason might he have been attempting to disguise?

2. What words or phrases in Harry Truman's letter show his realistic attitude toward his meeting with other world leaders?

3. Would Dolley Madison's letter be as interesting if written *after* her escape? Discuss.

Comment: The Art of Writing Letters

Letter writing, public and personal, goes back as far as history itself. Ancient Romans composed verse epistles (letters) to their friends, discussing philosophical or literary matters or satirizing people and government institutions. St. Paul's epistles, contained in the New Testament, provided spiritual guidance for the early Christians.

In the eighteenth century, letter writing rose to the status of fine art. Noted authors like British poet Alexander Pope followed the custom of the ancient Romans in directing verse epistles to friends, but most of these were, in fact, intended for public consumption. Rather than speaking directly to the person they were addressed to, such letters were generally essays satirizing some aspect of society, and many caused a great furor when they were published. The art of writing personal letters also flourished at this time. Originally written to family members and close friends, those that have survived exist now as historical documents, often providing unexpected insights into the world in which the correspondents lived.

Surprisingly, the modern novel owes much to letter writing. In eighteenth-century England Samuel Richardson, who had earlier published a book containing samples of the proper letters for various occasions, conceived the idea of telling a story through a series of letters written by and to the heroine. The result was *Pamela* (1740), sometimes called the first real English novel.

Perhaps the greatest influence on the decline of letter writing from the late nineteenth century to the present has been the telephone, admittedly a more direct form of communication. Nowadays public letters are no more exotic than letters to newspaper or magazine editors or to a columnist like "Dear Abby." Of these and the personal letters presently being written, it can be said with certainty that few display the grand style of the previous ages. In turning more to phone than pen, have people lost a valuable skill? An answer might be found in reviewing the preceding letters, which, with one exception, were written by twentieth-century figures.

Three Days to See!

Helen Keller USA

"I who am blind can give one hint to those who see: Use your eyes as if tomorrow you would be stricken blind."

I have often thought it would be a blessing if each human being were stricken blind and deaf for a few days at some time during his early adult life. Darkness would make him more appreciative of sight; silence would teach him the joys of sound.

Now and then I have tested my seeing friends to discover what they see. Recently I asked a friend, who had just returned from a long walk in the woods, what she had observed. "Nothing in particular," she replied. I was astonished.

How was it possible, I asked myself, to walk for an hour through the woods and see nothing worthy of note? I who cannot see find hundreds of things to interest me through mere touch. I feel the delicate symmetry of a leaf. I pass my hands lovingly about the smooth skin of a silver birch, or the rough, shaggy bark of a pine. In spring I touch the branches of trees hopefully in search of a bud, the first sign of awakening nature after her winter's sleep. Occasionally, if I am very fortunate, I place my hand gently on a small tree and feel the happy quiver of a bird in full song.

At times my heart cries out with longing to see all these things. If I can get so much pleasure from mere touch, how much more beauty must be revealed by sight. And I have imagined, selecting carefully, what I should most like to see if I were given the use of my eyes, say, for just a three-day period.

I should divide the period into three parts. On the first day, I should want to see the people whose kindness and companionship have made my life worth living. I do not know what it is to see into the heart of a friend through that "window of the soul," the eye. I can only "see" through my fingertips the outline of a face. I can detect laughter, sorrow, and many other obvious emotions. I know my many friends, not by sight, but only from the feel of their faces.

How much easier, how much more satisfying it is for you who can see to grasp quickly the essential qualities of another person by watching the subtleties of expression, the quiver of a muscle, the flutter of a hand. But does it ever occur to you to use your sight to see into the inner nature of a friend? Do not most of you seeing people grasp only casually the outward features of a familiar face and let it go at that?

For instance, can you describe accurately the faces of five good friends? As an experiment, I have questioned husbands about the color of their wives' eyes, and often they express embarrassed confusion and admit that they do not know.

Oh, the things that I should see if I had the power of sight for just three days!

The first day would be a busy one. I should call to me all my dear friends and look long into their faces, imprinting upon my mind the outward evidences of the beauty that is within them. I should let my eyes rest, too, on the face of a baby, so that I could catch a vision of the eager,

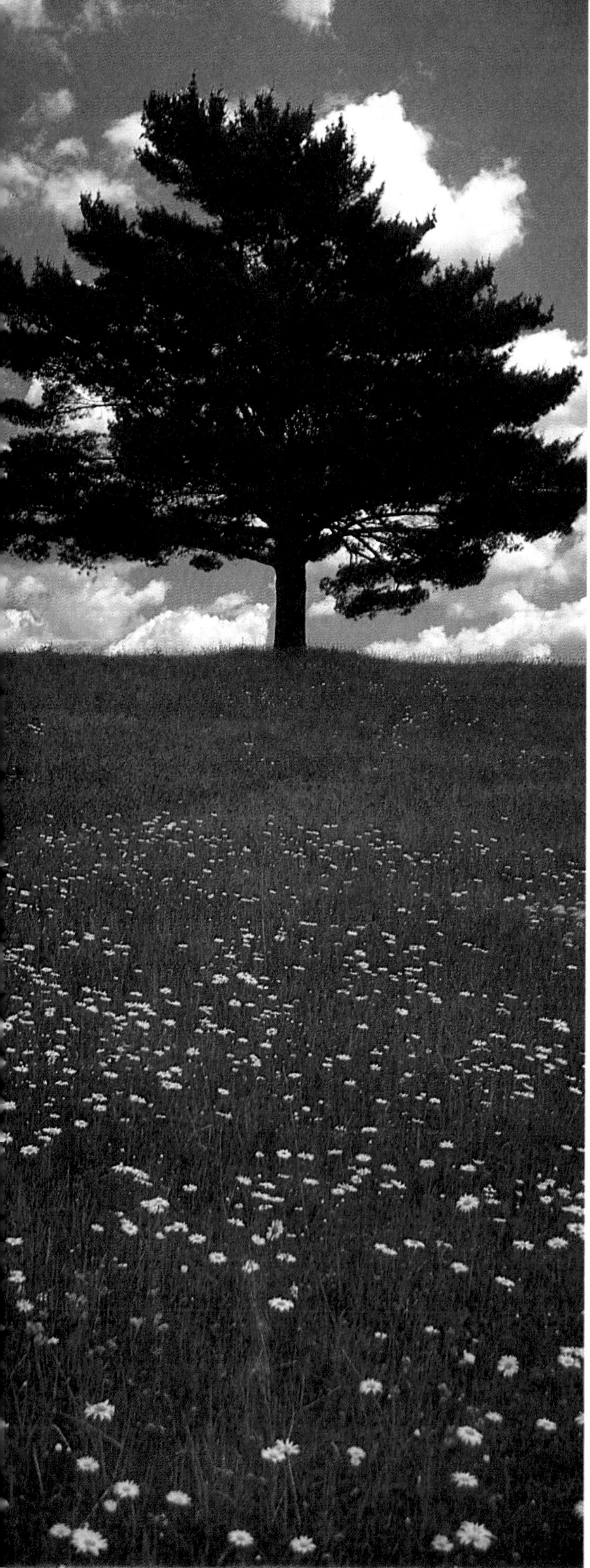

innocent beauty which precedes the individual's consciousness of the conflicts which life develops. I should like to see the books which have been read to me, and which have revealed to me the deepest channels of human life. And I should like to look into the loyal, trusting eyes of my dogs, the little Scottie and the stalwart Great Dane.

In the afternoon I should take a long walk in the woods and intoxicate my eyes on the beauties of the world of nature. And I should pray for the glory of a colorful sunset. That night, I think, I should not be able to sleep.

The next day I should arise with the dawn and see the thrilling miracle by which night is transformed into day. I should behold with awe the magnificent panorama of light with which the sun awakens the sleeping earth.

This day I should devote to a hasty glimpse of the world, past and present. I should want to see the pageant of man's progress and so I should go to the museums. There my eyes would see the condensed history of the earth—animals and the races of men pictured in their native environment; gigantic carcasses of dinosaurs and mastodons which roamed the earth before man appeared, with his tiny stature and powerful brain, to conquer the animal kingdom.

My next stop would be the museum of art. I know well through my hands the sculptured gods and goddesses of the ancient Nile land. I have felt copies of Parthenon friezes and I have sensed the rhythmic beauty of charging Athenian warriors. The gnarled, bearded features of Homer[1] are dear to me, for he, too, knew blindness.

So on this, my second day, I should try to probe into the soul of man through his art. The things I knew through touch I should now see. More splendid still, the whole magnificent world of painting would be opened to me. I should be able to get only a superficial impression. Artists

---

1. ***Parthenon friezes*** (frēz′əz) . . . ***Homer.*** The friezes, sculptures depicting historical and mythological figures, once decorated the Parthenon, an ancient Greek temple. They are now found in various museums. Homer, the great epic poet of Greece who lived during the ninth century B.C., overcame blindness to compose the *Illiad* and the *Odyssey*.

tell me that for a deep and true appreciation of art one must educate the eye. One must learn through experience to weigh the merits of line, of composition, of form, and color. If I had eyes, how happily would I embark on so fascinating a study!

The evening of my second day I should spend at a theater or at the movies. How I should like to see the fascinating figure of Hamlet, or the gusty Falstaff[2] amid colorful Elizabethan trappings!

I cannot enjoy the beauty of rhythmic movement except in a sphere restricted to the touch of my hands. I can vision only dimly the grace of a Pavlova,[3] although I know something of the delight of rhythm for often I can sense the beat of music as it vibrates through the floor. I can well imagine that cadenced motion must be one of the most pleasing sights in the world. I have been able to gather something of this by tracing with my fingers the lines in sculptured marble; if this static grace can be so lovely, how much more acute must be the thrill of seeing grace in motion.

The following morning I should again greet the dawn, anxious to discover new delights, new revelations of beauty. Today, this third day, I shall spend in the workaday world, amid the haunts of men going about the business of life. The city becomes my destination. There I must go at once!

First, I stand at a busy corner merely looking at people, trying by sight of them to understanding something of their daily lives. I see smiles and I am happy. I see serious determination and I am proud. I see suffering and I am compassionate.

I stroll down Fifth Avenue. I throw my eyes out of focus, so that I see no particular object but only a seething kaleidoscope of color. I am certain that the colors of women's dresses moving in a throng must be a gorgeous spectacle of which I should never tire. But perhaps if I had sight I should be like most other women—too interested in styles to give much attention to the splendor of color in the mass.

From Fifth Avenue I make a tour of the city—to the slums, to factories, to parks where children play. I take a stay-at-home trip abroad by visiting the foreign quarters. Always my eyes are open wide to all the sights of both happiness and misery so that I may probe deep and add to my understanding of how people work and live.

My third day of sight is drawing to an end. Perhaps there are many serious pursuits to which I should devote the few remaining hours, but I am afraid that on the evening of that last day I should again run away to the theater, to a hilariously funny play, so that I might appreciate the overtones of comedy in the human spirit.

At midnight permanent night would close in on me again. Naturally in those three short days I should not have seen all I wanted to see. Only when darkness had again descended upon me should I realize how much I had left unseen.

Perhaps this short outline does not agree with the program you might set for yourself if you knew that you were about to be stricken blind. I am, however, sure that if you faced that fate, you would use your eyes as never before. Everything you saw would become dear to you. Your eyes would touch and embrace every object that came within your range of vision. Then, at last, you would really see, and a new world of beauty would open itself before you.

I who am blind can give one hint to those who see: Use your eyes as if tomorrow you would be stricken blind. And the same method can be applied to the other senses.

Hear the music of voices, the song of a bird, the mighty strains of an orchestra, as if you would be stricken deaf tomorrow. Touch each object as if tomorrow your tactile sense would fail. Smell the perfume of flowers, taste with relish each morsel, as if tomorrow you could never smell and taste again. Make the most of every sense; glory in all the facets of pleasure and beauty which the world reveals to you through the several means of contact which nature provides. But of all the senses, I am sure that sight must be far and away the most delightful.

---

2. ***Hamlet . . . Falstaff,*** well-known characters from Shakespeare's plays.
3. ***Pavlova,*** Anna Pavlova, 1885–1931, famed Russian ballerina.

Discussion

1. **(a)** Identify the paradoxical statement about the condition of blindness made in the opening paragraph of the essay. **(b)** On what personal experiences did Helen Keller base this view?

2. Describe Keller's basic plan for each imaginary day of seeing.

3. Keller ends the description of her first day by saying, "That night, I think, I should not be able to sleep." Why not?

4. **(a)** What did Keller think the sense of sight might convey to her on the second day that her sense of touch could not? **(b)** What did she think she would learn from her activities on the third day?

5. Taking Keller's three days as a whole, what would you say she was most interested in seeing?

6. Consider her closing message to the sighted. Was the purpose of her essay to show what she as a sightless person felt deprived of? Explain.

Composition

Consider your actual physical condition and the things you most enjoy or take for granted about it. Then assume that you have lost the use of a particular sense, and, like Helen Keller, imagine that you could regain it for a three-day period. What would you do? To what greater understanding might such an experience lead you or others?

Try your hand at a five-paragraph essay in which you introduce your condition in the first paragraph, devote three paragraphs to describing your imagined period of restoration, and conclude with a paragraph that sums up the experience in some way. It might be helpful to review the structure and style of Helen Keller's essay, particularly her use of imagery. (See "Developing Your Style," page 660, in the Composition Guide.)

Helen Keller 1880–1968

Born in Tuscumbia, Alabama, Helen Keller contracted a disease as an infant that left her blind and deaf. Because of her disabilities she was unable to learn to speak. Through the efforts of her gifted and determined teacher, Anne Sullivan, Helen learned sign language and Braille, and, when she eventually earned a college degree, set about helping others.

Capable of speech from the age of sixteen, Keller became active in the American Foundation for the Blind and lectured extensively to educate the general public about the problems of the disabled. She also produced *The Story of My Life* (1903), the first of several accounts of her fascinating experiences. The story of Helen's early triumph is best known through William Gibson's play *The Miracle Worker* (1957). "Three Days to See!" has long been recognized for its literary value as well as its inspirational message.

Death of Grandmother Zabielska[1]

Zofia Starowieyska Morstin Poland

Even the final days of life can provide important lessons.

The death of Grandmother Zabielska was the first one experienced by the children. Both their grandfathers had died long before. None of the children remembered them. She was the first person whom they knew, whom they lived with, to leave this familiar life. For that reason her end became for them a kind of model death. It also explains how the seventy-second year, the age at which she died, came to mark for them the close of human life, just as the red line on a thermometer points to the normal temperature. They always believed that whoever died before that age died too young, while every additional year was a gift.

In the same way, through her death, their attitude towards that special moment of life was determined—and determined properly; although sad, the fact was simple and natural. There was nothing dramatic about it. It was, like Grandmother's life, well balanced, Christian, conducted intelligently and generously.

As soon as her condition was diagnosed as pneumonia, her bed was moved from the northern bedroom to the sunny living room. Treatment with oxygen was then unknown, and the disease was not accompanied, as it is now, by the threatening hiss of the oxygen tank. As much fresh air as possible was supplied for the congested lungs, but of course only natural sources were available. Here, in the red living room, air was plentiful. Also, there was enough space for an altar, in front of which Father Wojciech,[2] one of Grandmother's sons, said Mass every morning so she could share in the service and receive Holy Communion.

The sick woman, like everyone around her, fully realized that the end was near, for at that time there was no recovery from pneumonia for an old person. Grandmother Zabielska was not in the habit of deceiving herself; even this awesome fact she met as reasonably as she had always met all unavoidable events.

She did not complain, nor was she ever restive. On the contrary, she was gracious and grateful for the gentle care with which Emilia, her daughter-in-law, nursed her so efficiently. Nobody could please the sick woman as well as she did, for Pani Emilia,[3] though she had no natural leanings toward good Samaritanism, wanted to do everything well for those she loved.

Meanwhile, Grandmother Zabielska set about preparing for death in her orderly way. As Wojciech did not leave his mother's side, he would be on hand at the appropriate moment to administer the last rites.[4] In the Zabielski family it was not the custom when someone was dying to tell that person a white lie about recovering, but for Emilia's people, who loved talk, ornaments, and gentle ironies, these straightforward manners seemed brutal. They used to say that the Zabielskis died like peasants.

The sacrament of Extreme Unction was received by the patient in all the severity of truth.

---

1. ***Zabielska*** (zä byel′skə).
2. ***Wojciech*** (voi′cheн).
3. ***Pani*** (pä′nyi) ***Emilia.*** *Pani* is a complimentary title meaning "lady." [*Polish*]
4. ***last rites.*** Known also as Extreme Unction, these are religious rites performed for a dying person.

Zofia Starowieyska Morstin (zô′fyä stär′ō vyā′skä môr′stēn).

The business of the will was clear and decided ahead of time; it needed no explanation. The last instructions by Grandmother Zabielska, however, concerned matters so trivial that everyone was astonished that they were recalled at such a moment. But she, always tidy to the point of perfection, did not believe that small things should be forgotten on the doorstep of eternity. And so one day she called the eighteen-year-old sister of her daughter-in-law, and rather harshly ordered her to put the last stitches on the embroidery of a gray tablecloth. She herself would not have time, and she hated to leave a piece of work unfinished.

"But make sure that all the cross-stitches go in the same direction," she said.

And when Basia[5] began to reply that she could finish it herself upon recovering, Grandmother Zabielska interrupted. "I know what I'm talking about; you will finish the tablecloth. But you are messy and always mix up the stitches, and this time I want you to work carefully."

Basia kept her promise. Those were the only straight stitches she ever made.

A frequent guest at the sickbed was Emilia's mother, Pani Liza. The two old friends talked about the approaching parting. Pani Liza was very sorry to see her companion go, and with all her warm heart she tried to anticipate and understand the dejection and sorrow of her relative. The tearing-off process of death frightened her because—although reaching longingly for God—she had her roots deeply in life. Letting her thoughts out, she would say, more frankly than diplomatically, "How hard it must be to leave this world! To leave everything and everyone."

"Oh, no," the answer came. "When the dessert is to be passed, we don't want to go back to the soup."

But Pani Liza was not convinced that one could leave this world without regret. Not only was she more passionately attached to life, but also—being more pious—she was continuously stirred by feelings of doubt and guilt, never sure whether she had not committed a grave sin. That was why she could not understand her friend's composure. (Her own death, when it came, was very different: although she died in a nun's habit, and in a state of grace, her end was full of anguish, dreadful fears, and heart-rending sorrow. And perhaps in forewarning of these tortures she did not hesitate to say things which, presumably, would upset her friend.)

"It is so horrifying," she would say, "to know that soon one will face God's Judgment."

This prospect did not disturb Grandmother Zabielska either.

"But why?" she said soberly and reasonably. "When we knew that something was bad, we simply tried not to do it."

People are apt to judge themselves tolerantly; nevertheless in decisive moments panic seizes them. Then from the peaks of self-confidence, they fall into the depths of doubt. Not so Grandmother Zabielska; she never lost her balance. What she thought of herself no one knew, for she never talked about herself. Her one bit of self-praise in that last hour was a modest one. She simply stated that she did no wrong, or rather, tried to do no wrong. She was sure of it. Her moral standard was minimal: to avoid wrong. It was realized in full.

She imposed this peace-in-death on everyone around her. Everyone was sad—no one despaired.

Once a day the children were called to Grandmother's bedside. They would stand there a while, silent, suddenly hushed, and then they would go back to their rooms. Mrs. Zabielska looked at the children seriously—strictly, they thought. But this was entirely on the surface. She loved them very much and was proud of them. She was proud of their robust health, their tallness, their gaiety and brightness.

One afternoon Pani Emilia entered the nursery where they sat at the low table having their afternoon snack, and told them that Helenka and Maciej[6] were to come with her, because their grandmother was dying. She waited, leaning

5. ***Basia*** (bä'shə).
6. ***Helenka*** (hä län'kə) . . . ***Maciej*** (mä'chā).

down on the little table. From her neck hung a long, heavy chain the end of which, together with the watch, was tucked under the belt. Tears rolled down her face. The children got up quietly and went with her down to the living room, where everyone—family and servants—was kneeling in a circle around the bed, reciting the litany for the dying. The children knelt and prayed with the others—for the first time participating in the grave matter of death.

No shadow of terror fell on their lives. This "good death" they remembered many, many years later, when—quite grown-up—they followed the coffin of Grandmother Zabielska's son, Uncle Kazimierz.[7] Around them the Second World War was blazing and the terror of the German occupation raged. It was a time rife with death—dreadful, cruel, and unnatural. But Uncle Kazimierz escaped this fate. He died at a ripe old age in his own home, among his children and grandchildren. He died a sudden death, but not unexpected. His coffin was carried by his neighbors out of the place in which he had spent his life. According to ancient custom, the casket was lowered three times on every threshold: the dead man had to say good-by to his house.

Later on that sunny summer day, among the murmur of trees and flutter of flags, with ringing bells and wailing funeral chants, he was taken to the cemetery by his family, neighbors, and friends. And everyone felt, in spite of their sorrow at bidding farewell to this good and cheerful man, that they were taking part in something proper—not frightening at all. This was how a man should die, in his house, among his own people—by God's, not man's hand.

---

7. ***Kazimierz*** (kä zē′myesh).

Discussion

1. According to the author, what did Grandmother Zabielska's death symbolize for her family?

2. What attitudes toward dying and death were held by **(a)** Pani Emilia; **(b)** Pani Liza?

3. Grandmother Zabielska commented to Pani Liza, "When the dessert is to be passed, we don't want to go back to the soup." How does this statement express her ideas about death?

4. The author indicates at the beginning of the essay that sharing Grandmother Zabielska's experience would have long-range effects. **(a)** How does her description of Uncle Kazimierz's death support this assertion? **(b)** Do you think the mention of the period in which the latter death occurred in any way alters the essay's theme? Discuss.

Zofia Starowieyska Morstin 1895–1966

The product of a well-to-do, landowning family, Morstin was educated both in her homeland and abroad. Upon her return to Poland, she joined the staff of a newspaper and also produced several works of fiction. During World War II, when Germany occupied Poland, she devoted her time to writing a series of essays on the Italian Renaissance—a safe subject. After the war, she became a book reviewer and columnist for a popular Catholic weekly. "Death of Grandmother Zabielska" is taken from *Our Home,* a collection of memoirs of her early years.

The Bird and the Machine

Loren Eiseley USA

Faced with the "progress" of an automated world, this author clings to a wondrous memory of nature.

I suppose their little bones have years ago been lost among the stones and winds of those high glacial pastures. I suppose their feathers blew eventually into the piles of tumbleweed beneath the straggling cattle fences and rotted there in the mountain snows, along with dead steers and all the other things that drift to an end in the corners of the wire. I do not quite know why I should be thinking of birds over the *New York Times* at breakfast, particularly the birds of my youth half a continent away. It is a funny thing what the brain will do with memories and how it will treasure them and finally bring them into odd juxtapositions with other things, as though it wanted to make a design, or get some meaning out of them, whether you want it or not, or even see it.

It used to seem marvelous to me, but I read now that there are machines that can do these things in a small way, machines that can crawl about like animals, and that it may not be long now until they do more things—maybe even make themselves—I saw that piece in the *Times* just now. And then they will, maybe—well, who knows—but you read about it more and more with no one making any protest, and already they can add better than we and reach up and hear things through the dark and finger the guns over the night sky.

This is the new world that I read about at breakfast. This is the world that confronts me in my biological books and journals, until there are times when I sit quietly in my chair and try to hear the little purr of the cogs in my head and the tubes flaring and dying as the messages go through them and the circuits snap shut or open. This is the great age, make no mistake about it; the robot has been born somewhat appropriately along with the atom bomb, and the brain they say now is just another type of more complicated feedback system. The engineers have its basic principles worked out; it's mechanical, you know; and humans can always improve on nature once they get the idea. Well, they've got it all right and that's why, I guess, that I sit here in my chair, with the article crunched in my hand, remembering those two birds and that blue mountain sunlight. There is another magazine article on my desk that reads "Machines Are Getting Smarter Every Day." I don't deny it, but I'll still stick with the birds. It's life I believe in, not machines.

I'll never forget those birds—I was young then and left alone in a great desert—part of an expedition that had scattered its men over several hundred miles in order to carry on research more effectively. There had been talk of birds in connection with my duties. Birds are intense, fast-living creatures—reptiles, I suppose one might say, that have escaped out of the heavy sleep of time, transformed fairy creatures dancing over sunlit meadows. It is a youthful fancy, no doubt, but because of something that happened up there among the escarpments of that range, it remains with me a lifelong impression. I can never bear to see a bird imprisoned.

We came into that valley through the trailing mists of a spring night. It was a place that looked as though it might never have known the foot of man, but our scouts had been ahead of us and we knew all about the abandoned cabin of stone that lay far up on one hillside. It had been built in the

land rush of the last century and then lost to the cattlemen again as the marginal soils failed to take to the plow.

There were spots like this all over that country. Lost graves marked by unlettered stones and old corroding rim-fire cartridge cases lying where somebody had made a stand among the boulders that rimmed the valley. They are all that remain of the range wars; the men are under the stones now. I could see our cavalcade winding in and out through the mist below us: torches, the reflection of the truck lights on our collecting tins, and the far-off bumping of a loose dinosaur thighbone in the bottom of a trailer. I stood on a rock a moment looking down and thinking what it cost in money and equipment to capture the past.

We had, in addition, instructions to lay hands on the present. The word had come through to get them alive—birds, reptiles, anything. A zoo somewhere abroad needed restocking. It was one of those reciprocal matters in which science involves itself. Maybe our museum needed a stray ostrich egg and this was the payoff. Anyhow, my job was to help capture some birds and that was why I was there before the trucks.

The cabin had not been occupied for years. We intended to clean it out and live in it, but there were holes in the roof and the birds had come in and were roosting in the rafters. You could depend on it in a place like this where everything blew away, and even a bird needed some place out of the weather and away from coyotes. A cabin going back to nature in a wild place draws them till they come in, listening at the eaves, I imagine, peeking softly among the shingles till they find a hole and then suddenly the place is theirs and man is forgotten.

Sometimes of late years I find myself thinking the most beautiful sight in the world might be the birds taking over New York after the last person has run away to the hills. I will never live to see it, of course, but I know just how it will sound because I've lived up high and I know the sort of watch birds keep on us. I've listened to sparrows tapping tentatively on the outside of air conditioners when they thought no one was listening, and I know how other birds test the vibrations that come up to them through the television aerials.

"Is he gone?" they ask, and the vibrations come up from below, "Not yet, not yet."

Well, to come back, I got the door open softly and I had the spotlight all ready to turn on and blind whatever birds there were so they couldn't see to get out through the roof. I had a short piece of ladder to put against the far wall where there was a shelf on which I expected to make the biggest haul. I had all the information I needed just like any skilled assassin. I pushed the door open, the hinges squeaking only a little. A bird or two stirred—I could hear them—but nothing flew and there was a faint starlight through the holes in the roof.

I padded across the floor, got the ladder up and the light ready, and slithered up the ladder till my head and arms were over the shelf. Everything was dark as pitch except for the starlight at the little place back of the shelf near the eaves. With the light to blind them, they'd never make it. I had them. I reached my arm carefully over in order to be ready to seize whatever was there and I put the flash on the edge of the shelf where it would stand by itself when I turned it on. That way I'd be able to use both hands.

Everything worked perfectly except for one detail—I didn't know what kind of birds were there. I never thought about it at all, and it wouldn't have mattered if I had. My orders were to get something interesting. I snapped on the flash and sure enough there was a great beating and feathers flying, but instead of my having them, they, or rather he, had me. He had my hand, that is, and for a small hawk not much bigger than my fist he was doing all right. I heard him give one short metallic cry when the light went on and my hand descended on the bird beside him; after that he was busy with his claws and his beak was sunk in my thumb. In the struggle I knocked the lamp over on the shelf, and his mate got her sight back and whisked neatly through the hole in the roof and off among the stars outside. It all happened in fifteen seconds and you might think I would have fallen down the ladder, but no, I had a professional assassin's reputation to keep up, and the bird, of course, made the mistake of thinking the hand was the enemy and not the eyes behind it. He chewed my thumb up pretty effectively and lacerated my hand with his claws, but in the end I got him, having two hands to work with.

He was a sparrow hawk and a fine young male in the prime of life. I was sorry not to catch the pair of them, but as I dripped blood and folded his wings carefully, holding him by the back so that he couldn't strike again, I had to admit the two of them might have been more than I could have handled under the circumstances. The little fellow had saved his mate by diverting me, and that was that. He was born to it, and made no outcry now, resting in my hand hopelessly, but peering toward me in the shadows behind the lamp with a fierce, almost indifferent glance. He neither gave nor expected mercy and something out of the high air passed from him to me, stirring a faint embarrassment.

I quit looking into that eye and managed to get my huge carcass with its fist full of prey back down the ladder. I put the bird in a box too small to allow him to injure himself by struggle and walked out to welcome the arriving trucks. It had been a long day, and camp still to make in the darkness. In the morning that bird would be just another episode. He would go back with the bones in the truck to a small cage in a city where he would spend the rest of his life. And a good thing, too. I sucked my aching thumb and spat out some blood. An assassin has to get used to these things. I had a professional reputation to keep up.

In the morning, with the change that comes on suddenly in that high country, the mist that had hovered below us in the valley was gone. The sky was a deep blue, and one could see for miles over the high outcroppings of stone. I was up early and brought the box in which the little hawk was imprisoned out onto the grass where I was building a cage. A wind as cool as a mountain spring ran over the grass and stirred my hair. It was a fine day to be alive. I looked up and all around and at the hole in the cabin roof out of which the other little hawk had fled. There was no sign of her anywhere that I could see.

"Probably in the next county by now," I thought cynically, but before beginning work I decided I'd have a look at my last night's capture.

Secretively, I looked again all around the camp and up and down and opened the box. I got him right out in my hand with his wings folded properly and I was careful not to startle him. He lay limp in my grasp and I could feel his heart pound under the feathers but he only looked beyond me and up.

I saw him look that last look away beyond me into a sky so full of light that I could not follow his gaze. The little breeze flowed over me again, and nearby a mountain aspen shook all its tiny leaves. I suppose I must have had an idea then of what I was going to do, but I never let it come up into consciousness. I just reached over and laid the hawk on the grass.

He lay there a long minute without hope, unmoving, his eyes still fixed on that blue vault above him. It must have been that he was already so far away in heart that he never felt the release from my hand. He never even stood. He just lay with his breast against the grass.

In the next second after that long minute he was gone. Like a flicker of light, he had vanished with my eyes full on him, but without actually seeing even a premonitory wing beat. He was gone straight into that towering emptiness of light and crystal that my eyes could scarcely bear to penetrate. For another long moment there was silence. I could not see him. The light was too intense. Then from far up somewhere a cry came ringing down.

I was young then and had seen little of the world, but when I heard that cry my heart turned over. It was not the cry of the hawk I had captured; for, by shifting my position against the sun, I was now seeing further up. Straight out of the sun's eye, where she must have been soaring restlessly above us for untold hours, hurtled his mate. And from far up, ringing from peak to peak of the summits over us, came a cry of such unutterable and ecstatic joy that it sounds down across the years and tingles among the cups on my quiet breakfast table.

I saw them both now. He was rising fast to meet her. They met in a great soaring gyre that turned to a whirling circle and a dance of wings. Once more, just once, their two voices, joined in a harsh wild medley of question and response, struck and echoed against the pinnacles of the valley. Then they were gone forever somewhere into those upper regions beyond the eyes of humans.

I am older now, and sleep less, and have seen most of what there is to see and am not very much impressed anymore, I suppose, by anything. "What Next in the Attributes of Machines?" my morning headline runs. "It Might Be the Power to Reproduce Themselves."

I lay the paper down and across my mind a phrase floats insinuatingly: "It does not seem that there is anything in the construction, constituents, or behavior of the human being which it is essentially impossible for science to duplicate and synthesize. On the other hand . . ."

All over the city the cogs in the hard, bright mechanisms have begun to turn. Figures move through computers, names are spelled out, a thoughtful machine selects the fingerprints of a wanted criminal from an array of thousands. In the laboratory an electronic mouse runs swiftly through a maze toward the cheese it can neither taste nor enjoy. On the second run it does better than a living mouse.

"On the other hand . . ." Ah, my mind takes up, on the other hand the machine does not bleed, ache, hang for hours in the empty sky in a torment of hope to learn the fate of another machine, nor does it cry out with joy nor dance in the air with the fierce passion of a bird. Far off, over a distance greater than space, that remote cry from the heart of heaven makes a faint buzzing among my breakfast dishes and passes on and away.

Discussion

1. (a) What basic comparison does Eiseley make between birds and today's sophisticated machines? **(b)** Whose side is he on? Why?

2. (a) In what way was Eiseley "a professional assassin"? **(b)** What purpose does this exaggerated description of his role serve?

3. Reread the passage in which Eiseley tells how he released the hawk. **(a)** What factors foreshadow his almost subconscious decision to free it? **(b)** What is the first hint that he would do so?

4. Discuss Eiseley's style in describing the reunion of the two birds.

5. One reader has commented that this essay makes a strong case for the value of life. Explain why you agree or disagree.

Vocabulary

Roots, Combining Forms

Answer the following questions about the words from the selection.

1. What is the root word of *juxtaposition* (518, column 1)? What can you determine about the meaning of the word knowing that *juxta-* means "beside"?

2. What does *ecstatic* (521, column 1) mean? What is the noun related to it?

3. How does knowing the word *synthetic* aid in determining the meaning of *synthesize* (521, column 2)? Which syllable of *synthesize* is stressed?

4. From the Latin root *aer,* meaning "air," comes the combining form *aero-,* used in a number of English words. How is the meaning of *aer* incorporated in the meaning of *aerial* (519, column 2)? List at least three words formed from *aero-*.

Loren Eiseley 1907–1977

Though better known to his colleagues as an outstanding anthropologist and scientific writer whose books consistently won awards, Loren Eiseley also acquired renown as a poet and general writer. A brilliant student of American ancient history, the Lincoln, Nebraska, native served most of his teaching years at the University of Pennsylvania in its anthropology department. Besides writing for scientific journals, Eiseley contributed verse and prose to literary anthologies and edited a literary review, the *Prairie Schooner.* In such books as *The Immense Journey* (1957) and *All the Strange Hours* (1975), he combined a poetic style with a scholarly perspective. As "The Bird and the Machine" vividly asserts, he regarded the mysteries of nature with awe and reverence.

Comment: Structure and Formality in the Essay

Essays generally fall into two broad categories, the formal and the informal. A formal essay concentrates on the explication of ideas, is rigidly structured, is almost always written in the third person, and uses language and syntax intended for thoughtful, educated readers. An informal essay is concerned with the author's personality as well as ideas, is loosely structured and usually written in the first person, and uses the language and syntax of everyday educated speech.

What often determines the formality or informality of an essay is the degree to which these basic elements are utilized or combined. Of the essays in this unit, "Three Days to See!" is the most rigidly structured, proceeding in chronological order, yet its first-person narration and emotional quality keep it from being a formal essay. Another essay rendered informal by its point of view and appeal to emotions is "The Bird and the Machine," which you have just read. Here the shifts between past and present also informalize the structure. Less formal still is the personal memoir "Death of Grandmother Zabielska." It makes a point, then illustrates it by recounting the family's experience, and finally applies it to a future event. Though told in third person, the essay's loose time order keeps it informal.

The essay form can also be used for lighter prose, as exemplified by "The Backpacker." Although this essay is loosely structured, its idea is clearly and humorously expressed through the use of exaggeration and satire.

Unit 7 Review: 

Content Review

1. The first four selections in this unit are grouped under the heading "Events" because they focus more on what is occurring than on characterization or ideas. With the exception of "The Backpacker," each selection presents a person facing danger courageously. For each of the three, describe the danger, the character's reaction to it, and the outcome. Which character do you think was bravest? Explain.

2. Before reading the selection of letters, you probably had limited knowledge of the featured writers. Though each letter deals more with feelings than facts, each distinctly reveals the writer's unique personality. Give a brief character sketch of each person based only on the information in his or her letter and tell what you think makes that writer different from the others.

3. The last three selections in this unit focus on ideas. Although they have vastly different points to make, they all touch upon the value of life and the need for freedom to live it to the fullest. Briefly explain how each does this.

4. Why is "The Letter 'A' " classified under "People" and "Three Days to See!" grouped under "Ideas" when both are about people who surmounted severe physical disabilities? Discuss.

5. Who or what is the antagonist in "The Backpacker," "The Summit," and "The Bird and the Machine"? Defend your answer.

6. Every selection in this unit is to some degree *subjective;* that is, the feelings and personal biases of the writers affect their choice of words. On the other hand, an *objective* work is impersonal, unbiased, unemotional, and depends mostly on facts. Choose one selection you found to be the most subjective and one whose personal event or viewpoint is presented in the most objective manner possible. Explain your choices.

Concept Review: Interpretation of New Material

Read the account that follows. Then use the questions that come after it to review your understanding of the concepts and literary terms presented in this unit.

A Kiowa Grandmother • *N. Scott Momaday* USA

A single knoll rises out of the plain in Oklahoma, north and west of the Wichita Range. For my people, the Kiowas, it is an old landmark, and they gave it the name Rainy Mountain. The hardest weather in the world is there. Winter brings blizzards, hot tornadic winds arise in the spring, and in summer the prairie is an anvil's edge. The grass turns brittle and brown, and it cracks beneath your feet. There are green belts along the rivers and creeks, linear groves of hickory and pecan, willow and witch hazel. At a distance in July or August the steaming foliage seems almost to writhe in fire. Great green and yellow grasshoppers are everywhere in the tall grass, popping up like corn to sting the flesh, and tortoises crawl about on the red earth, going nowhere in the plenty of time. Loneliness is an aspect of the land. All things in the plain are isolate; there is no confusion of objects in the eye, but *one* hill or *one* tree or *one* man. To look upon that landscape in the early morning, with the sun at your back, is to lose

---

the sense of proportion. Your imagination comes to life, and this, you think, is where Creation was begun.

I returned to Rainy Mountain in July. My grandmother had died in the spring, and I wanted to be at her grave. She had lived to be very old and at last infirm. Her only living daughter was with her when she died, and I was told that in death her face was that of a child.

I like to think of her as a child. When she was born, the Kiowas were living the last great moment of their history. For more than a hundred years they had controlled the open range from the Smoky Hill River to the Red, from the headwaters of the Canadian to the fork of the Arkansas and Cimarron. In alliance with the Comanches, they had ruled the whole of the southern Plains. War was their sacred business, and they were among the finest horsemen the world has ever known. But warfare for the Kiowas was preeminently a matter of disposition rather than of survival, and they never understood the grim, unrelenting advance of the U.S. Cavalry. When at last, divided and ill-provisioned, they were driven onto the Staked Plains in the cold rains of autumn, they fell into panic. In Palo Duro Canyon they abandoned their crucial stores to pillage and had nothing then but their lives. In order to save themselves, they surrendered to the soldiers at Fort Sill and were imprisoned in the old stone corral that now stands as a military museum. My grandmother was spared the humiliation of those high gray walls by eight or ten years, but she must have known from birth the affliction of defeat, the dark brooding of old warriors.

Her name was Aho, and she belonged to the last culture to evolve in North America. Her forebears came down from the high country in western Montana nearly three centuries ago. They were a mountain people, a mysterious tribe of hunters whose language has never been positively classified in any major group. In the late seventeenth century they began a long migration to the south and east. It was a journey toward the dawn, and it led to a golden age. Along the way the Kiowas were befriended by the Crows, who gave them the culture and religion of the Plains. They acquired horses, and their ancient nomadic spirit was suddenly free of the ground. They acquired Tai-me, the sacred Sun Dance doll, from that moment the object and symbol of their worship, and so shared in the divinity of the sun. Not least, they acquired the sense of destiny, therefore courage and pride. When they entered upon the southern Plains they had been transformed. No longer were they slaves to the simple necessity of survival; they were a lordly and dangerous society of fighters and thieves, hunters and priests of the sun. According to their origin myth, they entered the world through a hollow log. From one point of view, their migration was the fruit of an old prophecy, for indeed they emerged from a sunless world.

Although my grandmother lived out her long life in the shadow of Rainy Mountain, the immense landscape of the continental interior lay like memory in her blood. She could tell of the Crows, whom she had never seen, and of the Black Hills, where she had never been. I wanted to see in reality what she had seen more perfectly in the mind's eye, and traveled fifteen hundred miles to begin my pilgrimage.

Yellowstone, it seemed to me, was the top of the world, a region of deep lakes and dark timber, canyons and waterfalls. But, beautiful as it is, one might have the sense of confinement there. The skyline in all directions is close at hand, the high wall of the woods and deep cleavages of shade. There is a perfect freedom in the mountains, but it belongs to the eagle and the elk, the badger and the bear. The Kiowas reckoned their stature by the distance they could see, and they were bent and blind in the wilderness.

Descending eastward, the highland meadows are a stairway to the plain. In July the inland slope of the Rockies is luxuriant with flax and buckwheat, stonecrop and larkspur. The earth unfolds and the limit of the land recedes. Clusters of trees, and animals grazing far in the distance, cause the vision to reach away and wonder to build upon the mind. The sun follows a longer course in the day, and the sky is immense beyond all comparison. The great billowing clouds that sail upon it are shadows that move upon the grain like water, dividing light. Farther down, in the land of the Crows and Blackfeet, the plain is yellow. Sweet clover takes hold of the hills and bends upon itself to cover and seal the soil. There the Kiowas paused on their way; they had come to the place where they must change their lives. The sun is at home on the plains. Precisely there does it have the certain character of a god. When the Kiowas came to the land of the Crows, they could see the dark lees of the hills at dawn across the Bighorn River, the profusion of light on the grain shelves, the oldest deity ranging after the solstices. Not yet would they veer southward to the caldron of the land that lay below; they must wean their blood from the northern winter and hold the mountains a while longer in their view. They bore Tai-me in procession to the east.

A dark mist lay over the Black Hills, and the land was like iron. At the top of a ridge I caught sight of Devil's Tower upthrust against the gray sky as if in the birth of time the core of the earth had broken through its crust and the motion of the world was begun. There are things in nature that engender an awful quiet in the heart of man; Devil's Tower is one of them. Two centuries ago, because they could not do otherwise, the Kiowas made a legend at the base of the rock. My grandmother said:

Eight children were there at play, seven sisters and their brother. Suddenly the boy was struck dumb; he trembled and began to run upon his hands and feet. His fingers became claws, and his body was covered with fur. Directly there was a bear where the boy had been. The sisters were terrified; they ran, and the bear after them. They came to the stump of a great tree, and the tree spoke to them. It bade them climb upon it, and as they did so it began to rise into the air. The bear came to kill them, but they were just beyond its reach. It reared against the tree and scored the bark all around with its claws. The seven sisters were borne into the sky, and they became the stars of the Big Dipper.

From that moment, and so long as the legend lives, the Kiowas have kinsmen in the night sky. Whatever they were in the mountains, they could be no more. However tenuous their well-being, however much they had suffered and would suffer again, they had found a way out of the wilderness.

My grandmother had a reverence for the sun, a holy regard that now is all but gone out of mankind. There was a wariness in her, and an ancient awe. She was a Christian in her later years, but she had come a long way about, and she never forgot her birthright. As a child she had been to the Sun Dances; she had taken part in those annual rites, and by then she had learned the restoration of her people in the presence of Tai-me. She was about seven when the last Kiowa Sun Dance was held in 1887 on the Washita River above Rainy Mountain Creek. The buffalo were gone. In order to consummate the ancient sacrifice—to impale the head of a buffalo bull upon the medicine tree—a delegation of old men journeyed into Texas, there to beg and barter for an animal from the Goodnight herd. She was ten when the Kiowas came together for the last time as a living Sun Dance culture. They could find no buffalo; they had to hang an old hide from the sacred tree. Before the dance could begin, a company of soldiers rode out from Fort Sill under orders to disperse the tribe. Forbidden without cause the essential act of their faith, having seen the wild herds slaughtered and left to rot upon the ground, the Kiowas backed away forever from the medicine tree. That was July 20, 1890, at the great bend of the Washita. My grandmother was there. Without bitterness, and for as long as she lived, she bore a vision of deicide.[1]

Now that I can have her only in memory, I see my grandmother in the several postures that were peculiar to her: standing at the wood stove on a winter morning and turning meat in a great iron skillet; sitting at the south window, bent above her beadwork, and afterwards, when her vision failed, looking down for a long time into the fold of her hands; going out upon a cane, very slowly as she did when the weight of age came upon her; praying. I remember her most often at prayer. She made long, rambling prayers out of suffering and hope, having seen many things. I was never sure that I had the right to hear, so exclusive were they of all mere custom and company. The last time I saw her she

---

1. ***deicide*** (dē′ə sīd), the killing of a god; in effect, the death of a religion.

prayed standing by the side of her bed at night, the light of a kerosene lamp moving upon her dark skin. Her long, black hair, always drawn and braided in the day, lay upon her shoulders like a shawl. I do not speak Kiowa, and I never understood her prayers, but there was something inherently sad in the sound, some merest hesitation upon the syllables of sorrow. She began in a high and descending pitch, exhausting her breath to silence; then again and again—and always the same intensity of effort, of something that is, and is not, like urgency in the human voice. Transported so in the dancing light among the shadows of her room, she seemed beyond the reach of time. But that was illusion; I think I knew then that I should not see her again.

Houses are like sentinels in the plain, old keepers of the weather watch. There, in a very little while, wood takes on the appearance of great age. All colors wear soon away in the wind and rain, and then the wood is burned gray and the grain appears and the nails turn red with rust. The windowpanes are black and opaque; you imagine there is nothing within, and indeed there are many ghosts, bones given up to the land. They stand here and there against the sky, and you approach them for a longer time than you expect. They belong in the distance; it is their domain.

Once there was a lot of sound in my grandmother's house, a lot of coming and going, feasting and talk. The summers there were full of excitement and reunion. The Kiowas are a summer people; they abide the cold and keep to themselves, but when the season turns and the land becomes warm and vital they cannot hold still; an old love of going returns upon them. The aged visitors who came to my grandmother's house when I was a child were made of lean and leather, and they bore themselves upright. They wore great black hats and bright ample shirts that shook in the wind. They rubbed fat upon their hair and wound their braids with strips of colored cloth. Some of them painted their faces and carried the scars of old and cherished enmities. They were an old council of warlords, come to remind and be reminded of who they were. Their wives and daughters served them well. The women might indulge themselves; gossip was at once the mark and compensation of their servitude. They made loud and elaborate talk among themselves, full of jest and gesture, fright and false alarm. They went abroad in fringed and flowered shawls, bright beadwork and German silver. They were at home in the kitchen, and they prepared meals that were banquets.

There were frequent prayer meetings, and great nocturnal feasts. When I was a child I played with my cousins outside, where the lamplight fell upon the ground and the singing of the old people rose up around us and carried away into the darkness. There were a lot of good things to eat, a lot of laughter and surprise. And afterwards, when the quiet returned, I lay down with my grandmother and could hear the frogs away by the river and feel the motion of the air.

Now there is a funeral silence in the rooms, the endless wake of some final word. The walls have closed in upon my grandmother's house. When I returned to it in mourning, I saw for the first time in my life how small it was. It was late at night, and there was a white moon, nearly full. I sat for a long time on the stone steps by the kitchen door. From there I could see out across the land; I could see the long row of trees by the creek, the low light upon the rolling plains, and the stars of the Big Dipper. Once I looked at the moon and caught sight of a strange thing. A cricket had perched upon the handrail, only a few inches away from me. My line of vision was such that the creature filled the moon like a fossil. It had gone there, I thought, to live and die, for there, of all places, was its small definition made whole and eternal. A warm wind rose up and purled like the longing within me.

The next morning I awoke at dawn and went out on the dirt road to Rainy Mountain. It was already hot, and the grasshoppers began to fill the air. Still, it was early in the morning, and the birds sang out of the shadows. The long yellow grass on the mountain shone in the bright light, and a scissortail hied above the land. There, where it ought to be, at the end of a long and legendary way, was my grandmother's grave. Here and there on the dark stones were ancestral names. Looking back once, I saw the mountain and came away.

1. According to Momaday, the Kiowa culture was **(a)** the last to evolve in America; **(b)** the first to evolve in America; **(c)** a great influence on the Crow culture; **(d)** a way of life his grandmother had always tried to put behind her.

2. Nearly three centuries ago, the Kiowas came down from **(a)** Oklahoma; **(b)** Wyoming; **(c)** Montana; **(d)** Rainy Mountain.

3. Why does the author travel fifteen hundred miles to begin his pilgrimage to his grandmother's grave?

4. The Kiowas acquired Tai-me, the Sun Dance doll, from **(a)** a hollow log; **(b)** Devil's Tower; **(c)** Rainy Mountain; **(d)** the Crows.

5. Momaday's grandmother, Aho, was **(a)** too old to be imprisoned at Fort Sill; **(b)** imprisoned at Fort Sill; **(c)** unaware that Fort Sill stood on the site of her birthplace; **(d)** born too late to be imprisoned at Fort Sill.

6. Although Yellowstone represented "the top of the world" to Momaday, he understands why the Kiowas did not settle there permanently. Explain.

7. According to the Kiowas' legend, which of the following was formed at the same time as Devil's Tower? **(a)** Rainy Mountain; **(b)** Tai-me; **(c)** the Big Dipper; **(d)** the Kiowas' destiny as a people.

8. The main reason for the end of the Sun Dance in 1890 was that **(a)** no buffalo head could be found to consummate the ceremony; **(b)** Tai-me had been lost; **(c)** the Kiowas could no longer remember the ritual; **(d)** soldiers from Fort Sill dispersed the Kiowa tribe and forbade the Sun Dance.

9. Aho retained her reverence for the sun even though **(a)** it caused many brush fires in her region; **(b)** the younger members of her family discouraged it; **(c)** it was rarely visible on Rainy Mountain; **(d)** she became a Christian in her later years.

10. Is the mood of the selection mournful, angry, or nostalgic? Explain.

Composition Review

Choose one of the following assignments.

1. With the possible exception of "The Backpacker," which may or may not be based on a real incident, the selections of this unit describe events that actually occurred. Select two or three of the events that you find particularly unusual. Then note how the author presents the event and whether he or she seems to recognize its extraordinary nature.

Write a short composition entitled "Truth Is Stranger Than Fiction," in which you discuss one or more of the out-of-the-ordinary things the authors describe.

2. Though the letters in this unit were originally created as personal correspondence, they have all been made public in various books. Review them, considering their varying tones and degrees of familiarity or intimacy. Arrange them in an order that reflects these differences.

Write a two- or three-paragraph explanation of the order you arrived at.

3. Informal essays are not difficult to write and often are quite enjoyable to read. A basic guideline to follow is to select a topic of interest to you that your audience would relate to. For example, if your audience is your class, your subject might be cafeteria food, designer jeans, peer-group pressure, and so on. "The Backpacker" is an example of an essay that employs exaggeration to make a point about a popular new trend. Think of other devices an essayist can use for effect.

Try your hand at a two- to three-hundred-word essay expressing your feelings about any of the above topics or about one of your own.

4. "Death of Grandmother Zabielska" and "A Kiowa Grandmother" both deal with the influence of grandmothers on the lives of their families. Review the specifics in each account about the grandmother's environment, cultural background, and what she handed down to her grandchildren.

In a two-paragraph essay, compare and contrast the grandmothers.

Unit 8 The Novel

One Day in the Life of Ivan Denisovich

Background

The publication in 1962 of *One Day in the Life of Ivan Denisovich* brought to light a little-known element of modern Russian life: the vast system of prison camps created during the reign of Soviet dictator Joseph Stalin and the living conditions within them. Some understanding of political background is necessary to see how Russian society evolved to this point.

The 1917 takeover of the Russian government by the Bolsheviks and their newly formed Communist Party was heralded as a great advance for the lower classes, who had been denied land and rights for hundreds of years under the rule of the czars. But it quickly became apparent that things would not change all that much. The first Communist to control the government, Nikolai Lenin, also became its first dictator by convincing the people that such a form of rule was temporarily necessary to achieve Party goals. During Lenin's years in power various areas or small countries that had been part of the hated Russian Empire were combined to form the new Union of Soviet Socialist Republics (U.S.S.R.). Even more importantly, however, steps taken in the name of improving the economic plight of the country also had the effect of exerting more control over the lives of the people. Central management bureaus to run virtually all industries and businesses were set up. Decrees forbidding the formation of opposition political parties were passed. A secret police force was installed.

When Joseph Stalin finally maneuvered himself into total power in 1929, the situation became even worse. One of his projects involved the forced combination of several million peasant farms into huge collective farms. When the wealthier peasants, or kulaks, rebelled at the collectivization because it meant losing the profits from their lands, Stalin sent millions of them as laborers to prison camps in the almost uninhabitable regions in the far north and Siberia. Thus began the widespread use of labor camps to silence dissenters, a practice which, as time passed, was employed to terrorize millions of people from all levels of society.

When Nikita Khrushchev (krüsh chôf′) came into power after Stalin's death, he tried to discredit his predecessor by, among other things, exposing the cruelty and corruption of the labor-camp system. It was solely for this reason that he allowed *One Day* to be published in the Soviet Union.

The Novel Itself

Though concerned with rather grim subject matter, *One Day in the Life of Ivan Denisovich* is not a depressing book. The author's own time in labor camps has familiarized him with the pettiness and corruption as well as the brutality of the life, and he portrays all in convincing detail. Most importantly, his indomitable nature seems to shine through his portrayal of the main character, making the novel ultimately a tale of the triumph of the human spirit.

One Day in the Life of Ivan Denisovich

Alexander Solzhenitsyn USSR

At five o'clock that morning reveille was sounded, as usual, by the blows of a hammer on a length of rail hanging up near the staff quarters. The intermittent sounds barely penetrated the windowpanes on which the frost lay two fingers thick, and they ended almost as soon as they'd begun. It was cold outside, and the campguard was reluctant to go on beating out the reveille for long.

The clanging ceased, but everything outside still looked like the middle of the night when Ivan Denisovich Shukhov[1] got up to go to the bucket. It was pitch dark except for the yellow light cast on the window by three lamps—two in the outer zone, one inside the camp itself.

And no one came to unbolt the barracks door; there was no sound of the barrack orderlies pushing a pole into place to lift the latrine barrel and carry it out.

Shukhov never overslept reveille. He always got up at once, for the next ninety minutes, until they assembled for work, belonged to him, not to the authorities, and any old-timer could always earn a bit—by sewing a pair of mittens for someone out of old sleeve lining; or bringing some rich loafer in the squad his dry valenki[2]—right up to his bunk, so that he wouldn't have to stumble barefoot round the heap of boots looking for his own pair; or going the rounds of the warehouses, offering to be of service, sweeping up this or fetching that; or going to the mess hall to collect bowls from the tables and bring them stacked to the dishwashers—you're sure to be given something to eat there, though there were plenty of others at that game, more than plenty—and, what's worse, if you found a bowl with something left in it you could hardly resist licking it out. But Shukhov had never forgotten the words of his first squad leader, Kuziomin—a hard-bitten prisoner who had already been in for twelve years by 1943—who told the newcomers, just in from the front, as they sat beside a fire in a desolate cutting in the forest:

"Here, men, we live by the law of the taiga.[3] But even here people manage to live. The ones that don't make it are those who lick other men's leftovers, those who count on the doctors to pull them through, and those who squeal on their buddies."

As for squealers, he was wrong there. Those people were sure to get through camp all right. Only, they were saving their own skin at the expense of other people's blood.

Shukhov always arose at reveille. But this day he didn't. He had felt strange the evening before, feverish, with pains all over his body. He hadn't been able to get warm all through the night. Even in his sleep he had felt at one moment that he was getting seriously ill, at another that he was getting better. He had wished morning would never come.

But the morning came as usual.

Anyway, where would you get warm in a place like this, with the windows iced over and the white cobwebs of frost all along the huge barracks where the walls joined the ceiling!

He didn't get up. He lay there in his bunk on the top tier, his head buried in a blanket and a

---

1. ***Ivan Denisovich Shukhov*** (i vän′ dyi nyi sô′vyich shü kôf′).
2. ***valenki*** (vä lyen′kyi), knee-length felt boots for winter wear.
3. ***taiga*** (tī′gə), the swampy forest land of subarctic Siberia.

coat, both feet stuffed into one tucked-under sleeve of his wadded jacket.

He couldn't see, but his ears told him everything going on in the barrack room and especially in the corner his squad occupied. He heard the heavy tread of the orderlies carrying one of the big latrine barrels along the passage outside. A light job, that was considered, a job for the infirm, but just you try and carry out the muck without spilling any. He heard some of the 75th slamming bunches of boots onto the floor from the drying shed. Now their own men were doing it (it was their own squad's turn, too, to dry valenki). Tiurin,[4] the squad leader, and his deputy Pavlo put on their valenki without a word, but he heard their bunks creaking. Now Pavlo would be going off to the bread-storage and Tiurin to the staff quarters to see the P.P.D.[5]

Ah, but not simply to report as usual to the authorities for the daily assignment. Shukhov remembered that this morning his fate hung in the balance: they wanted to shift the 104th from the building shops to a new site, the "Socialist Way of Life" settlement. It lay in open country covered with snowdrifts, and before anything else could be done there they would have to dig holes and put up posts and attach barbed wire to them. Wire themselves in, so that they wouldn't run away. Only then would they start building.

There wouldn't be a warm corner for a whole month. Not even a doghouse. And fires were out of the question. There was nothing to build them with. Let your work warm you up, that was your only salvation.

No wonder the squad leader looked so worried, that was his job—to elbow some other squad, some bunch of suckers, into the assignment instead of the 104th. Of course, with empty hands you got nowhere. He'd have to take a pound of salt pork to the senior official there, if not a couple of pounds.

There's never any harm in trying, so why not have a go at the dispensary and get a few days off if you can? After all, he did feel as though every limb was out of joint.

Then Shukhov wondered which of the camp-guards was on duty that morning. It was "One-and-a-half" Ivan's turn, he recalled. Ivan was a thin, weedy, dark-eyed sergeant. At first sight he looked like a real pig, but when you got to know him he turned out to be the most good-natured of the guards on duty: he didn't put you in the guardhouse, he didn't haul you off before the authorities. So Shukhov decided he could lie in his bunk a little longer, at least while Barracks 9 was at the mess hall.

The whole four-bunk frame began to shake and sway. Two of its occupants were getting up at the same time: Shukhov's top-tier neighbor, Alyosha the Baptist, and Buinovsky,[6] the ex-naval captain down below.

The orderlies, after removing both latrine barrels, began to quarrel about which of them should go for hot water. They quarreled naggingly.

"Hey you, cackling like a couple of hens!" bellowed the electric welder in the 20th squad. "Get going." He flung a boot at them.

The boot thudded against a post. The squabbling stopped.

In the next squad the deputy squad leader growled quietly: "Vasily Fyodorovich,[7] they've cheated us again at the supply depot, the dirty rats. They should have given us four twenty-five-ounce loaves and I've only got three. Who's going to go short?"

He kept his voice down, but of course everyone in the squad heard him and waited fearfully to learn who would be losing a slice of bread that evening.

Shukhov went on lying on his sawdust mattress, as hard as a board from long wear. If only it could be one thing or the other—let him fall into a real fever or let his aching joints ease up.

Meanwhile Alyosha was murmuring his prayers and Buinovsky had returned from the latrines, announcing to no one in particular but with a sort of malicious glee: "Well, sailors, grit your teeth. It's twenty below, for sure."

---

4. ***Tiurin*** (tē ů rēn′).
5. ***P.P.D.***, Production Planning Department.
6. ***Alyosha*** (äl yô′shä) . . . ***Buinovsky*** (bů ē nôf′skə i).
7. ***Vasily Fyodorovich*** (və syē′lyi fyô dô rô′vyich).

Shukhov decided to report sick.

At that very moment his blanket and jacket were imperiously jerked off him. He flung his coat away from his face and sat up. Looking up at him, his head level with the top bunk, was the lean figure of The Tartar.

So the fellow was on duty out of turn and had stolen up.

"S 854," The Tartar read from the white strip that had been stitched to the back of his black jacket. "Three days' penalty with work."

The moment they heard that peculiar choking voice of his, everyone who wasn't up yet in the whole dimly lit barracks, where two hundred men slept in bug-ridden bunks, stirred to life and began dressing in a hurry.

"What for, citizen chief?" asked Shukhov with more chagrin than he felt in his voice.

With work—that wasn't half so bad. They gave you hot food and you had no time to start thinking. Real jail was when you were kept back from work.

"Failing to get up at reveille. Follow me to the camp commandant's office," said The Tartar lazily.

His crumpled, hairless face was imperturbable. He turned, looking around for another victim, but now everybody, in dim corners and under the lights, in upper bunks and in lower, had thrust their legs into their black wadded trousers or, already dressed, had wrapped their coats around themselves and hurried to the door to get out of the way until The Tartar had left.

Had Shukhov been punished for something he deserved he wouldn't have felt so resentful. What hurt him was that he was always one of the first to be up. But he knew he couldn't plead with The Tartar. And, protesting merely for the sake of form, he hitched up his trousers (a bedraggled scrap of cloth had been sewn on them, just above the left knee, with a faded black number), slipped on his jacket (here the same digits appeared twice—on the chest and on the back), fished his valenki from the heap on the floor, put his hat on (with his number on a patch of cloth at the front), and followed The Tartar out of the barrack room.

The whole 104th saw him go, but no one said a word—what was the use, and anyway what could they say? The squad leader might have tried to do something, but he wasn't there. And Shukhov said nothing to anyone. He didn't want to irritate The Tartar. Anyway he could rely on the others in his squad to keep his breakfast for him.

The two men left the barracks. The cold made Shukhov gasp.

Two powerful searchlights swept the camp from the farthest watchtowers. The border lights, as well as those inside the camp, were on. There were so many of them that they outshone the stars.

With the snow creaking under their boots, the prisoners hurried away, each on his own business, some to the parcels office, some to hand in cereals to be cooked in the "individual" kitchen. All kept their heads down, buried in their buttoned-up coats, and all were chilled to the bone, not so much from the actual cold as from the prospect of having to spend the whole day in it. But The Tartar in his old army coat with the greasy blue tabs walked at a steady pace, as though the cold meant nothing to him.

They walked past the high wooden fence around the guardhouse, the only brick building in the camp; past the barbed wire that protected the camp bakery from the prisoners; past the corner of the staff quarters where the length of frosted rail hung on thick strands of wire; past another pole with a thermometer hanging on it (in a sheltered spot, so that the registered temperature shouldn't drop too low). Shukhov looked hopefully out of the corner of an eye at the milk-white tube—if it had shown −41° they ought not to be sent out to work. But today it was nowhere near −41°.

They walked into the staff quarters and The Tartar led him straight to the guardroom; and Shukhov realized, as he had guessed on the way there, that he wasn't being sent to the guardhouse at all—it was simply that the guardroom floor needed scrubbing. The Tartar told him he was going to let him off, and ordered him to scrub the floor.

Scrubbing the guardroom floor had been the job of a special prisoner who wasn't sent to work outside the camp—a staff orderly. The fellow had long ago made himself at home in the staff quarters; he had access to the offices of the camp commandant, the man in charge of discipline, and the security officer (the Father Confessor, they called him). When working for them he sometimes heard things that even the guards didn't know, and after a time he got a big head and came to consider scrubbing the floor for rank-and-file campguards a bit beneath him. Having sent for him once or twice, the guards discovered what was in the wind and began to pick on other prisoners for the floor-scrubbing.

In the guardroom the stove was throwing out a fierce heat. Two guards in grubby tunics were playing checkers, and a third, who had not bothered to remove his sheepskin and valenki, lay snoring on a narrow bench. In one corner of the room stood an empty pail with a rag inside.

Shukhov was delighted. He thanked The Tartar for letting him off and said: "From now on I'll never get up late again."

The rule in this place was a simple one: when you'd finished you left. And now that he'd been given work to do, Shukhov's aches and pains seemed to have gone. He picked up the pail and, barehanded—in his hurry he'd forgotten to take his mittens from under his pillow—went to the well.

Several of the squad leaders who were on their way to the P.P.D. had gathered near the pole with the thermometer, and one of the younger ones, a former Hero of the Soviet Union, shinnied up it and wiped off the instrument.

The others shouted advice from below:

"See you don't breathe on it. It'll push up the temperature."

"Push it up? Not very likely. *My* breath won't have any effect."

Tiurin of the 104th—Shukhov's squad—was not among them. Shukhov put down the pail, tucked his hands into his sleeves, and watched with interest.

The man up the pole shouted hoarsely: "Seventeen and a half. Not a rotten bit more."

And, taking another look to be sure, slid down.

"Oh, it's cockeyed. It always lies," someone said. "Do you think they'd ever hang one up that gave the true temperature?"

The squad leaders scattered. Shukhov ran to the well. The frost was trying to nip his ears under his earflaps, which he had lowered but not tied.

The top of the well was so thickly coated with ice that he only just managed to slip the bucket into the hole. The rope hung stiff as a ramrod.

With numb hands he carried the dripping bucket back to the guardroom and plunged his hands into the water. It felt warm.

The Tartar was no longer there. The guards—there were four now—stood in a group. They'd given up their checkers and their nap and were arguing about how much cereal they were going to get in January (food was in short supply at the settlement, and although rationing had long since come to an end, certain articles were sold to them, at a discount, which were not available to the civilian inhabitants).

"Shut that door, you scum. There's a draft," said one of the guards.

No sense in getting your boots wet in the morning. Even if Shukhov had dashed back to his barracks he wouldn't have found another pair to change into. During eight years' imprisonment he had known various systems for allocating footwear: there'd been times when he'd gone through the winter without valenki at all, or leather boots either, and had had to make shift with rope sandals or a sort of galoshes made of scraps of motor tires—"Chetezes" they called them, after the Chelyabinsk[8] tractor works. Now the footwear situation seemed better; in October Shukhov had received (thanks to Pavlo, whom he trailed to the warehouse) a pair of ordinary, hard-wearing leather boots, big enough for a double thickness of rags inside. For a week he went about as though he'd been given a birthday present, kick-

---

8. ***"Chetezes"*** (chi tyä'zyis) . . . ***Chelyabinsk*** (chi lyä'byinsk).

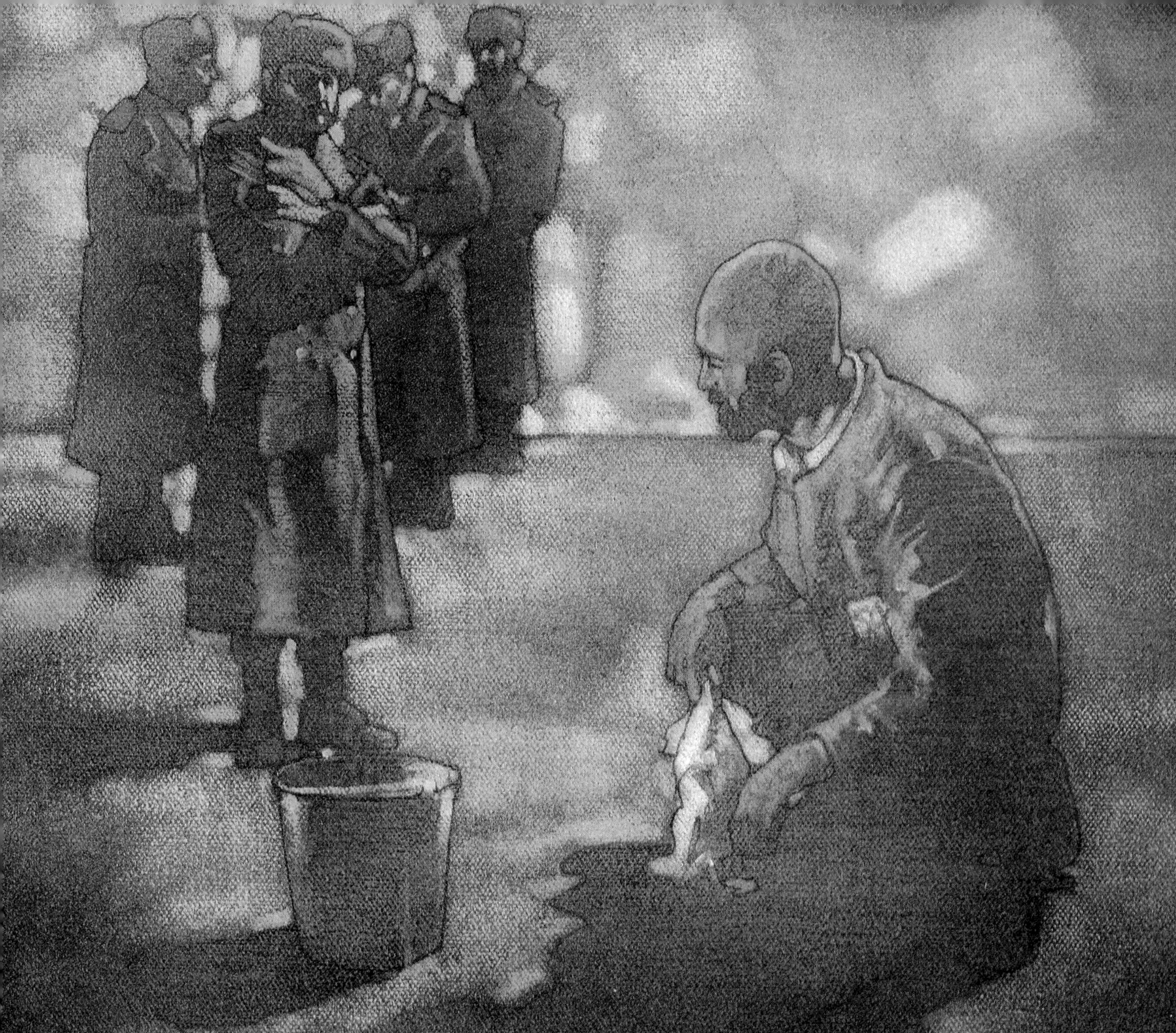

ing his new heels. Then in December the valenki arrived, and, oh, wasn't life wonderful?

But some devil in the bookkeeper's office had whispered in the commandant's ear that valenki should be issued only to those who surrendered their boots. It was against the rules for a prisoner to possess two pairs of footwear at the same time. So Shukhov had to choose. Either he'd have to wear leather throughout the winter, or surrender the boots and wear valenki even in the thaw. He'd taken such good care of his new boots, softening the leather with grease! Ah, nothing had been so hard to part with in all his eight years in camps as that pair of boots! They were tossed into a common heap. Not a hope of finding your own pair in the spring.

Now Shukhov knew what he had to do. He dexterously pulled his feet out of the valenki, put the valenki in a corner, stuffed his foot rags into them (his spoon tinkled on the floor—though he'd made himself ready for the guardhouse in a hurry, he hadn't forgotten his spoon), and, barefoot, sloshed the water right under the guards' valenki.

"Hey there, you slob, take it easy," one of the guards shouted, putting his feet on a chair.

"Rice?" another went on. "Rice is in a different category. You can't compare cereal with rice."

"How much water are you going to use, idiot? Who on earth washes like that?"

"I'll never get it clean otherwise, citizen chief. It's thick with mud."

"Didn't you ever watch your wife scrub the floor, pig?"

Shukhov drew himself up, the dripping rag in his hand. He smiled ingenuously, revealing the gaps in his teeth, the result of a touch of scurvy at Ust-Izhma[9] in 1943. And what a touch it was—his exhausted stomach wouldn't hold any kind of food, and his bowels could move nothing but a bloody fluid. But now only a lisp remained from that old trouble.

"I was taken away from my wife in '41, citizen chief. I've forgotten what she was like."

"That's the way the scum wash. . . . They don't know how to do a lousy thing and don't want to learn. They're not worth the bread we give them. We ought to feed them on dirt."

"Anyway, what's the sense in washing it every day? Who can stand the damp? Look here, you, 854. Just wipe it over lightly to make it moist and then get lost."

"No, you can't compare cereal with rice."

Shukhov knew how to manage anything.

Work was like a stick. It had two ends. When you worked for the knowing you gave them quality; when you worked for a fool you simply gave him eyewash.

Otherwise, everybody would have croaked long ago. They all knew that.

Shukhov wiped the floorboards with a damp rag so that no dry patches remained, tossed the rag behind the stove without wringing it out, pulled on his valenki near the door, threw out the rest of the water onto the path used by the camp authorities, and, taking short cuts, made a dash past the bathhouse and the dark, cold club to the mess hall.

He still had to fit in a visit to the dispensary. He ached all over. And there was that guard outside the mess hall to be dodged—the camp commandant had issued strict orders that prisoners on their own were to be picked up and thrown into the guardhouse.

That morning—a stroke of luck—there was no crowd, no lines, outside the mess. Walk in.

The air was as thick as in a Turkish bath. An icy wave blew in through the door and met the steam rising from the stew. The squads sat at tables or crowded the aisles in between, waiting for places to be freed. Shouting to each other through the crush, two or three men from each squad carried bowls of stew and oatmeal on wooden trays and tried to find room for them on the tables. Look at that crazy stiff-necked fool. He doesn't hear, he's bumped a tray. Splash, splash! You've a hand free, hit him on the back of the neck. That's the way. Don't stand there blocking the aisle, looking for something to swipe!

There at the table, before dipping his spoon in, a young man crossed himself. A West Ukrainian,[10] that meant, and a new arrival too.

As for the Russians, they'd forgotten which hand to cross themselves with.[11]

They sat in the cold mess hall, most of them eating with their hats on, eating slowly, picking out putrid little fish from under leaves of boiled black cabbage and spitting the bones out on the table. When the bones formed a heap and it was the turn of another squad, someone would sweep them off and they'd be trodden into a mush on the floor. But it was considered bad manners to spit the fishbones straight out on the floor.

Two rows of trestles ran down the middle of the hall and near one of them sat Fetiukov[12] of the 104th. It was he who was keeping Shukhov's breakfast for him. Fetiukov had the last place in his squad, lower than Shukhov's. From the outside, everyone in the squad looked the same—

---

9. *Ust-Izhma* (ůst ēzh mä'), a prison camp in which prisoners were used to cut timber.

10. *Ukrainian* (yü krā'nē ən), a person from the Ukraine, a republic within the southwestern Soviet Union.

11. *they'd forgotten . . . cross themselves with.* Traditionally, members of the Russian Orthodox Church bless themselves with the left hand as opposed to the right.

12. *Fetiukov* (fye tyů kôf').

their numbered black coats were identical—but within the squad there were great distinctions. Everyone had his grade. Buinovsky, for instance, was not the sort to sit keeping another zek's[13] bowl for him. And Shukhov wouldn't take on any old job either. There were others lower than him.

Fetiukov caught sight of Shukhov and with a sigh surrendered his place.

"It's all cold. I was just going to eat your helping. Thought you were in the guardhouse."

He didn't hang around—no hope for any leftovers to scrape out of Shukhov's bowl.

Shukhov pulled his spoon out of his boot. His little baby. It had been with him his whole time in the North, he'd cast it with his own hands in sand out of aluminum wire, and it was embossed with the words "Ust-Izhma 1944."

Then he removed his hat from his clean-shaven head—however cold it might be, he could never bring himself to eat with his hat on—and stirred the cold stew, taking a quick look to see what kind of helping they'd given him. An average one. They hadn't ladled it from the top of the kettle, but they hadn't ladled it from the bottom either. Fetiukov was the sort who when he was looking after someone else's bowl took the potatoes from it.

The only good thing about stew was that it was hot, but Shukhov's portion had grown quite cold. However, he ate it with his usual slow concentration. No need to hurry, not even for a house on fire. Apart from sleep, the only time a prisoner lives for himself is ten minutes in the morning at breakfast, five minutes over dinner, and five at supper.

The stew was the same every day. Its composition depended on the kind of vegetable provided that winter. Nothing but salted carrots last year, which meant that from September to June the stew was plain carrot. This year it was black cabbage. The most nourishing time of the year was June; then all vegetables came to an end and were replaced by grits. The worst time was July—then they shredded nettles into the pot.

The little fish were more bone than flesh; the flesh had been boiled off the bone and had disintegrated, leaving a few remnants on head and tail. Without neglecting a single fish scale or particle of flesh on the brittle skeleton, Shukhov went on chomping his teeth and sucking the bones, spitting the remains on the table. He ate everything—the gills, the tail, the eyes when they were still in their sockets but not when they'd been boiled out and floated in the bowl separately—big fish-eyes. Not then. The others laughed at him for that.

This morning Shukhov economized. Since he hadn't returned to the barracks he hadn't drawn his rations, so he ate his breakfast without bread. He'd eat the bread later. Might be even better that way.

After the vegetable stew there was *magara,* that disgusting "Chinese" oatmeal. It had grown cold too, and had set into a solid lump. Shukhov broke it up into pieces. It wasn't only that the oatmeal was cold—it was tasteless even when hot, and left you no sense of having filled your belly. Just grass, except that it was yellow, and looked like cereal. They'd got the idea of serving it instead of cereals from the Chinese, it was said. When boiled, a bowlful of it weighed nearly a pound. Not much of an oatmeal but that was what it passed for.

Licking his spoon and tucking it back into his boot, Shukhov put on his hat and went to the dispensary.

The sky was still quite dark. The camp lights drove away the stars. The broad beams of the two searchlights were still sweeping the zone. When this camp, this "special" (forced-labor) camp, had been organized, the security forces had a lot of flares left over from the war, and whenever there was a power failure they shot up flares over the zone—white, green, and red—just like real war. Later they stopped using them. To save money, maybe.

It seemed just as dark as at reveille but the experienced eye could easily distinguish, by various small signs, that soon the order to go to work

---

13. *zek's.* *Zek* is an abbreviation of the Russian word for prisoner.

would be given. Khromoi's assistant (Khromoi, the mess orderly, had an assistant whom he fed) went off to summon Barracks 6 to breakfast. This was the building occupied by the infirm, who did not leave the zone. An old, bearded artist shuffled off to the C.E.D.[14] for the brush and paint he needed to touch up the numbers on the prisoners' uniforms. The Tartar was there again, cutting across the parade ground with long, rapid strides in the direction of the staff quarters. In general there were fewer people about, which meant that everyone had gone off to some corner or other to get warm during those last precious minutes.

Shukhov was smart enough to hide from The Tartar around a corner of the barracks—the guard would stick to him if he caught him again. Anyway, you should never be conspicuous. The main thing was never to be seen by a campguard on your own, only in a group. Who knows whether the guy wasn't looking for someone to saddle with a job, or wouldn't jump on a man just for spite? Hadn't they been around the barracks and read them that new regulation? You had to take off your hat to a guard five paces before passing him, and replace it two paces after. There were guards who slopped past as if blind, not caring, but for others the new rule was a godsend. How many prisoners had been thrown in the guardhouse because of that hat business? Oh no, better to stand around the corner.

The Tartar passed by, and now Shukhov finally decided to go to the dispensary. But suddenly he remembered that the tall Lett[15] in Barracks 7 had told him to come and buy a couple of glasses of home-grown tobacco that morning before they went out to work, something Shukhov had clean forgotten in all the excitement. The Lett had received a parcel the previous evening, and who knew but that by tomorrow none of the tobacco would be left, and then he'd have to wait a month for another parcel. The Lett's tobacco was good stuff, strong and fragrant, grayish-brown.

Shukhov stamped his feet in vexation. Should he turn back and go to the Lett? But it was such a short distance to the dispensary and he jogged on. The snow creaked audibly underfoot as he approached the door.

Inside, the corridor was, as usual, so clean that he felt quite scared to step on the floor. And the walls were painted with white enamel. And all the furniture was white.

The surgery doors were all shut. The doctors must still be in bed. The man on duty was a medical assistant—a young man called Kolya Vdovushkin.[16] He was seated at a clean little table, wearing a small white cap and a snow-white smock. Writing something.

There was no one else in sight.

Shukhov took off his hat as if in the presence of one of the authorities and, letting his eyes shift, in the camp manner, where they had no business to shift, he noticed that Kolya was writing in even, neatly spaced lines and that each line, starting a little way from the edge of the page, began with a capital letter. He realized at once, of course, that Kolya was not doing official work but something on the side. But that was none of his business.

"Well, Nikolai Semyonich,[17] it's like this. . . . I'm feeling sort of . . . rotten. . . ," said Shukhov shamefacedly, as if coveting something that didn't belong to him.

Kolya Vdovushkin raised his big placid eyes from his work. His number was covered up by his smock.

"Why've you come so late? Why didn't you report sick last night? You know very well there's no sick call in the morning. The sick list has already been sent to the planning department."

Shukhov knew all this. He knew too that it was even harder to get on the sick list in the evening.

---

14. ***C.E.D.,*** Culture and Education Department.
15. ***Lett,*** member of a group of people living in Latvia, Lithuania, Estonia, and Germany, related to the Lithuanians.
16. ***Kolya Vdovushkin*** (kôl′yä vdô vůsh′kyin).
17. ***Nikolai Semyonich*** (nyi kə lī′ syi myô′nyich). Shukhov addresses Kolya Vdovushkin by his full first name and patronymic (pat′rə nim′ik), the name derived from the name of his father or a paternal ancestor.

"But after all, Kolya . . . You see, when I should have come . . . last night . . . it didn't ache."

"And now it does? And what is it?"

"Well, if you stop to think of it, nothing aches, but I feel ill all over."

Shukhov was not one of those who hung around the dispensary. Vdovushkin knew this. But in the morning he had the right to exempt from work two men only, and he'd already exempted them—their names were written down under the glass—it was greenish—on his desk, and he'd drawn a line across the page.

"Well, you ought to have considered that earlier. What are you thinking about? Reporting sick just before roll call. Come on, take this."

He pulled a thermometer out of one of the jars where they stood in holes cut in pieces of gauze, wiped it dry, and handed it to Shukhov, who put it in his armpit.

Shukhov sat on a bench near the wall, right at the very end, so that he nearly tipped it up. He sat in that uncomfortable way, involuntarily emphasizing that he was unfamiliar with the place and that he'd come there on some minor matter.

Vdovushkin went on writing.

The dispensary lay in the most remote and deserted corner of the zone, where no sounds of any sort reached it. No clocks or watches ticked there—prisoners were not allowed to carry watches; the authorities knew the time for them. Even mice didn't scratch there; they'd all been dealt with by the hospital cat, placed there for the purpose.

For Shukhov it was a strange experience to sit in that spick-and-span room, in such quietness, to sit under the bright lamps for five long minutes doing nothing. He cast his eyes around the walls and found them empty. He looked at his jacket—the number on the chest was almost rubbed off. That might be noticed. He ought to have it touched up. He ran his free hand over his chin and felt the stubble. His beard had grown fast since his last bath, over ten days back. But that didn't worry him. Next bath day was about three days off and he'd have a shave then. What was the sense in lining up at the barber's? Who did he have to doll himself up for?

Then as he eyed Vdovushkin's snow-white cap he remembered the hospital on the banks of the River Lovat where he'd been taken with a smashed jaw, and then—what a dope he was!—volunteered for the front again, though he could have lain there in bed for five days.

And now here he was dreaming of being ill for two or three weeks, not dangerously ill, of course, not so bad that they'd have to operate, yet bad enough to go to the hospital and lie in bed for three weeks without stirring; and let them feed him on nothing but that clear soup of theirs, he wouldn't mind.

But, he recalled, now they didn't let you lie in bed even in the camp infirmary. A new doctor had arrived with one of the latest replacements—Stepan Grigorych,[18] a fussy, loud-voiced fellow who gave neither himself nor his patients any peace. He invented jobs in and around the infirmary for all the patients who could stand on their feet—fencing the garden, laying paths, bringing soil to the flowerbeds, and, in wintertime, erecting snow barriers. Work, he said, was a first-rate medicine for any illness.

You can overwork a horse to death. That the doctor ought to understand. If *he*'d been sweating blood laying blocks he'd quiet down, you could be sure of that.

Vdovushkin went on with his writing. He was, indeed, doing some work "on the side," but it was something beyond Shukhov's understanding. He was making a fair copy of a long new poem that he'd finished the previous evening and had promised to show that day to Stepan Grigorych, the doctor who advocated work therapy.

As can happen only in camps, Stepan Grigorych had advised Vdovushkin to describe himself as a medical assistant, and had taken him on at the infirmary and taught him to make intravenous injections on ignorant prisoners, to whose innocent minds it could never occur that Vdovushkin wasn't a medical assistant at all. Vdovushkin had

---

18. ***Stepan Grigorych*** (styi pän′ gryi gô′ryich).

been a university student of literature, arrested while still in his second year. The doctor wanted him to write when in prison what he'd been given no opportunity to write in freedom.

The signal for the roll call was barely audible through the double-paned, frost-blurred windows. Shukhov heaved a sigh and stood up. He still had that feverish chill but evidently he wouldn't be able to skip work.

Vdovushkin reached for the thermometer and read it.

"H'm, neither one thing nor the other. Ninety-nine point two. If it had been a hundred it would have been clear to anyone. I can't exempt you. Stay behind at your own risk, if you like. The doctor will examine you. If he considers you're ill, he'll exempt you. If he finds you fit, he won't. Then you'll be locked up. You'd better go back to work."

Shukhov said nothing. He didn't even nod. Pulling his hat over his eyes, he walked out.

How can you expect a man who's warm to understand a man who's cold?

The cold stung. A murky fog wrapped itself around Shukhov and made him cough painfully. The temperature out there was −17°; Shukhov's temperature was +99°. The fight was on.

He ran at a jog trot to his barracks. The whole parade ground was deserted, the camp looked empty. It was that brief moment of relaxation when, although everything has been decided, everyone is pretending to himself that there will be no march to work. The sentries sit in warm quarters, their sleepy heads propped against their rifles—it's not all milk and honey for them either, lounging on the watchtowers in such cold. The guards at the main gate tossed coal into the stove. The campguards in their room smoked a last cigarette before searching the barracks. And the prisoners, now clad in all their rags, a rope around their waists, their faces bound from chin to eyes with bits of cloth against the cold, lay on their bunks with their boots on and waited, eyes shut, hearts aquake, for their squad leader to yell: "Out you go."

The 104th were with the rest in Barracks 7—all except Pavlo, the deputy squad leader, who moved his lips as he totted something up with a pencil, and Alyosha, Shukhov's clean and tidy neighbor, who was reading from a notebook in which he'd copied out half the New Testament.

Shukhov ran headlong, but without making any noise, straight to Pavlo's bunk.

Pavlo looked up.

"So they didn't put you in the guardhouse, Ivan Denisovich? All right?" he asked with a marked Ukrainian accent, rolling out the name and patronymic in the way West Ukrainians did even in prison.

Picking up Shukhov's bread ration, he handed it to him. A spoonful of granulated sugar lay in a small mound on top of the hunk. Shukhov had no time to spare but he answered properly (the deputy squad leader was also one of the authorities, and even more depended on him than on the camp commandant). And, though he was in a hurry, he sucked the sugar from the bread with his lips, licked it under his tongue as he put his foot on a support to climb up to make his bed, and took a look at his ration, weighing it in his hand and hastily calculating whether it reached the regulation sixteen ounces. He had drawn many a thousand of these rations in prisons and camps, and though he'd never had an opportunity to weigh them on scales, and although, being a man of timid nature, he knew no way of standing up for his rights, he, like every other prisoner, had discovered long ago that honest weight was never to be found in the bread cutting. There was short weight in every ration. The only point was how short. So every day you took a look to soothe your soul—today, maybe, they haven't snitched any.

He decided he was half an ounce short as he broke the bread in two. One half he stuck into a little clean pocket he'd specially sewn under his jacket (at the factory they make jackets for prisoners without pockets). The other half, which he'd saved by going without at breakfast, he considered eating on the spot. But food gulped down is no food at all; it's wasted; it gives you no feeling of fullness. He started to put the bread into his locker but again thought better of it—he recalled that two barrack orderlies had been beaten up for stealing. The barracks was a big place, like a public yard.

And so, still clutching the hunk of bread, he drew his feet out of his valenki, deftly leaving inside them his foot rags and spoon, crawled barefoot up to his bunk, widened a little hole in the mattress, and there, amidst the sawdust, concealed his half-ration. He pulled off his hat, drew out of it a needle and thread (hidden deeply, for they fingered the hats when they frisked you; once a guard had pricked his finger and almost broken Shukhov's skull in his rage). Stitch, stitch, stitch, and the little tear in the mattress was mended, with the bread concealed under it. Meanwhile the sugar in his mouth had melted. Every nerve was strained to breaking point. At any moment the roster guard would begin shouting at the door. Shukhov's fingers worked fast but his mind, planning the next move, worked faster.

Alyosha the Baptist was reading the Testament under his breath (perhaps especially for Shukhov—those fellows were fond of recruiting).

"If you suffer, it must not be for murder, theft, or sorcery, nor for infringing the rights of others. But if anyone suffers as a Christian, he should feel it no disgrace, but confess that name to the honor of God."

Alyosha was smart—he'd made a chink in the wall and hidden the little book in it, and it had survived every search.

With the same rapid movements as before, Shukhov hung up his coat on a crossbeam and pulled what he wanted from under the mattress: a pair of mittens, a second pair of old foot rags, a length of rope, and a piece of cloth with tapes at each end. He smoothed the sawdust in the mattress (it was lumpy and dense), tucked in the blanket, arranged the pillow, and slid down onto his bare feet and started binding them with the rags, first with the good ones, then, on top, with the torn.

Just then Tiurin stood up and barked: "Sleep's over, one hundred and fourth! Out you go."

And at once the entire squad, drowsing or not, got up, yawned, and went to the door. Tiurin had been in for nineteen years and never turned his men out for the roll call a moment too soon. When he said, "Out you go," it meant you'd better.

And while the men with heavy tread and tight lips walked into the corridor one by one and then onto the porch, and the leader of the 20th, following Tiurin's example, called in turn "Out you go," Shukhov drew his valenki over the double thickness of foot rags, slipped his coat over his wadded jacket, and fastened a rope tightly around him (leather belts had been removed from zeks who had them—leather belts weren't allowed in "special" camps).

So Shukhov managed to get everything done and to catch up with the last of his companions, just as their numbered backs were passing through the door onto the porch. Looking rather bulky, for they had wrapped themselves up in every garment they possessed, the men shuffled diagonally toward the parade ground in single file, making no attempt to overtake one another. The only sound was the crunch of their heavy tread on the snow.

It was still dark, though in the east the sky was beginning to glow with a greenish tint. A light but piercing breeze came to meet them from the rising sun.

There is nothing as bitter as this moment when you go out to the morning roll call—in the dark, in the cold, with a hungry belly, to face a whole day of work. You lose your tongue. You lose all desire to speak to anyone.

A junior guard was rushing around the parade ground.

"Well, Tiurin, how long do we have to wait for you? Late again?"

Maybe Shukhov might get scared of him, but not Tiurin, oh no. He wouldn't waste breath on him in the cold. Just stomped on in silence.

And the squad followed him through the snow. Shuffle, shuffle, squeak, squeak.

Tiurin must have greased them with that pound of salt pork, for the 104th had gone back to its old place in the column—that could be seen from the neighboring squads. So one of the poorer and stupider squads was being sent to the "Socialist Way of Life" settlement. Oh, it'd be cruel there today: seventeen degrees below zero, and windy. No shelter. No fire.

A squad leader needs a lot of salt pork—to take to the planning department, and to satisfy his own belly too. Tiurin received no parcels, but he didn't go short of pork. No one in the squad who received any lost a moment in taking him some as a gift.

Otherwise you'd never survive.

The senior roster guard glanced at a small piece of board.

"You have one away on sick leave today, Tiurin. Twenty-three present?"

"Twenty-three," said Tiurin with a nod.

Who was missing? Panteleyev[19] wasn't there. But surely he wasn't ill.

And at once a whisper ran through the squad: Panteleyev, that lousy scum, was staying behind again. Oh no, he wasn't ill, the security boys were keeping him back. He'd be squealing on someone.

They would send for him during the day, on the quiet, and keep him two or three hours. No one would see, no one would hear.

And they'd fix it all up with the medical authorities.

The whole parade ground was black with coats as the squads drifted forward to be searched. Shukhov remembered he wanted to have the numbers on his jacket touched up, and elbowed his way through the crowd to the side. Two or three prisoners stood waiting their turn with the artist. He joined them. They spelled nothing but trouble, those numbers: if they were distinct the guards could identify you from any distance, but if you neglected to have them repainted in time you'd be sure to land in the guardhouse for not taking care of your number.

There were three artists in the camp. They painted pictures for the authorities free of charge, and in addition took turns appearing at roll call to touch up the numbers. Today it was the turn of an old man with a gray beard. When he painted the number on your hat with his brush it was just like a priest anointing your brow.

The old man painted on and on, blowing from time to time into his glove. It was a thin, knitted glove. His hand grew stiff with cold. He only just managed to paint the numbers.

He touched up the S 854 on Shukhov's jacket, and Shukhov, holding his rope belt in his hand and without bothering to pull his coat around him—very soon he'd be frisked—caught up with the squad. At once he noticed that his fellow squad member Tsezar[20] was smoking, and smoking a cigarette, not a pipe. That meant he might be able to cadge a smoke. But he didn't ask straight away; he stood quite close up to Tsezar and, half turning, looked past him.

He looked past him and seemed indifferent, but he noticed that after each puff (Tsezar inhaled at rare intervals, thoughtfully) a thin ring of glowing ash crept down the cigarette, reducing its length as it moved stealthily to the cigarette holder.

Fetiukov, that jackal, had come up closer too and now stood opposite Tsezar, watching his mouth with blazing eyes.

Shukhov had finished his last pinch of tobacco and saw no prospects of acquiring any more before evening. Every nerve in his body was taut, all his longing was concentrated in that cigarette butt—which meant more to him now, it seemed, than freedom itself—but he would never lower himself like that Fetiukov, he would never look at a man's mouth.

Tsezar was a hodgepodge of nationalities: Greek, Jew, Gypsy—you couldn't make out which. He was still young. He'd made films. But he hadn't finished his first when they arrested him. He wore a dark, thick, tangled mustache. They hadn't shaved it off in the camp because

---

19. ***Panteleyev*** (pän tyi lyā′yef).
20. ***Tsezar*** (tse zär′).

that was the way he looked in the photograph in his dossier.

"Tsezar Markovich," slobbered Fetiukov, unable to restrain himself. "Give us a puff."

His face twitched with greedy desire.

Tsezar slightly raised the lids that drooped low over his black eyes and looked at Fetiukov. It was because he didn't want to be interrupted while smoking and asked for a puff that he had taken up a pipe. He didn't begrudge the tobacco; he resented the interruption in his chain of thought. He smoked to stimulate his mind and to set his ideas flowing. But the moment he lighted a cigarette he read in several pairs of eyes an unspoken plea for the butt.

Tsezar turned to Shukhov and said: "Take it, Ivan Denisovich."

And with his thumb he pushed the smoldering cigarette butt out of the short amber holder.

Shukhov started (though it was exactly what he had expected of Tsezar) and gratefully hurried to take the butt with one hand, while slipping the other hand under it to prevent it from dropping. He didn't resent the fact that Tsezar felt squeamish about letting him finish the cigarette in the holder (some had clean mouths, some had foul) and he didn't burn his hardened fingers as they touched the glowing end. The main thing was, he had cut out that jackal Fetiukov, and now could go on drawing in smoke until his lips were scorched. Mmm. The smoke crept and flowed through his whole hungry body, making his head and feet respond to it.

Just at that blissful moment he heard a shout:

"They're stripping our undershirts off us."

Such was a prisoner's life. Shukhov had grown accustomed to it. All you could do was to look out they didn't leap at your throat.

But why the undershirts? The camp commandant himself had issued them. No, something was wrong.

There were still squads ahead of them before it was their turn to be frisked. Everyone in the

104th looked about. They saw Lieutenant Volkovoi, the security chief, stride out of the staff quarters and shout something to the guards. And the guards who, when Volkovoi wasn't around, carried out the frisking perfunctorily, now flung themselves into their work with savage zeal.

"Unbutton your shirts," the sergeant shouted.

Volkovoi was as unpopular with the prisoners as with the guards—even the camp commandant was said to be afraid of him. God had named him appropriately.[21] He was a wolf indeed, and looked it. He was dark, tall, with a scowl, very quick in his movements. He'd turn up from behind a barracks with a "What's going on here?" There was no hiding from him. At first, in '49, he'd been in the habit of carrying a whip of plaited leather, as thick as his forearm. He was said to have used it for flogging in the cells. Or when the prisoners would be standing in a group near a barracks at the evening count, he'd slink up from behind and lash out at someone's neck with a "Why aren't you standing in line, slobs?" The men would dash away in a wave. Stung by the blow, his victim would put a hand to his neck and wipe away the blood, but he'd hold his tongue, for fear of the cells.

Now, for some reason, Volkovoi had stopped carrying his whip.

When the weather was cold the guards were fairly lenient in the morning, though not in the evening. The prisoners untied their belts, and flung their coats wide open. They advanced five abreast, and five guards stood waiting to frisk them. The guards slapped their hands down the belted jackets, ran over the right pants pocket, the only one permitted by regulation, and, reluctant to pull off their gloves, felt any object that puzzled them, asking lazily: "What's that?"

What was there to look for on a prisoner at the morning roll call? A knife? But knives weren't taken out of the camp, they were brought into it. In the morning they had to make certain a prisoner wasn't taking six pounds of bread with him, meaning to escape with it. There was a time when they were so scared of the quarter-pound hunks the prisoners took to eat with their dinner that each of the squads had to make a wooden case for carrying the whole ration, after collecting it, piece by piece, from the men. What they reckoned to gain by this stupidity was beyond imagining. More likely it was just another way of tormenting people, giving them something extra to worry about. It meant taking a nibble at your hunk, making your mark on it, so to speak, and then putting it in the case; but anyway the pieces were as alike as two peas—they were all off the same loaf. During the march it preyed on your mind: you tortured yourself by imagining that somebody else's bit of the ration might be substituted for yours. Why, good friends quarreled about it, even to the point of fighting! But one day three prisoners escaped in a truck from the work site and took one of those cases of bread with them. That brought the authorities to their senses—they chopped up all the boxes in the guardroom. Everyone carry his own hunk, they said.

At this first search they also had to make sure that no one was wearing civvies under the camp outfit. But, after all, every prisoner had had his civvies removed from him down to the very last garment, and they wouldn't be returned, they were told, until they'd served their terms. No one had served his term in this camp.

Sometimes the guards frisked you for letters that might have been sent through civilians. But if they were going to search every prisoner for letters they'd be fussing around till dinnertime.

Volkovoi, however, had shouted that they were to search for something, and so the guards peeled off their gloves, ordered everyone to pull up his jacket (where every little bit of barrack-room warmth was treasured) and unbutton his shirt. Then they strode up to run their paws over the zeks and find out whether any of them might have slipped on something against the rules. A prisoner was allowed to wear a shirt and an undershirt—he was to be stripped of anything

21. ***God had named him appropriately.*** *Volk* means "wolf" in Russian.

else: such were Volkovoi's instructions, passed down the ranks by the prisoners. The squads that had been frisked earlier were in luck. Some of them had already been passed through the gates. But the rest had to bare their chests. And anyone who had slipped on an extra garment had to take it off on the spot, out there in the cold.

That's how it started, but it resulted in a fine mix-up—a gap formed in the column, and at the gates the escort began shouting, "Get a move on, get a move on." So when it was the turn of the 104th to be frisked they had to ease up a bit: Volkovoi told the guards to take the name of anyone who might be wearing extra garments—the culprits were to surrender them in person to personal property that evening with a written explanation of how and why they had hidden the garments.

Shukhov was in regulation dress. Come on, paw me as hard as you like. There's nothing but my soul in my chest. But they made a note that Tsezar was wearing a flannel vest and that Buinovsky, it seemed, had put on a vest or a cummerbund or something. Buinovsky protested—he'd been in the camp less than three months, a former navy commander who still couldn't get his destroyer out of his system.

"You've no right to strip men in the cold. You don't know Article Nine of the Criminal Code."

But they did have the right. They knew the code. You, friend, are the one who doesn't know it.

"You're not behaving like Soviet people," Buinovsky went on saying. "You're not behaving like Communists."

Volkovoi had put up with the reference to the criminal code but this made him wince and, like black lightning, he flashed: "Ten days in the guardhouse."

And aside to the sergeant: "Starting from this evening."

They didn't like putting a man in the cells in the morning—it meant the loss of his work for a whole day. Let him sweat blood in the meantime and be put in the cells in the evening.

The prison lay just over there, to the left of the parade ground. A brick building with two wings. The second wing had been added that autumn—there wasn't room enough in the first. The prison had eighteen cells besides those for solitary confinement, which were fenced off. The entire camp was log-built except for that brick prison.

The cold had got under the men's shirts and now it was there to stay. All that wrapping up had been in vain.

Shukhov's back was really giving him trouble. How he longed to be in bed in the infirmary, fast asleep! He wanted nothing else. Under the heaviest of blankets.

The zeks stood in front of the gates, buttoning their coats, tying a rope around their bellies. And from outside the escort shouted: "Come on. Come on."

And from behind, the guard urged them on: "Move along. Move along."

The first gate. The border zone. The second gate. Railings along each side near the gatehouse.

"Halt!" shouted a sentry. Like a flock of sheep. "Form fives."

It was growing light. The escort's fire was burning itself out behind the gatehouse. They always lit a fire before the prisoners were sent out to work—to keep themselves warm and be able to see more clearly while counting.

One of the gate guards counted in a loud brisk voice: "First. Second. Third . . ."

And the prisoners, in ranks of five, separated from the rest and marched ahead, so that they could be watched from front and behind: five heads, five backs, ten legs.

A second gate guard—a checker—stood at the next rail in silence verifying the count.

And, in addition, a lieutenant stood watching.

That was from the camp side.

A man is worth more than gold. If there was one head short when they got past the barbed wire you had to replace it with your own.

Once more the squad came together.

And now it was the turn of the sergeant of the escort to count.

"First. Second. Third."

And each rank of five drew away and marched forward separately.

And on the other side of the wire the assistant head guard verified the count.

And another lieutenant stood by and watched.

That was from the side of the escort.

No one dared make a mistake. If you signed for one head too many, you filled the gap with your own.

There were escort guards all over the place. They flung a semicircle around the column on its way to the power station, their machine guns sticking out and pointing right at your face. And there were guards with gray dogs. One dog bared its fangs as if laughing at the prisoners. The escorts all wore short sheepskins, except for a half a dozen whose coats trailed the ground. The long sheepskins were interchangeable: they were worn by anyone whose turn had come to man the watchtowers.

And once again as they brought the squads together the escort recounted the entire power-station column by fives.

"You always get the sharpest frost at sunrise," said Buinovsky. "You see, it's the coldest point of the night."

Captain Buinovsky was fond of explaining things. The state of the moon—whether it was old or young—he could calculate it for any day of the year.

He was fading away under your very eyes, the captain, his cheeks were falling in. But he had guts.

Out beyond the camp boundary the intense cold, accompanied by a head wind, stung even Shukhov's face, which was used to every kind of unpleasantness. Realizing that he would have the wind in his face all the way to the power station, he decided to make use of his bit of rag. To meet the contingency of a head wind he, like many other prisoners, had got himself a cloth with a long tape at each end. The prisoners admitted that these helped a bit. Shukhov covered his face up to the eyes, brought the tapes around below his ears, and fastened the ends together at the back of his neck. Then he covered his nape with the flap of his hat and raised his coat collar. The next thing was to pull the front flap of the hat down onto his brow. Thus in front only his eyes remained unprotected. He fixed his coat tightly at the waist with the rope. Now everything was in order except for his hands, which were already stiff with cold (his mittens were worthless). He rubbed them, he clapped them together, for he knew that in a moment he'd have to put them behind his back and keep them there for the entire march.

The chief of the escort guard recited the "morning prayer," which every prisoner was heartily sick of:

"Attention, prisoners. Marching orders must be strictly obeyed. Keep to your ranks. No hurrying, keep a steady pace. No talking. Keep your eyes fixed ahead and your hands behind your backs. A step to right or left is considered an attempt to escape and the escort has orders to shoot without warning. Leading guards, on the double."

The two guards in the lead of the escort must have set out along the road. The column heaved forward, shoulders swaying, and the escorts, some twenty paces to the right and left of the column, each man at a distance of ten paces from the next, machine guns held at the ready, set off too.

It hadn't snowed for a week and the road was worn hard and smooth. They skirted the camp and the wind caught their faces sideways. Hands clasped behind their backs, heads lowered, the column of prisoners moved on, as though at a funeral. All you saw was the feet of two or three men ahead of you and the patch of trodden ground where your own feet were stepping. From time to time one of the escorts would cry: "U 48. Hands behind back," or "B 502. Keep up." But they shouted less and less; the slashing wind made it difficult to see. The guards weren't allowed to tie cloth over their faces. Theirs was not much of a job either.

In warmer weather everybody in the column talked, no matter how much the escort might shout at them. But today every prisoner hunched his shoulders, hid behind the back of the man in front of him, and plunged into his own thoughts.

The thoughts of a prisoner—they're not free either. They kept returning to the same things. A single idea keeps stirring. Would they feel that piece of bread in the mattress? Would he have any luck at the dispensary that evening? Would they put Buinovsky in the cells? And how did Tsezar get his hands on that warm vest? He'd probably greased a palm or two in the warehouse for people's private belongings. How else?

Because he had breakfasted without bread and eaten his food cold, Shukhov's belly felt unsatisfied that morning. And to prevent it complaining and begging for food, he stopped thinking about the camp and let his mind dwell on the letter he'd soon be writing home.

The column passed the wood-processing factory, built by prison labor, the workers' settlement (the huts had been assembled by prisoners too, but the inhabitants were civilians), the new club (convict-built in entirety, from the foundations to the mural decorations—but it wasn't they who saw the films there), and then moved out into the steppe, straight into the wind heading for the reddening dawn. Bare white snow stretched to the horizon, to the left, to the right, and not a single tree could be seen on the whole expanse of steppe.

A new year, 1951, had begun, and Shukhov had the right to two letters that year. He had sent his last letter in July and got an answer to it in October. At Ust-Izhma the rules had been different: you could write once a month. But what was the sense of writing? He'd written no more often then than now.

Ivan Shukhov had left home on June 23, 1941. On the previous Sunday the people who'd been to Polomnya to attend Mass had said: *War!* At Polomnya they'd learned it at the post office but at his village, Temgenovo, no one had a radio in those days. Now, they wrote, the radio roared in every cottage—it was piped in. There was little sense in writing. Writing now was like dropping stones in some deep, bottomless pool. They drop; they sink—but there is no answer. You couldn't write and describe the squad you were working with and what kind of squad leader Andrei Prokofievich[22] was. Just now he had a good deal more to talk about with Kilgas the Lett than with his family at home.

Neither did the two letters a year they sent him throw much light on the way they were living. The kolkhoz[23] had a new chairman—as if that hadn't happened regularly! It'd been amalgamated with neighboring farms—that'd happened before too, but afterward they'd reduced it to its former condition. And what else? The farmers were failing to fulfill their quota of work days—or the individual plots had been cut down to one-third acre, and some people's right back to the cottage walls.

What he couldn't take in was the fact that, as his wife wrote, the number of people in the kolkhoz hadn't grown by a single soul since the war. All the young men and women, without exception, had managed to get away to work in factories or in the peat-processing works. Half the men hadn't come back from the war at all and, among those who had, were some who cold-shouldered the kolkhoz. They lived in the village and worked on the side. The only men on the farm were Zakhar Vasilych, the manager, and Tikhon, the carpenter, who was turned eighty-four, had married recently, and already had children. The kolkhoz was kept going by the women who'd been there since 1930.

There was something about this that Shukhov couldn't understand—"living in the village and working on the side." He'd seen life in the days of private farming and in the days of the kolkhozes too, but that men weren't working in their own villages—this he couldn't swallow. Sort of seasonal workers, were they? Going out traveling? But then how did the village manage with the haymaking?

---

22. ***Andrei Prokofievich*** (än dryā′i prô kô fye′vyich), the first name and patronymic of Tiurin.
23. ***kolkhoz*** (kôl ʜôz′), a collective farm.

They'd given up seasonal work a long time back, his wife had replied. They didn't go out carpentering, for which that part of the country was famous; they didn't make osier baskets, for no one wanted them these days. But they did have a craft, a wonderful new craft—carpet painting. Someone had brought stencils back from the war and from that time it had become so popular that the number of those carpet painters grew and grew. They had no steady jobs, they didn't work anywhere, they helped the kolkhoz for a month or so, just at the haymaking or the harvesting, and for that the kolkhoz gave them a chit saying that so-and-so, a member of the kolkhoz, had been released to carry on his work and that the kolkhoz had no claim on him. And they traveled all over the country, they even flew in airplanes to save time, and they piled up rubles[24] by the thousand and painted carpets all over the place. Fifty rubles a carpet made out of any old sheet you could spare—and it didn't seem to take them more than an hour to make a carpet of it. And Shukhov's wife nursed the strong hope that when Ivan returned he too would become one of those painters. Then they'd raise themselves out of the poverty in which she was living and they'd send the children to a technical school and build a new cottage instead of the old broken-down one. All the carpet painters were building new cottages and now, near the railway station, the cottages had gone up in price from five thousand to all of twenty-five.

Then Shukhov asked his wife to explain to him how he, who'd never been able to draw in his life, was going to become a painter. And what were those beautiful carpets like? What did they have on them? His wife answered that you'd have to be an utter fool not to be able to paint the patterns; all you had to do was to put the stencil on and paint through the little holes with a brush. There were three sorts of carpets, she wrote: the "Troika," an officer of the hussars[25] driving a beautiful troika; the "Reindeer"; and a third with a Persian-style pattern. They had no other designs, but people all over the country were glad to get these and snatch them out of the painters' hands. Because a real carpet cost not fifty but thousands of rubles.

How Shukhov longed to see just one of those carpets!

During his years in prisons and camps he'd lost the habit of planning for the next day, for a year ahead, for supporting his family. The authorities did his thinking for him about everything—it was somehow easier that way. He still had another two winters, another two summers to serve. But those carpets preyed on his mind. . . .

There was easy money to be made, you see, and made fast. And somehow it seemed a pity to lag behind his fellow villagers. . . . But, frankly, he didn't want to turn carpet painter. For that a man needed to be free and easy with people, to be brash, to know how to grease a palm or two. And although Shukhov had trodden the earth for forty years, though he'd lost half his teeth and his head was growing bald, he'd never either given or taken a bribe, nor had he learned to do so in camp.

Easy money weighs light in the hand and doesn't give you the feeling you've earned it. There was truth in the old saying: pay short money and get short value. He still had a good pair of hands, capable hands. Surely, when he was out, he'd find work as a plumber, a carpenter, or a repairman.

Only if they deprived him of his civil rights and he couldn't be taken on anywhere, or if they wouldn't let him go home, would he turn to those carpets for a spell.

Meanwhile the column had come to a halt before the gatehouse of the sprawling site on which the power station stood. While the column was still on the move, two of the escort, clad in ankle-length sheepskins, had left their places and wandered across open country to their distant watchtowers. Until all the towers were manned the site was forbidden territory. The head guard,

---

24. ***rubles,*** at the time of this story, the Russian ruble was worth twenty-five cents in United States currency.
25. ***"Troika"*** (troi′kə) . . . ***hussars*** (hu̇ zärz′). A troika is a Russian carriage, wagon, sleigh, etc., pulled by three horses. A hussar is a light-armed cavalry soldier.

a machine gun slung over his shoulder, advanced to the gatehouse. Smoke, a great cloud of it, belched from its chimney—a civilian watchman sat there all night to prevent anyone stealing lumber or cement.

Far in the distance, on the other side of the site, the sun, red and enormous, was rising in haze, its beams cutting obliquely through the gates, the whole building site, and the fence. Alyosha, who was standing next to Shukhov, gazed at the sun and looked happy, a smile on his lips. What had he to be happy about? His cheeks were sunken, he lived strictly on his rations, he earned nothing. He spent all his Sundays muttering with the other Baptists. They shed the hardships of camp life like water off a duck's back.

During the march, Shukhov's face cloth had grown wet from his breath. In some spots the frost had caught it and formed an icy crust. He drew it down from his face to his neck and stood with his back to the wind. He'd managed to keep the cold out in most places though his hands were numb in his worn mittens. The toes of his left foot were numb too—that left boot was badly worn. The sole had been repaired twice.

The small of his back ached, and so did the rest of it, all the way up to his shoulders. Ached and throbbed. How could he work?

He looked around, and his eyes fell on the face of the squad leader, who had marched among the last five. Tiurin was a broad-shouldered man, broad in the face too. He looked morose as he stood there. He had no jokes or smiles for his squad, but he took pains to see they got better rations. He was serving his second term; he was a true son of the GULAG[26] and knew camp ways through and through.

In camp the squad leader is everything: a good one will give you a second life; a bad one will put you in your coffin. Shukhov had known Andrei Tiurin since the time they met at Ust-Izhma, though he hadn't been in his squad then. And when the prisoners who were in under Article 58[27] were transferred from general camps to "special" ones, Tiurin had immediately picked him out for his squad. Shukhov had no dealings with the camp commandant or the P.P.D., with foremen or engineers—that was the squad leader's job: he'd protect him with his own chest of steel. In return, Tiurin had only to lift an eyebrow or beckon with a finger—and you ran and did what he wanted. You can cheat anyone you like in camp, but not your squad leader. Then you'll live.

Shukhov would have liked to ask Tiurin whether they were to work at the same place as the day before or go somewhere else, but he was afraid to interrupt his lofty thoughts. He'd only just averted the danger of the squad being sent to work at the Socialist Way of Life settlement, and now he was probably deliberating over the "percentage"[28] on which the squad's rations for the next five days depended.

Tiurin was heavily pockmarked. He was facing the wind but not a muscle moved—his skin was as tough as the bark of an oak.

In the column the prisoners were clapping their hands and stamping their feet. The wind was nasty. It looked now as if the sentries, known to the prisoners as "parrots," were perched in all six watchtowers, but still they weren't letting the column in. They tormented the life out of you with their vigilance.

Here they are. The head guard came out of the gatehouse with the work checker. They posted themselves on each side of the gate. The gates swung wide open.

"Form fives. First. Second. Third . . ."

The prisoners marched as though on parade, almost in step. To get inside, that was all they wanted—there no one had to teach them what to do.

Just beyond the gatehouse was the office; near it stood the work superintendent, beckoning the squad leaders to turn in there, not that they didn't head that way anyway. Der too was

---

26. *GULAG* (gü′läg), Central Camp Administration, here used to mean Soviet prison camps in general.
27. *Article 58,* section of the Soviet Criminal Code dealing with "anti-Soviet" offenses. Under Stalin, the article was applied extensively without regard to guilt or innocence.
28. *"percentage,"* a paper stating the amount of work done and the percentage of the total work plan it amounts to.

there, a convict himself but a foreman, the swine, who treated his fellow prisoners worse than dogs.

Eight o'clock. Five minutes past (the whistle had just sounded the hour). The authorities were afraid that the prisoners might waste time and scatter into warm corners—and the prisoners had a long day ahead of them, there was time enough for everything. Everyone who steps onto the building site bends to pick up a scrap of firewood here and there—fuel for the stove. And they hoard it away in nooks and crannies.

Tiurin ordered Pavlo to go with him to the office. Tsezar turned in there too. Tsezar was well off. Two parcels a month. He greased every palm that had to be greased, and worked in the office in a cushy job, as assistant to the rate inspector.

The rest of the squad at once turned off to the side and vanished.

Discussion

1. From his years in labor camps, Ivan Denisovich Shukhov has learned how useful the early-morning hours can be. **(a)** What things might a prisoner do with these ninety "free" minutes? **(b)** Name at least two tasks or errands Shukhov hopes to take care of this particular morning.

2. Shukhov is not too upset when the Tartar promises him "three days' penalty with work," for he believes that "real jail was when you were kept back from work." **(a)** Explain his meaning. **(b)** Does he actually receive three days' penalty? Explain.

3. What do the following reveal about the hardship of prison life and the authorities' lack of humanity? **(a)** cobwebs of frost around the barracks ceiling; **(b)** the gaps in Shukhov's teeth; **(c)** the men's hiding places for personal possessions; **(d)** the need to always walk with a companion.

4. **(a)** Compare Fetiukov's and Shukhov's reactions as they watch Tsezar smoking a cigarette. **(b)** In what way does Fetiukov's reaction justify Shukhov's low opinion of him? **(c)** What important character trait does Shukhov's reaction reveal? **(d)** Name at least one other example that shows the same trait.

5. Buinovsky seems to be "fading away under [their] very eyes. . . . but he had guts." How does the episode of the extra clothing show both his courage and his possible weakness?

6. Shukhov believes that "in camp, the squad leader is everything." **(a)** What hardships has Tiurin already kept his men from this morning? **(b)** How does Shukhov infer that he's done it? **(c)** What other services does Tiurin generally supply, and how does his squad treat him in return?

7. Describe the special treatment given the following prisoners and tell in each case what seems to be the reason for it. **(a)** Kolya Vdovushkin, the medical assistant; **(b)** Tsezar; **(c)** Panteleyev.

8. During the march to the power-station site, Shukhov thinks about his most recent letter from his wife. **(a)** Explain the analogy used to describe Shukhov's feelings about letter writing. **(b)** Who seems to have more expectations for the future, he or his wife? Explain. **(c)** In what way is prison life responsible for Shukhov's attitude?

9. **(a)** What point of view is primarily used to tell Shukhov's story? **(b)** Do you agree that this point of view is more effective than the others that could have been used? Discuss.

Composition

Consider the main conflicts in the novel thus far. You have probably observed that both external and internal conflicts have been presented. Think of the details related to them: which conflicts appear to affect only Shukhov, which affect the prisoners in general, and which affect everyone in the labor camp.

Write a two- or three-paragraph composition describing the conflicts faced by Shukhov on this typical morning. Try to predict which conflicts will dominate as the novel continues to unfold.

Comment: The Art of Translation 2

The Comment article on page 189 should have made you aware of the difficulties involved in translating a piece of poetry from one language to another. Though prose may be easier to translate in that no rhyme or meter questions need be considered, it is still the translator's responsibility not only to make the selection sound natural in the new language, but also to convey such subtleties as mood or tone that were present in the original version. As with poetry, there is not necessarily a "right" way to translate a group of lines; compare the following translations of a scene from *One Day* and discuss the questions that follow them.

Shukhov looked up at the ceiling and said nothing. He didn't know any longer himself whether he wanted freedom or not. At first he'd wanted it very much and every day he added up how long he still had to go. But then he got fed up with this. And as time went on he understood that they might let you out but they never let you home. And he didn't really know where he'd be better off. At home or in here.

But they wouldn't let him home anyway. . . .

Alyoshka was talking the truth. You could tell by his voice and his eyes he was glad to be in prison.

"Look, Alyoshka," Shukhov said, "it's all right for you. It was Christ told you to come here, and you are here because of Him. But why am *I* here? Because they didn't get ready for the war like they should've in forty-one? Was that *my* fault?"

"Looks like they're not going to check us over again," Kilgas shouted from his bunk.

"Yeah," Shukhov said. "We ought to chalk that up on the chimney. Doesn't happen every day." And he yawned. "Time we got some sleep."

From *One Day in the Life of Ivan Denisovich* by Alexander Solzhenitsyn, translated by Max Hayward and Ronald Hingley, Frederick A. Praeger, 1963.

Shukhov gazed at the ceiling in silence. Now he didn't know either whether he wanted freedom or not. At first he'd longed for it. Every night he'd counted the days of his stretch—how many had passed, how many were coming. And then he'd grown bored with counting. And then it became clear that men like him wouldn't ever be allowed to return home, that they'd be exiled. And whether his life would be any better there than here—who could tell?

Freedom meant one thing to him—home.

But they wouldn't let him go home.

Alyosha was speaking the truth. His voice and his eyes left no doubt that he was happy in prison.

"You see, Alyosha," Shukhov explained to him, "somehow it works out all right for you: Jesus Christ wanted you to sit in prison and so you are—sitting there for His sake. But for whose sake am *I* here? Because we weren't ready for war in '41? For that? But was that *my* fault?"

"Seems like there's not going to be a recount," Kilgas murmured from his bunk.

"Yeah," said Shukhov. "We ought to write it up in coal inside the chimney. No second count." He yawned. "Might as well get to sleep."

From *One Day in the Life of Ivan Denisovich* by Alexander Solzhenitsyn. Translated by Ralph Parker. English translation

What differing effects are created by these word choices: *wanted—longed; how long he still had to go—days of his stretch; fed up—bored; they never let you home—they'd be exiled.* What other words would you substitute for any of these? What would be the effect?

What line was omitted in the Hayward-Hingley version? How do the effects of the two passages differ as a result? Which effect do you prefer?

Is the mood of the scene better complemented by having Kilgas *shout* or *murmur* his opinion about the bed check? In which version does Shukhov's response to this sound more like everyday informal English?

The sun rose red and hazy over the deserted area. At one place the panels of the prefabs lay under the snow; at another a start had been made on the brickwork, and abandoned when no higher than the foundations. Here lay a broken steam shovel, there a dredge, farther on a pile of scrap metal. A network of ditches and trenches crisscrossed the site with a hole or two here and there. The building of the automobile repair shop was ready for roofing. On a rise stood the power station itself, built up to the second story.

Now there was not a soul in sight. Only the six sentries on their watchtowers were visible—and some people bustling around the office. That moment belonged to the prisoners. The senior work superintendent, it was said, had long been threatening to save time by giving the squads their work assignments the evening before, but for all his efforts they never got around to it—because between the evening and the following morning all their plans turned upside down.

So that moment still belonged to the prisoners. While the authorities were sorting things out you stuck to the warmest place you could find. Sit down, take a rest, you'll have time enough to sweat blood. Good if you can get near a stove. Unwrap your foot rags and warm them a little. Then your feet will keep warm all day. And even without a stove it's good to sit down.

The 104th went into a big room in the repair shop where the windows had been glazed during the autumn and the 38th were pouring slabs of concrete. Some of the slabs lay in wooden forms, others, with mesh reinforcement, were stood up on end. The ceiling was high, the floor was of bare earth: a cold place it would've been if they hadn't heated it with lots of coal—not for the sake of the men working there, of course, but to help the slabs set faster. There was even a thermometer, and on Sundays, if for some reason or other no one was sent from the camp to work there, a civilian kept the stove going.

The 38th, naturally, wouldn't let any stranger near their stove. Their own men sat around it, drying their foot rags. Never mind, we'll sit here in the corner, it's not so bad.

Shukhov found a place for the seat of his wadded trousers—where hadn't they sat?—on the edge of a wooden form, and leaned against the wall. When he did so his coat and jacket tightened, and he felt something sharp pressing against the left side of his chest, near his heart. It was the edge of the hunk of bread in his little inner pocket—that half of his morning ration which he'd taken with him for dinner. He always brought the same amount with him to work and never touched it till dinnertime. But usually he ate the other half at breakfast. This time he hadn't. But he realized he had gained nothing by economizing—his belly called out to him to eat the bread at once, in the warmth. Dinner was five hours off—and time dragged.

And that nagging pain had now moved down to his legs, which felt quite weak. Oh, if he could only get to the stove!

He laid his mittens on his knees, unbuttoned his coat, untied the tapes of his face cloth, stiff with cold, folded it several times over, and put it away in his pants pocket. Then he reached for the hunk of bread, wrapped in a piece of clean cloth, and, holding the cloth at chest level so that not a crumb should fall to the ground, began to nibble and chew at the bread. The bread, which he had carried under two garments, had been warmed by his body. The frost hadn't caught it at all.

More than once during his life in the camps, Shukhov had recalled the way they used to eat in his village: whole pots full of potatoes, pans of oatmeal, and, in the early days, big chunks of meat. And milk enough to bust their guts. That wasn't the way to eat, he learned in camp. You had to eat with all your mind on the food—like now, nibbling the bread bit by bit, working the crumbs up into a paste with your tongue and sucking it into your cheeks. And how good it tasted—that soggy black bread! What had he eaten for eight, no, more than eight years? Next to nothing. But how much work had he done? Ah!

So he sat there, occupying himself with his hunk of bread, while near him on the same side of the room sat the rest of the 104th.

Two Estonians,[1] close as brothers, sat on a flat concrete slab taking turns smoking half a cigarette from the same holder. These Estonians were equally fair, equally tall, equally lean, and had equally long noses and big eyes. They hung on to each other so closely that you'd think one would suffocate unless he breathed the same air as the other. Tiurin never separated them. They shared their food, they slept in adjacent bunks in the top row. And when they stood in the column, waiting for work to start, or turned in for the night, they went on talking to each other in their quiet, deliberate manner. In fact they weren't brothers at all. They first met here in the 104th. One of them, they explained, had been a fisherman on the coast; the other had been taken as a child to Sweden by his parents when the Soviets were established in Estonia. But he'd grown up with a mind of his own and returned to Estonia to complete his education.

Well, it's said that nationality doesn't mean anything and that every nation has its bad eggs. But among all the Estonians Shukhov had known he'd never met a bad one.

The prisoners sat around, some on the slabs, some on forms, some straight on the ground. A tongue doesn't wag in the morning; everyone sat silent, locked in thought. Fetiukov, the jackal, had been collecting cigarette butts (he even fished them out of the spitoons, he wasn't fussy), and now he was breaking them up and filtering the unsmoked tobacco onto a piece of paper. Fetiukov had three children at home but when he was sentenced they'd disclaimed him and his wife had married again. So he got no help from anywhere.

Buinovsky, who kept stealing glances at him, finally barked: "Hey, you, what do you think you're doing? Picking up all kinds of diseases? Stop it."

The captain was used to giving orders. He spoke to everyone as if in command.

But Fetiukov didn't care what he said—the captain got no parcels either. And with a malicious grin on his drooling lips he replied: "You wait, Captain. When you've been in for eight years you'll be picking them up yourself. We've seen bigger men than you in the camp. . . ."

Fetiukov was judging by his own standards. Perhaps the captain would stand up to camp life.

"What? What?" asked Senka Klevshin, missing the point. Senka was deaf and thought they were talking about Buinovsky's bad luck during the frisking. "You shouldn't have shown your pride so much," he said, shaking his head in commiseration. "It could all have blown over."

Senka was a quiet, luckless fellow. One of his eardrums had been smashed in '41. Then he was captured; he escaped, was recaptured, and was sent to Buchenwald.[2] There he evaded death by a miracle and now he was serving his time here quietly. If you show your pride too much, he said, you're lost.

There was truth in that. Better to growl and submit. If you were stubborn they broke you.

Alyosha sat silent, his face buried in his hands. Praying.

Shukhov ate his bread down to his very fingers, keeping only a little bit of bare crust, the half-moon-shaped top of the loaf—because no spoon is as good for scraping a bowl of cereal clean as a bread crust. He wrapped the crust in his cloth again and slipped it into his inside pocket for dinner, buttoned himself up against the cold, and prepared for work. Let them send him out now! Though, of course, it would be better if they'd wait a bit longer.

The 38th stood up and scattered—some to the concrete mixer, some to fetch water, some to the mesh reinforcements.

But neither Pavlo nor Tiurin came back to their squad. And although the 104th had been sitting there barely twenty minutes and the working day—curtailed because it was winter—didn't end till six, everyone felt already they'd had a rare stroke of luck—now evening didn't seem so far off.

---

1. ***Estonians*** (e stō'nē ənz), Finnish people inhabiting Estonia, a republic within the Soviet Union near Finland.
2. ***Buchenwald*** (bü'kən wôld'), village in southern East Germany, site of a Nazi concentration camp during World War II.

"Curse it, it's a long time since we had a snowstorm," said Kilgas, a plump, red-faced Lett, gesturing. "Not one snowstorm all winter. What sort of winter do you call this?"

"Yes . . . a snowstorm . . . a snowstorm," the squad sighed in response.

When there was a snowstorm in those parts no one was taken out to work—they were afraid of letting the prisoners leave the barracks. They could get lost between the barrack room and the mess hall if you didn't put up a guide rope. No one would care if a prisoner froze to death, but what if he tried to escape? There had been instances. During the storms the snow was as fine as dust but the drifts were as firm as ice. Prisoners had escaped over them when they topped the barbed wire. True, they hadn't got far.

Come to think of it, a snowstorm was no use to anyone. The prisoners sat locked in; the coal was delivered late and all the warmth was blown out of the barracks. Flour didn't reach the camp, so there was no bread; and more often than not there was no hot food either. And as long as the storm lasted—three days, four days, even a week—those days were counted as holidays and had to be made up for by work on Sunday.

All the same, the prisoners loved snowstorms and prayed for them. Whenever the wind rose a little, every face was turned up to the sky. Let the stuff come! The more the merrier.

Snow, they meant. With only a ground wind, it never really got going.

Someone edged up to the stove of the 38th, only to be ousted.

Just then Tiurin walked in. He looked gloomy. His squad understood that there was something to be done, and quickly.

"H'm," said Tiurin, looking around. "All present, hundred and fourth?"

He didn't verify or count them because none of Tiurin's men could have gone anywhere. Without wasting time he gave his men their assignments. The two Estonians, Senka, and Gopchik were sent to pick up a big wooden box for mixing mortar nearby and carry it to the power station. They all immediately knew that they were being transferred to the half-completed building where work had been halted in late autumn. The other men were sent with Pavlo to get tools. Four were ordered to shovel snow near the power station and the entrance to the machine room, and inside and on the ramps. A couple of men were sent to light the stove in the machine room, using coal and such lumber as they could swipe and chop up. Another was to drag cement there on a sled. Two were sent to fetch water, two for sand, and yet another to sweep the snow off the sand and break it up with a crowbar.

The only two left without assignments were Shukhov and Kilgas, the leading workers of the squad. Calling them over, Tiurin said:

"Well, look here, boys—" he was no older than they were but he had the habit of addressing them like that—"after dinner you'll be laying cement blocks on the second-story walls, over there where the sixth stopped work last autumn. Now we have to figure how to make the machine room warmer. It has three big windows and the first thing to do is to board them up somehow. I'll give you people to help, but you must figure out what to board them up with. We're going to use the machine room for mixing the mortar, and for warming ourselves too. Unless we keep warm we'll freeze like dogs, understand?"

He'd have said more, maybe, but up came Gopchik, a Ukrainian lad, pink as a suckling pig, to complain that the other squad wouldn't give them the box. There was a scrap going on over it. So off went Tiurin.

Difficult as it was to start working in such cold, the important thing was to get going.

Shukhov and Kilgas exchanged looks. They'd worked as a team more than once as carpenter and mason, and had come to respect one another.

It was no easy matter to find something to board up those windows with in the bare expanse of snow. But Kilgas said: "Vanya, I know a little place over there where those prefabs are going up, with a fine roll of roofing felt. I put it aside with my own hands. Let's go and scrounge it."

Kilgas was a Lett but he spoke Russian like a native. There'd been a settlement of Old Believers[3] near his village and he'd learned Russian from childhood. He'd been in the camp only two years but already he understood everything: if you don't use your teeth you get nothing. His name was Johann and Shukhov called him Vanya.[4]

They decided to go for the roll, but first Shukhov ran over to where a new wing of the repair shops was under construction. He had to get his trowel. For a mason a trowel is a serious matter—if it's light and easy to handle. But there was a rule that wherever you worked you had to turn in every evening the tools you'd been issued that morning; and which tool you got the next day was a matter of chance. One evening, though, Shukhov had fooled the man in the tool store and pocketed the best trowel; and now he kept it hidden in a different place every evening, and every morning, if he was put to laying blocks, he recovered it. If the 104th had been sent to the Socialist Way of Life settlement that morning, Shukhov would of course have been without a trowel again. But now he had only to push aside a brick, dig his fingers into the chink—and presto! there it was.

Shukhov and Kilgas left the repair shops and walked over toward the prefabs. Their breath formed thick clouds of vapor. The sun was now some way above the horizon but it cast no rays, as in a fog. On each side of it rose pillars of light.

"Like poles, eh?" Shukhov said with a nod.

"It's not poles we have to worry about," said Kilgas casually, "so long as they don't put any barbed wire between them."

He never spoke without making a joke, that Kilgas, and was popular with the whole squad for it. And what a reputation he had already won for himself among the Letts in the camp! Of course, it was true he ate properly—he received two food parcels a month—and looked as ruddy as if he wasn't in camp at all. *You*'d make jokes if you were in his shoes!

This construction site covered an immense area. It took quite a long time to cross it. On their way they ran into men from the 82nd. Again they'd been given the job of chopping out holes in the ground. The holes were small enough—one-and-a-half feet by one-and-a-half feet and about the same in depth—but the ground, stone-hard even in summer, was now in the grip of frost. Just try and gnaw it! They went for it with picks—the picks slipped, scattering showers of sparks, but not a bit of earth was dislodged. The men stood there, one to a hole, and looked about them—nowhere to warm up, they were forbidden to budge a step—so back to the pick. The only way to keep warm.

Shukhov recognized one of them, a fellow from Viatka.

"Listen," he advised him. "You'd do better to light a fire over each hole. The ground would thaw out then."

"It's forbidden," said the man. "They don't give us any firewood."

"Scrounge some then."

Kilgas merely spat.

"How do you figure it, Vanya! If the authorities had any guts do you think they'd have men pounding away at the ground with pickaxes in a frost like this?"

He muttered a few indistinguishable oaths and fell silent. You don't talk much in such cold. They walked on and on till they reached the spot where the panels of the prefabs lay buried under snow.

Shukhov liked to work with Kilgas. The only bad thing about him was that he didn't smoke and there was never any tobacco in his parcels.

Kilgas was right: together they lifted a couple of planks and there lay the roll of roofing felt.

They lugged it out. Now, how were they going to carry it? They'd be spotted from the watchtowers, but that didn't matter: the "parrots' " only concern was that the prisoners shouldn't escape. Inside, you could chop up all those panels into firewood for all they cared. Nor would it matter if they happened to meet one of the

3. ***Old Believers,*** followers of the Russian Orthodox Church who did not accept reforms made in religious texts and ceremonies from the 1600s.

4. ***Vanya,*** nickname for both the names Ivan and Johann.

guards. He'd be looking about like the others to see what he could scrounge. As for the prisoners, they didn't give a hoot for those prefabs, and neither did the squad leaders. The only people who kept an eye on them were the superintendent, who was a civilian, that scum Der, and the lanky Shkuropatenko,[5] a mere goose egg, a trusty who'd been given the temporary job of guarding the prefabs from any stealing by the prisoners. Yes, it was Shkuropatenko who was most likely to spot them on the open ground.

"Look here, Vanya," said Shukhov, "we mustn't carry it lengthwise. Let's take it up on end with our arms around it. It'll be easy to carry and our bodies will hide it. They won't spot it from a distance."

It was a good idea. To carry the roll lengthwise would have been awkward, so they held it upright in between them and set off. From a distance it would look as if there were three of them, rather close to one another.

"But when Der notices the felt on the windows he'll guess where it came from," said Shukhov.

"What's it got to do with us?" asked Kilgas, in surprise. "We'll say it was there before. Were we to pull it down or what?"

That was true.

Shukhov's fingers were numb with cold under his worn mittens. He'd lost all sense of touch. But his left boot was holding—that was the main thing. The numbness would go out of his fingers when he started to work.

They crossed the stretch of virgin snow and reached a sled trail running from the tool store to the power station. Their men must have brought the cement along there.

The power station stood on a rise at the edge of the site. No one had been near the place for weeks and the approaches to it lay under a smooth blanket of snow; the sled tracks, and the fresh trails that had been left by the deep footsteps of the 104th, stood out boldly. The men were already clearing away the snow from around the building with wooden shovels and making a road for the trucks to drive up on.

It would have been good if the mechanical lift in the power station had been in order. But the motor had burned out, and no one had bothered to repair it. This meant that everything would have to be carried by hand to the second story—the mortar and the blocks.

For two months the unfinished structure had stood in the snow like a gray skeleton, just as it had been left. And now the 104th had arrived. What was it that kept their spirits up? Empty bellies, fastened tight with belts of rope! A splitting frost! Not a warm corner, not a spark of fire! But the 104th had arrived—and life had come back to the building.

Right at the entrance to the machine room the trough for mixing mortar fell apart. It was a makeshift affair, and Shukhov hadn't expected it to last the journey in one piece. Tiurin swore at his men just for form's sake, for he saw that no one was to blame. At that moment Kilgas and Shukhov turned up with their roll of roofing felt. Tiurin was delighted, and at once worked out a new arrangement: Shukhov was put to fixing the stovepipe, so that a fire could be quickly kindled; Kilgas was to repair the mixing trough, with the two Estonians to help him; and Senka was given an ax to chop long laths with—felt could then be tacked to them, two widths for each window. Where were the laths to come from? Tiurin looked around. Everybody looked around. There was only one solution: to remove a couple of planks that served as a sort of handrail on the ramp leading up to the second story. You'd have to keep your eyes peeled going up and down; otherwise you'd be over the edge. But where else were the laths to come from?

Why, you might wonder, should prisoners wear themselves out, working hard, ten years on end, in the camps? You'd think they'd say: No thank you, and that's that. We'll drag ourselves through the day till evening, and then the night is ours.

But that didn't work. To outsmart you they thought up work squads—but not squads like the

---

5. ***Shkuropatenko*** (shkü'rô pä tyen'kô).

ones outside the camps, where every man is paid his separate wage. Everything was so arranged in the camp that the prisoners egged one another on. It was like this: either you all got a bit extra or you all croaked. You're loafing, you swine—do you think I'm willing to go hungry just because of you? Put your guts into it, slob.

And if a situation like this one turned up there was all the more reason for resisting any temptation to slack. Regardless, you put your back into the work. For unless you could manage to provide yourself with the means of warming up, you and everyone else would give out on the spot.

Pavlo brought the tools. Now use them. A few lengths of stovepipe too. True, there were no tinsmith's tools, but there was a little hammer and a light ax. One could manage.

Shukhov clapped his mittens together, joined up the lengths, and hammered the ends into the joints. He clapped his hands together again and repeated his hammering. (He'd hidden his trowel in a nearby crack in the wall. Although he was among his own men, one of them might swap it for his own. That applied to Kilgas too.)

And then every thought was swept out of his head. All his memories and worries faded. He had only one idea—to fix the bend in the stovepipe and hang it up to prevent it smoking. He sent Gopchik for a length of wire—hang up the pipe near the window with it; that would be best.

In the corner there was another stove, a squat one with a brick chimney. It had an iron plate on top that grew red-hot, and sand was to be thawed and dried on it. This stove had already been lit, and the captain and Fetiukov were bringing up barrows of sand. You don't have to be very bright to carry a handbarrow. So the squad leader gave such work to people who'd been in positions of authority. Fetiukov had been a big shot in some office, with a car at his disposal.

At first Fetiukov had spat on the captain, bawled at him. But one punch on the jaw was enough. They got on all right after that.

The men bringing in the sand were edging over to the stove to warm up, but Tiurin drove them off.

"Look out, one of you is going to catch it in a hurry. Wait till we've got the place fixed up."

You've only to show a whip to a beaten dog. The frost was severe, but not as severe as the squad leader. The men scattered and went back to their jobs.

And Shukhov heard Tiurin say to Pavlo: "Stay here and keep them at it. I'm going to hand in the work report."

More depended on the work report than on the work itself. A clever squad leader was one who concentrated on the work report. That was what kept the men fed. He had to prove that work which hadn't been done had been done, to turn jobs that were rated low into ones that were rated high. For this a squad leader had to have his head screwed on, and to be on the right side of the inspectors. Their palms had to be greased too. But who benefited, then, from all those work reports? Let's be clear about it. The camp. The camp got thousands of extra rubles from the building organization and so could give higher bonuses to its guard-lieutenants, such as to Volkovoi for using his whip. And you? You got an extra six ounces of bread for your supper. A couple of ounces ruled your life.

Two buckets of water were carried in, but they had frozen on the way. Pavlo decided that there was no sense in doing it like this. Quicker to melt snow. They stood the buckets on the stove.

Gopchik brought along some new aluminum wire, used for electric leads.

"Ivan Denisovich," he said, as he turned it over to Shukhov, "it's good for making spoons. Teach me how to cast them."

Shukhov was fond of the kid. His own son had died young, and the two daughters he had left at home were grown up. Gopchik had been arrested for taking milk to the forest for Bendera's men,[6] and had been given an adult's term of imprisonment. He was like a puppy and he fawned on everyone. But he'd already learned cunning: he ate the contents of his food packages alone, sometimes during the night.

After all, you couldn't feed everyone.

They broke off a length of wire for the spoons and hid it in a corner. Shukhov knocked together a couple of planks into a stepladder and sent Gopchik up to hang the stovepipe. The boy, as nimble as a squirrel, climbed up into the beams, pounded in a nail or two, slipped the wire around them, and passed it under the pipe. Shukhov didn't begrudge him his energy; he made another bend in the pipe close to the end. Though there was little wind that day, there might be plenty tomorrow, and this bend would prevent the pipe from smoking. They mustn't forget that it was for themselves that they were fixing the stove.

Meanwhile, Senka had finished making the laths, and Gopchik was again given the job of nailing them up. The little devil crawled about up there, shouting down to the men.

The sun had risen higher, dispersing the haze. The two bright columns had gone. It was reddish inside the room. And now someone had got the stove going with the stolen wood. Made you feel a bit more cheerful.

"In January the sun warmed the flanks of the cow," Shukhov chanted.

Kilgas finished nailing the mortar trough together and, giving it an extra smash with his ax, shouted: "Listen, Pavlo, I won't take less than a hundred rubles from Tiurin for this job."

"You get three ounces," said Pavlo with a laugh.

"The prosecutor will make up the difference," shouted Gopchik from above.

"Stop that," Shukhov shouted, "stop." That wasn't the way to cut the roofing felt.

He showed them how to do it.

The men crept up to the stove, only to be chased away by Pavlo. He gave Kilgas some wood to make hods, for carrying the mortar up to the second story. He put on a couple more men to bring up the sand, others to sweep the snow off the scaffolding where the blocks were to be put, and another to take the hot sand off the top of the stove and throw it into the mortar trough.

A truck engine snorted outside. They were beginning to deliver the blocks. The first truck had got through. Pavlo hurried out and waved on

---

6. ***Bendera's men.*** Stepan Bendera was a leader from the West Ukraine who fought with the Germans against the Soviets in World War II.

the driver to where the blocks were to be dumped.

They put up one thickness of roofing felt, then a second. What protection could you expect from it? It was paper, just paper. All the same, it looked like a kind of solid wall. The room became darker, and this brightened the stove up.

Alyosha brought in some coal. Some of them shouted to tip it onto the stove, others not to. They wanted to warm up with the flames. Alyosha hesitated, not knowing whom to obey.

Fetiukov had found himself a cozy corner near the stove and, the fool, was holding his boots right up to the flames. The captain took him by the scruff of the neck and lugged him off to the barrow.

"You haul sand, you scum."

The captain might still have been on board ship—if you were told to do something you did it. He had grown haggard during the past month, but he kept his bearing.

In the end, all three windows were covered. Now the only light came through the door. And with it came the cold. So Pavlo had the upper half of the doorway boarded up but the lower left free, so that the men, by stooping, could get through it.

Meanwhile three trucks had driven up and dumped their loads of blocks. Now the problem was how to get the blocks up without the mechanical lift.

"Masons, let's go and look around," Pavlo called.

It was a job to be respected. Shukhov and Kilgas went up with Pavlo. The ramp was narrow enough anyhow, but now that Senka had robbed it of its rails you had to make sure you pressed close to the wall if you weren't going to fall off it. And still worse—the snow had frozen to the treads and rounded them; they offered no grip to your feet. How would they bring up the mortar?

They looked all around to find where the blocks should be laid. The men Pavlo had sent up were shoveling the snow from the top of the walls. Here was the place. You had to take an ax to the ice on the old workings, and then sweep them clean.

They figured out how best to bring up the blocks. They looked down. They decided that, rather than carry them up the ramp, four men would be posted down below to heave the blocks up to that platform over there, that another couple would move them on, and that two more would hand them up to the second story. That would be quicker than carrying them up the ramp.

The wind wasn't strong but you felt it. It would pierce them all right when they started laying. They'd have to keep behind the bit of wall that the old crew had begun on; it would give them some shelter. Not too bad—it'd be warmer that way.

Shukhov looked up at the sky and gasped—the sun had climbed almost to the dinner hour. Wonder of wonders! How time flew when you were working! That was something he'd often noticed. The days rolled by in the camp—they were over before you could say "knife." But the years, they never rolled by; they never moved by a second.

When they went down, they found that everyone had settled around the stove except the captain and Fetiukov, who were still hauling sand. Pavlo flew into a rage and sent eight men out at once to move blocks, two to pour cement into the box and mix it with sand, another for water, another for coal. But Kilgas gave his own orders:

"Well, men, we must finish with the barrows."

"Shall I give 'em a hand?" Shukhov volunteered.

"Yes, help them out," said Pavlo with a nod.

Just then they brought in a tank for melting snow. Someone had told the men that it was already noon.

Shukhov confirmed this.

"The sun's already reached its peak," he announced.

"If it's reached its peak," said the captain reflectively, "it's one o'clock, not noon."

"What do you mean?" Shukhov demurred. "Every old-timer knows that the sun stands highest at dinnertime."

"Old-timers, maybe," snapped the captain. "But since their day a new decree has been passed, and now the sun stands highest at one."

"Who passed that decree?"

"Soviet power."

The captain went out with a barrow. Anyway, Shukhov wouldn't have argued with him. Mean to say that the sun up in the sky must bow down to decrees too?

The sound of hammering continued as the men knocked together four hods.

"All right, sit down awhile and warm yourselves," said Pavlo to the two masons. "And you too, Senka. You can join them up there after dinner. Sit down."

So now they had a right to sit by the stove. Anyway they couldn't start laying the blocks before dinner and there was no point in carrying the mortar up there—it would freeze.

The coals were gradually glowing red-hot and throwing out a steady heat. But you felt it only when you were near them—everywhere else the shop was as cold as ever.

They took off their mittens. All four men held their hands up to the stove.

But you never put your feet near the flame if you're wearing boots. You have to remember that. If they're leather boots the leather cracks, and if they're valenki the felt becomes sodden and begins to steam and you don't feel any warmer. And if you hold them still nearer the flame then they scorch, and you'll have to drag along till the spring with a hole in your boot—getting another pair can't be counted on.

"What does Shukhov care?" Kilgas said. "Shukhov has one foot almost home."

"The bare one," said someone. They laughed (Shukhov had taken his mended boot off and was warming his foot rags).

"Shukhov's term's nearly up."

They'd given Kilgas twenty-five years. Earlier there'd been a spell when people were lucky: everyone to a man got ten years. But from '49 onward the standard sentence was twenty-five, irrespective. A man can survive ten years—but twenty-five, who can get through alive?

Shukhov rather enjoyed having everybody poke a finger at him as if to say: Look at him, his term's nearly up. But he had his doubts about it. Those zeks who finished their time during the war had all been "retained pending special instructions" and had been released only in '46. Even those serving three-year sentences were kept for another five. The law can be stood on its head. When your ten years are up they can say, "Here's another ten for you." Or exile you.

Yet there were times when you thought about it and you almost choked with excitement. Yes, your term really *is* coming to an end; the spool is unwinding. . . . Good lord! To step out to freedom, just walk out on your own two feet.

But it wasn't right for an old-timer to talk about it aloud, and Shukhov said to Kilgas: "Don't you worry about those twenty-five years of yours. It's not a fact you'll be in all that time. But that I've been in eight full years—now that is a fact."

Yes, you live with your feet in the mud and there's no time to be thinking about how you got in or how you're going to get out.

According to his dossier, Ivan Denisovich Shukhov had been sentenced for high treason. He had testified to it himself. Yes, he'd surrendered to the Germans with the intention of betraying his country and he'd returned from captivity to carry out a mission for German intelligence. What sort of mission neither Shukhov nor the interrogator could say. So it had been left at that—a mission.

Shukhov had figured it all out. If he didn't sign he'd be shot. If he signed he'd still get a chance to live. So he signed.

But what really happened was this. In February 1942 their whole army was surrounded on the northwest front. No food was parachuted to them. There were no planes. Things got so bad that they were scraping the hooves of dead horses—the horn could be soaked in water and eaten. Their ammunition was gone. So the Germans rounded them up in the forest, a few at a time. Shukhov was in one of these groups, and remained in German captivity for a day or two. Then five of them managed to escape. They stole through the forest and marshes again, and, by a miracle, reached their own lines. A machine gunner shot two of them on the spot, a third died of his wounds, but two got through. Had they been wiser they'd have said they'd been wandering in the forest, and then nothing would have happened. But they told the truth: they said they were escaped POWs. POWs, you pieces of garbage! If all five of them had got through, their statements could have been found to tally and they might have been believed. But with two it was hopeless. You've put your stupid heads together and cooked up that escape story, they were told.

Deaf though he was, Senka caught on that they were talking about escaping from the Germans, and said in a loud voice: "Three times I escaped, and three times they caught me."

Senka, who had suffered so much, was usually silent: he didn't hear what people said and didn't mix in their conversation. Little was known about him—only that he'd been in Buchenwald, where he'd worked with the underground and smuggled in arms for the mutiny; and how the Germans had punished him by tying his wrists behind his back, hanging him up by them, and whipping him.

"You've been in for eight years, Vanya," Kilgas argued. "But what camps? Not 'specials.' You had broads around. You didn't wear numbers. But try and spend eight years in a 'special'—doing hard labor. No one's come out of a 'special' alive."

"Broads! Boards you mean, not broads."

Shukhov stared at the coals in the stove and remembered his seven years in the North. And how he worked for three years hauling logs—for packing cases and railroad ties.

The flames in the campfires had danced up there too—at timber-felling during the night. Their chief made it a rule that any squad that had failed to meet its quota had to stay in the forest after dark.

They'd dragged themselves back to the camp in the early hours but had to be in the forest again next morning.

"N-no, brothers, . . . I think we have a quieter life here," he said with his lisp. "Here, when the shift's over, we go back to the camp whether our job's done or not. That's a law. And bread —three ounces more, at least, than up there. Here a man can live. All right, it's a 'special' camp. So what? Does it bother you to wear a number? They don't weigh anything, those numbers."

"A quieter life, do you call it?" Fetiukov hissed (the dinner break was getting near and everyone was huddling around the stove). "Men having their throats cut, in their bunks! And you call it quieter!"

"Not men—squealers." Pavlo raised a threatening finger at Fetiukov.

True enough, something new had started up. Two men, known to be squealers, had been found in their bunks one morning with their throats cut; and, a few days later, the same thing had happened to an innocent zek—someone must have gone to the wrong bunk. And one squealer had run off on his own to the head of the guardhouse and they'd put him inside for safety. Amazing. . . . Nothing like that had happened in the ordinary camps. Nor here, either, up till then.

Suddenly the whistle blew. It never began at full blast. It started hoarsely, as though clearing its throat.

Midday. Lay down tools. The dinner break.

Curse it, they'd waited too long. They should have gone off to the canteen long ago and taken their places in the line. There were eleven squads at work at the power station and there was room in the canteen for only two at a time.

Tiurin was still missing. Pavlo cast a rapid glance around the shop and said: "Shukhov and Gopchik, you come with me. Kilgas, as soon as I send Gopchik to you, bring the whole squad along."

Others took their places at the stove the moment any were vacated. The men all crept up to embrace it.

"Come on, don't spend all night!" others shouted. "Let's smoke."

They looked at one another to see who was going to light up. No one did. Either they had no tobacco or they were holding on to it, unwilling to let it be seen.

Shukhov went out with Pavlo. Gopchik loped behind like a hare.

"It's gotten warmer," Shukhov said at once. "Zero, no lower. Fine for laying the blocks."

They stole a glance at those blocks. The men had already thrown a lot of them up to the platform and quite a number had been shifted to the floor above.

Screwing up his eyes at the sun, Shukhov checked its position. He was thinking of the captain's "decree."

Out in the open the wind was still having its way and the cold was still fierce. Don't forget, it was telling them, this is January.

The zeks' canteen was no more than a shanty made of boards nailed together around a stove, with some rusty metal strips over the cracks. Inside, it was partitioned into a kitchen and an eating room. In neither was there a wood floor; it was pitted with the lumps and hollows that the men's feet had trodden into it. All that the kitchen consisted of was a square stove with a soup kettle stuck on top.

The kitchen was run by two men—a cook and a sanitation inspector. Every morning as he left the camp the cook drew an issue of grits from the main kitchen: about one-and-a-half ounces a head, probably. That made two pounds a squad, a little less than a pood[7] for the whole column. The cook didn't much like carrying the sack of grits the two miles himself, so he got a "helper" to carry it for him—better to give the "helper" an extra portion at the zeks' expense than burden his own back. There was water to be carried too, and firewood for the stove, and these were jobs the cook didn't much like either; so he found zeks to do them instead, for extra helpings at others' expense. What did it matter to him?

Then there was a rule that food must be eaten in the canteen; but the bowls couldn't be left there overnight, they'd have been swiped by civilians, so about fifty, not more, had to be brought in, and quickly washed after use and turned over to the next diners (an extra helping for the man who carried the bowls). To make sure that no one took bowls from the canteen, a man had to be posted at the door; but however careful he might be people took them just the same, either by distracting his attention or talking him into it. So someone else had to go over the whole site to collect the dirty bowls and bring them back to the kitchen. And *he* got an extra helping. And many others got one too.

All the cook himself did was this: he poured the grits into the pot, adding salt; he divided the fat between the pot and himself (good fat didn't reach the zeks, and the rancid all went into the soup kettle, so when there was an issue of rancid fat from the warehouse, the zeks welcomed it as an extra). Another thing he did: he stirred the kasha[8] when it was boiling.

The sanitation inspector had even less to do—he sat and watched: but when the oatmeal was ready he got his helping, as much as his belly would hold. And the cook too. Then the duty-squad leader arrived—the squad was changed every day—to have a taste and decide whether the stuff was good enough for the workers. He received a double portion.

The whistle sounded again. The squad leaders at once lined up, and the cook handed them bowls through the serving window. In the bottom of the bowls lay some oatmeal, how much you didn't ask, or try to judge by the weight. All you got if you opened your mouth was a bunch of swear words.

The steppe was barren and windswept, with a dry wind in the summer and a freezing one in winter. Nothing could ever grow in that steppe, less than nothing behind four barriers of barbed wire. Bread comes only from the bread cutter;

---

7. ***pood,*** a Russian weight equal to thirty-six pounds.
8. ***kasha,*** oatmeal.

oats are threshed only in the warehouse. And however much blood you sweat at work, however much you grovel on your belly, you'll force no food out of that earth; you'll get no more than the stinking authorities give you. And you don't even get that—because of the cook and the "help" and all the other trusties in soft jobs. They rob you here, they rob you in camp, they rob you even earlier—in the warehouse. And those who do the robbing don't swing picks. But you—you swing a pick and take what they give you. And get away from the serving window!

Pavlo and Shukhov, with Gopchik bringing up the rear, walked into the canteen. The men stood there so close to one another that you couldn't see either tables or benches. Some ate sitting down but most stood. The men of the 82nd, who'd been digging those holes half a day without a chance of getting warm, had been the first to get in after the whistle; now even after they'd finished eating they didn't leave. Where else could they warm up? The swearing fell off them like water off a duck's back—it was so much more comfortable here than in the cold. Pavlo and Shukhov elbowed their way in. They'd arrived at a good moment: one squad was being served, another was awaiting its turn, and there was only one deputy squad leader near the window. So they were well ahead of the rest.

"Bowls, bowls," the cook shouted through the window and people hurriedly handed them over. Shukhov was collecting another lot and turning them in, not to get extra oatmeal but to get what was coming to him quicker.

Behind the partition some "helpers" were already washing bowls—for extra oatmeal.

The cook began to serve the deputy squad leaders who stood ahead of Pavlo in the line.

"Gopchik," Pavlo shouted, over the heads of the men behind him.

"Here I am," came Gopchik's thin goatlike bleat from the door.

"Call the squad."

Off he went.

The main thing today was that the oatmeal was good—real oatmeal, the best sort. It wasn't often they had it. More often they got *magara* twice a day. But real oatmeal is filling, it's good.

How often had Shukhov in his youth fed oats to horses! Never had it occurred to him that there'd come a time when his whole soul would yearn for a handful of them.

"Bowls, bowls," shouted the cook.

Now the 104th was in line. That squad leader's deputy, up ahead, got his double helping and bounced away from the window.

This extra helping too was at the zeks' expense—but no one objected. The cook gave double helpings to all the squad leaders, and they either ate the extra helping themselves or gave it to their deputies. Tiurin gave his to Pavlo.

Shukhov's job now was to wedge himself in behind a table, oust two loafers, politely ask another prisoner to move, and clear a little space in front of him—for twelve bowls (to stand close together), with a second row of six, and two more on top. Next he had to take the bowls from Pavlo, repeating the number as he did so and keeping his eyes peeled—in case some outsider should grab a bowl from the table. And he had to see he wasn't bumped by someone's elbow so as to upset a bowl—right beside him people were leaving the table, stepping over the benches or squeezing in to eat. Yes, you had to keep your eyes peeled—was that fellow eating out of his own bowl? Or had he wormed his way up to one of the 104th's?

"Two, four, six," the cook counted at the window. He handed out the bowls two at a time—it was easier for him that way; otherwise he might count wrong.

"Two, four, six," Pavlo repeated quietly to himself, there at the window, in Ukrainian, and at once gave the bowls, in pairs, to Shukhov, who put them on the table. Shukhov didn't repeat the numbers aloud—but he counted more sharply than anyone.

"Eight, ten."

Why wasn't Gopchik bringing in the squad?

"Twelve, fourteen," the counting continued.

The kitchen ran out of bowls. Shukhov had a clear view through the window past Pavlo's head and shoulders. The cook put two bowls down on the counter and, keeping his hands on them, paused as though thinking. Must be bawling out the dishwashers. But just then another bunch of dirty bowls was pushed onto the counter. The cook let go of the two clean ones he'd filled and pushed back the pile of dirty ones.

Shukhov left the fourteen bowls he'd already stacked on the table, straddled a bench, took the two filled ones from the counter, and said quietly to Pavlo rather than to the cook: "Fourteen."

"Stop! Where are you taking those bowls?" shouted the cook.

"He's from our squad," Pavlo confirmed.

" 'Our squad,' but he's mixed up the count."

"Fourteen," Pavlo said with a shrug. Himself, he wouldn't have swiped the extra bowls, for as deputy squad leader he had to maintain his dignity; but now he was simply repeating what Shukhov had said—he could always blame him for the mistake.

"I've already counted fourteen," the cook expostulated.

"So you did, but you didn't pass them out. You kept your hands on them," Shukhov shouted. "Come and count for yourself if you don't believe us. Look, they're all here on the table."

As he spoke he'd noticed the two Estonians pushing through to him, and he shoved the two bowls into their hands as they passed. And he'd managed to get back to the table to see that all the bowls were in place—the next table hadn't swiped any, though they'd had plenty of opportunity to do so.

The cook's red face loomed large in the window.

"Where are those bowls?" he asked sternly.

"Here they are, at your service," yelled Shukhov. "Move along, scum, you're spoiling his view," he said to someone, giving him a shove. "Here they are, the pair of them." He picked up two bowls from the second row. "Here we have three rows of four, all nice and neat. Count them."

"Hasn't your squad come?" the cook asked, looking suspiciously around the small segment of the canteen he could see through the window—it had been kept narrow to prevent anyone looking into the kitchen and seeing how much was left in the kettle.

"No, none of 'em are here yet," said Pavlo, shaking his head.

"Then why the devil are you taking bowls when the squad's not here?"

"Here they come," yelled Shukhov.

And everyone heard the peremptory shouts of the captain at the door: "Why are you hanging around here?" he yelled, in his best quarterdeck voice. "If you've eaten, beat it and let others in."

The cook muttered something through the serving window. Then he drew himself up, and his hands could again be seen giving out the bowls: "Sixteen, eighteen."

Then he ladled the last portion, a double helping: "Twenty-three. That's all. Next squad."

The men of the 104th pushed through. Pavlo handed them bowls, passing them over the heads of the prisoners sitting at the second table.

In summer five could have sat on a bench, but now, as everyone was wearing thick clothes, four could barely fit in, and even they found it awkward to move their spoons.

Figuring that of the two bowls of oatmeal that had been swiped one at least would be his, Shukhov lost no time in applying himself to his first bowl. He drew his right knee up to his stomach, pulled his spoon ("Ust-Izhma, 1944") from under his boot top, removed his hat, put it in his left armpit, and ran his spoon under the edge of the kasha.

This is a moment that demands complete concentration, as you remove some of the scanty kasha from the bottom of the bowl, put it carefully into your mouth, and swirl it around there with your tongue. But Shukhov had to hurry, to show Pavlo he'd already finished and was waiting to be offered a second bowl. And there was Fetiukov to be dealt with. He had come into the canteen with the two Estonians and had witnessed the whole affair of the two extra bowls.

Now he stood there, straight in front of Pavlo, eying the four undistributed helpings as if to say that he ought to be given at least half a helping too.

Young swarthy Pavlo, however, went calmly on with his double portion, and there was no way of telling whether he noticed anyone standing there, or even remembered those extra bowls at all.

Shukhov finished his kasha. He had promised his belly two helpings, so one wasn't enough now to give him the full feeling he normally got from real oatmeal kasha.

He groped in his inside pocket for the scrap of clean rag, found the unfrozen crescent of crust, and meticulously used it to wipe off the last remnant of mush from the bottom of the bowl and any that still clung to the brim. Then he licked the crust clean, then repeated the whole process. The bowl looked now as if it had been washed, with a dull film, nothing more, on the inside surface. He handed it over his shoulder to one of the dish collectors and sat on, without replacing his hat.

Though it was Shukhov who had swindled the extra bowls, it was for Pavlo to distribute them.

Pavlo prolonged the agony a little longer while emptying his own bowl. He didn't lick it clean; he merely gave a lick to his spoon, tucked it away, and crossed himself. And then, very lightly, he touched—there wasn't room to move—two of the remaining four bowls. It meant he was giving them to Shukhov.

"Ivan Denisovich, take one for yourself and give the other to Tsezar."

Shukhov knew one of the bowls had to be taken to the office of Tsezar, who would never lower himself by going to the canteen or, for that matter, to the mess hall in camp. He knew it, but, all the same, when Pavlo touched the bowls his heart contracted. Could Pavlo be giving him both? And now, as Pavlo spoke, his heartbeat went back to normal.

Without losing any time he leaned over his lawful spoil and began to eat with deliberation, insensitive to the thumps on his back that the zeks in the next squad were dealing him. The only thing that vexed him was that the second bowl might still go to Fetiukov. Fetiukov was a past master at cadging, but he lacked the courage to swipe anything.

Nearby sat Captain Buinovsky. He had long finished his kasha. He didn't know the squad had two extra portions to dispose of. He didn't look around to see how much Pavlo still had left to hand out. He was simply relaxing, warming up. He was not strong enough to rise to his feet and go out into the cold or into that icy warming-up spot. He, like the very people he had just hounded out of the canteen with his rasping voice, was occupying a place he had no right to and getting in the way of the next squad. He was a newcomer. He was unused to the hard life of the zeks. Though he didn't know it, moments like this were particularly important to him, for they were transforming him from an eager, confident naval officer with a ringing voice into an inert, though wary, zek. And only in that inertness lay the chance of surviving the twenty-five years of imprisonment he'd been sentenced to.

People were already shouting at him and nudging him in the back to make him give up his place.

"Captain!" said Pavlo. "Hey, Captain."

Buinovsky shuddered as though he was being jerked out of a dream. He looked around.

Pavlo handed him a bowl of kasha. He didn't ask him whether he wanted it.

The captain's eyebrows shot up. He looked at the bowl as at something miraculous.

"Take it, take it," said Pavlo reassuringly, and picking up the last bowl—for the squad leader—went out.

An apologetic smile flitted over the captain's chapped lips. And this man, who had sailed around Europe and navigated the Great Northern Route, leaned happily over half a ladleful of thin oatmeal kasha, cooked entirely without fat—just oats and water.

Fetiukov cast angry looks at Shukhov and the captain and left the canteen.

But Shukhov thought Pavlo had been right. In time the captain would learn the ropes. Meanwhile, he didn't know how to live.

Shukhov still nursed a faint hope that Tsezar would give him his bowl of kasha. But it seemed unlikely, for more than two weeks had passed since Tsezar had received his last package.

After scraping the bottom and rim of the second bowl in the same way as the first, then licking the crust, Shukhov finally ate the crust itself. Then he picked up Tsezar's bowl of cold kasha and went out.

"It's for the office," he said, as he pushed past the man at the door who tried to stop him taking the bowl out.

The office was in a log cabin near the sentry house. As in the morning, smoke was curling out of the chimney. The stove was kept going by an orderly who worked as an errand boy too, picking up a few kopecks[9] here and there. They didn't begrudge him shavings or even logs for the office stove.

The outer door creaked as Shukhov opened it. Then came another door, caulked with oakum. Bringing with him a cloud of frosty vapor, he went in and quickly pulled the door shut (so that they wouldn't yell at him: "Hey, you scum, shut the door").

The office was as hot as a Turkish bath, it seemed to Shukhov. The sun, coming in through the icy windowpanes, played gaily in the room, not angrily as it did at the power station; and, spreading across the broad sunbeam, the smoke of Tsezar's pipe looked like incense in church. The stove glowed red right through. How they piled it on, the devils! Even the stovepipe was red-hot.

In an oven like that you only have to sit down a minute and you're fast asleep.

The office had two rooms. The door into the second one, occupied by the superintendent, was not quite closed, and through it the superintendent's voice was thundering:

"There's an overdraft on the expenses for labor and building materials. Right under your noses prisoners are chopping up valuable lumber, not to mention prefabricated panels, and using them for firewood at their warming-up spots. The other day the prisoners unloaded cement near the warehouse in a high wind. What's more, they carried it up to ten yards on barrows. As a result the whole area around the warehouse is ankle-deep in cement and the men are smothered in it. Just figure the waste!"

Obviously a conference was going on in there. With the foremen.

In a corner near the door an orderly sat lazing on a stool. Behind him, like a bent pole, stooped Shkuropatenko—B 219. That fathead—staring out of the window, trying to see, even now, whether anyone was pinching some of his precious prefabs! You didn't spot us *that* time, you snoop!

The bookkeepers, also zeks, were toasting bread at the stove. To prevent it from burning they'd fixed up a grill out of wire.

Tsezar was sprawling over his desk, smoking a pipe. His back was to Shukhov and he didn't notice him come in.

Opposite him sat X 123, a stringy old man who was serving a twenty-year sentence. He was eating kasha.

"No, my friend," Tsezar was saying in a gentle, casual way. "If one is to be objective one must acknowledge that Eisenstein is a genius. *Ivan the Terrible,* isn't that a work of genius? The dance of Ivan's guards, the masked *oprichniki!*[10] The scene in the cathedral!"

"Ham," said X 123 angrily, stopping his spoon in front of his lips. "It's all so arty there's no art left in it. Spice and poppyseed instead of everyday bread and butter! And then, the vicious political idea—the justification of individual tyranny. A mockery of the memory of three generations of Russian intelligentsia."

He ate as if his lips were made of wood. The kasha would do him no good.

"But what other interpretation could he have gotten away with?"

"Gotten away with? Ugh! Then don't call him a genius! Call him a toady, obeying a vicious dog's order. Geniuses don't adjust their interpretations to suit the taste of tyrants!"

"Hm, hm!" Shukhov cleared his throat. He hadn't the nerve to interrupt such a learned conversation. But there wasn't any sense in standing there, either.

Tsezar swung around and held out his hand for the bowl, not even looking at Shukhov, as though the kasha had materialized out of thin air.

"But listen," he resumed. "Art isn't a matter of *what* but of *how.*"

X 123 struck the table angrily with the edge of his hand.

---

9. *kopecks.* A kopeck is worth one one-hundredth of a ruble.

10. *Eisenstein* (ī′zen stīn′) ***. . . oprichniki*** (ô pryich′nyi kē). Tsezar and X 123 are discussing the artistic merit of Sergei Eisenstein, 1898–1948, a Russian film director and theorist. The classic film *Ivan the Terrible* (two parts, 1943–1946) is based on the life of the infamous first czar of a centrally governed Russian state. The *oprichniki* were the corps of Ivan's bodyguards who were used to crush any opposition.

"To the devil with your 'how' if it doesn't arouse any worthwhile feeling in me."

Shukhov stood there just as long as was decent for a man who had brought a bowl of kasha. After all, Tsezar might offer him a smoke. But Tsezar had quite forgotten his presence.

So Shukhov turned on his heel and went quietly out. The cold was bearable, he decided. The block-laying wouldn't go too badly.

As he walked along the path he caught sight in the snow of a short length of steel—a bit of a hacksaw blade.

He could conceive of no immediate use for it, but then you can never tell what you might need in the future. So he picked it up and slipped it into his pants pocket. He'd hide it at the power station. Waste not, want not.

The first thing he did on reaching the power station was to take his trowel out of its hiding place and slip it under the length of rope he wore around his waist. Then he took off for the machine shop.

After the sunlight the shop seemed quite dark and no warmer than outside. Sort of clammy.

All the men had crowded near the round iron stove that Shukhov had fixed, or near the one where the sand was steaming as it dried. Those who could find no room around the stoves sat on the edge of the mortar trough. Tiurin was seated against the stove, finishing the kasha that Pavlo had warmed up for him on it. The men were whispering to one another. They were in high spirits. One of them passed the news on to Shukhov: the squad leader had been successful in fixing the work report. He'd come back in a good mood.

What sort of work he'd found and how it had been rated was Tiurin's own business. What in fact had the squad done that first half of the day? Not a thing. They weren't paid for fixing the stoves, they weren't paid for arranging a place to warm up in—they had done that for themselves, not for the building site. But something had to be written in the report. Perhaps Tsezar was helping the squad leader to fix it up properly. It wasn't for nothing that Tiurin looked up to him. A cleverly fixed work report meant good rations for five days. Well, say four. Out of the five the authorities would wangle one for themselves by putting the whole camp onto the guaranteed minimum—the same for all, the best and the worst. Seems to be fair enough: equal rations for all. But it's an economy at the expense of our bellies. Well, a zek's belly can stand anything. Scrape through today somehow and hope for tomorrow.

This was the hope they all went to sleep with on the days they got only the guaranteed minimum.

But when you thought about it, it was five days' work for four days' food.

The shop was quiet. Zeks who had tobacco were smoking. The light was dim, and the men sat gazing into the fire. Like a big family. It was a family, the squad. They were listening to Tiurin as he talked to two or three of the men by the stove. Tiurin never wasted his words, and if he permitted himself to talk, then he was in a good humor.

He too hadn't learned to eat with his hat on, and when his head was bared he looked old. He was close-cropped like all of them, but in the light of the flames you could see how many white hairs he had.

"I'd be shaking in my boots before a battalion commander and here was the regimental commander himself. 'Red Army man Tiurin at your service,' I reported. The commander looked at me hard from under his beetle brows as he asked me my full name. I told him. Year of birth. I told him. It was in the thirties and I was, let's see, just twenty-two then, just a kid. 'Well, Tiurin, who are you serving?' 'I serve the working people,' I replied, with a salute. He blew up and banged both fists on the desk, bang! 'You're serving the working people, you pig, but what are you yourself?' I froze inside but I kept a grip on myself. 'Machine-gunner, first class. Excellent marks in military training and polit . . .' 'First class! What are you talking about, you scum? Your father's a kulak.[11] Look, this document has come from

11. ***kulak*** (kü läk'), a well-to-do peasant, farmer, or trader who opposed Soviet collectivization.

Kamen. Your father's a kulak and you've been hiding. They've been looking for you for two years.' I turned pale and kept my mouth shut. I hadn't written a line home for a year, to keep them from tracing me. I had no idea how they were living at home, and they knew nothing about me. 'Where's your conscience?' he shouted at me, all four bars on his collar shaking. 'Aren't you ashamed of yourself for deceiving the Soviet Power?' I thought he was going to hit me. But he didn't. He wrote out an order. To have me thrown out of the army at six o'clock that very day. It was November. They stripped me of my winter uniform and issued me a summer one, a third-hand one it must've been, and a short, tight jacket. I didn't know at the time that I didn't have to give up my winter uniform, just send it to them. . . . So they packed me off with a slip of paper: 'Discharged from the ranks . . . as a kulak's son.' A fine reference for a job! I had a four-day train journey ahead of me to get home. They didn't give me a free pass, they didn't provide me with even one day's rations. Just gave me dinner for the last time and threw me off the post.

"Incidentally, in '38, at the Kotlas deportation point, I met my former squadron commander. He'd been given ten years too. I learned from him that the regimental commander and the commissar were both shot in '37, no matter whether they were of proletarian or kulak stock, whether they had a conscience or not. So I crossed myself and said: 'So, after all, Creator, You do exist up there in heaven. Your patience is long-suffering but You strike hard.' "

After two bowls of kasha Shukhov so longed to smoke he felt he'd die if he didn't. And, reckoning he could buy those two glassfuls of home-grown tobacco from the Lett in Barracks 7, he said in a low voice to the Estonian fisherman: "Listen, Eino, lend me some for a cigarette till tomorrow. You know I won't let you down."

Eino gave him a hard look and then slowly turned his eyes to his "brother." They shared everything—one of them wouldn't spend even a pinch of tobacco without consulting the other. They muttered something together and Eino reached for his pink-embroidered pouch. Out of it he extracted a pinch of tobacco, factory-cut, placed it in Shukhov's palm, measured it with his eye, and added a few more strands. Just enough for one cigarette, no more.

Shukhov had a piece of newspaper ready. He tore off a scrap, rolled the cigarette, picked up a glowing coal from where it lay at Tiurin's feet—and drew and drew. A sweet dizziness went all through his body, to his head, to his feet, as if he had downed a glass of vodka.

The moment he began to smoke he felt, blazing at him from across the length of the shop, a pair of green eyes—Fetiukov's. He might have relented and given him a drag, the jackal, but he'd seen him pulling one of his fast ones already that day. No—better leave something for Senka instead. Senka hadn't heard the squad leader's tale and sat in front of the fire, poor guy, his head on one side.

Tiurin's pockmarked face was lit up by the flames. He spoke calmly, as if he were telling someone else's story:

"What rags I had, I sold for a quarter of their value. I bought a couple of loaves from under the counter—they'd already started bread rationing. I'd thought of hopping onto a freight train, but they'd just introduced some stiff penalties for that. And, if you remember, you couldn't buy tickets even if you had the money; you had to produce special little books or show travel documents. There was no getting onto the platform either—militiamen at the barrier, and guards wandering up and down the lines at both ends of the station. It was a cold sunset and the puddles were freezing over. Where was I going to spend the night? I straddled a brick wall, jumped over with my two loaves, and slipped into the public toilet. I waited in there for a while. No one was after me. I came out as though I were a soldier-passenger. The Vladivostok[12]-Moscow train was standing in the station. There was a crowd

---

12. ***Vladivostok*** (vlad′ə vos′tok).

around the hot-water faucet, people banging each other's heads with their teakettles. On the edge of the crowd I noticed a girl in a blue jersey—her kettle was a big one. She was scared of pushing through to the faucet. Didn't want her little feet stepped on or scalded. 'Look,' I said to her, 'hang on to these loaves and I'll get your kettle filled fast.' While I was doing so, off went the train. She was holding the loaves. She burst into tears. What was she going to do with them? She didn't mind losing the kettle. 'Run,' I called to her. 'I'll follow you.' Off she went, with me at her heels. I caught up with her and hoisted her onto the train with one arm. The train was going quite fast. I had a foot on it too. The conductor didn't slash at my fingers or shove me in the chest—there were other soldiers in the carriage and he took me for one of them."

Shukhov nudged Senka in the ribs—come on, finish this, you poor slob. He handed him the cigarette in his wooden holder. Let him take a drag, he's all right. Senka, the chump, accepted it like an actor, pressed one hand to his heart, and bowed his head. But, after all, he was deaf.

Tiurin went on:

"There were six, all girls, in a compartment to themselves—Leningrad students traveling back from technical courses. A lovely spread on their little table; raincoats swinging from coat hangers; expensive suitcases. They were going through life happily. All clear ahead for them. We talked and joked and drank tea together.

"They asked me what coach I was in. I sighed and told them the truth. 'I'm in a special coach, girls, heading straight for death.' "

There was silence in the shop. All you could hear was the stove roaring.

"Well, they gasped and moaned and put their heads together. And the result was they covered me with their raincoats on the top berth. They hid me all the way to Novosibirsk.[13] By the way, I was able to show my gratitude to one of them later—she was swept up by the Kirov wave[14] in '35. She had just about had it, working in a hard-labor team, and I got her fixed up in the tailoring shop."

"Shall we mix the mortar?" Pavlo asked Tiurin in a whisper.

Tiurin didn't hear him.

"I came up to our house at night, through the back garden. I left the same night. I took my little brother with me, took him to warmer parts, to Frunze. I'd nothing to give him to eat, and nothing for myself either. In Frunze some road workers were boiling asphalt in a pot, with all kinds of bums and stray kids sitting around. I sat down among them and said: 'Hey, you guys, take on my little brother as a learner. Teach him how to live.' They took him. I'm only sorry I didn't join the crooks myself."

"And you never saw your brother again?" asked the captain.

Tiurin yawned. "Never again."

He yawned once more. "Well, don't let it get you down, men," he said. "We'll live through it, even in this power station. Get going, mortar mixers. Don't wait for the whistle."

That's what a squad is. A guard can't get people to budge even in working hours, but a squad leader can tell his men to get on with the job even during the break, and they'll do it. Because he's the one who feeds them. And he'd never make them work for nothing.

If they were going to start mixing the mortar only when the whistle blew, then the masons would have to hang around waiting for it.

Shukhov drew a deep breath and got to his feet.

"I'll go up and chip the ice off."

He took with him a small hatchet and a brush and, for the laying, a mason's hammer, a leveling rod, a plumb, and a length of string.

Kilgas looked at him, a wry expression on his ruddy-cheeked face. Why should *he* jump up before his squad leader told him to? But after all, thought Shukhov, Kilgas didn't have to worry about feeding the squad. It was all the same to

---

13. ***Novosibirsk*** (nō'vō si birsk').
14. ***Kirov wave,*** refers to Sergey Kirov, a popular Communist leader. His assassination in 1934 was used by Stalin (who probably arranged it) as an excuse to remove suspected threats to Soviet leadership in the Great Purge (1934–1938).

him if he got a couple of ounces less—he'd manage on his parcels.

Even so, Kilgas stirred himself—you can't keep the squad waiting, he understood, just because of *you*.

"Wait a minute, Vanya, I'm coming too," he said.

"There you go, fathead. If you'd been working for yourself you'd have been on your feet in a hurry."

(There was another reason why Shukhov hurried—he wanted to lay his hands on that plumb before Kilgas. They'd drawn only one from the tool store.)

"Sure three are enough for the blocklaying?" Pavlo asked Tiurin. "Shouldn't we send another man up? Or won't there be enough mortar?"

Tiurin knitted his brows and thought.

"I'll be the fourth man myself, Pavlo. You work here on the mortar. It's a big box, we'll put six on the job. Work like this—take the mortar out from one end when it's ready and use the other for mixing some more. And see there's a steady supply. Not a moment's break."

"Ugh!" Pavlo sprang to his feet. He was young, his blood was fresh, camp life hadn't as yet worn him out. His face had been fattened on Ukrainian dumplings. "If *you're* going to lay blocks, I'll make the mortar for you myself. We'll see who's working hardest. Hey, where's the longest spade?"

That's what a squad leader is too. Pavlo had been a forest sniper, he'd even been on night raids. Try and make *him* break his back in a camp! But to work for the squad leader—that was different.

Shukhov and Kilgas came out onto the second story. They heard Senka creaking up the ramp behind them. So poor deaf Senka had guessed where they would be.

Only a start had been made with laying the blocks on the second-story walls. Three rows all around, a bit higher here and there. That was when the laying went fastest. From the knee to the chest, without the help of a scaffold.

All the platforms and trestles that had been there had been swiped by the zeks—some had been carried off to other buildings, some had been burned. Anything to prevent another squad getting them. But now everything had to be done right. Tomorrow they'd have to nail some trestles together; otherwise the work would be held up.

You could see a long way from up there—the whole snowclad, deserted expanse of the site (the zeks were hidden away, warming up before the dinner break ended), the dark watchtowers, and the sharp-tipped poles for the barbed wire. You couldn't see the barbed wire itself except when you looked into the sun. The sun was very bright; it made you blink.

And also, not far away, you could see the portable generator smoking away, blackening the sky. And wheezing too. It always made that hoarse, sickly noise before it whistled. There it went. So they hadn't, after all, cut too much off the dinner break.

"Hey, Stakhanovite![15] Hurry up with that plumb," Kilgas shouted.

"Look how much ice you've got left on your wall! See if you can chip it off before evening," Shukhov responded derisively. "*You* didn't have to bring your trowel up with you!"

They'd intended to start with the walls they'd been allocated before dinner, but Tiurin called from below: "Hey, men! We'll work in pairs, so that the mortar doesn't freeze in the hods. You take Senka with you on your wall, Shukhov, and I'll work with Kilgas. But to start with, you stand in for me, Gopchik, and clean up Kilgas's wall."

Shukhov and Kilgas looked at one another. Correct. Quicker that way.

They grabbed their axes.

And now Shukhov was no longer seeing that distant view where sun gleamed on snow. He was no longer seeing the prisoners as they wandered from the warming-up places all over the site, some to hack away at the holes they hadn't finished that morning, some to fix the mesh rein-

---

15. ***Stakhanovite*** (stə kä'nə vīt), worker who increases output under Stakhanovism, a Soviet system of rewarding individual enterprise.

forcement, some to put up beams in the workshops. Shukhov was seeing only his wall—from the junction at the left where the blocks rose in steps, higher than his waist, to the right to the corner where it met Kilgas's. He showed Senka where to remove ice and chopped at it energetically himself with the back and blade of his ax, so that splinters of ice flew all about and into his face. He worked with drive, but his thoughts were elsewhere. His thoughts and his eyes were feeling their way under the ice to the wall itself, the outer facade of the power station, two blocks thick. At the spot he was working on, the wall had previously been laid by some mason who was either incompetent or had stunk up the job. But now Shukhov tackled the wall as if it was his own handiwork. There, he saw, was a cavity that couldn't be leveled up in one row; he'd have to do it in three, adding a little more mortar each time. And here the outer wall bellied a bit—it would take two rows to straighten that. He divided the wall mentally into the place where he would lay blocks, starting at the point where they rose in steps, and the place where Senka was working, on the right, up to Kilgas's section. There in the corner, he figured, Kilgas wouldn't hold back; he would lay a few blocks for Senka, to make things easier for him. And, while they were puttering around in the corner, Shukhov would forge ahead and have half the wall built, so that his pair wouldn't be behindhand. He noted how many blocks he'd require for each of the places. And the moment the carriers brought the blocks up he shouted at Alyosha: "Bring 'em to me. Put 'em here. And here."

Senka had finished chipping off the ice, and Shukhov picked up a wire brush, gripped it in both hands, and went along the wall swishing it—to and fro, to and fro—cleaning up the top row, especially the joints, till only a snowy film was left on it.

Tiurin climbed up and, while Shukhov was still busy with his brush, fixed up a leveling rod in the corner. Shukhov and Kilgas had already placed theirs on the edges of their walls.

"Hey," called Pavlo from below. "Anyone alive up there? Take the mortar."

Shukhov broke into a sweat—he hadn't stretched his string over the blocks yet. He was rushing. He decided to stretch it for three rows at once, and make the necessary allowance. He decided also to take over a little of the outer wall from Senka and give him some of the inside instead; things would be easier for him that way.

Stretching his string along the top edge, he explained to Senka, with mouthings and gestures, where he was to work. Senka understood, for all his deafness. He bit his lips and glanced aside with a nod at Tiurin's wall. "Shall we make it hot for him?" his look said. We won't fall behind. He laughed.

Now the mortar was being brought up the ramp. Tiurin decided not to have any of it dumped beside the masons—it would only freeze while being shifted onto the hods. The men were to put down their barrows; the masons would take the mortar straight from them and get on with the laying. Meanwhile the carriers, not to waste time, would bring on the blocks that other prisoners were heaving up from below. As soon as the mortar had been scooped up from one pair of barrows, another pair would be coming and the first would go down. At the stove in the machine room, the carriers would thaw out any mortar that had frozen to their barrows—and themselves too, while they were at it.

The barrows came up two at a time—one for Kilgas's wall, one for Shukhov's. The mortar steamed in the frost but held no real warmth in it. You slapped it on the wall with your trowel and if you slowed down it would freeze, and then you'd have to hit it with the side of a hammer—you couldn't scrape it off with a trowel. And if you laid a block a bit out of true, it would immediately freeze too and set crooked; then you'd need the back of your ax to knock it off and chip away the mortar.

But Shukhov made no mistakes. The blocks varied. If any had chipped corners or broken edges or lumps on their sides, he noticed it at once and saw which way up to lay them and where they would fit best on the wall.

Here was one. Shukhov took up some of the steaming mortar on his trowel and slapped it into the appropriate place, with his mind on the joint below (this would have to come right in the middle of the block he was going to lay). He slapped on just enough mortar to go under the one block. He snatched it from the pile—carefully, though, so as not to tear his mittens, for with cement blocks you can do that in no time. He smoothed the mortar with his trowel and then—down with the block! And without losing a moment he leveled it, patting it with the side of the trowel—it wasn't lying exactly right—so that the wall would be truly in line and the block lie level both lengthwise and across. The mortar was already freezing.

Now if some mortar had oozed out to the side, you had to chop it off as quickly as possible with the edge of your trowel and fling it over the wall (in summer it would go under the next brick, but now that was impossible). Next you took another look at the joint below, for there were times when the block was not completely intact but had partially crumbled. In that event, you slapped in some extra mortar where the defect was, and you didn't lay the block flat—you slid it from side to side, squeezing out the extra mortar between it and its neighbor. An eye on the plumb. An eye on the surface. Set. Next.

The work went with a rhythm. Once two rows were laid and the old faults leveled up it would go quite smoothly. But now was the time to keep your eyes peeled.

Shukhov forged ahead; he pressed along the outside wall to meet Senka. Senka had parted with Tiurin in the corner and was now working along the wall to meet him.

Shukhov winked at the mortar carriers. Bring it up, bring it up. Steady. That's the ticket. He was working so fast he had no time to wipe his nose.

He and Senka met and began to scoop out of the same mortar hod. It didn't take them long to scrape it to the bottom.

"Mortar!" Shukhov shouted over the wall.

"Coming up!" shouted Pavlo.

Another load arrived. They emptied that one too—all the liquid mortar in it, anyhow. The rest had already frozen to the sides. Scrape it off yourselves! If you don't, you're the ones who'll be taking it up and down again. Get going! Next!

And now Shukhov and the other masons felt the cold no longer. Thanks to the urgent work, the first wave of heat had come over them—when you feel wet under your coat, under your jacket, under your shirt and your vest. But they didn't stop for a moment; they hurried on with the laying. And after about an hour they had their second flush of heat, the one that dries up the sweat. Their feet didn't feel cold, that was the main thing. Nothing else mattered. Even the breeze, light but piercing, couldn't distract them from the work. Only Senka stamped his feet—he had enormous ones, poor slob, and they'd given him a pair of valenki too tight for him.

From time to time Tiurin would shout "Mo-o-rtar," and Shukhov would shout "Mo-o-rtar"—he was shouting to his own men. When you're working all out, you're a sort of squad leader to your neighbors yourself. It was up to Shukhov to keep up with the other pair. Now, he'd have made his own brother sweat to hurry up with the mortar.

At first, after dinner, Buinovsky had carried mortar with Fetiukov. But the ramp was steep and dangerous, and the captain dragged his feet to begin with. Shukhov urged him on gently: "Quicker, Captain. Blocks, Captain."

Every time Buinovsky came up he worked faster. Fetiukov, on the other hand, grew lazier and lazier. He'd tilt the barrow as he came up, the lousy scum, so that the mortar would slop out of it and then it'd be lighter to carry.

Shukhov poked him in the back: "Hey, you filthy lowlife. When you were an overseer I'll bet you made your men sweat."

Buinovsky appealed to the squad leader: "Give me a man to work with. I won't go on working with this piece of garbage."

Tiurin agreed. He sent Fetiukov to heave up blocks from below; and made him work, on top of that, where the number of blocks he handled was counted separately. He told Alyosha to work with the captain. Alyosha was a quiet man; anyone could order him about.

"It's all hands on deck, sailor," the captain urged. "See how fast they're laying blocks?"

Alyosha smiled meekly. "If we have to work faster then let's work faster. Anything you say."

And tramped down for the next load.

Thank God for the man who does his job and keeps his mouth shut!

Tiurin shouted to someone down below. Another truckload of blocks had apparently arrived. Not one had been brought here for six months; now they were pouring in. You could work really fast as long as the trucks brought blocks. But this wouldn't go on. Later there'd be a holdup in the delivery and then you'd stand idle yourself.

Tiurin was bawling out someone else down below. Something about the lift. Shukhov would have liked to know what was up but he'd no time to find out—he was leveling his wall. The carriers came up and told him: a mechanic had come to repair the motor of the lift, and the superintendent of electrical repairs, a civilian, was with him. The mechanic was tinkering with the motor; the superintendent watched.

That was according to the rules: one man works, one man watches.

Good if they fixed the lift now. It could be used for both blocks and mortar.

Shukhov was laying his third row (Kilgas too was on his third), when up the ramp came yet another snoop, another chief—building-foreman Der. A Muscovite.[16] Used to work in some ministry, so they said.

Shukhov was standing close to Kilgas, and drew his attention to Der.

"Pfah!" said Kilgas contemptuously. "I don't usually have anything to do with the big shots. But you call me if he falls off the ramp."

And now Der took up his post behind the masons and watched them work. Shukhov hated these snoops like poison. Trying to make himself into an engineer, the fathead! Once he'd shown Shukhov how to lay bricks—and given him a belly laugh. A man should build a house with his own hands before he calls himself an engineer.

At Shukhov's village of Temgenovo there were no brick houses. All the cottages were built of wood. The school too was a wooden building, made from six-foot logs. But the camp needed masons and Shukhov, glad to oblige, became a

16. ***Muskovite*** (mus'kə vīt), a native or inhabitant of Moscow.

mason. A man with two trades to his credit can easily learn another ten.

No, Der didn't fall off the ramp, though once he stumbled. He came up almost on the double.

"Tiu-u-urin," he shouted, his eyes popping out of his head. "Tiu-u-urin."

At his heels came Pavlo. He was carrying the spade he'd been working with.

Der was wearing a regulation camp coat but it was new and clean. His hat was stylish, made of leather, though, like everyone else's, it bore a number—B 731.

"Well?" Tiurin went up to him trowel in hand, his hat tilted over one eye.

Something out of the ordinary was brewing. Something not to be missed. Yet the mortar was growing cold in the barrows. Shukhov went on working—working and listening.

"What do you think you're doing?" Der spluttered. "This isn't a matter for the guardhouse. This is a criminal offense, Tiurin. You'll get a third term for this."

Only then did Shukhov catch on to what was up. He glanced at Kilgas. He'd understood too. The roofing felt. Der had spotted it on the windows.

Shukhov feared nothing for himself. His squad leader would never give him away. He was afraid for Tiurin. To the squad Tiurin was a father; for *them* he was a pawn. Up in the North they readily gave squad leaders a second term for a thing like this.

Ugh, what a face Tiurin made. He threw down his trowel and took a step toward Der. Der looked around. Pavlo lifted his spade.

He hadn't grabbed it for nothing.

And Senka, for all his deafness, had understood. He came up, hands on hips. And Senka was built solid.

Der blinked, gave a sort of twitch, and looked around for a way of escape.

Tiurin leaned up against him and said quite softly, though distinctly enough for everyone to hear: "Your time for giving terms has passed, you swine. If you say one word, you bloodsucker, it'll be your last day on earth. Remember that."

Tiurin shook, shook uncontrollably.

Hatchet-faced Pavlo looked Der straight in the eyes. A look as sharp as a razor.

"Now, men, take it easy." Der turned pale and edged away from the ramp.

Without another word Tiurin straightened his hat, picked up his trowel, and walked back to his wall.

Pavlo, very slowly, went down the ramp with his spade.

Slo-o-owly.

Der was as scared to stay as to leave. He took shelter behind Kilgas and stood there.

Kilgas went on laying blocks, the way they count out pills at a drugstore—like a doctor, measuring everything so carefully—his back to Der, as if he didn't even know he was there.

Der stole up to Tiurin. Where was all his arrogance?

"But what shall I tell the superintendent, Tiurin?"

Tiurin went on working. He said, without turning his head: "You will tell him it was like that when we arrived. We came and that's how it was."

Der waited a little longer. They weren't going to bump him off now, he saw. He took a few steps and put his hands in his pockets.

"Hey, S 854," he muttered. "Why are you using such a thin layer of mortar?"

He had to get back at someone. He couldn't find fault with Shukhov for his joints or for the straightness of his line, so he decided he was laying the mortar too thin.

"Permit me to point out," Shukhov lisped derisively, "that if the mortar is laid on thick in weather like this, the place will be like a sieve in the spring."

"You're a mason. Listen to what a foreman has to tell you," Der said with a frown, puffing out his cheeks.

Well, here and there it might be a bit on the thin side. He could have used a little more—but only, after all, if he'd been laying the blocks in decent conditions, not in winter. The man ought to have a heart. You've got to show some results.

But what was the good of trying to explain? He didn't want to understand.

Der went quietly down the ramp.

"You get me that lift repaired," Tiurin sang out after him. "What do you think we are—pack horses? Carrying blocks up to the second story by hand."

"They'll pay you for taking them up," Der called back from the ramp, quite humbly.

"At the wheelbarrow rate? Child's play, pushing up a wheelbarrow. We've got to be paid for carrying them up by hand."

"Don't think I'm against it. But the bookkeepers won't agree to the higher rate."

"The bookkeepers! I've got a whole squad sweating to keep those four masons at work. How much do you think we'll earn?" Tiurin shouted, pressing on without a break.

"Mort-ar," he called down.

"Mort-ar," echoed Shukhov. They'd leveled off the whole of the third row. On the fourth they'd really get going. Time to stretch the string for the next row, but he could manage this way too.

Der went off across the open ground, looking haggard. To warm up in the office. Something must have been eating him. But he should have thought a bit before taking on a wolf like Tiurin. He should keep pleasant with squad leaders like that; then he'd have nothing to worry about. The camp authorities didn't insist on his doing any real hard work, he received top-level rations, he lived in a separate cabin—what else did he want? Giving himself airs, trying to be smart.

The men coming up with the mortar said the mechanic and superintendent had left. The motor was past repair.

Very well, haul 'em up by hand.

For as long as Shukhov had worked with machinery the machines had either broken down or been smashed by the zeks. He'd seen them wreck a log conveyer by shoving a beam under the chain and leaning hard on it, to give themselves a breather; they were stacking log by log with never a moment to stretch their backs.

"Curse the whole stinking lot of you!" shouted Tiurin, warming up.

"Pavlo's asking how you're fixed for mortar," someone called from below.

"Mix some more."

"We've got half a box mixed."

"Mix another."

What a pace they set! They were driving along the fifth row now. They'd had to bend over double when they were working on the first row, but now the wall had risen shoulder-high. And why shouldn't they race on? There were no windows or doors to allow for—just a couple of adjoining blank walls and plenty of blocks. Shukhov should have stretched a string higher but there was no time for it.

"The eighty-second have gone off to hand in their tools," Gopchik reported.

Tiurin looked at him witheringly. "Mind your own business, squirt. Bring some blocks."

Shukhov looked about. Yes, the sun was beginning to set. It had a grayish appearance as it sank in a red haze. And they'd got into the swing—couldn't be better. They'd started on the fifth row now. Ought to finish it today. Level it off.

The mortar carriers were snorting like winded horses. Buinovsky was quite gray in the face. He might not be forty but he wasn't far off it.

The cold was growing keener. Busy as were Shukhov's hands, the frost nipped his fingers through the shabby mittens. And it was piercing his left boot too. He stamped his foot. Thud, thud.

By now he needn't stoop to the wall, but he still had to bend his aching back for each block and each scoop of mortar.

"Hey, boys!" he pestered the men handling the blocks. "You'd better put them on the wall for me. Heave 'em up here."

The captain would gladly have obliged but lacked the strength. He wasn't used to the work. But Alyosha said: "All right, Ivan Denisovich. Show me where to put them."

You could count on Alyosha. Did whatever was asked of him. If everybody in the world was like that, Shukhov would have done likewise. If a man asks for help why not help him? Those Baptists had something there.

The rail clanged. The signal went dinning all over the site and reached the power station. They'd been caught with some unused mortar. Ugh, just when they'd got into the swing of it!

"Mortar! Mortar!" Tiurin shouted.

A new boxful had only just been mixed. They had to go on laying; there was no other way. If they left anything in the box, next morning they could throw the whole lot of it out—the mortar would have petrified; it wouldn't yield to a pickax.

"Don't let me down, brothers," Shukhov shouted.

Kilgas was fuming. He didn't like speedups. But he pressed on all the same. What else could he do?

Pavlo ran up with a barrow, a trowel in his belt, and began laying himself. Five trowels on the job now.

Now look out for where the rows meet. Shukhov visualized what shape of block was needed there, and shoving a hammer into Alyosha's hand egged him on: "Knock a bit off this one."

Haste makes waste. Now that all of them were racing one another Shukhov bided his time, keeping an eye on the wall. He pushed Senka to the left and took over the laying himself toward the main corner on the right. It would be a disaster if the walls overlapped or if the corner wasn't level. Cost him half a day's work tomorrow.

"Stop!" He shoved Pavlo away from a block and leveled it himself. And from his place in the corner he noticed that Senka's section was sagging. He hurried over to Senka and leveled it out with two blocks.

The captain brought up a load of mortar, enough for a good horse.

"Another two barrowsful," he said.

The captain was tottering. But he went on sweating away. Shukhov had had a horse like that once. He'd thought a lot of that horse but then they'd driven it to death. They'd worked the hide off it.

The top rim of the sun dipped below the horizon. Now, without Gopchik having to tell them, they saw that the squads had not only turned in their tools but were pouring up to the gates. No one came out into the open immediately after the signal—only a fool would go and freeze out there. They sat in the warmth. But the moment came, by agreement between the squad leaders, when all the squads poured out together. Without this agreement, the zeks, a stubborn lot, would have sat each other out in the warmth till midnight.

Tiurin himself realized that he'd cut things too fine. The man in charge of the tool store must be cursing him out.

"Hey," he shouted, "use enough of that stuff! Carriers! Go and scrape the big box. Throw what's left into that hole there and scatter some snow on it to keep it hidden. You, Pavlo, take a couple of men, collect the tools, and hand them in. I'll send Gopchik after you with the three trowels. We'll use up the last two loads of mortar before we knock off."

Everyone dashed to his job. They took Shukhov's hammer from him and wound up his string. The mortar carriers and the block lifters hurried down into the machine room. They'd nothing more to do up there. Three masons remained on top—Kilgas, Senka, and Shukhov. Tiurin walked around to see how much wall they'd built. He was pleased. "Not bad, eh? In half a day. Without any lift."

Shukhov noticed there was a little mortar left in Kilgas's hod. He didn't want to waste it, but was worried that the squad leader might be reprimanded if the trowels were handed in late.

"Listen, men," he said, "give your trowels to Gopchik. Mine's not on the list. So I won't have to hand it in. I'll keep going."

Tiurin said with a laugh: "How can we ever let you out? We just can't do without you."

Shukhov laughed too, and went on working.

Kilgas took the trowels. Senka went on handing blocks to Shukhov. They poured Kilgas's mortar into Shukhov's hod.

Gopchik ran across to the tool store, to overtake Pavlo. The rest were just as anxious to be in time, and hurried over to the gates, without Tiurin. A squad leader is a power, but the escort is a greater power still. They list latecomers, and that means the guardhouse for you.

There was a terrible crowd near the gates now. Everyone had collected there. It looked as if the escort had come out and started counting.

(They counted the prisoners twice on the way out: once before they unbolted the gates, to make sure they were safe in opening them, and again when the gates had been opened and the prisoners were passing through. And if they thought they'd miscounted, they recounted outside the gates.)

"To the devil with the mortar," said Tiurin, with a gesture of impatience. "Sling it over the wall."

"Don't wait, leader. Go ahead, you're needed there." (Shukhov usually addressed Tiurin, more respectfully, as Andrei Prokofievich, but now, after working like that, he felt equal to the squad leader. He didn't put it to himself, "Look, I'm your equal," he just knew it.) And as Tiurin strode down the ramp he called after him, jokingly: "Why do these swine make the workday so short? We were just getting into our stride when they call it off."

Shukhov was left alone now with Senka. You couldn't say much to him. Besides, you didn't have to tell him things: he was the wisest of them all; he understood without need of words.

Slap on the mortar. Down with the block. Press it home. See it's straight. Mortar. Block. Mortar. Block . . .

Wasn't it enough that Tiurin had told them himself not to bother about the mortar? Just throw it over the wall and forget about it. But Shukhov wasn't made that way—eight years in a camp couldn't change his nature. He worried about anything he could make use of, about every scrap of work he could do—nothing must be wasted without good reason.

Mortar. Block. Mortar. Block . . .

"Finish, you pig," shouted Senka. "Let's get out of here."

He picked up a barrow and ran down the ramp.

But Shukhov—and if the guards had put the dogs on him it would have made no difference—ran to the back and looked about. Not bad. Then he ran and gave the wall a good look over, to the left, to the right. His eye was as accurate as a carpenter's level. Straight and even. His hands were as young as ever.

Discussion

1. While awaiting work orders, a few of the 104th exhibit their own ways of coping with prison life. Explain what the behavior of each of the following characters reveals. **(a)** Shukhov's eating of the bread; **(b)** Fetiukov's sorting of scrounged cigarette butts; **(c)** Buinovsky's "commanding" Fetiukov to stop; **(d)** Senka's commenting about the captain's earlier show of pride.

2. In the prisoners' view, what advantages does a snowstorm have? What disadvantages?

3. **(a)** Give examples of how the zeks' work performance is hindered by the authorities. **(b)** What practices are used to disguise the inadequacies in the prison situation? **(c)** Do the zeks benefit from them? Explain.

4. Shukhov's nearness to the end of his sentence makes him the object of the others' kidding. **(a)** Why is he uneasy about his situation? **(b)** What is the actual story behind his arrest? **(c)** Do you agree or disagree with his view of the "quieter life" of his present camp? Give reasons for your answer.

5. **(a)** Why does Shukhov expect Pavlo to give him one of the stolen bowls of oatmeal? **(b)** Why does he agree with Pavlo's giving a bowl to Buinovsky? **(c)** What zeklike characteristic does Shukhov display in regard to Tsezar's share of the oatmeal?

6. Tiurin recalls the period of turmoil that occurred when he was branded as a "kulak's son." What do you think the following reveal about his character? **(a)** his reaction upon learning the fate of his regimental commander and commissar; **(b)** his success in boarding the Vladivostok-Moscow train; **(c)** his finding work for a victim of the Kirov wave; **(d)** his apparent detachment in relating his story.

7. Though the roofing felt is helpful to the squad at first, it becomes a point of conflict later. Explain.

8. Describe the transformation Shukhov undergoes while building the wall in terms of his **(a)** level of concentration; **(b)** sense of teamwork; **(c)** relationship to his superiors; **(d)** physical condition.

Vocabulary

Pronunciation

Use the Glossary and pronunciation key to answer the questions about the words listed below. Be sure you know the meanings of the words.

commiserate   proletarian
intelligentsia   expostulate
demur

1. Which word has a syllable with a vowel sound similar to the *er* in *term?*

2. Which word has a second syllable with a vowel sound similar to the *o* in *hot?*

3. Which word has a first syllable with a vowel sound similar to the *o* in *open?*

4. Which word has the most syllables?

5. Which words have both primary- and secondary-accented syllables?

Shukhov dashed down the ramp.

Senka was already out of the machine shop and running down the slope.

"Come on, come on," he shouted over his shoulder.

"Run ahead. I'll catch up," Shukhov gestured.

But he went into the machine shop. He couldn't simply throw his trowel down. He might not be there the next day. They might send the squad off to the Socialist Way of Life settlement. It could be six months before he returned to the power station. But did that mean he was to throw down his trowel? If he'd swiped it he had to hang on to it.

Both the stoves had been doused. It was dark, frightening. Frightening not because it was dark but because everyone had left, because he alone might be missing at the count by the gates, and the guards would beat him.

Yet his eyes darted here, darted there, and, spotting a big stone in the corner, he pulled it aside, slipped his trowel under it, and hid it. So that's that.

Now to catch up with Senka. Senka had stopped after running a hundred paces or so. Senka would never leave anyone in a jam. Pay for it? Then together.

They ran neck and neck, the tall and the short. Senka was a head taller than Shukhov, and a big head it was too.

There are loafers who race one another of their own free will around a stadium. Those devils should be running after a full day's work, with aching back and wet mittens and worn-out valenki—and in the cold too.

They panted like mad dogs. All you could hear was their hoarse breathing.

Well, Tiurin was at the gates. He'd explain.

They were running straight into the crowd. It scared you.

Hundreds of throats booing you at once, and cursing you up and down. Wouldn't *you* be scared if you had five hundred men blowing their tops at you?

But what about the guards? That was the chief thing.

No. No trouble with them. Tiurin was there, in the last row. He must have explained. Taken the blame on his own shoulders.

But the men yelled, the men swore. And what swearing! Even Senka couldn't help hearing and, drawing a deep breath, gave back as good as he got. He'd kept quiet all his life—but now, how he bellowed! Raised his fists too, ready to pick a fight right away. The men fell silent. Someone laughed.

"Hey, one hundred and fourth," came a shout. "Your deaf guy's a fake. We just tested him."

Everyone laughed. The guards too.

"Form fives."

They didn't open the gates. They didn't trust themselves. They pushed the crowd back from the gates (everyone stuck to the gates like idiots—as if they'd get out quicker that way!).

"Form fives. First. Second. Third . . ."

Each five, as it was called, took a few paces forward.

While Shukhov was recovering his breath he looked up. The moon had risen and was frowning, crimson-faced. Yesterday at this hour it had stood much higher.

Pleased that everything had gone so smoothly, Shukhov nudged the captain in the ribs and said: "Listen, Captain, where does this science of yours say the old moon goes afterward?"

"Where does it go? What do you mean? What stupidity! It's simply not visible."

Shukhov shook his head and laughed. "Well, if it's not visible, how d'you know it's there?"

"So, according to you," said the captain, unable to believe his ears, "it's another moon every month."

"What's strange about that? People are born every day. Why not a moon every four weeks?"

"Phaugh!" said the captain and spat. "I've never met a sailor as stupid as you in my life. So where do *you* think the old moon goes?"

"That's what I'm asking you. Where does it go?" Shukhov showed his teeth in a smile.

"Well, tell me. Where does it go?"

Shukhov sighed and said with a slight lisp: "In our village, folk say God crumbles up the old moon into stars."

"What savages!" The captain laughed. "I've never heard that one. Then you believe in God, Shukhov?"

"Why not?" asked Shukhov, surprised. "Hear Him thunder and try not to believe in Him."

"But why does God do it?"

"Do what?"

"Crumble the moon into stars. Why?"

"Well, can't you understand?" said Shukhov. "The stars fall down now and then. The gaps have to be filled."

"Turn around, you slob," a guard shouted. "Get in line."

The count had almost reached them. The twelfth five of the fifth hundred had moved ahead, leaving only Buinovsky and Shukhov at the back.

The escort was worried. There was a discussion over the counting boards. Somebody missing. Again somebody missing. Why can't they learn to count?

They'd counted 462. Ought to be 463.

Once more they pushed everybody back from the gates (the zeks had crowded forward again).

"Form fives. First. Second . . ."

What made this recounting so infuriating was that the time wasted on it was the zeks' own, not the authorities'. They would still have to cross the steppe, get to the camp, and line up there to be searched. The columns would come in from all sides on the double, trying to be first at the frisking and into the camp. The column that was back first was top dog in the camp that evening—the mess hall was theirs, they were first in line to get their packages, first at the private kitchen, first at the C.E.D. to pick up letters or hand in their own to be censored, first at the dispensary, the barber's, the baths—first everywhere.

And the escort too is in a hurry to get the zeks in and be off for the night. A soldier's life isn't much fun either—a lot of work, little time.

And now the count had come out wrong.

As the last few fives were called forward Shukhov began to hope that there were going to be three in the last row after all. No, curse it, two again.

The tellers went to the head guard with their tally boards. There was a consultation. The head guard shouted: "Squad leader of the hundred and fourth."

Tiurin took half a pace forward. "Here."

"Did you leave anyone behind in the power station? Think."

"No."

"Think again. I'll knock your head off. . . ."

"No, I'm quite sure."

But he stole a glance at Pavlo. Could anyone have dropped off to sleep in the machine shop?

"Form squads," the head guard shouted.

They had formed the groups of five just as they happened to be standing. Now they began to shift about. Voices boomed out: "Seventy-fifth over here," "This way, thirteenth," "Thirty-second here."

The 104th, being all in the rear, formed there too. They were empty-handed to a man, Shukhov noticed; like idiots, they'd worked on so late they'd collected no firewood. Only two of them were carrying small bundles.

This game was played every evening: before the job was over the workers would gather chips, sticks, and broken laths, and tie them together with bits of string or ragged tapes to carry back with them. The first raid on their bundles would take place near the gates to the work site. If either the superintendent or one of the foremen was standing there, he'd order the prisoners to throw down their firewood (millions of rubles had gone up in smoke, yet there they were thinking they'd make up the losses with kindling). But a zek calculated his own way: if everyone brought even a few sticks back with him the barracks would be warmer. Barrack orderlies were issued ten pounds of coal dust a stove and little heat could be squeezed out of that. So the men would break up sticks or saw them short and slip them under their coats.

The escort never made the zeks drop their firewood at the gates to the work site. For one thing, it would have been an offense to the uniform; and secondly they had their hands on machine guns, ready to shoot. But just before entering the zone several ranks in the column were ordered to throw their stuff down. The escort, however, robbed mercifully—they had to leave something for the guards, and for the zeks themselves, who otherwise wouldn't bring any with them.

So every zek brought some firewood along with him every evening. You never knew when you might get it through or when they'd grab it.

While Shukhov was scouring the ground in search of a few chips, Tiurin had finished counting the squad.

"One hundred and fourth all present," he reported to the head guard.

Just then Tsezar rejoined his own squad from the group of office workers. His pipe was glowing as he puffed away at it; his dark mustache was tipped with frost.

"Well, Captain, how'd it go?" he asked.

A man who's warm can't understand a man who's freezing. "How'd it go?" What a stupid question!

"If you really want to know," said the captain, his shoulders sagging, "worked so hard I can hardly straighten my back."

You might give me something to smoke was what he meant.

Tsezar gave him something to smoke. The captain was the only man in the squad he stuck to. He could unburden his heart to him—to no one else.

"There's a man missing from the thirty-second. From the thirty-second," everybody began to mutter.

The deputy squad leader of the 32nd scurried

off with another young fellow to search the repair shops. And in the crowd people kept asking: Who? How? Where? Soon it reached Shukhov's ears that it was the dark little Moldavian[1] who was missing. The Moldavian? Not the one who, it was said, had been a Rumanian spy, a real spy?

You could find up to five spies in each squad. But they were fakes, prison-made spies. They passed as spies in their dossiers, but really they were simply ex-POWs. Shukhov himself was one of these "spies."

But the Moldavian was genuine.

The head of the escort ran his eye down the list and grew black in the face. After all, if the spy were to escape what would happen to the head of the escort?

In the crowd everybody, including Shukhov, flew into a rage. Were they going through all this for that lowlife, that slimy little snake, that stinking worm? The sky was already quite dark; what light there was came from the moon. You could see the stars—this meant the frost was gathering strength for the night—and that runty swine was missing. What, haven't you had your bellyful of work, you miserable idiot? Isn't the official spell of eleven hours, dawn to dusk, long enough for you? Just you wait, the prosecutor will add something.

Odd that anyone could work so hard as to ignore the signal to knock off.

He completely forgot that he'd been working like that himself only an hour ago—that he'd been annoyed with the others for assembling at the gate too early. Now he was chilled to the bone and his fury mounted with everyone else's; were they to be kept waiting another half hour by that Moldavian? If the guards handed him over to the zeks they'd tear him apart, like wolves with a lamb.

Yes, the cold was coming into its own now. No one stood quiet. They either stamped their feet where they stood or walked two or three paces back and forth.

People were discussing whether the Moldavian could have escaped. Well, if he'd fled during the day that was one thing, but if he'd hidden and was simply waiting for the sentries to go off the watchtowers he hadn't a chance. Unless he'd left a trail through the wire the sentries wouldn't be allowed back in camp for at least three days. They'd have to go on manning the towers for a week, if necessary. That was in the regulations, as the old-timers knew. In short, if someone escaped, the guards had had it; they were hounded, without sleep or food. Sometimes they were roused to such fury that the runaway wouldn't get back alive.

Tsezar was arguing with the captain:[2] "For instance, when he hung his pince-nez on the ship's rigging. D'you remember?"

"Hm, yes," the captain said as he smoked.

"Or the baby carriage on the steps. Bumping down and down."

"Yes . . . But the scenes on board are somewhat artificial."

"Well, you see, we've been spoiled by modern camera technique."

"And the maggots in the meat, they crawl about like angleworms. Surely they weren't that size?"

"What do you expect of the movies? You can't show them smaller."

"Well, if they'd bring that meat here to camp instead of the fish they feed us and dumped it straight into the kettle, we'd be only too . . ."

The prisoners howled.

Three small figures were bursting out of the repair shop. So they'd found the Moldavian.

"Boooo!" went the crowd at the gates.

And they yelled, as the group drew nearer: "Scum! Filth! Idiot! Cow's udder! Lousy piece of garbage!"

And Shukhov joined in: "Rat!"

It's no joke to rob five hundred men of over half an hour.

Ducking his head, the Moldavian ran like a mouse.

---

1. ***Moldavian*** (mol dā'vē ən), native or inhabitant of Moldavia, a republic within the Soviet Union near Rumania.
2. ***Tsezar was arguing . . . captain.*** Their discussion is about several filmic effects in Eisenstein's *Battleship Potemkin* (1925).

"Halt!" a guard shouted. And, noting down "K 460," said: "Where were you?"

He strode over to the man and turned the butt of his rifle at him.

In the crowd people were still hurling curses: "Lowlife! Louse! Pig!"

But others, seeing the guard make ready to swing his rifle, held their tongues.

The Moldavian could hardly keep on his feet. He backed away from the guard.

The deputy squad leader of the 32nd advanced.

"The stupid fool crawled up to do some plastering. Trying to hide from me! Warmed up there and fell asleep."

And he hit the man hard in the face and on the neck, pushing him farther from the guard.

The Moldavian reeled back, and as he did so a Hungarian, one of his own squad, leaped up at him and kicked him hard from behind.

That wasn't like spying. Any fool can spy. A spy has a clean, exciting life. But try and spend ten years in a hard-labor camp!

The guard lowered his rifle.

The head of the escort shouted: "Back from the gates. Form fives."

Another recount, the dogs. Why should they count us now that everything's clear? The prisoners began to boo. All their anger switched from the Moldavian to the escort. They booed and didn't move.

"W-wha-a-at?" shouted the head of the escort. "Want to sit down on the snow? All right, I'll have you down in a minute and I'll keep you here till dawn."

He was quite capable of doing it too. He'd had them on the snow many a time. "Down on your faces!" And, to the escort: "Release safety catches!" The zeks knew all about that. They drew back from the gates.

"Back, back!" yelled the escort.

"What's the sense of shoving up to the gates anyhow, you morons?" men barked from the rear at the men in front as they were shoved back.

"Form fives. First. Second. Third . . ."

Now the moon was shining full. It cast its light all around and the crimson tint had gone. It had climbed a quarter of the way up the sky. The evening was lost. That stupid Moldavian. Those lousy guards. This stinking life.

As the prisoners in front were counted they turned and stood on tiptoe to see whether there were two men or three in the back row. It was a matter of life or death to them now.

Shukhov had the feeling that there were going to be four. He was numb with fear. One extra. Another recount. But it turned out that Fetiukov, after cadging a butt from the captain, had been wandering around and had failed to get into his five in time. So now he'd turned up in the back row as if he were an extra.

A guard struck Fetiukov angrily on the back of the neck.

Serves him right.

So they counted three in the back row. The count had come out right, thank God.

"Back from the gates," shouted a guard at the top of his voice. But this time the zeks didn't mutter—they'd noticed soldiers coming out of the gatehouse and forming a cordon on the other side of the gates.

So they were going to be let out.

None of the foremen was in sight, nor the superintendent, so the prisoners kept their firewood.

The gates swung open. And now the head of the escort, accompanied by a checker, came and stood on the other side, near some wooden railings.

"First. Second. Third . . ."

If the numbers tallied again the sentries would be removed from the watchtowers.

But what a distance they had to tramp along the edge of the site to reach the towers at the far end of it! Only when the last prisoner had been led off the site and the numbers had been found to agree would they telephone all the towers and relieve the sentries. If the head of the escort had his wits about him he'd put the column on the move right away, for he knew the zeks had nowhere to run to and the sentries would overtake the column. But some of the guards were so foolish, they feared they didn't have enough troops to handle the zeks; so they waited.

They had one of those idiots this evening.

A whole day in that freezing cold! The zeks were already chilled to the marrow; and now to stand around another shivering hour, when work was over! Yet it wasn't so much the cold and the fact that they'd lost an evening that infuriated them; the point was, there'd be no time now to do anything of their own in the camp.

"How is it you happen to know life in the British Navy so well?" Shukhov heard someone in the next five asking.

"Well, you see, I spent nearly a month on board a British cruiser. Had my own cabin. I was attached to a convoy as liaison officer. And imagine—after the war the British admiral—only the devil could have put the idea into his head—sent me a gift, a souvenir as 'a token of gratitude,' curse him! I was absolutely horrified. And now here we are, all lumped together. It's pretty hard to take, being imprisoned here with Bendera's men. . . ."

Strange! Yes, a strange sight indeed: the naked steppe, the empty building site, the snow gleaming in the moonlight. And the escort guards: they'd gone to their posts, ten paces apart, guns at the ready. And the black herd of prisoners; and among them, in a black coat like all the rest, a man, S 311, who'd never imagined life without gold shoulder straps, who had hobnobbed with a British admiral and now sweated at a barrow with Fetiukov.

You can push a man this way, and you can push a man that way.

Now the escort was ready. This time without any "prayer" the head guard barked at them: "Double time! Get a move on!"

To the devil with your "Get a move on!" All the other columns were ahead of them. What sense was there in hurrying? The prisoners didn't have to be in league with one another to figure the score: You kept us back; now it's our turn. The escort too, after all, was dying for a warm corner.

"Step lively!" shouted the guard. "Step lively, you in front."

To the devil with your "Step lively." The zeks marched with measured tread, hanging their heads as at a funeral. Now they'd nothing to lose—they'd be the last back anyhow. He

wouldn't treat them like human beings; now let him burst himself shouting.

On he went, "Step lively! Step lively!" But he realized it was futile. He couldn't order his men to shoot either. The prisoners were marching in fives, keeping in line, all correct. He had no power to hound them faster. (When they marched out to work in the morning the zeks walked slowly, to spare themselves. A man who's in a hurry won't live to see the end of his stretch—he'll tire and be done for.)

So on with regular, deliberate steps. The snow crunched under their boots. Some of them talked in low voices; others walked in silence. Shukhov asked himself whether there was anything he'd left undone in the camp that morning. Ah, the dispensary. Funny, he'd forgotten all about the dispensary while he'd been working.

This must be around the consulting hour. He'd manage it if he skipped his supper. But now somehow his back wasn't aching. And his temperature wouldn't be high enough. A waste of time. He'd pull through without benefit of the doctor. The only cure those docs know is to put you in your grave.

It wasn't the dispensary that appealed to him now; it was the prospect of adding something to his supper. His hopes were all pinned on that long-overdue parcel of Tsezar's.

A sudden change came over the column. It began to sway, to break out of its regular stride. The prisoners heaved forward with a buzz of excitement. And now the last five, which included Shukhov, were no longer treading on the heels of the five in front; they had to run to keep up. A few more paces, and again they were running.

When the rear of the column spilled over a rise Shukhov saw to the right, far away across the steppe, another dark column on the move, marching diagonally across their course. They too seemed to be forcing their pace.

It must be from the machine works, that column; there were about three hundred men in it. Another bunch with bad luck! Must have been held up—Shukhov wondered why. To finish assembling some piece of machinery? They could be kept after work hours for that. But what did it matter to them? They worked all day in the warmth.

Who'd get in first? The men ran, just ran. Even the escort broke into a jog trot: only the

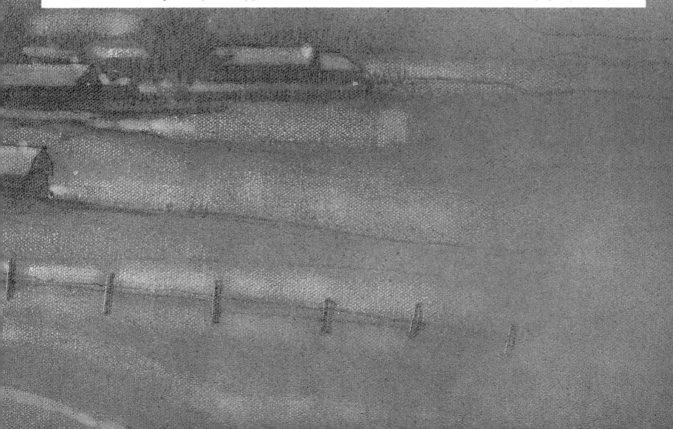

head guard remembered to shout, "Don't fall back. Keep up there, you in the rear. Keep up."

Oh, shut your trap. . . . What are you yapping about? As if they wouldn't keep up!

They forgot to talk; they forgot to think; everyone in the column was obsessed by one idea: to get back first.

Things were so lumped together, the sweet and the sour, that the prisoners saw the escort itself, now, as friend rather than foe. Now the enemy was the other column.

Their spirits rose, their anger passed.

"Get a move on, get a move on!" the rear shouted to the front.

Now their column had reached the street, while the other had passed out of sight behind the blocks of houses. They'd been racing blindly.

It was easier for Shukhov's column now; they were running down the middle of the street. And their escort had less to stumble over at the sides. This was where they ought to gain ground.

There was another reason why they simply had to reach the camp gates first: the guards there were unusually slow in searching the column from the machine works. Ever since zeks had been cutting one another's throats in the camp the authorities had arrived at one conclusion: that knives were being made at the machine works and smuggled in. So the zeks who worked there were gone over with special thoroughness on return to the camp. In late autumn, when the earth was already cold, the guards would shout at them: "Off with your boots, machine-works squad! Hold your boots in your hands."

And would frisk them barefoot.

Or, despite the frost, they'd pick men out at random, shouting: "You there, take off your right boot. And you, take off your left!"

A zek would pull off his boot and, hopping on one foot, turn it upside down and shake out the foot rag. No knife, curse you!

Shukhov had heard—he didn't know whether it was true or not—that back in the summer the zeks from the machine works had brought back two poles for a volleyball net and that there the knives were, there inside them. Ten long knives in each pole. And now knives would turn up occasionally, here and there.

So it was at a jog trot that they passed the new club and the residential block and the wood-processing plant, and reached the turning that led straight on to the gates.

"Hoooooo-ooo," shouted the whole column, in unison.

That was the turning they'd aimed at reaching before the others. The rival column was a hundred and fifty paces behind, on their right.

Now they could take things easy. Everyone was elated. As elated as a rabbit when it finds it can still terrify a frog.

There lay the camp, just as they'd left it in the morning: lights were on in the zone over the thick fence, specially powerful ones in front of the gatehouse. The entire area was flooded with light; it was as bright as day. They had to have it like that when they frisked the column.

But the column hadn't reached the gates yet.

"Halt!" shouted a guard and, handing his machine gun to a soldier, ran up close to the column (they weren't allowed to do that with their guns). "All those on the right carrying firewood dump it to their right."

He didn't have to guess about the firewood—the zeks were carrying it quite openly. A bundle fell, a second, a third. Some would have liked to conceal a stick or two inside the column, but their neighbors objected: "Throw it down as you're told! Do you want others to lose theirs because of you?"

Who's the zek's main enemy? Another zek. If only they weren't at odds with one another—ah, what a difference that'd make!

"Double time," shouted the head guard.

They advanced toward the gates.

Here five roads converged. An hour earlier all the other columns had met here. If they were paved, these roads, this would be just the place for the main square of a future city; and then processions would meet here, just as columns of zeks did now as they poured in from every direction, with sentries and guards all about.

The guards were already warming themselves indoors. They came out and formed a cordon across the road.

"Unbutton your coats. Unbutton your jackets."

They pulled the zeks' arms apart, the better to hug them and slap their sides. Same as in the morning, more or less.

It isn't so terrible to unbutton your coat now. We're going home.

That's what everyone used to say: "Going home."

They never had time to think of any other home.

While the head of the column was being frisked, Shukhov went over to Tsezar. "Tsezar Markovich, I'll run straight to the parcels office and keep a place in line for you."

Tsezar turned. The fringe of his dark mustache was tipped with frost.

"Why should you do that, Ivan Denisovich? Perhaps there won't be a parcel."

"Oh, well, it doesn't matter if there isn't. I'll wait ten minutes, anyway. If you don't turn up I'll go to the barracks."

(Shukhov reckoned like this: if Tsezar didn't come, maybe someone else would, then he could sell him his place in line.)

Obviously Tsezar was longing for his parcel.

"All right, Ivan Denisovich, run ahead and keep a place for me. Wait ten minutes, no longer."

And now Shukhov was on the point of being frisked. Today he had nothing to conceal. He would step forward fearlessly. He slowly unbuttoned his coat and undid the rope belt around his wadded jacket, and although he couldn't remember having anything forbidden, eight years in camp had given him the habit of caution: he thrust a hand into his pants pocket to make sure it was empty.

And there lay a small piece of broken hacksaw blade, the tiny length of steel that he'd picked up in his thriftiness at the building site without any intention of bringing it to camp.

He hadn't meant to bring it, but now, what a pity to throw it away! Why, he could make a little knife out of it, very handy for shoe repairing or tailoring!

If he'd intended to bring it with him he'd have thought hard of where to conceal it. But now the guards were only two rows ahead and the first of these rows was already stepping forward to be searched.

His choice had to be swift as the wind. Should he take cover behind the row in front of him and toss the bit of metal in the snow (it'd be noticed but they wouldn't know who the culprit was) or keep it on him?

For that strip of hacksaw he could get ten days in the cells, if they classed it as a knife.

But a cobbler's knife was money, it was bread.

A pity to throw it away.

He slipped it into his left mitten.

At that moment the next row was ordered to step forward and be searched.

Now the last three men stood in full view—Senka, Shukhov, and the man from the 32nd squad who had gone to look for the Moldavian.

Because they were three and the guards facing them were five, Shukhov could try a ruse. He could choose which of the two guards on the right to present himself to. He decided against a young pink-faced one and plumped for an older man with a gray mustache. The older one, of course, was experienced and could find the blade easily if he wanted to, but because of his age he would be fed up with the job. It must stink in his nose now like burning sulfur.

Meanwhile Shukhov had removed both mittens, the empty one and the one with the hacksaw, and held them in one hand (the empty one in front) together with the untied rope belt. He fully unbuttoned his jacket, lifted high the edges of his coat and jacket (never had he been so servile at the search but now he wanted to show he was innocent—Come on, frisk me!), and at the word of command stepped forward.

The guard slapped Shukhov's sides and back, and the outside of his pants pocket. Nothing there. He kneaded the edges of coat and jacket. Nothing there either. He was about to pass him through when, for safety's sake, he crushed the mitten that Shukhov held out to him—the empty one.

The guard crushed it in his hand, and Shukhov felt as though pincers of iron were crushing everything inside him. One such squeeze on the other mitten and he'd be sunk—the cells on nine ounces of bread a day and hot stew one day in three. He imagined how weak he'd grow, how difficult he'd find it to get back to his present condition, neither fed nor starving.

And an urgent prayer rose in his heart: "Oh Lord, save me! Don't let them send me to the cells."

And while all this raced through his mind, the guard, after finishing with the right-hand mitten, stretched a hand out to deal with the other (he would have squeezed them at the same moment if Shukhov had held them in separate hands). Just then the guard heard his chief, who was in a hurry to get on, shout to the escort: "Come on, bring up the machine-works column."

And instead of examining the other mitten the old guard waved Shukhov on. He was through.

He ran off to catch up with the others. They had already formed fives in a sort of corridor between long beams, like horse stalls in a market, a sort of paddock for prisoners. He ran lightly, hardly feeling the ground. He didn't say a prayer of thanksgiving because he hadn't time, and anyway it would have been out of place.

The escort now drew aside. They were only waiting for their chief. They had gathered for their own use all the firewood the 104th had dumped before being frisked; what the guards had removed during the frisking itself was heaped near the gatehouse.

The moon had risen still higher; the cold grew keener in the pale bright night.

The head guard walked to the sentry house—he had to get a receipt for the four hundred and sixty-three prisoners. He spoke briefly to Priakhov, Volkovoi's deputy.

"K 460," shouted Priakhov.

The Moldavian, who had buried himself deep in the column, drew in his breath and went over to the right of the corridor. He was still hanging his head and his shoulders were hunched.

"Come here," Priakhov ordered, gesturing for him to walk around the column.

The Moldavian did so. He was ordered to stand there, his arms behind his back.

That meant they were going to charge him with attempting to escape. They'd put him in the cells.

Just in front of the gates, right and left of the "paddock," stood two guards. The gates, three times the height of a man, opened slowly. The command rang out:

"Form fives!" (No need here to order the zeks back from the gates; all the gates opened inwards, into the zone. Let the zeks mass as they wished and push against the gates from within, they wouldn't be able to break out.) "First. Second. Third . . ."

It was at the evening recount on their return through the gates that the prisoners, freezing and famished, found the icy wind hardest to bear. A bowl of thin cabbage soup, half burned, was as welcome to them as rain to parched earth. They'd swallowed it in one gulp. That bowl of soup—it was dearer than freedom, dearer than life itself, past, present, and future.

They passed through the gates, those zeks, like soldiers back from a campaign, brisk, taut, eager—clear the road for 'em.

For a trusty with a soft job at staff quarters, those prisoners on the march must have been something to think about.

After the recount a prisoner became a free man again—for the first time in the day since the guards had given them the morning signal for roll call. They passed through the big gates (of the zone), through the small gates (of the intermediate zone), through two more gates (on the parade ground)—and then they could scatter where they liked.

But not the squad leaders. They were caught by the officer who assigned them their work: "All squad leaders to the planning office."

Shukhov rushed past the prison, between the barracks, to the parcels office. Tsezar, meanwhile, went at a dignified, even pace in the opposite direction, to where people were swarming around a pole with a board nailed to it. On it was the name of anyone for whom a parcel was waiting, written in indelible pencil.

Most writing in the camp was done on plywood, not on paper. It was surer, somehow, more reliable. The guards and turnkeys used wood too, for keeping tally of the zeks. You can scrape it clean for next day, and use it again. Economical.

Zeks who stay in camp all day can, among other odd jobs, read the names on the board, meet people who've got a parcel as they come in from work, and give them the number. Not much of a job, but it can earn you a cigarette.

Shukhov ran to the parcels office—a little annex to a barracks, to which in turn a small porch had been added. The porch had no door and was open to the weather. All the same, it was cozier that way; it had a roof, after all.

A line had formed along the walls of the porch. Shukhov joined it. There were some fifteen ahead of him. That meant over an hour's wait, to just before locking-up time. And there were others who'd be behind him in the line—the zeks of the powerhouse column who'd gone to look for their names on the board, and the machine-works column too. Looked as though *they* would have to come again. Tomorrow morning.

People stood in the line with little bags and sacks. On the other side of the door (Shukhov himself hadn't ever received a parcel at this camp but he knew from gossip) guards opened the parcels, which came packed in wooden boxes, with hatchets. They took everything out and examined the contents. They cut, they broke, they fingered. They tipped things out from one container into another. If there was anything liquid, in glass jars or tins, they opened them and poured it out, though you had nothing but your hands or a cloth bag to hold it in. They didn't give you the jars; they were scared of something. If there was anything home-baked, or some tasty sweetmeats or sausage or smoked fish, the guard would take a bite at it himself. (And just you try to get high and mighty and complain, and they'll immediately say that this and that are forbidden and won't issue them to you at all.) Every zek who got a parcel had to give and give, starting with the guard who opened it. And when they'd finished their search they didn't give you the stuff in the box it had come in; they just swept everything into your bag, even into the skirt of your coat and . . . off you go. Sometimes they'd whisk you out so fast you'd be sure to leave something behind. No good going back for it. It wouldn't be there.

When he was in Ust-Izhma Shukhov had got parcels a couple of times. But he wrote to his wife that it was a waste—don't send them. Don't take the food out of the kids' mouths.

Although when he had been at liberty Shukhov had found it easier to feed his whole family than it ever was to feed himself now, he knew what those parcels cost. He knew too that his family wouldn't be able to keep it up for ten years. Better do without them.

But though he'd decided that way, every time someone in the squad, or close by in the barracks, received a parcel (which was almost every day) his heart ached because there wasn't one for him. And though he'd strictly forbidden his wife to send him anything even for Easter, and though he never thought of reading the list except for some rich squad member, every now and then he felt himself longing for someone to run up and say: "Shukhov! Why don't you go for your parcel? There's one for you."

But no one ran up.

He had less and less cause to remember Temgenovo and his home there. Life in camp wore him out from reveille to bedtime, with not a second for idle reflections.

Now as he stood among men who were buoying themselves up with the hope of soon digging their teeth into bits of salt pork, or spreading butter on their bread, or sweetening their mugs of tea with lumps of sugar, Shukhov had one wish only—to reach the mess hall in time and to eat his stew hot. It was only half as good when it was cold.

He figured that if Tsezar's name hadn't turned up on the list he would have gone back to the barracks long ago to wash. But if he'd found it there he would now be collecting bags, plastic mugs, and a basin. That would take him ten minutes. And Shukhov had promised to wait.

There in line Shukhov learned some news. Again there wasn't going to be a Sunday this week; again they were going to steal one of their Sundays. He, like everyone else, had expected it, for if there happened to be five Sundays in a month, they gave them three and made them work the other two. Shukhov had expected it, but when he heard it a spasm of pain caught his heart: who wouldn't begrudge the loss of that sweet day? Though what they were saying in the line was right: they knew how to keep them jumping even on Sundays. They'd invent something—fixing up the baths, or building a wall somewhere, or cleaning up the yard. There were mattresses to be changed and shaken, bedbugs in the bunk frames to be exterminated. Or they'd have the idea of checking you with your photo. Or of carrying out an inventory—turning you with all your things into the yard and keeping you there half the day.

Nothing seems to make the authorities madder than zeks napping quietly after breakfast.

The line was moving, though slowly. People were coming in and shoving into the head of the line without even a pardon me, just elbowing through to the front—a camp barber, a bookkeeper, a man who worked in the C.E.D. But they weren't rank-and-file, they were respectable trusties, pigs of the first order with soft jobs in the camp. The zeks who worked outside thought them lower than dirt (a rating the trusties returned). But it was futile to protest—the trusties were a gang all their own, and were also in solid with the guards.

Now there were only ten ahead of Shukhov. Another seven had hurried in to line up behind him, when Tsezar, stooping, appeared in the doorway, wearing the new fur hat that had been sent him from outside.

Now take that hat. Tsezar must have tickled someone's palm to get permission for wearing a town hat so clean and new. They even robbed others of their bedraggled service hats. Here, wear the camp pig-fur model!

A strange-looking fellow with glasses was standing in line, his head buried in a newspaper. Tsezar at once made for him.

"Aha, Pyotr Mikhailych."[3]

They bloomed like a couple of poppies. The strange-looking fellow said: "Look what I've got! A fresh *Vechorka*.[4] They sent it by airmail."

"Really," said Tsezar, sticking his nose into the newspaper. How on earth could they make out such tiny print in the glimmer of that miserable lamp?

"There's a most fascinating review of a Zavadsky[5] premiere."

Those Muscovites can smell one another at a distance, like dogs: they sniff and sniff when they meet in a way of their own. They talk so fast too, each trying to outtalk the other. When they're jabbering away like that you hear practically no Russian; they might be talking Latvian or Rumanian.

However, Tsezar had all his bags with him—everything in order.

"So I can . . . er . . . Tsezar Markovich," lisped Shukhov, "I'll take off now."

"Of course, of course," said Tsezar, raising his dark mustache above the top of the newspaper. "Tell me though, who's in front of me? And who's behind me?"

Shukhov told him his place in the line and then, with a gentle hint, asked: "Do you want me to bring you your supper?"

(That meant from the mess hall to the barracks, in a mess tin. This was strictly against the rules—there'd been many made about it. When

---

3. ***Pyotr Mikhailych*** (pyô′tər myi нə ēl′yich).
4. ***Vechorka*** (vye chôr′kä), short for *Vecheruyaya Moska* (vye chi′ru-yä′yä môs′kä), a Moscow evening newspaper.
5. ***Zavadsky*** (zä väd′skē), a well-known Soviet theatrical producer connected with various Soviet theater groups.

they caught you they poured your food out of the mess tin onto the ground and put you in the guardhouse. All the same, food was carried and would go on being carried, because if a zek has anything to do he'll never find time to go to the mess hall with his squad.)

Shukhov asked: "Do you want me to bring you your supper?" but murmured to himself: "Surely he won't be stingy. Won't he give me his supper? After all, there's no kasha for supper, only thin stew."

"No, no," said Tsezar with a smile. "Eat it yourself, Ivan Denisovich."

That was just what Shukhov was expecting. And now, like a bird on the wing, he darted from the porch and ran from one zone to the other.

The prisoners were scurrying in all directions. There was a time when the camp commandant had issued yet another order: on no account were prisoners to walk about the camp on their own. Wherever possible, a squad was to go intact. But when there could be no business for a whole squad to do at once—at the dispensary, say, or at the latrines—then groups of four or five were to be formed and a senior appointed to head them and take them there and back in a body.

The camp commandant took a very firm stand on that order. No one dared contradict him. The guards picked up solitary prisoners, took down their numbers, yanked them off to the cells—yet the order was a flop. It flopped quietly, like many much-touted orders. Someone, say, is sent for by the security boys—must you take another four or five with you? Or you have to get your food from the warehouse. Why the devil should I go with you? Someone has the strange idea of going to the C.E.D. to read newspapers. Who wants to go with him? And this fellow goes to have his boots mended, another to the drying shed, a third merely from one barracks to another (that's forbidden more strictly than anything else)—how can you hold them all back?

With that rule of his the commandant would have robbed them of their last shred of freedom, but it didn't work out, much as he tried, the fat pig.

Hurrying along the path, meeting a guard on the way and, to be on the safe side, taking off his hat to him, Shukhov ran into the barracks. The place was in an uproar: someone's bread ration had been swiped during the day and the poor fellow was shouting at the orderlies and the orderlies were shouting back. But the 104th's corner was empty.

Shukhov was always thankful if, on returning to camp, he found that his mattress hadn't been turned over and that the guards hadn't been snooping around. So that's all right.

He hurried to his bunk, taking off his coat as he ran. Up with the coat, up with the mittens and the nice bit of blade. He probed the depths of his mattress—the bread was there. Good that he'd sewn it in.

And out he ran. To the mess hall.

He reached it without meeting a guard—only a couple of zeks arguing over their bread ration.

Outside the moon shone brighter than ever. The lamps seemed to be paler now. The barracks cast deep shadows. The door to the mess hall lay beyond a broad porch with four steps. Now the porch too lay in shadow. But above it a small lamp was swaying, and creaking dismally in the cold. The light it cast was rainbow-hued, from the frost maybe, or the dirt on the glass.

The camp commandant had issued yet another strict order: the squads were to enter the mess hall in double file. To this he added: on reaching the steps they were to stay there and not climb onto the porch; they were to form up in fives and remain standing until the mess orderly gave them the go-ahead.

The post of mess orderly was firmly held by "the Limper." Because of his lameness he'd managed to get classed as disabled, but he was a hefty piece of scum. He'd got himself a birch club, and standing on the porch would hit anyone who came up the steps without his say-so. No, not anyone. He was smart, and could tell, even in the dark, when it was better to let a man alone—anyone who might give him as good as he got. He hit the down-and-outs. Once he hit Shukhov.

He was called an orderly. But, looking closer into it, he was a real prince—he palled around with the cooks.

Today all the squads may have turned up together or there may have been delay in getting things in order, but there was quite a crowd on the porch. Among them was the Limper, with his assistant. The mess chief himself was there too. They were handling the crowd without guards—the bruisers.

The mess chief was a fat pig with a head like a pumpkin and a broad pair of shoulders. He was bursting with energy and when he walked he seemed nothing but a lot of jerks, with springs for arms and legs. He wore a white lambskin hat without a number on it, finer than any civilian's. And his waistcoat was lambskin to match, with a number on it, true, but hardly bigger than a postage stamp—thanks to Volkovoi. He bore no number at all on his back. He respected no one and all the zeks were afraid of him. He held the lives of thousands in his hands. Once they'd tried to beat him up but all the cooks—a prize bunch of thugs they were—had leaped to his defense.

Shukhov would be in hot water if the 104th had already gone in. The Limper knew everyone by sight and, with his chief present, wouldn't think of letting a man in with the wrong squad; he'd make a point of putting the finger on him.

Prisoners had been known to slip in behind the Limper's back by climbing over the porch railings. Shukhov had done it too. But tonight, under the chief's very nose, that was out of the question—he'd bust you so bad that you'd only just manage to drag yourself off to the doctor.

Get along to the porch and see whether, among all those identical black coats, the 104th was still there.

He got there just as the men began shoving (what could they do? it would soon be time to turn in) as though they were storming a stronghold—the first step, the second, the third, the fourth. Got there! They poured onto the porch.

"Stop, you swine," the Limper shouted and raised his stick at the men in front. "Get back or I'll bash your heads in."

"What can we do about it?" they yelled back at him. "The men at the back are pushing us."

That was true, but those up in front were offering little resistance. They hoped to dash through into the mess hall.

The Limper put his club across his chest—it might have been a barricade in a street battle—and rushed headlong at the men in front. His assistant, the trusty, shared the stick with him, and so did the mess chief—who had apparently decided to soil his hands with it.

They pushed hard—they had plenty of strength, with all that meat in them. The zeks reeled back. The men in front toppled down onto the men behind them, bowled them over like wheat stalks.

"You lousy Limper, we'll fix you," cried a man in the crowd, hiding behind the others. As for the rest, they fell without a word, they got up without a word—as quick as they could, before being stepped on.

The steps were clear. The mess chief went back to the porch but the Limper stayed on the top.

"Form fives, blockheads," he shouted. "How many times have I told you I'll let you in when I'm ready?"

Shukhov imagined that he saw Senka's head right in front of the porch. He felt wildly elated, and using his elbows made an effort to push through to him. But, looking at those backs, he knew that it was beyond his strength. He wouldn't get through.

"Twenty-seventh," the Limper called, "go ahead."

The 27th bounded up and made a dash for the door, and the rest surged after them. Shukhov, among them, was shoving with all his might. The porch quivered, and the lamp overhead protested shrilly.

"What again, you scum?" the Limper shouted in rage. Down came his stick, on a shoulder, on a back, pushing the men off, toppling one after another.

Again he cleared the steps.

From below Shukhov saw Pavlo at the Limper's side. It was he who led the squad to the mess hall—Tiurin wouldn't lower himself by joining in the hullabaloo.

"Form fives, hundred and fourth," Pavlo called from the porch. "Make way for them, friends."

Friends—just see them making way, the swine.

"Let me through, you in front. That's my squad," Shukhov grunted, shoving against a back.

The man would gladly have done so but others were squeezing him from every side.

The crowd heaved, pushing away so that no one could breathe. To get its stew. Its lawful stew.

Shukhov tried something else. He grasped the porch rail on his left, got his arms around a pillar, and heaved himself up. He kicked someone's knee and caught a blow in the ribs; a few curses, but he was through. He planted a foot on the edge of the porch floor, close to the top step, and waited. Some of his pals who were already there gave him a hand.

The mess chief walked to the door and looked back.

"Come on, Limper, send in two more squads."

"One hundred and fourth," shouted the Limper. "Where d'you think *you're* crawling, bloodsucker?"

He slammed a man from another squad on the back of the neck with his stick.

"One hundred and fourth," shouted Pavlo, leading in his men.

"Whew!" gasped Shukhov in the mess hall. And, without waiting for Pavlo's instructions, he started looking for free trays.

The mess hall seemed as usual, with clouds of steam curling in through the door and the men sitting shoulder to shoulder—like seeds in a sunflower. Others pushed their way through the tables, and others were carrying loaded trays. Shukhov had grown used to it all over the years and his sharp eyes had noticed that S 208 had only five bowls on the tray he was carrying. This meant that it was the last trayload for his squad. Otherwise the tray would have been full.

He went up to the man and whispered in his ear: "After you with that tray."

"Someone's waiting for it at the counter. I promised. . . ."

"Let him wait, the lazy filth."

They came to an understanding.

S 208 carried his tray to the table and unloaded the bowls. Shukhov immediately grabbed it. At that moment the man it had been promised to ran up and tried to grab it. But he was punier than Shukhov. Shukhov shoved him off with the tray—what the devil are you pulling for?—and threw him against a post. Then putting the tray under his arm, he trotted off to the serving window.

Pavlo was standing in the line there, worried because there was no empty tray. He was delighted to see Shukhov. He pushed the man ahead of him out of the way: "Why are you standing here? Can't you see I've got a tray?"

Look, there was Gopchik—with another tray.

"They were arguing," he said with a laugh, "and I grabbed it."

Gopchik will do well. Give him another three years—he has still to grow up—and he'll become nothing less than a bread cutter. He's fated for it.

Pavlo told him to hand over the second of the trays to Yermolayev,[6] a hefty Siberian who was serving a ten-year stretch, like Shukhov, for being caught by the Germans; then sent him to keep an eye on any table where the men might be finishing. Shukhov put his tray down and waited.

"One hundred and fourth," announced Pavlo at the counter.

In all there were five of these counters: three for serving regular food, one for zeks on special diets (ulcer victims, and bookkeeping personnel, as a favor), and one for the return of dirty dishes (that's where the dish-lickers gathered, sparring with one another). The counters were low—about waist level. The cooks themselves were out of sight; only their hands, and the ladles, could be seen.

The cook's hands were white and well cared for, but huge and hairy: a boxer's hands, not a cook's. He took a pencil and made a note on the wall—he kept his list there.

"One hundred and fourth—twenty-four portions."

Pantaleyev slopped into the mess hall. Nothing wrong with him, the scummy piece of garbage.

The cook took an enormous ladle and stirred, stirred, stirred. The soup kettle had just been refilled, almost up to the brim, and steam poured from it. Replacing the huge ladle with a smaller one he began serving the stew in twenty-ounce portions. He didn't go deep.

"One, two, three, four . . ."

Some of the bowls had been filled while the stuff from the bottom of the kettle hadn't yet settled after the stirring, and some were duds—nothing but soup. Shukhov made a mental note of which was which. He put ten bowls on his tray and carried them off. Gopchik waved from the second row of posts.

"Over here, Ivan Denisovich, over here."

No horsing around with bowls of stew. Shukhov was careful not to stumble. He kept his throat busy too.

"Hey you, H 920. Gently, uncle. Out of the way, my boy."

It was hard enough, in a crowd like this, to carry a single bowl without slopping it. He was carrying ten. Just the same, he put the tray down safely, on the end of the table that Gopchik had cleared. No splashes. He managed, too, to maneuver the tray so that the two bowls with the thickest stew were just opposite the place he was about to sit down in.

Yermolayev brought another ten bowls. Gopchik ran off and came back with Pavlo, the last four in their hands.

Kilgas brought the bread tray. Tonight they were being fed in accordance with the work they had done. Some got six ounces, some nine, and Shukhov twelve. He took a piece with a crust for himself, and six ounces from the middle of the loaf for Tsezar.

Now from all over the mess hall Shukhov's squad began streaming up, to collect their supper and eat it where they could. As he handed out the bowls, there were two things he had to take care of: he had to remember whom he'd served, and he had to watch out for the tray—and for his own corner of it. (He put his spoon into a bowl—one of the "thick" ones. Reserved, that meant.) Fetiukov was among the first to arrive. But he soon walked off, figuring there was nothing to be scrounged that particular evening; better to wander around the mess, hunting for leftovers (if someone doesn't finish his stew and pushes his bowl back, there are always people hustling to pounce on it, like vultures).

Shukhov counted the portions with Pavlo. Correct, apparently. He pushed across a bowl for Tiurin, one of the "thick" ones; and Pavlo poured his stew into a narrow German mess-tin, with a lid—you could carry it under your coat, close to your chest.

---

6. ***Yermolayev*** (yer mo lä′yef).

The empty trays were handed in. Pavlo sat there with his double helping, Shukhov with his two bowls. And now they had nothing more to say to one another—the sacred moments had come.

Shukhov took off his hat and laid it on his knees. He tasted one bowl, he tasted the other. Not bad—there was some fish in it. Generally, the evening stew was much thinner than at breakfast: if they're to work, prisoners must be fed in the morning; in the evening they'll go to sleep anyway.

He dug in. First he only drank the broth, drank and drank. As it went down, filling his whole body with warmth, all his guts began to flutter inside him at their meeting with that stew. Goo-ood! There it comes, that brief moment for which a zek lives.

And now Shukhov complained about nothing: neither about the length of his stretch, nor about the length of the day, nor about their swiping another Sunday. This was all he thought about now: we'll survive. We'll stick it out, God willing, till it's over.

He drained the hot soup from both bowls, and then tipped what was left in the second into the first, scraping it clean with his spoon. That set his mind at ease. Now he didn't have to think about the second and keep an eye or a hand on it.

Now that he could look freely he glanced at his neighbors' bowls. The one on his left was little more than water. The dirty snakes. The tricks they play! And on their fellow zeks.

He began to eat the cabbage with what was left of the soup. A potato had found its way into one of the bowls—Tsezar's. A medium-sized spud, frost-bitten, hard and sweetish. There wasn't much fish, just a few stray bits of bare backbone. But you must chew every bone, every fin, to suck the juice out of them, for the juice is healthy. It takes time, of course, but he was in no hurry to go anywhere. Today was a red-letter day for him: two helpings for dinner, two helpings for supper. Everything else could wait.

Except, maybe, that visit to the Lett for tobacco. None might be left in the morning.

He ate his supper without bread. A double helping *and* bread—that was going too far. The bread would do for tomorrow. The belly is a demon. It doesn't remember how well you treated it yesterday; it'll cry out for more tomorrow.

He ate up his stew without taking much interest in what was happening around him. No need for that: he wasn't on the lookout for extras, he was eating his own lawful portions. All the same, he noticed that when the fellow opposite got up a tall old man—U 81—sat down in his place. Shukhov knew he was in the 64th and had heard, while waiting in the parcels line, that the 64th had been sent to the Socialist Way of Life settlement that day instead of the 104th, and had spent the whole time without a chance of getting warm—putting up barbed wire, building their own zone.

He'd been told that this old man had spent years without number in camps and prisons, and that he hadn't benefited from a single amnesty. Whenever one ten-year stretch had run out they shoved another onto him right away.

Now Shukhov looked closely at the man. He held himself straight—the other zeks sat all hunched up—and looked as if he'd put something extra on the bench to sit on. There was nothing left to crop on his head: his hair had dropped out long since—the result of high living, no doubt. His eyes didn't dart after everything going on in the mess hall. He kept them fixed in an unseeing gaze at some spot over Shukhov's head. His worn wooden spoon dipped rhythmically into the thin stew, but instead of lowering his head to the bowl like everybody else, he raised the spoon high to his lips. He'd lost all his teeth and chewed his bread with iron gums. All life had drained out of his face but it had been left, not sickly or feeble, but hard and dark like carved stone. And by his hands, big and cracked and blackened, you could see that he'd had little opportunity of doing soft jobs. But he wasn't going to give in, oh no! *He* wasn't going to put his nine ounces on the dirty, bespattered table—he put it on a well-washed bit of rag.

However, he couldn't go on watching the old

man—he had other things to do. He finished his supper, licked his spoon clean, and put it in his boot. He pulled his hat over his eyes, got up, picked up his bread and Tsezar's, and went out. Another porch led from the mess hall. Two more orderlies stood there: they had nothing to do except unhook the door, let people through, and slip the hook on again.

Shukhov came out with a full belly. He felt pleased with himself and decided that, although it was close to curfew, he'd run over to the Lett all the same. Instead of taking the bread to his barracks, he strode to Barracks 7.

The moon was high—clean and white, as if chiseled out of the sky. It was clear up there and there were some stars out—the brightest of them. But he had even less time for stargazing than for watching people in the mess hall. One thing he realized—the frost was no milder. One of the civilians had said, and this had been passed on, that it was likely to drop to −25° in the night, and as low as −40° toward morning.

From far away in the settlement he heard the drone of a tractor. From the direction of the main thoroughfare an excavator squealed shrilly. And creak, creak, went every pair of boots in which people walked or ran about the camp.

There was no wind.

He meant to buy the tobacco at the price he'd paid before—one ruble a glassful, though, outside, that amount would cost three times as much, and for some cuts even more. In forced-labor camps all prices were local; it was quite different from anywhere else, because you couldn't save money and few had any at all, for it was very hard to come by. No one was paid a kopeck for his work (at Ust-Izhma he'd received at least thirty rubles a month). If anyone's relatives sent money by mail he didn't get it in cash anyway; it was credited to his personal account. You could draw on a personal account once a month at the commissary to buy soap, moldy biscuits, and "Prima" cigarettes. Whether you liked the wares or not, you had to spend the amount the chief had given you a slip for. If you didn't, the money was lost—simply written off.

Shukhov did private jobs to get money, making slippers out of customers' rags—two rubles a pair—or patching torn jackets, price by agreement.

Barracks 7, unlike Barracks 9, wasn't in two big halves. It had a long passage, with ten doors opening off it. Each room housed a squad, packed into seven tiers of bunks. In addition, there was a little cubbyhole for the bucket and another for the senior orderly. The artists had a cubbyhole to themselves too.

Shukhov headed for the Lett's room. He found him lying on a lower bunk, his feet propped on a ledge. He was talking to his neighbor in Latvian.

Shukhov sat down beside him. "Evening."

"Evening," replied the Lett, without lowering his feet. The room was small, everyone was listening. Who was he? What did he want?

Both Shukhov and the Lett realized that people were curious, so Shukhov let the conversation drag on. Well, how are you doing? Oh, not so bad. Cold today. Yes.

Shukhov waited until everyone had started talking again. (They were arguing about the Korean War—now that the Chinese had joined in, would that mean a world war or not?) He leaned closer to the Lett.

"Any t'bacca?"

"Yes."

"Let's see it."

The Lett dropped his feet off the ledge, put them on the floor, sat up. He was a mean fellow, that Lett—filled a glass with tobacco as if he was afraid of putting in a single pinch too many.

He showed Shukhov his tobacco pouch and slid open the fastener.

Shukhov took a pinch and laid the leaf on his palm. He examined it. Same as last time, brownish, same rough cut. He held it to his nose and sniffed. That was the stuff. But to the Lett he said: "Not the same, somehow."

"The same, the same," the Lett said testily. "I never have any other kind. Always the same."

"All right," said Shukhov. "Stuff some into a

glass for me. I'll have a smoke and perhaps take a second glassful."

He said "stuff" on purpose, because the Lett had the habit of dropping the tobacco in loosely.

The Lett brought out another pouch from under his pillow, fuller than the first. He took his glass out of a locker. It was really a plastic container, but Shukhov figured it held the same as an ordinary glass.

The Lett began to fray out the tobacco into the glass.

"Push it down, push it down," said Shukhov, laying his own thumb on it.

"I know how to do it," the Lett said sharply, jerking away the glass and pressing the tobacco, though lightly. He dropped in a little more.

Meanwhile, Shukhov had unbuttoned his jacket and was groping inside the cotton lining for a piece of paper that only he knew where to find. Using both hands he squeezed it along under the lining and forced it into a little hole in the cloth somewhere quite different, a small tear that he'd tacked with a couple of loose stitches. When the paper reached the hole he snapped the thread with a fingernail, folding the paper lengthwise (it had already been folded in a longish rectangle), and pulled it through the hole. Two rubles. Worn notes that didn't rustle.

In the room a prisoner shouted: "D'you mean to say you think Old Whiskers[7] will take pity on you? Why, he wouldn't trust his own brother. You haven't a chance, you fool."

One good thing about these "special" camps—you were free to let off steam. At Ust-Izhma you need only whisper that there was a shortage of matches outside, and they'd put you in the guardhouse and add another ten years to your stretch. But here you could bawl anything you liked from the top row of bunks—the squealers didn't pass it on, the security boys had stopped caring.

The trouble was, you didn't have much time to talk in.

"Ugh, you're making it lie too loose," Shukhov complained.

"Oh well, there you are," said the Lett, adding a pinch on top.

Shukhov took his pouch out of an inside pocket and poured in the tobacco from the glass.

"All right," he said, deciding not to waste the first precious cigarette by smoking it hurriedly. "Stuff it full again."

Wrangling a bit more, he poured the second glassful into his pouch, handed over the two rubles, and left with a nod.

As soon as he was outside again he doubled back to Barracks 9. He didn't want to miss Tsezar when he came back with that package.

But Tsezar was already there, sitting on his bunk and gloating over the parcel. Its contents were laid out on his bunk and on top of the locker, but as there was no direct light there—Shukhov's bunk was in the way—it wasn't very easy to see.

Shukhov stooped, passed between Tsezar's bunk and the captain's, and handed Tsezar his bread ration.

"Your bread, Tsezar Markovich."

He didn't say, "Well, did you get it?" That would have been to hint, "I kept that place in the line and now have a right to my share." The right was his, that he knew, but even eight years as a convict hadn't turned him into a jackal—and the longer he spent at the camp the stronger he made himself.

But his eyes were another matter. Those eyes, the hawklike eyes of a zek, darted to one side and slid swiftly over what was laid out there; and although the food hadn't been unpacked and some of the bags were still unopened, that quick look and the evidence of his nose told him that Tsezar had got sausage, condensed milk, a plump smoked fish, salt pork, crackers, biscuits, four pounds of lump sugar and what looked like butter, as well as cigarettes and pipe tobacco—and that wasn't all.

He learned all this during the brief moment it

---

7. ***Old Whiskers,*** Stalin. Incidentally, Solzhenitsyn's reference to Stalin as "the whiskered one" in a 1945 letter led to his imprisonment.

took him to say: "Your bread, Tsezar Markovich."

Tsezar, all excited and looking a bit tipsy (and who wouldn't, after getting a parcel like that!), waved the bread away: "Keep it, Ivan Denisovich."

His bowl of stew, and now this six ounces of bread—that was a full supper, and of course Shukhov's fair share of the parcel.

And he put out of his mind any idea of getting something tasty from what Tsezar had laid out. There's nothing worse than working your belly to no purpose.

Well, he had his twelve ounces and now this extra six, besides the piece in his mattress, at least another six ounces. Not bad. He'd eat six now and some more later, and still have next day's ration for work. Living high, eh! As for the hunk in the mattress, let it stay there! A good thing he'd found time to sew it in! Someone in the 75th had had a hunk pinched from his locker. That was a dead loss; nothing could be done about it.

People imagine that the package a man gets is a sort of nice, tight sack he has only to slit open and be happy. But if you work it out it's a matter of easy come, easy go. Shukhov had known cases when before his parcel arrived a fellow would be doing odd jobs to earn a bit of extra kasha, or cadging cigarette butts—just like anybody else. He has to share with the guard and the squad leader—and how can he help giving a little something to the trusty in the parcels office? Why, next time the fellow may mislay your parcel and a week may go by before your name appears again on the list! And that other fellow at the place where you hand in your food to be kept for you, safe from friskers and pilferers—Tsezar will be there before the morning roll call, with everything in a sack—he must have his cut too, and a good one, if you don't want him little by little swiping more than you gave him. Sitting there all day, the rat, shut up with other people's food—try to keep an eye on him! And there must be something for services like Shukhov's. And something to the bath attendant for issuing you decent underwear—not much but something. And for the barber who shaves you "with paper" (for wiping the razor on—he usually does it on your knee). Not much to him either but, still, three or four butts. And at the C.E.D., for your letters to be kept separate and not get lost. And if you want to goof off a day or two and lie in bed, instead of going to work, you have to slip the doctor something. And what about the neighbor you share a locker with (the captain, in Tsezar's case)? He must have his cut. After all, he sees every blessed ounce you take. Who'd be nervy enough not to give him his share?

So leave envy to those who always think the radish in the other fellow's hand is bigger than yours. Shukhov knows life and never opens his belly to what doesn't belong to him.

Meanwhile he pulled off his boots, climbed up to his bunk, took the strip of hacksaw out of his mitten, and decided that tomorrow he'd look around for a good pebble and start whetting down the blade to make a cobbler's knife. Four days' work, he figured, if he sat over it mornings and evenings, and he'd have a fine little knife with a sharp, curved blade.

But now he had to conceal that find of his, if only till morning. He'd slip it into the edge of the partition under the crossbeam. And as the captain hadn't returned yet to his bunk down below and the sawdust wouldn't fall on his face, Shukhov turned back the head of his mattress and set about hiding the thing.

His top-bunk neighbors could see what he was doing: Alyosha the Baptist and—across the aisle, in the next tier—the two Estonians. But he didn't worry about them.

Fetiukov walked through the barracks. He was sobbing, all hunched up, his mouth smeared with blood. So he'd been beaten up again—over the bowls! With no attempt to hide his tears, and looking at no one, he passed the whole squad, crawled into his bunk, and buried his face in his mattress.

When you thought about it, you couldn't help feeling sorry for him. He wouldn't live to see the end of his stretch. His attitude was all wrong.

Just then the captain turned up. He looked cheerful as he carried a pot of tea, special tea, you can bet! Two tea barrels stood in the barracks, but what sort of tea could you call it? Sewage: warm water with a touch of coloring, dishwater smelling of the barrel—of steamed wood and rot. That was tea for the workers. But the captain must have taken a pinch of real tea from Tsezar, put it in his pot, and hurried to the hot-water faucet. And now, well satisfied, he settled down beside his locker.

"Nearly scalded my fingers at the faucet," he boasted. Down there Tsezar spread a sheet of paper, and began laying this and that on it. Shukhov turned the head of his mattress back. He didn't want to see what was going on; he didn't want to upset himself. But even now they couldn't get along without him; Tsezar rose to his full height, his eyes level with Shukhov's, and winked.

"Ivan Denisovich! Er . . . lend me your 'ten days.' "

That meant a small penknife. Yes, Shukhov had one—he kept it concealed in the partition. A bit shorter than half a finger but it cut salt pork five fingers thick. He'd made the blade himself, mounted it and whetted it sharp.

He crawled to the beam. He fished the knife out. He handed it over. Tsezar nodded and ducked below.

That knife's a breadwinner too. After all, you can be put in the cells for keeping it, and only a man without a conscience would say: lend us your knife, we're going to slice some sausage, and you can go to the devil.

Now Tsezar was again in his debt.

Having settled the bread and knife business, Shukhov opened his tobacco pouch. First he took a pinch of tobacco out of it, equal to what he'd borrowed, and stretched a hand across the aisle to Eino the Estonian. Thanks.

The Estonian's lips stretched in a sort of smile. He muttered something to his "brother," and together they rolled the pinch of tobacco into a cigarette. Let's try Shukhov's tobacco.

No worse than yours. Try it, if you please. He'd like to try it himself, but some timekeeper in his brain told him that the evening count would very soon be starting. This was just the time the guards poked around the barracks. If he was going to smoke now he'd have to go into the corridor, but up there in his bunk he somehow felt warmer. The barracks was, as a matter of fact, far from warm—that film of frost was still on the ceiling. He'd shiver in the night, but now it was bearable.

Shukhov stayed in his bunk and began crumbling little bits off his bread. He listened unwillingly to Tsezar and Buinovsky, talking below over their tea.

"Help yourself, Captain. Help yourself, don't hold back. Take some of this smoked fish. Have a slice of sausage."

"Thanks, I will."

"Spread some butter on that bread. It's real Moscow bread."

"D'you know, I simply can't believe they're still baking pure white bread anywhere. Such luxury reminds me of a time when I happened to be in Archangel. . . ."[8]

The two hundred voices in Shukhov's half of the barracks were making a terrific din, but he fancied he heard the rail being struck. No one else seemed to have heard it. He also noticed that "Snubnose," the guard, had come into the barracks. He was no more than a boy, small and rosy-cheeked. He was holding a sheet of paper, and it was clear from this and his manner that he'd come, not to turn them all out for the evening count or catch smokers, but to get someone.

"Snubnose" checked something on his list and said: "Where's the hundred and fourth?"

"Here," they answered. The Estonians hid their cigarettes and waved away the smoke.

"Where's the squad leader?"

"Well?" said Tiurin from his bunk, lowering his feet reluctantly.

"Your people signed those forms—about the extra stuff they were wearing?"

8. ***Archangel*** (ärk′ān′jəl), seaport in the northwest Soviet Union, on the White Sea.

"They'll sign them," said Tiurin with assurance.

"They're overdue."

"My men haven't had much education. It's not an easy job. (This about Tsezar and the captain! What a squad leader! Never at a loss for an answer.) No pens. No ink."

"Ought to have them."

"They take them away from us."

"Well, look out, squad leader. If you go on talking like that I'll put you in the guardhouse with the rest," "Snubnose" promised Tiurin, but mildly. "Now about those forms—see they're handed in to the guardroom before roll call tomorrow morning. And give orders that all prohibited garments are to be surrendered to personal property. Get that?"

"I get it."

(The captain was in luck, thought Shukhov. He hadn't heard a word, he was having such a fine time with his sausage.)

"Let's see now," said the guard. "S 311. He one of yours?"

"Have to look at my list," said Tiurin vaguely. "Expect me to keep all those stupid numbers in my head?"

(He was playing for time. He wanted to save Buinovsky one night at least, by dragging things out till the count.)

"Buinovsky. He here?"

"Eh? Here I am," called the captain from his haven under Shukhov's bunk.

There you are; the quickest louse is always the first to be caught in the comb.

"You? Yes, that's right. S 311. Get ready."

"Where am I to go?"

"You know where."

The captain sighed. He grunted. Nothing more. It must have been easier for him to take out a squadron of destroyers into the dark, stormy night than to tear himself away from this friendly chat and set out for the icy cells.

"How many days?" he asked, his voice falling.

"Ten. Come on, come on. Get going."

At that moment the barracks orderlies shouted: "Evening count. All out for evening count."

This meant that the guard who was to count them had already entered the barracks.

The captain looked around. Should he take his coat? Anyway, they'd strip it off him when he got there, leaving him only his jacket. Better go as he was. He'd hoped that Volkovoi would forget (but Volkovoi never forgot anyone) and he had made no preparations, hadn't even hidden a pinch of tobacco in his jacket. And to carry it in his hands—that would be useless; they'd take it from him the minute they frisked him.

All the same . . . Tsezar slipped him a couple of cigarettes as he put on his hat.

"Well, brothers, good-by," said the captain with an embarrassed nod to his fellow prisoners, and followed the guard out.

A few voices shouted: Keep your chin up. But what could you really say to him? They knew the cells, the 104th did; they'd built them. Brick walls, cement floor, no windows, a stove they lit only to melt the ice on the walls and make pools on the floor. You slept on bare boards, and if you'd any teeth left to eat with after all the chattering they'd be doing, they gave you nine ounces of bread day after day and hot stew only on the third, sixth, and ninth.

Ten days. Ten days "hard" in the cells—if you sat them out to the end, your health would be ruined for the rest of your life. T.B. and nothing but hospital for you till you kicked the bucket.

As for those who got fifteen days "hard" and sat them out—they went straight into a hole in the cold earth.

As long as you're in the barracks—praise the Lord and sit tight.

"Come on now, out you get, before I count three," shouted the barracks commander. "Anyone who isn't out will have his number taken. I'll give it to the guard."

The barracks commander was one of the biggest swine. After all, just think, he's locked in with the zeks all night, but the way he acts, not afraid of anyone! On the contrary, everyone's afraid of him. Some of them he betrays to the

guards, others he wallops himself. He lost a thumb in a scrap and is classed as an invalid, but his face is the face of a thug. Actually he *is* a thug with a criminal record, but among the charges against him was one under Article 58, 14, and that's how he landed where he did.

He wouldn't think twice about taking your number and passing it to the guard—and that means two days in the guardhouse, with work. So instead of just trailing to the door one by one they all rushed out in a crowd, tumbling down from the bunks as if they were bears and pressing to the narrow exit.

Shukhov, the cigarette in his palm—he'd craved it so long and had already rolled it—sprang nimbly down, and slipped his feet into the valenki. He was on the point of leaving when he felt a twinge of pity for Tsezar. It wasn't that he wanted to make anything more out of the man; he felt genuinely sorry for him. For all his high opinion of himself, Tsezar didn't know a thing about life—after collecting his parcel he shouldn't have gloated over it; he should have taken it to the storeroom right away before the evening count. Eating's something that can wait. But now what was Tsezar going to do with all that stuff? He couldn't carry his sack with him to the count. What a horselaugh that would bring! Four hundred zeks roaring their heads off. But to leave it in the barracks no matter how briefly meant that the first to run back from the count would swipe it. (At Ust-Izhma it was even crueler: there, when the zeks came back from work, the crooks got in first and cleaned out all their lockers.)

Shukhov saw that Tsezar realized the danger. He was bustling here and there, but too late. He was stuffing the sausage and salt pork under his jacket. That at least he could save by taking it to the count.

Pityingly, Shukhov gave him some advice: "Sit here till the last moment, Tsezar Markovich. Hide here in the shadow and stay till everyone has left. And when the guard comes by the bunks with the orderlies and pokes into everything, come out and say you're feeling bad. I'll go out first and I'll be back first. That's the way. . . ."

And he ran off.

At first he elbowed his way through the crowd mercilessly (protecting his cigarette in his fist, however). In the corridor, which served both halves of the barracks, and near the door, the men in front were hanging back, the cagey beasts, clinging in two rows to the walls on each side, leaving just enough room for any fool who liked the cold to squeeze through. They were going to stay here; they've been out all day. Why should they freeze needlessly for another ten minutes? No fools here! You croak today but *I* mean to live till tomorrow.

At any other time Shukhov too would have clung to the wall. But now he strode to the door and even grinned.

"What are you scared of, you idiots? Never seen Siberian frost before? Come outside and warm yourselves by the wolf's sun. Give us a light, uncle."

He lit his cigarette at the door and moved out onto the porch. "Wolf's sun," that's what they'd called the moon in Shukhov's village.

The moon rode high now. As high again, and it would be at its zenith. The sky was greenish-white; the rare stars shone brilliantly. The snow gleamed white, the barracks walls gleamed white. The lamps had little effect.

There was a dense black crowd outside one of the barracks. The zeks had come out for the count. They were coming out over there too. But it wasn't the sound of voices you heard from the barracks—it was the creaking of boots on the snow.

Some prisoners were coming down the steps and lining up, opposite the barracks. Five in front, then three behind. Shukhov joined the three. After an extra bit of bread, and with a cigarette between your lips, it wasn't so bad standing there. Good tobacco—the Lett hadn't gypped him. Strong, and smelled good.

Gradually, other prisoners trailed through the door. Two or three more lines of five were forming behind him. They came out angry now. Why were those rats jostling in the corridor? Why weren't they coming out? Why should we have to freeze for them?

No zek ever saw a clock or a watch. What use were they to him anyway? All he needs to know is will reveille sound soon? How long to roll call? How long to dinner? To the last clanging of the rail?

The evening count, everyone said, was at nine. But it never finished at nine—they would sometimes recount two or even three times. You never got away before ten. And at five o'clock next morning they hounded you out of your bunk with the first clanging of the rail. No wonder that Moldavian had dozed off down at the shop before work was over today. Wherever a zek gets a bit of warmth into him he falls asleep on the spot. You lose so much sleep during the week that on a Sunday—provided they don't send you to work—whole barrackfuls of zeks sleep the day through.

Now they're streaming forward. At last! The barracks commander and the guard were dragging them out, kicking them in the tail. Serve 'em right, the tricky slobs.

"What?" the zeks in front shouted at the latecomers. "Pretty smart, huh? Want to lick the cream off the mud, you rats? If you'd come out earlier we'd be through now."

The whole barracks had been emptied. Four hundred men—eighty ranks of five. They lined up in a column, the ones in front strictly in fives, the others any old way.

"Get into line there, you at the back," the barracks commander shouted from the steps.

They didn't move, curse 'em.

Tsezar came out shivering, pretending he was sick. At his heels were four orderlies, two from each half of the barracks, and a prisoner who limped. They stood in front so that Shukhov was now a row farther back. Tsezar was sent to the rear of the column.

The guard came out too.

"Form fives!" he shouted to the rear of the column, furiously.

"Form fives!" shouted the barracks commander even more furiously.

The men didn't budge, curse 'em.

The barracks commander rushed from the porch to the rear of the column, swearing and hitting out.

But he was careful whom he hit. Only the meek ones.

The ranks formed. He came back. He shouted:

"First. Second. Third . . ."

As soon as they'd been counted the men broke away and rushed into the barracks. All square for today with the authorities.

All square, unless there's a recount. Those parasites were such morons, they counted worse than any herdsman. For all that he may be unable to read or write, a herdsman knows if there's a calf missing when he's driving the herd. And these parasites had been trained—whatever good it'd done them.

The previous winter there'd been no drying sheds at all for the boots, and the zeks had had to leave their valenki in the barracks night after night. So if the count was repeated, everyone had to be driven outside again, a second, a third, a fourth time—already undressed, just as they were, wrapped in blankets. Since then a drying shed had been built; it wasn't big enough for all the boots at one time, but at least each of the squads could get the benefit of it once every two or three days. So now any recount was held inside. They merely shifted the zeks from one half of the barracks to the other, counting them as they filed through.

Shukhov wasn't the first to be back, but he kept an eye on anyone ahead of him. He ran up to Tsezar's bunk and sat on it. He took off his boots, and climbed onto the top of a tier of bunks close by the stove. He put his boots on the stove—first-comer's prerogative—then back to Tsezar's bunk. He sat there cross-legged, one eye on the guard for Tsezar (they might swipe his packages from under the head of his bunk), the other for himself (they might push his boots off the stove).

"Hey," he shouted, "hey you, Red. Want to get that boot in your teeth? Put your own up but don't touch other people's."

The prisoners poured in like a stream.

The men in the 20th shouted: "Give us your boots."

As soon as they'd left the barracks with the boots the door was locked after them. When they ran back they shouted: "Citizen chief. Let us in."

And the guards gathered in their quarters with their boards and did the bookkeeping: had anyone escaped, or was everything in order?

Well, Shukhov needn't think about such things that evening. Here came Tsezar, diving between the tiers of bunks on his way back.

"Thank you, Ivan Denisovich."

Shukhov nodded, and shot up to his bunk like a squirrel. Now he could finish his bread, smoke a second cigarette, go to sleep.

But he'd had such a good day, he felt in such good spirits, that somehow he wasn't in the mood for sleep yet.

He must make his bed now—there wasn't much to it. Strip his mattress of the grubby blanket and lie on it (it must have been '41 when he last slept in sheets—that was at home; it even seemed odd for women to bother about sheets, all that extra laundering). Head on the pillow, stuffed with shavings of wood; feet in jacket sleeve; coat on top of blanket and—Glory be to Thee, O Lord. Another day over. Thank You I'm not spending tonight in the cells. Here it's still bearable.

He lay with his head near the window, but Alyosha, who slept next to him on the same level, across a low wooden railing, lay the opposite way, to catch the light. He was reading his Bible again.

The electric light was quite near. You could read and even sew by it.

Alyosha heard Shukhov's whispered prayer, and, turning to him: "There you are, Ivan Denisovich, your soul is begging to pray. Why don't you give it its freedom?"

Shukhov stole a look at him. Alyosha's eyes glowed like two candles.

"Well, Alyosha," he said with a sigh, "it's this way. Prayers are like those appeals of ours. Either they don't get through or they're returned with 'rejected' scrawled across 'em."

Outside the staff quarters were four sealed boxes—they were cleared by a security officer once a month. Many were the appeals that were dropped into them. The writers waited, counting the weeks: there'll be a reply in two months, in one month. . . .

But the reply doesn't come. Or if it does it's only "rejected."

"But, Ivan Denisovich, it's because you pray too rarely, and badly at that. Without really trying. That's why your prayers stay unanswered. One must never stop praying. If you have real faith you tell a mountain to move and it will move. . . ."

Shukhov grinned and rolled another cigarette. He took a light from the Estonian.

"Don't talk nonsense, Alyosha. I've never seen a mountain move. Well, to tell the truth, I've never seen a mountain at all. But you, now, you prayed in the Caucasus with all that Baptist society of yours—did you make a single mountain move?"

They were an unlucky group too. What harm did they do anyone by praying to God? Every one of them had been given twenty-five years. Nowadays they cut all cloth to the same measure—twenty-five years.

"Oh, we didn't pray for that, Ivan Denisovich," Alyosha said earnestly. Bible in hand, he drew nearer to Shukhov till they lay face to face. "Of all earthly and mortal things Our Lord commanded us to pray only for our daily bread. 'Give us this day our daily bread.' "

"Our ration, you mean?" asked Shukhov.

But Alyosha didn't give up. Arguing more with his eyes than his tongue, he plucked at Shukhov's sleeve, stroked his arm, and said: "Ivan Denisovich, you shouldn't pray to get parcels or for extra stew, not for that. Things that man puts a high price on are vile in the eyes of Our Lord. We must pray about things of the spirit—that the Lord Jesus should remove the scum of anger from our hearts. . . ."

"Listen to me. At our church in Polomnya we had a priest. . . ."

"Don't talk to me about your priest," Alyosha said imploringly, his brow furrowed with distress.

"No, listen." Shukhov propped himself up on an elbow. "In Polomnya, our parish, there isn't a man richer than the priest. Take roofing, for instance. We charge thirty-five rubles a day to ordinary people for mending a roof, but the priest a hundred. And he forks up without a whimper. And he keeps that bishop of his on a hook, I can tell you. Oh yes, he gives his fat hand to the bishop, all right. And he's thrown out every other priest they've sent there. Wouldn't share a thing with 'em."

"Why are you talking to me about priests? The Orthodox Church has departed from Scripture. It's because their faith is unstable that they're not in prison."

Shukhov went on calmly smoking and watching his excited companion.

"Alyosha," he said, withdrawing his arm and blowing smoke into his face. "I'm not against God, understand that. I do believe in God. But I don't believe in paradise or in hell. Why do you take us for fools and stuff us with your paradise and hell stories? That's what I don't like."

He lay back, dropping his cigarette ash with care between the bunk frame and the window, so as to singe nothing of the captain's below. He sank into his own thoughts. He didn't hear Alyosha's mumbling.

"Well," he said conclusively, "however much you pray it doesn't shorten your stretch. You'll sit it out from beginning to end anyhow."

"Oh, you mustn't pray for that either," said Alyosha, horrified. "Why do you want freedom? In freedom your last grain of faith will be choked with weeds. You should rejoice that you're in prison. Here you have time to think about your soul. As the Apostle Paul wrote: 'Why all these tears? Why are you trying to weaken my resolution? For my part I am not ready merely to be bound but even to die for the name of the Lord Jesus.' "

Shukhov gazed at the ceiling in silence. Now he didn't know either whether he wanted freedom or not. At first he'd longed for it. Every night he'd counted the days of his stretch—how many had passed, how many were coming. And then he'd grown bored with counting. And then it became clear that men like him wouldn't ever be allowed to return home, that they'd be exiled. And whether his life would be any better there than here—who could tell?

Freedom meant one thing to him—home.

But they wouldn't let him go home.

Alyosha was speaking the truth. His voice and his eyes left no doubt that he was happy in prison.

"You see, Alyosha," Shukhov explained to him, "somehow it works out all right for you: Jesus Christ wanted you to sit in prison and so you are—sitting there for His sake. But for whose sake am *I* here? Because we weren't ready for war in '41? For that? But was that *my* fault?"

"Seems like there's not going to be a recount," Kilgas murmured from his bunk.

"Yeah," said Shukhov. "We ought to write it up in coal inside the chimney. No second count." He yawned. "Might as well get to sleep."

And at that very moment the door bolt rattled to break the calm that now reigned in the barracks. From the corridor ran two of the prisoners who'd taken boots to the drying sheds.

"Second count," they shouted.

On their heels came a guard.

"All out to the other half."

Some were already asleep. They began to grumble and move about, they put their boots on (no one ever took his wadded trousers off at night—you'd grow numb with cold unless you wore them under your blanket).

"Curse them," said Shukhov. Mildly, because he hadn't gone to sleep yet.

Tsezar raised a hand and gave him two biscuits, two lumps of sugar, and a slice of sausage.

"Thank you, Tsezar Markovich," said Shukhov, leaning over the edge of his bunk. "Come on now, hand up that sack of yours. I'll put it under my mattress." (It's not so easy to swipe things from the top bunks as you go by. Anyway, who'd look for anything in Shukhov's bunk?)

Tsezar handed up his sack and Shukhov hid it under the mattress. Then he waited a little till more men had been sent out—he wouldn't have to stand barefoot so long in the corridor. But the guard scowled at him and shouted: "Come on, you there in the corner."

Shukhov sprang lightly to the floor (his boots and foot rags were so well placed on the stove it would be a pity to move them). Though he'd made so many slippers for others he hadn't a pair of his own. But he was used to this—and the count didn't take long.

They confiscate slippers too if they find them in daytime.

As for the squads who'd sent their boots to be dried, it wasn't so bad for them, now the recount was held indoors. Some wore slippers, some just their foot rags, some went barefoot.

"Come on, come on," growled the guard.

"Do you want to be carried out, you swine?" the barracks commander shouted.

They shoved them all into the other half of the barracks, and loiterers into the corridor. Shukhov stood against the wall near the bucket. The floor was moist underfoot. An icy draft crept in from the porch.

They had them all out now and once again the guard and the orderly did their round, looking for any who might be dozing in dark corners. There'd be trouble if they counted short. It would mean still another recount. Round they went, round they went, and came back to the door.

"One, two, three, four . . ." Now they released you faster, for they were counting one by one. Shukhov managed to squeeze in eighteenth. He ran back to his bunk, put his foot on the support—a heave, and he was up.

All right. Feet back into the sleeve of his jacket. Blanket on top. Then the coat. And to sleep. Now they'd be letting everybody from the other half of the barracks into our half. But that's not our worry.

Tsezar returned. Shukhov lowered his sack to him.

Alyosha returned. Impractical, that's his trouble. Makes himself nice to everyone but doesn't know how to do favors that get paid back.

"Here you are, Alyosha," said Shukhov, and handed him a biscuit.

Alyosha smiled. "Thank you. But you've got nothing yourself."

"Eat it."

(We've nothing but we always find a way to make something extra.)

Now for that slice of sausage. Into the mouth. Getting your teeth into it. Your teeth. The meaty taste. And the meaty juice, the real stuff. Down it goes, into your belly.

Gone.

The rest, Shukhov decided, for the morning. Before the roll call.

And he buried his head in the thin, unwashed blanket, deaf now to the crowd of zeks from the other half as they jostled between the bunk frames, waiting to be counted.

Shukhov went to sleep fully content. He'd had many strokes of luck that day: they hadn't put him in the cells; they hadn't sent his squad to the settlement; he'd swiped a bowl of kasha at dinner; the squad leader had fixed the rates well; he'd built a wall and enjoyed doing it; he'd smuggled that bit of hacksaw blade through; he'd earned a favor from Tsezar that evening; he'd bought that tobacco. And he hadn't fallen ill. He'd got over it.

A day without a dark cloud. Almost a happy day.

There were three thousand six hundred and fifty-three days like that in his stretch. From the first clang of the rail to the last clang of the rail.

Three thousand six hundred and fifty-three days.

The three extra days were for leap years.

Discussion

1. **(a)** Why is Shukhov the last of his squad to leave the power station? **(b)** What keeps the guards from giving him a hard time about his tardiness?

2. **(a)** What difficulties does the delay caused by the Moldavian create for the other prisoners? **(b)** Do you think it is only these difficulties that cause the men to get so angry? Discuss. **(c)** How do the prisoners get back at the escort guards for keeping them out so long?

3. **(a)** Why are the prisoners from the machine works subject to more thorough frisking? **(b)** Do the authorities have any justification for this action? Explain. **(c)** Why is Shukhov so reluctant to dispose of the hacksaw blade knowing that its discovery might cost him a term in the cells?

4. Shukhov had arranged long ago to have no parcels sent to him. **(a)** Why did he choose to do without them? **(b)** Is he happy with his decision? Explain. **(c)** Describe how his choice has shaped his relationship with Tsezar.

5. U 81, the elderly man opposite Shukhov in the mess hall, has been a prisoner for countless years. **(a)** What does Shukhov infer from the man's appearance? **(b)** Does he symbolize anything? Explain.

6. **(a)** Describe the situation Buinovsky is in prior to the appearance of "Snubnose" the guard. **(b)** How do some of the 104th show support for the captain in the light of what is about to happen to him? **(c)** Buinovsky would certainly be changed physically by the ordeal he faces. How else might he be different?

7. **(a)** Has Tsezar's privileged position in the camp eliminated every difficulty for him? Explain. **(b)** Discuss whether or not you think he deserves Shukhov's sympathy.

8. An internal conflict running throughout the novel emerges again when Alyosha preaches to Shukhov about the nature of freedom. **(a)** Why doesn't Alyosha want it? **(b)** Why is the prospect of freedom disturbing to Shukhov? **(c)** Shukhov recognizes an underlying purpose in Alyosha's situation but despairs at finding none in his own. Cite evidence to show how he has dealt with this conflict.

9. "Almost a happy day" is the way Shukhov characterizes this period. In your opinion, are the highlights he mentions particularly noteworthy? Discuss.

Composition

The author describes several hours of the thousands of days comprising Shukhov's term, focusing on routine activities: meals, marches to and from his work site, errands, and so on. This approach appears to be an alternative to one that would present Shukhov's experience over a longer period of time in a less detailed but more dramatic fashion. Review the novel for examples of the author's intensive description of a seemingly ordinary activity or incident. Then choose one for analysis.

In a four- or five-paragraph essay, evaluate this segment of material. What does it show about the author's technique? his attitude toward camp life? Would it be included if the novel covered a longer period of time? What insights would be lost if it were omitted? (See "Evaluating Your Evidence," page 662, in the Composition Guide.)

Alexander Solzhenitsyn 1918–

Within twenty-four hours after the publication of *One Day in the Life of Ivan Denisovich* in a Soviet literary magazine in 1962, Alexander Solzhenitsyn, an obscure writer and mathematician, achieved national prominence. The work revealed not only his artistry but a shameful period in his country's history. As translated versions of the work, as well as his public protestations against censorship, found a worldwide audience, he was hailed as both Russia's greatest living author and its "conscience."

Solzhenitsyn's former life constitutes the background of most of his work. Born in the Caucasus Mountains region and raised in the city of Rostov, he graduated from the university there and later became a twice-decorated army captain in World War II. In 1945, before the war's end, he wrote something that changed his life and brought purpose to his previously aimless literary aspirations—a personal letter in which he criticized Stalin's conduct of the war. The letter was obtained by Stalinist authorities and used to charge Solzhenitsyn with anti-Soviet agitation. During his subsequent eight-year imprisonment, he labored as a bricklayer, metalworker, and then mathematician. Teaching math became his means of support after his release in 1953.

At that time the ex-prisoner also began writing accounts of his camp experiences in a fictionalized form, not attempting to publish anything until 1961. Although under Khrushchev's regime he was allowed to publish not only *One Day* but also the short works "Matryona's Home" (1963), "For the Good of the Cause" (1963), and "Zakhar the Pouch" (1966), the political climate changed when Khrushchev was ousted. The outspoken Solzhenitsyn found himself pitted against Soviet authorities, who forbade the publication of his novels *The Cancer Ward* and *The First Circle* in 1968, prevented him from living in Moscow, and would not allow him to go to Stockholm to accept his 1970 Nobel Prize for Literature. His historical novel, *August 1914,* was published outside his homeland in 1971. The following year Soviet authorities confiscated the manuscript of his harshest portrayal of the prison camp system—*The Gulag Archipelago.* Within a brief period the author was arrested, charged with treason, and exiled from the Soviet Union. He and his family eventually settled in the United States, which had conferred honorary citizenship on him in 1974. Residing in his secluded compound in Vermont, Solzhenitsyn continues to produce material that upholds his place in the Russian literary tradition. Still controversial and uncompromising in his political views, he remains a celebrated symbol of free expression.

Unit 8 Review: *The Novel*

Content Review

1. Ivan Denisovich Shukhov is a simple peasant, yet shrewd enough to know the tricks of survival; an uneducated man, yet with much inborn wisdom and compassion. Give examples of each of these qualities, and then decide whether he ultimately comes across as a hero, a victim, or both. Give reasons for your answer.

2. Among the zeks are those who regard themselves as superior to the others. Describe what the following say or do to set themselves apart: **(a)** Tiurin; **(b)** Buinovsky; **(c)** Tsezar; **(d)** Pavlo.

3. Though fairly minor in the development of the plot, the characters listed at the top of the next column nevertheless have distinct backgrounds as well as attitudes about their situation. Give a one-sentence description of each character that presents him as a particular sort of prisoner. **(a)** Fetiukov; **(b)** Senka; **(c)** Alyosha; **(d)** Gopchik.

4. The question raised several times in the novel, "How can you expect a man who's warm to understand a man who's cold?" is also a problem Solzhenitsyn faced in conveying his setting to his audience. Give examples of how he was able to communicate the harshness of the life and of how his tone reveals his attitude toward it.

5. The characters in the novel are from different regions and represent various social classes. To what extent would you say that Solzhenitsyn intends the camp to stand for Russian society as a whole? Discuss.

6. Give at least three specific examples of how the workings of the bureaucracy affect camp life—through favoritism, bribery, inefficient work practices, and so on.

Concept Review: Interpretation of New Material

Read the introduction and the excerpt from the novella. Then use the questions following them to review your understanding of the concepts presented in the unit.

from Matryona's Home • *Alexander Solzhenitsyn* USSR

Matryona's Home is set in the isolated village of Talnovo, where, in 1953, the narrator comes in search of a teaching position. He finds lodgings with Matryona—an old and sickly woman with no pension and unsympathetic relatives and friends—and soon discovers how she manages to make her meager existence meaningful.

So I moved in with Matryona Vasilyevna.[1] We didn't divide the room. Her bed was in the corner between the door and the stove, and I unfolded my camp bed by one window and pushed Matryona's beloved rubber plants out of the light to make room for a little table by another.

Some of the better-off people in the village might not have thought Matryona's house much of a home, but it kept us snug enough that autumn and winter. The roof still held the rain out, and the freezing winds could not blow the warmth of the stove away all at once, though it was cold by morning, especially when the wind blew on the shabby side.

---

1. ***Matryona Vasilyevna*** (mä trē ô′nä və syēl′yev nə), the character's first name and patronymic.

In addition to Matryona and myself, a cat, some mice, and some cockroaches lived in the house.

The cat was no longer young, and gammy-legged as well. Matryona had taken her in out of pity, and she had stayed. She walked on all four feet but with a heavy limp: one of her feet was sore and she favored it. When she jumped from the stove she didn't land with the soft sound a cat usually makes, but with a heavy thud as three of her feet struck the floor at once—such a heavy thud that until I got used to it, it gave me a start. This was because she stuck three feet out together to save the fourth.

It wasn't because the cat couldn't deal with them that there were mice in the cottage: she would pounce into the corner like lightning, and come back with a mouse between her teeth. But the mice were usually out of reach because somebody, back in the good old days, had stuck embossed wallpaper of a greenish color on Matryona's walls, and not just one layer of it but five. The layers held together all right, but in many places the whole lot had come away from the wall, giving the room a sort of inner skin. Between the timber of the walls and the skin of wallpaper the mice had made themselves runs where they impudently scampered about, running at times right up to the ceiling. The cat followed their scamperings with angry eyes, but couldn't get at them.

Sometimes the cat ate cockroaches as well, but they made her sick. The only thing the cockroaches respected was the partition which screened the mouth of the Russian stove and the kitchen from the best part of the room.

They did not creep into the best room. But the kitchen at night swarmed with them, and if I went in late in the evening for a drink of water and switched on the light the whole floor, the big bench, and even the wall would be one rustling brown mass. From time to time I brought home some borax from the school laboratory and we mixed it with dough to poison them. There would be fewer cockroaches for a while, but Matryona was afraid that we might poison the cat as well. We stopped putting down poison and the cockroaches multiplied anew.

At night, when Matryona was already asleep and I was working at my table, the occasional rapid scamper of mice behind the wallpaper would be drowned in the sustained and ceaseless rustling of cockroaches behind the screen, like the sound of the sea in the distance. But I got used to it because there was nothing evil in it, nothing dishonest. Rustling was life to them.

Matryona got up at four or five in the morning. Her wall clock was twenty-seven years old, and had been bought in the village shop. It was always fast, but Matryona didn't worry about that—just so long as it didn't lose and make her late in the morning. She switched on the light behind the kitchen screen and moving quietly, considerately, doing her best not to make a noise, she lit the stove, went to milk the goat (all the livestock she had was this one dirty-white goat with twisted horns), fetched water and boiled it in three iron pots: one for me, one for herself, and one for the goat. She fetched potatoes from the cellar, picking out the littlest for the goat, little ones for herself, and egg-sized ones for me. There were no big ones, because her garden was sandy, had not been manured since the war,[2] and was always planted with potatoes, potatoes, and potatoes again, so that it wouldn't grow big ones.

I scarcely heard her about her morning tasks. I slept late, woke up in the wintry daylight, stretched a bit and stuck my head out from under my blanket and my sheepskin. These, together with the prisoner's jerkin round my legs and a sack stuffed with straw underneath me, kept me warm in bed even on nights when the cold wind rattled our wobbly windows from the north. When I heard the discreet noises on the other side of the screen I spoke to her, slowly and deliberately.

"Good morning, Matryona Vasilyevna!"

And every time the same good-natured words came to me from behind the screen. They began with a warm, throaty gurgle, the sort of sound grandmothers make in fairy tales.

"M-m-m . . . same to you too!"

And after a little while, "Your breakfast's ready for you now."

She didn't announce what was for breakfast, but it was easy to guess: taters in their jackets or tatty soup (as everybody in the village called it), or barley

---

2. ***the war,*** World War II.

gruel (no other grain could be bought in Torfoprodukt[3] that year, and even the barley you had to fight for, because it was the cheapest and people bought it up by the sack to fatten their pigs on it). It wasn't always salted as it should be, it was often slightly burned, it furred the palate and the gums, and it gave me heartburn.

But Matryona wasn't to blame: there was no butter in Torfoprodukt either, margarine was desperately short, and only mixed cooking fat was plentiful, and when I got to know it I saw that the Russian stove was not convenient for cooking: the cook cannot see the pots and they are not heated evenly all round. I suppose the stove came down to our ancestors from the Stone Age because you can stoke it up once before daylight, and food and water, mash and swill, will keep warm in it all day long. And it keeps you warm while you sleep.

I ate everything that was cooked for me without demur, patiently putting aside anything uncalled-for that I came across: a hair, a bit of peat, a cockroach's leg. I hadn't the heart to find fault with Matryona. After all, she had warned me herself.

"We aren't clever, we can't cook—I don't know how we shall suit. . . ."

"Thank you," I said quite sincerely.

"What for? For what is your own?" she answered, disarming me with a radiant smile. And, with a guileless look of her faded blue eyes, she would ask, "And what shall I cook you for just now?"

For just now meant for supper. I ate twice a day, like at the front. What could I order for just now? It would have to be one of the same old things, taters or tatty soup.

I resigned myself to it, because I had learned by now not to look for the meaning of life in food. More important to me was the smile on her roundish face, which I tried in vain to catch when at last I had earned enough to buy a camera. As soon as she saw the cold eye of the lens upon her, Matryona assumed a strained or else an exaggeratedly severe expression.

Just once I did manage to get a snap of her looking through the window into the street and smiling at something.

Matryona had a lot of worries that winter. Her neighbors put it into her head to try and get a pension. She was all alone in the world, and when she began to be seriously ill she had been dismissed from the kolkhoz[4] as well. Injustices had piled up, one on top of another. She was ill, but not regarded as a disabled person. She had worked for a quarter of a century in the kolkhoz, but it was a kolkhoz and not a factory, so she was not entitled to a pension for herself. She could only try and get one for her husband, for the loss of her breadwinner. But she had had no husband for twelve years now, not since the beginning of the war, and it wasn't easy to obtain all the particulars from different places about his length of service and how much he had earned. What a bother it was getting those forms through! Getting somebody to certify that he'd earned, say, three hundred rubles a month; that she lived alone and nobody helped her; what year she was born in. Then all this had to be taken to the Pensions Office. And taken somewhere else to get all the mistakes corrected. And taken back again. Then you had to find out whether they would give you a pension.

To make it all more difficult the Pensions Office was twenty kilometers east of Talnovo, the Rural Council Offices ten kilometers to the west, the Factory District Council an hour's walk to the north. They made her run around from office to office for two months on end, to get an *i* dotted or a *t* crossed. Every trip took a day. She goes down to the rural district council—and the secretary isn't there today. Secretaries of rural councils often aren't here today. So come in tomorrow. Tomorrow the secretary is in, but he hasn't got his rubber stamp. So come again the next day. And the day after that back she goes yet again, because all her papers are pinned together and some cockeyed clerk has signed the wrong one.

"They shove me around, Ignatich,"[5] she used to complain to me after these fruitless excursions. "Worn out with it I am."

But she soon brightened up. I found that she had a sure means of putting herself in a good humor.

---

3. ***Torfoprodukt*** (tôr′fô prô dukt′), the name of the station from which peat and other products could be obtained.
4. ***kolkhoz*** (kôl HÔZ′), collective farm.
5. ***Ignatich*** (ig nä′tyich).

She worked. She would grab a shovel and go off to lift potatoes. Or she would tuck a sack under her arm and go after peat. Or take a wicker basket and look for berries deep in the woods. When she'd been bending her back to bushes instead of office desks for a while, and her shoulders were aching from a heavy load, Matryona would come back cheerful, at peace with the world and smiling her nice smile.

"I'm on to a good thing now, Ignatich. I know where to go for it" (peat she meant), "a lovely place it is."

"But surely my peat is enough, Matryona Vasilyevna? There's a whole truckload of it."

"Pooh! Your peat! As much again, and then as much again, that might be enough. When the winter gets really stiff and the wind's battling at the windows, it blows the heat out of the house faster than you can make the stove up. Last year we got heaps and heaps of it. I'd have had three loads in by now. But they're out to catch us. They've summoned one woman from our village already."

That's how it was. The frightening breath of winter was already in the air. There were forests all round, and no fuel to be had anywhere. Excavators roared away in the bogs, but there was no peat on sale to the villagers. It was delivered, free, to the bosses and to the people round the bosses, and teachers, doctors, and workers got a load each. The people of Talnovo were not supposed to get any peat, and they weren't supposed to ask about it. The chairman of the kolkhoz walked about the village looking people in the eye while he gave his orders or stood chatting, and talked about everything you liked except fuel. He was stocked up. Who said anything about winter coming?

So just as in the old days they used to steal the squire's wood, now they pinched peat from the trust.[6] The women went in parties of five or ten so that they would be less frightened. They went in the daytime. The peat cut during the summer had been stacked up all over the place to dry. That's the good thing about peat, it can't be carted off as soon as it's cut. It lies around drying till autumn; or, if the roads are bad, till the snow starts falling. This was when the women used to come and take it. They could get six peats in a sack if it was damp, or ten if it was dry. A sackful weighed about two poods and it sometimes had to be carried over three kilometers. This was enough to make the stove up once. There were two hundred days in the winter. The Russian stove had to be lit in the mornings, and the "Dutch" stove in the evenings.

"Why beat about the bush?" said Matryona angrily to someone invisible. "Since there've been no more horses, what you can't heave around yourself you haven't got. My back never heals up. Winter you're pulling sledges, summer it's bundles on your back, it's God's truth I'm telling you."

The women went more than once in a day. On good days Matryona brought six sacks home. She piled my peat up where it could be seen, and hid her own under the passageway, boarding up the hole every night.

"If they don't just happen to think of it, the devils will never find it in their born days," said Matryona, smiling and wiping the sweat from her brow.

What could the peat trust do? Its establishment didn't run to a watchman for every bog. I suppose they had to show a rich haul in their returns, and then write off so much for crumbling, so much washed away by the rain. . . . Sometimes they would take it into their heads to put out patrols and try to catch the women as they came into the village. The women would drop their sacks and scatter. Or somebody would inform and there would be a house-to-house search. They would draw up a report on the stolen peat, and threaten a court action. The women would stop fetching it for a while, but the approach of winter drove them out with sledges in the middle of the night.

---

6. ***the trust,*** the state-owned organization administering the industry.

1. To Ignatich, the narrator, Matryona's home was **(a)** overcrowded; **(b)** unfit to live in; **(c)** snug; **(d)** the finest home in Talnovo.

2. She served him a lot of barley gruel because **(a)** he had expressed a liking for it; **(b)** she knew it was healthful; **(c)** barley was one of the few cheap foods available; **(d)** barley was very popular in that part of the country.

3. Matryona's character is shown primarily through **(a)** her thoughts and conversations; **(b)** the narrator's comments about her; **(c)** a description of her personal appearance; **(d)** all of the above.

4. Ignatich seems to most admire Matryona's **(a)** wallpaper; **(b)** boundless spirit; **(c)** feeling of helplessness; **(d)** ability to walk long distances.

5. An article of clothing is a clue to the narrator's past. Identify it and explain.

6. The troubles Matryona had in obtaining a pension were caused mostly by **(a)** the narrator; **(b)** her late husband; **(c)** the bureaucracy; **(d)** her jealous neighbors.

7. What means did Matryona have for putting herself in good humor?

8. The chairman of the kolkhoz ignored the workers' need for **(a)** healthier livestock; **(b)** heating fuel in the form of peat; **(c)** new farm equipment; **(d)** fewer working hours.

9. In order to survive Matryona was forced to **(a)** sell vegetables from her garden; **(b)** steal; **(c)** leave the kolkhoz; **(d)** raise her boarder's rent.

10. Which of the following elements of Soviet life is *not* shown in the excerpt? **(a)** difficulties caused by the bureaucracy; **(b)** poverty; **(c)** people's determination to survive and endure; **(d)** people's fear of being sent to prison camps.

Composition Review

Choose one of the following to write about.

1. Assume you are Buinovsky writing to your wife about the first few months in prison. You want to give her some idea of what the life is like, as well as how easy or difficult you find it to adjust to.

Write a several-paragraph letter, using a tone and language that you think would be appropriate for Buinovsky.

2. Though closely regimented, the zeks nevertheless can, through various means, enjoy certain small freedoms. Review the novel for examples of such freedoms; one example might be how Shukhov is able to get himself tobacco.

Write a composition presenting and discussing various instances of freedoms within the camp.

3. The novel several times suggests that a successful zek is a pragmatic, self-serving one. Decide whether you think that in general the prisoners subscribe to this code of behavior; then look for specifics to back up your opinion.

Write a short essay explaining why you agree or disagree with this evaluation of a good zek's attitude.

4. Matryona faces some of the same problems Shukhov does, but in certain respects her life is better than his. Review the excerpt for ways in which their situations are similar or different.

Write a composition comparing the ways of life of Matryona and Shukhov.

Handbook of Literary Terms

alliteration

> An Austrian army, awfully array'd,
> Boldly by battery besieged Belgrade;

What is the recurring initial sound in each word of the lines above? These lines contain extreme examples of *alliteration*, the repetition of identical or similar sounds at the beginnings of words or within the words themselves, particularly at the beginning of accented syllables. You are probably already familiar with alliteration as it is used in advertising: "Quick Clean Car Care" or "Buy Big Broiled Burgers." Many ordinary expressions contain alliteration: *wild west; through thick and through thin; merry month of May; rough and ready.*

Alliteration can draw attention to certain words in a poem:

> *S*afe upon the *s*olid rock the
> ugly hou*s*e*s* *s*tand:
> Come and *s*ee my *s*hining pala*c*e
> built upon the *s*and!
>
> Edna St. Vincent Millay,
> *Figs from Thistles*

It can link together words that are similar in thought or feeling:

> *C*old are the *c*rabs that *c*rawl on yonder hills,
> *C*older the *c*u*c*umbers that grow beneath. . . .
>
> Edward Lear, "Cold Are the Crabs"

It can point up contrasts:

> The *H*art loves the *h*igh wood,
> the *H*are loves the *h*ill. . . .

Alliteration in poetry gives pleasure, but a good poet may make the sound "an echo to the sense." How sound can echo sense or meaning is shown in the examples that follow:

> When he saw *Gr*endel's *gr*uesome footprints,
> that *gr*eat man *gr*ieved for his retainers.
>
> *Beowulf* (translated by Kevin Crossley-Holland)

Does the repeated *gr* sound help to make this line seem light or heavy?

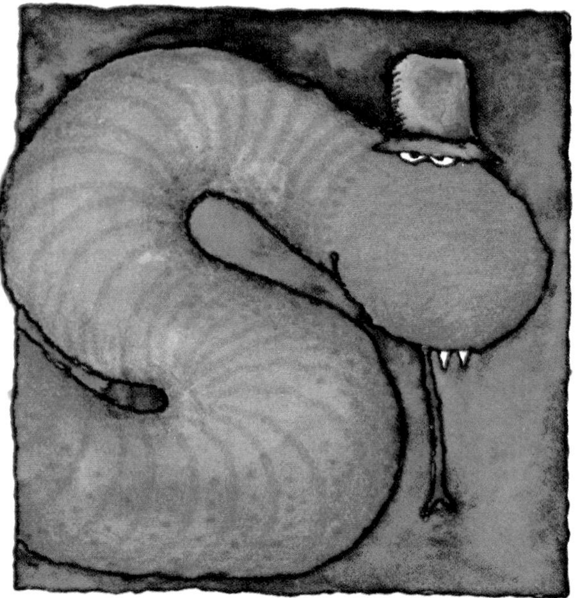

Sea-Weed

> Sea-weed sways and sways and swirls
> as if swaying were its form of stillness;
> and if it flushes against fierce rock
> it slips over as shadows do, without hurting itself.
>
> D. H. Lawrence

What effect does the repeated *s* sound have?

alliteration (ə lit′ə rā′shən)

The repetition of similar or identical sounds at the beginnings of words or in accented syllables. It is used to create melody, establish mood, emphasize certain words, and point up similarities and contrasts.

Apply to **"A Parrot"** on page 182.

allusion

March 15 hit hard this year—gray, rainy, and a chill wind that bit right through my jacket. By the time I reached school, my shoes were soaked, my socks damp and itchy, and my homework soggy. As I sat down in my first-period class, world history, Mr. Brutto told us to take out a clean sheet of paper and clear our desks. It meant only one thing: a pop quiz. I guess that old bird was right when he said to beware the ides of March. I should've stayed in bed.

Who is the "old bird" referred to in the above paragraph? What does the writer of the paragraph mean by referring to the "ides of March"? How does the reference relate to the events in the paragraph? (For the source of the *allusion,* see *Julius Caesar,* Act One, Scene 2.)

An allusion is a reference to any historical, cultural, mythical, or literary event or any other aspect of ancient or modern culture. Some allusions are so familiar that you may not think of them as such. For example, the Biblical figures David and Goliath are commonly alluded to in any kind of match which involves opponents of apparently unequal size or strength. A fantastic young hitter on a baseball team might be called "the new Hank Aaron" by sportswriters.

Allusions in literature may be used to increase meaning, beauty, or mood, or to add depth to a work. They are a concise means of strengthening atmosphere or clarifying tone. Allusions may be incidental to a work, or they may be crucial to its understanding. Sometimes they require research on the part of the reader.

In order to understand the cartoon, the reader must be familiar with a certain Mother Goose nursery rhyme. The reference to "Humpty" in the cartoon should prompt the memory of Humpty Dumpty, the character in the rhyme who was hurt beyond repair in a fall from a wall. Recalling that Humpty Dumpty was an egg should enhance the allusion the cartoon makes to the nursery rhyme. The reader can conclude that the hen is the object of the sympathetic message probably because Humpty Dumpty was her egg.

The requirements for allusions are that they be accurate and appropriate to the subject at hand. Unless one were being sarcastic, one would not call the last racehorse to cross the finish line "Pegasus," the winged horse of Greek mythology; nor, when speaking of a quick errand, would one allude to the quest of King Arthur's knights for the Holy Grail. No one reads simply to fill his or her head with sources of allusion, but the ability to recognize allusions is a satisfying and inevitable result of wide reading.

allusion (ə lü'zhən)

A reference to a historical or literary figure or event. It may allude to myth, religion, or to any other aspect of ancient or modern culture.

Apply to ***Medea*** on page 240.

Frank and Ernest
WE WERE ALL SORRY TO HEAR ABOUT HUMPTY.
3-5
THAVES

analogy

Aspirations
toward space
are not new.
Consider the worm
that becomes
a butterfly.

George Garrott

How does the poet make the point that our desire to fly into space is perfectly natural? By drawing an *analogy* between this desire and the innate ability of the caterpillar to change into a butterfly. An analogy is a comparison drawn between two basically unlike things that nonetheless have points of similarity. Analogy is often used when one thing being compared is somewhat unknown or hard to understand and the other is well known or easy to understand. Analogies are often stated like this: aspiration is to space as worm is to butterfly; or, more briefly, aspiration: space :: worm: butterfly.

Our Little Kinsmen

Our little kinsmen after rain
In plenty may be seen,
A pink and pulpy multitude
The tepid ground upon.

A needless life it seemed to me
Until a little bird
As to a hospitality
Advanced and breakfasted.

As I of he, so God of me,
Pondered, may have judged,
And left the little angleworm
With modesties enlarged.

Emily Dickinson

Who are "our little kinsmen"? Why are they not examples of "needless life"? If the "kinsmen" are half of the analogy, who is the other half? State this relationship in both analogy forms. Why is the poet humbled by the analogy?

analogy (ə nal′ə jē)

A comparison drawn between two basically different things that have some points in common, often used to explain a difficult idea in terms of a simpler one.

Apply to "The Rat Trap" on page 335.

assonance

While in the wild wood I did lie,
A child—with a most knowing eye.

Edgar Allan Poe, "Romance"

What words are accented in the above lines? What vowel sound is often repeated in those accented words? The recurring *i* sound is an example of *assonance:* identical or similar vowel sounds followed by different consonant sounds, and occurring generally in accented words or syllables. Assonance differs from rhyme in that rhyme is a similarity of both vowel and consonant sounds. *Wild* and *child* and *lie* and *eye* are rhyming words; *while* and *wild* illustrate assonance.

Point out the examples of assonance in the following lines.

Think from how many trees
Dead leaves are brought
To earth on seed or wing . . .

Vernon Watkins,
"The Compost Heap"

Not only are the assonant words stressed rhythmically, assonance emphasizes words whose meanings are already associated: *trees, leaves, seed.* Assonance can thus contribute not only to the sound or musical quality of a poem, but also to its meaning.

assonance (as′n əns)

The repetition of similar or identical vowel sounds followed by different consonant sounds in stressed words or syllables. Assonance can contribute to the meaning of a work, to its musical quality, and to its unity.

Apply to "Schoolmaster" on page 175.

blank verse

And at the threshold of her chamber door
The Carthage lords did there the queen await;
The trampling steed, with gold and purple decked,
Chawing the foamy bit, there fiercely stood.

Henry Howard, Earl of Surrey,
from *The Fourth Book of Virgil*

1. Do the above lines rhyme?

2. How many feet are there in each line?

3. What is the meter? (See RHYTHM for a discussion of meter and scansion.)

In the sixteenth century, English lyric poets discovered that the English language has a natural iambic beat. They also found that combinations of English words fall naturally into lines of five feet. Once the lyricists had recognized iambic pentameter as a natural English line, they used it extensively (though not exclusively) for rhymed verse.

Dramatists and narrative poets, however, aware that comparatively few English words end with the same sound, found it difficult to sustain rhymed iambic pentameter lines for five acts of a play or for several hundred lines of NARRATIVE poetry. Consequently, they began to write unrhymed iambic pentameter lines, or *blank verse*. Blank verse was later used in LYRIC poetry as well.

Read the following passages; explain whether or not each of them is in blank verse.

Come live with me and be my Love,
And we will all the pleasures prove
That hills and valleys, dales and fields,
Or woods or steepy mountain yields.

Christopher Marlowe,
"The Passionate Shepherd to His Love"

That time of year thou mayst in me behold
When yellow leaves, or none, or few, do hang
Upon those boughs which shake against the cold,
Bare ruined choirs where late the sweet birds sang.

William Shakespeare, "Sonnet 73"

Alas! for this gray shadow, once a man—
So glorious in his beauty and thy choice,
Who madest him thy chosen, that he seemed
To his great heart none other than a god!

Alfred, Lord Tennyson, "Tithonus"

William Shakespeare was a master of both rhymed verse and blank verse. He cast his dramas in blank-verse lines.

O, he sits high in all the people's hearts;
And that which would appear offense in us,
His countenance, like richest alchemy,
Will change to virtue and to worthiness.

William Shakespeare,
Julius Caesar, Act One, Scene 3

Occasionally a line or lines of a blank-verse passage may depart from a regular iambic pattern. The following lines are spoken by one of the conspirators against Caesar. What line deviates strongly from the iambic pentameter pattern?

Their minds may change. Besides, it were a mock
Apt to be rendered, for some one to say,
"Break up the Senate till another time,
When Caesar's wife shall meet with better dreams."
If Caesar hide himself, shall they not whisper
"Lo, Caesar is afraid"?

Julius Caesar, Act Two, Scene 2

Such shifts enabled Shakespeare to use blank verse to achieve a great variety of dramatic effects. Note how the last line of the passage above stands out because of its different line length. This dramatic line is the one which finally convinces Caesar to go to the Senate on the fateful ides of March, and so it is crucial to the play.

blank verse

Unrhymed poetry in iambic pentameter—ten-syllable lines with five unstressed syllables alternating with five stressed syllables. An unstressed syllable begins the line.

Apply to ***Julius Caesar*** on page 379.

characterization

People are interested in other people: how they act, where they go, what they think about in any number of situations. That interest is one of the reasons many people enjoy reading stories about imaginary people who seem real.

Characterization is the technique a writer uses to create lifelike characters. A writer may use any of various methods of characterization, but the most thorough depiction of a character will probably include all of the following.

(The examples are from the novel *Emma* by Jane Austen, 1816.)

An author may simply describe a character:

> Emma Woodhouse, handsome, clever, and rich, with a comfortable home and happy disposition, seemed to unite some of the best blessings of existence; and had lived nearly twenty-one years in the world with very little to distress or vex her.

With this method an author can tell the reader exactly what he or she wants the reader to know about a character's age, appearance, situation in life, or personality traits.

An author may choose to reveal a character's speech and behavior:

> "And you have forgotten one matter of joy to me," said Emma, "and a very considerable one—that I made the match myself. I made the match, you know, four years ago; and to have it take place, and be proved in the right, when so many people said Mr. Weston would never marry again, may comfort me for anything."

This method makes demands on the reader's ability to make INFERENCES or conclusions about a character. On another occasion with two other friends, Harriet Smith and Mr. Elton, Emma again reveals her taste for matchmaking:

> They now walked on together quietly, till within view of the vicarage pales, when a sudden resolution, of at least getting Harriet into the house, made her [Emma] again find something very much amiss about her boot, and fall behind to arrange it once more. She then broke the lace off short, and dexterously throwing it into a ditch, was presently obliged to entreat them to stop, and acknowledge her inability to put herself to rights so as to be able to walk home in tolerable comfort.
>
> "Part of my lace is gone," said she, "and I do not know how I am to contrive. I really am a most troublesome companion to you both, but I hope I am not often so ill-equipped. Mr. Elton, I must beg leave to stop at your house, and ask your housekeeper for a bit of ribband or string, or anything just to keep my boot on."

A writer may also describe opinions and reactions of some characters to another character. In the next passage two of Emma's close acquaintances, Mrs. Weston and Mr. Knightley, speak together about Emma and her friendship with someone of whom they faintly disapprove, Harriet Smith:

> ". . . One hears sometimes of a child being 'the picture of health'; now Emma always gives me the idea of being the complete picture of grown-up health. She is loveliness itself. Mr. Knightley, is not she?"

"I have not a fault to find with her person," he replied. "I think her all you describe. I love to look at her; and I will add this praise, that I do not think her personally vain. Considering how very handsome she is, she appears to be little occupied with it; her vanity lies another way. Mrs. Weston, I am not to be talked out of my dislike of her intimacy with Harriet Smith, or my dread of its doing them both harm."

"And I, Mr. Knightley, am equally stout in my confidence of its not doing them any harm. With all dear Emma's little faults, she is an excellent creature. Where shall we see a better daughter, or a kinder sister, or a truer friend? No, no; she has qualities which may be trusted; she will never lead any one really wrong; she will make no lasting blunder; where Emma errs once, she is in the right a hundred times."

Again, the readers must draw their own conclusions about the personality of Emma by noting what is said about her.

Finally, a writer can reveal a character's personality by disclosing his or her thoughts and feelings. The following excerpt finds Emma contemplating her relationship with a young man, Frank Churchill, who has been visiting his relatives, the Westons, at their estate, Randalls, and who has now left for his own home.

Emma continued to entertain no doubt of her being in love. Her ideas only varied as to the how much. At first, she thought it was a good deal; and afterwards, but little. She had great pleasure in hearing Frank Churchill talked of; and, for his sake, greater pleasure than ever in seeing Mr. and Mrs. Weston; she was very often thinking of him, and quite impatient for a letter, that she might know how he was, how were his spirits, how was his aunt, and what was the chance of his coming to Randalls again this spring. But, on the other hand, she could not admit herself to be unhappy, nor, after the first morning, to be less disposed for employment than usual; she was still busy and cheerful; and, pleasing as he was, she could yet imagine him to have faults; and farther, though thinking of him so much, and, as she sat drawing or working, forming a thousand amusing schemes for the progress and close of their attachment, fancying interesting dialogues, and inventing elegant letters; the conclusion of every imaginary declaration on his side was that she *refused him*. Their affection was always to subside into friendship. Everything tender and charming was to mark their parting; but still they were to part. When she became sensible of this, it struck her that she could not be very much in love; for in spite of her previous and fixed determination never to quit her father, never to marry, a strong attachment certainly must produce more of a struggle than she could foresee in her own feelings.

These selections represent but a small part of Jane Austen's characterization of Emma, but having read them, you have an idea of the sort of person Emma is.

1. Is Emma unattractive?

2. Has she had a difficult life?

3. What is something she prides herself on doing?

4. Is Emma self-confident or hesitant in making decisions?

5. What is her relationship with her father?

6. Will she stoop to deception to bring about something she desires? Support your opinion.

7. Is she honest with herself?

Not all written works emphasize characterization. When plot or setting is emphasized over character the characters are apt to be stereotypes. (See STEREOTYPE.)

characterization

The technique a writer uses to create and reveal the personalities of the characters in a written work. A writer may describe a character's physical appearance and situation, reveal a character's thoughts, or show the reactions of other characters.

Apply to "**A Visit to Grandmother**" on page 8.

connotation/ denotation

Below is a definition of the word *dentist* as it appears in a dictionary.

den tist (den′tist), *n.* doctor whose work is the care of teeth. A dentist fills cavities in teeth, cleans, straightens, or extracts them, and supplies artificial teeth.

Does the word *dentist* have any personal meaning or association for you? How does your own meaning for *dentist* differ from the dictionary definition? What might the word mean to someone with a toothache? to someone whose parent is a dentist? to a dentist?

Many words in everyday use do double duty. On the one hand they have a dictionary meaning, or *denotation*. On the other, they have a *connotation*, or significance and association beyond the dictionary meaning. A connotative word gathers its associations from people's experiences, both personal and universal.

Because many experiences are personal, the significance of a word such as *home*, for example, is different to different people. It might mean untidiness, bickering, or a lack of privacy to some, while to others it might connote good food, love, or security.

1. State possible connotations of the word *dog* to a **(a)** little child; **(b)** would-be thief; **(c)** person with allergies.

2. State possible connotations of the word *food* to **(a)** an overweight person; **(b)** a grocery-store owner; **(c)** a hungry person.

3. State possible connotations of the word *sky* to **(a)** a philosopher; **(b)** an airline pilot; **(c)** an astronomer.

What does the word *night* mean to you? Is it a time to go to sleep? a fearful time? a retreat from the day's work? Read the following poem to find the various ways the poet sees night.

Four Glimpses of Night

I. Eagerly
Like a woman hurrying to her lover
Night comes to the room of the world
And lies, yielding and content
Against the cool round face
Of the moon.

II. Night is a curious child, wandering
Between earth and sky, creeping
In windows and doors, daubing
The entire neighborhood
With purple paint.
Day
Is an apologetic mother
Cloth in hand
Following after.

III. Peddling
From door to door
Night sells
Black bags of peppermint stars
Heaping cones of vanilla moon
Until
His wares are gone
Then shuffles homeward
Jingling the grey coins
Of daybreak.

IV. Night's brittle song, sliver-thin
Shatters into a billion fragments
Of quiet shadows
At the blaring jazz
Of a morning sun.

Frank Marshall Davis

What different connotations does the word *night* take on in each stanza?

connotation

The interpretations of a word beyond its literal definition.

denotation

The literal meaning of a word as found in a dictionary.

"Four Glimpses of Night" by Frank Marshall Davis. From *The Poetry of the Negro 1746–1970.* Published by Doubleday & Company, Inc. Reprinted by permission of the author.

Apply to "The Secret Room" on page 462.

consonance

The moan of doves in immemorial elms,
And murmuring of innumerable bees.

Alfred, Lord Tennyson, "The Princess"

Read the above lines softly to yourself. What consonant sound is repeated several times? What effect does the repeated sound have on your reading of the lines?

The repeated *m* sound within the words is an example of *consonance:* the repetition of the same consonant sound preceded by a different vowel sound. In the above lines the repeated *m* sound has the effect of emphasizing the words in which it is found.

Consonance at the end of two or more lines of poetry is called *half rhyme* or *slant rhyme* because only the final consonant sounds are alike. (See RHYME.) Read the following stanza.

Nothing lovelier than that lonely call,
Bare and singular, like a gull,
And three notes or four, then that was all.
It drew up from the quiet like a well,
Waited, sang, and vanishing, was still.

Jon Swan, "In Her Song She Is Alone"

Consonance is also used to suggest associations between words. Note how the *l* sound effectively unites the key words of the stanza: *call* with *gull* and *well* with *still*. The *l* sound has a lingering, almost echoing effect. How is that appropriate to the stanza's TONE?

consonance (kon′sə nəns)

The repetition of similar or identical consonant sounds preceded by different vowel sounds. It is often used instead of rhyme at the end of lines of poetry. Consonance can stress important words and strengthen meaning through word association. It may add to the unity of sound and sense in a poem.

Apply to **"Hope Is the Thing with Feathers"** on page 220.

figurative language

Read each set of lines.

A. **a.** She has a pink-and-white complexion.
b. There is a garden in her face,
Where roses and lilies grow;

Thomas Campion, "Cherry-Ripe"

B. **a.** When I am old, wrinkled, chilly, and white-haired . . .
b. When age hath made me what I am not now;
And every wrinkle tells me where the plough
Of time hath furrowed; when an ice shall flow
Through every vein, and all my head wear snow;

Thomas Randolph, "Upon His Picture"

Which lines are literal? Which lines suggest associations or comparisons? What things are being compared in each case? All of the **b** items contain examples of *figurative language*. Figurative language is the use of words outside their usual, or literal, meanings. By suggesting new associations or comparisons, they can add beauty to and increase the impact or vitality of the lines and works in which they are found. Sometimes figurative language may seem even more direct than literal language because it enables the reader to grasp the idea quickly. The various elements of figurative language are called *figures of speech*. The most commonly used figures of speech are SIMILE, METAPHOR, and PERSONIFICATION.

To be successful, figurative language must be appropriate. Although figurative language compares basically different things, there must be a point of similarity between the objects for the figure of speech to be effective. For example, if a person said, "I've been shoveling snow for an hour, and my hands are like blocks of ice," most listeners would understand the connection—ice is cold and hard and hands can be cold and hard. If, however, the person compared his or her hands to daisies or cameras, the listener would very probably have no idea what was meant. There must be some recognizable point of simi-

larity for the figure of speech to be appropriate. Read the following lines and decide (1) what things are being compared and (2) whether the figurative language is effective and appropriate.

A. The lion's roar rolled like thunder.

B. The frightened lost child cowered in the aisle
like a golden eagle.

C. O my luve is like a red, red rose
That's newly sprung in June:
O my luve is like the melodie
That's sweetly played in tune.
Robert Burns, "A Red, Red Rose"

D. The tears on her cheeks were glistening rocks.

A figure of speech need not be limited to one phrase, line, sentence, or paragraph. It may often be extended to include any of these, or even the entire work. If a figure of speech extends through a paragraph, for instance, it should be consistent. That is, many different comparisons or associations should not be used to describe the same thing. For example, a lantern in the window may seem to a weary traveler to beam "a finger of light" that "points the way home," "beckons him in welcome," and "warmly strokes his cheek as he nears the house." It would be inconsistent then to change the image to compare the lantern to the sun or the moon.

Read the following lines. The main character, Macbeth, has just murdered his sleeping king.

Methought I heard a voice cry, "Sleep no more!
Macbeth does murder sleep," the innocent sleep,
Sleep that knits up the raveled sleave of care,
The death of each day's life, sore labor's bath,
Balm of hurt minds, great nature's second course,
Chief nourisher in life's feast—

William Shakespeare, *Macbeth*, Act Two, Scene 2

To what various things is sleep compared? What is Macbeth saying literally? How does the use of figurative language give the reader a clear idea about Macbeth's state of mind?

figurative language

The use of words outside their literal, or usual, meanings. Figurative language is used to add beauty, increase vitality and impact, suggest associations and comparisons, and develop conciseness.

Apply to "Those Winter Sundays" on page 171.

flashback

The following is from a novel about the experiences of an English schoolmaster. At the book's opening, the main character, Mr. Chips, is very old, under the care of his landlady, Mrs. Wickett, and long retired from teaching at Brookfield, a boys' school. Read the passage, paying close attention to the order of events.

from **Goodbye, Mr. Chips**

He was getting on in years (but not ill, of course); indeed, as Doctor Merivale said, there was really nothing the matter with him. "My dear fellow, you're fitter than I am," Merivale would say, sipping a glass of sherry when he called every fortnight or so. "You're past the age when people get these horrible diseases; you're one of the few lucky ones who're going to die a really natural death. That is, of course, if you die at all. You're such a remarkable old boy that one never knows." But when Chips had a cold or when east winds roared over the fenlands, Merivale would sometimes take Mrs. Wickett aside in the lobby and whisper: "Look after him, you know. His chest . . . it puts a strain on his heart. Nothing really wrong with him—only anno Domini,[1] but that's the most fatal complaint of all, in the end."

Anno Domini . . . by Jove, yes. Born in 1848, and taken to the Great Exhibition as a toddling child—not many people still alive could boast a thing like that. Besides, Chips could even remember Brookfield in Wetherby's time. A phenomenon, that was. Wetherby had been an old man in those days—1870—easy to remember because of the Franco-Prussian War. Chips had put in for Brookfield after a year at Melbury, which he hadn't liked, because he had been ragged there a good deal. But Brookfield he *had* liked, almost from the beginning. He remembered that day of his preliminary interview—sunny June, with the air full of flower scents and the plick-plock of cricket on the pitch. Brookfield was playing Barnhurst, and one of the Barnhurst boys, a chubby little fellow, made a brilliant century.[2] Queer that a thing like that should stay in the memory so clearly. Wetherby himself was very fatherly and courteous: he must have been ill then, poor chap, for he died during the summer vacation, before Chips began his first term. But the two had seen and spoken to each other, anyway.

Chips often thought, as he sat by the fire at Mrs. Wickett's: I am probably the only man in the world who has a vivid recollection of old Wetherby. . . . Vivid, yes; it was a frequent picture in his mind, that summer day with the sunlight filtering through the dust in Wetherby's study. "You are a young man, Mr. Chipping, and Brookfield is an old foundation. Youth and age often combine well. Give your enthusiasm to Brookfield, and Brookfield will give you something in return. And don't let anyone play tricks with you. I—er—gather that discipline was not always your strong point at Melbury?"

"Well, no, perhaps not, sir."

"Never mind; you're full young; it's largely a matter of experience. You have another chance here. Take up a firm attitude from the beginning—that's the secret of it."

Perhaps it was. He remembered that first tremendous ordeal of taking prep; a September sunset more than half a century ago; Big Hall full of lusty barbarians ready to pounce on him as their legitimate prey. His youth, fresh-complexioned, high-collared, and side-whiskered (odd fashions people followed in those days), at the mercy of five hundred unprincipled ruffians to whom the baiting of new masters was a fine art, an exciting sport, and something of a tradition. Decent little beggars individually, but, as a mob, just pitiless and implacable. The sudden hush as he took his place at the desk on the dais; the scowl he assumed to cover his inward nervousness; the tall clock ticking behind him, and the smells of ink and varnish; the last blood-red rays slanting in slabs through the stained-glass windows. Someone dropped a desk lid. Quickly, he must take everyone by surprise; he must show that there was no nonsense about him. "You there in the fifth row—you with the red hair—what's your name?" "Colley, sir." "Very well, Colley, you have a hundred lines." No trouble at all after that. He had won his first round.

And years later, when Colley was an alderman of the City of London and a baronet and various other things, he sent his son (also redhaired) to Brookfield, and Chips would say: "Colley, your father was the first boy I ever punished when I came here twenty-five years ago. He deserved it then, and you deserve it now." How they all laughed; and how Sir Richard laughed when his son wrote home the story in next Sunday's letter!

---

1. ***anno Domini*** (an′ō dom′ə nī), in the (specified) year since the birth of Christ. Used in the above context to suggest old age.
2. ***century,*** (in cricket) a score of one hundred or more points in one period of play.

And again, years after that, many years after that, there was an even better joke. For another Colley had just arrived—son of the Colley who was a son of the first Colley. And Chips would say, punctuating his remarks with that little "umph-um" that had by then become a habit with him: "Colley, you are—umph—a splendid example of—umph—inherited traditions. I remember your grandfather—umph—he could never grasp the Ablative Absolute.[3] A stupid fellow, your grandfather. And your father, too—umph—I remember him—he used to sit at that far desk by the wall—he wasn't much better, either. But I do believe—my dear Colley—that you are—umph—the biggest fool of the lot!" Roars of laughter.

A great joke, this growing old—but a sad joke, too, in a way. And as Chips sat by his fire with autumn gales rattling the windows, the waves of humor and sadness swept over him very often until tears fell, so that when Mrs. Wickett came in with his cup of tea she did not know whether he had been laughing or crying. And neither did Chips himself.

James Hilton

Arrange the following events of Mr. Chips's life in the order they actually occurred.

1. He assigns his very first punishment to red-haired Richard Colley.

2. He attends the Great Exhibition.

3. He meets Mr. Wetherby at Brookfield.

4. He teaches one year at Melbury.

5. He teases the grandson of the first student he ever punished.

You may know that you have arranged the events in *chronological order,* the order in which they happened in Mr. Chips's lifetime. Yet, did you notice that Mr. Chips is presented as very old at both the beginning and end of the passage? Did you realize that these events are not happening to Mr. Chips as you read them, but are incidents from his earlier life that he recalls while sitting by his fire? The author accomplishes these shifts in time through the use of *flashback,* an interruption in the narrative to show a scene or scenes that happened before that particular point.

A flashback can easily cover years of chronological time and give information that helps the reader better understand the characters and events of a story's present action. For example, you learned through a sequence of flashbacks that Mr. Chips's teaching career spanned at least three generations and provided years of memories that he continues to cherish.

This device also helps the reader anticipate what will occur when the major action is resumed. Mr. Chips's flashbacks at the beginning of the novel provide only a brief glimpse of his long career. Based on your knowledge of these flashbacks, what do you think will be the subject of the rest of the novel?

flashback

An interruption in the major action of a story, play, or nonfiction work to show an episode that happened at an earlier time. A flashback can shed light on characters and events of the present by providing background information.

Apply to *Our Town* on page 121.

3. ***ablative*** (ab′lə tiv) ***absolute,*** a grammatical construction in Latin.

foreshadowing

Shortly after the opening of the story "The Monkey's Paw," the White family questions their guest, Sergeant-Major Morris, about the mummified monkey's paw he acquired in India. After telling them of the spell put on the paw that allows three men three wishes each, Morris is asked if he has had his three wishes.

> "I have," he said quietly, and his blotchy face whitened.

At this point the reader does not know what the monkey's paw can or cannot do, but does learn that the very thought of it frightens a professional soldier. This hint, clue, or indication of what is to come is called *foreshadowing*.

Foreshadowing serves two purposes: (1) it stimulates interest on the part of the reader, listener, or viewer to learn what happens next; and (2) it prepares the reader, listener, or viewer, in part at least, for the direction the plot will take, thus making it seem more real.

In the first speech in *Medea* (page 240) the Nurse says of Medea's despairing mood,

> . . . This evil is not declining, it is just at dawn. I dread the lion-eyed glare of its noon.

Through this speech the reader or listener is alerted that the events to follow will probably be concerned with the actions prompted by Medea's mood.

As early as the second scene of Act One of *Julius Caesar* (page 382), the Soothsayer warns, "Beware the ides of March." Startled at first, Caesar laughs off the encounter. What is foreshadowed by this statement?

foreshadowing

The technique of giving the reader, listener, or viewer of a story or play hints of what is to come in that work.

Apply to "**Life Is Sweet at Kumansenu**" on page 57.

free verse

> I don't bother with rhymes. It is seldom
> That there are two trees equal, side by side.
>
> Alberto Caeiro, "XIV"
> (translated by Jonathan Griffin)

Free verse, a form of unrhymed English poetry, has become a favorite form of many modern poets. (See also BLANK VERSE.) Free verse is called "free" because the poet does not follow set patterns of rhyme, meter, or line length.

Free-verse poets believe rhyme is an inadequate poetic device. They point out that rhyme may restrict, even dictate, the meaning of a poem. For example, imagine a poet who is composing a serious tercet, a stanza of three rhyming lines, about a dove he once held in his hand and touched gently. The word *dove* suggests that his three lines will rhyme the *-ove* sound. He begins:

> A gray, white-throated dove
> Lay quivering in my glove;

In the next line, he wants to say, "I gave it a gentle touch." *Touch* does not rhyme with *dove* or *glove* so he casts about for a word that does, with this result:

> A gray, white-throated dove
> Lay quivering in my glove;
> I gave it a gentle shove.

The rhyme has drastically changed the poet's meaning. To avoid such a predicament, free-verse poets dispense with rhyme. If they regulate sound at all it is mainly through ALLITERATION and ASSONANCE.

Free-verse poets, unlike blank-verse poets, believe meter is an unnecessary poetic device since every word we use has a natural rhythm of its own. Depending upon the natural stress (or lack of stress) in words, free-verse lines such as these:

> Beautiful evening
> Calm, free

---

are just as rhythmical in their way as is this metrical version:

It is / a beau / teous eve / ning, calm / and free.

William Wordsworth, "It Is a Beauteous Evening"

Often the free-verse poet gives his reader a clue to the movement of his poem by beginning each rhythmical unit on a new line.

When I Heard the Learn'd Astronomer

When I heard the learn'd astronomer,
When the proofs, the figures, were
  ranged in columns before me,
When I was shown the charts and
  diagrams, to add, divide, and
  measure them,
When I sitting heard the astronomer
  where he lectured with much
  applause in the lecture-room,
How soon unaccountable I became
  tired and sick,
Till rising and gliding out I wander'd
  off by myself,
In the mystical moist night air, and
  from time to time,
Look'd up in perfect silence at the
  stars.

Walt Whitman, 1865–1867

free verse

Poetry that follows no set patterns of rhyme, meter, or line length.

Apply to "**Porcupine Fish**" on page 181.

hyperbole

When people use such commonplace expressions as "It's raining cats and dogs" or "He is as big as a house," they are deliberately exaggerating the truth and do not expect to be taken literally. Yet in each case they are expressing a genuinely felt emotion. The use of exaggeration for effect is called *hyperbole*.

Authors use hyperbole to give emphasis to their point. For example, the following lines by Gwendolyn Brooks show the power of the language used by Martin Luther King, Jr., and its effect on his listeners:

His word still burns the center of the sun,
  above the thousands and the
  hundred thousands.

A promise of undying love is emphasized in the lines from "A Red, Red Rose" by Robert Burns.

Till a' the seas gang dry, my dear,
  And the rocks melt wi' the sun!
I will luve thee still, my dear,
  While the sands o' life shall run.

What feeling about poetry do you think the speaker wishes to emphasize through hyperbole in the following poem?

from **The Secret**

Two girls discover
the secret of life
in a sudden line of
poetry.

Denise Levertov

hyperbole

A figure of speech involving great exaggeration. Hyperbole is used to emphasize strong feeling and to create a satiric, comic, or sentimental effect.

Apply to "**For Anne Gregory**" on page 174.

imagery

The Pond

Cold, wet leaves
Floating on moss-coloured water,

And the croaking of frogs—
Cracked bell-notes in the twilight.

Amy Lowell

Which words or phrases in this poem appeal to your senses of sight, sound, and touch? Sensory appeals made through descriptions and details are called *images*. Now look for images as you read the passage below from Charles Dickens's *A Christmas Carol.*

It was his own room. There was no doubt about that. But it had undergone a surprising transformation. The walls and ceiling were so hung with living green, that it looked a perfect grove; from every part of which, bright gleaming berries glistened. The crisp leaves of holly, mistletoe, and ivy reflected back the light, as if so many little mirrors had been scattered there; and such a mighty blaze went roaring up the chimney, as that dull petrification of a hearth had never known in Scrooge's time, or Marley's, or for many and many a winter season gone. Heaped up on the floor, to form a kind of throne, were turkeys, geese, game, poultry, brawn, great joints of meat, suckling-pigs, long wreaths of sausages, mince-pies, plum-puddings, barrels of oysters, red-hot chestnuts, cherry-cheeked apples, juicy oranges, luscious pears, immense twelfth-cakes, and seething bowls of punch, that made the chamber dim with their delicious steam.

To which senses does the passage appeal? What details does Dickens add to the recital of food that make it more than a holiday grocery list? Which images appeal particularly to your sense of taste? of smell?

A skilled writer can use imagery to convey to readers a sense of experiencing what they are reading about, and so involving them in the world of the written selection.

Read the following passage about Tayo, a young Indian home from the Korean War, and try to imagine the scene as you read.

Tayo stood near the horses, looking down the path over the way they had come. The plateaus and canyons spread out below him like clouds falling into each other past the horizon. The world below was distant and small; it was dwarfed by a sky so blue and vast the clouds were lost in it. Far into the south there were smoky blue ridges of the mountain haze at Zuni. He smoothed his hand over the top of his head and felt the sun. The mountain wind was cool; it smelled like springs hidden deep in mossy black stone. He could see no signs of what had been set loose upon the earth: the highways, the towns, even the fences were gone.

What images of sight, touch, and smell are depicted? In what part of the country would you say the story takes place? How is the sense of the vastness of the place communicated? What emotions or feelings are evoked?

In the following passage, Tayo is hurt and losing consciousness:

Black pebbles and the ancient gray cinders the mountain had thrown poked into his backbone. He closed his eyes but did not sleep. He felt cold gusts of wind scattering dry oak leaves in the grass. He listened to the cowboy collect tobacco juice in his mouth and the squirting liquid sound when he spat. He was aware of the center beneath him; it soaked into his body from the ground through the torn skin on his hands, covered with powdery black dirt. The magnetism of the center spread over him smoothly like rainwater down his neck and shoulders: the vacant cool sensation glided over the pain like feather-down wings. It was pulling him back, close to the earth, where the core was cool and silent as mountain stone . . .

What do you think is the most vivid image in this passage? How is the sensation of losing consciousness commmunicated?

imagery

The use of concrete details that appeal to the five senses. By appealing to a reader's senses, a writer can more easily communicate an experience.

Leslie Marmon Silko, *Ceremony*. New York: The Viking Press, 1977.

Apply to **"Drought"** on page 187.

inference

Thomas W. Cheney

"Very well, Your Honor. I shall rephrase the question."

What kind of question could have had such an effect on the witness? Do you think he was prepared for the question? In considering the clues in the cartoon and drawing a conclusion from them, you are making an *inference.*

Writers often give their readers only limited or indirect information and expect them to make their own inferences about time, setting, characters, and actions. Note the clues for making inferences in the passage below, from Sherwood Anderson's "I'm a Fool."

And so, there not being any work in our town any more than when I left there to go to the races, I went off to Sandusky and got a pretty good place taking care of horses for a man who owned a teaming and delivery and storage and coal and real-estate business there. It was a pretty good place with good eats, and a day off each week, and sleeping on a cot in a big barn, and mostly just shoveling in hay and oats to a lot of big good-enough skates of horses that couldn't have trotted a race with a toad. I wasn't dissatisfied and I could send money home.

And then, as I started to tell you, the fall races come to Sandusky and I got the day off and I went. I left the job at noon and had on my good clothes and my new brown derby hat I'd bought the Saturday before, and a stand-up collar.

First of all I went downtown and walked about with the dudes. I've always thought to myself, "Put up a good front," and so I did it. I had forty dollars in my pockets and so I went into the West House, a big hotel, and walked up to the cigar stand. "Give me three twenty-five-cent cigars," I said. There was a lot of horsemen and strangers and dressed-up people from other towns standing around in the lobby and in the bar, and I mingled amongst them. In the bar there was a fellow with a cane and a Windsor tie on, that it made me sick to look at him. I like a man to be a man and dressed up, but not to go put on that kind of airs. So I pushed him aside, kind of rough, and had me a drink of whiskey. And then he looked at me, but he changed his mind and didn't say anything. And then I had another drink of whiskey, just to show him something, and went out and had a hack[1] out to the races, all to myself, and when I got there I bought myself the best seat I could get up in the grandstand, but didn't go in for any of these boxes. That's putting on too many airs.

1. What details suggest the narrator is easily satisfied in life?

2. What details suggest the story takes place before automobiles were common?

3. What evidence is there that the coming of the fall races to Sandusky is a special occasion to the narrator?

4. When the narrator roughly pushes aside the fellow in the Windsor tie, the man does nothing but look at him. The speaker infers that the man is a coward. What other inference can you make?

5. The narrator does not like people "putting on . . . airs." What actions does the narrator take that reveal him to be the same as those he criticizes?

Notice that the author does not directly describe the narrator; he relies on the readers to read between the lines.

inference

A reasonable conclusion about the behavior of a character or the meaning of an event drawn from the limited details supplied by the author.

1. ***hack,*** horse-drawn carriage for hire.

Apply to **"The Other Wife"** on page 54.

inversion

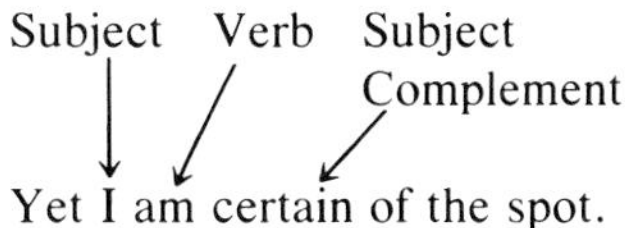

The above line follows the normal pattern of an English sentence: subject, followed by verb, followed by complement. Now read the two lines below.

Yet certain am I of the spot
As if the chart were given.

Emily Dickinson,
"I Never Saw a Moor"

The parts of the sentence in line 1 are not in the normal pattern. They are *inverted*—the complement and the verb both appear before the subject. Although the inverted line makes as much sense as the one following the normal pattern, there is a difference. Writers use *inversion* for emphasis or to achieve a certain poetic effect. What word is emphasized in the inverted line? How does this emphasis affect the meaning of the sentence?

In the normal pattern, an adjective is usually placed before the noun it modifies. The following are familiar examples of the adjective placed after the noun:

The bride traditionally wears something old, something new, something borrowed, and something blue.
The dancers were tripping the light fantastic.

Another normal pattern is the subject, followed by verb, followed by adverbial modifier:

New life comes with the arrival of spring.

But the exact reverse order will not harm the meaning:

With the arrival of spring comes new life.

Although an inverted line might cause initial difficulty or confusion, alert readers will have little trouble if they are aware of inversion and concentrate on the meaning.

Look for the use of inversion in the following poem.

Parting at Morning

Round the cape of a sudden came the sea,
And the sun looked over the mountain's rim:
And straight was a path of gold for him,
And the need of a world of men for me.

Robert Browning

The first two lines describe the sight someone in a boat might have as the boat moves out from a harbor. In what lines is inversion used? How would the lines read if they were not inverted? How would the rhyme scheme be affected? What words are given emphasis in the inverted lines?

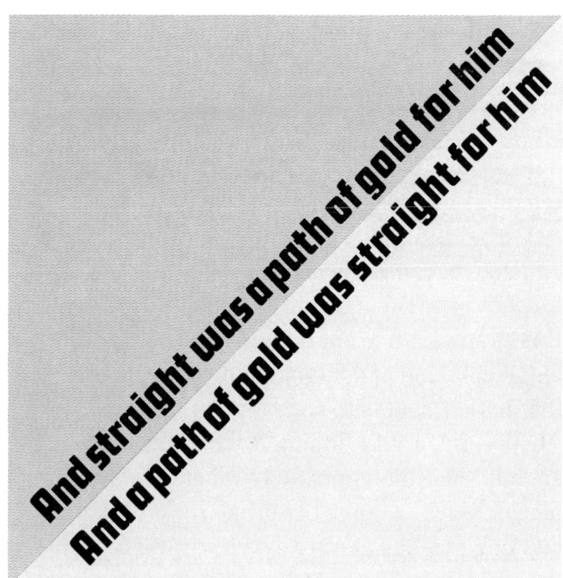

inversion

The reversal of the conventional order of words in a sentence to create a special effect or for emphasis.

Apply to "White in the Moon the Long Road Lies" on page 216

irony

In the following excerpt from *The Sketch Book,* Washington Irving, an early nineteenth-century American author, explains his reasons for wanting to visit Europe and England: to see great men.

> . . . for I had read in the works of various philosophers, that all animals degenerated in America, and man among the number. A great man of Europe, thought I, must therefore be as superior to a great man of America as a peak of the Alps to a highland of the Hudson; and in this idea I was confirmed by observing the comparative importance and swelling magnitude of many English travellers among us, who, I was assured, were very little people in their own country. I will visit this land of wonders, thought I, and see the gigantic race from which I am degenerated.

Does Irving really think the English are superior to Americans? What clues lead to your conclusions? Irving says one thing in this passage, but he means just the opposite. This is an example of *verbal irony*—the surface meaning of what one writes or says being the opposite of the intended meaning.

Verbal irony in everyday speech is easily recognized because the listener has the speaker's tone of voice and facial expression to aid him. For example, if you and a friend have planned a day picnicking and hiking, and when you step out the door it begins to rain, one of you might say, "Oh, good! I was hoping it would rain." This is actually just the opposite of what you were hoping and is an example of verbal irony. When reading, one must be alert to a writer's use of irony or the point may be missed entirely. Verbal irony is frequently used as a device of SATIRE.

Irony of situation occurs when events turn out contrary to what is expected or what seems appropriate. "The Gift of the Magi," a short story by O. Henry, turns on irony of situation. In it a penniless young couple want to buy each other special Christmas presents. The wife has her beautiful long hair cut off, sells it, and buys a chain worthy of her husband's prized gold pocket watch. The husband sells his watch to buy tortoise-shell combs for his wife's beautiful hair. What is the double irony of the story?

Irony may be gentle, sad, bitter, or, as in "The Gift of the Magi," bittersweet. The general TONE of the piece will indicate the author's intention.

The subway rider in the cartoon below is making a reasonable assumption. What do you know that she does not that makes her comment particularly humorous?

"I think something's coming now."

Dramatic irony occurs when the reader or viewer knows more about the actual situation than the characters do. It is often found in drama; for example, an offhand remark is made or a seemingly unimportant action occurs which has significance hidden from the character involved, but revealed to the audience. Dramatic irony may be humorous, as in the cartoon; poignant, as in *Our Town* (page 121); or ominous, as in *Julius Caesar,* when the audience knows Brutus is plotting Caesar's death but Caesar does not.

irony

A contrast between what is said and what is actually meant is called *verbal irony; irony of situation* occurs when things turn out contrary to what is expected; *dramatic irony* occurs when the reader or viewer is aware of something about which the character involved knows nothing. Irony is a common device in satire.

Apply to **"The Necklace"** on page 296.

lyric

Together

Because we do
All things together
All things improve,
Even weather.
Our daily meat
And bread taste better,
Trees greener,
Rain is wetter.

Paul Engle

What emotion is expressed in the poem? Do you think the poet is concerned primarily with telling a story or expressing a feeling?

The poem above belongs to a category of poetry called *lyric* poetry. Instead of telling a story, as a NARRATIVE poem does, a lyric is a short poem expressing a personal, basic emotion—love, sorrow, joy, patriotism, religious feeling, or any other sentiment sincerely felt by the poet.

The Rustling of Grass

I cannot tell why,
But the rustling of grass,
As the summer winds pass
Through the field where I lie,
Brings to life a lost day,
Long ago, far away,
When in childhood I lay
Looking up at the sky
And the white clouds that pass,
Trailing isles of grey shadow
Across the gold grass . . .
O, the dreams that drift by
With the slow flowing years,
Hopes, Memories, tears,
In the rustling grass.

Alfred Noyes

What emotion is expressed in this poem?

lyric

A short poem expressing a basic, personal emotion such as grief, happiness, love, or melancholy.

Apply to **"Who Is Silvia?"** on page 171.

metaphor

Life's but a walking shadow, a poor player
That struts and frets his hour upon the
stage. . . .

William Shakespeare,
Macbeth, Act Five, Scene 5

What two things is life compared with in the above lines? Are the comparisons appropriate? The lines contain examples of *metaphor,* a figure of speech that implies comparison between two basically dissimilar things. The comparison is implied because no connective word such as *like* or *as* is used. (See FIGURATIVE LANGUAGE.)

We all use metaphors daily without giving them much thought. A student who is finally understanding chemistry might say he is beginning to see the light, or a teacher who is explaining the basics of trigonometry might say that the explanation was just the tip of the iceberg. In each case, qualities of one thing are being assigned to completely different things.

Writers use metaphors to expand meanings through surprising associations. A metaphor need not be limited to a single line or sentence. Sometimes a writer will continue a metaphor throughout a paragraph, stanza, or entire work. This is called an *extended metaphor*.

Forgotten Dreams

The soft gray hands of sleep
Toiled all night long
To spin a beautiful garment
Of dreams;
At dawn
The little task was done.
Awakening,
The garb so deftly spun
Was only a heap
Of raveled thread—
A vague remembrance
In my head.

Edward Silvera

What things are being compared in the poem?

Is the metaphor extended throughout the poem? Do you think the comparisons are appropriate? Are the metaphors used effective in describing dreams? For a metaphor to be effective, it must reveal or suggest a common quality between the things compared. For example, what if the poet had begun the poem with "The rough red hands of sleep"? Why would that not be as effective as "soft gray"?

Not only must a metaphor be appropriate, it must also be consistent. A metaphor that is not consistent is called a *mixed metaphor*. The commentator Edwin Newman calls a mixed metaphor "a figure of speech that is out of control." For example: "With feline grace, Alice stretched and strolled across the room, a great golden canary ready to pounce." What is inconsistent about this metaphor?

The following quote is from a newspaper article.

"I personally resent it: this commission being asked to draw a budget for a plan we had no part in developing," Frank said. "The rug was pulled out from under us, leaving us to hang in limbo and at the end of a primrose path," he said.

St. Louis Globe-Democrat

What mixed metaphors do you find in this statement? What is Frank trying to say?

Egg

In this kingdom
the sun never sets;
under the pale oval
of the sky
there seems no way in
or out,
and though there is a sea here
there is no tide.

For the egg itself
is a moon
glowing faintly
in the galaxy of the barn,
safe but for the spoon's
ominous thunder,
the first delicate crack
of lightning.

Linda Pastan

What is the "sun"? the "pale oval of the sky"? the "sea"? What is meant by lines 15 and 16? Do you think the metaphors are appropriate? consistent?

metaphor

A figure of speech that implies comparison between two fundamentally different things. The qualities of one are ascribed to the other. An *extended metaphor* is a metaphor continued throughout a stanza, paragraph, or entire work. A *mixed metaphor* is an inconsistent comparison.

Apply to "**Water Picture**" on page 191.

mood

Dawn

Ecstatic bird songs pound
the hollow vastness of the sky
with metallic clinkings—
beating color up into it
at a far edge,—beating it, beating it
with rising, triumphant ardor,—
stirring it into warmth,
quickening in it a spreading change,—
bursting wildly against it as
dividing the horizon, a heavy sun
lifts himself—is lifted—
bit by bit above the edge
of things,—runs free at last
out into the open—! lumbering
glorified in full release upward—
songs cease.

William Carlos Williams

Does the poem describe an indoor or outdoor scene? Which words create an atmosphere of intensifying activity? To what senses does the author appeal? Would you characterize the poem as sad? joyous? mysterious?

Though the reader knows from the title that the poem describes a sunrise, the reader does note the additional detail—"the hollow vastness of the sky"—that sets the scene for some sort of happening. The sense of intensifying activity is communicated through such words as "rising," "stirring," "quickening," and "spreading." Various details produce the IMAGERY that appeals to the reader's senses: the changing color of the sky, the pound of ecstatic bird songs, the warmth of the sky. Such references create images that appeal to sight, sound, and touch.

All of the details, the descriptions, the imagery, the SETTING, and evocative words come together to create the *mood* of surging triumph that surrounds the poem.

mood

The atmosphere and feeling that a writer creates in a work through the choice of setting, imagery, details, descriptions, and other evocative words.

Apply to "**Gift**" on page 196.

narrative poetry

Read the following poem.

The Fifth Sense

A 65-year-old Cypriot Greek shepherd, Nicolis Loizou, was wounded by security forces early today. He was challenged twice; when he failed to answer, troops opened fire. A subsequent hospital examination showed that the man was deaf. NEWS ITEM, 30 December 1957.

Lamps burn all the night
Here, where people must be watched and seen,
And I, a shepherd, Nicolis Loizou,
Wish for the dark, for I have been
Sure-footed in the dark, but now my sight
Stumbles among these beds, scattered white
boulders,
As I lean towards my far slumbering house
With the night lying upon my shoulders.

My sight was always good,
Better than others. I could taste wine and bread
And name the field they spattered when the
harvest
Broke. I could coil in the red
Scent of the fox out of a maze of wood
And grass. I could touch mist, I could touch
breath.
But of my sharp senses I had only four.
The fifth one pinned me to my death.

Continued

The soldiers must have called
The word they needed: Halt. Not hearing it,
I was their failure, relaxed against the winter
Sky, the flag of their defeat.
With their five senses they could not have told
That I lacked one, and so they had to shoot.
They would fire at a rainbow if it had
A colour less than they were taught.

Christ said that when one sheep
Was lost, the rest meant nothing any more.
Here in this hospital where others' breathing
Swings like a lantern in the polished floor
And squeezes those who cannot sleep,
I see how precious each thing is, how dear,
For I may never touch, smell, taste or see
Again, because I could not hear.

Patricia Beer

Who is the speaker in the poem? Where is he as he speaks? Why is he there? What details does the poem relate that are not found in the news item?

"The Fifth Sense" is a *narrative* poem, a poem that tells a story or relates a series of events, usually leading to a climax. What does the poem tell the reader about the kind of person Nicolis Loizou is? What does the reader learn about the soldiers?

Unlike a LYRIC poem, which is shorter and usually expresses one basic emotion, a narrative is both story and poem. A story is told, but in the compressed, dramatic, and FIGURATIVE LANGUAGE of poetry. Pick out some examples of figurative language from the poem.

narrative poetry

Poetry that relates a story or series of events.

Apply to "My Father & The Figtree" on page 162

onomatopoeia

Onomatopoeia

The rusty spigot
sputters,
utters
a splutter,
spatters a smattering of drops,
gashes wider;
slash,
splatters,
scatters,
spurts,
finally stops sputtering
and plash!
gushes rushes splashes
clear water dashes.

Eve Merriam

What action is the poet describing in the poem? What words does she use to create the effect of water coming from a rusty faucet? Words such as *sputter, spatters, gushes, plash* are examples of *onomatopoeia,* the use of words whose sounds suggest their sense.

Read the following lines. Decide which words are examples of onomatopoeia.

When blood is nipp'd and ways be foul,
Then nightly sings the staring owl,
Tu-whit;
Tu-who, a merry note . . .

William Shakespeare,
"Winter," from *Love's Labours Lost*

The wind blew east: we heard the roar
Of Ocean on his wintry shore,
And felt the strong pulse throbbing there
Beat with a low rhythm our inland air.

John Greenleaf Whittier, "Snowbound"

Which words above strongly suggest their sense? Which more subtly suggest their sense?

Words such as *bam, pow,* and *clang,* and animal sounds such as *miaow, woof,* and *quack* are examples of onomatopoetic words used mainly when sound is the effect desired. Other words suggest their sense more subtly and may be used to create atmosphere, set the scene, or heighten IMAGERY. Examples of such words might be *slushing* through the melting snow, the *whistle* of the ball in the air, the *clatter* of horses' hooves on city streets.

from **Mrs. Small**

Mrs. Small went to the kitchen for her pocketbook
And came back to the living room with a peculiar
    look
And the coffee pot.
Pocketbook. Pot.
Pot. Pocketbook.

The insurance man was waiting there
With superb and cared-for hair.
His face did not have much time.
He did not glance with sublime
Love upon the little plump tan woman
With the half-open mouth and the half-mad eyes
And the smile half-human
Who stood in the middle of the living-room floor
    planning apple pies
And graciously offering him a steaming coffee pot.
Pocketbook. Pot.

Gwendolyn Brooks

What words in these stanzas imitate the sounds of coffee brewing? Which suggests that the insurance man is out to make a profit? Which suggests that Mrs. Small has no more to offer than her hospitality? Note how these words lose independent meaning when combined to create sound effect.

onomatopoeia (on′ə mat′ə pē′ə)

The use of words whose sounds suggest their sense.

Apply to **"Cheers"** on page 182.

paradox

What is meant by the saying, "The more we learn, the less we know"? It is a seemingly self-contradictory statement, and yet there is sense to be made of it. Such a statement that seems to say two opposite things is called a *paradox*. Writers employ paradoxical statements to concentrate the readers' attention or to emphasize a point.

The term paradox also applies to people or situations that seem to have two contradictory elements: a wealthy person who chooses to live in the conditions of severest poverty might be considered a paradox. Something extremely out of the ordinary such as a silent city street on a weekday noon or springlike temperatures occurring within a wintry season might be called paradoxes. The English author G. K. Chesterton wrote a collection of stories, *Tales of the Long Bow*, each of which unfolds from a paradoxical situation. In this book and in others where paradoxes are found, their use is to make readers stop and think about what they are reading and about any possible symbolism developed or emphasized by the use of apparent opposites.

paradox

A seemingly self-contradictory statement that is still true. It is also said of a person or situation that seems to incorporate two opposite elements.

Apply to **"The Soul of Goodness in Things Evil"** on page 206.

personification

Sunday Rain

The window screen
is trying to do
its crossword puzzle
but appears to know
only vertical words.

John Updike

Is the window screen in the poem really doing a crossword puzzle? Does having the screen described in human terms make it easier for you to understand the image the poet is trying to communicate?

We often give human characteristics to nonhuman things or events. If your car has a flat tire, you may say it "limped" into the nearest garage. Or you may hear someone say that the TV sat staring across the room. These figures of speech are called *personification.* Personification lets the reader see inanimate objects and abstract ideas in terms of familiar human qualities.

What is being personified in the lines below? Point out the word or words the poet uses to personify the subject in each example.

A. Bitter the storm tonight.
It hurls the white locks of the sea. . . .

Geoffrey Grigson from the Irish,
"The Vikings"

B. Winter sat tight on
our shoulder blades,

Ann Darr,
"The Stone Under the Skin"

C. Leaves don't fall. They descend.
Longing for earth, they come winging.

Malka Heifetz Tussman, "Leaves"

A poet may use personification throughout a poem as in "Sunday Rain," or there may be personification in only one stanza within a poem.

But vainly the fierce frost
Interns poor fish, ranks trees in an armed host,
Hangs daggers from house eaves
And on the windows ferny ambush weaves;
In the long war grown warmer
The sun will strike him dead and strip his armor.

Andrew Young, "Hard Frost"

1. How are the frost and the sun made to seem human?

2. To what human event does the poet compare the actions described here?

Writers of prose use personification too. Here are two examples from Charles Dickens's "The Holly Tree," a short story.

As we got into the country, everything seemed to have grown old and gray. The roads, the trees, the thatched roofs of cottages and homesteads, the ricks in farmers' yards . . .

. . . the midnight wind that rattled at my lattice windows came moaning at me from Stonehenge.

personification (pər son′ə fə kā′shən)
A figure of speech in which human characteristics are attributed to nonhuman things and events.

Apply to "Wind" on page 192.

plot

Grand Inquisitor

"Haunted, sir? No, not what you'd call haunted. Of course, one of the gentlemen who lived here last was murdered but still . . . Haunted's a nasty thing to say about nice rooms like these, isn't it, sir? And so you're two brothers, as well as the Mr. Farmiloes. Funny how things do repeat themselves."

The resident housekeeper of No. 82, Regency Chambers, paused and eyed the prospective owners with a certain pleasant relish oozing through her habitual melancholy. It would be her task to cook for them and look after them. She was a crooked wisp of a woman, fading into the late sixties, with eyes like a jugged hare; narrow in the shoulders, she was yet broad in the beam, like an old ship; and her movements, too, were clumsy like those of an old-fashioned ship, of which her face, startled yet wooden, might have been the figurehead.

As the two gentlemen had already signed the contract for No. 82, she felt that they might be admitted at once to its privileges; so she told them the story of the bachelor brothers Farmiloe:

The elder, Roger, was big and handsome in a beefy sort of way. He had a self-confident chest and a beaming red face; and nearly everything he did, he did well. "Bet you can't do this!" he was often heard boasting to his pathetic little junior, and always he was right: Leslie couldn't do "this."

Leslie Farmiloe was not at all handsome. He was timid and had a sort of impediment in his speech, which sounded like the ghost of a chuckle. He was partially bald, too, though he was not yet forty, whereas Roger's hair was thick as a doormat.

Roger, retired from the army, worked in the City; and Leslie studied geology at home. He was supposed to be writing a tome on various minerals, their strata and sub-strata, and was always surrounded by encyclopedias and dictionaries and maps. Endless notes he made on scraps of paper; but he never left these about, because Roger, his patron and hero, must not be annoyed by litter. At least, not by Leslie's litter; his own was different.

In the mornings, when they breakfasted together, Roger usually bullied him; but in the evenings he chaffed him. The two processes were very much alike. The legend stood that Leslie adored his bluff, genial brother, and would endure any amount of good-natured torment from him.

Sundays Roger spent in a knotted agony, sweating at every pore, over the *Weekly Scrutiny:* Leslie watching him with large mild blue eyes, the while thinking no doubt what a wonderful fellow this was, and what a shame that on every seventh day he should be so humiliated by the "Grand Inquisitor."

For this was Roger's one great weakness, and his only intellectual amusement—crossword puzzles. And of all crossword puzzles, the only ones he could not master with his usual swaggering facility were those set by Grand Inquisitor of the *Weekly Scrutiny*. They were devils, those Grand Inquisitor puzzles! Roger Farmiloe nearly burst his veins trying to solve them, but he had never yet succeeded in filling in the spaces of any one of them right up to the very end.

Occasionally he managed to wring out a quarter or even a third of the answers, and then he would sit for hours, staring and baffled; or else, in a boiling temper, flinging his dictionaries about; or resting his head helplessly against the cool varnished spaces of the Pacific Ocean on the old-fashioned globe of the world. Leslie was no help. Leslie would not even know that "yen" was a Japanese coin, or "emu" an Australian bird. Even the elementary mysteries of "eft" and "eli" were blank to Leslie. "To think," groaned Roger, "that my brother—my brother—should be a fool!"

Laboriously he set to work again, writhing a little in the ingenious web of clues, allusions, double meanings, anagrams, quotations, and beheaded syllables.

Leslie watched him with large mild blue eyes.

One Sunday afternoon Leslie Farmiloe was discovered lying dead on the carpet, his bald head and the globe of the world having come into too violent contact. The globe had hardly suffered at all.

There were three extraordinary things about the case. One was the expression on the face of the dead little man—sneering and triumphant. It was so unlike any that had ever been seen on him. The second thing that excited comment was the bits of paper strewn about the room, scrawled over and over—even the blotting paper; some crumpled up and hurled about, scribbled with amazing and incomprehensible messages, as though the unknown murderer had been surprised in the working out of some esoteric code: "Yolc" . . . "Cramoisy" . . . "Sckats" . . . "Ecaroh" . . . "Pachisi" . . . "Wolliw" . . .

And Roger Farmiloe had disappeared.

Eventually he was found and brought back, still apparently struggling under a terrific sense of grievance and anxious to tell the whole

---

English-speaking world, his judge and his jury, the spectators at the trial, and the journalists who visited him eager for a good story, exactly what had led him to slay poor harmless Leslie.

For there the little brother had sat, Sunday after Sunday, meekly in his corner, his feet resting on the crossbar of the chair, so that his knees were almost level with his chin. Outwardly meek, but inwardly gloating, gloating with ruthless revengeful ferocity, remembering the humiliations he had suffered from Roger all through the past week; gloating over the full-blooded successful big brother helplessly caught in the toils of Grand Inquisitor's wheel and rack and thumbscrew. For instance: "In opposition to jug-jug." . . . "More than one eight gives the ear the second half of this cheers, two-thirds of eleven are the first half." . . . "The oat is heard above me in Calydon." . . . "The forge of the flea." . . . Until Roger, glancing up too suddenly, on that fatal afternoon when the tragedy had occurred, had surprised on little Leslie's face a fleeting grin of mockery. This week's was a particularly malevolent example of the Grand Inquisitor's most fiendish art, and Roger was fractious. Immediately two dictionaries sped through the room and hit the wall, one on either side of the younger of the Farmiloe brothers.

"I suppose," bellowed Roger, "that you, being a half-wit and an imbecile and an idiot, imagine you can do this better than me?" and expected Leslie to shrink and cower, and to whisper his usual apologies after the usual challenge of "bet you can't do this."

But Leslie replied tranquilly, with that ghost of a chuckle bubbling through his speech: "Do you know—ch-ch—I rather think—ch-ch—I rather think I could."

"Come on, then," shouted Roger, marveling at the half-wit's effrontery. So little Leslie climbed down from his chair and tripped across the room, seized a pencil, bent over the folded page, the ruled squares of the crossword blurred already and indented by poor Roger's attempts and crossings out.

And with swift neatness, still smiling in that odd triumphant way, he filled in the whole solution, first across and then down.

It was Roger's turn to watch, which he did in dumb, fishlike bewilderment.

This was outrageous! This was incredible! It couldn't be true, and yet—it was true. Three more words—two—one—and Leslie had finished. "You see," he said, kindly explaining, but not bothering to hide the fact that he was patronizing that poor burly oaf, Roger Farmiloe, "you see: 'Seat renowned for its association with Arachnida' must be 'tuffet.' Of course you know that Arachnida is the class name of spiders, scorpions, and mites."

Either this was magic, or—

Suddenly Roger Farmiloe guessed.

With a roar like a bull, he flung down his accusation. "You! You're Grand Inquisitor!"

"Dear me, yes," replied little Leslie Farmiloe, sweetly and gently. "Fancy you only discovering that now! It's been such fun every Sunday, sitting here and watching you."

"Haunted, sir? No, not what you'd call haunted. Of course one of the gentlemen who lived here last was hanged. . . ."

Gladys Bronwyn Stern

The *plot* of a story is the series of related events that present a problem or *conflict*, lead to the *climax* or point at which the conflict must be resolved, and finally result in a *conclusion* of the conflict.

Who are the main characters of "Grand Inquisitor"? List some of the ways in which they differ. How have these differences affected their relationship?

In most stories there is a conflict of opposing forces that must be resolved. In "Grand Inquisitor" the conflict is between the two Farmiloe brothers: Roger, the bully, and Leslie, the bullied. Conflicts that pit character against character, character against nature (weather, animals), or character against the forces of society (opinion, convention) are called *external* conflicts.

Conflicts within the character such as between duty and desire, between opposing emotions, or between character and conscience are called *internal* conflicts. Conflict in a story is rarely entirely one or the other. Which sort of conflict do you find in "Grand Inquisitor"?

What is the conclusion of the conflict between Roger and Leslie? What brings it about? The climax of the story occurs when Roger realizes that Leslie is the author of the puzzles with which Roger wrestles each Sunday. At this point something has to happen. The conflict must be resolved. Why is Roger unable to accept his discovery about Leslie?

If, at the climax of the story, Roger had expressed his amazement and then gone on to admire Leslie's talent, how might the conclusion of the story have been different?

Roger cannot accept the knowledge that the brother he despises and bullies can best him at something and gloat over his victory. He murders Leslie. Given what you know of Roger, is this a logical conclusion to the story?

plot

A series of related events that present and resolve a conflict. The usual pattern of plot is conflict, climax, and conclusion.

Apply to "The Monkey's Paw" on page 14.

point of view

Every literary work is told to the reader by a *speaker* or *voice*, commonly called the *narrator*. The author, in choosing a narrator for fiction, does much more than select someone to tell the story; he or she determines what the reader will see through the narrator's eyes.

The relationship between the narrator of a story and the story he or she relates is called the *point of view*. There are basically two main points of view: *first person* and *third person*.

The following passage is from "The Secret Sharer" by Joseph Conrad.

> And I told him a little about myself. I had been appointed to take charge while I least expected anything of the sort, not quite a fortnight ago. I didn't know either the ship or the people. Hadn't had the time in port to look about me or size anybody up. And as to the crew, all they knew was that I was appointed to take the ship home. For the rest, I was almost as much of a stranger on board as himself, I said. And at the moment I felt it most acutely. I felt that it would take very little to make me a suspect person in the eyes of the ship's company.

The "I" in the passage refers to a young ship's captain, a major character who is telling the story of his almost dreamlike encounter with a mysterious stranger. The "I" indicates that the story is told from a *first-person point of view*.

First-person narrators are always characters in the story. If they are major characters, they tend to report mainly what happens to them; if they are minor characters, they generally tell what they see happening to others. The information they communicate may be limited by what they observe, but in many cases readers can draw INFERENCES from the information. (For another example of the first-person point of view see "The Boar Hunt.")

The passage on the following page is about the main character in Audrey M. Lee's "Waiting for Her Train."

Joseph Conrad, *'Twixt Land and Sea.* New York: Doubleday & Company, Inc., 1912.

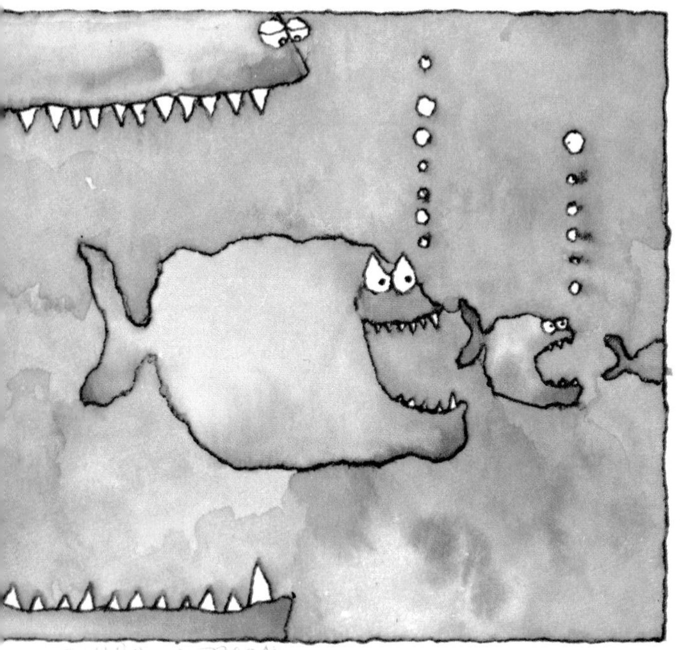

. . . She is giving the menu a respectable glance, demonstrating her discriminating taste with proper deliberation. Then with the same deliberating eye, she looks at the long line of people waiting to take advantage of the early morning special breakfasts. A glass of water will do until the line is shorter. That is her reasoning. . . .

The woman is sitting alone when this narrative takes place; no other character is with her to record her actions or speeches. Even if there had been, what is recorded in this passage is what is going on inside the woman's mind. It could only be told by an all-knowing or *omniscient* (om-nish′ənt) narrator. An omniscient narrator is not a character in the story, but is capable of relating what every character is saying, doing, and thinking. Sometimes, as in "Waiting for Her Train," the narrator knows and relates the thoughts of only one character. This is called the *limited omniscient* point of view. ("Lamb to the Slaughter" is another example.)

The second kind of third-person point of view occurs when the narrator acts as an anonymous reporter, relating only what he or she sees and hears and drawing no conclusions. This is called the *third-person objective* or *dramatic* point of view because the reader learns from the narrator only what he or she would learn from the characters in a play; that is, what they say and do, but not what they think (unless they say aloud what they are thinking).

The following passage is from "The Death of Ivan Ilych" by Leo Tolstoy.

Ivan Ilych had been a colleague of the gentlemen present and was liked by them all. He had been ill for some weeks with an illness said to be incurable. His post had been kept open for him, but there had been conjectures that in case of his death Alexeev might receive his appointment, and that either Vinnikov or Shtabel would succeed Alexeev. So on receiving the news of Ivan Ilych's death the first thought of each of the gentlemen in that private room was of the changes and promotions it might occasion among themselves or their acquaintances.

Is the above passage in the first or third person? Does the narrator relate only what is happening or also what any character is thinking? What point of view is represented in the passage?

point of view

The relationship between the narrator of a story and the characters and action in it. The two most common points of view are *first person* and *third person.* The first-person narrator might offer a personal account of his or her own experiences, past or present, or may focus on what happens to other characters. The third-person narrator stands anonymously outside a story's action, presenting an all-knowing or omniscient point of view, a limited omniscient point of view that centers on the thoughts and actions of only one character, or an objective or dramatic point of view that describes only what can be seen.

Leo Tolstoy, *The Death of Ivan Ilych*, 1884, translated by Aylmer Maude, Oxford University Press.

Apply to "Forgiveness in Families" on page 39

protagonist/ antagonist

The leading character of a short story, play, or novel is called the *protagonist.* The work mainly concerns or is about the protagonist. Thus, the protagonist of "The Piano" (page 27) is João de Oliveira; the protagonist of *One Day in the Life of Ivan Denisovich* (page 531) is the title character.

In most stories the protagonist is opposed by an adversary called the *antagonist.* The antagonist may be a villainous character or he or she may simply be the source of conflict in the story. The family members in "The Piano" who urge João to get rid of his cherished possession are the antagonists of that story. The antagonist need not be a character, however; in *One Day,* for example, the antagonist is the living conditions of a Russian labor camp. In a well-known story by Jack London, "To Build a Fire," the sole character is the protagonist; the antagonist is the weather that surrounds him. Fate, chance, a set of events, a character, or any combination of these may be the antagonist of a work.

protagonist/antagonist

(prō tag′ə nist); (an tag′ə nist)

The protagonist is the main character in a short story, play, or novel.
The adversary who opposes the protagonist is called the antagonist. The antagonist may be another character in the work, the forces of nature, fate, chance, or any combination of these.

Apply to "Twelve Angry Men" on page 86.

rhyme

The Swan and Goose

A rich man bought a Swan and Goose— *a*
That for song and this for use. *a*
It chanced his simple-minded cook *b*
One night the Swan for Goose mistook. *b*
But in the dark about to chop *c*
The Swan in two above the crop, *c*
He heard the lyric note, and stayed *d*
The action of the fatal blade. *d*

And thus we see a proper tune *e*
Is sometimes very opportune. *e*

Aesop
(translated by William Ellery Leonard)

Rhyme is the repetition of similar or identical sounds. Where are the rhyming words in the lines above? How many different rhyming sounds are there in the poem? Which words that rhyme are not spelled similarly?

Rhyme is among the sound devices poets use. One of its chief uses is the pleasure it gives the reader. This fable might have been written in prose, but the use of rhyme adds to its amusing tone.

Rhyme found at the ends of lines is called *end rhyme*. When there is a definite pattern to the end rhyme, as in the poem, it is called *rhyme scheme*.

If one were to chart the rhyme scheme of a poem, one would represent the first rhyming sound as *a* and the second rhyming sound as *b*. Thus the rhyme scheme for "The Swan and Goose" would be *a a b b c c d d, e e*. More intricate rhyme schemes are possible. Read the following poem. Chart the rhyme scheme.

The Craftsman

I ply with all the cunning of my art
This little thing, and with consummate care
I fashion it—so that when I depart,
Those who come after me shall find it fair

Continued

And beautiful. It must be free of flaws—
Pointing no laborings of weary hands;
And there must be no flouting of the laws
Of beauty—as the artist understands.
Through passion, yearnings infinite—yet dumb—
I lift you from the depths of my own mind
And gild you with my soul's white heat to plumb
The souls of future men. I leave behind
This thing that in return this solace gives:
"He who creates true beauty ever lives."

Marcus B. Christian

How does the rhyme scheme of the last two lines differ from that of the previous lines? Note how this difference emphasizes the last two lines and sets them apart from the rest of the poem. Notice also how the rhyme scheme divides the poem into four distinct parts. How many lines are there in the poem? The form of this poem and its rhyme is that of a Shakespearean sonnet.

Midsummer Jingle

I've an ingle, shady ingle, near a dusky bosky
dingle
Where the sighing zephyrs mingle with the purling
of the stream.
There I linger in the jungle, and it makes me thrill
and tingle,
Far from city's strident jangle as I angle, smoke
and dream.

Through the trees I'll hear a single ringing sound,
a cowbell's jingle,
And its ting-a-ling'll mingle with the whispers of
the breeze;
So, although I've not a single sou, no potentate or
king'll
Make me jealous while I angle in my ingle 'neath
the trees.

Newman Levy

Which words within the lines rhyme with the words at the ends of the lines? Rhyming sounds within lines are called *internal rhyme.*

Do *jingle, jangle,* and *jungle* rhyme? Words that sound similar but are not identical are called *half rhymes* or *slant rhymes.* (See also CONSONANCE.)

Half rhyme adds variety to the sound of poems and is much used by more recent poets. Poets who use half rhyme have a much wider selection of words from which to choose since the number of identically rhyming words is actually rather limited.

"And now there came both mist and snow,
And it grew wondrous cold;
And ice, mast-high, came floating by
As green as emerald.

"And through the drifts the snowy cliffs
Did send a dismal sheen;
Nor shapes of men nor beasts we ken—
The ice was all between."

Samuel Taylor Coleridge,
"The Rime of the Ancient Mariner"

Point out examples of internal rhyme. What example of half rhyme is in the first stanza?

rhyme

The repetition of similar or identical sounds. Its use may give pleasure to the ear, emphasize important words or lines, and unify parts of the poem or the whole poem.

Apply to **"A Poison Tree"** on page 167.

rhythm

Language has *rhythm* because we give words a certain stress, or accent, in pronouncing them. We say *beGIN* and *MERcy, interRUPT* and *BEAUtiful*. Both prose and poetry have rhythm, but in poetry the rhythm is regulated. What we call rhythm, or *meter,* in English poetry is the pattern of accented and unaccented syllables.

Rhythm alone does not make a poem, as these lines show:

> Birds GO rePAST the Ego YOU,
> DULL ROLLer SKATE sinCERE we DO.

Meter must echo sense. Poets who wrote solemnly of death do not want their lines to bounce along like a nursery jingle. They will use meter (in combination with other devices) to create a slow, solemn movement. The pace of a poem must be appropriate to the emotion.

The most common meter in English is *iambic*, an unaccented syllable followed by an accented syllable (˘/). The English language has many words that consist of two syllables. Because most of these two-syllable words, like *beGIN,* are accented on the final syllable, English speech has a natural iambic beat. As a result, the rhythm of an iambic line moves smoothly:

> Her deck, / once red / with he / roes' blood.
>
> Oliver Wendell Holmes, "Old Ironsides"

Trochaic meter, an accented syllable followed by an unaccented syllable, (/˘), as in *MERcy*, reverses the natural iambic beat. As such, a trochaic line seems to move roughly:

> Thou, when / thou re / turnst, wilt / tell me.
>
> John Donne, "Song"

Anapestic meter (˘˘/), as in *interRUPT*, tends to move in leaps:

> The As syr / ian came down / like
> the wolf / on the fold.
>
> George Gordon, Lord Byron, "The Destruction of Sennacherib"

Dactylic meter (/˘˘), as in *BEAUtiful*, moves in thrusts:

> O the wild / charge they made!
>
> Alfred, Lord Tennyson, "The Charge of the Light Brigade"

Spondaic meter (//) consists of two accented syllables.

Poets can manipulate any one of the basic meters so that it moves quickly or slowly. They adjust the motion of a poem by occasionally substituting a different meter in a line. Identify the substitute meter in each example.

1. The ship / was cheered, / the har / bor cleared,
Mer ri / ly did / we drop

Samuel Taylor Coleridge, "The Rime of the Ancient Mariner"

2. Can non to / right of them,
Can non to / left of them,
Can non be / hind them
Vol leyed and / thun dered;

Alfred, Lord Tennyson, "The Charge of the Light Brigade"

In the example from Coleridge, the pace quickens when the poet reverses the *accented* syllables. In the example from Tennyson the pace slows when the poet decreases the number of *unaccented* syllables. This is *how* the movement changes, but it is even more important to recognize *why* it changes. Tennyson, for example, slows the line so that it echoes (and emphasizes) the mournful tone of the stanza. Rhythm is part of a poem's meaning.

Much modern poetry frequently departs from a regular meter or rhythm, but all poems have rhythm; that is, there are always some words or syllables that are stressed more than others.

Scansion (skan′shən)

When we scan a line of poetry, we determine the kind of meter it contains and then count the number of metrical units, or *feet,* in a line. A *foot* is a group of syllables constituting a metrical unit of a verse.

Thus I

Pass by

And die

As one

Un known

And gone.

Robert Herrick,
"Upon His Departure Hence"

Because each line of Herrick's poem is written in the *iambic* meter, and because each line contains *one* iambic foot, we say the lines of the poem are basically *iambic monometer.*

The English word *monometer* (mə nom′i tər) is derived from the Greek prefix *mono-* ("one") and the Greek word *metron* ("measure"). Other words that indicate the length of lines are:

dimeter (dim′i tər) (two feet)
trimeter (trim′i tər) (three feet)
tetrameter (te tram′ə tər) (four feet)
pentameter (pen tam′ə tər) (five feet)

Scan the following examples. On a separate sheet of paper, copy the defining sentence. Then fill in the name of the meter *(iambic, trochaic, anapestic,* or *dactylic),* number of feet in the lines *(1, 2, 3, 4,* or *5),* and the scansion pattern (the name of the meter plus *monometer, dimeter, trimeter, tetrameter,* or *pentameter).*

1. Mor tal / man and / wo man,
Go up / on your / tra vel!

Elizabeth Barrett Browning,
"A Drama of Exile"

Each of Browning's lines is written in the ______ meter. Because each line contains ______ feet, the lines are ______ ______.

2. How like / a win / ter hath / my ab / sence been
From thee, / the plea / sure of / the fleet / ing year!

William Shakespeare, "Sonnet 97"

Each of Shakespeare's lines is written in the ______ meter. Because each line contains ______ feet, the lines are ______ ______.

3. Cold in hu / man i ty,
Burn ing in / san i ty.

Thomas Hood,
"The Bridge of Sighs"

Each of Hood's lines is written in the ______ meter. Because each line contains ______ feet, the lines are ______ ______.

rhythm

The arrangement of stressed and unstressed sounds in speech and writing.

Apply to "The Stone" on page 164.

satire

Drawing by Lorenz; © 1977 The New Yorker Magazine, Inc.

1. What situation is the cartoonist making fun of?

2. Do you think the cartoonist is trying to correct the situation, or is he simply commenting on it?

3. Is the general tone of the cartoon humorous or critical? (See TONE.)

S*atire* is a device used by writers (and cartoonists) to ridicule people and their institutions, whether social, political, religious, or commercial, in order to reveal their foolishness or vice. The aim of satire is to comment on the situation, often with an eye toward correcting it by making society more aware of the problem.

Satire is frequently a more successful means of bringing a situation to the public's notice than plain criticism. While the subject and the writer's intent may well be serious, satire itself is entertaining, whether gently humorous or savagely witty. Irony, humor, sarcasm, and exaggeration are common devices of satire. (See IRONY.)

Read the following poem. Try to determine whether the poet is gently, or bitterly, humorous.

We Are Going to See the Rabbit

We are going to see the rabbit.
We are going to see the rabbit.
Which rabbit, people say?
Which rabbit, ask the children?
Which rabbit?
The only rabbit,
The only rabbit in England,
Sitting behind a barbed-wire fence
Under the floodlights, neon lights,
Sodium lights,
Nibbling grass
On the only patch of grass
In England, in England
(Except the grass by the hoardings[1]
Which doesn't count.)
We are going to see the rabbit
And we must be there on time.

First we shall go by escalator,
Then we shall go by underground,
And then we shall go by motorway

Continued

---

1. ***hoardings,*** billboards. [*British*]

And then by helicopterway,
And the last ten yards we shall have to go
On foot.
And now we are going
All the way to see the rabbit.
We are nearly there,
We are longing to see it,
And so is the crowd
Which is here in thousands
With mounted policemen
And big loudspeakers
And bands and banners,
And everyone has come a long way.
But soon we shall see it
Sitting and nibbling
The blades of grass
On the only patch of grass
In—but something has gone wrong!
Why is everyone so angry,
Why is everyone jostling
And slanging and complaining?

The rabbit has gone,
Yes, the rabbit has gone.
He has actually burrowed down into the earth
And made himself a warren,[2] under the earth,
Despite all these people.
And what shall we do?
What *can* we do?

It is all a pity, you must be disappointed,
Go home and do something else for today,
Go home again, go home for today.
For you cannot hear the rabbit, under the earth,
Remarking rather sadly to himself, by himself,
As he rests in his warren, under the earth:
"It won't be long, they are bound to come,
They are bound to come and find me, even here."

Alan Brownjohn

Why is the rabbit so special? What do you suppose has happened to the other rabbits? the grass? What is the poet commenting on in the second stanza? Is the poet optimistic or pessimistic about the future of wildlife? Do you think the poem is meant solely to entertain the reader or to stir a feeling that "something must be done"?

When people, actions, or literary works are satirized by ridiculous exaggeration, it is called *burlesque*. Comedians on television often perform burlesques of old movies and soap operas. In writing, burlesque may be characterized by an inconsistency between the subject matter and the style: the struggle between a spider and a fly, for example, written in epic form.

Mimicking aimed at a particular writer or work is called *parody* (par′ə dē). In parody the outstanding characteristics of a work or writer are so exaggerated that anyone in the least familiar with the original will recognize the parodied style. For example, as you read the following, determine which writer and work are being parodied.

Wits, comics, funnymen, spare me your jeers;
I've come to help your humor, not to pan it.
Your skits are long, your repartee is dull;
Your jokes were old when Noah was a lad.

Do you recognize the original? If not, see page 423, lines 73-76. Try writing a parody of a well-known nursery rhyme.

satire

A technique that ridicules people and their institutions in an effort to expose their weaknesses and evils. The purpose of satire is often to bring about a change. Exaggeration and irony are frequent devices of satire. *Burlesque* is a means of making people, actions, or literary forms ridiculous through extreme exaggeration. *Parody* is mimicking aimed at making fun of a particular writer's style or work.

Apply to "**Action Will Be Taken**" on page 347.

2. ***warren,*** place underground where rabbits live.

setting

The following passage is from the opening pages of *Rebecca* by Daphne du Maurier.

> There was Manderley, our Manderley, secretive and silent as it had always been, the grey stone shining in the moonlight of my dream, the mullioned windows reflecting the green lawns and the terrace. Time could not wreck the perfect symmetry of those walls, nor the site itself, a jewel in the hollow of a hand.
>
> . . . When I thought of Manderley in my waking hours I would not be bitter. I should think of it as it might have been, could I have lived there without fear. I should remember the rose garden in summer, and the birds that sang at dawn. Tea under the chestnut tree, and the murmur of the sea coming up to us from the lawns below.

What is Manderley? Is the narrator still at Manderley? Is Manderley inland or on the coast? What do these lines tell the reader about the narrator?

The two paragraphs tell the observant reader a good deal about Manderley, the English country estate where most of *Rebecca* takes place. They describe the *setting* of the novel: an old, grand, stone house in the midst of fine green lawns situated above the sea. The time is not specified, but the reader can make an INFERENCE that the narrator has lived at Manderley at some time in the past, and that the memories of having lived there are not all happy ones.

The setting is the time and place in which the action of a narrative occurs. Setting helps in the understanding of character and action. Later in the story, which is told in FLASHBACK, the narrator meets the owner of Manderley, Maximilian de Winter.

> . . . I thought how unreal he would look against a Florida background. He belonged to a walled city of the fifteenth century, a city of narrow, cobbled streets, and thin spires, . . . a past of narrow stairways and dim dungeons, a past of whispers in the dark, of shimmering rapier blades, of silent, exquisite courtesy.

What does the narrator's imagined setting for Mr. de Winter tell you about him? Setting can help the reader understand character through association with familiar backgrounds.

A third function of setting is to help create the atmosphere and mood of the narrative. Consider the following paragraph from *Rebecca,* which describes the narrator's first ride up the drive to the great house.

> This drive twisted and turned as a serpent, scarce wider in places than a path, and above our heads was a great colonnade of trees, whose branches nodded and intermingled with one another, making an archway for us, like the roof of a church. Even the midday sun would not penetrate the interlacing of those green leaves, they were too thickly entwined, one with another, and only little flickering patches of warm light would come in intermittent waves to dapple the drive with gold. It was very silent, very still. On the high-road there had been a gay west wind blowing in my face, making the grass on the hedges dance in unison, but here there was no wind. Even the engine of the car had taken a new note, throbbing low, quieter than before. As the drive descended to the valley so the trees came in upon us, great beeches with lovely smooth white stems, lifting their myriad branches to one another, and other trees, trees I could not name, coming close, so close that I could touch them with my hands. On we went, over a little bridge that spanned a narrow stream, and still this drive that was no drive twisted and turned like an enchanted ribbon through the dark and silent woods, penetrating even deeper to the very heart surely of the forest itself, and still there was no clearing, no space to hold a house.

Is the atmosphere created cheerful or subdued? What are the elements that add a slightly sinister quality to the description? How does the setting affect what you expect of the story?

Finally, setting may aid the development of the plot. When the narrator goes to Manderley, she goes as the second Mrs. de Winter. The reader is told that the first Mrs. de Winter, a beautiful and vivacious woman, was drowned in the bay below the grounds. Mrs. Danvers, the housekeeper,

---

shows the narrator to her rooms in the east wing of the house overlooking the rose garden.

"You can't see the sea from here then," I said, turning to Mrs. Danvers.

"No, not from this wing," she answered, "you can't even hear it, either. You would not know the sea was anywhere near, not from this wing.

". . . the rooms in the west wing are very old. The bedroom in the big suite is twice as large as this, a very beautiful room too, with a scrolled ceiling."

. . . I did not know why she must speak with such an undercurrent of resentment, implying as she did at the same time that this room, where I found myself to be installed, was something inferior, not up to Manderley standard, a second-rate room, as it were, for a second-rate person.

. . . [Mrs. Danvers] paused an instant, feeling me with her eyes. "They used to live in the west wing and use those rooms when Mrs. de Winter was alive. That big room I was telling you about, that looked down to the sea, was Mrs. de Winter's bedroom."

The plot of *Rebecca* concerns the two wives, one dead and one the narrator. Do you see how the above passage foreshadows a rivalry between the women? Do you expect the sea to play an important role in the plot? One woman's room looks out over the sea and the rose garden; the other's room, only the rose garden. How do you think this might influence the plot?

setting

The time and place in which the action of a narrative occurs. The setting may serve simply as a background for characters and events or it may help create the atmosphere from which the story evolves. It may directly affect the plot's development, and it may help in the understanding of character, or even be vital to that understanding.

Apply to "The Boar Hunt" on page 2.

simile

My heart is like a singing bird
  Whose nest is in a water'd shoot

Christina Rossetti,
"A Birthday"

Fair as a star, when only one
  Is shining in the sky.

William Wordsworth,
"She Dwelt Among the Untrodden Ways"

In both examples above, comparisons are made. What is being compared in each? What word in each example tells you that a comparison is being made?

A *simile* is a stated comparison between two things that are literally unlike but share some quality or qualities that the writer wishes to emphasize. Similes are expressed by the use of the words *like* or *as*. In the first simile, the speaker's heart is like a singing bird. What feeling does this comparison suggest? The second simile compares the fairness of a beloved woman no longer alive to the shining of a single star. What qualities do the two elements of the comparison share?

Be careful not to confuse similes with literal comparisons. When we express such comparisons as "She looks like her mother" or "He writes as well as a professional writer," we are being literal.

simile

A figure of speech involving a direct comparison between two unlike things and using words such as *like* or *as*.

Apply to "Sunset" on page 188.

stereotype

Read the following passages about different characters. Decide which person each passage is describing.

A. Jeffrey Lombard was tall and dark with just a tinge of silver at his temples. Always impeccably dressed, he wore his clothes with a kind of lazy grace that belied his athletic prowess. Well-read, witty, and assured of the best tables, Lombard was a sought-after escort, but, as yet, no woman had managed to hold him for long.

Lombard is probably **(a)** coal miner; **(b)** truck driver; **(c)** secret agent; **(d)** jockey.

B. Grace Meadowes was smart, no doubt about that. When George had died, she'd invested wisely and was now nicely set up for life. If only her darling Billy hadn't married that silly Florence. What on earth had he seen in her anyway? Adjusting her best rose-trimmed hat, she resolutely set her shoulders as she glanced in the mirror. A plain face with a determined jaw gazed back at her.

Grace Meadowes is probably **(a)** a domineering mother-in-law; **(b)** a timid, retiring woman; **(c)** the heroine of a historical novel; **(d)** a duchess.

C. Herbie sweated profusely and seemed to shrink as he sagged against the wall. He was a weasel-faced little man with scanty hair and a pasty complexion. He was scared, but too out of breath to keep running. He hadn't worked these streets for all those years for nothing, though, so as they hovered close he blubbered out a deal.

Herbie is probably a **(a)** hardware salesman; **(b)** chef; **(c)** small-time crook; **(d)** veterinarian.

The above characters are examples of *stereotypes*. Stereotyped characters are those that embody a conventional idea about whatever character is being portrayed. Make a list of some other stereotyped characters.

Stereotypes in written works need to be recognized as stereotypes rather than as fully developed characters. Stereotypes are useful when the author wants to compare and contrast different reactions in a limited space or time as in "Twelve Angry Men" (page 86).

Secondary characters, too, are often presented as stereotypes; they are better foils if they remain one-dimensional.

Reading about stereotyped characters in popular fiction is often pleasurable because such characters are predictable, and the reader knows what to expect. Usually, however, a writer will try to develop characters more fully. (See CHARACTERIZATION.)

PLOTS and SETTINGS may be stereotyped also. Very likely as you have watched a program on television or read a book, you have suddenly realized that it is similar to something you have seen or read before. An example of a stereotyped plot might be one in which a doctor, a lawyer, or a policeman discovers that his best friend is taking drugs or bribes or kickbacks. Make a list of some other stereotyped plots you have seen on television or read.

Settings that for one reason or another are continually depicted in the same manner are stereotyped. Examples might be a wholesome farm, a wicked city, or the glamorous French Riviera. Anyone who lives in any of these places knows that such views are one-sided.

Stereotypes can be harmful if they lead a reader to accept certain standardized views about people, situations, or places. In real life they are all more complex.

stereotype (ster′ē ə tīp′)

Standardized, conventional ideas about characters, plots, and settings. An example of a stereotyped character might be an absent-minded professor; a stereotyped plot might be a story about a brave dog saving a small child; a stereotyped setting might be a smoke-filled newsroom.

Apply to **"Enemies"** on page 352.

style

As you read the following paragraphs, try to determine what makes them different.

A. At any time of year the view from the Paris bridges is very nice, especially in the evening. It is just like a picture-postcard scene with the buildings on both sides of the river, and the big trees that come right down to the water. Behind them, in the west, you can see the large Louvre, the famous museum. It sort of glows when the sun goes down. Toward the other direction you can see the outline of the also-famous Cathedral of Notre Dame.

B. At any season, and all year long, in the evening the view of the city from the bridges was always exquisitely pictorial. One's eyes became the eyes of a painter, because the sight itself approximated art, with the narrow, pallid façades of the buildings lining the river; with the tall trees growing down by the water's edge; with, behind them, the vast chiaroscuro[1] of the palatial Louvre, lightened by the luminous lemon color of the Paris sunset off toward the west; with the great square, pale stone silhouette of Notre Dame to the east.

Janet Flanner, from "That Was Paris"

What do you think is the purpose of the paragraphs? To entertain? to inform? to create a scene? All of these things?

Which paragraph has more difficult words? Longer sentences? Which paragraph is more conversational? Does one paragraph give you a clearer picture of the scene than the other? If so, which? Are IMAGERY and FIGURATIVE LANGUAGE employed?

Two elements are necessary when writing: ideas (or a subject) and the words to express those ideas. The manner in which writers make words fit their ideas is called *style*. Style is a combination of the many techniques and devices of writing and the way they are used to express the writer's ideas.

Both paragraphs are about the view from the bridges of Paris, but the styles are vastly different. The first paragraph mainly informs the reader about the view. The writer uses simple, informal language. The TONE might be described as conversational, much like what one might write in a letter home. No particular MOOD is established, though it is plain the writer is enjoying the view.

In the second paragraph the style is much more complex. The writer attempts to make the scene as real for the reader as it is for the viewer. There is a faintly reminiscent TONE, as though the writer were remembering how things looked rather than describing them as she now sees them. The language is more formal and ornate than that of the first paragraph, and the IMAGERY and FIGURATIVE LANGUAGE are more concrete: "narrow, pallid façades," "the palatial Louvre," "the luminous lemon color of the Paris sunset," and "the great square, pale stone silhouette of Notre Dame." A METAPHOR is found in the sentence "One's eyes became the eyes of a painter." There is ALLITERATION: "the palatial Louvre, lightened by the luminous lemon color . . ." The MOOD created is quiet, almost dreamy.

Some authors so consistently write in a particular manner that their style is immediately distinguishable from other writers; hence, people speak of James Thurber's style or E. E. Cummings's style. All people who write, however, have their own individual ideas and use the language that they think best expresses those ideas. Thus, everyone has his or her own style of writing.

1. ***chiaroscuro*** (kē är′ə skyůr′ō), pattern of light and shade.

style

The manner in which writers use words and sentences to fit their ideas. Style involves many choices on the part of the writer: types of words, placement of words in a sentence, the purpose of the written work, tone, mood, imagery, figurative language, sound devices, and rhythm.

Janet Flanner, "That Was Paris." *The New Yorker*, March 11, 1972.

Apply to **"Five Letters"** on page 504.

symbol

Judge not the play before the play be done.

The line above is literal advice that might be offered to any theatergoer. There is no reason to suppose "play" means or stands for anything except itself. Now read the line in the context of the poem.

My soul, sit thou a patient looker on;
Judge not the play before the play be done:
Her plot has many changes; every day
Speaks a new scene; the last act crowns the play.

Francis Quarles, from *Epigram*

1. What is the first indication that "play" now may mean more than just a theater production?

2. What might "play" refer to in this context?

3. What might the "plot" be?

4. What is the "last act"?

When read in context, "play" becomes a *symbol,* something that stands for or represents something else: in this case, a person's life.

Not all works employ symbolism. Readers should not try to force meaning that is not there, nor should they try to make symbols of things that have only literal meaning.

Are there any symbols in the following poem, in your opinion?

Plain

Out of Mobile I saw a 60 Ford
fingers wrapped like pieces of rope
around the steering wheel
foxtail flapping the head of the hood
of the first thing ever
he has called his own.

Between two Bardahls
above the STP
the flag flies backwards
Go To Church This Sunday
Support Your Local Police
Post 83
They say the same thing
They say
I am not alone.

Miller Williams

1. Some of the stickers obviously "stand for" a product, but what more abstract idea does the poet say they also represent? In which lines of the poem does the poet tell the reader what he thinks the stickers "stand for"?

2. How do you think the stickers might make the owner feel less alone?

3. Of what might the car itself be a symbol?

symbol

Something concrete, such as an object, person, place, or happening, that stands for or represents something abstract, such as an idea, a quality, a concept, or a condition.

Apply to **"The Sentimentality of William Tavener"** on page 313.

theme

One Hard Look

Small gnats that fly
In hot July
And lodge in sleeping ears
Can rouse therein
A trumpet's din
With Day of Judgment fears.

Small mice at night
Can wake more fright
Than lions at midday;
A straw will crack
The camel's back—
There is no easier way.

One smile relieves
A heart that grieves
Though deadly sad it be,
And one hard look
Can close the book
That lovers love to see.

Robert Graves

How can small gnats create more noise than a trumpet, according to the first stanza of the poem above? How might mice rustling at night be more frightening than lions during the day? How might a sad person's smiling or being smiled at help lessen his or her grief? What is the poet saying in the last three lines of the third stanza? (Keep in mind the expression "face like an open book.")

Which of the following statements best reveals the main idea of the poem? **(a)** Small sounds at night seem noisier than loud ones during the day; **(b)** Things seem different by the light of day; **(c)** Small things in general can make big differences in the way one feels; **(d)** Don't despise the little things.

The main idea underlying a literary work is called the *theme*. The theme of the above poem is revealed in statement **(c)**.

Statement **(d)** presents a moral: it tells the reader how to act. It is not the theme, because the poet does not tell the reader how to think or behave. He simply states various examples and leaves it up to the reader to make an INFERENCE about the theme: seemingly insignificant things

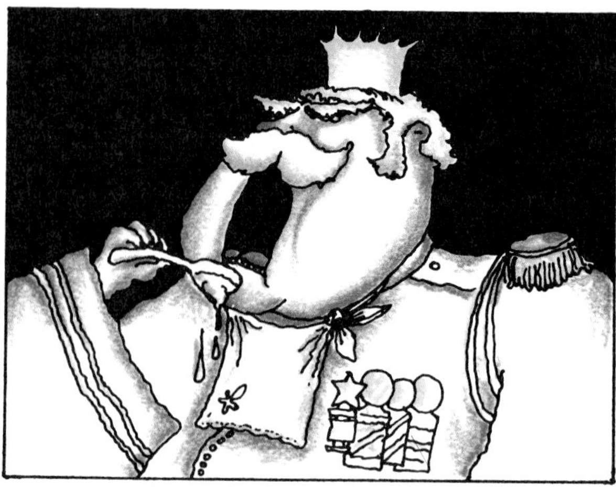

can make all the difference to the way one feels.

Statement **(a)** relates what plot there is in stanzas one and two. A PLOT is a pattern of events, things that happen in a narrative or poem. The theme is the central idea, what the work is about.

It is important to recognize the difference between the theme and the *subject* of a literary work. The subject is the topic about which the author has chosen to write. The theme, however, makes a statement about that topic or expresses an opinion about it. The subject of the above poem is suggested by the title, "One Hard Look"; the theme is the great effect small things can have.

Soup

I saw a famous man eating soup.
I say he was lifting a fat broth
Into his mouth with a spoon.
His name was in the newspapers that day
Spelled out in tall black headlines
And thousands of people were talking about him.

When I saw him,
He sat bending his head over a plate
Putting soup in his mouth with a spoon.

Carl Sandburg

1. What sets the man in the poem apart from most other people?

2. What impression of him do you have from this poem?

3. What do you think is the theme of this poem?

Not every work has a theme. Works with no theme are most likely to be those written entirely for the entertainment of the reader. Examples might be mystery or adventure stories. Some literary works—*Julius Caesar,* for example—have more than one theme.

theme

The underlying main idea of a literary work. The theme may be stated or implied. Theme differs from the subject of a literary work in that it involves a statement or opinion about that subject. Not every literary work has a theme. Some literary works have more than one theme.

Apply to "Through the Tunnel" on page 64.

tone

The following passage is from the novel *Oliver Twist* by Charles Dickens. It concerns the members of the board who administer the affairs of the local workhouse where the paupers, or poor people of the area, may find employment, food, and lodging.

As you read, try to determine Dickens's attitude toward his subject.

The members of this board were very sage, deep, philosophical men; and when they came to turn their attention to the workhouse, they found out at once, what ordinary folks would never have discovered—the poor people liked it! It was a regular place of public entertainment for the poorer classes; a tavern where there was nothing to pay; a public breakfast, dinner, tea, and supper all the year round; a brick and mortar elysium,[1] where it was all play and no work. "Oho!" said the board, looking very knowing; "we are the fellows to set this to rights; we'll stop it all, in no time." So, they established the rule, that all poor people should have the alternative (for they would compel nobody, not they), of being starved by a gradual process in the house, or by a quick one out of it. With this view, they contracted with the water-works to lay on an unlimited supply of water; and with a corn-factor to supply periodically small quantities of oatmeal; and issued three meals of thin gruel a day, with an onion twice a week, and half a roll on Sundays. They made a great many other wise and humane regulations, having reference to the

1. ***elysium*** (i lizh′əm, i liz′ē əm), paradise.

ladies, which it is not necessary to repeat; kindly undertook to divorce poor married people, in consequence of the great expense of a suit in Doctors' Commons; and, instead of compelling a man to support his family, as they had theretofore done, took his family away from him, and made him a bachelor! There is no saying how many applicants for relief, under these last two heads, might have started up in all classes of society, if it had not been coupled with the workhouse; but the board were long-headed men, and had provided for this difficulty. The relief was inseparable from the workhouse and the gruel; and that frightened people.

Further on, Dickens explains parenthetically that the board would "compel" no one to adopt one manner of starvation over the other. What is the INFERENCE the reader may draw from this statement?

When relating the arrangements for food, Dickens points out that the board contracted for an "unlimited supply of water," and "small quantities of oatmeal" with an onion "twice a week" and "half a roll on Sundays." He then notes that the board made "a great many other wise and humane regulations," implying that the aforementioned are wise and humane also. Is that the actual case?

Noting that relief from family responsibilities might have proved too popular with "all classes of society," Dickens refers to the board members as "long-headed" men who had foreseen and provided for that event; that is, "The relief was inseparable from the workhouse and the gruel; and that frightened people." What is the tone here?

Through his choice of words and the juxtaposition of the cruelties inflicted on poor people with the wisdom of the board in inflicting them, Dickens has created a passage that is ironic in tone with both humorous and serious overtones to it.

Determine the tone of this poem.

Daniel at Breakfast

His paper propped against the electric toaster
 (Nicely adjusted to his morning use),
Daniel at breakfast studies world disaster
 And sips his orange juice.

The words dismay him. Headlines shrilly chatter
 Of famine, storm, death, pestilence, decay.
Daniel is gloomy, reaching for the butter.
 He shudders at the way

War stalks the planet still, and men know hunger,
 Go shelterless, betrayed, may perish soon.
The coffee's weak again. In sudden anger
 Daniel throws down his spoon

And broods a moment on the kitchen faucet
 The plumber mended, but has mended ill;
Recalls tomorrow means a dental visit,
 Laments the grocery bill.

Then, having shifted from his human shoulder
 The universal woe, he drains his cup,
Rebukes the weather (surely turning colder),
 Crumples his napkin up
And, kissing his wife abruptly at the door,
Stamps fiercely off to catch the 8:04.

Phyllis McGinley

1. What terrible things are happening in the world?

2. What "terrible" things are happening at home to Daniel?

3. Which do you think upsets him more? Do you think the narrator is sympathetic to Daniel's trials?

4. What are some clues in the poem as to the way the narrator views Daniel's situation?

tone

The attitude of the writer toward his or her subject. Tone may be stated or implied. Tone may be revealed by the author's word choice and arrangement of ideas, events, and descriptions.

Apply to **"One Perfect Rose"** on page 198.

Composition Guide

This Guide offers practical advice for writing many of the composition assignments in this book. These articles by themselves will not make you a better writer, but they will give you useful tips and techniques. And they will underline, again and again, that writing is a process that begins before your pen touches paper and does not end with the period of your last sentence.

This Guide includes the following articles:

Prewriting

Why is it sometimes so hard to write that first sentence? Perhaps it's because you are distracted by too many concerns: conceiving, evaluating, and ordering ideas, fitting them into grammatically accurate sentences with correctly spelled words, and creating a beginning that makes the world take notice. The result of this overload? Blank paper and sweaty palms. The solution? Take it one step at a time. And use your brain before you use your pen.

1. Understand the assignment. Ask questions if you don't. Note the details. A "compare and contrast" assignment, for example, expects you to discuss likenesses and differences; be sure to do both. A "character sketch" involves more than physical appearance; be sure to focus on personality and character traits as well.

2. Think. If you have several days to complete an assignment, use one or two to think it over. (Not ignore—*think,* as in mull, muse, stew, and ruminate.) Most of your writing assignments will be based in some way on selections you have read. One way to feed your subconscious is to become completely familiar with the selection. You will find yourself reading in a different, hungrier way when you have a writing assignment.

To check on how your subconscious is doing, try brainstorming. For example, what comes to mind when you think of the Stage Manager in *Our Town?* Jot down every word, idea, fact, example, or opinion that occurs to you. Don't stop to evaluate; just stream your ideas onto paper. And save that paper.

3. Who is your audience? What is your purpose? On first impulse your answers probably are "my teacher" and "to pass." But the questions are more complicated, and more important, than that.

You vary your speaking style as you talk to a friend, a child, a parent, a police officer. Your tone of voice varies as you borrow five dollars, explain how to adjust a bike's brakes, tell a joke, or console an unhappy friend. The same holds true of your writing. Your audience and your purpose will influence your tone, vocabulary, choice of details, level of complexity, and a great deal more. So answer carefully: Who is your audience? What is your purpose?

4. Talk it over. Writing is sometimes called a lonely art. Prewriting isn't. Take advantage of class discussions to try out your ideas. Or, talk them over with a friend:

"To me, the falling snow in the Frost poem is not a reference to death; it's a weather report."

"But everyone knows that snow and winter are universal symbols of death."

"Yeah? Tell that to Santa Claus."

A friendly argument is a *great* prewriting activity.

5. Plan ahead. Some people are allergic to outlining. Too bad; it's worth trying. An outline is a writing road-map that will tell you where to go and when to stop. It will keep track of what is more and less important and help you give equal ideas equal attention. If the formality of Roman numerals and capital letters bothers you, try something else: a simple listing of key words, or a two-level set of headings and subpoints. Some writers put their ideas on cards to be shuffled into effective order. Whatever your method, you will find that time invested in "planning on paper" pays off as you write.

6. Write a rough draft. Promise yourself not to hand in your first version. This simple vow will give you a wonderful—if temporary—freedom from tidiness, correctness, and good penmanship. Get your ideas on paper! Can't think of a first sentence? Start with the second, or the second paragraph. Work fairly quickly; try to keep a flow of words going. Sometimes it helps concentration to set mini deadlines for completion of pages or paragraphs.

When you've completed your rough draft, you're ready for what many writers consider to be Real Writing. It's spelled r-e-v-i-s-i-n-g.

Revising

A teacher once said, "There's no such thing as a bad composition. There are only compositions that are handed in too soon." Revision (and if necessary re-revision) is the secret to avoiding the "too soon" problem.

The best way to begin the revision process is to do nothing. Give your first draft a rest—overnight at least. This will let you approach your work with fresh eyes; you will also be less reluctant to cut and rewrite.

As you examine your first draft, ask the following questions:

1. Is the main idea of the paper clearly stated in the first paragraph?

2. Does the paper have a clear sense of progression, a steady movement toward important ideas or details? Have you used transition words *(first, next, on the other hand, as a result)* to show how your ideas are related?

3. Have you chosen the appropriate tone (humorous, serious, etc.) and level of formality (formal or informal) to reach your intended audience?

4. Does the paper read well aloud? Where could sentences be combined, *and*'s be eliminated? Are there any monotonously repeated sentence patterns?

5. Has each paragraph been developed in sufficient detail? A short paragraph may be used occasionally for dramatic effect, but otherwise paragraphs should be equally well developed.

6. Are the opening and closing paragraphs forceful and interesting? Does the last paragraph drive home what the first paragraph promises?

7. Are your examples and details clear? Do they all directly relate to your purpose? Is each one necessary?

8. Is each sentence clear and complete? Will each phrase and word be understandable to your readers?

9. Have you used strong verbs and precise nouns wherever possible?

10. Does your composition completely fulfill the assignment? (Reread your original assignment.)

Editing and Proofreading. Before typing or copying your paper in its final form, check carefully for errors in grammar, mechanics, and usage.

1. Are all words spelled correctly?

2. Is your punctuation logical and helpful in making meaning clear?

3. Have you used capitals, underlining, numerals, and abbreviations correctly?

4. Have you checked pronouns and verbs for common errors such as faulty agreement, incorrect pronoun form or reference, incorrect form of the verb?

5. Can you spot any errors in word choice or usage?

After you have copied or typed your final "hand-in" version, only proofreading remains to ensure that you actually wrote what you meant to write. By now you're so familiar with the words that you can read them with your eyes closed. This does not lead to effective proofreading. Set the copy aside for a time (again, overnight if possible). Read slowly, word by word. You may find it helpful to use a ruler or a card with a narrow slot cut in it to help you focus on only one line or a few words at a time. Watch for two frequent copying errors: the omitted word ("Caesar to go to the Capitol anyway") and the doubled word ("Caesar decided to go to the the Capitol anyway").

Making Comparisons and Contrasts

"For your next paper, compare and contrast . . ." How do you begin to discuss likenesses and differences between two (or more) characters, incidents, objects, or ideas? Here are some basic guidelines.

1. Points of comparison. Whether your assignment is general ("Compare Brutus and Mark Antony") or specific ("Compare Brutus and Mark Antony as public speakers"), take time to set up points of comparison, issues or categories that apply to each subject.

For example, if you're comparing two characters as speakers your points of comparison might be:

purpose of speech
attitude toward audience
technique
effect on audience

As you study your material you will probably drop some points of comparison and add others. But having these in mind will get you organized.

2. Don't jump to conclusions. Wait until you've carefully examined your subjects before making judgments.

3. Make lists. As you study your subjects, jot down your notes in separate columns for each subject. Use your points of comparison as subheadings, and try (without being fanatical about it) to keep equivalent details on the same line in both lists. Like so:

Brutus	**Mark Antony**
	Purpose of Speech
to calm mob	to stir up mob
to justify killing of C.	to remind of C's goodness
	to "sneak" the spch. past conspirators

As the example shows, your lists won't always be equal line-for-line, but trying for parallelism will help you be complete and balanced.

Don't be stingy at this note-taking stage. Write down everything that occurs to you and save questions about importance or relevance for later.

4. Form a conclusion. Write your opinion on the comparison of your subjects in one or two sentences. This might become the opening or closing of your paper; you might not use it at all. But establishing your own conclusion will help you sift through your details and shape your paper.

5. Pick a pattern. There are a number of ways to organize a comparison/contrast paper.

• *Item-by-Item.* Basically, this is your comparison columns written in sentence form. "Brutus wanted to reassure the angry and excited Romans. Mark Antony, on the other hand, wanted to prod them into a vengeful rage. Brutus wanted to explain . . ." And so on. This method can be effective in short takes—one or two paragraphs. In longer papers, this pattern tends to create a monotonous, ping-pong effect. It's also difficult to steer your reader to an overall conclusion.

• *Whole-to-whole.* You may choose to completely discuss one of your subjects first, then turn to the second subject for similar scope and treatment. (You'll find that your second discussion will almost always be easier to write and take fewer words than the first.)

• *Likenesses-differences.* Here you discuss all the similarities of your subjects in one section and all the differences in another. In what order? Follow this simple rule: *The more important discussion goes last.* If you wish to emphasize the differences between your subjects, discuss differences last.

6. Look it over. Comparison/contrast papers tend naturally to have a balanced, parallel style. But watch out for dullness—a boring sameness of sentence pattern and length, wordy repetition. Also:

• Have you chosen an effective organizational pattern?

• Is the flow of your ideas made clear by transitions such as *similarly, likewise, but, on the other hand, in contrast?*

• Have you avoided a clogging overuse of these same transitions?

• Does your paper come to a conclusion or does it simply run out of ideas?

Writing a Description

"Describe your favorite relative."

"Describe the contents of your family's junk drawer or glove compartment."

"Describe what your city or town might look like if it had been abandoned by every living thing."

How do you handle such assignments? Start by remembering that a description is a series of written details that develop a picture in a reader's mind. Now:

1. Form the picture in your mind. You can't create a picture for someone else until you've fully imagined it for yourself. This is true whether you're describing the desk before your eyes or a domed city on the third moon of Jupiter. Hold the picture in your mind and let details and feelings soak in.

2. Find a purpose. Don't start writing, don't even jot down details, until you know what mood, feeling, idea, opinion—what dominant impression you want to share with your reader through the description. The shivery misery of a foggy day at the beach? The wonder of seeing an eagle in flight? The most important thing to know about your best friend?

The need to convey meaning will color and animate your description. You will be able to select details not because "they're there" but because they contribute to the particular effect you are aiming for. You will create not a random snapshot, but a focused, purposeful picture.

3. Arrange your details. You might present your description in space order, showing where things are in terms of left and right, north and south, front and back: "To the left of the door, on a scrap of rug, was a pile of orphaned shoes." You might present your details in the order that they impressed you: "The first thing I noticed about David was . . ." Or you might arrange details in order of increasing importance to your dominant impression: "But the most gruesome thing about the creature . . ."

Instinct and your purpose will usually make the choice of organization easy. Just remember to be consistent.

4. Show, don't tell. You are "telling" when you write "It was a hot day for biking." You are "showing" when you write "The air above the asphalt road wavered and wrinkled like molten glass." Which will create the stronger effect of a "hot day" in your reader's mind?

You are telling (and being lazy) when you use words like *beautiful, wonderful,* or *horrible*. You are showing when you use details that create a sense of beauty, wonder, or horror in the mind of your reader.

You are telling when you say "My grandfather was a shy man." You are showing when you describe an incident or quote a speech that demonstrates your grandfather's shyness.

You can't entirely avoid general statements and abstract words in description. But try always to pin them down with details. Remember, your purpose is not to summarize the picture in your mind, but to create that picture in your reader's mind. It makes a difference. You might be content with writing "The boat passed out of sight" because you've seen the boat. But what are you giving your reader to see? A canoe or an oil tanker? Is it sailing, cruising, buzzing, plunging, gliding, or drifting?

5. Use strong verbs and exact nouns. Verbs and nouns—not adjectives—are the snap and crackle of good description. Avoid the "is-was-were" pattern where possible and put the weight of your ideas on strong verbs. "Wrinkles were like stitches at the corners of her mouth" is a fine detail. But notice how more forceful and direct it becomes when a verb does the work: "Wrinkles stitched the corners of her mouth."

Use adjectives carefully. If you catch yourself stringing more than two together ("Ice formed a *brittle, glistening, transparent* jacket on each twig"), you can be fairly sure that you haven't found the right adjective ("Ice formed a *crystal* jacket on each twig").

6. Use "technique." Apply in your description the literary skills you've learned from reading.

• *Imagery*. Use words and details that help

your reader see, touch, hear, smell, and taste. What sensory experiences are shared in the following description? "The old outboard motor stuttered and snarled as it pushed the boat across the pond, briefly scarring the smooth surface of the water and tainting the morning air with the reek of blue exhaust."

• *Metaphors and similes.* Figurative comparisons can make a detail clearer or more vivid to your reader: "The mist over the pond was as wispy as pulled cotton."

• *Personification.* Giving objects human characteristics will give life to your description: "The dawning sun slipped into the sky and glowed with pride at its accomplishment."

7. Don't be trivial. In an effort to be specific, many writers make the mistake of stuffing their descriptions with "grocery lists" of petty details. They tell their reader the color of everything in sight (beginning with "blue sky") or reveal the brand name of every article of clothing worn.

Where do you draw the line? When is the knot in a shoelace a marvelously precise detail, and when is it trivial? Ask: Does this detail contribute to the dominant impression I want to create? Details that don't contribute are trivia.

8. Don't just stop; finish. Don't let your description wheeze to an end on its last exhausted detail. Your last sentence is a final chance to fix the picture in your reader's mind. Again, try to show rather than tell. Which of the following seems more effective?

"All in all, it was a good feeling to have won the game."

"The scoreboard is dark, the crowd now scattered home, but the smile will last all night."

Developing Your Style

Ideally, style expresses your uniqueness in writing as your voice expresses your uniqueness in speech. As your voice changes depending on whether you're giving a warning, soothing a child, or asking a question, so your style alters with your audience and your purpose.

Some elements of style are beyond your conscious control. Style is partly an expression of the way you see things, the way your mind works, the way you respond to words. But other elements of style result from deliberate decisions you make before you write, as you write, and as you revise.

How can you improve your style? Read as many books and authors as you can. Write often. And keep the following suggestions in mind.

1. Be yourself. Use words and images that are natural to you. When writing about literature it may be appropriate to use a slightly more formal style. But no tuxedos, please. Your purpose is to share ideas, not to prostrate your reader by the capaciousness of your verbal arsenal nor by the baroque felicities, or, as it were, the architectural symmetries of your sentential configurations. Language that distracts the reader from meaning (as in the previous sentence) is poor style.

Being a good reader can complicate the matter of "being yourself." You may find yourself unconsciously imitating the style of your favorite writer or, chameleonlike, adopting the style of whatever book you read last. This is not so much a problem as it is a phase that almost all writers go through. The trick is not to avoid such influence, but to absorb it. Keep reading, widely and often, and keep writing.

2. Be honest. Write what you believe. You cannot write with style while groping for what you think your teacher thinks you should think. A writing assignment is not an algebra problem; it's seldom a question of giving a correct or incorrect solution. What is wanted is a clear expression of *your* ideas.

You won't always have your choice of topics, nor will every assignment spontaneously ignite your interest and emotions. In those cases, light your own match: scratch at the assignment until you find some issue, some angle that you can discuss with conviction. Avoid writing anything with your mind and emotions on automatic.

3. Be direct. Say what you mean clearly and in the fewest possible words.

- Use direct words. Some synonyms are understood more quickly and intensely than others. *Lie* is more direct than *untruth* or *falsehood; home* is more direct than *dwelling* or *abode; book* more direct than *volume* or *publication.*
- Rely on verbs and nouns to carry your meaning. Be sparing in your use of adjectives and adverbs.
- Use passive verbs only for special reasons (when you don't know who does an action, or when it's unimportant who does the action). At all other times use active verbs.

> *Passive:* The bike was taken last night.
> *Active:* Doyle took the bike last night.

- Chop deadwood. It's good exercise.

> *Not:* It was during the month of July
> *But:* In July
> *Not:* Due to the fact that
> *But:* Because
> *Not:* true facts, join together, red in color
> *But:* facts, join, red

4. Be fresh. Your effort here is not to be original (hard to do), but to avoid laziness. Mistrust words and phrases that come too easily to mind. Clichés such as "white as a sheet" or "clean as a whistle" (what does that mean, by the way?) contribute only a tired predictability to your style. When you revise, don't tolerate a sentence like "His heart broke with grief." Try: "His heart splintered. . . ." Or leave his trite heart out altogether: "He wilted with grief." What about "His heart was freeze-dried with grief"? No, this will only puzzle your reader. Be fresh, but don't be bizarre.

5. Be emphatic. Emphasis involves far more than scattering exclamation marks and underlines. These devices are frequently overused. Before resorting to them, consider the following options:

- *Emphatic words.* A well-chosen, forceful word is worth a half-dozen exclamation marks.
- *Emphatic position.* First and last are positions of stress within a sentence, a paragraph, or an entire composition. Arrange your ideas and phrase your sentences accordingly. In revising, give particular polish to your first and last paragraphs, your first and last sentences.
- *Emphatic rhythms.* Skilled writers control the rhythms of their words to stress their ideas. A short, terse sentence amid longer sentences rivets a reader's attention, as does a short paragraph amid longer paragraphs. Occasionally inverting the usual grammatical order of a sentence can also create emphasis. "Lying in the mud puddle was Jane's lost mitten" has a stronger, fresher effect than if it were written in usual subject-verb order.
- *Emphatic repetition.* Stylistic repetition (as opposed to unnecessary, accidental, or boring repetition) can effectively emphasize ideas. A classic example is Lincoln's "government of the people, by the people, and for the people. . . ." Emphasis can be achieved by repeating words, phrases, or grammatical patterns.

Of course, overuse can weaken the impact of any of these techniques. Use them carefully.

Evaluating Your Evidence

Suppose you are asked to write on the following issue:

> Is Val in "Forgiveness in Families" justified in her low opinion of her brother? Or is her disdain for him an indication of some problem in her own character?

How would you respond? By stating "Val's opinion is justified because . . . I say so"? Mere assertion is seldom convincing (on paper, anyway), and it leads to a brutally short composition. What is wanted is evidence.

1. Know your evidence. Evidence can be considered in the following ways:

• *Strong evidence.* Your most solid evidence will be factual details about which there can be no disagreement:

> It is Val, not her brother, who calls the ambulance when their mother has a heart attack.

That is true; you can look it up; case closed.

Unfortunately (or fortunately) the really interesting issues in a work of literature are seldom resolved by a recitation of facts. Such evidence is important, but usually you will have to go beyond the facts in developing your case.

• *Weak evidence.* Your poorest evidence will be your own unsupported opinions. Such "evidence" often pulls you and your reader away from, rather than into, the story. The effect of one opinion chasing another is usually pointless and unpersuasive:

> Val suspects that her mother likes her brother more than she likes Val. Of course it's true that mothers always care more for their sons than their daughters.

Most writers know, even as they set them down, that such opinions are weak evidence, so they instinctively insert sweeping language ("Of course it's true," "always") to make them seem more convincing. But the usual effect of such exaggeration is to make the weakness more obvious and the "evidence" easier to dismiss.

When you spot *always, every, never, none, everybody knows, nobody believes,* or other blustery expressions in your first draft, you can be fairly sure your argument is on thin ice. Stop skating and find substantial evidence.

• *Inferential evidence.* Between the bedrock of factual detail and the thin ice of unsupported opinion is a broad middle ground of evidence based on inferences, generalizations, logic, and common sense. Handling such evidence is the best test of your abilities as a careful reader and a persuasive writer.

Val begins "Forgiveness in Families" by joking that if she told a psychiatrist about her brother, she'd be committed to a mental hospital. This opening establishes the basically humorous tone of the story. But doesn't it also alert the reader that the story is about Val's problems rather than her brother's? Such an inference does not carry the weight of fact, but it is valid and, used with other valid inferences, can create a convincing web of evidence.

Sometimes it is wise to use qualifying words (such as *perhaps, probably, seems, suggests*) in presenting inferential evidence. The right amount of such language shows that you are careful with evidence. But too many *perhaps*'s can create an impression of wordiness, weakness, and uncertainty.

• *Outside evidence.* Sometimes you may want to use evidence outside the immediate context of the story. In "Forgiveness in Families," for example, you might note that Val's mixed-up emotions about her mother's recovery are not unusual; relatives of critically ill patients often have similar feelings.

When you do go "outside the story," make sure this evidence is clearly related to your argument and presented as concretely as possible. (Not: "I once read somewhere . . ." or "They say that . . . ") The danger here is that you may find yourself smuggling in your own personal opinions disguised as "common knowledge."

2. Use evidence fairly. Misreading or careless analysis of the text can lead to a poor selection of evidence:

> In "Forgiveness in Families," the mother knows that her son is disturbed. In the fourth paragraph she suggests he is a lunatic; near the end, she calls him an idiot.

By missing or ignoring the mother's affectionate, joking tone, the writer has distorted the evidence.

Using evidence fairly means presenting information in context: considering the tone and intention of a speaker as well as his or her actual words, seeing each event as a part of the whole. Avoid the mistake of building your case on a single episode without considering what comes before and after:

> Cam finally settles down when he joins a religious cult.

This statement ignores the overall pattern of Cam's life and the clear indication at the end of the story that the cult, like Cam's other involvements, is only a temporary interest.

3. Double-check your ideas. Suppose, after carefully studying the story, you decide:

> The key to the story is Val's need to forgive herself for her mixed-up feelings when her mother survives.

You've got details to back up this inference. Val clearly feels guilty; she wants to change; she reads a book about loving; she no longer feels superior to her brother. Your statement seems to check out. But now double-check it against the story as a whole.

Important clues to meaning are often found in the title and the first few and last few paragraphs of a selection. Is personal forgiveness really the key? The final scene emphatically involves Val's mother and brother as well as Val. The story's last line and the title "Forgiveness in Families" (not simply "Forgiveness") seemingly suggest a broader meaning than personal forgiveness. Better think again.

Defending Your Position

You are frequently asked to express and defend a viewpoint about a work of literature:

> Is Mr. White an innocent victim of the curse of "The Monkey's Paw," or is he in some way responsible for the catastrophe that occurs? Support your opinion with details from the story.

You have two jobs here: to reach a conclusion about an issue and to convince your reader to share that conclusion. Here are some guidelines.

1. Go to the source. Don't come to any conclusions until you've reread and carefully considered the story, poem, or play in question.

2. State your position. Write it like a challenge, as clearly and as forcefully as you can. Such a tone will help to persuade others.

> Mr. White is *not* innocent; it is his greedy curiosity that starts the fatal chain of events.

This statement may eventually be refined into your opening sentence, but for now it functions as a magnet to help you pick out evidence from the selection.

3. List your evidence. Brainstorm: Quickly list everything you can think of—facts, reasons, inferences, opinions—that can possibly support your statement. Then skim through the selection for additional details you may have forgotten. Your purpose at this stage is just to get this material down on paper.

4. Select your evidence. Using the guidelines from "Evaluating Your Evidence" (662), choose the strongest and most convincing items from your list.

5. Consider opposing evidence. Before going further, ask, "What's the best evidence *against* my position? Why doesn't this evidence change my mind?" (It's possible you *will* change your mind. Better now than later. Go back to the evidence and reshape your position.)

If your position survives those two questions, plan on including a discussion of opposing evidence early in your own argument:

> It is true that the White family is portrayed as charming, loving, contented. White even says ". . . I've got all I want." But if he is content, why does he ask so many questions about the paw? Why does he literally reach into fire to save it? Why does he insist on paying for it? Why does he wish for money? White's greedy actions speak louder than his protestations of contentment.

In doing so, you're demonstrating that you are smart enough to see other sides to an issue, fair enough to consider them, and confident enough to overcome them. It's worth doing.

6. Arrange your evidence. As you outline (or think about) your first draft, remember that the places of emphasis are first and last. If you have only a few items of evidence, you might begin with the most important. The danger of leading off with your best evidence is that your argument loses force as it goes on, like a singer running out of breath. Try saving the best evidence for last. This allows your argument to develop momentum and virtually guarantees a strong conclusion.

7. Explain your evidence. A quotation or detail from the selection is not evidence until you make it so. Make sure your evidence relates clearly to your argument. "So what?" is a useful question to ask yourself each time you bring up a supporting detail.

Beware of fascinating but useless details and pointless summarizing of the plot:

> The paw twists "like a snake" when White makes his wish.

A detail like this one doesn't connect at all to your argument about White's responsibility. A quick "so what?" gets you back on track.

8. Finish strong and fast. Once you've made your final (and best) point, quickly bring your paper to a close. Summarize your evidence and restate your conclusion. Do *not* repeat or weakly echo your first paragraph. Leave your reader with a sense of completeness and finality.

9. Test your first draft. Stop being a writer; become a skeptic ("Who says? So what?").

- Read the first sentences of each of your paragraphs. Do these clearly express the points of your argument? Do you get a sense of flow and direction? Does the argument build or fade, or does it wander in a circle?
- Are there any skinny paragraphs? This is often a sign of scanty or nonexistent support for a point. Back up any unsupported opinions, or cross them out.
- Have you provided enough evidence? Too much? Are any of your details repetitive?
- Read the first paragraph and last paragraph together. Does the last deliver on the promise of the first?

Glossary

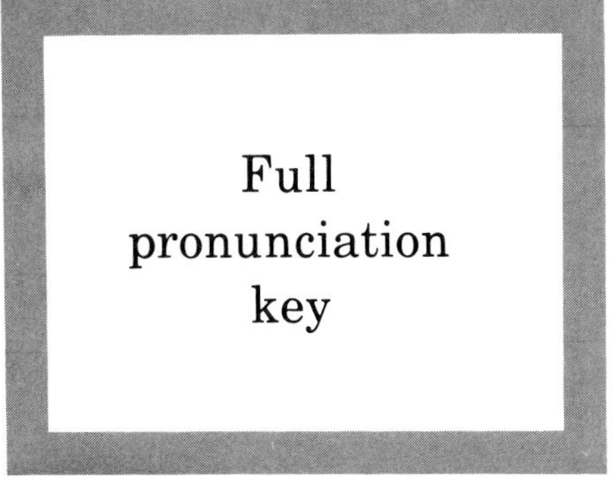

The pronunciation of each word is shown just after the word, in this way: **ab bre vi ate** (ə brē′vē āt). The letters and signs used are pronounced as in the words below. The mark ′ is placed after a syllable with primary or heavy accent, as in the example above. The mark ′ after a syllable shows a secondary or lighter accent, as in **ab bre vi a tion** (ə brē′vē ā′shən).

Some words, taken from foreign languages, are spoken with sounds that do not otherwise occur in English. Symbols for these sounds are given in the key as "foreign sounds."

a	hat, cap
ā	age, face
ä	father, far
b	bad, rob
ch	child, much
d	did, red
e	let, best
ē	equal, be
ėr	term, learn
f	fat, if
g	go, bag
h	he, how
i	it, pin
ī	ice, five
j	jam, enjoy
k	kind, seek
l	land, coal
m	me, am
n	no, in
ng	long, bring
o	hot, rock
ō	open, go
ô	order, all
oi	oil, voice
ou	house, out
p	paper, cup
r	run, try
s	say, yes
sh	she, rush
t	tell, it
th	thin, both
ŦH	then, smooth
u	cup, butter
u̇	full, put
ü	rule, move
v	very, save
w	will, woman
y	young, yet
z	zero, breeze
zh	measure, seizure
ə	represents: a in about, e in taken, i in pencil, o in lemon, u in circus

foreign sounds

Y as in French *du.* Pronounce (ē) with the lips rounded as for (ü).

à as in French *ami.* Pronounce (ä) with the lips spread and held tense.

œ as in French *peu.* Pronounce (ā) with the lips rounded as for (ō).

N as in French *bon.* The N is not pronounced, but shows that the vowel before it is nasal.

H as in German *ach.* Pronounce (k) without closing the breath passage.

Grammatical key

adj.	adjective	*prep.*	preposition
adv.	adverb	*pron.*	pronoun
conj.	conjunction	*v.*	verb
interj.	interjection	*v.i.*	intransitive verb
n.	noun	*v.t.*	transitive verb
sing.	singular	*pl.*	plural

a bash (ə bash′), *v.t.* embarrass and confuse; make uneasy and somewhat ashamed; disconcert: *I was not abashed by the laughter of my classmates.* [< Old French *esbaïss-*, a form of *esbaïr* astonish] **—a bash′ment,** *n.*

a bate (ə bāt′), *v.,* **a bat ed, a bat ing.** *—v.t.* 1 lessen in force or intensity; reduce or decrease: *Soft words did not abate her fury.* 2 put an end to; stop: *abate a nuisance.* *—v.i.* become less in force or intensity; diminish: *The storm has abated.* [< Old French *abatre* beat down < *a-* to + *batre* to beat] **—a bat′a ble,** *adj.*

a bor tive (ə bôr′tiv), *adj.* 1 coming to nothing; unsuccessful: *an abortive rebellion.* 2 born prematurely. 3 imperfectly formed or developed; rudimentary. **—a bor′tive ly,** *adv.*

ac cen tu ate (ak sen′chü āt), *v.t.,* **-at ed, -at ing.** 1 call special attention to; emphasize: *Her white dress accentuated her sunburn.* 2 pronounce with an accent. **—ac cen′tu a′tion,** *n.*

ac cost (ə kôst′, ə kost′), *v.t.* approach and speak to first; address: *The stranger accosted me and asked for directions.* [< Middle French *accoster* < Latin *ad-* to + *costa* side, rib]

ac qui esce (ak′wē es′), *v.i.,* **-esced, -esc ing.** give consent by keeping silent or by not making objections; accept (the conclusions or arrangements of others); accede: *acquiesce in a decision.* [< Latin *acquiescere* < *ad-* to + *quies* rest, quiet]

ac quit tal (ə kwit′l), *n.* a discharge; a release after considering evidence.

acrop o lis (ə krop′ə lis), *n.* the high, fortified part or citadel of an ancient Greek city. [< Greek *akropolis* < *akros* highest part + *polis* city]

Ae o li an (ē ō′lē ən), *adj.* 1 of Aeolus. 2 **aeolian,** of, produced by, or carried by the winds.

aer i al (er′ē əl, ar′ē əl; *adj. also* ā ir′ē əl), *n.* the antenna of a radio, television set, etc. *—adj.* 1 of, for, between, or used by aircraft: *aerial navigation.* 2 growing in the air instead of in soil: *The banyan tree has aerial roots.* 3 of the air; atmospheric. [< Latin *aer* air] **—aer′i al ly,** *adv.*

aer o nau ti cal (er′ə nô′tə kəl, ar′ə nô′tə kəl), *adj.* of or having to do with aeronautics, the science or art involved with the design, manufacture, and operation of aircraft.

af fa bil i ty (af′ə bil′ə tē), *n.* 1 condition or quality of being courteous and pleasant in responding to others. 2 graciousness. [< Latin *affabilis* easy to speak to < *affari* speak to < *ad-* to + *fari* speak] **—af′fa bly,** *adv.*

af flic tion (ə flik′shən), *n.* 1 condition of continued pain or distress; misery. 2 cause of continued pain or distress; misfortune.

af fray (ə frā′), *n.* a noisy quarrel; fight in public; brawl. [< Old French *effrei*]

af front (ə frunt′), *n.* word or act that openly and purposely expresses disrespect; open insult: *To be called a coward is an affront.* *—v.t.* 1 insult openly; offend purposely and to one's face. 2 face courageously and defiantly; confront. [< Old French *afronter* strike on the forehead, defy, face < *a front* against the forehead]

a ghast (ə gast′), *adj.* struck with surprise or horror; filled with shocked amazement. [past participle of obsolete *agast* terrify < Old English *on-* on + *gæstan* frighten. Related to GHOST.]

a kin (ə kin′), *adj.* 1 of the same kind; alike; similar: *Your opinions are akin to mine.* 2 of the same family; related: *Your cousins are akin to you.* [for *of kin*]

a lac ri ty (ə lak′rə tē), *n.* brisk and eager action; liveliness: *move with alacrity.* [< Latin *alacritatem* < *alacer* brisk]

al che my (al′kə mē), *n.* 1 the chemistry of the Middle Ages, which combined science, magic, and philosophy. Alchemy tried to find a means of transmuting cheaper metals into gold and silver. 2 any miraculous power of transformation. [< Old French *alkemie* < Medieval Latin *alchimia* < Arabic *al-kīmiyā'* the art of alloying metals]

al ien ate (ā′lyə nāt, ā′lē ə nāt), *v.t.,* **-at ed, -at ing.** turn away the normal feelings, fondness, or devotion of anyone; make unfriendly; estrange: *The colonies were alienated from England by disputes over trade and taxation.* **—al′ien a′tor,** *n.*

al lay (ə lā′), *v.t.,* **-layed, -lay ing.** 1 put at rest; quiet: *My fears were allayed by the news that my family was safe.* 2 relieve (pain, trouble, thirst, etc.); alleviate. [Old English *ālecgan* < *ā-* away, off + *lecgan* to lay] **—al lay′er,** *n.*

al le vi ate (ə lē′vē āt), *v.t.,* **-at ed, -at ing.** 1 make easier to endure (suffering of the body or mind); relieve; mitigate: *Heat often alleviates pain.* 2 lessen or lighten; diminish. [< Late Latin *alleviatum* lightened < Latin *ad-* up + *levis* light]

al lo cate (al′ə kāt), *v.t.,* **-cat ed, -cat ing.** set or lay aside for a special purpose; assign, allot, or apportion: *The Ford Foundation allocated millions of dollars among colleges and hospitals.* [< Medieval Latin *allocatum* located < Latin *ad-* to, at + *locus* place]

a mal gam ate (ə mal′gə māt), *v.,* **-at ed, -at ing.** *—v.t.* unite (distinct elements, ideas, etc.) so as to form a whole; blend; merge: *amalgamate two competing companies.*

am big u ous (am big′yü əs), *adj.* 1 having or permitting more than one interpretation or explanation; equivocal: *an ambiguous remark.* 2 of doubtful position or classification: *an ambiguous character.* [< Latin *ambiguus* < *ambigere* be uncertain, wander < *ambi-* + *agere* to drive] **—am big′u ous ly,** *adv.* **—am big′u ous ness,** *n.*

a mi a ble (ā′mē ə bəl), *adj.* having a good-natured and friendly disposition; pleasant and agreeable. [< Old French < Late Latin *amicabilis* < Latin *amicus* friend. Doublet of AMICABLE.] **—a′mi a ble ness,** *n.* **—a′mi a bly,** *adv.*

am i ca ble (am′ə kə bəl), *adj.* having or showing a friendly attitude; peaceable: *settle a quarrel in an amicable way.* [< Late Latin *amicabilis* < Latin *amicus* friend < *amare* to love. Doublet of AMIABLE.] **—am′i ca ble ness,** *n.* **—am′i ca bly,** *adv.*

am nes ty (am′nə stē), *n., pl.* **ties.** a general pardon or conditional offer of pardon for past offenses against a government: *The king granted amnesty to political prisoners.* [< Greek *amnēstia* a forgetting < *a-* not + *mimnēskesthai* remember]

am u let (am′yə lit), *n.* locket, carved image, or some other small object worn as a magic charm against evil, disease, etc. [< Latin *amuletum*]

an ar chist (an′ər kist), *n.* 1 person who seeks to bring about the destruction of government and law; advocate of anarchism. 2 person who promotes disorder and stirs up revolt.

an ar chy (an′ər kē), *n.* 1 absence of a system of government and law. 2 disorder and confusion; lawlessness. [< Medieval Latin *anarchia* < Greek < *an-* without + *archos* ruler]

an i mat ed (an′ə mā′tid), *adj.* 1 lively; vigorous: *an animated discussion.* 2 gay; joyful: *an animated smile.* 3 seeming to be alive: *animated dolls.* 4 living; alive; animate. **—an′i mat′ed ly,** *adv.*

an ni hi la tion (ə nī′ə lā′shən), *n.* complete destruction.

an o nym i ty (an′ə nim′ə tē), *n.* condition or quality of being unknown.

an te cham ber (an′ti chām′bər), *n.* anteroom.

an thro po log i cal (an′thrə pə loj′ə kəl), *adj.* of anthropology, the study of humans, especially their physical characteristics, cultures, customs, and beliefs. **—an′thro po log′i cal ly,** *adv.*

ap a thet ic (ap′ə thet′ik), *adj.* 1 lacking interest or desire for action; indifferent. 2 lacking in feeling; unemotional. **—ap′a thet′i cal ly,** *adv.*

ap a thy (ap′ə thē), *n.* 1 lack of interest in or desire for activity; indifference. 2 lack of feeling. [< Greek *apatheia* < *a-* without + *pathos* feeling]

ap er ture (ap′ər chər, ap′ər chůr), *n.* an opening; hole. [< Latin *apertura* < *aperire* to open.]

a pex (ā′peks), *n., pl.* **a pex es** or **ap i ces.** 1 the highest point; vertex: *the apex of a triangle.* 2 a tip; point. 3 climax; peak: *the apex of her career.* [< Latin]

a plomb (ə plom′), *n.* self-possession springing from perfect confidence in oneself; assurance; poise. [< French < *à plomb* according to the plummet]

ap pall or **ap pal** (ə pôl′), *v.t.,* **-palled, -pall ing.** fill with consternation and horror; dismay; terrify. [< Old French *apallir* make pale < *a-* to + *pale* pale]

ap pa ri tion (ap′ə rish′ən), *n.* 1 a supernatural sight or thing; ghost or phantom. 2 the appearance of something strange, remarkable, or unexpected. [< Late Latin *apparitionem*]

ap per tain (ap′ər tān′), *v.i.* belong as a part; be connected; pertain; relate: *Forestry appertains to geography, botany, and agriculture.* [< Old French *apartenir* < Late Latin *appertinere* < Latin *ad-* to + *pertinere* pertain]

ap prais al (ə prā′zəl), *n.* 1 estimate of the value, amount, quality, etc.: *Their appraisal of the stock was too low.* 2 an appraising; evaluating.

ar id (ar′id), *adj.* 1 having very little rainfall; dry: *an arid climate.* 2 unfruitful because of lack of moisture; barren: *arid soil.* [< Latin *aridus* < *arere* be dry] **—ar′id ly,** *adv.*

ar is toc ra cy (ar′ə stok′rə sē), *n., pl.* **-cies.** 1 class of people having a high position in society because of birth, rank, or title; nobility. 2 class of people considered superior because of intelligence, culture, or wealth; upper class. [< Late Latin *aristocratia* < Greek *aristokratia* < *aristos* best + *kratos* rule]

a hat	**i** it	**oi** oil	**ch** child		a in about
ā age	**ī** ice	**ou** out	**ng** long		e in taken
ä far	**o** hot	**u** cup	**sh** she	**ə** =	i in pencil
e let	**ō** open	**ů** put	**th** thin		o in lemon
ē equal	**ô** order	**ü** rule	**ᴛʜ** then		u in circus
ėr term			**zh** measure	**<**	= derived from

ar rest (ə rest′), *v.t.* 1 seize (a person) and keep in custody by legal authority; apprehend: *The police arrested the woman for shoplifting.* 2 cause to stop (in a course of action); halt: *A fallen tree arrested traffic on the road.* [< Old French *arester* < Latin *ad-* + *restare* remain]

ar ro gance (ar′ə gəns), *n.* excessive pride with contempt of others; haughtiness.

ar ro gant (ar′ə gənt), *adj.* excessively proud and contemptuous of others. [< Latin *arrogantem* < *ad-* to + *rogare* ask] **—ar′ro gant ly,** *adv.*

a skew (ə skyü′), *adv., adj.* out of the proper position; turned or twisted the wrong way; awry.

a sphyx i ate (a sfik′sē āt), *v.t., v.i.,* **-at ed, -at ing.** suffocate. **—a sphyx′i a′tion,** *n.* **—a sphyx′i a′tor,** *n.*

as pic (as′pik), *n.* kind of jelly made from meat or fish stock, tomato juice, etc., used as a garnish or in salads. [< French]

as sail (ə sāl′), *v.t.* 1 attack repeatedly with violent blows. 2 attack with hostile words, arguments, or abuse. 3 (of a feeling) come over (a person) strongly; beset; trouble: *No doubts ever assail them.* [< Old French *asalir* < Latin *ad-* at + *salire* to leap] **—as sail′a ble,** *adj.*

a the ist (ā′thē ist), *n.* 1 person who does not believe in the existence of God. 2 a godless person. [< Greek *atheos* denying the gods]

at trib ute (*v.* ə trib′yüt; *n.* at′rə byüt), *v.,* **-ut ed, -ut ing,** *n.* —*v.t.* 1 regard as an effect or product of; think of as caused by: *She attributes her great age to a carefully planned diet.* 2 think of as belonging to or appropriate to. —*n.* a quality considered as belonging to a person or thing; characteristic: *Patience is an attribute of a good teacher.* [< Latin *attributum* assigned < *ad-* to + *tribuere* divide]

au di ble (ô′də bəl), *adj.* that can be heard; loud enough to be heard. [< Latin *audire* hear] **—au′di bly,** *adv.*

aught (ôt), *n.* zero; cipher; nothing. Also, **ought.** [< *naught; a naught* taken as *an aught*]

aug ment (ôg ment′), *v.t., v.i.* make or become greater in size, number, amount, or degree; increase or enlarge. [< Late Latin *augmentare* < *augmentum* an increase < Latin *augere* to increase] **—aug ment′a ble,** *adj.*

aus tere (ô stir′), *adj.* 1 stern in manner or appearance; harsh: *a silent, austere man.* 2 severe in self-discipline; strict in morals: *The Puritans were austere.* 3 severely simple: *The tall, plain columns stood against the sky in austere beauty.* 4 grave; somber; serious. [< Greek *austēros* < *auos* dry] **—aus tere′ly,** *adv.*

av a ri cious (av′ə rish′əs), *adj.* greatly desiring money or property; greedy for wealth. **—av′a ri′cious ly,** *adv.*

a ver sion (ə vėr′zhən, ə vėr′shən), *n.* 1 a strong or fixed dislike, antipathy: *an aversion to working hard.* 2 thing or person disliked.

a vert (ə vėrt′), *v.t.* 1 keep (a disaster, misfortune, etc.) from happening; prevent; avoid: *She averted the accident by a quick turn of her car.* 2 turn away or turn aside (the face, eyes, mind, etc.). [< Latin *avertere* < *ab-* from + *vertere* to turn]

av id (av′id), *adj.* extremely eager or enthusiastic; greatly desirous: *an avid defender of human rights. The miser was avid for gold.* [< Latin *avidus* < *avere* desire eagerly] **—av′id ly,** *adv.*

a wry (ə rī′), *adv., adj.* 1 with a twist or turn to one side: *My hat was blown awry by the wind.* 2 wrong; out of order: *Our plans have gone awry.*

balm (bäm, bälm), *n.* 1 a fragrant, oily, sticky substance obtained from certain kinds of trees, used to heal or to relieve pain; balsam. 2 a healing or soothing influence. [< Old French *basme* < Latin *balsamum* < Greek *balsamon.*]

bar na cle (bär′nə kəl), *n.* a small, saltwater crustacean that attaches itself to rocks, the bottoms of ships, the timbers of wharves, etc. [Middle English *bernacle* < Old French]

bea dle (bē′dl), *n.* a minor church officer whose duties include keeping order and waiting on the clergy. [< Old French *bedel*]

bean curd (bēn′kėrd′), *n.* a soft vegetable cheese eaten extensively in the Orient.

be di zen (bi dī′zn, bi diz′n), *v.t.* dress or ornament with showy finery. [< *be-* + *dizen*] **—be di′zen ment,** *n.*

be guile (bi gīl′), *v.t.,* **-guiled, -guil ing.** 1 trick or mislead (a person); deceive; delude: *Your flattery beguiled me into thinking that you were my friend.* 2 take away from deceitfully or cunningly. 3 win the attention of; entertain; amuse.

be hind hand (bi hīnd′hand′), *adv., adj.* 1 behind time; late. 2 behind others in progress; backward; slow. 3 in debt; in arrears.

bel lig er ent (bə lij′ər ənt), *adj.* fond of fighting; tending or inclined to war; warlike; pugnacious. [< Latin *belligerantem* < *bellum* war + *gerere* to wage] **—bel lig′er ent ly,** *adv.*

be night ed (bi nī′tid), *adj.* 1 not knowing right from wrong; ignorant. 2 ARCHAIC. overtaken by darkness. [< obsolete verb *benight* <*be-* + *night*]

be queath (bi kwēᴛʜ′, bi kwēth′), *v.t.* 1 give or leave (especially money or other personal property) by a will. 2 hand down or leave to posterity; pass along. [Old English *becwethan* < *be-* to, for + *cwethan* say] **—be queath′er,** *n.*

be reave (bi rēv′), *v.t.,* **-reaved** or **-reft, -reav ing.** 1 leave desolate and alone: *The family was bereaved by the death of the father.* 2 deprive ruthlessly; rob: *bereaved of hope.* [Old English *berēafian* < *be-* away + *rēafian* rob] **—be reave′ment,** *n.*

be reft (bi reft′), *adj.* bereaved: *Bereft of hope and friends, the old man led a lonely life.* —*v.* a pt. and a pp. of **bereave.**

ber lin (bər lin′), *n.* a large, four-wheeled, closed carriage hung between two perches and having two interior seats. [< French *berline,* after Berlin, Germany, where it was first made]

be times (bi tīmz′), *adv.* ARCHAIC. 1 early. 2 before it is too late. 3 in a short time; soon.

be to ken (bi tō′kən), *v.t.* be a sign or token of; indicate; show.

bib u lous (bib′yə ləs), *adj.* fond of drinking alcoholic liquor. [< Latin *bibulus* < *bibere* to drink]

big ot (big′ət), *n.* person who is bigoted; intolerant person. [< Middle French]

black guard (blag′ärd, blag′ərd), *n.* a low, contemptible person; scoundrel.

blade (blād), *n.* the cutting part of an edged tool or weapon, as distinguished from the handle. 2 a smart, dashing fellow. 3 leaf of grass. [Old English *blæd*] **—blade′like′,** *adj.*

bog (bog, bôg), *n.* piece of wet, spongy ground, too soft to bear the weight of any heavy body on its surface; marsh; swamp. [< Irish or Scottish Gaelic, soft]

bois ter ous (boi′stər əs), *adj.* 1 noisily cheerful; exuberant: *a boisterous game.* 2 rough and stormy; turbulent: *a boisterous wind.* 3 rough and noisy; clamorous: *a boisterous child.* [< Middle English *boistrous*] **—bois′ter ous ly,** *adv.* **—bois′ter ous ness,** *n.*

bon ny or **bon nie** (bon′ē), *adj.,* **-ni er, -ni est.** 1 fair to see; rosy and pretty: *a bonny baby.* 2 gay or cheerful. [Middle English *bonne,* apparently < Old French *bone* good < Latin *bonus*]

borne (bôrn, bōrn), *v.* a pp. of **bear.** *I have borne it as long as I can.*

brach i o ce phal ic (brak′ē ə sə fal′ik), *adj.* having a short, broad skull. Also, **brachycephalic.** [< Greek *brachys* short + *kephalē* head]

brack et (brak′it), *n.* 1 a flat piece of stone, wood, or metal projecting from a wall as a support for a shelf, etc. 2 a small shelf supported by brackets. [< Middle French *braguette* < *brague* breeches < Latin *bracae*]

bra vo (brä′vō, brā′vō), *n., pl.* **-voes** or **-vos.** a hired fighter or murderer. [< Italian, literally, wild]

bra zen (brā′zn), *adj.* 1 having no shame; shameless; impudent. 2 loud and harsh; brassy. —*v.t.* 1 make shameless or impudent. 2 **brazen it out** or **brazen it through,** act as if one did not feel ashamed of it: *Although he was caught lying, he tried to brazen it out by telling another lie.* [< Old English *bræsen* < *bræs* brass] **—bra′zen ly,** *adv.* **—bra′zen ness,** *n.*

broach (brōch), *v.t.* 1 begin conversation or discussion about; introduce: *broach a subject.* 2 open by making a hole: *broach a barrel of cider.* [< Old French *broche* < Latin *broccus* projecting]

buf fet (buf′it), *v.t.* 1 strike with the hand or fist. 2 knock about; strike repeatedly; beat back: *The waves buffeted me.* 3 fight or struggle against: *The boat buffeted the heavy waves caused by the storm.* [< Old French, diminutive of *buffe* blow]

bull ock (bůl′ək), *n.* 1 a castrated bull; ox; steer. 2 (originally) a young bull. [< Old English *bulluc* bull calf]

ca coph o ny (kə kof′ə nē), *n., pl.* **-nies.** succession of harsh, clashing sounds; dissonance; discord. [< Greek *kakophōnia* < *kakos* bad + *phōnē* sound]

ca dence (kād′ns), *n.* 1 the measure or beat of music, dancing, marching, or any movement regularly repeating itself; rhythm: *the cadence of a drum.* 2 fall of the voice. 3 a rising and falling sound; modulation. [< French < Italian *cadenza* < Latin *cadere* to fall]

cadge (kaj), *v.t., v.i.,* **cadged, cadg ing.** INFORMAL. beg shamelessly. [< Middle English *caggen*] **—cadg′er,** *n.*

cairn (kern, karn), *n.* 1 pile of stones heaped up as a memorial, tomb, or landmark. 2 cairn terrier. [< Scottish Gaelic *carn* heap of stones]

ca jole (kə jōl′), *v.t.,* **-joled, -jol ing.** persuade by pleasant words, flattery, or false promises; coax. [< French *cajoler*]

cal dron (kôl′drən), *n.* a large kettle or boiler. Also, **cauldron.** [< Old French *caudron* < Late Latin *caldaria* < Latin *calidus* hot]

cal lig ra phy (kə lig′rə fē), *n.* 1 handwriting. 2 beautiful handwriting. [< Greek *kalligraphia* < *kallos* beauty + *graphein* write]

ca price (kə prēs′), *n.* 1 a sudden change of mind without reason; unreasonable notion or desire; whim. 2 tendency to change suddenly and without reason. [< French < Italian *capriccio,* literally, a shiver]

car a pace (kar′ə pās), *n.* shell or bony covering on the back of a turtle, armadillo, lobster, crab, etc. [< French < Spanish *carapacho*]

ca reer (kə rir′), *v.i.* rush along wildly; dash: *The runaway horse careered through the streets.* [< Middle French *carrière* racecourse < Latin *carrus* wagon]

car ni vore (kär′nə vôr, kär′nə vōr), *n.* any of an order of mammals that feed chiefly on flesh, characterized by large, sharp canine teeth and including cats, dogs, lions, tigers, bears, and seals.

car ri on (kar′ē ən), *n.* 1 dead and decaying flesh. 2 rottenness; filth. [< Old French *caroine* carcass < Popular Latin *caronia* < Latin *carnem* flesh.]

cas sock (kas′ək), *n.* a long outer garment, usually black, worn by a clergyman. [< French *casaque* < Italian *casacca*]

caste (kast), *n.* 1 one of the social classes into which Hindus are divided. By tradition, a Hindu is born into a caste and cannot rise above it. 2 an exclusive social group; distinct class. 3 a social system having distinct classes separated by differences of birth, rank, wealth, or position. [< Portuguese *casta* race, class, animal species < Latin *castus* pure, chaste]

cat a ract (kat′ə rakt′), *n.* 1 a large, steep waterfall. 2 a violent rush or downpour of water; flood. 3 an opaque condition in the lens of the eye, or its capsule, that develops from a cloudy film and may cause partial or total blindness. [< Latin *cataracta* < Greek *kataraktēs* < *kata-* down + *arassein* to dash]

cat e chist (kat′ə kist), *n.* person who catechizes.

caulk (kôk), *v.t.* fill up (a seam, crack, or joint) so that it will not leak; make watertight. Also, **calk.** [< Old French *cauquer* press in, tread < Latin *calcare* < *calcem* heel]

cav al cade (kav′əl kād′, kav′əl kād), *n.* procession of persons riding on horses, in carriages, or in automobiles. [< Middle French < Italian *cavalcata* < *cavalcare* ride horseback < Late Latin *caballicare* < Latin *caballus* horse]

ca vort (kə vôrt′), *v.* prance about; jump around: *The children cavorted about the field, racing and tumbling.*

cen sure (sen′shər), *n., v.,* **-sured, -sur ing.** *—n.* 1 expression of disapproval; unfavorable opinion; criticism. 2 penalty, as a public rebuke or suspension from office. *—v.t.* express disapproval of; find fault with; criticize. [< Latin *censura* < *censere* appraise]

ces sa tion (se sā′shən), *n.* a ceasing; a stopping. [< Latin *cessationem* < *cessare* cease]

cha grin (shə grin′), *n.* a feeling of disappointment, failure, or humiliation. *—v.t.* cause to feel chagrin. [< French, apparently < *chat* cat + *grigner* to purse (the lips)]

cham ber lain (chām′bər lən), *n.* 1 person who manages the household of a sovereign or great noble. 2 a high official of a royal court. [< Old French *chamberlenc*]

chasm (kaz′əm), *n.* 1 a deep opening or crack in the earth; gap. 2 a wide difference of feelings or interests between people or groups: *The chasm between England and the American colonies finally led to the Revolutionary War.* [< Latin *chasma* < Greek]

che mise (shə mēz′), *n.* 1 a loose, shirtlike undergarment worn by women and girls. 2 a loosely fitting dress without a belt. [< Old French < Late Latin *camisia* shirt]

chron ic (kron′ik), *adj.* 1 lasting a long time: *Rheumatism is often a chronic disease.* 2 suffering long from an illness: *a chronic invalid.* [< Greek *chronikos* of time < *chronos* time] **—chron′i cal ly,** *adv.*

cin na bar (sin′ə bär), *n.* 1 artificial mercuric sulfide, used as a red pigment in making paints, dyes, etc. 2 a bright red color; vermilion. *—adj.* bright-red; vermilion. [< Latin *cinnabaris*]

cite (sīt), *v.t.,* **cit ed, cit ing.** 1 quote (a passage, book, or author), especially as an authority: *I cited the encyclopedia to prove my statement.* 2 refer to; mention as an example: *The lawyer cited another case similar to the one being tried.* [< Latin *citare* summon < *ciere* set in motion]

clam or (klam′ər), *n.* 1 a loud noise or continual uproar; shouting. 2 a shout; outcry. 3 a noisy demand or complaint. Also, **clamour.** [< Latin < *clamare* cry out] **—clam′or er,** *n.*

cleav age (klē′vij), *n.* a cleaving or a being cleft; split; division.

clem en cy (klem′ən sē), *n., pl.* **-cies.** 1 gentleness in the use of power or authority; mercy or leniency: *The judge showed clemency to the prisoner.* 2 mildness: *the clemency of the weather.*

clench (klench), *v.t.* 1 close tightly together: *clench one's fists.* 2 grasp firmly; grip tightly: *The player clenched the bat to swing at the ball.* [< Old English *(be)clencan* hold fast]

cog ni zance (kog′nə zəns, kon′ə zəns), *n.* knowledge; perception; awareness. [< Old French *conoissance* < *connoistre* know < Latin *cognoscere.*]

col league (kol′ēg′), *n.* fellow worker; fellow member of a profession, organization, etc.; associate. [< Middle French *collègue* < Latin *collega* < *com-* together + *legare* to delegate]

com mis e rate (kə miz′ə rāt′), *v.t., v.i.,* **-rat ed, -rat ing.** feel or express sorrow for another's suffering or trouble; sympathize with; pity. [< Latin *commiseratum* pitied < *com-* + *miser* wretched] **—com mis′e ra′tion,** *n.*

com mis sar (kom′ə sär), *n.* 1 (formerly) head of a government department in the Soviet Union. 2 a Soviet government official representing the Communist Party in the army, etc. [< Russian *komissar*]

com mod i ty (kə mod′ə tē), *n., pl.* **-ties.** 1 anything that is bought and sold: *Groceries are commodities.* 2 a useful thing.

com mon wealth (kom′ən welth′), *n.* 1 the people who make up a nation; citizens of a state. 2 a democratic state; republic.

com pact (kom′pakt), *n.* agreement or contract. [< Latin *compactum* < *com-* together + *pacisci* make an agreement]

com pass (kum′pəs), *n.* 1 instrument for showing directions, consisting of a needle or compass card that points to the North Magnetic Pole. 2 boundary; circumference. 3 space within limits; extent; range: *There have been many scientific advancements within the compass of my lifetime.* [< Old French *compas* < *compasser* divide equally < Latin *com-* with + *passus* step]

com pla cent (kəm plā′snt), *adj.* pleased with oneself or what one has; self-satisfied. [< Latin *complacentem* < *com-* + *placere* please] **—com pla′cent ly,** *adv.*

com pressed (kəm prest′), *adj.* 1 squeezed together; made smaller by pressure. 2 flattened.

con (kon), *v.t.,* **conned, con ning.** 1 learn well enough to remember; study. 2 examine carefully; pore over. [< Old English *cunnian* test, examine]

con cave (kon kāv′, kon′kāv, kong′kāv), *adj.* hollow and curved like the inside of a circle or sphere; curving in. [< Latin *concavus* < *com-* + *cavus* hollow] **—con cave′ly,** *adv.* **—con cave′ness,** *n.*

con cep tion (kən sep′shən), *n.* 1 thought; idea; impression: *Your conception of the problem is different from mine.* 2 design; plan. **—con cep′tion al,** *adj.*

con dole (kən dōl′), *v.i.,* **-doled, -dol ing.** express sympathy; grieve; sympathize: *Their friends condoled with them at the funeral.* [< Latin *condolere* < *com-* with + *dolere* grieve, suffer]

con fab u late (kən fab′yə lāt), *v.i.,* **-lat ed, -lat ing.** talk together informally and intimately; chat. [ultimately < Latin < *com-* together + *fabulari* talk < *fabula* fable] **—con fab′u la′tion,** *n.*

con gen ial (kən jē′nyəl), *adj.* 1 having similar tastes and interests; getting on well together: *congenial companions.* 2 agreeable; suitable: *congenial work.* [< *con-* + Latin *genialis* < *genius* spirit] **—con gen′ial ly,** *adv.*

con nois seur (kon′ə sėr′), *n.* a critical judge of art or of matters of taste; expert: *a connoisseur of antique furniture.* [< Old French < *connoistre* know < Latin *cognoscere*]

con sci en tious (kon′shē en′shəs), *adj.* 1 careful to do what

a hat	i it	oi oil	ch child	ə = a in about
ā age	ī ice	ou out	ng long	e in taken
ä far	o hot	u cup	sh she	i in pencil
e let	ō open	ů put	th thin	o in lemon
ē equal	ô order	ü rule	ŦH then	u in circus
ėr term			zh measure	< = derived from

one knows is right; controlled by conscience. 2 done with care to make it right; painstaking: *conscientious work.* **—con′sci en′tious ly,** *adv.* **—con′sci en′tious ness,** *n.*

con sign ment (kən sīn′mənt), *n.* 1 act of consigning. 2 something consigned, especially a shipment sent to a person or company for safekeeping or sale.

con sort (*n.* kon′sôrt; *v.* kən sôrt′), *n.* 1 husband or wife. 2 an associate. *—v.i.* 1 keep company; associate: *consorting with a rough gang.* 2 agree; accord. [< Middle French < Latin *consortem* sharer < *com-* with + *sortem* lot]

con ster na tion (kon′stər nā′shən), *n.* great dismay; paralyzing terror: *To our consternation the child darted out in front of the speeding car.* [< Latin *consternationem* < *consternare* terrify]

con stit u ent (kən stich′ü ənt), *adj.* 1 forming a necessary part; that composes: *Carbon is a constituent element in all living cells.* 2 appointing; electing. 3 having the power to make or change a political constitution: *a constituent assembly.* *—n.* 1 part of a whole; necessary part; component. 2 voter.

con strained (kən strānd′), *adj.* 1 forced. 2 restrained; stiff; unnatural: *a constrained smile.* **—con strain′ed ly,** *adv.*

con straint (kən strānt′), *n.* 1 a holding back of natural feelings; forced or unnatural manner; embarrassed awkwardness. 2 force; compulsion. 3 confinement. 4 restraint.

con sum mate (*v.* kon′sə māt; *adj.* kən sum′it), *v.,* **-mat ed, -mat ing,** *adj.* *—v.t.* bring to completion; realize; fulfill: *My ambition was consummated when I won the first prize.* *—adj.* in the highest degree; complete; perfect. [< Latin *consummatum* brought to a peak < *com-* + *summa* peak] **—con sum′mate ly,** *adv.*

con ta gion (kən tā′jən), n. 1 the spreading of disease by direct or indirect contact. 2 disease spread in this way; contagious disease. 3 the spreading of any influence from one person to another: *At the cry of "Fire!" a contagion of fear swept through the audience.* [< Latin *contagionem* a touching < *contingere*]

con ten tion (kən ten′shən), *n.* 1 statement or point that one has argued for; statement maintained as true: *Galileo's contention that the earth goes around the sun proved to be true.* 2 an arguing; disputing; quarreling. [< Latin *contentionem* < *contendere*]

con tin gen cy (kən tin′jən sē), *n., pl.* **-cies.** a happening or event depending on something that is uncertain; possibility: *The explorer carried supplies for every contingency.*

con tor tion ist (kən tôr′shə nist), *n.* person who can twist or bend his or her body into odd and unnatural positions.

con tri tion (kən trish′ən), *n.* 1 sorrow for one's sins or guilt; being contrite; penitence. 2 deep regret.

con trive (kən trīv′), *v.t.,* **-trived, -triv ing.** 1 plan with cleverness or skill; invent; design: *contrive a new kind of engine.* 2 plan; scheme; plot: *contrive a robbery.* 3 manage: *I will contrive to be there by ten o'clock.* 4 bring about. [< Old French *controver* < Late Latin *contropare* compare] **—con triv′er,** *n.*

con tu me ly (kən tü′mə lē, kən tyü′mə lē; kon′tü mə lē, kon′tyə mə lē), *n., pl.* **-lies.** 1 insolent contempt; insulting words or actions; humiliating treatment. 2 a humiliating insult. [< Latin *contumelia,* related to *contumacia* contumacy]

con verge (kən vėrj′), *v.,* **-verged, -verg ing.** *—v.i.* 1 tend to meet in a point: *The sides of a road seem to converge in the distance.* 2 come together; center. [< Late Latin *convergere* < Latin *com-* together + *vergere* to incline]

con vex (kon veks′, kon′veks), *adj.* curved out like the outside of a circle or sphere; curving out: *The lens of an automobile headlight is convex.* [< Latin *convexus*] **—con vex′ly,** *adv.*

con vic tion (kən vik′shən), *n.* 1 act of proving or declaring guilty. 2 a being convinced. 3 firm belief; certainty.

con voy (kon′voi), *n.* 1 an escort; protection: *The payroll was brought by truck under convoy of armed guards.* 2 warships, soldiers, etc., that convoy; protecting escort. 3 ship, fleet, supplies, etc., that are convoyed. [< Middle French *convoyer* < *Old French conveier*]

con vulse (kən vuls′), *v.t.,* **-vulsed, -vuls ing.** 1 shake violently: *An earthquake convulsed the island.* 2 cause violent disturbance in; disturb violently: *His face was convulsed with rage.* 3 throw into convulsions; shake with muscular spasms: *The patient was convulsed before the doctor came.* [< Latin *convulsum* torn away < *com-* + *vellere* to tear]

con vul sion (kən vul′shən), *n.* 1 Often, **convulsions,** *pl.* a violent, involuntary contracting and relaxing of the muscles; spasm; fit. 2 a fit of laughter. 3 a violent disturbance: *The country was undergoing a political convulsion.*

con vul sive (kən vul′siv), *adj.* 1 violently disturbing. 2 having convulsions. 3 producing convulsions. **—con vul′sive ly,** *adv.*

co ny (kō′nē), *n., pl.* **-nies.** 1 rabbit fur. Cony is used to make or trim coats. 2 rabbit. 3 hyrax. 4 pika. Also, **coney.** [< Old French *conil* < Latin *cuniculus* rabbit]

co quet tish (kō ket′ish), *adj.* 1 of a coquette, or flirt. 2 like a coquette; like a coquette's: *coquettish behavior.* **—co quet′tish ly,** *adv.*

cor don (kôrd′n), *n.* line or circle of soldiers, policemen, forts, etc., enclosing or guarding a place. [< French]

cor nice (kôr′nis), *n., v.,* **-niced, -nic ing.** *—n.* 1 an ornamental, horizontal molding along the top of a wall, pillar, building, etc. 2 a molding around the walls of a room just below the ceiling or over the top of a window. *—v.t.* furnish or finish with a cornice. [< French *corniche* < Italian *cornice*]

co ro na tion (kôr′ə nā′shən, kor′ə nā′shən), *n.* ceremony of crowning a king, queen, emperor, etc.

co ro ner (kôr′ə nər, kor′ə nər), *n.* official of a local government whose principal function is to inquire in the presence of a jury into the cause of any death not clearly due to natural causes. [< Anglo-French *corouner* officer of the crown < *coroune*]

co ro net (kôr′ə net′, kor′ə net′), *n.* 1 a small crown, especially one indicating a rank of nobility below that of the sovereign. 2 a circle of gold, jewels, or flowers worn around the head as an ornament.

cor por al (kôr′pər əl), *adj.* of the body: *corporal punishment.* [< Latin *corporalem* < *corpus* body] **—cor′por al ly,** *adv.*

cor ru gat ed (kôr′ə gā′tid, kor′ə gā′tid), *adj.* bent or shaped into wavy ridges; wrinkled: *corrugated paper, corrugated iron.*

cor tege or **cor tège** (kôr tezh′, kôr tāzh′), *n.* 1 procession: *a funeral cortege.* 2 group of followers, attendants, etc.; retinue. [< French *cortège* < Italian *corteggio* < *corte* court < Latin *cohortem* crowd, enclosure.]

coun te nance (koun′tə nəns), *n.* 1 expression of the face: *an angry countenance.* 2 face; features: *a noble countenance.* 3 approval; encouragement: *They gave countenance to our plan, but not active help.* 4 calmness; composure: *lose countenance.* [< Old French *contenance* < Medieval Latin *continentia* demeanor < Latin, self-control < *continere*]

coun ter pane (koun′tər pān′), *n.* an outer covering for a bed; bedspread. [alteration of *counterpoint* quilt < Old French *cuilte-pointe* quilt stitched through]

cou pé (kü pā′), *n.* 1 coupe. 2 a four-wheeled, closed carriage with a seat for two people inside and a seat for the driver outside.

cou pling (kup′ling), *n.* 1 a joining together. 2 device for joining together parts of machinery. 3 a railroad coupler.

cour ti er (kôr′tē ər, kōr′tē ər), *n.* person often present at a royal court; court attendant.

cov et (kuv′it), *v.t.* desire eagerly (something that belongs to another). [< Old French *coveitier* < Popular Latin *cupiditare* < Latin *cupiditatem*]

cov et ous (kuv′ə təs), *adj.* desiring things that belong to others.

cow er (kou′ər), *v.i.* 1 crouch in fear or shame. 2 draw back tremblingly from another's threats, blows, etc. [apparently < Scandinavian (Old Icelandic) *kūra* doze, lie quiet]

cra ven (krā′vən), *adj.* cowardly. *—n.* coward. [< Old French *cravente* overcome < Popular Latin *crepantare* < Latin *crepare* crush; burst] **—cra′ven ly,** *adv.* **—cra′ven ness,** *n.*

cre du li ty (krə dü′lə tē, krə dyü′lə tē), *n.* a too great readiness to believe.

crest fall en (krest′fô′lən), *adj.* dejected; discouraged.

cum ber (kum′bər), *v.t.* 1 hold back (from running, doing, etc.); hinder. 2 block up; fill. [< Old French *combrer* impede < *combre* barrier]

cum mer bund (kum′ər bund), *n.* a broad sash worn around the waist. [< Hindustani *kamarband* < Persian *kamar* waist + *band* band, bandage]

cur ry (kėr′ē), *n., pl.* **-ries.** a peppery sauce or powder of spices, seeds, vegetables, etc. Curry is a popular seasoning in India. [< Tamil *kari* sauce]

cur tail (kėr/tāl′), *v. t.* cut short; cut off part of; reduce; lessen. [< obsolete *curtal,* adjective, cut short (especially of tails) < Old French *curtald* < *court* short < Latin *curtus* cut short]

cyn ic (sin′ik), *n.* 1 person inclined to believe that the motives for people's actions are insincere and selfish. 2 a sneering, sarcastic person.

cyn i cal (sin′ə kəl), *adj.* 1 doubting the sincerity and goodness of others. 2 sneering; sarcastic. **—cyn′i cal ly,** *adv.*

cyn i cism (sin′ə siz′əm), *n.* 1 cynical quality or disposition. 2 a cynical remark.

daunt (dônt, dänt), *v.t.* 1 overcome with fear; frighten; intimidate. 2 lessen the courage of; discourage; dishearten. [< Old French *danter* < Latin *domitare* < *domare* to tame]

de fer (di fėr′), *v.t., v.i.,* **-ferred, -fer ring.** put off to some later time; delay; postpone: *defer an exam.* [< Latin *differre*]

de file[1] (di fīl′), *v.t.,* **-filed, -fil ing.** 1 make filthy or dirty; make disgusting in any way. 2 destroy the purity or cleanness of (anything sacred); desecrate. 3 stain; dishonor. [< Old French *defouler* trample down or violate] **—de file′ment,** *n.*

de file[2] (di fīl′, dē′fīl), *n.,v.,* **-filed, -fil ing.** —*n.* a steep and narrow valley. —*v.i.* march in single file or a narrow column. [< French *défiler*]

de grade (di grād′), *v.,* **-grad ed, -grad ing.** —*v.t.* 1 reduce in rank, especially as a punishment. 2 bring into dishonor or contempt. 3 lower in character or quality; debase. [< Late Latin *degradare* < Latin *de-* down + *gradus* grade]

deign (dān), *v.i.* think fit; condescend. —*v.t.* condescend to give (an answer, a reply, etc.). [< Old French *deignier* < Latin *dignari* < *dignus* worthy]

de i ty (dē′ə tē), *n., pl.* **-ties.** 1 one of the gods worshiped by a people or a tribe; god or goddess. 2 divine nature; being a god. [< Old French *deite* < Latin *deitatem* < *deus* god]

de lib e ra tion (di lib′ə rā′shən), *n.* 1 careful thought: *After long deliberation, I decided not to go.* 2 discussion of reasons for and against something; debate: *the deliberations of Congress.* 3 slowness and care: *She drove the car over the icy bridge with great deliberation.*

de mean or (di mē′nər), *n.* way a person looks and acts; behavior; manner.

de mo ni a cal (dē′mə nī′ə kəl), *adj.* demoniac. **—de′mo ni′a cal ly,** *adv.*

de mur (di mėr′), *v.,* **-murred, mur ring,** *n.* —*v.i.* 1 show disapproval or dislike; take exception; object. 2 OBSOLETE. hesitate. —*n.* a demurring; objection; exception. [< Old French *demurer* < Latin *demorari* < *de-* + *morari* to delay]

de noue ment or **dé noue ment** (dā′nü mäɴ′, dā nü′mäɴ), *n.* 1 solution of a plot in a story, play, situation, etc. 2 outcome; end. [< French *dénouement* < *dénouer* untie]

de nounce (di nouns′), *v.t.,* **-nounced, -nounc ing.** 1 condemn publicly; express strong disapproval of. 2 give information against; accuse. [< Old French *denoncer* < Latin *denuntiare* < *de-* + *nuntius* messenger]

de ploy (di ploi′), *v.t.,* 1 spread out (troops, military units, etc.) from a column into a long battle line. 2 spread out, extend, or place, especially in a planned or strategic position: *deploy offensive missiles, deploy actors on a stage.* [< French *déployer* < *dé-* de- + *ployer* to fold]

dep re da tion (dep′rə dā′shən), *n.* act of plundering; robbery; ravaging. [< Latin *depraedationem* < *de-* + *praeda* booty]

der e lict (der′ə likt), *adj.* abandoned, deserted, or left by its crew, owner, or guardian; forsaken: *a derelict ship.* —*n.* 1 ship abandoned and afloat at sea. 2 any useless, discarded, or forsaken thing. [< Latin *derelictum* abandoned < *de-* + *re-* behind + *linquere* leave]

de ride (di rīd′), *v.t.,* **-rid ed, -rid ing.** make fun of; laugh at in scorn. [< Latin *deridere* < *de-* + *ridere* to laugh]

de ri sion (di rizh′ən), *n.* 1 scornful laughter; ridicule. 2 object of ridicule. [< Latin *derisionem* < *deridere.* See DERIDE.]

de ri sive (di rī′siv), *adj.* that ridicules; mocking: *derisive laughter.* **—de ri′sive ly,** *adv.* **—de ri′sive ness,** *n.*

der vish (dėr′vish), member of a Moslem religious order that practices self-denial and devotion. Some dervishes dance and spin about violently. [< Turkish *derviş* < Persian *darvīsh*]

de spond en cy (di spon′dən sē), *n.* loss of heart, courage, or hope; discouragement; dejection. Also, **despondence.**

de spond ent (di spon′dənt), *adj.* having lost heart, courage, or hope; discouraged; dejected. **—de spond′ent ly,** *adv.*

dex ter i ty (dek ster′ə tē), *n.* 1 skill in using the hands or body. 2 skill in using the mind; cleverness.

dex ter ous (dek′stər əs), *adj.* 1 skillful in using the hands or body. 2 having or showing skill in using the mind; clever. Also, **dextrous. —dex′ter ous ly,** *adv.*

dif fuse (*v.* di fyüz′; *adj.* di fyüs′), *v.,* **-fused, -fus ing,** *adj.* —*v.t.* spread out so as to cover a large space or surface; scatter widely: *The sun diffuses light and heat.* —*v.i.* scatter widely; spread. —*adj.* not concentrated together at a simple point; spread out: *diffuse light.* [< Latin *diffusum* poured forth < *dis-* + *fundere* to pour] **—dif fuse′ly,** *adv.*

di late (dī lāt′, də lāt′), *v.,* **-lat ed, -lat ing.** —*v.t.* make larger or wider: *When you take a deep breath, you dilate your nostrils.* —*v.i.* become larger or wider: *The pupil of the eye dilates when the light gets dim.* [< Latin *dilatare* < *dis-* apart + *latus* wide]

di lem ma (də lem′ə), *n.* situation requiring a choice between two alternatives, which are or appear equally unfavorable; difficult choice. [< Greek *dilēmma* < *di-* two + *lēmma* premise]

dil i gent (dil′ə jənt), *adj.* 1 hard-working; industrious. 2 careful and steady: *a diligent search.* [< Latin *diligentem* < *dis-* apart + *legere* choose] **—dil′i gent ly,** *adv.*

din (din), *n., v.,* **dinned, din ning.** —*n.* a continuing loud, confused noise. —*v.i.* make a din. —*v.t.* say over and over again; repeat in a tiresome way. [< Old English *dynn*]

dis com fit (dis kum′fit), *v.t.* 1 defeat the plans or hopes of; frustrate. 2 embarrass; confuse; disconcert. [< Old French *desconfit* discomfited < *des-* dis- + *confire* make, accomplish]

dis com fi ture (dis kum′fi chůr, dis kum′fi chər), *n.* 1 defeat of plans or hopes; frustration. 2 confusion.

dis course (*n.* dis′kôrs, dis′kōrs; *v.* dis kôrs′, dis kōrs′), *n., v.,* **-coursed, -cours ing.** —*n.* 1 a formal or extensive speech or writing: *Lectures and sermons are discourses.* 2 talk; conversation. —*v.i.* 1 speak or write formally or at length on some subject. 2 talk; converse. [< Latin *discursus* a running about < *dis-* + *cursus* a running]

dis creet (dis krēt′), *adj.* very careful and sensible in speech and action; having or showing good judgment; wisely cautious. [< Old French *discret* < Late Latin *discretus* discerning < Latin *discernere* discern] **—dis creet′ly,** *adv.* **—dis creet′ness,** *n.*

dis dain ful (dis dān′fəl), *adj.* feeling or showing disdain; scornful. **—dis dain′ful ly,** *adv.* **—dis dain′ful ness,** *n.*

di shev eled or **di shev elled** (də shev′əld), *adj.* not neat; rumpled; mussed; disordered: *disheveled hair.*

dis patch (dis pach′), *v.t.* send off to some place or for some purpose: *The captain dispatched a boat to bring a doctor on board ship.* —*n.* a written message or communication, such as special news or government business: *a dispatch from the ambassador in France.* Also, **despatch.** [< Italian *dispacciare* or Spanish *despachar*]

dis pen sar y (dis pen′sər ē), *n., pl.* **-sar ies.** place where medicines, medical care, and medical advice are given out.

dis perse (dis pėrs′), *v.,* **-persed, -pers ing.** —*v.t.* send or drive off in different directions; scatter. —*v.i.* spread in different directions; scatter: *The crowd dispersed when it began raining.* [< Latin *dispersum* dispersed < *dis-* apart + *spargere* to scatter]

dis pos sess (dis′pə zes′), *v.t.* 1 force to give up the possession of a house, land, etc.; oust: *The tenant was dispossessed for not paying rent.* 2 deprive. **—dis′pos ses′sor,** *n.*

dis sem ble (di sem′bəl), *v.,* **-bled, -bling.** —*v.t.* hide (one's real feelings, thoughts, plans, etc.); disguise: *She dissembled her anger with a smile.* [alteration (patterned after *resemble*) of obsolete *dissimule* dissimulate]

dis sim u late (di sim′yə lāt), *v.,* **-lat ed, -lat ing.** —*v.t.,* disguise or hide under a pretense; dissemble. —*v.i.* hide the truth; dissemble. **—dis sim′u la′tion,** *n.* **—dis sim′u la′tor,** *n.*

dis si pa tion (dis′ə pā′shən), *n.* 1 a scattering in different directions. 2 a wasting by misuse. 3 excessive indulgence in sensual or foolish pleasures; intemperance.

dis tract (dis trakt′), *v.t.* 1 turn aside or draw away (the mind, attention, etc.): *Noise distracts my attention from study.* 2 confuse; disturb. 3 make insane. —*adj.* ARCHAIC. insane; mad. [< Latin *distractum* drawn away < *dis-* + *trahere* to draw] **—dis tract′ing ly,** *adv.*

a hat	i it	oi oil	ch child	ə = a in about, e in taken, i in pencil, o in lemon, u in circus
ā age	ī ice	ou out	ng long	
ä far	o hot	u cup	sh she	
e let	ō open	ů put	th thin	
ē equal	ô order	ü rule	ᴛʜ then	
ėr term			zh measure	< = derived from

dis traught (dis trôt′), *adj.* 1 in a state of mental conflict and confusion; distracted. 2 crazed. [variant of obsolete *distract,* adjective, distracted]

di verge (də vėrj′, dī vėrj′), *v.,* **-verged, -verg ing.** —*v.i.* move or lie in different directions from the same point; branch off: *Their paths diverged at the fork in the road.* [< Late Latin *divergere* < Latin *dis-* off + *vergere* to slope]

di verse (də vėrs′, dī vėrs′), *adj.* 1 not alike; different: *diverse opinions.* 2 varied; diversified. [variant of *divers*] **—di verse′ly,** *adv.* **—di verse′ness,** *n.*

di vert (də vėrt′, dī vėrt′), *v.t.* 1 turn aside: *A ditch diverted water from the stream into the fields.* 2 amuse; entertain: *Listening to music diverted me after a hard day's work.* [< Latin *divertere* < *dis-* aside + *vertere* turn]

di vin i ty (də vin′ə tē), *n., pl.* **-ties.** 1 a divine being; god or goddess. 2 divine nature or quality.

di vulge (də vulj′, dī vulj′), *v.t.,* **-vulged, -vulg ing.** make known or tell openly (something private or secret); reveal. [< Latin *divulgare* make common < *dis-* + *vulgus* common people]

dog ged (dô′gid, dog′id), *adj.* not giving up; stubborn: *dogged determination.* [< *dog*] **—dog′ged ly,** *adv.*

do main (dō mān′), *n.* 1 territory under the control of one ruler or government. 2 land owned by one person; estate. 3 (in law) the absolute ownership of land. 4 field of thought, action, etc.; sphere of activity: *the domain of science, the domain of religion.* [< Middle French *domaine* < Latin *dominium* < *dominum* lord, master]

dos si er (dos′ē ā, dos′ē ər), *n.* collection of documents or papers about some subject or person. [< French, bundle of papers labeled on the back, ultimately < Latin *dorsum* back]

dote (dōt), *v.i.,* **dot ed, dot ing.** 1 be weak-minded and childish because of old age. 2 **dote on** or **dote upon,** be foolishly fond of; be too fond of. [Middle English *doten*] **—dot′er,** *n.*

dough ty (dou′tē), *adj.,* **-ti er, -ti est.** strong and bold; stout; brave; hearty. [Old English *dohtig* < *dugan* be of use] **—dough′ti ly,** *adv.* **—dough′ti ness,** *n.*

dow ry (dou′rē), *n., pl.* **-ries.** 1 money or property that a woman brings to the man she marries. 2 natural gift, talent, or quality; natural endowment: *Good health and intelligence are a precious dowry.* Also, **dower.** [< Old French *douaire.*]

drap er (drā′pər), *n.* 1 BRITISH. dealer in cloth or dry goods. 2 person who drapes.

dregs (dregz), *n.pl.* 1 the solid bits of matter that settle to the bottom of a liquid: *the dregs of a coffee pot.* 2 the least desirable part. [< Scandinavian (Old Icelandic) *dregg,* singular]

drom e dar y (drom′ ə der′ē, drum′ə der′ē), *n., pl.* **-dar ies.** a swift camel with one hump and short hair. [< Late Latin *dromedarius* < Greek *dromados (kamēlos)* running (camel) < *dromos* a running]

dromedary—7½ ft. (2.3 m.) high at the hump

du bi ous (dü′bē əs, dyü′bē əs), *adj.* 1 filled with or being in doubt; doubtful; uncertain: *a dubious compliment.* 2 feeling doubt; wavering or hesitating. 3 of questionable character; probably bad: *a dubious scheme for making money.* [< Latin *dubiosus* < *dubius* doubtful] **—du′bi ous ly,** *adv.*

dull ard (dul′ərd), *n.* person who is stupid and learns very slowly.

dy nast (dī′nast, dī′nəst), *n.* 1 member or founder of a dynasty. 2 any ruler.

eaves (ēvz), *n.pl.* the lower edge of a roof that projects over the side of a building. [Old English *efes* edge]

ec stat ic (ek stat′ik), *adj.* full of ecstasy: *an ecstatic look of pleasure.* **—ec stat′i cal ly,** *adv.*

ed dy (ed′ē), *n., pl.* **-dies,** *v.,* **-died, -dy ing.** —*n.* 1 water, air, smoke, etc., moving against the main current, especially when having a whirling motion; small whirlpool or whirlwind. 2 any similar current of fog or dust. [perhaps < Scandinavian (Old Icelandic) *itha*]

ef fa ble (ef′ə bəl), *adj.* utterable; expressible. [abstracted from INEFFABLE]

e jac u late (i jak′yə lāt), *v.t., v.i.,* **-lat ed, -lat ing.** say suddenly and briefly; exclaim. [< Latin *ejaculatum* thrown out < *ex-* out + *jacere* to throw]

e lat ed (i lā′tid), *adj.* in high spirits; joyful or proud. **—e lat′ed ly,** *adv.* **—e lat′ed ness,** *n.*

e la tion (i lā′shən), *n.* high spirits; joy or pride: *She was filled with elation at having won the first prize.*

el o quence (el′ə kwəns), *n.* 1 flow of speech that has grace and force. 2 power to win by speaking; the art of using language so as to stir the feelings.

el o quent (el′ə kwənt), *adj.* very expressive: *eloquent eyes.* [< Latin *eloquentem* speaking out < *ex-* out + *loqui* speak] **—el′o quent ly,** *adv.*

e lu ci date (i lü′sə dāt), *v.t.,* **-dat ed, -dat ing.** make clear; explain; clarify. [< Late Latin *elucidatum* made clear < Latin *ex-* out + *lucidus* bright] **—e lu′ci da′tion,** *n.* **—e lu′ci da′tor,** *n.*

em bas sy (em′bə sē), *n., pl.* **-sies.** 1 ambassador and his or her staff of assistants. 2 the official residence, offices, etc., of an ambassador in a foreign country. 3 person or group officially sent to a foreign government with a special errand. [< Old French *embassee* < Italian *ambasciata* embassy; trip down into the valley, ultimately < Popular Latin *in* + *bassus* down]

em boss (em bôs′, em bos′), *v.t.* 1 decorate with a design, pattern, etc., that stands out from the surface: *Our coins are embossed with letters and figures.* 2 cause to stand out from the surface: *The letters on the book's cover had been embossed.*

em u late (em′yə lāt), *v.t.,* **-lat ed, -lat ing.** 1 copy or imitate in order to equal or excel the achievements or qualities of an admired person. 2 vie with; rival. [< Latin *aemulatum* rivaled < *aemulus* striving to equal] **—em′u la′tion,** *n.*

en gen der (en jen′dər), *v.t.* bring into existence; produce; cause: *Filth engenders disease.* [< Old French *engendrer* < Latin *ingenerare* < *in-* in + *generare* create]

en mi ty (en′mə tē), *n., pl.* **-ties.** the feeling that enemies have for each other; hostility or hatred. [< Old French *enemistie* < Popular Latin *inimicitatem* < Latin *inimicus.*]

en trails (en′trālz, en′trəlz), *n.pl.* 1 the inner parts of the body of a human being or animal. 2 the intestines; bowels. [< Old French *entrailles* < Medieval Latin *intralia,* alteration of Latin *interanea* things inside < *inter* within]

en ven om (en ven′əm), *v.t.* 1 make poisonous. 2 fill with bitterness, hate, etc.

ep i gram (ep′ə gram), *n.* 1 a short, pointed or witty saying. EXAMPLES: "Speech is silver, but silence is golden." "Some people know the cost of everything, but the value of nothing." 2 a short poem ending in a witty or clever, and often satirical, turn of thought. [< Greek *epigramma* < *epigraphein* inscribe < *epi-* on + *graphein* write]

ep i taph (ep′ə taf), *n.* a short statement in memory of a dead person, usually put on a gravestone or tombstone. [< Greek *epitaphion* funeral oration < *epi-* upon + *taphos* tomb]

eq uer ry (ek′wər ē), *n., pl.* **-ries** officer of a royal or noble household who has charge of the horses. [< Old French *escuerie* stable]

ere (er, ar), ARCHAIC. —*prep.* before. —*conj.* 1 before. 2 sooner than; rather than. [Old English *ǣr*]

er rat ic (ə rat′ik), *adj.* 1 not steady; uncertain; irregular: *An erratic clock is not dependable.* 2 strange; odd; eccentric: *erratic behavior.* 3 having no certain course; wandering: *an erratic star.* [< Latin *erraticus* < *errare* wander] **—er rat′i cal ly,** *adv.*

es carp ment (e skärp′mənt), *n.* 1 a steep slope; cliff. 2 ground made into a steep slope as part of a fortification. [< French]

es sence (es′ns), *n.* that which makes a thing what it is; necessary part or parts; important feature or features: *Being thoughtful of others is the essence of politeness.* [< Latin *essentia* < *esse* be]

et al., 1 and others [for Latin *et alii* and other persons, or *et alia* and other things]. 2 and elsewhere [for Latin *et alibi*].

e ther e al (i thir′ē əl), *adj.* 1 light; airy; delicate: *the ethereal beauty of a butterfly.* 2 not of the earth; heavenly. Also, **aethereal.**

eu phe mism (yü′fə miz′əm), *n.* a mild or indirect expression used instead of one that is harsh or unpleasantly direct. "Pass away" is a common euphemism for "die." [< Greek *euphēmismos* < *euphēmizein* speak with fair words < *eu-* good + *phēmē* speaking < *phanai* speak]

e voc a tive (i vok′ə tiv, i vō′kə tiv), *adj.* tending to evoke.

ewe (yü), *n.* a female sheep. [Old English *ēowu*]

ex e crate (ek′sə krāt), *v.,* **-crat ed, -crat ing.** —*v.t.* 1 feel intense loathing for; abhor; detest. 2 pronounce a curse upon. —*v.i.* curse. [< Latin *exsecratum* declared accursed < *ex-* out + *sacer* sacred]

ex er tion (eg zėr′shən), *n.* 1 strenuous action; effort: *The exertions of the firefighters kept the fire from spreading.* 2 a putting into action; active use; use: *exertion of authority.*

ex e unt (ek′sē ənt), *v.i.* LATIN. they go out (a stage direction for two or more actors to leave the stage).

ex i gent (ek′sə jənt), *adj.* demanding prompt action or attention; urgent; pressing. —*n.* OBSOLETE. time of crisis or need. [< Latin *exigentem* < *ex-* out + *agere* to drive]

ex ploit (*n.* ek′sploit, ek sploit′; *v.* ek sploit′), *n.* a bold, unusual act; daring deed. —*v.t.* 1 make use of; turn to practical account: *A mine is exploited for its minerals.* 2 make unfair or selfish use of: *Nations used to exploit their colonies, taking as much wealth out of them as they could.* [< Old French *esploit* < Popular Latin *explicitum* achievement < Latin, an unfolding < *ex-* out + *plicare* to fold]

ex ploi ta tion (ek′ sploi tā′shən), *n.* 1 use: *the exploitation of the ocean as a source for food.* 2 selfish or unfair use.

ex pos tu late (ek spos′chə lāt), *v.i.,* **-lat ed, -lat ing.** reason earnestly with a person, protesting against something that person means to do or has done; remonstrate in a friendly way: *The teacher expostulated with the student about her poor work.* [< Latin *expostulatum* demanded < *ex-* + *postulare* demand]

ex pound (ek spound′), *v.t.* 1 make clear; explain, interpret, etc. 2 set forth or state in detail. [< Old French *espondre* < Latin *exponere* < *ex-* forth + *ponere* put] **—ex pound′er,** *n.*

ex trem i ty (ek strem′ə tē), *n., pl.* **-ties.** 1 the very end; farthest possible place; last part or point. 2 **extremities,** *pl.* the hands and feet. 3 an extreme degree: *Joy is the extremity of happiness.*

ex ult (eg zult′), *v.i.* be very glad; rejoice greatly. [< Latin *exsultare* leap out or up < *ex-* forth + *saltare* to leap] **—ex ult′ing ly,** *adv.*

fa cade or **fa çade** (fə säd′), *n.* 1 the front part of a building. 2 outward appearance: *a facade of honesty.* [< French *façade,* ultimately < Latin *facies* a form, face]

fa cil i tate (fə sil′ə tāt), *v.t.,* **-tat ed, -tat ing.** make easy; lessen the labor of; help bring about; assist; expedite: *A computer facilitates many tasks.* **—fa cil′i ta′tion,** *n.* **—fa cil′i tat′tor,** *n.*

fac tious (fak′shəs), *adj.* 1 fond of stirring up disputes; quarrelsome. 2 of or caused by faction. **—fac′tious ly,** *adv.*

fac ul ty (fak′əl tē), *n., pl.* **-ties.** 1 power of the mind or body; capacity; capability: *the faculty of hearing, the faculty of memory.* 2 power or ability to do some special thing, especially a power of the mind: *She has a great faculty for arithmetic.* 3 the teachers of a school, college, or university. [< Latin *facultatem* < *facilis.*]

fain (fān), *adv.* ARCHAIC. gladly; willingly. [< Old English *fægen*]

fa kir (fə kir′, fā′kər), *n.* 1 a Moslem holy man who lives by begging. 2 dervish. 3 a Hindu ascetic. Fakirs sometimes do extraordinary things, such as lying upon sharp knives. [< Arabic *faqīr* poor (man)]

fal low (fal′ō), *adj.* plowed and left unseeded for a season or more. [< Old English *fealg*] **—fal′low ness,** *n.*

fal ter (fôl′tər), *v.i.* 1 hesitate in action from lack of courage; draw back; waver: *falter before making a difficult decision.* 2 move unsteadily; stumble; totter. [Middle English *faltren*]

farce (färs), *n.* 1 a play full of ridiculous happenings and unreal situations, meant to be very funny. 2 a ridiculous mockery; absurd pretense; sham: *The trial was a mere farce.* [< French, literally, stuffing < Old French *farcir* to stuff < Latin *farcire*]

fa tal i ty (fā tal′ə tē, fə tal′ə tē), *n., pl.* **-ties.** 1 a fatal accident or happening; death: *Careless driving habits cause thousands of fatalities every year.* 2 condition of being controlled by fate; inevitable necessity; destiny: *We struggle against fatality in vain.*

fawn (fôn), *v.i.* try to get favor or notice by slavish acts: *Many flattering relatives fawned on the rich old woman.* [Old English *fagnian* < *fægen* fain] **—fawn′ing ly,** *adv.*

fel on (fel′ən), *n.* person who has committed a felony; criminal. [< Old French < Popular Latin *fellonem*]

fer ret (fer′it), *n.* species of weasel; polecat. —*v.t.* 1 hunt with ferrets. 2 hunt; search: *The detectives ferreted out new evidence.* —*v.i.* 1 hunt with ferrets. 2 search about; rummage. [< Old French *fuiret,* ultimately < Latin *fur thief*]

fes ter (fes′tər), *v.i.* 1 form pus: *The neglected wound festered and became very painful.* 2 cause soreness or pain; rankle: *Resentment festered in her mind.* [< Old French *festre* < *Latin fistula* ulcer]

fet lock (fet′lok), *n.* 1 tuft of hair above a horse's hoof on the back part of its leg. 2 the part of a horse's leg where this tuft grows. [Middle English *fetlak, fitlok*]

fet ter (fet′ər), *n.* 1 chain or shackle for the feet to prevent escape. 2 Usually, **fetters**, *pl.* anything that shackles or binds; restraint. —*v.t.* 1 bind with chains; chain the feet of. [Old English *feter.* Related to FOOT.]

flab ber gast (flab′ər gast), *v.t.* INFORMAL. make speechless with surprise; astonish greatly; amaze. [origin uncertain]

flay (flā), *v.t.* 1 strip off the skin or outer covering of; skin. 2 scold severely; criticize without pity or mercy. [Old English *flēan*]

fledge (flej), *v.,* **fledged, fledg ing.** —*v.t.* (of a young bird) grow the feathers needed for flying. —*v.t.* provide or cover with feathers. [Old English *(un)fligge* unfledged]

fledg ling or **fledge ling** (flej′ling), *n.* 1 a young bird that has just grown feathers needed for flying. 2 a young, inexperienced person.

flot sam (flot′səm), *n.* wreckage of a ship or its cargo found floating on the sea. [< Anglo-French *floteson* < Old French *floter* to float]

flu ent (flü′ənt), *adj.* 1 flowing smoothly or easily: *speak fluent French.* 2 speaking or writing easily and rapidly. 3 not fixed or stable; fluid. [< Latin *fluentem* < *fluere* to flow] **—flu′ent ly,** *adv.*

foal (fōl), *n.* a young horse, donkey, etc.; colt or filly. —*v.t., v.i.* give birth to (a foal).[Old English *fola*]

fod der (fod′ər), *n.* coarse food for horses, cattle, etc. Hay and cornstalks with their leaves are fodder. —*v.t.* give fodder to. [Old English *fōdor* < *fōda* food]

for bear ance (fôr ber′əns, fôr bar′əns), *n.* 1 act of forbearing. 2 patience; self-control.

fore bod ing (fôr bō′ding, fōr bō′ding), *n.* 1 prediction; warning. 2 a feeling that something bad is going to happen; presentiment. **—fore bod′ing ly,** *adv.*

fore stall (fôr stôl′, fōr stôl′), *v.t.* prevent by acting first: *The owner forestalled a strike by starting to negotiate early with the union.* [Middle English *forstallen* < Old English *foresteall* prevention]

for mi da ble (fôr′mə də bəl), *adj.* hard to overcome; hard to deal with; to be dreaded: *a formidable opponent.* [< Latin *formidabilis* < *formidare* to dread < *formido* terror, dread] **—for′mi da bly,** *adv.*

free think er (frē′thing′kər), *n.* one who forms opinions, especially on religion, independently of authority or tradition.

friv o lous (friv′ə ləs), *adj.* lacking in seriousness or sense; silly: *Frivolous behavior is out of place in a courtroom.* [< Latin *frivolus*] **—friv′o lous ly,** *adv.*

frond (frond), *n.* the leaf of a fern, palm, or cycad. [< Latin *frondem* leaf]

fur tive (fėr′tiv), *adj.* 1 done quickly and with stealth to avoid being noticed; secret: *a furtive glance into the forbidden room.* 2 sly; stealthy: *a furtive manner.*[< Latin *furtivus* < *furtum* theft < *fur* thief] **—fur′tive ly,** *adv.* **—fur′tive ness,** *n.*

fu sil lade (fyü′zə lād′), *n.* 1 a rapid or continuous discharge of many firearms at the same time. 2 any rapid discharge or burst: *The reporters greeted the mayor with a fusillade of questions.* [< French]

fu tile (fyü′tl, fyü′tīl), *adj.* 1 not successful; useless; ineffectual: *He fell down after making futile attempts to keep his balance.* 2 not important; trifling. [< Latin *futilis* pouring easily, worthless < *fundere* pour] **—fu′tile ly,** *adv.*

fu til i ty (fyû til′ə tē), *n.,pl.* **-ties.** 1 uselessness; ineffectiveness. 2 unimportance. 3 futile action, event, etc.

a hat	**i** it	**oi** oil	**ch** child	ə = a in about, e in taken, i in pencil, o in lemon, u in circus
ā age	**ī** ice	**ou** out	**ng** long	
ä far	**o** hot	**u** cup	**sh** she	
e let	**ō** open	**ů** put	**th** thin	
ē equal	**ô** order	**ü** rule	**ꟻH** then	
ėr term			**zh** measure	< = derived from

gab ble (gab′əl), *v.*, **-bled, -bling,** *n.* —*v.i.* talk rapidly with little or no meaning; jabber. —*n.* rapid talk with little or no meaning. [probably imitative] **—gab′bler,** *n.*

gab er dine (gab′ər dēn′, gab′ər dēn′), *n.* a man's long, loose outer garment or cloak, worn in the Middle Ages.

gall stone (gôl′stōn′), *n.* a pebblelike mass of cholesterol, mineral salts, etc., that sometimes forms in the gall bladder or its duct and can cause a painful illness.

gal va nize (gal′və nīz), *v.t.*, **-nized, -niz ing.** 1 arouse suddenly; startle. 2 cover (iron or steel) with a thin coating of zinc to prevent rust. [< Luigi *Galvani*]

gan gling (gang′gling), *adj.* awkwardly tall and slender; lank and loosely built.

gaunt (gônt, gänt), *adj.* very thin and bony; with hollow eyes and a starved look: *Sickness had made him gaunt.* [origin uncertain]

ge ne al o gist (je′nē al′ə jist, je′nē ol′ə jist; jen′ē al′ə jist, jen′ē ol′ə jist), *n.* person who makes a study of or traces genealogies; that is, descents of persons or families from their ancestors.

gen ial (jē′nyəl), *adj.* 1 smiling and pleasant; cheerful and friendly; kindly: *a genial welcome.* 2 helping growth; pleasantly warming; comforting: *a genial climate.* [< Latin *genialis,* literally belonging to the genius < *genius* genius] **—ge′ni al′i ty** (jē′nē al′ə tē), *n.* **—gen′ial ly,** *adv.* **—gen′ial ness,** *n.*

gen tile or **Gen tile** (jen′tīl), *n.* person who is not a Jew. [< Late Latin *gentilis* foreign < Latin, of a people, national.]

gen try (jen′trē), *n.* people of good family and social position, belonging to the upper class of society. [alteration of *gentrice* < Old French *genterise,* ultimately < *gentil.*]

ge o phys i cal (jē′ō fiz′ə kəl), *adj.* of or having to do with geophysics, the study of the relations between the physical feautres of the earth and the forces that change or produce them.

gild (gild), *v.t.*, **gild ed** or **gilt, gild ing.** 1 cover with a thin layer of gold or similar material; make golden. 2 make (something) look bright and pleasing. [Old English *-gyldan* < *gold* gold]

glean (glēn), *v.t.* 1 gather (grain) left on a field by reapers. 2 gather little by little: *glean information.* [< Old French *glener* < Late Latin *glennare*] **—glean er,** *n.*

gourd (gôrd, gōrd, gůrd), *n.* 1 any of various fleshy fruits that grow on vines and are related to squash. 2 cup, bowl, etc., made from the dried shell of a gourd. [< Old French *gourde,* ultimately < Latin *cucurbita*]

gra di ent (grā′dē ənt), *n.* 1 rate of upward or downward slope of a road, railroad track, etc.: *steep gradients.* 2 the sloping part of a road, railroad, etc.; grade. [< Latin *gradientem* walking, going, related to *gradus* step, degree]

grat i fy (grat′ə fī), *v.t.*, **-fied, -fy ing.** 1 give pleasure to; please: *Flattery gratifies a vain person.* 2 give satisfaction to; satisfy; indulge: *gratify one's hunger with a large meal.* [< Latin *gratificari* < *gratus* pleasing + *facere* make, do]

gra ting (grā′ting), *n.* framework of parallel or crossed bars.

grav i ty (grav′ə tē), *n., pl.* **-ties.** 1 the natural force that causes objects to move or tend to move toward the center of the earth and causes objects to have weight. 2 seriousness; earnestness. [< Latin *gravitatem* < *gravis* heavy]

guile less (gīl′lis), *adj.* without guile; honest; frank; straightforward. **—guile′less ly,** *adv.* **—guile′less ness,** *n.*

gull (gul), *v.t.* deceive; cheat. —*n.* person who is easily deceived or cheated. [origin uncertain]

gy rate (jī′rāt, jī rāt′), *v.i.*, **-rat ed, -rat ing.** move in a circle or spiral; whirl; rotate. [< Latin *gyrus* circle < Greek *gyros*]

gyre (jīr), *n.* 1 a circular or spiral form or motion. 2 a great, rotating area in an ocean. [< Latin *gyrus* < Greek *gyros*]

hag gle (hag′əl), *v.*, **-gled, -gling.** —*v.i.* dispute, especially about a price or the terms of a bargain. [< Scottish *hag* to chop < Scandinavian (Old Icelandic) *höggva*]

hal berd (hal′bərd), *n.* weapon of the 1400s and 1500s used both as a spear and as a battle-ax. [< Middle French *hallebarde* < Italian *alabarda*]

hard tack (härd′tak′), *n.* a very hard, dry biscuit that resists spoiling, formerly eaten on shipboard; sea biscuit. [< *hard*+*tack* food, of unknown origin]

har row (har′ō), *n.* a heavy frame with iron teeth or upright disks, used by farmers to break up ground into fine pieces before planting seeds. —*v.t.* 1 pull a harrow over (land, etc.). 2 hurt; wound. 3 cause pain or torment to; distress. [Middle English *harwe*]

haw ser (hô′zər, hô′sər), *n.* a large, stout rope or thin steel cable, used for mooring or towing ships. [< Old French *haucier* to hoist < Popular Latin *altiare* < Latin *altus* high]

hearth (härth), *n.* 1 stone or brick floor of a fireplace, often extending into the room. 2 fireside; home: *The travelers began to long for their own hearths.* [< Old English *heorth*]

her ni a (hėr′nē ə), *n., pl.* **-ni as, -ni ae** (-nē ē). protrusion of some tissue or organ of the body, especially a part of the intestine, through a break in its surrounding walls; rupture. [< Latin]

hi a tus (hī ā′təs), *n., pl.* **-tus es** or **-tus.** an empty space; space from which something necessary to completeness is missing; gap. [Latin, gap < *hiare* to gape]

hie (hī), *v.*, **hied, hie ing** or **hy ing.** —*v.i.* go quickly; hasten; hurry. —*v.t.* cause to hasten. [Old English *hīgian*]

high boy (hī′boi′), *n.* a tall chest of drawers on legs.

hind (hīnd), *n., pl.* **hinds** or **hind.** a female deer, especially a female red deer in and after its third year. [Old English]

hir sute (hėr′süt), *adj.* hairy. [< Latin *hirsutus*]

hod (hod), *n.* trough or tray set crosswise on top of a long, straight handle that is rested on the shoulder and used for carrying bricks, mortar, etc., up ladders, etc. [< Middle Dutch *hodde*]

hom i cide (hom′ə sīd, hō′mə sīd), *n.* a killing of one human being by another. Intentional homicide is murder. [< Old French, ultimately < Latin *homo* human being, man + *-cidium* act of killing or *-cida* killer]

hos tler (os′lər, hos′lər), *n.* person who takes care of horses at an inn or stable. Also, **ostler.** [Middle English < Old French *hostelier* < *hostel*]

hum mock (hum′ək), *n.* 1 a very small, rounded hill; knoll; hillock. 2 a bump or ridge in a field of ice. 3 a raised, often fertile, area surrounded by marsh or swampland. [origin unknown]

hus band (huz′bənd), *n.* man who has a wife; a married man. —*v.t.* 1 manage carefully; be saving of: *husband one's strength.* 2 marry. [Old English *hūsbōnda* < Scandinavian (Old Icelandic) *hūsbōndi* < *hūs* house + *bōndi* freeholder]

hy po thet i cal (hī′pə thet′ə kəl), *adj.* of or based on a hypothesis; assumed; supposed. **—hy′po thet′i cal ly,** *adv.*

ig no ble (ig nō′bəl), *adj.* 1 without honor; disgraceful; base: *To betray a friend is ignoble.* 2 not of noble birth or position; humble. [< Latin *ignobilis* < *in-* not + *nobilis* noble] **—ig no′bly,** *adv.*

il lim it a ble (i lim′ə tə bəl), *adj.* without limit; boundless; infinite. **—il lim′it a ble ness,** *n.* **—il lim′it a bly,** *adv.*

il lit er ate (i lit′ər it), *adj.* 1 unable to read and write: *People who have never gone to school are usually illiterate.* 2 showing a lack of education; not cultured: *illiterate writing.* —*n.* 1 person who is unable to read and write. 2 an uneducated person.

il lu mi nate (i lü′mə nāt), *v.t.*, **-nat ed, -nat ing.** 1 light up; make bright: *The room was illuminated by four large lamps.* 2 make clear; explain: *Our teacher could illuminate almost any subject we studied.* 3 decorate with lights: *The streets were illuminated for the celebration.* [< Latin *illuminatum* lit up < *in-* in + *lumen* light]

il lu sion (i lü′zhən), *n.* 1 appearance or feeling that misleads because it is not real; thing that deceives by giving a false idea. 2 a false impression or perception. 3 a false notion or belief: *They have the illusion that wealth is the chief source of happiness.* [< Latin *illusionem* < *illudere* mock < *in-* at + *ludere* play]

illusion (def. 2)

im me mo ri al (im′ə môr′ē əl, im′ə mōr′ē əl), *adj.* extending back beyond the bounds of memory; ancient beyond record or knowledge; extremely old. **—im′me mo′ri al ly,** *adv.*

im mi nent (im′ə nənt), *adj.* likely to happen soon; about to occur: *Black clouds show rain is imminent.* [< Latin *imminentem* overhanging, threatening] **—im′mi nent ly,** *adv.*

im mo late (im′ə lāt), *v.t.,* **-lat ed, -lat ing.** 1 kill as a sacrifice. 2 offer in sacrifice; sacrifice. [< Latin *immolaturm* sacrificed, (originally) sprinkled with sacrificial meal < *in-* on + *mola* sacrificial meal] **—im′mo la′tion,** *n.* **—im′mo la′tor,** *n.*

im pale (im pāl′), *v.t.,* **-paled, -pal ing.** pierce through with something pointed; fasten upon something pointed: *The dead butterflies were impaled on pins stuck in a sheet of cork.* [< Medieval Latin *impalare* < Latin *in-* on + *palus* stake]

im part (im pärt′), *v.t.* 1 give a part or share of; give: *The new furnishings imparted an air of newness to the old house.* 2 communicate; tell: *They imparted the news of their engagement to their families.* [< Latin *impartire* < *in-* in + *partem* part]

im pas sive (im pas′iv), *adj.* 1 without feeling or emotion; unmoved: *Her face was impassive when we told her the news.* 2 not feeling pain or injury; insensible. **—im pas′sive ly,** *adv.*

im ped i ment (im ped′ə mənt), *n.* 1 hindrance; obstruction. 2 some physical defect, especially a defect in speech.

im per a tive (im per′ə tiv), *adj.* 1 not to be avoided; that must be done; urgent; necessary: *It is imperative that this very sick child should stay in bed.* 2 (in grammar) having to do with a verb form which expresses a command, request, or advice. "Go!" and "Stop, look, listen!" are in the imperative mood. *—n.* something imperative; command: *The dog trainer issued sharp imperatives to the dog.* [< Latin *imperativus* < *imperare* to command] **—im per′a tive ly,** *adv.*

im per i ous (im pir′ē əs), *adj.* haughty or arrogant; domineering; overbearing. **—im per′i ous ly,** *adv.* **—im per′i ous ness,** *n.*

im per son al (im pėr′sə nəl), *adj.* not referring to any one person in particular; not personal: *impersonal criticism.* **—im per′son al ly,** *adv.*

im per ti nence (im pėrt′n əns), *n.* a being impertinent; impudence; insolence. 2 an impertinent act or speech.

im per turb a ble (im′pər tėr′bə bəl), *adj.* not easily excited or disturbed; calm.

im plic it (im plis′it), *adj.* 1 meant, but not clearly expressed or distinctly stated; implied: *implicit consent.* 2 without doubting, hesitating, or asking questions; absolute. 3 involved as a necessary part or condition. [< Latin *implicitum* implied, enfolded < *in-* in + *plicare* to fold]

im po tent (im′pə tənt), *adj.* not having power; helpless: *We were impotent against the force of the tornado.* **—im′po tent ly,** *adv.*

im preg na ble (im preg′nə bəl), *adj.* able to resist attack; not yielding to force, persuasion, etc.: *an impregnable fortress, an impregnable argument.* **—im preg′na bly,** *adv.*

im pru dence (im prüd′ns), *n.* lack of prudence, or good judgment before acting; imprudent behavior.

im pu dent (im′pyə dənt), *adj.* shamelessly bold; very rude and insolent. [< Latin *impudentem* < *in-* not + *pudere* be modest] **—im′pu dent ly,** *adv.*

in au di ble (in ô′də bəl), *adj.* that cannot be heard. **—in au′di bly,** *adv.*

in can des cent (in′kən des′nt), *adj.* 1 heated to such a high temperature that it gives out light; glowing with heat; red-hot or white-hot. 2 shining brightly; brilliant.

in can ta tion (in′kan tā′shən), *n.* set of words spoken as a magic charm or to cast a magic spell. [< Latin *incantationem* < *incantare* enchant < *in-* against + *cantare* to chant]

in cense (in sens′), *v.t.,* **-censed, -cens ing.** make very angry; fill with rage. [< Latin *incensum* inflamed, enraged, set on fire < *in-* (intensive) + *candere* glow white]

in ces sant (in ses′nt), *adj.* never stopping; continued or repeated without interruption; continual: *the incessant noise from the factory.* [< Late Latin *incessantem* < Latin *in-* not + *cessare* cease] **—in ces′sant ly,** *adv.* **—in ces′sant ness,** *n.*

in cip i ent (in sip′ē ənt), *adj.* just beginning; in an early stage; commencing. [< Latin *incipientem* < *in-* on + *capere* take]

in co her ent (in′kō hir′ənt), *adj.* 1 having or showing no logical connection of ideas; not coherent; disconnected; confused. 2 not sticking together; loose. **—in′co her′ent ly,** *adv.*

in com pat i bil i ty (in′kəm pat′ə bil′ə tē), *n., pl.* **-ties.** 1 quality of being incompatible; lack of harmony. 2 an incompatible thing, quality, etc.

in cred u lous (in krej′ə ləs), *adj.* 1 not ready to believe; doubting; skeptical: *If they look incredulous show them the evidence.* 2 showing a lack of belief: *an incredulous smile.* **—in cred′u lous ly,** *adv.*

in dif fer ent (in dif′ər ənt), *adj.* 1 having or showing no interest or attention: *indifferent to an admirer.* 2 not inclined to prefer one person or thing to another; impartial; neutral; fair: *an indifferent decision.* 3 not mattering much; unimportant. **—in dif′fer ent ly,** *adv.*

in dis creet (in′dis krēt′), *adj.* not discreet; not wise and judicious; imprudent. **—in′dis creet′ly,** *adv.*

in ef fa ble (in ef′ə bəl), *adj.* not to be expressed in words; too great to be described in words. [< Latin *ineffabilis* < *in-* not + *effari* express in words < *ex-* out + *fari* speak] **—in ef′fa bly,** *adv.*

in ert (in ėrt′), *adj.* 1 having no power to move or act; lifeless: *A stone is an inert mass of matter.* 2 inactive; slow; sluggish. [< Latin *inertem* idle, unskilled < *in-* without + *artem* art, skill] **—in ert′ly,** *adv.* **—in ert′ness,** *n.*

in es ti ma ble (in es′tə mə bəl), *adj.* 1 not capable of being estimated; incalculable. 2 too precious to be estimated; priceless; invaluable. **—in es′ti ma bly,** *adv.*

in ev i ta ble (in ev′ə tə bəl), *adj.* not to be avoided; sure to happen; certain to come: *Death is inevitable.* [< Latin *inevitabilis* < *in-* not + *evitare* avoid < *ex-* out + *vitare* shun] **—in ev′i ta bly,** *adv.*

in ex plic a ble (in′ik splik′ə bəl, in ek′splə kə bəl), *adj.* that cannot be explained, understood, or accounted for; mysterious. **—in′ex plic′a ble ness,** *n.* **—in′ex plic′a bly,** *adv.*

in fal li ble (in fal′ə bəl), *adj.* 1 free from error; that cannot be mistaken: *an infallible rule.* 2 absolutely reliable; sure: *infallible obedience, an infallible remedy.* **—in fal′li bly,** *adv.*

in fa my (in′fə mē), *n., pl.* **-mies.** 1 a very bad reputation; public disgrace: *Traitors are held in infamy.* 2 shameful badness; extreme wickedness. 3 an infamous or disgraceful act. [< Latin *infamia* < *infamis* of ill fame < *in-* without + *fama* fame, reputation]

in firm (in fėrm′), *adj.* lacking strength or health; physically weak or feeble, especially through age. **—in firm′ly,** *adv.*

in gen u ous (in jen′yü əs), *adj.* 1 free from restraint or reserve; frank and open; sincere. 2 simple and natural; innocent; naïve. [< Latin *ingenuus,* originally, native < *in-* in + *gignere* beget] **—in gen′u ous ly,** *adv.* **—in gen′u ous ness,** *n.*

in graft (in graft′), *v.t.* 1 graft (a shoot, etc.) from one tree or plant into another. 2 fix in; implant. Also, **engraft.**

in her ent (in hir′ənt, in her′ənt), *adj.* belonging to a person or thing as a permanent and essential quality or attribute; intrinsic: *inherent honesty, the inherent sweetness of sugar.* **—in her′ent ly,** *adv.*

in quis i tive (in kwiz′ə tiv), *adj.* 1 asking many questions; curious. 2 prying into other people's affairs; too curious. **—in quis′i tive ly,** *adv.*

in scru ta ble (in skrü′tə bəl), *adj.* that cannot be understood; so mysterious or obscure that one cannot make out its meaning; incomprehensible. [< Late Latin *inscrutabilis* < Latin *in-* not + *scrutari* examine, ransack < *scruta* trash]

in sid i ous (in sid′ē əs), *adj.* 1 seeking to entrap or ensnare; wily or sly; crafty; tricky. 2 working secretly or subtly; developing without attracting attention: *an insidious disease.* [< Latin *insidiosus* < *insidiae* ambush < *insidere* sit in < *in-* in + *sedere* sit] **—in sid′i ous ly,** *adv.* **—in sid′i ous ness,** *n.*

in sig nif i cant (in′sig nif′ə kənt), *adj.* 1 of no consequence, influence, or distinction: *an insignificant position, an insignificant person.* 2 too small to be important; unimportant; trivial; petty: *an insignificant detail, an insignificant amount of money.* **—in′sig nif′i cant ly,** *adv.*

in sin u ate (in sin′yü āt), *v.,* **-at ed, -at ing.** *—v.t.* 1 suggest in an indirect way; hint: *To say "That worker can't do the job; it takes skill" is to insinuate that the worker is not skilled.* 2 push in or get in by an indirect, subtle way: *The stray cat insinuated itself into our kitchen.* *—v.i.* make insinuations. [< Latin *insinuatum* wound or twisted into < *in-* in + *sinus* a curve, winding] **—in sin′u at′ing ly,** *adv.*

in so lent (in′sə lənt), *adj.* boldly rude; intentionally disregarding the feelings of others; insulting. [< Latin *insolentem* arrogant, contrary to custom < *in-* not + *solere* be accustomed]

in sti gate (in′stə gāt), *v.t.,* **-gat ed, -gat ing.** urge on; stir up: *instigate a quarrel.* [< Latin *instigatum* incited, urged on] **—in′sti ga′tion,** *n.* **—in′sti ga′tor,** *n.*

in su per a ble (in sü′pər ə bəl), *adj.* that cannot be passed over or overcome; insurmountable: *an insuperable barrier.*

a hat	**i** it	**oi** oil	**ch** child	ə = a in about
ā age	**ī** ice	**ou** out	**ng** long	e in taken
ä far	**o** hot	**u** cup	**sh** she	i in pencil
e let	**ō** open	**ů** put	**th** thin	o in lemon
ē equal	**ô** order	**ü** rule	**ᴛʜ** then	u in circus
ėr term			**zh** measure	< = derived from

in sup port a ble (in′sə pôr′tə bəl, in′sə pōr′tə bəl), *adj.* not endurable; unbearable; intolerable.

in tel li gent si a (in tel′ə jent′sē ə, in tel′ə gent′sē ə), *n.pl.* persons representing, or claiming to represent, the superior intelligence or enlightened opinion of a country; the intellectuals. [< Russian *intelligentsiya* < Latin *intelligentia* < *intelligentem* intelligent]

in tem per ate (in tem′pər it), *adj.* not moderate; lacking in self-control; excessive: *an intemperate appetite.* **—in tem′per ate ly,** *adv.*

in ter (in tėr′), *v.t.,* **-terred, -ter ring.** put (a dead body) into a grave or tomb; bury. [< Medieval Latin *interrare* < Latin *in-* in + *terra* earth]

in ter cede (in′tər sēd′), *v.i.,* **-ced ed, -ced ing.** 1 plead for another; ask a favor from one person for another: *Friends of the condemned man interceded with the governor for a pardon.* 2 act as an intermediary in order to bring about an agreement; mediate. [< Latin *intercedere* go between < *inter-* between + *cedere* go]

in ter ces sion (in′tər sesh′ən), *n.* 1 act or fact of interceding. 2 prayer pleading for others. [< Latin *intercessionem* < *intercedere.*]

in ter lop er (in′tər lō′pər), *n.* person who interferes, unasked and unwanted; intruder.

in ter lude (in′tər lüd), *n.* anything thought of as filling the time between two things; interval: *an interlude of sunshine between two showers.* [< Medieval Latin *interludium* < Latin *inter-* between + *ludus* a play]

in ter mi na ble (in tėr′mə nə bəl), *adj.* 1 never stopping; unceasing; endless. 2 so long as to seem endless; very long and tiring. **—in ter′mi na bly,** *adv.*

in ter pose (in′tər pōz′), *v.,* **-posed, -pos ing.** —*v.t.* 1 put between; insert. 2 put forward; break in with: *She interposed an objection at this point.* —*v.i.* 1 come or be between other things. 2 interrupt. 3 interfere in order to help; intervene; intercede. [< Middle French *interposer* < *inter-* between + *poser* to place]

in ter stice (in tėr′stis), *n., pl.* **-sti ces** (-stə sēz′). a small or narrow space between things or parts; narrow chink, crack, or opening. [< Late Latin *interstitium* < Latin *inter-* between + *stare* to stand]

in ter vene (in′tər vēn′), *v.i.,* **-vened, -ven ing.** 1 come between; be between: *A week intervenes between my sister's birthday and mine.* 2 come between persons or groups to help settle a dispute: *The President was asked to intervene in the coal strike.* [< Latin *intervenire* < *inter-* between + *venire* come]

in tra ve nous (in′trə vē′nəs), *adj.* 1 within a vein or the veins. 2 into a vein or veins. **—in′tra ve′nous ly,** *adv.*

in vin ci ble (in vin′sə bəl), *adj.* unable to be conquered; impossible to overcome; unconquerable: *an invincible fighter.* [< Latin *invincibilis* < *in-* not + *vincere* conquer]

in voke (in vōk′), *v.t.,* **-voked, -vok ing.** 1 call on in prayer; appeal to for help or protection. 2 appeal to for confirmation or judgment: *invoke an authority.* [< Latin *invocare* < *in-* on + *vocare* to call]

in vol un tar y (in vol′ən ter′ē), *adj.* 1 not voluntary; not done of one's own free will; unwilling: *involuntary consent.* 2 not done on purpose; not intended: *an involuntary injury.* 3 not controlled by the will: *Breathing is mainly involuntary.* **—in vol′un tar′i ly,** *adv.*

ir i des cent (ir′ə des′nt), *adj.* displaying changing colors; changing color when moved or turned. [< Latin *iris, iridis* rainbow] **—ir′i des′cent ly,** *adv.*

i ron i cal (ī ron′ə kəl), *adj.* 1 expressing one thing and meaning the opposite: *"Speedy" was the ironical name of our turtle.* 2 contrary to what would naturally be expected: *It was ironical that the man was run over by his own automobile.* **—i ron′i cal ly,** *adv.*

ir re deem a ble (ir′i dē′mə bəl), *adj.* 1 that cannot be redeemed or bought back. 2 that cannot be exchanged for coin: *irredeemable paper money.* 3 impossible to change; beyond remedy; hopeless: *an irredeemable mistake.* **—ir′re deem′a bly,** *adv.*

ir ref u ta ble (i ref′yə tə bəl, ir′i fyü′tə bəl), *adj.* that cannot be refuted or disproved; undeniable; unanswerable.

ir rel e vant (i rel′ə vənt), *adj.* not to the point; off the subject: *an irrelevant question.* **—ir rel′e vant ly,** *adv.*

ir re spec tive (ir′i spek′tiv), *adj.* without regard to particular persons, circumstances or conditions; regardless *(of): All students, irrespective of age, may join the club.* **—ir′re spec′tive ly,** *adv.*

ir rev o ca ble (i rev′ə kə bəl), *adj.* 1 not able to be revoked; final: *an irrevocable decision.* 2 impossible to call or bring back: *the irrevocable past.* **—ir rev′o ca bly,** *adv.*

jack al (jak′əl, jak′ôl), *n.* 1 any of several species of carnivorous wild mammals of the dog family, which hunt in packs at night and feed on small animals and carrion left by large animals. 2 person who does menial work for another. [< Turkish *çakāl* < Persian *shaghāl*]

jack straw (jak′strô′), *n.* 1 straw, strip of wood, bone, etc., used in the game of jackstraws. 2 **jackstraws,** *pl.* a children's game played with a set of jackstraws thrown down in a pile and picked up one at a time without moving any of the rest of the pile.

jade (jād), *n.* an inferior or worn-out horse. [origin uncertain]

jer kin (jėr′kən), *n.* a short, close-fitting coat or jacket without sleeves. [origin uncertain]

joc und (jok′ənd, jō′kənd), *adj.* feeling, expressing, or communicating mirth or cheer; cheerful; merry; gay. [< Latin *jocundus, jucundus* pleasant < *juvare* please]

jowl (joul, jōl), *n.* 1 jaw, especially the lower jaw. 2 cheek. [Old English *ceafl*]

ju di cious (jü dish′əs), *adj.* having, using, or showing good judgment; wise; sensible: *A judicious historian selects and weighs facts carefully and critically.* **—ju di′cious ly,** *adv.*

jux ta po si tion (juk′stə pə zish′ən), *n.* a putting close together; a placing side by side.

ka lei do scope (kə lī′də skōp), *n.* 1 tube containing bits of colored glass and two mirrors. As it is turned, it reflects continually changing patterns. 2 a continually changing pattern or object: *The circus was a kaleidoscope of colors.* [< Greek *kalos* pretty + *eidos* shape + English *-scope*]

ka pok (kā′pok), *n.* the silky fibers around the seeds of a tropical silk-cotton tree, used for stuffing pillows, mattresses, and life preservers, for insulation, etc.; silk cotton. [< Malay]

ken (ken), *n.* 1 range of sight. 2 range of knowledge: *Outer space is no longer beyond our ken.* [Old English *cennan* make declaration < *cann* know]

kit tle (kit′l), *v.t.* **kit tled, kit tling.** to give birth to a litter of rabbits, kittens, etc.

lab y rinth (lab′ə rinth′), *n.* 1 number of connecting passages so arranged that it is hard to find one's way from point to point; maze. 2 any confusing, complicated arrangement: *a labyrinth of dark and narrow streets.* [< Greek *labyrinthos*]

labyrinth (def. 1)

lac e rate (las′ə rāt′), *v.t.,* **-rat ed, -rat ing.** 1 tear roughly; mangle: *The bear's claws lacerated the hunter's arm.* 2 wound; hurt (the feelings, etc.). [< Latin *laceratum* torn, mangled]

lack ey (lak′ē), *n., pl.* **-eys.** 1 a male servant; footman. 2 a slavish follower; toady. [< Middle French *laquais* < Spanish *lacayo* foot soldier]

lair (ler, lar), *n.* 1 den or resting place of a wild animal. 2 secret or secluded retreat. [< Old English *leger* < *licgan*]

lan guor (lang′gər), *n.* 1 lack of energy; weakness; weariness: *A long illness causes languor.* 2 lack of interest or enthusiasm; indifference. 3 softness or tenderness of mood. 4 quietness; stillness: *the languor of a summer afternoon.* 5 lack of activity; sluggishness. [< Latin < *languere* be faint]

lap i dar y (lap′ə der′ē), *n., pl.* **-dar ies,** *adj.* —*n.* person who cuts, polishes, or engraves precious stones. —*adj.* 1 having to do with cutting or engraving precious stones. 2 engraved on stone. [< Latin *lapidarius* < *lapis* stone]

las si tude (las′ə tüd, las′ə tyüd), *n.* lack of energy; weariness; languor. [< Latin *lassitudo* < *lassus* tired]

lee (lē), *n.* 1 shelter; protection. 2 side or part sheltered or away from the wind: *the lee of a ship.* —*adj.* sheltered or away from the wind: *the lee side of a ship.* [Old English *hlēo*]

leg a cy (leg′ə sē), *n., pl.* **-cies.** money or other property left to a person by the will of someone who has died; bequest. [< Medieval Latin *legatia* < Latin *legatum* bequest < *legare* bequeath]

leth ar gy (leth′ər jē), *n., pl.* **-gies.** drowsy dullness; lack of energy; sluggish inactivity. [< Greek *lēthargia* < *lēthē* forgetfulness + *argos* lazy < *a-* not + *ergon* work]

li a bil i ty (lī′ə bil′ə tē), *n., pl.* **-ties.** 1 state of being susceptible: *liability to disease.* 2 state of being under obligation: *liability for a debt.*

li ai son (lē′ā zon′, lē ā′zon, lē′ə zon), *n.* 1 connection between military units, branches of a service, etc., to secure proper cooperation. 2 similar connection or communication between civilian bodies, such as government departments, companies, or schools. [< French < Latin *ligationem* a binding < *ligare* to bind]

li ba tion (lī bā′shən), *n.* 1 a pouring out of wine, water, etc., as an offering to a god. 2 the wine, water, etc., offered in this way. 3 INFORMAL. liquid poured out to be drunk; drink. [< Latin *libationem* < *libare* pour out]

lib er tar i an (lib′ər ter′ē ən), *n.* 1 person who advocates liberty, especially in thought or conduct. 2 person who maintains the doctrine of the freedom of the will.

liege (lēj), *n.* in the Middle Ages: lord having a right to the homage and loyal service of his vassals. [< Old French, ultimately of Germanic origin]

lim pid (lim′pid), *adj.* 1 clear or transparent: *limpid water, limpid eyes.* 2 free from obscurity; lucid. [< Latin *limpidus,* related to *lympha* clear water]

lin tel (lin′tl), *n.* a horizontal beam or stone over a door, window, etc., to support the structure above it. [< Old French, threshold, ultimately < Latin *limitem* limit]

lit a ny (lit′n ē), *n., pl.* **-nies.** 1 prayer consisting of a series of words or requests said by a minister or priest and the congregation's responses. 2 a repeated series. [< Greek *litaneia* litany, entreaty < *litesthai* entreat]

lithe (līᴛʜ), *adj.* bending easily; supple: *lithe of body, a lithe willow.* [Old English *līthe* mild] **—lithe′ly,** *adv.* **—lithe′ness,** *n.*

liv er y (liv′ər ē), *n., pl.* **-er ies.** 1 any special uniform provided for the servants of a household, or adopted by any group or profession. 2 the feeding, stabling, and care of horses for pay. 3 the hiring out of horses and carriages. 4 the keeping of cars, boats, etc., for hire. 5 livery stable. [< Old French *livree* provisions dispensed to servants < *livrer* dispense < Latin *liberare* liberate]

liv id (liv′id), *adj.* 1 flushed; reddish: *livid with rage.* 2 very angry: *Their insults made me livid.* [< Latin *lividus* < *livere* be bluish] **—liv′id ly,** *adv.*

loam (lōm), *n.* rich, fertile earth in which much humus is mixed with clay and sand. [Old English *lām*]

loath (lōth, lōᴛʜ), *adj.* unwilling or reluctant; averse: *The little girl was loath to leave her mother. They were loath to admit that their son had run away.* Also, **loth.** [Old English *lāth* hostile]

lor gnette (lôr nyet′), *n.* eyeglasses or opera glasses mounted on a handle. [< French < *lorgner* look sidelong at]

lu cid (lü′sid), *adj.* 1 marked by clearness of reasoning, expression, or arrangement; easy to follow or understand: *a lucid explanation.* 2 clear in intellect; rational; sane: *An insane person sometimes has lucid intervals.* 3 shining; bright; luminous. [< Latin *lucidus* < *lucere* to shine] **—lu′cid ly,** *adv.*

lu gu bri ous (lü gü′brē əs, lü gyü′brē əs), *adj.* too sad; overly mournful: *the lugubrious howl of a dog.* [< Latin *lugubris* < *lugere* mourn] **—lu gu′bri ous ly,** *adv.* **—lu gu′bri ous ness,** *n.*

lum ba go (lum bā′gō), *n.* form of rheumatism characterized by pain in the muscles of the small of the back and in the loins. [< Late Latin < Latin *lumbus* loin]

lu mi nar y (lü′mə ner′ē), *n., pl.* **-nar ies,** *adj.* —*n.* 1 a heavenly body that gives or reflects light. 2 anything that gives light. 3 a famous person. —*adj.* having to do with light. [< Late Latin *luminarium* < Latin *lumen* light]

lu mi nous (lü′mə nəs), *adj.* 1 shining by its own light: *The sun and stars are luminous bodies.* 2 full of light; shining; bright. 3 easily understood; clear; enlightening. **—lu′mi nous ly,** *adv.*

lyre (līr), *n.* an ancient stringed musical instrument somewhat like a small harp. [< Latin *lyra* < Greek]

mag a zine (mag′ə zēn′, mag′ə zēn′), *n.* 1 publication issued regularly, especially weekly, semimonthly, or monthly, which contains stories, articles, etc., by various contributors. 2 room in a fort or warship for storing gunpowder and other explosives. 3 chamber for cartridges in a repeating or automatic gun. [< Old French *magazin,* ultimately < Arabic *makhzan* storehouse]

mag got (mag′ət), *n.* the legless, wormlike larva of any of various kinds of two-winged flies, often living in decaying matter. [Middle English *magot*]

ma jor-do mo (mā′jər dō′mō), *n., pl.* **-mos.** 1 man in charge of a royal or noble household. 2 butler or steward. [< Spanish *mayordomo* or Italian *maggiordomo* < Medieval Latin *major domus* chief of the household]

ma lar i a (mə ler′ē ə, mə lar′ē ə), *n.* disease characterized by periodic chills, fever, and sweating. [< Italian < *mala aria* bad air]

mal ice (mal′is), *n.* active ill will; wish to hurt or make suffer; rancor. [< Old French < Latin *malitia* < *malus* bad, evil]

ma li cious (mə lish′əs), *adj.* 1 showing active ill will; wishing to hurt or make suffer; spiteful. 2 proceeding from malice: *malicious mischief.* **—ma li′cious ly,** *adv.* **—ma li′cious ness,** *n.*

ma lign (mə līn′), *v.t.* speak evil of; slander: *You malign an honest person whom you call a liar.* —*adj.* 1 evil; injurious. 2 hateful; malicious. [< Late Latin *malignare* < Latin *malignus* disposed to evil < *malus* evil + *-gnus* born]

man i fest (man′ə fest), *v.t.* 1 show plainly; reveal; display. 2 put beyond doubt; prove. [< Latin *manifestus* palpable < *manus* hand + *-festus* (able to be) seized]

man sard (man′särd), *n.* roof with two slopes on each side. [< François *Mansard,* 1598-1666, French architect]

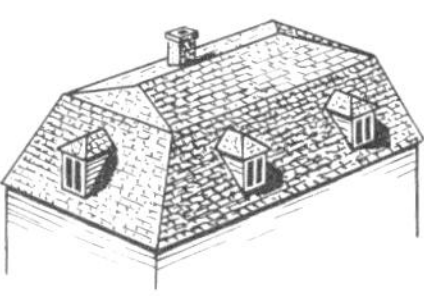
mansard

man til la (man til′ə, man tē′yə), *n.* veil or scarf, often of lace, covering the hair and falling down over the shoulders. [< Spanish, diminutive of *manta* cloak]

man tle (man′tl), *n., v.,* **-tled, -tling.** —*n.* 1 a long, loose cloak without sleeves. 2 anything that covers like a mantle: *The ground had a mantle of snow.* —*v.t.* 1 cover with a mantle. 2 cover or conceal; obscure; cloak: *Clouds mantled the moon.* [partly Old English *mentel,* partly < Old French *mantel;* both < Latin *mantellum*]

ma raud (mə rôd′), *v.i.* go about in search of plunder. —*v.t.* plunder. [< French *marauder*] **—ma raud′er,** *n.*

mar gin al (mär′jə nəl), *adj.* 1 written or printed in a margin: *a marginal comment.* 2 barely able to produce goods, crops, etc., profitably: *marginal income.* **—mar′gin al ly,** *adv.*

mar row (mar′ō), *n.* 1 the soft, vascular tissue that fills the cavities of most bones and is the source of red blood cells and many white blood cells. 2 the inmost or essential part. [< Old English *mearg*]

mas to don (mas′tə don), *n.* any of various large extinct mammals somewhat resembling mammoths and present-day elephants. [< New Latin < Greek *mastos* breast + *odōn* tooth (from the nipple-shaped projections on its teeth)]

ma ter i al ize (mə tir′ē ə līz), *v.i.,* **-ized, -iz ing.** 1 become an actual fact; be realized: *Our plans did not materialize.* 2 appear in material or bodily form: *A spirit materialized from the smoke of the magician's fire.* **—ma ter′i al i za′tion,** *n.*

ma ter nal (mə tėr′nl), *adj.* of or like a mother; motherly. [< Middle French *maternel* < Latin *maternus* < *mater* mother] **—ma ter′nal ly,** *adv.*

ma tri cide (mā′trə sīd, mat′rə sīd), *n.* 1 act of killing one's mother. 2 person who kills his or her mother.

maw (mô), *n.* 1 mouth, throat, or gullet, especially of a meat-eating animal. 2 stomach. [< Old English *maga*]

med ley (med′lē), *n., pl.* **-leys.** 1 mixture of things that ordinarily do not belong together. 2 piece of music made up of parts from other pieces. [< Old French *medlee, meslee* < *mesler* to mix, ultimately < Latin *miscere.*]

a hat	**i** it	**oi** oil	**ch** child	a in about
ā age	**ī** ice	**ou** out	**ng** long	e in taken
ä far	**o** hot	**u** cup	**sh** she	**ə** = i in pencil
e let	**ō** open	**ů** put	**th** thin	o in lemon
ē equal	**ô** order	**ü** rule	**ᴛʜ** then	u in circus
ėr term			**zh** measure	< = derived from

met al lur gy (met′lėr′jē), *n.* science or art of working with metals. [< New Latin *metallurgia,* ultimately < Greek *metallon* metal + *ergon* work] **—met′al lur′gist,** *n.*

me tic u lous (mə tik′yə ləs), *adj.* extremely or excessively careful about details. [< Latin *meticulosus* fearful, timid < *metus* fear] **—me tic′u lous ly,** *adv.* **—me tic′u lous ness,** *n.*

mod u la tion (moj′ə lā′shən), *n.* 1 a modulating. 2 an alteration in pitch, tone, or volume.

mol ten (mōlt′n), *adj.* 1 made liquid by heat; melted: *molten steel.* 2 made by melting and casting: *a molten image.* —*v.* a pp. of **melt.**

mo men tous (mō men′təs), *adj.* very important; of great consequence; weighty. **—mo men′tous ly,** *adv.*

mo nop o ly (mə nop′ə lē), *n., pl.* **-lies.** 1 the exclusive control of a commodity or service: *The only milk company in town has a monopoly on milk delivery.* 2 the exclusive possession or control of something: *a monopoly of a person's time.* [< Greek *monopōlion* < *mono-* + *pōlein* to sell]

moor ing (mür′ing), *n.* 1 act of tying up or securing a ship, etc. 2 rope, cable, anchor, etc., by which a ship is made fast. 3 Also, **moorings,** *pl.* anything to which a thing is attached or fastened.

mo rose (mə rōs′), *adj.* gloomy; sullen; ill-humored: *a morose person.* [< Latin *morosus,* originally, set in one's ways < *morem* custom, habit] **—mo rose′ly,** *adv.* **—mo rose′ness,** *n.*

murk y (mėr′kē), *adj.,* **murk i er, murk i est.** 1 dark; gloomy: *a murky prison.* 2 very thick and dark; misty; hazy: *murky smoke.* 3 hard to understand; obscure: *a murky argument.* Also, **mirky.** **—murk′i ly,** *adv.* **—murk′i ness,** *n.*

mus ing (myü′zing), *adj.* meditative. —*n.* meditation. **—mus′ing ly,** *adv.*

mus ter (mus′tər), *v.t.* 1 gather together; assemble; collect: *muster financial resources, muster soldiers.* 2 summon: *muster up courage.* 3 number; comprise: *The garrison musters eighty men.* [< Old French *mostrer* < Latin *monstrare* to show < *monstrum* portent]

mute (myüt), *adj., v.,* **mut ed, mut ing.** —*adj.* 1 not making any sound; silent: *The little girl stood mute with embarrassment.* 2 unable to speak; dumb. 3 not pronounced; silent: *The "e" in "mute" is mute.* 4 without speech or sound. —*v.t.* deaden or soften the sound of (a tone, voice, a musical instrument, etc.) with or as if with a mute. [< Latin *mutus*] **—mute′ly,** *adv.* **—mute′ness,** *n.*

mu ti late (myü′tl āt), *v.t.,* **-lat ed, -lat ing.** 1 cut, tear, or break off a limb or other important part of; injure seriously by cutting, tearing, or breaking off some part; maim. 2 destroy or ruin some part of: *mutilate a book.* [< Latin *mutilatum* maimed]

myr i ad (mir′ē əd), *n.* 1 ten thousand. 2 a very great number: *There are myriads of stars.* [< Greek *myriados* ten thousand, countless]

na dir (nā′dər, nā′dir), *n.* 1 the point in the celestial sphere directly beneath the observer or a given place; the point opposite the zenith. 2 the lowest point: *Efforts to achieve agreement reached their nadir.* [< Old French < Arabic *nazīr* opposite (that is, to the zenith)]

na ïve or **na ive** (nä ēv′), *adj.* simple in nature; like a child; not sophisticated; artless. Also, **naïf.** [< French *naïve,* feminine of *naïf* < Latin *nativus*] **—na ïve′ly, na ive′ly,** *adv.*

na per y (nā′pər ē), *n.* tablecloths, napkins, and doilies. [< Old French *naperie* < *nape* cloth]

naught (nôt), *n.* 1 nothing. 2 zero; 0. Also, **nought.** [Old English *nāwiht* < *nā* no + *wiht* thing]

net tle (net′l), *n.* any of a genus of herbs having sharp hairs on the leaves and stems that sting the skin when touched. [Old English *netele*]

noc tur nal (nok tėr′nl), *adj.* 1 of the night: *Stars are a nocturnal sight.* 2 active in the night: *The owl is a nocturnal bird.* [< Latin *nocturnus* of the night < *noctem* night] **—noc tur′nal ly,** *adv.*

no mad ic (nō mad′ik), *adj.* of nomads or their life; wandering.

no to ri ous (nō tôr′ē əs, nō tōr′ē əs), *adj.* 1 well-known, especially because of something bad; having a bad reputation: *a notorious gambler.* 2 well-known; celebrated: *a notorious court case.* [< Medieval Latin *notorius* < Latin *notus* known] **—no to′ri ous ly,** *adv.* **—no to′ri ous ness,** *n.*

nup tial (nup′shəl), *adj.* of marriage or weddings. [< Latin *nuptialis,* ultimately < *nubere* take a husband] **—nup′tial ly,** *adv.*

oa kum (ō′kəm), *n.* a loose fiber obtained by untwisting and picking apart old tarred hemp ropes, used for stopping up the seams or cracks in ships. [Old English *ācumba*]

o blique (ə blēk′; *military* ə blīk′), *adj.* 1 neither perpendicular to nor parallel with a given line or surface; slanting. 2 not straightforward; indirect: *She made an oblique reference to her illness, but did not mention it directly.* [< Latin *obliquus*] **—o blique′ly,** *adv.* **—o blique′ness,** *n.*

oc clude (o klüd′), *v.,* **-clud ed, -clud ing.** —*v.t.* 1 stop up (a passage, pores, etc.); close. 2 shut in, out, or off. [< Latin *occludere* < *ob-* up + *claudere* to close]

oc cult (ə kult′, ok′ult), *adj.* 1 beyond the bounds of ordinary knowledge; mysterious. 2 outside the laws of the natural world; magical: *Astrology and alchemy are occult sciences.* 3 not disclosed; secret; revealed only to the initiated. [< Latin *occultum* hidden < *ob-* up + *celare* to hide] **—oc cult′ly,** *adv.*

o di ous (ō′dē əs), *adj.* very displeasing; hateful; offensive. [< Latin *odiosus* < *odium* odium] **—o′di ous ly,** *adv.*

of fal (ô′fəl, of′əl), *n.* 1 the waste parts of an animal killed for food. 2 garbage; refuse. [< *off* + *fall*]

of fice (ô′fis, of′is), *n.* 1 place in which the work of a position is done; room or rooms in which to work. 2 position, especially in the public service; post. 3 duty of one's position; task; job; work. 4 act of kindness or unkindness; attention; service: *Through the good offices of a friend, I was able to get a job.* [< Latin *officium* service < *opus* work + *facere* do]

om i nous (om′ə nəs), *adj.* unfavorable; threatening: *ominous clouds.* **—om′i nous ly,** *adv.* **—om′i nous ness,** *n.*

o paque (ō pāk′), *adj.* 1 not letting light through; not transparent or translucent. 2 not conducting heat, sound, etc. 3 not shining; dark; dull. 4 hard to understand; obscure. 5 stupid. —*n.* something opaque. [< Latin *opacus* dark, shady] **—o paque′ly,** *adv.*

o ra to ry (ôr′ə tôr′ē, ôr′ə tōr′ē; or′ə tôr′ē, or′ə tōr′ē), *n., pl.* **-ries.** a small chapel, room, or other place set apart for private prayer. [< Late Latin *oratorium* < Latin *orare* plead, pray.]

or der ly (ôr′dər lē), *n., pl.* **-lies.** 1 soldier who attends a superior officer to carry out orders and perform other duties. 2 a male hospital attendant who keeps things clean and in order, often tends to patients, etc.

o ri ent (ôr′ē ent, ōr′ē ent), *v.t.* 1 put facing east. 2 find the direction or position of; determine the compass bearings of. 3 bring into the right relationship with surroundings; adjust to a new situation, condition of affairs, etc. [< Latin *orientem* the East, literally, rising (with reference to the rising sun)]

o sier (ō′zhər), *n.* 1 any of various willows with tough, flexible branches or shoots. 2 one of these branches, used in weaving baskets or other wickerwork. —*adj.* made of osiers. [< Middle French]

o ver se er (ō′vər sē′ər, ō′vər sir′), *n.* one who oversees others or their work.

o ver wrought (ō′vər rôt′), *adj.* 1 wearied or exhausted by too much work or excitement; greatly excited: *overwrought nerves.* 2 too elaborate. —*v.* a pt. and a pp. of **overwork.**

pach y derm (pak′ə dėrm′), *n.* 1 any of several thick-skinned mammals with hoofs, formerly classed together, such as the elephant, hippopotamus, and rhinoceros. 2 person who is not sensitive to criticism or ridicule; thick-skinned person. [< Greek *pachydermos* thick-skinned < *pachys* thick + *derma* skin]

pad dock (pad′ək), *n.* 1 a small, enclosed field near a stable or house, used for exercising animals or as a pasture. 2 pen at a racetrack where horses are saddled before a race. [variant of *parrock,* Old English *pearroc.* Related to PARK.]

pal lid (pal′id), *adj.* lacking normal color; wan; pale: *a pallid complexion.* [< Latin *pallidum.*]

pan o ram a (pan′ə ram′ə), *n.* 1 a wide, unbroken view of a surrounding region. 2 a complete survey of some subject: *a panorama of history.* 3 a continuously passing or changing scene: *the panorama of city life.* [< *pan-* + Greek *horama* view < *horan* to see]

par a pher nal ia (par′ə fər nā′lyə), *n., pl. or sing.* 1 personal belongings. 2 equipment; outfit. [< Medieval Latin < Greek *parapherna* a woman's personal property besides her dowry < *para-*[1] + *phernē* dowry]

par a site (par′ə sīt), *n.* 1 animal or plant that lives on or in another from which it gets its food, always at the expense of the host, which is often injured by the relationship. 2 person who lives on others without making any useful and fitting return; hanger-on. [< Greek *parasitos* feeding beside < *para-*[1] + *sitos* food]

parch ment (pärch′mənt), *n.* 1 the skin of sheep, goats, etc., prepared for use as a writing material. 2 manuscript or document written on parchment. [< Old French *parchemin,* alteration of Greek *pergamēnē* of Pergamum, where it came from]

par ish (par′ish), *n.* 1 district that has its own church and clergyman. 2 people of a parish. 3 members of the congregation of a particular church. [< Old French *paroisse* < Late Latin *parochia* < Late Greek *paroikia,* ultimately < *para-*[1] + *oikos* dwelling]

par ley (pär′lē), *n., pl.* **-leys.** 1 conference or informal talk. 2 an informal discussion with an enemy during a truce about terms of surrender, exchange of prisoners, etc. [< Old French *parlee,* past participle of *parler* speak < Late Latin *parabolare* < *parabola* speech, story]

par ry (par′ē), *v.,* **-ried, -ry ing,** *n., pl.* **-ries.** —*v.t.* 1 ward off or block (a thrust, stroke, weapon, etc.) in fencing, boxing, etc. 2 meet and turn aside (an awkward question, a threat, etc.); avoid; evade. —*n.* act of parrying; avoiding. [< French *parez,* imperative of *parer* ward off < Italian *parare* < Latin, prepare]

paunch (pônch, pänch), *n.* 1 belly; stomach. 2 a large, protruding belly; potbelly. [< Old French *panche* < Latin *pantex*]

pence (pens), *n.* a pl. of **penny.**

pen chant (pen′chənt), *n.* a strong taste or liking; inclination: *a penchant for taking long walks.* [< French, present participle of *pencher* to incline]

pen sive (pen′siv), *adj.* 1 thoughtful in a serious or sad way. 2 melancholy. [< Old French *pensif* < *penser* think < Latin *pensare* ponder < *pendere* weigh] **—pen′sive ly,** *adv.* **—pen′sive ness,** *n.*

pe remp tor y (pə remp′tər ē, per′əmp tôr′ē, per′əmp tōr′ē), *adj.* 1 leaving no choice; decisive; final; absolute: *a peremptory decree.* 2 imperious; dictatorial: *a peremptory teacher.* [< Latin *peremptorius* that puts an end to, ultimately < *per-* to the end + *emere* to take] **—pe remp′tor i ly,** *adv.*

per func tor y (pər fungk′tər ē), *adj.* done merely for the sake of getting rid of the duty; done from force of habit; mechanical; indifferent: *I gave my room a perfunctory cleaning.* [< Late Latin *perfunctorius* < Latin *per-* through + *fungi* execute] **—per func′tor i ly,** *adv.*

per il ous (per′ə ləs), *adj.* full of peril; dangerous. **—per′il ous ly,** *adv.* **—per′il ous ness,** *n.*

per i wig (per′ə wig), *n.* wig or peruke. [earlier *perewyke* < French *perruque.*]

per me ate (pėr′mē āt), *v.t.,* **-at ed, -at ing.** 1 spread through the whole of; pass through; pervade: *Smoke permeated the house.* 2 penetrate through pores or openings; soak through. [< Latin *permeatum* passed through < *per-* through + *meare* to pass]

per ron (per′ən; *French* pe rôn′), *n.* an outside platform upon which the entrance door to a building opens. It generally has steps leading up to it.

per se vere (pėr′ sə vir′), *v.i.,* **-vered, -ver ing.** continue steadily in doing something hard; persist. [< Latin *perseverare* < *per-* thoroughly + *severus* strict]

per son age (pėr′sə nij), *n.* 1 person of high rank, distinction, or importance. 2 person. 3 character in a book or play.

per vade (pər vād′), *v.t.,* **-vad ed, -vad ing.** go or spread throughout; be throughout: *The odor of pines pervades the air.* [< Latin *pervadere* < *per-* through + *vadere* go] **—per vad′er,** *n.*

pes ti len tial (pes′tl en′shəl), *adj.* 1 like a pestilence, or rapidly spreading epidemic disease; having to do with pestilences. 2 causing or likely to cause pestilence. **—pes′ti len′tial ly,** *adv.*

phan tasm (fan′taz′əm), *n.* 1 thing seen only in one's imagination; unreal fancy: *the phantasms of a dream.* 2 a supposed appearance of an absent person, living or dead. 3 a deceiving likeness (of something). [< Greek *phantasma* image, ultimately < *phainein* to show]

phan tas ma (fan taz′mə), *n., pl.* **-ma ta.** phantasm (defs. 1, 2).

pho bi a (fō′bē ə), *n.* a persistent, abnormal, or irrational fear of a certain thing or group of things. [< Greek *-phobia* < *phobos* fear] **—pho bic** (fō′bik), *adj.*

phos phate (fos′fāt), *n.* drink of carbonated water flavored with fruit syrup, and containing a little phosphoric acid.

pig iron, crude iron as it first comes from the blast furnace or smelter, used to make steel, cast iron, and wrought iron.

pil grim age (pil′grə mij), *n.* 1 a pilgrim's journey; journey to some sacred place as an act of religious devotion. 2 a long journey.

pil lage (pil′ij), *v.,* **-laged, -lag ing,** *n.* —*v.t.* rob with violence; plunder: *Pirates pillaged the towns along the coast.* —*v.i.* take booty; plunder. —*n.* act of plundering or taking as spoil; plunder, especially as practiced in war. [< Old French < *piller* to plunder]

pince-nez (pans′nā′, pins′nā′), *n., pl.* **pince-nez** (pans′nāz′, pins′nāz′). eyeglasses kept in place by a spring that clips onto the bridge of the nose. [< French, pinch-nose < *pincer* to pinch + *nez* nose < Latin *nasus*]

pince-nez

pin ion (pin′yən), *v.t.* bind the arms of; bind (to something); bind: *pinion a person's arms.* [< Middle French *pignon* < Popular Latin *pinnionem* < Latin *penna* feather and *pinna* wing]

pin na cle (pin′ə kəl), *n.* 1 a high peak or point of rock, ice, etc. 2 the highest point: *at the pinnacle of one's fame.* [< Old French *pinacle* < Latin *pinnaculum,* diminutive of *pinna* wing, point]

pi ous (pī′əs), *adj.* 1 having or showing reverence for God; righteous. 2 done under pretense of religion or of serving a good cause: *a pious fraud.* 3 sacred rather than secular. [< Latin *pius*] **—pi′ous ly,** *adv.* **—pi′ous ness,** *n.*

plac id (plas′id), *adj.* pleasantly calm or peaceful; quiet: *a placid lake, a placid temper.* [< Latin *placidus* < *placere* to please] **—plac′id ly,** *adv.*

plain tive (plān′tiv), *adj.* expressive of sorrow; mournful; sad. [< Old French *plaintif* < *plaint* plaint] **—plain′tive ly,** *adv.*

plau si ble (plô′zə bəl), *adj.* 1 appearing true, reasonable, or fair. 2 apparently worthy of confidence but often not really so: *a plausible liar.* [< Latin *plausibilis* deserving applause, pleasing < *plaudere* applaud] **—plau′si bil′i ty,** *n.* **—plau′si bly,** *adv.*

plumb (plum), *n.* a small weight hung on the end of a line, used to find the depth of water or to see if a wall is vertical. [< Latin *plumbum* lead]

plum met (plum′it), *n.* plumb. —*v.i.* plunge; drop. [< Old French *plommet* < *plomb* lead < Latin *plumbum*]

plu to crat ic (plü′tə krat′ik), *adj.* having power and influence because of wealth. **—plu′to crat′i cal ly,** *adv.*

poign ant (poi′nyənt), *adj.* 1 very painful; piercing: *poignant suffering.* 2 stimulating to the mind, feelings, or passions; keen; intense: *a subject of poignant interest.* [< Old French, present participle of *poindre* to prick < Latin *pungere*] **—poign′ant ly,** *adv.*

pon der ous (pon′dər əs), *adj.* 1 very heavy. 2 heavy and clumsy: *A hippopotamus is ponderous.* 3 dull; tiresome: *The speaker talked in a ponderous way.* **—pon′der ous ly,** *adv.*

por tent (pôr′tent, pōr′tent), *n.* 1 a warning of coming evil; sign; omen. 2 ominous significance. [< Latin *portentum* indicated beforehand]

por ten tous (pôr ten′təs, pōr ten′təs), *adj.* 1 indicating evil to come; ominous; threatening. 2 amazing; extraordinary. **—por ten′tous ly,** *adv.* **—por ten′tous ness,** *n.*

post chaise, a four-wheeled carriage used for carrying passengers and mail in the 1700s and early 1800s, usually having seats for two or four people.

poul tice (pōl′tis), *n.* a soft, moist mass of mustard, herbs, etc., applied to the body as a medicine. [< Latin *pultes,* plural of *puls* mush]

POW, prisoner of war.

pram (pram), *n.* BRITISH INFORMAL. baby carriage; perambulator.

prat tle (prat′l), *v.,* **-tled, -tling,** *n.* —*v.i.* 1 talk or tell freely and carelessly, as some children do. 2 talk or tell in a foolish way. —*n.* 1 childish or foolish talk. 2 babble. [< *prate*] **—prat′tler,** *n.*

pre am ble (prē′am′bəl), *n.* 1 a preliminary statement; introduction to a speech or a writing. 2 a preliminary or introductory fact or circumstance, especially one showing what is to follow.

a hat	**i** it	**oi** oil	**ch** child	ə = a in about
ā age	**ī** ice	**ou** out	**ng** long	e in taken
ä far	**o** hot	**u** cup	**sh** she	i in pencil
e let	**ō** open	**u̇** put	**th** thin	o in lemon
ē equal	**ô** order	**ü** rule	**ᴛʜ** then	u in circus
ėr term			**zh** measure	< = derived from

[< Medieval Latin *praeambulum* < Late Latin, walking before < Latin *prae-* pre- + *ambulare* to walk]

pre car i ous (pri ker′ē əs, pri kar′ē əs), *adj.* not safe or secure; uncertain; dangerous; risky: *Soldiers on the battlefield lead a precarious life.* [< Latin *precarius* obtainable by prayer, uncertain < *precem* prayer] **—pre car′i ous ly,** *adv.*

prec i pice (pres′ə pis), *n.* a very steep or almost vertical face of rock; cliff or steep mountainside. [< Latin *praecipitium* < *praecipitem* steep, literally, headlong < *prae-* pre- + *caput* head]

pre cip i tous (pri sip′ə təs), *adj.* **1** like a precipice; very steep: *precipitous cliffs.* **2** hasty; rash. **3** rushing headlong; very rapid. **—pre cip′i tous ly,** *adv.*

pre em i nent or **pre-em i nent** (prē em′ə nənt), *adj.* standing out above all others; superior to others. **—pre em′i nent ly, pre-em′i nent ly,** *adv.*

pre fab (prē′fab′), INFORMAL. *n.* something prefabricated, especially a house. *—adj.* prefabricated: *a prefab house.*

preg nant (preg′nənt), *adj.* **1** having an embryo or embryos developing in the uterus; being with child or young. **2** filled; full: *words pregnant with meaning.* **3** abounding with ideas; fertile; inventive: *a pregnant mind.* [< Latin *praegnantem* < *prae-* pre- + *gen-* to bear]

pre med i tate (prē med′ə tāt), *v.t.,* **-tat ed, -tat ing.** consider or plan beforehand: *The murder was premeditated.*

pre mon i to ry (pri mon′ə tôr′ē, pri mon′ə tōr′ē), *adj.* giving warning beforehand.

pre oc cu pied (prē ok′yə pīd), *adj.* absorbed; engrossed.

pre rog a tive (pri rog′ə tiv), *n.* right or privilege that nobody else has: *The government has the prerogative of coining money.* [< Latin *praerogativa* allotted to vote first < *praerogare* ask for a vote first < *prae-* pre- + *rogare* ask]

pres age (pres′ij; pri sāj′), *v.t.,* **pre saged, pre sag ing. 1** give warning of; predict: *Some people think that a circle around the moon presages a storm.* **2** have or give a presentiment or prophetic impression of. [< Latin *praesagium* < *prae-* pre- + *sagus* prophetic]

pre sump tu ous (pri zump′chü əs), *adj.* acting without permission or right; too bold; forward. **—pre sump′tu ous ly,** *adv.*

pri or i ty (prī ôr′ə tē, prī or′ə tē), *n., pl.* **-ties. 1** a being earlier in time. **2** a coming before in order or importance: *Fire engines and ambulances have priority over other traffic.*

pri va tion (prī vā′shən), *n.* **1** lack of the comforts or of the necessities of life: *Many children were hungry and homeless because of privation during the war.* **2** a being deprived; loss; absence. [< Latin *privationem* < *privatum* deprived]

pro cure (prə kyůr′), *v.t.,* **-cured, -cur ing.** obtain by care or effort; secure: *procure a job.* [< Latin *procurare* manage < *pro-* before + *cura* care]

pro di gious (prə dij′əs), *adj.* **1** very great; huge; vast: *The ocean contains a prodigious amount of water.* **2** wonderful; marvelous. [< Latin *prodigiosus* < *prodigium* prodigy, omen] **—pro di′gious ly,** *adv.* **—pro di′gious ness,** *n.*

prof fer (prof′ər), *v.t.* offer for acceptance; present; tender: *We proffered regrets at having to leave so early.* [< Anglo-French *proffrir* < Old French *pro-* forth + *offrir* to offer]

pro fu sion (prə fyü′zhən), *n.* **1** great abundance. **2** extravagance; lavishness.

pro le tar i an (prō′lə ter′ē ən, prō′lə tar′ē ən), *adj.* of or belonging to the proletariat, or working class. *—n.* person belonging to the proletariat. [< Latin *proletarius* furnishing the state only with children < *proles* offspring < *pro-* forth + *alescere* grow]

prom e nade (prom′ə nād′, prom′ə näd′), *n., v.,* **-nad ed, -nad ing.** *—n.* walk for pleasure or display: *a promenade in the park.* *—v.i.* walk about or up and down for pleasure or for display: *promenade on a ship's deck.* [< French < *promener* take for a walk < Latin *prominare* drive on < *pro-* forward + *minare* to drive]

prom on to ry (prom′ən tôr′ē, prom′ən tōr′ē), *n., pl.* **-ries.** a high point of land extending from the coast into the water; headland. [< Latin *promonturium,* probably < *pro-* forward + *montem* mountain]

pro pi tious (prə pish′əs), *adj.* **1** holding well; favorable: *propitious weather for our trip.* **2** favorably inclined; gracious. [< Latin *propitius,* originally, falling forward < *pro-* forward + *petere* go toward] **—pro pi′tious ly,** *adv.* **—pro pi′tious ness,** *n.*

pro sa ic (prō zā′ik), *adj.* like prose; matter-of-fact; ordinary; not exciting. **—pro sa′i cal ly,** *adv.* **—pro sa′ic ness,** *n.*

pro sce ni um (prō sē′nē əm), *n., pl.* **-ni a** (-nē ə). **1** the part of the stage in front of the curtain. **2** curtain and the framework that holds it. [< Latin < Greek *proskēnion* < *pro-* in front of + *skēnē* stage, scene]

pro scrip tion (prō skrip′shən), *n.* a proscribing or a being proscribed; banishment; outlawry.

pros e cu tion (pros′ə kyü′shən), *n.* **1** the carrying on of a lawsuit: *The prosecution will be abandoned if the stolen money is returned.* **2** side that starts action against another in a court of law.

pro spec tive (prə spek′tiv), *adj.* **1** that is looked forward to as likely or promised; probable; expected: *a prospective client.* **2** looking forward in time; future: *a prospective mother.*

pros trate (pros′trāt), *adj.* **1** lying flat with face downward: *She was humbly prostrate in prayer.* **2** lying flat: *I stumbled and fell prostrate on the floor.* [< Latin *prostratum* thrown down flat < *pro-* forth + *sternere* spread out]

prov o ca tion (prov′ə kā′shən), *n.* **1** act of provoking. **2** something that stirs up or provokes: *Their insulting remarks were a provocation.*

prox im i ty (prok sim′ə tē), *n.* nearness; closeness.

pru dent (prüd′nt), *adj.* **1** planning carefully ahead of time; sensible; discreet: *A prudent man saves part of his wages.* **2** characterized by good judgment or good management: *a prudent policy.* [< Latin *prudentem,* contraction of *providentem* provident] **—pru′dent ly,** *adv.*

pu is sant (pyü′ə sənt, pyü is′nt, pwis′nt), *adj.* having great power or strength; powerful; mighty. [< Old French < Popular Latin *possentem* < Latin *potentem* potent] **—pu′is sant ly,** *adv.*

pun gent (pun′jənt), *adj.* **1** sharply affecting the organs of taste and smell: *a pungent pickle, the pungent smell of burning leaves.* **2** sharp; biting: *pungent criticism.* **3** stimulating to the mind; keen; lively: *a pungent wit.* [< Latin *pungentem* piercing, pricking < *pungere* pierce, prick]

purl (pėrl), *v.i.* **1** flow with rippling motions and a murmuring sound: *A shallow brook purls.* **2** pass with a sound like this. [perhaps < Scandinavian (Norwegian) *purla* to ripple]

pur su ant (pər sü′ənt), *adj.* **1** following; carrying out; according. **2 pursuant to,** following; acting according to; in accordance with.

quad ran gle (kwod′rang′gəl), *n.* a four-sided space or court wholly or nearly surrounded by buildings: *the quadrangle of a palace, a college quadrangle.* [< Late Latin *quadrangulum* < Latin *quadr-* four + *angulus* angle]

quad ru ped (kwod′rə ped), *n.* something that has four feet. *—adj.* four-footed. [< Latin *quadrupedem* < *quadru-* four + *pedem* foot]

quay (kē), *n.* a solid landing place where ships load and unload, often built of stone. Also, FRENCH **quai.** [< Old French *cai;* of Celtic origin]

quell (kwel), *v.t.* **1** put down (disorder, rebellion, etc.): *quell a riot.* **2** put an end to; overcome: *quell one's fears.* [Old English *cwellan* to kill] **—quell′a ble,** *adj.* **—quell′er,** *n.*

queue (kyü), *n., v.,* **queued, queu ing** or **queue ing.** *—n.* **1** braid of hair hanging down from the back of the head. **2** a line of people, automobiles, etc.: *There was a long queue in front of the theater.* *—v.i.* **1** form or stand in a long line. **2 queue up,** line up. Also, **cue.** [< French < Latin *coda, cauda* tail]

quo rum (kwôr′əm, kwōr′əm), *n.* number of members of any society or assembly that must be present if the business done is to be legal or binding. [< Latin, of whom]

rab ble (rab′əl), *n.* **1** a disorderly, boisterous crowd; mob. **2 the rabble,** (in contemptuous use) the lower classes. [Middle English *rabel*]

rab ble ment (rab′əl mənt), *n.* rabble.
rag a muf fin (rag′ə muf′ən), *n.* a dirty, ragged person, especially a child. [probably < *rag*]
ram part (ram′part), *n.* 1 a wide bank of earth, often with a wall on top as a fortification, built around a fort to help defend it. 2 anything that defends; defense; protection. [< Middle French *rempart* < *remparer* fortify]
ran cid (ran′sid), *adj.* 1 stale; spoiled: *rancid butter.* 2 tasting or smelling like stale fat or butter: *rancid odor.* [< Latin *rancidus* < *rancere* be rank] **—ran′cid ly,** *adv.* **—ran′cid ness,** *n.*
ran cor ous (rang′kər əs), *adj.* bitterly malicious; spiteful. **—ran′cor ous ly,** *adv.* **—ran′cor ous ness,** *n.*
ra pa cious (rə pā′shəs), *adj.* 1 seizing by force; plundering. 2 grasping; greedy. 3 living by the capture of prey; predatory. [< Latin *rapacem* grasping < *rapere* seize] **—ra pa′cious ly,** *adv.* **—ra pa′cious ness,** *n.*
ra pi er (rā′pē ər), *n.* a long and light sword used for thrusting. [< Middle French *rapière*] **—ra′pi er like′,** *adj.*
rap port (ra pôr′, ra pōr′; ra pôrt′, ra pōrt′; *French* (rå pôr′), *n.* 1 relation; connection. 2 agreement; harmony. [< French]
rapt (rapt), *adj.* 1 lost in delight. 2 so busy thinking of or enjoying one thing that one does not know what else is happening. [< Latin *raptum* seized] **—rapt′ly,** *adv.* **—rapt′ness,** *n.*
rash (rash), *adj.* 1 too hasty and careless; impetuous. 2 characterized by undue haste: *a rash promise.* [Middle English *rasch* quick] **—rash′ly,** *adv.* **—rash′ness,** *n.*
ra tion al ize (rash′ə nə līz), *v.,* **-ized, -iz ing.** *—v.t.* 1 make rational or conformable to reason. 2 treat or explain in a rational manner. 3 find (often unconsciously) an explanation or excuse for: *I rationalized eating two desserts by thinking "I must eat enough to keep up my strength."* *—v.i.* find excuses for one's desires.
rea son a ble (rē′zn ə bəl), *adj.* 1 according to reason; sensible; not foolish. 2 not asking too much; fair; just. 3 able to reason. **—rea′son a ble ness,** *n.* **—rea′son a bly,** *adv.*
re buke (ri byük′), *v.,* **-buked, -buk ing,** *n.* *—v.t.* express disapproval of; reprove. *—n.* expression of disapproval; scolding. [< Anglo-French *rebuker* < Old French *rebuchier* < *re-* back + *buchier* to strike]
re cip ro cal (ri sip′rə kəl), *adj.* 1 in return: *Although she gave me a present, she expected no reciprocal gift from me.* 2 mutual: *reciprocal distrust.* [< Latin *reciprocus* returning] **—re cip′ro cal ly,** *adv.*
re coil (ri koil′), *v.i.* 1 draw back; shrink back: *Most people would recoil at seeing a snake in the path.* 2 spring back: *The gun recoiled after I fired.* [< Old French *reculer,* ultimately < Latin *re-* back + *culus* rump]
rec om pense (rek′əm pens), *v.,* **-pensed, -pens ing,** *n.* *—v.t.* 1 pay (a person); pay back; reward. 2 make a fair return for (an action, anything lost, damage done, or hurt received), *—n.* 1 payment; reward. 2 return; amends. [< Late Latin *recompensare* < Latin *re-* back + *compensare* compensate]
rec on cile (rek′ən sīl), *v.t.,* **-ciled, -cil ing.** 1 make friends again. 2 settle (a disagreement or difference). 3 make agree; bring into harmony: *I could not reconcile that story with the facts.* [< Latin *reconciliare* < *re-* back + *concilium* bond of union]
rec on cil i a tion (rek′ən sil′ē ā′shən), *n.* 1 a reconciling; bringing together again in friendship. 2 a being reconciled; settlement or adjustment of disagreements or differences.
re cu pe rate (ri kyü′pə rāt′, ri kü′pə rāt′), *v.,* **-rat ed, -rat ing.** *—v.i.* recover from sickness, exhaustion, loss, etc. *—v.t.* 1 restore to health, strength, etc. 2 get back; regain. [< Latin *recuperatum* recovered] **—re cu′pe ra′tion,** *n.*
red o lent (red′l ənt), *adj.* having a pleasant smell; fragrant; aromatic. [< Latin *redolentem* emitting scent < *re-, red-* back + *olere* to smell] **—red′o lent ly,** *adv.*
re dress (*v.* ri dres′; *n.* rē′dres, ri dres′), *v.t.* set right; repair; remedy. *—n.* 1 a setting right; reparation; relief: *Anyone who has been injured deserves redress.* 2 the means of a remedy. [< Middle French *redresser* < *re-* again + *dresser* straighten, arrange]
re fute (ri fyüt′), *v.t.,* **-fut ed, -fut ing.** show (a claim, opinion, or argument) to be false or incorrect; prove wrong; disprove. [< Latin *refutare* cause to fall back] **—re fut′er,** *n.*
re it e rate (rē it′ə rāt′), *v.t.,* **-rat ed, -rat ing.** say or do several times; repeat (an action, demand, etc.) again and again: *reiterate a command.* **—re it′e ra′tion,** *n.*
re ju ve nate (ri jü′və nāt), *v.t.,* **-nat ed, -nat ing.** make young or vigorous again; give youthful qualities to. [< *re-* + Latin *juvenis* young] **—re ju′ve na′tion,** *n.* **—re ju′ve na′tor,** *n.*
rel ish (rel′ish), *n.* 1 a pleasant taste; good flavor: *Hunger gives relish to simple food.* 2 something to add flavor to food, such as olives, pickles, or a highly seasoned sauce. 3 a slight dash (of something). 4 keen enjoyment or appetite; zest: *eat with great relish.* [earlier *reles* < Old French, remainder < *relesser, relaissier* release.]
re mon strate (ri mon′strāt), *v.i.,* **-strat ed, -strat ing.** speak, reason, or plead in complaint or protest: *The teacher remonstrated with us about our unruly behavior.* [< Medieval Latin *remonstratum* pointed out, ultimately < Latin *re-* back + *monstrum* sign] **—re mon stra tion** (rē′mən strā′shən), *n.*
ren dez vous (rän′də vü), *n., pl.* **-vous** (-vüz). 1 an appointment or engagement to meet at a fixed place or time; meeting by agreement. 2 a meeting place; gathering place: *The family had two favorite rendezvous, the library and the garden.* [< Middle French < *rendez-vous* present yourself!]
rent (rent), *n.* a torn place; tear; split. *—adj.* torn; split. *—v.* pt. and pp. of **rend.**
rep a ra tion (rep′ə rā′shən), *n.* 1 a giving of satisfaction or compensation for wrong or injury done. 2 **reparations,** *pl.* compensation for wrong or injury, especially payments made by a defeated country for the devastation of territory during war.
re past (ri past′), *n.* meal; food. [< Old French, ultimately < Latin *re-* again + *pascere* to feed]
re pute (ri pyüt′), *n., v.,* **-put ed, -put ing.** *—n.* 1 reputation: *a generous man by repute.* 2 good reputation. *—v.t.* suppose to be; consider; suppose: *They are reputed to be quite rich.* [< Latin *reputare* consider < *re-* over + *putare* think]
res ig na tion (rez′ig nā′shən), *n.* 1 act of resigning. 2 patient acceptance; quiet submission.
res o lute (rez′ə lüt), *adj.* 1 having a fixed resolve; determined; firm. 2 constant in pursuing a purpose; bold. [< Latin *resolutum* resolved] **—res′o lute′ly,** *adv.* **—res′o lute′ness,** *n.*
re spec tive (ri spek′tiv), *adj.* belonging to each; particular; individual: *The classes went to their respective rooms.*
res pite (res′pit), *n.* 1 time of relief and rest; lull: *a respite from the heat.* 2 a putting off; delay, especially in carrying out a sentence of death; reprieve. [< Old French *respit* < Late Latin *respectus* expectation < Latin, regard]
re splend ent (ri splen′dənt), *adj.* very bright; shining; splendid: *the resplendent sun, a face resplendent with joy.* [< Latin *resplendentem* < *re-* back + *splendere* to shine] **—re splend′ent ly,** *adv.*
res tive (res′tiv), *adj.* 1 restless; uneasy. 2 hard to manage. [< Old French *restif* motionless < *rester* remain.] **—res′tive ly,** *adv.*
re ten tive (ri ten′tiv), *adj.* 1 able to hold or keep. 2 able to remember easily. **—re ten′tive ly,** *adv.* **—re ten′tive ness,** *n.*
ret ri bu tion (ret′rə byü′shən), *n.* a deserved punishment; return for wrongdoing. [< Latin *retributionem,* ultimately < *re-* back + *tribuere* assign]
rev el (rev′əl), *v.,* **-eled, -el ing** or **-elled, -el ling,** *n.* *—v.i.* 1 take great pleasure *(in): The children revel in country life.* 2 make merry. *—n.* a noisy good time; merrymaking. [< Old French *reveler* be disorderly, make merry < Latin *rebellare.*] **—rev′el er, rev′el ler,** *n.*
rev el ry (rev′əl rē), *n., pl.* **-ries.** boisterous reveling or festivity.
re ver be rate (ri vėr′bə rāt′), *v.,* **-rat ed, -rat ing.** *—v.i.* 1 echo back: *His voice reverberates from the high ceiling.* 2 be cast back; be reflected a number of times, as light or heat. [< Latin *reverberatum* beaten back < *re-* back + *verber* a blow] **—re ver′be ra′tion,** *n.* **—re ver′be ra′tive,** *adj.*
rev er ie (rev′ər ē), *n.* 1 dreamy thoughts; dreamy thinking of pleasant things. 2 condition of being lost in dreamy thoughts. Also, **revery.** [< French *rêverie* < *rêver* to dream]
re vin di cate (rē vin′də kāt), *v.t.,* **-cat ed, -cat ing.** redefend successfully against opposition; uphold; justify: *The heir revindicated his claim to the fortune.*
re vul sion (ri vul′shən), *n.* a sudden, violent change or reaction, especially of disgust. [< Latin *revulsionem* < *re-* back + *vellere* tear away]
rife (rīf), *adj.* 1 happening often; common; numerous; widespread. 2 full; abounding: *The city was rife with rumors of political corruption.* [Old English *rīfe*] **—rife′ly,** *adv.*
rit u al is tic (rich′ü ə lis′tik), *adj.* 1 having to do with ritual or ritualism. 2 fond of ritual. **—rit′u al is′ti cal ly,** *adv.*
roe buck (rō′buk′), *n., pl.* **-bucks** or **-buck.** a male roe deer.
rolling mill, 1 factory where metal is rolled into sheets and bars. 2 machine for doing this.
rote (rōt), *n.* 1 a set, mechanical way of doing things. 2 **by rote,**

by memory without thought of the meaning: *learn a lesson by rote.* [Middle English]

ru bi cund (rü′bə kund), *adj.* reddish; ruddy. [< Latin *rubicundus* < *rubere* be red] **—ru′bi cun′di ty,** *n.*

rue (rü), *v.,* **rued, ru ing,** *n.* *—v.t.* be sorry for; regret. *—n.* sorrow; regret. [Old English *hrēowan*]

rup ture (rup′chər), *n., v.,* **-tured, -tur ing.** *—n.* 1 a breaking. 2 a being broken. *—v.t.* 1 break off; burst; break. 2 affect with hernia. *—v.i.* suffer a break. [< Latin *ruptura* < *rumpere* to break]

ruse (rüz, rüs), *n.* scheme or device to mislead others; trick. [< French < *ruser* to dodge < Old French.]

sac ra ment (sak′rə mənt), *n.* 1 any of certain religious ceremonies of the Christian church, considered especially sacred, such as baptism. 2 something especially sacred. [< Latin *sacramentum,* ultimately < *sacer* holy]

sa dism (sā′diz′əm, sad′iz′əm), *n.* an unnatural love of cruelty. [< French *sadisme* < Marquis de *Sade,* 1740-1814, who wrote about it]

sa dist (sā′dist, sad′ist), *n.* person who practices or is affected by sadism.

sal low (sal′ō), *adj.* having a sickly, yellowish or brownish-yellow color: *a sallow skin, a sallow complexion.* [Old English *salo*] **—sal′low ness,** *n.*

sanc tu ar y (sangk′chü er′ē), *n., pl.* **-ar ies.** 1 a sacred place. A church is a sanctuary. 2 the part of a church around the altar. 3 place of refuge or protection: *a wildlife sanctuary.* 4 refuge or protection: *The cabin provided sanctuary from the rain.*

sa ri (sär′ē), *n.* the principal outer garment of Hindu women, a long piece of cotton or silk wrapped around the body, with one end falling nearly to the feet and the other end thrown over the head or shoulder. [< Hindi *sārī* < Sanskrit *śāṭī*]

sari

sa vant (sə vänt′, sav′ənt), *n.* person of learning; sage; scholar. [< French, present participle of *savoir* know < Latin *sapere* be wise]

scar i fy (skar′ə fī), *v.t.,* **-fied, -fy ing.** 1 make scratches or cuts in the surface of (the skin, etc.). 2 loosen (soil) without turning it over. [< Old French *scarifier* < Late Latin *scarificare* < Latin *scarifare* < Greek *skariphasthai* to scratch < *skariphos* stylus]

scav en ger (skav′ən jər), *n.* 1 organism that feeds on decaying organic matter. Vultures are scavengers. 2 person who scavenges. [alteration of *scavager,* literally, inspector, ultimately < Old French *escauwer* inspect < Flemish *scauwen*]

scourge (skėrj), *n., v.,* **scourged, scourg ing.** *—n.* 1 a whip; lash. 2 some thing or person that causes great trouble or misfortune. *—v.t.* 1 whip; flog; punish severely. 2 trouble very much; afflict; torment. [< Old French *escorge,* ultimately < Latin *ex-* out + *corium* a hide]

scow (skou), *n.* a large, rectangular, flat-bottomed boat used to carry freight, especially in bulk, as coal, sand, etc. [< Dutch *schouw*]

scru ti nize (skrüt′n īz), *v.t.,* **-nized, -niz ing.** examine closely; inspect carefully: *The jeweler scrutinized the diamond for flaws.* **—scru′ti niz′er,** *n.* **—scru′ti niz′ing ly,** *adv.*

scud (skud), *v.,* **scud ded, scud ding,** *n.* *—v.i.* 1 run or move swiftly: *Clouds scudded across the sky driven by the high wind.* 2 (of a boat, etc.) run before a storm with little or no sail set. *—n.* 1 a scudding. 2 clouds or spray driven by the wind. [perhaps < Scandinavian (Danish) *skyde* shoot, glide]

scul lion (skul′yən), *n.* ARCHAIC. servant who does the dirty, rough work in a kitchen. [< Old French *escouillon* swab, cloth < *escouve* broom < Latin *scopa*]

scur vy (skėr′vē), *n., adj.,* **-vi er, -vi est.** *—n.* disease caused by a lack of vitamin C in the diet, characterized by swollen and bleeding gums, extreme weakness, bruises on the skin, and prostration. *—adj.* mean; contemptible; base: *a scurvy fellow, a scurvy trick.* [< *scurf*] **—scur′vi ly,** *adv.*

scythe (sīŦH), *n., v.,* **scythed, scyth ing.** *—n.* a long, thin, slightly curved blade on a long handle, for cutting grass, etc. *—v.t.* cut or mow with a scythe. [Old English *sithe;* spelling influenced by Latin *scindere* to cut]

sec u lar (sek′yə lər), *adj.* 1 not religious or sacred; worldly:

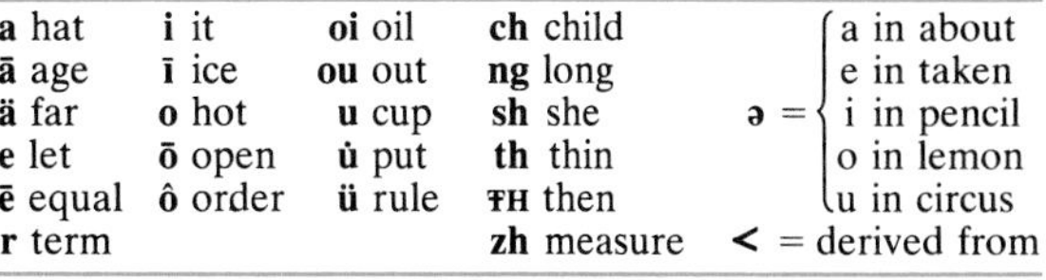

a hat	i it	oi oil	ch child	ə = a in about
ā age	ī ice	ou out	ng long	e in taken
ä far	o hot	u cup	sh she	i in pencil
e let	ō open	ů put	th thin	o in lemon
ē equal	ô order	ü rule	ŦH then	u in circus
ėr term			zh measure	< = derived from

secular music, a secular education. 2 living in the world; not belonging to a religious order: *the secular clergy, a secular priest.* *—n.* 1 a secular priest. 2 layperson. [< Latin *saecularis* < *saeculum* age, world] **—sec′u lar ly,** *adv.*

sedge (sej), *n.* any of a large family of monocotyledonous herbs growing chiefly in wet places, resembling grasses. [Old English *secg*]

sem blance (sem′bləns), *n.* 1 outward appearance: *Their story had the semblance of truth, but was really false.* 2 likeness: *These clouds have the semblance of a huge head.* [< Old French < *sembler* seem < Latin *similare* make similar < *similis* similar]

se nile (sē′nīl, sē′nl), *adj.* 1 of old age. 2 showing the mental and physical deterioration often characteristic of old age. 3 caused by old age. [< Latin *senilis* < *senex* old] **—se′nile ly,** *adv.*

sen ti nel (sen′tə nəl), *n.* person stationed to keep watch and guard against surprise attacks. [< Middle French *sentinelle* < Italian *sentinella* < Late Latin *sentinare* avoid danger wisely < Latin *sentire* to feel]

ser pen tine (*adj.* sėr′pən tēn′, sėr′pən tīn′; *n.* sėr′pən tēn′), *adj.* 1 of or like a serpent. 2 winding; twisting: *the serpentine course of a creek.* 3 cunning; sly; treacherous: *a serpentine plot.* *—n.* anything twisted or winding like a snake.

ser ried (ser′ēd), *adj.* crowded closely together. [< French *serré,* past participle of *serrer* press close]

ser vile (sėr′vəl), *adj.* 1 like that of slaves; mean; base: *servile flattery.* 2 of or having to do with slaves: *a servile revolt, servile work.* 3 fit for a slave. 4 yielding through fear, lack of spirit, etc.: *An honest judge cannot be servile to public opinion.* [< Latin *servilis* < *servus* slave] **—ser′vile ly,** *adv.* **—ser′vile ness,** *n.*

sex ton (sek′stən), *n.* person who takes care of a church building. [< Old French *secrestein* < Medieval Latin *sacristanus* sacristan.]

si es ta (sē es′tə), *n.* a nap or rest taken at noon or in the afternoon. [< Spanish < Latin *sexta (hora)* sixth (hour) of the Roman day, noon.]

sim u late (sim′yə lāt), *v.t.,* **-lat ed, -lat ing.** 1 put on a false appearance of; pretend; feign: *simulate interest.* 2 act like; look like; imitate: *Certain insects simulate flowers or leaves.* [< Latin *simulatum* simulated < *similis* like] **—sim′u la′tor,** *n.*

si mul ta ne ous (sī′məl tā′nē əs, sim′əl tā′nē əs), *adj.* existing, done, or happening at the same time: *The two simultaneous shots sounded like one.* [< Medieval Latin *simultaneus* simulated < Latin *similis* like; confused in sense with Latin *simul* at the same time] **—si′mul ta′ne ous ly,** *adv.* **—si′mul ta′ne ous ness,** *n.*

sire (sīr), *n., v.,* **sired, sir ing.** *—n.* 1 a male ancestor. 2 male parent; father: *Lightning was the sire of the racehorse Danger.* 3 title of respect used formerly to a great noble and now to a king. *—v.t.* be the father of. [< Old French < Latin *senior* older]

sir rah (sir′ə), *n.* ARCHAIC. fellow, used to address men and boys when speaking contemptuously, angrily, impatiently, etc. [apparently < *sir* + *ha*]

skep ti cal (skep′tə kəl), *adj.* 1 of or like a skeptic; inclined to doubt; not believing easily. 2 questioning the truth of theories or apparent facts. Also, **sceptical.** **—skep′ti cal ly,** *adv.*

skirl (skėrl), *v.t., v.i.* (of bagpipes) sound loudly and shrilly. *—n.* sound of a bagpipe. [< Scandinavian (dialectal Norwegian) *skrylla*]

slake (slāk), *v.,* **slaked, slak ing.** *—v.t.* 1 satisfy (thirst, revenge, wrath, etc.). 2 cause to be less active, vigorous, intense, etc. 3 put out (a fire). *—v.i.* become less active, vigorous, intense, etc. [Old English *slacian* slacken < *slæc* slack]

slat tern (slat′ərn), *n.* woman or girl who is dirty, careless, or untidy in her dress, her housekeeping, etc. [origin uncertain]

slouch hat, a soft hat, usually with a broad brim that bends down easily.

smelt er (smel′tər), *n.* 1 person whose work or business is smelting ores or metals. 2 furnace for smelting ores.

sniv el (sniv′əl), *v.,* **-eled, -el ing** or **-elled, -el ling,** *n.* *—v.i.* 1 cry with sniffling; whimper. 2 put on a show of grief; whine. 3 run at the nose; sniffle. *—n.* 1 pretended grief or crying; whining. 2 sniffling. [Middle English *snivelen,* related to Old English *snofl* mucus] **—sniv′el er, sniv′el ler,** *n.*

so lic i tous (sə lis′ə təs), *adj.* 1 showing care or concern; anxious; concerned: *Parents are solicitous for their children's progress in school.* 2 desirous; eager: *solicitous to please.* [< Latin *sollicitus* < *sollus* all + *ciere* arouse] **—so lic′i tous ly,** *adv.*

sol stice (sol′stis), *n.* either of the two times in the year when the sun is at its greatest distance from the celestial equator and appears to be farthest north or south in the heavens. [< Old French < Latin *solstitium* < *sol* sun + *sistere* stand still]

som nam bu list (som nam′byə list), *n.* sleepwalker.

sor rel (sôr′əl, sor′əl), *adj.* reddish-brown. —*n.* 1 a reddish brown. 2 horse having this color. [< Old French *sorel* < *sor* yellowish-brown]

sov er eign (sov′rən), *n.* 1 supreme ruler; king or queen; monarch. 2 person, group, or nation having supreme control or dominion; master: *sovereign of the seas.* —*adj.* 1 having supreme rank, power, or authority. 2 above all others; supreme; greatest: *Character is of sovereign importance.* 3 very excellent or powerful. [< Old French *soverain,* ultimately < Latin *super* over]

spe cious (spē′shəs), *adj.* 1 seeming desirable, reasonable, or probable, but not really so; apparently good, but without real merit: *The teacher saw through that specious excuse.* 2 making a good outward appearance in order to deceive: *a specious friendship, a specious flatterer.* [< Latin *speciosus* < *species* appearance, sort] **—spe′cious ly,** *adv.* **—spe′cious ness,** *n.*

spew (spyü), *v.t., v.i.* throw out; cast forth; vomit. Also, **spue.** [Old English *spīwan*] **—spew′er,** *n.*

spleen (splēn), *n.* 1 a ductless, glandlike organ at the left of the stomach in human beings that helps filter foreign substances from the blood. 2 bad temper; spite; anger. [< Greek *splēn*]

spo rad ic (spə rad′ik), *adj.* 1 appearing or happening at intervals in time; occasional: *sporadic outbreaks.* 2 being or occurring apart from others; isolated. 3 occurring in scattered instances; not epidemic: *sporadic cases of scarlet fever.* [< Medieval Latin *sporadicus* < Greek *sporadikos* scattered, ultimately < *spora* a sowing] **—spo rad′i cal ly,** *adv.*

squall (skwôl), *n.* 1 a sudden, violent gust of wind, often with rain, snow, or sleet. 2 INFORMAL. disturbance or commotion; trouble. —*v.i.* undergo or give rise to a squall. [apparently related to Swedish *skval* sudden rush of water]

stac ca to (stə kä′tō), *adj.* 1 (in music) with breaks between the successive tones; disconnected; detached. 2 abrupt: *a staccato manner.* —*adv.* in a staccato manner. [< Italian, literally, detached]

stal wart (stôl′wərt), *adj.* 1 strongly built; sturdy; robust. 2 strong and brave; valiant. 3 firm; steadfast. —*n.* 1 a stalwart person. 2 a loyal supporter of a political party. [Old English *stælwierthe* serviceable < *stathol* position + *wierthe* worthy] **—stal′wart ly,** *adv.* **—stal′wart ness,** *n.*

stealth (stelth), *n.* secret or sly action: *She obtained the letter by stealth, taking it while nobody was in the room.* [Middle English *stelthe.* Related to STEAL.]

stealth y (stel′thē), *adj.,* **stealth i er, stealth i est.** done in a secret manner; secret; sly: *The cat crept in a stealthy way toward the bird.* **—stealth′i ly,** *adv.* **—stealth′i ness,** *n.*

steppe (step), *n.* 1 one of the vast, treeless plains in southeastern Europe and in Asia. 2 any vast, treeless plain. [< Russian *step′*]

stol id (stol′id), *adj.* hard to arouse; not easily excited; showing no emotion; seeming dull; impassive. [< Latin *stolidus*] **—sto lid i ty** (stə lid′ə tē), *n.* **—stol′id ly,** *adv.* **—stol′id ness,** *n.*

strat a gem (strat′ə jəm), *n.* scheme or trick for deceiving an enemy; trickery. [< Greek *stratēgēma* < *stratēgein* be a general < *stratēgos* general.]

strip ling (strip′ling), *n.* boy just coming into manhood; youth.

stu pe fy (stü′pə fī, styü′pə fī), *v.t.,* **-fied, -fy ing.** 1 make stupid, dull, or senseless. 2 overwhelm with shock or amazement; astound: *They were stupefied by the calamity.* [< Latin *stupefacere* < *stupere* be amazed + *facere* to make] **—stu′pe fi′er,** *n.* **—stu′pe fy′ing ly,** *adv.*

stu por (stü′pər, styü′pər), *n.* 1 a dazed condition; loss or lessening of the power to feel: *He lay in a stupor, unable to tell what had happened to him.* 2 intellectual or moral numbness. [< Latin < *stupere* be dazed]

suave (swäv), *adj.* smoothly agreeable or polite. [< Latin *suavis* agreeable] **—suave′ly,** *adv.* **—suave′ness,** *n.*

sub lime (sə blīm′), *adj., n.* —*adj.* lofty or elevated in thought, feeling, language, etc.; noble; grand; exalted: *sublime devotion, sublime poetry.* —*n.* something that is lofty, noble, exalted, etc. [< Latin *sublimis,* originally, sloping up (to the lintel) < *sub-* up to + *liminis* threshold] **—sub lime′ly,** *adv.* **—sub lime′ness,** *n.*

sub mis sive (səb mis′iv), *adj.* yielding to the power, control, or authority of another; obedient; humble. **—sub mis′sive ly,** *adv.* **—sub mis′sive ness,** *n.*

sub se quent (sub′sə kwənt), *adj.* 1 coming after; following; later: *subsequent events.* 2 **subsequent to,** after; following; later than: *on the day subsequent to your call.* [< Latin *subsequentem* < *sub-* up to, near + *sequi* follow] **—sub′se quent ly,** *adv.*

sub ser vi ent (səb sėr′vē ənt), *adj.* 1 slavishly polite and obedient; tamely submissive; servile. 2 useful as a means to help a purpose or end; serviceable. **—sub ser′vi ent ly,** *adv.*

sub side (səb sīd′), *v.i.,* **-sid ed, -sid ing.** 1 grow less; die down; become less active; abate: *The storm finally subsided.* 2 sink to a lower level: *After the rain stopped, the floodwaters subsided.* [< Latin *subsidere* < *sub-* down + *sidere* settle]

sub tle ty (sut′l tē), *n., pl.* **-ties.** subtle—that is, delicate, faint, or discerning—quality. Also, **subtility** or **subtilty.**

suc ces sive (sək ses′iv), *adj.* coming one after another; following in order. **—suc ces′sive ly,** *adv.* **—suc ces′sive ness,** *n.*

suc cor (suk′ər), *n.* person or thing that helps or assists; help; aid. [< Old French *sucurs,* ultimately < Latin *succurrere* run to help < *sub-* up to + *currere* to run] **—suc′cor er,** *n.*

suf fuse (sə fyüz′), *v.t.,* **-fused, -fus ing.** overspread (with a liquid, dye, etc.): *eyes suffused with tears. At twilight the sky was suffused with color.* [< Latin *suffusum* poured under < *sub-* under + *fundere* to pour]

su per fi cial (sü′pər fish′əl), *adj.* 1 of the surface: *superficial measurement.* 2 on the surface; at the surface: *His burns were superficial and soon healed.* 3 concerned with or understanding only what is on the surface; not thorough; shallow: *superficial education, superficial knowledge.* [< Latin *superficialis* < *superficies* surface < *super-* above + *facies* form] **—su′per fi′cial ly,** *adv.* **—su′per fi′cial ness,** *n.*

sup ple (sup′əl), *adj.,* **-pler, -plest.** 1 bending or folding easily: *a supple birch tree, supple leather.* 2 moving easily or nimbly: *a supple dancer.* 3 readily adaptable to different ideas, circumstances, people, etc.; yielding: *a supple mind.* [< Old French *souple* < Latin *supplex* submissive < *supplicare* bend down, supplicate] **—sup′ple ly,** *adv.* **—sup′ple ness,** *n.*

sup pli ca tion (sup′lə kā′shən), *n.* 1 a supplicating, or asking humbly and earnestly. 2 Usually, **supplications,** *pl.* a humble prayer addressed to God or a deity.

sup press (sə pres′), *v.t.* 1 put an end to; stop by force; put down: *suppress a rebellion.* 2 keep in; hold back; keep from appearing: *Each nation suppressed news that was not favorable to it.* 3 subdue (a feeling, etc.): *suppressed desires.* [< Latin *suppressum* pressed down < *sub-* down + *premere* to press]

sur mount (sər mount′), *v.t.* 1 rise above: *That mountain surmounts all the peaks near it.* 2 be above or on top of: *A statue surmounts the monument.* 3 go up and across: *surmount a hill.* 4 overcome: *surmount difficulties.* [< Old French *surmonter* < *sur-* over + *monter* to mount] **—sur mount′a ble,** *adj.*

sur rep ti tious (sėr′əp tish′əs), *adj.* 1 stealthy; secret: *a surreptitious glance.* 2 secret and unauthorized; clandestine: *surreptitious meetings.* [< Latin *surrepticius* < *surripere* seize secretly < *sub-* under + *rapere* to seize] **—sur′rep ti′tious ly,** *adv.*

swain (swān), *n.* ARCHAIC. 1 lover. 2 a young man who lives in the country. [< Scandinavian (Old Icelandic) *sveinn* boy]

swarth y (swôr′ᴛʜē, swôr′thē), *adj.,* **swarth i er, swarth i est.** having a dark skin. **—swarth′i ly,** *adv.* **—swarth′i ness,** *n.*

swatch (swoch), *n.* sample of cloth or other material. [origin uncertain]

sym met ri cal (si met′rə kəl), *adj.* having symmetry; well-proportioned. **—sym met′ri cal ly,** *adv.*

sym me try (sim′ə trē), *n., pl.* **-tries.** a regular, balanced arrangement on opposite sides of a line or plane, or around a center or axis. [< Greek *symmetria* < *syn-* together + *metron* measure]

syn the size (sin′thə sīz), *v.t.,* **-sized, -siz ing.** 1 combine into a complex whole. 2 make up by combining parts or elements.

tab leau (tab′lō), *n., pl.* **-leaux** (-lōz), **-leaus.** 1 a striking scene; picture. 2 representation of a picture, statue, scene, etc., by a person or group posing in appropriate costume. [< French, diminutive of *table* table]

tac it (tas′it), *adj.* 1 implied or understood without being openly expressed; implicit: *His eating the food was a tacit confession that he liked it.* 2 unspoken; silent: *a tacit prayer.* [< Latin *tacitum* < *tacere* be silent] **—tac′it ly,** *adv.* **—tac′it ness,** *n.*

a hat	**i** it	**oi** oil	**ch** child	ə = a in about
ā age	**ī** ice	**ou** out	**ng** long	e in taken
ä far	**o** hot	**u** cup	**sh** she	i in pencil
e let	**ō** open	**ů** put	**th** thin	o in lemon
ē equal	**ô** order	**ü** rule	**ŦH** then	u in circus
ėr term			**zh** measure	**<** = derived from

tac tile (tak′təl), *adj.* 1 of or having to do with touch. 2 having the sense of touch. [< Latin *tactilis* < *tangere* to touch]

taint (tānt), *n.* a stain or spot; trace of decay, corruption, or disgrace. —*v.t.* give a taint to; spoil, corrupt, or contaminate. [< Old French *teint,* past participle of *teindre* to dye < Latin *tingere*] **—taint′less,** *adj.*

tal is man (tal′i smən, tal′iz mən), *n., pl.* **-mans.** stone, ring, etc., engraved with figures or characters supposed to have magic power; charm. [< French < Arabic *tilsam* < Greek *telesma* initiation into the mysteries < *telein* perform]

tap i o ca (tap′ē ō′kə), *n.* a starchy, granular food obtained from the root of the cassava plant, used in puddings and for thickening soups. [ultimately < Tupi *tipioca*]

taut (tôt), *adj.* tightly drawn; tense: *a taut rope.* [Middle English *tought*] **—taut′ly,** *adv.* **—taut′ness,** *n.*

tem pest (tem′pist), *n.* 1 a violent windstorm, usually accompanied by rain, hail, or snow. 2 a violent disturbance. [< Latin *tempestas* < *tempus* time, season]

te na cious (ti nā′shəs), *adj.* 1 holding fast: *the tenacious jaws of a bulldog, individuals tenacious of their rights.* 2 stubborn; persistent; obstinate: *The tenacious salesman would not take no for an answer.* 3 able to remember; retentive: *The bright child had a tenacious memory.* [< Latin *tenacem* holding fast < *tenere* to hold] **—te na′cious ly,** *adv.* **—te na′cious ness,** *n.*

ten ta tive (ten′tə tiv), *adj.* 1 done as a trial or experiment; experimental: *We made tentative plans to work together for six months.* 2 hesitating: *Her tentative laugh indicated that she hadn't understood the joke.* [< Medieval Latin *tentativus* < Latin *tentare* to try] **—ten′ta tive ly,** *adv.*

ten u ous (ten′yü əs), *adj.* 1 thin or slight; slender: *the tenuous thread of a spider's web.* 2 having slight importance; not substantial: *a tenuous claim.* [< Latin *tenuis* thin] **—ten′u ous ly,** *adv.* **—ten′u ous ness,** *n.*

ter mi nal (tėr′mə nəl), *adj.* 1 at the end; forming the end part: *a terminal appendage.* 2 coming at the end: *a terminal examination.* 3 marking a boundary, limit, or end. 4 resulting in death; fatal: *a terminal disease.* 5 INFORMAL. fatally ill: *a terminal patient.* [< Latin *terminalis* < *terminus* end] **—ter′mi nal ly,** *adv.*

tes ti mo ny (tes′tə mō′nē), *n., pl.* **-nies.** 1 statement used for evidence or proof: *A witness gave testimony that the defendant was at home all day Sunday.* 2 evidence: *The pupils presented their teacher with a watch in testimony of their respect and affection.* See synonym study below. [Old English *thanc,* originally, thought]

Syn. *n.* 1 **Evidence, testimony, proof** mean that which tends to demonstrate the truth or falsity of something. **Evidence** applies to facts that indicate, without fully proving, that something is so: *Running away was evidence of his guilt.* **Testimony** applies to any speech or action which serves as evidence of something: *Her testimony contradicted that of the preceding witness.* **Proof** means evidence so full and convincing as to leave no doubt or little doubt: *The signed receipt is proof that the letter was delivered.*

tes ty (tes′tē), *adj.,* **-ti er, -ti est.** easily irritated; impatient; petulant. [< Anglo-French *testif* headstrong < Old French *teste* head.] **—tes′ti ly,** *adv.* **—tes′ti ness,** *n.*

thews (thüz), *n.pl.* 1 muscles. 2 sinews. 3 bodily force; might; strength. [Old English *thēaw* habit]

thresh (thresh), *v.t.* 1 separate the grain or seeds from (wheat, etc.) with a flail, a machine, etc. 2 **thresh out,** settle by thorough discussion. 3 **thresh over,** go over again and again. [Old English *threscan*]

tim bre (tim′bər, tam′bər), *n.* the quality in sounds, regardless of their pitch or volume, by which a certain voice, instrument, etc., can be distinguished from other voices, instruments, etc. [< Old French, bell without a clapper, drum, ultimately < Greek *tympanon* kettledrum]

tinc ture (tingk′chər), *n., v.,* **-tured, -tur ing.** —*n.* 1 solution of medicine in alcohol: *tincture of iodine.* 2 trace; tinge. 3 color; tint. —*v.t.* 1 give a trace or tinge to. 2 color; tint. [< Latin *tinctura* < *tingere* to tinge]

toad y (tō′dē), *n., pl.* **toad ies,** *v.,* **toad ied, toad y ing.** —*n.* a fawning flatterer. —*v.i.* act like a toady. —*v.t.* fawn upon; flatter. [perhaps short for *toadeater*]

toque (tōk), *n.* hat without a brim or with a very small brim, worn by women. [< Middle French]

toque

tor por (tôr′pər), *n.* torpid condition or quality; apathy; lethargy. [< Latin < *torpere* be numb]

tor rent (tôr′ənt, tor′ənt), *n.* 1 a violent, rushing stream of water. 2 a heavy downpour: *The rain came down in torrents.* 3 any violent, rushing stream; flood: *a torrent of abuse.* [< Latin *torrentem* boiling, parching]

traipse (trāps), *v.i.,* **traipsed, traips ing.** walk about aimlessly, carelessly, or needlessly. [origin unknown]

trans lu cent (tran slü′snt, tranz lü′snt), *adj.* letting light through without being transparent: *Frosted glass is translucent.* [< Latin *translucentem* < *trans-* through + *lucere* to shine] **—trans lu′cent ly,** *adv.*

tra verse (*v.* trə vėrs′, trav′ərs; *n.* trav′ərs), *v.,* **-versed, -vers ing,** *n., adj.* —*v.t.* 1 pass across, over, or through: *We traversed the desert.* 2 go to and fro over or along (a place, etc.); cross. 3 ski or climb diagonally across. —*n.* something put or lying across. [< Old French *traverser* < Late Latin *transversare* < Latin *transversum* transverse.] **—tra vers′a ble,** *adj.*

trawl er (trô′lər), *n.* 1 boat used in trawling. 2 one who trawls.

tread mill (tred′mil′), *n.* 1 device used for exercise or to power a machine by having a person or animal walk or run on a sloping, endless belt. 2 any wearisome or monotonous round of activity.

trel lis (trel′is), *n.* frame of light strips of wood or metal crossing one another with open spaces in between; lattice, especially one supporting growing vines. [< Old French *trelis,* ultimately < Latin *trilix* triple-twilled < *tri-* three + *licium* thread]

trem u lous (trem′yə ləs), *adj.* 1 trembling; quivering: *a voice tremulous with sobs.* 2 timid; fearful. 3 that wavers; shaky: *tremulous writing.* [< Latin *tremulus* < *tremere* to tremble] **—trem′u lous ly,** *adv.* **—trem′u lous ness,** *n.*

tri fle (trī′fəl), *n., v.,* **-fled, -fling.** —*n.* 1 thing having little value or importance. 2 a small amount; little bit: *I was a trifle late.* 3 a small amount of money: *buy something for a trifle.* —*v.i.* talk or act lightly not seriously: *Don't trifle with serious matters.* [< Old French *trufle* mockery, diminutive of *truffe* deception]

trill (tril), *v.t., v.i.* 1 sing, play, sound, or speak with a tremulous, vibrating sound. 2 (in music) sing or play with a trill. [< Italian *trillare*]

trous seau (trü′sō, trü sō′), *n., pl.* **trous seaux** (trü′sōz, trü sōz′), **trous seaus.** a bride's outfit of clothes, linen, etc. [< French, originally, bundle]

trust y (trus′tē), *adj.,* **trust i er, trust i est,** *n., pl.* **trust ies.** —*adj.* trustworthy; reliable. —*n.* 1 convict who is given special privileges because of good behavior. 2 any trustworthy person or thing. **—trust′i ly,** *adv.* **—trust′i ness,** *n.*

tuft ed (tuf′tid), *adj.* 1 furnished with a tuft or tufts. 2 formed into a tuft or tufts.

tu reen (tə rēn′), *n.* a deep, covered dish for serving soup, etc. [< French *terrine* earthen vessel, ultimately < Latin *terra* earth]

ty coon (tī kün′), *n.* 1 businessman having great wealth and power. 2 title given by foreigners to the former hereditary commanders in chief of the Japanese army; shogun. [< Japanese *taikun* < Chinese *tai* great + *kiun* lord]

um bra geous (um brā′jəs), *adj.* 1 likely to take offense. 2 shady.

u nan i mous (yü nan′ə məs), *adj.* in complete accord or agreement; agreed: *The vote was unanimous.* [< Latin *unanimus* < *unus* one + *animus* mind] **—u nan′i mous ly,** *adv.*

un bri dled (un brī′dld), *adj.* 1 not having a bridle on. 2 not controlled; not restrained: *unbridled anger.*

un can ny (un kan′ē), *adj.* 1 strange and mysterious; weird: *The trees took uncanny shapes in the darkness.* 2 so far beyond what is normal or expected as to have some special power: *an uncanny knack for solving riddles.* **—un can′ni ly,** *adv.*

un der mine (un′dər mīn′, un′dər mīn′), *v.t.,* **-mined, -min ing.** 1 make a passage or hole under; dig under: *undermine a foundation.* 2 wear away the foundations of: *a cliff undermined by waves.* 3 weaken or destroy gradually: *Many severe colds have undermined her health.*

un du late (*v.* un′jə lāt, un′dyə lāt; *adj.* un′jə lit, un′jə lāt; un′dyə lit, un′dyə lāt), *v.*, **-lat ed, -lat ing,** *adj.* —*v.i.* 1 move in waves: *undulating water.* 2 have a wavy form or surface: *undulating hair, an undulating prairie.* —*adj.* wavy. [< Latin *undulatus* wavy < *unda* wave]

un gain ly (un gān′lē), *adj.* not gainly; awkward; clumsy.

un in tel li gi ble (un′in tel′ə jə bəl), *adj.* not intelligible; not able to be understood. **—un′in tel′li gi bly,** *adv.*

un mod u lat ed (un moj′ə lāt′əd), *adj.* not modulated; not adjusted so as to tone down or soften.

un ob tru sive (un′əb trü′siv), *adj.* not obtrusive; inconspicuous. **—un′ob tru′sive ly,** *adv.* **—un′ob tru′sive ness,** *n.*

un wont ed (un wun′tid, un wōn′tid, un wôn′tid), *adj.* 1 not customary; not usual: *unwonted anger.* 2 not accustomed; not used. **—un wont′ed ly,** *adv.* **—un wont′ed ness,** *n.*

up braid (up brād′), *v.t.* find fault with; blame; reprove: *The captain upbraided the guards for falling asleep.* [Old English *upbregdan* < *up* up + *bregdan* to weave, braid]

u sur er (yü′zhər ər), *n.* person who lends money at an extremely high or unlawful rate of interest.

vamp (vamp), *n.* an unscrupulous flirt. —v.t. flirt with. [short for *vampire*]

vaunt (vônt, vänt), *v.t.* boast of. —*v.i.* brag or boast. —*n.* a boasting assertion or speech; brag. [< Old French *vanter* < Late Latin *vanitare* be vain, boast < *vanus* vain]

veer (vir), *v.i.* change in direction; shift; turn: *The wind veered to the south. The talk veered to ghosts.* —*v.t.* change the direction of: *We veered our boat.* —*n.* a change of direction; shift; turn. [< Middle French *virer*] **—veer′ing ly,** *adv.*

veld or **veldt** (velt, felt), *n.* the open, grass-covered plains of southern Africa, often with bushes but having few trees. [< Afrikaans *veld* < Dutch, field]

ven om ous (ven′ə məs), *adj.* 1 poisonous: *a venomous bite, a venomous snake.* 2 spiteful; malicious. **—ven′om ous ly,** *adv.*

ver i fy (ver′ə fī), *v.t.*, **-fied, -fy ing.** 1 prove to be true; confirm: *The driver's report of the accident was verified by eyewitnesses.* 2 test the correctness of; check for accuracy: *You can verify the spelling of a word by looking in a dictionary.* [< Old French *verifier* < Medieval Latin *verificare* < Latin *verus* true + *facere* to make]

ves per (ves′pər), *n.* 1 evening. 2 an evening prayer, hymn, or service. 3 **vespers** or **Vespers,** *pl.* a church service held in the late afternoon or in the evening. [< Latin]

ves sel (ves′əl), *n.* 1 a large boat; ship. 2 airship. 3 a hollow holder or container. Cups, bowls, pitchers, bottles, barrels, and tubs are vessels. 4 tube carrying blood or other fluid. [< Old French < Latin *vascellum,* diminutive of *vas* vessel]

ves ti bule (ves′tə byül), *n.* 1 passage or hall between the outer door and the inside of a building. 2 the enclosed platform and entrance of a railroad passenger car. [< Latin *vestibulum*]

ves tige (ves′tij), *n.* a slight remnant; trace; mark: *Ghost stories are vestiges of a former widespread belief in ghosts.* [< French < Latin *vestigium* footprint]

ves ture (ves′chər), *n.* 1 clothing; garments. 2 covering.

vex (veks), *v.t.* 1 anger by trifles; annoy; provoke. 2 worry; trouble; harass. 3 disturb by commotion; agitate: *The island was much vexed by storms.* [< Latin *vexare*] **—vex′ing ly,** *adv.*

vex a tion (vek sā′shən), *n.* 1 a vexing. 2 a being vexed: *His face showed his vexation at the delay.* 3 thing that vexes.

vig i lance (vij′ə ləns), *n.* watchfulness; alertness; caution: *Constant vigilance is necessary in order to avoid accidents in driving.*

vig i lant (vij′ə lənt), *adj.* keeping steadily on the alert; watchful; wide-awake: *The dog kept vigilant guard.* **—vig′i lant ly,** *adv.*

vir ile (vir′əl), *adj.* 1 of, belonging to, or characteristic of a man; manly; masculine. 2 full of manly strength or masculine vigor. 3 vigorous; forceful. [< Latin *virilis* < *vir* man]

vis age (viz′ij), *n.* 1 face. 2 appearance or aspect. [< Old French < *vis* face < Latin *visus* sight < *videre* to see]

void (void), *n.* 1 an empty space; vacuum. 2 a feeling of emptiness or great loss: *The death of his dog left a void in the boy's life.* 3 emptiness; vacancy. —*adj.* 1 empty; vacant: *a void space.* 2 without legal force or effect; useless. 3 **void of,** devoid of; without; lacking: *words void of sense.* [< Old French *voide* < Popular Latin *vocitus* < Latin *vacuus* empty]

vo li tion (vō lish′ən), *n.* 1 act of willing; decision or choice: *She went away of her own volition.* 2 power of willing: *The use of drugs has weakened his volition.* [< Medieval Latin *volitionem* < Latin *volo* I wish]

vo ra cious (və rā′shəs), *adj.* 1 eating much; greedy in eating; ravenous. 2 very eager; unable to be satisfied; insatiable. [< Latin *voracis* greedy] **—vo ra′cious ly,** *adv.* **—vo ra′cious ness,** *n.*

vouch safe (vouch sāf′), *v.t.*, **-safed, -saf ing.** be willing to grant or give; deign (to do or give): *The proud man vouchsafed no reply when we spoke to him.*

vul gar (vul′gər), *adj.* 1 showing a lack of good breeding, manners, taste, etc.; not refined; coarse; low. 2 of the common people. 3 current or prevalent among people; popular; general: *vulgar prejudices.* [< Latin *vulgaris* < *vulgus* common people] **—vul′gar ly,** *adv.*

waft (waft, wäft), *v.t.* carry over water or through air: *The waves wafted the boat to shore.* —*v.i.* float. —*n.* 1 a breath or puff of air, wind, scent, etc. 2 a waving movement; wave. 3 act of wafting. [< earlier *wafter* convoy ship < Dutch and Low German *wachter* guard] **—waft′er,** *n.*

wamble (wom′əl), *v.i.*, **-bled, -bling.** DIALECT. move unsteadily.

wane (wān), *v.*, **waned, wan ing,** *n.* —*v.i.* 1 lose size; become smaller gradually: *The moon wanes after it has become full.* 2 decline in power, influence, or importance: *Many great empires have waned.* 3 decline in strength or intensity: *The light of day wanes in the evening.* 4 draw to a close: *Summer wanes as autumn approaches.* —*n.* act or process of waning. [Old English *wanian*]

war i ness (wer′ē nis, war′ē nis), *n.* caution; care.

wean (wēn), *v.t.* 1 accustom (a child or young animal) to food other than its mother's milk. 2 accustom (a person) to do without something; cause to turn away: *wean someone from a bad habit.* [Old English *wenian*]

weir (wir), *n.* dam erected across a river to stop and raise the water, as for conveying a stream to a mill. [Old English *wer*]

whelp (hwelp), *n.* 1 puppy or cub; young dog, wolf, bear, lion, tiger, etc. 2 an impudent young person. [Old English *hwelp*]

whet (hwet), *v.*, **whet ted, whet ting.** 1 sharpen by rubbing: *whet a knife.* 2 make keen or eager; stimulate: *The smell of food whetted my appetite.* [Old English *hwettan*]

wile (wīl), *n.* 1 a trick to deceive; cunning way: *The serpent by his wiles persuaded Eve to eat the apple.* 2 subtle trickery; slyness; craftiness. [Old English *wīgle* magic]

winch (winch), *n.* machine for lifting or pulling, turned by hand with a crank or by an engine. [Old English *wince*]

wont (wunt, wōnt, wônt), *adj.* accustomed: *He was wont to read the paper at breakfast.* —*n.* custom; habit: *She rose early, as was her wont.* [originally past participle of Old English *wunian* be accustomed]

wrath (rath), *n.* 1 great anger; rage. 2 vengeance or punishment caused by anger. [Old English *wrǣththu* < *wrāth* wroth]

wrest (rest), *v.t.* 1 twist, pull, or tear away with force; wrench away: *She wrested the knife from her attacker.* 2 take by force: *The usurper wrested the power from the king.* 3 obtain by persistence or persuasion; wring: *wrest a secret from someone.* [Old English *wrǣstan*] **—wrest′er,** *n.*

writhe (rīᴛʜ), *v.*, **writhed, writh ing.** —*v.i.* 1 twist and turn; twist about: *writhe in pain. The snake writhed along the branch.* 2 suffer mentally; be very uncomfortable. —*v.t.* twist or bend (something). [Old English *wrīthan*]

wrought (rôt), *v.* ARCHAIC. a pt. and a pp. of **work.** —*adj.* 1 made: *The gate was wrought with great skill.* 2 formed with care; not rough or crude. 3 manufactured or treated; not in a raw state. 4 deeply stirred; possessed of an excited state of mind.

wrought-up (rôt′up′), *adj.* stirred up; excited.

wry (rī), *adj.*, **wri er, wri est.** 1 turned to one side; twisted: *She made a wry face to show her disgust.* 2 ironic: *wry humor.* [ultimately < Old English *wrīgian* to turn] **—wry′ly,** *adv.*

yo kel (yō′kəl), *n.* (often considered offensive) awkward or unsophisticated person from the country; rustic. [origin uncertain]

ze nith (zē′nith), *n.* 1 the point in the heavens directly overhead; point opposite the nadir. 2 the highest point; apex: *At the zenith of its power Rome ruled most of Europe.* [< Old French or Medieval Latin *cenith* < Arabic *samt (ar-rās)* the way (over the head)]

Index of Reading and Literature Skills

Index of Vocabulary Exercises

Combined skills exercises

Index of Composition Assignments

Personal

Explanatory

Creative

Critical

Index of Authors and Titles

Illustration Acknowledgments

Illustrations not credited are from Scott, Foresman.

Unit 1

1-© David Hockney 1970; **5**-*The Living Forest—A World of Animals,* by Rien Poortvliet. English translation © 1979 Harry N. Abrams, Inc. **9**-James T. Warner from *The Darker Brother;* **15**-Mike Muir; **23**-James Teason; **33**-John Slobodnik; **43**-John Sandford; **51**-Gary Gianni; **55**-from the private collection of Dr. and Mrs. Raphael Warkel/Photo: Goffman Fine Art, NY and Bluebell, PA; **59**-Georg Gerster/Photo Researchers, Inc.; **65**-Robert Amft; **73**-Irish Tourist Board.

Unit 2

84,85-Michael de Camp; **91** through **105**-Museum of Modern Art/Film Stills Archive; **111**-Copyright The Frick Collection, New York.

Unit 3

160,161-Robert Amft; **163**-Grant Heilman Photography; **165**-Franz Altschuler; **173**-Dan Morrill; **175**-Scott Mutter; **176**-Wood sculpture by Chris Carsten (1863–1956) from the Schneider/Higgins Collection; **180**-© Gerald F. Jarosz; **182**-Batik by Diana Christiansen, Courtesy Marianne Ociepka; **183**-© R. Hamilton Smith; **187**-Dr. Robert G. Thompson; **191**-Robert Llewellyn; **192**-Dan Morrill; **198**-Robert Amft; **204**-*Primavera* (detail) by Botticelli/Uffizi Gallery, Florence; **207**-Prize-winning painting by teen Fen Lee of Elmhurst, NY, reprinted from *Seventeen*® Magazine, copyright © 1984 by Triangle Communications, Inc. All rights reserved; **211** through **213**-Robert Pierron; **215**-Tom Heflin, Rockford, IL; **219,220**-Harriet Kittay/Courtesy Sutton Gallery, 29 W. 57th St., NYC; **226,229**-Robert Amft; **234**-John H. Gerard.

Unit 4

236,237,247,257,271,279-Courtesy WQED/Pittsburgh and *Kennedy Center Tonight*, Photos by Kenneth Love.

Unit 5

294,295-Osage robe/Denver Art Museum; **297**-Linda M. Byrd, Indian Harbour Beach, FL; **303**-Dan Morrill; **315**-*Father and Mother* by John Steuart Curry, Collection IBM Corporation, Armonk, NY; **309**-Mukul Roy; **318,323**-Pat Nagel; **329**-*Jewish Wedding* by Mane Katz/Private Collection; **339**-*Now It Is Christmas Again* by Carl Larsson/ Private Collection; **343**-Don Nibbelink; **347**-Robert Amft; **355**-Dennis Stock/Magnum; **359**-Tom Petrillo; **365**-Nancy Turgeon.

Unit 6

374,375 and **383** through **452**-American Shakespeare Theatre/Photos: Martha Swope; **377,378**-The physical features of Shakespeare's Globe Playhouse, as described in the text and as shown in the illustrations, are based upon the data assembled by Dr. John Cranford Adams in his *Globe Playhouse* (Barnes & Noble) and upon the model of the Globe constructed by Dr. Adams and Irwin Smith.

Unit 7

460,461-Robert Wahlgren; **463**-Courtesy Ministries of Corrie ten Boom; **472**-From *My Early Life: A Roving Commission* by Winston S. Churchill, Copyright 1930 Charles Scribner's Sons; renewal copyright © 1958 Winston Churchill. Reproduced by permission; **479**-Courtesy *Life* Magazine; **487**-© Ray F. Hillstrom; **493**-From the book *Annapurna* by Maurice Herzog. Copyright 1952 by E.P. Dutton & Co., Inc., N.Y. Reproduced by permission of E.P. Dutton & Co., Inc. and Jonathan Cape Ltd., London; **499**-*Newsweek*/Marvin Kupfer; **504**-Culver Pictures, Inc.; **505**-Wide World Photos; **506**-Culver Pictures, Inc.; **508**-The Bettmann Archive; **509**-National Park Services-Abbie Rowe/Courtesy Harry S. Truman Library; **512**-© Art Pahlke; **519**-From *Eagles, Hawks and Falcons of the World* by Leslie Brown & Dean Amadon, Vol II, Sponsored by the National Audubon Society, Copyright Country Life Books, London, England.

Unit 8

528,529-Stockphotos Inc.;
535,543,557,572,584,585,593,601-Ron DiCianni.

Handbook

624,633,638-Robert Korta; **643**-© Robert Drea.

Glossary

671-H. Armstrong Roberts; **678**-Brown Brothers;
681-Government of India Tourist Board.